INTERNATIONAL ENCYCLOPEDIA OF

Marriage
and
Family

EDITOR IN CHIEF

James J. Ponzetti, Jr.
University of British Columbia

ASSOCIATE EDITORS

Raeann R. Hamon
Messiah College

Yvonne Kellar-Guenther
University of Colorado

Patricia K. Kerig
*University of North Carolina
at Chapel Hill*

T. Laine Scales
Baylor University

James M. White
University of British Columbia

INTERNATIONAL ENCYCLOPEDIA OF

Marriage and Family

SECOND EDITION

Volume 3: Ke–Se

James J. Ponzetti, Jr
Editor in Chief

**MACMILLAN
REFERENCE
USA™**

THOMSON
GALE

New York • Detroit • San Diego • San Francisco • Cleveland • New Haven, Conn. • Waterville, Maine • London • Munich

THOMSON

GALE

International Encyclopedia of Marriage and Family
James J. Ponzetti, Jr.

© 2003 by Macmillan Reference USA.
Macmillan Reference USA is an imprint of
The Gale Group, Inc., a division of
Thomson Learning, Inc.

Macmillan Reference USA™ and
Thomson Learning™ are trademarks used
herein under license.

For more information, contact
Macmillan Reference USA
300 Park Avenue South, 9th Floor
New York, NY 10010
Or you can visit our Internet site at
http://www.gale.com

Macmillan Reference USA
300 Park Avenue South, 9th Floor
New York, NY 10010

Macmillan Reference USA
27500 Drake Road
Farmington Hills, MI 48331-3535

LIBRARY OF CONGRESS CATALOGING-IN-PUBLICATION DATA

International encyclopedia of marriage and family / James J. Ponzetti, Jr.,
editor in chief. — 2nd ed.
    p. cm.
  Rev. ed. of: Encyclopedia of marriage and the family. c1995.
  Includes bibliographical references and index.
  ISBN 0-02-865672-5 (set : alk. paper) — ISBN 0-02-865673-3 (v. 1 : alk.
paper) — ISBN 0-02-865674-1 (v. 2 : alk. paper) — ISBN 0-02-865675-X
(v. 3 : alk. paper) — ISBN 0-02-865676-8 (v. 4 : alk. paper)
  1. Marriage—Encyclopedias. 2. Family—Encyclopedias. I. Ponzetti,
James J. II. Encyclopedia of marriage and family.

  HQ9 .E52 2003
  306.8'03—dc21

                        2002014107

Printed in the United States of America
10 9 8 7 6 5 4 3 2 1

KENYA

The population of Kenya includes forty-two traditional ethnic groups (CBS 1994), which can be broadly divided into three groups: the Bantu, Nilotes, and Cushites. These three categories of ethnic groups are spread all over the country, and no particular group can be tied to one region. The regional boundaries do little to separate the similarity of customs and beliefs possessed by each group, owing to their common heritage and contacts over hundreds of years. Commonly, then, cultural traits exhibited by one ethnic group of a broader group in one region are the same as those of another ethnic group of the same broader group in a different region.

With the advent of modernity—education, technology, urbanization, Western religion and changing socioeconomic factors—the Kenyan society has increasingly become universal, and ethnic identities and affiliations are steadily fading. This has brought a degree of universality in the way of life as contemporary society adapts to new situations that were totally unknown to traditional society. Family life has also changed, with many families caught between the traditional family system that advocates for solidarity and the modern system, which is characterized by individualism, a shift that developed because of changing religious, social, political, and economic factors.

Family relations are undergoing redefinition within the emerging structures of socially and economically viable domestic groups. The HIV/AIDS pandemic in the 1990s has also given a new dimension to the Kenyan concept of marriage and family by challenging African traditional beliefs, marital roles, familial obligations, morality, and sexuality. Nevertheless, although these changes are widespread, in view of the cultural diversity in the country and difference in pace of adaptation to the changing social and economic environment, family structures and forms are not uniform.

The Concept of Marriage and Family

Marriage in the traditional Kenyan context is defined as a rite of passage that every individual is expected to undergo in his or her lifetime, and the integral purpose of this institution is to widen the kinship network of the individual through procreation. Also, affinal relatives (relatives by marriage) are acquired in addition to consaguineal kin (blood relatives). Families are made of a wide network of members, including brothers, sisters, parents, grandparents, uncles, aunts, cousins, in-laws, unborn children, and deceased relatives. The wide network of family members functions as a social unit with norms and beliefs and as an economic unit for the survival of its members.

The family system in Kenya is mainly patriarchal (consisting of paternal lineage or descent) and patrilocal (consisting of paternal residence). This system is emphasized by the need for the groom or his family to pay dowry to the bride's family before marriage. Payment of dowry is usually in the form of money or in kind (livestock) and may be done a few days before the marriage or over a long period, from the time of birth to years after the marriage. Dowry serves to fulfill justice and legality in the eyes of the families involved. With marriages breaking down in the modern society, this tradition is seen as a factor that links the society to the strong moral standards of earlier days because the woman feels worthwhile to her husband and may, hence, stay faithful to the marriage.

On the other hand, modern, educated and urbanite Kenyans, who ardently believe in marriage based on love, view this tradition in the reverse, arguing that it builds the marriage on purely economic factors because the wife's motivation to stay faithful to the marriage is based on fear that her parents would be required to return the dowry to her husband's family should she fail in her marriage. The argument goes on to draw attention to the demeaning status that the wife is subjected to as she is viewed as a commodity to be bought and sold (Kilbride 1994). With women subject to this situation, men are favored to control property, income, and labor. Furthermore, dowry violates women's rights because it encourages early marriages in cases where parents are eager to collect dowry on marrying off their daughters. It is against this backdrop that the dowry tradition is slowly eroding.

The Extended Family

The extended family system is the most important indigenous African institution, forming the pillar on which rests the entire social organization. With some modification to the traditional system to suit modern Kenya, this family type is the most common in the country. Traditionally, the extended family system worked as a welfare system aimed at ensuring that all members were loved and cared for at all times. This type of family may be intergenerational, and it may be based on exogamous, endogamous, or polygynous unions. With modernization, the extended family has taken on different forms, which can be divided into the following categories:

(1) Stem families, which are made up of extended family, which in turn is made up of either a female-headed household with affines (relatives by marriage) and consaguines (blood relatives), or a man, children, and grandchildren, or in rare cases, a solitary person. In many cases in which the household head is a woman, the consaguines are usually grandchildren who are borne out of wedlock through their daughters' premar-

ital or adolescent pregnancies (Kilbride and Kilbride 1997).

(2) Composite extended families, which consist of at least two nuclear families (monogamous or polygynous) that may be extended by generation. A common case of this family type is when a man dies and his brother inherits his wife or wives, thereby making his dead brother's family part of his own. Although still widely practiced in some communities in Kenya, wife inheritance is slowly disappearing following massive government, community, health, and nongovernmental organizations' campaigns to end the practice in a bid to curb the spread of HIV/AIDS.

(3) Nuclear families and consaguines, which consist of parents, children, and grandchildren (Kilbride and Kilbride 1990).

Child fostering is an integral aspect of the extended family, and until the late 1980s, it was widespread because it was a necessary welfare system that was entwined in the family structure. The most common scenarios of fostering depict poor rural peasants sending their children to be fostered by richer relatives in the urban areas, and poor urban migrants sending their children back to their kin in the village (Nelson 1987). Child fostering is known to sustain large families (Isiugo-Abanihe 1994; Anonymous 1987), and it is therefore not surprising that, with a drop in child fostering, the national total fertility rate fell from 7.7 per woman in 1984 to 4.7 in 1998. However, it is important to note that the reduction in the national total fertility rate is not the sole achievement of the reduction in child fostering but is the result of many factors, with contraception taking the leading role. Evidence suggests fostering is being weakened by social and economic changes and the availability of alternate childcare options. Kenya's constitution calls for the state provision of care and protection of abused or neglected children, and the courts choose foster parents (Umbima 1991). Although well-defined regulations are in place to govern this process, Kenya does not have the resources to put them into effect. Furthermore, with an average of four children, Kenyan families have limited economic ability to take in foster children. One result seems to be that Kenya is experiencing an upsurge in the numbers of street children in urban centers. A report by the Kenyan government and the United Nations Children's Fund (UNICEF) estimated the national figure of children in need of special protection (CNSP) in Kenya at 300,000 (GOK/UNICEF, 1998).

The Nonextended Family

Because of the changing social and economic environment, individual relationships have gained popularity, and marriage has ceased to represent ties between social groups; rather, it is an alliance between individuals. The nonextended family system is now widespread, with the most common form being the monogamous nuclear family found in both urban and rural areas. The other forms of this family type are the composite polygynous, which consists of a man, his wife or wives, and their children (most common in rural areas), and the stem nonextended or single-parent family consisting of one parent and children (common in the urban areas). Most single-parent families consist of the woman as the parent, a trend increasingly emerging among urban and professional women. Many of these women view marriage as an option that is detrimental to their attempts to have careers, professional occupations, and independent lifestyles. Autonomy is first on the agenda as many single mothers choose to have children with married or younger men who will not have absolute influence or authority over them (Kilbride 1994). This suggests a redefinition, based on gender, of roles and practices and a new form of social relationship between family members. Also, the increase in single-parent families in Kenya is attributed to high incidences of teenage pregnancy and premarital and extramarital sex.

According to Andrev Ocholla-Ayayo (1997a; 1997b), a leading anthropologist in the Kenyan study of family systems, the society has devalued traditional sexual mores, and premarital and extramarital sexual relationships are gaining acceptance. With this societal attitude towards sexuality, it is not surprising that mortality as a result of HIV/AIDS is high, and the resulting widowhood is increasingly contributing to the cases of single parenthood. Another emerging pattern is that of child-headed or youth-headed families when children are orphaned when parents die of HIV/AIDS infection (National Council for Population and Development [NCPD] 2000).

Polygyny

Anthropological literature often reports that African cultures greatly value polygyny, the term used when one man has more than one wife. Traditionally, it is the woman who chooses a co-wife—someone with whom she can cope well, like a younger sister or cousin, and in cases where the husband needs a subsequent wife, the preceding wives get to pick their co-wife or wives (Whyte 1980; Lwanga 1976). A man was only qualified to be polygynous if he was rich enough to take care of several wives and children, and the number of wives a man had directly reflected his economic status.

In contemporary Kenya, evidence suggests that polygyny is still accepted, especially among men and, to a little extent, traditional African women. Modern urban women, educated in the West, apparently disdain this institution. They often view women in polygynous unions as being deprived of their basic rights within marriage, having to compete between themselves rather than being partners with their husbands. These families are also economically deprived and live in disharmony as they increasingly compete for the scarce resources at this time when poverty is on the increase in Kenya. However, there is argument that, surprisingly, the very women who disregard polygyny and opt for single parenthood have their children fathered by married men. Could this be, in fact, a reinvented form of polygyny for current times? (Kilbride 1994).

Among the circumstances resulting in polygyny is rural-urban migration in search of cash income. For many male migrants, polygyny is a solution to the problem of spending a lot of time and resources travelling upcountry to be with their families. Therefore, it is not surprising that in today's emerging forms of polygyny, men have latter wives living with them in the urban areas while the first wives take care of their rural homesteads. In some cases, the wives share labor and company in their rural home while the husband is away in town (Kilbride and Kilbride 1990; Kilbride 1994). Also, lack of forces to monitor and sanction who is eligible for polygyny has led to the current economic strife among polygynous families. Traditional leaders and elders who were commissioned to regulate and monitor family lives have lost their authority, and as a result, men who traditionally would not qualify to be polygynous on economic grounds are marrying freely. The erosion of the dowry tradition, which would have required men to pay for the acquisition of additional wives, also mitigates the economic implications that arise from polygyny.

Conclusion

Evidently, family and marriage relations in Kenya are gradually changing in response to the changing social and economic environment. In this regard, indigenously favored family systems are eroding, either through complete abandonment or evolution into more viable forms that are conventional with modern Kenya.

See also: EXTENDED FAMILIES; KINSHIP

Bibliography

Anonymous. (1987). "African Fertility Decline Will Not Happen Soon Without Major Attitudinal and Cultural Changes." *International Family Planning Perspectives.* 13(3):109–11.

Central Bureau of Statistics (CBS). (1994). *Kenya Population Census 1989.* Nairobi: Government Printer.

Government of Kenya. (GOK)/UNICEF (1998). *Situation Analysis of Children and Women in Kenya.* Nairobi: Reproduction and Distribution Section, United Nations Office.

Isiugo-Abanihe, U. C. (1994). "Parenthood in Sub-Saharan Africa: Child Fostering and Its Relationship with Fertility." In *The Onset of Fertility Transition in Sub-Saharan Africa,* ed. T. Locoh and V. Hertrich. Liege, Belgium: International Union for the Scientific Study of Population.

Kilbride, P. (1994). *Plural Marriage for Our Times: A Reinvented Option?* Westport, CT: Greenwood.

Kilbride, P. L., and Kilbride, J. C. (1990). *Changing Family Life in East Africa: Women and Children at Risk.* University Park: Pennsylvania State University Press.

Kilbride, P. L., and Kilbride, J. C. (1997). "Stigma, Role and Delocalization Among Contemporary Kenyan Women." In *African Families and the Crisis of Social Change,* ed. T. S. Weisner, C. Bradley, and P. L. Kilbride, in collaboration with A. B. C. Ocholla-Ayayo, J. Akong'a, and S. Wandibba. Westport, CT: Bergin and Garvey.

Lwanga, G. (1976). "Report on the Health of Clan Health Workers." Nangina, Kenya: Nangina Hospital.

National Council for Population and Development. (2000). *Sessional Paper No. 1 of 2000 on National Population Policy for Sustainable Development.* Nairobi, Kenya: Government Printer.

Nelson, N. (1987). "Rural-Urban Child Fostering in Kenya: Migration, Kinship Ideology and Class." In *Migrants, Workers, and Social Order,* ed. J. Eades. London: Association of Social Anthropologists.

Ocholla-Ayayo, A. B. (1997a). "The African Family Between Tradition and Modernity." In *Family, Population and Development in Africa,* ed. A. Adepoju. London: Zed Books.

Ocholla-Ayayo, A. B. (1997b). "HIV/AIDS Risk and Changing Sexual Practices in Kenya." In *African Families and the Crisis of Social Change,* ed. T. S. Weisner, C. Bradley, and P. L. Kilbride, in collaboration with A.B.C. Ocholla-Ayayo, J. Akong'a, and S. Wandibba. Westport, CT: Bergin and Garvey.

Umbima, K. J. (1991). "Regulating Foster Care Services: the Kenyan Situation." *Child Welfare* 70(2):169–74.

Whyte, S. (1980). "Wives and Co-wives in Marachi, Kenya." *Folk* 22:134-146.

SALOME NASIROLI WAWIRE

KIDNAPPING

See MISSING CHILDREN

KINSHIP

All human beings are connected to others by blood or marriage. Connections between people that are traced by blood are known as *consanguineal* relationships. Relationships based upon marriage or cohabitation between collaterals (people treated as the same generation) are *affinal* relationships. These connections are described by genealogies and/or academic kinship charts, which trace the consanguineal and affinal relationships among individuals. Theoretically, the kinds of relationships that these charts and genealogies describe are the same for all individuals in all cultures—that is, any person can in principle trace a relationship to a spouse, children, children's children, parents, parents' siblings, the spouses and children of parents' siblings, and so on. However, people in different societies customarily calculate genealogical connections differently, recognizing some kinds of relationships and ignoring others. The culturally determined genealogies turn objective relationships of blood and marriage between people into kinship. In no culture are all genealogical relationships recognized as kin relations. All people have kin relations about whom they know nothing, and everyone knows of relatives who have no importance in their lives. Genealogical relationships that have no social significance, either because the individuals whom they designate are unknown or because they are known but ignored, are not kin in the social sense. Genealogical ties that a culture chooses to recognize are what constitute an individual's kin.

Kinship relations have routinely captured the attention of students of human culture. This is especially true of anthropologists, whose major focus has traditionally been upon kin-based societies. Kinship, once a primary focus of cultural anthropology, has faded in centrality since the 1970s as many traditional societies have been drawn into the world system. The significance of kin relations begins to diminish only in large societies with mobile populations and money-based economies. By contrast, kin relations in most nonindustrial cultures underlie such critical domains as place of residence, inheritance customs, religious obligations, political power, economic relations, domestic life, and choice of spouse. People across cultures are more likely to turn to kin than to nonkin for help and are more likely to give aid and comfort to kin than to nonkin (Broude 1994).

If kin relations are the result of the selective interpretation of genealogies by cultures, how do societies accomplish this transformation of biological fact into social reality? The transformation is achieved in part by the way in which a particular culture establishes recognized kin groups and in part by the way in which a society comes to label relatives with respect to some target person. Recognized kin groups are established by and reflected in what are called descent rules. The labeling of relatives is described by a culture's kinship terminology. Further, in all societies, human beings often reside near or with kin. Different cultures, however, follow different rules regarding which kin will live with whom. The three major elements of kinship are rules of descent, kinship terminology, and residence rules. The incest taboo,

rules governing marriage choice, and family structure are also important (Fox 1967).

Descent

Descent rules define socially recognized kin groups by tracing connections through chains of parent-child ties. A society may focus exclusively on connections traced through the male parent (*patrilineal*) or through the female parent (*matrilineal*). In either case, the culture is employing a *unilineal,* or single-line, descent system.

When descent is patrilineal, the descent group is composed of people of either sex whose fathers belong to the group. Siblings belong to the descent group of their father, but their mother belongs to a different descent group, the group to which her father belongs. Therefore, a man's children will belong to his descent group, but a woman's children will not belong to her descent group. Analogously, if descent is matrilineal, siblings belong to the mother's group but their father does not. A woman's children will belong to her descent group, but a man's children will not belong to his. Sometimes a society will assign individuals to one unilineal descent group for one purpose and to the other for another purpose, resulting in a system of double descent. For example, the person's patrilineal descent group may be in charge of political functions, while inheritance operates through the matrilineal descent group.

In contrast to societies that trace descent unilineally, individuals in some cultures such as the United States are characterized by *bilateral* descent rules, tracing relationships through both parents. In these societies, other institutions, such as governments, churches, businesses, and voluntary organizations, provide the structure and perform the functions of other societies' kin-based groups. In some societies, descent is traced through one parent for some people and through the other parent for other people; this is *ambilineal* descent. For instance, males may trace descent through their fathers, and females may trace descent through their mothers.

Because unilineal descent rules produce bounded and nonoverlapping groups, unilineal descent is a more powerful organizing principle than bilateral descent in that unilineal descent groups are able to act as corporate groups on behalf of their members in a way that bilateral descent groups cannot. Each patrilineal descent group in a society that traces descent through the father has a particular identity and membership that is entirely different from the identity and membership of any other patrilineal descent group in the same society. Where descent is traced bilaterally, by contrast, only full siblings belong to precisely the same descent group because only full siblings have the same parents. Where descent is reckoned bilaterally, a person tends to single out some relatives within his or her kin group as more important than others. This close circle of kin is referred to as one's kindred. Who is included in one's kindred and who is not is a matter of individual choice based upon individual preference and sentiment. What is more, the definition of kindred shifts, depending upon circumstances. For instance, people in the United States are likely to count a smaller number of relatives as close when planning the guest list for Christmas dinner than when they are writing wedding invitations. In either case, because bilateral descent groups fan out indefinitely, it becomes hard to decide where to draw the line between kin who are close and kin who are not. Since each person belongs to a unique descent group and different bilateral descent groups in the same society have somewhat overlapping but also somewhat different memberships, these groups cannot function effectively as representatives of their members.

Unilineal descent, specifically patrilineal descent, is the most common system of reckoning (Ember and Ember 1988). Therefore, the majority of cultures around the world exploit blood and marriage connections to maximize the power and effectiveness of the kin group in supervising a wide variety of activities in which individuals participate. Unilineal descent groups are important sources of political power in many societies. The leaders can arbitrate disputes between individuals within the descent group or between different descent groups. They can go to war in support of a group member and retaliate for wrongs done to one of their own. Unilineal descent groups can delegate land rights and often act as a kind of government vis-à-vis the members. Unilineal descent groups also have important economic roles. Such groups can own land, money, houses, religious places and objects, songs, economic capital, and even personal names. Property is often inherited through the unilineal descent group. Unilineal

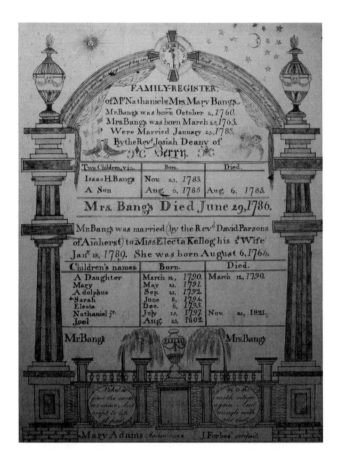

Family trees are one of the oldest ways to organize and display genealogical data on consanguineal and affinal relationships. This family tree traces lineages back to the 1760s. CATHERINE KARNOW/CORBIS

descent groups can lend money and maintain members who have no other means of support. The unilineal descent group is also commonly the center of religious activity. Often a descent group is identified with supernatural beings who may be ancestors or claimed ancestors of members of the group. Supernaturals may be believed to protect and otherwise affect the members of the group, and the members may, in turn, be required to engage in particular activities in an effort to influence the actions of the supernatural.

Particular descent groups can also be associated with particular sets of taboos that the members of the group are obligated to honor. Marriages, often regulated by the unilineal descent group, may be prohibited or preferred between members of the same descent group, depending upon the norms of the group. Unilineal descent groups may also take over the burden of providing what are sometimes very costly payments to the bride or bride's family when a member of the group is married.

Kinship Terminology

Cultures transform cross-culturally equivalent genealogies into socially defined kin relations by the way in which they name categories of individuals who are members of the kin group. Such naming results in the kinship terminology of the culture. There are two basic sets of kin terms: *terms of reference* and *terms of address.* A term of reference is how ego would refer to that relative in communications with others. For example, if ego were asked "Who is that person to you?" he or she might say "That is my father." A term of address is what one calls that person when interacting with him or her—e.g., "Hi, Dad." In all cultures, one or more of nine basic criteria are used in the system of kinship terminology particular to that culture (Kroeber 1909; Murdock 1949): generation, lineality and collaterality, sex, affinity, polarity, bifurcation, relative age, speaker's sex, and address versus reference. In the United States and most other Western societies, the first five criteria are commonly used. North Americans customarily distinguish among kin and assign kin terms on the basis of a person's generation, directness of relationship, sex, ties of blood versus marriage, and the use of different terms by interacting kin.

Different cultures collapse different relatives under one name that allows kinship terminology to transform objectively identical genealogies into different social constructions of kinship. For instance, the kinship terminology employed in the United States uses the term *aunt* to refer to all of the sisters of a person's mother but employs a different term for the mother herself. In some other cultures, by contrast, a person's mother and the mother's sister are referred to by the same term. Relatives who are called by the same label tend to be identified with similar roles, responsibilities, and privileges with regard to ego. Similarly, relatives who are distinguished from each other terminologically also tend to play distinctive roles with respect to ego. Kin names, therefore, act to reinforce cultural expectations about how kin will behave toward one another. While classificatory kin terms emphasize similarities in the relationships of different kin to ego, individuals distinguish between relatives who are called the same name and respond to them differently in a myriad of ways. Thus, in societies where mother and mother's sisters are called by the same term, children know the difference between their mothers and aunts, treat them

differently, and feel differently about them. The collapsing of different categories of relatives under one label facilitates certain kinds of interactions between kin but does not eradicate an individual's ability to appreciate that people called by the same name are, nevertheless, not the same people.

While kin terminology is not uniform across cultures, there are a number of systems of kin naming that appear over and over from one culture to the next. Six such systems of kinship terminology have been identified, based on the manner in which cousins and siblings are classified: Hawaiian, Eskimo, Sudanese, Iroquois, Crow, and Omaha (Murdock 1949). U.S. kin terms are of the Eskimo type. Cousins are distinguished from brothers and sisters, but cousins on the father's side are not distinguished from those on the mother's side—they are all referred to as *cousin.*

Cultures that share systems of kinship terminology also tend to be similar in residence patterns, descent rules, and family organization (Levinson and Malone 1980). These similarities in important features of social structure are thought to account for shared kin terminology systems. Societies with similar patterns of descent, residence, and family organization are likely to allocate roles, rights, and responsibilities similarly.

A shared system of kin terminology reflects and reinforces these similar role assignments. For example, in societies that trace descent through the father, a greater number of terminological distinctions are made regarding relatives from different generations for kin traced through the father than for kin traced through the mother. This may be because role, rights, and responsibilities depend upon the age of the relative vis-à-vis ego. As the interactions between an individual and the father's kin are more finely enumerated and distinguished in cultures where descent is traced through the male parent, the generation-based name distinctions on the father's side of the genealogy that are typical of these cultures reflect generation-based role distinctions. As interactions between an individual and relatives traced through the mother are not so finely drawn, terminological distinctions also tend to be less finely distinguished.

In societies that trace descent through the father, married couples also tend to live with or near the husband's family. This means that children of both sexes as well as married males will be interacting daily with relatives traced through the father, while no individuals will ever live where there is a concentration of relatives traced through the mother. The finer distinctions between the father's kin on the basis of age may reflect the far greater number of interactions that an individual will have with these relatives and, therefore, the greater need to distinguish these relatives on the basis of age. Societies that reverse this pattern of kin naming, distinguishing between mother's but not father's kin on the basis of generation, tend to trace descent through the female parent. In cultures of this kind, married couples are more likely to live with or near the wife's family. The greater role of the mother's kin in the life of the individual is mirrored in the more clearly differentiated kin labeling with respect to relatives traced through the mother.

Residence Rules

In all known cultures, at least some people—usually the majority—live near or with kin. Which kin live together differs from one society to the next and from family to family within a culture, but one particular kind of household tends to predominate in a given society. This is in part because many cultures have explicit rules that specify where a married couple will establish their new home.

In most societies around the world, newly married people are required or expected to live with or near the husband's family. This *patrilocal* residence pattern is found in 70 percent of a sample of 1,153 cultures (Levinson and Malone 1980). Residence is *matrilocal* in 11 percent of these societies, with a married couple living with or near the wife's family. Couples live apart from both the husband's and the wife's families in 5 percent of cultures. Husbands and wives are expected to live with or near the husband's mother's brother in 4 percent, a pattern known as *avunculocality,* or the uncle's place. Residence rules that require a couple to live with or near the family of one or the other spouse are known as *unilocal* rules. In 7 percent of cultures, a married couple can live with or near the family of either spouse, based on *bilocal* residence rules. Sometimes couples change households over the course of their marriage. *Patrimatrilocal* residence rules require couples to live first with the husband's family and then with the wife's parents. In *matri-patrilocal* cultures, the opposite occurs.

Particular rules of residence seem to occur more frequently in some kinds of cultures than in others. *Neolocal* residence is most common in societies whose economies depend upon money. The introduction of money into a culture means that individuals can obtain what they need on a flexible schedule, so that a husband and wife are no longer as dependent upon kin for the necessities of life. Further, in money-based economies, people are not as free to remain in one place; they may be required to move to where a job is available. Moving entire households composed of parents, aunts, uncles, and cousins is impractical. Therefore, as money economies make couples more independent and also more mobile, living with relatives becomes less necessary and less realistic (Ember and Ember 1983).

In most cultures, people live with relatives. Some theorists have suggested that the particular choice of relatives with whom to live is influenced by which sex makes the greater economic contribution in the culture (Levinson and Malone 1980; Murdock 1949). Residence would be patrilocal where men make the greater economic contribution and matrilocal where the contribution of women is greater. This theory is intuitively attractive, but in fact residence rules are not predictably related to the roles of men and women in the economy. However, residence rules are predictably related to warfare (Ember and Ember 1983). In particular, where wars tend to be waged between groups who live far apart from each other, interfering with the subsistence activities of the men, residence rules tend to be matrilocal. Perhaps this is because matrilocality allows a closely related and therefore cohesive group of women to take charge of subsistence tasks when the men are away. Where enemies are close to home, societies are more likely to be patrilocal. Perhaps under these circumstances, families wish to keep the men at home as a kind of militia. Bilocality also occurs in particular kinds of cultures. Societies that allow a married couple to live with either set of parents have often been recently depopulated by disease. Dramatic population reductions of this sort may mean that one parent or set of parents has died. The flexibility of the bilocal residence means that a particular couple can choose to live with whichever parents have survived (Ember and Ember 1983).

In most cultures around the world, people live in the company of kin. The particular patterning of household differs dramatically from culture to culture, but in all cultures, households are composed of relatives. This means that the most fundamental challenges of living are met with the help of kin. Human beings give and receive food from kin, accept the support of kin in the rearing of their children, go to kin when in need of help, and help kin who are in need. Human beings also treat kin preferentially and are, in turn, treated preferentially by kin. For instance, among the Philippine Ilongot, kin ties regulate all important interactions between people (Rosaldo 1980). Kin hunt together and cooperate in the performance of other subsistence activities. A man who must make a marriage payment receives contributions from his kin. Relatives visit each other, provide each other with food and medical knowledge, take care of one another, and tend each other's children. A man will request help from his nephew because he views the child as his own, and a woman will give a sister rice for her family because sisters should feed each other's children. This pattern of nepotism is captured in the familiar homily that "blood is thicker than water." Just as kin are favored over nonkin, closer kin are favored over those who are more distantly related. None of this is surprising. Biological evolutionary theory suggests that because relatives share genes, they should be disposed to be good to each other; contributing to the survival and reproduction of a blood relative results in the proliferation of genes identical to one's own. This is entirely consistent with the Darwinian claim that animals, including the human animal, act in ways that promote the representation of their own genes in the gene pool of their kind.

In the United States and other Western societies, the idealized kinship customs are monogamous marriage, neolocal residence, nuclear families, incest prohibitions within the nuclear family, bilateral descent, and Eskimo kinship terminology. However, there are often important intrasocietal variations in the overall importance of kinship and kin and specific customs, with the most notable ones involving social class and ethnic variation (Schneider 1973).

See also: AUNT; BRIDE-PRICE; CLAN; COUSINS; DOWRY; EXTENDED FAMILY; FAMILY, DEFINITION OF; FAMILY THEORY; FICTIVE KINSHIP; GENEALOGY; GREENLAND; HUSBAND; INCEST/INBREEDING TABOOS; INDONESIA; IN-LAW RELATIONSHIPS; INTERGENERATIONAL RELATIONS; KENYA; MIGRATION; NAMES FOR CHILDREN; NIGERIA; NUCLEAR FAMILY; PRIMOGENITURE; SIBLING RELATIONSHIPS; TOGO; UNCLE; WIFE

Bibliography

Barnes, J. A. (1971). *Three Styles in the Study of Kinship.* Berkeley: University of California Press.

Broude, G. (1994). *Marriage, Family, and Relationships.* Santa Barbara, CA: ABC-CLIO.

Ember, C., and Ember, M. (1988). *Anthropology,* 5th edition. Englewood Cliffs, NJ: Prentice Hall.

Ember, M., and Ember, C. (1983). *Marriage, Family, and Kinship: Comparative Studies of Social Organization.* New Haven, CT: HRAF Press.

Fox, R. (1967). *Kinship and Marriage.* London: Penguin Books.

Holy, L. (1996). *Anthropological Perspectives on Kinship.* London; Chicago: Pluto Press.

Kroeber, A. L. (1909). "Classificatory Systems of Relationship." *Journal of the Royal Anthropological Institute of Great Britain and Ireland* 39:77–84.

Levinson, D., and Malone, M. J. (1980). *Toward Explaining Human Culture.* New Haven, CT: HRAF Press.

Murdock, G. P. (1949). *Social Structure.* New York: Macmillan.

Parkin, R. (1997). *Kinship: An Introduction to the Basic Concepts.* Oxford, UK: Cambridge, MA.: Blackwell Publishers.

Rosaldo, M. Z. (1980). *Knowledge and Passion: Ilongot Notions of Self and Social Life.* Cambridge, UK: Cambridge University Press.

Schneider, D. M. (1973). *American Kinship: A Cultural Account.* Chicago: University of Chicago Press.

Stephens, W. N. (1963). *The Family in Cross-Cultural Perspective.* New York: Holt, Rinehart and Winston.

GWEN J. BROUDE (1995)
REVISED BY JAMES J. PONZETTI, JR. AND JAMES M. WHITE

KOREA

For centuries, Korea was the Hermit Kingdom, "The Land of the Morning Calm" in Asia, a country that was characterized as closed to the outside world. Nevertheless, throughout Korea's early history, neighboring nations such as China, Mongolia,

TABLE 1

Korean households by type of family

[Percent]

Year	Nuclear family			Extended family		Other family type
	Married couple	Married with children	Single parent with children	Married couple with parents	Married couple with parents and children	
1955	63.5	–	–	30.7	–	2.5
1966	64.7	–	–	20.6	–	12.4
1970	5.4	55.5	10.6	1.4	17.4	9.7
1975	5.0	55.6	0.5	0.5	10.9	17.9
1980	6.5	57.4	0.6	0.6	10.6	14.8
1985	7.8	57.8	9.7	0.8	9.9	14.0
1990	9.4	58.0	8.7	0.9	9.4	13.8
1995	12.6	58.6	8.6	1.1	8.0	11.2

SOURCE: National Statistical Office, Annual Report on Vital Statistics (1982–1997).

and Japan have invaded the country often. The twentieth century also brought Korea tremendous upheaval, such as the Japanese occupation (1910–1945), the Korean War (1950–1953), the partition of the country (1953–present), and the foreign-exchange crisis in 1997. Korea and the Korean family are both in a period of transition.

The concept of the contemporary Korean family dates from the 1960s, a period of transformation that affected the economic and political spheres, as well as cultural patterns and legal affairs. From the end of World War II until the 1960s, Korea experienced great social and economic difficulties such as the Korean war. After the 1960s, Korea began to industrialize rapidly, while also becoming more urban, and since then the Korean economy has grown faster than at any other time in its history. The standard of living has improved significantly: Per capita income rose from $87 in 1962 to $11,380 in 1996, although it dropped to $9,628 in 2000 after the financial crisis of 1997. Few countries have changed economically as rapidly as has Korea.

During these periods, the government made industrialization its top priority. This process brought about urbanization and changes in family type to nuclear families. As a result, the average household changed dramatically, especially the relationships among family members.

Traditional Korean Families

Families were very different among the three historical periods of the Shilla (57 B.C.E.–C.E.

935), Koryo (C.E. 918–1392), and Chosun (C.E. 1392–1910) Dynasties because of their religious orientation.

Buddhism was introduced in Korea during the Early Kingdoms (C.E. 372) and was adopted as the state religion for a millennium. With its emphasis on rejecting worldly values and concerns, including the family, Buddhism delivered a message contrary to that of Confucianism. But Buddhism's influence was limited to the sphere of individual self-enlightenment and discipline, and it appealed principally to the ruling class because the majority of people, who lived at a subsistence level, had few material possessions to renounce. As a result, relatively few people were affected by the self-abnegation and antifamilial monasticism that Buddhism taught (Han 1981; Park and Cho 1995a). The religion's influence declined further during the late Koryo Dynasty (918–1392) when Buddhist groups in Korea became corrupt. They constructed extravagant temples, and followers of the religion observed only superficial rituals (Lee 1973; Hong 1980).

When the Chosun Dynasty succeeded the Koryo in 1392, it adopted Confucianism as the familial and state philosophy, suppressing Buddhism. The term *Confucianism* is used to refer to the popular value system of China, Korea, and Japan. This system is derived from the synthesis of the traditional cultural values espoused by Confucius and his followers and subsequently influenced by elements of Taoism, Legalism, Mohism, Buddhism, and, in the case of Korea and Japan, Shamanism (Park and Cho 1995a). Confucianism declares the family the fundamental unit of society, responsible for the economic functions of production and consumption, as well as education and socialization, guided by moral and ethical principles (Lee 1990; Park and Cho 1995a). In its teachings, Confucianism has traditionally deified ancestors, institutionalized ancestor worship, and delegated the duties of ritual master to the head of the male lineage, that is, to the father and husband. Confucianism is a familial religion (Lee 1990). As Confucianism took hold, the ideal of male superiority within the patrilineal family became more prominent in the late Chosun dynasty than it had been during the early Chosun dynasty (1392–1650) (Park and Cho 1995a).

Values and functions of the family. The family is the basic component of social life in Korea, and its perpetuation has been of paramount importance under patriarchal Confucianism. In a Confucian patriarchal family, the family as an entity takes precedence over its individual members, and the family group is inseparably identified with the clan. The most important function of family members is to maintain and preserve the household within the traditional Confucian system (Lee 1960). Society became organized around two principles: that males shall dominate females and that elders shall dominate the young (Kim 1993). Growing old in Korea had advantages for both women and men, for age was respected. According to this perspective, women were often self-assertive and highly valued, as the family finance managers, decision-makers in family matters, and educators of children (Brandt 1971; Osgood 1951).

Traditionally, the ideal family type in Korea was a patrilocal stem family. The stem family typically consists of two families in successive generation, a father and mother living in the same household with married oldest son, his wife, and their children. The eldest son generally inherited the family estates. The other sons were expected to live in separate residences after their marriages (Cho and Shin 1996). The central familial relationship was not that between husband and wife, but rather between parent and child, especially between father and son. At the same time, the relationships among family members were part of a hierarchy. These relationships were characterized by benevolence, authority, and obedience. Authority rested with the (male) head of the household, and

differences in status existed among the other family members (Park and Cho 1995a).

Marital roles and women's roles. During the Shilla and Koryo period, among commoners, couples entered freely into marriage with their chosen partners (Choi 1971). This changed, however, during the Chosun dynasty; strict rules were imposed on the selection of partners, and all marriages were arranged. *Naehun* (Instruction for Women), compiled by the mother of King Seongjong in 1475, was the most important and influential textbook used to teach proper Confucian roles to girls and married women. The book emphasized the basics of womanly behavior such as chastity, and it prepared girls for their future functions as moral guardians of the domestic sphere and providers for the physical needs of their families. The book also elaborated on a married woman's role, including being a self-sacrificing daughter-in-law, an obedient and dutiful wife, and a wise and caring mother (Kim 1993; Deuchler 1983).

Based on Confucian values, families observed strict gender differentiation in married life. Traditional Korean women's responsibility was restricted to the domestic sphere. As an inside master, the woman established her own authority and became a financial manager, symbolized by the right to carry the family keys to the storage areas for rice and other foods (Kim 1992; Lee 1990). Also, husbands and wives strictly observed a hierarchical relationship. A wife would sacrifice herself completely to serve her husband and family in an exemplary manner. In accordance with the rule of three obediences, a woman was required to obey her father, husband, and son, in that order. Under this system of severe discrimination, women of the Chosun Dynasty were confined to the home. Nevertheless, the position of women, at least those with children, was not hopeless. Just as women occupied a subordinate position in relation to men, children were subordinate to their parents and were required to revere their mothers as well as their fathers (Choi 1982a; Park and Cho 1995a).

Traditionally, Korean society considered divorce and remarriage deviant and problematic family events. Only the husband had the right to divorce his wife; if he did so, she had to be expelled from her family-in-law according to the traditional marital code that held the husband's authority and absolute power to govern his wife. A husband could legally divorce his wife when she committed the following seven faults (*chilchul*); being disobedient to one's parents-in-law; not giving birth to a son; committing adultery; expressing jealousy of the concubine; contracting a serious illness; and being garrulous or thievish.

Three exceptions (*sambulgeo*), however, prohibited a husband from expelling a wife who committed the above faults: The husband was not allowed to divorce his wife if she spent more than a three-year mourning period for her parents-in-law; if she had no place to return after the divorce; or if she married in poverty and contributed to the wealth and the social position of the family. The woman was forced to serve the husband's family after her husband died. Thus, people blamed remarried women for denigrating the reputation of their kin as well as themselves. Although a husband could not divorce under these circumstances, he could make an alternative arrangement. If, for example, a wife bore no son, it was common for the couple to adopt one or for the husband to keep a concubine.

It was customary for a man seeking remarriage to select a spinster from a lower-class family, because women who had been married before were socially unacceptable. Also, according to the patriarchal norm, Korean women were socialized to break their relationships with birth families and be thoroughly absorbed into families-in-law, and to assimilate their traditions. This meant that a woman whose first marriage was to a previously married man occupied a very humble position. These women were likely to want their own children to insure marital stability and secure their own position in the family.

Parent-child relationships. One of the most important doctrines of Confucianism was the requirement that children be dutiful to their parents. Filial piety has been the highest moral principle of the parent-child relationship and has greatly influenced the Korean family system. It guided the socialization of children enforced the moral rule that adult children should obey and serve their elderly parents and to repay them for their work as parents by looking after them for the rest of their lives (Chung and Yoo 2000). Thus, the stem family began to be considered an ideal type.

But what constituted filial behavior changed from the Shilla to the Chosun Dynasty. In *Samganghangsil,* the most important expression of filial

TABLE 2

Traditional concepts of filial piety of Shilla, Koryo, and Chosun

[Frequencies, percent]

Category of filial piety	Shilla	Koryo	Chosun
Support and material services	3 (75)	5 (8.1)	55 (8.1)
Nursing	1 (25)	8 (12.9)	279 (41.2)
Self-sacrifice	0 (0)	11 (17.7)	136 (20.1)
Funeral services and worship	0 (0)	38 (61.3)	207 (30.6)
Total cases(percent)	4 (100)	62 (100)	677 (100)

SOURCE: H. Chung and K. Yoo. (2000). *Filial Piety and the New Generation in Korea.*

piety during the Shilla Dynasty was supporting the material needs of elderly parents. In contrast, in the Koryo and Chosun periods, filial piety was best demonstrated in formal and ritual services, such as funeral services and worship in the Koryo and nursing in the Chosun period (see Table 2). In particular, nothing was as important as worshiping of the spirits of one's ancestors as well as one's parents in the period of Chosun (Chung and Yoo 2000).

Contemporary Korean Families

The tremendous demographic changes, as well as changes in the family makeup itself, make it very hard to grasp the characteristics of the contemporary Korean family. Korea's traditional culture, including its religious heritage, was seriously undermined during Japan's colonial rule of Korea (1910–45) and during the Korean War (1950–53). Further complicating the question, since the 1960s, within a single generation, Korea has been transformed from an agrarian to an industrialized urban society. The adoption of not only Western science and technology, but also Western culture, has played a decisive role in bringing about this transformation. Swept into the country on the tides of westernization, industrialization, and economic development, Protestantism has taken root and expanded its reach (Park and Cho 1995a; Yoon 1964). All of these societal forces have transformed the traditional value system and demographic characteristics of Korean families.

Population and household composition. The industrialization of the 1960s accelerated the regional relocation of the population. The urban population has grown from 28 percent of the total population in 1960 to 74 percent in 1990 and to 81 percent in

TABLE 3

Korean households by type and average size
[Percent]

	One generation	Two generations	Three generations	More than four generations	Single household	Households w/ unrelated persons	Average size of household
1955	–	–	–	–	3.2	–	–
1966	7.5	64.0	26.9	1.6	–	–	5.5
1970	6.8	70.0	22.1	1.1	0.0	0.0	5.2
1975	7.0	71.9	20.1	1.0	4.2	0.0	5.0
1980	9.0	74.2	17.8	0.6	4.8	1.5	4.5
1985	10.5	73.3	15.8	0.5	6.9	1.7	4.1
1990	12.0	74.1	13.6	0.3	9.0	1.5	3.7
1995	14.7	73.7	11.4	0.2	12.7	1.4	3.3

SOURCE: Korean National Statistical Office, Annual Report on Vital Statistics (1982–1997).

2000 (KNSO 2000). Since 1945, the number of households has constantly increased, but the average number of people per household has decreased from 5.7 in 1960, to 4.5 in 1980, 4.16 in 1985, 3.77 in 1990, and 3.34 in 1995. During the same period, the difference in average family size between urban and rural areas disappeared because of changes in the nuclear family and the increase in the number households consisting of a single person.

Since 1960, the number of nuclear families in rural areas increased more rapidly than it did in urban areas because young rural adults migrated into cities (KNSO 1970, 1980, 1995). In particular, the increase in life expectancy and decrease in filial responsibility led to more elderly people (over sixty-five) living by themselves, an increase of 16.0 percent between 1990 and 1995. The elderly represented 7.1 percent of Korea's population in 2000 (KNSO 2000).

Families with two generations cohabiting comprised 73.7 percent of the total population in 1995 (see Table 2). The number of households that consisted of childless married couples increased (see Table 3). At the same time, the percentage of stem families, three-generation families cohabiting, decreased. Thus, the traditional extended family system is changing to that of the conjugal family composed of a couple and their children.

But this phenomenon does not mean that Korean nuclear family is seen as an ideological construct (Chang 1997). Because the Korean people still cherish the ideal image of the extended family, modified nuclear families are more popular in reality. Economic factors also play a role (Kweon 1998). A strong discrepancy, then, is evident be-

tween the ideal images of the extended family, commonly cherished by Korean people, and the actual reality of Korean families.

Fertility. During this same period, the birth rate in Korea dropped. This drop is explained by a massive family-planning program by the government that began in 1962, more women pursuing higher education, and more women working outside the home. In 2000, the college and university enrollment was 60.7 percent of women and 99.1 percent of men of college age (Ministry of Education 2000). Because of all these factors, the total fertility rate (the number of children a woman has if her childbearing rate follows national averages) has decreased to 1.4 in 1999 from 2.7 in 1980 and 6.0 in 1960.

Even as the fertility rate dropped, the sex ratio at birth showed unique features. In patriarchal societies, more male children are born. This demographic trend may be due to the societal preference for sons over daughters, which pressures couples to produce children until they have more sons than daughters. For example, the sex ratio at birth was 109.5 men per 100 women in 1970, reached a record high in 1995 of 113.2, and decreased to 109.6 in 1999. Still higher ratios have been reported from large cities such as Taegu and Pusan (Park and Cho 1995b). Moreover, the number of males born increases with the number of conceptions. From this perspective, Larson, Chung, and Gupta (1998) pointed out, even though the total fertility rate is declining, preference of male offspring and patriarchy are strong predictors of second, third, and fourth conceptions.

Marriage, divorce, and remarriage rates. Today, customs governing marriage have changed dra-

FIGURE 1

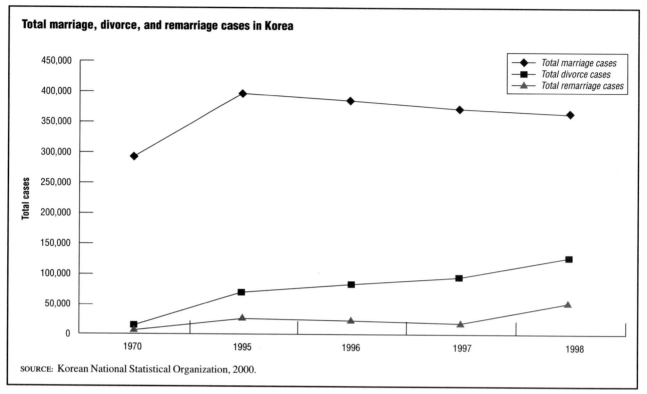

Total marriage, divorce, and remarriage cases in Korea

SOURCE: Korean National Statistical Organization, 2000.

matically. Young women and men mingle freely in parks and on the street, and far fewer parents choose mates for their children (Lee 1997). More and more people are postponing marriage, and the marriage rate is decreasing (see Figure 1). The average age of marriage for women in 1999 was 26.3 years; for men it was 29.1 years, higher than at any previous time. Comparing these figures to those of 1980 shows a very rapid increase; at that time, the ages were 24.1 and 27.3, respectively. These facts reflect the higher educational attainment of women and their increased participation in the job market.

From 1948, when the democratic consitution was adopted, in Korea divorce has been based on fault, or the assessment of blame against one of the spouses. Typically, both partners would be accused of committing adultery, desertion, or physical and mental cruelty; other grounds were cruel and inhuman treatment by in-laws, abandonment for two or more years, or long imprisonment for a felony. Thus, the changing pattern of divorce and remarriage can be seen as a symbol of a changing Confucian tradition.

After 1911, the earliest year for which statistics are available, Korea witnessed a steadily increasing

divorce rate except for the years from 1946 to 1966, a period that included the Korean War and post-World War II industrialization. Since the 1970s, the crude divorce rate has increased significantly every ten years, almost doubling from 0.67 per 1,000 population in 1970, to 1.16 in 1980 and again to 2.6 in 1999 (NSO 2000; see figure 2).

Divorce patterns in recent years have changed in several ways. First, the average duration of a marriage was 10.1 years in 1998 because of an increase in the number of couples who remained married for more than fifteen years. Second, divorce increased with 1997 financial crisis; in more cases, both parties agreed to part because of financial problems. Third, couples now divorce less often because of conflict with kin and more often for marital incompatibility. This suggests that conjugal ties have become more crucial in maintaining a marriage, while the traditional kin relationships have declined in importance (Chung and Yoo 1999).

Social changes such as alternatives to traditional marriage, the declining stigma attached to divorce, and the rising standard for happiness in marriage have occurred in Korea. Women's growing independence, the product of feminist ideas and employment outside the home, have significantly contributed to a continued rise in the divorce rate.

As the divorce rate rose, so did the number of remarriages, a figure that has grown continuously since the 1970s (Figure 1). Remarriage, however, has also changed (Figure 3). The proportion of men who married a woman who had never been married, the dominant remarriage type until the 1980s, has dropped from 48.2 percent in 1970 to 34.4 percent in 1998. During the same period, the proportion of remarriages in which both parties were remarrying for the second time increased from 41.2 percent to 52.2 percent. And the proportion also increased of women who had been married before and married, for their second marriage, men who had not been married before; these grew from 10.6 percent to 25.8 percent during the same period (KNSO 1999). Korean society thus seems more accepting of the egalitarian remarriage norm and less prone to traditional attitudes that discriminated against women. The change is not universal; some of the traditional negative images of remarried families still strongly persist in Korean society (Leem 1996; Yoo et al. 1998).

Women's Labor Force Participation

One of the biggest changes from the past is the increasing number of women in the work force.

Dual-income families, in which both partners work either in full time or part time, now represent 60 percent of families in Korea (KNSO 1997). Since 1987, the number of married women who were employed outside the home has exceeded the number of employed unmarried women.

These figures do not reflect the complete picture. Although most working women take jobs out of economic necessity (Korean Women's Development Center 2000; KNSO 2000), their contributions are not valued because men still play authoritarian roles in the family. In addition, the greatest cause of stress for employed women is society's expectation that they have complete responsibility for the raising of children. Women experience conflict about their dual roles and also feel overload of roles (Chung 1997; Ha and Kim 1996; Kim and Kim 1994; Ko 1994). The double standard continues in Korean society. Although Korean husbands prefer working wives (*Chungang Daily,* March 15, 1989), 26 percent of women office workers are forced to resign their jobs upon marriage (*Choson Daily,* January 9, 1991). Although many young husbands want working wives because they contribute to the family's finances, these same husbands still regard their wives' work as part-time. Although women's labor force participation rates are increasing, the reality is that most of housework and the rearing of children are left to women in Korean households (Chung 1997; Kim 1999).

FIGURE 2

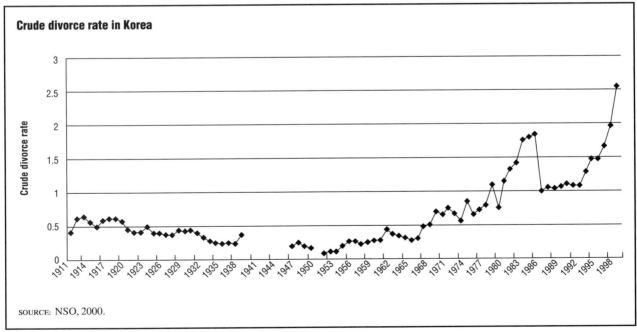

SOURCE: NSO, 2000.

FIGURE 3

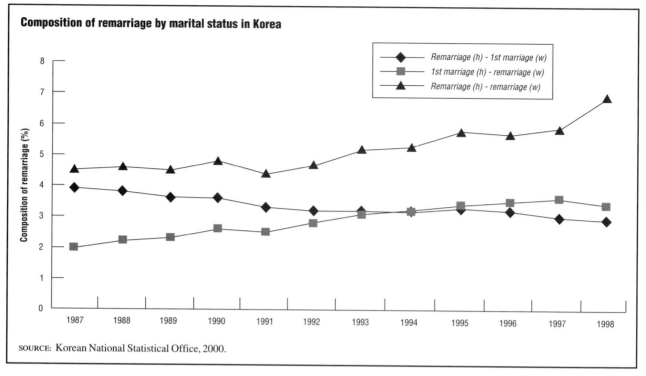

Composition of remarriage by marital status in Korea

SOURCE: Korean National Statistical Office, 2000.

Conclusion

Significant changes have occurred in recent times to the structure and dynamics of family life in Korea, yet some of the old patterns persist. In terms of structure, Korean families are very similar to those of Western countries. But Koreans' attitudes differ greatly from those of Westerners because of the society's dualistic mentality. For instance, Korean society includes both progressive and conservative trends, coexisting with the Western and Asian mentalities; a dual class system with the emergence of the middle and the poor classes alongside a very powerful rich class; a division among the generations, as with individualism of the younger generations nurtured on Western culture and the traditional patriarchy of older generations; and a duality between family centered on the relationships of couples and children and society composed of collective families centered on adults. Finally, Korean society shows discrepancies between action and mindset. Although many Koreans have a Western mentality, their actions reflect a very conservative tendency, which grows even more pronounced with age (Chung 1999). The Korean family is in transition, and one result of these opposing forces is confusion.

Despite these changes, family laws and policies in Korea still represent the traditional value systems in many aspects. Countering this have been recent movements toward improving individual and women's rights. The family law reform in 1991, for example, included an asset partition claim right for women and visitation rights for noncustodial parents. Also, new family law entitles a divorced woman to a share of the couple's property based on the extent of her contribution to it. Furthermore, custody of the children, which used to be automatically awarded to the father upon divorce, will now be decided in court. Drastic changes in the property inheritance system include eliminating discrimination against daughters. When her husband dies, a childless widow will be entitled to half of the inheritance, with the other half going to the husband's parents. The law was abolished that prohibited a woman's remarriage until six months after the end of a former marriage. However, the new family law does not completely abolish the controversial head-of-the-family system, which Confucians lobbied to preserve. More political and legal support is needed for the welfare of elderly and children, as well as for types of families that remain in the minority, such as singles, homosexuals, and remarried couples.

See also: ASIAN-AMERICAN FAMILIES; BUDDHISM; CONFUCIANISM; ETHNIC VARIATION/ETHNICITY

Bibliography

Brandt, S. J. (1971). *A Korean Village: Between Farm and Sea.* Seoul: Prospect Heights.

Cha, J-S. (1978). *A Study of Value Formation about Family Among College Students in Korea.* Seoul: Research Institute of Human Development, Ehwa Woman's University.

Chang, K-S. (1997). "The Neo-Confucian Right and Family Policies in Korea: The Nuclear Family as an Ideological Construct." *Economy and Society* 1:22–42.

Cho, B. E., and Shin, H-Y. (1996). "State of Family Research and Theory." *Marriage and Family Review* 22:101–135.

Choi, C-M. (1989). "The Confusion of Moral Values in Contemporary Society: A Way to Overcome This Confusion for the Believer." In *The Confusion in Ethics and Value in Contemporary Society and Possible Approaches to Redefinition.* Seoul: Christian Academy.

Choi, J-S. (1964). "The Pre-Modern Family Consciousness in Modern Korea." *Journal of Korean Academy* 4:1–18.

Choi, J-S. (1971). "Traditional Value Consciousness of Korean Families." *Asea Yungu* 14:19–41.

Choi, J-S. (1982). *Studies of Modern Families.* Seoul: Iljisa.

Choi, S-J. (1996). "The Family and Ageing in Korea: A New Concern and Challenge." *Ageing and Society* 16:1–25.

Chung, H. (1997). "Parenting Stress and Marital Satisfaction among Dual-Earner Families." *Journal of Korean Home Economics Association* 35:151–162.

Chung, H., and Yoo, K. (2000). "Filial Piety and the New Generation in Korea." Paper presented at the 62nd Annual Conference of National Council of Family Relations, Minneapolis, Minnesota.

Deuchler, M. (1983). "The Tradition: Women During the Yi Dynasty." In *Korean Women: View from the Inner Room,* ed. L. Kendall and M. Peterson. Cusing, ME: East Rock Press.

Ha, H-S, and D-S Kim. (1996). "A Study on the Relationships Between Role Conflict and Psychological Physical Distress of Dual-Earner Couples." *Journal of the Korean Home Economics Association* 34:309–326.

Han, S. B. (1981). *Modern Buddhism and Social Science.* Seoul: Dongkuk University Press.

Hong, Y. S. (1980). *Buddhism and Folk Religion.* Seoul: Dongkuk University Press.

Kim, J. M. (1992). "Patriarchal Disclosure and Power in Ritual and Daily Life: A Study of Damni Village in Korean's Honam Region." Ph.D. dissertation. Seoul: Seoul National University.

Kim, M. H. (1993). "Transformation of Family Ideology in Upper-Middle-Class Families in Urban South Korea." *Ethnology* 32:69–86.

Kim, S., and Kim, D. (1994). "An Effect of Cohesion and Adaptability on Role Conflicts of Dual Earner Couples." *Journal of the Korean Home Economics Association* 32:121–134.

Ko, J. J. (1994). "A Study on the Family Resources, the Level of Stress Recognition and Distress of Dual-Earner Families." *Journal of the Korean Home Economics Association* 32:97–116.

Korean Institute for Health and Social Affairs. (1998). *Health and Welfare Indicators in Korea.* Seoul: Korea Institute for Health and Social Affairs.

Korean National Statistical Office. (1970, 1975, 1980, 1985, 1990, 1995). *Population and Housing Census Report.* Seoul: Korean National Statistical Office.

Korean National Statistical Office. (1982, 1987, 1992, 1997). *Annual Report on the Vital Statistics.* Seoul: Korean National Statistical Office.

Korean National Statistical Office. (1999, 2000). *Social Indicators in Korea.* Seoul: Korean National Statistical Office.

Korean National Statistical Office. (1999, 2000). *Annual Report on Live Births and Deaths Statistics.* Seoul: Korean National Statistical Office.

Korean National Statistical Office. (1999). *Report on the Social Statistics Survey.* Seoul: Korean National Statistical Office.

Korean National Statistical Office. (1999). *Population Vital Statistics.* Seoul: Korean National Statistical Office.

Korean Women's Development Center. (2000). *Statistical Year Book on Women.*

Kweon, S-I. (1998). "The Extended Family in Contemporary Korea: Changing Patterns of Co-residence." *Korea Journal* 38:178–209.

Larson, U.; Chung, W.; and Gupta, M. D. (1998). "Fertility and Son Preference in Korea." *Population Studies* 52:317–326.

Lee H-J. (1960). *Family and Culture.* Seoul: Minhosa.

Lee, H-S. (1997). "Factors of Changing in Mate Selection Process." *Journal of the Korean Family Studies Association* 9:1–28.

Lee, K-K. (1990). *Korean Family and Religion*. Seoul: Minumsa.

Lee, K-K. (1990). *Structural Analysis of Korean Families*. Seoul: Iljisa

Lee, K-Y. (1973). *Buddhism and the Culture*. Seoul: Korean Institute for Buddhism Research Press.

Leem, C. (1996). "A Qualitative Study on the Stepmother's Stress and Adaptation to Her Stepfamily." Unpublished doctoral dissertation, Korea University, Seoul.

Osgood, C. (1951). *The Koreans and Their Culture*. New York: Ronald Press.

Park, C., and Cho, N. (1995). "Consequences of a Son Preference in a Low-Fertility Society: Imbalance of the Sex Ratio at Birth in Korea." *Population and Development Review* 21:59–84.

Park, I. H., and Cho, L-J. (1995a). "Confucianism and the Korean Family." *Journal of Comparative Family Studies* 26:117–134.

Yoo, G.; Leem, C.; Chun, C.; and Chun, H. (1998). *Another We, the Remarried Family: A Study on the Current State of Remarried Families and Development of Remarriage Preparation Program*. Seoul: Korean Institute of Family Counseling and Education.

Yoon, M. (1964). *Christianity and Korean Philosophy*. Seoul: Hankukgidokgyoseohae.

HYUNSOOK CHUNG

KURDISH FAMILIES

Kurdish traditions and languages distinguish Kurds from other ethnic groups in that they live within numerous linguistically homogeneous nation-states. Kurdish communities are divided by the borders of Iran, Iraq, Syria, and Turkey, and many Kurds also live in various diasporas in Europe. Although it is debated, some historians trace the origins of Kurds to the Medes. Kurds speak different but related dialects of Kurdish, a member of the Indo-European language group. Kurdish communities are affected by changes in the global capitalist system and by mass migrations due to economic and political pressures. While they struggle against countervailing cultural pressures, their old traditions are continuously revitalized and some are modified to reflect changing circumstances and outside pressures.

Kurdish Family and Households

A traditional Kurdish family is a peasant family. A Kurdish household is a patrilineal lineage, assembled around the male head of the family. Such a lineage depends on mutual support and defense while living in the same ancestral village. Although men are responsible for agricultural tasks and socioeconomic and political contacts with the outside world, Kurdish women also contribute to all social, economic, and political processes within their villages. The Kurdish household is a corporate entity whether the extended family lives under the same roof, *xani,* or breaks into nuclear family sub-units—consisting of mother, father, and their children—in the family compound. During their trans-humance—a seasonal movement organized around the migration of livestock from lowland winter to highland summer pastures—seminomadic pastoralist households may share a tent, live in a compound of tents, or both. The compound is called *zoma.* The extended Kurdish family includes not only parents and unmarried children, but also married male children, their wives, and their offspring. Unmarried sisters and brothers of the male head of the family may also live with them.

According to Kurdish traditions, marriage does not bring with it the creation of a new household. Kurdish traditions oblige the oldest brother and his wife and children to remain with his parents. As family resources expand, married younger brothers build their own houses and move into them, gradually enlarging the family compound. Household production refers to the production of all members of the family compound. The main building, the home for those members of the kin group who share a residence, is referred to as *mal.* All consumption activities take place in *mal.* The extended family continues to have meals together in the *mal,* even after younger sons move to their own houses within it. This is also the case for seminomadic pastoralists. Pastoralist households are united in their village compounds during some seasons and may be cyclically divided between pasture camps when they move to higher plateaus during the summer months.

A Kurdish household is a unit where production, reproduction, distribution, and consumption take place. *Mal* is an economic unit for about thirty million Kurds in the Middle East. *Mal* is also very important for urban families in transition and for diaspora families. Not only the first, but often the transitional second generation of migrant families in urban areas replicate this pattern. However, with the creation of permanent wage labor, young modernized urban families both challenge and reiterate traditional arrangements. They may independently decide not to pool their income with their extended families, while insisting on their traditional rights to resources, such as their share from the harvest and animals.

For hundreds of years, Kurdish households have relied on a broad range of economic activities to generate income. Within households in Kurdistan, noncapitalist forms of labor exchanges (reciprocal labor exchanges) transform all daily activities—agricultural work, animal husbandry, daily chores, and preparations for weddings and other celebrations. Intrahousehold exchanges expand to encompass interhousehold exchanges with kin who are living in the same villages and hamlets. A traditional form of reciprocal labor exchange, called *zebari* or *zebare,* is recognized as an obligation to be fulfilled between kin and neighbors, even in urban contexts. Another form of labor exchange, also called *zebari,* is a form of forced labor. Tribal Kurds are obliged to work for their tribal leaders and landlords. While fulfilling *zebari* obligations, men work in agriculture for a limited time, but the duration of women's work in the houses of their tribal leaders or landlords is never specifically defined.

Historically, most peasant Kurdish households occupy multiple class positions as merchants and petty producers, and according to their participation in capitalist relations as wage laborers. From the 1950s onward, the development of wage relations was tied to the monetization of the rural economy and was closely correlated with a household's access to land. Today, the families of seasonal workers continue to live in rural areas while their men return home for cultivation and harvest. Permanent wage employment is particularly important for urban Kurdish families. The jobs available for unskilled urban Kurds are in the construction industry and the service sector is attracting a growing number of Kurdish women as well as men. Successful urbanized families responding to socioeconomic changes are gaining a greater ability to live independently from rural, social, and economic networks and are distancing themselves from rural obligations.

For almost all Kurds—Sunni (Shafiis), Shii (Twelvers), Alevi (*Ahl-el* Haqqs), and Yezidi (a heterodox sect occurring only among Kirmanchi-speaking Kurds)—household relations define gender relations. Kurdish households have both a male, *malxî,* and female head, *kabanî,* with clearly defined duties concerning production, distribution, and consumption allocations. There are gender and intergenerational inequalities in patriarchal Kurdish households. In rural households, with the exception of female heads of households, women have a subordinate role in household decision-making. However, they are able to exercise power by negotiating with patriarchal structures, especially by choosing to socially isolate themselves from family affairs, thereby publicly damaging the reputation of the family. The women of seminomadic pastoral tribes enjoy privileges that allow them to be nominal equals with their husbands. Peasant women's engagement in wage labor in urban settings weakens the old patriarchal traditions and allows women to have decision-making power in their households.

Kurdish Marriage Patterns

Kurdish marriage arrangements are very complex and defined by tribal traditions. Almost all Kirmanji-, Sorani-, Zaza-, and Gorani-speaking Kurds are historically tribal people, and tribal traditions continue to affect the daily experiences of tribal, as well as nontribal Kurds, who live in both rural and urban areas. The term *mal* also means a lineage in Kurdish. A lineage is a group of people who descend from a common ancestor. According to tribal ideology, brothers, father, and sons are joined in a single group, creating a division within the tribe against the father's brother and his sons. They all unite against far removed patriarchal cousins. Although a tribe is segmented genealogically, all of the units described above are united as patrilineal kin against another tribe at times of conflict, such as blood feuds. Tribal membership exists both in terms of putative patrilineal kin groups (groups that trace their genealogy to a common ancestor of the main branch of the tribe) and fictive patrilineal kinship groups (groups created in circumstances when an individual was adopted as a tribal member; lineages are traced from this adopted individual). However, tribal kinship is described bilaterally (traced through both male and

Kurdish households may have both a male and female head, with separate family obligations. Kurdish traditions are being modified by outside forces, including global capitalism. ED KASHI/CORBIS

female lines). Kurdish kinship terminology consists of two categories: kin relations traced through blood (consanguine) and through marriage (affinal) relations. In each category, terms are very specific for ascending and descending generations; the categories define patrilineal kin and female affine, as well as social relations. Yezidi traditions are similar to the traditions of Muslim Kurds, yet are differentiated by the existence of social categories: *sheihks, peshimams, pirs, kawals,* and *faqirs.* These categories clearly define social, political, and economic positions, as well as responsibilities of these individuals within Yezidi societies.

Marriage is one of the most important events for establishing alliances and creating social hierarchies within and between tribes. Upon marriage, a woman leaves her birth homestead and moves to her husband's village. Traditionally, a woman did not move away from the territory of her lineage since most marriages were within the lineage where members live a short distance away. However, urban migration and diaspora relations resulted in contemporary marriages in which women

not only move from their paternal homes, but frequently cross national borders. Traditionally, Kurdish marriages are arranged marriages. Marriage arrangements may be completed even before children are born. For boys and girls, marriage establishes the passage to adulthood. The marriageable age of male and female children varies according to socioeconomic class and the specific needs of individual families. The average age for marriage increases in urban areas, where the parties involved are usually educated and employed. Although the marriage age of boys is slightly higher than girls, this depends on various social and economic strategies of households. Generally, girls' marriages are postponed when there is a labor shortage in the family. However, they may be given in marriage at an early age to settle a dispute in a case of kidnapping, taking an unmarried girl by force to marry against her will. That is, if a son of family *A* kidnaps a girl from family *B*, the resulting dispute between the two families can't be settled unless family *A* gives a girl to family *B*. The possibilities of both eloping and kidnapping also contribute to the desire to arrange early marriages for girls. Although kidnapping and eloping are relatively rare, both cause a social disruption and require mediation between lineages and families to recover from social and economic damages. These events highlight certain aspects of Kurdish family traditions.

Historically, tribal endogamy—the obligation to marry within the tribe—is followed in Kurdish marriages. Yezidi marriages similarly follow strict endogamy within well-defined social categories. Yezidi traditions do not allow marriages between the families of *sheihks, peshimams, pirs, kawals,* and *faqirs.* According to Kurdish traditions, a man has the right to marry his paternal uncle's daughter. Any arrangement contrary to this rule must be negotiated between the two brothers. Therefore, for all Kurds the preferred form of marriage is with patrilateral cousins (the children of siblings of the same sex, FBD/FBS—father's brother's daughter and son) while cross-cousin (the children of the siblings of opposite sex, FZD/FZS—father's sister's daughter and son) marriages are rarely practiced. The lineage endogamy is secured by marrying a first parallel cousin, and if this is not possible, a second or a more distant patrilateral cousin. The patrilateral cousins' marriage keeps property in the family and reinforces patriarchal and tribal solidarity.

Marriages are often arranged in the form of direct exchanges, *pê-guhurk.* Direct exchange marriages are made if one household head, who gives a daughter to another one as a wife for their son, demands a wife in return. The most common form of a direct exchange between two households is sister exchange. In rare cases, marriages are arranged between three families: family *A* gives a daughter to family *B,* family *B* gives a daughter to family *C,* and family *C* completes the circle of exchange by giving a daughter to family *A.* Direct wife and sister exchanges eliminate the payment of bride-price in marriages.

In Kurdistan, a widowed woman stays with her husband's family. If she is widowed when her children are young, she is obliged to marry her deceased husband's brother. This form of marriage is called *levirate. Sororate* is another custom: When a man loses his wife before she bears a child or she dies leaving young children, her lineage provides another wife to the man, usually a younger sister with a lowered bride-price. Both levirate and sororate are practiced to guarantee the well being of children and ensure that any inheritance of land will stay within the family.

Most Kurdish marriages are monogamous marriages. However, Islam allows polygynous marriages; a man may have as many as four wives at one time providing that he fulfills his obligations as prescribed in Islam. Although statistically rare, polygynous marriages are practiced by Kurdish men who have high economic and political status or claim to have such status. Patriarchal ideology justifies these marriages by emphasizing the Islamic prescription that asserts that social harmony will develop between wives who share household chores and childcare. In reality, polygyny complicates social relations between the members of extended households.

Bride-price is called *naxt* in Kurdish. It is given to the family of the bride at the time of betrothal or may be paid in increments until the wedding ceremony. It is paid in cash and gold and may include gifts to the bride and her family, the expenses of the wedding ceremony, a rifle, a revolver, jewelry, household goods, electronic equipment, and hoofed animals. The wedding expenses, including the bride-price and the construction and preparation of a room for the marrying couple, may be as much as one year's income for an average household. The amount of the bride-price varies according to the wealth and social standing of the groom's family. However, the bride-price is decreased if the marriage is an FBD/FBS marriage. The bride does not claim any of the bride-price. Generally, most fathers of young sons use the bride-price, which they receive from their daughter's marriages, to pay the family providing a bride for their sons. Fathers of young women are expected to prepare a trousseau and a dowry, which may include jewelry and livestock, for their marrying daughters. *Kaleb* or *sirdan,* so-called milk money, is not negotiated between families; rather, it is courteously presented to the mother of the bride, generally in the form of gold jewelry, for her loss of a daughter and a laborer.

Traditionally, peasant weddings include everyone living in the village of the groom and involve elaborate ceremonies. Most able members of the village contribute to wedding preparations in different ways. The wedding ceremonies may last several days. Following proper rules of conduct, a newly married couple avoids being in the same room with the groom's father for close to a week, although they are living in the same house. It is only after this period of prohibition that a bride can visit her parents to receive their blessings.

The preference for FBD/FBS marriages is one of the reasons why young men and women choose to elope. In urban areas, some young girls negotiate to marry a young man they choose by threatening their parents with the possibility of eloping. In both rural and urban areas, kidnapping may also be considered as an attempt on the part of young people to undermine this patriarchal imposition. Eloping and kidnapping also eliminate the problems of paying a high bride-price for the Kurds, but not for the Yezidis. Both eloping and kidnapping bring shame to families. However, kidnapping may have far more serious consequences. It may result in interlineage and intertribal feuds, since it is believed that the woman's *honor* is stained; she is no longer considered a virgin, and can't be returned to her family.

Traditionally, blood feuds are intertribal affairs. When a Kurd is murdered by someone from another tribe, not only the lineage of the dead man, but the whole tribe comes together for an extrajuridical form of punishment, usually provoking countermeasures that lead to escalated tribal warfare. Settlement between the tribes can be a lengthy process and is pursued until an agreement is reached about the payment of blood money, *bezh,* to the relatives of the victim. Blood feuds are more widespread in Northern Kurdistan than in other parts of Kurdistan, and incidents of it are decreasing as the power of tribal leaders decreases.

Among Muslim Kurds, despite the *sharia,* Islamic law, and civil inheritance laws where applicable, and among Yezidis, women are not given property, including land, pastures, houses, and livestock, as their inheritances. In addition, FBD/FBS marriages guarantee the continuity of patriarchal domination; it is less likely that her husband will support a woman's right to claim her inheritance. However, in urban areas, education, employment opportunities and nontraditional marriage arrangements situate women in more powerful positions to demand their legal inheritances.

Every birth in a Kurdish family is recognized with joy. In rural households, mothers do not discipline their children in the presence of their in-laws. Generally, breastfeeding continues until the baby is two years old. Although toddlers receive excessive care, as they grow up to understand the world around them, they also recognize that seniority is the organizing principle in Kurdish households. Children are expected to be obedient and submissive to their elders. Traditionally, they do not contest the decisions of the parents.

Sibling bonds, especially between sisters and brothers, are very strong among the Kurds. Brother-sister ties continue after her marriage. This bond guarantees the well being of the sister in her husband's household. In exchange, it secures the brother's right to keep all inherited property. Despite tribal ideology and the segmentary model, FBSs are usually close friends. Conflicts between the two of them, especially related to the division of landed property, are generally managed by the elder's mediation within village life. Cross-cousins (MBSs/MSSs) also usually have a close relationship and most often invest in trading activities together. Kurds are very clear in defining how close their relatives are with specific terms and references. The *distance* and the *closeness* of the kin are also strategically defined in terms of establishing ties with individuals who may be profitable to have as familial contacts. Kurds develop close relationships with their non-Kurdish neighbors through a mechanism called *tirib* relationships.

Circumcision is an important rite of passage in a man's life. Most boys are circumcised between the ages of six and ten. Kurds select a *tirib* from their neighbors who will comfort the young boy during his circumcision, with the hope that the two will have a lifelong relationship. Yezidis have a similar custom, selecting a Muslim man as *karif* or *kiniv* for the young boy, forming a blood-brotherhood between the two.

See also: IRAN; ISLAM; TURKEY

Bibliography

Ahmetbeyzade, C. (2000). "Kurdish Nationalism in Turkey and the Role of Peasant Kurdish Women." In *Gender Ironies of Nationalism: Sexing the Nation,* ed. T. Mayer. London and New York: Routledge.

Guest, J. (1987). *The Yezidis: A Study in Survival.* London and New York: KPI.

Gunter, M. (1990). *The Kurds in Turkey: A Political Dilemma.* Boulder, CO: Westview Press.

Izadi, M. (1992). *The Kurds: A Concise Handbook.* Washington, DC: Crane Russak.

Keyenbroek, P., and Allison, C., eds. (1996). *Kurdish Culture and Identity*. London: Zed Books.

Keyenbroek, P., and Sperl, S., eds. (1992). *The Kurds: Contemporary Overview*. London: Routledge.

Meiselas, S. (1997). *Kurdistan: In the Shadow of History*. New York: Random House.

Olson, R. (1989). *The Emergence of Kurdish Nationalism 1880–1925*. Austin: University of Texas Press.

Van Bruinessen, M. (1992). *Agha, Shaikh and State: The Social and Political Structures of Kurdistan*. London: Zed Books.

Yalçin-Heckmann, L. (1991). *Tribe and Kinship among the Kurds*. Frankfurt: Peter Lang.

MIHRI İNAL ÇAKIR

KYRGYZSTAN

The Kyrgyz Republic gained its independence from the Soviet Union in 1991. Since then, the family law of the former Kyrgyz Soviet Socialist Republic (KSSR) remains in effect. With the transition to a market economy that began in 1991, Kyrgyz children and families face many new social and economic problems. Independence brought a significant revival of Islamic tradition, especially in the south. These changes have brought with them a need to reform family law.

The evolution of Kyrgyz family law can be divided into three periods: The first was the time before the 1917 Russian Revolution. The second began with the family law reforms instituted in 1917. The third commenced in 1991, when Kyrgyz Republic achieved its independence from the Soviet Union, and prevails through the beginning of the twenty-first century.

Prerevolutionary Period

It is impossible to understand the role of the family in the Kyrgyz Republic without studying family relations in Kyrgyzstan in the second half of the nineteenth and beginning of the twentieth centuries. During this period, family law combined customary law, the norms of Muslim law, and the law of the Russian Empire. The three were interconnected, influenced each other, and contradicted each other. None of the three systems was dominant.

Customary, or traditional, law is a set of unwritten norms produced over a long period of time, regulating all kinds of activity and having a binding character. In Kyrgyzstan, the sources of customary law are custom (*adapt* or *urp*), the practice of courts (*biilerdin bytymy*), and the written decisions of the Congress of Judges (*Ereje*). Customary law was passed from generation to generation by word of mouth. Within this tradition, the standards of family law and inheritance varied among districts. In the south, customary law was strongly influenced by Muslim law. At the same time, traditional laws changed constantly as a region's economic relations developed and evolved.

In traditional Kyrgyz culture, almost all marriages are arranged, with the purpose of forming alliances between clans. Women, upon marriage, become part of the husband's clan; their status within the family depends on the number of male children they bear and their skills in performing their duties as wife, mother, and daughter-in-law. The pre-Soviet Kyrgyzs had no tradition of veiling or seclusion. Polygamy was common.

The oral folklore of the Kyrgyz people has its roots in ancient times; its prehistory remains alive in the legendary *Manas* epos (or body of traditional poems and stories on the same theme). *Manas* is an original encyclopedia for study of the customs, traditions, beliefs, and the worldview of the Kyrgyz people. As the historian V.V. Radlov notes, the epos, as a document of Kyrgyz history, presents a picture of family life, spiritual life, economy, ethics, popular philosophy, religious concepts, and matchmaking.

Soviet Period

In the Soviet period, the centralized government created a new family law when it presented countries with decrees, codes, and other acts. Turkestan, which included Kyrgyzstan, accepted the Soviet orders and decisions explaining the Family Code of 1918. The new legislation was carried out slowly because the population was still under the powerful influence of local clergy, aristocrats, and customary law judges (*biev*). The *biev* were wealthy elders informally chosen by the community, discretely maintained by the ruling class (*baev*) in the patriarchal-feudal aristocracy and imperial administration to keep peace between the classes. Their rulings were oral.

When they created the code, the Soviets did not take into account the conditions of the region. The people were used to living according to custom and Muslim law. Because of this situation, the Soviet Union subsequently permitted Islamic judges (*kaziev*) and the *biev* to decide family disputes by application of both the Family Code of 1918 and traditional norms, unless those norms were inconsistent with the Family Code. The Soviet Union also recognized household and national traditions in 1924 when the legal institution of adoption under customary law was restored in Turkestan. In general, however, Kyrgyzstan leaders were limited in their ability to regulate family relations and generally followed Soviet laws and rules.

The Marxist-Leninist government encouraged the "liberation" of women from the home and into the workforce, particularly in the urban areas. Under Soviet rule, women were given equal access to employment, protection under family law, and social-support provisions. Girls were required to attend school. The Soviets prohibited bride-price and dowry, but officials rarely enforced the prohibition, and the practice remained common.

During the Soviet era, public law, not civil or private law, governed family relations. Many government decisions show this policy. To encourage motherhood, the Soviet government prohibited abortion in a 1936 decision. Women who had abortions in violation of that prohibition were punished under the Criminal Code until 1955.

During World War II, the government opened many orphanages to care for children whose parents had been killed in the war. On September 8, 1943, the Decree of Presidium of the Supreme Soviet "On Adoption" was issued to encourage adoption of these children. The Presidium enacted an edict on July 8, 1944, that specified that only a marriage registered with the state was accorded rights and obligations. This edict also made divorce very difficult and abolished paternity proceedings. From February 15, 1947, to January 21, 1954, marriages between foreigners and Soviet citizens were prohibited.

The Supreme Soviet enacted completely new family legislation on October 1, 1968. These "Fundamental Principles of Legislation on Marriage and the Family" were followed in 1969 by new family codes in the fifteen Soviet Republics. This 1969 Family Code remains in effect in the Kyrgyz Republic at the beginning of the twenty-first century.

Under Soviet rule, the central marriage code was designed to establish equality between spouses, secularize marriage, and make divorce simple and accessible to both partners.

The constitution of the Kyrgyz Soviet Socialist Republic in 1978 established the protection of family as a constitutional principle. Other legislation mandated equality of men and women, the strengthening of the family, and the protection of children.

Independence

Kyrgyz Republic became sovereign and independent in 1991. Restoration of independence in Kyrgyzstan, as well as in its neighboring countries, was connected to the collapse of the USSR. With independence came the opportunity to continue the interrupted development of the market economy and institutions of the democratic state.

The Constitution of the Kyrgyz Republic, accepted by the Supreme Soviet in 1993, continues Soviet-era protection by providing in Article 26 that motherhood, fatherhood, and childhood will be under the defense of the State. The addition of fatherhood enlarges the provisions of the constitution.

Since independence, the Parliament of the Kyrgyz Republic (*Jokorku Kenesh*) has ratified many international conventions. Analysis of the conventions in the fields of women's and children's rights has shown that the existing base of Kyrgyz law as a whole agrees with international norms.

Development of family law after the restoration of independence has been determined by the common conception of civil or private law. A new civil code went into effect in 1996. According to Art.1 of this code, "Civil legislation shall be applied to family relationships, if such relationships are not regulated by family legislation." Portions of the 1969 family code have been moved into the 1996 civil code including trusteeship and the acts of a civil condition.

Legal regulation of marriage. In Kyrgyz law, marriage is the union of men and women, which brings legal consequences, creating a status for the married person and for the state. The only legal marriage ceremonies are state-sanctioned, although the participants may have religious ceremonies as well. Couples who plan to marry must file applications at a government office (the ZAGS bureau) one month in advance of the wedding. The waiting period may be reduced or extended by up to one month for justifiable reasons. In both cases, the ceremony must be preceded by a procedure before a civil registrar who issues written findings that there are no obstacles to the marriage. A civil wedding may be accompanied by a religious ceremony, but a religious ceremony without the civil ruling is not valid. Marriage is finalized by registration.

Under law, both parties to a marriage must be at least eighteen years old. The CMF Art.18 provides for the possibility of lowering the marriageable age, but only for the woman and not by more than one year. Couples who marry in religious ceremonies or under customary law at younger ages are not legally married and do not receive legal marriage benefits. The department of state generally decides questions about the lowering of marriageable age. Many marriages today are based on mutual consent of spouses; paternal consent is still a requirement by custom, maintaining a semblance of the tradition of arranged marriages.

According to civil wedding statistics from by the Ministries of Justice, the number of registered marriages has diminished. In 1996, 36,710 couples registered to marry; in 1997, the figure was 26,110; in 1998, 26,910; in 1999, 26,060; and in 2000, 26,557. There is an increasing number of unregistered, traditional unions or de facto marriages. De facto unions are popular especially in the south and among rich men in cities.

In Kyrgyzstan, bride-price, known as *kalym,* is again openly practiced in the post-Soviet era. According to Kyrgyz custom, the groom gives the bride's family a gift of livestock. Kyrgyz women sometimes bring family livestock into the marriage. The children of the marriage subsequently inherit the bride-wealth, not the husband and his family. De facto polygamous marriages have also increased in number. One statistic showed that as many as 70 percent of the men in the south had multiple wives. Polygamy typically takes the form of acquiring a woman over the age of twenty-five as a second wife. The second wife is called the *tokol* and is married in a religious ceremony conducted by the *iman,* or Muslim cleric. The *tokol* has no legal rights under Kygyz law.

Under the Criminal Code of 1997, bigamy and polygamy are punishable crimes and result in the annulment of the second marriage. Nevertheless, men take on additional wives under traditional and Muslim law. Traditional law permits more wives does Islamic law, which limits a man to four wives. These unions have created a conflict between traditional, religious, and civil law.

De facto marriage, or cohabitation, is of a personal and spiritual nature; it carries no legal family obligations (such as alimony or division of property) according to the civil code. De facto unions are not forbidden by law and are not prosecutable, but the law does not accord them any legal significance. Thus, men and women living together are not considered spouses and do not inherit from each other. Children born from these unions are considered illegitimate and bear the mother's surname. The relations between children and their natural fathers are not considered paternal in the same sense as those involving legitimate children. Although children have the right to receive child support from their natural father, the law does not provide for inheritance rights after his death. Nevertheless, many women who are second wives—who joined the household as a result of de facto marriage—apply to courts to defend the inheritance rights of their children. Such cases are a problem in legal practice.

There are two categories of de facto union. The first might be termed modern and voluntary. These unions exist as a result of a mutual agreement of the parties with little involvement of their families. They occur primarily in the cities. This is a contractual model as a voluntary union of two individuals. The second category, in which the family of the man or man himself pays a bride-price to woman's family, is consummated by the transfer of an agreed bride-wealth. These de facto unions are based on an agreement between families. A woman from a poor family may be forced to marry even if she believes that her rights are being violated. However, since the enactment of the 1997 criminal code, the purchase or ransom of bride-price by parents is no longer a criminal offense. The new code recognized this practice as a social custom and thus not punishable by criminal law.

The difficult question is determining the form of a relationship before its legal effects can be ascertained. Women in polygamous unions often believe that they are validly married under Islamic law, which recognizes these unions. Customary law in Kyrgyzstan also permitted polygamy. In the

Prior to a marriage ceremony, Kyrgyz couples are required by law to file applications at a government office. Without government approval this couple wouldn't be recognized as being legally married. CAROLINE PENN/CORBIS

south, a first wife may not protest against her husband's expressed intention to marry other women. Women and their families do not demand a marriage certificate because the ceremony (*nike*) is performed by an Islamic official (*moldo*—a man who works in a mosque under an *iman*). These traditions date back to the prerevolutionary era and belong to both the Islamic and traditional laws. Given these circumstances, parties may remain ignorant of their actual legal status until a marital dispute or the death of one person throws a dark shadow on the validity of their marriage.

The Code of Marriage and Family does not include legal rules to govern the distribution of property when one of the cohabitants dies intestate before the validity of the relationship is decided in court. The law has no provisions that give economic protection to the woman who lives with the man and her children. This brings consequences for the second wife and her children. Fathers' and children's rights and duties arise from the establishment of the children's parentage. A child's

parentage becomes legal when certified by the ZAGS. The parentage of a child born to unmarried parents may be established if the child's mother and father submit a joint declaration to the ZAGS. Based on the parents' free and willing declaration that they are the parents, ZAGS register the child's birth and issue the parents a birth certificate that indicates the child's father's and mother's name, patronymic, and surname.

The courts may determine a child's paternity if the child is born out of wedlock and if, at the time of birth, no joint declaration was submitted to the ZAGS. Paternity may be established based upon cohabitation and the running of a joint household by the mother and the respondent for at least six months prior to the birth of the child, the joint upbringing or maintenance of the child by the two, or documentary evidence authentically proving that the respondent recognizes his paternity. Paternity can be proved if only one of these is established. Cohabitation and running a joint household by the child's mother and the respondent before the child's birth may be proved if the two persons lived in the same household, ate together, took care of one another, and acquired property for mutual use and enjoyment or for the child. All these facts may be confirmed with various documents and witnesses' testimony. After the court exhaustively examines all evidence relevant to a paternity case, it declares whether the respondent is the child's father or not. The court's decision becomes the basis for the entry in the ZAGS registry, which brings about personal and property rights and obligations between the child and the father.

The process of establishing paternity may be difficult, particularly after the father has died. Documentary evidence is rarely available, and the illegal widow will have to offer proof of established cohabitation. In many cases, a de facto union may not last long enough to meet this test. Genetic evidence is accepted, but is expensive and only available in Moscow.

Experience shows that the woman usually loses when the second marriage is invalid under the general law. Since the Kyrgyz Republic republic gained its independence, polygamy and de facto marriage unions have spread in the neighboring republics of Kazakhstan, Uzbekistan, Tajikistan, and Turkmenistan. This has come about because of the interests of Muslim men and the revival of Central Asian traditions. Polygamy is against the law in all of these countries, but the governments do not enforce the laws. During the Soviet era, the criminal code prohibited both polygamy and the payment of bride-price. Even more important, a man with more than one wife (or a man who divorced) would lose his membership in the Communist Party and would lose prestige and even his job as a result.

Divorce. The Code of Marriage and Family required equal ownership and distribution of marital assets upon divorce. By the end of the twentieth century, the number of divorces exceeded 50 percent of the annual marriages.

Domestic violence increased in the post-Soviet era. Under the criminal code, husbands do not have a right to beat their wives, but domestic violence is only a crime if the abused partner complains. Hospital admission records indicate an increase in domestic violence injuries requiring medical attention.

Conclusion

The transition to independence and a market economy have brought a need for family law reform. Because of the large gap between the law on the books and the practices in Kyrgyz society, the shape of family law reform will be controversial. The 1969 Code on Marriage and the Family of the KSSR, which became effective on January 1, 1970, is still in force. A new family code for the Kyrgyz Republic will fundamentally change the system of family law in almost every aspect. The new family code will attempt to achieve an international standard of human rights, with particular emphasis on the rights of children In 1994, the country approved the International Convention on the Rights of the Child, but no legislation was passed to implement it.

The institution of family has undergone tremendous changes in the last century due to both societal and political upheaval. Marriage as an institution has diminished with the rise in cohabitation and illegitimate children. Further change is certain to occur.

See also: ISLAM

Bibliography

Achilova, R. (1986). *Family and Society.* Frunze, Kyrgyzstan.

Allworth, E. (1967). *Central Asia. A Century of Russian Rule.* New York: Columbia University Press.

Antokoliskay, M. B. (1997). *Family Law.* Moscow.

Constitution Kyrgyz Republic. (1993). Bishkek, Kyrgyzstan.

Civil Code Kyrgyz Republic. (1996). Bishkek, Kyrgyzstan.

Code of Marriage and Family. (1969). Frunze, Kyrgyzstan.

Frantz, D. (2001). "Central Asia Braces to Fight Islamic Rebels." *The New York Times,* May 3.

Hansen, K. J. (1981). *Mormonism and the American Experience.* Chicago: University of Chicago Press.

Heyat, F. (2000). "Azeri Professional Women's Life Strategies in the Post-Soviet Period." In *Gender and Identity Construction: Women of Central Asia, the Caucasus and Turkey,* ed. F. Acar and A. Gunes-Ayata. Leiden, The Netherlands: Brill NV.

Jakipova, A. (1975). Soviet Family Law. Kazaxstan.

Kerimbaeva A. K. (1976). *Soviet Law in Emancipation Women of Kyrgyzstan.* Moscow.

Kislykov, N. A. (1969). *Novels About History, Marriage, and Family in Central Asia.* Leningrad.

Law of Kyrgyzstan: Problems and Perspectives. (1997). Bishkek, Kyrgyzstan.

Lapidus, I. M. (1988). *A History of Islamic Societies.* Cambridge, UK: Cambridge University Press.

"Manas" epos and the World's Epic Heritage. (1995). Bishkek, Kyrgyzstan.

Moghadam, V. (2000). "Gender and Economic Reforms: A Framework for Analysis and Evidence from Central Asia, the Caucasus, and Turkey." In *Gender and Identity Construction: Women of Central Asia, the Caucasus and Turkey,* ed. F. Acar and A. Gunes-Ayata. Leiden, The Netherlands: Brill NV.

Poliakov, S. P. (1992). *Everyday Islam: Religion and Tradition in Rural Central Asia.* Armonk, NY: M. E. Sharpe.

Panteleeve, I. V. (1986). *Marriage in International Private Law.* Moscow.

Sykiynen, L. R. (1980). *Muslim Law.* Moscow.

Turgunbekov, R. (1992). Development Sovereign State of Kyrgyz People. Bishkek, Kyrgyzstan.

Tekeli, S., ed. (1995). *Women in Transition.* Florence: International Child Development Centre.

Walther, W. (1993). *Women in Islam.* New York: Markus Wiener.

Zaikov, F. A. (1982). *New Constitution about Marriage and Family.* Frunze, Kyrgyzstan.

Zaikovk, F. A., and Asanova, K. (1998). *Family Law of Kyrgyzstan.* Bishkek, Kyrgyzstan.

Other Resource

Human Rights Watch. (2001). *World Report 2001.* Available from http://www.hrw.org/hrw/wr2k1/.

KUNDUZ ASANOVA

LATER LIFE FAMILIES

Similar to their younger counterparts, families in later life experience both change and continuity. In addition to *retirement, grandparenthood,* and changing *intergenerational relationships,* members of later life families experience marital transitions, the onset of health problems, and changes in marital satisfaction and sexual relationships as well as emerging needs for the caregiving of older family members. Race, ethnicity, class, country of origin, age, and sexual orientation combine to further augment the diversity of experience within the family in later life.

Defining Later Life Families

Timothy Brubaker (1983; 1990) suggests that later life families are delineated by the fact that they have completed the child-rearing stage. In contrast, Ingrid Connidis (2001) asserts that definitions of the later life family should allow for the diversity of individual experience by focusing on familial relationships rather than a particular life-course stage or chronological age. Connidis (2001) points out that older childless couples do not fit Brubaker's definition of the later life family. Similarly, age is not always an accurate means of defining later life families as individuals may become grandparents in their twenties and thirties (Burton and Bengtson 1985). Undoubtedly, the term *family* implies a different set of meanings and relationships for each individual (Holstein and Gubrium 1999). Victoria Bedford and Rosemary Blieszner (1997) offer the most helpful means of defining later life familial relationships as they state:

> A family is a set of relationships determined by biology, adoption, marriage, and, in some societies, social designation and existing even in the absence of contact or affective involvement, and, in some cases, even after the death of certain members (526). Thus, familial relationships derive from biologically and socially defined relationships that transcend the finality of death and the exclusiveness of blood and marital kinship relationships.

Characteristics of Later Life Families

Brubaker (1990) notes that later life families are characterized by the presence of three, four, and even five generations. Family structures with four or five generations but relatively few people in each generation are referred to as *beanpole families* (Bengtson, Rosenthal, and Burton 1990). Families in which successive generations have children at an earlier age, resulting in smaller age differences between the generations, are referred to as *age-condensed families*. In contrast, families in which successive generations delay childbearing, resulting in larger age differences between the generations, are referred to as *age-gapped families*. The number of individuals in each generation—as well as the age differences between the generations—influences familial relationships in later life. For example, the beanpole family structure is associated with the concept of the *sandwich generation,* in which the middle generation, particularly women, experiences simultaneous demands to care for aging relatives and dependent children. The burden experienced by the sandwich generation is augmented by the lack of family members with whom caregiving tasks may be shared. Although it is thought to be the most common family form, Peter Uhlenberg (1993) states that the prevalence of the beanpole family structure has been exaggerated. Carolyn Rosenthal (2000) points out that relatively few women experience being sandwiched between the competing demands of their parents and children. Rosenthal (2000) asserts that daughters are more likely to be providing active help to their aged parents when they themselves are older and their children have been launched, thus there is a decreased likelihood of having conflicting roles. Nevertheless, smaller or larger age differences between the generations may influence the nature and duration of intergenerational relationships as well as the type and extent of help and care exchanged between the generations.

At the same time, family structures in later life vary as a result of social, demographic, and cultural differences. Although longevity continues to increase around the world, there are notable distinctions between developed and developing countries as well as between men and women. For example, the World Health Organization (2000) reports that healthy life-expectancy rates range from approximately 75 years in Japan to less than 26 years in Sierra Leone. Women tend to outlive men by seven or eight years in developed countries, whereas men and women have similar life expectancy rates in developing countries (World Health Organization 2000). Life-expectancy differences have an impact on later life familial relationships such that in some countries three- and four-generation families are more common than in others. With increasing longevity, later life becomes a normative life-course stage. In contrast, in some developing countries low life expectancy renders the experience of later life less common and the definition of *old age* is much younger than in developed countries (Albert and Cattell 1994). Moreover, differing cultural values lead to diversity in norms surrounding old age and intergenerational relations. In some countries, such as Japan and China, older relatives hold a special place of honor in the family and there are strong social norms that dictate that adult children provide care and shelter for aged family members (Thorson 2000).

Later life grandparents usually have teenage or young adult grandchildren. Using the Internet has been a popular way for grandparents and grandchildren to communicate. TOM STEWART/CORBIS

Despite differences in family structure, later life families tend to share another characteristic identified by Timothy Brubaker (1990), namely family history. Brubaker (1990) points out that later life families have a long and rich "reservoir of experience." As well as having well-established patterns of interactions, later life families may also be characterized by "unfinished business or tensions" (Brubaker 1990, p. 16) arising from events that happened earlier in the family's history.

Couple Relationships in Later Life

With increased longevity and barring divorce or separation, married and common-law couples can expect to be together into their later years. Relatively few older adults are either never married or divorced (Choi 1996). Although they are becoming increasingly visible and socially accepted, older lesbian and gay couples are also a minority. In contrast, most older adults are either currently married or widowed. Marriage has been found to have positive effects on the well-being of individuals in later life. Indeed, married individuals report greater well-being than never-married, divorced, separated, or widowed individuals (Mastekaasa 1994). However, at all stages of the marital relationship, men report higher levels of satisfaction and a greater sense of well-being than women.

In addition to gender differences, there are also differences in marital satisfaction in later life related to race, ethnicity, and nationality. For example, one study found that in the United States,

African-American adults tend to report lower levels of marital satisfaction across the life-course than white adults (Adelmann, Chadwick, and Baerger 1996). In another study, Mexican-American women experienced greater declines in marital satisfaction over the life-course than did Mexican-American men (Markides et al. 1999). Ed Diener, Carol Gohm, Eunkook Suh, and Shigehiro Oishi (2000) compared marital satisfaction across forty-two different countries. They define *collectivist countries,* such as China, South Korea, and Nigeria, as nations that tend to have strong norms about marriage, conformity, and supporting in-group members. *Individualist countries,* such as the United States, Great Britain, and the Netherlands, place greater emphasis on individual rights, attitudes, and choices. Diener and his colleagues (2000) found that although individuals derive greater satisfaction from marriage than cohabitation in collectivist countries, the relationship between marital status and subjective well-being is relatively similar cross-nationally.

Couples in later life experience a number of transitions as children leave home, individuals retire, and grandchildren are born. Previous research has suggested that marital satisfaction tends to follow a U-shaped curve with the highest levels of marital satisfaction reported in the beginning and later stages of the relationship and declines in marital satisfaction during the middle (and usually parental) years. Following the launching of adult children, couples may have more time to spend with each other, more privacy, and more financial resources. The bond between couples in later life may be enhanced by a lifetime of shared history and experiences. Some researchers have found that increased marital satisfaction in later life is largely explained by decreases in parenting and work responsibilities stemming from the launching of adult children and the transition to retirement (Orbuch et al. 1996). Similarly, Barbara Mitchell and Ellen Gee (1996) note that the return of adult children to the home following initial launching has a potentially negative impact on marital satisfaction. The presence of adult children in the home may augment existing marital tensions, particularly in the case where the parents are in a second marriage or in poor health. Returning adult children may also result in decreased marital satisfaction in cases where the adult child has made three or more departures from and returns to the

family home. However, Mitchell and Gee (1996) found that strong relationships between mothers and adult children are associated with fewer declines in marital satisfaction following the return of the adult child.

Later research on the U-shaped pattern of marital satisfaction across the life-course has generated conflicting findings. One longitudinal study found that marital satisfaction tends to decline over time "with the steepest declines in marital happiness occurring during the earliest and latest years of marriage" (VanLaningham, Johnson, and Amato 2001, p. 1313). In other words, they did not find any evidence of increases in marital satisfaction following the launching of adult children or the transition to retirement. Defining a lack of success in terms of marriages that ended in divorce or that were reported as being less than happy, Norval Glen's (1998) study of marital success also rebutted the U-shaped model of marital satisfaction. Glen's (1998) research suggests that differences in marital success across the life-course are due to cohort differences. Glen also contends that declines in marital success may be due to personal and health characteristics that occur over time and that serve to make couples less compatible or less well-matched.

Another way of examining marital satisfaction and marital quality in later life is in terms of conflict. Older couples have been found to have a decreased potential for marital conflict and an increased potential for deriving pleasure from their children and grandchildren, from shared activities, and from shared aspirations and vacations (Levensen, Carstensen, and Gottman 1993). In addition, older couples tend to be less emotionally negative and more affectionate in their resolution of conflict than their middle-aged counterparts (Carstensen, Gottman, and Levensen 1995). Thus, older couples may have developed strategies for avoiding conflict as well as resolving differences in a more amiable manner. Older couples' shared and long-term histories may serve to further strengthen their bonds as well as buffering the negative impact of marital tension and conflict.

Retirement and Couple Relationships

Retirement is one of the most significant changes that face later life families. As has been stated above, the U-shaped pattern of marital satisfaction suggests that retirement may enhance satisfaction with the marital relationship. However, the process of transition from employment to retirement may pose a difficult challenge to many couples. During the transition stage, both husbands and wives tend to describe losses in marital quality (Moen, Kim, and Hofmeister 2001). The timing of retirement may be a source of marital conflict as well as the result of negotiation between the spouses. Deborah Smith and Phyllis Moen (1998) report that the husband's decision to retire is more likely to influence the timing of the wife's retirement than the other way round. Couples in which one partner retires while the other continues to work tend to experience greater marital discord, regardless of gender (Moen, Kim, and Hofmeister 2001).

Upon retirement, couples may spend more time together, which will either enhance the marital relationship or lead to increased conflict. There are gender differences in the perception of marital conflict and satisfaction following retirement. Maximiliane Szinovacz and Anne Schaffer (2000) state that husbands—but not wives—tend to perceive a decrease in the number of "heated arguments" following the retirement of the wife. The retirement of the husband is associated with an increase in calm discussions about conflictual issues in relationships where the spouses are strongly attached to the marriage. In contrast, the retirement of the husband may culminate in a decrease in calm discussions where one or both of the spouses are not strongly attached to the marriage.

Unlike their younger counterparts, the majority of today's older women did not work outside the home. Thus, the retirement of the husband and his increased presence in the home may result in a wife's sense that she has lost personal freedom and autonomy (Rosenthal and Gladstone 1994). The retirement of one or both spouses may necessitate the negotiation of personal space and domestic duties. Although the wife may have been primarily responsible for domestic tasks, following retirement there is often a lessening of a traditional gendered division of labor (Szinovacz 2000). In addition to increasing the amount of time spent on their own chores, retired spouses tend to spend more time doing tasks formerly designated the responsibility of the other spouse. Nevertheless, wives continue to spend a significantly greater amount of time on household labor than do husbands. The division of domestic labor following retirement has been found to be related to marital satisfaction. Couples who divide household chores more equitably tend to report higher levels of marital satisfaction than couples who adhere to more traditional definitions of gender roles and behavior (Rosenthal and Gladstone 1994).

Sexuality in Later Life

Benjamin Schlesinger (1996) asserts that older adults are often perceived as being asexual. Indeed, the sexual behavior of older adults is frequently assumed to be nonexistent, funny, physically risky, embarrassing, or less satisfying and exciting. In reality, sexuality continues to be an important part of couple relationships in later life. However, sexual activity tends to decline with age as a result of changing health levels, the loss of partners, the declining interest of husbands, and the effects of prescription medications. At the same time, definitions of sexual behavior in later life expand beyond sexual intercourse as older adults refer to "kissing, touching, caressing, holding hands, and hugging" (Neugebauer-Visano 1995, p. 22) as important elements of sexual activity. In this way, sexual intercourse is only one facet of the sexual expression of couples in later life.

Sexual interest and activity have been found to be contributors to marital satisfaction and well-being in later life (Ade-Ridder 1995). Couples who report higher levels of sexual activity tend to describe their marriages as being happier than those in which sexual activity has declined. Levels of sexual activity in later life vary by gender, education, age, and marital status (Matthias et al. 1997). Older men report higher levels of sexual activity than older women. The strongest predictors of being sexually active for men are being younger and well-educated. In contrast, the strongest predictor of being sexually active among older women is marital status: married women tend to report higher levels of sexual activity than single older women.

Grandparenthood

Grandparenthood is a role that most people will experience in their lifetimes. Maximiliane Szinovacz (1998) notes that most people become grandparents in middle age rather than in later life. Thus, grandparents in later life will tend to have grandchildren who are in their teenage and young adult years (Connidis 2001). Women and members of ethnic minorities tend to become grandparents at earlier stages in their lives than men and Caucasians (Thorson 2000). Due to differences in life expectancy, the length of relationships between grandparents and grandchildren vary between developed and developing countries (Albert and Cattell 1994). Although grandparenthood is a lengthy life-course stage in developed countries, lower life expectancies in developing countries mean that grandparents and grandchildren will share fewer years together. Similarly, the longer life expectancies of women as compared to men result in grandchildren being more likely to have living grandmothers, particularly maternal grandmothers, than living grandfathers (Thorson 2000). With the growing rates of divorce both among the middle and later generations, step-grandparenthood is becoming increasingly common and roughly one-quarter of all grandparents will become step-grandparents (Thorson 2000). Finally, great-grandparenthood is becoming increasingly common and approximately one-quarter of older men and one-third of older women will have great-grandchildren (Rosenthal and Gladstone 1994).

The relationships that grandparents share with their grandchildren vary by age and gender (Connidis 2001). When grandchildren are younger, grandparents tend to be more involved in their lives. Contact between grandparents and grandchildren tends to decrease once the grandchildren reach their teenage years. Similarly, grandmothers tend to provide more emotional support, whereas grandfathers tend to give their grandchildren more instrumental support such as advice and financial assistance. Although they participate in relatively few activities with either of their grandparents, adult grandchildren spend more time with their grandmothers than with their grandfathers (Roberto and Stroes 1995). Grandmothers tend to report greater satisfaction with their relationships with their grandchildren than do grandfathers (Thomas 1995). Moreover, grandparents tend to perceive their relationships with grandchildren as being closer than do grandchildren (Connidis 2001). Regardless of the differences deriving from age and gender, grandparents play a stabilizing role in the family as they provide a sense of continuity for the younger generations.

Marital Transitions: Widowhood, Divorce and Remarriage

Among today's older adults, the death of a spouse is the typical way a marital relationship ends. Given that women tend to outlive men and to marry men who are the same age or older than themselves, women continue to be much more likely than men to be widowed (Connidis 2001). Approximately two-thirds of women aged 80 and over are widowed. In contrast, the majority of men aged 80 and over is married.

The loss of a spouse is among the most stressful life events that an individual will experience (Martin-Matthews 1991). Although widowhood is an "expectable life event" for older women, "the duration of the spouse's final illness and forewarning of the death" (Martin-Matthews 1991, p. 21) shape a widow's experience of the loss of her husband. Widowhood tends to be preceded by a period of time in which men and women provide care for their ailing spouse, usually the wife caring for the husband (Wells and Kendig 1997). Undoubtedly, the stress and anguish associated with the care of a failing spouse may account for the declines in marital satisfaction in later life (VanLaningham, Johnson, and Amato 2001). At the same time, Helena Lopata (2000) notes that an individual's experience of widowhood is shaped by the cultural importance given to marriage. In developing countries where women have less power and access to resources and where they derive social status and security from their husbands, widows may face financial and social adversity in addition to profound feelings of grief and loss.

Although remarriage following the death of a spouse in later life is uncommon, more men remarry than do women. Carolyn Rosenthal and James Gladstone (1994) suggest that the primary motivations for remarrying in later life are the desire for companionship and the wish to feel useful and able to contribute to another person's happiness. The higher remarriage rates of men may be due to the greater number of potential marriage partners (O'Bryant and Hansson 1995). Similarly, the overall low rates of remarriage among older men and women are due to fears of social disapproval, financial concerns, and the opposition of other family members (O'Bryant and Hansson 1995). Maria Talbott's (1998) study of attitudes towards remarriage reveals that older women are reluctant to remarry because they do not want to give up their freedom, they are not interested in establishing a new sexual relationship, they do not want to go through the loss of another husband, they fear the reactions of their children, they feel that it would be disloyal to their deceased husband, and/or they do not want to take on additional domestic responsibilities.

Divorce among later life couples continues to be rare, although the rates are increasing. Laurie Hatch (2000) notes that divorce in later life may be more disruptive to an individual's life than widowhood. Unlike widowhood, divorce in later life is unexpected and is often accompanied by a sense of social stigma. Charles Hennon (1995) states that divorced older adults report lower life satisfaction and physical well-being than do their widowed counterparts. William Aquilino (1994) reports that couples who divorce in later life tend to have less contact and poorer quality relationships with their adult children. The relationships between adult children and fathers tend to be more negatively impacted by later life divorce than the relationships between adult children and mothers.

Although later life divorce is rare, divorce among the younger generations is not uncommon. Older adults whose children divorce may feel caught in the middle between their biological offspring and their sons- and daughters-in-law. Depending upon custody arrangements, grandparents may have increased or decreased access to their grandchildren following the divorce of the middle generation. For example, should the grandchildren be placed in the primary custody of their mother, the paternal grandparents may see their grandchildren less often.

Conclusion

Later life families experience both change and continuity through marital, familial, social, and work transitions. At the same time, each individual's experience and definition of what constitutes the later life family and familial relationships varies. Despite the differences that derive from gender, race, class, country of origin, and the numerous transitions they encounter, families in later life are both adaptive and resilient.

See also: CAREGIVING: FORMAL; CAREGIVING: INFORMAL; CHILDLESSNESS; DEATH AND DYING; DIVORCE: EFFECTS ON COUPLES; ELDER ABUSE; ELDERS; FILIAL RESPONSIBILITY; GRANDPARENTHOOD; GRIEF, LOSS, AND BEREAVEMENT; INTERGENERATIONAL RELATIONS; MARITAL QUALITY; RETIREMENT; SANDWICH GENERATION; SEXUALITY IN ADULTHOOD; SUBSTITUTE CAREGIVERS; WIDOWHOOD

Bibliography

Adelmann, P. K.; Chadwick, K.; and Baerger, D. R. (1996). "Marital Quality of Black and White Adults over the Life Course." *Journal of Social and Personal Relationships* 13(3):361–384.

Ade-Ridder, L. (1995). "Sexuality and Marital Quality among Older Married Couples." In *Seniors and Sexuality,* ed. R. Neugebauer-Visano. Toronto: Canadian Scholars' Press.

Albert, S. M., and Cattell, M. G. (1994). *Old Age in Global Perspective: Cross-Cultural and Cross-National Views.* Toronto: Maxwell Macmillan.

Aquilino, W. S. (1994). "Later Life Parental Divorce and Widowhood: Impact on Young Adults' Assessment of Parent-Child Relations." *Journal of Marriage and the Family* 56:908–922.

Bedford, V. H., and Blieszner, R. (1997). "Personal Relationships in Later-life Families." In *Handbook of Personal Relationships,* 2nd edition, ed. S. Duck. New York: Wiley.

Bengtson, V. L.; Rosenthal, C. J.; and Burton, L. (1990). "Families and Aging: Diversity and Heterogeneity." In *Handbook of Aging and the Social Sciences,* ed. R. H. Binstock and L. K. George. New York: Academic Press.

Brubaker, T. H., ed. (1983). *Family Relationships in Later Life,* 2nd edition. Newbury Park, CA: Sage.

Brubaker, T. H. (1990). "An Overview of Family Relationships in Later Life." In *Family Relationships in Later Life,* 2nd edition, ed. T. H. Brubaker. Newbury Park, CA: Sage.

Burton, L., and Bengtson, V. L. (1985). "Black Grandmothers: Issues of Timing and Continuity of Roles." In *Grandparenthood,* ed. V. L. Bengtson and J. Robertson. Beverly Hills, CA: Sage.

Carstensen, L. L.; Gottman, J. M.; and Levensen, R. W. (1995). "Emotional Behavior in Long-Term Marriage." *Psychology and Aging* 10(1):140–149.

Choi, N. G. (1996). "The Never-Married and Divorced Elderly: Comparison of Economic and Health Status, Social Support, and Living Arrangement." *Journal of Gerontological Social Work* 26(1/2):3–25.

Connidis, I. A. (2001). *Family Ties and Aging.* Newbury Park, CA: Sage.

Diener, E.; Gohm, C. L.; Suh, E.; and Oishi, S. (2000). "Similarity of the Relations between Marital Status and Subjective Well-Being across Cultures." *Journal of Cross-Cultural Psychology* 31(4):419–436.

Glen, N. D. (1998). "The Course of Marital Success and Failure in Five American 10-Year Marriage Cohorts." *Journal of Marriage and the Family* 60(3):569–576.

Hatch, L. R. (2000). *Beyond Gender Differences: Adaptation to Aging in Life Course Perspective.* Amityville, NY: Baywood.

Hennon, C. B. (1995). "Divorce and the Elderly: A Neglected Area of Research." In *Seniors and Sexuality,* ed. R. Neugebauer-Visano. Toronto: Canadian Scholars' Press.

Holstein, J. A., and Gubrium, J. (1999). "What is Family? Further Thoughts on a Social Constructionist Approach." *Marriage and Family Review* 28(3/4):3–20.

Levensen, R. W.; Carstensen, L. L.; and Gottman, J. M. (1993). "Long-Term Marriage: Age, Gender, and Satisfaction." *Psychology and Aging* 8(2):301–313.

Lopata, H. Z. (2000). "Widowhood: Reconstruction of Self-Concept and Identities." *Studies in Symbolic Interaction* 23:261–275.

Markides, K. S.; Roberts-Jolly, J.; Ray, L. A.; Hoppe, S. K.; and Rudkin, L. (1999). "Changes in Marital Satisfaction in Three Generations of Mexican Americans." *Research on Aging* 21(1):36–45.

Martin-Matthews, A. (1991). *Widowhood in Later Life.* Toronto: Butterworths.

Mastekaasa, A. (1994). "Marital Status, Distress and Well-Being: An International Comparison." *Journal of Comparative Family Studies* 25:183–206.

Matthias, R. E.; Lubben, J. E.; Atchison, K. A.; and Schweitzer, S. O. (1997). "Sexual Activity and Satisfaction among Very Old Adults: Results from a Community-Dwelling Medicare Population Survey." *Gerontologist* 37(1):6–14.

Mitchell, B. A., and Gee, E. M. (1996). "'Boomerang Kids' and Midlife Parental Marital Satisfaction." *Family Relations* 45(4):442–448.

Moen, P.; Kim, J. E.; and Hofmeister, H. (2001). "Couples' Work/Retirement Transitions, Gender, and Marital Quality." *Social Psychology Quarterly* 64(1):55–71.

Neugebauer-Visano, R. (1995). "Seniors and Sexuality? Confronting Cultural Contradictions." In *Seniors and Sexuality,* ed. R. Neugebauer-Visano. Toronto: Canadian Scholars' Press.

O'Bryant, S. L., and Hansson, R. O. (1995). "Widowhood." In *Handbook of Aging and the Family,* ed. R. Blieszner and V. B. Bedford. Westport, CT: Greenwood Press.

Orbuch, T. L.; House, J. S.; Mero, R. P.; and Webster, P. S. (1996). "Marital Quality over the Life Course." *Social Psychology Quarterly* 59(2):162–171.

Roberto, K. A., and Stroes, J. (1995). "Grandchildren and Grandparents: Roles, Influences, and Relationships." In *The Ties of Later Life,* ed. J. Hendricks. Amityville, NY: Baywood.

Rosenthal, C. J., and Gladstone, J. (1994). "Family Relationships and Support in Later Life." In *Aging: Canadian Perspectives,* ed. V. Marshall and B. McPherson. Peterborough, Canada: Broadview.

Rosenthal, C. J. (2000). "Aging Families: Have Current Changes and Challenges Been 'Oversold'?" In *The Overselling of Population Aging: Apocalyptic Demography, Intergenerational Challenges, and Social Policy,* ed. E. M. Gee and G. M. Gutman. Toronto: Oxford University Press.

Schlesinger, B. (1996). "The Sexless Years or Sex Rediscovered." *Journal of Gerontological Social Work* 26(1/2):117–131.

Smith, D. B., and Moen, P. (1998). "Spousal Influence on Retirement: His, Her, and Their Perceptions." *Journal of Marriage and the Family* 60(3):734–744.

Szinovacz, M. E. (1998). "Grandparents Today: A Demographic Profile." *Gerontologist* 38(1):7–52.

Szinovacz, M. E. (2000). "Changes in Housework after Retirement: A Panel Analysis." *Journal of Marriage and the Family* 62(1):78–92.

Szinovacz, M. E., and Schaffer, A. M. (2000). "Effects of Retirement on Marital Conflict Tactics." *Journal of Family Issues* 21(3):367–389.

Talbott, M. M. (1998). "Older Widows' Attitudes towards Men and Remarriage." *Journal of Aging Studies* 12(4):429–449.

Thomas, J. L. (1995). "Gender and Perceptions of Grandparenthood." In *The Ties of Later Life,* ed. J. Hendricks. Amityville, NY: Baywood.

Thorson, J. A. (2000). *Aging in a Changing Society,* 2nd edition. Philadelphia: Brunner/Mazel.

Uhlenberg, P. (1993). "Demographic Change and Kin Relationships in Later Life." In *Annual Review of Gerontology and Geriatrics,* Vol. 13, ed. G. Maddox and M. P. Lawton. New York: Springer.

VanLaningham, J.; Johnson, D. R.; and Amato, P. (2001). "Marital Happiness, Marital Duration, and the

U-Shaped Curve: Evidence from a Five-Wave Panel Study." *Social Forces* 78(4):1313–1341.

Wells, Y. D., and Kendig, H. L. (1997). "Health and Well-Being of Spouse Caregivers and the Widowed." *Gerontologist* 37(5):666–674.

Other Resources

World Health Organization. (2000). "WHO Issues New Healthy Life Expectancy Rankings: Japan Number One in New 'Healthy Life' System." Press Release. Released in Washington, DC and Geneva, Switzerland, June 4, 2000. Available from www.who.int/inf-pr-2000/en/pr2000-life.html.

LAURA HURD CLARKE

LATIN AMERICA

It is not possible to make accurate generalizations about an area as large and diverse as Latin America. There are many different kinds of Latin Americans. This overview provides some background on family life in the Hispanic world, drawing mainly on the research done in a few key countries such as Mexico and Colombia, and with special focus on how the struggle for economic survival affects that life. It has been reported that 40 percent of families in Latin America have insufficient income for essential needs, and that another 28 percent can be categorized as "working poor" (David 1987). In 1980, 41 percent of the population was under fourteen. Population growth in the Western Hemisphere, and Latin America in particular, has exceeded that of the Old World for some time (Stycos 1968). With this trend continuing, poverty is the way of life for most Hispanic children.

Drawing on census data, Elsa M. Chaney (1984) gives the following snapshot: In looking at twenty different countries, the most common minimum age for marriage for females is fourteen. Colombia and Mexico have declared eighteen for both sexes, but the others range from twelve to sixteen for females, and fourteen to sixteen for males. Other research indicates that the average age of marriage for women is about eighteen, and that these young brides will give birth to an average of more than five children in the course of their married lives (Balakrishnan 1976).

Chaney also points out that childrearing is still the highest social status available to women. Because of the costs involved, many of the poor cannot afford to marry, and legal divorce is usually difficult to attain. Thirty percent of households are headed by females (similar to the United States), and the typical household has 3.5 to 5.3 members.

Especially among the lower classes, consensual unions may significantly outnumber formal marriages. For instance, among poor blacks in Venezuela, 57 percent of couples are not married, in spite of the influence of Catholicism. These families tend to be matrifocal (mother-centered) and characterized by early motherhood, migration, and poverty (Pollak-Eltz 1975).

In fact, migration appears to be an important factor in understanding the Hispanic family. Males often migrate to the United States or other places in search of work in order to support their families (Weist 1983). This allows the family to live better, but puts strains on the relationship. Wives rarely have affairs because if their husbands found out, the men could beat or abandon them. Even though the mother is responsible for the children, the usually absent father is the final decision-maker. This pattern holds in Mexico where patriarchal notions make it difficult for women to support themselves (Chant 1993).

In other subcultures, such as the black Caribs of Guatemala (Gonzalez 1983), women change companions fairly frequently in search of economic support. They have also discovered that they can provide for themselves as well as their migrating menfolk can, and as a result are less likely to look up to males as leaders than they used to.

When the Spaniards came to the Americas, they worked hard to impose their family ideals on the indigenous populations. That ideal was a patriarchal, monogamous, nuclear family (Munoz 1983). Before this pressure, there had been significant variety among local peoples, including polygyny, cousin marriages, extended clans, and the more familiar patriarchal power and strict separation of tasks by gender (Boremanse 1983).

Ignorance often goes with poverty, and one example of this is in the area of health. Anesthesia is often avoided in childbirth, as many Mexicans believe that the mother must endure pain in order to be a real mother. This has nothing to do with

A Kuna Native American family. The Kuna are a hardy group that has resisted pressure from Catholic missionaries and the Panamanian government in order to preserve their way of life. DANNY LEHMAN/CORBIS

the pros and cons of natural childbirth, but is related to the Biblical idea of women bringing forth children in sorrow. Some attribute miscarriages, and other problems, to *susto,* which means a terrible fright. Even when their health is in danger, some women will avoid birth control since their main purpose in life is to reproduce. Having children is proof of the husband's virility, and using birth control might tempt the wife to have affairs (Haffner 1992).

What, then, is the typical Latin American family like? Some research (Ingoldsby 1980) indicates that psychological intimacy is not as highly valued as it is in the United States. In comparing couples from the United States and Colombia, it was found that high satisfaction marriages in the United States were correlated with a high level of emotional expressiveness between spouses. This was not true for the Colombian couples. Their satisfaction was predicted by having a similar level of expressiveness, be it high, medium, or low. Also, Colombian women and men are equally likely to say what they feel and are at the same level as U.S. males, whereas females in the United States are significantly more expressive as a group than are their male counterparts.

This pattern appears similar to the one that prevailed in the preindustrial United States, where the marital focus was on agreement between spouses and task completion. As more women in Latin America enter the labor force, it may be that

marriages will shift from traditional to more companionate, as has occurred in the United States, where the emphasis is on emotional sharing.

In looking at the literature on Hispanic families, two general types are described. The first, called *familism,* is the cultural ideal, and it describes a close, loving, and religious family. The second type is a result of *machismo,* which is an abuse of patriarchy due in large part to poverty.

Familism

Familism places the family ahead of individual interests and development. It includes many responsibilities and obligations to immediate family members and other kin, including godparents. Extended family often live in close proximity to each other, with many often sharing the same dwelling. It is common for adult children to supplement their parents' income. In many ways, the Hispanic family helps and supports its members to a degree far beyond that found in individualistically oriented Anglo families (Ingoldsby 1991b).

William M. Kephart and Davor Jedlicka (1991) claim that a large majority of Mexican-American young people comply with parental rules in the following areas: (1) dating and marriage within their ethnic and religious group; (2) having parental approval and some supervision of dating; and (3) complete abstinence from sexual intercourse before marriage. American-born Hispanics are less likely to insist on the tradition of chaperoning their daughters on their dates, and it is not known how well the children adhere to the no sex rule. Nevertheless, the research findings paint a very positive picture of Latin American family life that includes lower mental illness and divorce rates, greater personal happiness, and a secure feeling about aging.

Studies support this picture of Latin America being less individualistic than is the United States. In ranking the characteristics of an ideal person of the opposite sex, adolescents from the United States gave higher rankings to such traits as having money and being fun, popular, and sexy. Teens from Mexico and Guatemala were more collectivistic in citing many of the above traits to be unimportant and preferring someone who is honest, kind, and helpful and someone who likes children (Stiles et al. 1990; Gibbons et al. 1996).

Machismo

Two principal characteristics appear in the study of machismo. The first is aggressiveness. Each *macho* must show that he is masculine, strong, and physically powerful. Differences, verbal or physical abuse, or challenges must be met with fists or other weapons. The true macho shouldn't be afraid of anything, and he should be capable of drinking great quantities of liquor without necessarily getting drunk.

The other major characteristic of machismo is hypersexuality. The impotent and homosexual are scoffed at—the culturally preferred goal is the conquest of women, and the more the better. To take advantage of a young woman sexually is cause for pride and prestige, not blame. In fact, some men will commit adultery just to prove to themselves that they can do it. Excepting the wife and a mistress, long-term affectionate relationships should not exist. Sexual conquest is to satisfy the male vanity. Indeed, others must know of one's potency, which leads to bragging and storytelling. A married man should have a mistress in addition to casual encounters. His relationship with his wife is that of an aloof lord-protector. The woman loves, but the man conquers—this lack of emotion is part of the superiority of the male (Ingoldsby 1991b).

Most women also believe in male superiority (Stycos 1955), and they want their men to be strong and to protect them. According to the dominant cultural stereotype, a man must protect his female relatives from other men because they should be virgins when they marry. Knowing that other men are like himself, the macho is very jealous and, as a result, allows his wife very few liberties.

In summary, machismo may be defined as: "[T]he cult of virility, the chief characteristics of which are exaggerated aggressiveness and intransigence in male-to-male interpersonal relationships and arrogance and sexual aggression in male-to-female relations" (Stevens 1973, p. 315).

Street Children

Young children living on their own in the streets is a widespread problem throughout Latin America. United Nations Children's Fund (UNICEF) estimates that more than forty million children are surviving on their own, without parental supervision. Lewis Aptekar (1990) claims that this is not as tragic and threatening as some claim that it is. His research indicates that the children are not so much abandoned as they are encouraged into early independence. This is a natural consequence of poor, matrifocal family life. Most scholars have seen it in a more negative light, however.

In one study by Paul Velasco (1992), in which 104 street boys in Guayaquil, Ecuador, were interviewed, the following profile emerged. The boys ranged in age from eight to eighteen, with thirteen as the most common age (31%, with twelve and fourteen year olds at about 15% each). The large majority, 62 percent, had been on the street for less than two years, and on average they had a third-grade education.

More than half of these boys had seen their parents within the last year. This supports most research, which indicates that these boys are not lost in the sense of not knowing where their home and family is. To survive, each boy has one or two jobs. Selling and begging are common, but shining shoes was the work most often mentioned (38.5%). Another 19 percent identified themselves as "artists," with about half of them acting like clowns for money and the others being comics or singers. Few admitted to being thieves, though they are feared by the community, especially for violence and stealing car parts. They typically stay within a certain part of town and sleep on the sidewalks, or even in the sewers, to avoid harassment by adults. That they form their own little communities is exemplified by the fact that four-fifths of them go by nicknames given to them by their comrades.

The Colombian term for runaway or abandoned children who live on their own and on the street is *gamine*. There are five thousand gamines in Bogota, the capital of Colombia, alone. They are mostly boys (there are girls as well, but they have received less attention by researchers and the media), and they live in small groups, controlling a territory where they sleep at night under cartons or sheets of plastic. They work hard each day to survive, by begging or stealing (Bikel 1979). In a country with no real social welfare program, this is a significant concern.

There are different types of *gamines,* and a boy may sometimes progress from one category to the next. The first is the *pre-gamine*—this boy still lives at home, but his mother works and is seldom there, so after school he spends his time on the street, occasionally staying away from home for two or three days at a time. The second is the *neighborhood gamine*—this boy lives in the street but has not left the general area of his home, and may visit his family from time to time. The third is the *street gamine*—the true gamine who has left his home and is learning to live by stealing. The fourth is the *pre-delinquent*—the older boy who, after about age fourteen, will become either a marginal unskilled worker (selling lottery tickets, for example) or part of organized crime—stealing with other boys, using and selling drugs, or both—a career he will carry with him into adulthood (de Nicolo, Irenarco, Castrellon, and Marino 1981).

But why do the boys leave their homes? Many possible explanations have been put forth: lack of love at home, child abuse, neglect of basic needs due to parental unemployment, too much free time and television, pornography, and escaping overwork by parents for the freedom of the streets. All of these ideas may contain some truth, but parental rejection appears to be the chief cause, and the family dynamic is based on the stress of economic poverty.

The predominant pattern resulting in a gamine appears to be as follows: A young man moves from the country to the city in search of a better life. He does not find it—the Colombian economy is structured so that unemployment is consistently and extremely high, creating widespread poverty. He does fall in love with a young woman and they get married. The husband cannot find work, becomes depressed, acts irresponsibly, and eventually leaves his wife and children. They can have sex, but they cannot eat (Ingoldsby 1991a).

Another man moves in with the children's mother. This *stepfather* (informally so, as divorce and remarriage are rare in Colombia) is not interested in the fruit of a previous union and pushes the boys away, generally when they are eight to twelve years old. Almost half (47%) of all street urchins have stepfathers. The child feels rejected and leaves for the street. The mother, for fear of her new husband, does not try to bring her sons back (Bikel 1979). To summarize, unemployment leads to poverty and desertion, which results in child abuse and neglect, which creates the

gamines. Similar conditions can result in abandoned children in any culture of poverty, and not only in Latin America.

For girls who become runaways, the situation is a little different. Half of those who do are escaping sexual abuse by their stepfather. They generally leave when they are ten to twelve years of age. Tragically, the most likely survival path for girl gamines is prostitution. Girls are less likely to run away because the street life is more dangerous for them, and parents are less likely to turn them away, as they are generally more useful than boys are at performing domestic tasks.

Family Violence

Spouse and child abuse are characteristics of family life that received very little attention in the United States before 1970. Leading researchers in this area have concluded that family violence is more common in marriages in which the male is dominant and in societies that condone violence in general. Another predictor is the privacy of the conjugal family, which could predispose Western societies towards violence, though it is widespread throughout the world (Strauss 1977). In one study of ninety different societies, wife beating was found to occur at least occasionally in 84.5 percent of them (Levinson 1989).

Wife abuse is consistently mentioned as commonplace in traditional Hispanic families. In one study (Straus and Smith 1989), almost one-fourth of Latino couples experienced violence in their relationship—a rate over 50 percent higher than it was for Anglo couples. This may not be surprising when we realize that the characteristics of machismo are some of the same ones mentioned in studies of spouse abuse. One is alcohol. Varying estimates suggest that from 40 to 95 percent of all wife-beating situations are ones in which the husband has been drinking. Another is male dominance, or the man's right to force compliance to his wishes within his family. The last is low self-esteem, often related to financial problems. All of these characteristics that predict spouse abuse are aspects of being a macho male.

Conclusion

The culture of poverty and the rejection by men of children not their own provides the context and tragic results of machismo. In fact, it may be that it is poverty that is breaking down the personal dignity necessary for traditional familism and replacing it with the excesses of machismo. Some evidence, however, suggests movement toward what Western clinicians would describe as a more functional or healthy family.

A survey of seventy-one married women in Panama (Stinnett; Knaub; O'Neal; and Walters 1983) revealed fairly egalitarian beliefs concerning marriage. Large majorities believed that women (1) should have an education of equal quality as men; (2) should receive equal pay for equal work; (3) are just as intelligent as men; (4) are just as capable of making important decisions as are men; and (5) should express their opinions even if their husbands do not ask for them, and should voice their disagreements with their husbands.

At the same time, most agreed that the husband is the head of the family, that the wife must obey her husband, and that the woman's place is in the home (even though 77% of the sample worked outside the home). This indicates a separate but equal attitude compatible with the familism construct.

Finally, Hispanic families that rate themselves as strong and in which couples are highly satisfied with their marriages emphasize that psychological factors—love and companionship—take precedence. Data collected from nine Latin American countries using Stinnett's Family Strengths Inventory yielded results that were virtually identical to studies conducted in the United States (Casas et al. 1984).

The most important factors for maintaining a happy family life were:

(1) love and affection;

(2) family togetherness;

(3) understanding and acceptance;

(4) mutual respect and appreciation;

(5) communication and relationship skills;

(6) religion.

Wives emphasized love and affection more than husbands did, and husbands were more likely than wives to mention the importance of religion.

Evidence also shows that a growing number of Latin American families value love and affection in the husband-wife and parent-child relationships more than they do the traditional authority-submissiveness approach. All of this bodes well for familism, which not only avoids the abuses of patriarchy, but also makes it more likely that Latin American families will not suffer the disengagement, in which individualism is more important than family, common in the West.

See also: ARGENTINA; ETHNIC VARIATION/ETHNICITY; EXTENDED FAMILIES; FAMILISM; GODPARENTS; HISPANIC-AMERICAN FAMILIES; MEXICO; PERU; SPAIN; VENEZUELA

Bibliography

Aptekar, L. (1990). "How Ethnic Differences Within a Culture Influence Child Rearing: The Case of Colombian Street Children." *Journal of Comparative Family Studies* 21(1):67–79.

Balakrishnan, R. (1976). "Determinants of Female Age at Marriage in Rural and Semi-Urban Areas of Four Latin American Countries." *Journal of Comparative Family Studies* 7(2):167–173.

Bikel, O. (1979). *World: Bogota, One Day*, transcript of PBS television program. Boston, MA: WGBH.

Boremanse, D. (1983). "A Comparative Study of the Family Lives of the Northern and Southern Lacandan Mayas of Chiapas (Mexico)." *Journal of Comparative Family Studies* 14(2):183–202.

Casas, C.; Stinnett, N.; Williams, R.; DeFrain, J.; and Lee, P. (1984). "Identifying Family Strengths in Latin American Families." *Family Perspective* 18(1):11–17.

Chaney, E. (1984). "Marital Status and Living Arrangements." In *Women of the World: Latin America and the Caribbean*, U.S. Bureau of the Census, 99–132.

Chant, S. (1993). "Family Structure and Female Labor in Queretaro, Mexico." In *Next of Kin*, ed. L. Tepperman and S. Wilson. Englewood Cliffs, NJ: Prentice Hall.

David, P. (1987). "Children in Despair: The Latin American Experience." *Journal of Comparative Family Studies* 18(2):327–337.

de Nicolo, J.; Irenarco, A.; Castrellon, C.; and Marino, G. (1981). *Musaranas*. Bogota, Colombia: Industria Continental Grafica.

Gibbons, J.; Richter, R.; Wiley, D.; and Stiles, D. (1996). "Adolescents' Opposite-Sex Ideal in Four Countries." *The Journal of Social Psychology* 136:(4)531–537.

Gonzalez, N. (1983). "Changing Sex Roles Among the Garifuna (black Carib) and Their Implications for the

Family." *Journal of Comparative Family Studies* 14(2):203–213.

Haffner, L. (1992). "Translation is Not Enough: Interpreting in a Medical Setting." *The Western Journal of Medicine* 157(3):255–259.

Ingoldsby, B. (1991a). "Street Children and Family Life." *Family Science Review* 4(2):73–77.

Ingoldsby, B. (1991b). "The Latin American Family: Familism vs. Machismo." *Journal of Comparative Family Studies* 22:57–61.

Ingoldsby, B. (1980). "Emotional Expressiveness and Marital Satisfaction: A Cross-Cultural Analysis." *Journal of Comparative Family Studies* 11(4):501–515.

Kephart, W., and Jedlicka, D. (1991). *The Family, Society, and the Individual.* 7th edition. New York: Harper-Collins.

Levinson, D. (1989). "Family Violence in Cross-Cultural Perspective." In Vol. 1: *Frontiers of Anthropology.* Newbury Park, CA: Sage Publications.

Munoz, J. (1983). "Changes in the Family Structure of the Pokaman of Petapa, Guatemala in the First Half of the 16th Century." *Journal of Comparative Family Studies* 14(2):215–227.

Pollak-Eltz, A. (1975). "Household Composition and Mating Patterns Among Lower-Class Venezuelans." *International Journal of Sociology of the Family* 5(1):85–95.

Stevens, E. (1973). "The Prospects for a Women's Liberation Movement in Latin America." *Journal of Marriage and the Family* 35:313–321.

Stiles, D.; Gibbons, J.; and Schnellmann, J. (1990). "Opposite-Sex Ideal in the U.S.A. and Mexico as Perceived by Young Adolescents." *Journal of Cross-Cultural Psychology* 21(2):180–199.

Stinnett, N.; Knaub, P.; O'Neal, S.; and Walters, J. (1983). "Perceptions of Panamanian Women Concerning the Roles of Women." *Journal of Comparative Family Studies* 14(2):273–282.

Straus, M. (1977). "Societal Morphogenesis and Intrafamily Violence in Cross-Cultural Perspective." *Annals of the New York Academy of Sciences* 285:719–730.

Straus, M., and Smith, C. (1989). "Violence in Hispanic Families in the United States: Incidence Rates and Structural Interpretations." In *Physical Violence in American Families: Risk Factors and Adaptations to Violence in 8,145 Families,* ed. M. Straus and R. Gelles. New York: Transaction Books.

Stycos, J. (1955). *Family and Fertility in Puerto Rico, A Study of the Lower Income Group.* New York: Columbia University Press.

Stycos, J. (1968). *Human Fertility in Latin America: Sociological Perspectives.* Ithaca, NY: Cornell University Press.

Velasco, P. (1992). Unpublished study. Guayaquil, Ecuador.

Wiest, R. (1983). "Male Migration, Machismo, and Conjugal Roles: Implications for Fertility Control in a Mexican Municipio." *Journal of Comparative Family Studies* 14(2)167–181.

BRON B. INGOLDSBY

LATVIA

Latvia is situated at the ancient waterway from the Baltic Sea to the Black Sea via lands inhabited by Eastern Slavs. Because of its location, the territory has, since the twelfth century, been conquered repeatedly—by German crusaders, Russians, Poles, and Swedes. The principal inhabitants of the region—the Balts, one of the ancient Indo-European tribes, and Livs—were oppressed for centuries.

Only in 1918, after World War I, was the independent Republic of Latvia proclaimed. World War II and occupation by the Nazis and then the Soviets interrupted the state's successful development. The latter lasted up to 1990 and left Latvia with enormous share of migrant Slavs from other republics of the former Union of Soviet Socialist Republics (USSR)—almost one-third of the population (Demographic Yearbook of Latvia 2000).

The invasions left the population of Latvia mixed by ethnicity and religion. The local tribes were converted to Christianity in the thirteenth century, but the upheavals of history and the influx of migrants resulted in many different denominations. A great proportion of the population are nonbelievers, a number that drastically increased under Soviets, when religion was considered to be incompatible with Communist ideology. In contrast to the regime representatives of different ethnic groups, believers, and nonbelievers remained mutually tolerant.

The diversity of the country's population has lead to a variety of habits and attitudes on family and marital behavior.

Legislation Affecting Families

After fifty years of occupations in Latvia, the Latvian Civil Code (1937) was restored though its norms on family were modernized. Many privileges of the husband were eliminated.

Marriages can be registered at the state's office or the licensed churches of traditional Christian and Jewish denominations, but couples must be divorced by the courts. Persons under eighteen are allowed to marry only with the permission of parents or guardians. Homosexual marriages are not allowed. Both spouses have the right to keep their family name and citizenship, to choose their place of residence and kind of employment, and to manage mutual or personal property. Couples may also sign an additional marital contract on property.

If a couple divorces after they have children, both parents continue to have equal rights and responsibilities. Children born in or out of wedlock have the same public and family rights as those born to married couples. All children born in marriage or with recognized paternity have equal inheritance rights (or half of it in case of a written wish of the late parent regarding his or her property) and are equally responsible for the support of their elderly parents. Paternity of children born out of wedlock may be recognized voluntarily or by court. Orphans are entitled to the state's allowance up to eighteen years of age.

Partner Relationships

At the end of the twentieth century, the distribution of the Latvian population by gender did not offer favorable prospects for lifelong partnerships for all adults: Among residents, 54 percent are women and 46 percent are men (Demographic Yearbook of Latvia). The proportion of sexes differs significantly by age. Up to thirty-five years of age, the numbers of men and women are close to equal, and each person could have a partner of the opposite gender. Beyond that age, however, the prevalence of women increases proportionally.

Two factors explain the disparity in gender in older groups. In most developed countries, males have shorter life expectancies, but Latvia has one of the greatest differences between males and females: only sixty-five years for newborn boys, compared to seventy-six for girls. World War II and the Stalinist repressions that followed also account for the gap in numbers. The victims were mainly young men, men who were of an age at which they were most likely to marry. In the mid-twentieth century there were only sixty-three men

per one hundred women. Due to such disproportion, the distribution of men and women by marital status is uneven. According to the census data in 1989 at above sixteen years old almost 68 percent of men and only 56 percent of women were married, while 7 percent of men and 11 percent of women were divorced, and 3 percent of men and 18 percent of women were widowed. In their thirties, both sexes have the highest marital rate—80 percent of men and 77 of women were married. The shortage of males affected sexual and marital behavior. Extramarital sexual relations became more frequent, and society acquired a more tolerant attitude to those involved. This also delayed the elimination of patriarchal gender roles as women were ready to comply with all the wishes of their husbands in order to prevent the husbands from leaving them for other women.

Political, economic, and demographic obstacles did not prevent people from forming partnerships and families. The number of marriages per thousand of population was nine to ten per year during most of the twentieth century. Only during the 1990s did the marriage rate decrease rapidly, down to four per thousand in 2000. During the 1990s, legal marriages were largely replaced by nonmarital cohabitation. According to the Fertility and Family Surveys of the ECE Region (1998), almost 17 percent of men and 16 percent of women eighteen to fifty years of age agree that marriage is an outdated institution. Women's opinions do not significantly differ by age, but among men, young men are much more likely to agree with this statement.

Among the generations born between 1945 and 1949, only 3 percent of men and 5 percent of women were living in a consensual union in 1999, but in generations born between 1970 and 1975 this proportion rose to 9 percent of men and 11 percent of women (Zvidrins 1999). The percentage of women who had started their first partnership by living with a partner to whom they were not married increased from 25 percent of all who entered any union among the older generations to 51 percent among younger one. Statistics also show a drastic increase in the share of those who entered their first partnerships when they were under twenty years of age. Among the older generations, 34 percent of the women and 13 of the percent of men were in this category. Among the younger generation, the figure was 50 percent of the women and 27 percent of the men (Zvidrins 1999).

The growing popularity of partnerships entered when the parties are young has not led to similar changes of age at marriage. During the Soviet occupation, the percentage of marriages among people under twenty increased to 6 percent among men and 23 percent among women. This trend was determined by two main reasons. Among the massive influx of migrants, the proportion of young people was twice that of the residents. Marriage rates among the young also rose because of the scarcity of contraceptives under the Soviets, which led to so-called forced marriages because of unwanted pregnancies. The average age at first marriage decreased between 1970 and 1990 from twenty-five to twenty-four years for men and from twenty-four to twenty-two years for women. This trend reversed after the collapse of the Soviet system. With the elimination of restrictions on human rights, exchange of information, and other aspects of life, people felt freer to become involved in premarital and nonmarital cohabitation and to delay marriage. At the end of the twentieth century, the average age at which people married had risen to the highest ever observed in Latvia: thirty-two for men and twenty-nine for women in 1999; the average age at *first* marriage was accordingly twenty-six and twenty-four years. But the proportion of first marriages has constantly decreased, down to 69 percent for men and 70 percent for women in 1999 (*Demographic Year Book of Latvia 2000*).

The overall marriage rate during the 1990s describes the trends in civil marriages; the number of church marriages was constant. The number of church marriages, as a proportion of the total, rose from 15 to 23 percent during the 1990s. One-fourth of new spouses, who marry in church, are not of the same denomination, a situation that is explained by the diversity of ethnic groups and religions in Latvia. One-fifth of ethnic Latvians, two-fifths of ethnic Russians, and nine-tenths of smaller minorities chose a spouse of another ethnicity (Demographic Yearbook of Latvia 2000). This reflects the aforementioned tolerance to immigrants to the country.

Marriages are not stable in Latvia. Since the mid-twentieth century, the divorce rate increased up to 5 per 1,000 inhabitants a year in the 1980s. Conditions that were common under the Soviet System explain this increase; these conditions include the economic independence of women, particularly high in Latvia, widespread alcoholism among men, poor housing, and the difficulties of everyday life, as well as scarce information on interpersonal communication, family roles, and other factors that influence the success of marriage.

As the divorce rate rose, the length of marriages tended to decrease. One reason for this was the instability of early marriages that had been forced by unwanted pregnancy. This trend changed during the 1990s. The prevalence of marriages after some period of premarital cohabitation and dissolution of some of these relationships before marriage led to a drastic decrease in the number of early divorces (after less than five years of marriage) from 35 percent in the 1980s to 13 percent at the close of the twentieth century. Accordingly, the average duration of a marriage at divorce increased from nine years in 1990 to twelve in 1999.

Because marriages lasted longer before the couples divorced, the percentage of couples with children also increased during the 1990s, from 62 to 67 percent, while the average number of their children remained almost the same—1.5 per couple.

Family

At the end of twentieth century, 88 percent of the Latvian population lived in families. The make-up of families varied, as couples had children at different stages of life. Thus, families consisted of both parents with children under eighteen (32 % of the population); those with older, unmarried children (16%); young couples with no children (those who had left their parental homes in their twenties) and couples whose adult children had moved out (26%); and single-parent families with underage children (8%). Fourteen percent of population lived in three-generation families, most in rural areas (30%). The proportion of single-parent families and one-person households (12%) corresponded to the high divorce rate and the disparities in gender in the older generations. More than half of those who live alone were older than sixty, and most of them were women (Eglite 2001).

Latvian families are small. The fertility surveys show that most couples want, on average, two children, although this varies slightly by age, sex, ethnicity, or education (1998). This would keep population numbers at steady replacement levels. The actual birth rate, however, does not correspond to the desired birth rate. After some increase between 1985 and 1989, the birth rate dropped in the 1990s—during the transition to a market economy—and in 1999 was two times lower than at the end of the 1980s. This drop happened mainly in civil marriages; the number of births in church marriages remained constant, while the number of extramarital births increased. The share of the latter in total births rose from some 12 percent in the 1980s to 39 percent in 1999 (Demographic Yearbook of Latvia 2000).

The principal reason the drop in birth rates is the low standard of living (Zarina 1995). During the 1990s, 47 percent of the households with one child and 74 percent with three or more children lived under the poverty line (approximately sixty U.S. dollars per member, per month) (Eglite 1999). To prevent a drop in population, the state supports childrearing. Employed mothers are entitled to four months' maternity allowance on full salary and a child's sickness benefit. For each child, if the caregiver does not have full-time employment, families receive a birth grant—a childcare allowance until the child is one and one-half years of age, and a monthly allowance proportional to order of birth up to fifteen years of age. Children also have free and mandatory education until grade nine, and secondary education if they choose (it is not mandatory). The total of these payments, however, does not compensate for the mothers' lost salary.

In contemporary Latvia, attitudes towards gender roles in the family are fluid. Stereotypes of husband as earner and wife as housekeeper are more popular among men than women (Rungule 1997). Younger generations and more educated groups tend to share responsibilities. At the end of the twentieth century 52 percent of men and women in their thirties recognized that there is no distinct leader in their family while 40 percent of men and 31 percent of women thought that the family was headed by the husband (Koroleva 1999).

In reality even employed women still spend almost twice as much time as men on unpaid domestic tasks and more than two times on childcare (*Time Use* 1998). The quality of family life could be improved by increasing fathers' participation and creating better possibilities to reconcile mothers' employment with childcare.

Bibliography

Demographic Yearbook of Latvia (since 1990 yearly). Riga: Central Statistical Bureau of Latvia.

Eglite, P. (2001). "Household Composition." In *Living Conditions in Latvia*: Norbalt—2, ed. E. Vaskis. Riga: Central Statistical Bureau of Latvia.

Eglite, P., Pavlina, I.; and I. M. Markausa. (1999). *Situation of Family in Latvia*. Riga: Institute of Economics, Latvian Academy of Science.

Fertility and Family Survey in Countries of the ECE Regions, Standard Country Report, Latvia. (1998). New York and Geneva: United Nations.

Koroleva, I. (1999). "The Views of Young People on the Role of the Man and the Woman in the Family." In *Man's Role in the Family,* ed. I. B. Zarina. Riga: Latvian Women's Studies and Information Center.

Rungule, R. (1997). "The Role of Parents—Fathers and Mothers—in the Family and in Society." In *Invitation to Dialogue: Beyond Gender (In)equality,* ed. I. Koroleva. Riga: Institute of Philosophy and Sociology, Latvian Academy of Sciences.

Time Use by the Population of Latvia. Statistical Bulletin. (1998). Riga: Central Statistical Bureau of Latvia, Institute of Economics, Latvian Academy of Sciences.

Zarina, I. B. (1995). "Actual and Desired Family Models in Latvia." *Humanities and Social Sciences. Latvia.* 2(7):48–61.

Zvidrins, P., and Ezera, L. (1999). "Dynamics and Differentiation of Cohabitation in Latvia." *Revue Baltique* 13:71–81.

PARSLA EGLITE

LEARNING DISABILITIES

Learning disabilities applies to difficulties in reading, mathematics, and written language. Although children with learning disabilities can have difficulty with spoken language and language comprehension, most of the research revolves around the ability to read and understand *written* information. For further information about oral communication one should look at material in speech and language, which is beyond the scope of this entry.

Learning difficulties can be present in *reading* (phonics, comprehension), *mathematics* (calculation, reasoning), *language* (receptive, expressive), and *written expression*. Learning disabilities are assumed to be due to central nervous system dysfunction (National Joint Committee for Learning Disabilities [NJCLD] 1991) and reflect a discrepancy between ability and achievement.

Diagnosis of Learning Disabilities

The diagnosis of learning disabilities varies depending on where one resides, with different states having different requirements for a learning disability diagnosis. Differences among states vary between psychometric measurement practices, which are called discrepancy models. However, most definitions share the requirement that a significant discrepancy exist between ability and achievement. The Intelligence Quotient (IQ) test becomes an important part of the diagnosis in these definitions. Such a discrepancy model leads to differing numbers of children identified as learning disabled (Sofie and Riccio 2002). Children and adolescents who are in the low average range of intelligence have a more difficult time qualifying for services as they must score very low on an achievement test in order to qualify (Semrud-Clikeman et al. 1992).

Children who have language difficulties frequently score poorly on the verbal portion of the IQ test, thus lowering their scores (Aaron 1997; Morris et al. 1998; Siegel 1992). These children and those from backgrounds other than the middle and upper class may be penalized by standardized tests that are far from culture-free (Greenfield 1997; Siegel 1990; Stanovich 1986). The highest concentration of poor readers has been found in certain ethnic groups and in poor urban neighborhoods (Snow, Burns, and Griffin 1998). Children from impoverished backgrounds or those from a different culture may not have acquired sufficient knowledge in order to answer the IQ test questions correctly. In fact, research has found that many of these children are not classified as learning disabled but rather as slow learners and often not considered bright enough to profit from remediation (Siegel 1990). The current methods of diagnosing children with learning disabilities assume that intelligence is a prerequisite for reading attainment. Research has indicated that IQ scores account for only 25 percent of the variance in reading scores and, as such, is not an important variable in predicting how a child will read (Aaron 1997; Swanson, Hoskyn, and Lee 1999). R. Valencia (1995) found that major achievement tests may underestimate the learning of minority children, particularly those whose primary language is not English. A study found that IQ explained only 6 percent of the variance of a Hispanic child's variance and only 10 percent of an African-American child's grades (Figueroa and Sassenrath, 1989).

Some authors suggest that children reading below grade level should be provided with reading support no matter what ability level they possess. Sally Shaywitz and her colleagues (1992) found that reading disabilities occur along a continuum with no clear difference between children with reading problems and those usually classified as *slow learners*. Further research has found more similarities than differences between slow learners and those with learning disabilities with few differences present between these two groups on measures of reading, spelling, and phonics knowledge (Siegel 1990). Linda Siegel concluded that the more the task is related to reading the less important intelligence is to reading achievement.

Assessment Issues

Given the above concerns, it is important to provide a comprehensive evaluation of a child with a possible learning disability. Reading is a multidimensional skill involving the ability to read words from sight, sound out words (phonological coding), read fluently and with good speed, and to understand what is read. In any part of this reading process problems can arise and disrupt the reading process. For example, a child who reads haltingly and needs to sound out almost every word will often experience difficulty with comprehension because it takes so long to read a passage and the child is concentrating on the words rather than the information. Evaluation of this child's *reading rate* and *sight-word vocabulary* are important aspects. Reading a passage to him/her and checking the comprehension of the passage assists one in understanding whether difficulties in comprehension are due to true comprehension problems or to the difficulty with the reading process. Similarly a child who has difficulty sounding out words may well have an intact sight-word vocabulary. In this case the child will benefit from using this strength with remediation in phonics.

Comorbidity Issues

Learning disabilities often occur in conjunction with other disorders or conditions. *Comorbidity* refers to multiple disorders within one individual. Learning disabilities occur concurrently with other conditions (for example, sensory impairment or serious emotional disturbance), but is not a result of the comorbid disorder (NJCLD 1991). For example, a child who is hearing-impaired would not

A special education teacher helps an ADHD student with a math assignment. The inattention and impulsivity characteristic of ADHD make it difficult to determine if academic difficulty is due to the presence of learning disabilities or is a consequence of attention deficits. PHOTO RESEARCHERS, INC.

qualify for LD services due solely to the hearing impairment.

Attention deficit hyperactivity disorders (ADHD) and learning disabilities are frequently comorbid. However, the inattention and impulsivity characteristic of ADHD make it difficult to determine if academic difficulty is due to the presence of learning disabilities or is a consequence of attention deficits (Semrud-Clikeman et al. 1992). *Language disorders, depression,* and *anxiety* are often experienced by those diagnosed with learning disabilities (American Psychiatric Association 1994). Social skills deficits are also frequently found in children diagnosed with learning disability (San Miguel et al. 1996).

Neuropsychology of Learning Disabilities

Learning disabilities is a heterogeneous disorder. The most common type of learning disability is language-based and due to difficulties with the sounding out of words—also called *phonological coding deficits* (Teeter and Semrud-Clikeman 1997). In this type of learning disability the child has difficulty hearing and/or understanding the differences in the sounds of a word (Mann 1991). For example, the word *cat* may not be heard as three different sounds—*c a t*. Reading requires that a

child learn the relationship between the written letters and the sound segments—also called *sound-symbol learning* (Torgesen 1993). This is the most common type of learning disability.

Another type of learning disability involves difficulty with the *visual* or *orthographic* features of a word (Stanovich 1992). For example the outward configuration of words such as *left* and *felt* are relatively similar—high letter, low letter, two high letters—and may be confused by a child with this type of learning disability. These types of learning disabilities are less common. *Visual memory* is important in reading and children with this type of learning disability seem to have difficulty recalling what they see (Terepocki, Kruk, and Willows 2002). Children are evaluated in their ability to discriminate phonetically similar words like *main* from *mane* and homonyms (e.g., *see* and *sea*).

The majority of learning disabilities are reading based and most of the research involves children with *reading disabilities* (or *dyslexia*). However, it is important to realize that learning disabilities can also be identified in mathematics and written language. These types of learning problems are not as commonly evaluated or reported as a reading disability. Written language disabilities can have profound effects on a child's ability to generate and organize ideas in written form (Nodine, Barenbaum, and Newcomer 1985). Less is known about written language disabilities than reading disabilities but a study that evaluated children with brain injuries found that these children had intact reading skills but deficits in mathematics and written language, particularly if the damage was in the right hemisphere.

The incidence of *math-based learning disabilities* suggests that approximately 6 percent of children show a learning disability in this area (Miles and Forcht 1995). Difficulties can be found in mathematics calculations that are often related to difficulties with visual-spatial skills. Children with this type of disability may also show difficulties with *social understanding.* When mathematics problems and visual-spatial delays occur together, the child may have a *nonverbal learning disability.* These difficulties involve the child's inability to understand the context of the social situation, to interpret facial and body gestures, and to act accordingly. The relationship between the mathematics difficulties and these social deficits is not fully understood and further research is needed in this area (Semrud-Clikeman and Hynd 1990).

Neuro-Imaging and Learning Disabilities

Differences in brain anatomy have been consistently found in the area where sound-symbol relationships are believed to take place. Neuro-imaging has now allowed further evaluation of the brain in living children. Studies found differences in the area of the brain responsible for sound-symbol interpretation (Hynd et al. 1990) as well as in the left hemisphere and frontal areas of the brain believed to be responsible for speaking (Jernigan et al. 1991; Semrud-Clikeman et al. 1991). Neurons were found to be out of place, additional neurons in places where they should not be were found, and smaller volumes of the planatemporale were found. This area is responsible for auditory processing (Hynd and Semrud-Clikeman 1989). Such regional differences imply a neurodevelopmental process that went awry during gestation rather than brain damage or environmental influences. It is important to note that this asymmetry/symmetry may not be solely responsible for learning disabilities, although it is likely a major contributor to such difficulties (Morgan and Hynd 1998; Steinmetz and Galaburda 1991).

Electrophysiology and Learning Disabilities

Electrophysiological techniques have also been used in the study of learning disabilities to examine the neurobiological mechanisms that underlie these disabilities. The brain has ongoing electrical activity whose waveform can be measured and recorded. Large populations of neurons are measured by electrodes placed on the scalp with changes in the ongoing waveform occurring in response to a cognitive event, such as attention or stimulus discrimination.

Several decades of research have demonstrated different patterns of activation in the brains of children with learning disabilities and those of control groups. Abnormal electrical responses have been found in populations with learning disabilities when they are asked to process phonological information. Studies of components not involving conscious processing have demonstrated that adults and children with reading disabilities process auditory information differently than do normal readers. These components occur later in subjects with learning disabilities, indicating low-level auditory processing deficits. (McAnally and Stein 1996; Baldeweg et al. 1999). This physiological abnormality has also found to be correlated with phonological deficits.

Genetics of Learning Disabilities

The genetics of learning disabilities became of an area of significant interest beginning in the 1990s. Reading disabilities run in families and this familiarity may be due in part to genetic influences and in part to environment. These genetic influences are likely to have a direct impact on the development of the brain or a specific region of the brain that is probably involved in language.

Genetic influences appear to be more prominent in children with phonological coding deficits than in those with visual coding deficits (Pennington 1991). These studies have been generally involved identical and fraternal twins. Deficits in specific processes have been found in *phonological coding* (the ability to discriminate sounds in words) and *phonemic analysis* (the ability to sound out words) compared to in visual-spatial deficits (DeFries et al. 1991). The concordance of phonetically based learning problems was 71 percent for identical twins but only 49 percent for fraternal twins. Bruce Pennington and his colleagues (1991) found evidence of a major gene transmission in a large sample of families with reading disabilities linking a small set of genes that indirectly affect reading. Although chromosomes 6 and 15 have been linked to reading problems, it is likely that the difficulty is due to several genes that have not been fully evaluated (Smith, Kimberling, and Pennington 1991). Genetic analysis of children with mathematics or written expression disabilities is another area that requires study.

Environmental influences also impact the brain and culture may change the development of neurons in a specific manner (e.g., reading left to right rather than right to left). Arabic and Hebrew readers have been found to show differences in hemispheric activation on reading tasks—particularly tasks that involve orthographic processing (Eviatar 2000). In addition, preliminary studies have indicated that those readers that read right to left do not show the same right hemispheric preference for the processing of faces and emotion as do those who read left to right (Eviatar 1997; Vaid and Singh 1989). Genetics and neuro-imaging studies may provide more information about these differences.

Familial risk for learning disabilities is clearly significant and substantial in many of the research findings (Gilger, Pennington, and DeFries 1991). Environment may play a role in the development of reading disabilities but no difference has been found between preschool literacy rate in children with reading problems and those without reading problems (Scarborough 1991). What has been found that within the family, the child with a predisposition for a reading problem is less interested in reading and reading-like activities than those without such a predilection (Scarborough, Dobrich, and Hager 1991). Moreover, differences in amount of time being read to, looking at books, and listening to stories were found between siblings with and without later reading difficulties.

Family Aspects of Learning Disabilities

The discussion of the genetics of learning disabilities leads into family aspects as many parents also have a learning disability. It is important to recognize this possibility, particularly when developing interventions and recommendations for these families. It may be unrealistic to ask a parent who also has a learning disability to read to their child, as the action may be fraught with anxiety and difficulty for the parent. It is also important to realize that parents who experienced difficulty in learning themselves may find coming to a school for a parent-teacher conference to be frightening and intimidating (Semrud-Clikeman 1994).

There are few studies in this area but prenatal and postnatal factors have been found to be important in the development of learning problems in the first two years of life (Werner and Smith 1981). Families that were characterized as chaotic or in poverty showed a higher probability of children experiencing learning problems than those without—these variables become more significant as the child becomes older (Teeter and Semrud-Clikeman 1997). Socioeconomic status, home conditions, and educational level of family members appear to act either as complicating factors or as compensatory factors for children with reading problems (Badian 1988; Keogh and Sears 1991).

Robert Jay Green (1992) draws from biological, sociological, and familial sources in evaluating the impact of families on achievement and learning. He suggests that each of these factors interact with one another and either improve learning or impede skill development. These factors work less strongly on biologically based difficulties (e.g., genetically based type of learning disability) than on those environmentally based. However, difficulties in learning and attention are due to the influences of many genes and may well respond to environmental changes that can assist the child in overcoming learning difficulties in an environment that is helpful and exacerbate the difficulties in a less than optimal environment. Green's (1992) model assumes that achievement difficulties can be partially caused or maintained by family factors as well as those present in the school system and social environments. Given these concerns it is important to link school-based interventions with family support.

Interventions

Children with phonological coding deficits appear to respond well to interventions that stress direct training of phonics and place the training within a context (Cunningham 1990). Such a context—*metacognitive* training—allows the child to learn when to use a particular tactic and how to decide if it is effective (Cunningham 1989). The *Reading Recovery Program* (Clay 1993) has shown good promise in assisting children with their learning. The program emphasizes understanding the reading process in addition to emphasizing decoding skills. Teaching word families within this context has also been found to be helpful (i.e., *an, in, fan, tan,* or *man*).

Early identification of children at risk for learning difficulties is also recommended with specific training in phonemic awareness, rhyming skills, and word families provided in preschool and kindergarten (Felton and Pepper 1995; Wise and Olson 1991). Such early intervention has been found to be most appropriate for children with a family history of learning disabilities (Scarborough 1991). These children demonstrate early on difficulties in language, both in understanding and expressing their thoughts, that later translates into problems in reading readiness (Wise and Olson 1991). Programs, such as *FastForword, Lindamood*

Auditory System, and the *Slingerland* or *Orton-Gillingham* method, are helpful to some children with learning disabilities. Websites can be readily found for each of these interventions.

Conclusion

Learning disabilities is a field that is constantly changing. With the advent of techniques that allow scholars to study the brain in action, we may understand not only the normal process of reading but also what happens when the system is not working. The hope is that we will be able to prevent learning disabilities or, at the least, to develop innovative and successful interventions. It is also hoped that we will become more adept at identifying children at earlier ages to prevent some of the emotional and social difficulties that can be associated with a learning disability. Neuroscience is now promising new avenues in our study of learning disabilities as is genetics. Families who have a history of learning disability need further study to provide appropriate support for them as well as to assist with early interventions. Schools are becoming more adept at working with children with differing types of learning disability and it is hoped that our ability to assess minority children appropriately will also improve.

See also: ACADEMIC ACHIEVEMENT; CHRONIC ILLNESS; DEVELOPMENT: COGNITIVE; SCHOOL

Bibliography

Aaron, P. G. (1997). "The Impending Demise of the Discrepancy Formula." *Review of Educational Research* 67:461–502.

American Psychiatric Association. (1994). *Diagnostic and Statistical Manual of Mental Disorders,* 4th edition. Washington, DC: Author.

Badian, N. (1988). "The Prediction of Good and Poor Reading before Kindergarten Entry: A Nine-Year Follow-Up." *Journal of Learning Disabilities* 21: 98–103.

Baldeweg, T.; Richardson, A.; Watkins, S.; Foale, C.; and Gruzelier, J. (1999). "Impaired Auditory Frequency Discrimination in Dyslexia Detected with Mismatch Evoked Potentials." *Annals of Neurology* 45:495–503.

Clay, M. M. (1993). *Reading Recovery: A Guidebook for Teachers in Training.* Portsmouth, NH: Heinemann.

Cunningham, A. (1989). "Phonemic Awareness: The Development of Early Reading Competency." *Reading Research Quarterly* 24:471–472.

Cunningham, A. (1990). "Explicit versus Implicit Instruction in Phonemic Awareness." *Journal of Experimental Child Psychology* 50:429–444.

DeFries, J. C.; Stevenson, J.; Gillis, J. J.; and Wadsworth, S. J. (1991). "Genetic Etiology of Spelling Deficits in the Colorado and London Twin Studies of Reading Disability." In *Reading Disabilities: Genetic and Neurological Influences,* ed. B. F. Pennington. Boston: Kluwer Academic.

Eviatar, Z. (1997). "Language Experience and Right Hemisphere Tasks: The Effects of Scanning Habits and Multilingualism." *Brain and Language* 58:157–173

Eviatar, Z. (2000). "Culture and Brain Organization." *Brain and Cognition* 42:50–52.

Felton, R. H., and Pepper, P. P. (1995). "Neuropsychological Prediction of Reading Disabilities." In *Neuropsychological Foundations of Learning Disabilities: A Handbook of Issues, Methods, and Practice,* ed. J. E. Obrzut and G. W. Hynd. San Diego, CA: Harcourt.

Figueroa, R. A., and Sassenrath, J. M. (1989). "A Longitudinal Study of the Predictive Validity of the System of Multicultural Pluralistic Assessment (SOMPA)." *Psychology in the Schools* 26:5–19.

Gilger, J. W.; Pennington, B. F.; and DeFries, J. C. (1991). "Risk for Reading Disability as a Function of Parental History in Three Family Studies." In *Reading Disabilities: Genetic and Neurological Influences,* ed. B. Pennington. Boston: Kluwer Academic.

Green, R. J. (1992). "Learning to Learn and the Family System: New Perspectives on Underachievement and Learning Disorders." In *The Handbook of Family-School Intervention,* ed. M. J. Fine and C. Carlson. Boston: Allyn and Bacon.

Greenfield, P. M. (1997). "You Can't Take It with You: Why Ability Assessments Don't Cross Cultures." *American Psychologist* 52:1115–1124.

Hynd, G. W., and Semrud-Clikeman, M. (1989). "Dyslexia and Brain Morphology." *Psychological Bulletin* 106: 447–482.

Hynd, G. W.; Semrud-Clikeman, M.; Lorys, A. R.; and Novey, E. S. (1990). "Brain Morphology in Developmental Dyslexia and Attention Deficit Disorder/Hyperactivity." *Archives of Neurology* 47(8):919–926.

Individuals with Disabilities Education Act. (Pub. L. No. 101–476) 20 U.S.C. Chapter 33. Amended by Pub. L. No. 105–17 in June 1997. Regulations appear at 34 C.F.R. Part 300.

Jernigan, T. L.; Hesselink, J. R.; Sowell, E.; and Tallal, P. A. (1991). "Cerebral Structure on Magnetic Resonance

Imaging in Language-and Learning-Impaired Children." *Archives of Neurology* 48:539–545.

Keogh, B. K., and Sears, S. (1991). "Learning Disabilities from a Developmental Perspective: Early Identification and Prediction." In *Learning about Learning Disabilities,* ed. B. Y. L. Wong. Orlando, FL: Academic Press.

Mann, V. (1991). "Why Some Children Encounter Reading Problems." In *Psychology and Educational Perspectives on Learning Disabilities,* ed. J. Torgesen and B. Y. L. Wong. Orlando, FL: Academic Press.

McAnally, K. I., and Stein, J. F. (1996). "Auditory Temporal Coding in Dyslexia." *Proceedings of the Royal Society of London* 263:961–965.

Miles, D. D., and Forcht, J. P. (1995). "Mathematics Strategies for Secondary Students with Learning Disabilities or Mathematical Deficiencies: A Cognitive Approach." *Intervention in School and Clinics* 31:91–96.

Morgan, A. E., and Hynd, G. W. (1998). "Dyslexia, Neurolinguistic Ability, and Anatomical Variation of the Planum Temporale." *Neuropsychology Review* 8(2): 79–93.

Morris, R. D.; Stuebing, K. K.; Fletcher, J. M.; Shaywitz, S. E.; Lyon, G. R.; Shankweiler, D. P.; Katz, L.; Francis, D. J.; and Shaywitz, B. A. (1998). "Subtypes of Reading Disability: Variability around a Phonological Core." *Journal of Educational Psychology* 90:347–373.

National Joint Committee on Learning Disabilities. (1991). "Learning Disabilities: Issues on Definition." *Asha* 33(Suppl. 5):18–20.

Nodine, B. F.; Barenbaum, E.; and Newcomer, P. (1985). "Story Composition by Learning Disabled, Reading Disabled, and Normal Children." *Learning Disability Quarterly* 8:167–179.

Pennington, B. (1991). *Reading Disabilities: Genetic and Neurological Influences.* Boston: Kluwer Academic.

Pennington, B. F.; Gilger, J.; Pauls, D.; Smith, S. A.; Smith, S. D.; and DeFries, J. (1991). "Evidence for Major Gene Transmission of Developmental Dyslexia." *Journal of the American Medical Association* 266: 1527–1535.

San Miguel, S. K.; Forness, S. R.; and Kavale, K. A. (1996). "Social Skills Deficits in Learning Disabilities: The Psychiatric Comorbidity Hypothesis." *Learning Disability Quarterly* 19(4):252–261.

Scarborough, H. S. (1991). "Antecedents to Reading Disability: Preschool Language Development and Literacy

Experiences of Children from Dyslexic Families." In *Reading Disabilities: Genetic and Neurological Influences,* ed. B. F. Pennington. Boston: Kluwer Academic.

Scarborough, H. S.; Dobrich, W.; and Hager, M. (1991). "Preschool Literacy Experience and Later Reading Achievement." *Journal of Learning Disabilities* 24(8): 508–511.

Semrud-Clikeman, M. (1994). *Child and Adolescent Therapy.* Boston: Allyn and Bacon.

Semrud-Clikeman, M.; Biederman, J.; Sprich-Buckminster, S.; Lehman, B. K.; Faraone, S. V.; and Norman, D. (1992). "Comorbidity between ADDH and Learning Disability: A Review and Report in a Clinically Referred Sample." *Journal of American Academy of Child and Adolescent Psychiatry* 31(3):439–448.

Semrud-Clikeman, M., and Hynd, G. W. (1990). "Right Hemispheric Dysfunction in Nonverbal Learning Disabilities: Social, Academic, and Adaptive Function in Adults and Children." *Psychological Bulletin* 107: 196–207.

Semrud-Clikeman, M.; Hynd, G. W.; Novey, E. S.; and Eliopulos, D. (1991). "Relationships between Neurolinguistic Measures and Brain Morphometry in Dyslexic, ADHD, and Normal Children." *Learning and Individual Differences* 3:225–242.

Shaywitz, S. E.; Escobar, M. D.; Shaywitz, B. A.; Fletcher, J. M.; and Makuch, R. (1992). "Evidence that Dyslexia May Represent the Lower Tail of a Normal Distribution of Reading Ability." *New England Journal of Medicine* 326:145–150.

Siegel, L. S. (1990). "IQ and Learning Disabilities: R.I.P." In *Learning Disabilities: Theoretical and Research Issues,* ed. H. L. Swanson and B. Keogh. Hillsdale, NJ: Erlbaum.

Siegel, L. S. (1992). "An Evaluation of the Discrepancy Definition of Dyslexia." *Journal of Learning Disabilities* 25:618–629.

Smith, S. D.; Kimberling, W. J.; and Pennington, B. F. (1991). "Screening for Multiple Genes Influencing Dyslexia." In *Reading Disabilities: Genetic and Neurological Influences,* ed. B. F. Pennington. Boston: Kluwer Academic.

Snow, C. E.; Burns, M. S.; and Griffin, P. (1998). *Preventing Reading Difficulties in Young Children.* Washington, DC: National Academy Press.

Sofie, C. A., and Riccio, C. A. (2002). "A Comparison of Multiple Methods for the Identification of Children with Reading Disabilities." *Journal of Learning Disabilities* 35:234–244.

Stanovich, K. E. (1986). "Matthew Effects in Reading: Some Consequences of Individual Differences in the Acquisition of Literacy." *Reading Research Quarterly* 21:360–407.

Stanovich, K. E. (1992). "Developmental Reading Disorder." In *Developmental Disorders: Diagnostic Criteria and Clinical Assessment,* ed. S. R. Hooper and G. Hynd. Hillsdale, NJ: Erlbaum.

Steinmetz, H., and Galaburda, A. M. (1991). "Planum Temporale Asymmetry: In-Vivo Morphometry Affords a New Perspective for Neuro-Behavioral Research." *Reading and Writing* 3(3):331–343.

Swanson, H. L.; Hoskyn, M.; and Lee, C. (1999). *Interventions for Students with Learning Disabilities: A Meta-Analysis of Treatment Outcomes.* New York: Guilford Press.

Teeter, P. A., and Semrud-Clikeman, M. (1997). *Child Neuropsychology: Assessment and Intervention.* Boston: Allyn and Bacon.

Terepocki, M.; Kruk, R. S.; and Willows, D. M. (2002). "The Incidence and Nature of Letter Orientation Errors in Reading Disability." *Journal of Learning Disabilities* 35:214–233.

Torgesen, J. K. (1993). "Variations on Theory in Learning Disabilities." In *Better Understanding Learning Disabilities: New Views from Research and Their Implications for Education and Public Policies,* ed. G. R. Lyon, D. Gray, J. Kavanagh, and N. Krasnegor. Baltimore, MD: Paul H. Brookes.

Vaid, J., and Singh, M. (1989). "Asymmetries in the Perception of Facial Affect: Is There an Influence of Reading Habits?" *Neuropsychologia* 27:1277–1287.

Valencia, R. R. (1995). "K-ABC Content Bias: Comparisons between Mexican American and White Children." *Psychology in the Schools* 32:153–158.

Werner, E. E., and Smith, R. S. (1981). *Vulnerable but Invincible: A Study of Resilient Children.* New York: McGraw-Hill.

Wise, B. W., and Olson, R. K. (1991). "Remediating Reading Disabilities." In *Neuropsychological Foundations of Learning Disabilities: A Handbook of Issues, Methods, and Practice,* ed. J. E. Obrzut and G. W. Hynd. Orlando, FL: Academic Press.

MARGARET SEMRUD-CLIKEMAN
KELLIE HIGGINS

LEBANON

See ETHNIC VARIATION/ETHNICITY

LEISURE

The family has been, and continues to be, important to the study of leisure. Conversely, research on leisure provides valuable insights in understanding families and how they function, However, although *family leisure* is a concept studied around the world (Freysinger and Chen 1993; Dijk, Betuw, and Kloeze 1993; McCabe 1993; Samuel 1996; Wearing and McArthur 1988), there has long been controversy in defining the concept (Shaw 1997). This entry reviews the research on family and leisure focusing predominantly, but not solely, on scholarship conducted within the field of leisure studies in North America.

Meanings of Leisure

Leisure in Western cultures has been defined in many ways, most commonly as time, activity, and a state of mind (Kelly and Freysinger 2000). Central to each of these definitions is the concept of freedom or choice: leisure is *discretionary time* (time when one is free from obligation). Leisure is activity that is not required. As a state of mind, leisure is the perception of choice or of the freedom to choose. Concomitant with this freedom is the perception that leisure is positive or beneficial to the individual and/or society. This notion of leisure has its roots in ancient Greece, where leisure was seen as both freedom from the necessity of *ponos* (work or sorrow) and freedom for engagement with *paideia* (culture). Engagement in leisure would allow man to develop virtue or his full potential and in so doing, prepare him to be a good citizen and wise and just leader. Ignored for the most part in discussions of the history of leisure was the fact that leisure as freedom was available primarily to a group of elite males and was possible only because of a slave economy and the subjugation of women.

Since the 1980s in the West, the notion of leisure as freedom has been continuously challenged by feminist, Marxist, cross-cultural, and critical sociological scholarship. Research in these areas suggests at least three problems with defining leisure as freedom of the individual:

(1) This is a conceptualization that does not apply to most of the world but rather reflects a specific culture (Western) and its development, economy, and ideologies (industrial/post-industrial capitalism, individualism).

(2) This notion of leisure is *androcentric* and ignores the gendered experience of leisure, everyday life, and aging across the life cycle.

(3) This is a predominantly social psychological (and North American) conceptualization of leisure that emphasizes individual experience and ignores social relationships and structures, cultural practices, and historical context.

Thus, more recent scholarship defines leisure as *legitimated pleasure,* a social construction and means of social reproduction (Rojek 1996), but also as a place where individuals may resist, challenge, and even transform oppressive or constraining social relations (Henderson et al. 1996).

This changing understanding of leisure in Western scholarship was influenced by research in North America and Great Britain on family leisure and differences in girls', boys', women's, and men's experiences of family and leisure (e.g., Henderson et al. 1996; Wimbush and Talbot 1988; Lynd and Lynd 1929; Rapoport and Rapoport 1975). However, despite the fact that the family has always been the major context of leisure, leisure was predominantly studied and defined in relationship to paid employment or work. In the aftermath of the Civil Rights and Women's Rights movements in the United States in the 1960s, the social roles of females and males started to change (e.g., a broader spectrum of women pursued higher education and/or paid employment) and research began to be directed towards the lives of women and girls. Such changes in girls' and women's opportunities, and thus in their family roles and leisure activities, has occurred more recently in other cultures as well (e.g., India and Korea) (Robertson 1995), though hegemonic patriarchal patterns in family and leisure continue to dominate in some countries (e.g., Bangladesh) (Khan 1997), and continue to exist in all countries. In countries where Women's Rights movements have altered educational and employment opportunities, sociology of leisure and leisure studies has increasingly focused on the family, and important insights have been gained about leisure, family, gender, and their interrelationships.

Family's Influence on Leisure

Family is the major context of leisure (Shaw 1998). When asked about most important leisure, individuals, regardless of age or culture, typically indicate that time spent or activities pursued with family are most valued. It is within families that individuals learn leisure skills, interests, attitudes, and behaviors, and research has indicated continuity of recreation and leisure interests learned in childhood and adolescence across the life course. In addition, family and family members are common or frequent leisure companions throughout the life cycle. Families also construct time and opportunities for leisure, as well as constraints. However, the family's influence on leisure is often distinguished by gender, social class, age, race/ethnicity, and culture.

Parents have a strong influence on children's and adolescents' play and recreation. They facilitate, constrain, and shape children's development of leisure skills, interests, and participation in numerous ways: through their own leisure activities, the toys made available, economic support for lessons and equipment, and transportation to and from practices, activities, and events. For example, in Canada and the United States mothers have been found to be important to children's ability to participate in recreation. Mothers, even when employed outside the home, are often the ones who actually transport (or organize the transportation of children) to various activities, events, and entertainment venues (Henderson et al. 1996). Research in Canada suggests, however, that children, in particular adolescents, do not passively accept leisure constraints imposed by parents. Rather, many adolescents negotiate constraints (e.g., parents' unavailability for transport) in ways that allow continued participation in valued leisure (Jackson and Rucks 1995). Further, the extent to which parents influence children's recreation and leisure, and how and why they do, varies by gender, social class, and/or race. Daughters are often more dependent than sons on parental approval and support for recreational activities; middle-class children have more independence and freedom from parents in their leisure than working-class children (e.g., McMeeking and Purkayastha 1995; Zeijl et al. 2000). Race and ethnicity are also important in shaping family's influence on children's leisure. For example, racial minority parents in the Netherlands and United States have been found to have concerns with children's leisure activities related to racism and being unwelcome that racial majority parents do not have (Phillip 1999; Zeijl et al. 2000). At the same time, recreation and leisure are also seen as ways to celebrate and pass on valued cultural and racial identities to children. The cultural values that shape racial and ethnic groups' leisure are not static, however. For example, Susan Juniu (2000), in a study of South American (Mexican or Hispanic) immigrants to the United States, found that cultural values surrounding work, social interaction, perceptions of time, and appropriate recreational activity changed with immigration, though this was mediated by the social class of the immigrants.

Adults' leisure is also strongly influenced by family. Much adult leisure is *role determined* (Kleiber 1999), that is, roles such as spouse, worker, parent, or caregiver have a tremendous influence on time, energy, economic resources, companions, and opportunities for, as well as the meaning of, leisure. The birth of the first child in particular—and the presence of dependent children in the home generally—has a dramatic impact on parental leisure. There is typically a shift from personal or joint (spouse/partner only) leisure to child-centered leisure. Women's leisure is especially affected by marriage and/or presence of dependent children. Research in Canada, the Netherlands, China and the United States suggests that women are more likely than men to give up personal leisure and to give priority to children's and/or spouse's (or partner's) leisure interests and engagements (Freysinger and Chen 1993; Shaw 1998). For example, in the Netherlands, despite research in the 1970s that suggested the family was becoming more *symmetrical* or *plastic* in terms of women's and men's roles, Simone van Dijk, Annita van Betuw, and Jan W. te Kloeze (1993) contend that such family structures exist in theory but not in practice. This is true regardless of age of the child (or children) and the mother's employment status. Further, based on her study of Canadian families' experiences of Christmas, Leslie Bella

(1992) found that women are most often the *organizers* and *providers* of family leisure. This gendered construction of family and leisure has resulted in women experiencing family leisure (particularly when dependent children are involved) as *semi-leisure* whereas men are more likely to experience the same interactions as *pure leisure*. This does not mean that family has an absolute or only a negative impact on women's leisure. Rather, women also negotiate family constraints to leisure, report important satisfactions from family leisure, and may derive different meanings from their leisure than do men. Further, in Canada, the United States, and Bangladesh, gender has been found to intersect with other identities such as race, social class, sexual orientation, and able-bodiedness in shaping family's impact on both women's and men's leisure (Allen and Chin-Sang 1991; Bialeschki and Pearce 1997; Henderson et al. 1995; Khan 1997; Tirone and Shaw 1997). Further, research in Canada, Great Britain, the United States, and other countries indicates the experience and impact of family on leisure changes with age, as the demands of and activities in family and other social roles shift and developmental changes occur (e.g., Bialeschki 1994; Dupuis and Smale 2000), and across time as cultures are altered by economic, social, and political changes. For example, changing family structures in Korea at the end of the twentieth century has led to decreased intergenerational and interfamilial activities and increased intrafamilial activities (Robertson 1995). In France, Nicole Samuel (1996) has documented changing notions of vacation time for French families.

In summary, the family shapes leisure meanings and participation across the course of life and time in a myriad of ways. Family is both a source of leisure opportunity and constraint, reflecting the tension between individual wants/self-determination and societal norms/expectations of others. This tension is perhaps best illustrated in the gendered experience of family leisure and in cultural differences in perceptions and notions of leisure. At the same time, individuals negotiate family constraints to leisure and report finding freedom or leisure within constraint. Finally, how and why family is important to individuals' experiences of leisure differs across cultures and changes across age and time as family roles, responsibilities, and structures change, development

A Sephardic family celebrates Passover by sharing a picnic in West Jerusalem. Individuals learn leisure skills, interests, attitudes, and behaviors within the family. Family members are common leisure companions throughout the life cycle.
ANNIE GRIFFITHS BELT/CORBIS

occurs, and societal norms and cultural practices are challenged.

Leisure's Influence on Family

In addition to investigating the impact that the family has on children's and adults' experiences of play, recreation and leisure, researchers have also examined the impact that leisure interests and participation has on family satisfaction, family interaction, and family stability or cohesion. Although a popular belief is that "the family that plays together stays together," the research in this area indicates that leisure can serve to both facilitate and undermine family satisfaction, interaction, and cohesion.

Leisure is a way through which the parental role is enacted. Although mothers and fathers do not enact the parental role in the same way, both mothers and fathers report that leisure is an important context for the development of children.

By teaching their children how to use free time constructively or by providing challenging and stimulating recreational activities, parents feel that they are facilitating the learning and growth of their children (Freysinger 1995). Further, leisure is seen as a context for the affirmation of family. Leisure with one's children and/or spouse provides a common interest and a context for interaction and is perceived by adults to strengthen bonds between family members and to provide a sense of family (Freysinger 1995; Orthner and Mancini 1990). At the same time, leisure interaction with children has been found to have a different impact on mothers' and fathers' satisfaction with being a parent. A study by Valeria Freysinger (1994) in the United States found that although mothers had more leisure interactions with their children than fathers, these had no effect on mothers' parental satisfaction. Other research (e.g., McClanahan and Adams 1987) indicates that mothers report both greater satisfaction with and stress from being a parent than fathers, which is one possible explanation for Freysinger's findings. On the other hand, leisure interaction with children was positively related to fathers' parental satisfaction. For both, however, marital satisfaction was the strongest and a positive predictor of parental satisfaction.

Indeed leisure has been found to positively related to marital satisfaction and stability and these relationships seem to be true across cultures (Orthner and Mancini 1990). Although preferences for joint or shared, parallel, and individual leisure vary over the marital career and differ somewhat by gender, in general the research suggests that the time spent in joint or shared activities is positively related to marital satisfaction for both husbands and wives. However, it is not just spending time together that is important to marital satisfaction. Rather, it seems to be the amount of communication that occurs during time together that is positively related to marital satisfaction.

Children affect the amount of leisure interaction spouses have with one another. Couples with children in the home tend to have less leisure interaction and that negatively affects satisfaction with the spousal/couple relationship. At the same time, children's effect on parental leisure is not uniformly negative. Children may provide new leisure interests and social networks for their parents. For example, adults with children involved in sport and physical activity are more likely than adults with no children or nonphysically active children to stay involved in recreational physical activity.

As suggested above, leisure may also be a source of tension or conflict within families. This may be because leisure connotes a freedom of choice that may contradict expectations that family members have of one another or that may challenge authority relations in some families. For example, in her study of the leisure of mid-life women and men, Valeria Freysinger (1995) found that leisure was a source of dissatisfaction with one's spouse and marriage when different leisure interests limited time for interaction. Some of the divorced men in this study reported that the different leisure interests they and their ex-wives had contributed to the dissolution of their marriages. Other reasons leisure may be a source of family conflict include inappropriate use of leisure or free

time, changing leisure patterns, and conflicting circadian rhythms (i.e., a *night person* and a *morning person*) (Orthner and Mancini 1990).

In summary, leisure is both a source of family satisfaction and cohesion as well as dissatisfaction and instability. The relationship between leisure and family satisfaction, interaction, and cohesion is complex. A number of other factors (e.g., presence, number, and age of children, educational and employment status, stage of the marital career) likely mediate these relationships. For example, Deborah Bialeschki (1994) found that although *leisure interruption* was a common experience of U.S. women with children at home, once children left the home and active mothering demands decreased, a focus on self through leisure re-emerged in a process she called *full-circle leisure*. Stephen Goff, Daniel Fick, and Robert Oppliger (1997), in a study of "serious runners" and their spouses, found that leisure-family conflict was moderated by spouses' level of support for running. Such factors must be considered when seeking to understand the significance of leisure to family.

Emerging Issues and Unanswered Questions

This review of the extant research on family and leisure points to a number of issues, questions, and directions for future scholarship in this area including:

(1) *Leisure* and *family* are historically situated concepts that cannot be separated from culture and society; that is, one's experience and understanding of leisure and family are constantly being constructed and reconstructed, challenged and transformed in the interactions of individuals and contexts. It will be important for future researchers to be aware of the diversity of people's experiences of leisure and family and to explore this diversity in the way the research is conceptualized, the questions that are asked, and the populations that are studied (e.g., Acock and Demo 1994; Cheal 1991).

(2) Jennifer Mactavish, Stuart Schleien, and Carla Tabourne (1997) in their study of patterns of recreation in families with developmentally disabled children, asked the question, "Who is involved in family recreation most of the

time?" They found that family leisure participants included both immediate family members and extended family members, all members of the family and subgroups (e.g., children only, parents only, one parent and all children) of the family. The most common pattern was subgroup leisure activity. However, much research on family leisure does not ask who is involved and in not asking this question what is meant by family leisure and the importance of family leisure is obscured.

(3) Most of the research on leisure and family has focused on adult perceptions and experiences. In one of the few studies that asked both parents and children about their perceptions of family leisure, Reed Larson, Sally Gillman, and Maryse Richards (1997) found that adolescent children experienced lower intrinsic motivation and less positive affect than parents during family leisure. Future research needs to further explore children's perceptions of family leisure, why they hold the perceptions that they do, and the developmental consequences of their experiences of family leisure.

(4) Although research has documented the interactive relationship between leisure and family, there has been little exploration of leisure as the expression or the creation of family. Research on *serious leisure* has revealed that in such leisure *small worlds* are created which provide individuals with a valued sense of identity and community (Stebbins 1992). An interesting question is to what extent leisure is pursued to create family—or whether families are created as a consequence of leisure. This question may become particularly relevant as 1) divorce, never marrying, and not having children become recognized as choices that people make rather than misfortunes that befall them; and 2) life expectancy continues to be extended and years not living within one's family of procreation increase.

See also: COMPUTERS AND FAMILIES; DIVISION OF LABOR; MARITAL QUALITY; PARENTING STYLES; RETIREMENT; TELEVISION AND FAMILIES; TIME USE

Bibliography

Acock, A. C., and Demo, D. H. (1994). *Family Diversity and Well-Being*. Thousand Oaks, CA: Sage.

Allen, K. R., and Chin-Sang, V. (1990). "A Lifetime of Work: The Context and Meanings of Leisure for Aging Black Women." *Gerontologist* 30:734–740.

Bella, L. (1992). *The Christmas Imperative*. Halifax, Canada: Fernwood.

Bialeschki, M. D. (1994). "Re-Entering Leisure: Transition within the Role of Motherhood." *Journal of Leisure Research* 26:57–74.

Bialeschki, M. D., and Pearce, K. D. (1997). "'I Don't Want a Lifestyle, I Want a Life': The Effect of Role Negotiations on the Leisure of Lesbian Mothers." *Journal of Leisure Research* 29:113–131.

Cheal, D. (1991). *Family and the State of Theory*. Toronto: University of Toronto Press.

Dijk, S. van; Betuw, A. van; and Kloeze, J.W. te (1993). "Familia Ludens: A Literature Study Focused on the Netherlands." *World Leisure and Recreation* 35:10–14.

Dupuis, S. L., and Smale, B. J. A. (2000). "Bittersweet Journeys: Meanings of Leisure in the Institution-Based Caregiving Context." *Journal of Leisure Research* 32:303–340.

Freysinger, V. J., and Chen, T. (1993). "Leisure and Family in China: The Impact of Culture." *World Leisure and Recreation* 35(3):22–24.

Freysinger, V. J. (1994). "Leisure with Children and Parental Satisfaction: Further Evidence of a Sex Difference in the Experience of Adult Roles and Leisure." *Journal of Leisure Research* 26:212–226.

Freysinger, V. J. (1995). "The Dialectics of Leisure and Development for Women and Men in Mid-Life: An Interpretive Study." *Journal of Leisure Research* 27:61–84.

Goff, S. J.; Fick, D. S.; and Oppliger, R. (1997). "The Moderating Effect of Spouse Support on the Relation between Serious Leisure and Spouses' Perceived Family-Leisure Conflict." *Journal of Leisure Research* 29:47–60.

Henderson, K. A.; Bedini, L. A.; Hecht, L.; and Shuler, R. (1995). "Women with Physical Disabilities and the Negotiation of Leisure Constraints." *Leisure Studies* 14:17–31.

Henderson, K. A.; Bialeschki, M. D.; Shaw, S. M.; and Freysinger, V. J. (1996). *Both Gains and Gaps: Feminist Perspectives on Women's Leisure*. State College, PA: Venture.

Jackson, E. L., and Rucks, V. C. (1995). "Negotiation of Leisure Constraints by Junior-High and High-School Students: An Exploratory Study." *Journal of Leisure Research* 27:85–105.

Juniu, S. (2000). "The Impact of Immigration: Leisure Experience in the Lives of South American Immigrants." *Journal of Leisure Research* 32:358–381.

Kelly, J. R. (1993). "Leisure-Family Research: Old and New issues." *World Leisure and Recreation* 35:5–9.

Kelly, J. R., and Freysinger, V. J. (2000). *21st Century Leisure: Current Issues.* Needham Heights, MA: Allyn and Bacon.

Khan, N. A. (1997). "Leisure and Recreation among Women of Selected Hill-Farming Families in Bangladesh." *Journal of Leisure Research* 29:5–20.

Kleiber, D. (1999). *Leisure Experience and Human Development: A Dialectical Interpretation.* New York: Basic Books.

Larson, R. W.; Gillman, S. A.; and Richards, M. H. (1997). "Divergent Experiences of Family Leisure: Fathers, Mothers, and Young Adolescents." *Journal of Leisure Research* 29:78–97.

Lynd, R. S., and Lynd, H. M. (1929). *Middletown: A Study in American Culture.* New York: Harcourt and Brace.

Mactavish, J.; Schleien, S.; and Tabourne, C. (1997). "Patterns of Family Recreation in Families that Include Children with a Developmental Disability." *Journal of Leisure Research* 29:21–46.

McCabe, M. (1993). "Family Leisure Budgets: Experience in the U.K." *World Leisure and Recreation* 35:30–34.

McClanahan, S., and Adams, J. (1987). "Parenthood and Psychological Well-Being." *Annual Review of Sociology* 5:237–257.

McMeeking, D., and Purkayastha, B. (1995). "I Can't Have My Mom Running Me Everywhere: Adolescents, Leisure and Accessibility." *Journal of Leisure Research* 27:360–378.

Orthner, D. K., and Mancini, J. A. (1990). "Leisure Impacts on Family Interaction and Cohesion." *Journal of Leisure Research* 22:125–137.

Phillip, S. F. (1999). "Are We Welcome? African American Racial Acceptance in Leisure Activities and the Importance Given to Children's Leisure." *Journal of Leisure Research* 31:385–403.

Rapoport, R., and Rapoport, R. N. (1975). *Leisure and the Family Life Cycle.* Boston: Routledge and Kegan Paul.

Robertson, B., ed. (1995). "Factors Impacting Leisure in Middle Aged Adults throughout the World." *World Leisure and Recreation* 37:30–38.

Rojek, C. (1996). *Decentring Leisure.* London: Sage.

Samuel, N. (1993). "Vacation Time and the French Family." *World Leisure* 35:15–16.

Samuel, N., ed. (1996). *Women, Leisure and the Family in Contemporary Society.* Wallingford, UK: C.A.B. International.

Shaw, S. M. (1997). "Controversies and Contradictions in Family Leisure: An Analysis of Conflicting Paradigms." *Journal of Leisure Research* 29:98–112.

Shaw, S. M. (1998). "Family Activities and Family Leisure." In *Canadian Families,* ed. L. C. Johnson. Toronto: Thompson.

Stebbins, R. (1992). *Amateurs, Professionals and Serious Leisure.* Montreal: McGill-Queen's University Press.

Tirone, S. C., and Shaw, S. M. (1997). "At the Center of Their Lives: Indo Canadian Women, Their Families and Leisure." *Journal of Leisure Research* 29:229–244.

Wearing, B., and McArthur, M. (1988). "The Family that Plays Together Stays Together: Or Does It?" *Australian Journal of Sex, Marriage, and Family* 9:150–158.

Wimbush, E., and Talbot, M., eds. (1988). *Relative Freedoms.* Philadelphia: Milton Keynes.

Zeijl, E.; te Poel, Y.; du Bois-Reymond, M.; Ravesloot, J.; and Meulman, J. J. (2000). "The Role of Parents and Peers in the Leisure Activities of Young Adolescents." *Journal of Leisure Research* 32:281–302.

VALERIA J. FREYSINGER

LESBIAN PARENTS

An increasing number of lesbians are choosing to become parents. Estimates of the number of gay and lesbian parents in the United States alone range from two to eight million, with the number of children of these parents estimated at four to fourteen million (Patterson 1995). Although more research exists on lesbian families than on gay male families, the lack of cross-cultural research is notable. Most research has been conducted in the United States using white lesbian samples. In many nations, the preponderance of negative attitudes toward homosexuality, the religious condemnation of homosexuality, or the complete invisibility of homosexuals accounts for the lack of cross-cultural research findings. Thus, the majority of the research findings presented below are from Euro-American perspectives.

Several terms are important to understanding the cultural environment of lesbian parents

(Gruskin 1999). *Homophobia* is often used to describe antigay feelings related to some type of action. Some argue that this term assumes that fear is the primary cause of antigay feelings, when many factors other than fear may be involved. As a result, some prefer the term *homonegative* to describe negative or hostile attitudes towards lesbians and gays. Another term relevant to establishing the climate in which lesbians live is *heterosexism*. Heterosexism essentially denies the existence of homosexuals under the assumption that all individuals are heterosexual. Whether the widespread lack of acceptance and support of lesbian families (Bigner 2000) is attributed to homophobia, homonegativity, or heterosexism, the effect on these families deserves attention.

Parenting Types and Legal Concerns

The quality of research involving lesbian relationships has evolved, yet participation rates are often constrained because lesbians fear reprisals if their sexual orientation becomes known. Cheryl A. Parks concluded in her review of seventeen studies on lesbian parents that respondents typically are "young, white, middle to upper class, highly educated, living in urban areas, and open about their sexual identity" (1998, p. 377). As a result, generalizing findings across diverse multicultural and socioeconomic backgrounds is not possible.

Lesbian parenting is hindered by several cultural barriers, and thus those who choose to undertake it must go through a careful decision-making process. In the United States and most European countries, lesbians are denied legal marriage. The Defense of Marriage Act in the United States formally prohibits government recognition of same-sex marriages (Allen 1997). As a result, lesbian couples lose tax, insurance, and medical benefits, as well as property rights (Friedman 1997; Griffin 1998). Hungary, on the other hand, allows same-sex marriage, and domestic partnerships are granted in Denmark, Sweden, Iceland, and Norway (Griffin 1998). Domestic partnerships provide more of the rights automatically granted to married heterosexual couples (Erickson and Simon 1996). Despite the legal limitations on marriage, lesbians who want to become parents can do so through various methods, including former heterosexual relationships, adoption, donor insemination, foster care, and step-parenting.

The Jensen-Wysinger family, from left to right, Hazel, Noah, Donna, and Mackenlie. Research indicates that children of lesbian parents are no more at risk for depression, adjustment difficulties, or behavior problems than children of heterosexual parents. A/P WIDE WORLD PHOTOS

Former heterosexual relationships. Although former heterosexual relationships are the most frequently used method for lesbians to become parents, Parks (1998) indicates that the introduction of the mother's new sexual identity presents both benefits and challenges for the mother and the children that often must be negotiated simultaneously with an upheaval in living arrangements. In these situations, lesbian parents frequently face the possibility of having their children taken away in custody battles. Child custody laws are not uniform in the United States. Thus, some states consider the sexual orientation of the mother unimportant, whereas, for other states, sexual orientation is the focus of the legal custody case (Patterson and Redding 1996). Lesbian parents in Europe often share similar fears of losing custody of their children if their sexual orientation is revealed (Griffin 1998).

Adoption. Some states prohibit lesbians and gay couples from seeking adoption. As a result, lesbians are forced to keep their sexual orientation a secret, either permanently or at least until completion of the adoption process. Policies on adoption vary by state in the United States (Human Rights Campaign Foundation 2001) and by country in Europe. Some states (Florida and New Hampshire) have legislation that disqualifies gays or lesbians from becoming foster or adoptive parents (Leiter

1997). In contrast, Israeli courts have approved legal parenting rights for lesbian mothers. (National Center for Lesbian Rights [NCLR] 2001). In cases of single-parent adoption, the partner or *second parent* petitions the court in hope of gaining recognition as a legal parent without terminating the first parent's rights (NCLR 2001). Second-parent or co-parent adoption typically occurs in cases of donor insemination. Second-parent adoptions are allowed in approximately seventeen states (NCLR 2001). Although a small number of jurisdictions permit third-parent adoptions, the option is not common (NCLR 2001).

In Europe, most countries deny legal adoption rights to the nonbiological parent (Griffin 1998). At this time, Iceland is the only country that allows lesbian couples to hold joint custody of their children. However, Iceland's regulations do not allow artificial insemination or adoption for lesbian couples (Griffin 1998). In England, some lesbian couples successfully obtained parental rights of their nonbiological children (Griffin 1998). In general, the majority of nonbirth or nonadopting parents have no legal relationship to their children (Savin-Williams and Esterberg 2000).

Donor insemination. Donor insemination appears to have become a popular option for a number of heterosexual, as well as lesbian, women who want to have children. As a precautionary measure, lesbians often request an anonymous sperm donor as a strategy for avoiding later claims of paternal rights.

Foster care. Acceptance of lesbian and gay couples is evolving. However, as a result of pejorative attitudes, lesbian women rarely serve as foster parents. On the basis of an increasing pressure to find suitable and loving homes for America's children, Crawford and Solliday (1996) point to the lack of evidence for current policies that exclude lesbian couples from providing foster care.

Step-parents. Information on lesbian step-parenting remains limited and is often the least discussed role in the literature. Lesbians in step-parenting roles may experience less validation from both partners and social networks (Parks 1998).

In summary, lesbian couples have several options for becoming parents. If they choose to exercise these options, they often confront legal complications that heterosexual parents do not face.

No available research suggests, however, that lesbian couples should not have the same opportunities that heterosexual couples enjoy.

Research on Children's Adjustment

Research concerning the lasting effects on children raised by lesbian parents centers on three primary concerns: sexual identity, psychological adjustment, and social development. Each of these concerns are presented below.

Sexual identity. One assumption behind the bias against lesbian parenthood is that children raised by lesbian parents will experience excessive difficulty in determining their own sexual orientation and gender identity. However, no evidence suggests that lesbian parents are more likely to raise lesbian or gay children than are heterosexual parents (Patterson and Redding 1996). Other research using projective testing, which involves responding to ambiguous pictorial stimuli, and interview procedures has documented normal gender identity development among children raised by lesbian parents (Patterson and Redding1996).

Psychological aspects. Another assumption is that children raised by homosexual parents are at increased risk for depression, adjustment difficulties, or behavioral problems. Again, research indicates that children of lesbian or gay parents are at no more risk for experiencing psychological difficulties than are the children of heterosexual parents. Although children of lesbian parents report higher levels of stress, their overall sense of well-being is not significantly different from that reported by children of heterosexual parents (Patterson 1994).

Social development. Still another assumption is that children raised by lesbian parents may experience more social isolation and peer rejection, which would have adverse effects on their development. Again, the evidence indicates that children of lesbian and gay parents report peer relationships that are similar in quality to those reported by the children of heterosexual parents (Parks 1998). Certainly, children of lesbian and gay parents report instances of harassment, but this harassment is not significantly different in content from that experienced by children of heterosexual parents.

Finally, a pervasive cultural myth is that homosexual parents are more likely than heterosexual parents to sexually abuse their children. No empirical evidence supports such a belief. In fact, males typically exhibit more pedophilic behavior, so the potential for lesbian parents to commit sexually abusive acts toward children is miniscule (Patterson and Redding 1996).

Benefits. Contradicting the negative assumptions regarding lesbian parenting, a number of benefits have been documented. Four benefits accrue for children of lesbian parents (Allen 1997). First, children of homosexual parents learn respect, empathy, and acceptance of diversity. Second, some authors have argued that children of lesbian parents are also more assertive in confronting traditional sex roles and in establishing egalitarian intimate relationships. Third, children raised by homosexual parents may also learn to negotiate and maintain a healthy family in the face of legal restrictions (Savin-Williams and Esterberg 2000), understanding that families are not necessarily confined to biological events, but can be created by choice. Fourth, children in lesbian families may gain appreciation for the strengths and social support available in the gay and lesbian community (Allen 1997).

In sum, children of lesbian parents do not experience any apparent developmental disadvantage when compared to children of heterosexual parents. Overall, the quality of the child-parent relationship, not the mother's sexual orientation, is important to healthy child development. Lesbian parents experience a multitude of obstacles to becoming parents; however, many are fighting for their rights and paving new legal pathways to benefit those who will follow them. Research should continue to focus on the strengths and resiliency of these families.

See also: ADOPTION; CHILDCARE; CHILD CUSTODY; FAMILY ROLES; FICTIVE KINSHIP; FOSTER PARENTS; GAY PARENTS; GENDER; GENDER IDENTITY; MOTHERHOOD; PARENTING STYLES; SEXUAL ORIENTATION; SURROGACY; WOMEN'S MOVEMENTS

Bibliography

Allen, K. R. (1997). "Lesbian and Gay Families." In *Contemporary Parenting: Challenges and Issues,* ed. T. Arendall. Thousand Oaks, CA: Sage.

Almeida, R. (1996). "Hindu, Christian, and Muslim Families." In *Ethnicity and Family Therapy,* ed. M. McGoldrick, J. Giordano, and J. K. Pearce. New York: Guilford Press.

Bigner, J. J. (2000). "Gay and Lesbian Families." In *Handbook of Family Development and Intervention,* ed. W. C. Nichols, M. A. Pace-Nichols, D. S. Becvar, and A. Y. Napier. New York: John Wiley and Sons.

Crawford, I., and Solliday, E. (1996). "The Attitudes of Undergraduate College Students Toward Gay Parenting." *Journal of Homosexuality* 30:63–77.

Erickson, B. M., and Simon, J. S. (1996). "Scandinavian Families: Plain and Simple." In *Ethnicity and Family Therapy,* ed. M. McGoldrick, J. Giordano, and J. K. Pearce. New York: Guilford Press.

Friedman, L. J. (1997). "Rural Lesbian Mothers and Their Families." *Journal of Gay and Lesbian Social Services* 7:73–82.

Griffin, K. (1998). "Getting Kids and Keeping Them: Lesbian Motherhood in Europe." In *Living "Difference": Lesbian Perspectives on Work and Family Life,* ed. G. A. Dunne. New York: Haworth Press.

Gruskin, E. P. (1999). *Treating Lesbians and Bisexual Women.* Thousand Oaks, CA: Sage.

Leiter, R. A. (1997). *National Survey of State Laws.* Detroit, MI: Gale Research.

Parks, C. A. (1998). "Lesbian Parenthood: A Review of the Literature." *American Journal of Orthopsychiatry* 68:376–389.

Patterson, C. J. (1994). "Children of the Lesbian Baby Boom: Behavioral Adjustment, Self-Concepts, and Sex-Role Identity." In *Contemporary Perspectives on Lesbian and Gay Psychology: Theory, Research and Applications,* ed. B. Green and G. M. Herek. Thousand Oaks, CA: Sage.

Patterson, C. J. (1995). "Lesbian Mothers, Gay Fathers, and Their Children." In *Lesbian, Gay, and Bisexual Identities Over the Lifespan: Psychological Perspectives,* ed. A. R. D'Augelli and C. J. Patterson. New York: Oxford University Press.

Patterson, C. J., and Redding, R. E. (1996). "Lesbian and Gay Families with Children: Implications of Social Science Research for Policy." *Journal of Social Issues* 52:29–50.

Savin-Williams, R C., and Esterberg, K. G. (2000). "Lesbian, Gay, and Bisexual Families." In *Handbook of Family Diversity,* ed. D. H. Demo, K. R. Allen, and M. A. Fine. New York: Oxford University Press.

Sullivan, G., and Leong, L. (1995). "Introduction." In *Gays and Lesbians in Asia and the Pacific: Social and Human Services,* ed. G. Sullivan and L. W. Leong. New York: Haworth Press.

Other Resources

Human Rights Campaign Foundation. (2001). *Adoption Laws in Your State.* Available from http://www.hrc.org.

National Center for Lesbian Rights. (2001). *Second Parent Adoptions: An Information Sheet.* Available from http://www.nclrights.org.

GINA OWENS
ASHLEY REED
SHARON SCALES ROSTOSKY

LIFE COURSE THEORY

Life course theory, more commonly termed the life course perspective, refers to a multidisciplinary paradigm for the study of people's lives, structural contexts, and social change. This approach encompasses ideas and observations from an array of disciplines, notably history, sociology, demography, developmental psychology, biology, and economics. In particular, it directs attention to the powerful connection between individual lives and the historical and socioeconomic context in which these lives unfold. As a concept, a life course is defined as "a sequence of socially defined events and roles that the individual enacts over time" (Giele and Elder 1998, p. 22). These events and roles do not necessarily proceed in a given sequence, but rather constitute the sum total of the person's actual experience. Thus the concept of life course implies age-differentiated social phenomena distinct from uniform life-cycle stages and the life span. Life span refers to duration of life and characteristics that are closely related to age but that vary little across time and place.

In contrast, the life course perspective elaborates the importance of time, context, process, and meaning on human development and family life (Bengtson and Allen 1993). The family is perceived as a micro social group within a macro social context—a "collection of individuals with shared history who interact within ever-changing social contexts across ever increasing time and space" (Bengtson and Allen 1993, p. 470). Aging and developmental change, therefore, are continuous processes that are experienced throughout life. As such, the life course reflects the intersection of social and historical factors with personal biography and development within which the study of family life and social change can ensue (Elder 1985; Hareven 1996).

Historical Development

Many researchers identify the life course perspective as a "new" paradigm in the behavioral sciences because it was not formally advanced until the 1990s. During this decade, rapid social change and population aging drew attention to historical influences and to the complexity of processes underlying family change and continuity. Advances in statistical techniques also prompted the continued growth of life course studies, including the creation of new methodologies to analyze longitudinal data.

Early applications of life course theorizing can be traced to the beginning decades of the twentieth century (Bengston and Allen 1993). Until the mid-1960s, however, no distinct field of life course studies, with a focus on the variability of age patterns, developmental effects, and the implications of historical change, gained prominence. At this time, researchers from diverse social science disciplines (e.g., Clausen 1991; Riley 1987; Hagestad and Neugarten 1985) examined various aspects of these themes, including the joint significance of age, period, and cohort in explaining the relationship between individual and social change. "Social timetables" and their variability were also used to study development, aging, and cohorts. For example, Bernice Neugarten pioneered a research program that considered individual deviations from widely shared age-expectations about the timing of major transitional events (for example, when to marry or to have children). Research conducted in the 1970s and 1980s continued to incorporate these themes, as well as to focus attention on historical changes in life patterns, the consequences of life course experiences (such as the Great Depression) on subjective well-being, the interlocking transitions of family members, and integrating kin and age distinctions, among others (Burton and Bengtson 1985; Clausen 1991; Elder 1974; Rossi and Rossi 1990). By the end of the twentieth century, the life course approach was commonly considered an "emerging paradigm" (Rodgers and White 1993) with both a distinctive theory and methods. Glen Elder, in particular, began to advance core principles of life course theory, which he describes as defining "a common field of inquiry by providing a framework that guides research on matters of problem identification and conceptual development" (1998, p. 4). This perspective has also been (and continues to be) synthesized with other theories or fields of study, such as family development (e.g., Bengston and Allen), human development (e.g., Elder), status attainment (e.g., Featherman; Blau; and Duncan), family history (e.g., Hareven), life span (e.g., Baltes), stress theory (e.g., Pearlin and Skaff), demography (e.g., Uhlenberg), gerontology (e.g., Neugarten), and Bronfenbrenner's ecological perspective (Moen et al. 1995).

Key Principles and Concepts

Several fundamental principles characterize the life course approach. They include: (1) socio-historical and geographical location; (2) timing of lives; (3) heterogeneity or variability; (4) "linked lives" and social ties to others; (5) human agency and personal control; and (6) how the past shapes the future. Each of these tenets will be described and key concepts will be highlighted. This will be followed by an overview of selected examples of empirical applications from an international and cross-cultural perspective.

Sociohistorical and geographical location. An individual's own developmental path is embedded in and transformed by conditions and events occurring during the historical period and geographical location in which the person lives. For example, geopolitical events (e.g., war), economic cycles (e.g., recessions), and social and cultural ideologies (e.g., patriarchy) can shape people's perceptions and choices and alter the course of human development. Thus, behavior and decisions do not occur in a vacuum, because people and families interact within sociohistorical time. Indeed, an understanding of the location of various cohorts in their respective historical contexts aids scholars and policy makers to identity circumstances that have differentially affected people's respective life histories.

Timing of lives. Three types of time are central to a life course perspective: *individual* time, *generational* time, and *historical* time (Price, McKenry, and Murphy 2000). *Individual* or *ontogenetic* time refers to chronological age. It is assumed that periods of life, such as childhood, adolescence, and old age, influence positions, roles, and rights in society, and that these may be based on culturally shared age definitions (Hagestad and Neugarten 1985). Generational time refers to the age groups or cohorts in which people are grouped, based upon their age. People born between 1946 and 1964, for example, are often referred to as the *baby boom* generation. Finally, historical time refers to societal or large-scale changes or events and how these affect individuals and families, such as political and economic changes, war and technological innovations (e.g., information access through the Internet).

Furthermore, Elder (1985) observes that time can also be envisioned as a sequence of transitions that are enacted over time. A *transition* is a discrete life change or event within a trajectory (e.g., from a single to married state), whereas a *trajectory* is a sequence of linked states within a conceptually defined range of behavior or experience (e.g., education and occupational career). Transitions are often accompanied by socially shared ceremonies and rituals, such as a graduation or wedding ceremony, whereas a trajectory is a long-term pathway, with age-graded patterns of development in major social institutions such as education or family. In this way, the life course perspective emphasizes the ways in which transitions, pathways, and trajectories are socially organized. Moreover, transitions typically result in a change in status, social identity, and role involvement. Trajectories, however, are long-term patterns of stability and change and can include multiple transitions.

Progress along trajectories is age-graded such that some transitions can be viewed as more age appropriate while others violate normative social timetables by occurring too early or too late (Hagestad and Neugarten 1985). An off-age transition might be leaving home at a very young age (e.g., age fifteen) or becoming a teenage parent. There is also the possibility of *transition reversals* or *countertransitions*. An example of a transition reversal is when a young adult returns after leaving home, while countertransitions can be produced by the life changes of other roles and statuses (e.g., parenthood creates grandparenthood). The timing of transitions also can decrease the chance of success in a particular trajectory, such as the likelihood of completing school.

Heterogeneity or variability. Heterogeneity or diversity in structures or processes is another life course principle. One must consider not only modal or average developmental and transitional trends, but also variability. Matilda Riley's (1987) research supported a model of age stratification—the different experiences of different cohorts—and so helped to overcome the fallacy of cohort centrism, the notion that cohorts share perspectives simply because they share a common age group. Indeed, generations or cohorts are not homogeneous collections of people. Rather, they differ in terms of influential dimensions such as gender, social class, family structure, ethnicity, and religion. Moreover, the ability to adapt to life course change can vary with the resources or supports inherent in these elements in the form of economic or cultural capital (e.g., wealth, education) or social capital (e.g., family social support). For example, Barbara A. Mitchell's (2000) research demonstrates that young adults with weak family ties may not have the option to return home during difficult economic times. Finally, there is also the recognition of increasing diversity associated with aging. The longer one lives, the greater the exposure to factors that affect the aging process.

Linked lives and social ties. A fourth tenet emphasizes that lives are interdependent and reciprocally connected on several levels. Societal and individual experiences are linked thorough the family and its network of shared relationships (Elder 1998). As a result, macro-level events, such as war, could affect individual behaviors (e.g., enrolling in military service), and this can significantly affect other familial relationships. Stressful events, such as the death of a family member, can also affect family relationships because these occurrences can trigger patterns of stress and vulnerability or, conversely, promote adaptive behaviors and family resilience. Moreover, personality attributes of individual family members can also affect family coping styles, functioning, and well-being.

In addition, family members can also synchronize or coordinate their lives with regard to life planning and matters related to the timing of life events. This can sometimes generate tensions and conflicts, particularly when individual goals differ from the needs of the family as a collective unit. Tamara Hareven (1996), for example, notes that historically, the timing of adult children's individual transitions (e.g., when to marry) could generate problems if it interfered with the demands and needs of aging parents.

Human agency and personal control. According to the life course perspective, individuals are active agents who not only mediate the effect of social structure but also make decisions and set goals that shape social structure. Individuals are assumed to have the capacity to engage in *planful competence,* which refers to the thoughtful, proactive, and self-controlled processes that underlie one's choices about institutional involvements and social relationships (Clausen 1991). However, it should be recognized that the ability to make specific choices depends on opportunities and constraints. Parallel to this idea is the concept of *control cycles* whereby families and individuals modify their expectations and behavior in response to changes in either needs or resources. Elder (1974) found that families in the Great Depression regained a measure of control over their economic hardship through expenditure reductions and multiple family earners. In this way, families and individuals can construct, negotiate, and traverse life course events and experiences.

How the past shapes the future. Finally, another hallmark of this perspective is that early life course decisions, opportunities, and conditions affect later outcomes. The past, therefore, has the potential to shape the present and the future, which can be envisioned as a ripple or domino effect. This can occur at various levels: the cohort/generational level and the individual/familial level. For example, one generation can transmit to the next the reverberations of the historical circumstances that shaped its life history (living through the feminist movement, for example). The timing and conditions under which earlier life events and behaviors occur (e.g., dropping out of school, witnessing domestic abuse) can also set up a chain reaction of experiences for individuals and their families (e.g., reproduction of poverty, a cycle of family violence). The past, therefore, can significantly affect later life outcomes such as socioeconomic status, mental health, physical functioning, and marital patterns. This long-term view, with its recognition of cumulative advantage or disadvantage, is particularly valuable for understanding social inequality in later life and for creating effective social policy and programs (O'Rand 1996).

Selected Research Applications

The life course perspective has been applied to several areas of family inquiry in North America (particularly in the United States), as well as internationally. Although space limitations do not permit full coverage of this vast body of work, several studies are highlighted to illustrate recent applications of the approach. In the United States, researchers have adopted this framework to investigate: men's housework (Coltrane and Ishii-Kuntz 1992); the timing of marriage and military service (Call and Teachman 1996); work history and timing of marriage (Pittman and Blanchard 1996); families, delinquency and crime (Sampson and Laub 1993) as well as many other substantive areas (Price et al. 2000).

In Canada, researchers have used a life course approach to study the transition to grandmotherhood (Gee 1991) and youth transitions into adulthood, especially leaving and returning to home (e.g., Mitchell 2000). It should also be noted that this perspective is becoming popular in studies of ethnic diversity, social inequality, and aging families (Stoller and Gibson 2000) and that numerous cross-national comparisons of life patterns have been conducted (e.g., between Germany and the United States—Giele and Elder 1998, p. 246).

Furthermore, the life course approach is being used more and more in countries such as Japan (Fuse 1996) and other East Asian countries, as well as Great Britain, Germany, Italy, Norway, the Netherlands, and India. Applications of the life course perspective are illustrated in research on generational relations and family support in Thailand and Sri Lanka (Hareven 1996), caregiver's marital histories in Britain (Lewis 1998), the German Life History Study (Brüchner and Mayer 1998; Elder and Giele 1998, p. 52), young adults from the Netherlands (Liefbroer and De Jong 1995), changing patterns of age, work, and retirement in Europe (Guillemard 1997), and patterns of household formation and inheritance in preindustrial northern Europe and in northern India (Gupta 1995).

Finally, a variety of quantitative and qualitative methodologies have been used in life course analyses. Common quantitative methodologies include: longitudinal designs, cohort and cross-sectional comparisons, and life event history analysis; whereas descriptive and qualitative approaches entail archival research, biographical approaches such as life history reviews and in-depth interviews, personal narratives, and life stories. This methodological pluralism is consistent with the multidisciplinary nature of the life course perspective and the recognition of the necessity to bridge macro and micro levels of theory and analysis (Giele and Elder 1998).

In summary, the flourishing area of life course theorizing and research offers unique opportunities to interconnect historical and cultural location and changes in societal institutions with the experiences of individuals and families. The challenge will be to refine and test a dynamic, emergent conceptual model that extends across multiple disciplines and multiple levels of analysis. Future advances will enable researchers to extend the frontiers of knowledge pertaining to continuity and discontinuity in family life amidst ever-changing social, economic and global environments.

See also: ADULTHOOD; FAMILY ROLES; FAMILY THEORY; RITES OF PASSAGE; TIME USE; TRANSITION TO PARENTHOOD

Bibliography

Bengtson, V. L., and Allen, K. R. (1993). "The Life Course Perspective Applied to Families over Time." In *Sourcebook of Family Theories and Methods: A Contextual Approach,* ed. P. Boss, W. Doherty, R. LaRossa, W. Schumm, and S. Steinmetz. New York: Plenum.

Brücher, E., and Mayer, K. U. (1998). "Collecting Life History Data: Experiences from the German Life History Study." In *Methods of Life Course Research: Qualitative and Quantitative Approaches,* ed. J. Z. Giele and G. H. Elder Jr. Thousand Oaks, CA: Sage.

Burton, L. M., and Bengtson, V. (1985). "Black Grandmothers: Issues of Timing and Continuity in Roles." In *Grandparenthood,* ed. V. L. Bengtson and J. Robertson. Beverly Hills, CA: Sage.

Call, V. R. A., and Teachman, J. D. (1996). "Life-course Timing and Sequencing of Marriage and Military Service and Their Effects on Marital Stability." *Journal of Marriage and the Family* 58:219–226.

Clausen, J. A. (1991). "Adolescent Competence and the Shaping of the Life Course." *American Journal of Sociology* 96:805–842.

Coltrane, S., and Ishii-Kuntz, M. (1992). "Men's Housework: A Life Course Perspective." *Journal of Marriage and the Family* 54:43–58.

Elder, G. H., Jr. (1974). *Children of the Great Depression: Social Change in Life Experience.* Chicago: University of Chicago Press.

Elder, G. H., Jr. (1985). *Life Course Dynamics*. Ithaca, NY: Cornell University Press.

Elder, G. H., Jr. (1998). "The Life Course as Developmental Theory." *Child Development* 69:1–12.

Fuse, A. (1996). "Status of Family Theory and Research in Japan." *Marriage and Family Review* 22:73–99.

Gee, E. M. (1991). "The Transition to Grandmotherhood: A Quantitative Study." *Canadian Journal on Aging* 10:254–270.

Giele, J. Z., and Elder, G. H., Jr. (1998). *Methods of Life Course Research: Qualitative and Quantitative Approaches*. Thousand Oaks, CA: Sage.

Guillemard, A. M. (1997). "Re-Writing Social Policy and Changes within the Life Course Organization: A European Perspective." *Canadian Journal on Aging* 16:441–464.

Gupta, M. D. (1995). "Life Course Perspectives on Women's Autonomy and Health Outcomes." *American Anthropologist* 97:481–492.

Hagestad, G. O., and Neugarten, B. L. (1985). "Age and the Life Course." In *Handbook of Aging and the Social Sciences,* ed. R. H. Binstock and E. Shanas. New York: Van Nostrand Reinhold.

Hareven, T. K., ed. (1996). *Aging and Generational Relations: Life Course and Cross-Cultural Perspectives*. New York: Aldine de Gruyter.

Lewis, R. (1998). "Impact of the Marital Relationship on the Experience of Caring for an Elderly Spouse with Dementia." *Aging and Society* 18:209–231.

Liefbroer, A. C., and De Jong Gierveld, J. (1995). "Standardization and Individualization: The Transition to Adulthood among Cohorts Born between 1903 and 1965." In *Population and Family in the Low Countries,* ed. H. van den Brekel and F. Deven. Netherlands: Kluwer Academic Publishers.

Mitchell, B. A. (2000). "The Refilled 'Nest': Debunking the Myth of Families in Crisis." In *The Overselling of Population Aging: Apocalyptic Demography, Intergenerational Challenges, and Social Policy,* ed. E. M. Gee and G. M. Gutman. Toronto: Oxford University Press.

Moen, P.; Elder, G. H., Jr.; and Lüscher, K., eds. (1995). *Examining Lives in Context: Perspectives on the Ecology of Human Development*. Washington, DC: American Psychological Association.

O'Rand, A. M. (1996). "The Precious and the Precocious: Understanding Cumulative Disadvantage and Cumulative Advantage over the Life Course." *The Gerontologist* 36:230–238.

Pittman, J. F., and Blanchard, D. (1996). "The Effects of Work History and Timing of Marriage on the Division of Household Labor: A Life Course Perspective." *Journal of Marriage and the Family* 58:78–90.

Price, S. J.; McKenry, P. C.; and Murphy, M. J., eds. (2000). *Families across Time: A Life Course Perspective*. Los Angeles: Roxbury.

Riley, M. W. (1987). "On the Significance of Age in Sociology." *American Sociological Review* 52:1–14.

Rodgers, R. H., and White, J. M. (1993). "Family Development Theory." In *Sourcebook of Family Theories and Methods: A Contextual Approach,* ed. P. Boss, W. Doherty, R. LaRossa, W. Schumm, and S. Steinmetz. New York: Plenum.

Rossi, A. S., and Rossi, P. H. (1990). *Of Human Bonding: Parent-Child Relationships across the Life Course*. New York: Aldine De Gruyter.

Sampson, R. J., and Laub, J. H. (1993). *Crime in the Making: Pathways and Turning Points through Life*. Cambridge, MA: Harvard University Press.

Stoller, E. P., and Gibson, R. C. (2000). *Worlds of Difference: Inequality in the Aging Experience*. Thousand Oaks, CA: Pine Forge Press.

BARBARA A. MITCHELL

LONELINESS

Nature did not construct human beings to stand alone. . . . Those who have never known the deep intimacy and intense companionship of happy mutual love have missed the best thing that life has to give. Love is something far more than desire for sexual intercourse; it is the principal means of escape from loneliness which afflicts most men and women throughout the greater part of their lives. (Russell 1929, 122–123)

To shed light on Bertrand Russell's proposition that love is the principle means to escape from loneliness, this entry will examine the links between loneliness and the family. In thinking about loneliness in a family and life cycle perspective, several questions come to mind. What is the relationship between marriage and loneliness? Is loneliness passed from parents to their children and, if so, how? From birth to death are there predictable fluctuations in loneliness due to parents and their children's life stages? Is it true, as is frequently depicted, that the loss of intimate relationships leads to loneliness? Since the mid-1970s social scientists have published a growing number of studies addressing these questions (Ernst and Cacioppo 1999).

Concept and Prevalence

Contemporary social scientists have defined loneliness as the unpleasant experience that occurs when a person's network of social relationships is deficient in some important way, either quantitatively or qualitatively (Peplau and Perlman 1982, p. 4). According to this conceptualization, loneliness stems from a discrepancy between the level of social contact a person needs or desires and the amount she or he has. The deficits can be in the person's intimate relationships, as Russell's quote implies, leading to emotional loneliness or in the individual's broader network of relationships leading to social loneliness (Weiss 1973). In either case, loneliness is a subjective experience—people can be alone without being lonely or lonely in a crowd.

Loneliness is widely prevalent. Although loneliness appears to occur in virtually all societies, its intensity varies by culture. In an eighteen-country survey (Stack 1998), the United States was in the top quarter of countries in terms of average levels of loneliness. Perhaps this in part reflects the individualistic, competitive nature of life in the United States. Individuals in European social democracies such as the Netherlands and Denmark were least lonely. Sociologists have associated national differences in loneliness with differences in social integration. The Dutch, for example, are socially well-integrated in terms of having more people in their social networks, such as being involved in civic organizations and volunteer work and receiving emotional support.

Loneliness and Marriage

One cultural universal found in a multinational study (Stack 1998) was that married men and women are less lonely than their unmarried counterparts. Cohabitation also buffered individuals from loneliness but not as much as marriage. When the unmarried are categorized into subgroups (never married, separated or divorced, widowed), the results vary somewhat by study. The general tendency appears to be for single people to be less lonely than the divorced or widowed (Perlman 1988, Table 3). In at least one Dutch study, single parents were also a group high in loneliness. Overall, loneliness seems to be more a reaction to the loss of a marital relationship rather than a response to its absence.

Differences in loneliness as a function of marital status can be explained either in terms of selection or what marital relationships provide. If selection is operating it means that the people who marry are different and would avoid loneliness even in the absence of getting married. This explanation is difficult to definitively test, although it is challenged to some extent by the relatively low levels of loneliness among never married respondents. The second view implies that the more the marital relationships provide, the less lonely the partners should be. Consistent with this explanation, low marital satisfaction is associated with greater loneliness. Similarly, compared with individuals who confide in their spouses, married individuals who talk most openly about the joys and sorrows of their lives with somebody besides their spouse are more prone to being lonely. One can conclude from the evidence that when marriages are working well, they provide partners with ingredients that buffer them from loneliness.

Parents, Children, and Loneliness

Social scientists frequently debate questions of heredity versus the environment. In the origins of loneliness, both appear to have a role. Consistent with there being an inherited component to loneliness, in a 2000 study (McGuire and Clifford 2000) both siblings and twins had some similarity in their levels of loneliness, but the similarity was greater for identical twins than for either fraternal twins or singleton siblings.

Researchers have also checked for an association between parents and their children in the likelihood of being lonely. Working with older parents (85 or older) and their mid-life children, M. V. Long and Peter Martin (2000) did not find evidence of intergenerational similarity. In contrast, J. Lobdell and Daniel Perlman (1986) administered questionnaires to 130 female undergraduates and their parents. As expected, they demonstrated that the parents' loneliness scores were modestly correlated with those of their daughters. Of course, such an association could be explained by either genetic or environmental factors.

To explore possible psychosocial factors, Lobdell and Perlman also had the university students in their study rate their parents' marriages and childrearing practices. Lonely students depicted their parents as having relatively little positive involvement with them. This is one of several studies showing the cold, remote picture of parent-child relations reported by lonely young adults. They also saw their parents as having lower than average marital satisfaction. This finding compliments other studies showing that children whose parents divorce are at risk for loneliness, especially if the divorce occurs early in the child's life. These findings can be interpreted within an environmental framework. In sum, the work on the origins of loneliness suggests that both genetic and family factors each play a role in levels of loneliness, although nonfamilial environmental influences are likely also critical.

The parental contribution to children's loneliness is not simply a one-time input. Instead, loneliness bidirectionally intertwines with parent-child relations over the life-cycle. A first noteworthy lifespan phenomenon is that in the transition to parenthood, women who are lonely during their pregnancy are at higher risk for postpartum depression.

In infancy, children are highly dependent upon their parents and caretakers. As they get older, peer relations become more important. Along with this shift comes a shift in what type of relations are most closely linked with loneliness. In the middle elementary years, it is the quality of children's relationships with their mothers. In late adolescence, it is the quality of university students' relationships with their peers.

Concerning more mature children, Pauline Bart (1980) has analyzed how children's leaving home affects middle-aged mothers. She concluded that women who adopt the traditional role of being homemakers devoted to their children are prone to experience greater loneliness and depression when their children leave home than are women less invested in a maternal, homemaker role.

For many people, one perceived benefit of having children in the first place is the notion that they will provide comfort and support in old age. As far as loneliness goes, there is evidence challenging

this view. Tanya Koropeckyj-Cox (1998) looked at older adults with and without children. Contrary to common belief, the results didn't show a clear advantage of having children. A second line of research has examined whether family or friends are more strongly associated with avoiding loneliness in old age. Martin Pinquart and Silvia Sorensen's (2001) meta-analysis, a technique for statistically combining the results of several studies, shows the primary role of friends as opposed to family members in buffering seniors from loneliness.

Relationship Endings and Loneliness

Having examined separation and loss in parent-child relationships, what happens when these phenomena occur in romantic relations? As young adult dating relationships end, presumably both partners experienced a decline in the social aspects of their lives. But in many couples, one person initiates the breakup whereas the other is "left behind." Charles Hill, Zick Rubin, and Letitia Peplau (1976) found that the initiators suffered significantly less loneliness than the partners who were spurned. Perhaps having control over such life changes helps reduce the distressing effects of loosing a partner.

After their young adult dating experiences, many individuals marry and eventually end those unions via divorce. In one study (Woodward, Zabel, and Decosta 1980) fifty-nine divorced persons were asked when, and under what circumstances, they felt lonely. For these respondents, the period of greatest loneliness occurred before (rather than after) the divorce decree became final. Both ex-husbands and ex-wives felt lonely when they felt out of place at a particular social event or excluded by others. For ex-wives, loneliness was also triggered when (1) they wanted to join an activity but were unable to do so; (2) they had no one with whom to share decision-making responsibilities and daily tasks; (3) they felt stigmatized by being divorced; and (4) they had financial problems.

A University of Tulsa study involving seventy-four men and women compared the divorce experiences of lonely versus nonlonely individuals. Lonely individuals blamed more of the marriage's problems on their former spouse. They also had more difficulties in their relationships with their ex-partners. They argued more over childrearing, felt less affection, and had less friendly interactions. In terms of adjusting to separation, lonely respondents drank more, experienced greater depression, and felt more cut-off from their friends. They spent more time with their children and were less likely to become romantically involved with a new partner.

For many North Americans, marriage lasts "till death do us part." If relationships end via death of a spouse, U.S. Census data show a 5 to 1 sex ratio with women predominantly being the individual left widowed. Helena Lopata (1969) has identified several ways that widows miss their husbands. For example, when their spouse dies, women lose a) a partner who made them feel important; b) a companion with whom they shared activities; c) an escort to public encounters as well as a partner in couple-based socializing; and d) a financial provider who enabled them to participate in more costly activities and enjoy a more expensive lifestyle. With such losses, it is not surprising that loneliness is a major problem in bereavement.

Robert Hansson and his associates (1986) found a general tendency for greater loneliness to be associated with a maladaptive orientation toward widowhood. Prior to the death of their husbands, the lonely widows engaged in less behavioral rehearsal (e.g., finding jobs, getting around on their own) for widowhood and instead engaged in more rumination about the negative consequences of their spouse's impending death. At the time of their spouse's death, subsequently lonely widows experienced more negative emotions and felt less prepared to cope. Lonely widows were also less likely to engage in social comparison with widowed friends.

If a spouse dies unexpectedly, loneliness is especially pronounced. To overcome loneliness, widows typically turn to informal supports (e.g., friends, children, and siblings) as opposed to formal organizations or professionals (e.g., their church, psychotherapists). In widowhood as in other transitions, time heals: Feelings of loneliness are greatest shortly after the loss of a spouse but decline over the months and years. As widows continue their lives, the quality of their closest friendship is more likely to be associated with their experiences of loneliness than is the quantity or quality of their quality of their closest kin relationship (Essex and Nam 1987).

Conclusion

In sum, the findings from contemporary social science research indicate that married individuals are less likely to be lonely. However, the picture is more complex than Russell's simple suggestion that love, at least as provided by marital and kin relations, provides a surefire escape from loneliness. At some ages and positions in life, kin relationships appear to be a less important aspect of the loneliness equation than friendships or other factors. Parents not only protect their children from being lonely but also they contribute to it. If siblings are close, they tend to be less lonely (Ponzetti and James 1997). Throughout adulthood, unsatisfying marriages and the endings of intimate relationships are associated with greater loneliness. Thus, it is not simply relationships but what happens in them that counts.

See also: DIVORCE: EFFECTS ON COUPLES; FRIENDSHIP; GRIEF AND BEREAVEMENT; POSTPARTUM DEPRESSION; SEPARATION ANXIETY; SINGLES/NEVER-MARRIED ADULTS; SINGLE-PARENT FAMILIES; WIDOWHOOD

Bibliography

Bart, P. (1980). "Loneliness of the Long-Distance Mother." In *The Anatomy of Loneliness,* ed. J. Hartog, J. R. Audy, and Y. A. Cohen. New York: International Universities Press.

Ernst, J. M., and Cacioppo, J. T. (1999). "Lonely Hearts: Psychological Perspectives on Loneliness." *Applied and Preventive Psychology* 8:1–22.

Essex, M. J., and Nam, S. (1987). "Marital Status and Loneliness among Older Women: The Differential Importance of Close Family and Friends." *Journal of Marriage and the Family* 49:93–106.

Hansson, R. O.; Jones, W. H.; Carpenter, B. N.; and Remondet, J. H. (1986). "Loneliness and Adjustment to Old Age." *International Journal of Aging and Human Development* 24:41–53.

Hill, C. T.; Rubin, Z.; and Peplau, L. A. (1976). "Breakups before Marriage: The End of 103 Affairs." *Journal of Social Issues* 32:147–168.

Koropeckyj-Cox, T. (1998). "Loneliness and Depression in Middle and Old Age: Are the Childless More Vulnerable?" *Journal of Gerontology: Series B: Psychological Sciences and Social Sciences* 53B:S303–S312.

Lobdell, J., and Perlman, D. (1986). "The Intergenerational Transmission of Loneliness: A Study of College Females and Their Parents." *Journal of Marriage and the Family* 48:589–595.

Long, M. V., and Martin, P. (2002). "Personality, Relationship Closeness, and Loneliness of Oldest Old Adults and Their Children." *Journal of Gerontology: Series B: Psychological Sciences and Social Sciences* 55B: P311–P319.

Lopata, H. Z. (1969). "Loneliness: Forms and Components." *Social Problems* 17:248–261.

McGuire, S., and Clifford, J. (2000). "Genetic and Environmental Contributions to Loneliness in Children." *Psychological Science* 11:487–491

Peplau, L. A., and Perlman, D., eds. (1982). *Loneliness: A Sourcebook of Current Theory, Research, and Therapy*. New York: Wiley.

Perlman, D. (1988). "Loneliness: A Life Span, Developmental Perspective." In *Families and Social Networks*, ed. R. M. Milardo. Newbury Park, CA.: Sage.

Pinquart, M., and Soerensen, S. (2001). "Influences on Loneliness in Older Adults: A Meta-Analysis." *Basic and Applied Social Psychology* 23:245–266.

Ponzetti, J. J., Jr., and James, C. (1997). "Loneliness and Sibling Relationships." *Journal of Social Behavior and Personality* 12:103–112

Russell, B. (1929). *Marriage and Morals*. New York: Liveright.

Stack, S. (1998). "Marriage, Family and Loneliness: A Cross-National Study." *Sociological Perspectives* 41: 415–432.

Weiss, R. S. (1973). *Loneliness: The Experience of Emotional and Social Isolation*. Cambridge, MA: MIT Press.

Woodward, J. C.; Zabel, J.; and Decosta, C. (1980). "Loneliness and Divorce." *Journal of Divorce* 4:73–82.

DANIEL PERLMAN

LOVE

Though I speak with the tongues of men and of angels,—and though I have all faith, so that I could remove mountains, but have not love, I am nothing. (1 Corinthians 13:1–2, Gideon Bible).

This widely quoted statement from the Christian Bible is not unique. More ink has been spilled about love than any other topic, except perhaps God. Speculation about the nature of love is very ancient; however, the scientific study of love only began in the twentieth century. Human love has been the primary focus, although love is not restricted to humans, as every pet owner knows. Harry Harlow (1974) demonstrated that *mother love* and nurturance is required for infant monkeys to develop normally. Infants deprived of mother contact became disturbed, unhappy adults, unfit for monkey society.

There are many kinds of love. The encompassing love of our parents begins our own life's journey of love, a journey that wends its way through love of parents, siblings, grandparents, friends, romantic partners, and eventually full circle to the encompassing love of our own children—and grandchildren. St. Paul was right—without love we are nothing!

The primary focus of this entry is *romantic love*. As Beverley Fehr (1995) noted, the emotions and feelings that underlie *companionate love* may be the foundation for all types of love. For example, *parent-child* and *friendship love* match this general concept of companionable love. Romantic, erotic love is a specialized love that may evolve out of a broader companionable love. But passionate, romantic love is very important to people, thus leading to strong interest by social scientists.

Passionate and Companionate Love

Ellen Berscheid and Elaine Walster (1969, 1978) proposed the distinction between love as *passion* and love as friendly *companionship*. These authors construed passionate love as a state of total absorption between two lovers, including mood swings, intense emotions (pleasurable and aversive), and obsessive thinking. Companionate love was construed as the affection two people feel for each other when their lives are deeply intertwined. According to Elaine and G. William Walster (1978), most passionate love affairs end in breakups. But if a couple is lucky, passion can change into the mild glow of companionate love. In essence, passion becomes friendship.

This early scientific theory of romantic love tended toward an either/or view, either passion or companionship, but not both at once. This view may well have had cultural validity during much of the twentieth century. However, Elaine Hatfield (formerly Elaine Walster) noted that people are capable of both types of love and may experience them intermittently during their lives (Hatfield 1988).

People appear to want both types of romantic love. Passion is pleasurable, but its associated strong emotion creates the potential for relationship instability. Lovers want stability and often desire friendship. Several recent studies show that romance and friendship are often combined in today's Western cultural milieu. Susan and Clyde Hendrick (1993) collected written accounts of love, and found that friendship with the lover was the most frequently desired characteristic. Susan Sprecher and Pamela Regan (1998) also found that both passion and companionship were related to relationship satisfaction and commitment. Pat Noller (1996) concluded that a mix of passionate and companionate love best supports the continuity of marriage and family. But passion *is* important; erotic love is one important predictor of relationship satisfaction, regardless of length of the relationship (Hendrick and Hendrick 2000). Passion alone may not be enough, however; perhaps we *must* be friends with the one we love in order for love to last. The recent research and theorizing on passionate and friendship love is consistent with the prototype theory of love developed by Fehr.

Prototypes of Love

People think in terms of concepts. For example, *love, sex,* and *intimacy* are concepts. But what is a concept and how is it defined? Recent theorizing in cognitive science treats a concept as either a best example, or as a best set of features. These *best sets* may be viewed as an abstract average of the characteristics that compose the concept. This abstract average is called a *prototype.*

In numerous studies, Fehr (1988; Fehr and Broughton 2001) has explored a prototype conception of love. For example, she (1988) had people list the features of love that they considered important. A list of sixty-eight features emerged, including both passionate and companionate features. The most frequent features that emerged were trust, caring, honesty, friendship, and respect (Fehr 1993).

So where was passion in this feature list? It was there, but low in importance. Other studies asked people to rate the importance of twenty different kinds of love.

Mother love, parental love, and friendship were the three most important types of love, and romantic love ranked fifth. However, passionate love and sexual love ranked low on the list.

The prototype approach indicates that people clearly distinguish between passionate and companionate love. Companionate love appears to be the foundational type of love. It is general in that it applies to many types of love relationships (e.g., parent, child, friend). Passionate love is more specialized, and its links to sexuality lead to societal restrictions on the people for whom this type of love is appropriate (e.g., lover, spouse).

Fehr's research was concerned with love in general. Another approach could focus only on romantic love and ask people to list its features. Pamela C. Regan, Elizabeth R. Kocan, and Teresa Whitlock (1998) did such a prototype analysis of romantic love. In this case, results showed that sexual attraction and passion were among the central features of romantic love. However, sexual attraction and passion ranked well below trust, honesty, and happiness in importance. When given a large list of features, people appear unwilling to rate passion and sexual feelings as important defining features of love—even when the focus is on passionate love!

What is going on in these studies? One answer was provided by Arthur Aron and Lori Westbay (1996) in a complex statistical reduction (factor analysis) of the sixty-eight features to the smallest possible number of independent factors. Three factors emerged that were identified as *passion, intimacy,* and *commitment.* Features on the intimacy factor were rated as more important to the meaning of love than the features of passion or commitment.

So love includes intimacy, commitment, and passion, but the greatest of these is intimacy—at least according to this theoretical tradition. These three prototypes of love form the basic concepts of another theory of love proposed by Robert Sternberg (1986).

Triangular Theory of Love

For Sternberg, the three components of love—intimacy, passion, and commitment—can be viewed as three points on a triangle and occur in people in different proportions (present or absent) to create eight different types of love. These eight

TABLE 1

Triangular theory of love			
	Three components of love (present or absent)		
Type of love	Intimacy	Passion	Commitment
1. Consummate	Present	Present	Present
2. Companionate	Present	Absent	Present
3. Romantic	Present	Present	Absent
4. Fatuous	Absent	Present	Present
5. Infatuated	Absent	Present	Absent
6. Empty	Absent	Absent	Present
7. Liking	Present	Absent	Absent
8. Nonlove	Absent	Absent	Absent

SOURCE: Based on Sternberg. (1986). "A Triangular Theory of Love." *Psychology Review* 93: 119-135.

types may be most easily visualized in table form (see Table 1).

This theory is elegant in its simplicity, yet consistent with everyday notions of love. Moreover, the theory is relevant to the development of relationships over time. For example, before meeting another person the three components of love would be absent (nonlove). After meeting, liking may develop (intimacy). Perhaps some degree of commitment develops also, suggesting companionate love. If passion develops as well, then full consummate love has flowered. Other developmental trajectories are possible. A sudden burst of passion and commitment may develop from an initial meeting. *Fatuous love* seems an appropriate name for such instant, committed attraction. Perhaps a full consummate relationship loses its passion and intimacy, but retains strong commitment. The concept of *empty love* captures this situation well.

More recently, Sternberg (1998) shifted his theorizing to focus on the narrative, developmental aspects of love. In fact, the progression of a love relationship is a kind of story, one commonly celebrated in novels and films. In *Love Is a Story*, Sternberg (1998) explicitly recognized the story-like nature of love, and described twenty-five love stories, each representing one kind of theme or metaphor of love. If people can understand their own love stories, perhaps they will be able to manage future outcomes of those stories more successfully.

The ubiquity of romantic love in human life may suggest that it is part of our genetic heritage for mating, a possibility noted by several theorists.

Attachment Theory and the Evolution of Love

Evolutionary psychology is a broad group of theories that include sex and mating practices as part of their domain (e.g., Buss and Kenrick 1998). Most mammals engage in a mix of emotional expressions and attachment behaviors that, in human terms, appear to be love. In fact, John Bowlby (1969) developed an elaborate evolutionary theory of human infant attachment as the precursor of and foundation for human love. Cindy Hazan and Phillip P. Shaver (1987) elaborated Bowlby's infant attachment theory into an adult model of romantic love. Sydney L. W. Mellen (1981) wrote an entire book on the evolution of love. Mellen speculated that species survival depended on primitive emotional bonding between breeding pairs of proto-humans. Such bonding enhanced survival rates, and in a few hundred generations passionate love emerged as a defining human attribute. Thus attachment processes and love may be closely linked.

The attachment behavior first identified by Bowlby was further explored by Mary D. S. Ainsworth and her colleagues (1978), whose research with infants and their mothers resulted in the articulation of three basic attachment styles. These include *secure attachment* (warmth and trust in relationships), *anxious/ambivalent attachment* (nervous dissatisfaction with either closeness or separateness in relationships), and *avoidant attachment* (discomfort with closeness in relationship).

Hazan and Shaver (1987) adapted the three infant attachment styles to adult romantic relationships, and Kim Bartholomew (1990) broadened the styles from three to four, essentially differentiating avoidance based on dismissal from avoidance based on fearfulness. Much research effort has gone into conceptualizing and measuring attachment over the last decade, and there is some consensus that there are indeed four rather than three styles. It is also possible to view attachment as *dimensions* rather than *styles,* meaning that instead of fitting into only one of four attachment boxes, everyone has aspects of all four attachment styles (Feeney, Noller, and Roberts 2000).

Attachment processes are clearly relevant for human socialization. Further, attachment does appear similar to various types of love, including some aspects of romantic love. As an area of scientific theory and research, however, attachment has become very complex. It is not known if there are different types of attachment, or if attachment varies in small steps on one or more *dimensions.* The stability of attachment processes over the life span is another area of controversy. Perhaps these and other issues will be sorted out as this research tradition matures.

The theories discussed so far capture a broad range of the human experience of love. But they do not capture all of it. To broaden the conception still further, this entry considers a sociological theory developed by John Alan Lee (1973), described in his book *The Colors of Love,* and commonly referred to as a theory of *love styles.*

The Love Styles

Although no one theory of love can capture all of love's characteristics in all of love's domains (e.g., parent-child love, love of friends), Lee's (1973) love styles approach proposes six major orientations to romantic, partnered love. These love styles include *Eros* (passionate love), *Ludus* (game-playing love), *Storge* (love based on friendship), *Pragma* (practical love), *Mania* (dependent, possessive love), and *Agape* (altruistic love). The *Love Attitudes Scale* (LAS) was originally developed with seven items to measure each of the six love styles (forty-two items total) (Hendrick and Hendrick 1986) and is now available in a short form of twenty-four items (Hendrick, Hendrick, and Dicke 1998). The LAS has been used to explore a number of questions about love.

For example, do women and men differ in their love styles? Men typically describe themselves as more game-playing, and women describe themselves as more friendship-oriented, practical, and dependent. Recent research also indicates that men endorse altruistic love more than women do, so sex differences may vary depending on such factors as the version of the LAS that is being used or the age and culture of the sample. In any case, because gender differences are typically small, sex similarities are probably more important. For example, men and women are similar on passionate love, and for both sexes, passionate love (as well as other qualities) predicts relationship satisfaction, across both ages and cultures (Contreras, Hendrick, and Hendrick 1996).

Are romantic partners similar in their love styles? Gregory D. Morrow, Eddie M. Clark, and Karla F. Brock (1995) found partner similarity on

love styles (consistent with previous research) and also found that people's love styles (and their partners' love styles) were related to a number of positive relationship qualities (e.g., commitment, investment). Is companionate or passionate love more important to a romantic relationship? Both companionate and passionate love appear to be related to satisfaction with one's relationship, and it is concluded "that passion and friendship/companionship are not consecutive in a romantic relationship but rather are concurrent. Both play a part in relationship initiation and development as well as in relationship maintenance" (Hendrick and Hendrick 1993, p. 465).

The LAS has been translated into many languages, probably because many cultures and countries are interested in romantic love, and also because different love styles may be congruent with different cultures.

Love Across Cultures

Although love needs to be framed within a cultural context, many scholars believe that romantic love is transcultural. Elaine Hatfield and Richard L. Rapson (1996) viewed passionate love as common to virtually all cultures, and indeed, romantic love has been found in most countries of the world, as described in the *Standard Cross-Cultural Sample* (Jankowiak and Fischer 1992). Love also appears to have been part of people's conscious experience for many centuries. Wenchun Cho and Susan E. Cross (1995) examined Chinese literature dating from 500 to 3,000 years ago and found themes that seemed to represent *passionate love, casual love, devoted love, obsessive love,* and *free choice of a mate,* all themes that are present in contemporary love theories. These authors then used the LAS to see whether these themes were found in current attitudes of Taiwanese students living in the United States. These students did indeed express six different love styles, but not exactly the six contained in the LAS. For example, passionate and altruistic love seemed to be combined in a "Romantic and Considerate love," and practical and altruistic love seemed to be combined in "Obligatory love."

Robin Goodwin and Charlotte Findlay (1997) compared Chinese, Hong Kong, and British respondents on the love styles and the Chinese concept of *yuan (fated and predestined love).* Although the Chinese participants were more endorsing of *yuan* as well as practical and altruistic love styles, British respondents also agreed strongly with several of the *yuan* items. Robert L. Moore (1998) used written narratives and interviews to document the importance of love to both Chinese and U.S. cultures but also emphasized that love in Chinese society is tempered by additional characteristics such as the need for parental approval and the importance of appropriate behavior.

In other research, Pacific Islanders, Japanese Americans, and European Americans (all Hawaii residents) were compared on various aspects of love and relationships (Doherty et al. 1994). Attachment was related to love similarly for all the groups, and the groups did not differ in either companionate or passionate love. Sprecher and her colleagues (1994) also found similarities across cultures. They compared Russians, Japanese, and Americans on love and relationships, and found that although some cultural differences were present—Russians less likely to require love as a basis for marriage, Japanese agreeing less with certain romantic beliefs, Americans more endorsing of secure attachment—"the young adults from the three countries were similar in many love attitudes and experiences" (p. 363).

Cross-cultural similarity in love attitudes was documented by Raquel Contreras and her colleagues (1996), who studied Mexican-American and Anglo-American couples in the United States. The Mexican-American couples were divided into bi-cultural (equally oriented to Hispanic and Anglo cultures) and Hispanic-oriented groups, because acculturation to a majority culture in a particular country may alter the relationship behavior that someone brings with them from a country of origin. In fact, there were only modest love attitude differences among the groups. The Anglo-American, bicultural, and Hispanic-oriented couples did not differ in passionate, altruistic, or friendship-based love, and they were also similar in relationship satisfaction. Modest cultural differences were shown by Bernard I. Murstein, Joseph R. Merighi, and Stuart A. Vyse (1991), who found in comparing French and American students on the LAS that the French students were more agapic, and American students were more manic and oriented to friendship love.

In considering what we know about love across cultures, it is likely that the propensity for romantic love is cross-cultural and may well be part of our genetic heritage. But love is also construed and constructed within contexts of culture and country. As William R. Jankowiak (1995) observed, "Romantic passion is a complex, multifaceted emotional phenomenon that is a byproduct of an interplay between biology, self, and society" (p. 4).

Love Across the Life Span

Love, in its romantic expression, is often thought to belong to the "young," just as sexuality is thought to belong to the young (and often the beautiful). Yet love spans all of human life. Nancy K. Grote and Irene Hanson Frieze (1994) have given particular attention to love and other relationship characteristics in middle-aged married couples. They found that game-playing love was a negative predictor of marital satisfaction, whereas friendship-based and passionate love were positive predictors of satisfaction. These findings were similar to those for younger couples. In another study with largely the same married sample, Grote and Frieze (1998) asked people to recall their love for their partner when the relationship was beginning, as well as assess their current love for their partner. Passionate love, though perceived as somewhat lower than it had been many years before, was still "moderately strong" (p. 104). Love based on friendship was perceived to be about the same as it had been when the relationship began. Interestingly, husbands perceived that their altruistic love for their wives had grown over the years.

Love across the life span was also explored by Marilyn J. Montgomery and Gwen T. Sorell (1997), who studied relationship characteristics and love styles in four different groups: (1) college-age adults who had never been married; (2) married adults under age 30 without children; (3) married adults (ages 24–50) with children in the home; and (4) married adults (ages 50–70) with no children in the home. The greatest differences between the groups were not based on age, but rather the presence or absence of the marital bond. The young, unmarried people reported less altruistic love and greater game-playing and manic love than the other three groups. Neither passionate love (often thought to be the property of the young) or friendship-oriented love (often thought to be the hallmark of older couples) differed across the groups. The authors noted that "individuals throughout the life-stages of marriage consistently endorse the love attitudes involving passion, romance, friendship, and self-giving love" (p. 61).

Conclusion

Love is fundamentally important to our humanity. Various expressions of love are important, including romantic, partnered love. No one theory captures all the nuances of love, but virtually all of the love theories help us to understand love better. Love may manifest somewhat differently across both cultures and ages, but overall, people are more similar than different.

See also: AFFECTION; ATTACHMENT: COUPLE
RELATIONSHIPS; ATTRACTION; DATING; FRIENDSHIP;
HONEYMOON; INTIMACY; MARITAL QUALITY;
MARITAL SEX; MARRIAGE, DEFINITION OF; MATE
SELECTION; SEXUALITY; TRUST

Bibliography

Ainsworth, M. D. S.; Blehar, M. S.; Waters, E.; and Wall, S. (1978). *Patterns of Attachment: A Psychological Study of the Strange Situation.* Hillsdale, NJ: Erlbaum.

Aron, A., and Westbay, L. (1996). "Dimensions of the Prototype of Love." *Journal of Personality and Social Psychology* 70:535–551.

Bartholomew, K. (1990). "Avoidance of Intimacy: An Attachment Perspective." *Journal of Social and Personal Relationships* 7:147–178.

Berscheid, E., and Walster, E. (1969). *Interpersonal Attraction.* Reading, MA: Addison-Wesley.

Berscheid, E., and Walster, E. (1978). *Interpersonal Attraction,* 2nd edition. Reading, MA: Addison-Wesley.

Bowlby, J. (1969). *Attachment and Loss: Vol. 1. Attachment.* New York: Basic Books.

Buss, D. M., and Kenrick, D. T. (1998). "Evolutionary Social Psychology." In *The Handbook of Social Psychology*: Vol. 2, 4th edition, ed. D. T. Gilbert, S. T. Fiske, and G. Lindzey. Boston, MA: McGraw-Hill.

Cho, W., and Cross, S. E. (1995). "Taiwanese Love Styles and their Association with Self-Esteem and Relationship Quality." *Genetic, Social, and General Psychology Monographs* 121:283–309.

Contreras, R.; Hendrick, S. S.; and Hendrick, C. (1996). "Perspectives on Marital Love and Satisfaction in Mexican American and Anglo Couples." *Journal of Counseling and Development* 74:408–415.

Doherty, R. W.; Hatfield, E.; Thompson, K.; and Choo, P. (1994). "Cultural and Ethnic Influences on Love and Attachment." *Personal Relationships* 1:391–398.

Feeney, J. A.; Noller, P.; and Roberts, N. (2000). "Attachment and Close Relationships." In *Close Relationships: A Sourcebook,* ed. C. Hendrick and S. S. Hendrick. Thousand Oaks, CA: Sage.

Fehr, B. (1988). "Prototype Analysis of the Concepts of Love and Commitment." *Journal of Personality and Social Psychology* 55:557–579.

Fehr, B. (1993). "How Do I Love Thee? Let Me Consult My Prototype." In *Individuals in Relationships,* Vol. 1, ed. S. Duck. Newbury Park, CA: Sage.

Fehr, B. (1995). "Love." In *Encyclopedia of Marriage and the Family,* ed. D. Levinson. New York: Macmillan.

Fehr, B., and Broughton, R. (2001). "Gender and Personality Differences in Conceptions of Love: An Interpersonal Theory Analysis." *Personal Relationships* 8:115–136.

Goodwin, R., and Findlay, C. (1997). "'We Were Just Fated Together' . . . Chinese Love and the Concept of Yuan in England and Hong Kong." *Personal Relationships* 4:85–92.

Grote, N. K., and Frieze, I. H. (1994). "The Measurement of Friendship-Based Love in Intimate Relationships." *Personal Relationships* 1:275–300.

Grote, N. K.; and Frieze, I. H. (1998). "'Remembrance of Things Past': Perceptions of Marital Love from its Beginnings to the Present." *Journal of Social and Personal Relationships* 15:91–109.

Harlow, H. F. (1974). *Learning in Love.* New York: Jason Aronson.

Hatfield, E. (1988). "Passionate and Companionate Love." In *The Psychology of Love,* ed. R. J. Sternberg and M. L. Barnes. New Haven, CT: Yale University Press.

Hatfield, E., and Rapson, R. L. (1996). *Love and Sex: Cross-Cultural Perspectives.* Boston: Allyn and Bacon.

Hazan, C., and Shaver, P. (1987). "Romantic Love Conceptualized as an Attachment Process." *Journal of Personality and Social Psychology* 52:511–523.

Hendrick, C., and Hendrick, S. S. (1986). "A Theory and Method of Love." *Journal of Personality and Social Psychology* 50:392–402.

Hendrick, C.; Hendrick, S. S.; and Dicke, A. (1988). "The Love Attitudes Scale: Short Form." *Journal of Social and Personal Relationships* 15:147–159.

Hendrick, S. S., and Hendrick, C. (1993). "Lovers as Friends." *Journal of Social and Personal Relationships* 10:459–466.

Hendrick, S. S., and Hendrick, C., eds. (2000). *Close Relationships: A Sourcebook.* Thousands Oaks, CA: Sage.

Jankowiak, W. R., ed. (1995). *Romantic Passion: A Universal Experience.* New York: Columbia University Press.

Jankowiak, W. R., and Fischer, E. F. (1992). "A Cross-Cultural Perspective on Romantic Love." *Enthnology* 31:149–155.

Lee, J. A. (1973). *The Colors of Love.* Don Mills, Ontario: New Press.

Mellen, S. L. W. (1981). *The Evolution of Love.* San Francisco: W. H. Freeman.

Montgomery, M. J., and Sorell, G. T. (1997). "Differences in Love Attitudes Across Family Life States." *Family Relationships* 46:55–61.

Moore, R. L. (1998). "Love and Limerence with Chinese Characteristics: Student Romance in the PRC." In *Romantic Love and Sexual Behavior: Perspectives from the Social Sciences,* ed. V. C. deMunck. Westport, CT: Praeger.

Morrow, G. D.; Clark, E. M.; and Brock, K. F. (1995). "Individual and Partner Love Styles: Implications for the Quality of Romantic Involvements." *Journal of Social and Personal Relationships* 12:363–387.

Murstein, B. I.; Merighi, J. R.; and Vyse, S. A. (1991). "Love Styles in the United States and France: A Cross-Cultural Comparison." *Journal of Social and Clinical Psychology* 10:37–46.

Noller, P. (1996). "What Is This Thing Called Love? Defining the Love That Supports Marriage and Family." *Personal Relationships* 3:97–115.

Regan, P. C.; Kocan, E. R.; and Whitlock, T. (1998). "Ain't Love Grand! A Prototype Analysis of the Concept of Romantic Love." *Journal of Social and Personal Relationships* 15·411–420.

Sprecher, S., and Regan, P. C. (1998). "Passionate and Companionate Love in Courting and Young Married Couples." *Sociological Inquiry* 68:163–185.

Sprecher, S.; Aron, A.; Hatfield, E.; Cortese, A.; Potapova, E.; and Levitskaya, A. (1994). "Love: American Style, Russian Style, and Japanese Style." *Personal Relationships* 1:349–369.

Sternberg, R. J. (1986). "A Triangular Theory of Love." *Psychological Review* 93:119–135.

Sternberg, R. J. (1998). *Love Is a Story.* New York: Oxford University Press.

Walster, E., and Walster, G. (1978). *A New Look at Love.* Reading, MA: Addison-Wesley.

CLYDE HENDRICK
SUSAN S. HENDRICK

MALAYSIA

Since the 1960s changes in population patterns and the economy have significantly affected Malaysian families. Over those four decades, economic development, modernization, and rural-urban migration together altered family ties and contributed to a more fragmented family structure. There was a corresponding steady and noticeable decline in the average size of the family in Malaysia over the same period. A related change is the increasing life expectancy in Malaysian society (Subbiah 1994; Tey 1994). This increase is related to economic and social improvements that Malaysians in general experienced during this period.

These changes have ushered in distinct developments in the population distribution and trends in the family that distinguish the experiences of the Malays, Chinese Malaysians, and Indian Malaysians, the three dominant ethnic groups in the country. Based on the 2000 census, the Malays who are predominantly Muslims comprised 65.1 percent of the population (estimated at 23.3 million). In turn, the Chinese Malaysians (who are primarily Buddhist, although smaller proportions of them are Christian, Taoist, or followers of Confucianism) make up 26 percent, and a largely Hindu Indian Malaysian population makes up 7.7 percent of the population. These data represent a shift from 1991; the Malay proportion of the total population increased by approximately 4.5 percent as the Chinese Malaysian and Indian Malaysian proportion declined by 2.1 percent and 0.2 percent of the population, respectively. This shift in the ethnic

distribution has occurred alongside a steady pattern of an average annual population growth of 2.6 percent, which dates to 1980 (Department of Statistics 2001). Along with the population growth rate, the 2000 census indicated an upward trend in the number of households that reached the 4.9 million mark, in contrast to the 1.9 million households reported in 1970. Since 1960, Malaysia has been experiencing a higher growth rate of households than of population, and this trend in part reflects the breakdown of the extended family pattern that had historically characterized the traditional rural-based Malaysian society (Tey 1994). However, household size shows a downward trend; the current household size stands at 4.5 persons, compared with 4.9 in 1991. The largely rural states such as Kelantan and Terengganu still show a large household and family size due to the high fertility rates in these states.

Marriage and Family Formation Patterns

Since the early 1970s social interaction between the three dominant ethnic groups has gradually increased, but intermarriage across ethnic lines remains very rare (Leete 1996). As such, marriage traditions and rituals and family life among the different ethnic groups have also remained distinct, reflecting the cultural and religious heritage of each of the ethnic groups (Subramaniam 1997). Compared to the Chinese Malaysian, the Malays and Indian Malaysians have historically been more inclined to marry at a younger age. For the Malays, this practice of marriage at a relatively early age reflects the strong influence of rural traditions and customs that shaped and dominated the lives of the historically rural-based Malay population. For example, in the 1950s more than 50 percent of Malay women married between the ages of fifteen and nineteen. This stands in stark contrast to an only 10 percent marriage rate for Chinese Malaysian women between those same ages during the same period. In large part, this marriage trend among Malay women was due to the fact that it was customary for Malay women to receive minimal, if any, formal education, and parents typically arranged marriages for their daughters shortly after the onset of puberty. However, increased educational and economic opportunities—particularly in urban areas—has lead to a significant shift of the Malay population to urban areas, and this shift affected the trend of marriage and family formation among Malay women. By 1991 only 5.1 percent of Malay women (and 2.5 percent of Chinese Malaysian women) married between the ages of fifteen and nineteen (Leete 1996).

Cutting across ethnic lines, Malaysians as a whole have been opting to marry later in life. Young male adults' age at marriage increased from 28.2 years in 1991 to 28.6 years in 2000, while for females the increase was from 24.7 years to 25.1 years over the same period. At marriage, there is an average of four to five years' difference in the age of the male and female. Furthermore, the proportion of never-married people aged twenty to thirty-four increased from 43.2 percent in 1991 to 48.1 percent in 2000. Among females between the ages of twenty and twenty-four, 68.5 percent were single in 2000, compared to only 60.2 percent in 1991. Similar patterns were observed for both men and women between the ages of twenty-five and thirty-four (Department of Statistics 2001; Tan and Jones 1990). This tendency to postpone marriage until later in life is most evident among men and women who are urban dwellers and have relatively high levels of education. This phenomenon of marrying later in life corresponds to the decline in the average number of children in Malaysian families as well. In 1974, for example, the average number of children born to a Malay and Chinese Malaysian household, respectively, was 4.2, while Indian households averaged 4.6 children. By 1988 the average had declined to 3.6 for Malays, 3 for Chinese Malaysian and 3.3 for Indian Malaysian (Tey 1994).

The nuclear family—consisting of two parents and at least one unmarried child—remains the predominant family arrangement in Malaysia. Where extended family household patterns persist (that is, where at least one elderly parent resides with an adult child), it is least likely among Malays and most likely among Chinese Malaysians. In part, this difference is a reflection of a strong cultural tradition among Chinese Malaysians that emphasizes filial piety and strong respect for elders. Indian Malaysians also have a strong cultural tradition upholding a son's commitment to care for his adult parents in old age. The influence of filial piety, respect for elders, and a cultural norm of support between parent and son creates a strong bond of social and economic commitment between different generations of Chinese Malaysians and Indian Malaysians, and translates into a higher proportion of parent-adult child living arrangements within Chinese Malaysian and Indian Malaysian families. At the same time, the historically rural-based Malay population created a set of property relations where Malay parents were more inclined to own their own dwellings independent of their children. In contrast, the historically more urban Indian Malaysian and, especially, Chinese Malaysian population would be more likely to encounter higher economic costs of maintaining independent households from their adult offspring (DaVanzo and Chan 1994). With life expectancy in 2001 reaching seventy years for men and seventy-five for women, it is highly likely that elder care by family members and parents residing with an adult child will be a significant concern for Malaysian families in the near future.

If marital dissolution is any indication of the stability of the Malaysian family structure, the majority of Malaysian families tend to be stable. In 1990 more than 90 percent of all first marriages remained intact. For those married less than ten years, 98 percent of marriages were intact. This figure dropped to 75 percent for those married for twenty years or more. Comparing the three dominant ethnic groups, Chinese Malaysians had the lowest divorce/separation rate (2.2 percent), followed by Indian Malaysians (2.9 percent), and Malays (8.4 percent). Malay women are also far more likely than their Chinese Malaysian or Indian Malaysian counterparts to remarry after a divorce. In 1989 only 19.9 percent of divorced women in general remarried, but the rate was 78.7 percent for Malay women. It is widely perceived that these higher rates of divorce and remarriage in large part simply reflect the fact that divorce and remarriage tend to be far more socially acceptable among Malays than among the other ethnic groups (Tom 1993). Another significant trend that has and will continue to affect Malaysian families is the rate of female participation in the labor force, which increased from 42 percent in 1980 to 45 percent in 1994. Malay women (65 percent during the mid-1980s) tended to have a far higher rate of participation in the labor force than women from the other major ethnic groups. Upon marriage, women's participation in the labor force declines significantly, although according to one estimate from the late 1980s, more than 44 percent of Malaysian households can be classified as dual income families (Razak 1993; Tey 1994).

See also: ISLAM

Bibliography

Brien, M. J., and Lillard, L. A. (2001). "Education, Marriage, and First Conception in Malaysia." *The Journal of Human Resources* 29:1167–1204.

Chattopadhyay, A. (1997). "Family Migration and the Economic Status of Women in Malaysia." *International Migration Review* 31:338–352.

DaVanzo, J., and Chan, A. (1994). "Living Arrangements of Older Malaysians: Who Coresides with Their Adult Children?" *Demography* 31:95–113.

Dixon, G. (1993). "Ethnicity and Infant Mortality in Malaysia." *Asia Pacific Population Journal* 8:23-54.

Hassan, M. K. (1994). "The Influence of Islam on Education and Family in Malaysia." In *The Role and Influence of Religion in Society,* ed. O. AlHadshi and S. O. S. Agil. Kuala Lumpur: Institute of Islamic Understanding Malaysia.

Leete, Richard. (1996). *Malaysia's Demographic Transition: Rapid Development, Culture, and Politics.* Kuala Lumpur: Oxford University Press.

Panis, C. W. A. and Lillard, L. A. (1995). "Child Mortality in Malaysia: Explaining Ethnic Differences and the Recent Decline." *Population Studies* 49:463–79.

Razak, R. A. (1993). "Women's Labour Force Participation in Peninsular Malaysia." In *Proceedings of the Seminar of the Second Malaysian Family Life Survey,* ed. J. Sine, N. P. Tey, and J. DaVanzo. Santa Monica, CA: Rand.

Subbiah, M. (1994). "Demographic Developments, Family Change and Implications for Social Development in Southeast Asia." In *Social Development under Rapid Industrialization: The Case of Southeast Asia,* ed. S. Chong and Cho Kah Sin. Kuala Lumpur: Institute of Strategic and International Studies.

Subramanian, P. (1997). *Malaysian Family, An Introduction.* Kuala Lumpur: National Population and Family Development Board.

Sudha, S. (1997). "Family Size, Sex Composition and Children's Education: Ethnic Differentials over Development in Peninsular Malaysia." *Population Studies* 51:139–51.

Tan, P. C., and Jones, G. (1990). "Changing Patterns of Marriage and Household Formation." *Sojourn* 5:163–93.

Tey, N. P. (1994). "Demographic Trends and Family Structure in Malaysia." In *Social Development under Rapid Industrialization: The Case of Southeast Asia,* ed. S. Chong and Cho Kah Sin. Kuala Lumpur: Institute of Strategic and International Studies.

Tom, K. M. (1993). "Marriage Trends among Peninsular Malaysian Women." In *Proceedings of the Seminar of the Second Malaysian Family Life Survey,* ed. J. Sine, N. P. Tey, and J. DaVanzo. Santa Monica, CA: Rand.

Other Resources

Department of Statistics, Malaysia. (2001). "Population and Housing Census 2000." In *Distribution and Basic Demographic Characteristics Report.* Available from http://www.statistics.gov.my/English/pageDemo.htm.

SUNIL KUKREJA

MARITAL DISSOLUTION

See CHILD CUSTODY; DIVORCE: EFFECTS ON CHILDREN; DIVORCE: EFFECTS ON COUPLES; DIVORCE: EFFECTS ON PARENTS; DIVORCE MEDIATION

MARITAL INTERACTION

See COMMUNICATION: COUPLE RELATIONSHIPS; CONFLICT: COUPLE RELATIONSHIPS; INTIMACY; MARITAL QUALITY; MARITAL SEX; POWER: MARITAL RELATIONSHIPS

MARITAL QUALITY

When people are asked to rate or rank their life goals, having a happy marriage is usually among the most important. People in most other modern societies seem to be somewhat less enamored of marriage than those in the United States, but with the possible exception of Scandinavians, who have often chosen nonmarital cohabitation over marriage, most adults throughout the modern world devote much effort to striving for a happy and satisfying marriage. Given the prominence and prevalence of this goal, family social scientists and psychologists could hardly avoid trying to assess the extent of its attainment and to identify the conditions under which it is likely to be attained. These efforts have been extensive, and the academic and clinical literature that deals with marital happiness and/or satisfaction is huge, with the number of relevant books, articles, and chapters published in the United States alone since the 1960s numbering in the thousands.

The terms *marital happiness* and *marital satisfaction* are closely related, but not synonymous (Campbell, Converse, and Rodgers 1976). Both refer to positive feelings that a spouse derives from a marriage, and both happiness and satisfaction are broader and more global in their meaning than such concepts as enjoyment, pleasure, and contentment. According to Angus Campbell, Philip Converse, and Willard Rodgers (1976), marital happiness is based on an affective evaluation, whereas marital satisfaction seems to have a more cognitive basis that involves a relation of one's circumstances to some standard. They found that marital happiness varied positively with formal education, while the most highly educated persons reported somewhat less marital satisfaction than those with less education. However, marital happiness and satisfaction are highly correlated and generally have been found to bear a similar relationship to other variables; thus, the common practice of using the two terms interchangeably in literature reviews is sloppy, but not a very serious error. This entry uses *marital quality* as a blanket term to cover either or both of these terms (see Lewis and Spanier 1979).

Marital quality is often used in a sense that includes marital adjustment as well as happiness and satisfaction. However, it is better to conceive of marital adjustment as something that may affect marital quality but is not part of it, since adjustment is an aspect of the relationship between spouses rather than a feeling experienced by each of them. Such indicators of adjustment as conflict, communication, and sharing of activities may relate differently to the spouses' feelings in different marriages, or even differently to the husband's and wife's feelings in the same marriage. The literature on marital adjustment is quite closely related to that on marital happiness and adjustment; the two literatures cannot be cleanly separated, since some marital quality scales (e.g., the widely used Dyadic Adjustment Scale) mix elements of adjustment with spouses' evaluations of their marriages (Spanier 1976). However, the focus in this entry is only on marital quality, as indicated by husbands' and wives' evaluations.

Measurement Issues

Marital happiness and satisfaction are often measured by single, straightforward questions that ask respondents to rate their marriages on a scale of happiness or satisfaction. There may be up to ten points on the scale, but often there are only three or four. It should be noted that individual satisfaction might be composed of different dimensions in different cultures. For example, a culture where arranged marriages and strong residential extended kinship is practiced might have satisfaction with in-laws as a significant dimension of marital quality and this dimension might not show up in cultures that practice voluntaristic mate selection and neolocal residence.

The prevailing view in family social science is that single-item indicators of marital quality are unsophisticated, and they are shunned by many researchers in favor of scales and multiple-item indices. Nevertheless, the best evidence on trends in and correlates of marital quality are based on responses to one, two, or three questions, since more complex measures have very rarely been used with large and representative samples. Furthermore, several critics have argued for the use of global measures of marital quality rather than multidimensional scales and indices that include variables that may influence or be influenced by spouses' evaluations of their marriages (e.g., Fincham and Bradbury 1987; Huston, McHale, and Crouter 1986; Huston and Robins 1982; Norton 1983). One may go beyond these critics and argue that one-item measures are sometimes superior to even two- and three-item scales and indices that might be multi-dimensional rather than unidimensional.

If a question has high face validity, as the straightforward questions about marital happiness and satisfaction do, then any other questions will have lower face validity and perforce must deal with something other than simply happiness or satisfaction. The purpose of multiple-item scales is to measure "latent" variables for which no direct measurement is possible and for which several indirect measures produce a higher degree of validity than a single one can. The usual assumption seems to be that there can be no simple, direct, and straightforward measure of feelings or other psychological characteristics, although single-item measures of date of birth, gender, and various demographic characteristics are routinely used. However, the correctness of this assumption is not self-evident, and the preference for multiple-item indicators for all psychological characteristics may grow primarily out of the researchers' need to feel sophisticated.

Nevertheless, most questions used to gauge marital happiness and satisfaction provide only crude measurement, if only because they offer only a few response alternatives, and the distribution of responses is usually highly skewed. For instance, the question about marital happiness most often used on national surveys in the United States offers only three degrees of happiness—"very happy," "pretty happy," and "not too happy"—and up to two-thirds of the respondents select the highest degree. Much of the variance in marital happiness must be among those who select the "very happy" alternative, but the measure is not finely calibrated enough to capture that variance. Furthermore, there is probably a systematic over-reporting of marital happiness and satisfaction, due not only to social desirability considerations—the most commonly discussed source of response bias—but also due to denial and a stoic tendency to put up a happy front. The extent of any such bias is unknown, and perhaps unknowable, but the likelihood that it is substantial is high enough to make it unwise to take reports of marital happiness and satisfaction at face value. Generally, only trends in the reports, and differences among categories of married persons, are worthy of interpretation. Of course, changes and differences in response bias may occasionally affect trend and comparative data.

Trends in Reported Marital Happiness

An essential part of the task of assessing the state of marriage in a modern society is to gauge change in the overall level of reported marital quality. Unfortunately, the data necessary for this task are quite limited for most societies, the United States being no exception. Until the early 1990s, about the only published evidence on this issue for the United States was from the Americans View Their Mental Health Surveys, conducted with national samples in 1957 and 1976. Joseph Veroff, Elizabeth Douvan, and Richard A. Kulka (1981) compared responses at the two dates to the question, "Taking things all together, how would you describe your marriage—would you say that your marriage was very happy, a little happier than average, just about average, or not too happy?" The "very happy" responses increased from 47 to 53 percent, and the combined "average" and "not too happy" responses declined from 32 to 20 percent—an indication of a moderate increase in marital happiness. The importance of not combining evaluations of specific aspects of marriages with global evaluations is illustrated by the fact that the percent of respondents who said "nothing" in response to a question about "not so nice things" about their marriage declined from 31 to 23, and the percent who reported problems with their marriage rose from 46 to 61. There apparently were specific aspects of marriages not covered by the questions that tended to improve from 1957 to 1976.

The most common reason given for the 1957-1976 increase in average marital happiness is that the steep increase in divorce beginning in 1965 improved the speed and effectiveness of the removal of persons in poor marriages from the married population. Since the divorce rate continued to rise after 1976 before leveling off at a very high level in the 1980s, there are reasons to suspect that the increase in marital happiness continued after 1976—a suspicion often voiced by commentators on marriage in the United States.

The best relevant data, however, indicate otherwise. The General Social Surveys conducted by the National Opinion Research Center have asked a simple marital happiness question of its married respondents annually since 1973, except in 1979, 1981, and 1992 (Davis and Smith, 1993). The question is worded, "Taking things all together, would you say that your marriage is very happy, pretty happy, or not too happy?" Fewer than 5 percent of the respondents have typically chosen the "not too happy" alternative, so the data are often collapsed into "very happy" versus less favorable responses. The 1973-1993 trend is shown in Figure 1, the linear trend line being distinctly downward, though only at the rate of .32 points per year.

The important thing about these findings is not that reported marital happiness declined moderately, but that it did not increase substantially, as it should have done if the main reason for the increase in divorce in recent decades was, as the sanguine view of U.S. marriage would have it, an increased reluctance of persons to endure poor marriages. Assuming the validity of the reports of marital happiness, the sanguine view is clearly indefensible; the increase in divorce must have resulted to a large extent from an increased tendency for marriages to go bad. This point is illustrated by the other two linear trend lines in Figure 1. The decline in the percent of persons in very happy marriages was steeper for all ever-married, nonwidowed persons (.60 points per year) and for all persons age thirty or older (.73 points per year) than for those currently married. Data on the trend in percent of ever-married, non-widowed persons in marriages in which they reported to be "very happy" at various lengths of time after the first marriage indicate that a decreasing proportion of the persons in the United States who marry at least once are finding the marital happiness they seek (Glenn 1991, 1993). In addition, the increase in divorce has not even decreased the proportion of persons who say they are in less than happy marriages at various lengths of time after the first marriage.

One might speculate that the apparent decline in the prospects of achieving a good marriage is illusory and has resulted from an increased tendency of persons in unsatisfactory marriages to report the quality of their marriages honestly. There is no definitive evidence that this explanation is not correct, but if the validity of reports of marital happiness had increased, the relationship of reported marital happiness to variables likely to be affected by marital happiness should have increased; that did not happen. For instance, the relationship of reported marital happiness to reported global (personal) happiness remained virtually stable from 1973 to 1993.

Why has the probability of attaining happy and satisfying marriages in the United States declined?

Since few commentators have recognized such a change or conceded that it has probably occurred, little has been written on the topic. Norval D. Glenn (1991) has speculated that a decline in the ideal of marital permanence has made persons less willing and less able to make the commitments, sacrifices, and "investments" of energy, time, and lost opportunities that are necessary to make marriages succeed. The breakdown in consensus about marital roles, whereby the terms of the marriage must be negotiated by each married couple and often must be renegotiated during the course of the marriage, has almost certainly contributed to the change, as have increased expectations of marriage. Disagreement over the division of household responsibilities has also emerged as a major cause of trouble in U.S. marriages (Berk 1985; Booth et al. 1984).

Bases of Marital Quality

Marriage counselors, ministers, various custodians of the folklore, and perhaps even family social scientists and psychologists may possess a great deal of wisdom about how to achieve and maintain happy and satisfying marriages. Many people probably know a great deal about how to achieve a happy marriage, but that knowledge is based hardly at all on systematic research. In spite of the enormous amount of research devoted to the topic, truly scientific evidence on the bases of marital happiness and satisfaction is meager. One reason may be that marital quality is inherently hard to study, but a more certain reason is that most of the research has been seriously deficient.

Consider, for instance, the many cross-sectional studies of samples of married persons in which various demographic and social variables have been related to the respondents' reports of their marital happiness or satisfaction. These studies have amassed a large body of evidence on the correlates of the measures of marital quality and have often inferred cause and effect from the correlational data. Even though some of the studies have used apparently sophisticated causal modeling, virtually none of the research has met the requirements for valid causal inference. An inherent limitation of studies concentrating on currently married persons, especially in a society with very high divorce rates, is that many of the persons among whom negative influences on marital quality have been the strongest have been selected out

FIGURE 1

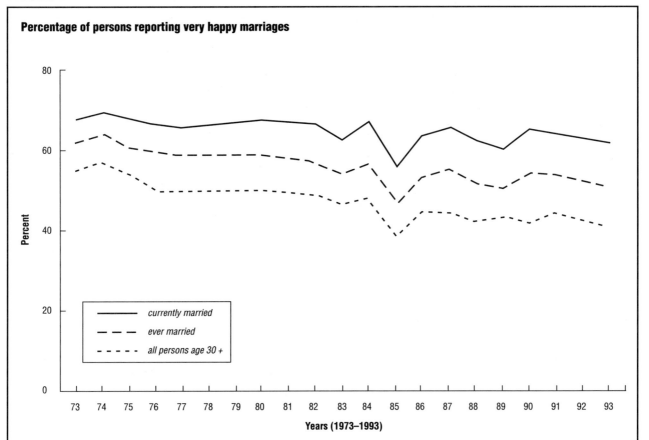

Percentage of persons reporting very happy marriages

Legend:
— currently married
– – – ever married
· · · · all persons age 30 +

Percent (y-axis: 0, 20, 40, 60, 80)

Years (1973–1993) (x-axis: 73, 74, 75, 76, 77, 78, 79, 80, 81, 82, 83, 84, 85, 86, 87, 88, 89, 90, 91, 92, 93)

of the sampled population through divorce. Therefore, the effects of the negative influences will be underestimated or not detected at all in analyses of data on married persons, or positive effects may even be attributed to the influences.

There are two aspects of the problem. First, divorce lessens the variance of marital quality, thus attenuating estimates of effects on that variable. Second, if variables that affect marital quality affect the probability of divorce in ways other than via marital quality, the estimates of the effects can be substantially biased in either direction. A hypothetical case will illustrate the point. Suppose that celebrity status typically has negative effects on marital quality and that it increases the probability of divorce (by providing numerous alternatives to the current marriage) at each level of marital quality. If the latter effect is very strong and the former is relatively weak, a causal analysis with cross-sectional data that does not take the selection factor into account will estimate the effect of celebrity status on marital quality to be positive. Suppose that adherence to a particular religious ideology

typically exerts positive influence on marital quality but decreases the probability of divorce at each level of marital quality. In this case, the straightforward testing of a simple causal model may indicate a negative effect of religious adherence on marital quality, or at least it will yield an attenuated estimated positive effect.

It is theoretically possible, of course, to incorporate selection processes into causal models to obtain unbiased estimates of effects (Berk 1983; Heckman 1979), but the methods developed to do this have been criticized as inadequate, and in any event, they require information the researcher rarely has. Given the limitations of corrections for "sample selection bias," it is hardly lamentable that they have rarely been used in studies of the bases of marital quality.

A more promising solution to the problems posed by the use of cross-sectional data from samples of married individuals to infer effects on marital quality is to use longitudinal data or cross-sectional data from samples including formerly married as well as currently married individuals. Except in those rare studies in which marital quality has been assessed at frequent intervals before divorces have occurred, such research requires the assumption that marital quality becomes low before divorce occurs, but that assumption seems generally justified. Overall, longitudinal data are, of course, better for the purpose at hand, but cross-sectional data can be used to assess the effects of background variables that can be measured with reasonable accuracy through retrospective reports. Unfortunately, research with these designs has been rare, and such research with data from large and representative national samples is only in its infancy. As it increases, a substantial increment in credible evidence on the effects of several demographic and social variables on marital quality can be expected.

In the meantime, the evidence on the bases of marital happiness and marital satisfaction from "mainstream" quantitative social science consists almost entirely of a body of weak correlations and estimates of weak effects. The lack of strong relationships no doubt results in large measure from some of the most important influences on marital quality not being amenable to measurement on large-scale surveys and thus not being taken into account. Individuals' feelings about their marriages are also subject to considerable short-term fluctuation, and the variance resulting from this fluctuation will not be explained by the major long-term influences on marital quality. There is also the attenuation of measured relationships resulting from the selection of many of the people with the least satisfactory marriages out of the population of married persons.

These limitations of the evidence do not mean that it is worthless, but only that it should be interpreted with caution. Most of the estimates of effects are probably in the right direction, and theory, common sense, and what is known about the phenomena studied from sources other than the data at hand (side information) can provide strong clues about when to suspect that the estimated direction is wrong. When theory and common sense suggest that the direction of the estimated effects is right, it should often be suspected that the real world effects are stronger than the estimated ones. Since correlational data not used to test explicitly specified causal models can suggest effects on

marital quality, it is useful to discuss briefly some of the frequently found correlates.

One of the most frequent findings concerning marital quality is that it bears a nonmonotonic relationship to family life stage, being high in the preparental stage, lower in the parental stages, and relatively high in the "empty nest" or postparental stage. Although every few years someone publishes an article challenging the existence of this nonmonotonic relationship, its cross-sectional existence is hardly in doubt; it has been found by numerous studies conducted over more than twenty years, and the data from large national samples reported in Table 1 clearly show it. The reasons for and meaning of this cross-sectional relationship are not clear, however, and it is much less than certain that marriages that survive through all of the stages typically follow the down-up pattern suggested by the cross-sectional data (Vaillant and Vaillant 1993).

Most of the data on family life stage and marital quality confound any effects of presence-absence of children with those of duration of marriage. However, research has shown that each of these variables bears a relationship to measures of marital quality when the other is held constant (e.g., Glenn 1989; McLanahan and Adams 1989; White and Booth 1985; White, Booth, and Edwards 1986). That average marital quality drops during the first few years of marriage is hardly in doubt, especially in view of the fact that a high divorce rate during those years eliminates many of the worst marriages and prevents many marital failures from being reflected in the cross-sectional data. That reported marital quality is typically lower after the birth of the first child than earlier is also not in doubt, but in spite of numerous studies of the transition to parenthood (e.g., Belsky, Spanier, and Rovine 1983; Feldman and Nash 1984; Goldberg, Michaels, and Lamb 1985; McHale and Huston 1985), it still is not certain that the addition of a child to the family typically brings about any permanent reduction in marital quality. At least one study has found evidence that the cross-sectional association of the presence of a child or children with low marital quality results to a large extent, though not totally, from the fact that children tend to prevent or delay divorce and keep unhappily married couples together, at least temporarily (White, Booth, and Edwards 1986). The apparent upturn in marital quality in the postparental stage

TABLE 1

Characteristics of married persons who reported very happy marriages

Characteristic	Husbands (%)	(n)	Wives (%)	(n)
Hours per week wife worked outside home				
0–9	68.4	(4,120)	63.7	(4,627)
10–29	65.9	(705)	63.1	(841)
30 or more	66.2	(2,580)	63.1	(2,836)
Race				
White	68.6	(6,691)	65.1	(7,482)
African American	54.5	(595)	48.3	(654)
Education				
Less than high school	66.4	(2,194)	56.7	(2,135)
High school	67.9	(3,503)	64.8	(4,761)
Junior college	61.4	(233)	62.4	(272)
Bachelor's degree	68.4	(938)	71.6	(844)
Graduate degree	69.1	(548)	67.6	(275)
Husband's occupational prestige*				
Low	64.9	(3,153)	60.2	(3,597)
Medium	69.3	(3,095)	64.9	(3,430)
High	70.8	(745)	74.6	(748)
Age at first marriage†				
12–19	65.2	(741)	62.6	(2,690)
20–22	69.6	(2,005)	65.7	(2,284)
23–39	67.5	(3,274)	65.0	(1,912)
Years since first marriage†				
0–2	75.0	(323)	78.8	(391)
3–5	63.8	(575)	66.6	(623)
6–8	63.2	(493)	64.4	(543)
9–11	63.7	(393)	61.6	(490)
12–14	68.2	(349)	64.1	(473)
15–19	63.5	(600)	58.5	(681)
20–24	63.6	(584)	59.6	(732)
25–29	69.3	(647)	62.0	(713)
30–39	68.6	(1,040)	67.1	(1,225)
40 or more	74.0	(1,074)	64.0	(1,046)
Family life stage				
Preparental	70.8	(994)	74.4	(1,094)
Parental	64.5	(3,771)	59.6	(4,375)
Postparental	70.2	(2,659)	65.1	(2,823)
Spend a social evening with relatives				
Never or infrequently	59.9	(484)	51.8	(463)
Several times a year	62.0	(876)	61.8	(880)
About once a month	64.5	(828)	62.8	(785)
Once or twice a week/several times a month	69.3	(2,139)	65.2	(2,534)
Almost daily	72.6	(246)	66.3	(334)
Religious preference				
Protestant	68.1	(4,743)	63.9	(5,493)
Catholic	69.5	(1,864)	62.6	(2,172)
Jewish	68.4	(152)	68.6	(188)
None	53.5	(518)	56.8	(337)
Identification with a religion or denomination				
Strong	75.1	(2,333)	69.1	(3,436)
Somewhat strong	65.3	(702)	62.5	(755)
Not very strong	64.0	(3,114)	57.5	(2,946)
Attendance of religious services				
Never	57.8	(978)	58.9	(855)
Infrequently	62.8	(1,792)	58.7	(1,418)
Several times a year	67.5	(1,006)	61.1	(1,067)
One to three times a month	67.8	(1,117)	59.2	(1,343)
Weekly or almost weekly	73.0	(1,968)	68.0	(2,746)
Several times a week	77.6	(532)	71.2	(836)

* Hodge-Siegel-Rossi scores: Low = 9-39; Medium = 40-59; High = 60-82
† Persons in first marriages only

SOURCE: The 1973–1991 General Social Survey Cumulative File (Davis and Smith 1993). Data are weighted on number of persons age 18 or older in the household.

is probably real, though small, but the existence of positive duration-of-marriage effects beyond the middle years is not at all certain, since the cross-sectional data confound any effects of marital duration with those of cohort membership and the divorces of unhappily married persons.

Some of the other data in Table 1 suggest influences stronger than those of family stage or duration of marriage. Since reported marital happiness varies directly with frequency of attendance of religious services and strength of identification with a religious group or denomination and is higher for persons who report a religious preference than for those who say they have no religion, religiosity is probably a rather strong positive influence on marital quality, especially since indicators of religiosity are also associated with low divorce rates (Glenn and Supancic 1984). However, more than religiosity may be involved in the relationship between frequency of attendance of religious services and marital quality. Such attendance is an indicator of social participation and social integration as well as religiosity, and there are many suggestions in literature that social integration is conducive to marital success. The data in Table 1 indicating that frequency of association with extended family members is positively related to marital happiness are also consistent with the social integration explanation of marital happiness.

The literature on African-American-white differences in the probability of marital success is extensive, yet there is no definitive evidence as to why reported marital quality is higher among whites (see Table 1) and divorce rates are lower. The measures of socioeconomic status usually included on social surveys do not account for much of the difference and in fact do not relate strongly to either reported marital quality or the probability of divorce (Glenn and Supancic 1984). Of course, this does not mean that past differences in economic conditions or differences in economic security are not important reasons for the racial difference in the probability of marital success, but their influence may be largely through such variables as the lower sex ratio among African Americans (Guttentag and Secord 1983).

The lack of even a moderately strong relationship between reported marital happiness and two of the independent variables included in Table 1 illustrates the danger of concluding that there is no

effect on marital quality on the basis of cross-sectional data. The indicated differences in marital happiness by age at first marriage (shown only for persons in their first marriages) are quite small, which might lead to the conclusion that early marriages are almost as successful on average as marriages of more mature persons. However, the divorce rate *does* vary substantially by age at marriage—an indication that early marriages are unusually likely to have failed, either by ending in divorce or being less than satisfactory (Bumpass and Sweet 1972; Schoen 1975). It appears that persons who find themselves in less than satisfactory marriages within a few years after marriage are more likely to divorce if they were married early, and this results in a very small difference in marital quality between early and late marriers in intact first marriages.

The data in Table 1 show virtually no relationship between the number of hours the wife worked outside the home and the reported marital happiness of either the wife or the husband. There is no definitive evidence that the wife's working outside the home *does* affect marital quality, but these cross-sectional data do not prove that it does not. Suppose that at each level of marital quality, the probability of divorce varies directly with the number of hours the wife works outside the home—not an unlikely relationship. If so, poor marriages will be more quickly ended among couples in which the wife works more hours outside the home, thus raising the average marital quality in the remaining marriages in that category. If so, marital quality should vary positively with number of hours worked by the wife unless wives' working outside the home has a negative effect on marital success.

Dozens of other variables have been related to measures of marital happiness and satisfaction, but the ones discussed here are among those to which the greatest attention has been devoted. The deficiencies in the evidence of the causal importance of these variables is illustrative of the weakness of the body of "scientific" study concerning the bases of marital quality.

Consequences of Marital Quality

In contrast to the literature on the bases of marital quality, that on its consequences is quite sparse. About the only variables likely to be affected by marital quality to which strong relationships have been shown to exist are global happiness and life satisfaction (Andrews and Withey 1976; Campbell, Converse, and Rodgers 1976; Glenn and Weaver 1981). Data from the 1982-1991 General Social Surveys show that the percent of married persons who said they were personally very happy varied from 57.2, for those who said they had "very happy" marriages, to 11.2 and 2.6, respectively, for those reporting "pretty happy" and "not too happy" marriages. Although this relationship may be partially spurious, it is likely to be largely causal, since theory and common sense predict strong effects of marital quality on life quality. If so, the data indicate that having a good marriage is virtually necessary, though not sufficient, for global happiness.

Research on the effects of marital quality is likely to increase along at least two different lines. There is already a great deal of evidence on the probable effects of marital status on physical and mental health (Umberson 1987; Verbrugge 1979), and researchers are beginning to perceive the need to do equally extensive and sophisticated research on the health effects of marital quality. Simply stated, the main question is: How bad does a marriage have to be before it is worse than no marriage at all? There is also much discussion, especially in the journalistic and policy literature, about the effects of marital quality on children, as conservatives and communitarians have challenged the orthodox liberal belief that it is better for the children if the parents divorce when a marriage goes bad. Virtually everyone agrees that a violent or extremely hostile marriage is bad for children, but how bad does a marriage have to be for the children to benefit from the parents' separation? Excluding the most hostile and conflict-ridden marriages, is there any close relationship between the quality of the parents' marriage and the children's well-being? So far, well-conducted research has provided hints, but no compelling evidence. We must also await comparative cross-cultural data to assist us in establishing the uniformity for both the causes and consequence of marital quality as they are currently viewed by North American academics.

See also: AFFECTION; ATTACHMENT: COUPLE RELATIONSHIPS; CODEPENDENCY; COMMUNICATION: COUPLE RELATIONSHIPS; COPARENTING; CONFLICT: COUPLE RELATIONSHIPS; DIVISION OF LABOR; DIVORCE: EFFECT ON COUPLES; DUAL-EARNER FAMILIES; FAMILY ROLES; FAMILY STRENGTHS; INFIDELITY; INTERPARENTAL CONFLICT—EFFECTS ON CHILDREN; INTERPARENTAL VIOLENCE—EFFECTS ON CHILDREN; LOVE; LATER LIFE FAMILIES; LEISURE; MARITAL SEX; MARITAL TYPOLOGIES; MOTHERHOOD; POWER: MARITAL RELATIONSHIPS; RELATIONSHIP MAINTENANCE; RELIGION; REMARRIAGE; RESEARCH: FAMILY MEASUREMENT; RETIREMENT; SEXUAL COMMUNICATION: COUPLE RELATIONSHIPS; SEXUAL DYSFUNCTION; SOCIAL NETWORKS; SPOUSE ABUSE: PREVALENCE; SPOUSE ABUSE: THEORETICAL EXPLANATIONS; STRESS; THERAPY: COUPLE RELATIONSHIPS; TRANSITION TO PARENTHOOD; WIDOWHOOD; WORK AND FAMILY

Bibliography

Andrews, F. M., and Withey, S. B. (1976). *Social Indicators of Well-Being: Americans' Perceptions of Life Quality.* New York: Plenum.

Belsky, J.; Spanier, G.; and Rovine, M. (1983). "Stability and Change in Marriage Across the Transition to Parenthood: A Second Study." *Journal of Marriage and the Family* 45:567–577.

Berk, R. A. (1983). "An Introduction to Sample Selection Bias in Sociological Data." *American Sociological Review* 48:386–398.

Berk, S. F. (1985). *The Gender Factory.* New York: Plenum.

Booth, A.; Johnson, D. R.; White, L.; and Edwards, J. N. (1984). "Women, Outside Employment, and Marital Instability." *American Journal of Sociology* 90:567–583.

Bumpass, L. L., and Sweet, J. A. (1972). "Differentials in Marital Instability: 1970." *American Sociological Review* 37:754–766.

Campbell, A.; Converse, P.; and Rodgers, W. (1976). *The Quality of American Life: Perceptions, Evaluations, and Satisfactions.* New York: Russell Sage Foundation.

Davis, J. A., and Smith, T. (1993). *The General Social Surveys, 1972–1993: Cumulative Data File.* Chicago: National Opinion Research Center.

Feldman, S., and Nash, C. S. (1984). "The Transition from Expectancy to Parenthood: Impact of the Firstborn Child on Men and Women." *Sex Roles* 11:84–92.

Fincham, F. D., and Bradbury, T. N. (1987). "The Assessment of Marital Quality: A Reevaluation." *Journal of Marriage and the Family* 49:797–809.

Glenn, N. D. (1989). "Duration of Marriage, Family Composition, and Marital Happiness." *National Journal of Sociology* 3:3–24.

Glenn, N. D. (1991). "The Recent Trend in Marital Success in the United States." *Journal of Marriage and the Family* 53:161–270.

Glenn, N. D. (1993). "The News is Bad, But Not Quite as Bad as First Reported: A Correction." *Journal of Marriage and the Family* 55:242–243.

Glenn, N. D., and Supancic, M. (1984). "The Social and Demographic Correlates of Divorce and Separation in the United States: An Update and Reconsideration." *Journal of Marriage and the Family* 46:563–575.

Glenn, N. D., and Weaver, C. N. (1981). "The Contribution of Marital Happiness to Global Happiness." *Journal of Marriage and the Family* 43:161–168.

Goldberg, W. A.; Michaels, G. Y.; and Lamb, M. E. (1985). "Husbands' and Wives' Patterns of Adjustment to Pregnancy and First Parenthood." *Journal of Family Issues* 6:483–504.

Guttentag, M., and Secord, P. F. (1983). *Too Many Women: The Sex Ratio Question.* Newbury Park, CA: Sage Publications.

Heckman, J. J. (1979). "Sample Selection Bias as a Specification Error." *Econometrica* 45:153–161.

Huston, T. L.; McHale, S. M.; and Crouter, A. C. (1986). "When the Honeymoon is Over: Changes in the Marital Relationship Over the First Year." In *The Emerging Field of Close Relationships,* ed. R. Gilmour and S. Duck. Hillsdale, NJ: Erlbaum.

Huston, T. L., and Robins, E. (1982). "Conceptual and Methodological Issues in Studying Close Relationships." *Journal of Marriage and the Family* 44:901–925.

Lewis, R., and Spanier, G. (1979). "Theorizing about the Quality and Stability of Marriage." In *Contemporary Theories about the Family,* Vol. 2, ed. W. R. Burr, R. Hill, F. I. Nye, and I. Reiss, New York: Free Press.

McHale, S. M., and Huston, T. L. (1985). "The Effect of the Transition to Parenthood on the Marriage Relationship: A Longitudinal Study." *Journal of Family Issues* 6:409–434.

McLanahan, S., and Adams, J. (1989). "The Effects of Children on Adults' Psychological Well-Being: 1957–1976." *Social Forces* 68:124–146.

Norton, R. (1983). "Measuring Marital Quality: A Critical Look at the Dependent Variable." *Journal of Marriage and the Family* 45:141–151.

Schoen, R. (1975). "California Divorce Rates by Age at First Marriage and Duration of First Marriage." *Journal of Marriage and the Family* 37:348–555.

Spanier, G. B. (1976). "Measuring Dyadic Adjustment: New Scales for Assessing the Quality of Marriage and Similar Dyads." *Journal of Marriage and the Family* 42:15–27.

Umberson, D. (1987). "Family Status and Health Behavior: Social Control as a Dimension of Social Integration." *Journal of Health and Social Behavior* 28:306–319.

Vaillant, C. O., and Vaillant, G. E. (1993). "Is the U-Curve of Marital Satisfaction an Illusion? A 40-Year Study of Marriage." *Journal of Marriage and the Family* 55:230–239.

Verbrugge, L. M. (1979). "Marital Status and Health." *Journal of Marriage and the Family* 41:267–285.

Veroff, J.; Douvan, E.; and Kulka, R. A. (1981). *The Inner American: A Self-Portrait from 1957 to 1976.* New York: Basic Books.

White, L. K., and Booth, A. (1985). "Transition to Parenthood and Marital Quality." *Journal of Family Issues* 6:435–450.

White, L. K.; Booth, A.; and Edwards, J. N. (1986). "Children and Marital Happiness: Why the Negative Correlation?" *Journal of Family Issues* 7:131–147.

NORVAL D. GLENN (1995)
REVISED BY JAMES M. WHITE

MARITAL RAPE

See RAPE

MARITAL ROLES

see FAMILY ROLES

MARITAL SATISFACTION

see MARITAL QUALITY; MARITAL SEX

MARITAL SEX

Marriage is a socially sanctioned long-term mating arrangement that typically involves economic, social, and reproductive cooperation between the partners. Although the norms that govern selection of a marriage partner and the customs surrounding the marriage ceremony vary from culture to culture, all known human societies practice and endorse this type of long-term pairing (Daly and Wilson 1983; Goodwin 1999). Marriage and sexuality share an intimate and universal connection: Across cultures, marriage represents the most socially accepted, legitimate context for sexual intercourse. It is important to recognize that most research on marital (and other types of) sexuality has been conducted with participants from industrialized western European (particularly North American) societies. Very little data are available about the sexuality of men and women in non-Western and/or aboriginal or tribal cultures.

Beliefs about Marital Sexuality

There have been relatively few empirical investigations of marital sexual attitudes. However, several general conclusions can be gleaned from the available literature. First, sexual intercourse is considered part of the marital relationship. Historically, marriage has been defined by secular and nonsecular forces as a socially sanctioned sexual and reproductive relationship. During the seventeenth century, for example, western European church doctrine identified sexual intercourse as a marital duty for both spouses (Leites 1982). Three hundred years later, social scientists continue to employ a similar definition: Noted sexologist Havelock Ellis defined marriage as "a sexual relationship entered into with the intention of making it permanent" ([1933] 1944, p. 256), a notion echoed by other theorists (e.g., Murstein 1974).

Second, whereas some cultures sanction extramarital sex, marital sex is assumed to be exclusive sex. That is, once an individual is married, the general presumption is that his or her sexual activities (if not his or her sexual desires) will be confined to the marital relationship (or, in polygamous mating systems, the marital relationships). Self-report survey and interview data do, however, reveal that marital infidelity actually is quite common. Nonetheless, a majority of individuals disapprove of extramarital sexual activity. Anthropologist Suzanne Frayser (1989) examined sexual behavior and customs in sixty-two different cultures and found that extramarital relationships ranked second after incestuous relationships as the most forbidden type of sexual liaison. Large-scale attitude surveys of

adults living in the United States found similar high levels of disapproval with regard to extramarital sex (Greeley 1991; Laumann et al. 1994).

As with most sexual attitudes, men and women differ slightly. Compared to women, men tend to hold more permissive attitudes about extramarital sex and are more likely to express an interest in having an extramarital sexual relationship (Oliver and Hyde 1993). Although men may possess more positive attitudes toward infidelity, they are not necessarily less likely to be punished for such behavior. Frayser's (1989) cross-cultural investigation revealed that 40 percent of societies punish both the husband and the wife about equally for extramarital sexual activity, 35 percent of societies punish the husband more severely than the wife, and 25 percent of societies punish the wife more severely than the husband.

A third belief about marital sexuality concerns the relative power accorded to each sex in the making of sexual and reproductive decisions. Traditionally, choices and decisions about the sexual aspects of married life—including when and how to initiate sexual activity, the amount and type of sex, the timing and number of children, and the use of contraception—were considered the exclusive province of the male partner. The following excerpt is from a popular guide to love, courtship, and marriage published in the United States over a hundred years ago:

> Usually marriage is consummated within a day or two after the ceremony, but this is gross injustice to the bride. In most cases she is nervous, timid, and exhausted by the duties of preparation for the wedding, and in no way in a condition, either in body or mind, for the vital change which the married relation brings upon her. . . . This, then, is the time for all approaches by the husband to be of the most delicate . . . Young husband! Prove your manhood, not by yielding to unbridled lust and cruelty, but by the exhibition of true power in self-control and patience with the helpless being confided to your care! (Jefferis and Nichols 1896, pp. 202–204)

The authors of this advice manual clearly view sexual decisions as the husband's duty and right—he is the one who must guard against yielding to "unbridled lust," determine the appropriate time for sexual initiation, and calmly and patiently guide the couple's first and subsequent physical interactions.

An examination of modern marriage manuals and guides to newlyweds reveals that this particular constellation of beliefs about marital sexuality has changed significantly over time, at least in the United States and western Europe. Martin Weinberg, Rochelle Swensson, and Sue Hammersmith (1983) analyzed forty-nine sex manuals published in the United States between 1950 and 1980. During the 1950s and 1960s, for example, writers continued to emphasize differences between male and female sexuality and complementarity in sexual roles (i.e., husband as sexual teacher and wife as sexual learner). By the late 1970s, both sexes were depicted as autonomous sexual beings in control of their own sexuality, capable (and desirous) of sexual pleasure, and equally able to enact the parts of sexual teacher and learner. In many other parts of the world (e.g., Africa, Central America, and India), however, men continue to be expected to make the major sexual and reproductive decisions (Bertrand et al. 1996; Karra, Stark, and Wolf 1997; Renne 1997; Villasmil Prieto 1997).

A fourth general belief relevant to marital sexuality concerns preferences for various partner attributes that are specifically related to sexuality, including a potential spouse's sexual history or level of sexual experience. In general, research indicates that low to moderate levels of sexual experience are considered more desirable than extensive sexual experience. For example, sociologist Susan Sprecher and her colleagues (1997) surveyed over 400 college students living in the United States and found that men and women preferred "chastity" more than "extensive sexual experience" when considering a potential marriage partner. Similarly, social psychologists Pamela Regan and Ellen Berscheid (1997) asked a group of participants to rank a list of characteristics, including several related to sexuality, in terms of their desirability in a long-term, romantic partner: Being sexually available or "easy" was the least desired attribute in a potential spouse.

Some cultures value chastity or sexual inexperience more than others. An international team of researchers led by psychologist David Buss (1989) surveyed over ten thousand men and women from a variety of countries and cultures (including

Africa, Asia, eastern Europe, North America, western Europe, and South America) about their preferences in a spouse. The characteristic "chastity" was highly valued in Asian cultures, including Taiwan, China, Indonesia, and India, and more so than in any other cultures. In western European cultures (e.g., France, Sweden, Norway), however, chastity was considered irrelevant (a few respondents even jotted down in the margins of their questionnaires that it was *un*desirable in a mate). These cultural differences notwithstanding, less rather than more sexual experience seems to be the rule governing marriage partner preferences.

Sexual Frequency

Rates of intercourse appear to have increased among married couples in recent decades. For example, pioneering sex researcher Alfred Kinsey and his colleagues (Kinsey et al. 1953) surveyed over eleven thousand men and women living in the United States during the late 1940s and early 1950s about a variety of sexual issues, including how often they had sex. The results of these large-scale surveys revealed that young married couples tended to have sex approximately twice weekly. Twenty years later, in 1974, social scientist Morton Hunt reported slightly higher frequencies—on average, young married men and women (ranging in age from eighteen to twenty-four) had sex 3.25 times a week. This seeming rise in sexual frequency may stem from a variety of social changes occurring in the 1960s and 1970s that liberalized marital sexuality, including the advent of sex therapy, the "sexual revolution," the increased availability of erotic or pornographic material, and the introduction of the birth control pill.

More recent data, however, suggest that the amount of sexual activity between spouses has not continued to rise. According to a U.S. national study headed by sociologists Edward Laumann and John Gagnon (Laumann et al. 1994), most married couples have sex an average of seven times a month (this amounts to less than twice a week). Only 7 percent, in fact, of the married respondents in their study reported having sex four or more times each week. Other U.S. national surveys of married couples in the 1990s provided similar results (Call, Sprecher, and Schwartz 1995; Donnelly 1993). In addition, there is tremendous variability in the frequency of sexual intercourse in marital relationships. Some couples are celibate or have sex very infrequently, whereas others engage in intercourse on a daily basis. For example, Cathy Greenblat (1983) interviewed eighty people who had been married five years or less. The number of times spouses reported having had sexual intercourse each month during their first year of marriage ranged from one (or an average of twelve times that year) to forty-five (or 540 times that first year).

Several researchers have explored whether certain long-term couple types have sex more frequently than others. In general, surveys reveal that cohabitation is a "sexier" living arrangement than is marriage. That is, cohabiting heterosexual couples and homosexual male couples tend to have sexual intercourse (defined as genital contact) more frequently than married couples (Blumstein and Schwartz 1983; Call, Sprecher, and Schwartz 1995; Rao and DeMaris 1995). Homosexual female (lesbian) couples, on the other hand, have sex less frequently than other couple types, although they engage in more nongenital physical contact (e.g., cuddling, hugging). Despite these differences, all forms of long-term, committed partnership—married or cohabiting, heterosexual or homosexual—are associated with greater sexual frequency than is singlehood (Laumann et al. 1994).

The Decline of Sexual Frequency Over Time

The frequency with which couples engage in sex is affected both by the partners' ages and by the duration of their relationship. In general, older couples have sex less frequently than younger couples. For example, sociologist Vaughn Call and colleagues (1995) surveyed over six thousand married people living in the United States and reported that sexual activity was highest among the youngest respondents (those ranging in age from nineteen to twenty-nine, who had sex approximately ten to twelve times per month), became progressively lower in older age groups (e.g., four to seven times a month among forty- and fifty-year-olds), and reached its nadir among respondents in their seventies (who engaged in intercourse with their spouses less than twice a month). The majority of studies also find that the longer couples have been married, the less often they have sex (Rao and DeMaris 1995; Samson et al. 1991). This decline may be greatest during the first year or the first few years of the relationship. For example, William James (1981) analyzed diaries kept by

newlywed couples over the course of their first year of marriage. Couples reported having sex on seventeen or more occasions during their first month of married life; however, by the end of the year, their rate of intercourse had declined to approximately eight times a month.

Because these two age-related factors are linked—as a relationship ages, so do the partners—it is difficult to know for certain whether it is chronological age that causes the decline in sexual frequency or habituation from being with the same sex partner year after year. Both factors probably play a role in producing lowered levels of sexual activity. For example, as men and women age, changes in their physical abilities, increased incidence of illness, and negative attitudes about sex in the elderly may contribute to a less active sex life. At the same time, the loss of novelty that results from having sexual intercourse with the same individual may reduce levels of activity.

Various events that occur during the course of a couple's relationship also are associated with changes in sexual frequency, including factors related to birth control and pregnancy (e.g., lack of interest during pregnancy), to children and child care (e.g., lack of privacy, fatigue), and to work (e.g., heavy work schedules, fatigue) (Greenblat 1983). All of these factors may play a role in limiting a couple's desire and opportunity for sex. Of course, some couples return to previous levels of sexual activity once they adjust to their circumstances or after the situation resolves itself. Other couples, however, become comfortable with the lowered levels of intercourse; they may cease to have sex altogether and/or they increasingly may engage in nonsexual forms of affection and contact.

Sexual Practices and Preferences

Married couples in today's society may not be having intercourse any more frequently than those living twenty or thirty years ago. However, they do seem to be engaging in a greater variety of sexual activities. For example, although vaginal intercourse remains the most common form of sexual expression among heterosexual couples (Laumann et al. 1994), a greater proportion report practicing oral-genital sex today than a generation or two ago. Studies indicate that a majority of married and cohabiting couples engage in oral-genital sex at least occasionally (Blumstein and Schwartz 1983;

Gagnon and Simon 1987; Laumann et al. 1994). Anal intercourse, while relatively uncommon, is tried at least once by 8 to 10 percent of heterosexual North American couples (Laumann et al. 1994; Voeller 1991), and many couples report experimenting with new sexual techniques or activities at least some of the time (Greeley 1991). Homosexual couples practice many of the same sexual activities as heterosexual couples, but report higher frequencies of particular behaviors. For example, lesbian couples engage in more kissing, caressing, holding, and breast stimulation during lovemaking than cohabiting or married heterosexual couples; gay male couples, in turn, incorporate more body contact, including nipple stimulation and caressing, into their lovemaking than heterosexual couples (Blumstein and Schwartz 1983; Masters and Johnson 1979). In addition, oral-genital and anal sex are more commonly used by homosexual than heterosexual couples (Blumstein and Schwartz 1983; Laumann et al. 1994).

In addition to exploring what people actually do sexually with their partners, some researchers have examined what people say they would *like* to do—in other words, their sexual preferences. Of all the possible sexual practices on the heterosexual menu, vaginal intercourse possesses the most universal appeal. Laumann and colleagues' (1994) survey revealed that nearly 80 percent of women and close to 85 percent of men prefer this particular sexual activity. Watching the partner undress was a distant second choice, followed by receiving and giving oral sex (with both men and women preferring to receive rather than to give this sexual act).

Sexual Satisfaction

The majority of modern North American couples expect that sexual activity will be pleasurable, and research indicates that most are in fact satisfied with the sexual aspects of their relationship. In a national survey of over 650 married couples, approximately one-third of the husbands and wives reported a "very great deal" of sexual satisfaction, and an additional one-third reported "a great deal" of satisfaction (Greeley 1991). Similarly, the majority (over 80 percent) of married or cohabiting respondents in Laumann and colleagues' (1994) study stated that they were "extremely" or "very" physically and emotionally satisfied by sexual activity with their partner.

Sexual satisfaction is associated with a variety of factors. One of these is sexual frequency. Specifically, couples who have more frequent sex report higher levels of sexual satisfaction than couples who have less frequent sex (Young et al. 1998). The experience of orgasm also is correlated with sexual satisfaction (Perlman and Abramson 1982; Pinney, Gerrard, and Denney 1987; Young et al. 1998). For example, women who experience orgasms before or at the same time as their partner report higher levels of sexual satisfaction than women who have orgasms after their partners do (Darling, Davidson, and Cox 1991). Another predictor of a married couple's degree of sexual satisfaction is the ratio of sexual rewards (aspects of the sexual relationship that are pleasing or gratifying) to sexual costs (aspects of the sexual relationship that require physical or mental effort or that produce pain, anxiety, or embarrassment) that each partner receives from the relationship (Lawrance and Byers 1995). Marital sexual satisfaction generally is greatest when sexual rewards are high, sexual costs are low, sexual rewards exceed sexual costs, the obtained sexual rewards and costs in the relationship compare favorably to the expected sexual rewards and costs, and one partner's sexual rewards and costs do not greatly exceed the other's.

Sexual Communication

Another factor that is closely connected to sexual satisfaction in marital relationships is communication. Effective communication about sex—about expectations, preferences, attitudes, or standards—plays an important role in determining sexual satisfaction. One aspect of sexual communication that has received a great deal of attention from researchers is the initiation and refusal of sexual requests. In the traditional heterosexual "sexual script," men are expected to initiate sexual activity, whereas women are expected to then accept or refuse these sexual requests (Gagnon and Simon 1973; Reiss 1981). Although the majority of couples endorse and demonstrate this interaction pattern (Byers and Heinlein 1989), their communication style may change over the course of the relationship as each partner becomes more comfortable with less traditional roles (Brown and Auerback 1981). What is most important in determining sexual satisfaction is that partners share a sexual script and agree about the balance of sexual initiation in their relationship.

How couples actually talk about sex—the specific words or phrases they use to communicate sexual interest (or disinterest) to each other or to indicate a preference for a particular type of activity—is also associated with their level of sexual satisfaction. Many couples develop their own idiosyncratic phrases, terms, or names for sexual body parts, activities, and preferences. For example, one partner may ask the other if he or she would like to have some "afternoon delight" (as opposed to formally requesting sexual intercourse) or to "go south" (as opposed to requesting oral-genital sex). The development of a special sexual vocabulary and the use of pet names, phrases, and euphemisms may enhance a couple's feelings of satisfaction (Bell, Buerkel-Rothfuss, and Gore 1987; Cornog 1986).

Additional research has revealed that married couples are more often indirect than direct when they communicate about sex. For example, spouses tend to reveal their interest in sexual activity through the use of such indirect, nonverbal strategies as kissing, suggestive glances, and playing music rather than through the use of direct, verbal techniques (Brown and Auerback 1981; Byers and Heinlein 1989). Indirect communication may serve an important function in the relationship. Partners do not always desire sex at the same time—by making a sexual invitation somewhat ambiguous, indirect communication strategies allow a partner who is not in the mood for sex to avoid overtly rejecting the invitation and hurting the initiator.

The Role of Sexuality in Married Life

Frequent, mutually rewarding sex, along with effective communication about sexual desires and preferences, clearly is associated with sexual satisfaction. In addition, all of these aspects of sexuality—frequency, practices and preferences, communication, and satisfaction—are related to nonsexual aspects of a couple's relationship. For example, there is a strong connection between sexual satisfaction and relationship satisfaction; couples who are happy with their sex lives tend to be happy with other areas of their relationship (Christopher and Sprecher 2000). The frequency with which a couple engages in sexual intercourse also is related to dimensions of relationship satisfaction. Specifically, the more often a couple has sex, the more generally satisfied they are with the relationship and their nonsexual interactions, the

more they enjoy spending time together and sharing activities and hobbies, and the more equitable and fair they perceive their relationship to be (Blumstein and Schwartz 1983; Call et al. 1995; Hatfield et al. 1982).

It makes intuitive sense that a good sex life is associated with a good overall relationship. What is less intuitive is the direction of that association. Does unsatisfying sex lead to an unsatisfying relationship, or does a bad relationship lead to bad sex? On the one hand, it is likely that an unhappy, stressed, or conflicted partner—one who is preoccupied, worried, or angry about various (nonsexual) aspects of the relationship—would have difficulty becoming sexually interested in and aroused by the other partner, particularly if that partner is viewed as a source of the conflict or unhappiness. On the other hand, it is equally likely that a person who is not satisfied with either the quantity or the quality of sex with the partner may become dissatisfied with other aspects of the marriage. Whatever the direction of the relationship between sexuality and general satisfaction, most researchers agree that the two are intimately connected.

Conclusion

Across cultures, sexuality plays an important role in marital and other types of long-term, established relationships. The attitudes that partners hold about marital sexuality, the amount of sex that they have, their preferences and the kinds of sexual activities in which they engage, and how they communicate with each other about their needs and desires can have an enormous impact upon their level of sexual satisfaction and on their happiness with the relationship in general. Although there is no "right" amount or type of sex that characterizes healthy relationships, research suggests that partners will be most satisfied—sexually and nonsexually—when they utilize sexual activity to express feelings of love, commitment, and intimacy (rather than to dominate, punish, or harm the partner) and when they agree about the role that sexuality should and does play in their relationship.

See also: HONEYMOON; INFIDELITY; INTIMACY; LOVE; MARITAL QUALITY; MARITAL TYPOLOGIES; SEXUAL COMMUNICATION: COUPLE RELATIONSHIPS; SEXUAL DYSFUNCTION; SEXUALITY; SEXUALITY IN ADULTHOOD; THERAPY: COUPLE RELATIONSHIPS

Bibliography

Bell, R. A.; Buerkel-Rothfuss, N. L.; and Gore, K. E. (1987). " 'Did You Bring the Yarmulke for the Cabbage Patch Kid?' The Idiomatic Communication of Young Lovers." *Human Communication Research* 14:47–67.

Bertrand, J. T.; Makani, B.; Edwards, M. P.; and Baughman, N. C. (1996). "The Male Versus the Female Perspective on Family Planning: Kinshasa, Zaire." *Journal of Biosocial Science* 28:37–55.

Blumstein, P., and Schwartz, P. (1983). *American Couples.* New York: William Morrow.

Brown, M., and Auerback, A. (1981). "Communication Patterns in Initiation of Marital Sex." *Medical Aspects of Human Sexuality* 15:105–117.

Buss, D. M. (1989). "Sex Differences in Human Mate Preferences: Evolutionary Hypotheses Tested in 37 Cultures." *Behavioral and Brain Sciences* 12:1–49.

Byers, E. S., and Heinlein, L. (1989). "Predicting Initiations and Refusals of Sexual Activities in Married and Cohabiting Heterosexual Couples." *Journal of Sex Research* 26:210–231.

Call, V.; Sprecher, S.; and Schwartz, P. (1995). "The Incidence and Frequency of Marital Sex in a National Sample." *Journal of Marriage and the Family* 57:639–650.

Christopher, F. S., and Sprecher, S. (2000). "Sexuality in Marriage, Dating, and Other Relationships: A Decade Review." *Journal of Marriage and the Family* 62:999–1017.

Cornog, M. (1986). "Naming Sexual Body Parts: Preliminary Patterns and Implications." *Journal of Sex Research* 22:393–398.

Daly, M., and Wilson, M. (1983). *Sex, Evolution, and Behavior,* 2nd edition. Belmont, CA: Wadsworth Publishing.

Darling, C. A.; Davidson, J. K.; and Cox, R. P. (1991). "Female Sexual Response and the Timing of Partner Orgasm." *Journal of Sex and Marital Therapy* 17:3–21.

Donnelly, D. A. (1993). "Sexually Inactive Marriages." *Journal of Sex Research* 30:171–179.

Ellis, H. ([1933] 1944). *Psychology of Sex.* New York: Emerson Books.

Frayser, S. G. (1989). "Sexual and Reproductive Relationships: Cross-Cultural Evidence and Biosocial Implications." *Medical Anthropology* 11:385–407.

Gagnon, J. H., and Simon, W. (1973). *Sexual Conduct: The Social Sources of Human Sexuality.* Chicago: Aldine.

Gagnon, J. H., and Simon, W. (1987). "The Sexual Scripting of Oral-Genital Contacts." *Archives of Sexual Behavior* 16:1–25.

Goodwin, R. (1999). *Personal Relationships Across Cultures.* London: Routledge.

Greeley, A. M. (1991). *Faithful Attraction: Discovering Intimacy, Love, and Fidelity in American Marriage.* New York: Doherty.

Greenblat, C. S. (1983). "The Salience of Sexuality in the Early Years of Marriage." *Journal of Marriage and the Family* 45:289–299.

Hatfield, E.; Greenberger, R.; Traupman, P.; and Lambert, M. (1982). "Equity and Sexual Satisfaction in Recently Married Couples." *Journal of Sex Research* 18:18–32.

Hunt, M. (1974). *Sexual Behavior in the 1970s.* Chicago: Playboy Press.

James, W. H. (1981). "The Honeymoon Effect on Marital Coitus." *Journal of Sex Research* 17:114–123.

Jefferis, B. G., and Nichols, J. L. (1896). *Search Lights on Health. Light on Dark Corners. A Complete Sexual Science and a Guide to Purity and Physical Manhood. Advice to Maiden, Wife, and Mother. Love, Courtship and Marriage;* 18th edition. Naperville, IL: J. L. Nichols.

Karra, M. V.; Stark, N. N.; and Wolf, J. (1997). "Male Involvement in Family Planning: A Case Study Spanning Five Generations of a South Indian Family." *Studies in Family Planning* 28:24–34.

Kinsey, A. C.; Pomeroy, W. B.; and Martin, C. E. (1948). *Sexual Behavior in the Human Male.* Philadelphia: W. B. Saunders.

Kinsey, A. C.; Pomeroy, W. B.; Martin, C. E.; and Gebhard, P. H. (1953). *Sexual Behavior in the Human Female.* Philadelphia: W. B. Saunders.

Laumann, E. O.; Gagnon, J. H.; Michael, R. T.; and Michaels, S. (1994). *The Social Organization of Sexuality.* Chicago: University of Chicago Press.

Lawrance, K., and Byers, E. S. (1995). "Sexual Satisfaction in Long-Term Heterosexual Relationships: The Interpersonal Exchange Model of Sexual Satisfaction." *Personal Relationships* 2:267–285.

Leites, E. (1982). "The Duty to Desire: Love, Friendship, and Sexuality in Some Puritan Theories of Marriage." *Journal of Social History* 15:383–408.

Masters, W. H., and Johnson, V. E. (1979). *Homosexuality in Perspective.* Boston: Little, Brown.

Murstein, B. I. (1974). *Love, Sex and Marriage through the Ages.* New York: Springer.

Oliver, M. B., and Hyde, J. S. (1993). "Gender Differences in Sexuality: A Meta-Analysis." *Psychological Bulletin* 114:29–51.

Perlman, S. D., and Abramson, P. R. (1982). "Sexual Satisfaction Among Married and Cohabiting Individuals." *Journal of Consulting and Clinical Psychology* 50:458–460.

Pinney, E.M.; Gerrard, M.; and Denney, N.W. (1987). "The Pinney Sexual Satisfaction Inventory." *Journal of Sex Research* 23:233–251.

Rao, K. V., and DeMaris, A. (1995). "Coital Frequency among Married and Cohabiting Couples in the United States." *Journal of Biosocial Science* 27:135–150.

Regan, P. C., and Berscheid, E. (1997). "Gender Differences in Characteristics Desired in a Potential Sexual and Marriage Partner." *Journal of Psychology and Human Sexuality* 9:25–37.

Reiss, I. L. (1981). "Some Observations on Ideology and Sexuality in America." *Journal of Marriage and the Family* 43:271–283.

Renne, E. P. (1997). "The Meaning of Contraceptive Choice and Constraint for Hausa Women in a Northern Nigerian Town." *Anthropology and Medicine* 4:159–175.

Samson, J. M.; Levy, J. J.; Dupras, A.; and Tessier, D. (1991). "Coitus Frequency Among Married or Cohabiting Heterosexual Adults: A Survey in French-Canada." *Australian Journal of Marriage and Family* 12:103–109.

Sprecher, S.; Regan, P. C.; McKinney, K.; Maxwell, K.; and Wazienski, R. (1997). "Preferred Level of Sexual Experience in a Date or Mate: The Merger of Two Methodologies." *Journal of Sex Research* 34:327–337.

Villasmil Prieto, M. C. (1997). "Social Representation of Feminine Sexuality: An Interpretation From a Gender Perspective." *Sociologica* 12:159–182.

Voeller, B. (1991). "AIDS and Heterosexual Anal Intercourse." *Archives of Sexual Behavior* 20:233–276.

Weinberg, M. S.; Swensson, R. G.; and Hammersmith, S. K. (1983). "Sexual Autonomy and the Status of Women: Models of Female Sexuality in U.S. Sex Manuals From 1950 to 1980." *Social Problems* 30:312–324.

Young, M.; Denny, G.; Luquis, R.; and Young, T. (1998). "Correlates of Sexual Satisfaction in Marriage." *Canadian Journal of Human Sexuality* 7:115–127.

PAMELA C. REGAN

MARITAL TYPOLOGIES

Part of the process of science is description. As an aid in this description process, some scholars have classified marriages into different typologies. *Typologies,* used in all fields of science, are artificial categories developed to demonstrate the similarities that exist within a group and highlight the differences between groups. Typologies enable marriage scholars to develop a shared language and are useful in describing the similarities and differences between marriages. For example, Walter F. Willcox (1892) identified two types of marriage: *despotic* and *democratic.* The despotic type of marriage, based on Roman law, viewed the wife as the property of the husband and, therefore, subject to him in all matters. The democratic type of marriage arose under the Teutones. They honored women and viewed the husband and wife as equals who made decisions on a democratic basis. This typology was developed as a simple way of bringing order to the study of marriage relationships.

Scholars have since developed numerous marriage typologies. In the 1940s, sociologists noted two types of marriage: *institutional* and *companionate* (Burgess and Locke 1948). The traditional institutional marriage emphasized the separate roles that husbands and wives played within the family. Husbands were the primary wage earners, decision makers, and the link between the family and the larger society. Wives were usually responsible for childrearing and homemaking and were subordinate to the desires of their husbands. However, a trend was noted toward companionate marriages, which emphasized shared, rather than separate, roles and decision-making responsibilities. In companionate marriages, wives often earned an income and husbands assisted with care of the children. The specific roles and responsibilities carried out within the companionate marriage were not based on a person's gender, but on a mutual agreement between equals.

Later, scholars criticized the institutional/-companionate typology because it was inadequate for describing many of the contemporary differences that existed within marriage relationships. Therefore, John F. Cuber and Peggy B. Harroff (1965), studying enduring marriages, developed one of the best-known marital typologies. They proposed three institutional (*conflict habituated, devitalized, passive-congenial*) and two companionate (*vital, total*) types of marriage.

Elements of a Good Typology of Marriage

A good typology should include five important characteristics. The typology must be: exhaustive; mutually exclusive; a reliable means of assigning couples to a type; developed through a systematic process; and able to economize thought.

Exhaustive means that all of the important dimensions of a marriage relationship are included when couples are assigned to a marital type. If communication is an important component of a marriage, then "communication" must be one of the criteria used to assign couples to a marriage type. However, if the typology is to be exhaustive, it must include other important dimensions of marriage relationships, not merely communication.

Mutually exclusive means that a couple should be assigned to only one type of marriage. Thus, a couple should be classified as either a vital or a total marriage, not a mixed type including characteristics common to both vital and total marriages. A reliable method of assigning couples means there must be no uncertainty in the typology assignment. A good typology will clearly outline why the marriage is assigned a specific type.

The typology should be developed through a systematic process rather than merely by intuition or logic. Some typologies have been developed in a fairly informal fashion when scholars, based on their own understanding of marriage, developed what they thought were the most important and logical characteristics to describe all marriages. For example, some scholars assumed that marital stability (how likely the couple is to stay married) and marital satisfaction (the degree of happiness within the marriage) were the best two dimensions to describe all marriages (Levinger 1965; Lewis and Spanier 1979). The logic of these scholars was therefore used to develop a typology that described all marriages. On the other hand, some scholars use sophisticated scientific procedures to observe marriages and, as a result of their observations, develop a typology. For instance, John M. Gottman (1999, 1994) and his colleagues observed marital partners as they discussed real relationship problems, and then developed five marital types based on their observations. Therefore, Gottman's

marital types are derived from systematic observations rather than logic and beliefs about marriage.

Finally, a good typology should be able to economize thought. It should concisely describe a great deal of information about a marriage. The typology should group together into one type all marriages sharing similar characteristics and separate into different types those marriages that differ from one another.

The Proliferation of Marriage-Related Typologies

Many of the recent studies of marriage typologies have focused on a limited collection of marital behaviors rather than focusing on a more exhaustive list of characteristics of all marriages. For example a range of typologies have been developed examining: extramarital affairs in Taiwan (Chang 1999); divorcing couples (Cohen, Finzi, and Avi-Yonah 1999); dual earner couples (Crouter and Manke 1997; Rosenfeld, Bowen, and Richman 1995); marriages lasting 50 years or more (Dickson 1995); and alcohol consumption habits of marriage partners (Roberts and Leonard 1998). Though this proliferation of unique typologies helps scholars understand certain marriages, they cannot be used to classify all marriage relationships. For example, in many marriages neither individual consumes alcohol, and in other marriages neither partner engages in an extramarital affair. Because some typologies focus on an incomplete set of marital characteristics and behaviors they have limited utility in describing all marriages. This entry will primarily address typologies that tend to be more inclusive rather than those typologies limited to a small subset of marriages.

Using Logical Methods to Create Typologies

Some scholars develop a typology based on the logical characteristics or pre-existing categories they believe describe most marriage relationships. The basis for the marital typology is therefore the scientist's own logic and reason. Some of the marriage typologies that have been developed have used this informal logical process.

George Levinger (1965) believed that marital stability and satisfaction were two of the most significant dimensions to consider when developing marital types; marriages could be either high or low on stability and marital satisfaction. He used these two dimensions of marriage to describe four different marital types. Full-shell marriages had high levels of satisfaction and stability; these couples rarely if ever considered divorce and were very happy with the relationship. No-shell marriages had low levels of stability and satisfaction; these couples were having difficulty staying together and were not happy with the relationship. Empty-shell marriages were low on satisfaction, yet there were high levels of stability; although these couples were not happy with their relationships, there was no consideration of divorce. Half-shell marriages had high levels of satisfaction, yet the couples were likely to terminate the marriage.

Researchers studying marriage in other cultures have used this logical process to examine specific aspects of marriage that are unique to a culture. For example, in some cultures parents and family members initiate "arranged" marriages. Thus parents select marriage partners for their children. In contrast, in most western cultures, the selection of a spouse is based on the individual's own choice and feelings of love for the partner. Arranged versus love marriages can therefore be viewed as two different marital categories. Noran Hortacsu (1999) studied 130 Turkish couples comparing couple initiated (love marriages) and family initiated (arranged) marriages. Although this study is useful in understanding some of the differences between love versus arranged marriages, this classification focuses only on one element of a marriage, the selection process.

Using Scientific Methods to Create Typologies

In more recent years, an effort has been made to classify marriages into one type or another based on systematic scientific observations of marriages. Probably the most comprehensive marriage typology was developed using a computer-scored questionnaire (Olson and Fowers 1993). David H. Olson and his colleagues used a questionnaire called ENRICH to evaluate marriage relationships along nine dimensions: personality issues, communication, conflict resolution, financial management, leisure activities, sexual relationship, children and parenting, family and friends, and religious orientation. This typology meets the "exhaustive" criteria because it examines nine areas of the relationship before determining the marital type. The couples' responses were also used to help specify which aspect of their relationship might be a

strength and which aspect of their relationship might be an area for growth. This study yielded five different types of marriages: devitalized, conflicted, traditional, harmonious, and vitalized.

The first and most common type was labeled a devitalized marriage. The devitalized marriage was primarily characterized as dissatisfaction with all nine dimensions of the relationship. These couples were overall more likely to be dissatisfied with their relationship and likely to have considered divorce. The second type was labeled a conflicted marriage. Partners in these marriages were dissatisfied with communication, conflict resolution, their partner's personality, and their sex lives. However, they were satisfied with their children, religious lives, and the use of leisure time within their marriages. Dissatisfaction stemmed most often from things within the relationship, and satisfaction was obtained from things outside the relationship. The third type of union was characterized as a traditional marriage. Traditional couples were dissatisfied with communication, conflict resolution, and sex, yet they were satisfied with family and friends, religion, and leisure time. They were one of the most satisfied of all types in how they handled their children and parenting duties. Partners in the fourth type, harmonious marriages, were self-focused and tended to be unions in which the couple was highly satisfied with their sex lives, leisure time, and finances. Dissatisfaction within harmonious marriages arose for the most part from interaction with their children and family, and their friendships with others. The last type, vitalized marriages, demonstrated the highest levels of satisfaction across all nine dimensions.

To examine the usefulness of this typology with different ethnic groups, William Allen (1997) sampled a group of 450 African-American couples who completed the ENRICH questionnaire. The study results yielded the same five couple types, with similar percentages of couples in each type. This lends credibility to the notion that Olson's typology is useful in describing more than merely Caucasian marriages.

One strength of this typology is that nine different marital dimensions are evaluated before a couple is assigned to a type. An additional strength is the ENRICH questionnaire. This assessment, used by thousands of couples since 1986, is accepted as a valid and reliable way to examine marital and premarital relationships. This typology can also be useful to clergy and marital counselors who are helping couples improve their marriages, because it highlights specific areas of the relationship that need work. It gives a clear understanding of both the strong and weak areas of a relationship. Finally, this typology demonstrates clearly that couples can be satisfied with some dimensions of their marriage, yet dissatisfied with other aspects.

It is evident by this brief discussion that the study of marriage has generated many different typologies that all attempt to describe marriage. Only one typology, however, has been practically useful in not only describing marriage but predicting marital stability, whether a couple will divorce or whether they will stay together (Gottman 1994).

Gottman and his colleagues observed couples in conflictual conversations, and from these observations divided couples into five different types (Gottman 1999; Gottman and Levenson 1992). Three of these marriage types (*validating, volatile,* and *avoidant*) were stable and, thus, not likely to divorce. The other two types (hostile-engaged and hostile-detached) were unstable and on the path toward divorce.

Validating couples avoided conflict unless there was a very serious issue in the marriage. When conflict did arise, there were high levels of validation. Validation was defined as minimal vocal responses from the listener such as "mmmmh-mmm" or "yeah" that provided feedback that the speaker should continue, and demonstrated the partner was listening and wanted to understand the point of view of the speaker. Volatile couples valued their individuality more than the marriage, and allowed each partner more time for privacy. They thrived on conflict and were free to express their disagreements. Husbands and wives expressed high levels of both positive and negative feelings within their conflict. Avoidant couples minimized marital conflict. They were distant from each other, with low levels of sharing and companionship. They valued their own separate space and desired high levels of independence. In all three of the stable types of marriages, partners had both positive and negative interactions with each other. However, the stable couples had much higher levels of positive than negative interaction.

Hostile-engaged couples experienced high levels of overt conflict. One partner complained and criticized, and the other responded defensively. Neither seemed to understand the point of view of the partner. Hostile-detached couples engaged in a type of guerrilla warfare. Although they typically led very emotionally separate and independent lives, they got into brief encounters of attack and defend. When not attacking, the listener would nonverbally communicate disinterest, coldness, and disapproval of the conflict. Disinterest was referred to as stonewalling, typically a male behavior showing a lack of interest in the message of the speaker.

The unstable couples resolved their conflicts in primarily negative ways. They rated their conflicts as more serious and felt more negative during their conflicts than the stable couples. Unstable couples were less satisfied with their marriages, more likely to have been thinking about divorce, and more likely to have already separated than were the stable couples.

Gottman's typology demonstrated that all stable marriages were not alike. Similarly, there were also considerable differences among unstable marriages. Neither intense conflict nor conflict avoidance were necessarily problematic marital patterns. For a marriage to be stable, negative communication needed to be offset by about five times as much positive communication. Still, a high level of negative interaction did not in itself lead to divorce unless there was little positive in the relationship. Even withdrawal and expressions of criticism and defensiveness did not lead to divorce if they were combined with high levels of positive interaction.

If the process of classifying marriages is to be useful, it must be able to describe marriages across cultures. In reality, few empirically derived typologies have attempted to test these classification systems across cultures. However, Guy Bodenmann, John Gottman, and John Backman (1997) explored the applicability of Gottman's typology with a sample of Swiss marriages. Although marriage relationships in the two cultures differed, with the divorce rate in Switzerland about half of that in the United States, the typology was useful in classifying the same five couple types. This study provided initial support that Gottman's typology of marriage was useful in classifying couples beyond North America.

Problems with Marital Typologies

Typologies are useful because they group similar types of marriages into one category. This process brings order to the study of marriage and provides a language that describes the similarities and differences among marriages. Though current typologies are useful, no marital classification system clearly meets all of the characteristics of a good typology.

Although marital scholars have made strides in creating and refining typologies, the scientific community has not come to a consensus on any one typology. In order for the typological study of marriage to progress there must be agreement on the behaviors and characteristics the typology should describe and the system needs to be adopted by a significant number of marital scholars. In contrast, classification systems have been more widely accepted in the natural sciences. For example, within the biological sciences there is agreement on a classification system that is widely adopted by biologists. Thus, each species can be classified by certain characteristics common to the kingdom, phylum, genus, and species. This classification system and common language is agreed upon within the biological community and is useful in the communication process. Similarly, those who study marriage relationships must develop a classification system that includes the important behaviors and characteristics of most marriages. If marital scholars could develop and agree upon such a typology, it would create a useful language that scholars could use in their study and treatment of marriage relationships.

The current marital typologies often fail to promote the clarity that a classification system should provide. For example, validating marriages share a group of common characteristics yet still differ along many dimensions, thus validating marriages are not all the same. When researchers assign a marriage within a typology, they often lose sight of the uniqueness of the marriages among that type. This being the case, some scholars believe that typologies actually blur reality rather than describe it more clearly (Hall and Lindzey 1985). Although a typology does help to describe marriage in an understandable way, it may simplify the complexity of marriage too much.

The difficulty of capturing several dimensions of a marriage creates difficult measurement challenges. To date, the two most widely used typologies are those developed by Gottman and Olson.

Gottman has combined multiple methods to assign couples to a type including self-report surveys, laboratory observations, physiological measurements, and couple interviews. However, his focus has been on one main dimension of marriage: how couples handle conflict. Gottman's typology could be strengthened if it examined a greater number of marital characteristics rather than only conflict. In contrast, Olson has surveyed large numbers of couples along the nine dimensions of marriage, but his only method to assign couples to a type has been self-report surveys. Olson's typology could be strengthened if he would use more than one method in the assignment of couples to the type. Focusing on core dimensions of the marriage relationship using multiple methods of measurement strengthens the typology because it recognizes the complexity in the assignment process.

An additional problem arises when the spouses disagree on which typology best describes their marriage. For example, Douglas Snyder and Gregory Smith (1986) found that almost 50 percent of couples disagreed about which typology most accurately described their marriage. This may be evidence of the fact that there are really two perspectives of the same marriage—his marriage, as the husband sees it, and her marriage, as the wife sees it. A good typology should place the couple into one category only.

Typologies also present only a still-life snapshot of marriage, when in reality marriages change over time and across situations. A relationship that is categorized as vital at one point in time may be characterized as conflict-habituated later on because of changes that have taken place. In fact, marriages are typically dynamic and can change considerably over time. Research done on the first year of marriage indicates that partners' feelings of love for each other (as well as their hugging, kissing, and affection) decrease, while conflict increases (Huston, McHale, and Crouter 1986). Marriages also change when new members are added to the family as a result of a birth, or when a spouse retires. Therefore, although a typology is useful to describe a marriage at a given point in time, it is not helpful for describing how marriages change over time.

Last, and potentially the most challenging issue facing those who study marriage, is the feasibility of a typology that is useful across cultures. Can a single typology adequately capture the differences that exist in marital relationships across cultures? Studies must continue to examine the usefulness of existing typologies in describing marriages beyond the boundaries of North America.

Conclusion

Though there are limitations to the existing marital typologies, the current systems are more useful in describing marriage relationships than no system at all. The ongoing challenge is to refine a classification system and encourage scholars to adopt the typology. Though these challenges may seem daunting, it is important to realize that marital scholarship is yet in its infancy. As the field refines its methods, develops more continuity, and wrestles with the challenges of developing a good typology, the ability to classify marriages in useful and a commonly accepted manner will emerge.

See also: ATTACHMENT: COUPLE RELATIONSHIPS; CONFLICT: COUPLE RELATIONSHIPS; EQUITY; FAMILY ROLES; INTIMACY; MARITAL QUALITY; POWER: MARITAL RELATIONSHIPS; MARITAL SEX; THERAPY: COUPLE RELATIONSHIPS

Bibliography

Allen, W. (1997). "Replication of Five Types with African American Couples Based on ENRICH." Ph.D. dissertation, University of Minnesota.

Bodenmann, G.; Gottman, J. M.; and Backman, H. (1997). "A Swiss Replication of Gottman's Couple Typology." *Swiss Journal of Psychology* 56:205–216.

Burgess, E. W., and Locke, H. J. (1945). *The Family: From Institution to Companionship.* New York: American Book Company.

Chang, J. S. (1999). "Scripting Extramarital Affairs: Marital Mores, Gender Politics, and Infidelity in Taiwan." *Modern China* 25:69–99.

Cohen, O.; Finzi, R.; and Avi-Yonah, O. (1999). "At Attachment-Based Typology of Divorcing Couples." *Family Therapy* 26:167–190.

Crouter, A. C., and Manke, B. (1997). "Development of a Typology of Dual-Earner Families: A Window into Differences between and within Families in Relationships, Roles, and Activities." *Journal of Family Psychology* 11:62–75.

Cuber, J. F., and Harroff, P. B. (1965). *Sex and the Significant Americans.* New York: Penguin Books.

Dickson, F. C. (1995). "The Best is Yet to Be: Research on Long-Lasting Marriages." In *Under-Studied Relationships: Off the Beaten Track,* ed. J. T. Wood and S. Duck. Thousand Oaks, CA: Sage Publications.

Gottman, J. M. (1994). *What Predicts Divorce: The Relationship Between Marital Processes and Marital Outcomes.* Hillsdale, NJ: Erlbaum.

Gottman, J. M., and Levenson, R. W. (1992). "Marital Processes Predictive of Later Dissolution." *Journal of Personality and Social Psychology* 63:221–233.

Gottman, J. M. (1999). *The Marriage Clinic.* New York: W.W. Norton.

Hall, C. S., and Lindzey, G. (1985). *Introduction to Theories of Personality.* New York: Wiley.

Hortacsu, N. (1999). "The First Year of Family- and Couple-Initiated Marriages of a Turkish Sample: A Longitudinal Investigation." *International Journal of Psychology* 34:29–41.

Huston, T. L.; McHale, S. J.; and Crouter, A. C. (1986). "When the Honeymoon's Over: Changes in the Marriage Relationship Over the First Year." In *The Emerging Field of Personal Relationships,* ed. R. Gilmour and S. Duck. Hillsdale, NJ: Erlbaum.

Levinger, G. (1965). "Marital Cohesiveness and Dissolution: An Integrative Review." *Journal of Marriage and the Family* 27:19–28.

Lewis, R. A., and Spanier, G. B. (1979). "Theorizing About the Quality and Stability of Marriage." In *Contemporary Theories About the Family,* Vol. 1, ed. W. R. Burr, R. Hill, F. Nye, and L. Reiss. New York: Free Press.

Olson, D. H., and Fowers, B. J. (1993). "Five Types of Marriage: An Empirical Typology Based on ENRICH." *Family Journal* 1:196–207.

Roberts, L. J., and Leonard, K. E. (1998). "An Empirical Typology of Drinking Partnerships and Their Relationship to Marital Functioning and Drinking Consequences." *Journal of Marriage and the Family* 60:515–526.

Rosenfeld, L. B.; Bowen, G. L.; and Richman, J. M. (1995). "Communication in Three Types of Dual-Career Marriages." In *Explaining Family Interactions,* ed. M. A. Fitzpatrick and A. L. Vangelisti. Thousand Oaks, CA: Sage Publications.

Snyder, D. K., and Smith, G. T. (1986). "Classification of Marital Relationships: An Empirical Approach." *Journal of Marriage and the Family* 48:137–146.

Willcox, W. F. (1892). *Studies in History, Economics, and Public Law*. New York: Columbia University.

EDGAR C. J. LONG
JEFFREY J. ANGERA

MARRIAGE CEREMONIES

Rituals or ceremonies that celebrate a newly achieved marital status are near universal. Why is that? The assumption of husband and wife roles, before and after the birth of a child, clearly marks the beginning of a new generation. The fulfillment of these roles—husband, wife, and parent—is fundamental to the continuity of a society. Therefore, both the larger social group and individual families have an investment in the institutions of mate selection, marriage, and parenthood. This investment is recognized and acknowledged with a variety of ceremonies, including engagement or betrothal rituals, marriage ceremonies, and christening or naming ceremonies.

Marriage ceremonies range across cultures from very elaborate ceremonies including the performance of religious rituals, dancing, music, feasting, oath taking, and gift exchange over several days to the virtual absence of ceremonies in the relatively few societies where individuals announce their marriage by simply acting married—that is, usually by living together and telling others that they are now married. Marriage ceremonies, along with those marking birth, death, and achievement of adult status in some cultures, are the major rites of passage in cultures around the world. Religion plays a role in ceremonies in most cultures. Prayers, sacrifices, and donations are often made and rituals performed to gain supernatural blessings or to ward off evil forces.

In a few societies, such as rural communities in the Balkans, people from communities, villages, or kin groups that are antagonistic to one another sometimes intermarry. In these situations, the marriage ceremonies often allow for the expression of hostilities between the groups through wrestling matches and the ritualized exchange of insults.

A key component of marriage ceremonies is the symbolic expression of the new status of the bride and groom through an alteration of their physical appearance. Change in clothing style or hairstyle, as among Hopi women in Arizona, and the exchange and wearing of wedding rings or other types of jewelry such as ankle bracelets, are a few of the ways this custom is played out in different cultures.

Marriage ceremonies are common across cultures for multiple reasons. First, marriage is an important emotional and social transition for the bride and groom, and participation of family and friends in the process can be a major source of emotional and financial support for the newlyweds. Second, marriage usually marks a dramatic change in social status for individual newlyweds. In most societies, marriage signifies adulthood and potential parenthood. The couple is expected to establish a new home apart from their natal families or, in some societies, one spouse is expected to join the community or home of the other spouse's family (in most cases, the bride moves to the groom's community). The marriage ceremony emphasizes the importance of these new statuses and the behavioral expectations associated with them, both for the individuals and the community. Third, ceremonies are often paid for by families of one spouse, sometimes both, and this emphasizes to the couple their parents' investment in them and their parents' expectation that they will produce and raise the next generation in the family. Fourth, in some societies, much wealth is exchanged between families at marriage. This exchange may take the form of bride-price, where the groom's family makes a payment to the bride's family or kin group, or dowry, where the bride brings wealth to the marriage. This exchange may also take the form of an expectation of a large inheritance in the future.

In the United States, marriage is a civil action licensed by each state, but most people use the occasion for a special ceremony to mark a couple's rite of passage from singlehood to marriage. Most states require the presence of one or more witnesses and a certified individual to oversee the vows. However, the majority of couples (80 percent) are married by a member of the clergy (Knox and Schacht 1991), thus ensuring the approval of their religious group as well as the state. The remaining 20 percent of couples who forego a religious ceremony are married by a judge or justice of the peace.

Unification church leader reverend Sun Myung Moon (right) and his wife marry 2,075 pairs of his followers at Madison Square Garden on New Years Day, 1982. BETTMANN/CORBIS

Wedding Traditions

With industrialization and the rapid expansion of technology the influence of Western culture has affected marriage ceremonies and rituals around the globe. However, remnants of traditional cultural customs are still an integral part of many weddings. In Mexico, weddings often combine Catholic and traditional rites. The priest blesses the wedding rings that are exchanged by the bride and groom as well as coins that the groom gives to the bride during the ceremony. These coins symbolize the husband's dedication to his home and his promise to provide for his new family. During the ceremony the bride and groom are loosely wrapped with a rope rosary, or *lazo,* as they kneel at the alter. This custom symbolizes the uniting of the couple in love (Mordecai 1999; Weyer 2000).

In most African nations, arranged marriages were historically the norm, and wedding ceremonies were sometimes as simple as the paying of a bride-price. While Western influence has resulted in men and women having more opportunity to select a spouse, in most tribes parents and other adult relatives must approve the selection, if they don't make the selection themselves. Traditional rites and rituals are still an important component of many African marriage ceremonies. During a Yoruba wedding ceremony in Nigeria, for example, the groom is presented with two different women in place of the bride-to-be. He nods his disapproval toward these women, and they are escorted from the room. A third woman, dressed in hand-loomed fabric and brass anklets, is then presented to him. This woman, the bride, is accepted by the groom. During the wedding ceremony the couple tastes ceremonial symbols of life. The bride and groom share honey to symbolize sweet love and happiness and peppercorn for the "heated times" and "growing pains" of family life ahead. The eldest woman at the wedding then uses gin, which symbolizes the ancestral spirits, to bless the couple, and other family members offer praise and affirmation of the marriage (Mordecai 1999).

Among the Ijo people of the Niger River delta there are two forms of marriage, both involving bride-wealth. The groom must offer a payment to the wife's parents and kinspeople in a *small-dowry* marriage. This typically is a cash payment, although in the past it was paid with cases of gin. The second type of marriage is a *large-dowry* marriage, and it involves a large payment. The difference between the two types of marriage involves inheritance. When a small-dowry marriage has taken place, the children trace their line of inheritance through their mother to her brother and kinsmen. This means that when they grow up, they have more choices as to where they can live: They can continue to live in their father's residence or move to any residence where they can trace their mother's line of descent. A large-dowry marriage means the children belong to the father. These marriages are rare, and wives are usually not local women. Among the Ijo people, polygyny is practiced, and the preferred form of marriage is to have two or more wives. However, each wife must have her own bedroom and kitchen, usually in a single house. Ijo wives are not ranked within a marriage, and ideally, each is treated equally and has equal access to her husband. Jealousy and conflicts can and do lead to divorce (Leis 1998).

In Japan, a traditional Shinto-style wedding is brief and very dignified. The bride wears a white silk kimono with red lining and an ornate headdress. The groom wears a black kimono with a striped *hakama* (loose pants) and a black jacket. A priest first offers prayers and blessings to assure that the couple do not experience ill fortune in their marriage, then waves a *haraigushi,* a sacred tree with streamers attached, to symbolize purification. The couple then drinks nine sips of rice wine, called *saki,* from three cups. It is a belief of the Shinto religion that the number three is lucky, thus the nine sips of wine (3 x 3) is as ritual for good luck. The exchanging of cups symbolizes the bonding of the husband and wife (Mordecai 1999; Fong 2001).

In Bali, Indonesia, adulthood (and the social responsibility that accompanies it) begins only with marriage. There are generally two types of weddings. The first, and most expensive, is a *wedding by proposal.* This type of wedding has three separate ceremonies. The first involves the boy's family asking the girl's family for her hand in marriage. The second is the wedding itself, and the third is a formal visit by the couple to the bride's family so that she may *ask leave* of her ancestors.

In former times this was the time the bride-price was delivered. However, most educated Balinese have dropped this custom. A wedding by proposal involves many expensive rituals and feasts, to which kin, neighbors, and members of the *banjar* (a small subvillage residential unit of sometimes up to 100 families) contribute.

A popular alternative to the wedding by proposal involves *elopement.* Here, a young man and woman spend the night together at the home of a friend. This public event means that they must now marry. The wedding ceremony is held at the home of the groom, but the bride's family is not invited. Her family is obliged to act angry, even if they had prior knowledge of the elopement and are happy with their daughter's choice. Soon the family of the groom pays a formal visit to the bride's family, bringing gifts and a desire to reconcile her parents to the union. After this visit the bride's family can publicly accept the marriage (Abalahin 1998).

Several rites and rituals make up the wedding ceremony in the United States. However, it is up to the individual couple whether they incorporate some or all of these into their wedding. Generally, the more formal the wedding, the more traditional it is and the more often these customs are followed. These traditions include the following: a bridal shower in which the bride receives personal gifts or gifts to help establish a household; a party for the groom given by male friends, meant to be a last fling before he gives up his state of bachelorhood; an exchange of wedding rings; and a white bridal gown with a veil to cover the bride's face. Another tradition is for the bride to throw her garter to the single men present at the wedding party and her bouquet to the unmarried women. Throwing away the bouquet symbolizes the end of girlhood, and the woman who catches it is supposed to be the next to marry. Rice thrown upon the departing couple symbolizes fertility (Knox and Schacht 1991). However, environmentally minded couples now provide birdseed as a substitute for rice because many birds died from eating the celebratory rice left behind on the ground. A traditional wedding ends with a reception or banquet for the wedding guests. Often, music and dancing accompany the feast, and an important ritual is the cutting of the wedding cake. It reenacts the custom of breaking bread and symbolizes the breaking of the bride's hymen to aid in first sexual intercourse and future childbirth (Chesser 1980).

The vows expressed at weddings are variable. Most marriage vows include the promise of a commitment, including permanency and fidelity. However, there have always been couples who create their own vows to express their individual philosophy toward marriage. Christian ceremonies emphasize marriage as a divine sacrament and call attention to the tie between the couple and God. In these cases, the marriage itself is under the jurisdiction of God (Saxton 1993). People of different ethnic, racial, and religious groups in the United States, such as Jews, Poles, Italians, Latinos, and African Americans, sometimes develop ceremonies that feature elements from both U.S. culture and the couple's specific ancestral cultures.

The average cost of a wedding in the United States in 2002 was approximately $19,000. This expenditure for a traditional wedding is often beyond the means of many young people and their families. Therefore, many weddings take place in less formal clothing and are held in backyards, civic gardens, and parks.

Marriage ceremonies around the world are as varied as the couples who marry. They may be formal or informal, religious or secular, expensive or modestly priced. In all cases the ceremony symbolizes a couple's transition from single to married status and represents a willingness on the part of the couple to become a family and begin a new generation.

See also: BRIDE-PRICE; DOWRY; FAMILY RITUALS; HONEYMOON; MARRIAGE, DEFINITION OF; MATE SELECTION; RELIGION; RENEWAL OF WEDDING VOWS; RITES OF PASSAGE; WEDDING RING

Bibliography

Abalahin, A. J. (1998). "Balinese." In *Worldmark Encyclopedia of Cultures and Daily Life*. Vol. 3: *Asia & Oceania,* ed. T. L. Call. Detroit, MI: Gale.

Chesser, B. J. (1980). "Analysis of Wedding Rituals: An Attempt to Make Weddings More Meaningful." *Family Relations* 29:204–209.

Knox, D., and Schacht, C. (1991). *Choices in Relationships,* 3d edition. St. Paul, MN: West Publishing.

Leis, P. E. (1998). "Ijo." *In Worldmark Encyclopedia of Cultures and Daily Life,* Vol. 1: *Africa,* ed. T. L. Call. Detroit, MI: Gale.

Mordecai, C. (1999). *Weddings: Dating and Love Customs of Cultures Worldwide.* Phoenix, AZ: Nittany.

Saxton, L. (1993). *The Individual, Marriage, and the Family,* 8th edition. Belmont, CA: Wadsworth.

Weyer, H. (2000). *LaBoda: The Wedding.* POV: Public Broadcasting System. New York: Border Pictures.

Other Resource

Fong, L. (2001). "Help! I'm a Wedding Guest: Japanese Ceremony." Wedding Bells Inc. Available from http://www.weddingbells.com/help/guestceremony7.html.

MARILYN IHINGER-TALLMAN
DEBRA A. HENDERSON

MARRIAGE COUNSELING

See: THERAPY: COUPLE RELATIONSHIPS

MARRIAGE, DEFINITION OF

The institution of marriage is found in all societies. In the United States, marriage means stabilized patterns of norms and roles associated with the mutual relationship between husband and wife. It joins together a man (or men) and a woman (or women) in a special kind of social and legal arrangement that serves several purposes for a society. While this definition fits what is meant by marriage in the United States and other Western nations, it is not broad enough to encompass the essential features of marriage across all cultures. However, because marriage as an institution may differ in structure, function, dynamics, and meaning from one culture to another, no all-encompassing definition of marriage is possible (Kottak 1991). In almost all societies, it entails a legal contract (written or verbal), and this contract varies in the degree to which it can be broken.

Why People Get Married

In most societies, marriages are formed to produce children. From the perspective of evolutionary biology and sociobiology, all individual human beings, as with other species, are driven to reproduce and invest in their offspring to ensure that their genes are passed on to future generations. For at least two million years and perhaps longer, marriage or some arrangement like it has been the social relationship that has proven most effective for this purpose. It is also in the interest of all social groups to maintain and reproduce themselves so that the group will continue. Through the marital union, a stable living unit is established (a family). In this unit, children are socialized into the society's norms and values. In some societies, the connection between marriage and reproduction is so strong that if conception does not occur a divorce is permissible, and often is automatic. In others, a marriage does not take place until after pregnancy occurs and fertility is proven (Miller 1987). For a society, the institution of marriage ensures the regulation of sexual activity for adults and the socialization and protection of children born as a result of that sexual activity. However, individuals living within a society need not comply with behavior that serves the needs of society. Why do they?

In the United States, the most often stated reason for marrying is for love—that is, a man and a woman perceive a mutual emotional and/or physical attraction that is satisfying enough to both that they decide to contract a lifelong relationship. Marriage is a socially sanctioned relationship from which children are born; thus, many people marry to have children. Some persons are premaritally pregnant, and they choose marriage to provide two parents for their child or to escape the negative sanctions or stigma they feel they may experience as an unwed parent. Other persons report that their motivation for entering into a marriage is for economic security, to escape the living situation they are in, or because the relationship has lasted so long that marriage is viewed simply as the "next logical step" (Knox and Schacht 1991).

The feelings called romantic love are nearly universal culturally. In some 85 percent of cultures, at least some people report feeling "in love" with another at some time in their lives (Jankowiak 1994). Love has not always been the basis for marriage in the United States, and it is not the basis for marriage in some societies around the world today. In the early Colonial period in the United States, marriages were arranged, based on the economic needs and the prospects of two families. Even when mutual attraction was the basis for a couple's desire to marry, social boundaries were rarely crossed among financially well-off families who sought to maintain their positions of status and power through appropriate marriages of their children. Marriages of individuals in other social classes varied according to the family's economic circumstances, whether it was a son or a daughter who wanted to marry, and the number of children in the family who needed a dowry or deed of land for marriage to occur. In the Colonial agrarian economy, fathers deeded land to sons to set up new households. Where sons were located in the sibling group (oldest, middle, youngest) and whether their labor was still needed at home to farm the family's land were strong considerations that determined whether a father would grant permission to marry. However, although marriages were based on economic rather than romantic considerations, this did not mean that romantic love was wholly absent from Colonial society. It was present but not linked directly or consistently to courtship or marriage. It did not become the basis for marriage until the late 1700s (Baca-Zinn and Eitzen 1990).

Rules and Regulations

In the United States, marriage is a legal contract, with the state regulating the economic and sexual exchanges between two heterosexual adults (McIntyre 1994). The fifty states vary somewhat in the regulations or criteria that must be satisfied before a couple can contract to marry. Most states specify that people must get a license to marry; must be a specific age before they can marry; must marry only people of the opposite sex; must not be married to someone else; cannot marry persons with whom they hold certain kin relationships (e.g., mother, father, sibling, in-laws [in some states]); and must be married by a legally empowered representative of the state with two witnesses present. In some states, the couple must have blood tests made to ensure that neither partner has a sexually transmittable disease in the communicable stage. Some states demand a waiting period between the time of purchasing a marriage license and the marriage ceremony (Knox and Schacht 1991). The nature of the legal contract is such that the couple cannot dissolve their marriage on their own; the state must sanction the dissolution of marriage, just as it sanctions the contracting of it.

In some other parts of the world, marriages are arranged and love is hoped for after the marriage occurs. Arranged marriages are the norm in many parts of the world. One cross-cultural survey indicates that marriages are arranged for girls in 44 percent of cultures and for boys in 17 percent (Broude 1994). Arranged marriages occur through the involvement of two sets of parents or through negotiations by professional marriage brokers with prospective families. However, even in most societies where marriage is arranged, the prospective bride and groom are consulted and have some veto power if they feel the proposed partner is absolutely unacceptable. Even in cultures where marriages are preferably arranged and the wishes of the parents and kin of the prospective couple are important, marriages based on love do occur. They typically take place through elopement followed by the grudging acceptance of the parents and kin. The motivation for arranged marriage is to assure the continuity of the family's political and economic well-being and growth. The desire is to provide the best possible match for the children, so educational level, personal skills, and family resources are all important considerations. Because many family resources may be exchanged through marriage, the reputation, resources, and knowledge of the marriage brokers are important (Saxton 1993).

Types of Marriage

To this point, the institution of marriage has been discussed as if all marriages were the same—a living arrangement legally contracted by or for two people of the opposite sex. However, this description has been limited insofar as it describes monogamous marriage. There are other types of marriage, which include more than one husband or wife at the same time (*plural marriage* or *polygamy*), several husbands and wives (*group marriage*), or ones that are not contracted on the basis of the state's rules and regulations specified earlier (*common-law marriage*).

Monogamy is the only legal type of marriage permitted in the United States. It is illegal to have more than one spouse at a time (*bigamy*), and most citizens comply with this rule. There are a few exceptions, however. In some western states, members of some fundamentalist Mormon groups practiced polygamy until the late nineteenth century (Hardy 1992). While those who practice group marriage and those in homosexual unions may wish to call themselves married and hold rites or ceremonies to make a public statement that they are married, the states do not recognize such

unions. In Vermont, however, homosexual couples can apply for a "civil union," through which they receive nearly all of the legal benefits and protections given to married heterosexual couples.

While having more than one spouse is illegal in the United States, *polygyny* (one husband with two or more wives at the same time) is the preferred form of marriage throughout most of the world. Seventy-five percent of the world's societies prefer this type of marriage (Saxton 1993). Preference, however, does not necessarily translate into practice, because the number of men and women of marriageable age in most cultures is about the same, meaning that there are rarely more than a few extra women available as second or third wives. Thus, even when polygyny is preferred, there are only a few men, mostly wealthy ones, who have more than one wife at a time (Broude 1994).

Very few societies have polyandrous marriages. *Polyandry* refers to one wife having several husbands at the same time. Such marriages occur only in a few cultures—probably no more than a dozen—and often take the form of fraternal polyandry, that is, when the husbands are brothers. The cause of such an arrangement is unclear but may be related to the need to keep scarce resources such as small parcels of land inherited by the brothers under the control of a single household.

Group marriage (when men and women living together consider themselves married to each other) is illegal, but there are examples of it throughout the history of the United States and in other societies as well. However, in no society is this type of marriage the primary form of marriage. It was practiced by members of the Oneida Company in the mid-1800s in Vermont and then in New York when the group was forced to move because of community disapproval. A study of more than 100 group marriages in the early 1970s showed that such arrangements do not last long: only 7 percent of the "multilateral marriages" studied lasted longer than five years (Constantine and Constantine 1973). Most of these groups consisted of two couples who lived together, sharing economic resources, services, and child care as well as sexual access. Communication and personality conflicts were the primary reasons for dissolving the group, and bonds between same-sex members of the group were the primary factor responsible for success.

In the United States, common-law marriage is recognized in fifteen states and the District of Columbia. These states are Alabama, Colorado, Georgia, Idaho, Iowa, Kansas, Montana, New Hampshire, Ohio, Oklahoma, Pennsylvania, Rhode Island, South Carolina, Texas, and Utah. If a heterosexual couple who are of legal age and legally competent to marry (e.g., they are not already married) make an agreement to live together as husband and wife and actually do cohabit, they are legally married. A ceremony is not necessary, nor is compliance with the other formal requirements governing marriage in their state (Knox and Schacht 1991). This practice stems from the tradition that marriage contracted between two adults was their own or their family's business. Historically in continental Europe and England (societies that are the source of much of U.S. law and custom), marriage needed neither civil nor religious sanction. However, the Catholic Church became more powerful during the Middle Ages and assumed control over marriage (Goody 1988). Even though private arrangements continued, these marriages were not recognized as valid by the church (Saxton 1993). In the United States, marriage became regulated by civil laws in the nineteenth century, but some "states took the position that private marriages were valid so long as they were not expressly forbidden by statute. Such unions were called common law" (Saxton 1993, p. 198). In all societies, a marriage is generally not recognized as such unless the couple is deemed married by the community. However, once a marriage is recognized by one state, it must be recognized by all other states (e.g., a common-law marriage officially recognized by Texas must be recognized in Oregon even though Oregon does not officially sanction common-law marriages).

Finally, some social groups have attempted to organize themselves and function without marriage. These include communes, religious orders, and special social or occupational categories such as warrior castes. In the United States, the best known of such groups are the Shakers, a religious community among whose central rules are celibacy and communal living without marriage. Although the group has lasted since the late 1700s, its numbers have now dwindled from a high of about 4,000 in some sixty communities in the mid-1800s to fewer than a dozen members in one community in 1991 (Foster 1991). Similarly, many communes founded in the 1960s either folded or instituted monogamous marriage. The two types of social groups that have survived without marriage are religious orders and caste or castelike groups such as the Hijras in India. However, all of these groups are institutionalized within a larger society and are able to attract new members from that society.

Conclusion

Marriage represents a multi-level commitment, one that involves person-to-person, family-to-family, and couple-to-state commitments. In all societies, marriage is viewed as a relatively permanent bond, so much so that in some societies it is virtually irrevocable. The stability provided by a life-long promise of remaining together makes marriage the institution most suited to rearing and socializing the next generation of members, a necessary task if the society's norms, values, and goals are to be maintained and if the society itself is to be perpetuated.

See also: COHABITATION; FAMILY LAW; FAMILY RITUALS; INTENTIONAL COMMUNITIES; LOVE; MARRIAGE CEREMONIES; MATE SELECTION

Bibliography

Baca-Zinn, M., and Eitzen, D. S. (1990). *Diversity in Families.* New York: HarperCollins.

Broude, G. (1994). *Marriage, Family, and Relationships.* Denver: ABC-CLIO.

Constantine, L. L., and Constantine, J. M. (1973). *Group Marriage.* New York: Macmillan.

Foster, L. (1991). *Women, Family, and Utopia.* Syracuse, NY: Syracuse University Press.

Goody, J. (1988). *The Development of the Family and Marriage in Europe.* Cambridge, UK: Cambridge University Press.

Hardey, B. C. (1992). *Solemn Covenant: The Mormon Polygamous Passage.* Urbana: University of Illinois Press.

Jankowiak, W., ed. (1994). *Romantic Passion: The Universal Emotion?* New York: Columbia University Press.

Knox, D., and Schacht, C. (1991). *Choices in Relationships.* St. Paul, MN: West Publishing.

Kottak, C. P. (1991). *Cultural Anthropology,* 5th edition. New York: McGraw-Hill.

McIntyre, L. (1994). *Law and the Sociological Enterprise.* Boulder, CO: Westview Press.

Miller, B. (1987). "Marriage, Family, and Fertility." In *Handbook of Marriage and the Family,* ed. M. B. Sussman and S. K. Steinmetz. New York: Plenum.

Saxton, L. (1993). *The Individual, Marriage, and the Family.* Belmont, CA: Wadsworth.

MARILYN IHINGER-TALLMAN (1995)
DAVID LEVINSON (1995)
REVISED BY JAMES M. WHITE

MARRIAGE ENRICHMENT

Marriage enrichment is a form of primary prevention in the area of human relationships. Begun in an organized way by David and Vera Mace in the mid-twentieth century, its objectives are to promote a mutual commitment to growth in the marital relationship; to develop and agree on a communication style of talking and listening that works for enhancement of the marital relationship; to learn how to use conflict in creative ways that helps, not hinders, the marital relationship, including the sharing of feelings; and to develop and maintain a desire for and the presence of intimacy in the marital relationship, utilizing a variety of positive interaction skills.

Marriage enrichment takes place when couples deem their marriage of primary importance. These couples are intentional about their marital growth and choose to do something about it. Couples who commit to an ongoing marriage enrichment group, through which they can practice quality interactive skills with each other and in the presence of other caring couples, tend to have more successful marriages. The longer the process is of practicing the skills that enhance the marriage, the greater the potential for behavioral change (Markman, Stanley, and Blumberg 1994).

Marriage enrichment programs teach spouses interpersonal skills in communication and conflict resolution. Couples can, in a group process, help couples. A sense of safety develops when the group's couples have a mutual commitment to growth. The individual couples in the group begin to recognize their issues are common to other couples.

Marriage enrichment uses multiple techniques to provide opportunities for couple growth. The focus of most enrichment events is each couple's marriage. Given the approach's effectiveness, its leaders most often help couples apply the material via experiential learning techniques. One such technique is the *couple dialogue,* where one spouse turns to the other and talks about their relationship while other couples in the group listen. This exercise provides a very different dynamic from a typical group discussion. It also encourages the couple to affirm good communication skills. Much of marriage enrichment depends upon peer relationship in a supportive environment.

A married couple provides the leadership for some marriage enrichment programs. In the A.C.M.E. (Association for Couples in Marriage Enrichment) model, couples are required to be trained as leader couples. They serve as *facilitator participants* and need not be experts on marriage. As they lead, they work on their own relationship and bring their issues to the group through their public dialogue. The leader couple's vulnerability encourages openness for the other couples. This couple revelation to other couples through the means of couple dialogue is the most disarming and effective tool for growth offered in marriage enrichment. In other marriage enrichment models, leadership couples recite scripted material, but for A.C.M.E. dialogue and interaction are authentic and powerful.

The marriage enrichment group *focuses on strengths and growth.* The guidelines suggested to couples by A.C.M.E. emphasize this positive focus:

- Sharing is voluntary; no individual or couple will be asked to share, nor will it be their turn after the couple next to them shares.

- Each spouse speaks for self; this illustrates equal partnership in the marriage.

- Each spouse shares his/her own experience; conversation or sharing is from the individual's perspective regarding the marriage.

- Focus is on the couple's relationship; regardless of the issue, the focus is turned to the impact on the couple or on either spouse.

- No advice or counseling is given; each couple is working on their own marriage, no experts are present.

- Celebrations and concerns are shared first; spouses or couples need to first share and manage preoccupying concerns. Any joy or good experience in the life of the couple is also shared during this brief segment of the group meeting.

- Confidentiality is essential; to build trust, couples are encouraged to let each couple's conversation or dialogue remain in the group.

Many couples are reluctant to participate in marriage enrichment programs because they think, by doing so, they are admitting some grave faction in their relationship. It is not uncommon for couples to say "we are not having any problems," "we do not need counseling," or "we are doing all right."

Marriage enrichment is not counseling and is probably contraindicated for couples who are going through serious relationship problems. Counseling or even giving advice to another couple is discouraged in the A.C.M.E. leader training. Marriage enrichment is not primarily for problem marriages, but it *is* for married couples who want their marriage to grow. Both members of the couples need to attend since marriage enrichment concentrates on the growth of the relationship. It is couples working on their own relationship alongside other couples working on their relationships.

Marriage enrichment is a process that over time creates positive changes as the couple practices healthy interaction skills. Marriage enrichment events serve as the beginning of the process for many couples. Once the couples see the benefits of the approach taken in marriage enrichment, they want to know how they can keep the healthy process going. It is then that they are ready for a marriage enrichment group that meets once a month.

Couples who want to work on their marriage begin by determining whether counseling or marital enrichment would be best for their relationship. Some brief guides regarding marriage enrichment and marriage counseling are suggested for couple consideration (Smith and Smith 1989). If a couple chooses to be involved in marriage enrichment, it usually means that:

- The couple wants to face or deal with whatever is unsettling in their relationship and they believe they have a potential for growth.

- The couple can identify their issues without the aid of professional assistance.

- The couple is intentionally motivated to work on their marriage. They believe they

have enough positives going for them to make their marriage work.

- The couple is open to new learning opportunities and interaction skills that assist them with their issues.

- The couple is able to identify their issues and willing to address the issues, one at a time.

- The couple recognizes that anger is a given in healthy relationships. Therefore, they mutually work on ways to deal with their anger so that it does not build up and destroy the relationship. In contrast, they use their anger as a positive tool to get closer to the feelings behind the anger.

If a couple wants to improve their marriage through marriage counseling, it can mean that:

- The couple senses that something is wrong in the relationship, but they tend to avoid facing it. Either or both of them may deny there is a problem.

- The couple finds it difficult to identify the problem.

- The couple feels overwhelmed by all of the negative verbal and nonverbal expressions in the relationship and feel it is not worth the effort to continue in the relationship.

- The couple does not feel good about talking about the issues with their partner because it is too painful or useless, or they cannot agree on the issue.

- The couple becomes anxious when a problem comes up because their pattern has been that the situation always gets worse.

- The couple becomes so angry that they want to hurt each other more than they want to focus on the issue itself.

The Marriage Movement

The true pioneers of the marriage enrichment movement are David and Vera Mace and Father Gabriel Calvo. The Maces, primarily David, helped to establish the Marriage Guidance Council in England following World War II. After coming to America to teach in 1949, David Mace began to work with the National Council on Family Relations

(NCFR) and the American Association of Marriage and Family Counselors (later to become the American Association of Marriage and Family Therapists, AAMFT). In the early sixties, the Maces began to define and shape marriage enrichment work, and by the early seventies, they launched a new organization, the Association for Couples in Marriage Enrichment (A.C.M.E.), a nonprofit, nonsectarian organization.

In January 1962, Father Gabriel Calvo began the Roman Catholic Marriage Encounter program in Spain. Father Calvo recognized that to make a difference in the families and the lives of the children in those families, one would have to start with the primary relationship of the couple. This organization came to the United States in 1967 and has remained connected to the Roman Catholic Church. However, other religious bodies have taken on the marriage encounter concepts and adapted them to their religious perspectives (Hof and Miller 1981). Both Marriage Encounter and A.C.M.E. seek to be change agents for couples who want their marriages to flourish. Although they differ in approach, they are similar in their emphasis on couple growth.

Developments

Research provides insight into a better understanding of why marriages succeed or fail (Gottman 1994); what makes a marriage worth fighting for (Markman, Stanley, and Blumberg 1994); and the impact of unresolved anger on the relationship (Williams 1993, 1997). David Olson (1998) has provided inventory or questionnaire tools to assist clergy and premarital counselors in determining the readiness of the engaged couple for marriage. This inventory is called PREPARE/ENRICH. Other inventories, tests, or questionnaires have been used as well, such as RELATE (a self-scored inventory) and FOCCUS (facilitating open couple communication, understanding, and study). These tools help engaged couples learn more about their differences and similarities in preparation for marriage.

A plethora of other helpful books and products provide a supplementary resource for any couple interested in learning how to have a better marriage. Some book titles include: *The Heart of Commitment* (Stanley 1998), *The Essential Humility of Marriage* (Hargrave 2000), *The Power of Two* (Heitler 1997), *Getting Ready for Marriage* (Mace 1985), *Fighting for Your Marriage* (Markman, Stanley, and Blumberg 1994), *Couple Communication II, Thriving Together* (Miller and Miller 2000), *Saving Your Marriage Before It Starts* (Parrott and Parrott 1995), *The Second Half of Marriage* (Arp and Arp 1996), *The Good Marriage* (Wallerstein and Blakeslee 1995), *Passionate Marriage* (Schnarch 1997), *Empowering Couples* (Olson and Olson 2000) and *Close Companions* (Mace 1982).

Two major conferences provide showcases that bring many of the therapists and marriage enrichment leaders together. The first A.C.M.E. International Marriage Enrichment Conference (IMEC) was in 1988. Because David Mace died in 1990, the Second IMEC was held in 1996, many years later than initially hoped, in Fort Worth, Texas. Then in 1997, the Smart Marriage conference was held in Washington, DC. The IMEC venue emphasizes couple participation, plus training for professionals. The Smart Marriage emphasizes programs for professionals and entrepreneurs.

In England, the marriage guidance program spearheaded by David Mace has changed its name to Relate (in the United States there is a premarital inventory called Relate; the two are not related). Also, in England, Couples for Marriage Enrichment (CME) was formed through the inspiration of the Maces. The CME is a similar organization to A.C.M.E., but quite different from Relate (in England). In Australia, the Maces helped form the Couples for Marriage Enrichment Australia (CMEA). The Maces introduced marriage enrichment to many countries and wrote more than thirty books on the subject. The only cultures the Maces did not work with were in the Middle Eastern countries. The Maces were honored by the United Nations in 1994, the International Year of the Family, as recipients of the Family Patron Award. A new wave of interest in marriage enrichment interest began in South American countries, Africa, and several European countries at the end of the twentieth century. Throughout the world, a primary A.C.M.E. goal is to have groups wherever possible to help fulfill the A.C.M.E. slogan of "building better marriages, beginning with our own."

Many religious bodies have seen the need for more emphasis on marriage enrichment. National

Marriage Encounter holds an annual conference for its members. Some denominations conduct regional conferences each year. These events, usually built around a theme, tend to design a product on the topic for its participants.

Not all approaches to marriage enrichment are the same, however. Some organizations approach marriage enrichment from a companionship approach, as the Mace model does, with both marriage partners being equal. Other approaches, primarily religious, emphasize that the husband is the head of the house and therefore gets the final vote. This one-vote system, as it is sometimes called, is also prevalent in Middle Eastern countries. Individuals or couples who want to investigate possible models should explore the approach taken by a particular group when choosing an affiliation with any organized effort in marriage enrichment.

The Future of Marriage Enrichment

At the same time that popular magazines describe a decline in marriage, primarily because of the increase in cohabitation or the postponement of marriage, there is a resurgence of interest from the family therapists and family professionals. In a sense, marriage has become a priority for many societies because of the high cost of divorce and its impact on children. This greater emphasis on the health of the marriage and the preparation for marriage will, in the long run, benefit couples. Findings suggest that a happy marriage is conducive to a long, healthy life, (Waite and Gallagher 2000).

Researchers have focused on problem marriages and ignored the special needs of racial minorities, remarrying couples, and cohabiting couples. But a concerted emphasis has begun to address issues of marital health and growth for the broader population. This interest in marriage enrichment and education is overdue. It is welcomed by the existing organizations that have served as the pioneers in the field. Ideally, the new marriage movement and the pioneer marriage enrichment movement will join hands in promoting couple strengths. The potential positive outcome of this resurgence is that more couples will marry with a realistic understanding of the work involved in building a strong marriage. They will also recognize the impact the couple relationship has on the children who are nurtured in their homes.

See also: FAMILY LIFE EDUCATION; FAMILY MINISTRY; MARRIAGE PREPARATION; THERAPY: COUPLE RELATIONSHIPS

Bibliography

Arp, D., and Arp, C. (1996). *The Second Half of Marriage.* Grand Rapids, MI: Zondervan Publishing House.

Catron, S. (1989). Association for Couples in Marriage Enrichment, *Marriage Enrichment Newsletter* 17(9).

Diskin, S. (1986). "Marriage Enrichment: Rationale and Resources." In *Marriage and Family Enrichment.* New York: Haworth Press.

Dyer, P., and Dyer, G. (1989). *Marriage Enrichment, Process, Methods and Techniques.* Winston-Salem NC: Association for Couples in Marriage Enrichment.

Dyer, P., and Dyer, G. (2001). "Education for Relationships and Marriage." In *Family Life Education: An Introduction,* ed Powell, L., and Cassidy, D. New York: McGraw-Hill.

Gottman, J. (1994). *Why Marriages Succeed or Fail...and How You Can Make Yours Last.* New York: Simon and Schuster.

Hargrave, T. D. (2000). *The Essential Humility in Marriage.* Phoenix, AZ: Zeig, Tucker and Theisen.

Heitler, S. (1997). *The Power of Two: Secrets to a Strong and Loving Marriage.* Oakland, CA: New Harbinger Publications.

Hof, L., and Miller, W. R. (1981). *Marriage Enrichment: Philosophy, Process and Program.* Bowie, MD: Robert J. Brady Co.

Institute for American Values. (2000). "The Marriage Movement, A Statement of Principles." New York: Author.

Mace, D. R. (1985). *Getting Ready for Marriage,* revised edition. Nashville, TN: Abingdon.

Mace, D. R. (1979). "Marriage and Family Enrichment...A New Field?" *The Family Coordinator* 28(3):409–413.

Mace, D. R. (1982). *Close Companions: The Marriage Enrichment Handbook.* New York: Continuum Publishing.

Mace, D. R., ed. (1983). *Prevention in Family Services: Approaches to Family Wellness.* Beverly Hills, CA: Sage.

Markman, H.; Stanley, S.; and Blumberg, S. L. (1994). *Fighting for Your Marriage.* San Francisco: Jossey-Bass.

Miller, S., and Miller, P. (2000). *Couple Communication II: Thriving Together.* Evergreen, CO: Interpersonal Communication Programs, Inc.

Miller, S.; Nunnally, E. W.; and Wackman, D. B. (1975). *Alive and Aware*. Minneapolis, MN: Interpersonal Communication Programs.

Olson, D. H., and Olson, A. K. (2000). *Empowering Couples,* 2nd edition. Minneapolis, MN: Life Innovations.

Olson, D. H. (1998) *PREPARE/ENRICH Counselor's Manual,* Minneapolis, MN: Life Innovations.

Parrott, L. and Parrott, L. (1995). *Saving Your Marriage Before it Starts*. Grand Rapids, MI: Zondervan Publishing House.

Schnarch, D. (1997). *Passionate Marriage*. New York: W. W. Norton.

Silliman, B., and Schumm, W. R. (1999). "Improving Practice in Marriage Preparation." *Journal of Sex & Marital Therapy* 25:23–43.

Smith, A., and Smith, L. (1989). "Enrichment and Counseling—Two Ways to Improve Marriage." Association for Couples in Marriage Enrichment, *Marriage Enrichment Newsletter* 17(7, 8).

Stanley, S. (1998). *The Heart of Commitment*. Nashville, TN: Thomas Nelson Publishers.

Waite, L., and Gallagher, M. (2000). *The Case for Marriage*. Cambridge, MA: Harvard University Press.

Wallerstein, J., and Blakeslee, S. (1995). *The Good Marriage*. New York: Warner Books.

Williams, R., and Williams,V. (1993). *Anger Kills*. New York: Harper Perennial.

Williams, R., and Williams, V. (1997). *Lifeskills*. New York: Times Book.

BRITTON WOOD

MARRIAGE PREPARATION

Marriage preparation programs are offered to adolescent, young adult, and remarrying partners to increase readiness for predictable tasks of married life and reduce their likelihood of distress and divorce. Under the broader rubric of *relationship enhancement,* training workshops, self-help materials, marital therapy, and/or support services are offered to individuals, dating couples, cohabitants, and married couples to improve knowledge of relational issues, interpersonal skills, personal insight, and behavior change. Marriage preparation programs typically target one or more of the following objectives: (1) Prevention of distress, including dating or domestic violence and conflict, and prevention of divorce by altering malleable risk factors (e.g., negative interpretations, conflict resolution skills); (2) competence-building, by enhancing self- and other-awareness (e.g., attitudes and behaviors that improve or erode marriage), knowledge of couple issues (e.g., finances, sexuality, parenting), interactive skills (e.g., communication, problem solving, stress management), and access to resources (e.g., self-help curricula, social services, mutual support networks); and (3) intervention, including individual or couple therapy as appropriate, to resolve conflict, promote healing, teach skills for growth, or to deter partners from entering a high-risk marriage.

Historical Context

During the twentieth century marriage rules changed, but the tools by which couples maintain stability and satisfaction changed little. Today's companionate marriages depend more on couple commitment and effort than on social roles and sanctions. Early in the nineteenth century, newspaper columns and marriage manuals began to replace or augment traditional socialization-to-adulthood by family and church. College and community premarriage courses began in the 1920s and 1930s, followed by the growth of marriage and family counseling and the marriage enrichment movement (Stahmann and Hiebert 1997). Publication of the first extensive outcome studies in the 1970s and 1980s initiated a period of expanded activity and attention to program results (for reviews see Bagarozzi and Rauen 1981; Guerney and Maxson 1990; Schumm and Denton 1979; Silliman and Schumm 2000). University-based programs of twelve to twenty-four (or more) hours significantly improved communication, conflict resolution, and problem solving skills of couples. Although participants were typically nondistressed, educated, middle-class, young adult volunteers, short- and long-term behavior changes and reduced divorce rates demonstrated the potential for divorce prevention and enhancement.

The most recent advancement in marriage preparation began with community-based testing of assessments (Larson et al. 1995) and training programs (Center for Marriage and Family 1995; Stanley et al. 2001). Training of local providers, including mentor couples, dissemination of research-based curricula, and strengthening of natural support networks shows promise of expanding benefits of laboratory-based programs to the estimated 60 percent of couples who currently participate in some premarital training (Stanley and Markman 1996). The past decade has seen the rise of a marriage movement, including community-based and state-mandated high school classes, and marriage preparation and support in the United States, Australia, and Britain (Ooms 1998). Some policies and programs have been published to limited audiences (e.g., university, conference, government) and developments can be tracked through the Coalition for Marriage, Family, and Couples Education web site news archive. On-site evaluations of programs in South Africa (Praetorius 1990), Canada (Boisvert et al. 1992; Farnden and Lyster 1992), Australia (Parish 1992), Czechoslovakia (Novok, and Pulkrobkova 1987), and the United States (Silliman and Schumm 2000) suggest participants enjoy and gain immediate knowledge or skill, yet few studies examine long-term benefits (Center for Marriage and Family 1995).

Components of Successful Programs

Howard Markman, Frank Floyd, Scott Stanley, and Ragnar Storaasli (1988) suggest that programs show impact when participants a) use conflict constructively, employing problem solving rather than withdrawing or overreacting; b) invest in growth; c) display optimism about changes in marriage; or d) remain confident about their abilities to maintain a healthy marriage. These positive outcomes are most typical of programs with one or more of the following traits:

- *Strengths-based.* A focus on affirming or improving capabilities rather than dwelling on problems tends to build confidence and openness to new learning. Helping partners utilize existing personal, couple, and family assets to meet life's challenges and encouraging their affection, fun, and togetherness sustains romance and cooperation.

- *Growth-oriented.* Although couples face predictable challenges with each life stage, adjustment rarely follows a prescribed pattern. Couples benefit most from training in interpersonal skills (communication, conflict resolution, problem solving), information (understanding issues such as sex, money, parenting), and insight (appreciating dilemmas of personality, commitment, balancing

work and family). Interactive skills help couples talk and listen more effectively, especially under stress. Information about issues enhances understanding and decision making. Insight about self, others, and relationships leads to improved perspective and maturity regarding core values and goals for marriage. No one component is sufficient for a strong marriage, but each complements the others. Experiential learning activities such as discussions, role-play, projects, and simulation games produce more effective learning and practice than lecture or classroom instruction. Activities that help couples help themselves, including quality time together, regular study of issues, knowledge and skill application, sharing in support networks, and celebrating commitments promote expectations of lifelong learning.

- *Intensive and extensive.* The traditional one- or two-session meeting of clergy and couple to make wedding arrangements can hardly be expected to produce long-term marital adjustment. Even a three- or four-session lecture or video training typically has little impact on attitudes and behaviors. Ironically, these limited efforts may imply that conforming to social ceremony or popular norms rather than lifelong learning, is enough to enjoy lifetime happiness. Research indicates that at least twelve hours, and ideally twenty-four to thirty hours, of intensive training with quality curricula and well-trained staff is needed for couples to understand and master basic skills for marital interaction (communication, conflict resolution, problem solving). A variety of methods better serves a wider variety of experience levels and learning styles. Repetition and rehearsal help couples to reverse old habits and teach healthy new patterns. One-on-one coaching is the most desired and effective skill training. In combination with peer coaching, lecture-discussion, and guided couple learning (e.g., workbook or audio/videotape), coaching can be cost-effective. Homework such as additional reading, mentoring with experienced couples, discussion of issues, or interpersonal skill application, tailored to couple needs and interests, can reinforce and extend learning in workshops.

Booster sessions, reteaching and extending lessons throughout the first three years of marriage, can reduce post-honeymoon disillusionment and help couples deal with real-life adjustments (Renick, Blumberg, and Markman 1992). Couples can benefit from education and enrichment at any point but gain most when they begin earlier and rehearse learning often.

- *Culturally appropriate.* Most marriage education is developed for Western audiences with companionate marriage ideals. However, expectations and interaction in marriage continue to be shaped by traditional ideas as well as diverse expressions of romantic love within ethnic, social, and age groups. Prevention-oriented programs funded by welfare reform and family support funds in the United States (see Oklahoma Marriage Iniative [2001]), Britain (see The Lord Chancellor Department [1998]), and Australia (see Commonwealth of Australia [2002]) typically assist community and religious organizations to reach specific populations of couples. Comprehensive reports on content, delivery, and impact are not available but online summaries suggest several thousand participants receive skill-based training adapted for setting and culture from models such as PREP (see below). Because males tend to be less interpersonally skilled, they tend to gain most from skill training. Differences in maturity, family background, and personal experience create cultural gaps even within social groups that are best bridged by programs that foster openness, dialogue, and skill application.

- *Outcome-focused.* Effective programs make a practical difference in the lives of participants. Problem solving, conflict resolution, and communication represent teachable skills that translate into everyday behaviors (e.g., mutual respect, cooperation) and perceptions (e.g., marital satisfaction and commitment). Knowledge of sexuality, finances, stress management, and other topics may indirectly improve couple life by shaping attitudes and choices. One-time programs can produce life-long attitude and behavior changes (Stanley et al. 2001), but positive differences more often result from consistent

training and self-growth, adapted to developmental needs.

Sample Programs

Of the many popular or research-based programs available, the most widely tested approaches include:

- *Relationship Enhancement* (RE). RE, using a humanistic model that teaches disclosure and empathy skills in a structured sixteen- to twenty-four-hour format, has shown short-term and sustained gains in empathy and problem solving among college students (Guerney and Maxson 1990). Structured training and practice focuses on speaking and listening processes known to be critical to positive interaction and satisfaction for couples. Expressive skills such as speaking for self, sharing negative emotions, and demonstrating affection are often "taken for granted" in relationships. Yet many partners experience difficulty in communicating love in an open, noncontrolling style due to childhood role models, personal maturity, or situational stress. Thus skills in active listening such as acknowledging feelings, clarifying ideas, and taking turns help couples defuse conflicts and demonstrate respect and good will. RE also teaches instrumental skills including problem solving and decision making, more effectively learned in a structured course than by personal experience. RE developed a training program by which lay couples as well as clinical psychologists could successfully teach skills.

- *Prevention and Relationship Enhancement Program* (PREP). PREP is the most thoroughly tested marriage education model, offering twelve- to twenty-four-hour training workshops that build upon many of the communication behaviors taught in Relationship Enhancement. In addition, PREP couples are challenged to explore marital issues and the spiritual and personal roots of their commitment. Results with dating, engaged, and married couples in the United States show participants have much lower divorce and dissatisfaction rates than nonparticipants up to twelve years after training. PREP workshops in Germany, Australia, and the Netherlands show a similar pattern of significant gains in communication, conflict management, and satisfaction up to three years after training. (Stanley et al. 2001). Based on *cognitive-behavioral theory,* PREP focuses on thinking and interacting processes critical to negotiating problem solving and conflict resolution in moment-to-moment and year-to-year tasks of married life. Results of such model programs suggest that dating and marriage education is a wise investment of public or private organization funding (Ooms 1998).

- *Couples Communication Program* (CCP). This family systems–based model helped couples develop better awareness of their own and partner emotions and ideas (Miller, Wackman, and Nunnally 1983). Although couple gains in CCP are not as dramatic as behavior-change programs, increased understanding of personal and partner ideas and feelings has been shown to improve communication and satisfaction among dating and married couples.

- *Safe Dates.* An ecological model, incorporating individual skill training, peer monitoring, and community awareness enhanced the success of this program in preventing dating violence among at-risk and violent middle school students (Foshee et al. 1998). A theater production and ten-session curriculum analyzed consequences of dating violence, gender stereotyping, and conflict management skills. Community-level activities included a crisis line, support groups, resources for parents, and training for service providers.

Several research-based books also became bestsellers. Clinical psychologist John Gottman (1999) most recently summarized his groundbreaking research in *Seven Principles for Making Marriage Work.* The book provides quizzes, exercises, and illustrations to support building a positive history, fostering mutual admiration, engaging rather than withdrawing from conflict, accepting a partner's influence, coping with unresolvable conflicts, and creating shared meaning.

Many practitioners use the PREPARE survey (Olson, Fournier, and Druckman 1989), a 125-item inventory of each partner's attitudes and practices in fourteen issue areas (e.g., communication, sexuality, money, leisure, religion). PREPARE's profile (similarities and differences, strengths and weaknesses relative to happily married couples) helps professionals coach couple discussion and skill learning. Like other widely used assessments such as FOCCUS (Williams and Jurich 1995) and RELATE (Busby, Holman, and Taniguchi 2001), couple participation in the process reduces the feeling of being analyzed and helps couples focus on issues perceived as relevant priorities.

Widely used approaches such as Caring Couples (Hunt and Hunt 1999), Marriage Enrichment (Dyer and Dyer 1999), and Saving Your Marriage before It Starts (Parrott and Parrott 1999) offer positive anecdotal reports but have not been systematically evaluated. For some couples, such insights and skills clearly enrich and revitalize, whereas for others information without intensive skill training may create unrealistic expectations and frustrated role performance (Berger and Hannah 1999).

Other Factors Influencing Marriage Preparation Success

Although research is beginning to reveal programs with promising potential, much remains to be done. Couples at high risk for distress, including those with personality disorders, individual or family problems with sex, violence, depression, and high-stress environments probably require more or different training than the well-adjusted middle-class volunteers in evaluation studies. Likewise, couples who cohabit and those who remarry are at higher risk for divorce and face issues—such as marital adjustment and parenting—not typical of first marriages. Programming and support targeted to high-risk partners is needed. In addition, relatively little is known about how couples sustain a legacy of positive adjustment in stressful conditions or reverse cycles of abuse and discord. Understanding the role of individual and couple resiliency in the learning and application of training could also improve marriage preparation program effectiveness.

Application of skill training and overall couple adjustment no doubt varies according to the attitudes, behavior norms, and support in a couple's family and community. Community marriage policies adopted by many religious and community groups encourage broader support for couples to stay together, avoid violence, and develop support and enrichment networks via mass-media campaigns to build awareness of marital strengths and resources (McManus 1993). Public and organizational policy initiatives aim to reduce domestic violence and encourage healthy marriages. In addition, employers and community organizations can commit to reducing demands that stress families, promoting fidelity and respect for marriage, supporting couples in crisis, and providing opportunities for continued learning. Educational providers, such as churches and schools, can commit to teaching interpersonal and problem-solving skills to children and teenagers, and to requiring premarital training for couples. Such steps toward reinforcing skills and social support could make a great difference for couples, but they remain largely unused and untested.

Conclusion

Marriage preparation includes efforts of professionals and lay persons to help partners build skills and awareness for satisfying marriages. Although many couples find happiness and positive interaction without strong parental or professional training, evidence suggests that quality training would enhance interaction and adjustment for most couples. Only a few research-based approaches (e.g., PREP, RE, PREPARE) have been widely implemented and most offered by national organizations in the United States and Australia vary in focus and quality (Silliman and Schumm 2000). Thus providers and couples benefit from understanding these best practices: (1) Effective programs teach how to communicate, problem solve, and resolve conflict and help couples learn about and discuss money, sex, parenting, and other issues; (2) programs of twelve to thirty hours with trained providers, follow-up classes, research-based learning materials, and evaluation are best equipped to facilitate change with couples; and (3) families and community organizations such as churches, clubs, and schools can enhance the transition-to-marriage by early skill training and modeling as well as ongoing support.

The benefits of vital marriage to both individuals and society's health and well being commends the expansion of higher-quality marriage preparation programming, targeted to general and special audiences.

See also: CATHOLICISM; FAMILY LIFE EDUCATION; FAMILY MINISTRY; MARRIAGE ENRICHMENT; MATE SELECTION

Bibliography

Bagarozzi, D. A., and Rauen, P. I. (1981). "Premarital Counseling: Appraisal and Status." *American Journal of Family Therapy* 9:13–27.

Berger, R., and Hannah, M. T., eds. (1999). *Preventive Approaches in Couples' Therapy*. Philadelphia: Brunner-Mazel.

Boisvert, A.; Ladouceau, R.; Bendry, M.; Freeston, M.; Turgeon, L.; Tardif, C.; Roussy, A.; and Loranger, M. (1992). "Perception of Marital Problems and Their Prevention by Quebec Young Adults." *Journal of Genetic Psychology* 156:33–44.

Busby, D. M.; Holman, T. B.; and Taniguchi, N. (2001). "RELATE: Relationship Evaluation of the Individual, Family, Cultural, and Couple Contexts." *Family Relations* 50(4):308–316.

Center for Marriage and Family. (1995). *Marriage Preparation in the Catholic Church: Getting It Right*. Omaha, NE: Author.

Dyer, P. M., and Dyer, G. H. (1999). "Marriage Enrichment: A.C.M.E-Style." In *Preventive Approaches in Couples' Therapy,* ed. R. Berger and M. T. Hannah. Philadelphia: Brunner/Mazel.

Foshee, V. A.; Bauman, K. E.; Arriaga, X. B.; Helms, R. W.; Koch, G. G.; and Fletcher-Linder, G. (1998). "An Evaluation of Safe Dates, an Adolescent Dating Violence Prevention Program." *American Journal of Public Health* 88(1):45–50.

Gottman, J. M. (1999). *The Seven Principles for Making Marriage Work*. New York: Simon and Schuster.

Guerney, B. G., Jr., and Maxson, P. (1990). "Marital and Family Enrichment Research: A Decade Review and a Look Ahead." *Journal of Marriage and the Family* 52:1127–1135.

Hunt, R. A., and Hunt, J. A. (1999). "Caring Couples Network." In *Preventive Approaches in Couples' Therapy,* ed. R. Berger and M. T. Hannah. Philadelphia: Brunner-Mazel.

Larson, J.; Holman, T. B.; Klein, D. M.; Busby, D. M.; Stahmann, R. F.; and Peterson, D. (1995). A Review of Comprehensive Questionnaires Used in Premarital Education and Counseling. *Family Relations* 44:245–252.

Markman, H. J.; Floyd, F. J.; Stanley, S. M.; and Storaasli, R. D. (1988). "Prevention of Marital Distress: A Longitudinal Investigation." *Journal of Consulting and Clinical Psychology* 56:210–217.

McManus, M. J. (1993). *Marriage Savers*. Grand Rapids, MI: Zondervan.

Miller, S.; Wackman, D. B.; and Nunnally, E. W. (1983). "Couple Communication: Equipping Couples to Be Their Own Best Problem Solvers." *Counseling Psychologist* 11:73–77.

Novok, T., and Pulkrobkova, E. (1987). "The Programmed Discussion Groups in Premarital Counseling with the Minor Engaged Couples." *Psychologia-a-Patosychologia Dietata* 22(6):527–533.

Olson, D. H.; Fournier, D. G.; and Druckman, J. (1989). *PREPARE, PREPARE-MC. ENRICH Inventories,* 3d ed. Minneapolis, MN: Life Innovations

Ooms, T., ed. (1998). *Toward More Perfect Unions: Putting Marriage on the Public Agenda.* Washington, DC: Family Impact Seminar.

Parish, W. E. (1992). "A Quasi-Experimental Evaluation of the Premarital Assessment Program for Premarital Counseling." *Australia-New Zealand Journal of Family Therapy* 134:33–36.

Parrott, L., and Parrott, L. (1999). "Preparing Couples for Marriage: The SYMBIS Model." In *Preventive Approaches in Couples' Therapy,* ed. R. Berger and M. T. Hannah. Philadelphia: Brunner/Mazel.

Praetorius, H. G.; van Wyk, J. D.; and Schepers, J. M. (1992). "The Evaluation of a Marital Preparation Programme." *South African Journal of Psychology* 22(3):140–146.

Renick, M. J.; Blumberg, S.; and Markman, H. J. (1992). "The Prevention and Relationship Enhancement Program (PREP): An Empirically-Based Preventive Intervention Program for Couples." *Family Relations* 41:141–147.

Russell, M., and Lyster, R. (1992). "Marriage Preparation: Factors Associated with Consumer Satisfaction." *Family Relations* 41(4):446–451.

Schumm, W. R., and Denton, W. (1979). "Trends in Premarital Counseling." *Journal of Marital and Family Therapy* 5(4):23–32.

Silliman, B., and Schumm, W. R. (2000). "Marriage Preparation Programs: Literature Review." *Family Journal* 8(2):128–137.

Stahmann, R. F., and Hiebert, W. J. (1997). *Premarital and Remarital Counseling: The Professional's Handbook,* 2d ed. San Francisco: Jossey-Bass.

Stanley, S. M., and Markman, H. J. (1996). "Marriage in the 90s: A Nationwide Random Phone Survey." Denver, CO: Prevention and Relationship Enhancement Program.

Stanley, S. M.; Markman, H. J.; Prado, L. M.; Olmos-Gallo, P. A.; Tonelli, L.; St. Peters, M.; Leber, B. D.; Bobulinski, M.; Cordova, A.; and Whitton, S. W. (2001).

"Community-Based Premarital Preparation: Clergy and Lay Leaders on the Front Lines." *Family Relations* 50(1):67–76.

Williams, L., and Jurich, J. (1995). "Predicting Marital Success after Five Years: Assessing the Predictive Validity of FOCCUS." *Journal of Marital and Family Therapy* 21(2):141–153.

Other Resources

Commonwealth of Australia. (2002). *Relate: Information on Relationships, Family, Love and Life.* Available from http://www.relate.gov.au/.

Lord Chancellor's Department, The (UK). (1998). *Marriage Support Services Directory.* Available from http://www.lcd.gov.uk/family/marsup/famtxtfr.htm.

Oklahoma Marriage Initiative. A Strategic Plan to Honor Marriage and Reduce Divorce. (2001). Available from http://www.governor.state.ok.us/policy.htm.

BENJAMIN SILLIMAN

MARRIAGE SQUEEZE

The phrase *marriage squeeze* refers to the demographic imbalance in which the number of potential brides does not approximately equal the number of potential grooms. When not everyone has an opportunity to marry, some will be squeezed out of the marriage market. An excess of eligible women is called a female marriage squeeze; an excess of eligible men is called a male marriage squeeze.

Three issues are examined. First, how are potential marriage partners defined and selected?

Second, what causes a marriage squeeze? Third, what are the consequences of a marriage squeeze for family systems and for the people who live in them?

Social Dimensions of the Pool of Eligibles

Mates are selected out of a *pool of eligibles*. Norms of *homogamy* dictate that a potential mate should have social characteristics similar to one's own: like marries like. Almost universal age norms dictate that couples are supposed to be of the same generation, with the husband slightly older. People seek others who are homogenous in salient aspects of social identity: race, religion, ethnicity, education, occupational prestige, affluence, and marital status.

Exemptions and exceptions. Some people have such special appeal for the opposite sex that they are considered eligible for marriage even if they do not meet conventional criteria. Alluring people include those of great beauty, talent, celebrity, rank, or achievement, as well as those of great wealth. Charismatic people are few in number but are desired by many, and their pool of eligibles is very large. Romantic love invests the loved one with alluring and unique features. A person in love may see any person as charismatic and may woo them regardless of circumstances.

People may be rejected from the pool of eligibles because of personal defects, disfigurements, or disabilities, whether physical, psychological, or social. Such people have, in effect, the opposite of charisma. Although a stigmatized person may be accepted in the role of friend or colleague, many are rejected for the role of spouse. People with debilities may still marry: however, their de facto pool of eligibles is restricted to those who can and do accept them as they are. The definitions of stigmata, and the degrees of social rejection associated with them, vary markedly among cultures.

The Mating Gradient

In choosing a marriage partner, the first requisite is homogamy. However, within those limits, it is almost universally accepted that *hypergamy,* a situation in which the woman marries up, is more common and more acceptable that *hypogamy,* a situation in which the woman marries down. Both husband and wife are most comfortable when the husband has higher status than the wife. The cultural preference for hypergamy results in a *mating gradient:* women prefer men who are of equal or higher status than themselves, and men prefer women who are of equal or lower status than themselves. The result is that two categories of people tend to be squeezed out of the marriage market: high status women and low status men.

The mating gradient is apparent in terms of height and weight. Tall women have trouble finding even taller men, and short men have trouble finding even shorter women. In more general terms, the mating gradient means that when men increase in status, they widen their pool of eligibles; when women increase in status, their pool of eligibles becomes narrower, leading to an exacerbation of the female marriage squeeze.

Sex Ratios: Measuring the Marriage Squeeze

The term *sex ratio* is calculated by dividing the number of males by the number of females and multiplying by 100. A ratio of 100 indicates equal numbers; a low ratio indicates an excess of females and a high number an excess of males. Researchers have operationalized a marriage squeeze in a variety of ways, taking into account age, race, labor force status, marital status, rates of homosexuality, and the census undercount (Veevers 1988). Sophisticated measures often yield results correlating with simple sex ratio measures, which in most instances serve as an adequate basis for research (Fossett and Kiecolt 1991).

How Do Sex Ratios Become Unbalanced?

The sex ratio at birth is almost even, with about 105 boy babies born for every 100 girls. By adolescence, higher male mortality usually results in balanced populations. In theory, if everyone picked a mate at that time, everyone would be able to marry. In reality, many demographic factors contribute to unbalanced outcomes.

Fertility rates: Baby booms. The phrase marriage squeeze was coined by the American demographer Paul Glick (1988). In the early 1960s, he observed declining marriage rates among young women and realized this outcome was in part due to the interaction of two factors: the sharp increase in fertility known as the baby boom and the reality of the mating gradient. Consider the Canadian example: in 1944, the crude birth rate was 24.0 per 1,000; in 1947, it was 28.9. Twenty years later, girls born in 1947 sought grooms two to four years older than themselves, but there were not enough for a one-to-one match. Glick observed that some of young women were squeezed out of the marriage market and predicted that some would never marry.

Fertility rates: Baby busts. In the 1970s, in the developed world, the baby boom became the baby bust. In the 1990s, young men of those cohorts sought wives two to four years younger than themselves and found them in scarce supply, creating a male marriage squeeze. Stable fertility rates yield stable sex ratios among young adults; it is fluctuations in them that produce a marriage squeeze. For a marriage squeeze, the most important factor is the stage of the population in terms of the *demographic transition.* Other things being equal, a sharp increase in fertility or in population growth leads to a female marriage squeeze, a circumstance found throughout the developing world. A sharp decline in fertility and a declining population, lead to a male marriage squeeze, a situation now emerging in industrialized countries.

Sex differences in mortality. In the developed world, mortality rates for males are generally higher than for females. From early adulthood, the sex ratio declines with advancing age. A contributing factor is that unmarried persons have higher mortality rates than do spouses, a difference more pronounced for men than for women. Males, especially young males, are more prone than females to institutionalization, incarceration, and violent death, an outcome that in the United States has lead to a much lower sex ratio among blacks than among whites. Male mortality is also disproportionately high in times of war, an outcome reflected in sex ratios in Vietnam and Cambodia (Goodkind 1997; Huguet et al. 2000).

Natal inequality: Missing girls in Asia. In Asian countries such as China, India, Taiwan, and South Korea, there is a strong cultural preference for sons rather than daughters. Traditionally, sex ratios in such countries have been kept low by high mortality among girl babies due to neglect, abandonment, and infanticide.

Within this cultural backdrop, two other factors have been added: the concerted effort to curb population growth and the availability of sex-selection technologies, which allow female fetuses to be identified and aborted. When the total number of children is reduced, as it is with China's one-child policy, it becomes increasingly important to not waste a pregnancy on girls. Sex-selection is most often used for second and third pregnancies (Chu 2001). In the 1980s, prenatal sex selection became widespread in spite of some official policies intended to control it. By 1992 in India, China, Taiwan, and South Korea, there were 110 to 119 boy babies born for every 100 girl babies. This practice alone, apart from other variables, guarantees a shortage of brides and a surplus of grooms, in subsequent generations.

Sex differences in migration. Migrating populations consist disproportionately of young unmarried men. In Vietnam, high male mortality due to war was further exacerbated by high out-migration of young men, creating a larger female marriage squeeze for the women left behind, and a male marriage squeeze for minority men in the host country (Goodkind 1997). In the United States, sex ratios among ethnic immigrants have been high for the first generation, but subsequently declined for second and third generations (McCaa 1993).

Regional variations: Local marriage markets. Sex ratios vary not only among countries, but also from one region to another. High sex ratios occur in areas devoted to primary industries, such as Newfoundland, Maine, Montana, and Utah (Hamilton and Otterstad 1998; Hooper and England 1988). Such regions provide good employment opportunities for young men, but few jobs for young women. Sex ratios are especially low in capital cities such as Ottawa or Washington, where government bureaucracies attract many women.

The smaller the unit of analysis, the more differences in sex ratio are observed. In Los Angeles, black women living in the inner city face a much more extreme marriage squeeze than other black women. In San Francisco, where male homosexuality is not uncommon, sex ratios calculated on the basis of male/female ratios may seem high, but in terms of heterosexual marriage, the actual sex ratio is considerable lower.

Demographic Consequences of a Female Marriage Squeeze

It could be argued that where there are women without marriage, there will be sex without marriage. Where there is sex without marriage, there will be babies without marriage. When there are enough illegitimate babies, the social significance of bastardy is eroded, which erodes the social significance of being married or not married.

A significant female marriage squeeze tends to destabilize traditional family systems based on universal marriage, lifelong monogamy, and babies born within wedlock. Breaking the sacrosanct link between fertility and marriage leads to changes in many interdependent demographic rates. Increases are observed in, *among other things,* women never married, premarital sex, premarital conceptions, common-law marriages, illegitimate births, and mother-child households. Age at first intercourse declines, but age at first marriage increases.

When the unmarried can act as if they were married, the married can act as if they were single. Redefining relationships leads to rising divorce rates. When divorce is defined as a right rather than as a privilege, grounds for divorce are widened, and eventually evolve to divorce on demand. The female marriage squeeze is again exacerbated by sex differences in remarriage: divorced men and widowers are more likely to remarry than are divorced women and widows, and they do so in a shorter period of time.

During a female marriage squeeze, unmarried women may be without a consort for a major period of their lives. The absence of financial support from men requires an investment in employment. Married women know that their marriages are vulnerable: marriage is difficult, divorce is easy, and remarriage is uncertain. An investment in employment provides some security. In either case, responsibility for children rests, or may rest, with the mother alone. A female marriage squeeze further reinforces two existing trends: an increase of women in the workforce and a decline in fertility.

Brides in India: A special case.   The rapid increase in population in India, and the subsequent increase in cohort size, has lead to an extreme female marriage squeeze, which as been extensively described and analyzed (Bhat et al. 1999). The scarcity of suitable grooms is associated with marked increase in the size of dowry given away with the bride. It involves, in effect, a "rising price of husband" (Rao 1993). This outcome reinforces the prevailing cultural devaluation of daughters in favor of sons. The incentive for sex selection has already increased the sex ratio at birth, and subsequent generations will experience a male marriage squeeze.

Black Americans: A special case.   The female marriage squeeze occurred much earlier, and much more intensely, among black Americans that among whites. "Approximately two-thirds of blacks are single. By contrast, approximately two thirds of whites are married" (Davis and Emerson 1997). Research on the demographic and interpersonal effects of the marriage squeeze draw heavily from research on them (Albrecht and Fossett 1997; Crowder and Tonlay 2000; and Fossett and Kiecolt 1991). The seminal work in this area is *Too Many Women? The Sex Role Question* (Guttentag and Secord 1983). Subsequently, this extensive literature has been integrated in *The Decline in Marriage Among African Americans* (Tucker and Mitchell-Kernan 1995) and *Family Life in Black America* (Taylor, Jackson, and Chatters 1997).

Unacceptable compromises: Exogamy.   When it comes to major issues, such as race and religion, rates of interracial or interreligious *exogamy* are not greatly increased. For example, Israeli women who married young, when they had many men to choose from, were no more likely to marry out that those who married later, when they had fewer options (Stier and Shavit 1994). In America, there have been only modest increases in black-white marriages (Crowder and Tonlay 2000).

Unacceptable compromises: Employability.   Among black women, the sex ratio is even lower than it seems, in that black women tend not to compromise on issues of employability. Usually they are willing to remain single rather than marry an economically unattractive man. "Market conditions— good or bad—have little to do with women's willingness to marry heterogamously. Generally, they are not willing to cast a wide net in the face of market constraints" (Lichter and Anderson 1995). The criterion that a potential husband should be employed, or at least employable, holds firm. In reality, the low sex ratio among blacks is even lower than it seems because men who are incarcerated, institutionalized, or unemployable are rejected. This is the distinction between the quantity of mates available, and the quality.

A survey in the United States found that, in every age category, available black women outnumbered available black employed men by two to one; they outnumbered black employed men, with earnings above the poverty line, by at least three to one (Crowder and Tolnay 2000).

Mixed marriages: Black husbands, white wives. Successful black men have disproportional rates of ignoring rules of homogamy and selecting white brides. The ones most likely to intermarry are those at the highest levels of education, income, and occupational prestige (Crowder and Tolnay 2000). For professional black women with high education and income, the mating gradient substantially reduces their pool of eligibles. Their prospects are further eroded when the most eligible men select themselves out of the pool by marrying white women.

Mixed marriages: Education.   Every person who marries makes some compromises by accepting a person who does not meet all of their ideal criteria. Black women do tend to compromise to some extent in that, compared with white women, they are more willing to accept a husband with less education than themselves, a husband who has been married before, or a husband who is much older (Albrecht and Fossett 1997).

Consequences of a Male Marriage Squeeze

A male marriage squeeze is less common than the female one and has received less attention. The social consequences are less clear (Hooper and England 1988). A female marriage squeeze tends to destabilize the traditional family, but a male marriage squeeze tends to reinforce it. In a male marriage squeeze, where all available women are taken in marriage, the distinction between an eligible woman and one who is already taken is crucial.

When there is an excess of males, increasing proportions do not marry, or marry at a later age (Lloyd and South 1996). Women are valuable in part because they are scarce. The proportion of ever-married people increases, the age at marriage decreases, and fertility increases. Nonmarital sexuality of respectable women is repressed, resulting in decreased rates of common-law marriage and illegitimacy and an increased proportion of children living in intact homes. There may be an increase in rates of male sexual violence (Pedersen 1991).

When there is a male marriage squeeze, the men who are most disadvantaged in competing are those who are too young or too poor. Familial success depends largely on economic resources, resulting in a clear motive towards financially success careers. When wives are valued as wives, the trend will be toward their decreased labor force involvement and increased fertility. Grounds for divorce will be stringent, and rates of divorce will be low. Rates of remarriage for women will be high.

The extent to which these projected outcomes will actually come about is not known. In Japan, there is a definite male marriage squeeze among young adults, but a definite female marriage squeeze among older cohorts (Kono 1991). More circumstances of a male marriage squeeze will emerge if and when developing countries experience a sharp decline in cohort size.

Interpersonal Consequences of Sex Ratio Imbalances

If it is assumed that most adults are heterosexual, and that their first preference is to be in a stable and monogamous marriage, then the imbalance of sex ratios results in a substantial, nonnegotiable, and pervasive double standard. The implications of a male marriage squeeze are not yet clear, but the implications of a female one are pervasive.

Odd woman out. Women in a marriage squeeze are often treated as superfluous, described as being extras, excess, a surplus, or simply as too many, all terms that minimize their intrinsic worth. They have been euphemistically described as *dyadically disadvantaged.* The minority sex, female or male, has the unique experience of intrasexual competition not only in early adulthood but also throughout the lifespan (Pedersen 1991).

Principle of least interest. A truism from social psychology, which reflects personal and political reality, is that: *The person who has the least interest in the continuation if a relationship is able to dictate the conditions of the relationship.* In a female marriage squeeze, men have a plethora of women who might be girlfriends, mistresses, or wives, a situation that applies to married men as well as the unmarried and the formerly married. With advancing age, men's pool of eligibles increases, whereas her small pool is made smaller still. Other things being equal, if marriage is a desired state, she will make more compromises than he does. To borrow a concept from economics, he exists in a buyer's market, while she is in a seller's market. What emerges is in effect a *demographic double standard* in role expectations, sexual norms, and power in general.

Antinuptialism: His. Men in a female marriage squeeze may find that marriage is not so much undesirable as it is unnecessary. If one relationship is less than perfect, other women are available. To take an extreme example, the marriage market in Brazil has been cogently described as: ". . . finding a balance by 'recycling' men through highly unstable informal unions" (Greene and Rao 1995).

Antinuptialism: Hers. If a woman is not able to find the kind of man she wants, or the egalitarian marriage she wants, she may withdraw from the market completely. The singles' subculture offers support and justification of a single lifestyle. The emergent attitude is summarized in an often-quoted aphorism: "It takes a hell of a man to be better than no man at all."

Extrafamilial roles. Single women anticipate a high probability of remaining single. Wives anticipate divorce without remarriage. Both are motivated to establish their independence with work roles. A cyclical effect is created: the greater the competence in extrafamilial roles, the less dependence on marriage; the less dependence of marriage, the greater the competence in extrafamilial roles. Taken to its logical extreme, the pattern emerging is that both men and women have, and expect to have, work roles, the only difference being a few years taken off for motherhood.

Conclusion

Racial differences in marriage-market conditions accentuate, but do not explain completely, black-white differences in marriage rates (Lichter et al. 1991; Lloyd and South 1996). The black experience suggests changes that might also appear in the white population, but there is no reason to expect they will be exactly the same. The consequences of a female marriage squeeze cannot be predicted independently of the culture in which it occurs.

For each of the outcomes that have been associated with a marriage squeeze, at the societal or at the interpersonal level, there are many other contributing factors. Thus, a marriage squeeze contributes to declining fertility, but declining fertility also reflects industrialization, medical advances in birth technology, education of women, and the population explosion. A marriage squeeze is an important factor in the continuation of traditional families or in their destabilization, but it is only *one* of many demographic and social forces in operation.

See also: MATE SELECTION

Bibliography

Albrecht, C., and Fossett, M. (1997). "Mate Availability, Women's Marriage Prevalence, and Husband's Education." *Journal of Family Issues* 18:429–453.

Bhat, P.; Mari, H.; and Shiva, S. "Demography of Bride-price and Dowry: Causes and Consequences of the Indian Marriage Squeeze." *Population Studies* 53:129–148.

Chu, J. (2001). "Prenatal Sex Determination and Sex-Selective Abortion in Rural Central China" *Population and Development Review* 27:259–281.

Crowder, K., and Tonlay, S. (2000). "A New Marriage Squeeze for Black Women: The Role of Racial Intermarriage by Black Men." *Journal of Marriage and Family* 62:792–808.

Davis, L. (2000). "Factors Contributing to Partner Commitment Among Unmarried African Americans." *Social Work Research* 24:4–16.

Davis, L., and Emerson, S. (1997). "Black Dating Professionals' Perceptions of Equity, Satisfaction, Power and Romantic Alternatives and Ideals." *Journal of Black Psychology* 23:148–165.

Fossett, M., and. Kiecolt, K. (1991). "A Methodological Review of the Sex Ratio: Alternatives for Comparative Research." *Journal of Marriage and the Family* 53:941–957.

Glick, P. (1988). "Fifty Years of Family Demography: A Record of Social Change." *Journal of Marriage and the Family* 50:861–873.

Goodkind, D. (1997). "The Vietnamese Double Marriage Squeeze." *International Migration Review* 31:108–27.

Greene, M., and Rao, V. (1995): "The Marriage Squeeze and the Rise in Informal Marriage in Brazil." *Social Biology* 42:65–82.

Guttentag, M., and Secord, P. F. (1983). *Too Many Women? The Sex Ratio Question.* Beverly Hills, CA: Sage.

Hamilton, L., and Otterstad, O. (1998). "Sex Ratio and Community Size: Notes from the Northern Atlantic." *Population and Environment* 20:11–22.

Hooper, D. A., and England, J. L. (1988). "Single Females in Rural Energy-Impacted Countries: The Effects of Rapid Growth and a Male Marriage-Market Squeeze." *Rural Sociology* 53:87–95.

Huguet, J. et al., (2000). "Results of the 1998 Population Census in Cambodia." *Asia-Pacific Population Journal* 18:1–18.

Kim, J. (1997). "The Relationship between Sex-ratio and Marital Behavior." *Health and Social Welfare Review* 17:99–120.

Kono, S. (1991). "A Treatise on Sex-Ratio in Population by Marital Status: Marriage Squeeze and Widowhood." *Journal of Population Problems* 47:1–6.

Lichter, D. (1990). "Delayed Marriage, Marital Homogamy, and the Mate Selection Process among White Women." *Social Science Quarterly* 71:802–811.

Lichter, D., and Anderson, R. (1995). "Marriage Markets and Marital Choice." *Journal of Family Issues* 16:412–420.

Lichter, D. et al. (1992). "Race and the Retreat from Marriage." *American Sociological Review* 57:781–799.

Lichter, D.; LeClere, F.; and McLaughlin, D. (1991). "Local Marriage Markets and the Marital Behavior of Black and White Women." *American Journal of Sociology* 96:843–867.

Lloyd, K., and South, S. (1996). "Contextual Influences of Young Men's Transition to First Marriage." *Social Forces* 74:1097–1119.

McCaa, R. (1993). "Ethnic Intermarriage and Gender in New York City." *Journal of Interdisciplinary History* 16:412–432.

Pedersen, F. (1991). "Secular Trends in Human Sex Ratios: Their Influence on Individual and Family Behavior." *Human Nature* 2:271–291.

Rao, V. (1993), "The Rising Price of Husbands: A Hedonic Analysis of Dowry Increases in Rural India." *Journal of Political Economy* 101:666–677.

South, S., and Lloyd, K. (1992), "Marriage Opportunities And Family Formation: Further Implications of Imbalanced Sex-ratios." *Journal of Marriage and the Family* 54:440–451.

Stier, H., and Shavit, Y. (1994) "Age At Marriage, Sex-ratios, And Ethnic Heterogamy." *European Sociological Review* 10:79–87.

Taylor, R.; Jackson, S.; and Chatters, L. (1997). *Family Life in Black America*. Thousand Oaks, CA: Sage.

Tucker, M., and Mitchell-Kerman, C. (1995). *The Decline in Marriage Among African Americans: Causes, Consequences and Policy Implications*. New York: Russell Sage.

Veevers, J. (1988). "The 'Real' Marriage Squeeze: Mate Selection, Mortality and the Marriage Gradient." *Sociological Perspectives* 31:169–189.

JEAN E. VEEVERS

MATE SELECTION

Choosing a mate is a problem that humans share with most other animals because successful reproduction is central to natural selection. Peahens choose among the most attractive peacocks, female elephant seals pick males who have already attracted large harems, and even promiscuous chimpanzees exercise choice about the other chimps with which they will be promiscuous. Among mammals, however, humans are in a small minority in one important way: for over 95 percent of other mammals, family arrangements involving male care of offspring are nonexistent (Geary 2000). Across human societies, though, men and women bond together in marriage (Broude 1994; United Nations 2000). Not all human mating occurs within such bonds; within and across societies, polygamous arrangements are relatively common

(Broude 1994). In considering how and why people choose mates, therefore, two points are significant: (1) there are variations as well as universalities across cultures, and (2) there is a distinction between selection of mates for short-term relationships versus long-term relationships.

The discussion below begins with research and theory focused on *proximal* causes, or immediate psychological triggers of mate choice (such as pleasant feelings in response to seeing a physically attractive other), and moves through progressively more *distal* factors (relationship exchange, cultural and historical factors, and evolutionary history). Like the single frames, scenes, and overall plot of a movie, these different approaches are complementary, and all are required to see the "big picture" of mate selection.

Factors within the Individual

Several theories of mate selection have focused on the psychological responses of the individual to potential mates. An influential early theory focused on reinforcement, emphasizing the observer's affective response to potential mates (Byrne and Clore 1970). The assumption was that a person is attracted to potential mates who make that person feel good. Researchers in this tradition focused on overt characteristics such as physical appearance and the expression of similar attitudes and values (Byrne 1971). People indeed tend to mate with others who have similar characteristics, including political attitudes, lifestyle values, personality, appearance, or ethnicity (Botwin, Buss, and Shackelford 1997; Keller, Thiessen, and Young 1996). Consistent with the theory that such features make the judge feel good, it was found that people do find it pleasant to interact with similar others (Byrne 1971).

There are exceptions to the similarity-attraction principle, however. Women at all ages tend to be attracted to men who are slightly older than themselves, and men shift their preferences throughout the lifespan, such that teenagers find older women most attractive, men in their twenties are most attracted to women their own age, and older men are most attracted to women who are younger than themselves (Kenrick et al. 1996; Kenrick and Keefe 1992). Besides this, women tend to emphasize status-linked characteristics in a partner, whereas men do not (Sadalla, Kenrick, and Vershure 1987). Men, on the other hand, place more emphasis on physical attractiveness (Townsend and Wasserman 1998). The cues for attractiveness are also slightly different for the two sexes. Although symmetry is attractive in both men and women, small noses and relatively smaller jaws are relatively more attractive in women, and medium noses and large jaws are attractive in men (Cunningham, Druen, and Barbee 1997). A small waist-to-hip ratio is attractive in a woman, but not in a man (Singh 1995).

Another interesting exception to the similarity-attraction rule is that individuals raised in the same home tend not to experience strong sexual attraction and romantic feelings towards one another, even when they are not related (Shepher 1983). Contrary to the general tendency for marriages to occur between neighbors and acquaintances, in a study of 211 kibbutzim, Joseph Shepher (1983) found no instances of marriage among adults who had been born on the same kibbutz and had stayed together in the same peer group without interruption during childhood.

Another theory focusing on individual psychological responses suggested that a person decides that he or she is feeling romantic attraction for another when he or she attributes feelings of arousal to that other (Berscheid and Walster 1974). Findings that people became attracted to others present when they were experiencing arousal due to fear of electric shock, standing on a shaky suspension bridge, or recent exercise were interpreted as support for that theory (Dutton and Aron 1974; White and Kight 1984). An alternative interpretation of those findings emphasizes that arousal simply boosts attraction, without any necessary misinterpretation of arousal (Allen et al. 1989).

Another set of factors that affects mate choice involves personality traits. One line of research examined differences between those adopting an *unrestricted* versus *restricted* approach to relationships (Simpson and Gangestad 1992). Unrestricted individuals, inclined to have sex without commitment and to be involved with more than one partner at a time, choose attractive and outgoing partners; restricted (or monogamously oriented) individuals favor partners manifesting personality characteristics associated with fidelity and good parenting.

Factors in the Relationship

Mate selection is a two-way street, involving more than the preferences of a single individual. A second wave of mate selection theories emphasized processes of dyadic exchange of costs and benefits. The most prevalent models emphasize *social exchange*: I seek a mate who brings a mix of assets and liabilities with comparable value to my own personal portfolio (e.g., Hatfield et al. 1985). Researchers focusing on *reciprocal exchange* have emphasized naturalistic studies of mate choice in relationships as they unfold over time (e.g., Cate, Huston, and Nesselroade 1986). Some of these approaches have suggested that, over the course of time, relationships go through different stages or phases. Bernard Murstein's (1970) *filter theory,* for example, suggested that partners are first selected based on obvious stimulus characteristics, such as attractiveness, and are then passed through finer filters based on similar values and role compatibility.

The earliest dyadic exchange models focused on *complementarity* (Winch 1955). So, for example, it was expected that socially dominant partners will seek socially submissive others for relationships. Although support for personality complementarity was not abundant, there is some degree of cross-sex complementarity in preferred traits. For example, females emphasize social dominance in their partners more than males do (Sadalla, Kenrick, and Vershure 1987). This is not a simple preference for complementarity, however, because dominant females do not seek out submissive males.

Support for general exchange theories, on the other hand, has been clearer. For example, there is evidence that physically attractive women tend to marry men of higher status, and that socially successful men tend to marry more attractive women (Taylor and Glenn 1976). There is also evidence that people of both sexes are attracted to others with personal characteristics that make them easy to get along with in long-term relationships (Jensen-Campbell, Graziano, and West 1995; Green and Kenrick 1994).

Sociocultural and Historical Factors

Taking still another step back from the isolated individual, some researchers have focused on the cultural and historical context of mate choice (e.g., Crook and Crook 1988; Hatfield and Rapson 1996). Adopting this perspective, one can ask both: How do human societies differ with regard to mate choice, and how are they similar? The range of differences is, at first glance, rather dazzling. As Gwen Broude (1994) noted, *exclusive monogamy*, the legally sanctioned form of mating in Europe and North America, is preferred in less than 20 percent of 238 cultures worldwide. *Polygyny* (more than one woman sharing the same husband) is practiced in most of the remainder (over 80%), and *polyandry* (more than one man sharing the same wife) is found in four societies. Although personal choice is emphasized in Western societies, males marry women chosen for them by third parties in 29.3 percent of 157 societies worldwide, and marriages are arranged for females in 44.1 percent of 161 societies (Broude 1994). Furthermore, there are cultural variations in norms about desirable features in mates, including amount of body fat desired, preferred size and shape of breasts, and other overt characteristics such as body markings (Anderson et al. 1992; Ford and Beach 1951; Broude 1994).

Looking across recent history, survey data on mate preferences among North American college students in 1939, 1956, 1967, 1977, 1985, and 1996, reveals regional as well as temporal variations. For example, students in Texas were more interested in chastity, religious background, and neatness than were students in Michigan. Over time, the value placed on chastity by both sexes dropped, and the value placed on mutual attraction and love increased (Buss et al. 2001).

In addition to cultural and historical variations in mate choice, there are many commonalities found across human societies. These range from preferred overt characteristics such as clear skin and lack of disfigurement to personality traits making for good parents and agreeable companions (Broude 1994; Ford and Beach 1951). A general preference for similarity in a mate is also widespread (Botwin, Buss, and Shackelford 1997). Moreover, a number of sex differences found in Western society are found across cultures and time periods, including the tendency to judge men on the basis of physical strength, social position, and economic worth, and to place more emphasis on a woman's physical attractiveness (Broude 1994; Buss 1989). The preference for older versus younger partners across the lifespan is also found across numerous societies and historical time periods (Otta et al. 1999; Harpending 1992; Kenrick and Keefe 1992).

It is sometimes suggested that, in Western societies, the relative emphasis on status and power in men and physical attractiveness in women might be related to women's relatively lower economic status, and that if opportunity and wage disparities were rectified, women would not prefer a man with higher socioeconomic status (Eagly and Wood 1999). Within the United States, however, there is evidence that women who gain social status do not shift to male-like preferences for relative youth and attractiveness, but instead continue to prefer older and higher status partners (Kenrick and Keefe 1992; Townsend 1987).

Due to warfare, migration, and random historical and geographic variations, there are sometimes relatively more available females than males in the pool of eligible mates, or the converse. Marcia Guttentag and Paul Secord (1983) found that a surplus of women (putting men in a "buyers' market") is associated with later marriage, more divorce, and more permissive sexual norms. A surplus of men, on the other hand, is associated with more stable relationships and male willingness to commit to monogamous relationships. Other research suggests that polyandry, though rare, is associated with conditions of extreme resource scarcity (as found in the high Himalayas in Nepal) under which survival rates for children of single males and their wives are low. In Nepal and a few other places, several brothers often combine their resources and marry a single wife, increasing survival rates for resultant children (Crook and Crook 1988). On the other hand, extreme polygyny (harems) is correlated with ecological conditions including a steep social hierarchy, a generally rich environment allowing higher status families to accumulate vast wealth, and occasional famines so lower-status families face possibilities of starvation (Crook and Crook 1988). Under these circumstances, a woman who absorbs the cost of sharing a wealthy husband reaps a survival insurance policy for herself and any resultant children.

Evolutionary Factors

Taking a still broader perspective, we can ask, "How does mate selection in humans compare with mate selection in other animals?" Looking across many animal species, evolutionary biologists have uncovered general principles that may help clarify some of the particulars of human mate selection.

At the broadest level, the *theory of inclusive fitness* suggests all animals are selected to behave in ways that, on average, benefit others sharing their genes (siblings and cousins as well as their own offspring). Sexual selection refers to a form of natural selection favoring characteristics that assist in attracting mates (e.g., peacock's feathers) or in competing with the same sex (e.g., rams' horns). Across species, females are more likely to be the selectors, and males are more likely to be found banging their heads against one another to win females' attention. According to *differential parental investment theory,* the sex with the initially higher investment in the offspring—generally the female—has more to lose from a poor mating choice and therefore demands more before agreeing to mate (Trivers 1972). In species in which males make the larger investment (e.g., by caring for the eggs and young, as in seahorses), males tend to be more selective about their mates (Daly and Wilson 1983). In mammals, the normal discrepancy between males and females is especially pronounced, because females carry the young inside their bodies and nurse them after birth. Male mammals can reproduce with little cost, and, frequently, the male's direct input does not go beyond the simple act of copulation. In such species, males tend to be nonselective about their mates, whereas females demand evidence of superior genetic potential before mating and will often mate only with males who have demonstrated superior capabilities. Humans also sometimes have sexual relations within less committed relationships, in the typical mammalian mode. Under those circumstances, males are less selective (Kenrick et al. 1990). Unlike most mammals, however, humans tend to form long-term pair-bonds, in which males invest many resources in the offspring. Under those circumstances, men's selectivity about mates approaches that of women (Kenrick et al. 1990).

Men and women make different contributions to the offspring. Women contribute their bodies, through internal gestation and nursing, and men consequently value indications of fertility including healthy appearance and a waist-hip ratio characteristic of youthful sexual maturity (Cunningham, Druen, and Barbee 1997). On the other hand, men primarily contribute their genes and indirect resources such as money and shelter. Women could appraise a man's genetic potential from physical attractiveness and position in a dominance hierarchy (Gangestad, Thornhill, and Yeo 1994). His ability to provide resources could be gauged indirectly by his ambition and directly by his social status and acquired wealth (Buss and Barnes 1986; Daly and Wilson 1983). Even with these differential tendencies, humans often cooperate in raising their offspring. Hence a number of characteristics should be (and are) desired by both sexes, such as agreeableness, kindness, and faithfulness (Buss 1989; Kenrick et al. 1990). People are not presumed to consciously calculate their genetic self-interest, but like all animals, to have inherited certain preferences that helped their ancestors reproduce successfully.

Conclusion

Individual psychological factors that influence mate choice must play out in the context of dyadic interaction, and those dyadic interactions unfold within a broader cultural context. The variations across individuals, dyads, and cultures are in turn affected by the preferences and proclivities inherited from ancestral humans, shaped by ecological forces common to all members of this particular species of social mammal. Thus, mate selection can be understood at several different, yet interconnected, levels of analysis.

The broader ecological factors discussed earlier provide a good example. Cultural variations in mate choice are not completely random, but often fit with general principles applicable to many animal species (Crook and Crook 1988; Daly and Wilson 1983). For example, polyandry is more common when the males are brothers in humans and other animals, in keeping with the general principle of inclusive fitness. Polygyny is more common than polyandry in humans and other mammals, as is the female preference for high status males, consistent with principles of differential parental investment (female mammals have less to gain from taking additional mates, so will demand more in a mate). Mate selection thus offers insight into fundamental questions about human nature and its interaction with human culture.

See also: ATTACHMENT: COUPLE RELATIONSHIPS;
ATTRACTION; BRIDE-PRICE; COHABITATION;
DATING; DOWRY; FAMILY LIFE EDUCATION;
HUSBAND; LOVE; MARRIAGE CEREMONIES;
MARRIAGE, DEFINITION OF; MARRIAGE
PREPARATION; MARRIAGE SQUEEZE; RELATIONSHIP
INITIATION; WIFE

Bibliography

Allen, J.; Kenrick, D. T.; Linder, D. E.; and McCall, M. A. (1989). "Arousal and Attraction: A Response Facilitation Alternative to Misattribution and Negative Reinforcement Models." *Journal of Personality and Social Psychology* 57:261–270.

Anderson, J. L.; Crawford, C. B.; Nadeau, J.; and Lindberg, T. (1992). "Was the Duchess of Windsor Right? A Cross-Cultural Review of the Sociobiology of Ideals of Female Body Shape." *Ethology and Sociobiology* 13:197–227.

Berscheid, E., and Walster, E. (1974). "A Little Bit About Love." In *Foundations of Interpersonal Attraction,* ed. T. Huston. New York: Academic Press.

Botwin, M.; Buss, D. M.; and Shackelford, T. K. (1997). "Personality and Mate Preferences: Five Factors in Mate Selection and Marital Satisfaction." *Journal of Personality* 65:107–136.

Broude, G. J. (1994). *Marriage, Family, and Relationships: A Cross Cultural Encyclopedia.* Santa Barbara, CA: ABC-CLIO.

Buss, D. M. (1985). "Human Mate Selection." *American Scientist* 73(1):47–51.

Buss, D. M. (1989). "Sex Differences in Human Mate Preferences: Evolutionary Hypotheses Tested in 37 Cultures." *Behavioral and Brain Sciences* 12(1):1–49.

Buss, D. M. (1999). *Evolutionary Psychology: The New Science of the Mind.* Boston: Allyn and Bacon.

Buss, D. M., and Barnes, M. (1986). "Preferences in Human Mate Selection." *Journal of Personality and Social Psychology* 50(3):559–570.

Buss, D. M.; Shackelford, T. K.; Kirkpatrick, L. A.; and Larsen, R. J. (2001). "A Half Century of Mate Preferences: The Cultural Evolution of Values." *Journal of Marriage and the Family* 63(2):491–503.

Byrne, D. (1971). *The Attraction Paradigm.* New York: Academic Press.

Byrne, D., and Clore, G. L. (1970). "A Reinforcement Model of Evaluative Responses." *Personality* 1:103–128.

Cate, R. M.; Huston, T. L.; and Nesselroade, J. R. (1986). "Premarital Relationships: Toward the Identification of Alternative Pathways to Marriage." *Journal of Social and Clinical Psychology* 4:3–22.

Crook, J. H., and Crook, S. J. (1988). "Tibetan Polyandry: Problems of Adaptation and Fitness." In *Human Reproductive Behaviour,* ed. L. Betzig, M. Borgerhoff-Mulder, and P. Turke. Cambridge, UK: Cambridge University Press.

Cunningham, M. R.; Druen, P. B.; and Barbee, A. P. (1997). "Angels, Mentors, and Friends: Tradeoffs among Evolutionary, Social, and Individual Variables in Physical Appearance." In *Evolutionary Social Psychology,* ed. J. Simpson and D. T. Kenrick. Hillsdale, NJ: Lawrence Erlbaum Associates.

Daly, M., and Wilson, M. (1983). *Sex, Evolution and Behavior,* 2nd edition. Belmont, CA: Wadsworth.

Dutton, D. G., and Aron, A. P. (1974). "Some Evidence for Heightened Sexual Attraction under Conditions of High Anxiety." *Journal of Personality and Social Psychology* 30(4):510–517.

Eagly, A. H., and Wood, W. (1999). "The Origins of Sex Differences in Human Behavior: Evolved Predispositions versus Social Roles." *American Psychologist* 54:408–423.

Ford, C. S., and Beach, F. A. (1951). *Patterns of Sexual Behavior.* New York: Harper.

Gangestad, S. W.; Thornhill, R.; and Yeo, R. A. (1994). "Facial Attractiveness, Developmental Stability, and Fluctuating Asymmetry." *Ethology and Sociobiology* 15(2):73–85.

Geary, D. C. (2000). "Evolution and Proximate Expression of Human Paternal Investment." *Psychological Bulletin* 126(1):55–77.

Green, B. L., and Kenrick, D. T. (1994). "The Attractiveness of Gender-Typed Traits at Different Relationship Levels: Androgynous Characteristics May Be Desirable after All." *Personality and Social Psychology Bulletin* 20(3):244–253.

Guttentag, M., and Secord, P. F. (1983). *Too Many Women: The Sex Ratio Question.* Beverly Hills, CA: Sage Publications.

Harpending, H. (1992). "Age Differences between Mates in Southern African Pastoralists." *Behavioral and Brain Sciences* 15:102–103.

Hatfield, E., and Rapson, R. L. (1996). *Love and Sex: Cross-Cultural Perspectives.* Boston: Allyn and Bacon.

Hatfield, E.; Traupmann, J.; Sprecher, S.; Utne, M.; and Hay, J. (1985). "Equity and Intimate Relationships: Recent Research." In *Compatible and Incompatible Relationships,* ed. W. Ickes. New York: Springer-Verlag.

Jensen-Campbell, L. A.; Graziano, W. G.; and West, S. G. (1995). "Dominance, Prosocial Orientation, and Female Preferences: Do Nice Guys Really Finish Last?" *Journal of Personality and Social Psychology* 68:427–440.

Keller, M. C.; Thiessen, D.; and Young, R. K. (1996). "Mate Assortment in Dating and Married Couples." *Personality and Individual Differences* 21:217–221.

Kenrick, D. T., and Keefe, R. C. (1992). "Age Preferences in Mates Reflect Sex Differences in Human Reproductive Strategies." *Behavioral and Brain Sciences* 15(1):75–133.

Kenrick, D. T.; Gabrielidis, C.; Keefe, R. C.; and Cornelius, J. S. (1996). "Adolescents' Age Preferences for Dating Partners: Support for an Evolutionary Model of Life-History Strategies." *Child Development* 67(4):1499–1511.

Kenrick, D. T.; Sadalla, E. K.; Groth, G.; and Trost, M. R. (1990). "Evolution, Traits, and the Stages of Human Courtship: Qualifying the Parental Investment Model." *Journal of Personality* 58:97–117.

Murstein, B. (1970). "Stimulus-Value-Role: A Theory of Marital Choice." *Journal of Marriage and the Family* 32:465–481.

Otta, E.; da Silva Queiroz, R.; de Sousa Campos, L.; da Silva, M. W. D.; and Silveira, M. T. (1999). "Age Differences between Spouses in a Brazilian Marriage Sample." *Evolution and Human Behavior* 20(2):99–103.

Sadalla, E. K.; Kenrick, D. T.; and Vershure, B. (1987). "Dominance and Heterosexual Attraction." *Journal of Personality and Social Psychology* 52(4):30–738.

Shepher, J. (1983). *Incest: A Biosocial View.* New York: Academic Press.

Simpson, J. A., and Gangestad, S. W. (1992). "Sociosexuality and Romantic Partner Choice." *Journal of Personality* 60(1):31–51.

Singh, D. (1995). "Female Judgment of Male Attractiveness and Desirability for Relationships: Role of Waist-to-Hip Ratio and Financial Status." *Journal of Personality and Social Psychology* 69(6):1089–1101.

Taylor, P. A., and Glenn, N. D. (1976). "The Utility of Education and Attractiveness for Females' Status Attainment through Marriage." *American Sociological Review* 41:484–498.

Townsend, J. M. (1987). "Sex Differences in Sexuality Among Medical Students: Effects of Increasing Socioecomic Status." *Archives of Sexual Behavior* 16:427–446.

Townsend, J. M., and Wasserman, T. (1998). "Sexual Attractiveness: Sex Differences in Assessment and Criteria." *Evolution and Human Behavior* 14:171–191.

Trivers, R. (1972). "Parental Investment and Sexual Selection." In *Sexual Selection and the Descent of Man,* ed. B. Campbell. New York: Aldine de Gruyter.

United Nations. (2000). *World Marriage Patterns 2000.* Population Division, Department of Economic and Social Affairs. DEV/2251, POP/771. New York: Author.

Walster, E., and Berscheid, E. (1971). "Adrenaline Makes the Heart Grow Fonder." *Psychology Today* 5(1):47–50, 62.

White, G. L., and Kight, T. D. (1984). "Misattribution of Arousal and Attraction: Effects of Salience of Explanations for Arousal." *Journal of Experimental Social Psychology* 20(1):55–64.

Winch, R. F. (1955). "The Theory of Complementary Needs in Mate Selection: Final Results on the Test of the General Hypothesis." *American Sociological Review* 20:552–555.

DOUGLAS T. KENRICK
SUSAN LEDLOW
JOSH ACKERMAN

MENARCHE

The word *menarche* is derived from the Greek words *mēn,* month, and *archē,* beginning. It is the term used to refer to the first menstrual period. This first sign that menstruation has begun is governed by a complex set of biological processes, genetic information, and psychosocial factors. In the human female, the usual age for menarche is between ages eleven and twelve (Martini 1992). Other studies, however, report figures between twelve and thirteen (Boaz and Almquist 1997).

Variables that influence the onset of menarche include body build or body mass, critical weight, height/weight ratio, skeletal maturation, and percentage of body fat. Other correlates are health history, protein intake, amount of daily exercise, and familial trends.

The Biological Process

At about age eight, the pituitary gland secretes hormones until the ovaries begin their own production of steroids (estrogens), the chemicals that are responsible for initiating puberty. These hormones (known as the follicle stimulating hormone [FSH] and luteinizing hormone [LH]) allow for an increase in adipose tissue (fat), and inhibit the growth hormone. They stimulate the ovary to produce estrogen and progesterone, which results in breast development and pubic hair.

At birth, the human female has approximately 750,000 primordial follicles (eggs). By puberty, 400,000 remain. At or soon after menarche, the first mature egg is released. Menstruation will recur each month until menopause when few or no follicles remain. (Guyton 1976).

Differing Ages of Onset Through History

By age thirteen, most girls in industrialized societies have attained menarche. Interestingly, this number has not been consistent throughout history. It appears that menstrual age has been decreasing from between fifteen and sixteen in the last half of the eighteenth century, to twelve to thirteen in the present day, at a rate of three months per decade (Tanner 1962). Various reasons have been hypothesized. Alarmists decry this trend and blame it on a multiplicity of factors from hormones in food to mass media. Since nutrition and the standard of living have improved in the last 200 years, one explanation is that the time for menarche has always been the same biologically, but was delayed because of the lack of essential nutrients for the chemical pathways to trigger hormone synthesis. Genetically, humans have always had the potential for certain biological phenomena to express themselves, but environmental conditions retarded both growth and development.

Meaning for Reproduction and Family

Menarche is an abrupt signal that marks a change in social status from child to adult. Cross-culturally, menarche has a variety of meanings that include adult responsibilities, freedoms, and expectations regarding reproduction. As with all cultural phenomena, there is a wide range of significance attached to menarche.

In the United States, ideally, there is an extended period of time from menarche to marriage and reproduction. Many families want their daughters to get an education beyond high school before they start families. After marriage, fecundity (reproductive potential) can be controlled by birth control technology in those social groups whose belief system accepts the ethics of these devices. However, the consequences of premarital sex are a concern for the modern family because as the age of menarche lowers, the time span between puberty and marriage increases. Many parents are conflicted about what kind of birth control information should be provided to their daughters. Education plays an important part in delaying the time of marriage. Education is highly correlated with family size: the greater the number of years of education, the smaller the family size (Ehrenreich and English 1978). Until early in the twentieth century, it was common belief that school weakened a woman's reproductive ability by physically stressing her body so that she could not have many children. Social scientists now acknowledge that time of marriage and family size are choices made by women, some of whom prefer to obtain an education before starting a family.

In tribal societies, where fertility is crucial, menarche is celebrated by a rite of passage. Where fertility is at a premium, it is cause for elaborate ritual and public knowledge. In other societies, menarche marks the time when the girl can be married (eHRAF 2001). Among the Western Apache, the ritual that accompanied menarche benefited the entire community through the girl's connection to a deity. She was also given an earthly sponsor who facilitated expanding social networks (Bonvillain 1995).

How Menarche is Treated in Different Societies

Anthropology is rich with descriptions of coming-of-age ceremonies for girls. The attitudes of societies toward menarche vary from delight and pride to fear and shame. Positive labels signify that the girl is an adult, capable of contributing to the ongoing society. *Menstrual pollution* is the term anthropologists use to describe fears of menstrual blood and its dangerous powers. Since the time of Pliny (23–79 C.E) myths and taboos have surrounded menarche. Societies in Brazil, British Columbia, India, Ceylon, and North America built menstrual huts to segregate menstruating women.

When the Bemba (from Rhodesia) were studied, the *chisungu* was held for each girl at menarche. The girl informed older women that she had started to bleed and they "brought her to the fire" to warm her. Seeds were cooked, and the girl was required to extract and eat them burning hot. Dances were performed to protect her against the magic dangers of her first intercourse. Pottery was painted and decorated with special symbols. Later the girl was isolated indoors and fed millet cooked in a new fire (Richards 1956). Menarche was a cause for celebration but recognized as a dangerous state.

In contrast to this public event, on the island of Inis Beag, Ireland, most girls were unaware and unprepared for menarche. Their mothers did not discuss menstruation with them. They were traumatized by the experience and had nowhere to turn for information or support. As a consequence, their adult reproductive life was fraught with half-truths and superstitions regarding their bodies and their sexual behavior (Marshall and Suggs 1962).

The Tiwi of Australia subjected menstruating girls to severe restrictions. The girl's mother and relatives chased her into the bush, where they built a menstrual hut for her. She could not dig up or touch food, or eat without a stick. She could not touch or look at water. Someone had to give it to her. She could not scratch herself with her fingers. She could not make a fire or break any sticks. She had to whisper instead of talk.

Among certain Jewish people, the mother slaps her daughter's face with a congratulatory statement such as "today you are a woman," or "may the blood run back to your face." One source reports the slap as an admonition that the daughter should not disgrace the family by becoming pregnant before marriage. The tradition is less common than it was before the 1950s. Certain mothers who were slapped have decided not to carry on the ritual because of its pejorative connotation (Appel-Slingbaum 2000).

See also: CHILDHOOD, STAGES OF: ADOLESCENCE; FERTILITY; MENSTRUAL TABOO; SEXUAL COMMUNICATION: PARENT-CHILD RELATIONSHIPS; RITES OF PASSAGE; SEXUALITY EDUCATION; SEXUALITY IN ADOLESCENCE

Bibliography

Boaz, Noel T., and Almquist, Alan J. (1997). *Biological Anthropology.* Upper Saddle River, NJ: Prentice Hall.

Bonvillain, N. (1995). *Women and Men: Cultural Constructs of Gender.* Englewood Cliffs, NJ: Prentice Hall.

Ehrenreich, B., and English, D. (1978). *For Her Own Good: 150 Years of the Expert's Advice to Women.* New York: Doubleday.

Guyton, A. C. (1976). *Textbook of Medical Physiology.* Philadelphia: W.B. Saunders Company.

Martini, F. (1992). *Fundamentals of Anatomy and Physiology.* 2nd edition. Englewood Cliffs, NJ: Prentice Hall.

Messenger, J. C. (1970). "Sex and Repression in an Irish Folk Community." In *Human Sexual Behavior,* ed. D. C. Marshall and R. C. Suggs. New York: Basic Books.

Richards, A .I. (1956). *Chisungu: A Girl's Initiation Ceremony among the Bemba of Northern Rhodesia.* London: Faber and Faber.

Tanner, J. M. (1962). *Growth at Adolescence,* 2d edition. Oxford: Blackwell.

Turner, V. (1968). *The Drums of Affliction.* New York: Oxford University Press.

Other Resources

Appel-Slingbaum, C. (2000). "The Tradition of Slapping Our Daughters." Available from http://www.mum.org/slap.htm.

eHRAF (Electronic Human Relations Area Files) (2001). Available from http://ets.umdl.umich.edu/reference.html.

LANA THOMPSON

MENNONITES

See ANABAPTISTS (AMISH, MENNONITE)

MENOPAUSE

Menopause refers to the cessation of menses. However, sociocultural definitions beyond the biological facts reflect differences between cultures. The feelings that a woman holds about herself and her social relationships, as well as the symptoms she experiences, can be defined by the culture in which she lives. It is the cultural definition that is the source of meaning women use to assess their expectations. Examples of such variance are described among women in the United States, Europe, the Middle Eastern, China, and Japan and among South African Indian women and rural Mayan Indians.

Cultural and Social Meanings

Women's specific concerns about menopause vary by culture (Datan 1987). Once thought of as a deficiency disease, menopause has been feared as well as welcomed (Lewis and Bernstein 1996). The sociocultural values about aging account for part of the diversity in meaning. In Asian cultures, for instance, age is regarded with respect. Women in menopause, therefore, may be accorded a higher status (Lock 1993). This may change, however, as Western values influence other parts of the world, and women may feel less satisfied as they enter this period of life (Berger 1999). In the United States and European countries, age is often associated with loss of attractiveness and value. In Western culture, the menopausal years are regarded as the enemy of youth, and they result in disqualification of the woman's feminine beauty (Scarf 1980). In other cultures, however, the biological processes are themselves qualifications for entry into the man's world. The end of menses is associated with a new freedom to participate in rituals previously closed to women (duToit 1990). In some Indian cultures, for example, women who have ceased menstruation are given more opportunity to move around the house in an unrestricted manner and to participate in prayers and funeral preparations (du Toit 1990).

In a study of women from different cultures residing in Israel, Nancy Datan (1987) found significant differences among her subjects. Some Moslem Arabs feared a decline in marital relations with the loss of fertility, while some European women were concerned about going crazy during menopause (Datan 1987).

Menopausal Symptoms

Women vary in their subjective experiences of symptoms. Not all of women's perceived changes in the body are reflected in the mirror; some are derived from a woman's perception of herself, based on the accounts of others. Expectations vary and are adjusted to actual experiences.

In the United States and Europe, symptoms of hot flashes and irritability are most commonly presented. Japanese women seem more worried about stiff shoulders, eyesight problems, fatigue, and irritability (Lock 1993). Indian women report hot flashes, weight gain, bloating of the stomach, headaches, lack of sexual interest, dizzy spells, loss of energy, and constipation (duToit 1993).

The differential report of symptoms supports the view that menopause is both a biological and subjective event defined by culture. Some Arab women report that they are not aware when they reach menopause. Many have been pregnant or

nursing since the onset of menses to menopause (Beyene 1986). Rural Mayan Indian women do not report any symptoms and in fact welcome menopause as a positive transition from childbearing and a time when they may pass many household chores to daughters-in-law (Martin et al. 1993). Lock (1993) reports that some Japanese women separate the experience of cessation of menses and the "change," which is known as *konenki*. Many believe the way in which a woman lives her life can control the symptoms. Interestingly, the view that menopause can be controlled was a belief previously accepted in Western thought before it arose in Japan (Lewis and Bernstein 1996). Some women do make a connection between the end of menstruation and *konenki*. Among Japanese women, neither educational level nor occupation seems to account for the differences. The women who associate the symptoms of *konenki* with the end of menstruation hold beliefs that are more closely related to those of North American women (Lock 1993).

Preparation for Menopause

Preparation for menopause evolves from stories a woman hears or reads about the experience (McAdams 1993). In cultures with taboos against intergenerational communication, communication between the sexes, and open discussions about physical functions, women have only limited opportunities for learning about menopause. Women among Indian South Africans are seldom prepared for menopause (du Toit 1993). There is little discussion or preparation for this women's issue, and consequently women become aware of many myths (duToit 1993). These include the idea that women with no children will have delayed menopause or none at all. Similarly, another myth is that women with many children will experience menopause at a younger age because the uterus is "exhausted" (p. 266). Gabriella Berger (1993) reported that Filipino women may feel less satisfied with themselves as they adopt the Western values of youth and beauty that have been imported from Australia. In many cultures, sometimes women may feel a lack of purpose in society when they are no longer able to reproduce (Spira and Berger 1999).

Women have the opportunity to experience several versions of menopause through relationships with mothers, aunts, grandmothers, and friends, as well as encounters with the culture, media, and health professionals (Spira and Berger 2000). They tend to make the explanations internally consistent with their self-understanding. They may focus on their lost capacity to bear children, the aging process and loss of memory, and the impact these have on their work and social life. Because of the stresses created by these events, some women may become more sensitive to their own adaptive abilities and self-esteem (Kaufert 1982).

Kathryn Hunter (1991) describes how difficult it is for doctors to diagnose menopause based solely on objective measurements of medical symptoms, without the woman's subjective account. Both are important in assessing the need for care. Health professionals must help women to communicate the symptoms in order to anticipate these natural changes. Those who suffer a loss in self-esteem and fear the end of their personal worth need to recognize the biological facts and the cultural influences on their responses. Most of the women report that freedom from childbearing responsibility and the discomfort of monthly periods are welcome aspects of menopause.

Medical Treatment

Most women experience perimenopausal symptoms between the ages of forty-five and fifty-five, with the actual cessation of menstruation as the final chapter. The slowdown of estrogen is thought to contribute to menopausal symptoms. However, culture clearly has a place in the construction of meaning of symptoms. Hot flashes are not prevalent enough in Japan to indicate *konenki,* whereas in the United States and Europe, this is the defining symptom of menopause.

In the United States, endocrine transitions are emphasized in the analysis of menopause, while in Japan, physicians understand the symptoms as functions of the autonomic nervous system. In Japan, medication may be prescribed to improve the hormone system, but treatments are given to improve circulation, which is seen as faulty (Lock 1993).

Medical treatment remains controversial because of the side effects of hormone replacement therapy (Spira and Berger 1999). Many women may be ashamed of their symptoms as an indication of advancing age (and implied loss of role and status). As women assume new roles, unaffected

Medical intervention for the symptoms of menopause remains controversial as all of the side effects of hormone replacement therapy are still unknown. STEPHEN WELSTEAD/CORBIS

by biological change, they may perceive the symptoms of menopause as less important (Spira and Berger 2001).

Conclusion

Menopause, viewed as part of aging, intricately relates the biological, cultural, and social aspects of a woman's life. Women in the cultures described all experience irregular periods and cessation of menses in midlife. However, women relate to the psychological and social aspects of menopause in less universal ways.

Symptomatic relief through medical interventions remains an important aspect of treatment. However, the focus on biomedical concerns does not outweigh the social and psychological expression of internalized cultural attitudes toward aging. The culture is a source of both language and images about aging from which individuals learn to describe their experience. Their concerns extend to the interpersonal realm of relationships between husbands and wives and mothers and daughters, as well as their status in the culture and social system. One aspect is clear: Despite the tangible marker of aging and the impact on identity, many women welcome the end of reproduction as a relief to their bodies and an opportunity for new experiences.

See also: ADULTHOOD; ELDERS; FERTILITY; SELF-ESTEEM; SEXUALITY IN ADULTHOOD

Bibliography

Beyene, Y. (1986). "The Cultural Significance and Physiological Manifestation of Menopause: A Biocultural Analysis." *Culture, Medicine & Psychiatry* 10:47–71.

Bowles, C. (1990). "The Menopausal Experience: Sociocultural Influences and Theoretical Models." In *The Meanings of Menopause,* ed. R. Formanek. Hillsdale, NJ: Analytic Press.

Daton, N. (1990). "Aging Into Transitions: Cross-cultural Perspective on Women at Midlife." In *The Meanings of Menopause,* ed. R. Formanek. New Jersey: Analytic Press.

DuToit, B. (1990). *Aging and Menopause Among Indian South African Women.* Albany, NY: State University of New York Press.

Formanek, R. (1990). "Continuity and Change and the 'Change of life'; Premodern Views of the Menopause." In *The Meanings of Menopause,* ed. R. Formanek. New Jersey: Analytic Press.

Hunter, K. (1991). *Doctors' Stories.* Princeton, NJ: Princeton University Press.

Kaufert, P. A. (1982). "Myth and Menopause." *Sociology of Health and Illness* 4:141–166.

Lewis, J., and Bernstein, J. (1996). *Women's Health: A Relational Perspective Across the Life Cycle.* Sudbury, MA: Jones and Barlett.

Lock, M. (1993). *Encounters with Aging: Mythologies of Menopause in Japan and North America.* Berkeley: University of California Press.

Martin, M.; Block, J.; Sanchez, S.; Arnaud, C.; and Beyene, Y. (1993). "Menopause Without Symptoms Among Rural Mayan Indians." *American Journal of Obstetrics and Gynecology* 168(6 part 1):1839–1845.

McAdams, D. (1993). *The Stories We Live By.* New York: Guilford Press.

Scarf, M. (1980). *Unfinished Business: Pressure Points in the Lives of Women.* Garden City, NY: Doubleday.

Spira, M., and Berger, B. (1999). "The Evolution of Understanding Menopause in Clinical Treatment." *Clinical Social Work Journal* 27(3):259–272.

Spira, M., and Berger, B. (2001). "The Penultimate: Understanding Adult Women Beyond Menopause." *Psychoanalytic Social Work* 8(1):23–37.

Other Resource

Berger, G. (1999) "Study Finds Culture and Menopause Linked." ABC Online News. Available from http://abc.net.au/science/news/stories/s31980.htm.

MARCIA K. SPIRA

MENSTRUAL TABOO

Menstruation, the approximately monthly shedding of the uterine lining in most women of reproductive age, is both a biological event and a cultural event. Biology cannot be separated from culture, and neither is a predetermined category with consistent impact on individual women's lives. Although menstruation is universal, the menstrual taboo is not, despite the claims of some writers. Anthropologists Thomas Buckley and Alma Gottlieb (1998) explain that this popular analysis is both partially true and overly simplistic:

> The "menstrual taboo" as such does not exist. Rather, what is found in close cross-cultural study is a wide range of distinct rules for conduct regarding menstruation that bespeak quite different, even opposite, purposes and meanings. . . . "The menstrual taboo," in short, is at once nearly universal and has meanings that are ambiguous and often multivalent. (p. 7)

Buckley and Gottlieb emphasize that particular practices surrounding menstruation must be interpreted within the cultural context of their enactment. For example, North Americans often assume that menstrual seclusion, the isolation of menstruating women from nonmenstruating members of society, is repressive, while in some practicing cultures, the women value the time away from their regular duties and in the company of other women, as among the Simbu people of Papua New Guinea (Appel-Slingbaum 2000).

In Western industrial societies, the basis of conduct norms and communication about menstruation is the belief that menstruation must remain hidden (Laws 1990). Menstruation must be concealed verbally as well as physically, and communication rules and restrictions permeate and define the concealment and activity taboos. A substantial majority of U.S. adults and adolescents believe that it is socially unacceptable to discuss menstruation, especially in mixed company. Many believe that it is unacceptable to discuss menstruation even within the family (Research & Forecasts 1981). More than one-third of the girls responding to a 1983 questionnaire did not believe that it was appropriate to discuss menstruation with their fathers, and nearly all believed that girls should not talk about menstruation with boys (Williams 1983). Talking about menstruation apparently provokes so much anxiety in adults that parents often delay preparing their pubescent daughters for their impending menarche, the first menstrual period (McKeever 1984; Whisnant and Zegans 1975).

In spite of this anxiety, research findings suggest that most girls get their early information about menstruation from their mothers, and fewer than 10 percent of North American girls begin menstruating without receiving any advance information (Kieren 1992; McKeever 1984). Other important sources of menstrual education and preparation are sex education classes and films at school, female friends, and mass media.

The importance of advance preparation for menarche should not be underestimated. Several studies suggest that girls and women who considered themselves adequately prepared for menarche experienced less distress at menarche and fewer painful menstrual symptoms. However, what counts as adequate preparation for menstruation is unclear, especially given that many girls and women who knew about menstruation and menstrual hygiene report that they did not feel well prepared for menarche (Golub 1992; Kieren 1992).

Interview research suggests that girls perceive a clear distinction between two kinds of menstrual knowledge: scientific knowledge about the anatomy and physiological functioning of menstruation, usually learned from institutional sources, and what they term realistic knowledge—pragmatic information about managing the lived experience of menstruation, always learned from other females. None of the girls interviewed felt that they were lacking in scientific, institutional knowledge about menstruation; but nearly all felt the need for more of the practical, personal menstrual knowledge they gained from mothers and friends. The two kinds of knowledge do not seem to be well integrated, even after girls experience their first periods (Kissling 1996).

For several girls, mothers were a valued source for the personal, pragmatic knowledge about menstruation that they craved. Some girls appreciated these talks, and some were embarrassed by them; all recognized the mother-daughter talk about menstruation as a cultural norm, whether they participated in it or not, referring to it casually as "the

talk." This norm is also illustrated in the commercial menstrual education booklet distributed in some schools, which states, "Of course it would be best to have discussed all this with your mother before your first period actually happens" (Tambrands 1990). Such prescriptions fail to recognize that not all girls have these kinds of conversations or the kinds of relationship with their mothers that promote candid conversations about menstruation and other aspects of sexuality and reproduction.

When interviewed, mothers are unanimous in believing that it is important to tell their daughters about menstruation, although some are frankly relieved that the schools provide information about the biological aspects. Mothers want their daughters to have concrete knowledge about menstrual physiology, but may not be equipped to provide it. Most mothers emphasize the importance of conveying a particular disposition toward menstruation. They are especially concerned that their daughters know that menstruation is a normal, natural part of being female with some variation in whether it is a positive, negative, or neutral experience.

Mothers are communicating attitudes toward menstruation not only in what they tell their daughters, but also in how they discuss it with their daughters. For example, when mothers pull daughters aside for a special facts-of-life talk, they are not only conveying factual information about menstruation, but they are communicating particular ways of thinking about menstruation. These implicit messages may challenge or contradict the explicit verbal messages. For instance, the talk is often overtly marked as an unusual communication situation, sometimes prefaced with a statement like, "We need to talk about some things, now that you're getting older." This marks menstruation as a special topic, not one for ordinary conversation. This special quality may be underscored by having the talk in an unusual setting instead of carrying on a discussion about menstruation during normal shared activities.

Other aspects of the talk reinforce the concealment norms of menstruation. The talk is nearly always one-on-one; younger siblings are excluded, especially brothers. One reason these mother-daughter talks sometimes take place in unusual settings is to enforce this exclusion. Some girls are asked specifically not to discuss menstruation with younger sisters and brothers, or with their fathers.

It is rare for fathers, even single fathers, to initiate the talk, and rarer still for a daughter to feel comfortable with a father who does. Sons may receive the talk about reproduction, but seldom learn much about menstruation from either parent.

Some parents provide their daughters with books or booklets about menstruation, instead of or as a supplement to the conventional mother-daughter talk. Parents also may provide printed material because of perceived complexity of the information. In most families, passing around reading material is not a primary method of communication, so asking a child to read a book about menstruation without prior discussion can suggest to her that the topic is too difficult to talk about, or that it is not appropriate to talk about.

One way mothers try to communicate to daughters the belief that menstruation is a normal, natural part of life is to treat it as one. For instance, one mother recalls that her daughter's menstrual education occurred in "bits and pieces, like if I was in the grocery store and I bought pads or something like that, I might say something like, 'You know, one day you will have to use these also'" (quoted in Kissling 1996). Mothers can answer their children's questions about her cycle, and even mark it on the family calendar.

Mothers who want to normalize menstruation and present it positively find themselves in an awkward position, caught between awareness of the culture's distaste for menstruation and negativity toward menstruating women and a mother's desire to instill positive self-esteem and attitudes toward her body in her daughter. In addition, mothers of adolescent daughters often find their situation an inherently difficult one, as Terri Apter's (1990) study of this relationship explicates:

Nothing shakes a woman's clear commitment to and confidence in motherhood as her children's, especially her daughter's, early adolescence. All studies I know show and repeatedly confirm that mothers and daughters during early adolescence endure increased stress—and there is more tension between mothers and early adolescent daughters than between mothers and early adolescent sons, or between fathers and either early adolescent sons or daughters. (p. 45)

Menarche, the physical marker of feminine maturity, can further complicate a complex relationship. A woman's quandary about preparing her daughter for menstruation may be confounded if she feels she was inadequately prepared for her own menarche. However, dissatisfaction with one's own menstrual education has also inspired women to do a better job with their daughters. Interviewed mothers frequently expressed the wish that their daughters have a better menarcheal experience than their own, and most women make concerted efforts to ensure that they did.

See also: MENARCHE; SEXUAL COMMUNICATION: PARENT-CHILD RELATIONSHIPS; SEXUALITY

Bibliography

Apter, T. (1990). *Altered Loves: Mothers and Daughters During Adolescence*. Hertfordshire, UK: Harvester Wheatsheaf.

Buckley, T., and Gottlieb, A., eds. (1988). *Blood Magic: The Anthropology of Menstruation*. Berkeley: University of California Press.

Gillooly, J. B. (1998). *Before She Gets Her Period: Talking with Your Daughter about Menstruation*. Glendale, CA: Perspective.

Golub, S. (1992). Periods: From Menarche to Menopause. Newbury Park, CA: Sage.

Laws, S. (1990). *Issues of Blood: The Politics of Menstruation*. London: Macmillan.

Kieren, D. K. (1992). Redesigning Menstrual Education Programs Using Attitudes toward Menstruation. *Canadian Home Economics Journal* 42(2):57–63.

Kissling, E. A. (1996). "Bleeding Out Loud: Communication about Menstruation." *Feminism and Psychology* 6:481–504.

McKeever, P. (1984). The Perpetuation of Menstrual Shame. *Women and Health,* 9(4):33–47.

Research & Forecasts, Inc. (1981). *The Tampax Report: Summary of Survey Results on a Study of Attitudes towards Menstruation*. New York: Research and Forecasts.

Tambrands. (1990). *What a Young Girl and Boy Should Know*. Lake Success, NY: Tambrands.

Whisnant, L., and Zegans, L. (1975). "A Study of Attitudes toward Menarche in White Middle-class American Adolescent Girls." *American Journal of Psychiatry* 132:809–814.

Williams, L. R. (1983). "Beliefs and Attitudes of Young Girls Regarding Menstruation." In *Menarche,* ed. Sharon Golub. Lexington, MA: Lexington.

Other Resource

Appel-Slingbaum, Caren. (2000). "The Tradition of Slapping our Daughters." Available from http://www. menstruation.com.au/contributors/slap.html.

ELIZABETH ARVEDA KISSLING

MEXICO

In the Mexican culture, family transcends individuals and generations. The family brings together the past, present, and future through kinship ties and the transmission of member identity. Some of the words used by Mexicans to describe the family evoke an infinite array of images and value representations such as: unity, children, love, home, well-being, parents, understanding, tenderness, education, happiness, and support (Salles and Tuirán, 1997) The family is the place where affection, solidarity, and providing care constitute everyday interaction. The central role given to the family in Mexico is a product of its historic and cultural heritage.

History of the Mexican Family

The pre-Hispanic families in Mexico were Aztec. Aztec families were typically monogamous in character, except in the noble caste, where polygamy was permitted. Marriage for the Aztecs was considered a family affair. Individuals did not have any say in the selection process, and the parents would normally consult a fortuneteller, who could, based on birth dates, predict the future of the marriage. Normally, a pair of older women, called *cihuatlanque*, would negotiate between the families. The tradition called then for a meeting of the girl's family to assess the proposal and obtain permission of all the family members.

After this, the marriage ritual would be celebrated next to the home, with the bride and groom sitting next to each other while they received gifts. The old women would tie a knot in the shirt of the groom and the blouse of the bride.

From that moment on, they were married, and their first activity would be to share a plate of *tamales* (corn-based food). Later, singing and dancing expressed the happiness of the moment, after which the couple would spend four days of prayer in the nuptial room. On the fifth day they would take a bath together in a *temazcal* (traditional bathroom), and a priest would shower them with holy water. A man would follow this ritual only with his first wife, although he could take other wives. Tradition also stressed that a woman should always worry about her appearance and that the male should be the undisputed head of the family (González Gamio 1997).

Clearly, during this period, Aztecs of high caste used polygamy to ensure a steady and growing reproductive rate. However, after the conquest, the Spanish imposed monogamy. By the middle of the eighteenth century, one-fourth of the population was *mestizo* (offspring of one Spanish and one indigenous parent).

The structure of the family in New Spain followed the Spanish tradition of an extended family, which assigned uncles and cousins on both sides of the family the same degree of closeness as parents and siblings. In fact, family identity prescribed, more than any other factor, the position of an individual within a social group, and family loyalty was held as the highest value of that society.

Marriage and family life were governed by the Catholic Church, which allowed individuals to choose their spouses, but required that the couple live together till death. According to the Christian faith, marriage sanctified the family, whose principal objective was to have children and care for them both morally and economically. Within the scheme that prevailed, the father had the divine right and obligation to guide his children toward Catholicism. The mother helped with this task by inculcating the values of love, honesty, and loyalty to the family. Children were expected to honor, love, obey, and respect their parents (González Gamio 1997).

Although the values, norms, and ways of the indigenous groups were never fully destroyed and have always permeated the country's culture, three centuries of Spanish colonization and the political and religious acculturation process imposed during this period carved deeply into the structure and

The contemporary Mexican family represents a mix of indigenous, pre-Hispanic ways of life and Spanish expectations and norms. Values that Mexicans ascribe to the family include unity, love, well-being, and tenderness. MACDUFF EVERTON/ CORBIS

character of the Hispanic-indigenous family (Ramos 1951).

The Contemporary Family

After five centuries of Spanish colonization, the Mexican contemporary family emerged with a distinct culturally hybrid character, which on the surface seemed to incorporate the institutionalization of the Judeo-Christian influence. However, this institution still holds within it an unfinished dialectic between the feelings of indigenous peoples (represented by the traditional feminine subculture), and Spanish expectations and norms (reflected in the masculine *machista* orientation). Thus, the Mexican family continues to live in the center of a national acculturation dialectic (González Pineda 1970), which is evidenced by the way Mexicans construe their interpersonal relationships (Díaz Guerrero 1994), their consciousness, attitudes,

thoughts, feelings, and behaviors towards interaction with other members of their society.

Although most Mexican families have characteristics in common, the Mexican family is not represented by one unique type; a variety of indigenous groups live in Mexico. By 1982, Luis Leñero, a Mexican sociologist, was able to identify more than twenty categories and at least fifty-four types of families by taking into account social context and heritage and its composition and structure, which creates very diverse family interactions and dynamics.

It is estimated that 74.2 percent of contemporary Mexican families fall into a nuclear marriage pattern, while the rest correspond to extended families types (Instituto Nacional de Estadística, Geografía e Informática 2000). Although the relations and structure appear to be nuclear, in practice, they continue to be extended (Sabau García and Jovane 1994). In fact, families are more like clans who give emotional and instrumental support and guidance at all times.

Marriage is so popular that by the time Mexicans are fifty years old, more than 95 percent of them have been married at least once (Salles and Tuirán 1997). The union of these couples is increasingly sanctioned by both church and state (80.5%). Some couples cohabitate without marrying (INEGI 2000). In the early twenty-first century, the average age for marriage was twenty-three for females and twenty-six for males (INEGI 2000). Until the 1980s, men used to wed women who liked to stay home and were feminine, hard working, honest, and simple; since then, attributes like submissiveness have declined in popularity. At the same time, there is a growing tendency to look for women who are faithful, understanding, responsible, and intelligent. The pattern reflects a new conceptualization of women and their role in couple relationships. At the same time, females have maintained their traditional search paradigm and are still looking for hard-working, faithful, good, understanding, and intelligent men (Consejo Nacional de Población 1995).

The profound changes in the attributes that males and females look for in a mate have had a major impact on the family life, which in turn has led to a reestablishment of the Mexican family. Mexicans are marrying older, are starting to forgo religious marriage in favor of legal or free unions, and perceive and interpret relationships in a more egalitarian form. In essence, there is a movement away from some of the traditions and rituals towards more individually based unions. In this world of transition, the families' everyday lives, dynamics, functioning, and organizations have been profoundly altered, creating new forms of conflict and crisis. Families increasingly see the lack of communication, financial difficulties, absence of respect for elders and parents, addictions, lack of closeness, and struggles with the upbringing of children and domestic chores as insurmountable problems (Espinosa Gómez 2000).

Changes of modern life have altered some families for the worse. Physical violence, emotional harassment, and sexual abuse have become more common in the home. Most agencies and researchers postulate that these problems are the product of a challenged machismo, the increase in power struggles within the family, and disputes related to women's double work days. In one in four households in the Mexico City region, both partners are employed (INEGI 1999). As a result of the growing participation of women in economic activities, new forms of family relationships, based on asymmetries and negotiations that were nonexistent in the traditional family structure, have become common. Unfortunately, males have not started to contribute to family chores and childrearing activities as fast as women have moved into the work force, placing a special burden on women. This load has had a negative effect on women's physical and mental health, as well as on the smooth organization, solidarity, and functioning of the family.

The problems of the modern Mexican family do have solutions. A national values survey (Beltrán et al. 1994) showed the emergence of positive beliefs and attitudes toward the gender work revolution. When asked who should take care of household chores, people with higher incomes and education indicated that both males and females should share in the activities. In addition, males with an androgynous personality—a personality that includes at the same time instrumental (intelligent, capable, active) and expressive (courteous, romantic, tender) positive traits—placed a higher value on egalitarian relations and are more willing to share family household responsibilities. With all the changes and the emphasis on individual well-being and personal growth, more nuclear families are separating from their extended families, and second and third marriages are becoming more common.

Stereotypes and Myths about the Mexican Family

The Mexican family has been subject to popular stereotypes, including an extreme machismo and a submissive and powerless woman. This vision is real in some families but is not the norm. In many cases, the moral and psychological strength of women withstands the initial pledge for power of their mates, and women end up with control and authority in all family matters. In a growing number of families, the men do the housework, and the women earn part of the family income (Leñero 1982).

Other stereotypes center on the role of religion in the family, giving it a sacred and ideal tone.

This is reflected in proverbs such as, "what God has united cannot be separated by man," or "you must have as many children as God sends you." These statements have affected the behavior of Mexicans for ages, but are more strongly held in the rural areas, towns, and small cities. However, in spite of the official religious character of the Mexican family, there is a large disparity between religious fervor and the practice of religious values in everyday life. Many do not practice the religion they profess (Bermúdez 1955; Lafarga 1975).

Along with stereotypes there are myths about the Mexican family. These tend to be deeply rooted in the collective memory and are expressed in the form of feelings of cognitive structures that guide the interpretation of events or traditions that confirm group identity. Thus, myths are the vehicles for the creation of beliefs and behavioral patterns of family life. Their origin is in the culture and they influence the values, feelings, and perception of how one should conduct oneself in everyday family activities. Among the most popular and widespread myth systems are:

- Families in the past were more stable and harmonious.
- The only place to satisfy the vital needs of love and protection is the family.
- Family agreement and consensus is natural.
- Virginity should be kept until marriage.
- He who is married wants a house.
- Until death do us part.
- Fidelity exists in marriage.
- Men always say the last word. (Salles and Tuirán 1997)

Mexican Family Historic Sociocultural Premises

The norms that regulate the thoughts, feelings, and behaviors within the Mexican culture, as well as the formation of national character, have been deeply researched and described by Rogelio Díaz Guerrero (1986). His analyses suggest that interpersonal behavior is directed and determined, in part, by the extent to which each subject addresses and believes the cultural dictates. To assess the adherence to the Mexican sociocultural norms, Díaz Guerrero (1982) extracted the historic-sociocultural premises from sayings, proverbs, and other forms of popular communication. Content analysis showed that these proverbs depicted the central position that family plays within this culture. Two basic propositions describe the Mexican family: (a) the power and supremacy of the father, and (b) the love and absolute and necessary sacrifice of the mother. More than 80 percent of those surveyed indicated that these premises were correct and guided their life. Analyses of the responses to the statements yielded a central traditionalism factor called *affiliative obedience versus active self-affirmation*, stressing that "children and people in general should always obey their parents," and that "everyone should love their mother and respect their father," which means children should never disobey parents and should show respect in exchange for security and love from them. From this point of view, Mexico is built on a strict hierarchical structure, where respect for a person reflects the power offered to people with higher social status. In contrast, in the United States, respect was found to be what a person who is on equal terms deserves (Díaz Guerrero and Peck 1963).

The changes related to gender in contemporary Mexican families and the sense of traditionalism are both evident in the *machismo versus virginity-abnegation* factor, which refers to the degree of agreement with statements such as "men are more intelligent than women," "docile women are better," "the father should always be the head of the home," and "women should remain virgins until marriage." This attitude of abnegation reflected that both men and women believed that it was important to first satisfy the needs of others and then of themselves. That is, self-modification is preferred over self-affirmation as a coping style in relationships.

Finally, the importance of *family status quo* and *cultural rigidity* in relation to the roles played by men and women in the family appears in such proverbs as "women always have to be faithful to their husbands," "most girls would prefer to be like their mothers," "women should always be protected," "married women should be faithful to the relationship," "young women should not be out alone at night," and "when parents are strict, children grow up correctly."

Factors that form the sociocultural premises of the Mexican family include not only the rules and norms that specify the relationship patterns, but also the expectations and stereotypes formed by people outside the group. Premises and stereotypes are tendencies in particular groups; they give a general idea of the character of a group, but there are also individual differences. Not all Mexicans defend and live by the sociocultural premises; some rebel against the traditional culture. Mexican students expressed countercultural beliefs when they called for liberty and equality in a culture based on interdependence and respect.

See also: ETHNIC VARIATION/ETHNICITY; GODPARENTS; HISPANIC-AMERICAN FAMILIES; LATIN AMERICA; SPAIN; UNITED STATES

Bibliography

Beltrán, U.; Castaños, F.; Flores, J.; and Meyenberg, Y. (1994). *Los Mexicanos de los noventa: Una encuesta de actitudes y valores.* Parte I, México (mimeograph).

Bermúdez, Ma. E. (1955). *La Vida Familiar del Mexicano.* México: Antigua Librería Robredo.

Consejo Nacional de Población (1995). *Informe preliminar.* México.

Díaz Guerrero, R. (1982). "The Psychology of the Historic-Sociocultural Premises." *Spanish Language Psychology* 2:383–410.

Díaz Guerrero, R. (1986). "Historio-sociocultura y personalidad. Definición y características de los factores en la familia mexicana." *Revista de psicología social y personalidad* 2(1):15-42.

Díaz Guerrero, R. (1994). *La psicología del mexicano: Descubrimiento de la etnopsicología.* México, D.F.: Trillas.

Díaz Guerrero, R., and Peck, R. F. (1963). *Respeto y posición social en dos culturas.* Proceedings of the VII Inter-American Psychology Congress, Mexico City.

Espinoza Gómez, M. M. (2000). "Exploración de los problemas familiares." *La psicología social en México* 8:217–224.

González Gamio, M. de los A. (1997). "Aspectos históricos de la familia en la ciudad de México." In *La familia en la ciudad de México: Presente, pasado y devenir,* ed. L. Solís Pantón. México, D.F.: Miguel Ángel Porrúa.

González Pineda, F. (1970). *El Mexicano: Psicologia de su destructividad.* México, D.F.: Pax México.

Lafarga, J. (1975). "Religiosidad y familia." In *La familia: medio propiciador o inhibidor del desarrollo humano,* ed. E. Dulanto Gutiérrez. México, D.F.: Ediciones Médicas del Hospital Infantil de México.

Leñero Otero, L. (1982). "Familia, sociedad, y cultura." In *El niño y la familia,* ed. F. Nava Saavedra. Compendio del XI Congreso Mundial de la Federación Internacional para la Educación de los Padres organizado por la Asociación Científica de Profesionales para el Estudio Integral del Niño, A. C. México.

Molina, S. (1994). "La historia de la familia como novela". In *Estampas de la familia Mexicana,* ed. Ma. L. Sabau García and Ana Jovane. México, D.F: Impresora Formal, S. A. de C. V.

Ramos, S. (1951). *El perfil del hombre y la cultura en México.* Buenos Aires: Espasa-Calpe.

Sabau García, M. L., and Jovane, A. (1994). *Estampas de la familia Mexicana.* México: Impresora Formal, S. A. de C. V.

Salles, V., and Tuirán, R. (1997). "Mitos y creencias sobre la vida familiar." In *La familia en la ciudad de México: Presente, pasado, y devenir,* ed. L. Solis Panton. México, D.F.: Miguel Ángel Porrúa.

Other Resources

Instituto Nacional de Estadística, Geografía e Informática (INEGI) (1998, 1999, 2000). Censo Nacional de Población. Available from http://www.inegi.gob.mx.

ROZZANA SÁNCHEZ-ARAGÓN

MIDDLE EASTERN FAMILIES

See BEDOUIN-ARAB FAMILIES; EGYPT; ETHNIC VARIATION/ETHNICITY; IRAN; ISLAM; ISRAEL; KURDISH FAMILIES; KYRGYZSTAN; TURKEY

MIGRATION

Migration is a difficult concept to define because it includes people who move for different reasons across different spaces. A migrant can be a person who moves to another city or town within a nation; a refugee who crosses an international border to escape religious or political persecution; a job-seeker who moves to another country for better economic opportunities; a slave who is forcibly moved; or a person displaced by war or natural disaster. Demographers lack a single, operational definition for migration because it occurs under different conditions.

The causes of migration are related to the specific contexts in which they take place. First, the composition of migration streams are characterized by structural forces such as the global economy. Second, sociocultural differentials (gender, class, caste, etc.) have important implications for individual mobility.

Because migration occurs under different circumstances, the demographic implications for receiver populations change accordingly. For example, when large numbers of rural residents migrate to cities, infrastructure problems may arise in urban areas.

Given the variation possible in the migration process, all migrants cannot be analyzed with the same theoretical framework. However, although heterogeneous factors make a universal definition impossible, in general, migration is a process in which an individual or a group shifts their residence from one population (or place) to another. Apart from its spatial dimension, migration also implies the disruption of work, schooling, social life, and other patterns. A migrant is someone who breaks off activities and associations in one place and reorganizes their daily life in another place. A move within the same area is considered mobility, not migration, because the mover can continue day-to-day life (keep the same job or school, shop at the same stores, and socialize with the same people) without significant disruption (Weeks 1999).

Most demographers argue that migration must involve an essentially *permanent* territorial shift in residence to be distinguished from mobility. Hence, travelers and commuters are excluded from migration studies because they move across boundaries on a temporary basis and because their movement does not generally cause major change in any population. Categorizing movers strictly in terms of the permanence of their move can be problematic, however, because this method tends to disregard the social context of population movement. Temporary moves are typically absent from the census, and therefore do not register in demographic terms. In this perspective, a software engineer who makes a permanent move from San Francisco to Los Angeles is classified as a migrant,

while a Mexican arriving in California as a seasonal agricultural laborer is not. However, the agricultural laborer's move is probably the most socially significant given language barriers, culture shock, and race discrimination encountered.

Just because a mover is not *measured* as a member of a population does not mean that their movement has had no measurable social impact on populations. Under the United States's *bracero* program (a system created in 1942 to help solve U.S. agricultural labor shortages), for example, the number of temporary Mexican laborers reached a point that U.S. policy makers reacted with mass deportations and the creation of a restrictive immigration act meant to keep Mexicans out. This policy created severe unemployment problems in Mexico, whose economy was not strong enough to reabsorb these workers. Hence, the program that previously encouraged mobility into the United States contributed to Mexican poverty after it was terminated in 1964. Even though they would not be counted as migrants, the mobility of Mexican agricultural workers left a deep impression on the Mexican economy, and it initiated changes to U.S. immigration policy.

Types of Migration

The relatively permanent movement of people across territorial boundaries is referred to as *in-migration* and *out-migration,* or *immigration* and *emigration* when the boundaries crossed are international. The place of in-migration or immigration is called the *receiver population,* and the place of out-migration or emigration is called the *sender population.* There are two basic types of migration studied by demographers:

(1) *Internal migration.* This refers to a change of residence within national boundaries, such as between states, provinces, cities, or municipalities. An internal migrant is someone who moves to a different administrative territory.

(2) *International migration.* This refers to change of residence over national boundaries. An international migrant is someone who moves to a different country. International migrants are further classified as legal immigrants, illegal immigrants, and

refugees. Legal immigrants are those who moved with the legal permission of the receiver nation, illegal immigrants are those who moved without legal permission, and refugees are those crossed an international boundary to escape persecution.

Jay Weinstein and Vijayan Pillai (2001) denote a third classification: forced migration. Forced migration exists when a person is moved against their will (slaves), or when the move is initiated because of external factors (natural disaster or civil war). The distinction between internal and international migration is crucial because they happen for different reasons. Because structural barriers are more likely to impede the mobility of a potential international migrant than an internal migrant—international migration involves more administrative procedures, greater expense, and more difficulties associated with obtaining employment, accessing state services, learning a new language, and the like—the motivations behind international migration are usually stronger than those behind internal migration (Weeks 1999).

Theories of Migration

People move for different reasons. These differences affect the overall migration process. The conditions under which a migrant enters a receiver population can have broad implications for all parties involved. The expression *migration experience* refers to the fact that different causes for migration will produce different outcomes observable from a sociological perspective. For example, a person who moves within a nation will not have the same migration experience as a political refugee. In most cases, refugees need special services from the receiver population such as emergency shelter, food, and legal aid. The psychological trauma of fleeing their homeland and leaving family members behind can also complicate refugees' adjustment to their new environment. Considering that a migrant can be a slave, refugee, or job-seeker, or have some other reason for moving, no single theory can provide a comprehensive explanation for the migration process.

Although a comprehensive theory is unattainable, it remains a crucial task of demographers to explain why people migrate. Theories of migration are important because they can help us understand population movements within their wider political

and economic contexts. For example, if out-migration from Third World nations is shown to be a result of economic problems caused by the global economy, then such migration could be managed with better international economic agreements instead of restrictive immigration acts. Indeed, rather than slowing Mexican in-migration to the United States, termination of the *bracero* program actually increased the amount of illegal immigration because it exacerbated Mexican poverty.

Ernest Ravenstein is widely regarded as the earliest migration theorist. Ravenstein, an English geographer, used census data from England and Wales to develop his "Laws of Migration" (1889). He concluded that migration was governed by a "push-pull" process; that is, unfavorable conditions in one place (oppressive laws, heavy taxation, etc.) "push" people out, and favorable conditions in an external location "pull" them out. Ravenstein's laws stated that the primary cause for migration was better external economic opportunities; the volume of migration decreases as distance increases; migration occurs in stages instead of one long move; population movements are bilateral; and migration differentials (e.g., gender, social class, age) influence a person's mobility.

Many theorists have followed in Ravenstein's footsteps, and the dominant theories in contemporary scholarship are more or less variations of his conclusions. Everett Lee (1966) reformulated Ravenstein's theory to give more emphasis to internal (or push) factors. Lee also outlined the impact that *intervening obstacles* have on the migration process. He argued that variables such as distance, physical and political barriers, and having dependents can impede or even prevent migration. Lee pointed out that the migration process is selective because differentials such as age, gender, and social class affect how persons respond to push-pull factors, and these conditions also shape their ability to overcome intervening obstacles. Furthermore, personal factors such as a person's education, knowledge of a potential receiver population, family ties, and the like can facilitate or retard migration.

Several theories have been developed to treat international patterns of migration on their own terms, but these too are variants of push-pull theory. First, *neoclassical economic theory* (Sjaastad 1962; Todaro 1969) suggests that international migration is related to the global supply and demand for labor. Nations with scarce labor supply and high demand will have high wages that pull immigrants in from nations with a surplus of labor. Second, *segmented labor-market theory* (Piore 1979) argues that First World economies are structured so as to *require* a certain level of immigration. This theory suggests that developed economies are dualistic: they have a primary market of secure, well-remunerated work and a secondary market of low-wage work. Segmented labor-market theory argues that immigrants are recruited to fill these jobs that are necessary for the overall economy to function but are avoided by the native-born population because of the poor working conditions associated with the secondary labor market. Third, *world-systems theory* (Sassen 1988) argues that international migration is a by-product of global capitalism. Contemporary patterns of international migration tend to be from the periphery (poor nations) to the core (rich nations) because factors associated with industrial development in the First World generated structural economic problems, and thus push factors, in the Third World.

Migration and the Family

Explanatory frameworks premised on the push-pull hypothesis tend to overemphasize the role of the individual in the migration process. Critics of this perspective argue that the decision to migrate is based on group experience, in particular the costs and benefits to the family. Rather than being an isolated calculation, an individual's decision to migrate is conditioned by multiple social and economic factors. For example, a member of a rural family may be motivated to migrate if urban employment translates into the diversification and amelioration of the family economy, or if rural productive resources are not enough to sustain an extended family. Such out-migration probably would not occur if it was likely to produce an economic deficit for the family unit. Apart from this, the decision to migrate is not calculated from an exclusively economic standpoint. An individual can have an economic opportunity in another place, but not take it up if their departure would cause emotional hardship in the sender community. In Sarah Harbison's words, the family "is the structural and functional context within which motivations and values are shaped, human capital is accrued, information is received and interpreted, and decisions are put into operation" (1981, p. 226).

The family is the crucial agent of an individual's capacity and motivation to migrate. Harbison argues that the complexities of the family structure characterize the migration process because the family unit mediates between the individual and society, and thus it can prioritize its needs over the individual's in many instances. Three factors give the family unit significant importance in the migration process (Harbison 1981; Boyd 1989).

(1) Because migration requires resources for transportation and to establish a new home, family support is paramount, especially because most migrants are young and lack sufficient personal savings to finance a move. In most cases, the family unit is the essential unit of economic production and thus determines the allocation of resources to individuals and specifies economic roles. Apart from the economic needs of the family, differential access to family resources and the social division of labor have important implications for individual mobility. The socioeconomic framework of the family can facilitate or restrict migration. In a situation where males control family resources, and females are assigned strict domestic roles in the division of labor, women's mobility will be structurally limited or at least determined by men.

(2) The family is the primary socializing unit. Through the framework of kinship, customs, values, social obligations, and the like, the family unit conditions the individual to fill a basic role in society. For example, in societies where migration is crucial for the putative well-being of the group, patterns of socialization will develop to prepare certain individuals to migrate. The primogeniture system—under which real estate passes to first-born sons—assisted the mobility of later-born sons because they were often provided an education or military placement in lieu of inheritance.

(3) The family is an enabling economic and social network. The geographic dispersion of kin members partially determines the migration destination. Many people move to where they have family members (rather than where economic opportunities are most fruitful) because they can be relied upon to provide food, shelter, and information,

which help them cope with their new environment. The presence of kin will also reduce the psychological impact of culture shock through the perpetuation of old customs in the new place. For these reasons, ethnic groups have tended to concentrate in specific regions and neighborhoods.

Harbison (1981) points out that while the family's function as a subsistence unit, agent of socialization, and support network shapes the motivations and incentives for migration, these are also conditioned by sociocultural factors, such as marriage rules and kinship rights. Of particular importance is the *gender* division of labor. For the most part, migration studies have been gender-blind, and this obviously has serious implications from both a theoretical and an empirical perspective. Many studies (Bjerén 1997; Chant 1992; Kelson and DeLaet 1999) have shown that women's migration experience is fundamentally different from men's. Because gender is a primary organizing principle of the family and society, it follows that gender structures the migration process to a significant degree.

Migration and the Global Economy

Before the international economic downturns that began in the 1970s, the composition of international migration generally held to Ravenstein's hypothesis that the primary motivation for migration was economic, and that young males predominated long-distance travel. Since the 1970s, the pattern of migration has transformed with global economic changes. Moreover, the composition of migration streams transformed because earlier waves of migration created support networks that helped more recent migrants overcome intervening obstacles and difficulties associated with adjusting to a new environment (Boyd 1989). As people settled in new places, they became valuable sources of information and economic assistance for prospective migrants to draw upon. As Monica Boyd (1989) notes, while structural forces form the basic incentives for migration, push-pull factors are filtered through social networks that connect sender and receiver populations. Various patterns of migration (e.g., Mexican immigration to the United States) have become institutionalized as these networks took root.

However, while family contacts often determine *where* migrants move, structural forces remain powerful causal factors. Douglas Massey and colleagues (1994) point out that most empirical evidence suggests that a crucial impetus for international migration is the combination of systemic unemployment in the sender population and good employment prospects in the receiver population. World-systems theorists argue that one effect of globalization has been to keep Third World economies dependent on agriculture and the exportation of raw materials and simple commodities. Slow industrialization and relatively high fertility rates have generated acute unemployment in these nations, and this partially explains why net migration streams have generally flowed in a unilateral (from periphery to core nations) under the global economy. Economic problems associated with globalization have made labor migration an important survival strategy for many Third World families. For some nations labor has become a major export economy, and states have facilitated migration to capitalize on its economic benefits. Shu-Ju Cheng (1999) notes that there were over two million documented Filipino migrant workers worldwide by 1995, and they remitted U.S. $18 billion between 1975 and 1994. Massey and colleagues (1994) point out that Mexican remittances were so great in certain communities that there were more U.S. dollars in circulation than their peso equivalent. In 1995, the total of world remittances from migrant laborers amounted to U.S. $70 billion (Taylor 1999).

Migration connections between rural economies and urban and international labor markets are particularly important for Third World consumption and production. Out-migration from rural populations to external labor markets has stimulated consumption and productivity in many Third World countries. As Massey and colleagues (1994) note, one study of two Mexican rural communities showed that remittances from domestic urban centers and the United States sustained a level of consumption 37 percent higher than gross production therein. J. Edward Taylor (1999) remarks that for every dollar Mexican migrant laborers sent home from the United States, Mexico's Gross National Product (GNP) increased between $2.69 and $3.17. Contrary to neoclassical theory, these studies demonstrate the potential nonunitary impact of labor migration. Besides increasing household consumption, income transfers have had a dynamic impact on some Third World economies. Remittances often initiate economic improvements because they are used for productive investments, and thus increase household incomes, productivity, and the GNP.

See also: GLOBAL CITIZENSHIP; HOME; HOMELESS FAMILIES; IMMIGRATION; INDUSTRIALIZATION; KINSHIP; POVERTY; RURAL FAMILIES; SOCIALIZATION; SOCIOECONOMIC STATUS; STRESS; UNEMPLOYMENT; URBANIZATION; WAR/POLITICAL VIOLENCE; WORK AND FAMILY

Bibliography

Bjerén, G. (1997). "Gender and Reproduction." In *International Migration, Immobility, and Development: Multidisciplinary Perspectives,* ed. T. Hammer, G. Bruchmann, K. Tomas, and T. Faist. Oxford, UK: Berg.

Boyd, M. (1989). "Family and Personal Networks In International Migration: Recent Developments and New Agendas." *International Migration Review* 23:638–70.

Chant, S., ed. (1992). *Gender and Migration in Developing Countries.* London: Belhaven Press.

Cheng, S. A. (1999). "Labor Migration and International Sexual Division of Labor: A Feminist Perspective." In *Gender and Immigration,* ed. G. A. Kelson and D. L. DeLaet. New York: New York University Press.

Harbison, S. F. (1981). "Family Structure and Family Strategy in Migration Decision Making." In *Migration Decision Making: Multidisciplinary Approaches to Microlevel Studies in Developed and Developing Countries,* ed. G. F. DeJong and R. W. Gardner. New York: Pergamon Press.

Kelson, G. A., and D. L. Delaet, eds. (1999). *Gender and Immigration.* New York: New York University Press.

Lee, E. (1966). "A Theory of Migration." *Demography* 3:47–57.

Massey, D. S.: Arango, J.; Hugo, G.; Kouaouci, A.; Pellegrino, A; and Taylor, J. (1994). "An Evaluation of International Migration Theory: The North American Case." *Population and Development Review* 20:699–751.

Piore, M. J. (1979). *Birds of Passage: Migrant Labour in Industrial Societies.* New York: Cambridge University Press.

Ravenstein, E. G. (1889). "The Laws of Migration." *Journal of the Royal Statistical Society* 52:245–301.

Sassen, S. (1988). *The Mobility of Labour and Capital: A Study in International Investment and Labour Flow.* Cambridge, UK: Cambridge University Press.

Sjaastad, L. A. (1962). "The Costs and Returns of Human Migration." *Journal of Political Economy* 70:80–93.

Taylor, J. E. (1999). "The New Economics of Labour Migration and the Role of Remittances in the Migration Process." *International Migration* 37:63–88.

Todaro, M. P. (1969). "A Model of Labor Migration and Urban Unemployment in Less-Developed Countries." *The American Economic Review* 59:138–48.

Weeks, J. R. (1999). *Population: An Introduction to Concepts and Issues.* Boston: Wadsworth.

Weinstein, J., and Pillai, V. K. (2001). *Demography: The Science of Population.* Boston: Allyn and Bacon.

ZHENG WU

MISSING CHILDREN

A missing child is the ultimate nightmare for parents of every nation—a nightmare imprinted on parents' consciousness by widely publicized abductions in the late twenty and early twenty-first centuries. However, missing persons rarely become the victims of foul play, because although missing-person cases are reported in record numbers, these cases have also been resolved in record numbers.

Several highly publicized abductions and murders in the United States during the 1970s and 1980s brought increased attention to missing children and made it a national concern (Gentry 1988). In response, the U.S. Congress enacted the Missing Children Act in 1982 and the Missing Children's Assistance Act in 1984 (Welsberg 1984). These acts required the Office of Juvenile Justice and Delinquency Prevention (OJJDP) to collect data. The first National Incidence Studies of Missing, Abducted, Runaway and Thrownaway Children (NISMART 1) was conducted in 1988, followed by NISMART 2 in 2000 (Hanson 2000). In the second study, missing children were classified into the following categories: runaway/thrownaway, nonfamily abduction, family abduction, custodial interference, lost and involuntarily missing, missing due to injury, missing due to false alarm situations, and sexually assaulted.

Thrownaways are children who did not leave home voluntarily, but were abandoned or forced from their homes by parents or guardians. *Nonfamily abductions* are children taken by nonrelatives without the knowledge or consent of parents or legal guardians. *Family abductions* are children taken from or not returned to their residence by a parent or relative (or their agent) in violation of legal or custody agreements. Children who are lost and *involuntarily missing* and who fail to return home or contact their parents or guardians are classified as missing if the caretaker becomes alarmed and tries to locate them. Children *missing due to injury* are children who fail to return or make contact with their parents or guardians because they have suffered serious injuries that require medical attention. Children *missing due to false alarm situations* are so labeled when caretakers report them missing because of a miscommunication between caretakers (Hanson 2000).

Throwaways are theoretically different but in practice are almost impossible to distinguish from runaways. Children missing because they are lost, injured, or because of miscommunication are usually in situations difficult to avoid and are found quickly. The majority of the 450,000 children reported to police as missing each year are lost or have run away and their cases resolved with minimal effort by law enforcement (Lord, Boudreaux, and Lanning 2001). The categories of missing children examined in this entry are nonfamily and family abductions.

Abductions by strangers understandably receive the most attention and generate the most fear; however, such kidnappings are only a small proportion of the number of missing children reported in the United States. Runaway is the largest category, followed by family abductions, and nonfamily abductions. Abductions by family members, ranging from 183,200 to 354,100 annually, represent the most prevalent child abduction type. In contrast, child abductions perpetrated by nonfamily members are significantly fewer, ranging from 3,200 to 4,600 cases annually, with 62 percent of these committed by strangers. Long-term stranger abductions of children from birth to eighteen, where serious risk of victim mortality exists, only account for 200 to 300 cases annually (Lord, Boudreaux, and Lanning 2001).

The absence of reliable statistics about kidnapping in the United States, which are not included in the Federal Bureau of Investigation's Uniform Crime Report (UCR), makes determining the threat of kidnapping to juveniles difficult. However, a comprehensive national database on kidnapping and other crimes is beginning to emerge. In partnership with the Bureau of Justice Statistics, the Federal Bureau of Investigation (FBI) is replacing the UCR with the more comprehensive National Incident-Based Reporting System (NIBRS), which collects information on crimes known to the police, such as the inclusion of specific data on kidnapping. When only kidnapping of juveniles is considered, 49 percent is by a family member, 27 percent by an acquaintance, and 24 percent by a stranger (Finkelhor and Ormrod 2000).

Family Abductions

Although U.S. custody laws vary from state to state, abducting one's own child is a crime in every state. When a family member takes or keeps a child away from the parent with custody or visitation rights, that person may have committed a crime. However, some states require that a custody order be in place for the act to be considered criminal. More importantly, seeing open conflict in their family, spending life on the run, and being deprived of a parent is psychologically harmful to a child (Johnston et al. 2001).

Family abductions are most frequently motivated by domestic discord and custody disputes. Abducting parents typically fit one of six different profiles.

Profile 1 abductors are family members who have made credible threats in the past and/or have a history of withholding visitation or kidnapping the child. The parent may be unemployed and have no emotional or financial ties to the area. Alternatively, the parent may have divulged plans to abduct the child and have the financial and emotional resources to survive in hiding. The abducting parent may have liquidated assets and borrowed the maximum from all sources.

The *Profile 2 abductor* is one who believes the other parent is abusing, molesting, or neglecting the child and will continue to do so. Family and friends support the parent in this belief. The allegations of sexual abuse by a parent or stepparent that motivate the noncustodial parent to abduct are frequently unsubstantiated.

The *Profile 3 abductor* suffers from paranoid delusions, and represents the greatest risk of harm or death to the child. Although these are the smallest percentage of abductors, they have psychotic delusions that the other parent will definitely harm them or the child. They perceive the child not as a separate entity but either as a part of themselves needing rescue or as a part of the other parent, which can lead to murder and suicide.

Profile 4 abductors are severely sociopathic and relatively rare. Characterized by a long history of flagrant violations of the law and contempt for authority, they relate to others in a self-serving, exploitative, and manipulative manner. They feel superior and would have no qualms about abusing or abducting their child and feel they should not be punished for it.

Profile 5 abductors are parents in a mixed-culture family with strong ties to their country of origin and to extended family there. During times of separation or divorce, they feel abandoned in their new culture and wish to return to their ethnic or religious roots to find emotional support and to reconstitute their self-identity. Returning with the child to the family and country of origin is a way of giving the abducting parent's cultural identity preeminent status in the child's upbringing.

Profile 6 abductors feel isolated from the judicial system in several different ways. They may be indigent and uneducated without knowledge of custody and abduction laws. They may not be able to afford the court system or have had negative experiences with it. Some parents belong to religious or ethnic groups that hold views about rearing children and custody rights contrary to law. A mother who had a transient, unmarried relationship with the child's father may be unaware that the father has any rights and may be supported in that belief by her family and friends. Parents who have been the victims of domestic violence and who received no help through the law are also likely abductors (Johnston et al. 2001).

Nonfamily Abductions

Although *nonfamily abductions* are relatively rare, they are the worst fear of most relatives of children. Long-term nonfamily abductions are typically motivated by sexual gratification, retribution, financial gain, desire to kill, and maternal desire. *Sexually motivated abductions* represent the most common type of nonfamily abduction and pose the highest risk of victim mortality (Lord, Boudreaux, and Lanning 2001).

The National Center for Missing and Exploited Children in the United States reports that most abductors tend to be white males between the ages of twenty and forty. They are loners who have difficulty interacting with adults and tend not to be married (Stepp 1994). For example, a former Long Island policeman who trains police officers for NCMEC says the typical kidnapper is a twenty-seven-year-old white male, a transient construction worker or day laborer with marginal social skills, often the "guy next door" (Ragavan 2001).

Examining the profile of the victims reveals that nearly 60 percent are juveniles, and 55 percent are female (Ragavan 2001). Due to their physical, emotional, and cognitive dependence on adults, children remain uniquely susceptible to abuse, neglect, and exploitation, which makes them vulnerable to a variety of offenders who may abuse and exploit them for such reasons as sex, revenge, and/or profit (Lord, Boudreaux, and Lanning 2001). Girls and adolescents twelve and older are more vulnerable than boys and young children (Stepp 1994).

Research (Lord, Boudreaux, and Lanning 2001) supports the following child abduction typologies by age:

Newborn (birth to one month) abductions take two forms. The first, *maternal desire abduction,* generally involves a female stranger abducting a young victim to rear as her own. These abductions usually occur at a hospital that the perpetrator has repeatedly walked through. She usually fakes a pregnancy to prepare others for the baby's sudden appearance. Therefore, the race of the victim must match that of the abductor. The second type of infant abduction, *emotion-based abduction,* usually results from anger, frustration, revenge, or retribution. The biological mother, the most frequent offender, may seek revenge on the other parent by abducting the child. The abduction often hides the death of the child—usually disposed of close to home.

Infants (1–12 months) comprise the second category of child abduction. Maternal desire abductions become less frequent, as a two-month-old infant is more likely to draw the attention of outsiders to the actual age of the baby. Most of these abductions are emotion based. Males face a higher risk of victimization, and males, usually the biological father, are the perpetrators in these

A bulletin board at a police station in Haight Ashbury in 1967, filled with pictures of missing juveniles sent by parents worried that their children were "flower children" living on the streets of San Francisco. BETTMANN/CORBIS

cases. These abductions usually result in the death of the child, usually on impulse, and the body of the child is disposed of close to home in a familiar, yet private, area of the family's property.

Preschool children (3–5 years) comprise the third category. Preschoolers are not always in parental view because of their increased mobility. Sexual crimes are one of the causes of abductions usually by strangers or acquaintances, not by parents. The victims are usually female, and the race of the child and abductor usually match the local demographics. The preschool child is usually abducted from their yard by a male who is an acquaintance of the victim, commonly a neighbor with a history of sexual misconduct. Profit based offenses—drug related or ransom—involving preschool children are rare. Some are emotion based, usually involving the father or boyfriend. When the

offender kills the child, the body is usually found within a hundred yards of the home.

Elementary and middle-school children (6–14 years) constitute the fourth category. Victimization rates triple for this age, and school-age females are at least three times more likely than males to be abducted and murdered. Sex is the major reason for abduction, usually by a male perpetrator with a history of sexual misconduct, violence, and substance abuse. The abductor may be an acquaintance or a stranger but rarely a family member. With middle-school children, the abductors are mostly likely to be strangers. Schoolyard access, physical maturity, and vulnerability help facilitate these abductions by strangers. Unlike familial abductions, the bodies of these children are usually found unconcealed or only slightly covered.

High school children and older teens (15–17 years) comprise the final category. Profit-

and emotion-based offenses are more prevalent in this group, perhaps due to the possession of money or other valuables, as well as an increase in the availability of drugs. Profit-based abduction usually victimizes males and involves the sale and distribution of drugs. Emotion-based crimes are similar to domestic violence and typically involve teenage females abused by boyfriends, ex-boyfriends, or stalkers. Sexually motivated crimes involve a female victim and a male offender—usually either a stranger or an acquaintance of the victim—who abducts the victim in a public area away from the victim's home. When murdered, the victim's remains are usually found within five miles of the home, slightly covered or not covered at all (Lord, Boudreaux, and Lanning 2001).

International

International abductions increased dramatically in 2000 with 1,697 cases, a 67 percent increase over 1999. In such cases the FBI, the Customs Service, the Secret Service, and Interpol become involved. 1,374 children of the 1,697 abducted were located (Ragavan 2001). Interpol is a 178-nation police communications network that enables police forces around the world to coordinate international criminal investigations. The FBI is the U.S. law enforcement agency responsible for investigating international parental kidnapping cases. The FBI legal attaché stationed at U.S. embassies abroad may try to confirm the location of the abductor and the child and may request assistance from local law enforcement personnel in that country (National Criminal Justice Reference Service [NCJRS] 2002).

The International Centre for Missing and Exploited Children (ICMEC) was launched in 1999 as a global response to the problems of international child abduction and child sexual exploitation. This global network transmits images, which are updated daily, of missing and exploited children via the Internet. It currently features over 2,600 children from eleven participating countries (Allen 2001). Because ICMEC includes exploited children in their data, these numbers do not correspond directly to the Interpol figure of 1,697 international cases.

Although some juveniles are abducted for prostitution or domestic help, most international abductions consist of family abductions. Children are vulnerable to international abduction when relations between parents are problematic and one spouse has close ties to another country—particularly one with laws prejudicial against the gender or citizenship of the other parent. It is important to know the laws and customs of a country before visiting. Abduction may occur when the abducting parent visits his or her (usually his) homeland and decides he wants to stay, making it extremely difficult for the mother to return with the children. Many countries, including the United States, consider both parents to have equal legal custody if there is no custody decree prior to the abduction. Therefore, ensuring that the custody decree prohibits a child traveling abroad without the custodial parent's permission is important.

The parent whose child has been abducted cannot expect much help from his or her own government. Since the late 1970s, the Department of State's Office of Children's Issues have been contacted in the cases of approximately 16,000 children either abducted from the United States or prevented from returning to the United States by one of their parents. However, the U.S. State Department only acts as a information resource by attempting to locate and contact the child, providing the parent information about the other country, and completing applications for The Hague Convention on the Civil Aspects of International Child Abduction. The U.S. government does not intervene in civil legal matters, enforce U.S. custody agreements overseas, pay legal fees, act as a lawyer, or take custody of children (U.S. Department of State 2001).

However, twenty-three nations agreed to draft a convention to deter international child abduction at the Hague Conference on Private International Law in 1976, and by July 2001 fifty-four other countries had accepted the Convention, including the United States. These countries agreed that a child who is habitually resident in one party country, and who has been removed to or retained in another party country in violation of the other parent's custodial rights, shall be promptly returned to the country of habitual residence (not necessarily that of citizenship). Thus, the Convention is a legal mechanism available to parents seeking the return of or access to their child; it can also help a parent exercise visitation rights abroad. Parents do not need a custody decree to use the Convention, but there is a time limit of one year, so the parent should contact their government immediately after the abduction.

A new U.S. law took effect in July 2001 that requires the signature of both parents prior to issuance of passports to children under the age of fourteen, but the United States cannot revoke a passport already issued (U.S. Department of State 2001). Without exit controls at the border, there is no way to stop someone with valid travel documents from leaving. Many countries do not require passports, so a birth certificate may allow a child to travel outside the country without parental consent. Although many children in these multinational families possess dual citizenship, those with only U.S. citizenship may have a request written in their passport that no visa be offered for that country. No international law requires compliance with such requests.

Abductions in progress can sometimes be stopped at a border or airport. Interdiction usually depends upon the existence of a criminal warrant for the abductor. Governments may be responsive to a Hague application if it is transmitted as urgent (NCJRS 2002).

Although some abducting parents return the child voluntarily when they learn that a Hague application has been or will be filed, the majority of Hague cases require the custodial parent to hire an attorney in the country where the child has been retained and petition the court there for the child's return. Children are recovered through private lawsuits in countries not party to the Hague Convention. Parents generally retain lawyers in the foreign country as well as their home country to assist with the proceedings (NCJRS 2002).

Causes

Changes facilitating the increase in abductions in the United States are (1) the increase in two-career parents and single heads of households that leave more children home alone; (2) urbanization, suburbanization, and the geographic mobility of today's workforce that lead families to move into communities with no family or friends to provide a safety net for children; (3) inadequate criminal data banks that make running background checks on would-be abusers difficult for schools, daycare, and youth organizations; and (4) the lack of cooperation between governmental agencies

that impedes tracing abductors across state lines (Stepp 1994).

Prevention and Recovery

To prevent abductions, a parent or caregiver should

- Know where the child is;

- Never leave a small child alone at home or in the car;

- Know the child's friends, their parents, and where they live; and

- Be alert to people paying special attention to the child.

If a child is abducted, it is important for the parent to give the best description of the child, clothes, jewelry, along with any pictures of the same, to law enforcement officials. Nothing should be touched or removed from the child's room or from the home that might have the child's fingerprints, DNA, or scent on it. (Fairview Heights Police Department 2002).

The International Centre for Missing and Exploited Children (ICMEC) website is helpful here. It receives more than 2.8 million hits per day. The network, made up of numerous websites sharing multilingual search databases, serves as an international resource for families and for law enforcement. It connects to websites in Belgium, Brazil, Canada, Chile, Italy, the Netherlands, South Africa, the United Kingdom, and the United States. These websites allow the filing of missing child descriptions within each of the above-listed countries and for searches in those countries.

If each nation and the international community work out cooperative agreements to track, find and retrieve missing children, work to strengthen families that protect women and children, alleviate abuse and teach precautions, fewer children will appear in the *missing* categories, and many of those who do will remain there for a shorter period of time.

See also: GRIEF, LOSS, AND BEREAVEMENT; RUNAWAY YOUTHS

Bibliography

Finkelhor, D., and R. Ormrod. (2000). "Kidnapping of Juveniles: Patterns from NIBRS." *Juvenile Justice Bulletin* (June 2000):1–7.

Gentry, C. (1988). "The Social Construction of Abducted Children as a Social Problem." *Sociological Inquiry* 58:413–425.

Hanson, L. (2000). "Second Comprehensive Study of Missing Children." *Juvenile Justice Bulletin.* (April 2000):1–5.

Johnston, J .R.; Sagatun-Edwards, I.; Blomquist, M. E.; and Girdner, L. K. (2001). "Early Identification of Risk Factors for Parental Abduction." *Juvenile Justice Bulletin.* (March 2001):1–11.

Loken, G. (1995). "Missing Children." In *Encyclopedia of Marriage and Family,* ed. David Levinson. New York; London: Macmillan.

Lord, W. D.; Boudreaux, M. C.; and Lanning, K. V. (2001). "Investigating Potential Child Abduction Cases: A Developmental Perspective." *FBI Law Enforcement Bulletin* 70:1–10.

Ragavan, C. (2001). "Lost and Found." *U.S. News and World Report* 131:12–18.

Stepp, L. S. (1994). "Missing Children: The Ultimate Nightmare." *Parents* 69:47–52.

Welsberg, D. K. (1984). "Children of the Night: The Adequacy of Statutory Treatment of Juvenile Prostitution." *American Journal of Criminal Law* 12:1–67.

Other Resources

National Criminal Justice Reference Service [NCJRS]. (2002). *Report to the Attorney General on International Parental Kidnapping*: "Section 3." Available from http://www.ncjrs.org/html/ojjdp/ojjdp_report_jp_kidnapping/section3b.html.

Fairview Heights Police Department. "Protecting Our Children from Abductions." Available from http://www.fhpd.co.st-clair.il.us/.

U.S. Department of State. (2001). *International Parental Child Abduction.* Available from http://travel.state.gov/int'lchildabduction.html.

TILLMAN RODABOUGH
ELIZABETH KELLY

MORMONISM

The Church of Jesus Christ of Latter-day Saints was established in 1830. By the year 2000, there were more than 11 million church members, who are commonly referred to as Latter-day Saints (LDS) or Mormons. International expansion of the church has been significant since 1960 when 90 percent of the membership lived in the United States. In 1999, only 12 percent of Latter-day Saints lived in Utah, the world headquarters of the church; 52 percent of members lived outside the United States in more than 160 countries. South America, Central America, and Mexico contain more than 60 percent of new church members; 9 percent also come from Asian countries (Heaton 1992). In 2000, the church reached an historic milestone of having more non-English-speaking than English-speaking members (Todd 2000).

Mormon Beliefs and Practices

One of the distinctive aspects of the Church of Jesus Christ of Latter-day Saints is the centrality of marriage and the family in its theological doctrine. The church teaches that all humankind are brother and sister—literally spiritual offspring of heavenly parents—and that life on earth ideally follows this heavenly pre-earth pattern. One of the church's primary purposes is to teach family ideals and preserve traditional family relationships through gospel ordinances, including eternal marriage. "The family is ordained of God. Marriage between man and woman is essential to His eternal plan. . . . Happiness in family life is most likely to be achieved when founded upon the teachings of the Lord Jesus Christ" (The Family 1995, p.102).

Eternal marriage. Most prominent among Mormon family-centered beliefs is the conviction that the family unit can be eternal. Eternal marriage is necessary to fulfill one's highest spiritual potential as a son or daughter of God. To achieve this goal, couples must have their wedding performed in a Latter-day Saint temple (or have their marriage solemnized in a temple, if they were previously married elsewhere). In temples, authorized temple workers join couples in matrimony "for time and all eternity" rather than "till death do us part." This highest of all temple rites, temple sealing, symbolizes that the husband and wife become bound to each other in a union that even death cannot dissolve. If couples remain true to their spiritual covenants, they are promised that their marriage can last throughout eternity.

Those who never married during their lives or who never had their marriage solemnized in a temple may still have an eternal marriage. Although

Joseph Smith founded the Church of Jesus Christ of Latter-Day Saints in 1830. THE LIBRARY OF CONGRESS

Jesus taught that individuals do not marry in the next life, the Mormon doctrine holds that he has provided a way for the living to do this work vicariously for the deceased. The Church is known for its vast genealogical resources that help Latter-day Saint members identify ancestors for whom essential ordinances (like baptism or the temple sealing) were never performed. Members stand as temple proxies for those who did not receive the ordinances during life. This *work for the dead* is a critical aspect of salvation: "For their salvation is necessary and essential to our salvation . . ." (Doctrine and Covenants 128:15). The Mormon belief is that God provides opportunities for all of his children, alive and deceased, to receive these essential ordinances.

Premarital preparation. Latter-day Saint youth are encouraged to prepare for future temple sealing. They are counseled to avoid dating before the age of sixteen. They are taught to reserve sex for marriage because premarital and extramarital sex is a violation of the sacred use of one's sexuality.

Latter-day Saint youth have lower rates of premarital sex than do their peers who are not Latter-day Saints (Heaton, Goodman, and Holman 1994). LDS youth are also cautioned against activities that may negatively affect their desire and spiritual worthiness to serve as missionaries when they reach young adulthood.

For a period of eighteen to twenty-four months, young men and women in their late teens and early twenties postpone their personal interests (including dating) to devote their time entirely to gospel teaching. The experience of missionary service can be life-altering, giving young people a more solid foundation upon which to build a successful marriage and family (Parry 1994). Allen W. Litchfield, Darwin L. Thomas, and Bing Dao Li (1997) found that private religious behavior, rather than public practice, is the best predictor of future religious plans. LDS missions were found to facilitate internalization of religious values.

Gender roles and parenthood. The Church of Jesus Christ of Latter-day Saints teaches that gender roles of men and women are distinct but equal. Fathers preside as the providers and protectors of their families. Mothers are the primary caregivers to nurture children with love, sensitivity, and spirituality. Men are taught that their highest calling is their role as a father. Fathers bless, heal, comfort, and guide their family members. Likewise, nothing in a woman's life is to take higher priority than family responsibilities.

Though separate, male and female gender roles complement one another. Spouses are encouraged to help one another as equals. Similarly, raising children is a sacred stewardship, a privilege that draws couples nearer to God and brings life's greatest blessings and responsibilities. The church does not give specific direction to couples about the number and spacing of children, including contraceptive use in family planning. The church also does not teach that sexual intimacy in marriage is only for procreation. Couples are taught that they should welcome children into their family circle. As a result, the Latter-day Saints are known as a childbearing people, with higher fertility rates than couples who are not Latter-day Saints (Heaton 1986). In cross-national comparisons on fertility, Tim B. Heaton (1989) found that although pronatalism is a persistent theme in Mormonism, "the expression of that theme is different in each country" (p. 410).

Myths about Mormon Beliefs and Practices

Since many of the teachings of the Church of Jesus Christ of Latter-day Saints about marriage and family are unique, misunderstanding and confusion about Mormon beliefs and practices may arise. Some of the myths about the church include those of polygamy and subjugation of women.

Polygamy. One of the church's "most controversial and least understood" (Bachman and Esplin 1992, p. 1091) practices was the polygamous marriage of a man to more than one wife, which was practiced in the church as early as the 1840s. Mormons, like the ancient patriarchs of biblical times, practiced plural marriage in obedience to God. Church leaders strictly regulated plural marriage within its membership. It was not a license for illicit sexual relationships; only 20 to 25 percent of LDS adults practiced polygamy. "At its height, plural marriage probably involved only a third of the women reaching marriageable age" (Bachman and Esplin 1992, p. 1095).

Latter-day Saints believed that the practice of plural marriage was protected under the United States Constitution's First Amendment guarantee of free exercise of religion. However, the United States Supreme Court in 1890 upheld the antipolygamy policies of the Edmunds-Tucker Act of 1887. Civil rights were denied to people living in polygamous unions; fines and imprisonment were imposed; Mormons were barred from public office and voting. The Edmunds-Tucker Act disincorporated the church and authorized confiscation of church properties. Seizure of Latter-day Saint temples was threatened. The church faced political and economic destruction (Davis 1992).

President Wilford Woodruff in the Manifesto of 1890 (Official Declaration 1) formally discontinued the church practice of polygamy. Members accepted discontinuance of the practice of plural marriage as the will of God. Since the early 1900s, those within the church who enter into polygamous marriages have been subject to excommunication.

Subjugation of women. One of the unique beliefs of the Church of Jesus Christ of Latter-day Saints is that neither gender can obtain the highest ordinances and spiritual blessings without the other.

Husband and wife receive these highest temple ordinances "together and equally, or not at all" (Nelson 1999, p.38). Neither man nor woman can attain their full divine potential without the other. Linking the woman with the man in marriage is perceived by some as relegation of women to the private rather than the public sphere and is interpreted as patriarchal subjugation of women (Cornwall 1994).

From the earliest days of the church, both women and men have participated in all church matters presented to the membership for vote (Smith and Thomas 1992). Although Utah women were enfranchised in 1870, the antipolygamy Edmonds-Tucker Act of 1887 disenfranchised all Utah women. It was believed that Utah women were oppressed by patriarchy and would vote as instructed by their husbands. Mormon women joined with eastern suffragists, such as Susan B. Anthony, to oppose the section of the antipolygamy legislation that repealed Utah women's suffrage. In 1896, Utah became the third state to join the Union with equal voting rights for women (Madsen 1992).

Marie Cornwall (1994) purports that there was more institutional responsibility and autonomy for women in early Mormonism. She suggests that the church's "hierarchical structure and emphasis on distinct gender roles restricts women's contribution, assigns them to a particular sphere, and adds to their silence and invisibility" (p. 262). Lawrence R. Iannaccone and Carrie A. Miles (1990) examined how the church responded to U.S. women's change in gender roles and conclude that "the Church has managed to accommodate change without appearing to abandon its ideals . . . [and to] exercise flexibility in practice while maintaining purity of doctrine" (p. 1245).

Although the stereotypic image of the Mormon woman is that of the "unquestioning and dutiful housewife," the reality is more complex. Not all LDS women fit the stereotype. Rather, they vary in political beliefs, party affiliations, and attitudes toward authority (Presley, Weaver, and Weaver 1986). LDS women differentially find ways to negotiate their identity and place in religious congregations and society. "To view the religious participation of LDS women in a static manner would fail to capture the rich diversity of the different ways in which they exercise agency at multiple levels, and in diverse ways over the course of their lives" (Beaman 2001, p. 84).

Although employment participation rates for LDS women have been found to be similar to the national average, research by Bruce A. Chadwick and H. Dean Garrett (1995) supports "the hypothesis that religiosity, as measured by beliefs and private worship, is moderately related to lower employment among LDS women" (p. 288). Employment by LDS women is also related to lower participation in religious activities. This should not be interpreted however to "mean that all religious women are housewives or that all employed women have lost their faith and left the church. . . . [Some women are able to] maintain their religiosity in spite of the time demands of full-time employment" (p. 291).

Strengthening LDS Families

The Church of Jesus Christ of Latter-day Saints is unapologetic in declaring its divine mandate to preserve what it views as the traditional family unit. The ideal family composition is believed to be a faithful husband and wife sealed eternally together with their children in the temple, who then each lovingly magnify their divinely appointed gender roles (Scott 2001). However, as church membership becomes increasingly international, family structure is becoming more diverse. For example, statistics show that the idealized family sealed in the temple describes only one in five LDS families in the United States and less than 5 percent of LDS families in Mexico (Heaton 1992). To nurture the ideal LDS family, the church doubled its number of operating Latter-day Saint temples worldwide from fifty temples in 1997 to one hundred temples in 2000. With the complexity and challenges of present-day reality, no family lives perfectly true to the ideal. Adaptations are required due to individual circumstances, such as divorce, disability, or death (The Family 1995).

Despite falling short of the ideal, research (Heaton, Goodman, and Holman 1994) finds that Mormons, compared to other U.S. families, are more likely to marry, less likely to divorce, less likely to have cohabited, and more disapproving of extramarital sex. Other comparisons, however, show similarities between Mormons and those of other religious traditions in marital interaction, time spent with children, evaluation of roles, disagreement, and conflict.

The church holds up the ideal, counseling its members to reach toward it through obedience to gospel principles (Scott 2001). The church, however, does not only teach principles; it provides support and resources to assist families to approach the ideal. This is consistent with cautions raised decades earlier by Darwin L. Thomas (1983) as he looked to the future of the Mormon family. He recommended that the church provide additional support and resources to families coping with the strain of increasing differences between Mormon beliefs and contemporary societal beliefs.

Latter-day Saints are taught to integrate gospel principles into everyday family life, through daily family prayer and scripture study. Families are encouraged to gather on Monday nights for family home evening to participate in spiritual and educational lessons, music, family activities, fun, planning, and councils to build family unity and to solve special challenges and needs. In addition to receiving regular instruction at church and in other meetings, Latter-day Saints receive monthly personal contacts from assigned home visitors offering teachings and support in fulfilling family duties. All age groups in the church are further supported through activities in their respective priesthood quorums and auxiliaries. Leaders counsel, assess special needs, and match Latter-day Saint members with resources that support family growth. Church resources supplement the self-reliant efforts of individuals and families to meet their own family needs. Families take care of themselves and share their resources in caring for others in need.

Promoting Family Well-Being Worldwide

The church not only supports Latter-day Saint families with its programs and activities, but it also promotes traditional family well-being worldwide. One of the church's initial family outreach efforts was its public service radio and television spots advocating for family solidarity. These continuing messages, entitled *Homefront,* began in 1971 and have helped establish the church worldwide as a pro-family proponent. The church's promotion of family well-being has become bolder, despite criticism and hostility by some individuals and groups. For example, O. Kendall White, Jr., (1986) identifies the Mormon belief that neither the man or woman is complete without the other as the ideology that places the church in opposition to modern feminist and gay social movements.

The church believes it has a God-given mandate to preserve the traditional family unit worldwide. Church President Gordon B. Hinckley defends the church's opposition to efforts to legalize same-sex marriage: "This is not a matter of civil rights; it is a matter of morality. . . . We believe that defending this sacred institution by working to preserve traditional marriage lies clearly within our religious and constitutional prerogatives. Indeed, we are compelled by our doctrine to speak out" (1999, p. 52).

As responsible citizens, church members are encouraged to voluntarily join with other like-minded religious and secular groups in coalitions to advocate and defend the traditional family through donation of time, talent, and means. Church members have been key players in national and international efforts to promote traditional marriage and family. Such efforts include the Defense of Marriage Act legislation passed by the U.S. Congress in 1996 and the establishment of the Family Studies Center and the World Family Policy Center at the church-sponsored Brigham Young University (Wardle, Williams, and Wilkins 2001).

The leaders of the Church of Jesus Christ of Latter-day Saints warn its members and the world that "[d]isintegration of the family will bring upon individuals, communities, and nations the calamities foretold by ancient and modern prophets. . . . We call upon responsible citizens and officers of government everywhere to promote those measures designed to maintain and strengthen the family as the fundamental unit of society" (The Family 1995, p. 102).

See also: RELIGION

Bibliography

Bachman, D. W., and Esplin, R. K. (1992). "Plural Marriage." *Encyclopedia of Mormonism,* Vol. 3. New York: Macmillan.

Beaman, L.G. (2001). "Molly Mormons, Mormon Feminists and Moderates: Religious Diversity and the Latter Day Saints Church." *Sociology of Religion* 62(1):65–86.

Chadwick, B. A., and Garrett, H. D. (1995). "Women's Religiosity and Employment: The LDS Experience." *Review of Religious Research* 36(3):277–293.

Cornwall, M. (1994). "The Institutional Role of Mormon Women." In *Contemporary Mormonism: Social Science Perspectives,* ed. M. Cornwall, T. B. Heaton, and L.A. Young. Chicago: University of Illinois.

Davis, R. J. (1992). "Antipolygamy Legislation." *Encyclopedia of Mormonism,* Vol. 1. New York: Macmillan.

The Doctrine and Covenants, Section 128:15; Official Declaration 1.

"The Family: A Proclamation to the World." (1995). *Ensign* (November):102.

Heaton, T. B. (1986). "How Does Religion Influence Fertility? The Case of Mormons." *Journal for the Scientific Study of Religion* 25(2):248–58.

Heaton, T. B. (1989). "Religious Influences on Mormon Fertility: Cross-national Comparisons." *Review of Religious Research* 30(4):401–411.

Heaton, T. B. (1992). "Vital Statistics." *Encyclopedia of Mormonism,*Vol. 4. New York: Macmillan.

Heaton, T. B.; Goodman, K. L.; and Holman, T. B. (1994). "In Search of a Peculiar People: Are Mormon Families Really Different?" In *Contemporary Mormonism: Social Science Perspectives,* ed. M. Cornwall, T. B. Heaton, and L. A. Young. Chicago: University of Illinois.

Hinckley, G. B. (1999). "Why We Do Some of the Things We Do." *Ensign* (November):52.

Iannaccone, L. R., and Miles, C.A. (1990). "Dealing with Social Change: The Mormon Church's Response to Change in Women's Roles." *Social Forces* 68(4):1231–1250.

Litchfield, A. W.; Thomas, D. L.; and Li, B. D. (1997). "Dimensions of Religiosity as Mediators of the Relations Between Parenting and Adolescent Deviant Behavior." *Journal of Adolescent Research* 12(2):199–226.

Madsen, C. C. (1992). "Woman Suffrage." *Encyclopedia of Mormonism,* Vol. 4. New York: Macmillan.

Nelson, R. M. (1999). "Our Sacred Duty to Honor Women." *Ensign* (May):38.

Parry, K. (1994). "The Mormon Missionary Companionship." In *Contemporary Mormonism: Social Science Perspectives,* ed. M. Cornwall, T. B. Heaton, and L. A. Young. Chicago: University of Illinois.

Presley, S.; Weaver, J.; and Weaver, B. (1986). "Traditional and Nontraditional Mormon Women: Political Attitudes and Socialization." *Women and Politics* 5(4):51–77.

Scott, R. G. (2001). "First Things First." *Ensign* (May):6.

Smith, B. B., and Thomas, S. W. (1992). "Gospel Principles and the Roles of Women." *Encyclopedia of Mormonism.* Vol. 4. New York: Macmillan.

Thomas, D. L. (1983). "Family in the Mormon Experience." In *Families and Religions: Conflict and Change in Modern Society,* ed. W. V. D'Antonio and J. Aldous. Beverly Hills, CA: Sage.

Todd, J. M. (2000). "News of the Church." *Ensign* (September):76.

Wardle, L. D; Williams, R. N; and Wilkins, R. G. (2001). "Defending Marriage and Family through Law and Policy." In *Strengthening Our Families: An In-depth Look at the Proclamation on the Family Strenthening Our Families,* ed. D. C. Dollahite. Salt Lake City, UT: Bookcraft.

White, O. K., Jr. (1986). "Ideology of the Family in Nineteenth-Century Mormonism." *Sociological Spectrum* 6:289–306.

DENNIS T. HAYNES
MARK O. JARVIS

An Achomawi mother and child. Motherhood is one of the few universal roles assigned to women. THE LIBRARY OF CONGRESS

MOTHERHOOD

Contemporary mothering and motherhood are viewed from a much broader perspective than in previous decades by emphasizing the relational and logistical work of childrearing. *Mothering* is defined as the social practices of nurturing and caring for people, and thus it is not the exclusive domain of women (Arendell 2000). In most societies, however, women not only bear children but also are primary caretakers of infants and children. Motherhood is one of the few universal roles assigned to women. Historically, despite changes in women's labor force participation, fertility rates, and age at first marriage, the experience of motherhood has remained a central aspect of most women's lives. Therefore, the description that follows is limited to women's motherhood practices and experiences.

Major issues about motherhood are divided into five interrelated contexts: transition to motherhood, maternal role in child rearing, the extent of maternal employment and its impact on child outcomes, the relationship between motherhood and marital quality, and mothers' psychological well-being.

Transition to Motherhood

In the United States, women are under tremendous pressure to bear children, and motherhood is often associated with their maturity and achievement in life. Becoming a mother is also considered to be a "normal" life course stage for women. This perception is also common in other societies. For example, Angelina Yuen-Tsang (1997) reported that many Chinese women accepted without question the view that childbearing was a natural and necessary part of their family life course; therefore, few ever considered the option of not having children. The pressure for women's childbearing is derived not only from their personal network of relatives and friends but also from society. In Japan, where low fertility rates have been of great governmental concern, young women are frequently accused of being selfish when they pursue higher education or prolong employment that distracts women from their "primary" duty of motherhood (Jolivet 1997).

Despite these societal and familial pressures, an increasing number of women today are either choosing not to have children or delaying childbearing until midlife. According to U.S. Bureau of Census data (1998), 23 percent of women between the ages of thirty-five and forty-four remained childless in 1992. This figure increased to 26.5 percent in 1999. Moreover, the percentage of mothers who gave birth at age twenty-four or younger decreased during the 1990s (U.S. National Center for Health Statistics 2001). In 1992, approximately 39 percent of total live births came from women younger than twenty-four, whereas 59 percent of live births came from mothers in between the ages of twenty-five and thirty-nine. In 1999, 36 percent of mothers were younger than twenty-four when they gave birth whereas 61 percent of live births came from mothers in between the ages of twenty-five and thirty-nine. Many women who choose to delay the birth of their first child wish to enjoy an autonomous life for themselves and achieve career objectives before beginning the tasks of parenting (Wilkie 1987).

Although contemporary motherhood can be seen as a choice for many women, some pregnancies occur without a conscious decision. Many of these unplanned pregnancies occur among teenage women. The causes of unplanned pregnancy are often complicated. Despite the availability of information about reproduction, many teenagers do not seem to understand how conception takes place and believe that they are somehow immune to pregnancy. Some researchers have attributed adolescent pregnancy to the individual's self perception, and have suggested that low self-esteem is a factor, or to social causes such as family problems and poverty. Most importantly, however, adolescents become pregnant because they frequently lack the judgment necessary to deal with their sexuality.

In a number of studies focusing on teenage mothers, poverty and child abuse have been found to be persistent problems (Geronimus and Korenman 1992). Children of teen parents are also found to be disadvantaged in terms of cognitive performance, and daughters of teen mothers are likely to give birth in their teens (Manlove 1997).

Maternal Role in Childrearing

Mothers are likely to be a constant presence throughout their children's lives. Mothers frequently refer to the use of common sense and intuition in raising children—as if no special knowledge is required and as if many of their practices are grounded in some biological instinct. However, almost all mothers admit that they seek at least

some explicit advice on how to raise their children. Childrearing manuals are one of the most important sources of advice. These advice books for mothers, to a large extent, represent cultural expectations for motherhood. For example, in a cross-cultural study comparing mothering books in Japan and the United States, Arlie Russell-Hochschild and Kazuko Tanaka (1997) found that compared to their U.S. counterparts, Japanese advice books emphasize collective life such as rites and rituals, whereas U.S. books focus more on individual aspects of childrearing. Further, it was found that Japanese books praise mothers for their attention to beauty, deference, and motherliness whereas U.S. books praise women for their creativity and brilliance in mothering.

With respect to styles of parenting, an attentive and hands-on approach is reported to be more common among mothers than fathers. For example, a six-nation study on children and their parents found whereas fathers are more likely to be involved in intrinsically fun activities with children, such as playing or taking a walk with them, mothers are often involved in routine care of children such as bathing, changing, and helping with homework (Japanese Association for Women's Education 1995). According to this study, 64 percent of parents in the United States reported that providing meals and feeding children are mainly the responsibility of the mother. The figures reported in other countries were 88.3 percent (Japan), 58 percent (Korea), 65.3 percent (Thailand), 75.5 percent (UK), and 67.4 percent (Sweden). Among various parental activities included in the survey, fathers in all of the aforementioned countries are most likely to report "playing with children" as one of their major parental roles.

Different styles of interaction with children between mothers and fathers are reflected by children's affection toward their parents. In a comparative study, it was found that children report liking and respecting their fathers more than their mothers. This may be due to the infrequent father-child interaction and children's "idealizing" of fathers' roles (Ishii-Kuntz 1993). Despite these findings, mothers continue to influence their children in numerous ways and mothering styles are affected by several demographic and psychological factors surrounding mothers. Using a sample of working- and middle-class African-American mothers, Cheryl Bluestone and Catherine Tamis-LeMonda (1999) found that maternal education contributed to child-centered parenting, and that maternal depression was negatively associated with child-centered parenting styles. In Japan, mothers' childcare stress and anxiety were found to negatively influence the child's social development (Makino 1988).

Extent and Effects of Maternal Employment

During the past few decades the proportion of women in labor force has increased dramatically in all industrialized societies. In the United States, the married mothers' employment rate increased from 39.7 percent in 1970 to 70.1 percent in 1999 (U.S. Bureau of Labor Statistics, 2000). Among mothers of children aged six to seventeen, 49.2 percent and 77.1 percent were employed in 1970 and 1999, respectively. Among mothers with children under the age of six, their employment rate doubled from 1970 (30.3%) to 1999 (61.8%). The increasing trend of maternal employment is seen in other industrialized countries such as Japan and Canada.

The above figures indicate that the majority of mothers in the United States experience dual roles of being a parent and a paid worker. A number of studies also show that women still bear more responsibility for childcare than their male counterparts (e.g., Hochschild 1989). Working mothers, therefore, are engaged in a second shift of caring for their children and families upon returning from their first shift of paid work (Hochschild 1989). Since mothers are more likely to prepare their children for day care and school in the morning hours than fathers, working mothers, in reality, are engaged in three shifts combining family carework and paid work.

An increase of labor-force participation among mothers also suggests that being a mother—even of an infant—is no longer a major deterrent to women's employment (Moen 1992). According to Moen, the three types of mothers most likely to return to work before their infants are a year old are the young mother (a married mother under age twenty-four with a high school education), the delayed childbearer (a mother with at least some college education who postponed starting her family until after age twenty-four), and the unmarried mother (a white high school graduate who already has two or more children and has been divorced or separated). It should be noted, however, that although the American public has shown more acceptance of the employment of married women,

the employment of mothers with young children has not enjoyed the same level of endorsement (Moen 1992). This is largely due to beliefs that maternal employment has harmful effects on young children.

A number of studies in the early 1990s explored the effects of maternal employment on child outcomes but yielded inconsistent results. Whereas some studies reported that maternal employment was a negative influence on children's cognitive and social development, others found enhanced cognitive outcomes for children as a function of early maternal employment (Vandell and Ramanan 1992). Studies in late 1990s report that neither early maternal employment status nor the timing and continuity of maternal employment were consistently related to a child's developmental outcome (Harvey 1999). A few significant findings reported that mothers' working more hours in the first three years was associated with slightly lower vocabulary scores up through age nine (Harvey 1999). Among low-income adolescent mothers, maternal employment was also associated with their children's lower verbal development (Luster et al. 2000). However, maternal employment during the first year of the child's life is slightly more beneficial for the children of single mothers, and early parental employment was related to more positive child outcomes for low-income families (Harvey 1999).

Although these results suggest that maternal employment status has few negative effects on young children, other research in the 1990s reported some of the conditions under which maternal work makes a difference in family relations. For example, when mothers frequently engaged in shared activities with children such as reading books and telling stories, the potentially disruptive effects of changes in maternal employment status on children's social and cognitive competence were mitigated. Additionally, less secure attachment relationships between mothers and children were more common when the quality of alternative childcare was poor and unstable (NICHD Early Child Care Research Network 1997).

The mothers' struggle of balancing work and family has also been reported in developing regions (such as Latin America), post-socialist regions (such as Russia), and industrialized countries (such as Great Britain and Japan). Helen Safa (1992), for example, reports that despite increased employment of married women in Puerto Rico and the Dominican Republic, housework and childcare are still perceived as women's responsibility, even when they are making major contributions to the household economy. Similarly, for many women in Great Britain, the absence of choices concerning childcare poses a major problem in pursuing outside employment (MacLennan 1992). Compared to these countries, mothers in Nordic countries have a less stressful experience in balancing motherhood and paid work due to the comprehensive maternity-parental leave system in which parents of children under the age of one are financially supported for childcare by governmental policies (Haavio-Mannila and Kauppinen 1992). It should be noted, however, this does not mean that gender-based discrimination in the larger social context does not exist in Nordic countries as evidenced by sex segregation in the workplace.

Motherhood and Marital Quality

One issue that has been studied extensively is the relationship between marital quality and parental satisfaction. The assumption that parenting satisfaction is primarily an outcome of marital satisfaction has not been firmly established. With respect to the relationship between motherhood and marital quality, studies during the last two decades found that women's relationships with their children are richer and more complex than men's (Umberson 1989) and thus women will experience both more strain and greater rewards from the parental role. The complex nature of parental satisfaction among mothers is reflected in their marital satisfaction. Overall findings suggest that the marital and parenting relationships are more closely linked for fathers than for mothers, although no significant gender differences in this relationship were noted by Stacy Rogers and Lynn White (1998).

Mothers and Psychological Well-Being

Women's psychological well-being is influenced by many factors including mothering performance. Mothers frequently assume the caretaker role in the family, which may increase the likelihood that they are attentive to, and thus possibly receivers of, emotions from other family members. In contrast to fathers' experiences, the emotions mothers experienced at their jobs did not foreshadow their emotional states at home in the evening (Larson

and Richards 1994). This suggests either that mothers are more capable of compartmentalizing work and home (i.e. leaving work behind) than are fathers, or that the urgent tasks they must perform when they come home readily overwhelm what happened that day at work.

Mothers' psychological well-being, however, is more likely to be influenced by the daily routine of childrearing activities. Mothers report greater satisfaction with parenting than fathers, and they are more supportive than fathers of their children (Starrels 1994). At the same time, however, mothers of infants report higher levels of stress and anxiety when they evaluate their own performance as mothers than do their male counterparts (Arendell 2000). Compared with fathers, mothers are more involved with the responsibility for daily childcare, which exposes them to a wider range of disagreements and tension with their children (Hochschild 1989). David Almeida, Elaine Wethinton, and Amy Chandler (1999) found that mothers reported almost twice as many days of parental tension as fathers. The number of children in the household are also important predictors of family tension for mothers. Having more children in the household was associated with more mother-child tension (Almeida, Wethinton, and Chandler 1999).

Additionally, the extent of mother's child-care related stress level is frequently affected by the societal expectations for women to be "good mothers" (Villani 1997). Shari Thurner (1994) asserts that the contemporary "Good Mother" myth in Western society sets standards that are unattainable and self-denying. In Japan, Katsuko Makino (1988) also found the unrealistic expectations (on the part of society as a whole and mothers in particular) on what it means to be a good mother, and a mother's social isolation from the support networks are the major cause of maternal stress and anxiety.

See also: ADOLESCENT PARENTHOOD; ATTACHMENT: PARENT-CHILD RELATIONSHIPS; CHILDCARE; CONFLICT: PARENT-CHILD RELATIONSHIPS; COPARENTING; DUAL-EARNER FAMILIES; FAMILY LIFE EDUCATION; FAMILY ROLES; FATHERHOOD; FERTILITY; GRANDPARENTHOOD; LESBIAN PARENTS; MARITAL QUALITY; NONMARITAL CHILDBEARING; PARENTING EDUCATION; PARENTING RESPONSIBILITIES: PARENTING STYLES; PREGNANCY AND BIRTH; SEPARATION-INDIVIDUATION; SINGLE-PARENT FAMILIES; STEPFAMILIES; STRESS; SUBSTITUTE CAREGIVERS; SURROGACY; TRANSITION

TO PARENTHOOD; WIFE; WOMEN'S MOVEMENTS; WORK AND FAMILY

Bibliography

Almeida, D. M.; Wethinton, E.; and Chandler, A. L. (1999). "Daily Transmission of Tensions between Marital Dyads and Parent-Child Dyads." *Journal of Marriage and the Family* 61:49–61.

Arendell, T. (2000). "Conceiving and Investigating Motherhood: The Decade's Scholarship." *Journal of Marriage and the Family* 62:1192–1207.

Bluestone, C., and Tamis-LeMonda, C. S. (1999). "Correlates of Parenting Styles in Predominantly Working- and Middle-Class African American Mothers." *Journal of Marriage and the Family* 61:881–893.

Geronimus, A., and Korenman, S. (1992). "The Socioeconomic Consequences of Teen Childbearing Reconsidered." *Quarterly Journal of Economics* 107:1187–1214.

Haavio-Mannila, E., and Kauppinen, K. (1992). "Women and the Welfare State in the Nordic Countries." In *Women's Work and Women's Lives: The Continuing Struggle Worldwide,* ed. H. Kahne and J. Z. Giele. Boulder, CO: Westview.

Harvey, E. (1999). "Short-Term and Long-Term Effects of Parental Employment on Children of the National Longitudinal Survey of Youth." *Developmental Psychology* 35:445–459.

Hochschild, A. (1989). *The Second Shift.* New York: Avon Books.

Ishii-Kuntz, M. (1999). "Children's Affection toward Fathers: A Comparison between Japan and the United States." *International Journal of Japanese Sociology* 8:35–50.

Japanese Association for Women's Education. (1995). *International Comparative Research on Home Education.* Tokyo: Author.

Jolivet, M. (1997). *Japan: The Childless Society?* New York: Routledge.

Larson, R., and Richards, M. H. (1994). *Divergent Realities: The Emotional Lives of Mothers, Fathers, and Adolescents.* New York: Basic Books.

Luster, T.; Bates, L.; Fitzgerald, H.; Vandenbelt, M.; and Key, J. P. (2000). "Factors Related to Successful Outcomes among Preschool Children Born to Low-Income Adolescent Mothers." *Journal of Marriage and the Family* 62:133–146.

MacLennan, E. (1992). "Politics, Progress, and Compromise: Women's Work and Lives in Great Britain." In *Women's Work and Women's Lives: The Continuing Struggle Worldwide,* ed. H. Kahne and J. Z. Giele. Boulder, CO: Westview.

Makino, K. (1988). "Child Care Anxiety: Reconsideration of Definitions and Influential Factors." *Journal of Family Education Research Center* 10:52–55.

Manlove, J. (1977). "Early Motherhood in an Intergenerational Perspective: The Experiences of a British Cohort." *Journal of Marriage and the Family* 59:263–279.

Moen, P. (1992). *Women's Two Roles: A Contemporary Dilemma.* New York: Auburn House.

NICHD Early Child Care Research Network. (1997). "The Effects of Infant Child Care on Infant-Mother Attachment Security: Results of the NICHD Study of Early Child Care." *Child Development* 68:860–879.

Rogers, S. J., and White, L. K. (1998). "Satisfaction with Parenting: The Role of Marital Happiness, Family Structure, and Parents' Gender." *Journal of Marriage and the Family* 60:293–308.

Russell-Hochschild, A., and Tanaka, K. (1997). "Light and Heavy Culture in American and Japanese Advice Books for Women." In *Unresolved Dilemmas: Women, Work and the Family in the United States, Europe and the Former Soviet Union,* ed. K. Kauppinen and T. Gordon. Brookfield, VT: Ashgate.

Safa, H. I. (1992). "Development and Changing Gender Roles in Latin America and the Caribbean." In *Women's Work and Women's Lives: The Continuing Struggle Worldwide,* ed. H. Kahne and J. Z. Giele. Boulder, CO: Westview.

Starrells, M. E. (1994). "Gender Differences in Parent-Child Relations," *Journal of Family Issues* 15:148–165.

Thurner, S. L. (1994). *The Myths of Motherhood: How Culture Reinvents the Good Mother.* Boston: Houghton Mifflin.

Umberson, D. (1989). "Marriage as Support or Strain: Marital Quality Following the Death of a Parent." *Journal of Marriage and the Family* 57:709–723.

U.S. Bureau of the Census. (1998). *Current Population Reports.* Series p20–526. Washington, DC: U.S. Government Printing Office.

U.S. Bureau of Labor Statistics. (2000). "Employment Status of Women by Marital Status and Presence and Age of Children: 1970–1999." Bulletin 2307. Washington, DC: U.S. Government Printing Office.

Vandell, D. L., and Ramanan, J. (1992). "Effects of Early and Recent Maternal Employment on Children from Low-Income Families." *Child Development* 63:938–949.

Wilkie, J. R. (1987). "Marriage, Family Life, and Women's Employment." In *Women Working*, 2nd edition, ed. A. H. Stromberg and S. Harkess. Mountain View, CA: Mayfield.

Yuen-Tsang, A. W. K. (1997). *Towards a Chinese Conception of Social Support*. Brookfield, VT: Ashgate.

Other Resource

U.S. National Center for Health Statistics. (2001). *Vital Statistics of the U.S.* Available from http://www.census .gov/prod/2001pubs/statab/sec02.pdf.

MASAKO ISHII-KUNTZ

MUNCHAUSEN SYNDROME BY PROXY

Munchausen Syndrome by Proxy (MSbP) is the name that has been given to a situation in which one person fabricates an illness in a second person and presents the second person to a doctor. The term was first used in the title of an article by Roy Meadow, a professor of pediatrics (Meadow 1977). MSbP has usually been used to refer to a situation involving a mother and child. Other adults, occasionally the father, have been reported to fabricate illnesses in a child under their care.

There has been controversy about MSbP, including usage of the term. MSbP refers to a *situation* comprising behaviors and psychological states of the fabricator, a victim, and a medical professional in a triadic interaction. MSbP is not a psychiatric diagnosis applicable to the fabricator, although many reports indicate consistent findings regarding the psychology of fabricators.

Recognition of fabrication is usually made by the doctor following bewilderment at the medical presentation, which may be one of a series of similar presentations. Following strong suspicion or confirmation of MSbP, multidisciplinary action under local child protection procedures is usually appropriate, with the paramount task being to ensure the health and safety of the child.

A psychiatrist or a clinical psychologist will usually carry out a detailed assessment of the fabricator. The importance of consulting the health records of the fabricator (as well as the victim and siblings) and meeting with reliable relatives or

friends of the fabricator who will act as informants cannot be over-emphasized.

The fabricator psychopathology (abnormal psychology) has been found to range in type and severity across a spectrum. Usually there will have been a history of presentations of physical symptoms, which are the result of a somatizing process (a tendency to experience emotional problems as physical symptoms detached from the emotional aspect of the problem). This may be extreme as in chronic factitious disorder (sometimes known as Munchausen's Syndrome, as described by Richard Asher in 1951) in which the adult lives a life centered around the fabrication of illness and gaining access to hospitals. In some cases the fabricator has been found to have a history of criminal behavior (especially involving deception, such as fraud), repeated self-harm, or misuse of medications or alcohol (Bools et al. 1994). The diagnosis made by a psychiatrist will often be of a personality disorder.

The child victim of MSbP may come to serious physical harm if, as part of the fabrication, physical signs of illness are actually caused in the child. Many methods of such *illness induction* have been reported: smothering to produce fits, poisoning to produce drowsiness or diarrhea, and abrading skin. Clearly such action constitutes physical child abuse. In situations in which illness is fabricated in the child without direct physical harm, the child may undergo medical investigations and procedures, such as surgery or toxic medications, so that in the end some physical harm results. In the absence of physical harm the child is likely to suffer psychological harm, including the effect of substantial school nonattendance (Bools et al. 1993). The relationship between the mother and child is usually highly pathological with the attachment needs of the child not being met, resulting in emotional and behavioral disturbance as well as the risk of abnormal personality development. The actions of the mother are likely to constitute some degree of emotional (psychological) child abuse.

Teresa Parnell (1998) noted that the majority of the fabricators gave histories consistent with emotional, physical, or sexual abuse in their own childhoods, which, together with constitutional factors, are likely to be important in the development of the abnormal relationship with the child and the eventual fabrication. Moreover, the husbands/

partners of fabricating mothers typically reported minimal involvement in family life. The distance between the partners may be emotional, physical, or both, and when the mother is over-involved with the child, the father becomes peripheral in the family system. This situation allows the mother to develop the fabricated illness in the child with little challenge—or even knowledge—of the father. Therefore, using a family systems perspective, treatment will require therapeutic work with both parents, later including the child victim, to complement the individual treatments. One aspect of the treatment is likely to include work to bring the father and child(ren) closer, improve the emotional environment for the child, and increase the protective role of the father.

In a number of cases, psychiatric treatment of fabricators has been successful enough to allow the rehabilitation of the fabricator as a caregiver of the child (Berg and Jones 1999). Important aspects in the assessment in this respect are the acknowledgement of the fabricating behavior and its impact on the child victim, and a capacity to tolerate an intensive psychotherapeutic treatment regime. Unfortunately, in many cases treatment was not found to be possible.

Most reports of MSbP have come from English-speaking countries; however, reports from non-English-speaking countries are growing in number (Brown and Feldman 2001). An estimate of incidence of MSbP in the United Kingdom—based on an epidemiological study—was at least 0.5 per 100,000 of children under sixteen years of age, and at least 2.8 per 100,000 of children ages under one year (McClure et al. 1996). There are no epidemiological data available from other countries.

See also: CHILD ABUSE: PSYCHOLOGICAL MALTREATMENT; CHILD ABUSE: SEXUAL ABUSE; CHILD ABUSE: PHYSICAL ABUSE AND NEGLECT; DEVELOPMENTAL PSYCHOPATHOLOGY; THERAPY: FAMILY RELATIONSHIPS

Bibliography

Asher, R. (1951). Munchausen's Syndrome. The *Lancet* 1:339–341.

Berg, B., and Jones, D. P. H. (1999). "Outcome of Psychiatric Intervention in Factitious Illness by Proxy (Munchausen's Syndrome by Proxy)." *Archives of Disease in Childhood* 81:465–472.

Bools, C. N. (1993). "Follow up of Victims of Fabricated Illness (Munchausen Syndrome by Proxy)." *Archives of Disease in Childhood* 69:625–630.

Bools, C. N.; Neale, B. A.; and Meadow, S. R. (1994). "Munchausen Syndrome by Proxy: A Study of Psychopathology." *Child Abuse and Neglect* 18:773–788

Brown, R., and Feldman, M. (2001). "International Perspectives on Munchausen Syndrome by Proxy." In *Munchausen's Syndrome by Proxy: Current Issues in Assessment, Treatment and Research,* ed. G. Adshead and D. Brooke. London: Imperial College Press.

Meadow, S. R. (1977). "Munchausen Syndrome by Proxy: The Hinterland of Child Abuse." *Lancet* 2:343–345

McClure, L. J.; Davis, P. M.; Meadow, S. R.; and Sibert, J. R. (1996). "Epidemiology of Munchausen Syndrome by Proxy, Non-Accidental Poisoning and Non-Accidental Suffocation." *Archives of Disease in Childhood* 75:57–61.

Parnell, T. F. (1998). "Guidelines for Identifying Cases." In *Munchausen by Proxy Syndrome: Misunderstood Child Abuse,* ed. T. F. Parnell and D. O. Day. Thousand Oaks, CA: Sage Publications.

CHRISTOPHER N. BOOLS

N

Nagging and Complaining

> Your room is filthy! I want you to clean it now.
>
> I am tired of saying this–clean your room.
>
> How many times do I have to tell you? Pick up your room!
>
> You are driving me crazy! What do I have to do to get you to do what I ask?

Nagging and complaining are common features of family life. A complaint is a statement of grievance, discomfort, discontent, or dissatisfaction (Doelger 1984). *Nagging* refers to repeated or persistent complaints. Though complaint behavior is common, *how* couples and families manage their complaints is connected to their overall adjustment and satisfaction. To understand the role nagging and complaining play in family relationships, it is helpful to explore the purposes and types of complaints as well as how complaining functions as an element of conflict.

Purposes and Types of Complaints

People complain because their dissatisfaction reaches a critical threshold (Kowalski 1996). When they feel that they can no longer endure their dissatisfaction, people attempt to determine what they can do to reduce the discrepancy between their ideal for a situation and the reality of the situation. Verbalization of one's dissatisfaction in the form of nagging or complaining occurs when this behavior is perceived as a possible means to reduce the discrepancy. In addition, complaining can alleviate feelings of distress. For instance, it can serve a cathartic role in cleansing people of their dissatisfaction, it can help them to present themselves in a way that influences other's impressions of them, it can help people to gauge themselves in comparison to others, and it can compel others to give accounts for their behavior.

Several factors influence the likelihood that individuals will choose to nag or complain as a means of reducing their dissatisfaction. Individuals' level of social anxiety, their degree of introversion versus extroversion, and their perception of control (whether it is internal to them or external to them) all affect whether they will complain. Those who are anxious about how others view them, who are introverts, or who perceive that they have no control over a situation are less likely to feel that complaining will resolve their dissatisfaction (Kowalski 1996). Power also plays a critical role in whether or not complaining and nagging are chosen as forms of redress. Complaining is typically viewed as a low power strategy. If one has the ability to change a situation, one simply makes the change. However, if one cannot effect change, then one must attempt to persuade others to enact the change. Thus, complaining and nagging often function as attempts to persuade or cajole others into changing.

Gender also may affect the likelihood one will nag or complain. Women appear to be slightly more likely to nag, complain, and whine than men (Conway and Vartanian 2000), and this verbal behavior has been found to be more stable for women over the course of a relationship than it is for men (Gottman and Levenson 1999). However, Jess K. Alberts (1988) found that while wives complained more often than husbands, this difference was not statistically significant. If women do complain and nag more often, it may be that they feel less able to effect change themselves, or they may have more cause for dissatisfaction (Macklin 1978).

What causes dissatisfaction within families? One study of romantic couples' interactions (Alberts 1989) discovered five broad categories of complaint topics: *behavior* (about another's actions or lack thereof), *personal characteristics* (about another's personality or beliefs), *performance* (about how others performed an action), *complaining* (about another's complaint behavior), and *personal appearance* (about how the other looked). Although this study focused specifically on husbands and wives, these categories likely encompass most complaints within the family.

Recognizing what causes individuals to nag and complain, as well as what they nag and complain about, is important to understanding the function of nagging and complaining. However, to better understand the affect of these behaviors on relationships, it is important to examine how individuals respond to the complaint behaviors of family members.

Complaints and Complaint Responses as Elements of Conflict

Conflict typically occurs when interdependent people perceive they have incompatible goals (Frost and Wilmot 1978). Complaints are a pervasive and natural aspect of conflict. Individuals do not need to express discontent, grievance, or dissatisfaction if their goals are not being interrupted by another individual. Complaining or nagging is often the first indication that a conflict exists; complaints make the other party aware that he or she is interfering with the speaker's goals. Even when complaints do not evolve into a full-scale conflict, the slow build-up and repetitive pattern of daily complaints and nagging can have a corrosive effect on a relationship. However, whether complaining and nagging serve a relationship well or poorly depends upon how the individuals involved manage the complaint interaction.

Family members can manage their complaints six different ways (Alberts and Driscoll 1992). First, complaint recipients may choose to *pass* or ignore

the complaint. Although conflict avoidance can negatively impact relationships in some instances, ignoring complaints that are relatively unimportant and will pass on their own may actually increase relational harmony. Second, the complainer and complaint recipient together may choose to *refocus* the complaint, placing responsibility for the cause of the complaint on a third party rather than upon the individuals themselves. This response allows the disagreement to be aired, but it also restores relational harmony by uniting the individuals against a common "enemy." Similarly, individuals can respond by *mitigating* the complaint. Again, in this instance individuals are able to voice their dissatisfaction, but ultimately are able to agree that the issue is not a weighty one that warrants sustained conflict. Fourth, participants can manage the complaint episode by *validating* one another's complaints and working through them to manage unsatisfactory elements of their relationship.

These four responses to complaints have the potential to downplay the complaint and to foster positive relational feelings. However, the two remaining responses to complaints are less effective at decreasing the level of conflict and may actually increase the occurrence of persistent complaining (such as nagging) and intense arguments. For example, some individuals respond to conflicts by *escalating* the situation; that is, they respond in a hostile fashion and expand the complaint episode by broadening the focus of the complaint. Thus, a complaint about forgetting to pick up the milk becomes a broader complaint about thoughtlessness in the entire relationship. Others are *unresponsive* to the complaint or the relational needs of the complainer. Although an ignoring response similarly does not address the complaint, it is done in the overall interest of the relationship. Unresponsiveness, however, shuts out both the complaint and the other person; it is a response that devalues the relationship and can easily lead to further conflict or relational distress. How a complaint is managed once it is voiced is pivotal in whether more complaints, nagging, and conflict are likely to follow or understanding and relational harmony will result.

Effects of Complaining on Familial Relationships

Unfortunately, virtually all of the research on complaining and nagging has focused on married or romantic couples. Thus, most of what we know about the connection between nagging and relationship adjustment or satisfaction concerns dyadic, not family, functioning. However, other research indicates that parental satisfaction and adjustment are key to overall family health and functioning (Noller and Fitzpatrick 1993). Thus, when parents manage their complaints effectively, family adjustment is likely increased.

The various studies that have examined relationship satisfaction and complaining have produced several consistent findings. It is known that satisfied and dissatisfied couples manage their complaints differently. One of the most consistent findings (Gottman 1979; Alberts 1988) is that dissatisfied couples are more likely to cross-complain; that is, they are more likely to respond to a complaint with a complaint. In addition, satisfied couples are more likely to complain about specific behaviors rather than general personality characteristics, they are more positive in their affect when they do complain, and they are more likely to respond to their partners' complaints with agreement or apologies. Overall, happy couples manage their complaints more effectively and are less likely to escalate complaint episodes.

Does this mean happy couples complain less? Not necessarily. Alberts (1988) did not find a statistically significant relationship between *number* of complaints and couples' satisfaction. In fact, she found that both the happiest and unhappiest couples had the fewest complaints. However, the very unhappy couples' lack of complaining was attributed to the *chilling effect* (Roloff and Cloven 1990). The chilling effect describes the tendency for individuals to withhold complaints due to their perception that they will not be received well or will have little effect.

Although the research on nagging/complaining and relationship satisfaction has not been extended to family relationships, it is likely that similar findings would hold. One may expect that in families where individuals use specific complaints delivered in a positive fashion and respond with agreement or apologies, family members will be happier and more satisfied.

See also: COMMUNICATION: COUPLE RELATIONSHIPS; COMMUNICATION: FAMILY RELATIONSHIPS; CONFLICT: COUPLE RELATIONSHIPS; CONFLICT: FAMILY RELATIONSHIPS; CONFLICT: PARENT-CHILD RELATIONSHIPS; DECISION MAKING; DIALECTICAL THEORY; PROBLEM SOLVING; RELATIONSHIP MAINTENANCE

Bibliography

Alberts, J. K. (1988). "An Analysis of Couples' Conversational Complaint Interactions." *Communication Monographs* 55:184–197.

Alberts, J. K. (1989). "A Descriptive Taxonomy of Couples' Complaints." *Southern Communication Journal* 54:125–143.

Alberts, J. K., and Driscoll, G. (1992). "Containment versus Escalation: The Trajectory of Couples' Conversational Complaints." *Western Journal of Communication* 56:394–412.

Conway, M., and Vartanian, L. R. (2000). "A Status Account of Gender Stereotypes: Beyond Communality and Agency." *Sex Roles* 43:181–199.

Doelger, J. (1984). "A Descriptive Analysis of Complaints and Their Use in Conversation." Unpublished master's thesis. Lincoln: University of Nebraska.

Frost, J. H, and Wilmot, W. W. (1978). *Interpersonal Conflict.* Dubuque, IA: William C. Brown.

Gottman, J. M. (1979). *Marital Interaction.* New York: Academic Press.

Gottman, J. M., and Levenson, R. W. (1999). "How Stable Is Marital Interaction Over Time?" *Family Process* 38:159–165.

Kowalski, R. M. (1996). "Complaints and Complaining: Functions, Antecedents, and Consequences." *Psychological Bulletin* 119:179–196.

Macklin, E. D. (1978). "Review of Research on Non-marital Cohabitation in the United States." In *Exploring Intimate Lifestyles,* ed. B. I. Burstein. New York: Springer.

Noller, P., and Fitzpatrick, M. A. (1993). *Communication in Family Relationships.* Englewood Cliffs, NJ: Prentice Hall.

Roloff, M. E., and Cloven, D. H. (1990). "The Chilling Effect in Interpersonal Relationships: The Reluctance to Speak One's Mind." In *Intimates in Conflict,* ed. D. D. Cahn. Hillsdale, NJ: Erlbaum.

JESS K. ALBERTS
CHRISTINA GRANATO YOSHIMURA

NAMES FOR CHILDREN

Personal names are one of the few cultural universals. Families in all societies provide personal names for the children born into them. By naming children, families are inducting their children into the family and the society. At the same time, they are expressing their hopes and desires for those children in the names they select. Names are both messages to children about who they are expected to be and messages to society at large about just who this child is.

Although personal names are universal, the components that make up a personal name and the ways names are bestowed vary widely from society to society. Within many societies, too, how children are named from subgroup to subgroup and from one historical period to the next varies greatly.

In every society children receive personal names. Such names always include a given name that distinguishes a child from all other individuals. These names may include surnames, which distinguish members of one family line from another, or patronyms, which distinguish the offspring of one man from those of another. Personal names may also include middle names, name suffixes (like *Jr., II,* or *III*), or sacred names. The components that make up a child's name may be ordered differently. North Americans are familiar with surnames coming last in a complete name, but in Korea, China, Japan, and other Asian societies, surnames are placed first in the child's complete name.

The idea of given names is much too old to have a discernible origin. In the earliest records of the earliest societies, people were provided given names. It is a reasonable assumption that given names probably date from the origin of language itself; when humans began naming their world, they possibly began with themselves.

North American given names can be traced back through its history and further through British history. According to George Stewart (1979), a small, highly traditional stock of Anglo-Saxon names was dominant in England until the Norman Conquest in 1066. Gradually, over the next century, a traditional stock of Norman names (William, Henry, Richard, Robert; Matilda, Heloise, Emma) became prominent in England. By the late Middle Ages the use of saints' names became popular (John, James, Thomas, Stephen; Mary, Elizabeth, Katherine, Margaret). The name pool was too small to distinguish people adequately, however, and nicknames became a common device for differentiating people. After the Protestant Reformation a new pattern emerged. Women were given names from the New Testament and non-Biblical saints' names, while men were given names from the New Testament and traditional Norman names.

The first immigrants to the southern colonies of America brought their naming practices with them. The Puritan immigrants to New England, however, began looking to the Old Testament for names, and the traditional Norman names disappeared for a period. At the same time, extensive contact with two culturally distinct groups had little effect on North American naming practices. Although the white settlers interacted with Native Americans, they did not adopt Native American naming practices. Instead, Native Americans gradually adopted those of the colonists. In addition, the African Americans brought to America as slaves were given traditional English names, although at first they were not given surnames. After they were emancipated, African Americans were highly traditional in their naming practices. This began to change in the 1960s and 1970s when African-American parents began to coin, or create, new given names for their children at an unprecedented rate. By creating new names, they are most likely exhibiting a diminished need to assimilate to white culture and a desire to express their distinctiveness and racial pride.

During the 1800s, Old Testament names began to drop in popularity and non-Biblical names became more the fashion. The Norman names, which became less popular during the Puritan era, returned, and new names flourished. Immigrant groups introduced some of these new names (German, Scotch-Irish); others were family names used as given names; and still others were coined by using diminutive forms of traditional given names. Increasingly for girls, masculine names were transformed by the addition of feminine suffixes (e.g., Roberta, Michelle). The stock of given names was growing dramatically.

In the twentieth century, this expansion accelerated. More and more, parents began creating names by changing the spelling of traditional names (e.g., Debra), by recombining syllables from traditional names (e.g., Kathann), and by making up completely new names. Over the course of the twentieth century, an increasing percentage of North American children were being given new names.

The same expansion of the pool of given names is occurring in other societies, including

Japan, China, and India. Although multiple reasons may explain this growing variety, it is likely that at least one is the general loosening of the grip of tradition and the accompanying desire on the part of young parents to provide their children with names that suggest that they are a new generation, rather than emphasizing continuity with the past.

In about two-thirds of all societies given names convey the gender of a child (Alford 1988). This may be done in several ways. First, names that are semantically meaningful may refer to activities that are gender specific (e.g., *keeper of the hearth,* or *hunter of leopard*) or may refer to qualities ideally belonging to one gender (e.g., beauty, strength, valor). Japanese given names for girls typically employ characters with such meanings as flower, beauty, and grace; names for boys use characters with such meanings as strong, firm, or winning. The same is true of Chinese given names.

Second, given names may distinguish girls and boys by using prefixes or suffixes. Among the Ojibwa, for example, women's names are distinguished from men's by a suffix that refers to the female genitalia. In several societies, including Native American societies, these suffixes can be used alone to refer to as yet unnamed children. In many societies the endings of girls' names differ from those of boys' names. North American given names for girls often end in *y, ie,* or *sha;* given names for boys often end in hard consonants.

Third, given names may distinguish boys and girls purely by tradition. This is true of given names in India, in Russia, in Nigeria, and in the United States. In these societies, although a few names may be gender-ambiguous, most are not. In the United States only 1 to 3 percent of men's names and 3 to 7 percent of women's names fall into this ambiguous category (e.g., Lee, Robin, Sandy, Leslie).

Surnames

Although the origin of surnames is unclear, they also have a long history. According to Christopher Andersen (1977), the ancient Greeks, Hebrews, and Romans had surnames. After the fall of the Roman Empire, however, surnames disappeared until the eleventh century. English surnames did not become common until after the Crusades. By 1465, King Edward IV decreed that the Irish should take and transmit surnames; before this the Irish did not typically use them. The possession of a

surname came to be seen as a sign of modernization. By the twentieth century colonization had spread the use of surnames to many non-Western nations that did not already use surnames.

Surnames are not a Western invention, but are traditional to many Asian societies and often appear first in an individual's complete set of names. In Korea, for example, the first component in a man's name is his surname, followed by a middle name, and then by a given name. All males in a particular generation in a surname group share the same middle name. These middle names occur in series, thus linking different generations. The names of the five classic elements in order (wood, fire, earth, metal, and water) or a cyclic series of animal names might be used as middle names. Thus, for the Korean man, surnames denote lineage, middle names generation, and given names individuality. In earlier times Korean women used personal names only until puberty, after which they were addressed in reference to their roles of sister, daughter, wife, and mother (e.g., *wife of, mother of*). Today, Korean women keep their given names after marriage and take the surnames of their husbands, although a tendency lingers to refer to Korean women by their family relationships.

In some societies, only aristocrats or important people used surnames originally. In some societies only royalty were allowed to transmit surnames; in many, surnames became a sign of status.

English surnames came from numerous sources, but most were derived from an individual's occupation (Smith, Baker, Taylor); place of origin or residence (London, Washington); or physical characteristics (White, Brown). In addition, many surnames are converted patronyms created by adding an "s" to the father's name (Abrams, Edwards), or by adding a suffix (Johnson). North American surnames are transmitted along the male line, and women, usually, at marriage, assume their husband's surname. The trend for some women to retain their own surname after marriage or to hyphenate their surname with their husband's reflected the resurgence of feminism in the 1970s.

Middle names, although they existed earlier in the Chinese and Korean cultures, started to be used in the United States and England at the end of the eighteenth century. By the end of the nineteenth century most people in the United States were given middle names, and today only 1 to 4 percent of U.S. children do not have middle

In Korea, a boy's name is made up of his surname, followed by a middle name, and then by a given name. All males in a particular generation in a surname group have the same middle name. NATHAN BENN/CORBIS

names. Middle names, which served to convey status, first became popular among the upper classes and then were adopted by the general population. Middle names are useful in distinguishing one generation from the next when sons are named after their fathers, and sometimes they preserve a mother's maiden name.

Many societies have prescribed systems for selecting children's names. In others, name givers are free to select any name they desire. In the United States, systems for selecting names exist for two subgroups, Catholics and Jews. U.S. Catholics are theoretically bound by Canon 761, set forth by Pope Benedict XV in 1917, to choose names for their children from the list of acceptable saints' names. If such names are not selected as first names, then they are supposed to be recorded as baptismal names. Increasingly, however, U.S. Catholics are ignoring this prescription. Jewish parents are expected to name their children after deceased relatives, never living relatives. Like Catholics, Jews in the United States are increasingly ignoring this rule, although many Jewish parents do try to give their child a name beginning with the same letter as the name of a deceased relative.

Various systems for selecting names exist in different societies. In a few, divination is used to choose the name for a child. Among the Lozi of Africa the names of ancestors will be mentioned in front of the newborn child one by one. When the child cries, the name givers believe that the ancestor just mentioned had been reincarnated in that child.

Other fixed systems also continue. Among the Ashanti of southern Ghana, one component of a child's personal name is a "day name," a name corresponding to the day of the week on which the child was born (there are separate sets of day names for boys and girls). Among the Hausa of northern Nigeria and southern Niger, a Qur'anic day name is given to each child according to the day of the week of the birth. Among some groups in Malaya, seven specific names are given in order to a couple's first seven children. If the couple has more than seven children, these same names are used again, with the addition of a prefix meaning *little*. Thus, the birth order of a child is evident from his or her name.

The first daughter of a Highland Scot couple will be named after the maternal grandmother, the first son after the paternal grandfather, the second daughter after the paternal grandmother, and the second son after the maternal grandfather. Among the Santal of West Bengal in India, first and second sons and daughters are named after paternal and maternal grandparents, and third sons and daughters are named after paternal and maternal great-uncles and great-aunts.

In some African and Africa-origin societies, fixed systems apply only to particular categories of children. The Wolof apply specific names to twins, as do the Bush Negroes, descendants of runaway slaves in South America. The Hausa, too, have specific names for twins, as well as a special name for a boy born after a number of girls or for a girl born after a number of boys. The Ganda, too, not only have special names for twins, but even the parents of twins are given special names, which they use thereafter. The subsequent siblings of twins also receive special names. The Ashanti give particular names to children born on holidays.

In most societies parents are free to select any name they choose for a child, but name selection usually follows certain principles. The most common tendency is for parents to select family names, and especially names of grandparents. On the eastern edge of Polynesia, Lau boys are often named for grandfathers or for grandfather's brothers, while girls are often named for grandmothers. Among the Ifugao of the Philippines, names are often chosen from the names of deceased ancestors. In Malaysia, Iban children are named after maternal or paternal grandparents, depending on their gender. This is to keep the memory of the grandparent alive. Among the Kanuri, children are often named after paternal, then maternal grandparents. This is to prevent jealousy. Parents are not allowed to speak their parents' names, however, so they have to call their children *little father* or *little mother*. Among the Senussi, nomads of western Egypt and eastern Libya, it is a man's obligation to perpetuate the name of the person (usually his father) who has provided him with his bride-price. Thus, sons are usually named after their grandfathers. But if a man dies without wealth, even his sons might not pass on his name.

The North American practice of naming children after their parents, and especially naming sons after their fathers, is very rare in other societies. Of all relatives, grandparents are typically the preferred name sources. In a few societies, even grandparents are considered too closely related to be name sources. The Garo of northern India always name their children after ancestors who have been dead for many years, since it is thought unlucky to mention the name of a recently dead person. On the Indonesian island of Celebes, Toradja children cannot be named after parents, grandparents, or even great-grandparents. The names of great- great-grandparents, however, are given to children.

Most North Americans are free to select their children's names in whatever manner they choose. They may name a child after a family member, living or dead, and they may bestow this name as either a first or middle name. Two different studies

of given names (Rossi 1965; Alford 1988) have estimated that more than half of all children get at least one name from a relative, although it is more likely to be a middle name than a first name. This pattern of naming children after family members is very old in North American society and does not appear to be waning. A small percentage of names (perhaps 6–10%) are taken from people special to the parents (friends or famous people). The remainder of names, more than half of all first names, are chosen on the basis of aesthetic preference, usually from the pool of given names available. An increasing percentage of North American parents make up new, unique names for their children by changing the spelling of a traditional name or by recombining name elements.

Research has revealed a number of patterns in name preference that suggest the influences that underlie name selection in the United States, four of which are particularly noteworthy. First, boys are much more likely to be named after a relative than are girls. In turn, girls' names are more often selected for their aesthetic appeal. Second, there is a much larger pool of girls' names than boys' names, and girls are less likely to share popular names. Stanley Lieberson and Eleanor Bell (1992) found that 20 percent of all girls born in 1985 in New York had the ten most popular girls' names, while 35 percent of all boys born had the ten most popular boys' names; this was 50 percent or higher in the 1800s. Girls' names change more from generation to generation as well. Preferences in boys' names change more slowly. Third, girls' and boys' names differ phonetically. Leiberson and Bell found that nearly 34 percent of girls' names ended in a *schwa* sound (Jessica, Sarah), while only 1 percent of boys' names ended with that sound. Some 28 percent of girls' names ended in an *ee* sound (Mary, Amy), but only 10 percent of boys' names ended with that sound. In contrast, boys' names usually end in a consonant. Fourth, many popular girls' names (Danielle, Michelle, Stephanie) are adapted from boy's names, but few if any boy's names are adapted from girls' names.

Alice Rossi (1965), Richard Alford (1988), and Lieberson and Bell (1992) have offered some interpretations of these gender differences. Rossi suggested that boys more than girls are seen as symbolic carriers of family continuity and so are more likely to receive family names. Alford and Lieberson and Bell suggest that girls' names, in contrast, are seen as a form of decoration, verbal jewelry. Since the aesthetics of girls' names is more important, fashions in girls' names change more. An apt analogy can be made between gender differences in clothing and in names. Men's clothing varies less than do women's clothes. Further, over time, men's fashions change more slowly and less dramatically than women's fashions. This analogy can be extended from names and clothes to North American gender roles themselves. It can be argued that female gender roles permit greater variation from woman to woman than male gender roles. So, too, female gender roles have changed more over time than have male gender roles. Despite these changes, however, two important elements of the female role have always been beauty and fashion, while two important elements of the male role have always been stability and tradition.

By the end of the 1990s a new trend appeared in boys' names. Boys' names are becoming as subject to fashion as girls' names have long been. Between 1985 and 1995 the top ten boys' and girls' names have almost completely changed. Increasingly, parents name boys based on aesthetic preferences, rather than family honor and continuity. Girls' names, too, are increasingly subject to fashion, turning over more completely from one generation to the next. This greater sensitivity to fashion for both boys' and girls' names very likely reflects the increasing pace of change in North American society as a whole, and the desire of parents to provide their children with names that sound current, not old-fashioned. This trend is even extending to middle names. In other words, fewer children appear to be named after relatives.

Social class, measured either by education or occupation, is the second most important factor after gender in determining name selection. Rex Taylor (1974), Rossi (1965), Alford (1988), and Lieberson and Bell (1992) have all uncovered pronounced class differences in naming. First, parents with higher socioeconomic status (SES) are more likely to select more traditional names than are parents of lower SES. Lower SES parents have a greater preference for new and unique names than do higher SES parents. Higher SES parents are more likely to give family names (especially the father's and grandfather's) to boys and to give less feminine names to girls than are lower SES parents. Finally, names that first become popular among higher SES parents gradually trickle down to lower SES parents, evidence of status diffusion.

These social class differences have stimulated some interesting interpretations. First, it seems clear that higher-status parents use names as a vehicle to convey status to their children. They do so by conferring a name of a high-status relative or a traditional, high-status name. Higher-status fathers are especially likely to name their firstborn sons after themselves. For example, Taylor (1974) found that 77 percent of lawyers, 52 percent of doctors, and 23 percent of teachers gave their names to their firstborn sons. In addition, high-status parents are more likely to bestow traditional names, especially upon boys. These names connote stability and tradition. Lower-status parents, in contrast, choose a different route to status. In their less frequent use of names of relatives and their rejection of more traditional names for new and more unusual names, lower SES parents are expressing their desire for change and for a new status system.

Name Use in the Family

In all societies one can address or refer to a member of one's family in a variety of ways, using: kin terms (e.g., mother, father, sister, brother), teknonyms (e.g., mother of . . ., father of . . .), nicknames, various forms of personal names (e.g., complete personal names, given names, surnames), honorific or respect terms (e.g., Mr., Mrs.), or some combination of the above. In many societies, custom dictates the use of a particular form of address or reference in particular relationships, and the individual has little latitude in choosing a form of address. In all societies, however, individuals sometimes have the latitude to choose a form or address or reference that serves their particular needs.

In most preindustrial societies individuals must use kin terms when addressing certain relatives (Alford 1988). This is especially true when individuals address their parents, aunts, uncles, and grandparents. A number of anthropologists have noted the important functions of requiring the use of kin terms. According to Martha Kendall (1980), in a discussion of the Yuman Indians:

> One appeals to others with generalized vocatives or kinship terms, thereby playing on all the structural and moral dicta governing appropriate reciprocal behavior between particular categories of actors. As

my respondent put it, "If you call someone *maya* (parallel cousin), they have to treat you right." Calling someone by name makes no such general appeal to institutionalized rights and obligations, rather, it does just the opposite. Since personal names make no direct reference to the place of a person in a social network, they leave the actor unconstrained when used in address. (p. 266)

Laura and Paul Bohannan (1953) make similar observations about the use of names and kin terms among the Tiv. "Everybody is referred to by personal name, including the parents, *unless* you are trying to call up specific types of kinship activity, in which case kinship terms are useful." Societies that require the use of kin terms with a variety of relatives, then, are emphasizing the aspects of that relationship that are governed by a particular role. In many societies it is considered disrespectful for a child to address a parent, aunt, uncle, or grandparent by name. In some groups, a child will not even know the names of these relatives.

Not only in preindustrial societies do children address parents, aunts, uncles, and grandparents by kin terms. This is also true in India, Japan, China, Russia, Nigeria, and the United States. The required use of kin terms in these relationships emphasizes the role-governed nature of these relationships as well as the greater authority of the older relative. In many societies where children must use kin terms with senior relatives, those senior relatives can use personal names when addressing their junior relatives.

In the United States, according to David Schneider and George Homans (1995), children have a wide variety of alternative terms available for addressing parents (e.g., father, pop, pa, papa, dad, daddy), and the selection of one term rather than another varies with the context and with the quality of the particular relationship. *Father* suggests greater formality, distance, and respect. *Dad* suggests less formality and distance. Shifts in the use of parental terms as one grows up reflect changes in the quality of the relationship. The continued use of the preferred early childhood terms, *Mommy* and *Daddy,* suggests a relatively unchanging relationship.

In Japan, too, parental terms vary in formality. A child might call his mother: *okaachan* (most childish), *okaasan,* or *okaasama* (most formal). Similarly, a child might call his father: *otoochan* (most childish), *otoosan,* or *otosame* (most formal). In Russia, while a child will use the same kin term for a parent throughout life, in rural areas a child will use the formal form of *you* with parents, while in cities a child will use the informal form of *you* with parents, reflecting slightly greater informality.

When addressing brothers and sisters, people in more traditional societies often use kin terms, especially with elder siblings. Japanese children must address elder siblings *older sister* or *older brother,* while younger siblings may be addressed by name. The same is true in India. In Nigeria a sibling senior by two or more years must be addressed by kin term plus name, while a younger sibling can be addressed by name only. This pattern occurs especially in societies where sibling seniority is important.

Between husbands and wives the use of kin terms or teknonyms (father of . . ., mother of . . .) is typical of preindustrial societies. In many societies husbands and wives are not allowed to use each other's names. This custom has the effect of emphasizing and reinforcing how the role governs their relationship. In some traditional societies husbands and wives in the past addressed each other with kin terms, but today, they more commonly call one another by personal names. In India, for example, in the past husbands and wives used kin terms with each other. Today, especially more educated people use personal names instead. In Nigeria, too, in the past husbands and wives addressed each other as *father of* and *mother of.* Today, more educated Nigerians increasingly use personal names or terms of endearment. According to Schneider and Homans, the practice of using personal names or terms of endearment between husbands and wives reflects a new attitude toward marriage, such that the husband-wife relationship is outside of the realm of kinship and centers instead on the unique relationship between marriage partners. The use of personal names de-emphasizes the parts of the relationship that are governed by role and emphasizes the open-ended, negotiable nature of modern marriage.

See also: GENDER; GENDER IDENTITY; KINSHIP; SOCIOECONOMIC STATUS

Bibliography

Alford, R. (1988). *Naming and Identity: A Cross-Cultural Study of Personal Naming Practices.* New Haven, CT: Human Relations Area File Press.

Andersen, C. P. (1977). *The Name Game.* New York: Jove Publications.

Bohannan, L., and Bohannan, P. (1953). *The Tiv of Central Nigeria.* London: International African Institute.

Evans-Pritchard, E. E. (1964). "Nuer Modes of Address." In *Language In Culture and Society,* ed. D. Hymes. New York: Harper & Row.

Kendall, M. B. (1980). "Exegesis and Translation: Northern Yuman Names as Texts." *Journal of Anthropological Research* 36:261–273.

Lieberson, S., and Bell, E. O. (1992). "Children's First Names: An Empirical Study of Social Taste." *American Journal of Sociology* 98:511–554.

Rossi, A. S. (1965). "Naming Children in Middle-Class Families." *American Sociological Review* 30:499–513.

Schneider, D. M., and Homans, G. C. (1955). "Kinship Terminology and the American Kinship System." *American Anthropologist* 57:1194–1208.

Stewart, G. R. (1979). *American Given Names.* New York: Oxford University Press.

Taylor, R. (1974). "John Doe, Jr.: A Study of His Distribution in Space, Time, and the Social Structure." *Social Forces* 53:11–21.

RICHARD ALFORD

NEIGHBORHOOD

The definition of *neighborhood* includes a territorially organized population with common ties and social interaction. It is a group of people living within a specific area, sharing common bonds, interacting with one another, and often having a common cultural and historical heritage (Lyon 1999). The amount and quality of the ties and interaction among those living in the neighborhood varies with each community. The basis of the common ties can include family, ethnicity, proximity, school, social class, or religion, yet the depth of these bonds ranges from considerable involvement to disassociation with the neighborhood (Lyon 1999).

Neighborhoods are as varied and different as people, yet throughout the world a common theme can be found with people living in and identifying with the neighborhood. Examples of this can be found in immigrant neighborhoods in the United States (i.e., China Town, Little Italy, Spanish Harlem), inner-city neighborhoods in overcrowded downtown areas, shantytowns in developing countries, wealthy gated communities, and the suburbs. In Mexico, along the U.S.–Mexican border, neighborhoods have sprung up rapidly due to the *maquiladoras* program—an enterprise area of multinational corporations with factories that employ cheap labor and hope to increase industrial development within the country (Macionis and Parrillo 2001). As the types of neighborhoods are varied, the roles that neighborhoods fulfill also differ.

The neighborhood plays an important role in the lives of families and children. A neighborhood that has strong ties and a supportive system can benefit the family, while a neighborhood without a network system, connection to others, or available programs can be detrimental to the family. The ecological model of human development (Bronfenbrenner 1977) is an approach that focuses on families' and children's behavior within a social context. This model examines the design of physical space, the roles and relationships of other people to the family and children in the setting, and the activities in which the family and child are involved in the neighborhood. The overall level of organization within a neighborhood and community directly affects the level of integration of families and the stress levels of family life. The neighborhoods can have a powerful role in serving as a family support system, relieving the stress of social isolation, reinforcing group values, providing resources, and even connecting families to professionals and referrals to programs (Garbarino and Kostelny 1992). Although the role of the neighborhood is integral to the well being of families and children, some have experienced a loss of neighborhood connections.

Loss of the Neighborhood

The idea that Western societies lose connection to their neighborhoods as they modernize has been a continuing theme in sociology. Ferdinand Tönnies, Georg Simmel, Louis Wirth, and, to a lesser degree, Emile Durkheim, Karl Marx, and Max Weber all concluded that, on balance, the quantity and quality of the neighborhood and community is reduced when a society becomes more urban, more industrial, with fewer connections. Simmel's famous observation that "one nowhere feels as lonely and lost as in the metropolitan crowd" illustrates a common theme of alienation and lost community in classic social theory. Often, then, assessments of modern and even postmodern societies include the "loss of" community and neighborhood (Lyon 1999). The loss of community and loss of connection to the neighborhood can be harmful to the family and children.

Although only a few attempts have been made to measure the decline of relationships and connections to the neighborhood in the United States and other Western societies, there is nonetheless a wide acceptance of this decline. Thus, when sociologists speak of the "loss" of neighborhood and community, two distinct meanings arise. The psychological meaning focuses on the social interaction dimension of the neighborhood and analyzes the alienation that can come from the loss of neighborhood. The territorial meaning focuses more on the specific area and identification of components of the neighborhood definition, with analysis of the economic dependence and political impotence of the local community. Both meanings are related in that they see the same primary source for the loss of neighborhood—the urban, industrial mass society—and both describe similar problems—excessive individualism, alienation, and a resultant lower quality of life for the family (Bateman and Lyon 2000).

Although the two types of neighborhoods that are "lost" can be conceptually distinct and are treated as separate phenomena in most literature, they are, nonetheless, closely related. Robert Nisbet (1976) relates the decline in identification with the place and the territorial neighborhood to the more psychological alienation from close, personal interaction. In short, the decline in the relevance of and identification with the territorial neighborhood is related to the decline in interpersonal relations; both reinforce one another, and both are seen as symptoms of a modern society and the problems of families.

The observation that isolating, alienating, individualism is replacing neighborhood communities typically receives broad popular acceptance. According to Robert Bellah (1996), many of the ills of society result from too great an emphasis on individualism and too weak a commitment to the neighborhood. As individualism, selfishness, and greed in

the United States have grown, civic commitment and a sense of responsibility to society have declined. Participation in the neighborhood will reduce alienation and allow neighbors to belong and contribute to the community (Bellah 1996).

Robert Putnam (2000) claims that a decline in the traditions of civic engagement is weakening U.S. society and sense of community and neighborhoods. Putnam documents the noticeable absence of Americans' involvement in voluntary associations and the reduced patterns of political participation. Thus, Putnam (2000) concludes that Americans are less trusting, and the social capital of society is eroding.

Robert Wuthnow (1998) states that neighborhood-mindedness is eroding, civic involvement is indeed declining in voluntary clubs, and "loose connections" now tend to suit people in the United States. People are still connected to some extent, but in different ways. Organizational membership is not necessarily decreasing, but rather shifting from traditional voluntary organizations to new types of groups. A rise in support groups and specialized hobby groups demonstrates that these have become a poor substitute for traditional neighborhoods and the loose connections that define them (Wuthnow 1998).

Ties to the Neighborhood

Barry Wellman's (1979) "community saved" argument maintains that neighborhoods have survived despite urbanization, industrialization, and technological advances. Residents still have a sense of local ties for social support and sociability. The local neighborhood serves various functions for its residents; it provides primary relationships, social support, organizations, and numerous facilities and services near their place of residence. According to Wellman (1979), the thesis of the saved community includes heavy involvement of residents in a single neighborhood; strong network ties; extensive networks that are densely knit; solidarity of activities and sentiments; and the mobilization of assistance.

New emphasis is being given to geographically located, neighborhood-based interactions influenced by issues of locally defined power groups, social organizations, and neighborhood improvement efforts to weave the fabric of the community. Research shows that communities still exist in which residents identify with an area, known as the neighborhood, and personal interactions may still be examined within the boundaries of the neighborhood (Chaskin 1997). Residents who define the neighborhood in terms of network interactions and personal relationships tend to identify with the geographic unit compared with those considering the neighborhood in terms of the institutions and facilities.

The neighborhood community provides families with a way to deal with large-scale, urban institutions. Community theories stress the importance of preserving existing neighborhoods against the destructive effects of urban growth. Neighborhood residents committed to combating the problems of urban society have been forming local groups at a high rate. Neighborhood improvement associations seek to protect the quality of life in the local community. Membership and participation in these neighborhood associations develop a bond among the residents and attachment to the community (Oropesa 1992).

Neighborhood sentiment is often dependent on the social integration of the residents and in turn, the social integration has a significant impact on the attachment to the neighborhood for the family (Austin and Baba 1990). Various factors, such as social statuses and "who you know," will influence the level of involvement and attachment to the neighborhood (Oropesa 1992), but it is usually argued that whenever social involvement can be enhanced, it is beneficial to the residents, families, and children as well as the neighborhood. In sum, neighborhoods remain the place for meaningful social interaction, important political organization, and significant psychological attachment for families and children.

Effects of Violent Neighborhoods

Violent or disorganized neighborhoods can negatively affect children and families. The level of disorganization may produce both economic stress for families and abusive behavior in some situations. Families within these violent neighborhoods do not have adequate support or the resources to help alleviate familial problems. The combination of poverty with neighborhood violence exacerbates the problems of the family. More children are being maltreated in urban communities of highly concentrated poverty due to lack of resources and support (Garbarino and Kostelny 1992).

According to James Garbarino (1996), children who experience extreme and chronic danger are more likely to be psychologically damaged. However, the effect of parental buffering was shown to be significant in the development of a healthy psyche. In his observations, Garbarino found that there is a general "contagion effect" with regard to danger and violence in the neighborhood. Aggression breeds further aggression among youth. Finally, children exposed to violence and danger within their community were more likely to have more fears of violence (Garbarino 1996). Violence, danger, and trauma in the neighborhood can increase the stress levels of families and the difficulties of childhood. One solution to combating violent neighborhoods is through effective program, policies, and community development.

Neighborhood Programs and Policies

Although community development and neighborhood improvement projects are traditionally associated with attempts to modernize U.S. communities and Third World villages, a more recent trend has been combating the effects of modernization in the small towns and urban neighborhoods in the United States. During the 1960s, community development models were created to battle the effects of modernization by transforming socially isolated, politically powerless individuals into organized, territorially based neighborhoods pursuing common goals, thus empowering the family to make positive changes in the community.

A primary reason for the relative success of famed community organizer Saul Alinsky (1971) was his recognition that local neighborhoods retained important elements of a socially organized community. The ghetto or slum was not devoid of a neighborhood and was not a disorganized community. Alinsky's strategies for community development are usually viewed as among the most successful attempts ever made at practical neighborhood organization (Reitzes and Reitzes 1982), and a key to his success was the recognition of existing community organization and the ability to combine and build upon these local organizations. Still, Alinsky's strategies are difficult to put into effect. They require vigorous, time-consuming, and continuous efforts on the part of shrewd community organizers, and even then their success is limited.

Garbarino (1996) advocates policies with organized service delivery that allocate the scarce resources and intervene in the high-risk areas. Policies need to be based on a family-community-government relationship of joint responsibility that develops informal networks aimed at resource exchange. Successful policies need to strengthen networks and interdependence that empower the community as a family support system (Garbarino 1996).

Conclusion

The idea that nonspatial voluntary organizations can replace the territorial community as the primary basis for the psychological feelings of community is questionable. A base level of community rises naturally from living in proximity to one another. Although professional associations, labor unions, religious groups, and other voluntary organizations can provide a measure of the sense of neighborhood, the territorial neighborhood seems certain to remain a primary basis for the psychological community. Benjamin Zablocki (1979) maintains that when people live near one another, a level of interaction and common identification is naturally forced upon them. Voluntary organizations can and do supplement the territorial neighborhood, but it is difficult to foresee a time when neighborhood relationships are no longer associated with the territorial place.

Communities still exist in which residents identify with the territorial area, often known as the neighborhood, and personal interactions are still important within the boundaries of the neighborhood. Overall, both the territorial and psychological versions of the neighborhood are still relevant and still matter (Bateman and Lyon 2000). Neighborhoods continue to evolve as the traditional memberships in voluntary associations shift, yet the territorial neighborhood continues to provide the basis for much psychological community for families.

See also: GANGS; HUMAN ECOLOGY THEORY; INTERGENERATIONAL PROGRAMMING; JUVENILE DELINQUENCY; POVERTY; SOCIAL NETWORKS; URBANIZATION

Bibliography

Alinsky, S. D. (1971). *Rules for Radicals*. New York: Random House.

Austin, D. M., and Baba, Y. (1990). "Social Determinants of Neighborhood Attachment." *Sociological Spectrum* 10:59–78.

Bateman, R., and Lyon, L. (2000). "Losing and Finding Community: The Quest for Territorial and Psychological Community from the Neighborhood to Cyberspace." In *Research in Community Sociology,* Vol. 10, ed. D. Chekki. Stamford, CT: JAI Press.

Bellah, R. (1996). *Habits of the Heart: Individualism and Commitment in American Life.* Berkeley: University of California Press.

Bronfenbrenner, U. (1977). "Toward an Experimental Ecology of Human Development." *American Psychologist* 32:513–531.

Chaskin, R. J. (1997). "Perspectives on Neighborhood and Community: A Review of the Literature." *Social Service Review* (December):521–545.

Garbarino, J. (1996). "Youth in Dangerous Environments: Coping with the Consequences." In *Social Problems and Social Contexts in Adolescence: Perspectives Across Boundaries,* ed. K. Hurrelmann and S. Hamilton. New York: Aldine de Gruyter.

Garbarino, J., and Kostelny, K. (1992). "Child Maltreatment as a Community Problem." *Child Abuse and Neglect* 16(4):455–464.

Lyon, L. (1999). *The Community in Urban Society.* Prospect Heights, IL: Waveland Press.

Macionis, J., and Parrillo, V. (2001). *Cities and Urban Life,* 2nd edition. Upper Saddle River, NJ: Prentice Hall.

Nisbet, R. (1976). *The Quest for Community*. New York: The Free Press.

Oropesa, R. S. (1992). "Social Structure, Social Solidarity and Involvement in Neighborhood Improvement Associations." *Sociological Inquiry* 62(1):108–117.

Putnam, R. D. (2000). *Bowling Alone: The Collapse and Revival of American Community*. New York: Simon and Schuster.

Reitzes, D. C. and Reitzes, D. C. (1982). "Alinsky Reconsidered: A Reluctant Community Theorist." *Social Science Quarterly* 63(2):256–79.

Wellman, B. (1979). "The Community Question: The Intimate Network of East Yorkers." *American Journal of Sociology* 84 (March):1201–31.

Wuthnow, R. (1998). *Loose Connections: Joining Together in America's Fragmented Communities*. Cambridge: Harvard University Press.

Zablocki, B. (1979). "Communes, Encounter Groups, and the Search for Community." In *Search for Community*, ed. K. Black. Boulder, CO: Westview Press.

ROBYN BATEMAN DRISKELL

NEW ZEALAND

New Zealand families have experienced changes similar to those of families in other developed nations, including falling marriage and birth rates, more de facto relationships, rising divorce rates, more solo mothers, and increased maternal employment. Yet the cultural composition, isolation, and small population of these islands (less than four million people) have made families different from other English-speaking nations. Because New Zealand is officially bicultural, it is necessary to understand both the family patterns of the original inhabitants (Maori) and the settlers who arrived since the nineteenth century. In addition, we must acknowledge the impact of recent policy reforms on family life, as well as changing public discourse about welfare and families.

Historical Background

According to the 1996 census, Maori comprised about 14.5 percent of the population, which is much larger than the indigenous population of Australia, Canada, or the United States. Historically, Maori lived in extended families, or *whanau*. Stewart-Hawira (1995, p. 2) notes that *whanau* is the most fundamental unit of Maori social life and identity. Maori were positioned within their *whanau* according to birth order, generation, and senior or junior relationship between people of the same gender. These relationships, combined with genealogy, determined who held positions of status and authority (Cram and Pitama 1998).

When British missionaries and settlers came to Aotearoa/New Zealand in the early nineteenth century, they confronted a different family and economic system, one that included extended families, arranged marriages, and tribal guardianship of land rather than ownership by nuclear families. British colonial families consisted mainly of husbands, wives, and their children. Some households contained unmarried siblings, aging parents, and hired help, but migration often isolated families from their kin. Legally, the husband headed the household, and family roles were distinguished by gender and age. Colonial family law largely overlooked the Maori family system, privileging the British nuclear family.

Most early settlers came from Britain in the late nineteenth and early twentieth centuries to find work, establish financial security, and own homes. Not all migrants were voluntary, as some wives came because their husband and relatives wanted to migrate. Women and children were expected to follow (Dalziel 1991; Toynbee 1995). British husbands, wives, and children worked hard to earn a living, as did their Maori neighbors, and many parents raised their children on isolated subsistence farms in rural communities with few services. Birth rates were high, especially among Maori.

Although New Zealand women had won the right to vote in 1893, before other industrialized nations, family roles were determined by gender, and women's participation in paid work was limited after marriage. Both sexes were expected to marry and raise children, and there was little tolerance of nonconformity (Dalziel 1977). Stable, hard-working families were valued, along with physical prowess, masculine sport, gender differentiation, and British culture. Urbanization and industrialization came later to New Zealand than to Britain, and New Zealanders saw themselves as a rural society well into the twentieth century.

Over the years, laws have been reformed to give men and women equal legal rights, and both husband and wife now typically own the family home and other marital property. Nevertheless, symbolic vestiges remain of the patriarchal family, such as the bride being "given away" by her father at the wedding and using her husband's surname after marriage. Despite urbanization and feminism, the social pressure to reproduce remains strong; birth rates are relatively high; and many married mothers with young children still give primacy to family. Nevertheless, many mothers work outside the home, especially part-time, while their children are young.

Cultural Variations

Since the 1970s, immigration increased from various Pacific Islands (including Samoa, Cook Islands, Tonga, Niue, and Fiji), and after the 1980s more Asians came to New Zealand from many countries.

A family plays baseball in Tauranga, North Island, New Zealand. Two-parent families are the most prevalent in New Zealand, but they make up less than half of all families. MICHAEL POLE/CORBIS

Cultural variations remain evident in family structure and practices, and as well as in socioeconomic status. In contemporary New Zealand, two major variations in family structure remain, based on who is considered to be part of the family unit, who is most worthy of loyalty, and how resources will be divided (Fleming 1997). Pakeha (New Zealanders with European origins) tend to organize their families around the married couple and their children sharing the same household. Maori and to an even greater extent Pacific Island peoples (who together comprise about 20% of the population) are more likely than Pakeha to retain extended family ties. For example, the 1996 census indicates that 12.2 percent of Maori and 37 percent of New Zealand Samoans (the largest Pacific group) live in extended family households, compared to 4.3 percent of all New Zealanders.

Family structure also affects perceptions of obligations and priorities and the allocation of financial resources. For Pakeha, family money and household money are essentially the same, and money tends to flow from males to females and from parents to children (Fleming 1997). Paying household bills is given priority over other expenses, such as assistance to relatives or community donations. For Maori couples, the boundaries of the family economy could stretch to include other kin such as cousins and married siblings. For Pacific Island couples, extended family demands often take precedence over household bills and individual needs.

Two-parent families are the most prevalent in New Zealand, yet they accounted for only 45 percent of all families in the 1996 census. Couples without children living in the household comprised 37.3 percent, and one-parent families comprised 17.7 percent of all families. Living with other families or individuals was more prevalent among lone parents, as about one-third of one-parent families shared a household with others. Furthermore, about one-third of Maori lived in one-parent families in 1996 compared to only 12.3 percent of non-Maori New Zealanders. Jackson and Pool (1996) note that Maori family demography differs from Pakeha, which has important policy implications. Maori tend to bear children at an earlier age, and to have higher fertility rates, higher unemployment rates, lower incomes, and lower life expectancy than Pakeha.

In the 1996 census, 6 percent of New Zealanders identified themselves as "Pacific Islands" ethnicity. Meleisea and Schoeffel (1998) suggest that the term is problematic because it ignores the cultural specificity and identities of these groups. The Samoan community comprises half of the Pacific Island population in New Zealand. Census data show a youthful population with a high birth rate. Shared households containing three or more generations are a common feature. Furthermore, about 37 percent of all Samoan children lived in families with no parent employed, which reflects the high poverty rates of many Pacific Island families.

About four-fifths of New Zealanders are of European origin. Increasingly, however, immigrants from Asian countries are bringing new family forms that include overtly patriarchal families and arranged marriages. Yet new immigrants often have fewer children, reducing their fertility to improve their economic status and accommodate wives' employment.

Social Benefits for Families

Before the 1950s, New Zealand was seen as a generous welfare state because it was among the first to introduce a fully state-funded old-age pension (in 1898) and a family allowance (in 1926). New Zealand governments also introduced benefits for widows and deserted wives before Australia did (Baker and Tippin 1999, p. 32). A close examination of how much was being paid and to whom reveals that New Zealand was not as generous as its politicians claimed (McClure 1998). The original family allowance covered only a fraction of child-rearing costs and was paid only to low-income families with three or more children. Furthermore, it was only for married mothers, who needed their husband's signature upon application because this allowance was seen as a supplement to the family wage rather than a payment for care. New Zealand introduced a universal family allowance in the 1940s (along with other English-speaking nations) and in 1973 improved benefits for lone mothers (as did Australia).

In the mid-1980s, the Labor government began a series of reforms designed to improve the flagging economy and reduce public debt. When the conservative National government came to power in the 1990s, they introduced more privatization, electoral reform, university tuition fees, user fees for health services, and major cuts to social assistance (Kelsey 1995; Cheyne et al. 2000). Policy reform was rapid and motivated by economic concerns, but families were expected to adapt. Low-wage workers and people on benefits, in particular, felt the negative effects of cost cutting, including relatively deprived Maori and Pacific Island families and low-income mothers (Shirley et al. 1997).

The National government accelerated social program restructuring throughout the 1990s and gave it an overtly moral emphasis (Higgins 1999). In 1998, the coalition government proposed a Code of Social and Family Responsibility that gave directives to parents in child raising and appeared to blame the poor for their circumstances (Higgins 1999; Larner 1999). A wide consultation process was initiated, but the Code was never enacted into legislation because of public opposition. Nevertheless, the political exercise gave the clear message that the National government did not intend to expand social provision, but rather would focus on welfare-to-work strategies (Baker and Tippin 1999).

Since then, the Labor government has made minor improvements to childcare subsidies, but childcare remains expensive by international standards. There was no paid maternity or parental leave in New Zealand until 2002, which encouraged mothers to opt out of the workforce. Housing standards, child safety records, and average family income are lower than most member countries of the Organization for Economic Cooperation and Development (OECD), and social benefits tend to be targeted to the poorest families. Walter Korpi (2000) studied eighteen industrialized countries and found that New Zealand ranked eighteenth in terms of government support for dual-earner families and seventeenth in terms of general family support.

Continuing Family Concerns

About 12 percent of New Zealand couples now live together without legal marriage. The divorce rate is now similar to Australia's and Canada's, but many New Zealanders perceive divorce to be rampant and an indication, along with de facto marriage and falling birth rates, of the decline of the family. Conservative political discourse tends to see contemporary families as too small and unstable. In fact, the birth rate tends to be relatively high compared to European nations, and the divorce rate is moderate compared to the United States. Both lone and partnered mothers are less likely to be employed full-time than in North America and many European nations. Although New Zealand families appear traditional to some outsiders, many New Zealanders see family trends as disturbing.

As in other countries, New Zealand youth are moving to cities (especially Auckland) to further their education or to find work, but many remain financially dependent on parents for longer than in previous decades. Most leave New Zealand to travel or live abroad, and many do not return. An increasing percentage of young people acquire large student loans for postsecondary education, but many will be unable to repay this debt until midlife. This is seen as a particular problem for women, Maori, and Pacific Islanders, who tend to receive lower wages. There is considerable public concern that the emigration of young people and the crippling burden of student debt could have future implications for family formation, home ownership, and economic prosperity.

New Zealand families are also becoming diverse. More couples live together without legal marriage, but less than half of one percent reports to be gay or lesbian in the census. Families are also becoming culturally diverse, as immigration draws from more nations. Pacific Island peoples tend to have higher birth rates, which, combined with high Maori rates, will eventually change the face of New Zealand, but many Asian families have low fertility. Nevertheless, public opposition to immigration has encouraged the government to focus on immigrants with employment skills rather than family reunification.

In summary, New Zealand trends in family demography look similar to those in other industrialized countries, but there are also differences. The income gap between families is growing, with lone mothers and Maori and Pacific Island families increasingly disadvantaged. Public discourse emphasizes the importance of marriage, reproduction, and child rearing, and New Zealanders tend to see themselves as a family-friendly society. In fact, the New Zealand approach emphasizes the family as a private institution, offering little material support for parenting or combining work and family.

See also: EXTENDED FAMILIES; FAMILY POLICY

Bibliography

Adair, Vivienne, and Dixon, Robin, eds. (1998). *The Family in Aotearoa New Zealand.* Auckland: Addison Wesley Longman.

Baker, Maureen. (2001). *Families, Labour and Love.* Sydney: Allen & Unwin; Vancouver, University of British Columbia Press.

Baker, Maureen, and Tippin, David. (1999). *Poverty, Social Assistance and the Employability of Mothers: Restructuring Welfare States.* Toronto: University of Toronto Press.

Cheyne, Christine; O'Brien, Mike; and Belgrave, Michael. (2000). *Social Policy in Aotearoa New Zealand. A Critical Introduction,* 2nd edition. Auckland: Oxford University Press.

Cram, Fiona, and Pitama, Suzanne. (1998) "Ko toku whanau, ko toku mana." In *The Family in Aotearoa New Zealand,* ed. V. Adair and R.Dixon. Longman: Auckland: Addison Wesley Longman.

Dalziel, Raewyn. (1977). "The Colonial Helpmeet: Women's Role and the Vote in Nineteenth-Century New Zealand" *New Zealand Journal of History* 2(2):112–123.

Dalziel, Raewyn. (1991) "Emigration and Kinship: Migrants to New Plymouth 1840–1843." *New Zealand Journal of History* 25(2):112–128.

Fleming, Robin. (1997). *The Common Purse.* Auckland: Auckland University Press.

Higgins, Jane. (1999). "From Welfare to Workfare." In *Redesigning the Welfare State in New Zealand,* ed. J. Boston, P. Dalziel, and S. St. John. Auckland: Oxford University Press.

Jackson, N., and Pool, I. (1996). "Will the Real New Zealand Family Please Stand Up? Substantive and Methodological Factors Affecting Research and Policy on Families and Households." *Social Policy Journal of New Zealand,* 6 (July):148–163.

Kelsey, Jane. (1995). *Economic Fundamentalism.* London: Pluto Press.

Korpi, Walter. (2000). "Faces of Inequality: Gender, Class, and Patterns of Inequalities in Different Types of Welfare States." *Social Politics* 7(2):127–191.

Larner, Wendy. (1999). "Post-Welfare State Governance: Towards a Code of Social and Family Responsibility." *Social Politics* 7(2):244–265.

McClure, Margaret. (1998). *A Civilised Community: A History Of Social Security In New Zealand 1898-1998.* Auckland: Auckland University Press.

Meleisea, M., and Schoeffel, P. (1998). "Samoan Families in New Zealand: The Cultural Context of Change." In *The Family in Aotearoa New Zealand, ed.* Vivienne Adair and Robin Dixon. Auckland: Addison Wesley Longman.

Shirley, Ian; Koopman-Boyden, Peggy; Pool, Ian; and St. John, Susan. (1997). "Family Change and Family Policy in New Zealand." In *Family Change and Family Policies in Great Britain, Canada, New Zealand and the United States, ed.* S. Kamerman and A. Kahn. Oxford: Clarendon Press.

Stewart-Hawira, M. (1995). *Whakatupurango ngaro ki te whei ao ki te ao marama: The Impact of Colonisation on Maori Whanau.* Unpublished Master's thesis, University of Auckland.

Toynbee, Claire. (1995). *Her Work and His: Family, Kin, and Community in New Zealand, 1900-1930.* Wellington: Victoria University Press.

MAUREEN BAKER

NIGERIA

Nigeria is a multitribal, multilingual, and, consequently, multicultural country in the West African subregion. It occupies an area of 923,770 square kilometers with an estimated population of more than 100 million people. The capital of Nigeria is Abuja; the official language is English. Nigerians speak more than 300 languages and dialects; the major ones are Hausa, Igbo, and Yoruba. Nigeria has about equal numbers of Christians and Muslims (about 45% of each). The remaining 10 percent of the population follows traditional religions or are atheist and freethinkers.

Families in Nigeria

A family, which is usually made up of people who are related by blood, marriage, or adoption, is very important to most Nigerians. There are two major family types; the nuclear family, which is made up of one man, his wife, and their unmarried children, and the extended family, which is usually made up of a series of nuclear families. Culturally, most Nigerian cultural groups practice patrilineal descent, have patriarchal authority, have patrilocal rule of residence, and are generally patricentric in outlook. The children are socialized with this arrangement in mind, and female children are consciously socialized to serve and be subordinate to males. This hierarchical structure has sometimes led to dissolution of marriages on the grounds of the birth of only or mostly female children (Omokhodion 1996).

In Nigeria, having many children is fashionable and is a status symbol. For example, although a large family brings a greater economic burden, many families in the eastern part of Nigeria have ten or more children. Thus, the national fertility rate was estimated at 6.31 children per woman in 1995. The birth rate was 43.26 births per 1,000 people, while the death rate was 12 deaths per 1,000 population. However, the infant mortality rate was 72.6 deaths per 1,000 live births due to the poor medical facilities and the poverty of most Nigerians. This rate is one of the highest in the world and had a negative influence on the birth rate. The maternal mortality rate is also high.

A unique feature of the Nigerian family is the existence of a loose matrilineage and use of various terms to describe households and unions. For example, some households are headed by women. This may be the result of the women being widowed or divorced. The women might also be *outside wives*. This term describes women who function as wives to married men who live with their original wives and have extra wives outside their homes. These men are mobile husbands who move among their various partners, spending nights, having sex with their partners, and supporting them financially. These outside wives use the surname of their "husbands," and in many cases, are known to the man's original wife. Those who are not part of the culture may find this confusing, but the practitioners seem to manage well. The Nigerian legal system has improvised ways of accommodating such women and their children. In many cultures in Nigeria, there is no such status as illegitimate child.

Nigerian families are also distinctive in their loose use of the word *uncle* when referring to all older male relatives and sometimes nonrelatives as well. Also, all older female relatives and nonrelatives may be referred to as "aunty." Similarly, women above the age of forty-five are loosely called "mommy," while men who are about fifty or older are loosely called "daddy." People of greater social status, regardless of age, are addressed as sir or madam. This may be based on the traditional cultural deference to elders or superiors, which is very important to most Nigerian cultures.

The Yorubas of southwestern Nigeria practice bilateral descent. Thus, many of the current traditional rulers (Obas) have ascended the throne from their mother's lineage. In most parts of Nigeria, family linkage and consanguinity are very important. Thus, people have fourth, fifth, sixth, or even seventh cousins. They may refer to people from their village or town as brothers or sisters and create associations to perpetuate the linkage.

As a result of urbanization and migration and associated economic factors, however, the nuclear family is gradually becoming the dominant family type. It functions slightly differently from the typical nuclear family in Western countries. This may be the result of traces of the extended family system of being "our brothers' keepers."

Marriages in Nigeria

Two major types of marriage exist in Nigeria: monogamy, a marriage of one man to one woman, and polygyny, a marriage of one man to two or more wives. In most cultural groups in Nigeria, traditional marriage is usually an arrangement between two families as opposed to an arrangement between two individuals. Accordingly, there is pressure on the bride and bridegroom to make the marriage work as any problem will usually affect both families and strain the otherwise cordial relationship between them. In most Nigerian cultures, the man usually pays the dowry or bride-price and is thus considered the head of the family. Adultery is acceptable for men, but forbidden for women. Marriage ceremonies vary among Nigerian cultures.

Idoma marriage. The Idoma people live in central Nigeria, in the Benue State. The myth of their origin states that they are descended from the Zulu tribe of South Africa. They are mainly warriors. Some of their subgroups are the Adors, Otupas, Ogbanibos, Apas, Ofokanus and Owukpas. Marriage in Idoma land is considered a lifelong state, although divorce is possible on the grounds of

A Nigerian bride and groom at their wedding ceremony. In most cultural groups in Nigeria, traditional marriage is an arrangement between two families rather than an arrangement between two individuals. KERSTIN GEIER/ CORBIS

adultery or other concrete reasons. When an Idoma man is at least twenty-five years old and has the financial and physical capacity to maintain a wife and children, he searches for and finds a woman of his choice, who is at least eighteen years old. He reports his findings to his family, which then chooses a go-between, a person who is familiar with the girl's family. The go-between investigates the family of the prospective bride to ascertain that the family has no history of mental disease, epilepsy, or similar problems. If the result of this investigation is positive, the prospective groom's family visits the woman's family with gifts of kola nut and hot drinks. After the first visit, another visit is scheduled for the woman to meet her future husband, after which a final visit is scheduled for the future groom and his family to pay the bride-price and offer other gifts. If the woman refuses to marry the man after these gifts have been provided, the groom's family keeps them (Omokhodion 1998).

On the wedding day, in addition to the bride-price, the groom must pay a dowry first to the bride's mother and then another dowry to the father; this involves a significant amount of bargaining. Also every member of the bride's mother's family must be given money, with the groom's family determining the amount. The bride's age group and her more distant relatives also are given money, with the amount varying with level of the bride's education and productivity. Then the groom's family gives the bride a rooster and some money. If she accepts these gifts and gives them to her mother, she indicates her acceptance of the groom, but if she refuses, she signifies her refusal. If she accepts him, she is showered with gifts and money, and the two families eat and drink together. Before the bride is finally handed over to her husband, however, her age group will pose as a mock barrier to those who want to take her and extort money from the anxious groom's family. The bride's mother buys her cooking utensils and food because she is not expected to go to the market for the first five market days after her marriage. At the end of the eating and drinking, the wife is finally handed over to her husband's family. (Omokhodion 1998).

Ideally the bride should be a virgin at marriage, which brings pride and joy to her family. If she is found not to be a virgin, she is taken to the husband's family' ancestral shrine for cleansing. After this the *Ije* is put on her to invoke fertility on her. This marks the beginning of married life among the Idoma tribe.

Marriage in Okrika land. Okrika is located in the eastern part of the Niger Delta of Nigeria, in the Rivers State. The Okrika clan is made up of nine major towns and more than fifteen villages. The fifteen villages are known as *Iwoama* (new towns). Okrika is the largest town with the largest population and is the administrative and traditional headquarters of the clan. In the Wakirike area, there are two main types of marriages—the *Ya* or *Iyaye* and the *Igwa*.

The Ya marriage ceremony involves certain customary functions that precede the consummation of

the marriage. Here the bride and groom must come from the same tribe. When the husband is ready, members of the family assemble for the essential marriage rites, including the tying of the knot. The man is required to produce three to five pieces of kano cloth or *Ikpo,* one piece of real India cloth, or *injiri,* four yards of raffia palm cloth sewn together (*okuru*), and another separate yard of the same material. If the husband is wealthy, he adds additional kinds of cloth. He also provides three or four large pots of palm wine and twenty-two or twenty-four manila. These offerings are placed in the shrine of the family ancestors, and an elderly person in the family takes up the single yard of raffia cloth and ties the knot. The husband and wife stand before the shrine, side by side. The elder then ties the raffia cloth round the waist of the wife seven times, each time uttering some words that invoke blessings on the couple. Palm wine is poured into a drinking cup, and the bride and groom drink from it simultaneously. The knot has thus been tied, and divorce becomes virtually impossible. The single yard of raffia cloth is the essential thing to make the marriage binding. In case of unavoidable divorce as a result of adultery on the woman's part, the parents of the wife are bound to return double the cumulative expenses of the husband (Ikiriko 1984).

The second system, *Igwa,* means mixed; the woman and the man may marry even though they are from different families. A woman married under the *Ya* system can be married under *Igwa* if the *Ya* husband is not living with her as husband and wife under the same roof. All offspring of this second marriage belong not to the biological father but to the *Ya* husband, who by custom is regarded as their legal father. If the woman has not been previously married to any man under the *Ya* system, children from the *Igwa* marriage belong either to the lawful husband of the wife's mother or to her brothers. However, the once unchangeable custom of the possession of children born under the *Igwa* system of marriage is relaxing under the pressure of modern times. Many adult men and young people engage in *Igwa* marriage if their previous marriage produced no children (Omokhodion 1998).

Marriage among the Ibos. The Ibos are a very class-conscious group. They have a caste system and encourage endogamy. In the Ibo society, the castes include the Nwadiani, who are the upper caste of freeborn and land owners, and the Osu, who are the lower caste and descendants of former slaves. In the past, the Osu were used in human sacrifices. (Though the Osus are no longer slaves, yet they are still discriminated against by the freeborn, who will usually oppose any of their children marrying an Osu.)

Within the Nwadiani are three groups:

(1) The freeborn, who are able to trace their lineage to the founder of a segment of the community.

(2) The Omoru, whose ancestors came from elsewhere to settle and become attached to the founder of the community. Their descendants are accepted as full members of the village or town because of their freeborn status in their place of origin.

(3) The descendants of the autonomous groups who lived in the area before the founders of the state arrived and incorporated them into the structure of the community, which they established.

Intermarriage among Nwadiani has united these three categories in a closely knit kinship system. All the lineages in the village were believed to have descended from one ancestor or the other. Kinship links were sometimes invoked to create special relationships with neighboring village groups or village. Owing to their close kinship ties, men had to find their wives outside the village. One kind of link is between villages and village groups. Villages in a group, as well as neighboring villages, were linked by bonds forged by marriage alliances.

Endogamous marriage seemed to have served to perpetuate the Osu status, which is inferior. At Oguta, Osomari, Onitsha, and Abo, Osu could only marry an Osu because of their outcast status. They are thus despised by the freeborn. This discrimination was carried further at Osamari where the Osu class had their exclusive residential quarters (ebo) in each division. This also gave the servile quarters a sense of corporate solidarity in opposition to the "Freeborn" quarters. Through the intermarriage between members of different Ogbe, Ebo and the Osu of a community they have developed a web of kinship similar to that, which characterizes the Nwadiani. However, permitted intermarriage between Osu and Nwadianins and children born of such mixed marriages are allowed to have the status of Nwadiani. (Note that though this caste system is historical, the descendants of these castes

have inherited their ancestors' classes and are therefore stratified along that line even today.)

Marriage ceremonies in traditional Ibo society are elaborate affairs celebrated with much fanfare and merriment. The couple must have had some period of courtship during which the prospective groom informs his parents of his intention to take a woman of a certain village as wife. The parent of his intended wife must be known to his parents, and the courtship requires the prospective bride to pay at least one courtesy call on her potential in-laws to enable them to get to know her. After getting acquainted with the woman, the parents of the bridegroom will give their approval if they are satisfied that their prospective daughter-in-law has an unblemished reputation. Such courtships usually become public knowledge. The day of the marriage must be mutually agreed upon by both families (Omokhodion 1998).

On the day of marriage, the bride proceeds to her future spouse's village, accompanied by her mother, many girls of her own age, and her mother's female friends. An Ibo bride may also carry with her a "bride's dowry," which usually consists of kitchen utensils, mortar, palm oil, cassava, locust beans, and other condiments. The bride's dowry is usually contributed by her parents, their friends, and her own friends. The bridegroom and the two families, including friends and well-wishers, sit in their compound to eagerly await the arrival of the bride. When she comes, several young, unmarried women of the host village attend to her as a sign of welcome. An Ibo bride is usually colorfully decorated and given a beauty mark and other embellishments to set her apart. *Jigida,* which are waist beads of different colors (as many as fifteen or eighteen), adorn her waist. The young women dance in a circle around her, while her future husband and in-laws occasionally break through the circle one or two at a time and stick money on her forehead. As the money falls to the ground, one of the young women picks it up for her. As she dances, the jigida that covers her waist and the upper part of her buttocks jingle. After the feasting, the mother and others from her village return home, while the bride remains in her husband's village.

Marriage in the Hausa culture. The Hausas live in northern Nigeria. They are also found in Ghana, Togo, and Benin. The Hausas generally attach great importance to premarital chastity. A Hausa husband who discovers that the girl he has married is not a virgin will proclaim her shame to the entire town by breaking a pot outside his house. Among most Fulani, and other subtribes of the Hausa, custom forbids sexual intercourse between young people who are betrothed. Other tribes, however, view premarital intercourse as a kind of trial marriage. The *Piri* suitor cohabits with his fiancée for a period of four months in her mother's compound. Some of them may bear children before marriage, depending on the length of courtship. The young men are usually happy to marry these young mothers. Among tribes who accept premarital sex, no stigma is attached to the young woman girl who bears a child before marriage. The child is claimed by the girl's family, except where the father of the child is the girl's betrothed and has paid the bride-price in full. Kona boys and girls who are betrothed may cohabit. If the girl conceives, the boy has to make additional payments to her father, presumably on the ground that her fertility has been proven.

Some tribes practice the custom of placing young women under the care of their betrothed before they reach marriageable age; this is common among the Kona, Margi, Mumuye, and Mumbake, as well as the Mosi tribe. The objective appears to be twofold (Omokhodion 1996, 1998). First, the responsibility for the girl's upbringing and chastity is thrown on the fiancé's family, and second, the appropriation of the girl by her betrothed is clearly signified. As a result of pre-nuptial relations, a man can repudiate his betrothal at any time without the payment of damages in Hausaland.

Types of marriages in Hausaland. The Hausas practice various kinds of marriage. They include junior levirate marriage, whereby a younger brother may marry his late senior brother's wife or wives, and sororate marriage, whereby a man may marry his late wife's sister. Other types of marriage in Hausaland include cousin marriage known as *auren zumunta*, whereby a man or woman may marry anyone from a second cousin onward. Polygyny is also very popular, while many of the women, especially among the Muslims, are kept in the harems. The Hausas also practice a special type of polyandry that is a counterpart of concubinage. Among the Fulani pagan nomads, "wife lending" to a husband's brother or son is regarded as an act of reciprocal hospitality. The Munshi, Amgula, Yergurn, Rukuba, and Lungu practice marriage by "wife abduction." Other types of marriages in Hausaland include "marriage by purchase" (women are seen as transferable property) and "marriage by exchange" (one man gives his sister or daughter to a friend for a wife in exchange for a wife for himself). Marriage can also be by "capture," in most cases with the girl's consent, or by elopement.

Marriage Ceremony

If a man desires to marry a woman who is a virgin, he will first ask her. If she agrees, he goes to her father, and if he gives his consent, the prospective husband gives the father money. This money is divided into two parts, with half going to the girl's mother and half to her father. This is the preliminary part of the marriage ceremony.

About two or three months later, if the woman is still willing to marry, the groom may go to her father and discuss the bride-price with him. Once he knows the amount, he then tries to gather the money, which is usually handed over to the bride's father as soon as it is ready. The father then passes the money to the girl's mother to buy clothes and food for the marriage feast, including the white cloth that the bride will wear during the marriage ceremony. Also, part of the money will be used to purchase the food that the bride will eat after marriage for at least two weeks.

For about five to seven days after the ceremony, the bride remains in her father's house. She wears a white cloth and covers up her face, while her fingers are printed with henna. Usually, other young women come to play with her, while she is taught various homemaking skills. These girls usually eat food provided by the bride's father at the husband's expense. After about seven days, her relatives come to her house and take her to her husband's house, where the husband's friend (grooms men) try to get her to enter the house. Traditionally, she is supposed to refuse. At this stage, some money is usually given to the bridesmaids while a struggle ensues, with some pushing the bride while others pull her until she eventually enters her husband's house. All the women usually enter with her, singing, clapping, and dancing. At this stage the bridegroom's friends enter the house and distribute money to the dancing young women, who then spend some nights with the bride before returning home.

While the above is taking place, the bridegroom is not usually there, but in his best man's house. He only returns to his own house after five or seven days. If he decides to come home before this time, the bridesmaids will drive him away, but from the sixth day he can come and give the bridesmaids money and urge them to return to their homes, thus marking the end of the marriage ceremonies. Thereafter, the newly married couple will be free to live together as husband and wife (Omokhodion 1998).

Conclusion

The cultural diversity, richness, and distinctive qualities of Nigerian society are reflected in the various family types within the country. Culturally, Nigerian society is patrilineal, and the average man is socialized to have an inflated image of himself and other men. The desirability and permanence of marriage is the ideal of all the cultural groups in Nigeria. The payment of at least token dowry or bride-price is a cultural prescription cherished by most Nigerian cultural groups because it depicts the value of a properly socialized wife and conveys respect and appreciation for her family. Thus, marriage and family types in Nigeria are one major area of cultural similarity among the more than 300 diverse tribes and cultural groups that make up Nigeria.

See also: KINSHIP; YORUBA FAMILIES

Bibliography

Ikiriko, I. Okrika. (1984). *Okrika People.* Oragold Publishers Porthacort, Nigeria.

Omokhodion, J. O. (1996). *Sociology of Education: An African Experience.* Lagos, Nigeria: Tropical Publications.

Omokhodion, J. O (1998). *Socialization in Some Nigerian Communities: Readings in Sociology of Education.* Lagos, Nigeria: John Odionuwa Publishers.

JULIA O. OMOKHODION

NONMARITAL CHILDBEARING

Nonmarital childbearing is a part of the reproductive experience of many women, but much more so in some cultures than others. Nonmarital births are of two basic types. Some births, especially among younger women, are to those who never have been married. The other type of nonmarital childbearing occurs among women who were previously married, but who were divorced or widowed at the time of the birth. Among other factors, increasing diversity in marriage and family forms have contributed to the prevalence of nonmarital births. Specifically, *cohabiting unions,* where partners live in an informal, marriage-like relationship, often result in nonmarital births. Such unions are common in many cultures (Alan Guttmacher Institute 1998). Changing social and cultural norms including increased acceptance of premarital sex, out-of-wedlock childbearing, abortions, divorce, decisions to never marry, and greater labor force participation by women are thought to contribute to upward trends in nonmarital childbearing (Thornton 1995).

Nonmarital Childbearing in Developing Nations

Where strong cultural norms link marriage and fertility, nonmarital childbearing is likely to be especially visible among adolescents. Worldwide trends such as younger age of reproductive maturity, later age of marriage for women, improvements in women's reproductive (and overall) health, and changing social norms and attitudes have contributed to an increase in premarital sexual activity among adolescents. These trends are clearly visible for example, in Kenya, Ghana, Colombia, and Côte d'Ivoire (Ivory Coast). A common consequence of these trends is a high level of nonmarital fertility among adolescents. For example, in Botswana and Namibia, three-fourths of births to adolescents are nonmarital (Alan Guttmacher Institute 1998).

Several factors influence the prevalence of nonmarital childbearing among adolescents in developing nations. In some cultures, nonmarital childbearing among adolescents is a means to prove fertility and might even be a prerequisite to marriage (Alan Guttmacher Institute 1998). The prevalence of nonmarital childbearing among adolescents in developing nations also is influenced by the availability of modern contraceptive methods. Sexually active unmarried adolescents are more likely than those who are married to seek and use birth control. For example, in Côte d'Ivoire, 47 percent of unmarried adolescents use contraception whereas only 8 percent of married adolescents do so (Alan Guttmacher Institute 1998). The availability of reliable methods of contraception is not uniform across developing nations; moreover, cultural norms may deny contraceptive access to adolescents. A vast majority of sexually active adolescents in developing nations can, therefore, be at risk for nonmarital childbearing.

Research documenting trends in nonmarital childbearing in developing nations is inadequate for a comprehensive understanding. Some developing nations have strict norms against premarital and extramarital sexual activity, and, as a result, respondents may be unwilling to disclose nonmarital childbearing. In some developing countries (e.g., in North Africa and the Middle East), national surveys do not collect data on sexual activity among unmarried women, because cultural norms perpetuate the assumption that sexual activity is confined to marriage. In such nations, it is difficult to estimate the trends and patterns of nonmarital childbearing. However, it may be speculated that the level of nonmarital sexual activity is indeed low within developing nations, where there are strict cultural norms and taboos that regulate sexual activity. For example, less than 10 percent of adolescents in India reported being sexually active during adolescence (Alan Guttmacher Institute 1998).

Nonmarital Childbearing in Developed Nations

An examination of nonmarital childbearing trends in developed nations dramatic increase between 1970 and 1999 (see Table 1 and Figure 1). The United States, Canada, Denmark, Germany, the Netherlands, and Sweden have witnessed their nonmarital childbearing rates tripling, and in some cases (Denmark, France, Italy, and the United Kingdom), quadrupling or more during this period.

Nonmarital childbearing trends in some developed nations (especially Canada and the United Kingdom) are comparable to those in the United States. In 1995, the proportion of all births to unmarried women was about one-third in the United States and Canada, but was as high as 55 percent in Sweden, and 45 percent in Denmark. Developed countries with lower nonmarital births were: Japan (1% in 1995), Italy (9%), Germany (20%), and the Netherlands (23%). However, the United States has relatively higher nonmarital childbearing among teenagers, even compared with countries

TABLE 1

Percentage of nonmarital births in selected industrialized nations: 1970–1999

Country	Percentage of nonmarital births				
	1970	1980	1990	1995	1999
United States	11	18	28	32	33
Canada[1]	10	13	24	26	35[3]
Denmark	11	33	46	46	45
France	7	11	30	37	40[3]
Germany[2]	6	8	11	16	20[4]
Italy	2	4	6	8	9
Japan	1	1	1	1	
Netherlands	2	4	11	16	23
Sweden	18	40	47	53	55
United Kingdom	8	12	28	34	39

[1]1980 through 1990 excludes Newfoundland. After 1990 a significant number of births are not allocated according to marital status, resulting in an understatement of the proportion of births to unmarried women. [2]Prior to 1990, data are for former West Germany. [3]1997 [4]1998

SOURCE: U.S. Bureau of Census, *Statistical Abstract of the United States: 1998*. Council of Europe, *Recent Demographic Developments in Europe, 2000*. Statistics Canada, *Canada Year Book 2001*. S. J. Ventura and C. A. Bachrach, "Nonmarital Childbearing in the United States, 1940–99." *National Vital Statistics Reports*.

where the total nonmarital childbearing rates are higher than those in the United States (Singh and Darroch 2000).

International trends of increasing nonmarital childbearing have not been observed in some developed nations. The nonmarital childbearing rate in Japan is among the lowest in developed nations and had remained stable between 1970 and 1995. Cultural influences that serve to distinguish Japan from the nations discussed above may be an important explanation for this finding. In addition to an emphasis on fertility within marriage, Japan is also experiencing a decline in total fertility due to sociocultural changes and women's increased labor force participation (Iwao 2001).

Nonmarital births in the United States. Increasing numbers of births to unmarried mothers began to be a major concern in the United States in the late 1960s. There were about 224,000 children born in 1960 to unmarried mothers (Furstenberg 1991), but by 1991, that number had risen to more than 1.2 million (Ventura and Martin 1993). Nonmarital births increased from 11 percent of all births in 1970 to 33 percent in 1994 (Ventura and Bachrach 2000). The nonmarital birthrate in the United States

FIGURE 1

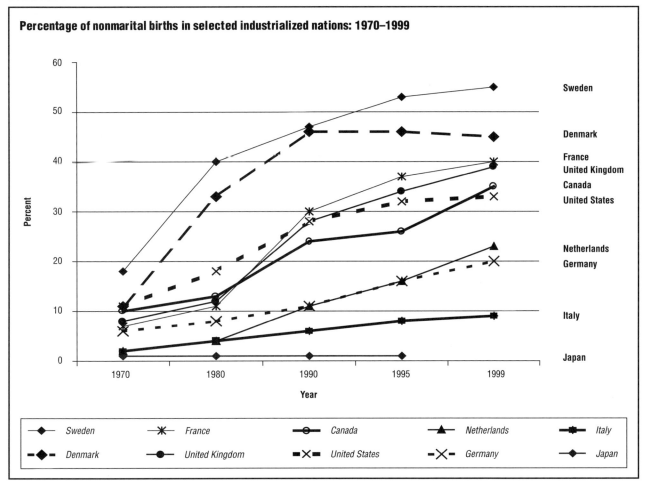

Percentage of nonmarital births in selected industrialized nations: 1970–1999

has remained approximately the same from 1994 to 1999 (Terry-Humen, Menlove, and Moore 2001).

The United States has traditionally had a high birthrate among adolescents (Singh and Darroch 2000). Approximately 80 percent of teenage births in the United States are nonmarital (Terry-Humen et al. 2001), but teens account for only 29 percent of all nonmarital births in this country. The teenage percentage of all nonmarital births has fallen from 50 percent in 1970 to 29 percent in 1999. On the other hand, the percentage of all nonmarital births that occurred among women aged twenty-five and older rose from 18 percent in 1970 to 34 percent in 1999 (Ventura and Bachrach 2000).

Nonmarital childbearing in the United States varies across ethnic groups. In 1970, the nonmarital birthrate was 13.9 per 1,000 women for white women and 95.5 for African-American women; this large racial difference has narrowed over time. In 1998, the nonmarital birthrate per 1,000 women

was 37.5 for white women, 73.3 for African-American women, and 90.1 for Latina women (Ventura and Bachrach 2000). Latina women have the highest nonmarital birthrate among all racial and ethnic groups in the United States (Ventura and Bachrach 2000).

One explanation for the nonmarital birth trends in the United States is the rise of cohabiting unions. The proportion of cohabiting unions increased from 29 percent in the 1980 to 1984 period to 39 percent in the 1990 to 1994 period. The percentage of nonmarital births from cohabiting unions varies by ethnic group. In 1994, Latinos had the highest rate (53%) of nonmarital births resulting from cohabiting unions, followed by whites (50%), and African Americans (22%) (Bumpass and Lu 2000). Another explanation for the high nonmarital birthrate in the United States is the decline in marriage rates for women aged eighteen to forty-four, especially among women in the twenty and older age category. For example, the percentage of unmarried women in the twenty-five to twenty-nine age group increased from 16 percent in 1970 to 45 percent in 1998 (Ventura and Bachrach 2000). Declining marriage rates for women are an indication of broad socioeconomic changes. The rise in cohabiting unions, later age of marriage, and a growing tendency to never marry (Abma et al. 1997) are some of the changes that have contributed to increasing trends in nonmarital childbearing. In addition, when faced with a nonmarital pregnancy, fewer women today marry before the birth of the child than in the past (Terry-Humen et al. 2001).

Risk Factors Associated with Nonmarital Childbearing in Developed Nations

An understanding of risk factors associated with nonmarital childbearing is vital for policy makers who are concerned with reducing rates. Childhood experiences, environmental contexts, neighborhoods, socioeconomic opportunities, family structure, parents' marital status, and parental educational and income levels are some of the common risk factors thought to be associated with nonmarital childbearing.

Risk factors for nonmarital childbearing in the United States. Research on the risk factors for nonmarital childbearing in the United States reveals that instability in family living arrangements due to parents' divorce, remarriage, job loss, and frequent migration is associated with children's nonmarital childbearing later in life. In addition, children in single parent homes who experience poverty and inadequacy of resources face a higher likelihood of being involved in nonmarital fertility. Further, individuals who suffer physical or sexual abuse as children are more likely to have nonmarital births in their adolescent or early adult years (Burton 1995).

Nonmarital fertility is also influenced by neighborhood contexts. Women in neighborhoods with a higher concentration of public assistance recipients experience higher levels of nonmarital fertility (Hill and O' Neill 1993), possibly because the receipt of public assistance is related to poverty, the absence of positive role models, and a lack of community resources (Duncan 1995).

Nonmarital fertility is also influenced by marital opportunities. Marriage rates are often lower among women who live in areas with relatively fewer numbers of employed men (South and Lloyd 1992). In addition, marriage and nonmarital fertility rates are affected by the economic position of men and their ability to support a family (Duncan 1995).

Research on adolescents suggests that the absence of social and economic opportunities, along with disadvantaged socioeconomic contexts, often leads to teenage pregnancy and childbirth (Alan Guttmacher Institute 1994). Adolescents who grow up in resource-deprived neighborhoods, those who lack positive role models in their families and neighborhoods, and those whose parents have lower educational and income levels are more likely to engage in early sexual intercourse and nonmarital childbearing (Brooks-Gunn et al. 1993; Duncan 1995). Other risk factors associated with the early onset of sexual activity and nonmarital fertility in adolescents include: early onset of puberty (Morris 1992), being African-American (Brewster 1994), and exhibiting psychosocial deviance (Costa et al. 1995). Research also indicates that warmth, connectedness, and communication between parents and children, parental monitoring and supervision of children, and parents' values against sexual intercourse or unprotected intercourse by their children are related to a reduction in the risk of adolescent pregnancy (Miller, Benson, and Galbraith 2001). In addition, teenagers who perform poorly at school, have low future aspirations, and who belong to disadvantaged families and communities face a higher risk of becoming sexually active at a younger age and of experiencing nonmarital childbearing (Miller 1995). Female adolescents who have traditional views about gender roles and family, and those with low self-esteem face a higher possibility of being involved in nonmarital childbearing (Plotnick 1992).

Consequences of Nonmarital Childbearing in Developed Nations

Nonmarital childbearing has implications for women, children, and entire societies across the world. One of the most pervasive consequences of nonmarital childbearing is the altered life trajectories of women and children who experience it. The exact consequences of nonmarital childbearing may vary from one nation to another depending on economic, social, and political conditions, but some general consequences have been documented in research.

Consequences of nonmarital childbearing in the United States. Research in the United States suggests that nonmarital childbearing has several negative consequences for women and their children. Women who experience nonmarital births attain lower levels of education and income, and are more likely to be dependant on governmental support (Driscoll et al. 1999). Further, women who experience nonmarital childbearing are likely to experience poverty. This is often due to the fact that the fathers of their children are unable or unwilling to pay child support (Garfinkel 1993; Garfinkel, McLanahan, and Robins 1994). Experiencing early single parenthood can hinder women from realizing their educational and career goals and may also limit the scope of future mate selection or family structure choices (Miller 1995). Teenagers who experience nonmarital fertility are less likely to complete high school or obtain college education (McLanahan 1995), and are thus more likely to experience poverty in their lives.

Nonmarital childbearing has negative consequences for children. Children of unmarried mothers are more likely to live in poverty. They are also likely to experience other risks such as a higher school dropout rate, a higher possibility of engaging in premarital sex, and experiencing teenage nonmarital pregnancy (Aquilino 1996; Moore, Morrison, and Glei 1995; Wu 1996). Children of unmarried mothers are also more likely to grow up in single parent, typically female-headed, households and to experience instability in living arrangements (Aquilino 1996; Bumpass and Lu 2000).

Nonmarital childbearing can have negative behavioral and cognitive outcomes for children, such as: delinquent behaviors, lower scores on standardized tests, and lower school grades (McLanahan 1995). Children of unmarried mothers may receive lower levels of parental supervision and involvement (McLanahan and Sandefur 1994). Children who grow up in neighborhoods with a high prevalence of single parent families might also consider nonmarital fertility to be a viable option in the future, and are more likely to engage in it themselves (McLanahan 1995). Children of young, unmarried teenage mothers also tend to experience a lower quality of home environment. Many of the negative consequences of nonmarital childbearing

are partially due to the poverty that often accompanies nonmarital fertility (McLanahan 1995).

Conclusion

Nonmarital fertility has become prevalent in many countries of the world. Due to social and cultural norms against nonmarital childbearing in developing nations, and because reliable data are not available to document rates and trends of nonmarital fertility in some cases, little is known about nonmarital childbearing in developing nations. On the other hand, among developed nations, nonmarital childbearing clearly has increased dramatically between 1970 and 1999, in most cases by a factor of 3 or 4. In the United States nonmarital births increased from about 1 in 10 in 1970 to about 1 in 3 in 1999. Although 80 percent of births to U.S. teenagers are nonmarital, teenagers account for only 29 percent of all nonmarital births, whereas women aged twenty-five and older account for 34 percent of nonmarital births in the United States. Nonmarital childbearing in the United States varies across racial and ethnic groups. In 1998, Latina women had the highest nonmarital birthrate, followed by African-American and white women respectively. The postponement of marriage, reflected in declining marriage rates and increasing cohabitation, as well as broad socioeconomic changes have contributed to increases in nonmarital childbearing. At a more specific level, unstable family arrangements, the experience of physical or sexual abuse, negative neighborhood contexts, the scarcity of marital opportunities, and disadvantaged socioeconomic contexts are all key risk factors associated with nonmarital childbearing. Among adolescents in particular, parental values about sexual activity, warmth and connectedness between parents and children, and parental monitoring of children are associated with nonmarital childbearing. Adolescent nonmarital childbearing often results in reduced educational attainment and income, and less stable ongoing marital and family structures for women and children. Nonmarital childbearing also results in negative cognitive, environmental, and behavioral outcomes for children. Policies to discourage nonmarital births among women and adolescents might help arrest these trends. Increased economic opportunities for women, economic initiatives for educational attainment, and policies supporting deferred childbearing among teenagers are examples of such policies.

See also: ABORTION; ADOLESCENT PARENTHOOD; COHABITATION; MOTHERHOOD; PREGNANCY AND BIRTH; RELIGION; SEXUALITY IN ADOLESCENCE, SINGLE-PARENT FAMILIES

Bibliography

Abma, J.; Chandra, A.; Mosher, W.; Peterson, L.; and Piccinino, L. (1997). "Fertility, Family Planning, and Women's Health: New Data from the 1995 National Survey of Family Growth." *Vital and Health Statistics* 23(19):1–114.

Alan Guttmacher Institute. (1998). *Into a New World: Young Women's Sexual and Reproductive Lives.* New York: Author.

Alan Guttmacher Institute. (1994). *Sex and America's Teenagers.* New York: Author.

Aquilino, W. S. (1996). "The Life Course of Children Born to Unmarried Mothers: Childhood Living Arrangements and Young Adult Outcomes." *Journal of Marriage and the Family* 58(2):293–310.

Brewster, K. (1994). "Race Differences in Sexual Activity among Adolescent Women: The Role of Neighborhood Characteristics." *American Sociological Review* 59:408–424.

Brooks-Gunn, J.; Duncan, G. J.; Klebanov, P.; and Sealand, N. (1993). "Do Neighborhoods Affect Child and Adolescent Development?" *American Journal of Sociology* 99(2):353–395.

Bumpass, L., and Lu, H. (2000). "Trends in Cohabitation and Implications for Children's Family Contexts in the United States." *Population Studies* 54(1):29–41.

Burton, L. M. (1995). "Family Structure and Nonmarital Fertility: Perspectives from Ethnographic Research." *Report to Congress on Out-of-Wedlock Childbearing.* Hyattsville, MD: U.S. Department of Health and Human Services.

Costa, F. M.; Jessor, R.; Donovan, J. E.; and Fortenberry, J. D. (1995). "Early Initiation of Sexual Intercourse: The Influence of Psychosocial Unconventionality." *Journal of Research on Adolescence* 5:91–121.

Council of Europe. (2000). *Recent Demographic Developments in Europe.* Strasbourg, Belgium: Author.

Driscoll, A. K.; Hearn, G. K.; Evans, V. J.; Moore, K. A.; Sugland, B. W.; and Call, V. (1999). "Nonmarital Childbearing among Adult Women." *Journal of Marriage and the Family* 61(1):178–187.

Duncan, G. J. (1995). "How Nonmarital Childbearing is Affected by Neighborhoods, Marital Opportunities, and Labor Market Conditions." *Report to Congress on Out-of-Wedlock Childbearing.* Hyattsville, MD: U.S. Department of Health and Human Services.

Furstenberg, F. F., Jr. (1991). "As the Pendulum Swings: Teenage Childbearing and Social Concern." *Family Relations* 40:127–138.

Garfinkel, I. (1993). "Assuring Child Support." New York: Russell Sage Foundation Press.

Hill, A., and O'Neill, J. (1993). "Underclass Behaviors in the United States: Measurement and Analysis of Determinants." New York: Center for the Study of Business and Government, Baruch College, City University of New York.

Iwao, S. (2001). "Japan's Battle of the Sexes: The Search for Common Ground." In *Family in Transition,* ed. A. S. Skolnick and J. H. Skolnick. Needham Heights, MA: Allyn and Bacon.

McLanahan, S. S. (1995). "The Consequences of Nonmarital Childbearing for Women, Children, and Society." *Report to Congress on Out-of-Wedlock Childbearing.* Hyattsville, MD: U.S. Department of Health and Human Services.

McLanahan, S. S., and Sandefur, G. D. (1994). "Growing Up with a Single Parent." Cambridge, MA: Harvard University Press.

Miller, B. C. (1995). "The Risk Factors for Adolescent Nonmarital Childbearing." *Report to Congress on Out-of-Wedlock Childbearing.* Hyattsville, MD: U.S. Department of Health and Human Services.

Miller, B. C.; Benson, B.; and Galbraith, K. A. (2001). "Family Relationships and Adolescent Pregnancy Risk: A Research Synthesis." *Developmental Review* 21:1–38.

Moore, K. A.; Morrison, D. R.; and Glei, D. (1995). "Welfare and Adolescent Sex: The Effects of Family History, Benefit Levels and Community Context." *Journal of Family and Economic Issues* 16(2/3):207–237.

Morris, N. M. (1992). "Determinants of Adolescent Initiation of Coitus." *Adolescent Medicine: State of the Art Reviews* 3(2):165–180.

Plotnick, R. D. (1992). "The Effects of Attitudes on Premarital Teenage Pregnancy and its Resolution." *American Sociological Review* 57:800–811.

Singh, S., and Darroch, J. E. (2000). "Adolescent Pregnancy and Childbearing: Levels and Trends in Developed Countries." *Family Planning Perspectives* 32(1):14–23.

South, S. J., and Lloyd, K. M. (1992). "Marriage Opportunities and Family Formation: Further Implications of Imbalanced Sex Ratios." *Journal of Marriage and the Family* 54:440–451.

Statistics Canada. (2001). *Canada Yearbook 2001*. Ottawa: Author.

Terry-Humen, E.; Manlove, J.; and Moore, K. A. (2001). "Births Outside of Marriage: Perceptions vs. Reality." *Child Trends Research Brief*. Washington, DC: Child Trends.

Thornton, A. (1995). "Attitudes, Values, and Norms Related to Nonmarital Fertility." *Report to Congress on Out-of-Wedlock Childbearing*. Hyattsville, MD: U.S. Department of Health and Human Services.

U.S. Bureau of Census. (1998). *Statistical Abstract of the United States: 1998*. Washington, DC: Government Printing Office.

Ventura, S. J., and Bachrach, C. A. (2000). "Nonmarital Childbearing in the United States, 1940–99." *National Vital Statistics Reports* 48(16):1–40.

Ventura, S. J., and Martin, J. (1993). "Advance Report of Final Natality Statistics, 1991." *Monthly Vital Statistics Report from the Centers for Disease Control* 42(3):1–48.

Wu, L. L. (1996). "Effects of Family Instability, Income, and Income Instability on the Risk of a Premarital Birth." *American Sociological Review* 61(2):386–406.

BRENT C. MILLER
KYUNG-EUN PARK
ANNE THOMAS

NORWAY

see SCANDINAVIA

NUCLEAR FAMILIES

The term *nuclear family* can be defined simply as a wife/mother, a husband/father, and their children. However, this straightforward structural definition is surrounded by a cloud of ambiguity and controversy. Most of the debates have centered around three questions. First, is the nuclear family universal—found in every known human society? Second, is the nuclear group the essential form of family—the only one that can carry out the vital functions of the family (especially, rearing the next generation) or can other family patterns (e.g., single mothers, single fathers, two women, or two men) be considered workable units for fulfilling these functions? The third issue concerns the link between the nuclear family household and industrial society. In the old days, before work moved outside the home to factories and offices, did parents and children live together under one roof with grandparents and other relatives? Did the nuclear family break away from this extended family system as a result of industrialization?

The debate over the universality and necessity of the nuclear family began in the early twentieth century. Pioneer anthropologist Bronislaw Malinowski (1913) stated that the nuclear family had to be universal because it filled a basic biological need—caring for and protecting infants and young children. No culture could survive, he asserted, unless the birth of children was linked to both mother and father in legally based parenthood. Anthropologist George P. Murdock (1949) elaborated on the idea that the nuclear family is both universal and essential: "Whether as the sole prevailing form of the family . . . or as the basic unit from which more complex families form, [the nuclear family] exists as a distinct and strongly functional group in every known society" (p. 2).

The debate about the nuclear family and industrialism centered around the writings of one of the leading sociologists of the post-World War II era, Talcott Parsons (1955). The nuclear unit, he argued, fits the needs of industrial society. Independent of the kin network, the "isolated" nuclear family is free to move as the economy demands. Further, the intimate nuclear family can specialize in serving the emotional needs of adults and children in a competitive and impersonal world.

In later years, the assumptions about the family held by Malinowski, Murdock, and Parsons have been challenged by family sociologists as well as by anthropologists, historians, feminist scholars, and others. Research in these fields has emphasized the diversity of family not only across cultures and eras but also within any culture or historical period.

Anthropologists have pointed out that many languages lack a word for the parent-child domestic units known as *families* in English. For example, the Zinacantecos of southern Mexico identify the basic social unit as a *house,* which may include one to twenty people (Vogt 1969). In contrast, historical studies of Western family life have shown that nuclear family households were extremely common as far back as historical evidence can reach, particularly in northwestern Europe—England, Holland, Belgium, and northern France (Gottlieb 1993). These countries have long held the norm that a newly married couple moves out of their parents' homes and sets up their own household. Despite the continuity of form, however, different social classes, ethnic groups, religious persuasions, and geographical regions have had different practices and beliefs with regard to parent-child relations, sexuality, family gender roles, and other aspects of family life.

Family life also has changed in response to social, economic, and political change. Many scholars believe that in the eighteenth century and the early nineteenth century, the modernizing countries of Western Europe witnessed a transformation of family feeling that resulted in "the closed domesticated nuclear family." The new family ideal, Lawrence Stone (1977) argued, prescribed domestic privacy and strong emotional attachments between spouses and between parents and children. On the other hand, some scholars have argued that strong emotional bonds between family members have existed for centuries, and others have argued that the "closed domesticated nuclear family" was a middle-class ideal that came to be applied slowly and incompletely outside that class. In Eastern Europe, however, the nuclear norm did not prevail. Households were expected to contain other relatives besides the nuclear unit (i.e., a third generation or a parent's sibling and possibly that person's spouse and children). It is true that in those parts of Europe about half of the households at any particular time were nuclear, but this unit served as just a stage the family might pass through.

As these examples show, it is important to distinguish between the nuclear family as a cultural symbol and as an observable domestic group (Schneider 1968). The nuclear family is a symbol deeply rooted in Western culture; it is represented in art, family photographs, advertising, and television. However, the family ideal of any particular culture does not necessarily describe the social realities of family life. For example, the nuclear family remains the preferred cultural pattern in the United States despite the fact that the proportion of

nuclear family households is smaller than in the past (Skolnick 1991). The persistence of this ideal is reflected in the fact that most divorced people remarry. Further, there is no evidence that most single mothers prefer to raise their children by themselves. In most Western nations, particularly the United States, the wish to become a parent at some time in one's life is virtually universal. Today's longevity means that the parent-child relationship can last fifty years or more. It remains a central attachment in most people's lives.

In any particular time and place, families have always been more varied than the prevailing image of what the ideal family should be. However, although family types are even more diverse than in the past, most contemporary families are still variations on the traditional nuclear family pattern (e.g., the two-job family, the empty nest couple with grown children, or the blended family). An unsettled period of family transition has resulted from major shifts in economic, demographic, political, and cultural trends in the industrialized world and beyond. These changes have altered people's lives dramatically, but other institutions of society—government, business, religion—have not yet caught up with the new realities.

The traditional Western concept of the nuclear family as the only normal, natural family has had a profound influence on research, therapy, and public policy. It has encouraged the tendency to define any departure from that arrangement as unhealthy or immoral. This concentration on a single, universally accepted pattern has blinded students of behavior to historical precedents for multiple legitimate family arrangements.

See also: EXTENDED FAMILY; FAMILY, DEFINITION OF; FICTIVE KINSHIP; KINSHIP

Bibliography

Bernardes, J. (1999). "We Must Not Define 'The Family.'" *Marriage and Family Review* 28(3/4):21–41.

Chester, R. (1986). "The Myth of the Disappearing Nuclear Family." In *Family Portraits,* ed. D. Anderson and G. Dawson. Exeter, UK: Short Run Press, Ltd.

Gottlieb, B. (1993). *The Family in the Western World.* New York: Oxford.

Malinowski, B. (1913). *The Family Among the Australian Aborigines.* London: University of London Press.

Murdock, G. P. (1949). *Social Structure.* New York: Macmillan.

Parsons, T. (1955). "The American Family: Its Relations to Personality and the Social Structure." In *Family Socialization and Interaction Process,* ed. T. Parsons and R. F. Bales. New York: Free Press.

Schneider, D. M. (1968). *American Kinship: A Cultural Account.* Englewood Cliffs, NJ: Prentice Hall.

Schneider, D. M., and Smith, R. T. (1973). *Class Differences and Sex Roles in American Kinship and Family Structure.* Englewood Cliffs, NJ: Prentice Hall.

Skolnick, A. (1991). *Embattled Paradise: The American Family in an Age of Uncertainty.* New York: Basic Books.

Stacey, J. (1996). *In the Name of the Family.* Boston, MA: Beacon Press.

Stone, L. (1977). *The Family, Sex, and Marriage in England, 1500–1800.* New York: Harper & Row.

Uzoka, A. (1979). "The Myth of the Nuclear Family: Historical Background and Clinical Implications." *American Psychologist* 34:1095–1106.

Vogt, E. Z. (1969). *Zinacantan: A Maya Community in the Highlands of Chiapas.* Cambridge, MA: Harvard University Press.

ARLENE SKOLNICK (1995)
BIBLIOGRAPHY REVISED BY JAMES J. PONZETTI, JR.

OLD AGE

ONLY CHILDREN

Only children are people who grow up without siblings. They have been stereotyped as "selfish," "lonely," and "maladjusted." Early in the twentieth century, the emerging discipline of psychology portrayed only children as inevitably pathological. However, since that time, hundreds of studies about only children have been conducted, and the overall conclusion is that only children are no more selfish, lonely, or maladjusted than people who grow up with siblings. Thus, the maturing discipline of psychology no longer views only children as inevitably pathological (Falbo and Poston 1993).

The highest percentage of one-child families in the United States can be found among families formed during the Great Depression. Among white women who began their families during this period, as many as 25 percent had only one child. Immediately after World War II, the average rose to four children per couple. This so-called Baby Boom ended in the late 1960s, and the one-child family gradually became more common again, especially among single-parent families (Falbo 1984).

Researchers have evaluated only children in terms of five main developmental outcomes: intelligence, achievement, personality, sociability, and psychological adjustment. Intelligence (usually measured in terms of standardized ability tests, such as IQ tests) and achievement (measured typically in terms of the number of years of education attained or the prestige of occupations) are the two most commonly studied outcomes. Only children generally score slightly better than others on intelligence when they are young. However, during adolescence, the small advantage in intelligence disappears (Falbo and Polit 1986). On the other hand, only children appear to have and maintain an advantage in achievement. Even when the socioeconomic characteristics of their parents are controlled, analyses indicate that only children tend to complete more years of education than others and are likely to have more prestigious jobs (Blake 1989).

One of the concerns about only children is that their lack of sibling relationships might lead them to have less desirable personalities than those who grew up with siblings. However, the results of hundreds of personality studies suggest that only children are generally like children with siblings in most personality dimensions, including autonomy, generosity, and cooperativeness (Polit and Falbo 1987).

Research into the sociability of only children has yielded mixed results (Falbo and Polit 1986).

Although a few large, longitudinal studies suggest that children without siblings may be prone to more solitary recreational activities than children with siblings (Claudy 1984), other studies indicate that only children marry at about the same age as others and are no more likely to divorce (Groat, Wicks, and Neal 1984).

Many studies have also examined the psychological adjustment of only children, typically basing assessments on omnibus adjustment inventories, such as the Junior Eysenck Personality Inventory. Taken as a whole, these studies indicate that only children tend to score much like people with siblings. A few studies have reported that many only children receive services at psychological clinics; however, this type of finding should not be construed to mean that only children are more likely to be maladjusted. Instead, the most plausible interpretation is that the parents of only children are more likely to get services for their children when they need them than are other parents (Falbo and Polit 1986).

In 1979, the People's Republic of China initiated policies that were designed to promote the number of one-child families. These policies were most successful among urban families. In the late 1980s and 1990s, one-child families predominated in urban China. During this time, more than 90 percent of the students in urban elementary schools were only children (Falbo and Poston 1993). Soon after the one-child policy began, people in the United States and some in China predicted that China would become a country filled with "little emperors," Chinese slang for spoiled brats.

Many studies have been done in China about the characteristics of only children to determine if, indeed, they are little emperors. However, these studies have, in turn, found that only children are similar to, inferior to, and superior to other children (Falbo and Poston 1993). Given the mix of these results, the consequences of the one-child policy on the development of children will likely remain a controversial subject.

See also: ACADEMIC ACHIEVEMENT; CHILDHOOD; DEVELOPMENT: SELF; SIBLING RELATIONSHIPS

Bibliography

Blake, J. (1989). *Family Size and Achievement.* Berkeley: University of California Press.

Claudy, J. G. (1984). "The Only Child as a Young Adult: Results from Project Talent." In *The Single-Child Family,* ed. T. Falbo. New York: Guilford.

Falbo, T. (1984). "Only Children: A Review." In *The Single-Child Family,* ed. T. Falbo. New York: Guilford.

Falbo, T., and Polit, D. F. (1986). "A Quantitative Review of the Only Child Literature: Research Evidence and Theory Development." *Psychological Bulletin* 100:176–189.

Falbo, T., and Poston, D. L. (1993). "The Academic, Personality, and Physical Outcomes of Only Children in China." *Child Development* 64:18–35.

Groat, H. T.; Wicks, J. W.; and Neal, A. G. (1984). "Without Siblings: The Consequences in Adult Life of Having Been an Only Child." In *The Single-Child Family,* ed. T. Falbo. New York: Guilford.

Polit, D. F., and Falbo, T. (1987). "Only Children and Personality Development: A Quantitative Review." *Journal of Marriage and the Family* 49:309–325.

Roberts, L. C., and Blanton, P. W. (2001). "I Always Knew Mom and Dad Loved Me Best: Experiences of Only Children." *Journal of Individual Psychology* 57(2):125–140.

TONI FALBO (1995)
BIBLIOGRAPHY REVISED BY JAMES J. PONZETTI, JR.

OPPOSITIONALITY

Children learn to resist and, if necessary, oppose the will of others as part of their normal development. The refusal to conform to the ordinary requirements of authority and a willful contrariness is called *oppositionality,* and manifests itself during childhood with behaviors such as stubbornness, argumentativeness, tantrums, noncompliance, and defiance.

Children's prosocial impulses become apparent in the first year of life through cooperative interactions and sharing. Learning how to tolerate frustration is an important aspect of the socialization process, but a degree of defiance and noncompliance is normal during the preschool years (e.g., the *terrible twos*). After the age of three children start to learn that they do not always need to be "good." Defiance and noncompliance, particularly in boys, may increase at that time. Oppositionality may accentuate again during adolescence when teenagers try to break away from the influence of their parents and develop their own identity. It shows in adolescents wanting to do "their own thing," in the way they dress or cut their hair and in their propensity to challenge authority. Most parents know this and allow young people some room to manifest their individuality, and usually it does not cause major problems. Occasionally, this drive becomes so intense that it creates difficulties at home and school.

It is not clear what happens to oppositional children when they grow up. The majority are likely to become well-functioning adults, some may develop antisocial behavior, and others may continue showing difficulties in their interpersonal relationships, mostly by showing passive resistance and covert hostility (Fergusson 1998). Some of the characteristics of these children, such as stubbornness, single-minded determination, and nonacceptance of social rules or expectations, can be harnessed constructively and may result in considerable individual achievement.

These developmental changes have been observed in all cultures, although their manifestations and intensity vary. Behaviors such as temper tantrums and disobedience are reported to have similar prevalence in most countries (Crijnen, Achenbach, and Verhulst 1999).

Oppositionality and Oppositional Defiant Disorder

The boundaries between oppositionality—displayed by most young people at one time or another—and the psychiatric condition called oppositional defiant disorder are blurred. Whether oppositionality is considered maladaptive, that is, a disorder, largely depends on the intensity, frequency, and duration of the behaviors and if they interfere with the young person's psychosocial functioning. Defiance and noncompliance can cause impairment through frequent arguments at home, reduced school performance, school detention, or suspension.

Children and adolescents with oppositional defiant disorder display a pattern of negativistic and hostile conduct towards people in authority, typically parents or teachers. They lose their temper and swear with little provocation, especially if they cannot get what they want. They are stubborn and cannot give in. When asked to do something, they

simply do not do it ("I will do it later," "I forgot"). They are touchy, blame others for their mistakes, and often seem to get enjoyment from provoking and annoying people. They hold grudges and can be vindictive. Oppositional children justify their behavior by saying that what they are asked to do is unreasonable or unfair (American Psychiatric Association 1994).

These problems occur more often at home where they can result in extreme family tension, but can be seen at school also. Parents and teachers feel frustrated with these young people and this leads to angry confrontations. However, these defiant young people seldom carry out serious antisocial or delinquent acts and their conduct can be normal in many situations, for example at school or in social settings (Angold and Costello 1996).

Causal Factors

Stubbornness, noncompliance, and aggressiveness are traits largely determined genetically. Some children have by nature a difficult temperament (Sanson and Prior 1999). They are irritable, difficult to soothe, and have numerous and more severe tantrums than other children during infancy or the preschool years. Parents or teachers are often drawn into power battles with these young people, which can create a vicious cycle of increasing attempts to control the young person that lead to more anger and rebelliousness.

Conversely, oppositional behaviors are highly context-sensitive. Many factors can reinforce or exacerbate normal oppositionality so that it becomes a problem. Parents of noncompliant, defiant children seem to have less effective problem-solving skills, particularly in tasks that involve conflict, and are more likely to criticize, belittle, and blame their children. Oppositional behavior is also believed to be more common in children living in families in which there have been several parental figures, due to separation or divorce, or in which parents were very strict, particularly if discipline was inconsistent or not accompanied by warmth and care. Children who have been abused or neglected are often aggressive and defiant.

Childrearing practices that are caring, nonpunitive, and that encourage strong group loyalty and respect for authority may reduce oppositional behavior. These are observed in some Eastern cultures. For example, Chinese people tend to be very lenient toward infants and children under six years of age. This is in marked contrast to the strict, even harsh, discipline they impose upon older children. Traditionally, Chinese parents were more concerned with impulse control and less tolerant of aggressive behaviors in children than their Western counterparts. By emphasizing filial piety, they tended to discourage independence, assertiveness, and creativity (Ho 1986).

Young people with learning difficulties and mental health problems, such as *attention deficit/hyperactivity disorder,* and those who are depressed often show marked oppositionality and irritability. Oppositional defiant disorder can be an early stage in the development of the more serious conduct disorder. In that case, as children become older, their behavior escalates into breaking rules, truancy, stealing, and physical fights.

Epidemiology

Some degree of oppositionality is very frequent in two- to five- year-olds. Oppositional defiant disorder is a common problem displayed by 3 to 5 percent of young people in affluent Western countries such as the United States and Australia. Prevalence increases with age and is higher in males and among the poor and disenfranchised.

There is little epidemiological data about prevalence of this condition in non-Western cultures. Given the variation in child-rearing practices and the importance these have in the development and maintenance of oppositionality, it may be assumed that societies that discourage individualism have lower rates of oppositional disorder. However, epidemiological studies have revealed similar rates of behavioral problems to those reported in Western countries (Crijnen, Achenbach, and Verhulst 1999; Shen and Wang 1995).

Treatment

In practice, oppositional young people are treated with a variety of psychological and behavioral interventions targeting the child and the family. The broad aim of treatment is to increase compliance and reduce conflict. Working with one or both parents (or a parental figure) is desirable. The therapist usually tries to help parents understand the way they perceive and respond to the child; teach them more effective, nonviolent discipline strategies; find ways to reduce the frequency and intensity of arguments; and encourage parents to increase cooperative and leisure activities. The most promising way of achieving most of these goals appears to be parent management training (Kazdin 1998).

Parent management training refers to a set of procedures in which parents are taught to alter their child's behavior. It is based on the view that defiance and noncompliance are inadvertently developed or maintained by maladaptive patterns of parent-child interaction. These include harsh discipline, inconsistency, lack of satisfactory resolution of conflict, directly reinforcing deviant behavior, and not reinforcing appropriate behaviors. The treatment has been evaluated in controlled trials with prepubertal children and adolescents with oppositional problems of varying severity. Parent management training results in marked improvement in oppositional behavior, treatment gains are maintained up to three years, and there may also be improvements in areas not directly targeted by treatment, such as *sibling adjustment* and *maternal depression* (Scott et al. 2001; Kazdin 1998).

This therapy teaches parents to identify problem behaviors, to introduce prompts, instructions, and modeling to facilitate desirable behavior, and to use positive reinforcement. On average, programs run for six to eight weeks. Only one parent is required to attend in many of them. Traditionally, parent management training has been administered to individual families in a clinical setting. However, group delivery, often using videotaped material, and self-administration by manuals have made these treatments more accessible while remaining effective (Sanders and Markie-Dadds 1996).

An extensive range of medications has been tried for children with behavior problems, if not specifically for oppositionality. There are limited data about the response of oppositional defiant behaviors to psychotropic drugs. Therefore, medication should usually be reserved for cases with a concurrent (comorbid) disorder that is amenable to drug treatment (such as *depression* or attention deficit/hyperactivity disorder), and to children where oppositionality is the manifestation of another condition, such as depression (Rey and Walter 1999).

Family's Response to Oppositionality

Oppositional problems have often been present for a long time and parents become unable to differentiate matters in which they need to take a stand from issues that are trivial and not worth the fuss. In these situations, parents are afraid that if they give in or ignore something, their child will get out of control and walk all over them. Consequently, parents end up nagging, saying "no" all the time, or constantly trying to set more limits. This usually increases the child's defiance. In these cases the therapist may help parents identify what is important and what is not, what is really worth a fight and what is not.

Another common scenario is that parents just give in and think their child is too strong-willed for them. These parents lose confidence and the young person increasingly takes control. This can happen more easily in single-parent families or families in which parents do not support each other. When these patterns are well established, change is difficult and requires time.

Prevention

Oppositionality can be minimized and oppositional defiant disorder can be prevented. The optimal approach would identify and lessen risk factors—such as coercive parenting, marital conflict, and parental depression—prior to the development of disruptive behaviors and clinical disorder. At present, however, most interventions target families where children already exhibit problem behaviors and aim to prevent further deterioration. In this type of intervention children are selected because of the severity of their disturbance at day care center or preschool, or by measures of family adversity or dysfunction.

Preventative programs basically involve modifications of parent management training programs and are delivered to groups of children at risk for these problems (e.g., children with difficult temperament or those who display marked oppositionality by the age of four or five years). There are other types of preventive interventions that also seem promising, for example classroom programs such as the "Good Behavior Game" (Kellam et al. 1994).

See also: CHILDHOOD, STAGES OF: ADOLESCENCE; CHILDHOOD, STAGES OF: MIDDLE CHILDHOOD; CHILDHOOD, STAGES OF: PRESCHOOL; CHILDHOOD, STAGES OF: TODDLERHOOD; CONDUCT DISORDER; CONFLICT: PARENT-CHILD RELATIONSHIPS; DEVELOPMENTAL PSYCHOPATHOLOGY; DISCIPLINE; JUVENILE DELINQUENCY; PARENTING STYLES; SUBSTITUTE CAREGIVERS; TEMPERAMENT

Bibliography

American Psychiatric Association (1994). *Diagnostic and Statistical Manual of Mental Disorders,* 4th edition. (DSM-IV). Washington, DC: Author.

Angold, A., and Costello, J. (1996). "Toward Establishing an Empirical Basis for the Diagnosis of Oppositional Defiant Disorder." *Journal of the American Academy of Child and Adolescent Psychiatry* 35:1205–1212.

Crijnen, A.; Achenbach, T. M.; and Verhulst, F. C. (1999). "Problems Reported by Parents of Children in Multiple Cultures: The Child Behavior Checklist Syndrome Constructs." *American Journal of Psychiatry* 156:569–574.

Fergusson, D. M. (1998). "Stability and Change in Externalising Behaviours." *European Archives of Psychiatry and Clinical Neuroscience* 248:4–13.

Ho, Y. F. (1986). "Chinese Patterns of Socialization: A Critical Review." In *The Psychology and Behaviour of the Chinese People,* ed. M. H. Bond. Hong Kong: Oxford University Press.

Kazdin, A. (1998). "Parent Management Training: Evidence, Outcomes, and Issues." *Journal of the American Academy of Child and Adolescent Psychiatry* 36:1349–1356.

Kellam, S. G.; Rebok, G. W.; Ialongo, N.; and Mayer, L. S. (1994). "The Course and Malleability of Aggressive Behavior from Early First Grade into Middle School: Results of a Developmental Epidemiologically-Based Preventive Trial." *Journal of Child Psychology and Psychiatry* 35:259–289.

Rey, J. M., and Walter, G. (1999). "Oppositional Defiant Disorder." In *Disruptive Behavior Disorders in Children and Adolescents: Review of Psychiatry,* Vol. 18, ed. R. L. Hendren. Washington DC: American Psychiatric Press.

Sanders, M. R., and Markie-Dadds, C. (1996). "Triple P: A Multilevel Family Intervention Program for Children with Disruptive Behaviour Disorders." In *Early Intervention and Prevention in Mental Health,* ed. P. Cotton and P. H. Jackson. Melbourne: Australian Psychological Society.

Sanson, A., and Prior, M. (1999). "Temperamental and Behavioral Precursors to Oppositional Defiant Disorder and Conduct Disorder." In *Handbook of Disruptive Behavior Disorders*, ed. H. C. Quay and A. E Hogan. New York: Plenum Press.

Scott, S.; Spender, Q.; Doolan, M.; Jacobs, B.; and Aspland, H. (2001). "Multicentre Controlled Trial of Parenting Groups for Childhood Antisocial Behavior in Clinical Practice." *British Medical Journal* 323:1–7.

Shen, Y., and Wang, Y. (1995). "Behaviour Problems of Schoolchildren in Beijing: A Study of Prevalence and Risk Factors." In *Chinese Societies and Mental Health*, ed. T. Lin, W. Tseng, and E. Yeh. Hong Kong: Oxford University Press.

JOSEPH M. REY
SE-FONG HUNG

ORPHANS

Researchers and social policy makers have long been interested in the developmental impact of institutionalization. Are young children who have experienced extreme deprivation in the first year or two of their lives ever able to overcome such poor developmental beginnings? Children in orphanages have been studied in many parts of the world (e.g., Iran, Lebanon, United States, Greece, Romania, Russia, and Canada). The early work on institutionalization demonstrated that deprivation resulted in *developmental insult* but made no attempt to establish what it was about deprivation that caused such deficits. Intellectual assessments were often used as outcome measures and social emotional variables were used to explain these outcomes. In the late twentieth century, researchers examined larger samples of orphanage children using standardized developmental assessments and measures of all aspects of development (i.e., physical, intellectual, behavioral, and social-emotional). This entry presents a review of both the early literature and late-twentieth-century research on institutionalized children. In most studies children with orphanage experience are compared to children reared in foster care, adopted children, or children who were home-reared from birth. Typically orphanage children fare less well on most measures than children in these other groups.

Early Literature on Institutionalization

Research interest in the developmental consequences of extreme deprivation in infancy began in the early 1940s and 1950s with the work of researchers such as Rene Spitz (1945a; 1945b), William Goldfarb (1945; 1955), and John Bowlby (1953). Researchers became interested in this topic as a result of the high infant mortality rate in institutions from no known physical cause (Spitz 1945a; 1945b). Rene Spitz coined the term *hospitalism* to describe the physical and psychological characteristics of infants housed in institutions. He described conditions in the institution as dire. For example, children spent most of their days in cubicles with drab walls wherein sheets often hung over the sides of the infants' cribs, obstructing their view. Spitz suggested that this lack of stimulation explained the rapid deterioration in children's intellectual development. He found a drastic drop in infants' *developmental quotients* (DQ) over the first few months of life in institutions, and by the end of the second year Spitz reported that infants' DQs had dropped to a low of 45, where an average DQ is 100. Spitz concluded from his study that the damage inflicted on children during their first year of life was irreparable.

William Goldfarb (1955) studied fifteen children who had been reared in an institutions for the first three years of their lives and were subsequently placed in foster care. He compared these children to a group of children who had been in foster care since early infancy. Goldfarb found that the institution group, even in adolescence, were delayed intellectually relative to the foster care group, displayed significantly greater problem behaviors, were socially less mature and appeared emotionally removed in terms of their capacity to form relationships. Goldfarb claimed that early institutional rearing resulted in developmental deficits that were not overcome once children were placed in more stimulating and loving environments. He clearly stated that, given his findings, "babies should be kept out of institutions" (Goldfarb 1947, p. 457).

Clearly, this early work suggested that institutionalized children would be irreparably damaged as a result of such experience. This work has been criticized, however, largely because of methodological limitations (Longstreth 1981; Pinneau 1955). Critics reported that much of this early literature provided scant details regarding not only conditions in orphanages but also the assessments used to evaluate children. The number of children who were tested, the ages at which they were

Young Rwandan refugees sit on a blanket outside an orphanage in Goma, Democratic Republic of the Congo. Research has shown that improvements in the orphanage environment, such as lowering child-caregiver ratios and providing perceptual stimulation reduce the negative impact of institutional living. HOWARD DAVIES/CORBIS

tested, and how often assessments were carried out was often unclear. These limitations made it difficult for later researchers to have strong confidence in the early data on institutionalized children.

Not all early studies, however, predicted such dire outcomes for institutionalized children. In many parts of the world researchers conducted intervention studies attempting to ascertain the kinds of interventions that might prevent poor developmental outcomes. Researchers began demonstrating that many of the cognitive and social deficits among these children were ameliorated after improvements in their environment (Broussard and DeCarie 1971; Dennis 1960; Hunt et al. 1976; see Rosenblith and Sims-Knight 1985 for a review; Skodak and Skeels 1945, 1949). Such interventions included placing infants as *houseguests* with older children (Skodak and Skeels 1945, 1949), improving child-to-caregiver ratios (Hunt et al. 1976), and early-adoption (Dennis 1973). All of these studies

showed that simple changes, even within the orphanage environment (e.g., lowering child-caregiver ratios, providing perceptual stimulation), resulted in increases in children's intelligence quotient (IQ) scores. More importantly, this research showed that the effects of deprivation were not irreparable, although the length of institutionalization could make a difference in developmental outcomes.

Further support for the idea that institutionalized children were not destined for developmental compromise came from the work of Barbara Tizard and her colleagues with children who had spent the first two years of their lives in high-quality institutions in the United Kingdom (Tizard 1977). In these institutions child-to-caregivers ratios were 3:1 and the children experienced adequate social interaction, were taken on outings, and fed well. The caregivers, however, were discouraged from forming intimate relationships with the children. This was the major way in which orphanage children's lives differed from the lives of home-reared children. Tizard first assessed these children at two years of age and compared them to a sample of home-reared children from a working-class background. She found that at this time the institution children's IQs were slightly lower than the IQs of the working class children, and their language was slightly delayed, but their social development was normal. Tizard followed her sample of children up to sixteen years of age and found that the majority of parents claimed their children had developed a deep attachment toward them. These data were in contrast to Goldfarb's earlier work in which he claimed that previously institutionalized children would be unable to form subsequent attachment relationships. As noted previously, however, the children in Tizard's sample had not experienced the extreme deprivation that the children in Goldfarb's sample had. Therefore Tizard's more positive outcomes may be partially the result of less severe deprivation.

Later Deprivation Studies

It was not until late 1989 and early 1990 that researchers once again could address the impact of extreme deprivation on young children, when the Ceausescu regime in Romania was overthrown. At this time the outside world became aware of thousands of children who had been housed in Romanian state-run orphanages. The conditions in Romanian orphanages were similar to or worse than the conditions described by Goldfarb (Ames 1990; Groze and Ileana 1996). Children spent from twenty to twenty-four hours a day in their cribs, with little visual or auditory stimulation (Ames 1990, 1997), and child-to-caregiver ratios ranged from 10:1 for infants to as high as 20:1 for children over three years of age (Chisholm et al. 1995). Therefore researchers were once again permitted the opportunity to evaluate the developmental impact of extreme deprivation. Sandra Kaler and Betty Jo Freeman (1994) examined the cognitive and social-emotional developmental status of children within an orphanage in Romania and found that the majority of orphanage children were severely delayed.

Since the early 1990s three major studies have examined the developmental outcomes of children who had spent their first year or two of life in a Romanian orphanage and were subsequently adopted. Two studies in Canada (Ames 1997; Marcovitch et al. 1997) and one in the United Kingdom (Rutter et al. 1998) have followed these children postadoption. These studies represent an improvement on the earlier literature given they have used large samples of children, comparison groups, and standardized measures that evaluate several aspects of children's development. We now know more about the impact of institutionalization on children's physical, intellectual, behavioral, and social-emotional development.

Intellectual Development

Elinor Ames and her colleagues (Morison, Ames, and Chisholm 1995) examined children's development, eleven months postadoption, assessing delays in four areas: fine motor, gross motor, personal-social, and language. They found that when their parents first met them the vast majority of adoptees were delayed in all four areas of development. Eleven months postadoption, however, adoptees displayed clear developmental catch-up in that now only close to half the adoptees showed delays in each area of development. This is consistent with the work of Michael Rutter and his colleagues in the United Kingdom (Rutter et al. 1998).

In both of these studies of Romanian adoptees intellectual development was also examined (Morison and Ellwood 2000; Rutter et al. 1998). In Ames's sample, when the adopted children had been in their adoptive homes for approximately three years, orphanage children had significantly lower IQs than both Canadian-born and early-adopted children (Morison and Ellwood 2000). This was particularly the case for children who were adopted after two years of age. Therefore, the longer that children had been institutionalized the more likely such institutionalization had an impact on intellectual development. It is important to note, however, that there was wide variability in IQ scores within each group of children, with some orphanage children scoring in the superior range for IQ (Ames 1997).

Rutter and his colleagues compared Romanian adoptees' intellectual development to a group of within-country adoptees (Rutter et al. 1998). Rutter and his colleagues (1998) found that by the age of four, the Romanian adoptees who had been adopted before six months of age did not differ in terms of IQ from the sample of within-country adoptees. For those children adopted after six months of age, their mean IQ scores were only slightly below 100 but they did score significantly lower than either the within-country adoptees or the early-adopted Romanian children.

These findings are consistent with findings from a study comparing orphanage and home-reared children in Russia. Vladimir Sloutsky (1997) assessed differences in IQ scores between six- and seven-year-old children reared in an orphanage with home-reared children and found that the orphanage children scored significantly lower in IQ than home-reared children.

Behavior Problems

Behavior problems have also been examined in recent studies of institutionalized children. These studies have found that orphanage children display rather unique behavior problems when compared with either home-reared nonadopted children or within country-adoptees.

Ames and her colleagues attribute most of the behavior problems of orphanage children to their orphanage experience given that early-adopted children who were adopted before two months of age did not appear different from Canadian-born children in any problem area (Ames 1997; Fisher et al. 1997). The most troublesome problems for adoptive parents were in the areas of eating, sleeping, stereotyped behavior, and sibling and peer relationships. Eleven months postadoption, one-third of orphanage children in their sample would not eat solid food or ate too much, both behaviors that were likely the result of orphanage experience. Although orphanage children did not differ from Canadian-born children in the number of sleeping problems they had, the kind of sleeping problems that adoptive parents experienced with their orphanage children differed. The sleeping problem of most concern to adoptive parents was the fact that children would not signal when they were awake, another behavior that was likely the result of institutionalization.

Stereotyped behavior concerned adoptive parents. The majority of orphanage children (84%) displayed stereotyped behavior, mostly in the form of rocking. Three years after adoption adoptive parents reported improvements in all behavior areas. At this time orphanage children did not look different from Canadian-born and early-adopted

children in eating problems, sleeping problems, or sibling problems. However, they still displayed more stereotyped behavior than children in the other two groups, although this behavior had improved as well from Time 1 to Time 2. Clearly these recent results suggest that much of the difficulties linked to orphanage experience are overcome when children's environments improve.

Children's behavior problems were also examined using the Child Behavior Checklist (CBCL), a standardized behavior problem questionnaire developed by Thomas Achenbach, Craig Edelbrook, and Catherine Howell (1987). Romanian orphanage children scored significantly higher on the CBCL than did Canadian-born or early-adopted children, and a large percentage of orphanage children scored above the clinical cut-off for the CBCL (Fisher et al. 1997). This finding is consistent with work in a Greek residential group care facility with nine-year-old children (Vorria et al. 1998). In comparing residential group care children to children reared in two-parent families Panyiota Vorria and colleagues (1998) found that the group care children were more inattentive, passive, and participated less in group activities at school than did their family-reared peers. In general, institution-reared children typically display more behavior problems than home-reared children.

Social-Emotional Development

For many reasons *indiscriminate friendliness* is a behavior that is particularly relevant to any study of institutionalized children. References to indiscriminately friendly behavior are evident in the early literature on the social development of institutionalized children who were later fostered or adopted (Goldfarb 1955; Provence and Lipton 1962). Tizard (1977) characterized indiscriminate friendliness as behavior that was affectionate and friendly toward all adults (including strangers) without the fear or caution characteristic of normal children. In these cases a child's behavior toward other adults could not be discriminated from his or her behavior toward caregivers.

Studies of institutionalized children have also examined indiscriminate friendliness. In Ames's study parents were asked five questions assessing (a) whether their child wandered without distress; (b) whether their child was willing to go home with a stranger; (c) how friendly their child was with new adults; (d) whether their child was ever shy; and (e) what their child typically did upon meeting new adults. These researchers found that orphanage children displayed significantly more indiscriminate friendliness than both early-adopted and Canadian-born children, and orphanage children were just as indiscriminate three years postadoption as they were initially (Chisholm 1998). Similarly, Thomas O'Connor, Michael Rutter, and their colleagues in the United Kingdom (2000) found that indiscriminate friendliness was associated with length of deprivation in their sample of Romanian adoptees.

Attachment

Indiscriminate friendliness is particularly relevant to the study of attachment because some researchers have suggested that indiscriminately friendly behavior may be indicative of *nonattachment,* a term used to describe an attachment disorder that results from an infant not having had the opportunity to form an attachment relationship (Lieberman and Pawl 1988) or a *reactive attachment disorder.* (Zeanah 1996). A. F. Lieberman and J. H. Pawl (1988) have used the term *nonattachment* to describe an attachment disorder that results from an infant not having had the opportunity to form an attachment relationship. This is precisely the situation of children reared in institutions, so researchers have focused on linking this behavior to children's attachment. Kim Chisholm (1998) found that the more extreme indiscriminate behaviors (i.e., wandering without distress and being willing to go home with a stranger) were associated with insecure attachment in Ames's sample.

The question of whether orphanage children are able to form attachment relationships with their adoptive families has been of concern to both researchers and adoptive parents. Researchers have examined attachment using standard separation reunion procedures and validated coding systems.

Chisholm (1998), using Ames's sample of Romanian adoptees, found that one-third of orphanage children were securely attached to their adoptive parent, one-third were insecurely attached to their parent but in a way that is not uncommon in normative samples of children, and one-third of orphanage children displayed atypical insecure attachment patterns. Some researchers have suggested that such atypical patterns may be indicative of future psychopathology (Carlson and Sroufe

1995; Crittenden 1988a). Although all of the orphanage children formed attachments, significantly more of them displayed insecure attachment patterns than children in both the Canadian-born and early-adopted groups. This is consistent with other research on a sample of Romanian adoptees living in the Toronto area (Handley-Derry et al. 1995) and the UK sample of Romanian adoptees (Marvin and O'Connor 2000).

These findings taken together contradict claims in the early literature on institutionalized children (Goldfarb 1955; Spitz 1945), showing that orphanage children in all three of these studies were able to form attachment relationships with their adoptive parents. It is important to note, however, that these recent findings further suggest that when the attachment process does go wrong in previously institutionalized children, it may go very wrong. In Chisholm's study (1998) significantly more orphanage children than Canadian-born or early-adopted children displayed atypical attachment patterns, which some researchers have suggested are risk factors in the development of psychopathology (Carlson and Sroufe 1995; Crittenden 1988).

Summary

How does one attempt to summarize the recent literature on institutionalized children? Most of the studies show, perhaps unsurprisingly, that children who have spent an extended period of time in orphanage display deficits in all areas of development when compared to any other group (i.e., early-adopted, within-country adopted, and/or home-reared children). Although this sounds like the same pessimistic picture that both Goldfarb and Spitz painted, when one examines the data beyond mere group differences, a different picture emerges. Ames (1997) extended the work with her sample by going beyond group differences and examining the data within her orphanage group. As reported earlier, orphanage children in Ames's sample displayed significantly more behavior problems, they had significantly lower IQs, more social problems, and they displayed significantly more insecure attachment patterns, particularly more atypical or extreme attachment patterns than children in the other groups. On each of these measures, however, there was substantial within-group variation. Not all of the orphanage children were experiencing all of these problems. This raises a risk and resiliency question. Why do some children recover from such extreme deprivation seemingly unscathed, whereas other children carry scars into their futures? Ames examined the correlates that were associated with particular problems, and whether it was the same orphanage children experiencing each of these problems. She defined four areas of serious problems: having an IQ of eighty-five or lower, having an atypical insecure attachment pattern, having severe behavior problems, or continued presence of stereotyped behavior.

Ames then grouped her sample in terms of the number of serious problems and compared her groups in this way. She found only one early-adopted child had as many as three serious problems, and none of her Canadian-born group had three serious problems, but 30 percent of the orphanage group had three or four of these serious problems. This third of the orphanage group accounted for 68 percent of all the individual serious problems that orphanage children had. Ames then reanalyzed all of the data excluding those orphanage children with three or four serious problems from the analyses. She found there were no longer group differences on behavior problems as assessed by the CBCL or insecure attachment patterns. Nevertheless, orphanage children still had significantly lower IQs than Canadian-born children.

This is a more positive picture than earlier work on institutionalization and speaks to the strength in young children of overcoming tremendous adversity. Fully two-thirds of orphanage children were doing well given their poor start. One-third of the children, even three years postadoption, were doing poorly.

Ames then examined factors that were associated with a child having three or more serious problems. She considered characteristics of the institution, child characteristics, and family characteristics. Although length of time in the orphanage was associated with more problems, no characteristics of the institution or the child were associated with a child having serious problems.

There were, however, family characteristics that were associated with children having more problems. One factor that seemed to predict whether a child would have serious problems was the number of Romanian children adopted. Families who adopted two children had more serious problems than families who only adopted one

child. A number of other family characteristics were associated with children having serious problems and all of these appear to be tapping the resources available to a family. The higher the family income, the older the mother, and the higher the *socioeconomic status* (SES) of the family, the fewer problems they were experiencing with their child. A final—rather surprising—correlate of children who were experiencing many problems involved the parent who had traveled to Romania to adopt a child. Children who were selected by the father alone experienced more problems postadoption than children who had been selected by either the mother alone or both parents. Ames (1997) suggested that the parent who is going to be the parent providing most of the day-to-day caregiving should have been the parent to travel to Romania.

These correlates seem to suggest that resiliency is not something within a child. It develops as a result of the particular interactions a child experiences with his or her environment. Therefore, institutionalization represents a risk factor that initially sets a child on a less than optimal developmental pathway. Where a child ends up developmentally, however, will depend on what happens after the initial trauma.

Children's experience in orphanages clearly constitutes a risk factor for their optimal development. Given an optimal postorphanage environment with few stressors, however, orphanage children appear to do well and overcome early adversity. Institutionalization appears to contribute to less than optimal development only when coupled with other stressors (for example, low SES, high parenting stress). This is consistent with the suggestion that one risk factor in isolation does not lead to an increased probability for psychopathology. It is the combination of several risk factors working together that substantially increases the likelihood of future difficulty (Belsky, Rosenberger, and Crnic 1995; Rutter 1985).

Clearly, children who experience institutionalization and are subsequently adopted generally arrive in their adoptive homes in poor condition. Parents are dealing simultaneously with an array of problem areas, which requires an exceptionally high level of commitment from parents. The fact that many parents are successful in promoting optimal developmental outcomes in their children is truly a laudable achievement.

See also: ADOPTION; CHILDREN'S RIGHTS; FAILURE TO THRIVE; FOSTER PARENTING

Bibliography

Achenbach, T. W.; Edelbrock, C.; and Howell, C. T. (1987). "Empirically-Based Assessment of the Behavioral/Emotional Problems of 2–3-Year-Old Children." *Journal of Abnormal Child Psychology* 15:629–650.

Ames, E. W. (1990). "Spitz Revisited: A Trip to Romanian 'Orphanages.'" *Canadian Psychological Association Developmental Section Newsletter* 9(2):8–11.

Ames, E. W. (1997). *The Development of Romanian Orphanage Children Adopted to Canada.* Ottawa: Human Resources Development Canada.

Bowlby, J. (1953). *Child Care and the Growth of Love.* Baltimore, MD: Penguin Books.

Broussard, M., and Decarie, T. G. (1971). "The Effects of Three Kinds of Perceptual-Social Stimulation on the Development of Institutionalized Infants: Preliminary Report of a Longitudinal Study." *Early Child Development and Care* 1:111–130.

Carlson, E. A., and Sroufe, A. L. (1995). "Contributions of Attachment Theory to Developmental Psychopathology." In *Developmental Psychopathology,* Vol. 1: *Theory and Methods,* ed. D. Cicchetti and D. J. Cohen. New York: Wiley.

Chisholm, K. (1998). "A Three Year Follow-Up of Attachment and Indiscriminate Friendliness in Children Adopted from Romanian Orphanages." *Child Development* 69(4):1092–1106.

Chisholm, K.; Carter, M.; Ames, E. W.; and Morison, S. J. (1995). "Attachment Security and Indiscriminately Friendly Behavior in Children Adopted from Romanian Orphanages." *Development and Psychopathology* 7:283–294.

Crittenden, P. M. (1988a). "Relationships at Risk." In *Clinical Implications of Attachment,* ed. J. Belsky and T. Nezworski. Hillsdale, NJ: Lawrence Erlbaum Associates.

Crittenden, P. M. (1992). "Quality of Attachment in the Preschool Years." *Development and Psychopathology* 4:209–243.

Dennis, W. (1960). "Causes of Retardation among Institutional Children: Iran." *Journal of Genetic Psychology* 96:47–59.

Dennis, W. (1973). *Children of the Crèche.* New York: Appleton-Century-Croft.

Fisher, L.; Ames, E. W.; Chisholm, K.; and Savoie, L. (1997). "Problems Reported by Parents of Romanian Orphans Adopted to British Columbia." *International Journal of Behavioral Development* 20(1):67–82.

Goldfarb, W. (1945a). "Psychological Privation in Infancy and Subsequent Adjustment." *American Journal of Orthopsychiatry* 14:247–255.

Goldfarb, W. (1947). "Variations in Adolescent Adjustment of Institutionally Reared Children." *American Journal of Orthopsychiatry* 17:449–457.

Goldfarb, W. (1955). "Emotional and Intellectual Consequences of Psychologic Deprivation in Infancy: A Re-Evaluation." In *Psychopathology of Childhood,* ed. P. Hoch and J. Zubin. New York: Grune and Stratton.

Groze, V., and Ileana, D. (1996). "A Follow-Up Study of Adopted Children from Romania." *Child and Adolescent Social Work Journal* 13(6):541–565.

Handley-Derry, M.; Goldberg, S.; Marcovitch, S.; McGregor, D.; Gold, A.: and Washington, J. (1995). "Determinants of Behavior in Internationally Adopted Romanian Children." Paper presented at the annual meeting of the Society for Behavioral Pediatrics, Philadelphia, September 1995.

Hunt, J. M.; Mohandessi, K.; Ghodessi, M.; and Akiyama, M. (1976). "The Psychological Development of Orphanage-Reared Infants: Interventions with Outcomes (Tehran)." *Genetic Psychological Monographs* 94:177–226.

Kaler, S. R., and Freeman, B. J. (1994). "Analysis of Environmental Deprivation: Cognitive and Social Development of Romanian Orphans." *Journal of Child Psychology and Psychiatry* 35(4):769–781.

Lieberman, A. F., and Pawl, J. H. (1988). "Clinical Applications of Attachment Theory." In *Clinical Implications of Attachment,* ed. J. Belsky and T. Nezworski. Hillsdale, NJ: Lawrence Erlbaum Associates.

Longstreth, L. E. (1981). "Revisiting Skeels' Final Study: A Critique." *Developmental Psychology* 17:620–625.

Marcovitch, S.; Goldberg, S.; Gold, A.; Washington, J.; Wasson, C.; Krekewich, K.; and Handley-Derry, M. (1997). "Determinants of Behavioral Problems in Romanian Children Adopted in Ontario." *International Journal of Behavioral Development* 20(1):17–31.

Marvin, R. S., and O'Connor, T. G. (1999). "The Formation of Parent-Child Attachment Following Privation." Paper presented at the biennial meetings of the Society for Research in Child Development, Albuquerque, New Mexico, April 15–18.

Morison, S. J.; Ames, E. W.; and Chisholm, K. (1995). "The Development of Children Adopted from Romanian

Orphanages." *Merrill-Palmer Quarterly* 41(4): 411–430.

Morison, S. J., and Ellwood, A. L. (2000). "Resiliency in the Aftermath of Deprivation: A Second Look at the Development of Romanian Orphanage Children." *Merrill-Palmer Quarterly* 46(4):717–737.

O'Connor, T. G.; Rutter, M.; and the English and Romanian Adoptees Study Team (2000). "Attachment Disorder Behavior Following Early Severe Deprivation: Extension and Longitudinal Follow-Up." *Journal of the American Academy of Child and Adolescent Psychiatry* 39(6):703–712.

Pinneau, S. (1955). "The Infantile Disorders of Hospitalism and Anaclitic Depression." *Psychological Bulletin* 52:429–451.

Provence, S., and Lipton, R. C. (1962). *Infants in Institutions.* New York: International Universities Press.

Rosenblith, J. F., and Sims-Knight, J. E. (1985). "Deprivation and Enrichment." In *In the Beginning: Development in the First Two Years.* Monterey, CA: Brooks/Cole.

Rutter, M. (1985). "Resilience in the Face of Adversity: Protective Factors and Resistance to Psychiatric Disturbance." *British Journal of Psychiatry* 147:598–611.

Rutter, M., and the English and Romanian Adoptees Study Team. (1998). "Developmental Catch-Up, and Deficit, Following Adoption after Severe Global Privation." *Journal of Child Psychology and Psychiatry* 39(4):465–476.

Skodak, M., and Skeels, H. M. (1945). "A Follow-Up Study of Children in Adoptive Homes." *Journal of Genetic Psychology* 66:21–58.

Skodak, M., and Skeels, H. M. (1949). "A Final Follow-Up Study of One Hundred Adopted Children." *Journal of Genetic Psychology* 75:85–125.

Sloutsky, V. M. (1997). "Institutional Care and Developmental Outcomes of 6- and 7-Year-Old Children: A Contextual Perspective." *International Journal of Behavioral Development* 20(1):131–151.

Spitz, R. (1945a). "Hospitalism: An Inquiry into the Genesis of Psychiatric Conditions in Early Childhood." *Psychoanalytic Study of the Child* 1:53–74.

Spitz, R. (1945b). "Hospitalism: A Follow-Up Report." *Psychoanalytic Study of the Child* 2:113–118.

Tizard, B. (1977). *Adoption: A Second Chance.* London: Open Books.

Tizard, B., and Hodges, J. (1978). "The Effect of Early Institutional Rearing on the Development of Eight-Year-Old Children." *Journal of Child Psychology and Psychiatry* 19:99–118.

Vorria, P.; Wolkind, S.; Rutter, M.; Pickles, A.; and Hobsbaum, A. (1998). "A Comparative Study of Greek Children in Long-Term Residential Group Care and in Two-Parent Families: I. Social, Emotional, and Behavioral Differences." *Journal of Child Psychology and Psychiatry* 39(2):225–236.

Zeanah, C. H. (1996). "Beyond Insecurity: A Reconceptualization of Attachment Disorders in Infancy." *Journal of Consulting and Clinical Psychology* 64(1):42–52.

KIM MACLEAN

PALLIATIVE CARE

See HOSPICE

PANAMA

See LATIN AMERICA

PARENT–CHILD RELATIONS

See COMMUNICATION: PARENT-CHILD RELATIONSHIPS;
    CONFLICT: PARENT-CHILD RELATIONSHIPS; FILIAL
    RESPONSIBILITY; INTERGENERATIONAL RELATIONS;
    INTERGENERATIONAL TRANSMISSION;
    INTERPARENTAL CONFLICT—EFFECTS ON CHILDREN;
    INTERPARENTAL VIOLENCE—EFFECTS ON CHILDREN

PARENTING

See COPARENTING; DISCIPLINE; FATHERHOOD; FOSTER
    PARENTING; GAY PARENTS; GRANDPARENTHOOD;
    LESBIAN PARENTS; MOTHERHOOD; PARENTING
    EDUCATION; PARENTING STYLES; SINGLE-PARENT
    FAMILIES; STEPFAMILIES; SUBSTITUTE CAREGIVERS;
    TRANSITION TO PARENTHOOD

PARENTING EDUCATION

Parenting education may be defined as any deliberate effort to help parents be more effective in caring for children. There are many different processes for educating parents, including group meetings, resource centers, newsletters, radio programs, home visits, mentoring, Internet resources, support groups, and books. The content of these different efforts varies substantially, ranging from behavior-management approaches to relationship-enhancement approaches. What the programs have in common is the conviction that parents play a vital role in the development of children and that it is possible to help parents be more effective through training and education.

Parenting education is conducted in many settings: school, health and religious organizations, and the community. It is conducted by people with different backgrounds including human development, nursing, psychology, social work, and education.

There is a growing awareness in society that many social problems are the result of inadequate parenting education; parents are not automatically equipped to deal with the challenges of childrearing. Moreover, many social changes put additional pressures on families and limit their connections with family members and others. For example, since World War II there have been increased numbers of mothers working outside the home, increased rates of divorce, greater distances from extended family, increased involvement with negative electronic media, and more overloaded family schedules. All of these changes can make the job of parenting more challenging.

Content of Parenting Education

There are many different approaches to parenting education, each with different assumptions about the nature of humans (Are people basically good or bad?), the optimal outcome (Do we want an obedient child or an independent thinker?), and the process of change (Are people motivated by command or by invitation?). Advice given to parents centuries ago emphasized that children should submit to parents. With the growth of serious research on child development in the twentieth century, the definition of effective parenting has changed dramatically. Since the 1930s, there has been a clear recommendation that parents provide loving, supportive, involved care.

Research on parenting shows that parents who are supportive of their children and provide reasonable controls are more likely to have socially competent children. *Social competence* includes confidence, independence, responsibility, and achievement. Low levels of parental support are related to low self-esteem, deviance, and risk-taking behaviors. The vital role of parental support is well established.

Although the need for support has been clear for many years, research has been less clear on what constitutes reasonable control. At times experts have recommended a nonrestrictive role for parents. Recent research suggests that some control is necessary, but the type of control—and not just the amount—is important for effective parenting.

In research on parenting behavior, methods of control have commonly been divided into three categories. The first type of control is the use of *power* by parents. Such techniques, in which parents attempt to force or pressure their children to behave in certain ways, are associated with children who are less socially competent. When parents use power to control their children, the children are likely to see their choices as governed by external forces. They do as they are told but only as long as there is a power to make them. They may become passive or rebellious.

A second type of control is *love withdrawal,* in which parents show disapproval for behavior that displeases them. It may include ignoring, shaming,

or isolating the child. The use of love withdrawal shows mixed results in its effects on children; some studies have found it to be acceptable, whereas other studies have found it resulted in dependent or depressed children. New research on parents' use of psychological control may have identified what parts of love withdrawal are especially toxic. When parents use guilt or manipulation to control their children, the result is anxiety and depression for children. In contrast, when parents use reasonable monitoring and negotiated control of behavior, children are less likely to get in trouble.

The third type of control is *induction.* Induction includes reasoning with children and helping them understand the effects of their behavior on others. For example, a parent might say, "When you yell at your sister, she feels very afraid and sad. She feels that you don't like her." Induction is the type of control that is most likely to result in socially competent children.

There are also clear benefits for a child's moral development when a parent uses induction because induction teaches children to think about the effect of their behavior on others. Induction both activates and cultivates the child's own logic and compassion. Children raised with induction are more likely to have internalized standards for behavior, better developed moral sensitivities, and less vulnerability to external influence.

Each traditional school of thought in parenting has a different emphasis. For example, Rudolf Dreikurs (1964) stressed meeting the needs of children, a democratic family, and avoiding power struggles. Thomas Gordon (1970) emphasized the importance of appropriate communication and of allowing children to make their own decisions. Haim Ginott (1965) underscored understanding and respect for the child. A more recent and controversial approach developed by Lee Canter and Marlene Canter (1985) has stressed control of behavior.

The content of many parenting education programs remains similar to the roots of the programs in the 1960s and is based more on clinical wisdom than empirical research. The programs are largely based on their authors' assumptions about human nature and on commonsense recommendations that may or may not be in harmony with research. Many of the commercial programs have not yet

Parents meet to discuss obstacles in raising and educating schoolchildren. Parent education may provide solutions by equipping parents with skills for overcoming these challenges. ROGER RESSMEYER/CORBIS

applied recent research to their curricula. For instance, there is new interest in fathering, family time, marriage, character education, and parental beliefs. Many new research findings have not been incorporated into popular parenting programs. Parenting programs sponsored by universities or research-based organizations are more likely to incorporate the new discoveries of research.

Many child-rearing issues remain subjects of debate. For example, Sandra Scarr (1992) has suggested that children are born with strong adaptive capacities; if parents provide basic opportunities and a good enough environment, children will develop into healthy, capable adults. Some scholars are concerned that parents need to be actively and directly involved with their children in order to facilitate their development. This controversy is really another form of the longstanding nature-nurture debate.

The content of a parenting education program should allow for the diversity of life circumstances and values of parents. Some of the needs of limited-resource teenage mothers of infants will be different from the needs of middle-aged parents of teenagers. Information on feeding, changing diapers, dealing with sickness, and using community resources will be vital for parents of newborns; parents of teenagers are more likely to be interested in communication, limit setting, and problem solving.

As society becomes more diverse, program developers need to take into account a growing

number of varying populations. Different parenting circumstances, such as step, single, divorced, noncustodial, teenage, foster, urban, rural, and low-income, call for different parenting education. When parents participate actively in the process of parenting education, including the choice of program, they are more likely to be invested in the outcome.

Some models of parenting education also include initiatives for larger social change. For example, one youth development model that seeks to educate parents while building community capacity is the asset model that seeks to reduce risk factors and enhance protective factors. Several asset or positive youth development models exist, including those developed by the Search Institute, the Asset-Based Community Development Institute, America's Promise, and Communities that Care (see Bibliography for web addresses), but all focus on creating social change through the involvement of community-members, including parents, teachers, mentors, coaches, businesspeople, and ministers. Every member of the community is seen as a potential asset builder.

To discuss the content of parenting programs in more detail, it is necessary to divide them into two broad categories: behavior-management approaches and relationship-enhancement approaches.

Behavior-Management Approaches

Based on *social learning theory,* these approaches use *behavior modification,* including reinforcement, punishment, and modeling. Reinforcers may be material or social rewards. Reinforcers are provided contingent upon appropriate behavior. Punishment, in the form of withheld social attention (e.g., ignoring the child) or other penalties, is provided in response to inappropriate behavior.

Modeling involves showing the child the desired behavior. Modeling is based on the idea that children observe and imitate the interactions of others they view as successful. Children are more likely to imitate models whom they observe to be powerful, competent, and prestigious.

Gerald R. Patterson (1982), a leader in social learning approaches, asserts that children naturally produce certain undesirable behaviors, which are reinforced when they attract parental attention. Nagging by parents may teach children that they only get attention when they misbehave. It is easy for parents and children to get caught in a destructive cycle: The parents try to control the child; the child resists; the parents become more aversive; the child becomes more resistant or rebellious; the parents relent; the child continues the destructive behavior. Behavior-management approaches attempt to break this cycle with sensible behavior-management tools.

In behavior-management programs, parents commonly focus on two or three problem behaviors in their children and are taught to reinforce appropriate behavior and to ignore or punish inappropriate behavior. Parents learn, usually through play sessions, to recognize, acknowledge, and reward appropriate child behavior. Parents receive immediate feedback from trainers. They also learn to communicate clear instructions and to reward the child or give a *time-out,* depending on child compliance. Evaluation of effectiveness, usually based on parent report or observation of child behavior, generally supports a decrease in problem behaviors.

Behavior modification is accepted as an effective method for controlling specific problem behaviors. Some form of behavior modification is present in most parenting education programs. Due in part to its relatively quick results, its systematic focus on changing behavior, and the relative ease with which researchers can evaluate its effects, behavior modification has been a credible model in parenting education since the early 1970s.

However, the behavioral approaches have also drawn substantial criticism. Some people fault such approaches for making the parent the source of authority: Parents define desirable behavior and manipulate children's experience to assure certain outcomes. Such approaches may not encourage mature autonomy and decision making in children. Reliance on behavioral approaches does not lead to mature, internalized moral behavior. A child may become focused on the rewards rather than internalized standards or sensitivity to others.

Because of their ability to manage specific behaviors, behavior-management approaches are likely to have some role in effective parenting. Yet they may be most effective when combined with relationship-enhancement approaches.

Relationship-Enhancement Approaches

In contrast to behavior-modification programs, *relationship-enhancement approaches* place more emphasis on relationship quality and the emotional needs of the parents and their children. Such approaches teach parents to develop an accepting, supportive atmosphere for their children using such skills as active listening. Most of the humanistic, communication, and democratic parenting programs, such as those based on the works of Dreikurs (1964), Ginott (1965), and Gordon (1970), can be seen as relationship-enhancement approaches.

It is common for parents to react to their children's behavior with lectures. Relationship-enhancement approaches suggest a different reaction. Parents who use active listening skills might say things like the following: "I would like to understand how you are feeling. Will you tell me more?" "Let me see if I understand how you feel. Do you feel like . . . ?" Taking time to understand the child's feelings helps the child feel loved and helps the child deal with emotions. It also helps the parent and child work together for solutions. It is clear from research that a supportive parent-child relationship as endorsed by relationship-enhancement approaches is important for the developing child.

John Gottman (1997) has emphasized a helpful way of responding to children's emotions. Rather than responding to a child's emotions by dismissing them, disapproving of them, or being confused by them, a parent can be an emotion coach. *Emotion coaching* involves understanding the child, accepting the emotion, and helping them label and make sense of the emotion. Emotion coaching helps a child learn to understand and regulate his or her feelings and helps the child learn to solve problems.

Support, which is the basis of the parent-child relationship, is more than telling children that they are loved; it is behavior that helps a child feel comfortable and valued. Support might also be called acceptance, affection, love, nurturance, or warmth. One important way to help a child feel support is through efforts to understand their feelings.

Relationship-enhancement approaches have different strategies for dealing with misbehavior. For example, Ginott (1965) recommended that parents set clear limits, but also take time to understand what children feel rather than blaming or lecturing. His emphasis on compassionate understanding combined with clear limits is a reason that his books still remain popular and respected.

In some programs such as those developed by Gordon (1970), parents are trained to use *I-messages* in order to describe nonjudgmentally the problem behavior and its effects on the parent. The general outline for an *I-message* is: "When you (*child behavior*), I feel (*statement of emotion*) because (*effects*)." Properly used, *I-messages* can minimize blame and allow parent and child to identify the problem, list alternatives, choose a solution, decide on an implementation strategy, and evaluate the results.

Dreikurs (1964) suggested that parents understand the need expressed through the child's behavior and then help the child meet that need. In most relationship-enhancement approaches, control may be maintained by some combination of clear limit setting, reasoning, natural or logical consequences, and helping the child meet needs appropriately. The development of a warm, trusting relationship is expected to prevent many behavior problems. In addition, parents can improve their management of a child's behavior by being aware of what specific behaviors are developmentally appropriate or normal for that particular child.

Many programs emphasize parents' use of consequences for child misbehavior so that children learn to understand the connection between their behavior and the outcomes. An example of a natural consequence might be that children who fail to clean their bedrooms suffer messy rooms. On the other hand, a logical consequence might be that the children are not allowed to go out and play until their rooms are in order. Parents are encouraged to reduce their own power by avoiding spanking, shaming, or criticizing children. Parents can facilitate the children's self-control by allowing them to be responsible for their own actions and experience the results of their behavior. This is in contrast to the use of rewards and punishment in the behavior-management approaches that make parents the controlling agent in the child's life.

The debate continues about whether spanking has any place in the effective parent's repertoire. Murray Strauss (1994) argues that spanking is always unhelpful and unnecessary. Diana Baumrind (1996) has suggested that appropriate spanking may be used without serious consequences. She defined appropriate spanking as mild, immediate, calm, private, and combined with reasoning. She also suggests that the child must be older than eighteen months and younger than puberty.

In considering both behavior-management and relationship-enhancement approaches, it is clear that some common recommendations, such as monitoring children's behavior and providing an environment, support good behavior. Nevertheless, the language and focus of the two schools of thought are different. Behavior-management approaches emphasize parental control; relationship-enhancement approaches emphasize a caring relationship. Effective parenting programs should draw on the sensible response to problem behavior, as suggested in the former, and on the communication and relationship skills, as stressed in the latter.

The National Model of Parenting Education

To better define the essentials of effective parenting, the U.S. Cooperative Extension Service gathered a team of parent educators to develop a model of parenting education called the National Extension Parent Education Model (NEPEM) (Smith, Cudaback, Goddard, Myers-Walls 1994) that is intended to provide a common ground and common language for any person involved in parenting education. The heart of the model is a summary of critical parenting practices. Parent educators can draw on this core to structure and guide their program efforts.

The report identifies six categories of critical parenting practices:

- Care for self;
- Understand;
- Guide;
- Nurture;
- Motivate; and
- Advocate.

Care for self includes self-knowledge and management of life demands, as well as developing and using support systems. Parents who have learned to care for themselves effectively are more likely to provide a secure, supportive, and predictable environment for childrearing.

To understand a child includes the parents' knowledge of child development in general as well as insight into the style and preferences of each of their children individually. Understanding developmental issues, specific preferences, and circumstantial presses for each child, can help parents tune into and respond helpfully to the needs of each child.

To guide includes behavior that establishes boundaries or limits. Because flexibility and balance are vital to effective guidance, the most effective parenting will allow the child to make as many decisions as possible.

Nurture includes the expression of affection in ways that are effective with each child; basic caregiving, listening, and providing a sense of heritage are also elements of nurture.

To motivate a child means to stimulate imagination, curiosity, and ambition. Effective parenting performance in this area is presumed to develop children who are more effective in school and who are more likely to be lifelong learners.

Advocate, which stresses the identification and use of community resources to benefit children, recognizes that parents are in a unique role to advocate for their own children specifically, and for social change in general.

Each of these six categories in the model is discussed in the report along with a summary of key research findings.

NEPEM is an attempt to focus the content of parenting education on core issues. The model with accompanying discussion was distributed to county Extension offices and is available on the web (see Bibliography for web address).

Processes of Parenting Education

There are many ways to reach parents with messages for more effective parenting. *Group meetings* are the traditional way of teaching parents new skills. Meetings may include lectures, discussions, videos, role-playing, and opportunities for practicing skills. It seems likely that, if group meetings are to help parents be more caring and understanding, they must be conducted by leaders who are caring and understanding (Orgel 1980; Powell and Cassidy 2001). Although group meetings may be difficult for parents to attend regularly, the group can offer much-needed social support.

Many parents turn to books to inform their child-rearing efforts. There are classic books such as Ginott's *Between Parent and Child* (1965), and Spock's *Common Sense Book of Baby and Child Care* (1946) that are still useful. Unfortunately, there are also many books on the market that are not in tune with research recommendations. Parents can find help in identifying good books and web sites through use of books such as *Authoritative Guide to Self-Help Resources in Mental Health* (Norcross et al. 2000).

The Internet is becoming an increasingly important avenue for delivering parenting education. Courses, articles, and parenting tips are available at many sites. As the versatility and sophistication of web-based technologies increase, parenting education resources on the Internet will likely incorporate more sound and video components. The Internet has not only become a significant source for parenting resources, it has also created opportunities for virtual conferencing and training. Webcasting will allow parent educators to provide or participate in conferences or training over the Internet. Web-based tracking and diagnostic tools are increasingly being used to customize information. As this evolving technology is incorporated into parenting information databases, users will have easy access to information that is relevant to their own needs and preferences. One challenge will be to clearly distinguish between parenting education and virtual counseling or therapy.

Resource centers are another way of providing parenting information. Sometimes a community center, library, or public school develops a special collection of books, tapes, or other materials to help parents. Resource centers are especially likely to be useful when they are easily accessible to parents.

Newsletters make an important contribution to parenting education. Newsletters are commonly used with parents of newborns and include information about development, feeding, and caring for young children. They can be educational, supportive, and affordable. Even the most isolated families can be reached through the use of newsletters.

Some communities provide radio programs in order to reach parents who might not otherwise receive parenting information. The most effective radio programs provide a series of carefully planned and related messages.

Parents at risk for neglecting their children seem to benefit from one-on-one home visits that focus on childcare issues. Although home-based parenting education may be costly, the visits offer a good opportunity to monitor a child's environment, teach highly relevant skills, and provide support to isolated families.

Mentoring programs have been one response to shrinking budgets and a desire to invest a broader volunteer base in social programs. Mentoring programs draw on trained volunteers to provide information and support. Mentoring programs include such models as *godparent programs,* where trained volunteers visit with mothers of newborns in the hospitals, or *Big Brother/Big Sister programs,* where mentors work directly with children and youth, and indirectly with parents. *Grand mentor programs* establish a grandparent figure in the lives of children and youth. Though some parents may resist this direct involvement, they may benefit from the example and instruction of mentors who are working with their children. In the best mentoring programs, volunteers have regular opportunities to provide support and guidance over an extended period of time.

Support groups provide an opportunity for parents to meet and share experiences and information. Specialized parent-support groups can gather parents with a common challenge to learn from each other and to provide support for each other. Effective support groups facilitate the establishment of support both outside and inside the group. They teach parents ways to use social support in coping, and promote parents' problem-solving abilities.

Some programs bring parenting classes to work sites during regularly scheduled lunch hours. Creative ways of getting parenting education to parents will be increasingly important as parents struggle with crowded schedules.

Family resource programs attempt to provide a variety of services so that families do not need to go from one agency to another. They allow families to become comfortable with staff and maintain better access to services such as parenting education, latchkey programs, childcare, and social welfare programs. The traditional ideal of a self-supported, closely knit family may generate feelings of isolation for many families. Family resource programs are based on several premises: parenting can be challenging; parents can benefit from parenting education; support should focus on family strengths and enhance skills parents already have; and parents can serve as important sources of support for each other.

Cross-Cultural Perspective

Virtually all of the research on parenting education is based on modern Western culture. In fact, most of the research that has been done on parents and children has relied on a Western perspective (Bennett and Grimley, 2001). There are many differences between such an orientation and those in different places and at different times. For example, the desired outcomes of childrearing are reported to be more oriented toward obedience and compliance in economically disadvantaged countries whereas the desired outcomes in more prosperous countries favor independence and risk-taking (Harkness and Super, 1995). For the most disadvantaged cultures, training focuses on working together to merely sustain life (Bennett and Grimley, 2001), which is highly adaptive in a culture where survival is a continuing struggle. In contrast, "the main preoccupation of families in Western societies is not basic survival, but rather the pursuit of happiness" (Bennett and Grimley 2001, p. 101).

Substantial differences have also been discerned between geographically proximate ancient cultures. Valerie French (1995) compares parenting in various ancient Mediterranean cultures. Egyptians delighted in children, granted them prominence in family life and assigned fathers a vital role in training them. In contrast, Mesopotamian parents considered children a difficult burden and were more emotionally distant from their children.

Different cultural perspectives have also resulted in differences in processes for training parents. Traditional cultures favor apprenticeship in which parenting is learned by observation whereas modern Western orientations favor direct training through books, classes, and formal training (Rogoff 1990). Some cultures even minimize the parental role and seek to increase the socializing influence of professionals such as school teachers.

It is not possible to make simple generalizations about the training of parents and the prescribed manner of child-rearing but it is clear that cultural differences span both time and place. Even within countries, such as the United States, there are clearly observed differences in parenting styles and valued child outcomes (Lamborn, Dornbusch, and Steinberg, 1996) reflected in parenting education programs. Still, John Bennett and Liam Grimley (2001) found information about age-specific development and basic human needs to be relevant and adaptable across cultures. They describe ways a developmental parenting program was adapted for use in countries as diverse as the United States, Northern Ireland, Spain, and Macedonia. They also describe the delivery and focus of parenting programs in France, Turkey, China, and the Philippines.

Looking to the Future

There are challenges related to parenting education. For example, no established standards exist for parent educators. Groups from the National Council on Family Relations (NCFR) and U.S. Cooperative Extension are grappling with issues of certification and professional standards. In some models of certification, a bachelor's degree in a related subject is required. Some argue that such a requirement unnecessarily eliminates people who could be effective in working with parents. According to criteria of progress toward professional status (Czaplewski and Jorgensen 1993), parenting education has a long way to go to become fully professionalized.

Other problems in parenting education include the wide range of approaches and orientations, including some programs that are not in harmony with research; it is difficult for parenting education to be sensitive to differences in cultures and values; it is also increasingly difficult to motivate parents to participate in group meetings. There is still much to be learned about how to change parent behavior.

Nonetheless, parenting education continues to play a vital role in preparing people for parenting. In the challenging tasks of parenting, most parents welcome the help that it offers. As research continues, both the content and process of parenting education can be expected to improve, resulting in better family relationships and healthier, more balanced children.

See also: ADOLESCENT PARENTHOOD; ATTACHMENT: PARENT-CHILD RELATIONSHIPS; CHILDHOOD; CONDUCT DISORDER; CONFLICT: PARENT-CHILD RELATIONSHIPS; COPARENTING; DISCIPLINE; DIVORCE: EFFECTS ON CHILDREN; FAMILY LIFE EDUCATION; FAMILY LITERACY; FAMILY MINISTRY; FATHERHOOD; MOTHERHOOD; PARENTING STYLES; SEXUAL COMMUNICATION: PARENT-CHILD RELATIONSHIPS; SPANKING; THERAPY: PARENT-CHILD RELATIONSHIPS; TRANSITION TO PARENTHOOD

Bibliography

Baumrind, D. (1996). "A Blanket Injunction against Disciplinary Use of Spanking Is Not Warranted by the Data." *Pediatrics* 98:828–832.

Bennett, J., and Grimley, L. K. (2001). "Parenting in the Global Community: A Cross-Cultural International Perspective." In *Handbook of Diversity in Parent Education: The Changing Faces of Parenting and Parent Education,* ed. M. J. Fine and S. W. Lee. San Diego, CA: Academic Press.

Canter, L., and Canter, M. (1985). *Assertive Discipline for Parents.* New York: Harper and Row.

Czaplewski, M. J., and Jorgensen, S. R. (1993). "The Professionalization of Family Life Education." In *Handbook of Family Life Education: Foundations of Family Life Education,* ed. M. E. Arcus, J. D. Schvaneveldt, and J. J. Moss. Newbury Park, CA: Sage.

Dreikurs, R. (1964). *Children: The Challenge.* New York: Hawthorn Books.

French, V. (1995). "History of Parenting: The Ancient Mediterranean World." In *Handbook of Parenting,* Vol. 2: *Biology and Ecology of Parenting,* ed. M. H. Bornstein. Mahwah, NJ: Erlbaum.

Ginott, H. (1965). *Between Parent and Child.* New York: Macmillan.

Gordon, T. (1970). *Parent Effectiveness Training.* New York: Peter H. Wyden.

Gottman, J. (1997). *The Heart of Parenting: Raising an Emotionally Intelligent Child.* New York: Simon and Schuster.

Harkness, S., and Super, C. (1995). "Culture and Parenting." In *Handbook of Parenting,* Vol. 2: *Biology and Ecology of Parenting,* ed. M. H. Bornstein. Mahwah, NJ: Erlbaum.

Lamborn, S.; Dornbusch, S.; and Steinberg, L. (1996). "Ethnicity and Community Context as Moderators of the Relation between Family Decision-making and Adolescent Adjustment." *Child Development* 66:283–301.

Norcross, J. C.; Santrock, J. W.; Campbell, L. F.; Smith, T. P.; Sommer, R.; and Zuckerman, E. L. (2000). *Authoritative Guide to Self-Help Resources in Mental Health.* New York: Guilford.

Orgel, A. (1980). "Haim Ginott's Approach to Parent Education." In *Handbook on Parent Education*, ed. M. J. Fine. New York: Academic Press.

Patterson, G. R. (1982). *A Social Learning Approach,* Vol. 3: *Coercive Family Process.* Eugene, OR: Castalia.

Powell, L. H., and Cassidy, D. (2001). *Family Life Education: An Introduction*. Mountain View, CA: Mayfield.

Rogoff, B. (1990). *Apprenticeship in Thinking: Cognitive Development in Social Context*. New York: Oxford University Press.

Scarr, S. (1992). "Developmental Theories for the 1990s: Development and Individual Differences." *Child Development* 63:1–19.

Smith, C. A.; Cudaback, D.; Goddard, H. W.; and Myers-Walls, J. A. (1994). *National Extension Parent Education Model of Critical Parenting Practices.* Manhattan: Kansas State University Press.

Spock, B. (1946). *The Common Sense Book of Baby and Child Care.* New York: Duell, Sloan, and Pearce.

Strauss, M. (1994). *Beating the Devil Out of Them: Corporal Punishment in American Families.* New York: Lexington Books.

Other Resources

America's Promise. Available from http://www.americaspromise.org.

Asset-Based Community Development Institute. Available from http://www.northwestern.edu/ipr/abcd.html.

Children, Youth, and Families Education and Resource Network. Available from http://cyfernet.org.

Communities that Care. Available from http://www.preventionscience.com.

National Extension Parent Education Model. Available from http://www.cyfernet.org/parenting_practices/preface.html.

Search Institute. Available from http://www.search-institute.org.

H. WALLACE GODDARD
STEVEN A. DENNIS

PARENTING STYLES

The study of human development is centrally concerned with understanding the processes that lead adults to function adequately within their cultures. These skills include an understanding of—and adherence to—the moral standards, conventional rules, and customs of the society. They also include maintaining close relationships with others, developing the skills to work productively, and becoming self-reliant and able to function independently. All of these may be important to successfully rear the next generation. Researchers studying human development have assumed that the family is a particularly important context for developing these competencies, and therefore, they have examined how parents socialize their children to understand variations in adult outcomes. They have attempted to find associations between the way parents raise their children and children's social, emotional, and cognitive development. It has been assumed that variations in parents' discipline style, warmth, attention to the needs of the child, and parenting attitudes and beliefs all can be characterized in terms of consistent patterns of child-rearing, referred to as *parenting styles,* that are systematically related to children's competence and development. Research that began in the mid-1980s has focused more on the particular dimensions of parenting that underlie the different parenting styles to provide a more detailed understanding of how parenting influences healthy child and adolescent development.

Parenting Styles

Alfred Baldwin and his colleagues provided one of the most important early attempts to describe systematic patterns of child rearing. This research, conducted in the 1930s and 1940s, followed a group of children and their families longitudinally over time. They observed parents and children interacting together in their homes, and they also assessed progress in children's development at different ages. They identified two sets of parental childrearing dimensions that were related to differences in children's outcomes. As others had done, they distinguished parents along a dimension of emotional involvement versus detachment. They also distinguished between democratic and autocratic parents. Autocratic parents were more likely to simply hand down their rules, while democratic parents were more likely to involve the child in family decision making and provide explanations for their expectations. Their research demonstrated that democratic parents had children who were less hostile and who worked more effectively in the absence of adult supervision (Maccoby 1992; Maccoby and Martin 1983).

There have been many subsequent attempts to improve on Baldwin's descriptions of parenting styles. The most influential has been the research of Diana Baumrind, who believed that the democratic style as defined by Baldwin was not sufficient to produce culturally competent adults and that democracy must be combined with authority to produce optimal competence. Beginning in the 1960s, Baumrind identified a set of characteristics that she believed defined competence for children in North American society (Baumrind 1971), and then she examined parents' childrearing beliefs and practices to determine the parenting styles that were associated with those outcomes. She initially developed a typology of three distinct parenting styles that were related to child outcomes, but research from 1980 onward has expanded to include four distinct parenting styles.

Baumrind's widely used typology describes parenting styles as varying along two completely independent dimensions of demandingness and responsiveness that, when crossed, yield four parenting styles. *Authoritative* parents are both responsive and demanding. They set clear, reasonable standards for responsible behavior that are consistent with children's developing abilities, are firm in their enforcement, and provide explanations for their positions. They are also kind, warm, and responsive to children's needs and will negotiate their expectations. *Authoritarian* parents are demanding but not responsive. These parents place high values on obedience to rules, discourage give-and-take between parents and children, and do not take their child's needs into consideration. *Permissive* or indulgent parents are responsive but not demanding. These parents are warm and accepting and tolerant of the child's impulses. They also make few demands on the child for mature behavior, do not use much punishment, and avoid exerting their authority. More recently, permissive parents have been distinguished from *rejecting-neglecting* parents, who also do not make many demands on their children, primarily because they are disengaged, and thus are neither demanding nor responsive (Baumrind 1989).

Baumrind's research indicates that authoritative parenting is most effective in leading to healthy adjustment for children. Authoritative parenting consistently has been associated with a wide range of positive adolescent outcomes, including better academic performance, increased competence, autonomy, and self-esteem, more advanced moral development, less deviance, anxiety, and depression, and a more well-rounded orientation to peers (Maccoby and Martin 1983; Steinberg 2001). Baumrind has proposed that authoritative parenting is most effective because of parents' high expectations and support for mature behavior. Much of the research on parenting styles in relation to child and adolescent adjustment has been conducted on white middle-class families, but since the start of the 1990s, researchers have become increasingly interested in ethnic and cultural variations.

Cultural and Ethnic Variations in Parenting Styles

Laurence Steinberg (2001) has asserted that the benefits of authoritative parenting in childhood and adolescence "transcend the boundaries of ethnicity, socioeconomic status, and household composition" (p. 12) and that research from around the world also demonstrates the beneficial effects of authoritative parenting. Numerous studies have examined parenting in a very diverse set of countries with different value systems using measures of parenting derived from Baumrind's work. These studies have shown that authoritative parenting is associated with better psychosocial development and mental health across cultures.

Research has suggested that authoritative parenting is more prevalent in European-American parents than in ethnic minority parents and that African-American and Asian-American parents are more authoritarian in their parenting practices than are white parents. Some researchers have suggested that authoritarian parenting may have positive effects on ethnic minority children's psychosocial adjustment and, in particular, academic achievement. In reviewing the available research, Steinberg (2001) has concluded that although African-American and Asian-American children are not as negatively affected by authoritarian parenting as are children from other ethnic groups, authoritarian parenting is not associated overall with positive adjustment. Authoritative parenting appears to confer some benefits in protecting Asian-American and black adolescents from engaging in deviant behavior and in promoting psychosocial development. However, authoritative parenting is not clearly associated with better academic achievement among ethnic minority youths.

Studies suggest that the parenting styles of European Americans differ from those of African Americans and Asian Americans. However, more research is needed to understand how culture and ethnicity interact with situational demands and the characteristics of individual children.
TODD GIPSTEIN/CORBIS

Ruth Chao (1994) has argued that the authoritarian parenting style does not capture the essence of Chinese (and more broadly, Asian) parenting and that the control and restrictiveness that are seen as characteristic of Chinese families reflect a different set of underlying beliefs than for European-American parents. For many white families, strictness is located in Protestant Christian beliefs, whereas for Chinese parents, strictness is rooted in a notion of training (*chiao shun* and *guan*) that reflects role relationships defined by Confucianism. The goal is to assure harmonious family relationships rather than to dominate or control the child. Therefore, she argues that parenting styles developed on North American samples cannot be simply translated to other cultures, but instead must reflect their sociocultural contexts.

Concerns about the generalizability of parenting styles across diverse ethnic and cultural contexts, as well as a more general movement towards understanding the dimensions that underlie different parenting styles, has lead to a great deal of research that has focused on disaggregating Baumrind's parenting styles into their component parts. The goal of this research is to better understand how different parenting processes and behaviors interact to affect various child outcomes in different social contexts. Later theorizing and research have focused on separating parenting styles from parenting practices and differentiating forms of parental control.

Differentiating Parenting Styles and Parenting Practices

One proposition is that parenting styles affect child adjustment because they provide an emotional context in particular parenting practices have different meanings. For instance, Nancy Darling and Steinberg (1993) proposed that authoritative parenting may be effective because the warmth and involvement that characterizes this style may create an emotional climate in which the child is more receptive to parenting, which in turn influences its effectiveness. Also, authoritative parents' willingness to engage children in decision making provides them with negotiation skills that may be useful in their social interactions with others outside the family, for instance, with peers. Therefore, these skills may facilitate children's competence in different settings. Finally, the combination of support and structure that characterizes authoritative parenting may be important to children's ability to regulate their behavior (Steinberg 2001). The same parenting practices, in the emotional climate of authoritarian or indulgent parenting, may have different meanings and therefore have different consequences for adjustment.

Differentiating Forms of Parental Control

The research on parenting styles has viewed parental control as a single dimension that ranges from excessive control to insufficient control, but research that began in the early 1990s has focused on distinguishing among different forms of parental control. The primarily distinctions are between psychological control and behavioral control. As described by Steinberg (1990) and elaborated by Brian Barber and his colleagues (Barber 1996, 2002), psychological control refers to parents' attempts to control children's activities in ways that negatively affect their psychological world. Psychological control, including parental intrusiveness, guilt induction, and love withdrawal, undermines psychosocial development by interfering with children's ability to become independent and develop a healthy sense of self and personal identity. In contrast, behavioral control refers to the rules, regulations, and restrictions that parents have for their children and their supervision and management of their activities. One aspect of behavioral control that has been extensively investigated is parental supervision and monitoring, or parents' awareness of where their children are, who they are with, and what they are doing. Parental monitoring is increasingly important in adolescence, as adolescents spend less time with their parents and more time with peers. This distinction between psychological and behavioral control further distinguishes the parenting styles described by Baumrind. Authoritative parents, who have firm rules for their children's behavior, use a great deal of behavioral control but little psychological control. In contrast, authoritarian parents use both.

Research has demonstrated that high levels of psychological control are associated with children's internalizing problems, such as anxiety, depression, loneliness, and confusion. Both inadequate behavioral control and high levels of psychological control also have been found to be associated with externalizing problems, such as acting out, drug use, truancy, and antisocial behavior.

Barber (2002) provides evidence that psychological control (or closely related constructs) is relevant cross-culturally. Psychological control has been found in males and females in a range of cultures (including Mexico, China, India, Russia, Israel, Colombia, Australia, and South Africa, as reviewed by Barber 2002). These cultures vary in degree of industrialization, extent of individualism versus collectivism, religion, and exposure to political violence. Psychological control is related to internalizing and externalizing problems in a variety of cultures, much as has been found in the United States. Summarizing the available research, Barber (2002) found higher levels of psychological control reported by males than females, by younger than older children, among lower than upper socioeconomic status families, and by ethnic minority than European American families. However, these conclusions are based on a relatively small number of studies that typically employ a single method to assess psychological control, so these conclusions must be confirmed by further research.

Differentiating Parenting as a Function of Children's Behavior

The research on parenting styles assumes that parents have a consistent mode of parenting that is applied across contexts and situations. However, research has demonstrated that parenting practices are affected by situational factors. As reviewed by Judith Smetana (1995, 1997), observational studies

of responses to transgressions indicate that North American caregivers (for instance, parents and teachers) naturally coordinate their choice of discipline strategy with the nature of children's misdeeds. Caregivers are more likely to provide explanations that focus children on the consequences of their actions for others in response to transgressions that entail fairness, physical or psychological harm, lack of consideration of others, or violations of others' rights. All of these have been defined as moral transgressions, or actions that have intrinsic consequences for others' rights or welfare. Other-oriented reasoning, in turn, has been associated with greater moral internalization, greater resistance to temptation, and the development of concern for others. Caregivers are more likely to issue commands and directives, without explaining why actions are wrong, when children violate more arbitrary and contextually relative conventional norms, such as rules of etiquette and manners.

Similar findings have emerged from research examining parents' short-term and long-term socialization goals. Parents tend to use more power assertion when their goal is to obtain immediate compliance. Leon Kuczynski (1984) found that such responses are effective in terminating unwanted behavior, but they do not lead to moral internalization, because they do not provide children with an understanding of why their actions are wrong. When parents' goals are to enhance long-term socialization, parents report using more reasoning and induction. Therefore, although reasoning and induction may facilitate children's development, it does not lead to immediate child compliance, perhaps because while parental reasoning may make the parents' perspective clearer, it also may encourage children to negotiate and assert their choices. This notion is consistent with the speculation about why authoritative parenting is effective for children's development.

Differentiating Parents' Use of Affect: Anger, Shame, and Guilt

Parents also use different affective strategies to socialize their children. Research has shown that parents are more likely to employ negative affect, including dramatizations of distress and greater anger, in response to moral than other types of transgressions. When used with explanations that focus on others' welfare and rights, this may enhance the effectiveness of reasoning because it helps focus children on the harm or injustice their actions caused and therefore may lead them to experience other-oriented emotional reactions such as sympathy. However, parental anger may be effective only when it is moderate and not too negatively arousing, because highly arousing negative affect may become aversive and lead children to focus on the self, rather than on the consequences of their acts for others. A great deal of recent work by Nancy Eisenberg and her colleagues (reviewed in Eisenberg 1998) on vicarious emotional arousal has distinguished between other-oriented emotional reactions (such as sympathy) and self-oriented aversive emotional reactions.

In examining children's emotional reactions to parenting, researchers also have distinguished between shame and guilt. It is assumed that guilt and shame differ in their effects on children's development and the internalization of societal standards and that they are influenced by different parenting practices. June Tangney (2001) proposed that shame pertains to the self, whereas guilt pertains to the behavior. Children experience shame when they discover themselves to be deficient, unacceptable, or incompetent in relation to a social norm and when they see interpersonal relationships as being damaged or threatened. In contrast, guilt has been associated with feelings of responsibility to others, acknowledgement of misdeeds, and the desire to make the situation better. According to Tangney, guilt is constructive for children's development because it is associated with empathic responsiveness and perspective taking. In turn, parenting that displays high levels of parental warmth and open expression of emotions while displaying low levels of power assertion appears to be conducive to the development of internalized guilt feelings (Maccoby and Martin 1983). According to Martin Hoffman (1982, 1983), this type of parenting capitalizes on children's internal discomfort associated with wrongdoing and produce high levels of moral internalization. Moreover, there is empirical support for the relationship between this form of parenting and children's prosocial and moral behavior.

At the same time, research reviewed in Tangney and Fischer (1995) demonstrates that parenting that displays high levels of restrictive or coercive discipline, such as threats or physical discipline and/or high levels of love withdrawal, produces a fear-based sense of guilt and in some cases, expressions of shame. In turn, these have been associated with children's distress, lack of empathy, arousal of anger, and maladjustment. This type of parenting is assumed to induce an external moral orientation by shifting children's focus away from the internal discomfort produced by their wrongdoing and towards the consequences to them. Fear-based guilt and shame have been associated with less resistance to temptation and lower self-esteem (Grusec and Lytton 1988). Furthermore, guilt appears to be more associated with hostility and anger, while shame has been associated with depression and obsessive-compulsiveness.

Cultural Differences in Guilt and Shame

Research has also investigated cultural differences in parents' socialization of shame and guilt. Harald Wallbott and Klaus Scherer (1995) have asserted that in cultures that are collectivist and high in power distribution and uncertainty-avoidance, parents use typical or true shame, whereas in individualistic cultures that are low in power distribution and uncertainty-avoidance, shame more closely resembles guilt. In collectivist cultures, the experience of shame is more acute, less immoral, and has fewer negative consequences for self-esteem and social relationships than in individualistic cultures. Across the thirty-seven countries studied, Wallbott and Scherer found overall support for Tangney's distinction between shame and guilt. These researchers interpreted their findings as demonstrating that shared societal values are strongly related to the emotional experiences of individuals within the society.

Ethnographic research on Chinese culture suggests that it is a *shame-socialized culture.* Children are socialized to be conscious of what others think of them and are expected to act so as to get the most out of the approval of others while trying to avoid their disapproval. This begins when Chinese parents shift from being highly indulgent during infancy and toddlerhood to using parenting practices such as scolding, shaming, and physical punishment at the *age of understanding,* which is seen to occur around four to six years of age. Shame is used to teach children right from wrong, and Chinese parents appear to understand that shame should be used only when necessary, because too much shame may harm the child's self-esteem (Fung 1999). Observational research by Peggy

Miller and her colleagues (Miller; Fung; and Mintz 1996) using small samples of Chinese mothers and children has shown that Chinese mothers' narrative retelling of young children's transgressions focuses on inducing both guilt and shame. This has been found to differ from comparable observational studies of European-American middle-class mothers, whose disciplinary practices are more focused on maintaining and enhancing children's self-esteem (Wiley et al. 1998). These findings suggest that cultural differences in parenting may be more complex than the simple dichotomy between guilt and shame suggests and that more research examining parent-child interactions in different cultures is needed.

Conclusion

Starting with the 1960s, the research on parenting has evolved from a focus on global parenting styles, which were assumed to be employed consistently by parents across situations and to vary in systematic ways across cultures, ethnic groups, and socioeconomic statuses. This notion has given way to a more differentiated and transactive view of parenting and child development. In current research, it is assumed that parents may use different disciplinary techniques, parenting practices, and emotional strategies that are affected by the contexts of parenting, cultural beliefs, situational demands, and characteristics of the child. More research will be needed to understand how these interact and moderate each other to influence children's competence and development.

See also: ACADEMIC ACHIEVEMENT; ANXIETY DISORDERS; ATTACHMENT: PARENT-CHILD RELATIONSHIPS; ATTENTION DEFICIT/HYPERACTIVITY DISORDER (ADHD); BOUNDARY DISSOLUTION; CHILD ABUSE: PHYSICAL ABUSE AND NEGLECT; CHILD ABUSE: PSYCHOLOGICAL MALTREATMENT; CHILD ABUSE: SEXUAL ABUSE; CONDUCT DISORDER; CONFLICT: PARENT-CHILD RELATIONSHIPS; COPARENTING; DEVELOPMENT: MORAL; DEVELOPMENT: SELF; DISCIPLINE; FAMILY LIFE EDUCATION; FATHERHOOD; GAY PARENTS; LEISURE; LESBIAN PARENTS; MOTHERHOOD; OPPOSITIONALITY; PARENTING EDUCATION; POWER: FAMILY RELATIONSHIPS; SELF-ESTEEM; SPANKING; STEPFAMILIES; TEMPERAMENT; THERAPY: PARENT-CHILD RELATIONSHIPS

Bibliography

Barber, B. K. (1996). "Parental Psychological Control: Revisiting a Neglected Construct." *Child Development* 67:3296–3319.

Barber, B. K. (2002). *Intrusive Parenting: How Psychological Control Affects Children and Adolescents*. Washington, DC: American Psychological Association Press.

Baumrind, D. (1971). "Current Patterns of Parental Authority." *Developmental Psychology Monographs* 4 (I, part 2).

Baumrind, D. (1989). "Rearing Competent Children." In *Child Development Today and Tomorrow*, ed. W. Damon. San Francisco: Jossey-Bass.

Chao, R. (1994). "Beyond Parenting Control and Authoritarian Parenting Style: Understanding Chinese Parenting Through the Cultural Notion of Training." *Child Development* 65:1111–1119.

Darling, N., and Steinberg, L. (1993). "Parenting Style as Context: An Integrative Model." *Psychological Bulletin* 113:486–496.

Eisenberg, N. (1998). "Prosocial Development." *Handbook of Child Psychology,* 5th edition, Vol. 3: *Social, Emotional, and Personality Development,* ed. N. Eisenberg (W. Damon, Series Editor). New York: John Wiley and Sons.

Fung, H. (1999). "Becoming a Moral Child: The Socialization of Shame among Young Chinese Children." *Ethos* 27:80–209.

Grusec, J. E., and Lytton, H. (1988). *Social Development: History, Theory, and Research*. New York: Springer-Verlag.

Hoffman, M. L. (1982). "Development of Prosocial Motivation: Empathy and Guilt." In *Development of Prosocial Behavior,* ed N. Eisenberg. New York: Academic Press.

Hoffman, M. L. (1983). "Empathy, Guilt, and Social Cognition." In *The Relationship Between Social and Cognitive Development,* ed. W. F. Overton. Hillsdale, NY: Erlbaum.

Kuczynski, L. (1984). "Socialization Goals and Mother-Child Interaction: Strategies for Long-Term and Short-Term Compliance." *Developmental Psychology* 20:1061–1073.

Maccoby, E. E. (1992). "The Role of Parents in the Socialization of Children: An Historical Overview." *Developmental Psychology* 28:1006–1017.

Maccoby, E. E., and Martin, J. (1983). "Socialization in the Context of the Family: Parent-Child Interaction." In *Handbook of Child Psychology*, Vol. 4: *Socialization, Personality, and Social development,* ed. E. M. Hetherington. New York: John Wiley and Sons.

Miller, P. J.; Fung, H.; and Mintz, J. (1996). "Self-Construction Through Narrative Practices: A Chinese and American Comparison of Early Socialization." *Ethos* 24:237–280.

Smetana, J. G. (1995). "Morality in Context: Abstractions, Ambiguities, and Applications." In *Annals of Child Development,* Vol. 10, ed. R. Vasta. London: Jessica Kinglsey Publishers.

Smetana, J. G. (1997). "Parenting and The Development of Social Knowledge Reconceptualized: A Social Domain Analysis." In *Parenting and the Internalization of Values,* ed. J. E. Grusec and L. Kuczynski. New York: John Wiley and Sons.

Steinberg, L. (1990). "Interdependency in the Family: Autonomy, Conflict, and Harmony in the Parent-Adolescent Relationship." In *At the Threshold: The Developing Adolescent,* ed. S. S. Feldman and G. R. Elliot. Cambridge, MA: Harvard University Press.

Steinberg, L. (2001). "We Know Some Things: Parent-Adolescent Relationships in Retrospect and Prospect." *Journal of Research on Adolescence* 11:1–19.

Tangney, J. P. (2001). "Constructive and Destructive Aspects of Shame and Guilt." In *Constructive and Destructive Behavior: Implications for Family, School, & Society,* ed. A. C. Bohart and D. J. Stipek. Washington, DC: American Psychological Association Press.

Tangney, J. P., and Fischer, K. W. (1995). *Self-Conscious Emotions: The Psychology of Shame, Guilt, Embarrassment, and Pride.* New York: Guilford Press.

Walbot, H. G., and Scherer, K. R. (1995). "Cultural Determinants in Experiencing Shame and Guilt." In *Self Conscious Emotions: The Psychology of Shame, Guilt, Embarrassment, and Pride,* ed. J. P. Tagney and K. W. Fischer. New York: Guilford Press.

Wiley, A. R.; Rose, A. J.; Burger, L. K.; and Miller, P. J. (1998). "Constructing Autonomous Selves Through Narrative Practices: A Comparative Study of Working-Class and Middle-Class Families." *Child Development* 69:833–847.

JUDITH G. SMETANA
NICOLE CAMPIONE

PEER INFLUENCE

The successful formation and navigation of interpersonal relationships with peers is a process central to adolescent development in all cultures. In European-American cultural contexts, an ever-increasing amount of each day is spent in the company of peers, from 10 percent as early as two years of age to 40 percent between the ages of seven and eleven (Voydanoff and Donnelly 1999). By high school, teens are spending more than half of their time in the company of their peers (Updegraff et al. 2001). Because adolescents spend a large amount of their time with peers, it is not surprising that they play a highly influential role in adolescents' lives. The credibility, authority, power, and influence of peers is greater during adolescence than at any other time in life.

Although the process of socialization and individuation occurs in all cultures, the developmental time frame, goals, and practices are often unique (Cooper 1994). In the United States, the adolescents' developmental path is characterized by a transfer in closeness from parents to peers. In comparison with the emphasis placed by European-American cultures on individualism, other cultures, Asian and African cultures in particular, accentuate the socialization of "interdependence, self-control, social inhibition, and compliance" (Chen et al. p. 771). For example, Catherine Cooper (1994) notes that the peer-like mutuality with which adolescents negotiate with their parents during their high school years is a uniquely European-American construct. In contrast, the universes of family and friends remain more distinct for Asian and Mexican immigrants (Cooper et al. 1994). Studies on parent-child and adult mate relationships in Japan and the United States by Fred Rothbaum and colleagues (Rothbaum et al. 2000) suggest that each culture has a different path of development. In Japan, adolescence is characterized by more stable relationships with parents and peers.

Development of Peer Influence

Normal adolescent development in European-American cultures involves a gradual movement from the importance of relationships with family towards those with peers for socialization, self-definition, friendship, and support. Adolescent peer groups function more autonomously than children's peer groups, with less guidance or control provided by adults. As teens distance themselves from adults, they simultaneously draw closer to their peers (Brown 1999). In middle school, individuals begin to form small groups of friends based on mutual attraction, called cliques, which

Children between the ages of seven and eleven spend about 40 percent of their time with peers. MUG SHOTS/CORBIS

can help bolster self-confidence and provide a sense of identity or belonging. In adolescence, these smaller peer groups associated with childhood expand to recognize larger peer collectives referred to as crowds. Bradford Brown (1999) suggests that crowds are large, loosely defined groups of youths who choose to associate with each other based primarily on a common identification with certain characteristics or activities. Crowds help adolescents to decide with whom to associate. Through these crowds and cliques, adolescents demonstrate their identity to others and to themselves (Brown 1999). Margaret Spencer and Sanford Dornbusch (1990) found that adolescents in the United States who are members of an ethnic minority, recent immigrants in particular, rely more heavily on the support of peer groups than European-American adolescents. The threat of not being accepted by their peers and the strain of belonging to two cultures can be especially difficult. Siu Kwong Wong (1998) found that Chinese Canadian youths who associate with Chinese Canadian friends are less likely to be involved in delinquent behavior than those who have cross-ethnic friendships. These various peer associations exert increasing pressure on the adolescent to adopt certain behaviors and attitudes—pressure to conform.

Peer conformity, sometimes referred to as *peer pressure,* occurs when individuals choose to adopt the attitudes or behaviors of others because of real or imagined pressure. In Western cultures, as the amount of time spent with peers increases, so does the influence and support they provide. Thomas Berndt (1979) traced the developmental patterns of

family and peer influence in American families and found that in the third grade, the influence of parents and peers are often in opposition to each other. However, these children are influenced more by their parents than their peers. By sixth grade, the influence of peers rises dramatically, but it tends to be found in different situations from those of parents. Consequently, the influence of parents and peers are not in opposition. In ninth grade, conformity to peers peaks and is again in strong opposition to parents. At this time, peers often endorse the adoption of antisocial standards that inevitably conflict with parental values and standards. American adolescents' movement towards independence peaks around ninth grade and is met with maximal opposition from parents (Scholte, van Lieshout, van Aken 2001). Adolescent conformity to peer influence declines through late high school and college-age years, and the influence of parents and peers begins to coincide in a number of areas.

Negative Peer Influence

Popular conceptions regarding the influence of peers in adolescence often focus on their negative effects—peer pressure—to the exclusion of current empirical research attesting to the myriad positive aspects of peer influence. Supportive relationships between socially skilled adolescents confer developmental advantages while coercive and conflictual relationships confer disadvantages. Willard H. Hartup (1996) summarizes the situation with the following statement: "Knowing that a teenager has friends tells us one thing, but the identity of his or her friends tells us something else" (p. 2).

Across a variety of cultural settings, adolescents tend to be friends with those who are most like them. In fact, sociodemographic characteristics are usually the strongest predictors of friendship formation. Different types of peer groups have unique capacities to encourage negative or positive behaviors in their members. Adolescent misconduct most often occurs in groups. In the United States, cliques are often distinguished from other peer groups through the pressure they exert on their members to conform to certain norms in school orientation, drug use, and sexual behavior. Researchers found clear differences among six different cliques in their participation in high-risk health behaviors, including smoking cigarettes, alcohol use, marijuana use, and engagement in illicit sexual behavior (Prinstein, Fetter, and La Green 2001). Furthermore, members of "deviantly ordered" cliques are more likely to drop out of high school (Cairns and Cairns 1994). Across many cultures, perceived behavior and sanctions of friends are among the strongest predictors of an adolescent's misconduct (Greenberger et al. 2000). Jill V. Hamm (2000) found that when compared with European-American and Asian-American adolescents, African-American adolescents chose friends who were *less* similar in terms of academic orientation or substance use, but more similar in terms of ethnic identity.

Positive Peer Influence

Peer relationships can be a powerful positive influence in the lives of adolescents. Natural observations of adolescents indicate that most adolescents discuss options with their friends before reaching a consensus about what to do. Rarely is one adolescent pressured to conform to the rest of the group. Moreover, high school students in several large samples reported that their friends discouraged drug and alcohol use, delinquent activities, and other types of antisocial behavior more than they encouraged them; they also claimed their friends encouraged studying for school subjects more than they discouraged it (Brown, Clasen, and Eicher 1986). Some adolescents even display anticonformity, rejecting their peer's judgments, and making different decisions altogether. Friendships inherently limit the use and effectiveness of coercive pressure because they are relationships based on equality and mutual respect; consequentially, decisions are made by negotiation, not domination.

Adolescents choose friends who have characteristics or talents that they admire, which motivates them to achieve and act as their friends act. Friends encourage adolescents to study hard at school and can also help them think more creatively (Brown et al. 1986). High-achieving peers have positive effects on adolescents' satisfaction with school, educational expectations, report-card grades, and standardized achievement test scores (Epstein 1983). In Canada, 80 percent of graduates from high school had friends who believed completing high school was important, and only 2 percent had friends who thought this was unimportant (Statistics Canada 1993). Students with friends who like school, get good grades, and are interested in

school are more likely to graduate high school (Ekstrom et al. 1986). Hence, having friends who believe that academic achievement is important is beneficial for adolescents.

Family Relationships and Peer Influence

Outside of the classroom, adolescents who have friends have better family relationships and more positive attitudes toward family relationships. Friendships can also compensate for inadequate families. For example, adolescents who have low levels of family cohesion but have close and supportive friends have levels of self-worth and social competence equal to their peers who come from cohesive families (Guaze et al. 1996). Friends allow for high self-esteem (which includes freedom from depression) and self-worth, thereby promoting the exploration and development of personal strengths (Hartup 1999). Furthermore, adolescents who are engaged in friendships are more likely to be altruistic, display affective perspective-taking skills, maintain positive peer status (Savin-Williams and Berndt 1990), and have continued involvement in activities such as sports or arts (Patrick et al. 1999). Finally, having close same-sex friendships in adolescence forecasts success in early romantic relationships in early adulthood (Collins et al. 1997).

Although peers are very important for adolescents during this developmental stage, parents also play an influential role in adolescents' lives. Laurence Steinberg and his colleagues (1992) found that adolescents whose friends and parents support academic achievement perform better than adolescents who receive support from only one, or neither. Hence, both parents and friends are important for adolescents' development. Moreover, adolescents are less influenced by friends when they have close and involving relationships with their parents (Steinberg and Silverberg 1986). The ability of friends to influence the behaviors and attitudes of adolescents is magnified when adolescents perceive that their parental relationship is negative or deficient in support and guidance (Savin-Williams and Berndt 1990). Parenting styles can also affect peer influence. Authoritative parenting encourages adolescents to be less susceptible to peer influence specifically in domains in which peers are engaging in unacceptable behaviors, but more susceptible to peer influence in domains that are approved by adults (Mounts and Steinberg 1995). Hence, parents can adjust their style of parenting to reflect these favorable outcomes.

In summary, peers are more influential in adolescence than at any other time in life. The quality of the relationship between adolescents and their peers, as well as the type of peers they associate with, play important roles in aiding or impeding their current and future functioning. There are aspects of all peer relations that are unique to the culture and environment in which they exist. The relationship parents have with their adolescents influences their children's susceptibility to negative peer influence.

See also: CHILDHOOD, STAGES OF: ADOLESCENCE; CHILDHOOD, STAGES OF: MIDDLE CHILDHOOD; CHILDHOOD, STAGES OF: PRESCHOOL; CONDUCT DISORDER; FRIENDSHIP; PLAY; SHYNESS

Bibliography

Berndt, T. J. (1979). "Developmental Changes in Conformity to Peers and Parents." *Developmental Psychology* 15(6):608–616.

Brown, B. B. (1999). "You're Going Out with Who?: Peer Group Influences on Adolescent Romantic Relationships." In *The Development of Romantic Relationships in Adolescence,* ed. W. Furman and B. B. Brown. New York: Cambridge University Press.

Brown, B. B.; Clasen, D. R.; and Eicher, S. A. (1986). "Perceptions of Peer Pressure, Peer Conformity Dispositions, and Self-Reported Behavior among Adolescents." *Developmental Psychology* 22:521–530.

Cairns, R. B., and Cairns, B. D. (1994). *Lifelines and Risks: Pathways of Youth in Our Time.* New York: Cambridge University Press.

Chen, C.; Greenberger, E.; Lester, J.; Dong, Q.; and Guo, M. (1998). "A Cross-Cultural Study of Family and Peer Correlates of Adolescent Misconduct." *Developmental Psychology* 34(4):770–781.

Collins, W. A.; Hennighausen, K. C.; Schmit, D. T.; and Sroufe, L. A. (1997). "Developmental Precursors of Romantic Relationships: A Longitudinal Analysis." In *Romantic Relationships in Adolescence: Developmental Perspectives,* ed. S. Shulman and W. A. Collins. San Francisco: Jossey-Bass.

Cook, T. D.; Anson, A. R.; and Walchi, S. B. (1993). "From Causal Description to Causal Explanation: Improving Three Already Good Evaluations of Adolescent Health Programs." In *Promoting the Health of Adolescents,* ed. S. G. Millstein, A. C. Petersen, and E. O. Nightingale. New York: Oxford University Press.

Cooper, C. R. (1994). "Cultural Perspectives on Continuity and Change in Adolescents' Relationships." In *Personal Relationships during Adolescence,* ed. R. Montemayor and G. R. Adams. Thousand Oaks, CA: Sage.

Cooper, C. R.; Azmitia, M.; Garcia, E. E.; Ittel, A.; Lopez, E.; Rivera, L.; and Martinez-Chavez, R. (1994). "Aspirations of Low-Income Mexican American and European American Parents for Their Children and Adolescents." In *Promoting Community-Based Programs for Socialization and Learning,* ed. F. A. Villarruel and R. M. Lerner. San Francisco: Jossey-Bass.

Devereaux, M. S., ed. (1993). *Leaving School: Results from a National Survey Comparing School Leavers and High School Graduates 18 to 20 Years of Age.* Ottawa: Minster of Supplies and Services Canada.

Ekstrom, R. B.; Goertz, M. E.; Pollack, J. M.; and Rock, D. A. (1986). "Who Drops Out of High School and Why? Findings from a National Study." *Teachers College Record* 87:356–373.

Epstein, J. L. (1983). "The Influence of Friends on Achievement and Affective Outcomes." In *Friends in School: Patterns of Selection and Influence in Secondary Schools,* ed. J. L. Epstein and N. Karweit. New York: Academic Press.

Fuligni, A. J.; Eccles, J. S.; Barber, B. L.; and Clements, P. (2001). "Early Adolescent Peer Orientation and Adjustment during High School." *Developmental Psychology* 37(1):28–36.

Greenberger, E.; Chen, C.; Beam, M.; Whang, S.; and Dong, Q. (2000). "The Perceived Social Contexts of Adolescents' Misconduct: A Comparative Study of Youths in Three Cultures." *Journal of Research on Adolescence* 10(3):365–388.

Guaze, C.; Bukowski, W. M.; Aquan-Assee, J.; and Sippola, L. K. (1996). "Interactions Between Family Environment and Friendship and Associations with Self-Perceived Well-Being during Early Adolescence." *Child Development* 67:2201–2216.

Hallinan, M. T. (1983). "Commentary: New Directions for Research on Peer Influence." In *Friends in School: Patterns of Selection and Influence in Secondary Schools,* ed. J. L. Epstein and N. Karweit. New York: Academic Press.

Hamm, J. V. (2000). "Do Birds of a Feather Flock Together? The Variable Bases for African American, Asian American, and European American Adolescents' Selection of Similar Friends." *Developmental Psychology* 36(2):209–219.

Hartup, W. W. (1996). "The Company They Keep: Friendships and Their Developmental Significance." *Child Development* 67(1):1–13.

Hartup, W. W. (1999). "Peer Experience and Its Developmental Significance." In *Developmental Psychology: Achievements and Prospects,* ed. M. Bennett. Philadelphia: Psychology Press.

Mounts, N. S., and Steinberg, L. (1995). "An Ecological Analysis of Peer Influence on Adolescent Grade Point Average and Drug Use." *Developmental Psychology* 31(6):915–922.

Patrick, H.; Ryan, A. M.; Alfeld-Liro, C.; Fredricks, J. A.; Hruda, L. Z.; and Eccles, J. S. (1999). "Adolescents' Commitment to Developing Talent: The Role of Peers in Continuing Motivation for Sports and the Arts." *Journal of Youth and Adolescence* 28(6):741–763.

Prinstein, M. J.; Boergers, J.; and Spirito, A. (2001). "Adolescents' and Their Friends' Health-Risk Behavior: Factors That Alter or Add to Peer Influence." *Journal of Pediatric Psychology* 26(5):287–298.

Rothbaum, F.; Pott, M.; Azuma, H.; Miyake, K.; and Weisz, J. (2000). "The Development of Close Relationships in Japan and the United States: Paths of Symbiotic Harmony and Generative Tension." *Child Development* 71(5):1121–1142.

Savin-Williams, R. C., and Berndt, T. J. (1990). "Friendships and Peer Relations during Adolescence." In *At the Threshold: The Developing Adolescent,* ed. S. S. Feldman and G. R. Elliott. Cambridge, MA: Harvard University Press.

Scholte, R. H. J.; van Lieshout, C. F. M.; and van Aken, M. A. G. (2001). "Perceived Relational Support in Adolescence: Dimensions, Configurations, and Adolescent Adjustment." *Journal of Research on Adolescence* 11(1):71–94.

Spencer, M. B., and Dornbusch, S. M. (1990). "Challenges in Studying Minority Youth." In *At the Threshold: The Developing Adolescent,* ed. S. S. Feldman and G. R. Elliott. Cambridge, MA: Harvard University Press.

Steinberg, L.; Dornbusch, S. M.; and Brown, B. B. (1992). "Ethnic Differences in Adolescent Achievement: An Ecological Perspective." *American Psychologist* 47:723–729.

Steinberg, L., and Silverberg, S. B. (1986). "The Vicissitudes of Autonomy in Early Adolescence." *Child Development* 57:841–851.

Updegraff, K. A.; McHale, S. M.; Crouter, A. C.; and Kupanoff, K. (2001). "Parents' Involvement in Adolescents' Peer Relationships: A Comparison of Mothers' and Fathers' Roles." *Journal of Marriage and Family* 63(3):655–668.

Voydanoff, P., and Donnelly, B. W. (1999). "Multiple Roles and Psychological Distress: The Intersection of the Paid Worker, Spouse, and Parent Roles with the Role of the Adult Child." *Journal of Marriage and the Family* 61(3):725–738.

Wong, S. K. (1998). "Peer Relations and Chinese-Canadian Delinquency." *Journal of Youth and Adolescence* 27(5):641–659.

Other Resources

"Dealing with Peer Pressure." In KidsHealth. Available from http://kidshealth.org/kid/feeling/friend/peer_pressure.html.

"Developmental Psychology—The Peer Context." In The Psi Café: A Psychological Resource Site. Available from http://www.psy.pdx.edu/PsiCafe/Areas/Developmental/PeerContext.

"Peer Pressure." In Focus on the Family. Available from http://www.family.org/topics/a0017858.cfm.

"Society for Research in Adolescence: Peer Special Interest Group." In Society for Research in Adolescence. Available from http://www.personal.psu.edu/faculty/n/x/nxd10/peesig.htm.

PETER T. HAUGEN
SHARON C. RISCH
DEBORAH P. WELSH

PERU

Peru has a population of 26 million people, of whom 72 percent are concentrated in urban areas. Poverty is a major characteristic, with half of the population (48% in 2000) living in poverty. Even this striking statistic hides the extreme situations, especially in the mountains and rural areas of the Andes Mountains. According to 2000 data, 37 percent of people in urban areas live under the poverty line and 4 percent experience extreme poverty. Conversely, in rural areas, 70 percent of people live under the poverty line, and 36 percent are extremely poor (INEI 2000).

Peru is also characterized by its structural heterogeneity and its cultural pluralism. The Indian population make up between one-third and two-thirds of the population (Le Bot 1994; Weismantel 1998). Socioeconomic inequalities, including those based on class, race, and gender, are present in the social order and daily life (Henríquez 1995).

In the social history of the country, the colonial period gave rise to ethnic and cultural discrimination against the Indian population. The colonial period also saw the beginning of the domination of an oligarchic elite in the political and economic sectors. This domination is reflected today by the Lima centralism and the dominance of the coast over the mountains. The dichotomies of white/Indian, rich/poor, exploiter/exploited began with the same root, which over time, produced different inequalities (Figueroa et al. 1996).

One form of inequality is reflected in the monthly average income. The upper stratum have incomes of between US$2,200 to $4,700 monthly, the low and the very low levels earn only US$270 and $123 monthly (Henríquez 1995). In another example of inequality, although illiteracy decreased, on average, from 18 percent to 12 percent between 1981 and 2000, large differences in literacy rates persist between men (6%) and women (17%). These differences are more pronounced between *urban women* who are not poor (6%) and *poor rural women* (43%) (INEI 2000).

Family Representation

The ideal historical model of family is monogamous and patriarchal. That is, in the urban culture, the sexual division of work is based on separate and complementary spheres. The father is the authority of the family and represents it in the public space, while the wife is responsible for the education of children and is subordinate to her husband's authority (Fuller 1997).

Men must adhere to the ethics of protection and responsibility; women must remain chaste. These aspects constitute the global concept of family honor. The lack of chastity in women endangers the honor of the family. From this belief emerges the image of *Marianismo,* that in Peru is associated with the Virgin Mary and represents the notion of the moral superiority of women, the elevation of motherhood, the denial of sexuality, and the spirit of sacrifice (Fuller 1993).

In contrast, masculinity is based on the idea that sexuality is uncontrollable and that men must affirm their virility through its free exercise and the control of the sexuality of the women in their families. Men can establish sexual relationships throughout their lives without a conjugal or reproductive commitment. This double standard of morality, along with the strict ethnic and class hierarchy, allows the head of the family in the middle- and upper-class sectors (who already has his "official wife" and his "official children") to have sexual relationships with women of lower classes and thereby form secondary families (Fuller 1993).

Consequences

Fertility. The total fertility rate in Peru has decreased from an average of seven children per family at the beginning of 1950 to three children per family in 2002. This reduction is primarily a result of a sharp decrease in fertility among urban women, who had a fertility rate of 2.4 in 2002, compared with 4.6 among rural women (INEI 2002).

Some qualitative studies reveal that patriarchal ideology and the low status of women in Peruvian society have a direct effect on the fertility of women. There is a general belief, held particularly by men, that giving birth to many children is a sign of faithfulness in a woman and that family planning is strongly associated with infidelity (Ruiz-Bravo 1995). In addition, a large number of children is believed to attest to male virility (Chueca 1985).

Moreover, having children is a way for women to keep their husbands, whom they need for financial support. Children are a means for men to keep women at home and to prevent them from being approached by other men. Some women consider wife-beating (which is common especially when a man has been drinking or when he is having affairs outside the home) to be an accepted part of heterosexual relationships. At the same time, women see the sexual freedom of their partners as a normal reflection of men's "different nature" (Sara-Lafosse 1998; Fort 1989).

Furthermore, children represent an economic value, an investment for the future. Having many children is important for parents' security in later years. Sons will support them, and daughters will provide company and care. This is especially important in a country such as Peru where organized

Poverty is prevalent in Peru. In rural areas, 70 percent of people live under the poverty line, and 36 percent are extremely poor. CAROLINE PENN/CORBIS

social security plans cover only a small proportion of the population. (Chueca 1985; Fort 1989).

Female-headed households. Women head at least 20 to 25 percent of families in Peru. Some authors define a household as headed by a female if the father is absent, the result of the father abandoning the family (Sara-Lafosse 1995; Fuller 2000). The census definition of "head of the family" considers the head to be "the person, man or woman, who other members of the family recognize to be the head" (p.16). It has been argued that this definition is subjective, given that it is based on the perception of the other members of the family, and it does not consider the shared responsibility of heading a family. Furthermore, given the patriarchal ideology, the very presence of a man (i.e., a retired father, a partner, or an unemployed uncle) would be enough to declare him the head of the family even the woman has the major economic responsibility (Ponce and Francke 1985).

Violeta Sara-Lafosse (1998) associated female-headed households with the subculture of machismo, which is internalized and legitimized by the family as well as by the social, legal, and police institutions. Machismo is "a form of masculine behavior which comprises the man's desire to take sexual advantage of women, the failure to assume responsibility for the consequences of such actions, and the self-praise for sexual exploits within the subculture of the peer group" (p.107). Machismo and patriarchy are forms of sexist behavior; they treat the women as sexual objects, subject to domination. But while the patriarch becomes responsible for his children, the *macho* man does not take care of them or simply does not recognize them as his offspring.

One characteristic of families abandoned by fathers is the informal nature of the couple's conjugal arrangement, which was established on a verbal or implied common agreement. Under these circumstances, children face the stigma of illegitimacy (Sara-Lafosse 1995; 1998). Marcella Chueca (1985) argued that rather than divorcing or leaving their original families, men form other families parallel to their original families. By doing this, they are able to avoid the economic burden because there is no formal desertion.

Explanations

Sara-Lafosse's thesis (1995, 1998), supported by other authors' (Burkett 1985; Stein and Stein 1979; Montecino 1993; Mannarelli 1993), is that irresponsible fatherhood in Latin America and the Caribbean has its origins in the colonial conquest. Rape of indigenous women was used to subjugate and oppress. Violence was continuous during this period. After the conquest (1492 to the early 1800s), violence manifested itself in other forms of oppression. During the fifteenth century, to facilitate pacification, the Spanish Crown encouraged Spanish men to marry the Indians' daughters. This policy changed in the 1600s, when Indians and Spaniards were prohibited from marrying one another. In addition, the ratio of immigrant Spanish men to immigrant Spanish women was nine to one, pushing men toward interracial relationships. Furthermore, children of European fathers could not be considered Indians and therefore, they were not subject to the oppression, prohibitions, or taxes imposed on the conquered population. Although the father did not recognize his offspring, the son had progressed in social position and brought his mother on this relative ascent.

Cecilia Blondet (1990) argues that, for women who migrate from rural to urban Peru, children played a determinant role for developing roots and constructing a social identity in Lima. The possibility of having a partner and children was an incentive to settle down in their new situation, given that for a woman, forming a family meant having something belonging to her and gave her courage to go ahead. Thus, even though marriage was an ideal for immigrant women, to have children was the ultimate goal of these unions. In this way, faced with the difficulty of having or retaining partners, women accepted the irregular presence or the absence of the family father.

Fatherhood and femininity in urban areas. The second half of the twentieth century brought changes that particularly affected urban areas in Peru. Since the early 1960s, urban women have increasingly entered the labor market. By the beginning of the 1990s, women made up 40 percent of the active workforce (INEI 2000). They also reached secondary and postsecondary education and decreased their fertility rate. Other factors that have influenced changes in representations of masculinity and femininity and raised questions the traditional model of male-female relations include the equality of the genders established by the political constitution of 1981, as well as the cultural globalization of new images of paternity and discourses about women (feminism, citizenship, sexual liberation, etc.) (Fuller 1993). Machismo is criticized, and the image of the distant and authoritarian father has been replaced with the image of the close and loving father (Fuller 1997).

Machismo and marianismo persist in many practices and attitudes of the Peruvian middle-class culture, but they have lost legitimacy as absolute values. Female representations are now characterized by the coexistence of different models of femininity. Their values and their representations are modern but their practices and some fundamental definitions of femininity, including the relationship between the sexes and motherhood, remain traditional and correspond to the marianismo code (Fuller 1993).

Families and migration. Female-headed families experience more difficult economic conditions. They have inferior legal protection given that women are especially concentrated in the informal sector of the labor market. Social security affiliation rates are higher in male-headed families. Families headed by women tend to live in inferior housing, and they have less access to public services (Velez and Kaufmann 1985). As a result of these conditions, a large number of women are involved in the international migration process (Chant and Radcliffe 1992).

The following findings are based on a qualitative study of the way of life of Latin American women who live illegally in Switzerland (Carbajal 2002). The findings are based on the life histories of these women, who work in domestic service and childcare.

In Europe various social changes have influenced the family structure of Latin American immigrants. Changes in demographics and women's social and economic roles have brought increased demand for migrant female work in the domestic service, babysitting, and the care of seniors. These changes include an increase in employment among middle-class European women, the decline of the extended family in southern Europe and the reduction of the welfare state in northern Europe. Employing migrant women appears to be a strategy to combine work and family. (Henshall 1999; Ackers 1998; Sassen, 1984; Stier and Tienda 1992; Kofman 1999). In this way, the double burden of middle-class working European mothers is reduced at the expense of the work of domestic immigrant employees who, themselves, are frequently mothers.

Women and illegality. "Illegality means to live always with limits. Illegality marginalizes you, for example related to the type of work: I can't think of being a secretary in a firm. . . . Illegality is the psychological insecurity of always thinking that the police watch us" (Carbajal 2002). The closure of national borders to immigrants since the 1970s by European Union countries because of the economic crisis produced illegal immigrants, people who do not have a legal resident status and who lack all rights. The possibilities of having a legal status are thus reduced for non-European people, and they are often in illegal situations.

The study focused on women who work with the goal of saving money to improve living conditions for their families. They want to provide for their children's education, pay debts, build a house, establish a small savings, and have economic independence for the future. These women also want to send money regularly to their parents, children, or husbands.

Myrian Carbajal Mendoza distinguished between two profiles of illegal women: First, there are women with primary or secondary education, who are mothers, forty to fifty years old, come from the lower classes, and entered the labor market during their adolescence doing domestic work, babysitting, or working in the public market.

An example of this group are Peruvian women who are in Switzerland with their families (partners and children), as well as single mothers whose children stayed in their countries of origin.

Being in Switzerland represents the opportunity to escape insufficient living conditions and replace them with improved conditions. Women relate this to their role and identity as mothers: "We can't regret the fact of having come to Switzerland; a mother wants always to give the best to their children . . . it's for my children" (Carbajal 2000). This accomplishment, as they understand it, enables a woman to feel able to face poverty and to believe that the "sacrifice" she made was worthwhile, "Despite the fact of being far from my children I always have money to send them, they are not going to suffer because of a lack of meals or housing." They justify and validate their experience by defining the hardships and sacrifices, including being far from their children, in another country where they do not speak the language, as making it possible for their children to have another type of life, especially better education.

In the second profile are women with a higher educational level, twenty to thirty-five years old, who come from the middle class, and have professional training, higher education (secretary, university student, etc.) or who were occupying positions in public administration.

These women are single mothers whose children stayed in their origin country or single women who are responsible for helping their parents. These women feel a loss of their professional and social status: "In my country, I had a position at work where I was esteemed; here, I am a domestic. Just to think that in my house, we had somebody who worked for us, it's very hard."

Nevertheless, this identity is viewed as temporary. They do not use Switzerland but their country of origin as their reference. In this way, they construct an identity as courageous mothers who sacrifice themselves to give their children the possibility of a better life or an identity of the oldest courageous daughters who sacrifice their studies to help their parents. In addition to benefiting the family economically, these women also look to have some personal benefits such as the opportunity to travel, to save their own money, and to buy things for themselves.

Conclusion

It is from their role of mother that this identity is constructed. However, this role of mother is lived with tension. Even when economic needs are met, emotional needs are not. Consequently, these women work to bring their children to Switzerland, even though their children will share their illegal status. "I have always wanted to take my son with, until today I couldn't do it but the majority of my friends have already done it. They are here with two children and me, who has only one, why would I be the only one who is without her son?" (Carbajal 2002).

The children either have to face the absence of their mothers or their illegal status without understanding the reasons. Finally women, who are away from their own children may project their maternal love on others' children for whom they are paid to care. In this way, they accomplish the fact of being mothers from a distance, "I am always around children and I take care of them as if they were my son; they fill my life and it is more bearable." To Latin American immigrant women, motherhood continues to be an important aspect of their identity.

See also: HISPANIC-AMERICAN FAMILIES; LATIN AMERICA

Bibliography

Ackers, L. (1998). *Shifting Spaces Women, Citizenship, and Migration Within the European Union,* Bristol, Great Britain: The Policy Press.

Andersen, B. (1999) "Overseas Domestic Workers in the European Union" In *Gender, Migration and Domestic Service,* ed. J. Henshall. New York: Routledge.

Blondet, M. C. (1990). "Establishing an Identity: Women Settlers in a Poor Lima Neighbourhood." In *Women and Social Change in Latin America,* ed. E. Jelin. Geneva: UNRISD (United Nations Research Institute for Social Development). London: Zed Books.

Carbajal, M. Myrian. (2002). "Femmes latino-américaines clandestinisées: vie quotidienne et projet d'avenir." Unpublished doctoral dissertation. Université de Fribourg.

Chant, S., and Radcliffe, S. (1992). "Migration and Development: The Importance of Gender." In *Gender and Migration in Developing Countries,* ed. S. Chant. New York: Belhaven Press.

Chueca, M. (1985). "Sexualidad, fecundidad y familia en Villa El Salvador." In *Hogar y Familia en el Perú,* ed. Pontificia Universidad Católica del Perú. Lima: Fondo Editorial de la Pontificia Universidad Católica del Perú.

Figueroa, A., et al. (1996). *Exclusión social y desigualdad en el Perú.* Lima: Organización Internacional del Trabajo/Instituto Internacional de Estudios Laborales.

Fort, A. (1989). "Investigating the Social Context of Fertility and Family Planning: A Qualitative Study in Peru." *International Family Planning Perspectives* 15 (3):88-95.

Fuller, N. (1993). *Dilemas de la femineidad. Mujeres de clase media en el Perú.* Lima: Fondo Editorial Pontificia Universidad Católica del Perú.

Fuller, N. (1997). *Identidades masculinas, Varones de clase media en el Perú.* Lima: Editorial Pontificia Universidad Católica del Perú.

Fuller, N. (2000). *Significados de paternidad y reproducción entre varones urbanos del Perú.* Lima: Fondo Editorial Pontificia Universidad Católica del Perú.

Henríquez, N. (1995). "La sociedad diversa, hipótesis y criterios sobre la reproducción social." In *El Perú frente al siglo XXI,* ed. G. Portocarrero and M. Valcarcel. Lima: Fondo Editorial Pontificia Universidad Católica del Perú.

Henshall, M. J. (1999). "Maids on the Move Victim or Victor." In *Gender, Migration and Domestic Service,* ed. J. Henshall. New York: Routledge.

Kofman, E. (1999). "Birds of Passage' a Decade Later: Gender and Immigration in the European Union." *International Migration Review* (summer) 33(2):269–299.

Le Bot, Yvon. (1994). *Violence de la modernité en Amérique Latine, Indianité, société et pouvoir.* Paris: Editions Karthala.

Mujeres latinoamericanas en cifras: Perú. (coordinated by) T. Valdés and E. Gomáriz. Madrid: Instituto de la mujer; Chile: FLACSO (Facultad Latinoamericana de Ciencias Sociales).

Ponce, A. (1995). "Perú: Perfil sociodemográfico de la población (1972-1993)." In *El Perú frente al siglo XXI,* ed. G. Portocarrero and M. Valcarcel. Lima: Fondo Editorial Pontificia Universidad Católica del Perú.

Ponce, A., and Francke, M. (1985). "Hogar y Familia: Problemas para el estudio sociodemográfico." In *Hogar y Familia en el Perú,* ed. Pontificia Universidad Católica del Perú. Lima: Fondo Editorial de la Pontificia Universidad Católica del Perú.

Radcliffe, S. (1992). "Mountains, Maidens, and Migration: Gender and Mobility in Peru." In *Gender and Migration in Developing Countries,* ed. S. Chant. New York: Belhaven Press.

Ruiz-Bravo, P. (1995). "Estudios, prácticas y representaciones de género. Tensiones, desencuentros y esperanzas." In *El Perú frente al siglo XXI,* ed. G. Portocarrero and M. Valcarcel. Lima: Fondo Editorial Pontificia Universidad Católica del Perú.

Sara-Lafosse, V. (1995). "Familias peruanas y paternidad ausente. Aproximación sociológica." In *El Perú frente al siglo XXI,* ed. G. Portocarrero and M. Valcarcel. Lima: Fondo Editorial Pontificia Universidad Católica del Perú.

Sara-Lafosse, V. (1998). "Machismo in Latin America and the Caribbean." In *Women in the Third World: An Encyclopedia of Contemporary Issues,* ed. N. P. Stromquist. New York: Garland.

Sassen, S. (1984). "Notes on the Incorporation of Third World Women in to Wage-labor through Immigration and Off-shore Production." *International Migration Review* 18(4):1144–1167.

Stier, H., and Tienda, M. (1992). "Family, Work and Women: The Labor Supply of Hispanic Immigrant Wives." *International Migration Review* 26(4): 1291–1313.

Velez, E., and Kaufmann, D. (1985). "La heterogeneidad de los sectores marginados: El caso de los hogares con jefe femenino." In *Mujer y familia en Colombia,* ed. A. C. de S.; D. N. de P.; UNICEF. Bogotá: Plaza & Janes.

Weismantel, M., et al. (1998). "Race in the Andes: Global Movements and Popular Ontologies." *Bulletin of Latin American Research* 17(2):121–142.

Other Resource

Instituto Nacional de Estadística e Informática del Perú (INEI). Available from http: //www.inei.gob.pe/inei4/percifra/percifra.asp.

MYRIAN CARBAJAL MENDOZA

PHENOMENOLOGY

Phenomenology began as a primarily twentieth-century philosophical movement that argued that the best way to come to know the world is to rigorously examine how we apprehend the world through conscious experience (Spiegelberg 1982). Evidence for the influence of phenomenology on the practice of social science can be found in the widespread use of the term *phenomenology* for the description of human experience (e.g., the phenomenology of mothering refers to the description of mothering experiences of real women). Nevertheless, phenomenology also entails a distinct theoretical approach to the study of human life. It is an especially useful approach to the study of families and a vital element of any attempt to achieve a cross-cultural understanding of families.

Phenomenology is the study of *phenomena* or the study of the world as experienced. Beginning with Edmund Husserl (1913–1931), phenomenologists have sought to understand how the things of the world are ordinarily experienced. They have therefore focused their attention on the study of the *lifeworld,* or everyday life of the human subject, and how it is experienced in the *natural attitude.* The natural attitude, the common mode of experience in everyday life, assumes and takes for granted the constitution of the social world. Through the natural attitude, individuals encounter the world as a naturally given external reality and engage the world in terms of practical, everyday life concerns. One of the aims of phenomenology is to achieve accurate descriptions of how individuals experience the world in the natural attitude.

Phenomenologists do not, however, attempt to present the experience of the subject solely from the perspective of and in the language of the subject. Since its early beginnings in continental philosophy, phenomenology has sought a more objective knowledge of the world. This knowledge can be achieved through the *reduction* of human experience to those elements without which the experience could not be. Reduction entails using the subject's perspective (i.e., the researcher's own experience or accounts of other's experiences) as a means to delineating the conditions of experience. To accomplish this reduction phenomenologists attempt to *bracket* or suspend belief in the taken-for-granted assumptions common to the natural attitude. Through bracketing, phenomenologists replace the natural attitude with a scientific attitude or an attitude of calling into question the familiar experience of the world. For early phenomenologists, reduction would lead to an explication of the necessary and universal elements of experience, while for contemporary phenomenologists, reduction leads to the formation of prototypical descriptions of experiences.

Phenomenological analysis of experience has contributed to the linguistic turn in twentieth-century philosophy and social science. Early phenomenological studies demonstrated that human experience is fundamentally informed and constituted by and through language (Heidegger 1962). Therefore, for phenomenologists, any analysis of the essential elements of experience necessitates a thorough examination of how language enables human beings to experience the world in the ways that they do. Language both enables human beings to experience their world, and it constrains how they come to experience that world. Language discloses (some of) the features of experience (while simultaneously veiling others), and in so doing alters how we experience things (Aho 1998). By bringing to reflective awareness just how language both enables and constrains experience, phenomenologists aim to show how linguistic systems not only come to stand *for* things, but they also come to stand *between* things and us (Crotty 1998). An important aim of phenomenology is to bracket the already linguistically constituted ways of encountering things and thereby facilitate encountering those things directly through experience, perhaps even bringing forth new words through which previously hidden features of experience might be revealed. In this way, phenomenologists seek to examine and displace the givenness of the natural attitude and enable experiencing things anew or re-appropriating experiences in a new way. Whereas before the experiences were taken for granted, now they can be appreciated, esteemed, and valued, or resisted, overcome, and changed in significant ways.

Although phenomenology lacks clearly demarcated schools of thought, it is useful to indicate how phenomenological analysis of the family has taken different forms. These forms vary from those approaches that seek to merely describe individual experience (mundane phenomenology) to those that focus so extensively on language that individual experiences remain in the background (family discourse analysis).

Mundane Phenomenology (Everyday Life)

Mundane phenomenology refers to those studies that aim to describe human experience as it is experienced, understood, and communicated by the subject. Such studies often do not refer to their approach as phenomenological, and when they do they merely use it in a cursory and superficial way. Methodologically, these studies aim to render human experience precisely as it is experienced in the natural attitude. The social scientist attempts to incite retrospective accounts that are faithful to the experience without imposing any researcher biases or inauthentic structure on the subject's account of

the experience. Although for most phenomenologists such studies are exemplars of ethnographic research and not rigorous phenomenological analysis, they can often add important insights to our understanding of familial experience (e.g., Vaughn 1986).

Existential Phenomenology

Existential phenomenology is the most common form of phenomenology in psychology. Perhaps the most faithful to Husserlian philosophical phenomenology, the term reflects the influence of existentialist philosophical anthropology on phenomenological studies. With a heavy focus on understanding individual experience, existential phenomenology often incorporates a reliance upon the *phenomenological method* and/or the infusion of existentialist thought into the analysis of individual experience. The phenomenological method, as developed by Husserl and others (Spiegelberg 1982), has been adapted to fit the needs of social scientific research (Boss, Dahl, and Kaplan 1996; Giorgi 1985; Pollio, Henley, and Thompson 1997). Although psychological proponents of phenomenology do not subscribe to one single system of procedures, they do focus their efforts on developing methods that will enable the psychologist to capture the essential meaning of an experience. In contrast to more sociological forms of phenomenology, existential phenomenologists do not venture much further than an elaboration of the lived experience of the individual.

Some analysts use a phenomenological approach and incorporate forms of existential thought to study aspects of familial experience. Here, they draw on the work of Sigmund Freud, Martin Heidegger, Jean-Paul Sartre, Maurice Merleau-Ponty, Rollo May, Erich Fromm, and others to assist the in analysis of human experience. For example, Howard Pollio, Tracy Henley, and Craig Thompson (1997) contrast psychoanalytic and attachment theory conceptualizations of the human experience of other people with their own existential phenomenological perspective as well as analyzing the reparation of breaches in relationships and other experiences such as falling in love, loving others, and death. Other existential phenomenological studies of family life have focused on child development (Briod 1989), informal care of aged parents (Paul 1999a, 1999b), disturbed families (Laing 1971), and intimate relationships (Becker 1992).

Ethical Phenomenology

Some family scholars have begun to use the work of French phenomenologist Emmanuel Levinas in their study of familial relationships. Through an extensive examination of the phenomenology of our experience of others, Levinas concludes that our relation to the other is fundamentally grounded in an ethical responsibility for the other. Levinas uses a phenomenological approach to challenge most of the assumptions that underlie psychological and sociological theories of human relations, suggesting an alternative understanding of human experience as essentially moral. The implications of such a phenomenology are only beginning to be understood for the analysis of social life (Bauman 1993; Kunz 1998). Family scholars have introduced a Levinasian phenomenological approach to the study of parent-child relations (Knapp 1999), child development (Vandenberg 1999), intimacy (Beyers and Reber 1998; Williams and Gantt 1998), and family relationships (Knapp 2000).

Social Phenomenology

Building upon the work of Alfred Schutz, sociologists have emphasized the social and intersubjective nature of our experience of others. Here the focus is on understanding how shared meanings, social contexts, and social interaction enable the construction of intersubjective experience. Schutz argued that people depend upon language and the *stock of knowledge* they have acquired to enable social interaction. All social interaction requires that individuals *typify* others and their world, and the stock of knowledge assists them in this task. The particularity of the shared understandings achieved through social interaction will vary depending upon the social distance between the actors involved. The closer the position of others in the lifeworld, the more particular, rich, and full will be the understandings of the meaning of other's actions. If the lifeworld of the other person is more distant, then the understanding or typification of their actions will be narrower, more invariant, and more inflexible.

In a classic application of social phenomenology, Peter Berger and Hansfried Kellner (1964) examined the social construction of a marital reality. According to their analysis, marriage brought together two individuals from different lifeworlds and thrust them into such close proximity to one another that the lifeworld of each would be brought into dialogue with the other. Out of these two divergent realities would emerge a convergent marital reality that would become the primary social context from which the individual would engage in other social interactions and function in society. This construction of a new social reality (i.e., the marriage) was achieved largely through conversation between the couples in private, but it was also strengthened significantly through the couple's interaction with others outside the marriage in ways that took for granted the social reality of the marriage. Over time a new marital reality would emerge that would be of such consequence for each of the spouses that it would contribute to the formation of new social worlds within which each spouse would function.

Other approaches to family that exemplify a social phenomenological approach include Raymond McLain and Andrew Weigert's (1979) analysis of the basic features of the experience of family and Louise Levesque-Lopman's (1988) interpretation of women's experience, particularly pregnancy and childbirth.

Ethnomethodology and Family Discourse

Ethnomethodology, an approach developed by Harold Garfinkel, emerged out of social phenomenology as a reaction against Parsonian functionalism. Ethnomethodology refers to people's (ethno) methods for making sense of their world. Although building upon a phenomenological foundation, ethnomethodology extends the phenomenological concern for explicating what constitutes an experience to an analysis of how an experience is accomplished.

This subtle shift in focus moves ethnomethodology away from an analysis of experience per se to an analysis of how people make sense of their experience. The end result of such a shift is that ethnomethodologists focus on everyday language use and examine how everyday language in use both constitutes its context and is constituted by its context.

For ethnomethodologically inspired scholars, the study of familial experience becomes the study of how *family* is produced through language use or discourse (Gubrium and Holstein 1993). Family emerges whenever it is talked about, whenever the discourse constructs social relations as familial. Enacting family through talk does not mean one can make family any way she pleases. Rather, family discourse always depends on context and is sensitive to the situation. Therefore, scholars must carefully examine how the social organization of the context within which family discourse is evoked conditions the use of family discourse and also how family discourse serves to construct the context itself. Understanding family as a discursive production enables scholars to examine family as an organizationally embedded social reality. Family can be studied wherever family discourse occurs. Through this approach, family scholars have examined how family is enacted in family therapy clinics, nursing homes, the judicial system, and a wide variety of organizational settings (Gubrium and Holstein 1990; Holstein and Gubrium 1995).

Although future developments in phenomenological studies of family life are likely to occur, phenomenology remains an underutilized theoretical resource in the study of the family. It holds great promise for assisting scholars in understanding various aspects of familial experience and how family realities are constructed through language use in a wide variety of contexts. In particular, phenomenological approaches can facilitate a greater understanding of the cultural diversity of familial experience that characterizes social life at the beginning of the new millennium.

See also: FAMILY THEORY

Bibliography

Aho, J. A. (1998). *The Things of the World: A Social Phenomenology.* Westport, CT: Praeger.

Bauman, Z. (1993). *Postmodern Ethics.* Cambridge, MA: Blackwell.

Becker, C. S. (1992). *Living and Relating: An Introduction to Phenomenology.* Newbury Park, CA: Sage.

Berger, P. L., and Kellner, H. (1964). "Marriage and the Construction of Reality." *Diogenes* 46:1–25.

Beyers, M. S., and Reber, J. S. (1998). "The Illusion of Intimacy: A Levinasian Critique of Evolutionary Psychology." *Journal of Theoretical and Philosophical Psychology* 18:176–192.

Boss, P.; Dahl, C.; and Kaplan, L. (1996). "The Use of Phenomenology for Family Therapy Research: The Search for Meaning." In *Research Methods in Family Therapy,* ed. D. H. Sprenkle and S. M. Moon. New York: Guilford Press.

Briod, M. (1989). "A Phenomenological Approach to Child Development." In *Existential-Phenomenological Perspectives in Psychology: Exploring the Breadth of Human Experience,* ed. R. S. Valle and S. Halling. New York: Plenum Press.

Crotty, M. (1998). *The Foundations of Social Research: Meaning and Perspective in the Research Process.* Thousand Oaks, CA: Sage.

Giorgi, A. (1985). *Phenomenology and Psychological Research.* Pittsburgh, PA: Duquesne University Press.

Gubrium, J. F., and Holstein, J. A. (1990). *What is Family?* Mountain View, CA: Mayfield.

Gubrium, J. F., and Holstein, J. A. (1993). "Phenomenology, Ethnomethodology, and Family Discourse." In *Sourcebook of Family Theories and Methods: A Contextual Approach,* ed. P. Boss, W. Doherty, R. LaRossa, W. Schumm, and S. Steinmetz. New York: Plenum.

Heidegger, M. (1927/1962). *Being and Time,* trans. J. Macquarrie and E. Robinson. New York: Harper & Row.

Holstein, J. A., and Gubrium, J. F. (1995). "Deprivatization and the Construction of Domestic Life." *Journal of Marriage and the Family* 57:894–908.

Husserl, E. (1913/1931). *Ideas: General Introduction of Pure Phenomenology,* trans. W. Gibson. New York: Collier Books.

Knapp, S. J. (1999). "Facing the Child: Rethinking Models of Agency in Parent-Child Relations." *Contemporary Perspectives on Family Research* 1:53–75.

Knapp, S. J. (2000). "Emmanuel Levinas and the Moral Displacement of Knowledge: Rethinking the Relation between the Moral and Social Orders." *Current Perspectives in Social Theory* 20:187–213.

Kunz, G. (1998). *The Paradox of Power and Weakness: Levinas and an Alternative Paradigm for Psychology.* Albany, NY: SUNY Press.

Laing, R. D. (1971). *The Politics of the Family: And Other Essays.* New York: Vintage Books.

Levesque-Lopman, L. (1988). *Claiming Reality: Phenomenology and Women's Experience.* Totowa, NJ: Rowman & Littlefield.

McLain, R., and Weigert, A. (1979). "Toward a Phenomenological Sociology of Family: A Programmatic Essay." In *Contemporary Theories about the Family,* Vol. 2., ed. W. R. Burr; R. Hill; F. I. Nye; and I. L. Reiss. New York: Free Press.

Paul, L. J. (1999a). "Phenomenology as a Method for the Study of Informal Care." *Journal of Family Studies* 5:192–206.

Paul, L. J. (1999b). "Caring for Aged Parents: Phenomenology and Relationships." *Journal of Family Studies* 5:207–219.

Pollio, H. R.; Henley, T. B.; and Thompson, C. J. (1997). *The Phenomenology of Everyday Life*. New York: Cambridge University Press.

Spiegelberg, H. (1982). *The Phenomenological Movement: A Historical Introduction*. Boston: Martinus Nijhoff Publishers.

Vandenberg, B. (1999). "Levinas and the Ethical Context of Human Development." *Human Development* 42:31–44.

Vaughn, D. (1986). *Uncoupling: Turning Points in Intimate Relationships*. New York: Oxford University Press.

Williams, R. N., and Gantt, E. E. (1998). "Intimacy and Heteronomy: On Grounding Psychology in the Ethical." *Theory and Psychology* 8:253–267.

STAN J. KNAPP

PHILIPPINES, THE

Like other social formations of traditional Asia and Europe, Filipino society has, in the post-Cold War era, moved from being a predominantly agricultural society to a modern one. Economic transformations have brought new social changes as the concept of the traditional family continues to be reinvented and transformed. Globalization has created international employment opportunities for migrant workers, especially females, as increasing numbers of Filipinos are "sacrificing" themselves to work abroad to support their families back home. The function of the family changes when a husband and wife are separated for long periods of time. When the wife decides to work overseas and leaves her family behind, it changes the structure at home: Children are cared for by aunts and grandparents, and the husband's traditional role as breadwinner is threatened. Before discussing the dynamic and changing meaning of the concept of the Filipino family, it may be instructive to briefly look at some of the historical transformations that have occurred in Philippine society.

During several centuries of colonization by Spain and the United States, the Philippines produced crops and mined minerals for export and sale on the world market. Since gaining independence in 1946, it has experienced economic growth, decline, and recovery. In the 1960s, neighboring countries perceived it as a showcase for development. At that time, the Philippines had a newly burgeoning middle class and one of the highest literacy rates in the region. However, the economy began to go down when Ferdinand Marcos declared martial law (1972–1981) to prolong his power. Subsequently, the economy entered a period of some positive growth and recovery as Gross National Product (GNP) rates began to increase steadily. The GNP, however, is only a measure of improvements being made at the level of the infrastructure (e.g., increasing rates of electricity being used, new construction, improvements in transportation, increasing numbers of tourists). Consequently, changes in the GNP are not a clear indication that the quality of life for the majority of families has improved.

Politically, the Philippines has long been striving to institute a free and democratic way of life. It was one of the first nations to gain independence from colonial rule. It succeeded in overthrowing an authoritarian dictator (Ferdinand Marcos) in 1987, and it did this through an actively nonviolent people's power revolution. Again, the Philippines peacefully ousted an inept and corrupt president (Joseph Estrada) from office in 2001. Although traditional leading families and new military elites still hold and control powerful governmental posts, a fresh resurgence of people's movements continues from below, supported by nongovernment organizations, calling for a more equitable, just, and democratic society. In the face of these changing circumstances, the Filipino family has proved resilient.

The traditional regime of the Filipino family has been written about before (Mendez and Jocano 1974; Medina 1995; Miralao 1997). Filipinos trace their family relations bilaterally through the mothers' and fathers' lines. Relations between husbands and wives, and between men and women generally, tend to be more egalitarian in the Philippines than in many other cultures and societies. This may be because the Philippines was a matrilineal society before being colonized by Spain (1565–1898) and the United States (1898–1946). The precolonial family line was traced through the female side of the family, while males inherited their political titles and followings from their mother's brother. The close relationships between

Filipino members of both the nuclear and the extended family gather for a photograph. Households in the Philippines are commonly made up of extended family members, which may included grandparents, aunts, uncles, nephews, and nieces.
BENNETT DEAN; EYE UBIQUITOUS/CORBIS

brothers and sisters, husbands and wives, and men and women in general, are typically filled with dignity, protectiveness, and respect. Although the male-centered colonization processes effected some significant changes in the traditional gender regime, Filipino women in comparison to their Euro-American counterparts have enjoyed a relatively high status that can be traced to these early beginnings.

According to Paz Policarpio Mendez and F. Landa Jocano (1974), the traditional Filipino family acknowledges the importance of both consanguineal (blood) and affinal (marriage) ties. Ritual kinship in terms of godparents is recognized as being special because it is embedded in the Filipino community, although the Spanish introduced the practice. Consanguineal or biological ties, however, remain by far the most important relations. The blood bond is so close that even distant relatives are recognized. Mendez and Jocano found

that some rural Filipinos, when choosing friends and possible spouses, carefully examined genealogies to assess virtues and shortcomings because they believed that a person's hereditary character shows. Belen Medina (1995) found that blood bonds are so important, traditionally, that a person can be judged on the basis of who her or his relatives are. It follows that parents and children share an exceptionally strong and intimate bond. They give each other much mutual affection and respect. Children are taught by their parents to be gentle and deferential to elders, and this is carried on after they get married.

Gelia Castillo and Juanito Pua (1963, p. 116) classify the Filipino family as "residentially nuclear but functionally extended." This means that the household tends to be nuclear in form, but the family is extended in so far as relationships among members of the wider kin group are concerned. Members of the same kin group assist one another in times of need, and they participate in joint family activities even if they do not live together in the same household.

If the family living together in the same residential unit includes members other than a husband, wife, and their children, it is an extended family household. Many Filipino families living in the Philippines and abroad, such as in Canada or Southern California, actually live in extended family households. The family household may include grandparents, an unmarried aunt, an uncle, a cousin, a niece, or a nephew. Medina suggested that by the end of the twentieth century, the Filipino nuclear family household was more commonly found in the rural areas than in the cities. This is because it is quite expensive for a typical Filipino family or single person, starting a new life in the city, to rent, build, or purchase a home right away. It is much easier for a family to construct a dwelling made of light materials such as bamboo and other natural plants that are freely available in a barrio setting. These simple homes are considered by many educated Filipinos today to be elegant and environmentally attuned. This appreciation for traditional dwellings was not the case during the American colonial and postcolonial period when concrete homes with corrugated steel roofs were introduced to replace them. Also, in rural communities, kin members can build their household dwellings close to each other, which may not be possible in the city. Moreover, Filipinos who move away to study or work in cities, locally and abroad, tend to stay with their more affluent relatives, and this increases the size of the family household.

Virginia Miralao (1997) following Johan Gultang (1995) examines the transformation of Philippine society in relation to modernization theories that were first introduced by the sociologists Emile Durkheim and Max Weber. These evolutionary models posited that as societies modernize, social relationships become more impersonal and businesslike. At the same time, Durkheim and Weber characterized modern societies as being less religiously oriented and more scientifically grounded. Philippine society, however, does not work in accordance with Western-derived notions of modernization, although such models continue to dominate development circles. Although society is indeed becoming characterized by more impersonal relationships, popular religious and social movements for an alternative, holistic development

paradigm are widespread and growing stronger. Moreover, the modern Filipino family continues to be close knit and centered on the family. Relationships among extended kin continue to be marked by reciprocal obligations and privileges even across great geographic distances.

Familism and personalism are all-pervasive in Philippine society. Filipinos typically try to make their friendships into family-like relationships that are mutually supportive. They prefer to have smooth interpersonal relationships with one another and go out of their way to create an atmosphere in which the people around them feel comfortable and accepted. Filipinos generally try to avoid confrontations and make use of indirect speech and mediators in situations of potential conflict. As elsewhere in Asia, there is a strong concept of face in the Philippines. This means that Filipinos are taught to be sensitive to other people's feelings and, generally, do not say words that may embarrass or shame a fellow human.

Filipino parents consider it their duty to provide for the material and educational needs of their children. Children, in turn, are expected to obey and respect their parents and to take care of their parents when they grow old. Also, older children, until they marry and have families of their own, are expected to help younger siblings with school, and to assist them in getting a job after graduation.

Beginning in the 1970s, the Philippine government implemented an overseas employment program to absorb the increasing numbers of Filipino workers. This has led to new conceptualizations of the Filipino family and changing gender roles, as many married females have decided to migrate abroad to work, and their husbands stay home to care for the children. Today, most Filipino families are maintaining and reproducing transnational household connections and networks. The Filipino family continues to be adaptive and functional in these new and changing circumstances.

See also: ASIAN-AMERICAN FAMILIES; FAMILISM; GODPARENTS

Bibliography

Castillo, G., and Pua, J. (1963). "Research Notes on the Contemporary Filipino Findings in a Taglog Area." *University of the Phillipines Digest* 2(3):29–30.

Galtung, J. (1995). "Anomie/Atomie: On the Impact of Secularization/Modernization on Moral Cohesion and

Social Tissue." *International Journal of Sociology and Social Policy* 15(8–10).

Medina, B. (1995). *The Filipino Family, A Text with Selected Readings*. Diliman, Quezon City: The University of the Philippines Press.

Mendez, P. P., and Jocano, F. L. (1974). *The Filipino Family, in Its Rural and Urban Orientation: Two Case Studies*. Mendiola, Manila: Centro Escolar University.

Miralao, V. (1997). "The Family, Traditional Values and Sociocultural Transformation of Philippine Society." *Philippine Sociological Review* 45(1–4):189–215.

KATHLEEN NADEAU

PLAY

Play serves different purposes at different ages. Jean Piaget (1962) delineated play into three major periods: (1) *imitation and practice play*; (2) *symbolic play*, which is pure assimilation or distortion of reality and implies representation of an absent object; and (3) *games with rules*, such as board games or marbles.

Imitation and practice, the earliest form of play, occurs in the sensory-motor period from birth to approximately twenty-four months. The infant copies the sounds and actions of the persons or animals in the environment. Practice games leading to mastery are evidenced by the infant or toddler swatting a mobile in the crib to make it move, stacking cubes or blocks, or putting plastic sticks into a jar. Fine motor skills develop as the toddler explores the many objects in the crib or playroom. As the baby gets older, large motor skills are practiced through walking, climbing, and through play with push and pull toys.

Symbolic or pretend play emerges around age two, although researchers such as Greta Fein (1981) have found evidence of pretend play among eighteen-month-old toddlers.

Play is at peak during the *preoperational stage*, especially from ages three to six. Children move from *solitary pretend play* to *social play*, where they interact with other children. In simple solitary pretend play, a child may move a truck along the floor, imitate a cat or dog by crawling along the floor, put a teddy bear to sleep, or rock a doll in a cradle. Two toddlers may even play side by side (*parallel play*) without playing with each other. They may occasionally exchange a toy or a word, but their major focus is on their own play game.

At about age three, *cooperative social pretend play* begins and reaches its peak by ages four and five. Carolee Howes (1985) makes a distinction between *social play* and *social pretend play*. Social play involves turn-taking and sharing, but may not involve the make-believe elements found in symbolic play episodes.

The use of symbolic play continues even past the preschool years. When first, third, and fifth grade children played with representational objects such as cars and figures compared to children playing with tranformational objects (a vehicle changes into a robot), those children who played with the representational objects displayed more social play and symbolic play (Bagley and Chaille 1996). Low structured toys such as dress-up materials, toy doctor kits, blocks, stuffed animals, and puppets lead to more imaginative play than structured objects such as crayon, chalk, and puzzles that are more conducive to nonpretend play (Singer and Singer 1990, 2001).

Not only the kind of toy, but parental support and encouragement help to promote children's engagement in fantasy, imagination, and pretend play (Taylor and Carlson 2000). It is interesting to note that mood also affects the involvement in symbolic play. For example, researchers found differences between the play of depressed and nondepressed children (Lous et al. 2000). The depressed children played significantly less in general than the nondepressed children, and much less symbolic play was evident.

Games with rules is the last stage in Piaget's theory of play. Around age seven, the stage of *concrete operations*, children begin to move away from pretend play and involve themselves with board games. As children move from the preoperational stage to the stage of concrete operations, they begin to think more logically and can understand that rules are constant and cannot be modified. Observation of children in this stage, however, reveals that rules are sometimes changed by the leaders in the game to suit themselves. Only later, as children become older and move into Piaget's last developmental stage of formal operations, do children truly abide by rules and see them as inviolate.

Children play jump rope on South Caicos Island. These children are forming and developing social skills for later life as they interact with their peers. PHIL SCHERMEISTER/CORBIS

Gender Differences in Play

The literature indicates that same-gender children prefer to play with each other during their toddler years. When play interactions between parents and children are studied, differences in styles emerge. Mother-child relationships revolve around social interactions; mothers are generally more responsive and facilitative, especially if there is a secure mother-child relationship. Father-child relationships appear to be at a higher level of play particularly when children are securely attached to their fathers (Kazura 2000).

In an interesting study examining the content and structure of children's play narratives, Kai von Klitzing and colleagues (2000) used a sample of 652 same-sex twins whose parents completed a *Child Behavior Checklist* when their children were aged five and seven years. Teachers also completed a report when the children were seven years old. Girls told more narratives with less aggression than boys. Aggressive themes, however,

were related to behavior problems, and this correlation held for girls but not boys. Gender of the child as well as content and coherence of the story may be useful in identifying children who may be at risk for behavior problems.

Advertisers know that there are differences between boys and girls and the attitudes toward toys. This was borne out in a study of play themes of preschoolers by Dorothy Singer and Jerome Singer (1981). Adventure themes, fantasy characters, superheroes, and spacemen were the favored pretend play of boys. Girls indicated a clear preference for family pretend roles (mother, father, baby), playing "house," and dress-up clothes.

Children as young as eighteen months have shown preference for sex-stereotyped choices (Caldera, Huston, and O'Brien 1989), and as they get older, this preference for same-sex-typed toys continues (Eisenberg, Tryon, and Cameron 1984).

Rena Repetti (1984) found that children aged five and one-half to seven and one-half who chose more traditionally sex-linked toys were more likely to be those whose parents responded to gender-role questionnaires in a traditional way. The labeling of sex-typed toys was significantly related to a child's tendency to stereotype occupations. In an earlier study, Brian Sutton-Smith (1968) asked kindergartners to give alternative uses for male- and female-sex typed toys. The children were familiar with these toys, but their play experiences with them were different. If the toy was same-sex, the child ascribed more unique responses to the toy. It appears that toys manufactured for girls tend to be of a more passive nature—dolls, toy stoves, tea sets, carriages—whereas boys receive the cars, trucks, rocket ships, boats, mechanical sets, miniature tools, and toy weapons.

Cultural Differences in Play

When studying the various aspects of play it is essential to take cultural variations into account. Carolyn Edwards (2000) performed a qualitative and quantitative re-analysis of data derived from the *Six Cultures Study* of Beatrice Whiting (1963) on children's play that was collected in the 1950s when the sample communities were more isolated from mass markets and the media than they are today. Examination of the play of 140 children aged three to ten years was carried out looking at creative-constructive play, fantasy play, role play, and games with rules. Results indicated that children from Kenya and India were the lowest scoring in overall play. The children from the Philippines and Mexico scored on the intermediate level, whereas those from Japan and the United States scored highest. The cultural norms concerning work versus play, and the notion of freedom for exploration and motivation to practice adult roles through play are factors influencing the scores. In addition, if there are role models and access to materials there will be more creative and constructive play.

In another study comparing four communities in Guatemala, Turkey, India, and the United States, using fourteen children between the ages of twelve to twenty-four months, Artin Goencue, Jayanthi Mistry, and Christine Mosier (2000) found that social play occurred in all four communities, although the frequency and variation was influenced by the culture. In addition there were cultural variations in the numbers of children who engaged in the different kinds of play examined.

Interactions of 341 mothers and fathers in India were examined as they played with their one-year-old infants in their homes. Mothers were more likely to engage in object-mediated play than were fathers. The data do not support the contention that Indian fathers engage in rough play with their infants. The authors also state that parent-infant rough play in nonindustrialized countries may be culture-specific and not related to biological underpinnings (Roopnarine et al. 1992).

When we examine a sample of studies carried out with Asian children it is interesting to look at specific Asian groups. Two studies, for example, comparing thirty Korean-American children and thirty U.S. children (Farver, Kim, and Lee-Shinn 2000; Farver and Lee-Shin 2000) suggest that individual factors related to pretend play transcended the culture. However, there were similar patterns for pretend play between the two groups of mothers. In Jo Ann Farver and Yoolim Lee-Shin's study, the acculturation of immigrant Korean mothers played a part in the encouragement and acceptance of creativity and play. As mothers became more assimilated into U.S. culture, their children's play changed and became more creative. Jonathan Tudge, Soeun Lee, and Sarah Putnam (1995) also studied play of two- to four-year-olds using two samples in South Korea and two samples in North Carolina with middle-class and working-class parents represented in the samples. Children of working-class parents in Korea were less likely to initiate play than children in the other three groups. In the United States, middle-class and lower-class children did not differ in their initiation of play, but boys in the United States were more likely to initiate play themselves or in conjunction with another person. In all communities the mother was the single most likely partner in their children's play, particularly in middle-class Korea and in the middle-class U.S. community where the mother was not employed outside of the home. Mothers in Korea engaged more with their children than mothers in the United States, but the engagement was more of a passive nature than as a very active participant in play.

When we turn to play in China, we find that the beliefs of Chinese and U.S. early-childhood teachers relative to curriculum are similar in overall structure and organization (Wang et al. 2001). Teachers in both cultures emphasize child-initiated learning as well as teacher-directed learning. U.S. teachers are more supportive of child-initiated approaches and this may be reflected in their tolerance for play.

Using longitudinal data from five Irish-American families in the United States and nine Chinese families in Taiwan, Wendy Haight and her colleagues (1999) proposed that in studying groups from different cultures, it is important to consider such variables such as partner initiations, objects used in play, the extent of child initiations of pretend play, and the themes used in play.

Linda Sperry and Douglas Sperry (2000) found that among the African-American two-year-olds they studied, both nonverbal and verbal domains are functional during the third year of life. Pretend play objects are not always necessary for mental representations. Rhoda Redleaf and Audrey Robertson (1999) also suggest that children's play is often nonverbal and of a bodily character. These authors state that 70 percent of communicative interactions are nonverbal and that kind of communication is worthy of further sociological and linguistic concern.

Conclusion

Play, especially symbolic or pretend play, may be the training ground for the inventive mind and the attitude toward the possible. Parents or caregivers can foster play through their willingness to give a child space to play in, a few unstructured toys or props to play with, encouragement to use imagination and pretense, and most of all the sanction to enjoy the fantasies and fun of childhood without the threat of shame or embarrassment.

See also: ATTACHMENT: PARENT-CHILD RELATIONSHIPS; CHILDHOOD; CHILDHOOD, STAGES OF: INFANCY; CHILDHOOD, STAGES OF: PRESCHOOL; CHILDHOOD, STAGES OF: TODDLERHOOD; DEVELOPMENT: COGNITIVE; DEVELOPMENT: MORAL; GENDER; GENDER IDENTITY; PEER INFLUENCE; TELEVISION AND FAMILY; TIME USE

Bibliography

Bagley, D. M., and Chaille, C. (1996). "Transforming Play: An Analysis of First-, Third-, and Fifth-Graders' Play." *Journal of Research in Childhood Education* 10:134–142.

Caldera, Y.; Huston, A.; and O'Brien, M. (1989). "Social Interactions and Play Patterns of Parents and Toddlers with Feminine, Masculine, and Neutral Toys." *Child Development* 60:70–76.

Edwards, C. P. (2000). "Children's Play in Cross-Cultural Perspective: A New Look at the Six Cultures Study." *Cross-Cultural Research* 34:318–338.

Eisenberg, N.; Tryon, K.; and Cameron, E. (1984). "The Relation of Preschoolers' Peer Interaction to Their Sex-Typed Toy Choices." *Child Development* 55:1044–1050.

Farver, J. M.; Kim, Y. K.; Lee-Shin, Y. (2000). "Within Cultural Differences: Examining Individual Differences in Korean American and European American Preschoolers' Social Pretend Play." *Journal of Cross-Cultural Psychology* 31:583–602.

Farver, J. M., and Lee-Shin, Y. (2000). "Acculturation and Korean-American Children's Social and Play Behavior." *Social Development* 9:316–336.

Fein, G. G. (1981). "Pretend Play in Childhood: An Integrative Review." *Child Development* 52:1095–1118.

Goencue, A.; Mistry, J.; and Mosier, C. (2000). "Cultural Variations in the Play of Toddlers." *International Journal of Behavioral Development* 24:321–329.

Golomb, C., and Kuersten, R. (1996). "On the Transition from Pretense Play to Reality: What Are the Rules of the Game?" *British Journal of Developmental Psychology* 14:203–217.

Haight, W. L.; Wang, X.; Fung, H. H.; Williams, K.; and Mintz, J. (1999). "Universal, Developmental, and Variable Aspects of Young Children's Play: A Cross-Cultural Comparison of Pretending at Home." *Child Development* 70:1477–1488.

Howes, C. (1985). "Sharing Fantasy: Social Pretend Play in Toddlers." *Child Development* 56:1255–1258.

Kazura, K. (2000). "Father's Qualitative and Quantitative Involvement: An Investigation of Attachment, Play, and Social Interactions." *Journal of Men's Studies* 9:41–57.

Lewis, A. (1991). "Developing Social Feelings in the Young Child through His Play Life." *Individual Psychology: Journal of Adlerian Theory, Research, and Practice* 47:72–75.

Lous, A. M.; de Wit, C. A. M.; de Bruyn, E. E. J.; Riksen-Walraven, J. M.; and Rost, H. (2000). "Depression and Play in Early Childhood: Play Behavior of Depressed and Nondepressed 3- to 6-Year-Olds in Various Play Situations." *Journal of Emotional and Behavioral Disorders* 8:249–260.

Piaget, J. (1962). *Play, Dreams, and Imitation in Childhood*. New York: Norton.

Redleaf, R.; and Robertson, A. (1999). *Learn and Play the Recycled Way: Homemade Toys that Teach*. St. Paul, MN: Redleaf Press.

Repetti, R. (1984). "Determinants of Children's Sex Stereotyping: Parental Sex-Role Traits and Television Viewing." *Personality and Social Psychology Bulletin* 10:457–468.

Roopnarine, J. L.; Ahmeduzzaman, M.; Hossain, Z.; and Riegraf, N. B. (1992). "Parent-Infant Rough Play: Its Cultural Specificity." *Early Education and Development* 3:298–311.

Roskos, K. A., and Christie, J. F., eds. (2000). *Play and Literacy in Early Childhood: Research from Multiple Perspectives.* Mahwah, NJ: Erlbaum.

Russ, S. W.; Robins, A. L.; and Christiano, B. A. (1999). "Pretend Play: Longitudinal Prediction of Creativity and Affect in Fantasy in Children." *Creativity Research Journal* 12:129–139.

Singer, D. G. (1993). *Playing for Their Lives: Helping Troubled Children through Play Therapy.* New York: Free Press.

Singer, D. G., and Singer, J. L. (1990). *The House of Make Believe.* Cambridge, MA: Harvard University Press.

Singer, D. G., and Singer, J. L. (2001). *Make Believe: Games and Activities for Imaginative Play.* Washington, DC: Magination Press.

Singer, J. L., and Singer, D. G. (1981). *Television, Imagination, and Aggression: A Study of Preschoolers.* Hillsdale, NJ: Erlbaum.

Sperry, L. L., and Sperry, D. E. (2000). "Verbal and Nonverbal Contributions to Early Representation: Evidence from African American Toddlers." In *Communication: An Arena of Development. Advances in Applied Developmental Psychology,* ed. N. Budwig and I. C. Uzgiris. Stamford, CT: Ablex.

Sutton-Smith, B. (1968). "Novel Responses to Toys." *Merrill-Palmer Quarterly* 14:151–158.

Taylor, M., and Carlson, S. M. (2000). "The Influence of Religious Beliefs on Parental Attitudes About Children's Fantasy Behavior." In *Imagining the Impossible: Magical, Scientific, and Religious Thinking in Children,* ed. K. S. Rosengren and C. N. Johnson. New York: Cambridge University Press.

Tudge, J.; Lee, S.; and Putnam, S. (1995). "Young Children's Play in Socio-Cultural Context: South Korea and the United States." Paper presented at the biennial meeting of the Society for Research in Child Development, Indianapolis, IN.

van Oers, B. (1999). "Teaching Opportunities in Play." In *Learning Activity and Development,* ed. M. Hedegaard and J. Lompscher. Aarhus, Denmark: Aarhus University Press.

von Klitzing, K.; Kelsay, K.; Emde, R. N.; Robinson, J.; and Schmitz, S. (2000). "Gender-Specific Characteristics of 5-Year Olds' Play Narratives and Associations with Behavior Ratings." *Journal of the American Academy of Child and Adolescent Psychiatry* 39:1017–1023.

Wang, J.; Elicker, J.; McMullen, M.; and Mao, S. (2001). "American and Chinese Teachers' Beliefs about Early Childhood Curriculum." Poster presented at the biennial meeting of the Society for Research in Child Development, Minneapolis, MN.

Whiting, B. B. (1963). *Six Cultures: Studies of Child Rearing.* New York: Wiley.

Wyver, S. R., and Spence, S. H. (1999). "Play and Divergent Problem Solving: Evidence Supporting a Reciprocal Relationship." *Early Education and Development* 10:419–444.

DOROTHY G. SINGER

POLAND

Since 1989, Poland has gone through extraordinary social changes. It has made a complex transition from socialism to democracy and capitalism and has joined the European Union (EU). The formerly implemented Marxist ideology of equality for all (including idioms of equal opportunities and rights, equal access to privileges and positions, etc.) is being replaced by the development of a free market, which has introduced intense competition and a disparity between the rich and the poor (Łobodzińska 1995). Unemployment, inflation, layoffs, and the closure of nonprofitable plants all contribute to tensions in the labor force, economic insecurity, and lower family budgets. Poles are very concerned about high interest rates, rising crime, and the expanding underground economy, but their main concern is jobs (Jobs 2001). These differences influence behavior, attitudes, values, and opinions, and represent social change (Łobodzińska 2000b).

Changes in Population and Demographic Structure since the 1960s

Because of rural-urban migration after 1945, by the 1980s, the Polish population was transformed from a predominantly rural one into an urban one. The rural family was characterized as a three-generational, extended family, often living in the same household and working together on the farm. Rural people marry at relatively earlier ages and have higher birth and lower divorce rates.

The consequences of the industrialization and urbanization processes include changes in the composition of the family, in marital stability, in childbirth patterns, and in the number of children per family. Rural families tend to have more children than do urban ones. In socialist Poland, abortion was legal and served as a primary means of birth control. In postsocialist Poland, the aging of the population, decreasing birth rate and natural increase rate all contribute to the changing demographic structure. (The natural increase rate is calculated from the difference between the total numbers of births and deaths during one calendar year. Depending on which number is larger, the rate can be positive or negative.) People are marrying less, they are postponing their first marriages, and they are divorcing more frequently (see Table 1). Such trends resemble the vital statistics in other Western societies.

Legislation Applied to Marriage, the Family, and Working Mothers

The intention of lawmakers to meet high standards of equality for all people has resulted in legislation to protect the family and secure women's equal rights. Such ideas have a long tradition in Poland, initiated at the end of the eighteenth century. Legally introduced in socialist Poland, they were manifested by socialist fringe benefits: free access to health care for all, free access to education on all levels of schooling, and retirement benefits. This trend is continued in the most recent, postsocialist Constitution of 1997. The constitution emphasizes eight articles: equality; protection of marriage and the family; protection of children and their rights; protection of pregnant women, working mothers and their offspring; protection of the elderly; and the right to health care are emphasized. Reality, however, falls short of these intentions. Limited family aid, shortages of family services and fixed—but insufficient—family and retirement allowances, and discrimination against women in the labor force confine constitutional rights to aspirations (Malinowska 1995). Legislation evidenced by the Constitution is supplemented by several Legal Codes, amendments and bills, which regulate many aspects of employment and earnings, equal rights, and property.

Among factors modifying family structure and mothers' employment is family planning regulated by the law. Abortion was gradually limited after 1989 and in 1997 was made illegal (except in cases of rape or if the mother's health is at risk). This bill coincides with restrictions in family planning, expensive birth control devices, and limited birth control instructions. Those who perform an illegal procedure face heavy penalties, including imprisonment.

Right-wing, conservative politicians influenced by the Catholic Church who favor larger families argue that this is necessary to secure replacement in the labor force; with the present birth rate labor shortages will occur in the future. They also cite nationalistic reasons: to increase the size of the Polish population. This faction also wants to keep women out of the work force and argues that combining work and motherhood is a burden for the economy because of necessary expenses on family allowances and child care, as well as paid maternal leave of absence, and paid health care for the expectant mother and her child. Such arguments attempt to justify keeping women away from the labor market and persuading them to have more children while staying at home and taking care of the family. In reality, narrowing of the number of women in the labor force increases the chances for male workers' employment under the free market competition. Officially, the most often recommended method of birth control was either total abstinence or the rhythm method. The Catholic Church supported such recommendations. Feminist organizations are few, with small membership. Their influence on family law, politics, and women's employment is secondary.

Other significant aspects of the law regarding family life and women's employment are family violence and sexual harassment. Traditionally, Polish legislation abstained from addressing those issues, and laws were not always clear. Changes introduced in 2000 in divorce law included formal separation for the purpose of reducing the number of divorces granted. Instituting an official separation allows only for the temporary protection of marriage, justifying it as a benefit to the children. In case of divorce, absent parents had to pay child support.

Age of retirement is determined according to gender: women retire at age sixty, men at sixty-five. The law protects working women in general, pregnant working women, and working mothers and allows them to combine employment and motherhood. As a result of such protective laws,

TABLE 1

Population and demographic indications of marital status and the family, Poland

				Year			
Indications	1964	1970	1980	1990	1998	1999	Comments
Poland: population - total	31,3	32,6	35,7	38,1	38,7	38,7	in millions
Population - urban	49.5	52.3	58.8	61.5	61.8	61.8	in %
Population - rural	50.5	47.7	41.2	38.5	38.2	38.2	in %
Population**: age 60+	10.8	13.0	13.2	15.0	16.2	16.5	in % of total
Population***: age 65+	6.6	8.4	10.0	10.2	11.9	12.0	in % of total
Marriages contracted	7.6	8.5	8.6	6.7	5.4	5.7	per 1000 population
Median age at marriage****: men	25.6	24.1	24.9	24.9	24.9 (1996)	–	
Median age at marriage****: women	22.3	21.6	22.7	22.7	22.6 (1996)	–	
Divorces granted	0.7	1.05	1.1	1.1	1.2	1.1	per 1000 population
Live births	15.5	16.6	19.5	14.3	10.2	9.9	per 1000 population
Infant mortality rates - total	47.3	33.4	21.3	15.9	9.5	8.9	per 1000 live births
urban	41.7	31.6	21.0	15.7	9.7	9.2	per 1000 live births
rural	51.4	34.8	21.7	16.2	9.4	9.4	per 1000 live births
Non-marital births	4.6 (1966)	4.9	4.7	4.7	6.1	11.0 (1997)	in % of total births
Natural increase	8.5	10.5	9.6	4.1	0.5	0.0	per 1000 population
Families – single mothers	–	11.3	11.8	13.6 (1988)	15.0 (1995)	–	in % of total families (data include never married, divorced, and widowed)
Families – single fathers	–	1.4	1.5 (1978)	1.7	1.8 (1995)		in % of total families (data include never married, divorced, and widowed)

** - Retirement for women = 60 years of age
*** - Retirement for men = 65 years of age
**** Marriage and remarriage

SOURCES: Based on the author's calculations using the folowing sources: Publications of the Główny Urzad Statystyczny (Central Statistical Office) in Warsaw.
Rocznik Statystyczny 2000 (Statistical Yearbook 2000). pp. XXXVIII-XXXIX; 96; 102-103; 128; 248; 269; 271.
Rocznik Statystyczny 1999 (Statistical Yearbook 1999). pp. XXXVI-XXXVII; 97, 100, 103.
Rocznik Statystyczny 1998 (Statistical Yearbook 1998). pp. LXXVI; XXXIX; 97; 100-104; 126-27; 182; 271; 291; 293.
Rocznik Statystyczny 1997 (Statistical Yearbook 1997). p. 103.
Rocznik Statystyczny 1992 (Statistical Yearbook 1992). pp. 45.
Rocznik Statystyczny 1991 (Statistical Yearbook 1991). pp. XXXII-XXXIII, 49-50.
Rocznik Statystyczny 1990 (Statistical Yearbook 1990). pp. XXIV-XXV, 39-41.
Rocznik Statystyczny 1987 (Statistical Yearbook 1987). pp. 49.
Rocznik Statystyczny 1981 (Statistical Yearbook 1986). pp. 51.
Rocznik Statystyczny 1981 (Statistical Yearbook 1981). pp. XXXIII, 54-6.
Rocznik Statystyczny 1971 (Statistical Yearbook 1971). pp. 84, 90-1, 94.
Rocznik Statystyczny 1966 (Statistical Yearbook 1966). pp. 50.
Rocznik Statystyczny 1965 (Statistical Yearbook 1965). pp. 29; 44-5; 63; 247.
Rocznik Demograficzny 1967-68 (Demographic Yearbook 1967-68). pp. 238.
Rocznik Demograficzny 1971 (Demographic Yearbook 1971). pp. 166.
Rocznik Demograficzny 1987 (Demographic Yearbook 1987). pp. 122.
Rocznik Demograficzny 1993 (Demographic Yearbook 1993). pp. 140.

employers consider women unreliable workers. Patterns of discrimination carried over from the pre-1989 period include a largely sex-segregated labor market and a preference for hiring male workers, followed by inferior jobs and lower incomes for women, aggravated by a higher unemployment rate (which reached 17.4% in December 2001) and by a disproportionate increase in women's unemployment. In 2001, women's unemployment reached approximately 60 percent of the total unemployment. Seventy-five percent of working women earn average salaries below the national level ("Wydarzenia" 2001).

Family Planning and Number of Children Per Family

During the 1990s, birth rates were below replacement level (zero population growth, see Table 2) and marriage rates were on the decline. The population was getting older. In 2001 the birth rate indicators reached a level below zero population growth. In spite of restrictions and penalties, according to estimates, about 20 percent of all pregnancies end in artificially induced abortion (Montgomery 2001). Although there are fewer marriages and they are contracted at a later age, and the older generation makes up a greater proportion of the society, there has been no increase in family services or family allowances (childcare and family benefits policy). In other European countries, expanded family allowances and services have been implemented to stimulate higher birthrates. In Poland, the distribution of expenditures by the government suggests different priorities, which they consider aiding more urgent economic needs. Values that affect having children are changing; young couples delay the birth of their first child so that they may first achieve a more adequate level of economic stability. Fewer children and an older population are the case in Poland, as they are in most of the postsocialist countries. The number of children in an urban setting fluctuates between one and two; in the rural areas, it is more often two or three, and, fairly commonly, more than three. In urban areas, families with more than three children are rare (see Table 2).

The reduction in fertility since 1980 goes against the official postsocialist family policy statements. It is, however, consistent with Western values of a better life. In spite of limited means of family planning and abortion being illegal, practicing birth control results in smaller families. According to a public opinion poll (CBOS 2000, 2001), almost all respondents want to have children. The majority—62 percent—want two children; 21 percent want three children, the officially preferred model. Respondents said that the reasons preventing them from having larger families included inadequate housing conditions, insufficient state assistance, working women's fear of being fired, and concern about decrease in standard of living.

Three-Generational, Extended Family versus Nuclear Family

In the Polish tradition, maintaining close relationships within the family is well established. This applies to siblings and three-generational, extended family members.

Among factors limiting number of children in urban families is the housing shortage, which has been a problem since World War II. Despite the shortage, three-generational, extended families are common, even in urban areas. Housing shortages are especially stressful for young couples who intend to start families. A study conducted in 1999 pointed out that 23.0 percent of the adults—including young couples—in the research sample lived with their parents. In urban areas, approximately 33 percent of respondents aged eighteen to thirty-four lived with parents or other relatives (Wciórka 1999). Under such circumstances, conveying ideas from one generation to another and influencing them would be common and understandable. Even those grandparents who live separately from their adult children frequently supervise grandchildren whose mothers have daily full-time employment.

Under socialism, inexpensive childcare (state subsidized) and numerous family benefits policies were among the advantages for women in being employed. After 1989, the benefits that had been available under the socialist government were reduced. They included free tuition at universities and other schools, free medical care and medications, and subsidized child-care institutions. These circumstances, combined with inflation, have put family budgets under pressure and have made assistance from extended family members appreciated.

Many families share housing with several generations because the persistent housing shortage, low incomes, and high rents leave them no choice. Such arrangements not only provide care for grandchildren, but also serve as a factor in decreasing financial burdens for the retirees who are limited to their small pensions (Trafiałek 1997; Dyczewski, 1994). Such arrangements are determined by economic conditions and serve all generations involved. They also enable adult children (mostly women) to serve as caregivers to their ailing parents.

Several studies conducted before 1989 pointed out that families were characterized by a similarity of values that persisted across generations. This phenomenon was interpreted as an outcome of intergenerational transmission of values prompted by long years of hardships and adversity (e.g., political instability, wars, control by foreign rulers, low standard of living). As the country makes the transition to democracy and capitalism, it is expected that people will modify their values and emphasize self-expression, a better quality of life, and more

TABLE 2

Urban and rural families by number of children in percent, Poland						
		Families by number of children				
Year	Total = 100%	No children	1 child	2 children	3 children	4 children & more
1970 - total	8,197,000	20.5	30.8	27.1	12.6	9.0
urban	4,361,000	20.0	34.7	29.4	10.6	5.1
rural	3,836,000	21.0	26.5	24.5	15.0	13.0
1978 - total	9,435,000	22.2	34.9	28.1	9.6	5.2
urban	5,530,000	36.9	27.4	23.2	8.4	4.1
rural	3,836,000	20.9	26.6	24.5	15.0	13.0
1988 - total*	10,226,191**	29.3	24.6	24.7	8.1	3.3
urban	6,344,000	29.0	24.6	24.7	8.1	3.3
rural	3,862,000	43.1	19.4	21.3	10.5	5.7
1995 - total	10,533,428	23.6	36.2	29.0	8.2	2.8
urban	6,644,186	23.8	36.2	29.0	8.2	2.8
rural	3,889,242	23.2	28.7	26.0	13.6	8.5

* - Data for 1988 include children 24 years of age and younger, living with parents in the same household
** - Excludes children over 24 years of age (adults in the same, or a separate household)

SOURCE: Based on data from the following sources:
  Rocznik Statystyczny 1981 (Statistical Yearbook 1981). Warsaw: Central Statistical Office, 1981: 54.
  Rocznik Statystyczny 1990 (Statistical Yearbook 1990). Warsaw: Central Statistical Office, 1990: 53.
  Rocznik Statystyczny 2000 (Demographic Yearbook 2000). Warsaw: Central Statistical Office, 2000: 93.

significance of individuals' rights and privileges than duties and obligations. Such a switch in values is expected to widen the generation gap.

Mate Selection

The Polish population, socially, is highly heterogeneous (the same race, the same ethnic origin, the same nationality; the majority are practicing Catholics). The population is also highly socially mobile, mainly from rural to urban areas (horizontal mobility). Among the main characteristics for mate selection is similarity of urban or rural origin, similar educational level, and emotional involvement. Poles believe in love. Young rural men have difficulties finding spouses because more young women migrate to the cities to avoid the hard work of farming.

Young people are sexually active. A 1999 public opinion survey reported that 66 percent of secondary school pupils admitted to having sexual intercourse (CBOS [*Młodzież*] 1999). Compared with Western numbers, out-of-wedlock births are low (see Table 1). If a young woman becomes pregnant, the couple generally marries. Some tend to interpret those figures as an indication of being faithful to traditional family values. Those who experiment in alternative lifestyles face ethical and religious scorn; these lifestyles include living together (cohabiting couples in 1995 constituted 1.7 percent of the total) and same-sex couples. They are exceptions. The prevailing tradition is of heterogeneous and formally married couples, mostly in a church ceremony. The housing shortage adds another constraint to these experiments.

The younger generations of school graduates encounter obstacles in finding their first jobs. In a 2001 survey, a high percentage (68%) of people between the ages of eighteen and twenty-four wanted to emigrate to Western European countries to find more job opportunities (Bińczak 2001). This trend will make young people's choice of mates even less predictable and will weaken family ties.

Gender Roles and the Family; Spouses as Coproviders

In Polish families, traditionally, home is the stage for gender-related division of labor in spite of the high rate of women's full-time employment outside the home, including married women with children. Under socialism, usually both spouses were gainfully employed as the norm. Almost exclusively, the household chores and childcare responsibilities were and are placed on shoulders of women. Husbands assist working wives with household chores only sporadically. The higher the educational level of spouses, the more men are involved in household duties. Judging by studies on time budget, women have less available leisure time than do men, while men work longer hours at paid employment (CBOS [*Kobiety*] 1999).

Before 1989, almost all working-age citizens were expected to work, with few exceptions (e.g., university studies, illness). Women, however, continue to face a conflict between their maternal role and their occupational pursuits. The incentives and benefits offered for having a family and children resulted in a reverse effect on women's occupational roles, placing them in positions of constant role conflict, caused by combined family and employment responsibilities. After 1989, some women are rebelling against being forced to work and are trying to take advantage of *the free choices* that arrived with democracy by not working and having to cope without the state's assistance. However, low incomes, inflation, and unemployment forced many women (including those who are married with children) to seek work. According to a comparative study (1964–1998) among the most appreciated values of married life were having children and working (earning money) together with a spouse, to make ends meet. This manifests an expectation that both, husband and wife, will be working outside the home. In spite of an existing division of labor at home, most of the mothers opt for partnership in marriage, where the husband shares equally the decision-making and household duties with his wife (Łobodzińska 1970; OBOP 1998).

Occupational success is identified with higher education. Parents tend to influence children to pursue their schooling. Parents' intention is to secure their daughters' future economic independence through education (which will make them eligible for employment). Simultaneously, they urge the girls into types of education that ensure their future secondary roles in the economy. Young women tend to select occupations less in demand and with lower pay. Division of labor is thus passed from one generation to the next. More women attend universities, and more of them graduate. Among employees (also among the unemployed) are higher numbers of women with secondary education and with university degrees.

Working Mothers, Working Women

Women's employment, in comparison with that of men, increased steadily after World War II. National statistics indicated that in 1950 women constituted 30.6 percent of the total number of employees. In 1960 the figure was 33.1 percent; in 1970 it was 39.4 percent; in 1980 it was 43.5 percent; in 1990 it was 46.0 percent; and in 1999 it was 48.2 percent (*Rocznik Statystyczny* 2000). Although women represent a growing percentage of all workers, there are higher numbers of unemployed women than unemployed men (in 2001 unemployed women represented 60 percent of the total number of unemployed). Polish legislation, when applied to working conditions, protects all women, including pregnant women and working mothers, from circumstances interfering with their (present or future) maternal roles. This plan creates a bias among employers who try to avoid hiring women because they are stereotyped as unreliable workers. It is a long tradition in Poland that women's individual needs and interests were secondary to the needs of the family, the nation, and the state. After 1989, such trends intensified. Polish men, dominating the public and political domain, are inefficient in managing the challenges of democracy and the free market (Łobodzińska 2000a). During intense political competition, reproductive rights became a bone of contention, moving the focus away from solutions to political and economic problems associated with women's employment. Under the circumstances of failure, it was easier to shift responsibility for unacceptable changes onto the shoulders of women. This translates into an informally sanctioned lack of occupational retraining programs for women, which escalates their unemployment. There is a silent acceptance of discriminatory hiring practices, limited sources of childcare and kindergartens, and obstruction of regulations aimed at protecting working pregnant women and working mothers taking care of small children. When businesses must reduce the numbers of workers, women are first to go. New and developing plants hire only a limited number of women (Titkow 2000; Malinowska 1995).

Women, in spite of achieving higher educational levels than men, are mainly occupied in lower priority industries: in food and clothing industries, in services, as mid-level clerical and health care personnel, teachers, and selected types of professionals (physicians, teachers in higher education, economists, etc.). Women's salaries on the average are about 30 percent lower then men's wages.

When comparing women's employment in particular age groups, in the same age category, a lower percentage of women are working than are men (see Table 3). Besides unemployment, women's maternal roles interrupt their employment (between 20–24) to take care of small children. They return to work when the children are older. Also, a proportionally lower percentage of women are economically active in older age categories because they cannot find work or must retire early.

Women's organizations try to retrain women to improve their marketable skills to prepare them for occupations that are more in demand and assure higher pay. At present, family policy and social services addressing family needs and securing equal opportunities for working mothers appears at the bottom of the political agenda (Karpiński 1995; Majman 2000).

Bibliography

Bińczak, H. (2001). "Migracje zarobkowe. Młodzi liczą na pracę w Unii" (Economic migration. The young ones expect to find work in European Union). *Rzeczpospolita* 95.

CBOS (Public Opinion Research Centre). (1999). *Kobiety o podziale obowiązków domowych w rodzinie* (Women about division of labor in household chores). Bulletin no. 16. Warsaw: Author.

CBOS (Public Opinion Research Centre). (1999). *Młodzież o życiu seksualnym* (Youth about sexual behavior). Bullletin no. 98. Warsaw: Author.

CBOS (Public Opinion Research Centre). (2001). *Chłopiec czy dziewczynka? Polacy o dzieciach* (Boy or girl? Poles about children). Bulletin no. 26. Warsaw: Author

Domański, H. (1999). *Zadowolony niewolnik idzie do pracy* (A satisfied slave goes to work). Warsaw: The Institute of Philosophy and Sociology of The Polish Academy of Sciences.

Dyczewski, L. (1994). *Ludzie starzy i staro w społeczeństwie i kulturze* (Old people and old age in society and culture). Lublin: KUL

"Jobs, please." (2001). *The Economist* 358(8215):49.

Karpiński, E. C. (1995). "Do Polish Women Need Feminism? Recent Activity of the Parliamentary Women's Group." *Canadian Woman Studies* 16(1):91–94.

Łobodzińska, B. (1970). *Małżeństwo w miecie* (Marriage in the city). Warsaw: PWN

Łobodzińska, B., ed. (1995). *Family, Women and Employment in Central-Eastern Europe. Contributions in Sociology No. 112*. Westport, CT: Greenwood Publishing Group.

Łobodzińska, B. (1997). "Family, Women and Employment in Poland and Other Central European Countries: Ideology of Equality and Reality of Discrimination." *The Polish Review* 42(4):447–470

Łobodzińska, B. (2000a). "Polish Women's Gender-Segregated Education and Employment." *Women's Studies International Forum* 23(1):49–71.

Łobodzińska, B. (2000b) "Domestic and External Perception of Family and Women's Issues in Poland and in Other Post-Socialist Countries." *The Polish Review* 45(3): 258–302.

Malinowska, E. (1995). "Socio-Political Changes in Poland and the Problem of Sex Discrimination." *Women's Studies International Forum* 18(1):35–43.

Rocznik Statystyczny (Statistical Yearbook). (2000).Warsaw: Central Statistical Office.

Titkow, A. (2000). "Kobieta pod presją, super kobieta, czy kobieta dokonująca wyborów" (A woman under pressure, a super-woman, or a woman making decisions). Paper presented at the 58th Annual Meeting of the Polish Institute of Arts and Sciences in America, June 16-18, Kraków.

Trafiałek, E. (1997). "Główne wyznaczniki statusu ekonomicznego ludzi starszych w Polsce" (Leading indicators of the economic status of the elderly in Poland). In *Przygotowanie do staroci*, ed. M. Dzięgielewska. Łódz: Zakład Owiaty Dorosłych Uniwersytetu Łódzkiego.

Wciórka, B. (1999). *Sytuacja mieszkaniowa w Polsce* (Housing situation in Poland). Bulletin no. 2451.Warsaw: CBOS (Public Opinion Research Centre).

Wciórka, B. (2001). *Co zawdzięczamy swoim babciom i dziadkom?* (What do we owe to our grandmas and

TABLE 3

Employment in Poland, 1999*

Age	Men (%)	Women (%)
15-17	5.2	1.9
18-19	28.3	31.7
20-24	75.0	61.3
25-29	93.0	74.5
30-34	95.1	79.5
35-39	94.0	83.3
40-44	89.2	82.5
45-49	84.4	75.6
50-54	70.9	57.8
55-59	49.1	29.2
60-64	29.2	10.9
65 +	12.2	5.4

* - These figures include currently employed and those registered as unemployed and seeking employment.

SOURCE: Kobiety na rynku pracy (Women in the workforce) Warsaw: Central Statistical Office (GUS), October 2000.

grandpas?). Bulletin no. 102. Warsaw: CBOS (Center for Social Opinion Research).

Other Resources

CBOS (Public Opinion Research Centre). (2000). *o pols-kich rodzinach: preferowany model z dwojgiem dzieci* (About Polish families: A preferred model with two children). Warsaw: ONET—Wiadomoci. Available from http://www.onet.pl.

Centre for Europe's Children. (1999). *MONEE Regional Monitoring Report 6: Women in Transition.* Available from http://eurochild.gla.ac.uk/Documents/monee/.

Majman, S. (2000). "I Am Polish Woman, Hear Me Roar." *The Warsaw Voice* 21(604). Available from http://www.warsawvoice.pl/v604/View01.html.

Montgomery, K. (2001). "Raport jest, aborcje też są" (The report is here, abortions are here also). *Gazeta Wyborcza.* Available from http://www.gazeta.pl.

OBOP. (1998). *Małżeństwo i życie rodzinne w opiniach Polaków* (Marriage and family life in the Poles' opinions). Available from http://www.obop.com.pl.

"Wydarzenia" (Events). (2001). *Oka Biuletyn,* April. Available from http://www.oska.org.pl/biuletyn.

BARBARA ŁOBODZIŃSKA
(WITH ASSISTANCE FROM MIROSŁAWA ŁUKASZEWICZ,
WIESŁAW ŁAGODZIŃSKI, AND BOŻENA GŁÓWCZYŃSKA)

POLYANDRY

See MARRIAGE, DEFINITION OF

POLYGAMY

See MARRIAGE, DEFINITION OF

PORTUGAL

Lying at the far southwestern corner of Europe, with 10 million inhabitants and one-fifth of the Iberian Peninsula's space, Portugal is diminutive in terms of population and territory, and comparatively homogeneous in ethnic terms. Yet it remains noteworthy for the variability of its social life, and no less so in marriage and the family than in other social domains. Analysts of marriage practices and family structures in Portugal have attended to two main axes of variability: those based in social class and regional differentiation. This traditional framework provides the structure for the current discussion, as well. The most important aspects of family and marriage that vary along these axes are the relative position of women, the shape taken by households, inheritance patterns, and the extent of genealogical knowledge.

In a pioneering article from 1962, Emilio Willems posited class as the basic social division and region as the secondary social division influencing variation in marriage and the family in Portugal. Regarding class, the urban *bourgeoisie* was distinctive in being what he termed *family-ridden.* That is, this class contrasted with the lower classes in its focus on controlling the social relations of its members through kinship. One form of control was *particularized homogamous mating,* or the practice of restricting marriage not just to the bourgeoisie, but to a limited number of kinship groups within the class known to have comparable stores of wealth and attitudes toward its disposition. A special focus of control was women, who were kept secluded as part of what Willems labeled *the virginity complex.* In fact, only in the context of their restricted courtship groups were women allowed any real freedom of movement outside their own households. On the lower side of the class divide, proletarian and peasant men could not afford to sequester their wives, daughters, and sisters in the household, and with wider social exposure came significant premarital sexual intercourse and even what Willems called *matripotestal* tendencies, meaning tendencies for women to have significant power of decision within families. Still, he saw peasant families as relatively solid because they were anchored in landed property. Proletarian families, on the other hand, he considered *anomic,* due to their lack of such a material basis for continuity.

Willems made no hard regional distinctions, but his examples of peasant families came mainly from the north of Portugal, whereas his proletarian examples came from the south. The illustrative material is divided neatly, then, according to regional differences that have structured much of the social scientific literature on Portugal at least since Orlando Ribeiro's 1945 geographical masterpiece on the distinction between a wet, mountainous "Atlantic" and a dry, rolling "Mediterranean" Portugal,

Various studies of social structure in Portugal have shown that women in the lower socioeconomic classes—including small farmers, sharecroppers, and agricultural laborers—are not as restricted in their movements and have more decision-making power within families than their upper-class counterparts. OWEN FRANKEN/CORBIS

which corresponds roughly to a north/south division. The Tagus River forms the boundary. It runs from the northeast to the southwest, emptying into the Atlantic at the country's metropolitan center, Lisbon, bisecting the country into nearly equal parts. For Ribeiro, these basically ecological divisions had consequences for land ownership and settlement patterns, with large holdings in the south setting wealthy owners off from the landless proletarians who worked them, whereas in the north there were smaller, more evenly distributed holdings in land. Anthropologists connected these to differences in family structure and marriage patterns. Jorge Dias (1963) pointed out that in the south kinship ties were weaker and less extensive than in the north, and cohabitation without marriage was more frequent. Corresponding to this, the southern father had comparatively less power within the family. It is interesting to note that the "spiritual family"—made up of godparents and godchildren—intensified in compensation. Still, it was a fiction (often firming up relations across

class boundaries—between landowner and laborer), and had virtually no effect on the formation of new families.

In his groundbreaking ethnography of the Alentejo region, south of the Tagus River, Jose Cutileiro (1971) provided dense detail on the relation between the rich and the poor in the region, deepening Dias's insights and providing nuance to some of Willems's claims. He delineated a range of social classes in the region—estate owners, smaller farmers, sharecroppers, and agricultural laborers—and observed that the position of women varied across them. In the two upper groups, women's exposure to public space was much more controlled. As both smaller farmers and sharecroppers can be likened to Willems's peasants, we can see that peasant status alone did not determine the position of women in the family. Premarital virginity for women was a core value shared by all groups, but women from the lower groups were less likely to adhere to it rigidly. If marriage to the first sex partner was somehow prevented, women's *impure* status made marriage to another highly unlikely. This contributed to the relatively high rates of cohabitation outside of marriage in the region. In Cutileiro's Alentejo region the class division affected family life most notably: not only did women's position differ significantly by class, but the family was differentially organized around connections through women. In wealthy families, control of women consigned them to a hazy role in family integration; in poor families, "mothers, daughters, and sisters form[ed] the only operative groupings based on kinship found" (Cutileiro 1971, p. 127) In more general terms, landed families had a keen sense of kinship outside of the nuclear circle due to competing claims to inheritance, whereas poorer families were comparatively ignorant of the family tree. Naming, a practice crucial to family formation, varied much more among the poor than among the landed. Although the norm in Portuguese practice is that the father's surname end the child's full name, giving it special emphasis, among the poor the mother's surname was often given emphasis, or other names from the eight possibilities provided by the pool of grandparents were used. Thus, in the Alentejo region increasing property holdings corresponded with increasing patriarchy, which provided, in turn, a more fixed notion of family membership across the generations.

Later analyses turned northward in their regional focus, and provided for synthetic accounts of Portuguese marriage and family in regional terms. The north is divided roughly between the Minho, in the humid northwest, and Trás-os-Montes, in the dry northeast. Caroline Brettell (1986) turned both her historical and ethnographic attention to the Minho in large part because it was a region long characterized by heavy male emigration. This emigration contributed to the *matricentic*—or *mother-centered*—character of small land-holding families in the area studied. In accordance with this focus came a significant autonomy among women in such families. This was indexed by the practice of men being identified with reference to their mothers and wives (for example, Josés were distinguished by such designations as "Maria's José" or "Olinda's José"). Women's relative autonomy was also registered in the practice of giving daughters the family name of their mothers, and men that of their fathers (also noted for the Beira Baixa region, in the center of the country, by Santos [1992]). The families of larger

landowners were more patriarchal. João de Pina-Cabral (1986) drew a similar conclusion in his study of Minho social life: households based in farming, often combined with male emigration, were associated with women, and kin groups were centered on groups of sisters. In bourgeois families, male dominance was the norm. Among small farming families premarital sex was not condemned, though the formation of households outside of wedlock was considered shameful. (Brettell, in contrast, described more calibrated local judgements about the degree of shame to be attached to particular households.) Sally Cole's (1991) monograph on the Minho is consistent with many of the findings of Brettell and Pina-Cabral, though she focused her attention on fishing women, and discerned a *women-centered*—not just a *mother-centered*—character among their families; landed families were decidedly patriarchal.

Studies located east of the Minho, in Trás-os-Montes, have emphasized the principle of the household and its durability through the generations. Brian O'Neill's (1987) work is one of the key texts, with its finding that historically in this area matrimony has been far weaker as a social objective than retaining the patrimony intact. There has been significant effort to prevent—or at least postpone—marriages of individuals in order that the land fragmentation associated with inheritance by multiple sets of heirs legitimated by marriage be avoided. This has led, in O'Neill's view, to high levels both of formal celibacy and of birth outside of wedlock, something that analysts such as Brettell attribute to other causes in their regions of focus, namely the imbalance between women and men in combination with women's need for social security in their old age. The commitment to patrimony in O'Neill's Trás-os-Montes has also led to *natolocality* (also known as *night marriage*), in which spouses continue to reside with their birth families, changing their premarital activities only by sleeping together in the natal home of the bride (a practice confirmed later by Brito [1995]). Heirs inherit property only at the death of parents, with favored heirs buying the shares in the inheritance possessed by the (often unmarried) co-heirs in order to consolidate the original holding. This is achieved in spite of the Portuguese law specifying equal inheritance among all heirs. There is no gender bias involved in favoring an heir. The bourgeoisie plays no role in local village life, though there are divisions that approach social classes— the crucial inequality generated by inheritance practices that exclude family members.

Though an argument could be made that the variation in marriage and the family noted in the north is basically rooted in class differences, thus making it of a piece with the south, in synthetic accounts of marriage and the family in Portugal, writers like Pina-Cabral and O'Neill argue that there are regional differences irreducible to class structure. For Pina-Cabral (1991), northern Portugal forms part of a *Galician-Portuguese Regional Complex,* whereas significant parts of southern Portugal belong to a *Mediterranean Regional Complex.* In the former, the principle of the house predominates, whereas in the latter, the principle of conjugality is emphasized. An emphasis on the principle of the house means that those who make specific households durable through time are accorded social respect by their communities and more or less egalitarian relations hold among houses (Pina-Cabral 1992); such an emphasis also means higher rates of celibacy. Emphasis on the principle of conjugality leads to an emphasis on social hierarchy between domestic groups and lower rates of celibacy. This contradicts Willems and Cutileiro, who emphasized the class basis of cohabitation outside of marriage in the south. (The issue remains controversial.) It is consistent, however, with O'Neill's (1987) claim that in significant parts of northern Portugal patrimony is emphasized over matrimony, as well as with his (1995) correlation in northern Portugal between a stress on patrimony and relatively equal relations between the genders, and his findings that in southern Portugal an emphasis on marriage is related to the subordination of women. The issue of how class relates to region in shaping marriage and family life in southern Europe as a whole awaits resolution (Kertzer and Brettell 1987), and Portugal is no exception.

The early 1980s and 1990s saw the popularization of the notion that progressive urbanization and movement in the countryside towards industrial and service jobs will modernize the family forms traditionally found in different parts of Portugal; regional and class distinctions will be erased by the increasing occurrence of uniformly nuclear family households—*simple households,* that is, as opposed to *complex households* made up of both nuclear families and residents (such as grandparents, aunts, or uncles) not belonging to the nuclear family. Many recent analyses of marriage and the family in Portugal, by both sociologists and anthropologists, were written in conscious engagement with this belief. Thus M. Villaverde Cabral (1992) discusses survey data confirming the ongoing importance of north/south social distinctions in the context of increasing Portuguese integration into the European economy and polity. Examples of more locally focused empirical research finding against the nuclearization thesis are Karin Wall's (1998) historically informed ethnography and Antónia Lima's ethnographic investigations. Wall argues that in the Baixo Minho subregion of northern Portugal, the 1980s brought industrialization and closer averages in family size across social groups (between three and five individuals), as well as a greater emphasis on conjugal units. Yet these conjugal units were as likely to be found in complex domestic groups as they were in the 1930s (around 20% of the time). Lima (1999) shows how in the 1990s elite business families in Lisbon have remained as committed to extended family connections as they have been in the past, with gatherings of 200 family members considered ordinary annual occurrences, and individuals able to trace, extemporaneously, the connections between 350 to 400 family members. The work of Wall and Lima is but a sample of a treasure trove of work demonstrating that region and class continue to affect marriage and kinship reckoning even as economic modernization occurs. Understanding ongoing continuity and change in Portuguese marriage practices and family relations promises to remain an exciting and complicated affair.

See also: GODPARENTS

Bibliography

Brettell, C. (1986). *Men Who Migrate, Women Who Wait: Population and History in a Portuguese Parish.* Princeton, NJ: Princeton University Press.

Brito, J. P. de (1995). *Retrato de Aldeia com Espelho: Ensaio sobre Rio de Onor.* Lisbon: Publicações Dom Quixote.

Cabral, M. V. (1992). "Portugal e a Europa: Diferenças e Semelhanças." *Análise Social* XVII(118–119):943–954.

Cole, S. (1991). *Women of the Praia: Work and Lives in a Portuguese Coastal Community.* Princeton, NJ: Princeton University Press.

Cutileiro, J. (1971). *A Portuguese Rural Society.* Oxford, UK: Clarendon Press.

Dias, J. (1963). "Algumas Considerações acera da Estrutura Social do Povo Português." In *Actas do 1.ʃ Congresso da Etnografia e Folclore,* Vol. 1. Lisbon: Biblioteca Social e Corporativa.

Kertzer, D. I., and Brettell, C. (1987). "Advances in Italian and Iberian Family History." *Journal of Family History* 12(1–3):87–120.

Lima, A. P. de (1999). "Sócios e Parentes: Valores Familiares e Interesses Económicos nas Grandes Empresas Familiares Portuguesas." *Etnográfica* III(1):87–112.

O'Neill, B. J. (1987). *Social Inequality in a Portuguese Hamlet: Land, Late Marriage, and Bastardy, 1870–1978.* Cambridge, UK: Cambridge University Press.

Pina-Cabral, J. de (1986). *Sons of Adam, Daughters of Eve: The Peasant Worldview of the Alto Minho.* Oxford, UK: Clarendon Press.

Pina-Cabral, J. de (1991). *Os Contextos da Antropologia.* Lisbon: DIFEL.

Pina-Cabral, J. de (1992). "Family and Neighborhood in Portugal Today." In *The New Portugal: Democracy and Europe,* ed. R. Herr. Berkeley: Regents of the University of California.

Ribeiro, O. (1963 [1945]). *Portugal: O Mediterrâneo e o Atlântico.* Lisbon: Sá da Costa.

Santos, A. dos (1992). *Heranças: Estrutura Agraria e Sistema de Parentesco numa Aldeia da Beira Baixa.* Lisbon: Publicações Dom Quixote.

Wall, K. (1998). *Famílias no Campo: Passado e Presente em Duas Freguesias do Baixo Minho.* Lisbon: Publicações Dom Quixote.

Willems, E. (1962). "On Portuguese Family Structure." *International Journal of Comparative Sociology* 3(1):65–79.

SHAWN S. PARKHURST

POSTPARTUM DEPRESSION

There has been considerable clinical and research interest in postpartum depression. This has been largely provoked by the accumulating evidence that postpartum depression is associated with disturbances in child socioemotional development. This evidence has renewed concern about the epidemiology of postnatal depression, its etiology, methods of prediction and detection, and the most appropriate form of management.

The Nature of Postpartum Depression

Postpartum depression must be distinguished from two other mood disorders which occur after the birth of a child. The first is the *maternity blues,* a common disturbance in mood, which arises in the first few days following delivery and usually remits within a week or two, and is characterised by marked swings in mood (*lability*). It is not, in itself, of psychiatric significance. The second category of disorder is the postpartum psychoses which arise in the early weeks following delivery. These disorders affect around one in one thousand postpartum women. They cover a wide spectrum of psychiatric conditions, the most common being manic in form. They are of major psychiatric significance and frequently require hospital admission. In terms of severity, postpartum depression lies between these two classes of disturbance. The clinical profile is the same as depressions arising at other times (Cooper et al. 1988; O'Hara 1997). Thus, central to the depression is a protracted period of low mood accompanied, in varying combinations and to varying degrees, by a loss of interest and pleasure, sleep and appetite disturbance, concentration problems, irritability, feelings of guilt and worthlessness, anxiety symptoms, and, on occasion, suicidal thoughts.

Epidemiology and Course

Epidemiological studies of postpartum samples have consistently revealed that approximately 10 percent of women experience a non-psychotic major depressive disorder in the early weeks following delivery (O'Hara 1997). Although this does not represent an increase over the non-postpartum rate (Cooper et al. 1988; O'Hara et al. 1990), the inception rate for depression in the first three months postpartum does appear to be elevated compared to the succeeding nine months. The duration of postpartum depression is similar to that of depressions arising at other times; in other words, episodes typically remit spontaneously within two to six months. Some residual depressive symptoms are, however, not uncommon, and can persist up to a year following delivery (O'Hara et al. 1990; Cooper et al. 1988). Some cultural variation in the rate of postpartum depression is apparent. Thus, although a rate similar to that found in Western groups has been reported for a Chinese sample (Lee et al. 2001) and for a Nigerian sample (Aderbrigbe, Gureje, and Omigbodun 1993), a substantially lower rate has been found in a Malaysian sample (Grace et al. 2001), and in an indigent urban South African postpartum sample the rate was found to be as high as 34 percent (Cooper et al. 1999). The high prevalence in the latter sample probably reflects a response to the endemic levels of extreme socioeconomic adversity.

Etiology

There is little evidence to support a biological cause for postpartum depression (O'Hara 1997). Despite extensive research on steroid hormones in women after birth, no firm evidence has emerged linking these hormones to the development of postpartum depression

Several studies have found that the presence of maternity blues in the immediate postpartum period is related to the subsequent development of postpartum depression, but no hormonal basis to this association has been identified (O'Hara 1997). Obstetric factors are important in a vulnerable subgroup of women: amongst those with a previous history of depressive disorder, delivery complications are associated with a raised rate of postpartum depression (Murray and Cartwright 1993; O'Hara 1997).

Epidemiological studies have consistently shown that the major factors of etiological importance are largely psychosocial (O'Hara 1997). Thus, the occurrence of stressful life events, including unemployment, a dysfunctional marital relationship, and the absence of support from family and friends, has been found to raise the risk of postpartum depression. A psychiatric history is also commonly reported to be a risk factor for postnatal depression, especially a history of depressive disorder. The importance of this latter association was clarified in a five-year follow-up study of two subgroups of primiparous women who had had a postpartum depression: those for whom the postpartum depression was a recurrence of previous non-postpartum mood disorder, and those for whom the postpartum depression was their first experience of affective disturbance (Cooper and Murray 1995). The former group was found to be at raised risk for subsequent non-postpartum depression, but not to be at risk for depression following a subsequent delivery. Conversely, the latter group was found to be at raised risk for subsequent postpartum depression but not for subsequent non-postpartum depression. This suggests that for a subgroup of those with postpartum depression the birth of a child carries specific biological or psychological risks.

Prediction

Although a number of studies have reported on antenatal factors associated with postpartum depression, the samples used have usually been too small to derive a reliable predictive index. By the end of the twentieth century the only large-scale predictive study conducted revealed that the most reliable predictors of postpartum depression—such factors as the absence of social support or a previous history of depression—each approximately doubled the odds over the base rate risk (Cooper et al. 1996). The predictive index derived from this study is somewhat useful: at a cutoff score of twenty-six about a third of those who will develop postpartum depression are identified, and about a third of those scoring above this cutoff become depressed. It is unlikely, given the modest elevation of odds conferred by all antenatal risk factors identified to date, that an antenatal predictive index could be produced with substantially better predictive power.

The prediction of postpartum depression could probably be improved if account were taken of certain postpartum factors. For example, a study that examined the impact of early postpartum factors on the course of maternal mood (Murray et al. 1996b) found that, beyond the predictive contribution of antenatal factors, both a high maternity blues score and certain neonatal factors (infant irritability and poor motor control) were significantly related to the onset of postnatal depression. Because both the maternity blues and the neonatal infant factors contribute predictively over and above antenatal variables, the predictive value of critical antenatal factors could be improved by taking account of these postpartum variables.

Detection

Although postpartum depression is frequently missed by the primary care team (Seeley, Murray, and Cooper 1996), its detection does not present any special clinical problem. As noted above, the disorder's symptoms are not distinctive and its assessment is straightforward. Indeed, a simple self-report measure, the Edinburgh Postnatal Depression Scale (EPDS), has been developed as a screening device (Cox, Holden, and Sagovsky 1987). The questionnaire has sound psychometric properties (Murray and Carothers 1990), is easy to administer and simple to interpret, and could readily be incorporated within the routine services provided to all postpartum women. Sensitive clinical inquiry with those who have high EPDS scores would be sufficient to confirm the presence of a depressive disorder.

Impact on Family Life, Parenting, and Child Outcome

Little research has been conducted on the impact of postpartum depression on family life. However, in a study of a non-postpartum group of depressed patients, the impact on partners was found to be considerable and far-reaching, including restrictions in social and leisure activities (going out less frequently, seeing people less often), a fall in family income, and a considerable strain on the marital relationship (Fadden, Bebbington, and Kuipers 1987). A questionnaire study of a small sample found the same adverse impact in the case of postpartum depression (Boath, Pryce, and Cox 1998). Interestingly, the partners of women with postpartum depression have been found to have a significantly elevated rate of depression themselves (Ballard et al. 1994).

There have been a number studies on the impact of postpartum depression on the early mother-infant relationship. These have consistently shown difficulties in the interactions between depressed mothers and their infants, most notably either withdrawn and disengaged behavior in the mother, or intrusive and hostile mother-infant communication (Field et al. 1990). These difficulties are most apparent in groups with high adversity levels, but even in low risk samples depressed mothers have been found to respond less sensitively to their infants than well mothers (Murray et al. 1993; Murray et al. 1996a), particularly when the mood disturbance persists (Campbell, Cohn, and Meyers 1995). Follow-up studies also indicate an association between the maternal mood disorder and aspects of child development. Thus, one study conducted in Cambridge, U.K., found an adverse effect

on child cognitive performance among eighteen-month-old infants of mothers who had had a postpartum depression (Murray 1992; Murray et al. 1996b). Although cognitive disturbance was not found to persist in this study, two London studies found cognitive deficit persisting in boys of mothers with postpartum depression when the children were aged four to five (Cogill et al. 1986; Sharp et al. 1995). Poor emotional adjustment in children has reliably been shown to be associated with postpartum depression. Thus, the majority of studies which have systematically examined infant attachment in the context of postpartum depression have found an elevated rate of insecure attachments (Martins and Gaffan 2001). There is evidence that these emotional problems persist into later childhood. A follow-up study of the Cambridge cohort found that the five-year-old children of mothers who had had postpartum depression were significantly more likely than controls to be rated—by both their teachers and their mothers—as behaviorally disturbed (Sinclair and Murray 1998; Murray et al. 1999). One major conclusion from these studies is that the mechanism mediating the association between postpartum depression and adverse child developmental outcome is the impaired pattern of communication between the mother and her infant.

Treatment

There has been little systematic research on pharmacological treatment of postnatal depression. Although progesterone treatment has been enthusiastically advocated (Lawrie, Herxheimer, and Dalton 2000), there has been no systematic evaluation of its clinical utility. By the end of the twentieth century, there has been only one controlled trial of an antidepressant medication, and it showed significant antidepressant effect for both the active drug and the comparison psychological treatment (Appleby et al. 1997). However, there was no additive effect of the two treatments, and the drug treatment was not found to be superior to the psychological treatment. It should be noted that less than half of those invited to take part in the study agreed, mainly because of reluctance to take the medication. This suggests that this line of treatment is not appropriate as a first line treatment, especially in view of the positive results obtained using other forms of intervention which are highly acceptable to women, and that pharmacological treatment should be reserved for those with particularly severe depression or those whose mood disturbance fails to respond to other measures.

There have been a number of controlled trials of psychological treatment of postpartum depression. In an early study, whose findings were later replicated, Holden and her colleagues (Holden, Sagovsky, and Cox 1989) found that improvement in maternal mood in women visited an average of nine times in thirteen weeks by Health Visitors trained in non-directive counselling was substantially greater than in the control group who received routine primary care. Similar positive benefits to maternal mood have been reported for other forms of psychological intervention, such as cognitive behavior therapy, psychodynamic therapy (Cooper and Murray 1997; Cooper and Murray 2001), and interpersonal psychotherapy (O'Hara et al. 2000).

Few studies have examined the impact of treating postpartum depression on the quality of the mother-infant relationship and child development. One controlled psychological treatment trial found that intervention was associated with significant improvement in maternal reports of infant problems, both immediately after treatment (4 to 5 months postpartum) and at a follow-up at eighteen months postpartum; these benefits were confirmed by independent teacher reports of behavior problems at age five (Cooper and Murray 1997; Murray and Cooper 2001). Moreover, early remission from depression, itself significantly associated with treatment, was related to a reduced rate of insecure infant attachment at eighteen months. Similar benefits have been reported in a study of Health Visitor practice (Seeley, Murray, and Cooper 1996). Training was provided to all the Health Visitors working in one National Health Service sector and a cohort study was conducted to assess Health Visitors' clientele before their training and then during a post-training period. Again, significant benefits were apparent in terms of both maternal mood and maternal reports of the quality of the mother-infant relationship.

Marital therapy has been proposed as a treatment for postpartum depression (Apfel and Handel 1999) and as "the treatment of choice" in cases where the marital relationship is in crisis because of the partner's inability to respond empathically to their spouse's distress (Whiffen and Johnson 1998).

However, there is no reliable evidence to support such a proposal. Indeed, such an approach is likely to be appropriate only in a selected subgroup of those with postpartum depression where the spouse is available and willing to engage in a therapeutic process of this sort.

Conclusion

Postpartum depression has a significant adverse impact, not just on the affected woman, but on her partner and the family as a whole. This is of special importance to the infant who is so dependent on the mother for its care. It is of great concern that follow-up studies of the children of mothers who have experienced postpartum depression reveal an enduring adverse impact on the child's socioemotional development. It appears that these adverse child outcomes are driven by disturbances in the mother-child relationship which begin in the early postpartum period. This highlights the importance of early detection and treatment by the primary care health team. It also suggests that efforts should be directed to the identification of high risk samples and to the development and evaluation of preventive interventions.

See also: ATTACHMENT: PARENT-CHILD RELATIONSHIPS; DEPRESSION: ADULTS; LONELINESS

Bibliography

Aderbrigbe, Y. A.; Gureje, O.; and Omigbodun, O. (1993). "Postnatal Emotional Disorders in Nigerian Women." *British Journal of Psychiatry* 163:645–650.

Apfel, R. J., and Handel, M. H. (1999). "Couples therapy for postpartum mood disorders." In *Postpartum mood disorders,* ed. L. J. Miller. Washington, DC: American Psychological Association.

Appleby L.; Warner, R.; Whitton, A.; and Faragher, B. (1997). "A Controlled Study of Fluoxetine and Cognitive-Behavioural Counselling in the Treatment of Postnatal Depression." *British Medical Journal* 314:932–936.

Ballard, C. G.; Davis, R.; Cullen, P. C.; Mohan, R. N.; and Dean, C. (1994). "Prevalence of Postpartum Psychiatric Morbidity in Mothers and Fathers." *British Journal of Psychiatry* 164:782–788.

Boath, E. H.; Pryce, A. J.; and Cox, J. L. (1998). "Postnatal Depression: The Impact on the Family." *British Journal of Psychiatry* 16:199–203.

Campbell, S. B.; Cohn, J. F.; and Meyers, T. (1995). "Depression in First-Time Mothers: Mother-Infant Interaction and Depression Chronicity." *Developmental Psychology* 31:349–357.

Cogill, S.; Caplan, H.; Alexandra, H.; Robson, K.; and Kumar, R. (1986). "Impact of Postnatal Depression on Cognitive Development of Young Children." *British Medical Journal* 292:1165–1167.

Cooper, P. J.; Campbell, E. A.; Day, A.; Kennerley, H; and Bond, A. (1988). "Non-Psychotic Psychiatric Disorder after Childbirth: A Prospective Study of Prevalence, Incidence, Course and Nature." *British Journal of Psychiatry* 152:799–806.

Cooper, P. J., and Murray, L. (1995). "The Course and Recurrence of Postnatal Depression." *British Journal of Psychiatry* 166:191–195.

Cooper, P. J., and Murray, L. (1997). "The Impact of Psychological Treatments of Postpartum Depression on Maternal Mood and Infant Development." In *Postpartum Depression and Child Development,* ed. L. Murray and P. J. Cooper, 201–220. New York: Guilford Press.

Cooper, P. J., and Murray, L. (2001). "A Controlled Trial of the Long Term Effect of Psychological Treatment of Postpartum Depression: Impact on Maternal Mood." *British Journal of Psychiatry.* Forthcoming.

Cooper P. J.; Murray, L.; Hooper, R.; and West, A. (1996). "The Development and Validation of a Predictive Index for Postpartum Depression." *Psychological Medicine* 26:627–634.

Cooper, P. J.; Tomlinson, M.; Swartz, L.; Woolgar, M.; Murray, L.; and Molteno, C. (1999). "Postpartum Depression and the Mother-Infant Relationship in a South African Peri-Urban Settlement." *British Journal of Psychiatry* 175:554–558.

Cox, J. L.; Holden, J. M.; and Sagovsky, R. (1987) "Detection of Postnatal Depression: Development of the 10-Item Edinburgh Postnatal Depression Scale." *British Journal of Psychiatry* 150:782–786.

Fadden, G.; Bebbington, P.; and Kuipers, L. (1987). "Caring and Its Burdens: A Study of The Spouses of Depressed Patients." *British Journal of Psychiatry* 15:660–667.

Field, T.; Healy, B.; Goldstein, S.; and Guthertz, M. (1990). "Behavior-State Matching and Synchrony in Mother-Infant Interactions in Nondepressed versus Depressed Dyads." *Developmental Psychology* 26:7–14.

Grace, J.; Lee, K. K.; Ballard, C.; and Herbert, M. (2001). "The Relationship between Postnatal Depression, Somatization and Behaviour in Malaysian Women." *Transcultural Psychiatry* 38:27–34.

Holden, J. M.; Sagovsky, R.; and Cox, J. L. (1989). "Counselling in a General Practice Setting: Controlled Study of Health Visitor Intervention in Treatment of Postnatal Depression." *British Medical Journal* 298:223–226.

Lawrie T. A.; Herxheimer. A.; and Dalton, K. (2000). "Oestrogens and Progestogens for Preventing and Treating Postnatal Depression." *The Cochrane Library,* no. 2. Oxford.

Lee, D. T. S.; Yip, A. S. K.; Chiu, H. F. K.; Leung, T. Y. S; and Chung, T. K. H. (2001). "A Psychiatric Epidemiological Study of Postpartum Chinese Women." *American Journal of Psychiatry* 158:220–226.

Martins, C., and Gaffan, E. A. (2000). "Effects of Early Maternal Depression on Patterns of Infant-Mother Attachment: A Meta-Analytic Investigation." *Journal of Child Psychology and Psychiatry* 41:737–746.

Murray, L. (1992). "The Impact of Postnatal Depression on Child Development." *Journal of Child Psychology and Psychiatry* 33:543–561.

Murray, L., and Carothers, A. D. (1990). "The Validation of the Edinburgh Postnatal Depression Scale on a Community Sample." *British Journal of Psychiatry* 157:288–290.

Murray, L., and Cartwright, W. (1993) "The Role of Obstetric Factors in Postpartum Depression." *Journal of Reproductive and Infant Psychology* 11:215–219.

Murray, L., and Cooper, P. J. (2001). "A Controlled Trial of the Long Term Effect of Psychological Treatment of Postpartum Depression: Impact on the Mother Child Relationship and Child Outcome." *British Journal of Psychiatry.* Forthcoming.

Murray, L.; Fiori-Cowley, A.; Hooper, R.; and Cooper, P. J. (1996a). "The Impact of Postnatal Depression and Associated Adversity on Early Mother-Infant Interactions and Later Infant Outcome." *Child Development* 67:2512–2526.

Murray, L.; Kempton, C.; Woolgar, M.; and Hooper, R. (1993). "Depressed Mothers' Speech to Their Infants and Its Relation to Infant Gender and Cognitive Development." *Journal of Child Psychology and Psychiatry* 34:1083–1101.

Murray, L.; Sinclair, D.; Cooper, P.; Ducournau, P.; Turner, P.; and Stein, A. (1999). "The Socio-Emotional Development of Five Year Old Children of Postnatally Depressed Mothers." *Journal of Child Psychology and Psychiatry* 40:1259–1272.

Murray, L.; Stanley, C.; Hooper, R.; King, F.; and Fiori-Cowley, A. (1996b). "The Role of Infant Factors in

Postnatal Depression and Mother-Infant Interactions." *Developmental Medicine Child Neurology* 38:109–119.

O'Hara, M. W. (1997). "The Nature of Postpartum Depressive Disorders." In *Postpartum Depression and Child Development,* ed. L. Murray and P. J. Cooper. New York: Guilford Press.

O'Hara, M. W.; Stuart, S.; Gorman, L. L.; and Wenzel, A. (2000). "Efficacy of Interpersonal Psychotherapy for Postpartum Depression." *Archives of General Psychiatry* 57:1039–1045.

O'Hara, M. W.; Zekoski, E. M.; Phillips, L. H.; and Wright, E. J. (1990). "A Controlled Prospective Study of Postpartum Mood Disorders: Comparison of Childbearing and Non-Childbearing Women." *Journal of Abnormal Psychology* 99:3–15.

Seeley, S.; Murray, L.; and Cooper, P. J. (1996). "Postnatal Depression: The Outcome for Mothers and Babies of Health Visitor Intervention." *Health Visitor* 69:135–138.

Sharp, D.; Hay, D.; Pawlby, S.; Schmucher, G.; Allen, H.; and Kumar, R. (1995). "The Impact of Postnatal Depression on Boys' Intellectual Development." *Journal of Child Psychology and Psychiatry* 36:1315–1337.

Sinclair, D., and Murray, L. (1998). "The Effects of Postnatal Depression on Children's Adjustment to School: Teacher Reports." *British Journal of Psychiatry* 172:58–63.

Whiffen, V. E., and Johnson, S. M. (1998). "An Attachment Theory Framework for the Treatment of Childbearing Depression." *Clinical Psychology Science and Practice* 5:478–493.

PETER J. COOPER
LYNNE MURRAY

POSTTRAUMATIC STRESS DISORDER (PTSD)

The essential feature of posttraumatic stress disorder (PTSD) is the development of characteristic symptoms following exposure to a traumatic event that arouses "intense fear, helplessness, or horror," or in children, "disorganized or agitated behavior" (American Psychiatric Association 1994, p. 428). A host of stressors, both natural and manmade, can be traumatizing. Naturally occurring stressors include, for example, natural disasters and medical illnesses.

Man-made events include accidents and acts of violence. Some of these are single events with acute effects; others involve repeated or chronic exposure. Exposure can occur through direct experience with personal victimization or through witnessing or learning about a traumatic event.

Symptoms are categorized into three clusters: persistent re-experiencing of the stressor, persistent avoidance of reminders and emotional numbing, and persistent symptoms of increased arousal (American Psychiatric Association 1994). Intrusive re-experiencing may involve intrusive distressing recollections or dreams about the trauma, "acting or feeling" as if the event were recurring, and intense distress or physiological reactivity when exposed to reminders (American Psychiatric Association 1994, p. 428). In children, re-experiencing may be evident in repetitive play with themes of the traumatic experience, generalized nightmares, and trauma-specific reenactment. At least one re-experiencing symptom is required for the diagnosis.

The avoidance/numbing cluster includes both purposeful actions and unconscious mechanisms: efforts to avoid thoughts, feelings, or conversations related to the trauma; efforts to avoid activities, places, or people reminiscent of the trauma; inability to recall important aspects of the trauma; greatly decreased interest in important activities; feeling detached or estranged; restricted affect; and a "sense of a foreshortened future" (American Psychiatric Association 1994, p. 428). At least three avoidance/numbing symptoms, not present before the trauma, are required for the diagnosis.

The arousal cluster requires increased generalized arousal, including sleep disturbance, irritability or outbursts of anger, difficulty concentrating, hypervigilance, and exaggerated startle response. At least two arousal symptoms, not present before the trauma, are required.

To qualify for a diagnosis, symptoms must continue for more than one month; they may persist for months to years. Symptoms usually begin within three months after exposure, but may be delayed, and specific symptoms and their intensity or severity may vary over time (American Psychiatric Association 1994). The symptoms must cause "clinically significant distress" or impaired functioning (American Psychiatric Association 1994, p. 429), which may be evident at home, work, or school, or in other settings and in interpersonal relationships.

Endorsement of some PTSD symptoms may be normal following trauma exposure, partial symptomatology may be disabling, and the full symptom complex may develop over time. Treatment may be necessary even if all criteria are not met.

Prevalence, Epidemiology, and Comorbidity

Exposure to traumatic events and situations is increasingly common, especially in some environments. The estimated lifetime prevalence of PTSD in the general U.S. population ranges from 1 percent to 14 percent (American Psychiatric Association 1994). Rose Giaconia and colleagues (1995) found that by the age of eighteen years, more than two-fifths of youths in a community sample had been exposed to trauma severe enough to qualify for diagnosis, and over 6 percent met criteria for a lifetime diagnosis of PTSD. Co-morbid conditions are common with PTSD. They include anxiety, somatization (when psychological distress is translated to physical complaints or ailments), and substance-use disorders (American Psychiatric Association 1994; Giaconia et al. 1995).

Etiology

PTSD "is defined by its cause" (Davidson 1995, p. 1230) requiring exposure to a traumatic event or stressor that results in physiological changes associated with the fight-or-flight response, a complex interplay among several systems of the body that leads to increased blood pressure, pulse, and respiratory rate; increased blood supply to the muscles; and vigilance (Guyton and Hall 1997; Perry and Pollard 1998). This response dissipates with time except in cases of severe, prolonged, or chronic stress, in which it may persist and may have potentially detrimental consequences, especially for the developing child (Perry and Pollard 1998).

Risk Indicators and Factors That Promote Resilience

The factors that contribute to posttraumatic stress may be categorized into those occurring before, during, and after exposure to the stressor. Prestressor factors include characteristics of the victim, family, and sociocultural environment. Stressor factors include aspects of the event and exposure. Poststressor factors include aspects of the recovery environment, coping, and treatment.

Pre-event factors. Rates of PTSD are higher in women than men (Ballenger et al. 2000), though gender differences are less clear in children (Foy et al. 1996; Pfefferbaum 1997). The influence of age and ethnicity is not well established. Age and developmental differences may be evident in the symptoms of the disorder, and may reflect prior experience, coping, and the availability of support. Ethnic minorities may be at risk for trauma exposure, but this may reflect differences in socioeconomic status or family influences rather than ethnicity. Other individual factors important in trauma response are preexisting psychopathology and prior exposure to trauma (American Psychiatric Association 1994; Asarnow et al. 1999; Ballenger et al. 2000; Davidson 1995).

Prestressor family and social factors that may influence outcome include relationships within the family and social environment, family organization, and the family's long-term adaptation (Boney-McCoy and Finkelhor 1996; McFarlane 1987; Solomon 1989). Positive family relationships are generally considered protective for traumatized children. Specifically, problems in children appear to be associated with irritable, depressed, and overprotective families (Green et al. 1991; McFarlane 1987). Family adaptability—the capacity for change—and family cohesion—the flexibility of emotional bonds—are likely to affect trauma response. Both extremes of cohesion, too distant and too close, create risk for maladaptive outcome (Laor et al. 1996), although more research is needed to help clarify these family factors.

PTSD has been described in individuals from many cultures. In fact, one would expect high rates of exposure to trauma and PTSD in individuals from those parts of the world where war, crime, and poverty prevail and in refugee populations (American Psychiatric Association 1994). Race, ethnicity, and culture shape conceptualization of events, reactions to trauma, expectations, and treatment (Parson 1994). The biologic response to trauma appears to be consistent across cultures, while the psychosocial aspects of symptom expression are influenced by pre-event, stressor, and poststressor factors (Parson 1994). Of particular concern when Western concepts of trauma are applied in non-Western cultural contexts are potential differences in notions of illness and health, symptom expression, and the phenomenology of the disorder (Marsella et al. 1994).

Stressor factors. Characteristics of the stressor and one's exposure to it influence response. For example, man-made events are thought to be more traumatizing than natural ones (American Psychiatric Association 1994). Exposure can be direct or indirect. Direct exposure involves physical presence or direct victimization; indirect exposure occurs through witnessing or learning of an event experienced by a family member or close associate (American Psychiatric Association 1994). Severity, duration, and proximity are the most important aspects of exposure in predicting the likelihood of developing the disorder (American Psychiatric Association 1994). The role of interpersonal exposure through relationship to direct victims has also been established (American Psychiatric Association 1994). Television viewing as a form of indirect exposure may be associated with posttraumatic stress reactions (Pfefferbaum et al. 2001; Schuster et al. 2001), but no studies link television exposure to the diagnosis of PTSD. One's reaction at the time of the trauma is an important predictor of posttraumatic stress (Asarnow et al. 1999; Ballenger et al. 2000; Schwarz and Kowalski 1991).

Poststressor factors. Family and social factors may influence adjustment following exposure to trauma. For example, within a family, there may be an association between child and parent symptomatology (Foy et al. 1996; Green et al. 1991; Laor et al. 1996; McFarlane 1987) that in some cases may reflect similar exposure. Parental symptoms and poor parental functioning constitute important risk factors for symptom development in traumatized children (Green et al. 1991; McFarlane 1987). Consistency in reaction and mood between parents (Handford et al. 1986), and the quality of the parent-child relationship (Boney-McCoy and Finkelhor 1996) may also affect the intensity of the child's reaction.

When a traumatic event affects large numbers, social factors, such as community disruption, competition for resources, and community response, may influence adjustment (Pfefferbaum 1998; Quarantelli and Dynes 1985; Solomon 1989). Secondary adversities associated with a traumatic event such as displacement and relocation, property and economic loss, family and social problems, and loss of interpersonal support networks affect recovery (Freedy et al. 1992; Laor et al. 1996; Pfefferbaum 1998; Shaw et al. 1995). Traumatic reminders—stimulus cues that activate symptoms—may also interfere with recovery.

Assessment and Treatment

Assessment. Clinical assessment of posttraumatic stress involves the traditional methods of evaluation. The history of exposure, prior trauma, and pre-existing and co-morbid conditions must be assessed. In some situations, such as natural disasters or reported criminal victimization, exposure to trauma is obvious, and the clinician quite naturally inquires about the signs and symptoms of PTSD. In other situations, however, exposure is obscure, and the need for evaluation may be less obvious. Children may not spontaneously report their symptoms, and adults may underestimate trauma in children (Almqvist and Brandell-Forsberg 1997; Handford et al. 1986; Yule and Williams 1990), making it essential to ask children themselves about their experiences and reactions. In addition, children may have difficulty understanding concepts such as avoidance and numbing; therefore, evaluation of them should include observation and reports by parents, teachers, and/or other adults.

Treatment. Treatment involves transforming the individual's self-concept from victim to survivor as the trauma is resolved in a safe setting in which painful and overwhelming experiences can be explored (Amaya-Jackson and March 1995; Gillis 1993; Hollander et al. 1999). Avoidance, a core symptom of PTSD, may prevent the victim from seeking or continuing treatment (Ehlers 2000). The therapist, therefore, must consider omitted information and associated feelings and affects. Avoidance can be protective, decreasing suffering temporarily, but it may be interrupted by intrusive experiences and heightened arousal that occur spontaneously or with exposure to traumatic cues. Educational information is an important aspect of the treatment of PTSD, especially when anxiety and avoidance discourage the patient from seeking or continuing treatment. Prior traumatic experiences must be explored and co-morbid symptoms such as anxiety and depression must be identified and treated. A variety of modalities are used to treat PTSD, although the comparative effectiveness of various modalities has received little attention.

Psychotherapeutic and cognitive-behavioral approaches. The literature suggests that crisis intervention, individual and group therapy, play

A pediatrician and a young patient participate in art therapy. Projective treatment methods such as art therapy allow victims of PTSD to explore traumatic events in a less threatening manner. ED ECKSTEIN/CORBIS

therapy for children, therapeutic exposure, desensitization, relaxation, other cognitive-behavioral techniques, and pharmacotherapy are beneficial in treating PTSD (Davidson 1995; Terr 1989). Exposure therapy that involves repeated review of the traumatic experience is a component of many approaches. Use of projective techniques such as play in children and art may provide access to traumatic themes without threatening the victim's defensive structure. Relaxation techniques may decrease arousal, tension, physical symptoms, anxiety, and sleep disturbance (Hollander et al. 1999). Hypnosis can also be effective (Davidson 1995; Ehlers 2000; Hollander et al. 1999; Terr 1989).

Pharmacotherapy. Pharmacotherapy is an adjunctive treatment that may be needed if symptoms are disabling (Amaya-Jackson and March 1995; Hollander et al. 1999; Marmar et al. 1994). A variety of drugs are potentially effective, most notably anxiolytics (agents that dispel anxiety) and antidepressants. Specific symptoms and the stage of the illness determine whether to use a drug, what drug to use, and the duration of use. Positive symptoms of re-experiencing and arousal may be more responsive to medication than negative symptoms of avoidance (Marmar et al. 1994). Co-morbid conditions should be considered in selecting an agent.

Family therapy. Family work is an excellent means of providing education about trauma and what to expect over time. Parents of traumatized children may benefit from psychoeducation about their children's symptoms and how to effectively manage them. Often, more than one family member will be traumatized though individual exposure and the course of the illness and recovery may differ. Parental trauma may be so great that the needs of a young child may be overlooked. Helping parents resolve their own emotional distress can increase their perceptiveness and responsiveness to their children. The focus of family work includes validating the experiences and emotional reactions of each family member, helping family members regain a sense of security, anticipating situations in which additional support will be needed, and exploring ways to decrease traumatic reminders and secondary stresses.

Group treatment. Group work is ideal for educating victims about symptoms and the posttraumatic course. Sharing with others who have experienced the same or similar trauma can be reassuring, but some are uncomfortable sharing in a group. Group discussions may be re-traumatizing through re-exposure to one's own experiences or through exposure to the experiences of others. Group work also provides an expedient means of reaching individuals in need of more intensive individual assistance.

School-based efforts. School-based interventions are effective for traumatized children or children at risk for trauma. They provide access in developmentally appropriate settings that encourage normality and minimize stigma.

Long-term treatment and pulsed interventions. Long-term treatment may be necessary for those with intense or enduring exposure and symptoms, pre-existing or co-morbid conditions, prior or subsequent trauma, or family problems. Treatment during the acute phase of trauma may be followed by planned interventions at strategic points. These may be especially important following mass casualty events when many have been exposed and can be reached for follow-up in groups. Periodic, brief interventions are useful during developmental transitions and at anniversaries.

Conclusion

The diagnosis of PTSD requires exposure to a traumatic stressor and can be challenging to make if exposure is not obvious or if the victim does not reveal it. Symptoms fall into three clusters—intrusive re-experiencing, avoidance/numbing, and arousal. An array of treatment modalities is used to treat the disorder, although the comparative effectiveness of these modalities has not been well examined.

See also: ANXIETY DISORDERS; ATTACHMENT: PARENT-CHILD RELATIONSHIPS; CHILD ABUSE: PHYSICAL ABUSE AND NEGLECT; CHILD ABUSE: SEXUAL ABUSE; CODEPENDENCY; DEVELOPMENTAL PSYCHOPATHOLOGY; INCEST; INTERPARENTAL VIOLENCE—EFFECTS ON CHILDREN; RAPE; SPOUSE ABUSE: PREVALENCE; SPOUSE ABUSE: THEORETICAL EXPLANATIONS; WAR/POLITICAL VIOLENCE

Bibliography

Almqvist, K., and Brandell-Forsberg, M. (1997). "Refugee Children in Sweden: Posttraumatic Stress Disorder in Iranian Preschool Children Exposed to Organized Violence." *Child Abuse and Neglect* 21(4):351–366.

Amaya-Jackson, L., and March, J. S. (1995). "Posttraumatic Stress Disorder." In *Anxiety Disorders in Children and Adolescents,* ed. J. S. March. New York: Guilford Press.

American Psychiatric Association. (1994). *Diagnostic and Statistical Manual-IV,* 4th edition. Washington, DC: American Psychiatric Association.

Asarnow, J.; Glynn, S.; Pynoos, R. S.; et al. (1999). "When the Earth Stops Shaking: Earthquake Sequelae among Children Diagnosed for Pre-earthquake Psychopathology." *Journal of the American Academy of Child and Adolescent Psychiatry* 38(8):1016–1023.

Ballenger, J. C.; Davidson, J. R. T.; and Lecrubier, Y.; et al. (2000). "Consensus Statement on Posttraumatic Stress Disorder from the International Consensus Group on Depression and Anxiety." *Journal of Clinical Psychiatry* 61(Suppl 5):60–66.

Boney-McCoy, S., and Finkelhor, D. (1996). "Is Youth Victimization Related to Trauma Symptoms and Depression after Controlling for Prior Symptoms and Family Relationships? A Longitudinal, Prospective Study." *Journal of Consulting and Clinical Psychology* 64(6):1406–1416.

Davidson, J. R. T. (1995). "Posttraumatic Stress Disorder and Acute Stress Disorder." In *Comprehensive Textbook of Psychiatry,* Vol. 1, 6th edition, ed. H. I. Kaplan and B. J. Sadock. Baltimore: Williams & Wilkins.

Ehlers, A. (2000). "Post-traumatic Stress Disorder." In *New Oxford Textbook of Psychiatry,* Vol. 1, ed. M. G. Gelder, J. J. López-Ibor, and N. Andreasen. New York: Oxford.

Foy D.W.; Madvig, B.T.; and Pynoos, R.S.; et al. (1996). "Etiologic Factors in the Development of Posttraumatic Stress Disorder in Children and Adolescents." *Journal of School Psychology* 34(2):133–145.

Freedy, J. R.; Shaw, D. L.; and Jarrell M. P. et al. (1992). "Towards an Understanding of the Psychological Impact of Natural Disasters: An Application of the Conservation Resources Stress Model." *Journal of Traumatic Stress* 5(3):441–454.

Giaconia, R. M.; Reinherz, H. Z.; and Silverman, A. B.; et al. (1995). "Traumas and Posttraumatic Stress Disorder in a Community Population of Older Adolescents." *Journal of the American Academy of Child and Adolescent Psychiatry* 34(10):1369–1380.

Gillis, H. M. (1993) "Individual and Small-Group Psychotherapy for Children Involved in Trauma and Disaster." In *Children and Disasters,* ed. C. F. Saylor. New York: Plenum Press.

Green, B. L.; Korol, M.; and Grace, M. C.; et al. (1991). "Children and Disaster: Age, Gender, and Parental Effects on PTSD Symptoms." *Journal of the American Academy of Child and Adolescent Psychiatry* 30(6):945–951.

Guyton, A. C., and Hall, J. E. (1997). "The Autonomic Nervous System; Cerebral Blood Flow; and Cerebrospinal Fluid." In *Human Physiology and Mechanisms of Disease,* 6th edition, ed. A. C. Guyton and J. E. Hall. Philadelphia: W.B. Saunders Company.

Handford, H. A.; Mayes, S. D.; and Mattison, R. E.; et al. (1986). "Child and Parent Reaction to the Three Mile Island Nuclear Accident." *Journal of the American Academy of Child Psychiatry* 25(3):346–356.

Hollander, E.; Simeon, D.; and Gorman, J. M. (1999). "Anxiety Disorders." In *The American Psychiatric Press Textbook of Psychiatry,* 3rd edition, ed. R. E. Hales, S. C. Yudofsky, and J. A. Talbott. Washington, DC: American Psychiatric Press.

Laor, N.; Wolmer, L.; and Mayes, L. C.; et al. (1996). "Israeli Preschoolers under Scud Missile Attacks." *Archives of General Psychiatry* 53:416–423.

Marmar, C. R.; Foy, D.; and Kagan, B.; et al. (1994). "An Integrated Approach for Treating Posttraumatic Stress." In *Posttraumatic Stress Disorder: A Clinical Review,* ed. R. S. Pynoos. Lutherville, MD: Sidran Press.

Marsella, A. J.; Friedman, M. J.; and Spain, E. H. (1994). "Ethnocultural Aspects of Posttraumatic Stress Disorder." In *Posttraumatic Stress Disorder: A Clinical Review,* ed. R. S. Pynoos, J. D. Bremner, D. S. Charney, et al. Lutherville, MD: The Sidran Press.

McFarlane, A. C. (1987). "Family Functioning and Overprotection Following a Natural Disaster: The Longitudinal Effects of Post-traumatic Morbidity." *Australian and New Zealand Journal of Psychiatry* 21:210–218.

Parson, E. R. (1994). "Post-traumatic Ethnotherapy (P-TET): Processes in Assessment and Intervention in Aspects of Global Psychic Trauma." In *Handbook of Post-traumatic Therapy,* ed. M. B. Williams and J. F. Sommer Jr. Westport, CT: Greenwood Press.

Perry, B. D., and Pollard, R. (1998). "Homeostasis, Stress, Trauma, and Adaptation: A Neurodevelopmental View of Childhood Trauma." *Child and Adolescent Psychiatric Clinics of North America* 7(1):33–51.

Pfefferbaum, B. (1997). "Posttraumatic Stress Disorder in Children: A Review of the Past 10 Years." *Journal of the American Academy of Child and Adolescent Psychiatry* 36(11):1503–1511.

Pfefferbaum, B. (1998). "Caring for Children Affected by Disaster." *Child and Adolescent Psychiatric Clinics of North America* 7(3):579–597.

Pfefferbaum, B.; Nixon, S. J.; and Tivis, R. D.; et al. (2001). "Television Exposure in Children After a Terrorist Incident." *Psychiatry* 64(3):202–211.

Quarantelli, E.L., and Dynes, R. A. (1985). "Community Responses to Disasters." In *Disasters and Mental Health: Selected Contemporary Perspectives,* ed. B. J. Sowder. (DHHS Publication No. (ADM) 85–1421). Rockville, MD: National Institute of Mental Health.

Schuster, M. A.; Stein, B. D.; and Jaycox, L. H.; et al. (2001). "A National Survey of Stress Reactions after the September 11, 2001, Terrorist Attacks." *New England Journal of Medicine* 345(20):1507–1512.

Schwarz, E. D., and Kowalski, J.M. (1991). "Malignant Memories: PTSD in Children and Adults after a School Shooting." *Journal of the American Academy of Child and Adolescent Psychiatry* 30(6):936–944.

Shaw, J. A.; Applegate, B.; and Tanner, S.; et al. (1995). "Psychological Effects of Hurricane Andrew on an Elementary School Population." *Journal of the American Academy of Child and Adolescent Psychiatry* 34(9):1185–1192.

Solomon, S. D. (1989). "Research Issues in Assessing Disaster's Effects." In *Psychosocial Aspects of Disaster,* ed. R. Gist and B. Lubin. New York: John Wiley and Sons.

Terr, L. C. (1989). "Treating Psychic Trauma in Children: A Preliminary Discussion." *Journal of Traumatic Stress* 2(1):3–20.

Yule, W. and R. M. Williams. (1990). Post-traumatic Stress Reactions in Children. *Journal of Traumatic Stress* 3(2):279–295.

BETTY PFEFFERBAUM

POVERTY

The plight of poor people throughout the world continues to be much the same as what was described by the Brandt Commission in 1980. The words sound hauntingly similar to the description of the people living in today's global poverty.

Many hundred of millions of people in the poorer countries are preoccupied solely with survival and elementary needs. For them work is frequently not available or, when it is, pay is low and conditions often barely tolerable. Homes are constructed of impermanent materials and have neither piped water nor sanitation. Electricity is a luxury. Health services are thinly spread and in rural areas only rarely within walking distance. Primary schools, where they exist, may be free and not too far away, but children are needed for work and cannot be easily spared for schooling. Permanent insecurity is the condition of the poor. There are no public systems of social security in the event of unemployment, sickness or death of a wage earner in the family. Flood, drought or disease affecting people or livestock can destroy livelihoods without hope of compensation.

The poorest of the poor . . . will remain . . . outside the reach of normal trade and communication. The combination of malnutrition, illiteracy, disease, high birth rates, underemployment and low income closes off the avenues of escape. (Brandt Commission 1980, p. 49)

Definition of Poverty

No one common definition of poverty is accepted by all countries. Poverty is generally categorized as material deprivation. Generally, poverty is defined as the state of being poor or deficient in money or means of subsistence (Barker 1995).

Increasingly, the concept of basic subsistence is measured by the availability of infrastructure services, such as safe water, sanitation, solid-waste collection and disposal, storm drainage, public transportation, access roads and footpaths, street lighting, and public telephones. In some countries, other neighborhood amenities such as safe play areas, community facilities, electrical connections, and social services become important in helping increase the standard of living so that the poor can break the cycle of poverty (World Bank 2001).

Defining poverty solely as being deprived of money is, however, not sufficient. Social indicators and indicators of risk and vulnerability must also be considered and understood to obtain a clear picture of poverty.

Global Poverty

The world may be categorized into seven major areas for ease of study and understanding. They are: Latin America and the Caribbean; the Middle East and North Africa; Africa—Sub-Sahara; Europe, and Central Asia; East Asia and the Pacific; South Asia; and North America.

In a major study of global poverty, the World Bank (2001) estimated that 1.2 billion people lived in poverty in these seven major areas. Additionally, UNICEF (2001) reported that in a $30 trillion global economy, this figure represents one-fourth of the human race that is living in conditions of almost unimaginable suffering and want. Nearly 1 billion people in the world are illiterate. Approximately 1.3 billion people lack safe water. Over one-half of the developing world's population (2.6 billion people) is without access to adequate sanitation.

The United Nations Department of Public Information (1996) estimated that more than two-thirds of the world's poor people live in only ten African and Asian countries: Bangladesh, Brazil, central and western China, Ethiopia, India, Indonesia, Nigeria, Pakistan, the Philippines, and Vietnam. In Africa, the majority of the countries that are poor gained their independence from European colonial powers in the second half of the twentieth century. In Asia, most of the poverty is concentrated in the southern and eastern areas.

More than a billion people still live on less than $1 a day (World Bank 2001). The majority of the world's poor people are women and children. Most of these reside in rural areas. More than 110 million children of school age do not attend school. Easily preventable diseases (pneumonia, diarrhea, malaria, and measles) account for the deaths of nearly eleven million children under the age of five each year. Between 600 million and 700 million children, representing about 40 percent of all those in the developing world, are poor (World Summit for Social Development and Beyond web site).

Measuring Poverty

Each country measures poverty according to its level of development, societal norms, and values. Because of these differences, the poverty level may change from country to country; thus, there is no uniformity in the poverty line. The poverty line is a measure of the amount of money a government or a society believes is necessary for a person to live at a minimum level of subsistence or standard of living (Barker 1997).

In the United States, the poverty line measurement was developed in the mid-1960s by Mollie Orshansky (1965). Essentially, a poverty level (line) was determined by figuring out how much a family needed to maintain a minimally adequate diet and then multiplying by three (represents the number in a family). The United States government adopted this standard, and, with minor yearly adjustments, has used it ever since (Ellwood 1988).

The establishment of a poverty line has political implications. Poverty lines are established at given points of time, and they are usually adjusted, minimally, on a yearly basis. The question of who to count and what to count remains important because a poverty line reveals what a country does and does not do in addressing the needs of its poor citizens.

When estimating global poverty, the United States poverty line is not used. Although there are disagreements on its use, the World Bank uses poverty lines that are set at $1 and $2 per day (U.S. dollars) in 1993 Purchasing Power Parity (PPP) terms. The PPPs measure the relative purchasing power of currencies across countries. It was estimated that in 1998, 1.2 billion people worldwide had consumption levels below $1 a day—24 percent of the population of the developing world—and 2.8 billion people lived on less than $2 a day. For purposes of analysis, the World Bank uses the poverty lines that are based on the norms for respective countries (World Bank 2001).

Welfare Response

Welfare is defined as a condition of physical health, emotional comfort, and economic security. The term also characterizes the efforts of a society to help its citizens achieve that condition, and is used as a synonym for public assistance or other programs that provide for the economic and social services needs of poor people (Barker 1997). Welfare refers to government efforts that provide money, programs, medical care, food, and housing, for instance, to those who are poor. All countries differ, however, on how much they spend on welfare as compared to social insurance or the size of the overall economy (Garfinkel and Waldfogel 2001).

Typically, European countries have universal programs that provide free medical and hospital care, family allowances, and retirement pensions. The Scandinavian countries, such as Norway and Sweden, have extensive government programs; these are so comprehensive that poverty is considered practically nonexistent. Canada, Australia, New Zealand, and the United Kingdom all spend large shares of their economies on the needs of the poor. Aid is provided by employers and families in East Asian countries, such as Japan, South Korea, and Singapore.

Less developed countries in Africa, Latin America, and Asia have lower overall budgets for welfare than other nations. South Africa, however, has one of the most developed social welfare systems, with a particularly comprehensive health care system. Uruguay has a well-developed welfare system. India and Sri Lanka provide smaller benefits and serve fewer recipients (Garfinkel and Waldfogel 2001).

Categories of Dependence

Dependence can be divided into two categories: generational welfare dependence and situational welfare dependence. Welfare families who raise children who, in turn, become welfare recipients are the generational welfare dependent. Generational welfare dependency is the hardest type of poverty for a family to overcome. Over time, this kind of poverty creates a poverty of spirit that can affect a person's and family's entire being. The last thirty years of social welfare history in the United States, for example, reveal that such poverty usually destroys the family unit. In the worst cases, poverty of this sort overtakes entire neighborhoods, towns, and communities by thrusting them into hopelessness and despair (Carlson 1999).

Situational welfare-dependent families are those who have moved from a state of financial independence to welfare dependence, generally due to crises. Causes of sudden financial hardship include abandonment, divorce, debilitating illness, economic recession, natural disasters, and civil strife (Carlson 1999).

Weakened Families and Kinship Systems

In the early 1900s, a U.S. social worker, Mary Richmond, referred to the family as "the great social unit, the fundamental social fact." She demanded changes in agency and government practices, action in regard to child labor laws, industrial safety regulations, and protection of working women, as well as administrative changes in industrial operations to strengthen family life. She constantly challenged people to ask themselves: "Have we at least set plans in motion that will make the children better heads of families than their parents have been?" Her challenge was based on a new recognition of "the overwhelming force of heredity plus the environment we inherit" (1908, pp. 76–79).

A century later, the world's traditional family and kinship systems continued to undergo profound changes. These changes were driven mainly by such economic forces as repeated failures in subsistence agriculture, the availability of relatively higher-paying jobs in urban factories, and new economic opportunities in neighboring and distant countries. Social and political forces also figured centrally in the changes affecting traditional family forms—for example, continuing high rates of population increase, an aging population, increasing numbers of women who need to work outside the home, and recurrent wars and civil conflict (Edwards 1997).

Most of these changes occur in an environment of shrinking social welfare and other support services to help families. Services such as child-care assistance and care for the dependent elderly become paramount in importance to a world of women who carry these responsibilities.

All nations value the family unit. Poor, undeveloped countries are not able to absorb the high costs, however, associated with weakened family and kinship systems.

A Welfare Program Example

In the United States, federal cash assistance for dependent children began in 1935 with the enactment of the Social Security Act. At that time, most poor single mothers were widows, and the cash assistance appropriation was designed to help mothers stay home with their children. Through the years, that initial program, which was called Mother's Pension, changed in both the titles of the cash assistance programs and the requirements placed on the mothers who participate in these programs.

During the 1960s, the United States Congress passed laws that provided incentives to poor mothers to find jobs or to be in job skills training programs. Efforts were also made by the federal government to require fathers of poor children receiving governmental aid to pay child support. By the 1980s, the generalized picture of most poor single mothers revealed that they had never been married or were separated or divorced.

Two decades of moderate to conservative governmental leadership resulted in the U.S. Congress making major changes in the nation's welfare system in 1996. It passed the Personal Responsibility and Work Opportunity Reconciliation Act (PRWORA). Within this act, the Temporary Assistance to Needy Families (TANF) program also replaced the former federal program of Aid to Families with Dependent Children (AFDC). Under AFDC, the federal government required the states to provide aid to families whose income was below the poverty line. Under TANF, the federal government distributed cash payments directly to the states. The respective states determined the recipients of the cash assistance. The major shift in

TANF from AFDC was that recipients must be working within two years, with five years being the maximum time that poor families could remain on government aid.

The results of this ideological paradigm shift were mixed. Some statistics reveal decreases in the welfare caseload. Other statistics revealed that more poor people, especially women, were employed although many of the jobs paid only minimum wage. Anecdotal evidence abounded about to the number of poor women with children who had to choose between paying their utilities and purchasing food. Some estimates suggested that by the early twenty-first century, TANF would result in 2.6 million more people living below the federal poverty line (OneWorld web site).

Regional Disparities Still Exist

In the last decades of the twentieth century, according to the World Bank (2001), living standards improved all over the world. The proportion of the developing world's population living in extreme economic poverty—defined as living on less than $1 per day (in 1993 dollars, adjusted to account for difference in purchasing power across countries)—fell from 28 percent in 1987 to 23 percent in 1998. Improvement in social indicators accompanied growth in average incomes. Infant mortality rates fell; growth occurred in food production; governments reported rapid progress in primary school enrollment; adult literacy rose; gender disparities also narrowed.

In some countries, the increasing poor population overshadowed the improvement in social indicators. Poverty continued to rise in Sub-Saharan Africa. Child mortality rose quickly because of the AIDS epidemic. On average, 151 of every 1,000 African children died before the age of five. Burkina Faso, Ethiopia, Mali, and Niger have fewer than half of their children enrolled in primary school.

In South Asia, it is estimated that four in ten households (more than 500 million people) remained in poverty. Countries such as India made tremendous positive strides in educating their poor women. Gender disparities still existed in education. Female disadvantage in education remained large in Western and Central Africa, North Africa, and South Asia (World Bank web site).

See also: ADOLESCENT PARENTHOOD; CHRONIC ILLNESS; FAILURE TO THRIVE; FAMILY LITERACY; FAMILY

POLICY; GLOBAL CITIZENSHIP; HOMELESS FAMILIES; HOUSING; INDUSTRIALIZATION; JUVENILE DELINQUENCY; MIGRATION; NEIGHBORHOOD; RESOURCE MANAGEMENT; RUNAWAY YOUTHS; RURAL FAMILIES; SINGLE-PARENT FAMILIES; STRESS; UNEMPLOYMENT; URBANIZATION; WAR/POLITICAL VIOLENCE; WIDOWHOOD; WOMEN'S MOVEMENTS; WORK AND FAMILY

Bibliography

Axinn, J., and Levin, H. (1997). *Social Welfare: A History of the American Response to Need,* 4th edition. New York: Longman.

Barker, R. L. (1997). *The Social Work Dictionary,* 3rd edition. Washington, DC: NASW Press.

Brandt Commission. (1980). *North-South: A Programme for Survival.* London: Pan Books.

Carlson, D. L. (1999). *The Welfare of My Neighbor.* Washington, DC: Family Research Council.

Coulton, C. J., and Chow, J. (1995). "Poverty." In *Encyclopedia of Social Work.* 19th edition, ed. R. L. Edwards. Washington, DC: NASW Press.

Edwards, R. L., ed. (1998). *Encyclopedia of Social Work,* 19th edition, 1997 supplement. Washington, DC: NASW Press.

Ellwood, D. (1986). *Poor Support.* New York: Basic Books.

Estes, R. J. (1988). *Trends in World Social Development.* New York: Praeger.

Midgley, J. (1995). *Social Development: The Developmental Perspective in Social Welfare.* London: Sage.

Orshansky, M. (1965). "Counting the Poor: Another Look at the Poverty Profile." *Social Security Bulletin* 28:3–20.

Richmond, M. (1908). "The Family and the Social Worker." New York: Proceedings, NCCC.

United Nations Development Programme (UNDP). (1997). "Human Development Report, 1997." New York: Oxford University Press.

Wilson, W. J. (1988). *The Truly Disadvantaged.* Chicago: University of Chicago Press.

Wilson, W. J. (1996). *When Work Disappears: The World of the New Urban Poor.* New York: Vintage Books.

World Bank. (2001). "Annual Report, 2000-2001." New York: Oxford University Press.

Other Resources

International Monetary Fund. Web site. Available from http://www.imf.org.

OneWorld. Web site. Available from http://www.oneworld.net.

United Nations Children's Fund. Web site. Available from http://www.unicef.org.

United Nations Department of Public Information (UNDPI). (1996). "The Geography of Poverty." Available from http://www.rrojasdatabank.org/pvgeo.htm.

United Nations Development Programme. Web site. Available from http://www.undp.org.

World Bank Group, The. Web site. Available from http://www.worldbank.org

World Health Organization. Web site. Available from http://www.who.int/home-page/.

World Summit for Social Development and Beyond: Copenhagen +5. Web site. Available from http://www.unicef.org/copenhagen5/factsheets.htm.

GAYNOR YANCEY

POWER

FAMILY RELATIONSHIPS *Brian Jory*
MARITAL RELATIONSHIPS *Carrie L. Yodanis*

FAMILY RELATIONSHIPS

Family power is important to those who want to understand how families function as a unit to make decisions about how to manage money, about where to live, about occupational and educational choices, about parenting practices, about where to go on a vacation, and so on. Family scientists define power in terms of who is able to influence others to get their way in the family, and who is able to block others from getting their way. In most cases, family power is a property of the family system, not of a single individual, because it is almost impossible for one individual to have their way all of the time. Although the rules that govern power in a particular family may evolve as children are born, grow up, and move out, as the marital relationship changes or dissolves, or as the circumstances of the family changes, power is deemed to be fairly predictable within these stages. This predictability can be a comfort to those family members who are happy with the power arrangements or a matter of disdain, perhaps even a matter of personal health and safety, for those who find themselves dominated by others.

Ronald Cromwell and David Olson (1975) classified family power into three areas: *power bases, power processes,* and *power outcomes.*

Power Bases

J. R. P. French and Bertran Raven (1959) took a *microsystemic* view of family power. That is, they examined power strictly from inside the family and suggested that there are six bases of family power. *Legitimate power* is sanctioned by the belief system within the family, such as the belief that the husband should be the head of the household, that parents should have control over raising small children, or that adolescents should have control over what they wear. In the United States, an uncle who tries to impose his will on his nieces and nephews might be viewed as a meddler who is trying to exercise illegitimate power. In other cultures uncles are accorded legitimate power over nieces and nephews and might be respected for this kind of guidance.

Informational power has its foundation in specific knowledge that is not available or is unknown to others in the family and in one's ability to verbally present the pertinent information in a persuasive way. For example, if the man in the household is the only one who knows his income, or if he is viewed as knowledgeable about money, then he is likely to make decisions about how money is spent in the family. Alternatively, if a wife can assemble pertinent information about the benefits of purchasing a new car, she may be able to convince her reluctant husband.

Referential power is based on affection, mutual attraction, friendship, and likeability within the family. Positive feelings can be a powerful force in making alliances with others, if others want to make those they care about happy and, conversely, not to disappoint them. A parent's desire to please a favored child, a husband's desire to please his wife, a child's desire to please a grandparent are examples of referential power.

Coercive power involves the use of physical or psychological force in imposing one's way on others in the family, assuming that others are resistant or opposed. Parental discipline, threats, aggression, conflict, and competition are inherent in the use of coercive power because getting one's way is usually realized at the expense of others getting theirs. An example of coercive power: a parent forces a child to attend a school or college he or she does not wish to attend by threatening to withdraw the child's support.

Expert power is based on education, training, or experience that is relevant to the issue at hand. For example, if the woman of the household is a licensed real estate agent, she may have the most influence on where the family lives. If a child has studied the attractions of Florida, he or she may use the expert power accumulated to wield influence on decisions about a Florida vacation. Expert power can also be derived from the specific knowledge and experience of one individual in dealing with a specific issue. For example, if the husband was raised in Mexico, he is likely to be considered the expert about what relatives to visit in Mexico and where to stay on a visit there. Although he may not be considered an expert on Mexico outside the family, within the family he is.

Reward power is the ability to influence others by providing physical and psychological benefits to those who comply with one's wishes. With small children, parents often influence behavior with candy or sweets. With older children and adolescents, the price of power might be more expensive—a new outfit or bicycle. Adults in families often strike bargains, exchange pleasing behaviors, and "sweet talk" others to get their way.

The power bases articulated by French and Raven are often unclear in actual families. For example, if one family member has used coercion in the past, others may have learned that it is best to give in and keep their opinions to themselves. Although it may not be apparent to outsiders, those inside the family may feel coerced even though they do not signal their resistance in visible ways.

Robert Blood and Donald Wolfe (1960) took a *macrosystemic* view when they presented their *resource theory* of family power. That is, they looked for associations between power inside the family and power outside the family, and argued that power was apportioned between husbands and wives based on the relative resources that each contributed to the family. Blood and Wolfe specifically focused on the resources of income, occupational prestige, and educational attainment and, based on interviews with hundreds of white, middle-class wives in Detroit, Michigan, demonstrated that the greater the men's resources in these three areas, the greater the men's perceived power within the family.

The resource theory of family power was influential because the idea suggested that men do not become heads of households by divine right or natural biological processes, but because they have more and easier access to educational, financial, and occupational resources in society. The idea suggested that opening up women's access to resources outside the family could result in a more evenly balanced distribution of power within the family.

There has been considerable research support for resource theory in the United States and in Third World countries. Philip Blumstein and Pepper Schwartz (1983) conducted a study in the United States and found that when men made substantially more income than their wives, they were more likely to exert greater power in financial decision-making when compared with husbands that made about the same income as their wives. A study conducted in Mexico by R. S. Oropesa (1997) found that wives with higher education were equal to their husbands in family power, felt more satisfaction with their influence in the family, and were less likely to be a victim of domestic violence. A study of 113 nonindustrialized nations conducted by Gary Lee and Larry Petersen (1983) found that the more wives contributed to food production, the more power they exerted in marriage.

There has also been substantial criticism of resource theory. It has been pointed out that income, occupation, and education are only three among many resources that influence family power. Edna Foa and U. G. Foa (1980) suggested that in addition to *tangible resources* such as money, education, and occupation, *intangible resources* such as intelligence, physical attractiveness, likeability, love, and comfort impact family power. Actually, any trait or behavior that is valued by others in the family can be a resource that is exchanged for influence and power. For example, in immigrant families it has been observed that the ability to speak the host language can increase one's power if other family members depend on that ability to translate and interpret messages (Alvarez 1995). Among the Fulani tribes of West Africa, who primarily practice the religion of Islam, family members, especially women, can increase their power in the family by practicing traditional Fulani customs of conjuring the spirits of dead ancestors and others who have passed on to the other world (Johnson 2000).

Most family scientists take a *macrosystemic* view, first articulated by Constantina Safilios-Rothschild (1967), that the bases of family power are a reflection of culturally defined gender ideologics and gender-segregated resources in the wider society in which a family is embedded. In practically all societies, this means that males have more power in families because of patriarchal beliefs about male authority. For example, a 1996 Gallup Poll conducted in twenty-two countries found that women are almost universally perceived as more emotional, talkative, and patient than men, whereas men are perceived as more aggressive, ambitious, and courageous than women. Even though there may be little scientific justification for these perceptions, they exert a strong influence in favor of male dominance in families that might be diminished through women's resources, but not completely muted.

Power Processes

An examination of power processes reveals that getting one's way in the dynamic interaction of families entails an ongoing set of complex and subtle maneuvers involving communication, commitment, bargaining and negotiation, coalition formation, conflict and conflict resolution, and parenting styles. Moreover, an examination of power processes reveals that in virtually all cultures, variables like the number of children and where the family lives make family power processes more complex.

Willard Waller (1938) is credited with first articulating the idea that family power is sometimes affected by commitment: The *principle of least interest* states that in disputes involving power, the individual who is least interested in continuing the relationship usually has more power than the one who is more interested in continuing the relationship. In dating relationships, the threat to break up can level the playing field of relative power. In some cases, an individual who feels "one-down" can make the threat and gain an equal footing if the other wants to stay together. In worse cases, an individual who is already "one-up" can threaten to break up and gain an even stronger hand in future disputes. In marriage, the principle of least interest can involve threatening to divorce, or in parent-child relationships, by parents threatening to send a child to foster care, to boarding school, or to live with a relative. Children and adolescents sometimes invoke the principle of *least interest* by threatening to run away or, in cases where parents are divorced, by threatening to go live with the noncustodial parent. In order to increase power, however, threats to leave must be feared by those one is threatening. Otherwise, they may say, "Go ahead and leave." If this happens, the tables of power could be turned against the one making the threat.

The principle of least interest applies mostly in societies where marriage is a free choice rather than arranged, and where it is possible for men and women to dissolve marriage through divorce. In many cultures, divorce is restricted by social and religious tyranny that makes personal selectivity in one's partner irrelevant to the establishment or continuation of marriage (Swidler 1990). For example, in societies that are ruled by intolerant legalists or religionists, the courts might allow a husband to obtain a divorce simply because he has lost emotional interest in his wife or because she has done something of which he disapproves. In the same society, a wife might not be granted a divorce even if she has legitimate reasons, such as her husband's abuse, desertion, criminal behavior, or, in polygamous societies, if he were to take another wife without the permission of the wife or wives he already has. In these societies, family power processes are so structured along gender and generational lines that *selectivity* has little to do with the establishment and maintenance of marital and family relationships. Alternatively, selectivity may be applied unfairly, allowing men to make choices that are not accorded to women or children. As previously discussed, family power processes reflect power bases in society: Without power in society, it is difficult to get power in the family.

Anthropologist Janice Stockard (2002) analyzed the power processes of married couples in four cultures and found that *parent-child alliances* had a strong impact on family power. For example, girls of the !Kung San tribe of South Africa were traditionally married around age 10, usually to men who were much older. Marriages were arranged by the girls' parents, who expected the bridegroom to live with them for a few years following the marriage and help out by hunting for food. Although one might think that these young girls would be

powerless in relation to their older husbands, the fact that brides and grooms lived with the girls' parents permitted the girls to maintain strong alliances with their parents. These strong alliances tended to equalize power between husbands and wives, to the degree that !Kung San girls had strong veto powers over the marriage arrangement, which they often exercised.

In sharp contrast, girls in traditional Chinese societies were required to abandon alliances with their parents, grandparents, and siblings following marriage. On her wedding day, a traditional Chinese girl would be transported to live with her husband's family, where her mother-in-law would hold authority over her. The restriction of Chinese girls, who seemingly were not permitted to make many personal choices about their lives, was rationalized with the understanding that they would be compensated in later years by gaining rule over their own daughters-in-law. Because young girls were temporary participants in their families as they were growing up, it was difficult for Chinese girls to form deep, lasting alliances with their parents, grandparents, and siblings.

In Western culture, Theodore Caplow (1968) hypothesized that powerful male heads of households might find themselves at a power disadvantage in families with older children and adolescents because mothers and children might form *coalitions* to neutralize and override the fathers' power. A study conducted by Brian Jory and his colleagues (1996) found substantial support for coalition theory by observing the power processes of middle class families in the midwestern United States in moderately stressful problem-solving situations. In these families mothers were five times more likely to form power alliances with adolescent sons and daughters than with their husbands. These fathers, who were mostly in high power occupations, were at a clear disadvantage in family power negotiations. The importance of gender in family power processes was evident in another way: The study found that adolescent boys were more active in communication and bargaining than adolescent girls, and mothers offered more supportive communication to adolescent sons than daughters.

Diana Baumrind (1971) studied the balance between power and support in the childrearing behavior of parents in the United States and identified three *parenting styles*. The *authoritarian* style of parenting emphasizes obedience, giving orders, and discipline. Parents who exercise this style relate to their children with little emotional warmth because they view the child as a subordinate whose primary need is discipline. Children raised by authoritarian parents often feel rejected because their ideas are not welcomed, and these children may have trouble in tasks that demand autonomy, creativity, and reflection.

The *permissive* parenting style de-emphasizes parental control of children in favor of absolute acceptance and approval of the child. Permissive parents encourage children to make decisions on their own and to exercise creativity and independence in whatever they do. In the absence of parental guidance and limits, children raised by permissive parents may feel neglected and may struggle with tasks where focus, self-control, and perseverance are required.

The *authoritative* style of parenting combines a balance of parental control and parental warmth and support. Authoritative parents set limits on acceptable behavior in children, yet do so in an affectionate environment that encourages autonomy, values expression of opinions, and encourages participation in family decision-making. In reviewing a number of studies, Lawrence Steinberg and his colleagues (1991) demonstrated that children raised by authoritative parents—whatever their race, social class, or family type—develop better moral reasoning, do better academically, have less anxiety and depression, feel that their families are happier, are more self-confident, and are less likely to become delinquent.

A study by Brian Jory and his colleagues (1997) discovered that, in families with adolescents, power is not limited strictly to parental behavior, but is a property that affects the family system as a whole in terms of communication, bargaining, how affect is expressed, and how solutions to problems are generated. The study found four types of *family locus of control*. In families with *individualistic* locus of control, power resided in individuals who looked out for themselves. In these families, communication was egocentric and calculated, affect could turn negative or aggressive, and individuals sought solutions that benefited themselves at the expense of others.

In families with *authoritarian* locus of control, power was located in the parents, particularly

the father whose role as head of household was pronounced. Communication in these families was directed one-way from fathers to mothers and mothers to children, affect was stilted, and bargaining was nonexistent as solutions to problems took the form of parental pronouncements, exclusively by fathers.

In families with *external* locus of control, nobody in the family was viewed as having power, and control seemed to be located in circumstances, fate, or the control of others. Communication in these families was chaotic, affect was directed towards others outside the family, and solutions to problems were sought from authority figures and others who were viewed as having control.

In families with *collaborative* locus of control, communication was systematically elicited from each family member, ideas were valued, affection was warm, supportive, and caring, and great effort was dedicated to find solutions to problems that had the least negative impact on individuals and would benefit the group as a whole.

As each of these studies shows, power processes in families involve a large number of complex cultural and family-related variables, many of which are yet to be discovered by family scientists. Making matters more complex, those variables that have been discovered are subtle and difficult to measure. For example, keeping secrets—an intentional withholding of information—is a form of communication that affects power in families. Withholding information takes away the power of others to make reasonable decisions because they lack pertinent information. How does a scientist measure secrets? This reveals the scientific challenge of studying power in families, but also the importance.

Power Outcomes

Power is an underlying dimension of every family relationship and virtually every family activity, and its importance lies in the fact that having a sense of control over one's life is necessary for the health and happiness of humans, including children, adults, and the elderly. In the studies already discussed, it is evident that power should be fairly apportioned to every family member, from the youngest infant to the most elderly person. If every member of a family has a sense of personal control, balanced with family control, the family can be a source of power and strength through its guidance, support, and care. When someone in the family abuses power, however, the damage to trust, loyalty, and freedom can have long-term negative effects for everyone in the family.

In the last quarter of the twentieth century, Western society began paying attention to the dark side of family power. A new set of concepts developed that are common in the language of the twenty-first century: child abuse and neglect, child sexual abuse, elder abuse, marital rape, date rape, psychological abuse, wife abuse, and domestic violence. In a volume entitled, *The Public Nature of Private Violence* (1994), editors Martha Fineman and Roxanne Mykitiuk assembled a number of articles by scholars who suggest that our discovery of family abuse has created a new conception of the nature of family life for the twenty-first century. The old conception that families are guided by a higher moral law or a natural order of compassion has been replaced by a more realistic conception that, for many, the family is a place of anguish, worry, pain, and trauma. These scholars argue that the abuse of family power is not simply a private matter, but is a public matter that needs to be part of the public agenda to be addressed by policy-makers, police officers, judges, social workers, clergy, teachers, physicians, and counselors.

The abuse of power in families is not strictly a Western idea. Judy DeLoache and Alma Gottlieb (2000) compiled imagined childcare guides for seven societies. The variation in parental practices—the do's and don'ts of raising children—from society to society is astounding. For example, it may be difficult to understand why Turkish mothers keep their babies restrictively swaddled for several months following birth (to show that the baby is covered with care). It may seem odd, if enticing, that Beng mothers paint pretty designs on the faces of their infants every day (to protect the baby against sickness). Should parents clean and bathe children? That, according to the childcare guides, depends on what society the child is born into. Although parenting practices vary around the world, one principle underlies all cultural variations. In no extant culture are mothers or fathers legitimately granted absolute power to mistreat their children. There is a general ethical principle that is universal: the abuse of power in families is not socially condoned.

Building on the idea that family power should be subjected to the same ethical principles as other forms of social power, Brian Jory and his colleagues have conducted a number of studies exploring how the abuse of power in families is rooted in ethical beliefs about power (Jory, Anderson, and Greer 1997; Jory and Anderson 1999; Jory and Anderson 2000). In studies of abusive men (and their women partners) conducted in the United States, Jory concluded that interventions that change the ethical beliefs of those who abuse power in their families can result in a positive transformation of their values and behavior. The abuse of power in families is a challenge for those who shape all societies to transcend the bounds of culture and custom and work towards balancing the scales of *intimate justice* in all societies by fostering ethical beliefs about equality, freedom, respect, fairness, and caring in families, and by showing compassion for those who are suffering the anguish of victimization, whatever their cultural heritage.

See also: CHILD ABUSE: PHYSICAL ABUSE AND NEGLECT; CHILD ABUSE: PSYCHOLOGICAL MALTREATMENT; CHILD ABUSE: SEXUAL ABUSE; COMMUNICATION: FAMILY RELATIONSHIPS; DECISION-MAKING; FAMILY AND RELATIONAL RULES; GENDER; PARENTING STYLES; POWER: MARITAL RELATIONSHIPS; PROBLEM SOLVING; SPOUSE ABUSE: PREVALENCE; SPOUSE ABUSE: THEORETICAL EXPLANATIONS

Bibliography

Alvarez, L. (1995). "Pint-size Interpreters of World for Parents." *New York Times,* October 1: A16.

Baumrind, D. (1971). "Current Patterns of Parental Authority." *Developmental Psychology Monographs* 4:1–102.

Blumstein, P., and Schwartz, P. (1983). *American Couples: Money, Work, and Sex.* New York: Morrow.

Blood, R., and Wolfe, D. (1960). *Husbands and Wives: The Dynamics of Married Living.* New York: Free Press.

Caplow, T. (1968). *Two against One: Coalitions in Triads.* Englewood Cliffs, NJ: Prentice Hall.

Cromwell, R., and Olson, D., eds. (1975). *Power in Families.* Newbury Park, CA: Sage.

DeLoache, J., and Gottlieb, A., eds. (2000). *A World of Babies: Imagined Childcare Guides for Seven Societies.* Cambridge, UK: Cambridge University Press.

Fineman, M., and Mykitiuk, R. (1994). *The Public Nature of Private Violence: The Discovery of Domestic Abuse.* New York: Routledge.

French, J., and Raven, B. (1959). "The Basis of Power." In *Studies in Social Power,* ed. D. Cartwright. Ann Arbor: University of Michigan Press.

Foa, E., and Foa, U. (1980). "Resource Theory: Interpersonal Behavior as Exchange." In *Social Exchange: Advances in Theory and Research,* ed. K. Gergen, M. Greenberg, and R. Willis. New York: Plenum Press.

Gallup Poll. (1996). *Gender and Society: Status and Stereotypes.* Princeton, NJ: Gallup Organization.

Johnson, M. (2000). "The View from the *Wuro*: A Guide to Child Rearing for Fulani Parents." In *A World of Babies: Imagined Childcare Guides for Seven Societies,* ed. J. DeLoache and A. Gottlieb. Cambridge, UK: Cambridge University Press.

Jory, B., and Anderson, D. (1999). "Intimate Justice II: Fostering Mutuality, Reciprocity, and Accommodation in Therapy for Psychological Abuse." *Journal of Marital and Family Therapy* 25:349–363.

Jory, B., and Anderson, D. (2000). "Intimate Justice III: Healing the Anguish of Abuse and Embracing the Anguish of Accountability." *Journal of Marital and Family Therapy* 26:329–340.

Jory, B.; Anderson, D.; and Greer, C. (1997). "Intimate Justice: Confronting Issues of Accountability, Respect, and Freedom in Therapy for Abuse and Violence." *Journal of Marital and Family Therapy* 23:399–420.

Jory, B.; Rainbolt, E.; Xia, Y.; Karns, J.; Freeborn, A.; and Greer, C. (1996). "Communication Patterns and Alliances between Parents and Adolescents during a Structured Problem Solving Task." *Journal of Adolescence* 19:339–346.

Jory, B.; Xia, Y.; Freeborn, A.; and Greer, C. (1997). "Locus of Control and Problem Solving Interaction in Families with Adolescents." *Journal of Adolescence* 20:489–504.

Lee, G., and Petersen, L. (1983). "Conjugal Power and Spousal Resources in Patriarchal Cultures." *Journal of Comparative Family Studies* 14:23–28.

Oropesa, R. S. (1997). "Development and Marital Power in Mexico." *Social Forces* 75:1291–1317.

Safilios-Rothschild, C. (1967). "A Comparison of Power Structure in Marital Satisfaction in Urban Greek and French Families." *Journal of Marriage and the Family* 29:345–352.

Steinberg, L.; Mounts, N.; Lamborn, S.; and Dornbusch, S. (1991). "Authoritative Parenting and Adolescent Adjustment across Varied Ecological Niches." *Journal of Research on Adolescence* 1:19–36.

Stockard, J. (2002). *Marriage in Culture: Practice and Meaning across Diverse Societies.* New York: Harcourt.

Swidler, A. (1990). *Marriage among the Religions of the World.* Lewiston, NY: Mellen Press.

Waller, W. (1938, revised 1951). *The Family: A Dynamic Interpretation.* New York: Dryden.

BRIAN JORY

MARITAL RELATIONSHIPS

Power is a fundamental aspect of all human relationships, including family and marital relationships. Since 1960, there has been a continuing dialogue among social scientists seeking to define, measure, explain, and understand the consequences of power differentials in marriage relationships.

Definitions and Measurement

Power in marriage has been defined and measured in various ways. The first and most common definition of power is the ability of one person to get another to do what she or he wants even in the face of resistance. Based on this definition, Robert Blood and Donald Wolfe (1960) developed the *Decision Power Index.* To measure power, respondents are asked to report whether wives, husbands, or both have the *final-say* on a number of decisions within the marriage, including selecting a car, home or apartment, vacation, doctor, husband's job, and whether or not the wife should work. Who has power in the relationship is measured based on who has the final-say.

This index has remained at the core of the dialogue on marital power. Being a short and easily administered instrument, this index continues to be included in surveys worldwide, although occasionally with adaptations. It has also been critiqued, developed, and improved. Nearly once a decade since its development, a review is written that raises methodological questions and concerns about the *final-say* decision-making measures (Mizan 1994). Many of these problems have been tested empirically.

One problem cited is the discrepancy between the answers given by husbands and wives. However, data from such countries as the United States, India, and Panama have tested this issue and found that wife and husband answers tend to be parallel

(Allen and Straus 1984; Danes, Oswald, and De Esnaola 1998).

Another set of problems involves the types of decisions and assumptions about decisions that are included in measures. Merlin Brinkerhoff and Eugen Lupri (1978) and Vanaja Dhruvarajan (1992) present data from Canada to show that decisions are of varying importance and frequency and are made according to gender roles. Women tend to have final-say in some areas, particularly those decisions relating to care work—children, food, entertaining friends, and calling the doctor—which tend to be defined by both men and women as not very important. Thus, it is argued that a measure that gives each decision equal weight results in a flawed power score.

Furthermore, measures of power tend to be outcomes or consequences of power. The outcome serves as a *proxy measure of power*. For example, the individual with the most power in a relationship may or may not be most likely to make the decisions. Similarly, the division of household labor is an outcome of power differentials but is used in some studies as a measure of power.

It has been argued that it is important to define and measure power as a dynamic process, examining such issues as influence strategies and attempts (Aida and Fablo 1991; Zvonkovic, Schmiege, and Hall 1994). Using a multidimensional definition of power, Aafke Komter (1989) defines power as "the ability to affect consciously or unconsciously the emotions, attitudes, cognitions, or behaviors of someone else" (p. 192) and distinguishes between *manifest power, latent power,* and *invisible power.* As the usual conceptualization of marital power, manifest power refers to decision-making and associated conflict and influence strategies. Latent power refers to a lack of decision-making, conflict, or influence strategies as a result of one partner anticipating and deferring to the position of the other. This can result from the less powerful partner believing that they are unable to have influence or fearing negative reprisal. Finally, invisible power refers to an unconscious process in which social and psychological systems of inequality result in one partner being unable to even conceive of the possibility of having input in decision making, engaging in conflict, or using power strategies. In her study of Dutch couples, Komter found that although the couples share equally in decision making, there were uncovered hidden power mechanisms and strategies that result in women wanting more change in the relationship but being less successful in gaining it. As a result, an ideology of husbands' power over their wives was confirmed and justified.

Explanations

Resources. Like their measure of power, Blood and Wolfe's (1960) *resource theory* has had a prominent role in explanations of marital power. According to their theory, power in marriage results from the contribution of resources—particularly education, income, and occupational status—to the relationship. The spouse who contributes the most will have the greater decision-making power. As with the measurement of power, theoretical and empirical work on explanations of marital power has often emanated from a critique and extension of Blood and Wolfe's theory.

Considerable work has been done within the realm of resources. Some researchers have added additional dimensions to the concept of resources. In a study of marital power in Israel, Liat Kulik (1999) found that not only *material resources* but also *health and energy resources, psychological resources* (problem-solving and social skills), and *social resources* (access to social networks) are directly or indirectly related to power in marriage. Particular attention has been paid to the impact of extended families and *kin support resources* on power in marriage. In Turkey and Mexico, a wife's ties to her family of origin can translate into power in marriage (Bolak 1995; Oropesa 1997). On the other hand, living in a joint residence with the family of the husband, as in India, has been found to be associated with higher levels of power for husbands (Conklin 1988). In a study of over a hundred nonindustrial societies, in general women have somewhat more power in nuclear than extended families. Nevertheless, in societies where extended families are the norm, women have substantially more power when residence practices are matrilocal and descent is matrilineal rather than patrilocal and patrilineal (Warner, Lee, and Lee 1986).

Greater attention has been paid to the meaning tied to the resources, and not just the amount of resources contributed. A spouse may contribute resources but if this contribution is not recognized as significant and valuable within the couple, the contribution is not likely to result in greater power (Bolak 1995; Blaisure and Allen 1995). From this perspective, unpaid family work can also be a valued contribution to the relationship and not working for pay may reflect women's power rather than lack of power (Pyke 1994).

Resources can also be thought of as alternatives to the relationship. Adding to Blood and Wolfe's theory, David Heer (1963) developed an *exchange theory* of marital power, arguing that the individual who has the greatest access to alternative resources outside of the marriage relationship will have the most power. In a related argument, Willard Waller's (1951) *principle of least interest theory* proposes that the spouse who is least interested in maintaining the relationship will have the greater power. Karen Pyke (1994) found that women's reluctance to marry after divorce is associated with their greater power in remarriage. Based on a study in the United Kingdom, Pat O'-Conner (1991) argues for the need to also consider a *principle of high mutual interest*. Results show that women are powerful in relationships where dependence is high and balanced for both women and men. Using data from Israel, Liat Kulik (1999) developed the concept of *anticipated dependence,* defined as the extent to which one spouse expects to need the other at later points in life, and found greater anticipated dependence to be related to reduced power in the current relationship.

Culture. One of the most significant developments of Blood and Wolfe's resource theory came from Hyman Rodman (1967, 1972). Trying to understand cross-cultural inconsistency in the relationship between resources and marital power in Germany, United States, France, Denmark, Belgium, Greece, and Yugoslavia, Rodman developed the *theory of resources in cultural context.* This theory explains that the distribution of marital power results not only from an unequal contribution of resources, but also from the larger cultural context within which the marital relationship exists. Cultural gender norms affect the impact that resource contribution has on the distribution of power. In particular, he predicted that in patriarchal and egalitarian societies, the dominant norms would outweigh the influence of resources on marital power. So regardless of wife and husband's contribution, marriages will be male-dominated in

patriarchal societies and equal in egalitarian societies. He predicted that the contribution of resources has the most significant impact on the balance of marital power in *transitional egalitarianism,* societies that are moving from patriarchal toward egalitarian norms, and among the upper classes in *modified patriarchal societies,* societies in which egalitarian values are new and common only among the upper strata.

The theory of resources in cultural context has been applied and tested in countries throughout the world. Some studies have focused on Scandinavian countries, which are considered egalitarian societies. A comparison of Danish and U.S. couples revealed that although couples in both countries often report equality in decision making, Danish marriages were even more likely to be described as equal. Within this egalitarian society, the resource contribution of spouses still has an impact on the balance of power (Kandel and Lesser 1972). Studies in Sweden and Norway show that even within these relatively egalitarian societies, male power may not be blatant but is widespread in marital relations (Calasanti and Bailey 1991; Thagaard 1997).

Latin American countries are often assumed to be characterized by *machismo* cultures and families. However, data from Chile, Mexico, and Panama show that although husbands may have somewhat greater power in marriage, many marriages tend toward egalitarianism and the contribution of resources is related to power (Alvarez 1979; Cromwell, Corrales, and Torsiello 1973; Oropesa 1997; Danes, Oswald, and De Esnaola 1998). This tendency toward egalitarianism has been discussed in terms of wider societal change, resulting from social movements, including the women's movement, and economic development.

The connection between culture and resources in the balance of marital power has been examined in a wide range of societies, including Turkey, India, Israel, Romania, Russia, and China. As Turkey and other Muslim countries combine modernity and traditionalism and become *modified patriarchies,* women are better able to negotiate power, with their contribution of resources having an impact on their success (Fox 1973; Bolak 1995). In Eastern Europe under communist regimes, both spouses worked outside of the home and tended to be egalitarian in decision making, but women remained primarily responsible for household work (Lapidus 1978; Elliot and Moskoff 1983). Today in some Eastern European countries, such as Russia, the woman's role as head of household and breadwinner does not necessarily result in greater power but is a result of necessity and lack of alternatives (Kiblitskaya 2000). In China, where the influence of Western ideology has increased the acceptance of egalitarian relationships, education and occupation are related to the distribution of marital power (Tang 1999).

Structure. The patriarchal and egalitarian differences between societies described above can be considered as not only cultural but also structural differences. Gender inequality is not merely found in norms and ideologies but characterizes the structure and practices of a society's political, legal, religious, educational, and economic institutions. Discrimination and male domination of these institutions result in women's lower access to resources, including income, occupational status, and education; condone and reinforce patriarchal ideology; and thereby contribute to the maintenance of gender inequality in marriage. As Dair Gillespie (1971) argued, marital power can be described as a caste/class system because husbands as a class have power over wives as a class as a result of male-dominated societal structures rather than any specific resources they contribute to the marriage.

Interaction. Researchers have looked beyond resources and culture to examine how marital power is part of the unconscious construction of gender categories and identity during interaction. Veronica Jaris Tichenor (1999) studied couples in which wives had higher income and occupational status than their husbands and found that wives did not tend to have greater marital power. Rather, women and men in these couples act to ignore or minimize the status and income differences and construct the husband in a powerful position, through such acts as upholding male veto power and redefining the provider role to fit the activities of the husband. Examining conversations of women and men, Caroline Dryden (1999) found that wives act to construct their marriage as equal and blamed themselves for aspects of the relationship that were not equal. Husbands, on the other hand, act to construct the marriage as unequal and also blamed their wives for the existing inequality. The outcome of these constructions is the reinforcement of

A couple sit at the Old City Bazaar in Turkey, a country where people may falsely present their egalitarian relationship as male-dominated to comply with dominant cultural norms. RICHARD T. NOWITZ/CORBIS

the genders as unequal, with the man in the position of power. Tove Thagaard (1997) also found that power differences displayed during Norwegian couples' interactions served to confirm male and female identity, including gender inequality.

Another aspect of the growing interactionist perspective includes an examination of how couples publicly present marital power. The presentation may or may not correspond with the actual power dynamics in the relationship. In Turkey, couples who are equal in power may present their relationship as male-dominated to outsiders as a way to appear to be in compliance with dominant cultural norms (Bolak 1995). Another study found that couples who define themselves as feminist act to publicly present themselves as equal. Strategies used include maintaining different last names and putting the wife's name first on tax returns or car registration (Blaisure and Allen 1995). In a similar study, couples who claim to be egalitarian were found not to be in practice. However, they used language to create a "myth of equality" (Knudson-Martin and Mahony 1998).

Multivariate models. Attempts have been made to integrate many of these theories into comprehensive multivariate models. Rae Blumberg and Marion Tolbert Coleman's (1989) is one of the most complete. Starting with women's resource contribution, the model factors in societal and individual characteristics that can enhance or diminish women's ultimate economic power and then outlines the path through which women's net economic power translates into multiple dimensions of marital power.

Consequences

Inequality in marriage is related to a number of consequences, many of which are interrelated and, in turn, reinforce gender inequality. This section focuses on two related categories of consequences: health and happiness.

Health. A lack of power in marriage is a threat to women's mental and physical health. Wives who have power in marriage report lower rates of depression (Mirowsky 1985) and less stress (Kaufman 1988). In India and Kenya, women's power in marriage is related to lower fertility rates and greater use of methods of family planning (Sud 1991; Gwako 1997).

Violence against women is also related to unequal power between women and men. Studies show that women are less likely to be victims of physical and verbal abuse in egalitarian relationships (Coleman and Straus 1986; Tang 1999). However, a loss of men's power relative to women's may also result in a greater likelihood for violence. According to Craig Allen and Murray Straus's (1980) *ultimate resource theory,* when husbands lack economic or interpersonal skill resources to maintain a dominant position in marriage, they may fall back on physical size and strength—resources that, on average, husbands tend to have more of than their wives.

Happiness. In addition to individual mental health and happiness, the distribution of power in marriage is also related to marital quality and satisfaction. Some older studies found that wives' satisfaction was highest in egalitarian marriages (Alvarez 1979), whereas others found that quality and satisfaction were highest in male-dominated marriages (Buric and Zecevic 1967). These findings may well reflect pressure to correspond with previously dominant gender ideologies. More recent studies in countries such as Norway and China are quite consistent in finding that marital satisfaction is highest in egalitarian marriages (Thagaard 1997; Tang 1999; Pimental 2000). Not only is equality directly related to increased satisfaction but also indirectly related through the development of closer emotional ties and perceptions of a spouse as fair and sympathetic. In addition, marital satisfaction is related not only to the distribution of power between spouses but also the types of power strategies and attempts used. Although the use of any influence strategy has been found to be related to lower marital satisfaction, indirect and emotional strategies, including negative affect and withdrawal, seem to have particularly negative effects (Aida and Falbo 1991; Zvonkovic, Schmiedge, and Hall 1994).

Conclusion

Marital power has been the topic of a dialogue among social scientists from diverse perspectives, cultures, and methodological approaches who build on the past and add to the future. The dialogue has been international, using cultural and societal differences to test and advance theory. The result of this dialogue is rich theoretical and empirical work on marital power. Still, participation in the dialogue waxes and wanes over time. Although since 1990 new insights and approaches have been brought to the debate, as Jetse Sprey (1999) outlines, there is still a need to revisit and rethink longstanding approaches and assumptions to studying and understanding power in marital relationships.

See also: CONFLICT: COUPLE RELATIONSHIPS; DECISION MAKING; DEPRESSION: ADULTS; DIVISION OF LABOR; DUAL-EARNER FAMILIES; EQUITY; FAMILY LIFE EDUCATION; FAMILY ROLES; GENDER; MARITAL QUALITY; MARITAL TYPOLOGIES; POWER: FAMILY RELATIONSHIPS; PROBLEM SOLVING; RAPE; RESOURCE MANAGEMENT; RETIREMENT; RICH/WEALTHY FAMILIES; SELF-ESTEEM; SPOUSE ABUSE: PREVALENCE; SPOUSE ABUSE: THEORETICAL EXPLANATIONS; STRESS; THERAPY: COUPLE RELATIONSHIPS; WORK AND FAMILY

Bibliography

Aida, Y., and Falbo, T. (1991). "Relationships between Marital Satisfaction, Resources, and Power Strategies." *Sex Roles* 24:43–56.

Allen, C. A., and Straus, M. A. (1984). "'Final Say' Measures of Marital Power: Theoretical Critique and Empirical Findings from Five Studies in the United States and India." *Journal of Comparative Family Studies* 15:329–344.

Alvarez, M. D. L. (1979). "Family Power Structure in Chile: A Survey of Couples with Children in Primary Schools." *International Journal of Sociology of the Family* 9:123–131.

Blaisure, K. R., and Allen, K. R. (1995). "Feminists and the Ideology and Practice of Marital Equality." *Journal of Marriage and the Family* 57:5–19.

Blood, R. O., and Wolfe, D. M. (1960). *Husbands and Wives: The Dynamics of Married Living.* Glencoe, IL: Free Press.

Blumberg, R. L., and Coleman, M. T. (1989). "A Theoretical Look at the Gender Balance of Power in the American Couple." *Journal of Family Issues* 10:225–250.

Bolak, H. C. (1995). "Towards a Conceptualization of Marital Power Dynamics: Women Breadwinners and Working-Class Households in Turkey." In *Women in Modern Turkish Society,* ed. S. Tekeli. London: Zen Books.

Brinkerhoff, M., and Lupri, E. (1978). "Theoretical and Methodological Issues in the Use of Decision-Making as an Indicator of Conjugal Power: Some Canadian Observations." *Canadian Journal of Sociology* 3:1–20.

Buric, O., and Zecevic, A. (1967). "Family Authority, Marital Satisfaction, and the Social Network in Yugoslavia." *Journal of Marriage and the Family* 29:325–336.

Calasanti, T. M., and Baily, C. A. (1991). "Gender Inequality and the Division of Household Labor in the United States and Sweden: A Socialist-Feminist Approach." *Social Problems* 38:34–53.

Coleman, D. H., and Straus, M. A (1986). "Marital Power, Conflict, and Violence in a Nationally Representative Sample of American Couples." *Violence and Victims* 1:141–157.

Conklin, G. H. (1988). "The Influence of Economic Development on Patterns of Conjugal Power and Extended Family Residence in India." *Journal of Comparative Family Studies* 19:187–205.

Cromwell, R. E.; Corrales, R.; and Torsiello, P. M. (1973). "Normative Patterns of Marital Decision Making Power and Influence in Mexico and United States: A Partial Test of Resource and Ideology Theory." *Journal of Comparative Family Studies* 4:177–196.

Danes, S. M.; Oswald, R. F.; and De Esnaola, S. A. (1998). "Perceptions of Couple Decision Making in Panama." *Journal of Comparative Family Studies* 29:570–583.

Dhruvarajan, V. (1992). "Conjugal Power among First Generation Hindu Asian Indians in a Canadian City." *International Journal of Sociology of the Family* 22:1–34.

Dryden, C. (1999). *Being Married, Doing Gender: A Critical Analysis of Gender Relationships in Marriage.* London: Routledge.

Elliot, J. E., and Moskoff, W. (1983). "Decision-Making Power in Romanian Families." *Journal of Comparative Family Studies* 14:39–50.

Fox, G. L. (1973). "Another Look at the Comparative Resource Model: Assessing the Balance of Power in Turkish Marriages." *Journal of Marriage and the Family* 35:718–730.

Gillespie, D. L. (1971). "Who Has the Power? The Marital Struggle." *Journal of Marriage and the Family* 33:445–458.

Gwako, E. L. M. (1997). "Conjugal Power in Rural Kenya Families: Its Influence on Women's Decisions about Family Size and Family Planning Practices." *Sex Roles* 36:127–147.

Heer, D. M. (1963). "The Measurement and Bases of Family Power: An Overview." *Marriage and Family Living* 25:133–139.

Kandel, D. B., and Lesser, G. S. (1972). "Marital Decision-Making in American and Danish Urban Families: A Research Note." *Journal of Marriage and the Family* 34:134–138.

Kaufman, G. M. (1988). "Relationship between Marital Power and Symptoms of Stress among Husbands and Wives." *Wisconsin Sociologist* 25:35–44.

Kiblitskaya, M. (2000). "Russia's Female Breadwinners: The Changing Subjective Experience." In *Gender, State and Society in Soviet and Post-Soviet Russia,* ed. S. Ashwin. London: Routledge.

Knudson-Martin, C., and Mahony, A. R. (1998), "Language and Processes in the Construction of Equality in New Marriages." *Family Relations* 47:81–91.

Komter, A. (1989). "Hidden Power in Marriage." *Gender and Society* 3:187–216.

Kulik, L. (1999). "Marital Power Relations, Resources and Gender Role Ideology: A Multivariate Model for Assessing Effect." *Journal of Comparative Family Studies* 30:189–206.

Lapidus, G. W. (1978). *Women in Soviet Society: Equality, Development, and Social Change.* Berkeley: University of California Press.

Mirowsky, J. (1985). "Depression and Marital Power: An Equity Model." *American Journal of Sociology* 91:557–592.

Mizan, A. N. (1994). "Family Power Studies: Some Major Methodological Issues." *International Journal of Sociology of the Family* 24:85–91.

O'Conner, P. (1991). "Women's Experience of Power within Marriage: An Inexplicable Phenomenon?" *Sociological Review* 39:823–42.

Oropesa, R. S. (1997). "Development and Marital Power in Mexico." *Social Forces* 75:1291–1317.

Pimentel, E. E. (2000). "Just How Do I Love Thee?: Marital Relations in Urban China." *Journal of Marriage and the Family* 62:32–47.

Pyke, K. D. (1994). "Women's Employment as a Gift or Burden? Marital Power across Marriage, Divorce, and Remarriage." *Gender & Society* 8:73–91.

Rodman, H. (1967). "Marital Power in France, Greece, Yugoslavia, and the United States: A Cross-National Discussion." *Journal of Marriage and the Family* 29:320–324.

Rodman, H. (1972). "Marital Power and the Theory of Resources in Cultural Context." *Journal of Comparative Family Studies* 3:50–69.

Sprey, J. (1999). "Family Dynamics: An Essay on Conflict and Power." In *Handbook of Marriage and the Family,* 2nd ed., ed. M. B. Sussman, S. K. Steinmetz, and G. W. Peterson. New York: Plenum.

Sud, S. L. (1991). *Marital Power Structure, Fertility, and Family Planning in India.* New Delhi, India: Radiant.

Tang, C. S-K. (1999). "Marital Power and Aggression in a Community Sample of Hong-Kong Chinese Families." *Journal of Interpersonal Violence* 14:586–602.

Thagaard, T. (1997). "Gender, Power, and Love: A Study of Interaction between Spouses." *Acta Sociologica* 40:357–376.

Tichenor, V. J. (1999). "Status and Income as Gendered Resources: The Case of Marital Power." *Journal of Marriage and the Family* 61:638–650.

Waller, W. (1951). *The Family: A Dynamic Interpretation.* New York: Dryden.

Warner, R. L; Lee, G. R.; and Lee, J. (1986). "Social Organization, Spousal Resources, and Marital Power: A Cross-cultural Study." *Journal of Marriage and the Family* 48:121–128.

Zvonkovic, A. M.; Schmiege, C. J.; and Hall, L. D. (1994). "Influence Strategies Used when Couples Make Work-Family Decisions and Their Importance for Marital Satisfaction." *Family Relations* 43:182–188.

CARRIE L. YODANIS

PREGNANCY AND BIRTH

A woman's decision to begin a pregnancy carries with it the acceptance of the lifelong responsibility to be a parent. Ideally, effective parenting begins even before the moment of conception, when the woman confirms her desire to have a child and is physically and mentally prepared for the challenges of pregnancy, birth, and parenting.

Pregnancy and birth are not isolated from the woman's surroundings and circumstances. The woman's family, community, and culture typically influence her decisions and behaviors. Diverse beliefs, taboos, expected behaviors, and cultural rituals surrounding the childbearing experience are handed down from generation to generation. A common cultural expectation is that children will be conceived when a woman is in a committed sexual relationship. Pregnancy out of wedlock is sometimes frowned upon, and men and, especially, women can be ostracized for their sexual behavior. Regions of a single country also can have an influence. For example, pregnancy and birth in an urban region often involve the use of high technology and delivery in a large medical center hospital, whereas pregnancy and birth in a rural region may involve no technology and delivery at home.

Pregnancy

In many cultures, procreation is the primary reason for marriage. Motherhood may be considered the woman's most socially powerful role, and pregnant women have elevated status. Enormous pressure may be exerted on newly married couples to have a family as soon as possible. When pregnancy does not occur within a certain time period, the marital contract may be dissolved, permitting the man to take another wife who will give him children, preferably sons.

The physiological aspects of pregnancy are universal. Conception occurs when a sperm from a male fertilizes an egg from a woman. Fertilization typically results from sexual intercourse between a woman and a man, but it also may be the result of such technological alternatives as in vitro fertilization or artificial insemination. The product of conception is referred to as an ovum for the first fourteen days. During the next six weeks, it is referred to as an embryo. During the remainder of the pregnancy, the embryo of conception is called a fetus.

The ovum implants in the wall of the woman's uterus (womb) about seven days after fertilization. Following implantation, the ovum grows through cell division, and a separate structure—called the placenta—develops. The blood vessels of the placenta serve as a link between the woman and the developing baby, bringing oxygen and nourishment to the baby and removing its carbon dioxide and waste products.

Physical and Psychological Changes of Pregnancy

A full-term pregnancy lasts approximately forty weeks, or nine calendar months, and is divided into three phases, called trimesters, of three months each. During each trimester, the pregnant woman experiences various physical and psychological changes.

As the baby grows, the uterus enlarges, which produces an obvious change in the shape and appearance of the woman's body. Uterine enlargement is responsible for some of the physical and psychological changes that develop during the woman's pregnancy. High levels of two hormones that are present during pregnancy—estrogen and progesterone—trigger other physical and psychological changes.

During the first trimester, the woman may have morning sickness, which refers to persistent nausea or vomiting during the morning hours. Sometimes, though, the nausea can occur throughout the day or only in the evening. Other common changes during the first trimester are tender breasts and nipples, fatigue, and a desire for more sleep than usual, as well as frequent urination. Headaches and sensitivity to odors also may occur. In addition, the woman may notice that the skin surrounding her nipples has become darker and that a thin line of darker skin has appeared on her abdomen. During the second trimester, many of the physical changes disappear. Toward the end of the fifth month of pregnancy, the woman first feels the fetus move, an event that is called *quickening*. During the third trimester, the woman may have frequent backaches and may feel clumsy or awkward due to the change in her posture caused by the enlarging uterus. Other third-trimester physical changes include shortness of breath, heartburn or indigestion, more frequent urination, hemorrhoids, leg cramps, swollen ankles, and varicose veins. Shortness of breath is, however, frequently relieved about two to three weeks before birth, when *lightening* occurs, that is, when the uterus moves downward from the abdominal cavity into the pelvic cavity.

Psychological changes and associated behaviors are triggered not only by uterine enlargement and hormone levels, but also by the woman's culture. Studies of Western women indicate that during the first trimester, common feelings include excitement about the pregnancy or anger that an unplanned pregnancy has occurred. Feelings of ambivalence about a planned pregnancy are also common. On the one hand, the woman feels that she has achieved a much-desired goal, whereas on the other hand, she feels overwhelmed by the thought of caring for another human being. The woman also may feel worried or anxious about how she will cope with the birth and the care of a baby. The second trimester is frequently characterized as a time of psychological well-being. As the pregnancy progresses, the woman may have both positive and negative feelings about the changes in the size and shape of her body. The psychological changes of the third trimester may include a return of anxiety about the birth; concerns about changes in relationships with a partner, family, and friends; and financial worries. At the same time, the woman may feel excited about the forthcoming birth of her baby and the start of a new phase in her life.

Throughout pregnancy, dietary practices frequently are influenced by culture and folk beliefs. Foods and herbs may be used in rituals to ward off evil spirits. Pregnant women may be encouraged to eat certain foods, foods of a certain temperature, or foods of certain colors, and may be discouraged from eating other foods. Some foods are thought to be shocking to the woman's body or to cause a rash or other problem in the infant. Other foods are thought to influence the position in which the baby is born. In some cultures, the amount of food eaten is prescribed in the belief that less food will produce a smaller infant and, therefore, an easier birth. Food cravings may occur, especially during the second trimester, and then continue throughout the pregnancy.

The Woman's Partner

Although the majority of women throughout the world become pregnant through sexual intercourse with a male partner, some women have female partners, and some other women choose to be single parents. The available literature focuses primarily on reactions of the woman's male partner to her pregnancy.

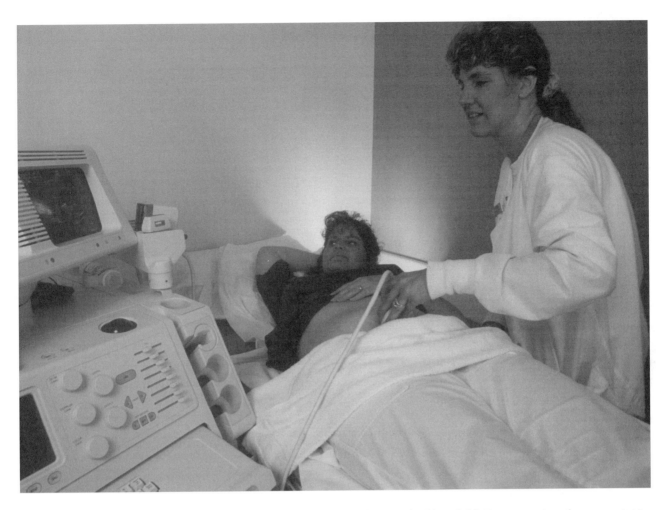

A physician carefully monitors this pregnant women's health and the growth of her child. Pregnancy in urban areas typically involves the use of high technology, while in rural areas such equipment might not be used. PHOTO RESEARCHERS, INC.

The male partner also may experience physical and psychological changes during the pregnancy. He may experience the same ambivalence as the woman once the pregnancy is confirmed. On the one hand, the male partner feels very pleased that he is capable of procreation, whereas on the other, he feels overwhelmed by the thought of his responsibility for his child.

Many of the physical and psychological changes experienced by the male partner, which are referred to as the *couvade syndrome,* are an expression of rituals associated with various cultures. Physical changes that appear throughout the pregnancy include indigestion, nausea and/or vomiting, bloating, changes in appetite, food cravings, increased urination, constipation, diarrhea, hemorrhoids, abdominal pain, backache, headache, toothache, difficult breathing, sensitivity to odors,

skin rashes, itching, fatigue, leg cramps, unintentional weight gain, and even fainting spells. Psychological changes include changes in the man's feelings about his body, and such mood changes as irritability, restlessness, insomnia, nervousness, inability to concentrate, anxiety, depression, or conversely, an enhanced sense of well-being.

Interestingly, studies of men in Western cultures have shown that the presence or absence of a physiological or psychological change in the man is directly related to the presence or absence of that change in his pregnant partner. That is, if the pregnant woman experiences a particular physical or psychological change, her partner most likely will also experience that change. In contrast, if the pregnant woman does not experience a particular change, her partner most likely will also not experience that change.

Studies also have shown that men who are members of certain cultures, have blue collar jobs, have limited financial resources, had health problems before the pregnancy, and who feel very involved in the pregnancy may be especially susceptible to the development of the couvade syndrome. In contrast, men who do not develop the couvade syndrome may feel hostility about the pregnancy or, conversely, may feel a special empathy for the pregnant woman.

Several theories have been proposed to explain why the couvade syndrome develops. One theory proposes that the syndrome is a result of the man's unconscious envy of the woman's ability to create a child. Another theory proposes that the couvade syndrome is a result of the man's ambivalence about the pregnancy. Still another theory proposes that the couvade syndrome is a result of the man's identification with his pregnant partner. Research has not, however, supported any of these theories.

Developmental Tasks of Pregnancy

Pregnancy and the birth of a woman's first child mark her entry to true adulthood in many cultures. As pregnancy progresses, the woman faces the challenge of two developmental tasks. One developmental task is to accept the fetus as part of herself, yet as a separate being that is a product of conception. The woman achieves this task when she accepts her pregnancy, begins to think of herself as a mother, and prepares for childbirth. Another task for the woman is to change her child-mother relationship with her own mother to a peer, or adult, relationship. The woman will achieve this task more readily when a partner or friend is willing to provide the psychological support previously provided by her mother, and when the mother is ready to accept her daughter as an autonomous adult and accept herself as a grandparent.

Additional Developmental Tasks of Women in Partner Relationships

Pregnant women who have partners must face three other developmental tasks. One developmental task for the woman and her partner is the commitment to make each other and the coming child a priority in their lives. That task may involve adjustments in their usual social life with family members and friends, as well as adjustments in the

family budget to provide for another family member. Another developmental task is the division of household responsibilities and responsibilities related to work. The pregnant woman may, for example, need help with household activities, such as heavy cleaning and care of pets. Furthermore, women and partners who both have careers may decide that one of them will take an extended leave from work after the baby is born. A third developmental task is the formation of a relationship that is emotionally and sexually satisfying to both the woman and her partner and that is characterized by open, honest communication.

Birth

Birth is the end of the pregnancy. It encompasses two major phases, referred to as labor and delivery. Labor typically begins with mild contractions of the uterus that occur five to thirty minutes apart. Each contraction lasts approximately thirty to forty seconds. As labor progresses, the contractions become stronger, occur more frequently, and last up to one minute. Throughout labor, the cervix (the opening of the uterus to the vagina, or birth canal) dilates progressively and the baby moves downward into the birth canal. Delivery occurs when the baby is born by being expelled from the birth canal or when a cesarean section is performed. Although the cesarean section rate varies from country to country, an increase in the cesarean method of birth is evident in both developed and developing countries. Cesarean birth requires a cut to be made through the abdominal wall and into the uterus. The woman receives medication so that she does not feel the cut. The physician then removes the baby and the placenta. When the baby is born through the birth canal, the placenta detaches from the uterine wall and is expelled through the birth canal. In some cultures, the placenta is considered sacred and is given a ceremonial burial at the family home. For example, some Maori people of New Zealand bury the placenta because they regard it as a twin who gave up life so the other twin, the live baby, could live.

In some cultures, pregnancy is viewed as a gift from God, and reliance on the spiritual aspects and sacredness of birth for a positive outcome is common. Throughout labor, the woman experiences sensations ranging from mild discomfort to intense pain. Cultural norms and expectations vary, such as acceptable vocalizations of pain, who may attend the birth and/or provide comfort and support, and the mother's birthing position. The belief that to give birth one must endure some pain is universal. Cultural norms about expressions of that pain vary from silence to frequent crying out. Herbal remedies; massage; relaxation and breathing exercises; medications administered by a physician, midwife, or nurse; and various rituals typically are employed to help alleviate the pain of labor and birth.

In many cultures, female members of the woman's extended family, especially mothers and mothers-in-law, provide comfort and support, with a lay midwife present for the birth. In other cultures, a nurse midwife is present for the labor and birth. In still other cultures, a registered nurse may be present for the labor and birth, and a physician delivers the infant. The woman's position varies from standing and/or walking to reclining in bed during labor, and from squatting to reclining in bed for the baby's birth.

The setting for birth also varies across cultures. In many cultures, the woman's home or the home of a relative is regarded as the most psychologically safe and comfortable birth environment. In other cultures, a hospital is viewed as most appropriate. In still other cultures, women and their partners may plan to have their baby at home but are ready to go to a hospital if a difficulty is encountered.

The role of a male partner during birth varies among cultures. In many cultures, norms about modesty may prohibit a male partner or other men from being with the woman during labor and delivery. In other cultures, the male partner is expected to be present, if only to observe the woman's suffering and be more willing to participate in family planning. In still other cultures, the male partner is regarded as a provider of much support and comfort to the laboring woman.

Women and their partners or such other support persons as family members or friends who plan to be together for the labor and birth can learn the proper relaxation and breathing exercises in childbirth preparation classes taught by trained childbirth educators. These classes also help the woman and support person to understand what happens during labor and delivery and to learn how the woman's support person can be present at the birth to coach her throughout labor and delivery.

Conclusion

Pregnancy and birth can be a very special time in the life of a woman. The nine months of pregnancy, as well as labor and delivery, are filled with many physical and psychological changes, as well as changes in lifestyle. Each change poses a challenge that can be met successfully when the woman shares her feelings and experiences with a partner or other supportive person and with her physician, midwife, nurse, and childbirth educator. The importance of health care throughout pregnancy is emphasized, because proper health care increases the likelihood of a healthy pregnancy, a healthy baby, and satisfied parents. Many references, particularly the *Human Relations Area Files,* describe cultural variations in beliefs about pregnancy and birth and associated behaviors.

See also: ABORTION; ADOLESCENT PARENTHOOD; FAMILY PLANNING; FERTILITY; GENETIC COUNSELING; MOTHERHOOD; NONMARITAL CHILDBEARING

Bibliography

Callister, L. C. (1995). "Cultural Meanings of Childbirth." *Journal of Obstetric, Gynecologic and Neonatal Nursing* 24:327–331.

Chalmers, B. (1996). "Cross-Cultural Comparisons of Birthing: Psycho-social Issues in Western and African Birth." *Psychology and Health* 12:11–21.

Chalmers, B. (1997). "Childbirth in Eastern Europe." *Midwifery* 13:2–8.

Davis-Floyd, R. (1992). *Birth as an American Rite of Passage.* Berkeley: University of California Press.

DePacheo, M. R., and Hutti, M. H. (1998). "Cultural Beliefs and Health Care Practices of Childbearing Puerto Rican American Women and Mexican American Women." *Mother Baby Journal* 3(1):14–22.

DeSevo, M. (1997). "Keeping the Faith: Jewish Traditions in Pregnancy and Childbirth." *AWHONN Lifelines* 1(4):46–49.

Harrison, A. (1991). "Childbirth in Kuwait: The Experiences of Three Groups of Arab Mothers." *Journal of Pain and Symptom Management* 6:466–475.

Hayba, P. (1996). "Childbirth in New Zealand: A Tribute from an American Educator." *International Journal of Childbirth Education* 12(1):18–22.

Jeng, S. J. (1997). "Chinese Traditional Childbearing Culture." *Chinese Culture Monthly* (212):1–26.

Jimenez, S. (1995). "The Hispanic Culture, Folklore, and Perinatal Health." *Journal of Perinatal Education* 4(1):9–16.

Jordan, B. (1993). *Birth in Four Cultures,* 4th ed. Prospect Heights, IL: Waveland Press.

La Torra, G. (1996). "Cultural Beliefs about Pregnancy and Birth." *International Journal of Childbirth Education* 11(2):36–38.

Lee, S. H., and Kuo, B. J. (2000). "Chinese Traditional Childbearing Attitudes and Infertile Couples in Taiwan." *Journal of Nursing Scholarship* 32:54.

Manio, E., and Renouf, R. (1987). "Asian Family Traditions and Their Influence in Transcultural Health Care Delivery." *Children's Health Care* 15:172–177.

Mattson, S. (2000). "Ethnocultural Considerations in the Childbearing Period." In *Core Curriculum for Maternal Newborn Nursing,* 2nd edition. ed. S. Mattson and J. Smith. Philadelphia: W. B. Saunders.

Nichols, F. (1996). "The Meaning of the Childbirth Experience: A Review of the Literature." *Journal of Perinatal Education* 5(4):71–77.

Nilsson, L. (1990). *A Child is Born.* New York: Delacorte Press/Seymour Lawrence.

Peritham, U. (1993). "Korean Women's Attitudes toward Pregnancy and Prenatal Care." *Health Care for Women International* 14:145–153.

Tuttle, C. R. (1997). "Experiences of Perinatal Care and Childbirth in New Zealand: A Model in Transition." *International Journal of Childbirth Education* 12(4):30–32.

Twiggs, F. T. (1988). "Expectant Fathers: Couvade Syndrome and Stress." *Dissertation Abstracts International* 48:2112B.

Wagner, M. (1996). "The Future of Birthing around the World." *International Journal of* Childbirth Education 12(2):7.

Other Resources

ABCbirth.com. (1999). *The ABCs of Pregnancy. An Online Textbook About Pregnancy, Childbirth, and Early Parenting.* Available from http://www.abcbirth.com.

BabyCenter, L.L.C. (2002). Available from http://www.babycenter.com.

Human Relations Area Files: Cultural Information for Education and Research. Information on HRAF available from http://www.yale.edu/hraf/.

Nestlé. (2002). *Very Best Baby.* Available from www.verybestbaby.com.

Pregnancy-Info.Net. (2002). Available from www.pregnancy-info.net.

U.S. National Library of Medicine. (2002). *MEDLINEplus Health Information. Pregnancy and Reproduction Topics.* Available from http://www.nlm.nih.gov/medlineplus/pregnancyandreproduction.html.

JACQUELINE FAWCETT
CYNTHIA ABER
VIRGINIA BOWEN SILVA

PREMARITAL AGREEMENTS

Premarital agreements are contracts made by prospective spouses in contemplation and consideration of marriage. They date back to sixteenth-century England, where prospective spouses used them in attempts to modify the legal rules that would otherwise govern their property rights during and after marriage. By the mid-seventeenth century, premarital agreements were so important that Parliament required them to be in writing. By 1700, they were so commonplace as to be the subject of jokes in the English popular theater. Today in the United States, these agreements are still useful; the rich and famous make them, as do other people. The emerging statutes and cases dealing with their validity recognize the differences between them and other contracts and, therefore, treat them differently.

Most countries enforce premarital agreements if they comply with specified procedural requirements. If, however, the agreement conflicts with some important public policy that overrides the parties' freedom to contract, the agreement will be modified or denied effect. For example, divorce courts in England do not consider themselves bound by premarital agreements regulating the economic incidents of divorce. English law takes the position that the courts' power to do economic justice at divorce is so important that it may not be limited by premarital agreement of the parties. Several Canadian provinces agree. Reliable information about specific rules in countries other than England and Canada is not available.

Premarital Agreements in the United States

The first difference between premarital agreements and ordinary contracts is their subject matter. Premarital agreements typically deal with one, or a combination, of three things: (1) property and support rights during marriage and on its dissolution by death of a spouse or divorce; (2) personal rights and obligations of the spouses during marriage; and (3) the education, care, and rearing of children who may later be born to the marrying couple. These subjects are of greater interest to the state than are those of ordinary contracts. The state wishes to protect the welfare of the couple and their children during and after marriage and to preserve the privacy of the family relationship. It passes laws to achieve these goals.

The second difference between premarital agreements and ordinary contracts is the relationship of the parties to each other. Prospective spouses are in a confidential relationship. They are often unevenly matched in bargaining power. The possibility, therefore, that one party may overreach the other is greater than in the case of ordinary contracts.

The third difference between premarital agreements and ordinary contracts is that premarital agreements are to be performed in the future, in the context of a marriage that has not yet begun, but which may continue for many years after the agreement is executed and before it is enforced. The possibility that unforeseen events may make enforcement of the agreement unwise, unfair, or otherwise undesirable, is greater than in the case of ordinary contracts.

These differences create a dilemma for the law. Prospective spouses have an interest in making their own bargains. As freely made bargains settling rights that might otherwise become a source of litigation, premarital agreements should be encouraged and enforced. To the extent, however, that these agreements vary or diminish the state-prescribed protections for the couple, their children, or their marital status; are likely to be the product of overreaching; or may become unfair by the time they are sought to be enforced, the law is wary of giving them validity. This built-in conflict makes premarital agreements less stable than ordinary contracts and explains why ordinary contract rules alone are insufficient to regulate them.

Like ordinary contracts, premarital agreements must be voluntary, made by competent parties, supported by consideration (the impending marriage is sufficient to satisfy this requirement), and consistent with public policy. However, they are subject to a more stringent review for procedural and substantive fairness than that accorded ordinary contracts. Courts review the fairness of ordinary contracts only at the time of execution but review premarital agreements for fairness at the time of enforcement as well.

Subjects of Effective Agreement

The state's interest in the subject matter of premarital agreements makes them more vulnerable to attack than ordinary contracts on the ground that they conflict with public policy. The net result is to limit the subjects on which prospective spouses can effectively contract.

Property and support rights. When a marriage dissolves by death of a spouse, state laws attempt to protect the financial interests of the survivor in a number of ways, including provisions for forced shares of each other's estates, homestead rights, exempt property, and family allowances. In most states, couples may alter these protections by premarital agreements. Some states consider certain protections more important than others and thus make it more difficult, or impossible, to waive or alter them—for example, widow's allowance or homestead rights when there are minor or dependent children, intestate shares, or rights to community property.

State law attempts to protect spouses on divorce as well, by providing for property division and for continued support in the form of alimony or maintenance. Premarital agreements altering these protections have been slower to win approval than those altering protections on death of a spouse and, before 1970, were almost universally held contrary to public policy. Courts thought they promoted divorce and commercialized marriage and that enforcing them would turn economically dependent spouses into public charges.

Since 1970, premarital agreements altering the incidents of divorce have gained wider acceptance. Divorce has become a common occurrence, and many married women have joined the labor force. Courts and legislatures now see these agreements, setting forth the parties' expectations and responsibilities, as devices for promoting marital stability and, accordingly, encourage them.

The states that enforce premarital agreements altering the incidents of divorce divide on provisions altering support rights. Some consider support a subject that couples cannot control by premarital agreement. Others allow premarital agreements altering support rights but refuse to enforce them if they are oppressive or unconscionable.

Employee benefits.   Employee benefits, including pension rights, can be the subject of premarital agreements between prospective spouses except for those emanating from plans covered by ERISA (the Employee Retirement Income Security Act of 1974, as amended by the Equity Retirement Act of 1984). This act of Congress preempts state laws and requires covered employee benefit plans to pay benefits to both the worker and his or her nonparticipating spouse unless the spouse waives them in the manner prescribed by the act. There is doubt about the validity of such waivers in premarital agreements, which are executed before the parties marry, because ERISA requires waiver by a "spouse."

Structure of marriage.   Sometimes the contracting couple, instead of, or in addition to, agreeing to alterations of property and support rights on death or divorce, uses a premarital agreement to structure the relationship by spelling out their personal rights and obligations. Courts have held such agreements unenforceable on the ground that it is improper for the judiciary to intervene in married couples' daily affairs.

Children.   Minor children are, of course, subjects of special interest to the state, which stands in the role of *parens patriae* to them. As subjects of premarital agreements, children retain their special status. A number of states have statutes that prohibit couples from making premarital agreements adversely affecting their children's support rights. Provisions for children's custody, care, or education also get careful scrutiny from the courts. Those in derogation of the child's best interests will not survive challenge.

Rules of Fairness

To be upheld, premarital agreements must satisfy local tests of procedural and substantive fairness.

As always, procedure and substance are closely related, and legislatures and courts considering the validity of premarital agreements often fail to separate the two. If the substantive terms of an agreement seem fair to the reviewing court, operating with or without statutory guidance, procedural niceties become less important. Conversely, if the agreement seems unfair, the procedures surrounding its execution become more important. The inquiry into procedure is made as of the time the agreement was executed. The question is whether the agreement was fairly procured. The inquiry into substantive fairness may be made at execution or reserved to, or repeated at, the time of enforcement. It is impossible to reduce the search for substantive fairness, whenever it is made, to a single question; the standards vary considerably from jurisdiction to jurisdiction and sometimes from case to case within a single jurisdiction.

Procuring the agreement.   According to most courts, parties to premarital agreements are in confidential relationships. In addition they are often ill-matched in terms of bargaining power. Before courts will uphold the validity of premarital agreements, therefore, they must be satisfied that the agreements were fairly procured. As courts and state legislatures describe them, fairly procured agreements are those that the parties enter into voluntarily after making financial disclosure to each other.

The requirement of financial disclosure is closely related to that of voluntariness and follows from the nature of premarital agreements calling for waivers of, or alterations in, property rights prescribed by the state. These rights take on, or lose, value on the bases of spouses' earning power and assets. A waiver of, or alteration in, such rights can hardly be voluntary and therefore fair, if the waiving spouse does not know the other's financial status. Accordingly, most jurisdictions require some kind of financial disclosure before the agreement is signed. They describe its extent variously: *fair, full, full and fair, full and frank,* or *fair and reasonable.* An agreement that the court finds substantively fair and reasonable may overcome a lack of disclosure; so may a spouse's actual knowledge of the other's assets or a spouse's waiver of the right to disclosure. The extent of required disclosure or knowledge varies from case to case, depending upon the relative sophistication of the parties, the apparent fairness or unfairness of the substantive terms of the agreement, and other circumstances unique to the parties and their situation. In every case, disclosure should be enough to give each contracting party a clear idea of the other's property and resources. The best device for proving disclosure is to attach schedules of assets and income to the agreement itself. A mere recital of disclosure in the agreement does not preclude a showing that there was none in fact.

Substantive terms of agreement. In passing on the validity of premarital agreements, courts state that they will not substitute their own notions of what is right for the provisions of the parties' freely made bargains. However, neither courts nor state legislatures, whose mandates they are obliged to follow, are oblivious to the substantive fairness of these agreements. This is an amorphous concept, which courts determine on a case-by-case basis. Unequal provisions for the parties do not alone make an agreement substantively unfair and therefore invalid.

The standard of substantive fairness, like the extent of required disclosure, is described variously: for example, *reasonableness in the circumstances, not so outrageous as to come within unconscionability principles as developed in commercial contract law, fair and equitable, equitable, fair and reasonable at the time of the making of the agreement, not unconscionable at the time of judgment,* and *not unconscionable at execution or enforcement.* Some states apply different standards to property provisions than those they apply to support provisions. Some distinguish between short marriages and long ones.

The states divide on the appropriate time for measuring substantive fairness—at execution of the agreement, at enforcement, or both. Measuring the substantive fairness of premarital agreements as of the time they were made gives maximum effect to the parties' freedom to contract but does not protect against unforeseen changes in circumstances that may affect the parties' financial status and put one or the other of them at risk if the agreement is enforced. Accordingly, an increasing number of states are assessing the fairness of premarital agreements at the time of enforcement. Provisions waiving or altering support rights are particularly vulnerable under this kind of review. Those that leave

a spouse unable to provide for reasonable needs, at a drastically reduced standard of living, or a public charge or close to it, will not be enforced; neither will those that are otherwise unconscionable. This does not lead to a wholesale rewriting of agreements, but it does protect parties against one-sidedness, oppression, or unfair surprise.

The Uniform Premarital Agreement Act

The Uniform Premarital Agreement Act (UPAA), some version of which has now been adopted in twenty-five states and the District of Columbia, lists eight subjects that may be included in premarital agreements. Six deal with property and support rights, a seventh deals with choice of law, and the eighth includes personal rights and obligations and other matters not in violation of public policy or a statute imposing a criminal penalty. It is not clear whether courts will read this provision as overriding earlier judicial decisions refusing to enforce agreements structuring couples' marriages.

UPAA provides for review of procedural and substantive fairness at the time of execution. Under it, an agreement is not enforceable if it either lacked voluntariness or was unconscionable and if the challenging party did not get fair and reasonable disclosure, or waive it, or have adequate actual knowledge of the other's finances. UPAA provides as well for a review of the substantive fairness of spousal support provisions at divorce or separation and empowers courts to modify any such provisions that cause parties to be eligible for support under a public assistance program. This review does not extend to other provisions of the agreement, nor does it extend to agreements effective on the death of a spouse.

Principles of the Law of Family Dissolution

The American Law Institute Principles of the Law of Family Dissolution take a position consistent with that of the UPAA and most U.S. jurisdictions. In a nutshell, it is that premarital agreements are generally enforceable if they comply with ordinary contract rules, meet specified procedural requirements, and do not work substantial injustice at enforcement.

See also: FAMILY LAW

Bibliography

Becker, L., and Kosel, J. E. (1989). "Property Disposition, Antenuptial, Postnuptial, and Property Settlement Agreements," In *Valuation and Distribution of Marital Property,* ed. J. P. McCahey. New York: Matthew Bender.

Clark, H. H. (1988). "Antenuptial Agreements," In *The Law of Domestic Relations in the United States.* St. Paul, MN: West Publishing.

Lindey, A. (1995). *Separation Agreements and Antenuptial Contracts.* New York: Matthew Bender.

National Conference of Commissioners on Uniform State Laws. (2001). *Uniform Laws Annotated,* Vol. 9C. West Group.

Winer, E. L., and Becker, L. (1993). *Premarital and Marital Contracts: A Lawyer's Guide to Drafting and Negotiating Enforceable Marital and Cohabitation Agreements.* Chicago: American Bar Association.

Younger, J. T. (1988). "Perspectives on Antenuptial Agreements." *Rutgers Law Review* 40:1059–1091.

Younger, J. T. (1992). "Perspectives on Antenuptial Agreements: An Update." *Journal of the American Academy of Matrimonial Lawyers* 8:1–44.

Younger, J. T. (2001). "Antenuptual Agreements." *William Mitchell Law Review* 28:697–721.

JUDITH T. YOUNGER

PREMARITAL PREGNANCY AND CHILDBIRTH

See ADOLESCENT PARENTHOOD; NONMARITAL CHILDBEARING

PREMARITAL SEX

See NONMARITAL CHILDBEARING; SEXUALITY; SEXUALITY EDUCATION; SEXUALITY IN ADOLESCENCE

PRENUPTIAL AGREEMENTS

See PREMARITAL AGREEMENTS

PRIMOGENITURE

Primogeniture has two closely related meanings: (1) a principle of seniority and authority whereby siblings are ranked according to their ages, with the eldest coming first; and (2) a principle of inheritance, in which the firstborn child receives all or his parents' most significant and valuable property upon their death. In most cases, the rules have been applied primarily or exclusively to males. But even where this is the case, the rule has often been interpreted flexibly. The Crown of England, for instance, has passed to the eldest daughter when a male heir was not available, as was the case with Elizabeth II in 1953.

Primogeniture as a principle of seniority exists in a wide range of societies where it forms an important element of social organization and cosmology. The Maori people of New Zealand, like many Polynesians, believed that human beings were descended from the gods and partook in divine potency (*mana*). The eldest clans and lineages, being closer to the gods, bore a higher degree of sacredness than junior lines. The chief of a group was always the most capable—and ideally the eldest—male of the eldest family line (Goldman 1970). Similar assumptions about the internal relationship between hierarchy and sacredness pervade Indian society, taking social expression in the caste system, the joint family, and marriage arrangements. The joint family of northern India, in its most mature and idealized form, consists of an elderly man and wife, their sons and daughters-in-law and grandchildren. The large family shares a single house, cooks at the same hearth, worships at a common altar, and works the same fields. Every male in the household holds an equal share in the estate until it is formally and legally dissolved. However, the senior male is the ultimate authority, a role that passes upon his death to the eldest son (Kolenda 1968).

Primogeniture in the second sense—as the eldest child's exclusive right to inherit his father's property—provides a means for keeping an estate unified. It tends to be found in agricultural societies where a person's status and economic prosperity is tied to ownership of land. In medieval Western Europe, the land-owning aristocracy developed practices and laws meant to prevent the splitting of estates and the titles and privileges that went with them. The lord of a manor would typically pass down his undivided lands, titles, and rights over peasants to his eldest son. Usually the younger sons received support from their families, allowing them to pursue careers in the military, church, or state bureaucracy. Daughters received a dowry upon their marriage in lieu of any rights over their father's estate (Goody 1983). Over time, many landholding peasants also adopted forms of primogeniture, although they appear to have often exercised the rule flexibly. One of the best known local adaptations is the *stem family* of rural Ireland in which the head of the household and his wife shared their home with one married son (usually the eldest) and his descendents. Other sons were expected to move away upon marriage (Arensberg and Kimball 1968).

Primogeniture is the most common inheritance rule used to maintain undivided property, but there are others. Parts of England prior to 1925 and Germany during the Nazi period had laws of *ultimogeniture,* where property passed to the youngest son. Other even rarer variations serving the same end include *seniorate* and *juniorate* rules where property passes to the eldest or youngest member of an extended family; and *secundogeniture, tertiogeniture* (and so forth), where property is reserved for the second or succeeding sons.

The primogeniture system came under attack from several quarters in the Western world in the latter part of the eighteenth century in part because of a growing resistance against the privileges of the landed aristocracy and a desire to release land into the open market. It was first abolished in New England and then all of the United States following the American Revolution. The French Revolution brought the system to a halt in France, and the Napoleonic Code, which specified minimal amounts of estates to be given to each child, prevented its resurrection. In England, laws were modified first to allow life tenants to mortgage or sell their lands. In 1925, the British Parliament abolished primogeniture as the governing rule in the absence of a valid will (Rheinstein and Glendon 1994–2002). It was and is still possible in many places for parents to reserve most or all of an estate for an eldest child in their will. Many countries have enacted estate taxes meant to encourage parents to share their property among their descendents (as well as a means of securing government revenues). Various countries, however, have at

times amended or created new laws meant to discourage or prevent the partitioning of farms as part of public policies aimed at maintaining a viable rural economy.

See also: BIRTH ORDER; KINSHIP; SIBLING RELATIONSHIPS

Bibliography

Arensberg, C. M., and Kimball, S. T. (1968). *Family and Community in Ireland,* 2nd edition. Cambridge, MA: Harvard University Press.

Goldman, I. (1970). *Ancient Polynesian Society.* Chicago: University of Chicago Press.

Goody, J. (1983). *The Development of the Family and Marriage in Europe.* Cambridge, UK: Cambridge University Press.

Kolenda, P. (1968). "Region, Caste, and Family Structure: A Comparative Study of the Indian 'Joint' Family." In *Structure and Change in Indian Society,* ed. M. Yinger and S. Cohn. Chicago: Aldine.

Other Resource

Rheinstein, M., and Glendon, M. A. (1994–2002). "Inheritance." *Britannica 2002 Deluxe Edition CD-ROM.* Britannica.com Inc.

JOHN BARKER

PRIVACY

See SELF-DISCLOSURE; HOME; HOUSING

PROBLEM SOLVING

Family problems come in many sizes and shapes. They range from minor annoyances, such as spats between children, to life-threatening situations such as physical abuse by a parent. They may be brief events that disappear in minutes or recurring disputes that last a lifetime. Whatever their form and duration, problems are distinguished by the presence of negative experiences for some family members. Such experiences provide natural motivation to eliminate the problem. Solving a family problem means finding a way to remove the negative experiences without creating new difficulties.

Humans have a variety of innate capabilities that are used for solving problems (Pinker 1997; Ellis and Seigler 1994). These include the abilities to recognize patterns in human situations, to recall relevant events from the past, to visualize events that may occur in the future, and to weigh the likely consequences of alternate future actions. One particular combination of abilities, *rational problem solving*, is especially important. It was initially identified in studies of the human thought process (Dewey [1910] 1982) and has been widely applied in work with couples and families (Forgatch and Patterson 1989; Vuchinich 1999). This form of problem solving occurs in a sequence of stages: (1) the problem is clearly defined; (2) several alternative possible solutions are generated; (3) each alternative is evaluated in terms of potential costs and benefits; (4) one alternative is selected as having the best potential to solve the problem; and (5) the solution is applied and adjusted as necessary.

These stages are generally recognized as being logical and based on elements of *common sense.* Indeed, they may be seen as essential to adaptation in the process of evolution (Pinker 1997; Vuchinich 1999). Using some variation of them provides a way to make changes that are likely to help eliminate the problem. However, individuals do not always use a rational approach to dealing with the difficulties in their lives. Other approaches to problem solving are prevalent and are often linked to couple and family dysfunctions.

Emotion and Problem Solving

To understand family efforts at problem solving it is first necessary to address the basic nature of problems and how they arise in family life. Since John Dewey's early formulations (1938) it has been acknowledged that the essence of problems is *blocked goal attainment* (Tallman 1988). *Goals* are physical or psychological states that individuals or groups seek. These include such things as sexual gratification, a sense of self-esteem, a full stomach, parental approval, or religious salvation. When attainment of such goals is blocked, individuals sense some form of frustration. At a certain level, such frustration creates a negative experience for the individual. Those experiences can be transformed into a perceived problem. When that happens, the individual feels dissatisfied and attempts to remove the blockage and reach the goal. If the

individual finds a way to reach the goal, the problem is solved. Because of the negative affect in this process, *emotional regulation* is a key element in how couples and families try to solve their problems. Certain types of emotional regulation can short-circuit problem solving.

One of these types of emotional regulation is denial. *Denial* is a normal defense mechanism that allows the individual to avoid the pain of facing negative experiences. The negative emotion is regulated by denying its existence. With denial, an individual or family has negative affective experiences but tries to ignore them and takes no action to eliminate them. For example, a wife who is physically abused by her husband may think and act as though nothing is really wrong with her marriage. Although it may be psychologically useful in certain contexts, denial is a hallmark of a variety of couple and family dysfunctions. Denial stops any problem solving before it can even get started. From the individual's viewpoint, there is no problem. When denial is present, problem solving can only occur after there is some acknowledgement that a problem exists and something needs to be done about it. This may require some form of confrontation in which family members or professionals assertively display the problem or create consequences for not addressing the issues.

A second common type of emotional regulation is *conflict engagement* (Kurdek 1995). Here the frustration of blocked goal attainment is transformed into anger and aggression, usually against someone in the family. This represents a low level of emotional regulation. Someone is often blamed for the difficulties and becomes the target for verbal or physical aggression. Although a perceived problem may be identified, the impulsive expression of anger and the aroused emotional state forestalls any movement toward a meaningful solution. As a result, the conditions that created the underlying problem are not improved. Thus, negative experiences continue to accumulate and ultimately lead to more aggressive outbursts. This pattern can become dangerous as verbal aggression worsens and is supplemented by physical aggression. In such cases it is typically necessary to improve anger management skills of some family members before problem solving can begin.

Individuals have their own styles of responding to problems. But solving problems in couples and families must take individual styles into account. One particularly damaging combination of styles has been found to be prevalent in U.S. couples. It is known as the *demand/withdraw pattern* (Heavey, Layne, and Christensen 1993; Gottman 1995). In such cases one partner (*the demander*), often the wife, pursues discussion of a problem sometimes by demanding or complaining. The other partner (*the withdrawer*) responds to this by withdrawing and refusing to talk about it. This increases the intensity of the first partner's demands, which leads to further withdrawal by the other. The result, of course, is that nothing is solved, one partner is increasingly frustrated and the other is pushed further into a noncommunicative state. This pattern can also take place between parents and their children. Typically it is the parent who demands and the child who withdraws. The demand/withdraw pattern can be overcome by persuading each party to use different strategies when problems arise (Gottman 1995). For example, the demander may learn to initiate discussions more subtly. The withdrawer may learn to acknowledge the other's concerns and communicate more openly.

Who Defines Couple and Family Problems?

The demand/withdraw pattern highlights the fundamental importance of how a family problem is defined. Is something a problem if one partner perceives it to be a problem but the other does not? In the family context, Does any family member have the right to declare that a problem exists and that changes need to be made to solve it? Ideally if anyone in a couple or family senses that a problem exists, then the others would consider it a problem and seek a solution. This ideal is the basis for models of *open communication, regular family meetings,* and similar practices (Vuchinich 1999). In reality, *power dynamics* in couples and families often determine what is defined as a problem. Those with the most power decide whether an issue is a problem or not, and what can be done about it. In healthy couples and families those with power are sensitive to the needs of all members. They acknowledge legitimate problems and seek appropriate solutions. However, in some families, power is used to suppress dealing with important problems based on negative experiences of weaker family members. This is part of a more general pattern of *dominance.*

The question of whether something is a problem can extend beyond the boundaries of the family. If a couple seeks counseling for marital problems then a professional is involved in determining what problems exist. Resistance to therapeutic efforts is often based on an unwillingness to accept the therapist's definition of problems. Success in therapy can be a result of reformulating the problems that cannot be solved into problems that can be solved. Defining problems is also a common issue in social services work. A family may not view the father's physical beatings of their young son as a problem. But evidence of broken bones and psychological symptoms makes those beatings a problem as defined by the medical, social work, and legal professionals. Solutions to such problems may need to be imposed from outside the family.

It is often said that admitting that a problem exists is half of the solution, but that may be an understatement. If a real problem is not acknowledged, there may be little chance for a solution. But family members who sense a problem tend to take a "wait and see" approach. There is a stigma attached to couple and family problems in U.S. culture. Bringing up problems risks a negative reaction from loved ones, or even making matters worse. Indeed, minor difficulties do disappear without professional help. So there are some reasons why addressing problems is avoided. The average troubled couple waits six years before seeking marital counseling (Gottman 1999). But as a consequence, problems are usually well developed by the time any action is taken. This is not inevitable. Couples who regularly "check in" with how each other are doing can resolve problems quickly. Weekly family meetings serve the same purpose for family groups (Forgatch and Patterson 1989). These practices acknowledge that minor problems are normal. They can draw families closer together by opening lines of communication with an orientation toward helping all family members solve problems that concern them.

The Problem-Solving Process in Couples and Families

Once a problem is defined, elements of the rational process can be used to seek solutions. However, the rhetoric of problem solving can be somewhat deceptive when applied to couples and families. It is important to recognize that problems in couples and families are not like math problems. There is no single correct solution. There are many different solutions that might help eliminate the negative experiences at the core of the problem. One solution might solve only part of the problem, and components may be needed. Moreover, it may not be clear in advance whether a given solution will be helpful or not. It may seem like a good idea at the time; it may not work. Furthermore, individuals, couples, and families change over time. Such changes mean that solutions that worked at one point in time may not work at a later point.

Thus, effective family problem solving is an ongoing process that involves more than pure logic and reasoning. Couples and families must have certain minimal levels of communication skills and cohesion. They must be willing to change some of their behaviors for the well-being of others. Possible solutions must be tried out to see what happens. The results must be evaluated to see how well a given solution worked and whether other parts of solutions are needed. Family members must have enough patience and willingness to persevere through negotiations that, at times, may seem tedious or unpleasant. These are endured because of the rewards associated with living in a healthy functioning family that solves its problems.

Some family problems may not have a complete solution. For example, a family in poverty may have many problems associated with not having enough resources to meet basic family needs. Or a parent may acquire a serious disability that prevents them from fulfilling their roles as spouse and parent. In such circumstances family members may have to accept that some of their goals can not be attained. It is important to acknowledge that some problems have no solution and further efforts to solve them is counterproductive (Gottman 1999). Problem solving can still be used to find ways of making the best of the situation.

The involvement of issues such as emotional regulation and power dynamics complicates the problem solving process. However, the rational model remains at the core. Teaching couples, parents, and children to use it has proven beneficial in both prevention and therapeutic applications (Vuchinich 1999). Specific issues emerge within each stage when working with couples and families.

First, constructing a clear definition of a problem is often difficult. Yet this is a crucial step in starting the process. Problem definitions are often expressed initially as complaints, and complaints are often met by immediate denials or countercomplaints. In the *definition stage* it is important to avoid such instantaneous negative reactions that engender conflict. Complaints deserve a fair hearing and some displays of empathy. One family member may have to facilitate this and later stages.

Once a problem is defined, possible solutions are suggested. Again, there is a tendency for proposals to be met with immediate negative response. But this stage should follow a *brainstorming session* in which various proposals are solicited, one after another, with neither criticism nor approval. Unrealistic or humorous proposals are allowed. This format promotes novel or creative approaches to the problem and participation from everyone.

The *evaluation stage* is facilitated by considering the potential consequences of each realistic proposed solution. By discussing the pros and cons of each proposed solution, family members can project what implications it would have for each of them. There are still disagreements here, but they should focus more on specific details of a solution rather than direct interpersonal conflict. In some cases it is useful to have someone write down each solution and its pros and cons. In this format the most severe objections of some family members get aired and acknowledged. It usually becomes apparent that only one or two solutions have a realistic chance of working. Ideally, the final selection of one solution is a consensual decision. This is not always possible. In such cases family cohesion and commitment to solving the family problems provide the motivation for everyone to try one solution, even if it wasn't everyone's first choice. Social skills can be especially valuable in this phase in reassuring everyone that their interests will be taken into account and the solution will not exploit them.

Once a solution is chosen, a detailed *implementation plan* is needed to specify exactly who will do what and when they will do it. Following through with a solution may be difficult. Talk is one thing—action is another. It is essential to plan for meetings or discussions to assess how well the solution worked. Typically an initial solution is only partially implemented and is only partially effective. Later meetings are used to revisit the solution and consider adjustments that will improve it. When family members begin seeing the benefits of solving their problems, their motivation for participating in problem solving activities increases.

The extent to which formal meetings are needed for problem solving varies from family to family. Family members do need to communicate about perceived problems in some way. Where and how often they do it depends on their communication patterns. The family meeting provides an effective structured format. It is important that such meetings do not degenerate into mere "gripe sessions," and some planning and facilitation may be necessary. A family meeting should include other activities besides problem solving. This can include such activities as sharing recent positive experiences, sharing news or feelings about extended family members, playing games, or eating snacks. This involves setting aside some time for the couple or family to be together and affirm their positive bonds. This can occur before or after the problem solving and helps integrate it into other aspects of family life.

See also: COMMUNICATION: COUPLE RELATIONSHIPS; COMMUNICATION: FAMILY RELATIONSHIPS; CONFLICT: COUPLE RELATIONSHIPS; CONFLICT: FAMILY RELATIONSHIPS; CONFLICT: PARENT-CHILD RELATIONSHIPS; DECISION MAKING; FAMILY LIFE EDUCATION; NAGGING AND COMPLAINING; POWER: FAMILY RELATIONSHIPS; POWER: MARITAL RELATIONSHIPS; RESOURCE MANAGEMENT; THERAPY: COUPLE RELATIONSHIPS

Bibliography

Dewey, J. ([1910] 1982). *How We Think.* Lexington, MA: Heath.

Dewey, J. (1938). *Logic: The Theory of Inquiry.* New York: Henry Holt

Ellis, S., and Siegler, R. S. (1994). "Development of Problem Solving." In *Thinking and Problem Solving,* ed. R. J. Sternberg. San Diego, CA: Academic Press.

Forgatch, M. S., and Patterson, G. R. (1989). *Family Problem Solving,* part 2 of *Parents and Adolescents Living Together.* Eugene, OR: Castalia.

Gottman, J. M., and Silver, N. (1995). *Why Marriages Succeed or Fail.* New York: Simon and Schuster.

Gottman, J. M., and Silver, N. (1999). *The Seven Principles for Making Marriage Work.* New York: Crown.

Heavey, C. L.; Layne, C.; and Christensen, A. (1993). "Gender and Conflict Structure in Marital Interaction." *Journal of Consulting and Clinical Psychology* 61:16–27.

Kurdek, L. A. (1995). "Predicting Change in Marital Satisfaction from Husbands' and Wives' Conflict Resolution Styles." *Journal of Marriage and the Family* 57: 153–164.

Pinker, S. (1997). *How the Mind Works.* New York: Norton.

Tallman, I. (1988). "Problem Solving in Families: a Revisionist View." In *Social Stress and Family Development,* ed. D. M. Klein and J. Aldous. New York: Guilford.

Vuchinich, S. (1999). *Problem Solving in Families: Research and Practice.* Thousand Oaks, CA: Sage.

SAM VUCHINICH

PROTESTANTISM

The sixteenth-century Protestant Reformation was a watershed in the history of the Western theology and law of marriage—a moment and movement that gathered several streams of classical and Catholic legal ideas and institutions, remixed them and revised them in accordance with the new Protestant norms and forms of the day, and then redirected them in the governance and service of the Christian West.

Medieval Catholic Background

Prior to the sixteenth century, marriage was principally subject to the theology and law of the Roman Catholic Church. The medieval Church treated marriage and the family in a threefold manner—at once as a natural, contractual, and sacramental unit. First, marriage was a natural association, created by God to enable man and woman to "be fruitful and multiply" and to raise children in the service and love of God. Since the fall into sin, marriage had also become a remedy for lust, a channel to direct one's natural passion to the service of the community and the church. Second, marriage was a contractual unit, formed in its essence by the mutual consent of the parties. This contract prescribed for couples a life-long relation of love, service, and devotion to each other and proscribed unwarranted breach or relaxation of their connubial and parental duties. Third, marriage, when properly contracted and consummated between Christians, rose to the dignity of a sacrament. The temporal union of body, soul, and mind within the marital estate symbolized the eternal union between Christ and His Church, and brought sanctifying grace to the couple, their children, and the church. This sacramental perspective helped to integrate the natural and the contractual dimensions of marriage and to render marriage a central concern of the church.

Although a sacrament and a sound way of Christian living, however, marriage was not considered to be particularly spiritually edifying. Marriage was a remedy for sin, not a recipe for righteousness. Marital life was considered less commendable than celibate life, propagation less virtuous than contemplation. Clerics, monastics, and other servants of the church were thus to forgo marriage as a condition for ecclesiastical service. Those who could not do so were not worthy of the church's holy orders and offices. Celibacy was something of a litmus test of spiritual discipline and social superiority.

From the twelfth century forward, the Catholic Church built upon this conceptual foundation a comprehensive canon law of marriage that was enforced by church courts throughout much of Western Christendom. Until the sixteenth century, the canon law of marriage was the law of the West. A civil law or a common law of marriage, where it existed at all, was generally considered supplemental and subordinate. Consistent with the naturalist perspective on marriage, the church's canon law punished contraception and abortion as violations of the created marital functions of propagation and childrearing. It proscribed unnatural relations, such as incest and polygamy, and unnatural acts such as bestiality, buggery, and sodomy. Consistent with the contractual perspective, the canon law ensured voluntary unions by dissolving marriages formed through mistake, duress, fraud, or coercion, and granting husband and wife alike equal rights to enforce conjugal debts that had been voluntarily assumed. Consistent with the sacramental perspective, the church protected the sanctity and sanctifying purpose of marriage by declaring valid marital bonds to be indissoluble, and by dissolving invalid unions between Christians and non-Christians or between parties related by various legal, spiritual, blood, or familial ties. This canon law of marriage, grounded in a rich sacramental theology and ecclesiastical jurisprudence, was formalized and systematized by the Council of Trent in 1563.

Reformation Response

The Lutheran, Calvinist, and Anglican branches of the Reformation gave birth to three Protestant models of marriage. Like Catholics, Protestants retained the naturalist perspective of marriage as an association created for procreation and mutual protection. They also retained the contractual perspective of marriage as a voluntary association formed by the mutual consent of the couple. Unlike Catholics, however, Protestants rejected the subordination of marriage to celibacy and the celebration of marriage as a sacrament. According to common Protestant lore, the person was too tempted by sinful passion to forgo God's remedy of marriage. The celibate life had no superior virtue and was no prerequisite for ecclesiastical service. It led too easily to concubinage and homosexuality and impeded too often the access and activities of the clerical office. Moreover, marriage was not a sacrament. It was instead an independent social institution ordained by God and equal in dignity and social responsibility with the church, state, and other estates of society. Participation in marriage required no prerequisite faith or purity and conferred no sanctifying grace, as did true sacraments.

From this common critique, the Lutheran, Calvinist, and Anglican traditions constructed their own models of marriage. Each Protestant tradition provided a different theological formula for integrating the inherited contractual, natural, and religious perspectives on marriage. Lutherans emphasized the social dimensions of marriage; Calvinists, the covenantal dimensions; and Anglicans, the commonwealth dimensions. Each Protestant tradition also assigned principal legal responsibility for marriage quite differently. Lutherans consigned legal authority mostly to the state, Calvinists to both state and church, and Anglicans mostly to the church. These differences in emphasis and authority among early Protestants were based, in part, on differences among their theological models of marriage.

Lutheranism

The Lutheran tradition, from 1517 forward, developed a social model of marriage, grounded in Martin Luther's doctrine of the heavenly and earthly kingdoms. Marriage, Luther and his colleagues taught, was a social estate of the earthly kingdom of creation, not a sacred estate of the heavenly kingdom of redemption. Though divinely ordained, marriage was directed primarily to human ends, to the fulfilling of civil and spiritual uses in the lives of the individual and of society. Marriage revealed to persons their sin and their need for God's marital gift. It restricted prostitution, promiscuity, and other public sexual sins. It taught love, restraint, and other public virtues. Any fit man and woman were free to enter such unions, clerical and lay alike. Indeed, all persons were encouraged to marry when they came of age, unless they had the rare gift of continence. This was especially imperative for Christian clergy, for a pastor's experience of marriage would enhance his pastoral ministry to the married, and his marital parsonage would serve a model for proper Christian living in the community.

As part of the earthly kingdom, Lutheran reformers argued, marriage was subject to the civil law of the state, not to the canon law of the church. To be sure, marriage was still subject to God's law, but this law was now to be administered by Christian magistrates who were God's vice-regents in the earthly kingdom. Church officials were required to counsel the magistrate about God's law and to cooperate with him in publicizing and disciplining marriage. All church members, as part of the priesthood of believers, were required to counsel those who contemplated marriage, to admonish those who sought annulment or divorce, and to aid in the rearing of all children as their collective baptismal vows prescribed. But principal legal authority over marriage and family life lay with the state, not with the church.

This new social model of marriage was reflected in the transformation of marriage law in Germany and other Lutheran polities of Western Europe. Civil marriage courts replaced church courts. New civil marriage statutes replaced traditional canon law rules. Lutheran jurists published scores of treatises on marriage law, affirming and embellishing the new Lutheran theology of marriage. The new Lutheran marriage law, like the new Lutheran marriage theology, remained indebted to the Catholic canon law tradition. Traditional marriage laws, like prohibitions against unnatural sexual relations and against infringement of marital functions, remained in effect. Impediments that protected free consent, that implemented biblical prohibitions against marriage of relatives, and that governed the couple's physical relations were largely retained. Such laws were as consistent with the Catholic sacramental model as with the Lutheran social model of marriage.

But changes in marriage theology also yielded changes in marriage law. Because the Lutheran reformers rejected the subordination of marriage to celibacy, they rejected laws that forbade clerical and monastic marriage, that denied remarriage to those who had married a cleric or monastic, and that permitted vows of chastity to annul promises of marriage. Because they rejected the sacramental nature of marriage, the reformers rejected impediments of crime and heresy and prohibitions against divorce in the modern sense. Marriage was for them the community of the couple in the present, not their sacramental union in the life to come. Where that community was broken, for one of a number of specific reasons (such as adultery or desertion), the couple could sue for divorce and the right to remarry. Because persons by their lustful nature were in need of God's remedy of marriage, the reformers removed numerous impediments to marriage not countenanced by Scripture. Because of their emphasis on the Godly responsibility of the prince, the pedagogical role of the church and the family, and the priestly calling of all believers, the reformers insisted that both marriage and divorce be public. The validity of marriage promises depended upon parental consent, witnesses, church consecration and registration, and priestly instruction. Couples who wished to divorce had to announce their intentions in the church and community and to petition a civil judge to dissolve the bond.

Calvinism

The Calvinist tradition, established in mid-sixteenth century Geneva, set out a covenantal model of marriage. This model confirmed many of the Lutheran theological and legal reforms, but cast them in a new ensemble. Marriage, John Calvin and his followers taught, was not a sacramental institution of the church, but a covenantal association of the entire community. A variety of parties participated in the formation of this covenant. The marital parties themselves swore their betrothals and espousals before each other and God—rendering all marriages triparty agreements, with God as third party witness, participant, and judge. The couple's parents, as God's lieutenants for children, gave their consent to the union. Two witnesses, as God's priests to their peers, served as witnesses to the marriage. The minister, holding God's spiritual power of the Word, blessed the couple and admonished them in their spiritual duties. The magistrate, holding God's temporal power of the sword, registered the couple and protected them in their person and property. Each of these parties was considered essential to the legitimacy of the marriage, for they each represented a different dimension of God's involvement in the covenant. To omit any such party was, in effect, to omit God from the marriage covenant.

The covenant of marriage was grounded in the order of creation and governed by the law of God. At creation, God ordained the structure of marriage to be a lifelong union between a fit man and a fit woman of the age of consent. God assigned to this marriage the interlocking purposes of mutual love and support of husband and wife, mutual procreation and nurture of children, and mutual protection of both parties from sexual sin. Thereafter, God set forth, in reason, conscience, and the Bible, a whole series of commandments and counsels for proper adherence to this ideal created structure and purpose of marriage.

God's moral law for the covenant of marriage set out two tracks of marital norms—civil norms, which are common to all persons, and spiritual norms, which are distinctly Christian. This moral law, in turn, gave rise to two tracks of marital morality—a simple morality of duty demanded of all persons regardless of their faith, and a higher morality of aspiration demanded of believers in order to reflect their faith. It was the church's responsibility to teach aspirational spiritual norms for marriage and family life. It was the state's responsibility to enforce mandatory civil norms. This division of responsibility was reflected in sixteenth-century Geneva in the procedural divisions between the church consistory and the city council. In marriage cases, the consistory was the court of first instance, and would call parties to their higher spiritual duties, backing their recommendations with threats of spiritual discipline. If such spiritual counsel and discipline failed, the parties were referred to the city council to compel them, using civil and criminal sanctions, to honor at least their basic civil duties for marriage.

This Calvinist covenantal model mediated both sacramental and contractual understandings of marriage. On the one hand, this covenant model confirmed the sacred and sanctifying qualities of marriage—without ascribing to it sacramental functions. Marriage was regarded as a holy and loving fellowship, a compelling image of the bond between Yahweh and His elect, Christ and His church. But marriage was no sacrament, for it confirmed no divine promise. On the other hand, this covenant model confirmed the contractual and consensual qualities of marriage—without subjecting it to the personal preferences of the parties. Marriage depended for its validity and utility on the voluntary consent of the parties. But marriage was more than a mere contract, for God was a third party to every marriage covenant, and He set its basic terms in the order and law of creation. Freedom of contract in marriage was thus effectively limited to choosing maturely which party to marry—with no real choice about the form, forum, or function of marriage once a fit spouse was chosen.

Anglicanism

The Anglican tradition, of the sixteenth and seventeenth centuries, brought forth a commonwealth model of marriage. This model embraced the sacramental, social, and covenantal models inherited from the Continent but went beyond them. Marriage was at once a gracious symbol of the divine, a social unit of the earthly kingdom, and a solemn covenant with one's spouse. But the essential cause, condition, and calling of the family was that it served and symbolized the common good of the couple, the children, the church, and the state all at once. Marriage was appointed by God as "a little commonwealth" to foster the mutual love, service, and security of husband and wife, parent and child. It was likewise appointed by God as a "seedbed and seminary" of the broader commonwealth to teach church, state, and society essential Christian and political norms and habits.

At first, this commonwealth model served to rationalize the traditional hierarchies of husband over wife, parent over child, church over household, state over church. After decades of experimentation, England in the mid-sixteenth century had formally rejected most Protestant legal reforms of marriage introduced on the Continent. It returned to much of the medieval canon law of marriage administered by the church, but now under the supreme headship of the English crown. To call the marital household "a little commonwealth" was to signal its subordinate place within the new hierarchy of social institutions of which "the great commonwealth" of England was composed. It was also to call the household to an internal hierarchy of offices that matched the royal and episcopal offices of the great commonwealth. The commonwealth model was thus used to integrate a whole network of parallel domestic and political duties rooted in the Bible and English tradition. Anglican divines and moralists expounded at great length the reciprocal duties of husband and wife, parent and child, master and servant, that would produce a well-ordered little commonwealth. In keeping with the tradition of stability of the great political commonwealth of England, these same Anglican writers prohibited the dissolution of this little domestic commonwealth of the family by divorce.

As the political concept of the English commonwealth was revolutionized and democratized in the seventeenth century, however, so was the English commonwealth model of marriage. The traditional hierarchies of husband over wife, parent over child, and church over family were challenged with a revolutionary new principle of equality. The biblical duties of husband and wife and of parent and child were recast as the natural rights of each household member against the other. The traditional idea of a created natural order of marriage, society, and state met with a new idea of marriage, society, and state formed voluntarily by contracts by individuals in the state of nature. Just as the English commonwealth could be rent asunder by force of arms when it abused the people's natural rights, so the family commonwealth could be put asunder by suits at law when it abused the couple's marital rights. Just as the king could be beheaded for abuses in the commonwealth, so the paterfamilias could be removed from the head of the little commonwealth for abuses in the household. This revolutionary construction of the commonwealth model provided

the rationale for the incremental liberalization of English marriage law in the course of the next two centuries. It also provided a stepping stone for the development of a more overtly contractarian model of marriage slowly developed by Enlightenment reformers in the eighteenth and nineteenth centuries.

Legacy

From the later sixteenth to the early nineteenth centuries, these Catholic and Protestant models lay at the heart of Western marriage and family life, lore, and law. The medieval Catholic model, confirmed and elaborated by the Council of Trent in 1563, flourished in southern Europe, Spain, Portugal, and France, and their many colonies in Latin and Central America, in the U.S. south and southwest, in Quebec and the Canadian Maritimes, and, eventually, in parts of East and West Africa. A Protestant social model rooted in the Lutheran two-kingdoms theory dominated portions of Germany, Austria, Switzerland, and Scandinavia together with their North American and, later, African colonies. A Protestant social model rooted in Calvinist covenant theology came to strong expression in Geneva, and in portions of Huguenot France, the Pietist Netherlands, Presbyterian Scotland, Puritan New England, and South Africa. A Protestant social model that treated marriage as a little commonwealth at the core of broader ecclesiastical and political commonwealths prevailed in Anglican England and its many colonies in North America and eventually in Africa and the Indian subcontinent as well.

See also: ANABAPTISTS (AMISH, MENNONITE); CATHOLICISM; EVANGELICAL CHRISTIANITY; FAMILY, HISTORY OF; FAMILY LAW; FAMILY MINISTRY; INTERFAITH MARRIAGE; RELIGION

Bibliography

Brundage, J. A. (1987). *Law, Sex, and Christian Society in Medieval Europe*. Chicago: University of Chicago Press.

Carlson, E. J. (1994). *Marriage and the English Reformation*. Oxford: Blackwell.

Harrington, J. F. (1995). *Reordering Marriage and Society in Reformation Germany*. Cambridge, UK: Cambridge University Press.

Johnson, J. T. (1970). *A Society Ordained by God: English Puritan Marriage Doctrine in the First Half of the Seventeenth Century*. Nashville, TN: Abingdon Press.

Kingdon, R. M. (1995). *Adultery and Divorce in Calvin's Geneva*. Cambridge, MA: Harvard University Press.

Ozment, S. E. (1983). *When Fathers Ruled: Family Life in Reformation Europe*. Cambridge, MA: Harvard University Press.

Ozment, S. E. (2001). *Ancestors: The Loving Family in Old Europe*. Cambridge, MA: Harvard University Press.

Stone, L. (1979). *The Family, Sex, and Marriage in England, 1500–1800*. New York: Harper and Row.

Witte, J., Jr. (1997). *From Sacrament to Contract: Religion, Marriage, and Law in the Western Tradition*. Louisville, KY: Westminster/John Knox Press.

Witte, J., Jr. (2002). *Law and Protestantism: The Legal Teachings of the Lutheran Reformation*. New York: Cambridge University Press.

JOHN WITTE JR.

PUERTO RICO

See ETHNIC VARIATION/ETHNICITY; HISPANIC-AMERICAN FAMILIES

QUALITY OF RELATIONSHIPS

See AFFECTION; EQUITY; FRIENDSHIP; FORGIVENESS;
INTIMACY; LOVE; MARITAL QUALITY; RELATIONSHIP
MAINTENANCE; SELF-DISCLOSURE; TRUST

RAPE

When people hear the word *rape,* it often conjures a mental image: perhaps a stranger with a knife jumping out of the bushes at night and forcing a woman to engage in sexual intercourse. Defining rape is no easy matter, however. Definitions come from the law, the media, research, and political activism. Even within any one of these domains, definitions vary.

Historically, in English common law, rape was defined as a man's engaging in sexual intercourse with a woman other than his wife against her will and without her consent by using or threatening force (Muehlenhard and Kimes 1999). Today, legal definitions of rape differ widely across nations.

Researchers studying rape must decide what definition to use (Muehlenhard et al. 1992). Much of the research on rape has taken place in the United States, and many researchers have relied on the legal definition used in a particular state. Others, however, have decided that the legal definitions are too narrow. Some feminist political activists have offered definitions of rape to highlight the social and economic pressures placed on women to engage in sex.

Incidence and Prevalence

Perhaps even more difficult than defining rape is the task of identifying the frequency of its occurrence. *Incidence* refers to the number of rapes occurring during a given period of time; *prevalence* refers to the percentage of persons who have been raped. Estimates of incidence and prevalence of rape depend on the definition used, the population studied, and the methods used to gather data (see Muehlenhard et al. 1994).

In the United States, several studies have provided estimates of rape incidence and prevalence. The National Institute of Justice and the Centers for Disease Control and Prevention sponsored the National Violence Against Women (NVAW) Survey. The survey consisted of telephone interviews with eight thousand women and eight thousand men in the United States regarding their experiences with various forms of violence. In this study rape was defined as "an event that occurs without the victim's consent and involves the use of threat or force to penetrate the victim's vagina or anus by penis, tongue, fingers, or object, or the victim's mouth by penis. The definition includes both attempted and completed rape" (Tjaden and Thoennes 2000, p. 5). The researchers found that 7.7 percent of women and 0.3 percent of men over age eighteen had experienced such an event (Tjaden and Thoennes 2000).

Reviewing international research, Lori L. Heise and her colleagues reported that between 19 and 27.5 percent of college-aged women in Canada, Korea, New Zealand, the United Kingdom, and the United States reported being the victim of a completed or attempted rape (Heise et al. 1994). The 1989 International Crime Survey collected data from fourteen countries in North America, Europe, and Australia. They found that 2.3 percent of women in the United States reported sexual assault (including rape and attempted rape), the highest percentage of any of the fourteen countries. Canada and Australia followed with 1.7 percent and 1.6 percent, respectively (Dijk, Mayhew, and Killias 1991).

Cross-nationally, acquaintance, date, and marital rape seem to be more common than stranger rape. Similar to research conducted in the United States, research in Chile, Peru, Malaysia, Mexico, Panama, and Papua New Guinea indicates that most rapes are perpetrated by someone known to the victim (Heise et al. 1994).

Rape is also a common form of war violence. There is evidence that rape rates are often drastically high in war-torn nations (Human Rights Watch 1995). For example, mass rape in war has been documented in Liberia, Uganda, Peru, Cambodia, Somalia, Bosnia, and Yugoslavia (Heise et al. 1994).

Rape is a widespread international problem. In particular, date rape and marital rape are highly prevalent in many countries. Most information about the rates of rape pertains to men raping women. Sometimes men rape men and women rape women or men, but little information about incidence or prevalence is available.

Characteristics of Rape Victims and Rapists

Internationally, girls and women seem to be at greater risk for being raped than are boys and men. Little research exists on characteristics of male victims.

In the United States, African-American women and European-American women seem to be at similar risk for being raped. In comparison, Native American women may be at greater risk, and Asian-American women may be at lower risk (Tjaden and Thoennes 2000). However, more research is needed to determine whether these differences are due to social and cultural differences or to a differential willingness to report rape. Although girls and women of all ages are raped, the greatest risk occurs in their teens and early twenties, approximately between the ages of sixteen and twenty-four years (Bureau of Justice Statistics 2000). Women who were sexually abused as girls are at greater risk for rape than are those who were not abused (Muehlenhard et al. 1998; Testa and Derman 1999). Additionally, experiences with rape are correlated with high rates of alcohol consumption and engagement in casual sex (Testa and

Derman 1999). However, it is unclear whether these activities make women more vulnerable to rape or whether rape results in alcohol abuse and casual sex.

Reports from numerous countries indicate that most rapists are male, although women sometimes rape (Sarrel and Masters 1982). In the United States, most rapists are below the age of thirty and are slightly older than their victims. Rape occurs mainly between members of the same ethnic group. Compared with other men, men who rape tend to be more accepting of violence, have a more authoritarian approach to relationships, and feel more hostility toward women (Drieschner and Lange 1999).

Causes of Rape

Different rapists commit rape for different reasons, and any one rapist may rape for different reasons at different times (Muehlenhard, Danoff-Burg, and Powch 1996). Thus, no one theory can explain all rapes. However, many cultural factors seem to contribute to rape.

Commonly held myths such as these contribute to date and marital rape:

- A man must have sex to prove his masculinity;
- When women say no to sex, they really mean yes, so men should ignore women's refusals;
- If a woman engages in kissing or petting, she is obligated to engage in sexual intercourse;
- What goes on between a husband and a wife is no one else's business; and
- The man should be head of the household.

These are dangerous myths that can lead to rape (Burt 1991).

Traditional gender roles prescribing female submission and male dominance are linked to rape. In Australia, Germany, and Japan, rates of violent sexual offenses were related to national levels of dominant masculinity (Neapolitan 1997). Studies in several countries have suggested that rigid gender roles and promotion of an ideology of male toughness are related to violence against women (Heise et al. 1994; Sanday 1981).

Characteristics of the culture and gender role socialization, however, do not explain why most men do not rape, why some women rape men, or why rape occurs in gay and lesbian relationships in which both people have experienced similar gender role socialization. Individual differences are also important.

Some people hold beliefs justifying rape more strongly than others. Men who rape tend to believe more strongly in myths about rape, and they are more likely to engage in fantasies about coercive sex (Drieschner and Lange 1999). Compared with other men, rapists drink more heavily, begin having sexual experiences earlier, and are more likely to have been physically or sexually abused as children (Berkowitz 1992; Ullman; Karabatsos; and Koss 1990).

Consequences of Rape

Rape victims often suffer from postassault depression, feelings of betrayal and humiliation, problems with trust and intimacy, guilt, anxiety, fears, anger, physical problems, sexual difficulties, and lowered self-esteem in many areas of their lives (Muehlenhard; Goggins; Jones; and Satterfield 1991; Shapiro and Schwarz 1997).

Additionally, rape often results in physical injury to the victim or leads to medical difficulties (RAINN 2001; Tjaden and Thoennes 2000). For example, rape victims can contract sexually transmitted diseases from rapists. Female victims may also become pregnant (Heise et al. 1994).

In the United States, the consequences of rape have been conceptualized as post-traumatic stress disorder (PTSD), which focuses on the victim's repeatedly re-experiencing the rape (e.g., in dreams or flashbacks); feeling numb and attempting to avoid stimuli associated with the rape; and experiencing increased physiological arousal (e.g., difficulty sleeping or concentrating, outbursts of anger, or an exaggerated startle response).

In many cultures the stigma associated with rape is extremely damaging to victims. In some Asian cultures, women are driven to suicide or are killed by family members in order to relieve the family of their shame (Heise et al. 1994). Similarly, in Alexandria, Egypt, 47 percent of women murdered were killed by a family member following a rape, and almost 8 percent of all suicides were committed by women following a rape (Heise et al. 1994).

Male and female rape victims experience many of the same consequences (Mezey and King 1989). Although both genders may have difficulty seeking help from crisis intervention services or the police, men may have more because being a rape victim is inconsistent with the male stereotype. Gay and lesbian rape victims may have greater difficulty than heterosexuals obtaining help from social service agencies, which are often not publicized for or geared toward gay and lesbian clients (Waterman, Dawson, and Bologna 1989).

Rape Prevention

There are many approaches to rape prevention. One approach has been to warn women not to go out alone at night, talk to strangers, or wear certain types of clothing. Unfortunately, such advice limits women's freedom and is ineffective because it is based on the myth that most rapists are strangers.

Another approach involves self-defense training. This approach has the advantage of helping women defend themselves while not limiting their freedom. Active resistance strategies such as physically fighting, yelling, screaming, and fleeing are generally more effective in resisting rape attempts than more passive strategies such as begging, pleading, or crying; furthermore, these active strategies do not seem to increase a woman's chance of being injured (Zoucha-Jensen and Coyne 1993).

Particularly on college campuses in the United States, attempts have been made to create educational rape prevention programs to change attitudes that seem to contribute to rape among young adults. There is some evidence that such programs may effectively reduce students' beliefs in myths about rape (e.g., Pinzone-Glover, Gidycz, and Jacobs 1998). However, more research is needed to determine whether changes in attitude are maintained and to determine whether changes in attitude result in changes in rape rates among program participants.

Most important is the need to address the causes of rape. Working for gender equality and against the ideas that violence against women is sexy and that violence is a good way to solve problems could help to decrease the prevalence of rape. Both men and women can work for changes in the media, laws, and public opinion so that rape is treated as unacceptable, even when it occurs within dating or family relationships.

See also: ABORTION; CHILD ABUSE: SEXUAL ABUSE; FAMILY ROLES; GRIEF, LOSS, AND BEREAVEMENT; POSTTRAUMATIC STRESS DISORDER (PTSD); POWER: MARITAL RELATIONSHIPS; SEXUALLY TRANSMITTED DISEASES; SPOUSE ABUSE: PREVALENCE; SPOUSE ABUSE: THEORETICAL EXPLANATIONS; SUICIDE; WAR/POLITICAL VIOLENCE

Bibliography

Berkowitz, A. (1992). "College Men as Perpetrators of Acquaintance Rape and Sexual Assault: A Review of Recent Research." *Journal of American College Health* 40:175–181.

Bureau of Justice Statistics. (2000). *Sourcebook of Criminal Justice Statistics, 1999.* Washington, DC: U.S. Government Printing Office.

Burt, M. R. (1991). "Rape Myths and Acquaintance Rape." In *Acquaintance Rape: The Hidden Crime,* ed. A. Parrot and L. Bechhofer. New York: John Wiley and Sons.

Drieschner, K., and Lange, A. (1999). "A Review of Cognitive Factors in the Etiology of Rape: Theories, Empirical Studies, and Implications." *Clinical Psychology Review* 19:57–77.

Heise, L. L.; Raikes, A.; Watts, C. H.; and Zwi, A. B. (1994). "Violence Against Women: A Neglected Public Health Issue in Less Developed Countries." *Social Science and Medicine* 39:1165–1179.

Human Rights Watch. (1995). *The Human Rights Watch Global Report on Women's Human Rights.* New York: Author.

Mezey, G., and King, M. (1989). "The Effects of Sexual Assault on Men: A Survey of 22 Victims." *Psychological Medicine* 19:205–209.

Muehlenhard, C. L.; Danoff-Burg, S.; and Powch, I. G. (1996). "Is Rape Sex or Violence? Conceptual Issues and Implications." In *Sex, Power, Conflict: Feminist and Evolutionary Perspectives,* ed. D. M. Buss and N. Malamuth. New York: Oxford University Press.

Muehlenhard, C. L.; Goggins, M. F.; Jones, J. M.; and Satterfield, A. T. (1991). "Sexual Violence and Coercion in Close Relationships." In *Sexuality in Close Relationships,* ed. K. McKinney and S. Sprecher. Hillsdale, NJ: Erlbaum.

Muehlenhard, C. L.; Highby, B. J.; Lee, R. S.; Bryan, T. S.; and Dodrill, W. A. (1998). "The Sexual Revictimization of Women and Men Sexually Abused as Children: A Review of the Literature." *Annual Review of Sex Research* 9:1–47.

Muehlenhard, C. L., and Kimes, L. A. (1999). "The Social Construction of Violence: The Case of Sexual and Domestic Violence." *Personality and Social Psychology Review* 3:234–245.

Muehlenhard, C. L.; Powch, I. G.; Phelps, J. L.; and Giusti, L. M. (1992). "Definitions of Rape: Scientific and Political Implications." *Journal of Social Issues* 48(1):23–44.

Muehlenhard, C. L.; Sympson, S. C.; Phelps, J. L.; and Highby, B. J. (1994). "Are Rape Statistics Exaggerated? A Response to Criticism of Contemporary Rape Research." *The Journal of Sex Research* 31:144–146.

Neapolitan, J. L. (1997). *Cross-National Crime: A Research Review and Sourcebook.* Westport, CT: Greenwood.

Pinzone-Glover, H. A.; Gidycz, C. A.; and Jacobs, C. D. (1998). "An Acquaintance Rape Prevention Program: Effects on Attitudes Toward Women, Rape Related Attitudes, and Perceptions of Rape Scenarios." *Psychology of Women Quarterly* 22:605–621.

Sanday, P. R. (1981). "The Socio-Cultural Context of Rape: A Cross-Cultural Study." *Journal of Social Issues* 37(4):5–27.

Sarrel, P. M., and Masters, W. H. (1982). "Sexual Molestation of Men by Women." *Archives of Sexual Behavior* 11:117–131.

Shapiro, B. L., and Schwarz, J. C. (1997). "Date Rape: Its Relationship to Trauma Symptoms and Sexual Self-Esteem." *Journal of Interpersonal Violence* 12:407–419.

Testa, M., and Dermen, K. H. (1999). "The Differential Correlates of Sexual Coercion and Rape." *Journal of Interpersonal Violence* 14:548–561.

Tjaden, P., and Thoennes, N. (2000). *Extent, Nature, and Consequences of Intimate Partner Violence: Findings From the National Violence Against Women Survey* (NCJ181867). Washington, DC: U.S. Department of Justice, National Institute of Justice.

Ullman, S. E.; Karabatsos, G.; and Koss, M. P. (1999). "Alcohol and Sexual Assault in a National Sample of College Women." *Journal of Interpersonal Violence* 14:603–625.

van Dijk, J. J. M.; Mayhew, P.; and Killias, M. (1991). *Experiences of Crime Across the World.* Boston: Kluwer Law and Taxation Press.

Waterman, C. K.; Dawson, L. J.; and Bologna, M. J. (1989). "Sexual Coercion in Gay Male and Lesbian Relationships." *Journal of Sex Research* 26:118–124.

Zoucha-Jensen, J. M., and Coyne, A. (1993). "The Effects of Resistance Strategies on Rape." *American Journal of Public Health* 83:1633–1634.

Other Resource

"RAINN Statistics." (2001). *Rape, Abuse, & Incest National Network.* Washington, DC. Available from http://www.rainn.org/statistics.html.

ZOË D. PETERSON
CHARLENE L. MUEHLENHARD

RELATIONSHIP DISSOLUTION

Relationship dissolution refers to the process of the breaking up of relationships (friendship, romantic, or marital relationships) by the voluntary activity of at least one partner. Such a definition excludes such eventualities as bereavement and refers to the conscious and intentional ending of relationships. Nonetheless, there is some dispute about the nature of "intentionality" and whether to include those relationships that end simply by default (e.g., friends who drift apart and purposely just let their contacts drop off) or incompetence (e.g., inability of one partner to be supportive or disclosive or to handle intimacy). This entry will focus on cases where one or other person purposefully ends a relationship. It does not deal with friendship breakup, because this happens largely by (one of) the parties just allowing the relationship to wither on the vine. In romantic or marital relationships, such neglect is not normally enough to end relationships and they must typically be *declared* to have ended not only by the activities of the partners themselves but also by some formal action recognized by society at large, such as divorce or separation. Such declarations render both partners "available" again for similar sorts of relationships with new partners.

Older scholarly models of dissolution (Davis 1973) tended to look for "causes" of breakup and tried to locate them in the partners or the processes of the relationships. Thus some explanations rested on the mismatch of characteristics of partners (their personalities were not compatible), flaws in mechanics of relationships (there was too much conflict), and dissolution as "sudden death" (an event created by the precipitate and inconsiderate action of one partner). Such accounts tended to treat the breakup as an event, announced by one partner to the other or brought about at a particular time by a specific occurrence or by the final

recognition that incompatibility was insuperable. *Social Penetration Theory* (Altman and Taylor 1973) has suggested that breakdown of relationships is something like the development of relationships, only backwards, such that partners gradually withdraw from the relationship in ways similar to those in which they enter the relationship. Later work (Johnson 1982) considered the accoutrements to such an event and noted the effects of such *barrier forces* as the presence of children on marriage and the ways in which partners may first consider the effects of divorce on their children rather than on their own personal feelings alone. Some research suggested that fears of neighbors' and family's reactions might outweigh the unhappiness felt in a relationship and so the partners would soldier on.

The above views all take it as a given that a divorce is a "failed" relationship, and that a breakup is inherently a bad thing that violates social expectations about the nature of marriage and romance. Although there are different views on this in the research, many researchers now see the rescuing of individuals from otherwise bad relationships (such as abusive marriages) as a success rather than a failure. Such approaches have tended to move away from the simple equation of endurance of a marriage as a measure of its success, although our society specifically continues to equate stamina with accomplishment (for example, by celebrating twenty-fifth, fiftieth, and sixtieth wedding anniversaries). However, people facing the prospect of divorce or breakup very often must contend with the added stress of the feeling that they have somehow "failed" if their relationship is ended. This sense is often based in the normativity of "couplehood" and the fact that by a certain age or stage in life a person is "expected" to have a stable life partner.

More recently, scholars have chosen to examine the long-term processes of separating and the ways in which third parties (children, relatives, friends) inflect the whole process. These models of dissolution recognize that a relationship always takes place within a set of other relationships: members of any given couple know other people, have their own relatives and friends, and are likely to discuss their relationship problems and successes with these people. These networks of other folks can be powerful influences on whether and how the relationship between the couple breaks up. For example, acquaintances and friends may bring out standard advice that there are always difficulties in marriages and that these will often pass away with time, or, alternatively, they may reveal that they did not ever like the partner and could not understand how the marriage would work out anyway!

Another thread of research is to treat dissolution as something negotiated over time between partners, and involving strategies by which partners persuade one another out of the relationship. Such proposals treat dissolution as a complex and multifaceted activity with several phases and aspects, and, in particular, treat dissolution as partly a network activity (or at least as an activity involving outsiders also). Such approaches focus less on the relationship difficulties that led to the wish to separate and more on the ways in which dissolution is managed. Such researchers note that everyone has a *social face,* a sense of their own personal dignity and worth. These approaches treat dissolution as involving issues of *facework,* where both partners hope to come out of the experience with some sense of their own dignity sustained, so that they can make themselves available for future relationships without being seen as "damaged goods." In some cases, dissolution may be treated as a matter of *teamwork.* Here the goal is that the partners should create a dissolution that manages to leave both people with their *social faces* undamaged. For example, the partners could make clear to everyone else that they agreed amicably to split up, that they are seriously attempting to remain friends, and that neither of them was at fault: things just didn't work out.

In this account of breakup of relationships, dissolution is treated as a time-framed process extending over several episodes of interaction and not as a single event (although scholars recognize that such instant breakups do of course occur as a result of some sudden mischance). The approach here is to treat dissolution as involving strategies and choices between them. For example a partner wishing to dissolve a relationship may simply announce *Bald On Record* (i.e. without redress) that the relationship is over, although this does not in itself mean that the partner will accept the news quietly or without debate. Another strategy used in breakups is to convince the partner that a mature and intelligent person would see that it is in her or his best interests to breakup (*positive altercasting*). Gerry Miller and Mac Parks (1982) listed

sixteen different strategies like this that could be used by persons wishing to convince another person to let them go.

A major development in more recent approaches to relationship dissolution is to treat dissolution as an integral part of the partners' lives and activities, not as a separate process. This development sees the negotiations and completion of a breakup as something intimately intertwined with the other projects and activities that the two people conduct in their daily lives, involving the same sorts of conversational processes.

Duck's Model

Steve Duck (1998, 1982) suggested that the dissolution of relationships is an extended process composed of several different parts, which might be either sequential or compounded. In this approach the breakup of a relationship is not simply an event that occurs and to which two partners react. Rather it is a long-term psychological process involving internal reflection, discussion with a partner, consultation with social networks, and the creation of personally satisfying stories about the history of the relationship from beginning to end.

The first *Intrapsychic Phase* of this process involves an individual brooding on the fact that the relationship is not satisfactory in some way from his or her perspective. Although the complaints may be voiced to other people, the point here is that the persons complained *to* do not personally know the partner complained *of.* The point of this stage is mostly to vent (for example, to a hairdresser, bartender, or distant colleague at work), but not to convey to the partner that dissatisfaction is felt. Such dissatisfaction may be about such things as partner's habits, feeling trapped in a relationship, a sense of injustice about distribution of effort, or a sense of hopelessness about resolution of an argument. In fact nothing more may come of the brooding: The person feels a sense of grievance but does not necessarily proceed to the next stage if the process of venting or reflection is adequate to relieve the sense of negativity about the relationship. Such brooding may be a recurrent activity, and probably occurs in most relationships at some time or another without leading to breakup. Alternatively, if the brooding Intrapsychic Phase does not result in satisfaction of the grievance by itself then the person moves to the next stage.

The *Dyadic Phase* emerges when the couple is confronted with the dissatisfaction experienced by one or both partners such that the dyad needs to discuss and evaluate it. Again, such discussions can be constructive and might lead to a rapprochement in the relationship or they can be threatening and unpleasant. Likewise, they could be recurrent complaints extended over a long period or sudden announcements of new concerns. Such discussion might be a shock to one partner, but in any case, it is likely that each person will be confronted with unknown perspectives on the relationship presented by the other person. Each person will have a view of the relationship and when challenged to present it as an individual, the person may break ranks from the usual points of view of the relationship that both members of the couple have previously shared. The tenor and outcome of the Dyadic Phase will be a large factor in the way that things proceed from it. One person may be determined to leave and proceed to do so, or both may want to give things another shot. It is only if things proceed to the next stage that the relationship gets into very serious difficulty that begins an almost unstoppable process of dissolution.

The next phase, a *Social Phase,* involves the social networks in which the dyad is necessarily embedded—all those other people whose lives intertwine with the couple or one of its members. Such people are not neutral observers but tend to comment on relationships and on the ways in which they are conducted, voicing opinions and common wisdom about how people "should" react to marital transgressions or to difficulties in relationships. Any dyad needs to exist within such groups and is therefore accountable to them to some extent. Such accounting, advice, and comparison go on throughout a relationship, not only when it is in trouble, but also are particularly important when a relationship hits the rocks. Dyad members then urgently consult with their associates to account for the breakdown of the relationship, or receive advice on how to stay together and deal with the difficulties. At this point, however, the breakdown becomes a social event—not merely something between the two members of the couple—and therefore becomes "official." As soon as other people know that the relationship is broken up then either partner becomes socially available as a partner to new people. However, it is important to note that the breakup of a given dyad in a relationship network has fallout for other relationships also. Relationships with couple friends, the partner's work associates, the partner's family, and so on may all dissolve because of the termination of the primary relationship. Of course, relationship dissolution creates a psychological toll on one or both members, members of the network (who do not want to see the relationship end), and children. Rarely does a relationship end that has no consequence for anyone else.

Last comes the *Grave-Dressing Phase.* An important and under-recognized feature of the breakup of relationships is the need for people to publish a record of the relationship and its death. For various reasons, both psychological and social, people "need" to justify themselves to other people and, in particular, to offer an account of the breakup that shows them in a favorable light relative to relational standards in the society. Such stories typically suggest that the breakup was inevitable and necessary for the person to bring about, or else maturely and mutually agreed, or else that the speaker was somehow duped or betrayed by the other person. Such stories serve a social function in placing the speaker in a good light that does not negatively affect their "face" for future relationships, as well as indicating that they are thinking and mature relaters—or innocent victims—who have learned a useful lesson. This sort of story is important for those people who seek to negotiate future relationships of a similar sort to the one lost. It is important that people are not perceived as irresponsible partners, damaged goods, or relationally naïve, all of which would be negative characteristics to take into a future relationship.

Relationships after Breakup

When researchers have examined relationships of couples after divorce or breakup they have most often examined the relationships of noncustodial parents with their children, although there is also work on the consequences of broken dating relationships (e.g., Metts, Cupach, and Bejlovec 1989). Most research suggests that relationships between ex-spouses have typically been acrimonious or difficult but the existence of children gives them little choice about meeting. If they take their roles as parents seriously then they will need to continue to interact in order to consider and discuss the future of the children or to see one another at social or educational events involving the children. Recent research has shown a more complicated picture with several examples of good relationships between ex-partners, some of whom report closer friendships after divorce than when they were married. Many people stay friends after the end of their romance and discover that one of the most difficult tasks is to work out a plausible account of their current friendship to tell other people. They must find a way in which to handle people's typical suspicion that the friendship is really a disguised sexual relationship. Such recent evidence strongly suggests that the process of relationship dissolution is not simply an emotional decision but a long-term process with consequences for accounting to other people.

Conclusion

Breakup of relationships should not be seen as a single event or an individual choice but a long-term process involving negotiation and communication between not only the partners themselves but also the rest of the network within which the relationship is conducted.

See also: COMMUNICATION: COUPLE RELATIONSHIPS; CONFLICT: COUPLE RELATIONSHIPS; DIVORCE: EFFECTS ON COUPLE; DIVORCE MEDIATION; EQUITY; INFIDELITY; SOCIAL NETWORKS

Bibliography

Altman, I., and Taylor, D. (1973). *Social Penetration: The Development of Interpersonal Relationships.* New York: Holt, Rinehart and Winston.

Battaglia, D. M.; Richard, F. D.; Datteri, D. L.; and Lord, C. G. (1998). "Breaking Up is (Relatively) Easy to Do: A Script of the Dissolution of Close Relationships." *Journal of Social and Personal Relationships* 15(6):829–845.

Davis, M. S. (1973). *Intimate Relations.* New York: Free Press.

Duck, S. W. (1982). "A Topography of Relationship Disengagement and Dissolution." In *Personal Relationships 4: Dissolving Personal Relationships,* ed. S. W. Duck. London: Academic Press.

Duck, S. W. (1998). *Human Relationships,* 3rd edition. Newbury Park, CA: Sage.

Johnson, M. (1982). "Social and Cognitive Features of Dissolving Commitment to Relationships." In *Personal Relationships 4: Dissolving Personal Relationships,* ed. S. W. Duck. London: Academic Press.

Metts, S.; Cupach, W. R.; and Bejlovec, R. A. (1989). "'I Love You Too Much to Ever Start Liking You.'" *Journal of Social and Personal Relationships* 6:259–274.

Miller, G. R., and Parks, M. R. (1982). "Communication in Dissolving Relationships." In *Personal Relationships 4: Dissolving Personal Relationships,* ed. S. W. Duck. London: Academic Press.

O'Connor, T. G; Pickering, K.; Dunn, J.; and Goldin, J. (1999). "Frequency and Predictors of Relationship Dissolution in a Community Sample in England." *Journal of Family Psychology* 13(3):436–499.

Specher, S., and Fehr, B. (1998). "The Dissolution of Close Relationships." In *Perspectives on Loss: A Sourcebook. Death, Dying, and Bereavement,* ed. J. H. Harvey. Philadelphia: Brunner/Mazel.

STEVE DUCK
STEPHANIE ROLLIE

RELATIONSHIP INITIATION

Romantic relationships and marriages have to start somewhere. People need to meet, find one another attractive and interesting, and decide to move further into a relationship.

Why do people initiate relationships in the first place? Research suggests that four reasons are especially important. First, individuals initiate relationships with those they see as attractive. Physical appearance is a critical cue in forming first impressions. When people are in social settings where they are likely to meet a potential partner, they worry a great deal about their appearance. Some evidence in the field of evolutionary psychology suggests that males view the physical attractiveness of potential partners as more important than do females (Buss 1989; Sprecher, Sullivan, and Hatfield 1994), but it is clear that both men and women see appearance as an important criterion for meeting others (Berscheid and Walster 1974; Hatfield and Sprecher 1986). Second, individuals tend to develop relationships based on proximity. People are far more likely to meet, date, and marry someone who is geographically close to them than someone who lives a great distance away. Third, individuals often initiate relationships with partners who are useful to them. For instance, someone may pursue a relationship with a medical specialist not because of her attractiveness or proximity, but because she knows things that individual needs to know. Finally, people develop relationships with others because humans are naturally social. Being alone, for long periods of time, is not appealing to most people. Indeed, most individuals see solitary confinement as a particularly cruel form of punishment.

Theories of Relationship Initiation

More than thirty years ago, Irwin Altman and Dalmas Taylor (1973) explored how people come to know one another. Their explorations led them to develop *Social Penetration Theory*. Social Penetration Theory portrays relationship development as like an onion—suggesting that when individuals "peel off" one layer of information about a relational partner, there is always another layer. Altman and Taylor noted that as people become acquainted, their relationship becomes broader and deeper. When individuals first meet, they exchange very impersonal information and limit the number of different topics they discuss. As they come to know and trust one another more, they will explore more topics (breadth) and share more intimate information about those topics (depth). An enduring romantic relationship would be marked by both breadth and depth. A "spring break fling" typically is one that has great depth but little breadth. Long-term neighbors might share much breadth but little depth.

How do people decide to move from acquaintanceship to an enduring, deep relationship? Drawing from Social Exchange Theories (Burgess and Huston 1979; Homans 1961; Thibaut and Kelley 1959), Altman and Taylor tell us that people move further into a relationship as long as the perceived rewards associated with the relationship exceed the costs. Individuals first meet. If the exchange is pleasing, they continue the relationship. If it is not, they stop. People are constantly calibrating their ratio of rewards and costs. In some relationships, one or both partners may reach a point where they say "that's far enough; this is fun, but if we get any closer, bad things might happen." At that point, partners will not move to deepen or broaden their relationship any further. According to Social Exchange Theories, in addition to assessing how rewarding their relationships are, individuals also consider what other alternative relationships might be available to them and how those potential relationships compare to their current one.

In 1975, Charles Berger and Richard Calabrese expanded Altman and Taylor's notion of social penetration. Berger and Calabrese suggested that during acquaintanceship people try to reduce their uncertainty about one another. When individuals first meet, they discuss relatively innocuous items—the weather, where they are from, what they do for a living (Berger et al. 1976). Normally, people do not discuss highly charged personal matters such as their fears, anxieties, or fantasies. As their relationship progresses, individuals begin exchanging more intimate information because they have come to "know" each other. Their uncertainty about each other has faded.

Gerald Miller and Mark Steinberg (1975) added to these ideas by suggesting that in relationships individuals make predictions about each other based on three types of information: cultural, sociological, and psychological. Cultural information typically provides only a very general level of prediction: People anticipate how an individual will act based upon his or her culture. There is still a great deal of uncertainty at this level. Sociological information emphasizes a person's group memberships. Someone may make predictions about a person based on the knowledge that the individual is a college freshman, came from a large city, is majoring in mathematics, and plays the violin. Sociological information offers better predictability than cultural information, but it is still stereotypic. Most people who are acquaintances know each other at the sociological level. When individuals know someone at the psychological level, they know him or her so well as to understand how that person differs from the groups he or she belongs to. Thus, for example, someone might know that one of his or her friends plays the violin, loves math, and comes from a big city, but also that the friend is only happy when he is hiking in the wilderness. The fact that the friend is devoted to hiking shows how he is unique or different from individuals in most of the social groups he belongs to. People know relatively few individuals at the psychological level because to know someone at this level requires a great deal of communication. It is important to note that relationships, over time, can exist at different levels of prediction. A college senior may discover that her parents really only know her at the sociological level when once they knew everything about her (i.e., they knew her at the psychological level).

The theories of Altman and Taylor, Berger and Calabrese, and Miller and Steinberg are helpful in understanding the underlying processes involved in relationship development. People meet and try to reduce their uncertainty about each other; they continue to get to know each other as long as their interactions are more pleasurable than punishing, and as long as the alternatives available to them are not as palatable as what they currently have.

Stages of Relationship Development

Other specialists have taken a different tack in describing relationship development. Mark Knapp and Anita Vangelisti (2000) have proposed that relationships go through certain stages from first meeting to deep intimacy. The first stage is labeled the *initiating* stage. This is when people initially meet and assess each other's attractiveness and availability. At this point in the relationship, people work very hard to present themselves as likeable and interesting. They tend to select their words with caution, knowing that a single mistake (e.g., asking someone about a sensitive topic) may spoil their chances to continue a conversation.

The second stage in Knapp and Vangelisti's formulation is the *experimenting* stage. This is the time people attempt to reduce their uncertainty about one another. In this stage people may begin testing one another. Indeed, some researchers have argued that people use "secret tests" to evaluate the other's interest in them and in the relationship (Baxter and Wilmot 1984). Is she polite to me? Does he laugh at my jokes? Does she respect the limits I put on intimacy? At the start of any relationship individuals have certain expectations about what should, and should not, happen. Others need to meet those expectations or people often decide not to spend more time with them. For instance, in the early stages of a relationship most individuals expect the other person to be upbeat and positive (not morose and depressed), to look good (not dress sloppily), and to be polite (not boorish). If, on a first date, a person is depressed, sloppy, and boorish, that individual is unlikely to get a second date.

Assuming the other person passes the initial tests, one moves on to the *intensifying* stage. In this stage, partners start disclosing extremely personal information to one another, they develop nicknames for each other, and often talk using the word "we." Couples develop routines and private symbols (e.g., "our special place," a nonverbal cue that means we like each other) and become more willing to make direct verbal statements of commitment. It is at this stage when couples move from saying "I really like you" to "I really love you." The intensifying stage is often a very passionate time in the relationship. Partners are highly attracted to each other and they find themselves thinking about each other all the time. They often idealize each other, even finding flaws in the other person particularly attractive (e.g., "I love those little handlebars that wrap around your tummy").

The fourth stage in Knapp and Vangelisti's model is called the *integrating* stage. This is the time when the two individuals become a couple. They emphasize to themselves, and others, how much they share in common—they are certain that they share similar attitudes, interests, and opinions. Their network of friends begins to merge and they often develop friendships with other couples. They start sharing property: The CD player is no longer "mine" but is now "ours." They also start to share what scholars call *intimacy trophies* (e.g., the room key to the first hotel they stayed at together).

If all goes well, at some point, couples move to the fifth, and final, stage of relationship development, that of *bonding*. The bonding stage is marked by a public ritual, typically marriage. Couples' willingness to engage in this sort of public commitment signifies their desire to obtain social and sometimes even institutional support for their relationship. After bonding, the two people are publicly tied to one another.

Obviously, the five-stage model offered by Knapp and Vangelisti simplifies what is a very complex process. In fact, Knapp and Vangelisti argue that in real life, people in relationships may skip stages, repeatedly move back and forth between stages, or even move backwards from a more advanced stage to one that appears to be less advanced. Throughout the development of their relationship, couples make decisions about whether to stay at one stage, move forward, or end the relationship.

Relationship Openers

Some of the more interesting work done on the early stages of relationship development has highlighted the "pick-up" process. Sociologist Murray

Davis (1973) suggests that there are several steps in the typical "pick up." First, people assess how "qualified" the other is. Individuals hoping to meet a potential partner try to show their qualifications. Davis breaks qualifications into two sorts: extraordinary and esoteric. Extraordinary qualifiers are special objects or characteristics people have that make them both attractive and different from others. For instance, a young man might walk into a party wearing a lapel pin of the Olympic gold medal that he won a year ago. Very few people have such a pin, yet most people know what it signifies. Esoteric qualifiers are a bit different. While they are distinctive, like extraordinary ones, they are not recognizable by most people. Only those who share a common interest, knowledge base, or experience would recognize how impressive an esoteric qualifier is. For example, a woman may enter a social environment in her military uniform, wearing a prestigious ribbon that signifies exceptional bravery. Few people in the room would have any idea what the ribbon signifies, but for the few who do, it is an important qualifier.

The next step noted by Davis is that the two people have to assess each other's availability. A man who is wearing a wedding ring and who enters a social situation with his arm around a woman probably is not available for a romantic encounter. Similarly, a woman who is involved in a serious conversation with two or three close friends may not be perceived as interested in starting a romantic relationship.

After assessing the availability of a potential partner, Davis suggests that people have to find opening lines—they have to figure out a way to begin a conversation. Psychologist Chris Kleinke (1981) collected hundreds of "pick-up" lines and categorized them into three clusters: (1) cute/flip (e.g., "You know, all my friends think you'll never spend the night with me. Want to help me out by showing them how wrong they are?"); (2) innocuous (e.g., "Excuse me, do you know what time it is?"); and (3) direct (e.g., "Hi, I happened to notice you coming in. Do you come here often?"). Kleinke found that both men and women prefer the latter two sorts of lines to the cute/flippant sort. Most opening lines do not really reveal what the person uttering them actually is thinking. Asking someone for the time, or querying them about how frequently they come to the bar, is not what people really want to know. What they are trying to do is start a conversation.

Assuming that the opening line works, Davis notes that the next step is finding an integrative topic—something that both individuals can easily discuss (e.g., the weather, the entertainment, the traffic). If people cannot find an integrative topic, the conversation quickly grinds to an uncomfortable halt. Davis's final step in first meeting someone is the scheduling of a second encounter. This is when individuals see whether the other person would like to meet again and ask if they can have the other person's phone number.

Strategies that Influence Relationship Initiation

Davis's description of the steps people take to "pick up" a relational partner suggests that individuals actively engage in behaviors to initiate relationships. Relationships, in other words, do not just happen. People encourage relationships to develop by observing potential partners, approaching them, and starting conversations with them.

Robert Bell and John Daly (1984) further suggest that people intentionally engage in strategies to generate affinity. That is to say, individuals do things to make themselves attractive and likable to others. Traditionally, attraction had been seen as a passive variable: People were either attractive or unattractive; others either were drawn to them or they were not. By contrast, Bell and Daly argued that there are a number of strategies individuals employ to get others to like them. Using a four step conceptual model (antecedent factors, constraints, strategic activity, target response), these researchers identified strategies people typically use to actively initiate relationships. The many strategies clustered into seven: focusing on commonalities (e.g., highlighting similarities, demonstrating equality), showing self-involvement (e.g., finding ways of regularly "running into" the other), involving the other (e.g., participating in activities the other person enjoys, including the other in activities), demonstrating caring and concern (e.g., listening, being altruistic), displaying politeness (e.g., letting the other have control over plans, acting interested), encouraging mutual trust (e.g., being honest, being reliable), and demonstrating control and visibility (e.g., being dynamic, looking good). The formulation Bell and Daly offer provides a catalog of rules for the active initiation of relationships. For instance, people beginning a relationship should be polite, demonstrate interest in the other person, try to look attractive, and so on. Indeed, later work by Vangelisti and Daly (1997) on relationship standards suggests that people are dissatisfied when their partners fail to meet their expectations. Like Bell and Daly's affinity seeing strategies, expectations or standards provide information about rules for relationships.

The communication processes people go through in meeting and engaging the interest of another are a vital part of any relationship. If social interaction is rewarding and successful, a relationship may progress into permanency. If it is awkward and uncomfortable, what might have been a promising relationship may not happen.

See also: ATTRACTION; COMMUNICATION: COUPLE RELATIONSHIPS; DATING; DIALECTICAL THEORY; INTIMACY; MATE SELECTION; SOCIAL EXCHANGE THEORY; SOCIAL NETWORK; TRUST

Bibliography

Altman, I., and Taylor, D. A. (1973). *Social Penetration: The Development of Interpersonal Relationships.* New York: Holt, Rinehart & Winston.

Baxter, L. A., and Wilmot, W. (1984). "'Secret Tests': Social Strategies for Acquiring Information About the State of the Relationship." *Human Communication Research* 11:171–201.

Bell, R. A., and Daly, J. A. (1984). "The Affinity-Seeking Function of Communication." *Communication Monographs* 51:91–115.

Berger, C. R., and Calabrese, R. J. (1976). "Toward a Developmental Theory of Interpersonal Communication." *Human Communication Research* 1:99–112.

Berger, C. R.; Gardner, R. R.; Clatterbuck, G. W.; and Schulman, L. S. (1976). "Perceptions of Information Sequencing in Relationship Development." *Human Communication Research* 3:34–39.

Berscheid, E., and Walster, E. (1974). "Physical Attractiveness." In *Advances in Experimental Social Psychology,* ed. L. Berkowitz. New York: Academic Press.

Burgess, R. L., and Huston, T. L., eds. (1979). *Social Exchange in Developing Relationships.* New York: Academic Press.

Buss, D. M. (1989). "Sex Differences in Human Mate Preferences: Evolutionary Hypotheses Tested in 37 Cultures." *Behavioral and Brain Sciences* 12:1–49.

Davis, M. (1973). *Intimate Relations.* New York: Free Press.

Hatfield, E., and Sprecher, S. (1986). *Mirror, Mirror: The Importance of Looks in Everyday Life.* Albany: State University of New York Press.

Homans, G. C. (1961). *Social Behavior: Its Elementary Forms.* New York: Harcourt.

Knapp, M. L., and Vangelisti, A. L. (2000). *Interpersonal Communication and Human Relationships.* Boston: Allyn and Bacon.

Miller, G. R., and Steinberg, M. (1975). *Between People: A New Analysis of Interpersonal Communication.* Palo Alto, CA: Science Research Associates.

Sprecher, S.; Sullivan, Q.; and Hatfield, E. (1994). "Mate Selection Preferences: Gender Differences Examined in a National Sample." *Journal of Personality and Social Psychology* 66:1074–1080.

Thibaut, J. W., and Kelley, H. H. (1959). *The Social Psychology of Groups.* New York: John Wiley & Sons.

Vangelisti, A. L., and Daly, J. A. (1997). "Gender Differences in Standards for Romantic Relationships." *Personal Relationships* 4:203–219.

ANITA L. VANGELISTI
JOHN A. DALY

RELATIONSHIP MAINTENANCE

Scholars define *relational maintenance* in various ways (Dindia and Canary 1993; Montgomery 1993). At the most basic level, relational maintenance refers to a variety of behaviors used by partners in an effort to stay together. Accordingly, researchers would examine relational longevity or *stability*. At a second level, relational maintenance means engaging in behaviors that help to sustain the *quality* of the relationship. In other words, being together and stable is not enough—one must also consider the quality of the relationship. Thus, maintenance researchers would be interested in examining relational properties such as satisfaction, love, and trust. A third definition of relational maintenance refers to keeping the relationship *status quo*. This definition would point to keeping a particular stage or state (e.g., keeping the current level of intimacy, keeping a friendship platonic). Fourth, maintenance refers to *repair*. This definition leads one to examine how people overcome problems and (perhaps) transgressions. Finally, maintenance refers to managing the *dialectical tensions* that naturally occur in every close involvement. For example, researchers investigate how people manage their desires for feeling connected to someone while also having an independent identity.

These alternative definitions point to behaviors that function differently to keep close relationships stable, satisfying, in a particular state, and in repair despite natural tensions that inhere in close involvements. This entry briefly highlights research that has examined relational maintenance using each of the alternative definitions (see Canary and Zelley 2000 for a review of alternative research programs on relational maintenance).

Maintaining Stability

For many people, relational longevity equals success. Certainly, silver and golden wedding anniversaries symbolize success. They also reflect years of interaction patterns that have somehow led to stability. Perhaps the most widely cited research with regard to predicting stability comes from the work of John Gottman (1994). Gottman emphasizes behaviors that determine whether or not a couple gets divorced.

Gottman's (1994) theory of marital success versus failure reflects a causal process model that specifies alternative paths that satisfied versus dissatisfied married partners take. Specifically, Gottman argues that marital partners' negative message behavior causes a shift in perceptions of each other that lead to unfavorable beliefs about the partner. In particular, negative message behavior (e.g., sarcasm, accusations) predicts relational instability; conversely, the ratio of positive-to-negative messages indicates stability. Whereas stable couples have a 5:1 positive-to-negative message ratio, unstable couples enact a 1:1 positive-to-negative message ratio. Unstable couples, however, exhibit an equal number of positive and negative messages. According to Gottman, negative conflict behaviors lead to negative emotional reactions. Called the "Four Horsemen of the Apocalypse," these four behaviors are deadly and are believed to occur in a general sequence; initially, partners complain/criticize, which leads to contempt, which leads to defensiveness, which leads to stonewalling (Gottman 1994).

Differences between stable and unstable couples also are evident in the attributions made regarding partners' negative behavior (Gottman 1994). For example, stable partners rely on positive or benign attributions to explain negative behaviors (e.g., he is tired, she has been under a lot of pressure). Unstable partners, on the other hand, explain the causes of their problems using hostile attributions, or explanations that reflect internal, stable, global, and intentional features of the partner (e.g., he is self-centered, which also explains why he never calls when he is late). Once hostile attributions are in place, partners tend to distance themselves from one another, re-cast the history of the marriage, and, finally, separate.

The primary strategies for maintaining stability would be to use cooperative messages, avoid negative reciprocity, and attempt to explain the partner's negative behavior using benign attributions. If one cannot alter defensive beliefs about the partner, then the assistance of a marital counselor, therapist, or spiritual leader would appear to be in order.

Maintaining Quality

For many people, simply staying together is not sufficient; instead, the quality of the relationship is important. For researchers, this means examining behaviors that are linked to relational satisfaction and other indicators of quality. Laura Stafford and Daniel J. Canary (1991) set out to determine a finite set of behaviors that would lead to increases in relational quality. By *quality,* Stafford and Canary referred to satisfaction, trust, control mutuality (i.e., the extent to which both partners agreed on who has the right to influence the other), and commitment. Using various methods, these authors uncovered a finite set of relational maintenance behaviors.

Stafford and Canary (1991) derived five relational maintenance strategies, or approaches to keeping the relationship in a satisfactory condition. These strategies are *positivity,* or being cheerful and upbeat, not criticizing the partner; *assurances,* such as stressing one's commitment and love; *openness,* which refers to directly discussing the nature of the relationship; *social networks,* or attempts to involve friends and family in various activities; and *sharing tasks,* which refer to doing one's fair share of chores and other work that needs to be done. Stafford and Canary found that positivity was most strongly related to satisfaction while control mutuality and assurances were most powerfully linked to commitment. These findings suggest that maintenance behaviors have varying functional utility in promoting different indicators of quality.

Relevant research has also found that perceptions of equity affect the desire to maintain quality relationships (Canary and Stafford 1992, 2001). Equity refers to whether the distribution of rewards divided by costs is fair. More precisely, an equitable relationship occurs when partners perceive the same ratio of rewards/costs. An inequitable relationship occurs when one person is overbenefited (i.e., one person perceives that, on balance, they get more than the partner does) or underbenefited (i.e., one person perceived that, on balance, they get less than the partner does). Canary and Stafford found that both self-reported maintenance strategies and perceptions of partner use of maintenance strategies were highest when the person felt the relationship was fair. However, people who felt overbenefited or underbenefited were less likely to use and perceive the use of the maintenance strategies indicated previously. In addition, self-reported inequity combined with perceptions of partners' maintenance strategies to affect important relationship characteristics, such as commitment. That is, maintenance behaviors would positively affect relational quality, but a lack of equity (especially underbenefitedness) would negatively affect relational quality.

Maintaining the Status Quo

Once a relationship has reached a particular level (e.g., a certain level of intimacy or satisfaction), people might try to sustain the *status quo*. That is, there should be no changes in the fundamental nature of the relationship. Accordingly, current levels of intimacy, for example, should remain within a predictable and low level of fluctuation around a set point. Dramatic fluctuation—whether they reflect increases or decreases in intimacy—is not desired.

Joe Ayres (1983) examined hypothetical reactions of participants who imagined that their partners wanted either to increase or decrease the level of intimacy they had. Ayers derived three maintenance strategies, or approaches to dealing with the situation: *directness,* or discussing the nature of the

relationship; *avoidance* of the partner and behaviors that might change the relationship; and *balance,* or behaving in ways that would counteract what the other person does (e.g., balance favors with favors). When imagining a partner who wanted to escalate intimacy, people reported they would use directness *and* avoidance. When imagining a partner who wanted to reduce intimacy, participants reported that they would use directness and attempt to balance the situation. Clearly, Ayres provides evidence that people respond to changes in the status quo with particular communication strategies and that these strategies might vary as a function of how the partner wants to change the status quo.

In an examination of a particular relationship context, Susan J. Messman, Daniel J. Canary, and Kimberly Hause (2000) investigated how opposite-sex friends maintained their relationships as platonic. Messman and her colleagues found that opposite-sex friends used several strategies to sustain the platonic nature of the relationship. These include *positivity* (e.g., be nice and cheerful), *support* (i.e., show one's support by comforting and giving advice), *share activity* (e.g., share routine activities), *openness* (e.g., discuss the relationship), *no flirting* (e.g., discourage familiar behaviors such as eye gazing), among others. The most commonly used strategies to keep a relationship platonic were alike for men and women: first came positivity, followed by support, share activity, openness, and no flirting.

Noting that many researchers have presumed that opposite-sex relationships are ripe with sexual tension, Messman and her colleagues (2000) also wanted to link different motives for having a platonic friendship to relational maintenance strategies. Motives included *safeguard relationship,* which refers to keeping the positive benefits afforded by the relationship (e.g., obtains information about how members of the opposite sex think); *not attracted* (e.g., never thought about the friend in a sexual manner); *third party* (e.g., the platonic friend was involved with someone else); *network disapproval* (e.g., others would disapprove of the relationship becoming romantic), as well as other less commonly reported motives. The desire to *safeguard relationship* was the strongest predictor of all the maintenance strategies. This finding underscores the power that wanting to keep a relationship in a particular state can have.

Repairing Troubled Relationships

Occasionally, there is trouble in paradise. The trouble may involve a problem that is acute (e.g., a single affair) or chronic (e.g., alcoholism). The question of how to repair a relationship that has gone through a severe test—or an ongoing series of tests—has lead various researchers to identify behaviors that function primarily to overcome problems. In terms of repairing relationships that have experienced acute problems, we turn to research on repairing a transgression. In discussing the more chronic problems, we turn to research on reactions to problems.

Not surprisingly, in romantic relationships the most offensive transgression involves sexual infidelity, followed by behaviors such as other forms of unfaithfulness, lying, physical violence, lack of trust, an unsavory past, and lack of consideration (Emmers and Canary 1996; Metts 1994). Although transgressions vary in the extent to which they challenge relational contracts, they all can raise doubts in the mind of the partner who assesses the transgression. In other words, transgressions lead to uncertainty about the person who has committed the behavior as well as about the relationship itself.

Researchers have uncovered various strategies that people use to repair a relationship following a transgression. Relying on *Uncertainly Reduction Theory* (Berger and Calabrese 1975), Tara Emmers and Canary (1996) coded relational repair strategies into four types: *passive,* which includes giving partner space, doing nothing, and simply contemplating the event; *active,* which include behaviors that do not involve the partner directly (e.g., giving gifts, asking friends to talk with partner); *interactive,* or direct discussion with the partner (e.g., apologizing, spending time together, seeking concessions); and *uncertainty acceptance,* which simply means accepting one's uncertainty by ignoring the event and possibly dating others. These authors found that partners relied on interactive behaviors most to repair their relationships. Kathryn Dindia and Leslie Baxter (1987) reported a similar finding—people tend to want to talk about issues when making attempts to repair their relationships.

In terms of which behaviors led to actual repair, less obvious results were reported. Emmers and Canary (1996) found that repair (measured in terms of retained intimacy) was greater when men did not use passive behaviors. Interestingly, women's intimacy was higher when they reported using active behaviors; however, men's intimacy was lower when their female partners reported using the same active behaviors. It appears that, to repair relationships, men should not avoid the issue and women should not attempt to use alternative sources to persuade the partner. This study also suggests that both men and women would be wise to use integrative behaviors that are direct and cooperative to repair their relationships following a transgression.

In terms of responses to everyday problems, Caryl Rusbult's *investment model* is perhaps the most widely cited (Rusbult 1987; Rusbult, Drigotas, and Verette 1994). *Commitment* is a critically important element of the model, where commitment reflects a desire to remain in the relationship and feelings of attachment. More precisely, the investment model holds that, in response to problematic events, a three-step course of action occurs. First, individuals examine their relationship in terms of its (a) rewards and costs (i.e., comparison levels, such as a previous partner); (b) quality of alternatives (e.g., number of potentials in the field); and (c) investments already made (e.g, time, money). Second, these three factors then determine how committed an individual is; higher levels of satisfaction and investment coupled with lower levels of desired alternatives should associate positively with commitment. Finally, one's commitment level then affects responses to everyday relational problems.

According to Rusbult and her colleagues (1994), reactions to problematic events involve the following factors: decision to remain with one's partner; tendencies to accommodate; derogation of alternatives; willingness to sacrifice; and perceived superiority of one's relationship. In terms of relational maintenance, the decision to remain with the partner is essential; beyond deciding to stay in the relationship, the other responses listed above may follow. Tendencies to accommodate refer to constructive minus destructive responses that people use. These responses to relational problems—exit, voice, loyalty, and neglect—vary according to their activity versus passivity as well as valence (constructive v. destructive): *exit* is active and destructive; *voice* is active and constructive; *loyalty* is passive and constructive; and *neglect* is passive and destructive. Exit behaviors include threatening the partner, intimidating the partner, and leaving;

voice entails the use of disclosure and discussion; loyalty refers to waiting and hoping for things to improve; and neglect behaviors include stonewalling and avoidance of the partner. Thus, the sum of accommodating behaviors can be reflected in voice and loyalty minus neglect and exit responses.

As one might expect, commitment is positively tied to accommodating behaviors; that is, commitment is positively associated with loyalty and voice and is negatively associated with exit and neglect. In addition, willingness to sacrifice on behalf of the partner is positively linked to one's commitment (e.g., forfeiting one's personally important activities for the partner) (Van Lange et al. 1997). Also, people engage in psychological distortion to enhance their relationships when commitment level is high. For example, people think less of relational alternatives (i.e., derogation of alternatives), especially when the alternative is attractive and one's commitment is high. In other words, a committed person is more likely to believe that her or his relationship is better than other entanglements (Rusbult et al. 1994).

In sum, people who are committed are more likely than others to remain in the relationship and engage in constructive responses to problems. Committed people also tend to derogate third party alternatives, sacrifice for the sake of the relationship, and believe that their relationship is superior to the norm. Less committed individuals have the opposite reactions to problems.

Managing Dialectical Tensions

A dialectical approach argues that relationships are dynamic entities. Consequently, partners are faced with the continuous management of opposing tendencies as they attempt to answer the question of how relationships operate in the midst of partners being drawn together as well as pushed apart. The dialectical perspective also holds that relationships cannot exist without the interplay between its contradictory parts.

A dialectical approach differs from other maintenance views. People might even find "maintenance" impossible to obtain in the face of ongoing contradiction, change, and tension. Barbara Montgomery (1993) noted that the term *maintenance* appears to counter a dialectical approach because maintenance denotes change as an anomaly

rather than as an inherent construct. Montgomery argued that dialectics involve the term relational *sustainment.*

According to a dialectical viewpoint, relational partners are said to experience three central contradictions: autonomy/connectedness, openness/closedness, and predictability/novelty (Baxter 1988). Autonomy/connectedness refers to the tension experienced due to the pull between wanting to connect as a partner and wanting to preserve an independent identity. Openness/closedness refers to the tension between desiring to engage in self-disclosure versus retaining boundaries of privacy. Predictability/novelty involves the pull between seeking behavioral patterns that have stability versus a desire for spontaneity. Fluctuation between each of these three poles is a natural and necessary task of every relational partner.

Accordingly, to sustain a relationship, partners must somehow manage these tensions. Baxter (1988) reported four primary strategies used by partners to manage these contradictions: *selection* of one pole over another (e.g., selection of autonomy over interdependence); *separation* through either cyclic alternation (e.g., women's night out) or topical segmentation (e.g., golf involves both parties but poker does not); *neutralization* through either moderation or disqualification (e.g., "I'm just going through a phase"); and *reframing,* or redefining the problem in terms of dialectical thinking (e.g., "I feel anxious because of the need to be less predictable"). Baxter (1990) discovered that separation through topical segmentation and separation through cyclic alternation exist as the most frequently used strategies to manage relational tensions. Interestingly, Baxter (1990) reported that partners underutilize more sophisticated and possibly more satisfactory strategies, such as reframing the tension so that it no longer functions as a contradiction, thereby suggesting that couples do not necessarily understand the flux of relational tensions and are therefore unable to cope most effectively.

In conclusion, it should be clear that the manner in which scholars define the terms *relational maintenance* plays a crucial role in determining the types of behaviors studied. As the above review shows, various kinds of behaviors perform relational maintenance–supposed functions. That scholars would attempt to uncover types of behavior that promote the welfare of close, personal relationships constitutes the single principle that unites this new domain of inquiry.

See also: AFFECTION; ATTRACTION; COMMUNICATION: COUPLE RELATIONSHIPS; COMMUNICATION: FAMILY RELATIONSHIPS; COMMUTER MARRIAGES; DATING; DIALECTICAL THEORY; EQUITY; INFIDELITY; INTIMACY; MARITAL QUALITY; NAGGING AND COMPLAINING; RELATIONSHIP METAPHORS; RENEWAL OF WEDDING VOWS; SOCIAL NETWORKS; TRANSITION TO PARENTHOOD; TRUST

Bibliography

Ayres, J. (1983). "Strategies to Maintain Relationships: Their Identification and Perceived Usage." *Communication Quarterly* 31:62–67.

Baxter, L. A. (1988). "A Dialectical Perspective on Communication Strategies in Relationship Development." In *Handbook of Personal Relationships: Theory, Research and Interventions,* ed. S. Duck. New York: John Wiley & Sons.

Baxter, L. A. (1990). "Dialectical Contradictions in Relationship Development." *Journal of Social and Personal Relationships* 7:69–88.

Berger, C. R., and Calabrese, R. (1975). "Some Explorations into Initial Interaction and Beyond: Toward a Developmental Theory of Interpersonal Communication." *Human Communication Research* 1:99–112.

Canary, D. J., and Stafford, L. (1992). "Relational Maintenance Strategies and Equity in Marriage." *Communication Monographs* 59:243–267.

Canary, D. J., and Stafford, L. (2001). "Equity in the Preservation of Personal Relationships." In *Maintenance and the Enhancement of Close Relationships,* ed. J. Harvey and A. Wenzel. Mahwah, NJ: Erlbaum.

Canary, D. J., and Zelley, E. D. (2000). "Current Research Programs on Relational Maintenance Behaviors." *Communication Yearbook* 23:305–339.

Dindia, K., and Canary, D. J. (1993). "Definitions and Theoretical Perspectives on Maintaining Relationships." *Journal of Social and Personal Relationships* 10:163–173.

Duck, S. (1988). *Relating to Others.* Chicago: Dorsey.

Emmers, T. M., and Canary, D. J. (1996). "The Effect of Uncertainty Reducing Strategies on Young Couples' Relational Repair and Intimacy." *Communication Quarterly* 44:166–182.

Gottman, J. M. (1994). *What Predicts Divorce? The Relationship Between Marital Processes and Marital Outcomes.* Hillsdale, NJ: Erlbaum.

Messman, S. J., Canary, D. J., and Hause, K. S. (2000). "Motives to Remain Platonic, Equity, and the Use of Maintenance Strategies in Opposite-Sex Friendships." *Journal of Social and Personal Relationships* 17:67–94.

Metts, S. (1994). "Relational Transgressions." In *The Dark Side of Interpersonal Communication,* ed. W. R. Cupach and B. H. Spitzberg. Hillsdale, NJ: Erlbaum.

Montgomery, B. M. (1993). "Relationship Maintenance versus Relationship Change: A Dialectical Dilemma." *Journal of Social and Personal Relationships* 10:205–223.

Rusbult, C. E. (1987). "Responses to Dissatisfaction in Close Relationships: The Exit-Voice-Loyalty-Neglect Model." In *Intimate Relationships: Development, Dynamics, and Deterioration,* ed. D. Perlman and S. Duck. Newbury Park, CA: Sage.

Rusbult, C. E.; Drigotas, S. M.; and Verette, J. (1994). "The Investment Model: An Interdependence Analysis of Commitment Processes and Relationship Maintenance Phenomena." In *Communication and Relational Maintenance,* ed. D. J. Canary and L. Stafford. San Diego, CA: Academic Press.

Stafford, L., and Canary, D. J. (1991). "Maintenance Strategies and Romantic Relationship Type, Gender, and Relational Characteristics." *Journal of Social and Personal Relationships* 8:217–242.

Van Lange, P. A. M.; Rusbult, C. E.; Drigotas, S. M.; Arriaga, X. B.; Witcher, B. S.; and Cox, C. L. (1997). "Willingness to Sacrifice in Close Relationships." *Journal of Personality and Social Psychology* 72:1373–1395.

DANIEL J. CANARY
ELAINE D. ZELLEY

RELATIONSHIP METAPHORS

A *metaphor* is a figure of speech in which a word or phrase that ordinarily applies to one kind of experience or phenomenon is applied to another, thereby suggesting a similarity or likeness between them. Metaphors have the general form *A is B,* in which *A* serves as the metaphor's *tenor* and *B* serves as the metaphor's *vehicle*. Tenors and vehicles can be related explicitly through a declarative sentence, but they often are related implicitly in discourse. For example, a person could say "Dating is a game," in which the tenor, *dating,* and the vehicle, *game,* are explicitly related. Alternatively, someone could talk about dating experiences and refer to "winning some and losing some," "the fun of the chase," and "scoring points"—all references that evoke implicitly the vehicle of a game. A *relationship metaphor* is an expression in which a personal relationship, or some associated experience or emotion, serves as the tenor. Scholarly attention has focused on the various vehicles of relationship metaphors.

Metaphors, including relationship metaphors, function as important mechanisms for the expression of experience and emotion. Andrew Ortony (1975) described three communicative functions of metaphors. First, metaphors allow us to express experiences that are difficult or impossible to describe literally. Second, metaphors are succinct and efficient, affording us an economical means of communication. Third, metaphors communicate the vividness and richness of experience in a manner less easily captured in the literal use of language.

In addition, George Lakoff and Mark Johnson (1980), among others, have argued that metaphors are central to the human thought process. Metaphors are not only poetic devices that enable us to communicate about social reality; in addition, they serve as organizing frameworks through which our thoughts about social reality are shaped.

Relationship scholars and practitioners have approached relationship metaphors in three ways. First, they have examined the metaphors used by relationship parties to describe their relationship experiences. Second, they have examined the metaphors of relating employed by researchers and theorists studying relationships. Third, they have employed relationship metaphors as interventions in family therapy contexts to facilitate behavioral change.

Metaphors Used by Relationship Parties

Some scholars have focused on one of the most frequently experienced emotions in the content of personal relationships: love. In one of the most comprehensive studies, Zoltan Kovecses (1988) examined conventional English expressions about love and identified about three dozen metaphors of love, including, among others: *love as a journey* ("We're at the crossroads."); *love as a physical force* ("There were sparks."); *love as a nutrient* ("I can't live without him."); *love as unity* ("We were made for each other."); *love as heat* ("She set my heart on fire."); *love as sport* ("He fell for her hook, line, and sinker."); and *love as disease* ("He's lovesick.").

Other scholars have examined the metaphors used by relationship parties in capturing specific kinds of relational experiences. Thus, for example, one can describe people's metaphors of interpersonal conflict (McCorkle and Mills 1992), battered women's metaphors for domestic violence (Eisikovitz and Buchbinder 1999), romantic partners' metaphors for relationship development (Baxter 1992), and former partners' metaphors for relationship break-up (Owen 1993).

Metaphors of relationships and relating in general have also been the focus of scholars. Across romantic relationships, marriages, and families, several metaphors frequently appear (Katriel and Philipsen 1981; Owen 1990; Quinn 1991). *Relationship as a thing* is a common metaphorical image. A thing is a bounded entity, separate from other entities. It is an object whose characteristics supercede the individuals who belong to it. In the context of two-person relationships, this metaphor encourages us to appreciate that there are three parts: "you," "me," and "it." The "it" is the relationship as entity. Relationship entities take on a life of their own, often making the parties feel as if they are responding to a force beyond their control.

Relationship as machine is another common metaphor. Like a machine, relationships have parts that need to be assembled or coordinated through the expenditure of time and energy. Like machines, relationships are oriented toward the output of some manufactured product—typically a stable, satisfactory relational outcome. Relationships, like machines, can break down and need ongoing maintenance and repair work.

Relationship as investment is a third common metaphor. Entailed in this image is the notion that parties invest in the "bank account" of their relationship in order to reap mutual benefits. Parties can stockpile "assets" of affection, they can "make withdrawals" that see them through difficult times, and so forth. Individuals may abandon relationships when the "return on their investment" is deemed unsatisfactory.

Relationship as journey is another typical metaphor used by relationship parties in capturing their relating process. The focus of this metaphor is not outcomes but process—the journey or relational trip itself. Like any journey, relationships are a process of ongoing change and discovery along the way. Detours are taken. Crossroads are encountered where one path is selected instead of alternative paths. The parties may lose sight of their destination, or it may change as a result of where the journey takes them.

Relationship as container is a common metaphorical image. Like containers, relationships have a distinct inside and outside. Containers also imply a stability or permanence of form. Things are kept in containers, and we can similarly refer to the parties who are "in" a relationship. For example, we can refer to being "in" a family. Social services agencies talk of pumping resources "into" the family unit. Containers can function both to protect their "contents" from outside forces and to limit or "box in" those contents.

Finally, parties often invoke the metaphorical image of *relationship as living organism*. Relationships are perceived to develop in a natural progression from infancy to maturity. They are born, they grow, they mature, they require nurturing, and they can wither and die. Relationships can be vibrant and healthy, or they can be sick.

This list of relationship metaphors is far from exhaustive, but it provides a sense of some of the principle ways in which relationships are figuratively described by the parties involved. Each metaphorical image highlights unique features about the relating process.

Metaphors Used by Relationship Scholars

Metaphors guide thinking, both for relationship parties and for the scholars who study relationships. Thus, some theorists have made a reflexive turn to focus on the metaphors that organize scholars' sense-making of the relating process. Paul Rosenblatt (1994) provides a detailed examination of the various metaphorical images used by family system theorists, identifying five dominant metaphors: *family as entity, family as container, family as living entity, family as primary group,* and *family as machine.* Steve Duck (1987) similarly examined the implicit assumptions of personal-relationship scholars through their metaphorical images, identifying three primary metaphors: *relationship as film,* in which early scenes in a relationship are thought to permit prediction of later outcomes; *relationship as horticulture,* a view close to the living-organism metaphor discussed

above; and *relationship as mechanical model,* a view similar to the machine metaphor discussed above. Both Rosenblatt (1994) and Duck (1987) note that the metaphors used by scholars function as both lenses and blinders. Metaphors encourage researchers to look in certain ways at relationships, leading to new insights, understandings, and discoveries. At the same time, however, metaphors blind researchers to alternative ways of seeing.

Metaphors and Family Therapy

Family therapists have a long tradition of recognizing the importance of understanding client metaphors of their relationship experiences (Sims and Whynot 1998). The metaphors used by family clients may limit their ability to explore alternative ways of relating more constructively. Family therapists strive to locate new metaphors for families, thereby giving them alternative language with which to construct different ways of being. Sometimes, these metaphors are idiosyncratic to the particular client family. At other times, therapists identify metaphors that can function as useful interventions for a number of families. Linda Wark and Shilpa Jobalia (1998), for example, discuss an intervention with stepfamilies based on the metaphor of building a bridge. Stepfamily development can be plagued with adjustment problems. By framing this process as the construction of a bridge, stepfamily members can temper their desire to rush to instant closeness and understand the slow, step-by-step process required to build a strong family structure.

Conclusion

Are relationship metaphors helpful or harmful to relationship parties? They are neither intrinsically good nor bad but simply inherent in the human experience (Lakoff and Johnson 1980). Are some metaphors more accurate than others? This question presumes that a single relationship reality exists as a benchmark against which to assess a given metaphor's adequacy. Relationships are different for different people, and different for the same people from one time to the next. Further, relationships are multifaceted, with many layers of meaning and function. Lakoff and Johnson (1980) suggest a different question to pose about any metaphor: "What does this metaphor illuminate and what does it obscure about relationships?"

See also: COMMUNICATION: COUPLE RELATIONSHIPS; FAMILY AND RELATIONAL RULES; FAMILY STORIES AND MYTHS; RELATIONSHIP MAINTENANCE; THERAPY: FAMILY RELATIONSHIPS

Bibliography

Baxter, L. A. (1992). "Root Metaphors in Accounts of Developing Romantic Relationships." *Journal of Social and Personal Relationships* 9:253–276.

Duck, S. (1987). "Adding Apples and Oranges: Investigators' Implicit Theories About Personal Relationships." In *Accounting for Relationships: Explanation, Representation and Knowledge,* ed. R. Burnett, P. McGhee, and D. D. Clarke. New York: Methuen.

Eisikovits, Z., and Buchbinder, E. (1999). "Talking Control: Metaphors Used by Battered Women." *Violence Against Women* 5:845–868.

Katriel, T., and Philipsen, G. (1981). "'What We Need is Communication': 'Communication' as a Cultural Category in Some American Speech." *Communication Monographs* 48:301–317.

Kovecses, Z. (1988). *The Language of Love: The Semantics of Passion in Conversational English.* Cranbury, NJ: Bucknell University Presses.

Lakoff, G., and Johnson, M. (1980). *Metaphors We Live By.* Chicago: University of Chicago Press.

McCorkle, S., and Mills, J. L. (1992). "Rowboat in a Hurricane: Metaphors of Interpersonal Conflict Management." *Communication Reports* 5:57–66.

Ortony, A. (1975). "Why Metaphors are Necessary and Not Just Nice." *Educational Theory* 25:45–53.

Owen, W. F. (1990). "Delimiting Relational Metaphor." *Communication Studies* 41:35–53.

Owen, W. F. (1993). "Metaphors in Accounts of Romantic Relationship Terminations." In *Interpersonal Communication: Evolving Interpersonal Relationships,* ed. P. J. Kalbfleisch. Hillsdale, NJ: Erlbaum.

Quinn, N. (1991). "The Cultural Basis of Metaphor." In *Beyond Metaphor: The Theory of Tropes in Anthropology,* ed. J. W. Fernandez. Stanford, CA: Stanford University Press.

Rosenblatt, P. C. (1994). *Metaphors of Family Systems Theory: Toward New Constructions.* New York: Guilford Press.

Sims, P. A., and Whynot, C. A. (1998). "Hearing Metaphor: An Approach to Working with Family-Generated Metaphor." *Family Process* 36:341–355.

Wark, L., and Jobalia, S. (1998). "What Would It Take to Build a Bridge?: An Intervention for Stepfamilies." *Journal of Family Psychotherapy* 9:69–77.

LESLIE A. BAXTER

RELATIONSHIP THEORIES— SELF–OTHER RELATIONSHIP

Most people have an implicit theory about how relationships work. Some people are more aware of or at least talk more about their viewpoint on relationships than others. Regardless of an individual's awareness or one's own theory of relationships, most people tend to treat their view of relationships as reality. Because of this egocentric view of reality, how one views Self and Others in relational contexts is of fundamental importance.

Communication in families and relationships is profoundly influenced by sources of cultural variability. The primary source of cultural-level variability explored here is an individual's orientation to the concepts of *Self, Other,* and *Relationship.* William W. Wilmot's (1995) conceptualization of three paradigmatic views of relationships is at the heart of this discussion. The concepts of individualism and collectivism augment this discussion illustrating the unique impact cultural-level variations have on individual's communicative behavior in interaction. This discussion should be tempered by cautioning that although there are general patterns of behavior consistently associated with paradigmatic views of relationships and individualism/collectivism, not every individual's behavior is guided by these cultural level factors. For example, William Gudykunst and Young Kim (1992) note that "Although most people in the United States have individualistic tendencies, some people do have collectivistic tendencies. Similarly, although most people in Japan have collectivistic tendencies, some people do have individualistic tendencies" (p. 55). In short, we must keep in mind the distinction between cultural-level behaviors and unique individual behavior within a given social setting. The following discussion begins with Paradigm I views of relationships common in individualistic cultures, continues with Paradigm II views common in collectivistic cultures, and explores the possibilities of a Paradigm III view for all cultures.

Figure 1 illustrates the *Paradigm I: Individual Selves Loosely Connected* view of relationships. Self and Other are viewed as separate units loosely coupled by a fragile relational thread. This view is the most common view of relationships in the individualistic culture of the United States. It is not an accident that the circle for Self is larger than the circle for Other. Individualistic cultures emphasize individual achievement and initiative (Gudykunst and Kim 1997), and view the Self as an independent, self-contained, and causative force guiding events (Harre 1989). Gudykunst and Kim (1997) note that individualistic cultures favor individual goals over group goals, look out for themselves and their immediate family only, are guided by many specific in-groups that individually exert minimal influence on behavior, and place a high value on materialism, success, work and activity, progress, and rationality.

Wilmot (1995) notes that the Paradigm I view "emphasizes the self, de-emphasizes the other, and reduces the relationships to a fragile connecting mechanism" (p. 37). This view of relationships is consistent with *Social Exchange* (Roloff 1981) models of relationships (e.g. equity theory) where individuals try to maximize their outcomes (Hatfield, Utne, and Traupmann 1979). The social exchange metaphor conjures up images of costs, rewards, profit margin, mergers and acquisitions, where the relationship is viewed as something exterior to the Self. If profits are not high enough, restructure your portfolio, change your investment, file for bankruptcy, but save yourself. In this view self-satisfaction is the prime value, not relationship enhancement.

There is of course, considerable debate about the applicability of Social Exchange theories to more intimate relations such as marriage and family. Elaine Hatfield, Mary Utne, and Jane Traupmann (1979) provide an excellent review of the research (most of the research was conducted in the United States) and conclude that equitable relations appear more stable than non-equitable relations and that the theory is useful for understanding the dynamics of these more intimate relations. Despite the unsavory taste that this view of relationships leaves in the mouths of many lay people and scholars alike, the cultural imperative of individualism has a significant impact on communication in these relationships. In fact, as couples in the United States experience relational difficulties, the first line of defense is often "Blame the Other" (Wilmot

FIGURE 1

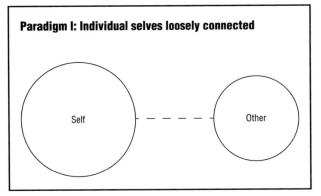

1995). Blame is seen as a problem of individuals, not the relational process. Of course, if both partners are blaming the other, the fragile thread of the relationship is more likely to be cut. We now turn to Paradigm II views of relationships, which emphasize connectedness between Self and Other.

Figure 2 illustrates the *Paradigm II: The Embedded Self* view of relationships. This paradigm makes a fundamental shift in its conceptualization of Self. Within this paradigm, Self cannot be seen as a separate identity, but must always be examined within the context of Relationship. Thus, the Self is not an independent, findable entity, and we begin to see people forming and reforming their selves within each unique relational context. In this view, the relationship itself is treated as a separate entity: Relationship has identity (Hecht 1993). Paradigm II views focus on interconnections and interdependencies that have created the Self. In other words, we only have Self because we have Others who support that view. Our very definition of Self is cast within a broader framework of family, friends, lovers, work, and the broader culture. Paradigm II views of relationships are more common in collectivistic cultures.

Gudykunst and Kim (1997) note that groups (i.e. relationships and families) take precedence over individuals' goals in collectivistic cultures. In contrast to individualistic cultures, collectivistic cultures have fewer in-groups but these in-groups have a strong influence on individual behavior across situations. "Collectivistic cultures emphasize goals, needs, and views of the in-group over those of the individual; the social norms of the in-group, rather than individual pleasure; shared in-group beliefs, rather than unique individual beliefs; and cooperation with in-group members, rather than maximizing of individual outcomes" (Gudykunst

FIGURE 2

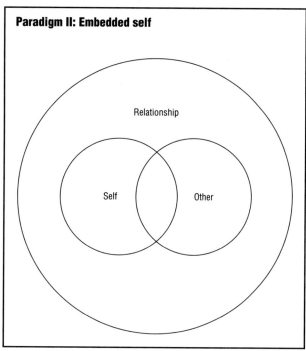

Paradigm II: Embedded self

and Kim 1997, p. 57). Thus, these collectivistic views are more in line with Paradigm II views of relationships that emphasize the Other and give the relationship itself pre-eminent status.

Wilmot (1995) argues that male/female communication problems could arise from variations in paradigm preferences. In the United States, males are more likely to rely on a Paradigm I view and females are likely to rely on a Paradigm II view. It has been clearly demonstrated that females do value and monitor their relationships more than males. Therefore, males might note the "suffocating" or "constricting" nature of a particular relationship and complain about the possibilities of making independent choices, while females might argue for more relationship rejuvenation work per se because they are more likely to hold a Paradigm II view of relationships. That is, females are more likely to treat the relationship as having a definable essence of its own that transcends the two individuals.

The theoretical perspective of dialectics is reflective of Paradigm II views of relationships. We briefly review it here because it challenges some of the assumptions of an independent Self in Paradigm I views and also helps to further understand the dynamics of male/female communication illustrated above. The dialectical approach to relationships stresses that phenomena that appear to be opposites are actually bound together, and that there is a

dynamic interplay between such opposites (Baxter 1984, 1994). People raised in individualistic cultures are often not sensitized to thinking in terms of the dialectics of opposites. Instead, they tend to think in an either/or fashion, whereas collectivistic cultures are more likely to think in terms of both/and. An individualistic cultural frame promotes the view that elements are opposite and not connected, rather than seeing the dialectical interrelation of opposites. A dialectical perspective emphasizes process and contradiction and lets us focus on the swings (now close, now far) that are present in all relationships. Figure 2A illustrates how the dialectic perspective aids our understanding of these relational swings within a Paradigm II view of relationships. The example of male/female communication mentioned above is a good illustration of how the relationship can serve a transcendent function in this view.

A male who notes the "suffocating" or "constricting" nature of a particular relationship and complains about the possibilities of making independent choices is illustrating the most frequently cited set of opposites in personal relationships, autonomy-connection or independence-interdependence. As noted above, males are more likely to hold a Paradigm I view of relationships and thus stress independence, while females are more likely to hold a Paradigm II view of relationships and thus stress interdependence. A dialectical perspective would allow both males and females to recognize the transcendent function of the relationship and recognize that natural fluctuations in autonomy-connection are normal, useful, and temporary processes. Furthermore, Paradigm II views of relationships recognize that each individual has a stake in self-interests, the Other's interests, and the relationship as the interplay between the two.

Understanding of Paradigm II views of relationships has been greatly aided by postmodern thinking. Postmodern writers challenge the notions of independence and individualism that dominate individualistic cultures and Paradigm I views of relationships. While Paradigm II views of relationships move us from emphasis on Self to recognition of Others in context of Relationship, these views of relationships are still bound in individualistic cultures by dualistic thinking. Note that even Figure 2A, while moving away from dualistic thinking and incorporating dialectical thoughts, still clearly separates Self, Other, and Relationship. Our understanding of relationships often suffers from

FIGURE 2A

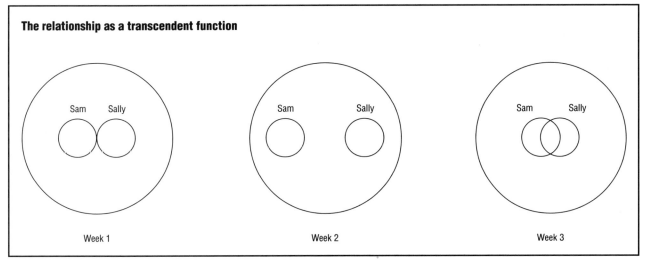

The relationship as a transcendent function

Sam   Sally   Sam   Sally   Sam   Sally

Week 1   Week 2   Week 3

the exactitude of our factual language, our ability to speak from only one point of view at a time, and limitations inherent in two-dimensional models of the process! The introduction of Paradigm III views of relationships is our attempt to stretch theorizing about, and understanding of, relationships.

Figure 3 illustrates the *Paradigm III: Nonseparable Self/Other/Relationship* view of relationships. In this view, the individual is not taken as a separate, sacred entity, but rather it challenges the very notion of an identifiable Self. Proponents of this paradigm would view Self, Other, and relationships as so inextricably tied that talking about one entity would necessitate talking about the other two. That is, any change in Self necessarily changes Other and relationship. In other words we are constructed in our transactions with others. We are not something that exists before contact with others, we "come-into-being" in our transactions. A view of relationships from the Paradigm III perspective suggests we cannot separate Self, Other, and relationships and that duality itself is an illusion.

Paradigm III is difficult to understand for many of us raised in individualistic cultures and/or have Paradigm I or II views of relationships. For many, it is difficult not to default to "I" language and concerns about self-satisfaction in relationships. Paradigm III adherents recognize that relationship work (and relationships are work!) is not undertaken to benefit the Self, but rather is done to enhance relationship, Other, and Self, all interwoven. In a very real sense, we don't "do" relationships, they "do" us! Given that people with individualistic tendencies and Paradigm I views of relationships

have trouble not defaulting to thinking in terms of Self and self-interests, and that people with collectivistic tendencies and Paradigm II views of relationships are still limited by their language and conceptions of a separate Self and Other, it is not surprising that researchers have yet to investigate any variations on Paradigm III views of relationships. We conclude by examining the potential improvement in our understanding of communication in personal relationships when relationships are viewed from a Paradigm III perspective.

An individual's lay or implicit theory of relationships, where ever it falls along the continuum from Paradigm I to Paradigm III, dramatically impacts the role communication plays in a relationship. Paradigm I adherents often talk about the Self as if it were a relationless entity, moving through time and space as an independent unit. Paradigm II adherents, with a large focus on Other, still mentally conceive of separate Self and Other entities, albeit bound in the context of a relationship. We argue that a shift to Paradigm III views of relationships and a conceptualization of communication as a conjoint reality created by two people in relation to each other is advantageous in relationships. Even though we have an impoverished language of relatedness, a shift to Paradigm III views allows us to see the real power of communication and uncovers blind spots in our relational realities.

Seeing communication as the joint product of two persons in relation, opens our eyes to (1) the transformative potential of communication; and (2) seeing dialogue, not monologue, as the heart of the process. Communication is transformative for

FIGURE 3

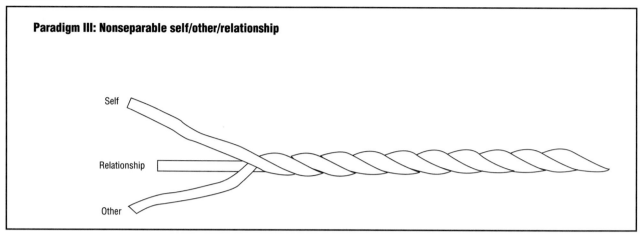

Paradigm III: Nonseparable self/other/relationship

both participants. Even if one person is doing all the talking in a relationship, the other's presence and actions as listener impact communication. All parties in a relationship undergo significant change when they participate and express themselves within a relationship. Simply put, transformation equals expression plus connection. This conception of communication in relationships shifts our thinking from two people trying to send accurate verbal and nonverbal messages to each other to two people generating meaning conjointly—it is hoped that this view will lead to productive development of Self/Other/Relationship.

See also: COMMUNICATION: COUPLE RELATIONSHIPS;
DIALECTICAL THEORY; SOCIAL EXCHANGE THEORY

Bibliography

Baxter, L. A. (1984). "Trajectories of Relationship Disengagement." *Journal of Social and Personal Relationships* 1:29–48.

Baxter, L. A. (1994). "Thinking Dialogically about Communication in Personal Relationships." In *Uses of Structure in Communication Studies,* ed. R. Conville. New York: Praeger.

Gudykunst, W. B., and Kim, Y. Y. (1992). *Communicating with Strangers: An Approach to Intercultural Communication.* New York: McGraw-Hill.

Harre, R. (1989). "Language Games and Texts of Identity." In *Texts of identity,* ed. J. Shotter and K. J. Gergen. Thousand Oaks, CA: Sage.

Hatfield, E.; Utne, M. K.; and Traupmann, J. (1979). "Equity Theory and Intimate Relationships." In *Social Exchange in Developing Relationships,* ed. R. L. Burgess and T. L. Huston. New York: Academic Press.

Hecht, M. L. (1993). "2002—A Research Odyssey: Toward the Development of a Communication Theory of Identity." *Communication Monographs* 48:201–216.

Roloff, M. E. (1981). *Interpersonal Communication: A Social Exchange Approach.* Thousand Oaks, CA: Sage.

Wilmot, W. W. (1995). *Relational Communication.* New York: McGraw-Hill

WILLIAM W. WILMOT
MARK J. BERGSTROM

RELATIONSHIPS

RELIGION

Religion may be defined as (1) a recognition of or belief in a superhuman power or god(s) commanding obedience and worship; (2) a feeling of reverence or spiritual awareness of such a power expressed in life conduct and/or ritual obser-vances; and (3) a system of faith including beliefs, worship, conduct, and perhaps a code of ethics or philosophy. Individuals with an awareness of a di-vine or higher power develop a view of life that is different from those who have no faith position. Religion may affect all of life because of the per-spective individuals use to interpret life experi-ences, to set personal and family goals, and to make value-based decisions. The particular ways in which religion will make a difference in life de-pend on many factors or dimensions of religion, including, but not limited to, the importance of re-ligion to the individual (salience), devotional prac-tices and sense of relationship with the divine, specific beliefs and emphases, the degree of sup-port and shared activities by the religious commu-nity, congregational worship, the rewards ex-pected for faith and the acting out of its values, and views of and behaviors toward significant oth-ers (family, friends, etc.).

The intersection of religion with family life is important to families and to society. Many contro-versial political and social issues are grounded in religious arguments or attitudes. The role of reli-gion in family functioning is being recognized, as is its potential importance in family life education, psychological counseling, and marriage and family therapy.

Religiosity may be categorized along two global dimensions. One dimension captures the depth of one's religious experience. At the more superficial or peripheral (distal) end of this contin-uum, researchers might assess religious affiliation of one or more family members or individual par-ticipation and devotion. At the more in-depth (proximal or core aspect) end of the continuum, researchers might measure an increasing internal-ization of religion, shared religious interaction such as praying together, a shared sense of the sacred or divine within family relationships, and the expres-sion of religion in attitudes and behaviors. Typi-cally, the more distal aspects of religion are ex-plored in large, nationally representative surveys, while the more proximal aspects are investigated in smaller, more detailed, but less representative studies. The second continuum is that of the qual-ity of the religious experience from toxic (nega-tive) to enhancing (positive). Some may experi-ence religion as fearful and rigid, abusive, violent, guilt-inducing, or patriarchal (Haj-Yahia 1998).

Others may experience religion as loving, egalitar-ian, and nonviolent (Rahim 2000), even though they depend upon the same religious traditions and scriptures. The best research on religion and the family will assess both global dimensions in ways that are theoretically pertinent to the family variables being considered. The ambiguous results of some past research (Booth et al. 1995) may re-flect incomplete assessment of both dimensions. In contrast, Annette Mahoney and colleagues (1999) investigated family outcomes with both distal (individual religiousness and religious homogamy) and proximal religious measures. Stronger relationships were found with proximal measures than with distal measures. Family out-comes (marital adjustment, reduced conflict, im-proved conflict resolution strategies) were more positive with enhancing proximal factors involved than with toxic or distal associations.

Religion and Family Composition

Religious variables appear to affect several issues involving family composition: mate selection, in-terfaith or intrafaith marriage, fertility, contracep-tion, and abortion. In some countries, parents arrange marriages. In many Muslim and African na-tions, as well as in India, polygamy is common, and some African nations have had polygynous marriages as a part of their religious heritage (Fu 1996). In the United States, mate selection is less likely to be religiously homogamous if people be-long to a small religious group, have an unbal-anced sex ratio (few people from whom to choose), and develop cultures and values similar to those outside the religious group. Apparently the more assimilated people become, the more likely intermarriage is. Evelyn Lehrer (1998) noted that the greater the religiosity and the commitment to their faith, the less likely people are to inter-marry. Bernard Lazerwitz (1995) found that Jewish intermarriages increased with the number of gen-erations since immigration, a finding also reported for Muslim immigrants to North America (Hogben 1991). By 1990, 25 percent of Jewish adults were living in interfaith marriages. Marriages depend upon many relational factors, but those who marry within their general faith community have one less arena of differences to resolve.

In North American society, cohabitation has in-creased, although it remains controversial. Low levels of religious participation and commitment have been correlated with higher rates of cohabitation (Thornton 1992). Religious participation typically decreases with cohabiting and increases with marriage. In addition, more conservative attitudes about premarital sexuality generally accompany more proximal measures of religiosity, findings that appear worldwide among a variety of religions. In recent decades, liberalization of sexual attitudes has occurred among many, especially in northern Europe, where cohabitation has increased to approximately 20 percent of couples in some countries (Fu 1996). Despite such changes, same-sex unions remain very controversial, with negative views frequently held by those with conservative beliefs.

Fertility (the birthrate of various groups) appears to be associated with aspects of religiosity. More traditional religiosity, both in the United States and around the world, seems to be correlated with both marriage and with desiring and having a greater number of children after marriage (Arnett 1998). Traditionalists may focus more on possible long-term rewards of rearing children as opposed to the more obvious short-term costs. Nevertheless, both Roman Catholic and Protestant fertility rates have been decreasing, and some couples choose not to have children. This choice was not practical until contraceptive options became available. Religious beliefs influence their use around the world.

Religious variables seem to predict strong attitudes about abortion (Jenkins 1991). Frequent worship attendance and religiosity had a significant negative relationship with abortion. This correlation may be related to the strong pro-life advocacy of some religious groups (such as Catholicism and fundamentalist Protestantism in the United States). Those who get abortions in spite of their religious beliefs to the contrary may be stressed by guilt.

Religion and the Marital Relationship

Two common areas of family research are marital quality (satisfaction and adjustment) and stability (whether marriages remain intact or end in separation or divorce). Virtually all research finds a significant relationship between most aspects of religion and stability (e.g., marginal affiliation or toxic religion may help dysfunctional marriages remain intact) (Call and Wheaten 1997). Satisfaction is

most often associated with more proximal and enhancing religious factors (Mahoney et al. 1999).

One theory suggests that religion gives couples the opportunity for shared values and norms (such as fidelity), joint participation in activities, and supportive joint social networks which promote marital satisfaction. This theory fits the research on couples married fifty years or more by Howard Bahr and Bruce Chadwick (1985), who found higher marital satisfaction among those who frequently attended worship services than among those who did not. A study of Seventh Day Adventists' homogamous marriages also showed that higher marital satisfaction was associated with more frequent worship attendance. (Dudley and Kosinksi 1990).

Among reasons for staying together (stability) are the belief that marriage is a lifetime commitment, love, and religious commitment and values (Kaslow and Robison 1996). Some religious groups emphasize the importance of a lifetime commitment to one's partner (e.g., Judaism, Catholicism and fundamentalist Protestantism, Islam, Confucianism). If people internalize such values and/or religious cultural pressures are great, the risk of divorce is reduced. Perhaps the Hindu, Catholic (such as Italy), and Eastern (e.g., Japan) cultures are largely responsible for their low divorce rate (Fu 1996). In contrast, Muslim countries have high divorce rates (e.g., divorce because of infertility). Vaughn Call and Tim Heaton (1997), in a national survey of the United States, found that when couples regularly attending religious activities together, it lowered the risk of divorce, but wide differences in spouses' attendance patterns increased the risk. Wives' religious beliefs about commitment and nonmarital sex correlated to stability more highly than did husbands' beliefs. Patriarchal religious groups in which wives are not allowed to work outside the home also have a low divorce rate (e.g., lack of income without family support).

Couples do not always agree or understand each other's viewpoints. In times of conflict, attitudes and the way partners resolve their differences (including religious differences) can affect marital satisfaction and stability. Mark Butler, Brandt Gardner, and Mark Bird (1998) investigated the effects of prayer during couples' conflicts with a small homogamous sample. Respondents reported that using prayer reduced hostility and increased empathy for partners. When the divine view of the problem was sought, a shift in focus from getting one's own way to considering the spouse's view and seeking mutual satisfaction allowed more satisfactory resolution. Howard Wineberg (1994) explored marital reconciliation for those in very troubled marriages. Of the wives who remained married for a year after attempting to reconcile (approximately one-third), religion had the strongest association with reconciliation. More research needs to be done to find how religion makes a difference.

Unfortunately, domestic abuse is one reaction to conflict. Patriarchal family and gender role values sometimes raise the risk of abuse, but the patriarchal values of Islam and Hinduism, for instance, do not support domestic violence. Christopher Ellison, John Bartkowski, and Kristin L. Anderson (1999) found self-reported perpetration of domestic violence to be inversely related to regular attendance at religious services in the United States.

Parenting and Family Relationships

General consensus affirms that parents influence children and having children affects couples. In general, religiosity of parents appears to have a positive impact on the quality of parent-child relationships (Varon and Riley 1999), including those within ethnic minorities (Barbarin 1999). Becoming a parent may increase some people's affiliation with or commitment to religion (Palkovitz and Palm 1998). Two specific areas related to religious variables are styles of parenting, particularly regarding discipline, and the transmittal of values and faith heritage. Discipline methods can be controversial. For instance, conservative and fundamentalist Protestants emphasize that parents are responsible for taming the sinful nature of their children and shaping their wills as they believe their bible requires. Spanking is often the discipline method used to promote submission to a God who is just, merciful, and forgiving but who also punishes sins (Bartkowski and Ellison 1995). Others believe that spanking or corporal punishment of any kind can and does lead to abuse some of the time and is harmful to the development of children. Jean Giles-Sims, Murray Straus, and David Sugarman (1995) found that young, single mothers and members of some ethnic groups are more likely to spank and that spanking is most likely to

escalate into abuse among single parents and stepparents and adults with severe stress (such as unemployment) or social-psychological problems.

Parents and grandparents influence their children's values, behavior, and religion. Scott Myers's (1996) longitudinal study suggested parents' religiosity, traditional family structure, and family relationships influence the transmission of religious beliefs and practices to children. Parents' marital satisfaction and warmth, emotional closeness, and sense of acceptance accentuated behavioral imitation by children. Religious grandparents seem to keep modeling their faith: High religiosity predicts grandparents willing to care for sick grandchildren.

Divorce can affect children's perception of God and religion. Children of divorced parents often have to cope with the absence of a loved parent, less income, less time with the custodial parent who is working, and time alone. Young adult children of divorce recalled for Joianne L. Shortz and Everett L. Worthington, Jr. (1994) their thoughts when as children they tried to make sense of and cope with their parents' divorce. Some were angry with God, asked faith questions or avoided religion, and pleaded with God for a miracle. Others leaned on their faith, seeking God's guidance; attending worship regularly; sought support from clergy and congregation; and tried to live their faith by performing good deeds.

Prevention and Coping with Special Problems

Troubled or hurting members affect the whole family. Although not the only factor, religion seems to deter some negative behaviors and give strength and comfort promoting health and well-being. Religion may make the lives of parents less stressful: Higher levels of religiosity have been correlated to many beneficial outcomes including lower use of drugs and alcohol (Corwyn and Benda 2000; Bahr et al. 1998); a reduced risk of suicide (Stack 1998); lower rates of delinquency (Evans et al. 1996); buffering of stress (Kendler, Gardner, and Prescott 1997); and delays in starting sexual activity (Plotnick 1992). It is possible that frequent involvement in religious organizations deters undesirable behaviors by providing students with a belief system and values to guide decisions, positive reinforcement, and wholesome activities with friends who share the same values.

Although sexual activity among adolescents has increased since the 1980s, conservative religious groups emphasizing chastity are less likely to have members involved in premarital sex. The risk of premarital sexual activity is less in the countries in which girls marry close to the age of puberty and are closely chaperoned until wed. Those adolescents who cohabit in spite of their religious values of chastity are likely to feel guilt and stress, but high levels of religiosity seem to protect many U.S. high-school students from the ordinary psychological stress more often felt by students with low religiosity (Sorenson, Grindstaff, and Turner 1995).

Participation in religious activities deters adult crime (Evans et al. 1995) and domestic violence. The positive side of religion also appears in its apparent ability to help families cope with health problems and death. Patients' attitudes and families' emotions and care interact for family well-being. Bernard Spilka, William Zwartjes, and Georgia Zwartjes (1991) found that highly religious families were able to work together, developing even closer family relationships to deal with a child's cancer. Of course, families can also blame God for painful experiences if they see God as judgmental and punishing (toxic religion), which is not helpful. Susan McFadden (1995) noted that religion can offer a sense of meaning to life, the calming effect of prayer, and services such as economic and social support to nursing home residents, all of which help residents' family members to cope.

Health itself seems at times to be influenced by religion. Christopher Ellison's and Jeffrey Levin's (1998) review of literature indicated that a high level of religious involvement correlated with positive health status across groups, different religions, cultures, socioeconomic status, race, and ethnicity. Positive mental health and psychological well-being also benefit from religious involvement. Several pathways are used: social support, frameworks of meaning, coping resources such as healthful lifestyles and emotional strengthening through religion, and prayer for and by others (positive relationship with health outcomes). Even death's timing seems to be influenced by religion. Ellen Idler and Stanislav Kasl (1992) found that fewer religious people died a month or so before special religious holidays, but more died immediately afterwards. A study of mortality (Hummer et al. 1999) even

found a correlation between longer life (months and years) and frequent religious participation.

Conclusion

Religion is a multidimensional concept that has often been used simplistically by researchers to show correlations with family life outcomes, even though the theories behind the associations were not always understood. Researchers are increasing their efforts to focus on theories to explain the complex religion-family relationships and to design and use more proximal (core) measures of religiosity as well as to assess the positive and/or negative qualities of religious experiences. While recognizing that religious groups differ in many ways, researchers need to discover more about the processes by which the social, cognitive, emotional, spiritual, and behavioral aspects of religion are translated into relationships and behaviors in the family context.

See also: ABORTION; ANABAPTISTS (AMISH, MENNONITE); BUDDHISM; CATHOLICISM; CIRCUMCISION; CONFUCIANISM; DISCIPLINE; DIVORCE: EFFECTS ON CHILDREN; EVANGELICAL CHRISTIANITY; FAMILY MINISTRY; FAMILY VALUES; FICTIVE KINSHIP; FOOD; HEALTH AND FAMILIES; HINDUISM; INFIDELITY; INTERFAITH MARRIAGE; ISLAM; JUDAISM; MARITAL QUALITY; MARRIAGE CEREMONIES; MORMONISM; NONMARITAL CHILDBEARING; PROTESTANTISM; SEXUALITY EDUCATION; SIKHISM

Bibliography

Arnett, J. J. (1998). "Risk Behavior and Family Role Transitions During the Twenties." *Journal of Youth and Adolescence* 27(3):301–320.

Bahr, S. J., and Chadwick, B. (1985). "Religion and Family in Middletown, USA." *Journal of Marriage and the Family* 47:407–414.

Bahr, S. J.; Maughan, S. L., Mareos, A. C., and Li, B. (1998). "Family, Religiosity, and the Risk of Adolescent Drug Use." *Journal of Marriage and the Family* 60:979–992.

Bao, W.; Whitbeck, L. B.; Hoyt, D. R.; and Conger, R. (1999). "Perceived Parental Acceptance as A Moderator of Religious Transmission among Adolescent Boys and Girls." *Journal of Marriage and the Family* 61:362–374.

Barbarin, O. A. (1999). "Do Parental Coping, Involvement, Religiosity, and Racial Identity Mediate Children's

Psychological Adjustment to Sickle Cell Disease?" *Journal of Black Psychology* 25:391–426.

Bartkowski, J. P. (1995). "Spare the Rod . . . or Spare the Child? Divergent Perspectives on Conservative Protestant Child Discipline." *Review of Religious Research* 37:97–116.

Bartkowski, J. P., and Ellison, C. G. (1995). " Divergent Models of Childrearing in Popular Manuals: Conservative Protestants vs. the Mainstream Experts." *Sociology of Religion* 56:21–34.

Bartkowski, J. P., and Xiaohe, X. (2000). "Distant Patriarchs or Expressive Dads? The Discourse and Practice of Fathering in Conservative Protestant Families." *The Sociological Quarterly* 41:465–485.

Benda, B. B., and Corwyn, R. F. (1997). "Religion and Delinquency: The Relationship after Considering Family and Peer Influences." *Journal for the Scientific Study of Religion* 36:81–92.

Booth, A., and Amato, P. R. (2001). "Parental Predivorce Relations and Offspring Postdivorce Well-Being." *Journal of Marriage and the Family* 63:197–212.

Booth, A.; Johnson, D. R.; Branaman, A.; and Sica, A. (1995). "Belief and Behavior: Does Religion Matter in Today's Marriage?" *Journal of Marriage and the Family* 57:661–671.

Bottoms, B. L.; Shaver, P. R.; Goodman, G. S.; and Qin, J. (1995). "In the Name of God: A Profile of Religion-Related Child Abuse." *Journal of Social Issues* 51:85–111.

Brewster, K. L.; Cooksey, E. C.; Guilkey, D. K.; and Rindfuss, R. R. (1998). "The Changing Impact of Religion on the Sexual and Contraceptive Behavior of Adolescent Women in the United States." *Journal of Marriage and the Family* 60:493–504.

Browning, D. S.; Miller-McLemore, B. J.; Couture, P. D.; Lyon, K. B.; and Franklin, R. M. (1997). *From Culture Wars to Common Ground: Religion and the American Family Debate.* Louisville, KY: Westminster John Knox Press.

Burton, L. A., ed. (1992). *Religion and the Family: When God Helps.* New York: Haworth Pastoral Press.

Butler, M.; Gardner, B. C.; and Bird, M. H. (1998). "Not Just a Time-Out: Change Dynamics of Prayer for Religious Couples in Conflict Situations." *Family Process* 37:451–478.

Call, V. R. A., and Heaton, T. B. (1997). "Religious Influence on Marital Stability." *Journal for the Scientific Study of Religion* 36:382–392.

Commerford, M. C., and Reznikoff, M. (1996). "Relationship of Religion and Perceived Social Support to Self-Esteem and Depression in Nursing Home Residents." *Journal of Psychology* 130(1):35–50.

Corwyn, R. F., and Benda, B. B. (2000). "Religiosity and Church Attendance: The Effects on Use of 'Hard Drugs' Controlling for Sociodemographic and Theoretical Factors." *International Journal for the Psychology of Religion* 10(4):241–258.

Cunningham, J. L., and Scanzoni, L. D. (1993). "Religious and Theological Issues in Family Life Education." In *Handbook of Family Life Education,* Vol. 1, ed. M. E. Arcus, J. D. Schvaneveldt, et al. Thousand Oaks, CA: Sage.

Dudley, M. G., and Kosinski Jr., F. A. (1990). "Religiosity and Marital Satisfaction: A Research Note." *Review of Religious Research* 32(1):78–96.

Ellison, C. G.; Bartkowski, J. P.; and Anderson, K. L. (1999). "Are There Religious Variations in Domestic Violence?" *Journal of Family Issues* 20:87–113.

Ellison, C. G.; Bartkowski, J. P.; and Segal, M. L. (1996). "Conservative Protestantism and the Parental Use of Corporal Punishment." *Social Forces* 74:1003–1028.

Ellison, C. G., and Levin, J. S. (1998). "The Religion-Health Connection: Evidence, Theory, and Future Directions." *Health Education and Behavior* 25:700–720.

Evans, T. D.; Cullen, F. T.; Dunaway, R. G.; and Burton Jr., V. S. (1995). "Religion and Crime Reexamined: The Impact of Religion, Secular Controls, and Social Ecology on Adult Criminality." *Criminology* 33:195–224.

Fu, Xuanning. (1996). "A Macro-level Longitudinal Analysis of Marriage and Divorce Rates: The Effects of Modernization and Religious Affiliation." *Family Perspective* 30(2):103–130.

Giblin, P. R. (1997). "Marital Spirituality: A Quantitative Study." *Journal of Religion and Health* 36:321–332.

Giles-Sims, J.; Straus, M. A.; and Sugarman, D. B. (1995). "Child, Maternal, and Family Characteristics Associated with Spanking." *Family Relations* 44:170–176.

Haj-Yahia, M. M. (1998). "Beliefs about Wife Beating among Palestinian Women: The Influence of Their Patriarchal Ideology." *Violence Against Women* 4(5):533–558.

Heaton, T. B.; Jacobson, C. K.; Fu, X. N. (1992). "Religiosity of Married Couples and Childlessness." *Review of Religious Research* 33:244–255.

Heller, P. E., and Wood, B. (2000). "The Influence of Religious and Ethnic Differences on Marital Intimacy: Intermarriage versus Intramarriage." *Journal of Marital and Family Therapy* 26:241–252.

Hogben, W. Murray. (1991). "Marriage and Divorce among Muslims in Canada." In *Muslim Families in North America,* ed. E. H. Waugh, S. McIrwin Abu-Laban, and R. Burckhardt Qureshi. Edmonton: University of Alberta Press.

Hummer, R. A.; Rogers, R. G.; Nam, C. B.; and Ellison, C. G. (1999). "Religious Involvement and U. S. Adult Mortality." *Demography* 36(May):273–285.

Idler, E. L., and Kasl, S. V. (1992). "Religion, Disability, Depression, and the Timing of Death." *American Journal of Sociology* 97(4):1052–1079.

Jenkins, K. W. (1991). "Religion and Families." In *Family Research: A Sixty-Year Review, 1930–1990,* Vol. 1, ed. S. J. Bahr. New York: Free Press.

Kaslow, F., and Robison, J. A. (1996). "Long-Term Satisfying Marriages: Perceptions of Contributing Factors." *The American Journal of Family Therapy* 24:153–170.

Kendler, K.; Gardner, C. O.; and Prescott, C. A. (1997). "Religion, Psychopathology, and Substance Use and Abuse: A Multimeasure, Genetic-Epidemiologic Study." *American Journal of Psychiatry* 154(3):322–329.

King, V., and Elder Jr., G. H. (1999). "Are Religious Grandparents More Involved Grandparents?" *Journals of Gerontology* 54B:S317–S328.

Krishnan, V. (1998). "PreMarital Cohabitation and Marital Disruption." *Journal of Divorce and Remarriage* 28:157–170.

Lawson, E. J., and Thompson, A. (1995). "Black Men Make Sense of Marital Distress and Divorce." *Family Relations* 44:211–218.

Lazerwitz, B. (1995). "Jewish-Christian Marriages and Conversions, 1971 and 1990." *Sociology of Religion* 56:433–443.

Lehrer, E. (1996). "Religion as a Determinant of Marital Fertility." *Journal of Population Economics* 9:173–196.

Lehrer, E. (1998). "Religious Intermarriage in the United States: Determinants and Trends." *Social Science Research* 27:245–263.

Lynch, E. W., and Hanson, M. J., eds. (1992). *Developing Cross-Cultural Competence: A Guide for Working with Young Children and Their Families.* Baltimore, MD: Paul H. Brooks.

Mackey, R. A.; Diemer, M. A.; and O'Brien, B. A. (2000). "Conflict-Management Styles of Spouses in Lasting Marriages." *Psychotherapy* 37:134–148.

Mahoney, A.; Pargament, K.; Jewell, T.; Swank, A. B.; Scott, E.; Emery, E.; and Rye, M. (1999). "Marriage and the Spiritual Realm: The Role of Proximal and Distal Religious Constructs in Marital Functioning." *Journal of Family Psychology* 13:321–338.

McFadden, S. H. (1995). "Religion and Well-Being in Aging Person in an Aging Society." *Journal of Social Issues* 51:161–175.

Mosher, J. P., and Handal, P. J. (1997). "The Relationship Between Religion and Psychological Distress in Adolescents." *Journal of Psychology and Theology* 25:449–457.

Musick, M., and Wilson, J. (1995). "Religious Switching for Marriage Reasons." *Sociology of Religion* 56:257–270.

Myers, S. (1996). "An Interactive Model of Religiosity Inheritance: The Importance of Family Context." *American Sociological Review* 61:858–866.

Palkovitz, R., and Palm, G. (1998). "Fatherhood and Faith in Formation: The Developmental Effects of Fathering on Religiosity, Morals, and Values." *Journal of Men's Studies* 7:33–51.

Pargament, K. I.; Kmaton, K. I.; and Hess, R. E., eds. (1993). *Religion and Prevention in Mental Health: Research, Vision, and Action.* New York: Haworth Press.

Pearce, L., and Axinn, W. G. (1998). "The Impact of Family Religious Life on the Quality of Mother-Child Relations." *American Sociological Review* 63:810–828.

Plotnick, R. D. (1992). "The Effects of Attitude on Teenage Premarital Pregnancy and Its Resolution." *American Sociological Review* 57(6):800–811.

Rahim, H. (2000). "Virtue, Gender and the Family: Reflections on Religious Texts in Islam and Hinduism." *Journal of Social Distress and the Homeless* 9(3):187–199.

Shortz, J. L., and Worthington Jr., E. L. (1994). "Research Note: Young Adults' Recall of Religiosity, Attributions, and Coping in Parental Divorce." *Journal for the Scientific Study of Religion* 33:172–179.

Snow, T. S., and Compton, W. C. (1996). "Marital Satisfaction and Communication in Fundamentalist Protestant Marriages." *Psychological Reports* 78(June Pt.1):979–985.

Sorenson, A. M.; Grindstaff, C.; and Turner, R. J. (1995). "Religious Involvement among Unmarried Adolescent Mothers: A Source of Emotional Support?" *Sociology of Religion* 56:71–81.

Spilka, B.; Zwartjes, W. J.; and Zwartjes, G. M. (1991). "The Role of Religion in Coping with Childhood Cancer." *Pastoral Psychology* 39:295–304.

Stack, S. (1998). "The Relationship Between Culture and Suicide: An Analysis of African Americans." *Transcultural Psychiatry* 35:253–269.

Thornton, A. (1992). "Reciprocal Effects of Religiosity, Cohabitation, and Marriage." *American Journal of Sociology* 98:628–651.

Vakalahi, H. F.; Harrison, R. S.; and Janzen, F. V. (2000). "The Influences of Family-Based Risk and Protective Factors on Adolescent Substance Use." *Journal of Family Social Work* 4:21–34.

Varon, S. R., and Riley, A. W. (1999). "Relationship Between Maternal Church Attendance and Adolescent Mental Health and Social Functioning." *Psychiatric Services* 50(6):799–805.

Wineberg, H. (1994). "Marital Reconciliation in the United States: Which Couples Are Successful?" *Journal of Marriage and the Family* 56:80–88.

RUTH CORDLE HATCH
WALTER R. SCHUMM

REMARRIAGE

In the United States, approximately 75 percent of divorced people legally remarry, and they usually do so less than four years after divorce. Nearly one-third, however, remarry within a year after their divorce is legal. Consequently, almost one-half of the marriages in the United States include a remarriage for at least one of the spouses; the remarriage is most likely to be a second marriage, but it could also be a third, fourth, or more. One important change in remarriage rates between the 1980s and the 1990s has been observed—a decrease in rates of legal marriage and a concomitant increase in rates of cohabitation. Further, most remarrying couples cohabit prior to legal marriage; the length of cohabitation ranges from a few days to many years.

Internationally, research on remarriage focuses on rates of remarriage after divorce. In general, reports from Western cultures—Canada, Europe, and Australia—and South Korea show remarriage trends that are similar to the United States. However, in some Asian countries divorced and remarried families still experience more stigma than in Western cultures, making it difficult to collect accurate statistics on stepfamilies, who can present themselves as a first-married, nuclear family in many situations. In Nigeria, where marital unions are relatively stable, and fertility is high, men and women remarry very quickly and at high rates after death or divorce. The traditional Muslim Hausa society of northern Nigeria has one of the highest rates of divorce and remarriage in the world. Apparently this is due to wives' fleeing oppressive family situations within a society that expects them to be married. Reports from the Dominican Republic explain that marriage and remarriage rates have decreased in the 1990s for economic reasons; women are choosing single parenting over marriage to men who are increasingly finding themselves unemployed due to a worsening job market. In much of the world, very little is known about divorce and remarriage patterns or about any other types of marital transitions; often this is due to religious or secular laws that forbid divorce.

Factors Affecting Likelihood of Remarriage after Divorce or Death of Spouse

In the United States where research on families is extensive, remarried life is understood better. Sex differences and race differences exist in rates of remarriage in the United States. Compared with women, men remarry sooner and more often and generally marry someone a few years younger. The more education and resources a man has, the more likely he is to remarry. Conversely, for women, having more education and resources and being older mean less likelihood of remarriage in general. However, women with high status employment who divorce when they are older tend to remarry more quickly. Hispanic/Latino Americans remarry slightly less frequently and African Americans remarry much less frequently than white, non-Hispanic Americans. It is not clear if these differences are a due to cultural, religious, or economic factors, or some combination of the three.

Being a parent lowers the likelihood of remarriage for women and men, but the effect of parenthood is greater for women. With respect to parenthood in the remarriage, about half of women in remarriages give birth to at least one child, and this usually happens within the first two years of the remarriage. Not surprising, as people age, the frequencies of remarrying and of re-divorcing decrease. However, in the twenty-first century, the numbers of later-life remarriages are expected to increase, as the baby boom generation will be living longer and healthier lives. When remarriage occurs after the death of a spouse, widowed men marry much sooner than widowed women, but all widowed people are much slower to remarry than divorced people.

In addition to the above statistics, which are based on the heterosexual population, unknown numbers of gay, lesbian, and bisexual couples have similar patterns of coupling, uncoupling, and re-coupling. Because there is no legal record of the coupling transitions of these groups, since they cannot legally marry or divorce, virtually nothing is known about the demographics of couple transitions among gays and lesbians, although many have wedding ceremonies and consider themselves to be married.

Marital Relationships

Although some studies of marital quality find no differences between first-married and remarried couples, other studies find remarried couples have lower quality relationships than first-marrieds. This could be because remarried couples express more disagreement, criticism, and anger; this negativity is usually focused on issues related to stepchildren. Indeed, when both spouses are stepparents, marital relationships are poorer than in families with a child or children of one spouse only. In addition, emotional attachment to a former spouse is also related to lower marital satisfaction. However, no differences in marital satisfaction have been found between stepmother and stepfather families, or between remarried couples in which children live in the home as compared to couples with children living in the ex-spouse's home.

Many studies have compared marrieds and remarrieds on various aspects of the marital relationship. Compared to first-married, remarried husbands and wives are more egalitarian in general, but have been found to be no different in decision-making power regarding issues directly related to their marriage; remarrieds do not avoid talking about marital problems more than first-marrieds. Further, remarried husbands and wives report being more autonomous with respect to childrearing and finances. Although remarried spouses are much more likely to have separate financial accounts, there is no difference in the marital satisfaction between those with separate accounts and those who pool their monies in one account. Also, remarried wives report having more autonomy regarding friendships and family and having more power in general in the marital relationship than

wives in first marriages. Although household duties tend to be based on traditional sex roles in both first marriages and remarriages, remarried husbands do more housework than first-married husbands. In addition, remarried spouses are less similar in age than first-married spouses, and they are not as emotionally close to extended family members. It is important to keep in mind that these differences between first-marrieds and remarrieds may be, at least in part, due to the age differences between the adults in these two groups; by definition, remarrieds are older than first-marrieds on average. The effect of remarriage on the physical and psychological well-being of men and women is not known. Studies comparing divorced adults to remarried adults, and remarried men to remarried women have been done, but the results of these studies are inconsistent.

Remarriage in Later Life

Given increasingly longer life expectancies, late-life (over age sixty) remarriage and cohabitation are on the rise. This phenomenon has major implications for eldercare of aging parents and stepparents, and for inheritance of assets passed down to children and stepchildren. Preliminary research shows that adult children feel more obligated to help parents than to help stepparents, especially stepmothers, unless the relationship with the stepparent is strong. Apparently, this phenomenon is reciprocal—remarried parents have been found to provide less support to adult children, in general, than parents who remain in first marriages. Further, elderly parents tend to favor biological kin over any other relationships in their wills. Although much needs to be learned about late-life remarriage, research has shown tentatively that late-life remarrieds have higher marital satisfaction than mid-life remarrieds; apparently this is due to very high marital satisfaction among late-life remarried men.

Divorce in Remarriages

Although remarrieds report being more willing than first-marrieds to leave a marriage, first-marrieds and remarrieds actually divorce at similar rates (about 60%). However, the divorce rate is higher if the couple is African American, if the husband is in his early twenties, or if stepchildren are present. Conversely, when a baby is born into a remarriage, the couple is less likely to divorce. When remarrieds do divorce, the divorce occurs sooner than it does for first-marrieds. There are two main sociological explanations for the high divorce rate among remarried couples: (1) a lack of social norms and support for remarrieds in our society in which the majority of the population idealizes the nuclear family as the ideal family, and (2) a smaller number of potential marriage partners with similar values and interests for divorced adults than for the younger group of never-married, single adults. The psychological explanation is that, on average, there are more adults with poor relationship skills or with psychological problems among the population of divorced persons.

Conclusion

Although divorce is prevalent in many countries of the world, people are not remaining single after a problematic marriage. Both men and women are remarrying, or at least cohabiting, at high rates. However, it appears that women who can financially support themselves choose not to remarry as frequently as other women. Although first marriages and remarriages are similar in many respects, remarried husbands and wives are more liberated from traditional sex roles than spouses in first marriages. The high rates of remarriage and recoupling suggest that men and women continue to seek to find a compatible partner with whom to share daily life.

See also: CONFLICT: COUPLE RELATIONSHIPS; DIVORCE: EFFECTS ON CHILDREN; GRANDPARENTS' RIGHTS; HONEYMOON; INTERPARENTAL CONFLICT—EFFECTS ON CHILDREN; MARITAL QUALITY; STEPFAMILIES; WIDOWHOOD

Bibliography

Allen, E. S.; Baucom, D. H.; Burnett, C. K.; Epstein, N.; and Rankin-Esquer, L. S. (2001). "Decision-making Power, Autonomy, and Communication in Remarried Spouses Compared with First-married Spouses." *Family Relations* 50:326–334.

Berger, R. (1998). *Stepfamilies: A Multi-dimensional Perspective.* New York: Haworth Press.

Booth, A., and Dunn, J. (1994). *Stepfamilies: Who Benefits? Who Does Not?* Hillsdale, NJ: Erlbaum.

Coleman, M.; Ganong, L.; and Fine, M. (2000). "Reinvestigation Remarriage: Another Decade of Progress." *Journal of Marriage and the Family* 62:1288–1307.

Crosbie-Burnett, M., and Helmbrecht, L. (1993). "A Descriptive Empirical Study of Gay Male Stepfamilies." *Family Relations.* Special Issue on Family Diversity 42:243–248.

Ganong, L. H., and Coleman, M. (1994). *Remarried Family Relationships.* Thousand Oaks, CA: Sage.

Ganong, L. H., and Coleman, M. (2000). "Remarried Families." In *Close Relationships: A Sourcebook,* ed. C. Hendrick and S. Hendrick. Thousand Oaks, CA: Sage.

Hetherington, E. M., ed. (1999). *Coping with Divorce, Single Parenting, and Remarriage: A Risk and Resiliency Perspective.* Mahwah, NJ: Erlbaum.

Ihinger-Tallman, M., and Pasley, K. (1997). "Stepfamilies in 1984 and Today: A Scholarly Perspective." *Marriage and Family Review* 26:19–40.

Pasley, K., and Ihinger-Tallman, M., ed. (1994). *Stepparenting: Issues in Theory, Research, and Practice.* Westport, CT: Greenwood.

MARGARET CROSBIE-BURNETT
KATRINA MCCLINTIC

RENEWAL OF WEDDING VOWS

Weddings are an ancient cultural practice that has great meaning for its participants. However, couples in the United States have been holding another kind of wedding ceremony for the purpose of renewing their wedding vows. There has been little research on this ritual, prompting researchers to reflect on what occurs when couples renew their wedding vows, and what the various forms of the vow renewal ritual accomplish for the couple and people in their social network.

Renewal of Wedding Vows Ritual

There is a dearth of information on the renewal of wedding vows. The research that is available was done in the United States (Braithwaite and Baxter 1995). Like wedding ceremonies, vow renewals are social events in which personal feelings and commitments between partners are witnessed by friends and family. The ceremonies are held in churches, public secular spaces (e.g., hotel or hall), or residential homes.

Dawn O. Braithwaite and Leslie Baxter (1995) asked participants to describe their vow renewal experiences. Couples described why they decided to hold a vow renewal, the setting, participants, and activities of the event, and the outcome of the event. Many of the interviewees kept and displayed meaningful artifacts from the ritual, such as invitations to the ceremony, copies of the text of renewal vows, pictures and photo albums, videotapes of the ceremony, and objects involved in the vow renewal (including special clothing worn during the ceremony and rings exchanged between spouses).

Although a few couples report renewing their vows alone and informally, the vast majority of these vow renewal rituals are carried out in a public setting with witnesses. The number of witnesses can range from two persons to several hundred. The renewal events typically involve two phases that occur either in the same setting or in different settings: the vow renewal ceremony and the celebratory reception/party. These events typically involve an officiating person who administers the vows of renewal to the couple, usually the couple's pastor, minister, priest, or judge.

Participants in the ceremonies enact a variety of roles in the event: helping with planning and preparations, serving as members of a traditional *wedding party* (e.g., ushers or bridesmaids), performing as part of the renewal ceremony (e.g., performing a song or reading a poem), serving in a *witness* role; and, in the case of *mass ceremony* renewals, coenactor of vows. Many of these vow renewal ceremonies take the form of a traditional wedding; an observer would be hard-pressed to tell the difference between a wedding and vow renewal event. Some couples reunite their original wedding party; other couples have their adult children serve as attendants.

Couples who renew their vows consider the witnessing function of family and friends in attendance important. They are aware that stating their vows in front of others also makes them accountable to the promises and commitments made: "[Having others present] adds verification that in a sense, we're willing to be held accountable for this commitment to each other because we promised [it] in front of the witnesses. We can't say to the witnesses now 'Well, we've broken that promise'

without real due cause. It's nothing casual." (Baxter and Braithwaite 1995)

Types of Vow Renewal Ceremonies and Their Purposes

Researchers have identified three different types of vow renewal events: (a) *couple or family initiated events,* where the couple or members or their families planned and carried out a renewal of vows ceremony; (b) *relational repair events,* where the couple came together after a separation or severe relational challenges and renewed their vows; and (c) *group or mass renewal of vows events,* an event usually planned by a church where multiple couples would renewal their vows (Braithwaite and Baxter 1995). Reasons for holding the vow renewal event differ within these three types.

The first type of renewal ritual is initiated by the couple or their family. Although a couple may renew their wedding vows at any time during their marriage, the majority hold this ceremony as a way to commemorate a *milestone* wedding anniversary, such as their twenty-fifth, fortieth, or even fiftieth anniversary. Several different motivations or goals are reflected within the couple-initiated ritual. Couples use the ceremony as an opportunity to publicly express their love and commitment to one another. Other couples pay homage to their marriage by giving themselves the "real wedding" that they never had. For some, their original wedding ceremonies were often found lacking in emotional and/or material ways. These include couples who had eloped, had limited financial means when they married, or married during wartime, and they opt for a large, formal renewal ceremony with all the traditional wedding trimmings (e.g., formal clothing, flowers, and wedding cake).

Some couples choose to enact the vow renewal event to pay homage to friends and family. These couples recognize that their marriages are embedded in communal webs of family and friends and believe these significant others should be honored through the celebration of the vow renewal event. (Baxter and Braithwaite 2001). Another function performed by the vow renewal ceremony is to pay homage to the institution of marriage. Some couples feel that the public renewal of their marriage testifies to the endurance, strength, and beauty of the institution of marriage.

In honoring their own successful marriage, couples feel that they are serving as role models to others, particularly members of the younger generation. Finally, for many of the couples, the renewal demonstrates a reverence for God and testifies to God's presence in their marriage.

A second type of vow renewal ritual is one that reflects *relational repair,* most often after a separation or severe relational challenge. The couple chooses to renew their vows to mark a turning point in their relationship, such as signifying the successful resolution of a crisis in the relationship (e.g., after an extramarital affair) or marking the transition to another stage in the relationship's history (e.g., after the children have left home).

The third type of vow renewal event is a *mass ceremony* in which a member of the clergy administers a common set of vows to an assembled group of couples who simultaneously renew their respective marriages. In some instances, a presiding minister or priest simply asks couples to stand up during part of a regular church service. In other instances, couples sign up for a special church service during which the mass ceremony will take place. These mass ceremonies recognize the central role of marriage in the institution of the church. Other mass ceremony renewal events involve marriage enrichment programs such as *Marriage Encounter,* in which couples participate in a structured program intended to enhance communication skills between spouses, and culminates in a group-enacted renewal of marital vows. Although most couples participating in mass ceremonies report they are glad they participated, some couples report that these mass vow renewals are somewhat impersonal and less meaningful than couple-initiated and repair vow renewal ceremonies.

In short, the marriage vow renewal event is a communication ritual that pays homage to both the unique marital bond between partners as well as the broader institution of marriage. The public nature of the marriage vow renewal event and the function of witnesses stresses the importance of understanding marriage, not as simply a relationship of two people, but as embedded in webs of social relationships including family, friends, and the community.

See also: AFFECTION; COMMUNICATION: COUPLE RELATIONSHIPS: DIALECTICAL THEORY; MARRIAGE CEREMONIES; RELATIONSHIP MAINTENANCE; SOCIAL NETWORKS

Bibliography

Baxter, L. A., and Braithwaite, D. O. (2001). "Performing Marriage: Marriage Renewal Rituals as Cultural Performance." *Southern Communication Journal* 67:94–109

Braithwaite, D. O., and Baxter, L. A. (1995). "'I do' Again: The Relational Dialectics of Renewing Marriage Vows." *Journal of Social and Personal Relationships* 12:177–198.

DAWN O. BRAITHWAITE

REPRODUCTION

See ABORTION; ASSISTED REPRODUCTIVE TECHNOLOGIES; BIRTH CONTROL: CONTRACEPTIVE METHODS; FAMILY PLANNING; FERTILITY; GENETIC COUNSELING; NONMARITAL CHILDBEARING; PREGNANCY AND BIRTH

RESEARCH

FAMILY MEASUREMENT *Murray A. Straus, Susan M. Ross*

METHODOLOGY *Alan Acock, Yoshie Sano*

FAMILY MEASUREMENT

A 1964 review of tests and scales used in family research found serious deficiencies (Straus 1964), and subsequent reviews showed very little improvement (Straus 1992; Straus and Brown 1978). However, changes in the nature of the field have contributed to an increase in the use of standardized tests to measure characteristics of the family. This is an important development because standardized tests are vital tools for both clinical assessment and research. New tests tend to produce a flowering of research focused on the newly measurable concept. Examples of tests that have fostered much research include measures of marital satisfaction (Spanier 1976), adequacy of family functioning

(Olson, Russell, and Sprenkle 1989), and family violence (Straus 1990a). Hundreds of family measures are abstracted or reproduced in compendiums such as *Family Assessment* (Grotevant and Carlson 1989), *Handbook of Measurements for Marriage and Family Therapy* (Fredman and Sherman 1987), and *Handbook of Family Measurement Techniques* (Touliatos, Perlmutter, and Straus 2001). There is also a growing methodological literature on techniques for constructing measures of family characteristics, such as those by Karen S. Wampler and Charles F. Halverson, Jr. (1993) and Thomas W. Draper and Anastascios C. Marcos (1990). The state of testing in family research, however, is not as healthy as these publications might suggest. In fact, the data indicate that the validity of tests used in family research is rarely known.

For purposes of this entry, the term *measure* includes test, scale (such as Likert, Thurstone, Guttman, and Semantic Differential scales), index, factor score, scoring system (when referring to methods of scoring social interaction such as Gottman 1994 or Patterson 1982), and latent variables constructed by use of a structural equation modeling program. The defining feature is that they "combine the values of several items [also called indicators, questions, observations, events] into a composite measure . . . used to predict or gauge some underlying continuum which can only be partially measured by any single item or variable" (Nie et al. 1978, p. 529).

Advantages of Multiple-Item Measures

Multiple-item measures are emphasized in this entry because they are mor ely to be valid than single-item measures. Although one good question or observation may be enough and thirty bad ones are useless, there are reasons why multiple-item measures are more likely to be valid. One reason is that most phenomena of interest to family researchers have multiple facets that can be adequately represented only by use of multiple items. A single question, for example, is unlikely to represent the multiple facets of marital satisfaction adequately.

A second reason for greater confidence in multiple-item measures occurs because of the inevitable risk of error in selecting items. If a single item is used and there is a conceptual error in formulating or scoring it, hypotheses that are tested by using that measure will not be supported even if they are true. However, when a multiple-item test is used, the adverse effect of a single invalid item is limited to a relatively small reduction in validity (Straus and Baron 1990). In a fifteen-item scale, for example, a defective item is only 6.6 percent of the total, so the findings would parallel those obtained if all fifteen items were correct.

Multiple items are also desirable because measures of internal consistency reliability are based on the number of items in the measure and the correlation between them. Given a certain average correlation between items, the more items, the higher the reliability. If only three items are used, it is rarely possible to achieve a high level of reliability. Reliability needs to be high because it sets an upper limit on validity.

Status and Trends in Family Measurement

To investigate the quality of measurement in family research, all empirical studies published in two major U.S. family journals (*Journal of Marriage and the Family* and *Journal of Family Psychology*) were examined. To determine trends in the *Journal of Marriage and the Family,* issues from 1982 and 1992 were compared. For the *Journal of Family Psychology,* issues from 1987 (the year the journal was founded) and 1992 were compared. Of the 161 empirical research articles reviewed, slightly fewer than two-thirds used a multiple item measurement. This increased from 46.9 percent initially to 68.1 percent in 1992. A typical article used more than one such instrument, so that a total of 219 multiple item measures were used in these 161 articles. Reliability was reported in 79.4 percent of these articles. Reliability reporting increased from 53.3 percent initially to 90.6 percent in 1992. Six percent of the articles had as their main purpose describing a new measurement instrument or presenting data concerning an existing instrument.

How one interprets these statistics depends on the standard of comparison. Articles in sociology journals and child psychology and clinical psychology journals are appropriate comparisons because these are the disciplines closest to family studies and in which many family researchers were trained. For sociology, the findings listed above can be compared to those reported in a study by Murray A. Straus and Barbara Wauchope (1992), in which they examined empirical articles from the

1979 and 1989 issues of *American Sociological Review, American Journal of Sociology,* and *Sociological Methods and Research*. This comparison shows that articles in family journals pay considerably more attention to measurement than articles in leading sociological journals. None of the 185 articles in sociology journals was on a specific measure, whereas 6 percent of the articles in the family journals were devoted to describing or evaluating an instrument. This portends well for family research because it is an investment in tools for future research. Only one-third of the articles in the sociology journals used a multiple-item measure, compared to more than two-thirds (68%) of articles in the family journals. The record of family researchers also exceeds that of sociologists in respect to reporting reliability. Only about 10 percent of the articles in sociology journals, compared to 80 percent of the articles in family journals, reported the reliability of the instruments. The main problem area is validity; only 12.4 percent of the articles in family journals described or referenced evidence of validity. The fact that this is three times more than in sociology is not much consolation because 12 percent is still a small percentage. Moreover, reporting or citing information on validity did not increase from the base period. Since validity is probably the most crucial quality of an instrument, the low percentage and the lack of growth indicate that more attention needs to be paid to measurement in family research.

There is no comparable study of measures in child or clinical psychological journals.

Reasons for Underdevelopment of Measures

The limited production of standard and validated measures of family characteristics is probably the result of a number of causes. Conventional wisdom attributes it to a lack of time and other resources for instrument development and validation. This is not an adequate explanation because it is true of all the social sciences. Why do psychologists devote the most resources to developing and validating tests, sociologists the least, and family researchers fall in between?

One likely reason is a difference in rewards for measurement research. A related reason is a difference in the opportunities and constraints. In psychology, there are journals devoted to psychological measures in whole or in part, such as *Educational and Psychological Measurement* and *Journal of Clinical and Consulting Psychology.* There are no such journals in sociology or family studies. Moreover, there is a large market for psychological tests, and several major firms specialize in publishing tests. It is a multimillion-dollar industry, and authors of tests can earn substantial royalties. By contrast, sociology lacks the symbolic and economic reward system that underlies the institutionalization of test development as a major specialization in psychology. The field of family studies lies in between. In principle there should be a demand for tests because of the large number of family therapists, but few family therapists actually use tests.

A second explanation for the differences among psychology, family studies, and sociology in attention to measurement is a situational constraint inherent in the type of research done. A considerable amount of family research is done by survey methods—for example, the National Survey of Families and Households. Surveys of this type usually include measures of many variables in a single thirty- to sixty-minute interview. Clinical psychologists, on the other hand, often can use longer and therefore more reliable tests, because their clients have a greater stake in providing adequate data and will tolerate undergoing two or more hours of testing.

Third, most tests are developed for a specific study and there is rarely a place in the project budget for adequate measure development—test/retest reliability, concurrent and construct validity, and construction of normative tables. Even when the author of a measure does the psychometric research needed to enable others to evaluate whether the measure might be suitable for their research, family journals rarely allow enough space to present that material.

Fourth, the optimum procedure is for the author to write a paper describing the test, the theory underlying the test, the empirical procedures used to develop the test, reliability and validity evidence, and norms. This rarely occurs because of the lack of resources indicated above. In addition, most investigators are more interested in the substantive issues for which the project was funded.

Another reason why standardized tests are less frequently used in family research is that many studies are based on cases from agencies. A researcher studying child abuse who draws the cases from child protective services might not need a method of measuring child abuse. However, standardized tests are still needed because an adequate understanding of child abuse cannot depend solely on officially identified cases. It is important also to do research on cases that are not known to agencies, because such cases are much more numerous than cases known to agencies and because general population cases typically differ in important ways from the cases known to agencies (Straus 1990b).

The Future of Family Research Measures

There are grounds for optimism and grounds for concern about the future of family tests. The grounds for concern are, first, that in survey research on the family, concepts are often measured by a single interview question. Second, even when a multiple-item test is used, it is rarely on the basis of empirical evidence of reliability and validity. Third, the typical measure developed for use in a family study is never used in another study. One can speculate that this hiatus in the cumulative nature of research occurs because of the lack of evidence of reliability and validity and because authors rarely provide sufficient information to facilitate use of the instrument by others.

The grounds for optimism are to be found in the sizable and slowly growing number of standardized instruments, as listed in compendiums (e.g., Grotevant and Carlson 1989; Fredman and Sherman 1987; Touliatos, Perlmutter, and Straus 1990). A second ground for optimism is the rapid growth in the number of psychologists doing family research, because psychologists bring to family research an established tradition of test development. Similarly, the explosive growth of family therapy is grounds for optimism, because it is likely that more tests will gradually begin to be used for intake diagnosis. A third ground for optimism is the increasing use of some family measures in cultures other than those in which the measures were initially developed. For example, David H. Olson's Family Adaptability and Cohesion Evaluation Scales (FACES) (1993) have been used to research Chinese families (Philips, West, Shen, and Zheng 1998; Tang and Chung 1997; Wang, Zhang, Li, and Zhao 1998; Zhang et al. 1995), immigrants to Israel (Ben-David and Gilbar

1997; Gilbar 1997), and Ethiopian migrants (Ben-David & Erez-Darvish 1997). The cross-cultural use of measures allows for assessments of validity and reliability outside of the background assumptions of the cultures in which they were developed.

There is a certain irony in the second source of optimism, because basic researchers usually believe that they, not clinicians, represent quality in science. In respect to measurement, clinicians tend to demand instruments of higher quality than do basic researchers because the consequences of using an inadequate measure are more serious. When a basic researcher uses an instrument with low reliability or validity, it can lead to a Type II error—that is, failing to accept a true hypothesis. This may result in theoretical confusion or a paper not being published. But when a practitioner uses an invalid or unreliable instrument, the worst-case scenario can involve injury to a client. Consequently, clinicians need to demand more evidence of reliability and validity than do researchers. As a result, clinically oriented family researchers tend to produce and make available more adequate measures. Hubert M. Blalock (1982) argued that inconsistent findings and failure to find empirical support for sound theories may be due to lack of reliable and valid means of operationalizing concepts in the theories being tested. It follows that research will be on a sounder footing if researchers devote more attention to developing reliable and valid measures of family characteristics.

See also: FAMILY ASSESSMENT; FAMILY DIAGNOSIS/DSM IV; MARITAL QUALITY; RESEARCH: METHODOLOGY

Bibliography

Ben-David, A., and Erez-Darvish, T. (1997). "The Effect of the Family on the Emotional Life of Ethiopian Immigrant Adolescents in Boarding Schools in Israel." *Residential Treatment for Children and Youth* 15(2):39–50.

Ben-David, A., and Gilbar, O. (1997). "Family, Migration, and Psychosocial Adjustment to Illness." *Social Work in Health Care* 26(2):53–67.

Blalock, H. M. (1982). *Conceptualization and Measurement in the Social Sciences.* Newbury Park, CA: Sage.

Burgess, E. W., and Cottrell, L. S. (1939). *Predicting Success or Failure in Marriage.* Englewood Cliffs, NJ: Prentice Hall.

Cronbach, L. J. (1970). *Essentials of Psychological Testing.* New York: Harper & Row.

Draper, T. W., and Marcos, A. C. (1990). *Family Variables: Conceptualization, Measurement, and Use.* Newbury Park, CA: Sage.

Fredman, N., and Sherman, R. (1987). *Handbook of Measurements for Marriage and Family Therapy.* New York: Brunner/Mazel.

Gilbar, O. (1997). "The Impact of Immigration Status and Family Function on the Psychosocial Adjustment of Cancer Patients." *Families, Systems and Health* 15(4):405–412.

Gottman, J. M. (1994). *What Predicts Divorce? The Relationship Between Marital Process and Marital Outcome.* Hillsdale, NJ: Erlbaum.

Grotevant, H. D., and Carlson, C. I. (1989). *Family Assessment: A Guide to Methods and Measures.* New York: Guilford.

Nie, N. H.; Hull, C. H.; Jenkins, J. G.; Steinbrenner, K.; and Bent, D. H. (1978). *SPSS: Statistical Package for the Social Sciences.* New York: McGraw-Hill.

Olson, D. H. (1993). "Circumplex Model of Marital and Family Systems: Assessing Family Functioning." In *Normal Family Process,* ed. F. Walsh. New York: Guilford Press.

Olson, D. H.; Russell, C. S.; and Sprenkle, D. H. (1989). *Circumplex Model: New Scales for Assessing Systematic Assessment and Treatment of Families.* New York: Haworth Press.

Patterson, G. R., ed. (1982). *Coercive Family Processes: A Social Learning Approach.* Eugene, OR: Castalia.

Philips, M. R.; West, C. L.; Shen, Q.; and Zheng, Y. (1998). "Comparison of Schizophrenic Patients' Families and Normal Families in China, Using Chinese Versions of FACES-II and the Family Environment Scales." *Family Process* 37:95–106.

Spanier, G. B. (1976). "Measuring Dyadic Adjustment: The Quality of Marriage and Similar Dyads." *Journal of Marriage and the Family* 38:15–28.

Straus, M. A. (1964). "Measuring Families." In *Handbook of Marriage and the Family,* ed. H. T. Christenson. Chicago: Rand McNally.

Straus, M. A. (1990a). "The Conflict Tactics Scales and Its Critics: An Evaluation and New Data on Validity and Reliability." In *Physical Violence in American Families: Risk Factors and Adaptations to Violence in 8,145 Families,* ed. M. A. Straus and R. J. Gelles. New Brunswick, NJ: Transaction.

Straus, M. A. (1990b). "Injury and Frequency of Assault and the 'Representative Sample Fallacy' in Measuring Wife Beating and Child Abuse." In *Physical Violence in American Families: Risk Factors and Adaptations to Violence in 8,145 Families,* ed. M. A. Straus and R. J. Gelles. New Brunswick, NJ: Transaction.

Straus, M. A. (1992). "Measurement Instruments in Child Abuse Research." Paper prepared for the National Academy of Sciences panel of child abuse research. Durham, NH: Family Research Laboratory, University of New Hampshire.

Straus, M. A., and Baron, L. (1990). "The Strength of Weak Indicators: A Response to Gilles, Brown, Geletta, and Dalecki." *Sociological Quarterly* 31:619–624.

Straus, M. A., and Brown, B. W. (1978). *Family Measurement Techniques,* 2nd edition. Minneapolis: University of Minnesota Press.

Strauss, M. A., and Wauchope, B. (1992). "Measurement Instruments." In *Encyclopedia of Sociology,* ed. E. F. Borgatta and M. L. Borgatta. New York: Macmillan.

Tang, C. S., and Chung, T. K. H. (1997). "Psychosexual Adjustment Following Sterilization: A Prospective Study on Chinese Women." *Journal of Psychosomatic Research* 42(2):187–196.

Touliatos, J.; Perlmutter, D.; and Straus, M. A. (2001). *Handbook of Family Measurement Techniques,* 4th edition. Thousand Oaks, CA: Sage.

Wampler, K. S., and Halverson, C. F., Jr. (1993). "Quantitative Measurement in Family Research." In *Source Book of Family Theories and Methods: A Contextual Approach,* ed. P. G. Boss, W. J. Doherty, R. LaRossa, W. R. Schumm, and S. K. Steinmetz. New York: Plenum.

Wang, Z.; Zhang, X.; Li, G.; and Zhao, Z. (1998). "A Study of Family Environment, Cohesion, and Adaptability in Heroin Addicts." *Chinese Journal of Clinical Psychology* 6(1):32–34.

Zhang, J.; Weng, Z.; Liu, Q.; Li, H.; Zhao, S.; Xu, Z.; Chen, W.; and Ran, H. (1995). "The Relationship of Depression of Family Members and Family Functions." *Chinese Journal of Clinical Psychology* 3(4):225–229.

MURRAY A. STRAUS (1995)
SUSAN M. ROSS (1995)
REVISED BY JAMES M. WHITE

METHODOLOGY

Four characteristics shape the research methods that family scholars use. First, family scholarship has conceptual roots in a variety of disciplines, including anthropology, family and consumer science, economics, history, human ecology, psychology, and sociology. Second, the subject matter studied by family scholars overlaps the subject matter studied by a variety of content specialty areas such as women's studies, human development, gerontology, education, nutrition, and counseling. Third, although other fields often focus on isolated individuals, family scholars study individuals who are embedded in family systems. Fourth, families have a shared past and future (Copeland and White 1991). Being responsive to these characteristics requires multiple perspectives from quantitative and qualitative methods, experimental and survey methods, and cross-sectional and longitudinal methods (Schumm and Hemesath 1999).

Some family scholars approach their study of families from a large-scale/historical perspective or a large-scale/comparative perspective. Others approach it from an individual perspective. Some scholars seek to discover family pattern in ancient culture; others seek to solve current social problems. The unit of analysis—that is, the smallest unit about which a scholar draws a conclusion—may be an individual (child, mother, nonresident father), a dyad (husband and wife, siblings), a family (nuclear, stem, lesbian, single parent), a culture, or a historical period.

A researcher may want to explain how a hyperactive child influences outcomes for families, such as conflict or chance of divorce. Other researchers may explain hyperactivity in children in terms of family or cultural factors. For the first researcher, the child's hyperactivity is the independent variable (predictor). For the second researcher, the child's hyperactivity is the dependent variable (outcome).

The intricate relationship between root disciplines and specialty areas on the one hand, and research methodology of groups of scholars on the other hand, has been detailed in a more complete exposition by Robert E. Larzelere and David M. Klein (1987).

Strategies for Data Collection

Data is the empirical information researchers use for drawing conclusions. Often they will use a cross-sectional design when data are collected only once. This is a snapshot of how things are at a single time. Less common are longitudinal designs, where the data are collected at least twice. Although each collection point provides a snapshot, it is possible to make inferences about changes. With time-series designs, you have many snapshots, often more than thirty data collection points.

Cross-sectional design. A cross-sectional design can be used in a survey, experiment, in-depth interview, or observational study. The justification for this design is usually cost.

Suppose researchers are interested in the effects of divorce on children. A cross-sectional design could take a large sample of children and measure their well-being. The children would be divided by whether they experienced divorce. If the children who had experienced divorce fared worse on well-being, the researcher would conclude that divorce had adverse effects.

Cross-sectional analysis requires the researcher to examine covariates (related variables) to minimize alternative explanations. Children who experienced divorce probably lived in families that had conflict, and may fare worse because of this conflict rather than because their parents divorced. Researchers would ask for retrospective information about marital conflict before the divorce, income before and after the divorce, and so on. These covariates would be controlled to clarify the effects of divorce, as distinct from the effects of these other variables, because each covariate is an alternative explanation for the children's well-being.

Longitudinal design. By collecting data at different times, causal order is clear; the variables measured at time one can cause the variables at time two, but not the reverse. When variables are measured imperfectly, however, the errors in the first wave are often correlated with the errors in the second and third waves. Therefore, statistical analyses of longitudinal data are typically very complex.

The question concerning the influence of divorce on the well-being of children illustrates advantages and disadvantages of longitudinal strategies. The well-being of children is measured at one time. Five years later the researcher would contact the same children and measure their well-being. Some of the children's parents would have gotten divorced. Children who experienced divorce could have their well-being at time two compared to time one. The difference would be attributed to the effects of divorce. By knowing the well-being of these children five years earlier, some controls for the influence of conflict would be automatically in place.

Although longitudinal designs are very appealing, they present some basic problems. After five years, the researcher may locate only 60 or 70 percent of the children. Those who vanished in the interval might have altered the researcher's conclusions. Second, five years is a long time in the life of a child, and many influences could have entered his or her life. Statistically these problems can be minimized, but the analysis is quite complex.

Time-series design. Although some people use time-series and longitudinal labels interchangeably, measures are made many times, usually thirty times or more, for time-series analyses. By tracking the participants over time, changes are described and attributed to life events.

Using the example of the effects of divorce on children, a researcher may be interested in how effects vary over time. Perhaps there is an initial negative effect that diminishes over time. Alternatively, initial adverse effects may decrease over time for girls but increase for boys.

Design for Collecting Data

Researchers have a variety of approaches and designs for collection of data. Three common designs are surveys, experiments and quasi-experiments, and observation and in-depth interviews.

Surveys. The most common data collection strategy is the survey. For example, the National Longitudinal Survey of Youth 1997 (NLSY97) is a sample of nearly 9,000 twelve- to sixteen-year-old adolescents and their families. This survey will be completed each year for this panel of youth, as they become adults. Such surveys allow researchers to generalize to a larger population, such as that of the United States, and to use longitudinal methods such as growth curves. Because these surveys are large, researchers can study special populations such as adolescents in single-parent families, teen mothers, and juvenile delinquents. These are "general-purpose" surveys, and independent scholars who had nothing to do with the data collection may have access to it to analyze the results.

A second type of survey focuses on special populations. Researchers with a particular interest—for example, middle-aged daughters caring for aged mothers—focus all of their resources on collecting data about a special group. In many cases, these surveys are not probability samples. Credibility for generalizing comes from comparing the profile of participants to demographic information. An advantage of these surveys is that they

can ask questions the researcher wants to ask. There might be a twenty-item scale to measure the physical dependency of an aged mother. Such detailed measurements are not usually available in general-purpose surveys. Because the subject of specialized studies is focused, it is often possible to include more open-ended questions than would be practical in a general-purpose survey.

Experiments and quasi-experiments. Experimental designs are used when internal validity is critical (Brown and Melamed 1990). Experiments provide stronger evidence of causal relationship than surveys because an experiment involves random assignment of subjects to groups and the manipulation of the independent variable by the researcher. Nevertheless, experimental designs give up some external validity as they gain internal validity. Because of the difficulty or impossibility of locating subjects who will volunteer to be assigned randomly to groups, many experiments are based on "captive" populations such as college students. Captive populations are fairly homogeneous regarding age, education, race, and socioeconomic status, making it difficult to generalize to a broader population. Experiments that involve putting strangers together for a short experience provide groups that differ qualitatively from naturally occurring groups such as families (Copeland and White 1991).

Many research questions are difficult to address using experiments. Suppose a survey result shows a negative correlation between husband-wife conflict and child well-being. A true experiment requires both randomization of subjects and manipulation of the independent variable. The researcher cannot randomly assign children to families. Nor can the level of husband-wife conflict be manipulated.

Observation and in-depth interviews. Both qualitative and quantitative researchers use observation and in-depth interviews. This may be done in a deliberately unstructured way. For instance, a researcher may observe the interaction between an African-American mother and her child when the child is dropped off at a childcare facility, comparing this to the mother-child interaction for other ethnic and racial groups. The researcher may structure this observation by focusing on specific aspects such as counting tactile contact (i.e., touching or hugging). For many qualitative researchers, however, the aspects of interaction that are recorded emerge after a long period of unstructured observation.

A quantitative researcher may have an elaborate coding system for observing family interaction. This may involve videotaping either ordinary (real life) or contrived situations. A researcher interested in family decision making might give each family a task, such as deciding what they would do with $1,000. Alternatively, the researcher might record family interaction at the dinner table. The videotape would be analyzed using multiple observers and a prearranged system. Observers might record how often each family member spoke, how often each member suggested a solution, how often each member tried to relieve tension, and how often each member solicited opinions from others (Bates 1950).

In-depth interviews are widely used by qualitative researchers. When someone is trying to understand how families work, in-depth interviews are an important resource. In-depth interviews vary in their degree of structure. A white researcher, who is married, has a middle-class background and limited experience in interracial settings, may want to understand the relationship between nonresident African-American fathers and their children. Such a researcher would gain much from unstructured in-depth interviews with nonresident African-American fathers and their children, including knowledge to replace assumptions and stereotypes. It may take a series of extended, unstructured interviews before the researcher is competent to develop a structural interview, much less design a survey or an experiment.

Many scholars would limit in-depth interviews and observational studies to areas where knowledge is limited. A major advantage of such designs, however, is that they open up research to new perspectives precisely where survey or experimental researchers naively believe they have detailed knowledge. By grounding research in the behavior and interactions of ordinary people, researchers may be less prone to impose explanations developed by others.

Two major problems are evident with observation and in-depth interviews. First, these approaches are time-consuming and make it costly to have a large or representative sample. Second, there are dangers of the researcher losing objectivity. When a researcher spends months with a group either as a participant or an observer, there is a danger of identifying so much with the group that objectivity is lost.

Selected other strategies. Case studies are used on rare populations such as families in which a child has AIDS. Content analysis and narrative analysis are used to identify emergent themes. For example, a review of the role of fathers in popular novels of the 1930s, 1960s, and 1990s will tell much about the changing ideology of family roles. Historical analysis has experienced a remarkable growth in the past several decades (Lee 1999), as evidenced by a major journal, the *Journal of Family History.* Demographic analysis is sometimes done to provide background information (economic well-being of continuously single families— see Acock and Demo 1994), document trends (demographic change of U.S. families—see Teachman, Tedrow, and Crowder 2000), and comparative studies (development of close relationships in Japan and the United States—see Rothbaum, Pott, Azuma, Miyake, and Weisz 2000). Increasingly, studies are using multiple approaches: quantitative, qualitative, and historical. Using multiple methods is called triangulation.

Measurement

All methodological orientations share a common need for measurement. Scientific advancement in many fields is built on progress in measurement (Draper and Marcos 1990). Good measurement is critical to family studies because of the complexity of the variables being measured. Most concepts have multiple dimensions and a subjective component. A happy marriage for the husband may be a miserable marriage for the wife. A daughter may have a positive relationship with her father centered on her performance in sports but a highly negative relationship with her father centered on her sexual activity. Ignoring multiple dimensions and the subjective components of measurement is a problem for both quantitative and qualitative researchers.

Scales. The most common, the Likert scale, gives the participant a series of statements about a concept, and the participant checks whether he or she strongly agrees, agrees, does not know, disagrees, or strongly disagrees with each of the statements. Often fewer than ten questions are asked, but they are chosen in a way that represents the full domain of the concept. Thus, to measure marital happiness, several items would be used to represent various aspects of the marriage.

The following is becoming a minimum standard for evaluating a scale. First, a factor analysis is done to see if the several questions converge on a single concept. Second, the reliability of the result (whether the scales gives a consistent result when administered again) is measured. This is done by using the scale twice on the same people and seeing if their answers are consistent or by using the alpha coefficient as a measure on reliability. The alpha coefficient indicates the internal consistency of the scale and should have a value of .70 or greater. This minimum standard has been emerging since the early 1980s. Few studies met these minimum standards before 1980. There has been progress, but this is still a problem today.

Additional procedures are done to assess the validity of the scales—that is, whether a scale measures what it is intended to measure (Carmines and McIver 1979). This is most often evaluated by correlating a new scale with various criteria such as existing scales of the same concept or outcomes that are related to the concepts.

Questionnaires and interviews. Questionnaires are the most commonly used methods of measuring the variables in a study. A questionnaire may be designed so that it can be self-administered by the participant, asked in a face-to-face interview, or administered by telephone.

Computer-assisted interviews can be used for all three collection procedures. Self-administered questionnaires are now completed by putting the participant in front of a computer. After the participant answers a question, the computer automatically goes to the next appropriate question. This allows each participant to have an individually tailored questionnaire. The use of Web-based questionnaires is becoming more common.

Difficulties of cross-cultural comparative analysis. Common sources of measurement error stem from insensitivity to gender, race, and culture (Van de Vijver and Leung 1996). Constructing culturally sensitive instruments is particularly salient when a researcher and subjects do not share the same language (Rubin and Babbie 2000; Hambleton and Kanjee 1995). Direct translation of a particular

word may not hold the same connotation in another language. Validity of questions can be also an issue. A researcher trying to measure parenting skills in Japan and the United States may ask: "How do you rate your parenting skills? Would you say they are: (a) excellent, (b) good, (c) fair, or (d) not good?" Because of a cultural value on humbleness, Japanese parents may rate themselves lower than do American parents. The findings from this question might be reliable, but certainly not valid to make a comparison between two cultures. Social desirability and how participants react to particular questions should be carefully examined in an appropriate cultural context.

It is not possible to completely avoid cultural biases, but there are some steps to minimize the effect of them. A rule of thumb for researchers is to become immersed in the culture before selecting, constructing, or administering measures. A researcher may utilize knowledgeable informants in the study population, use translation and back-translation of instruments, and pretest measures for reliability and validity before conducting the study.

Missing data. Regardless of the approach to measurement or research design, missing data is a problem. In longitudinal strategies missing data often comes from subjects dropping out of the studies. In cross-sectional strategies missing data often comes from participants refusing to answer questions. Readers should pay special attention to the amount of missing data. It is not unusual for studies to have 20 percent or more of the cases missing from the analysis. If those who drop out of a study or those who refuse to answer questions are different on the dependent variable, then the results will be biased.

There is no simple solution to missing data. Researchers often impute a value for missing cases. For example, if 10 percent of the participants did not report their income, the researchers might substitute the median income of those who did not report their income. A slightly better solution is to substitute the median for homogeneous subgroups. Instead of using the overall median, the researcher might substitute a different median, depending on the participant's gender and education. There are many other imputation methods, involving more complex statistical analysis (see Robin 1987; Acock 1997, Roth 1994; Ward and Clark 1991). In any case, it is important to report information about participants who have missing data.

Quantitative Analysis

The variety of statistical analysis techniques seems endless. The statistical procedures range from descriptive (e.g., means, standard deviations, percentage) to multivariate (e.g., ANCOVA, MANOVA, logistic regression, principal component and factor analysis, structural equation modeling, hierarchical linear modeling, event history analysis, and latent growth curves). Most analysis involves several independent variables. OLS regression is widely used as a basic statistical model. It allows researchers to include multiple independent variables (predictors) and systematically control for important covariates. Many of the procedures are either special cases of OLS regression (e.g., ANOVA, ANCOVA) or extensions (e.g., logistic regression, structural equation modeling). There is also clear evidence that factor analysis procedures and their extensions, such as confirmatory factor analysis, play a major role in evaluating how well variables are measured.

Special Problems and Ethical Issues

Family researchers study the issues that concern people the most—factors that enhance or harm the well-being of people and families. This often involves asking sensitive questions. Most studies have a high compliance rate, with 80 percent to 90 percent of the people answering most questions. When studies begin by asking questions that participants are willing to answer, the participants buy into their role and later report intimate information. The reality is that participants will tell interviewers, who are strangers, personal information they would never share with members of their own family.

Although researchers can get people to cooperate with studies, a crucial question is how the researchers should limit themselves in what they ask people to do. All universities have committees that review research proposals where human subjects are involved. Researchers need to demonstrate that the results of their study are sufficiently promising to justify any risks to their subjects. Researchers must take precautions to minimize risks. Sometimes this involves anonymity for the participants (no name or identification associated with participants); sometimes it involves confidentiality (name or identification known only to the project's staff). It also involves informed consent, wherein people agree to participate after they are told about the project. Informed consent is a special problem with qualitative research. The design of qualitative research is emergent in that the researcher does not know exactly what is being tested before going into the field. Consequently, it is difficult to have meaningful informed consent. The participants simply do not know enough about the project when they are asked to participate.

Even with the best intentions, subjects can be put at risk. Asking adolescents about their relationship with a nonresident father may revive problems that had been put to rest. In some cases, the effect of this can be positive; in some cases, it can be negative. Observational studies and participant observation studies are especially prone to risks for subjects. A scholar interested in interaction between family members and physicians when a family member is on an extraordinary life-support system is dealing with very important questions. Who decides to turn the machine off? What is the role of the physician? What are the roles for different family members? All these are important questions. The presence of the researcher may be extremely intrusive and may even influence the decision-making process. This potential influence involves serious ethical considerations.

Another special risk for qualitative work is unanticipated self-exposure (Berg 2001). As the project develops, the participant may reveal information about self or associates that goes beyond the original informed consent agreement.

Feminist methodology is not a particular research design method or data collection method (Nielsen, 1990). It is distinguished by directly stating the researchers' values, explicitly recognizing the influence research has on the researcher, being sensitive to how family arrangements are sources of both support and oppression for women, and having the intention of doing research that benefits women rather than simply being about women (Allen and Walker 1993). Given this worldview, feminist methodology presents complex ethical issues to researchers, and it demands that all family scholars be sensitive to these concerns.

Conclusion

The diversity of strategies, designs, and methods of analysis used by marriage and family researchers reflects the equally diverse root disciplines and content areas that overlap the study of marriage and family. In view of this, cross-sectional surveys remain the most widely used strategy, and quantitative analysis is dominant in the reporting of research results in the professional literature. However, experiments, longitudinal, time-series, and qualitative strategies also remain crucial tools for research.

See also: RESEARCH: FAMILY MEASUREMENT

Bibliography

Acock, A. C. (1997). "Working with Missing Data." *Family Science Review* 10(1):76–102.

Acock, A. C., and Demo, D. (1994). *Family Diversity and Well-Being.* Newbury Park, CA: Sage.

Allen, K. R., and Walker, A. J. (1993). "A Feminist Analysis of Interviews with Elderly Mothers and Their Daughters." In *Qualitative Methods in Family Research,* ed. J. F. Gilgun, K. Daly, and G. Handel, Newbury Park, CA: Sage.

Bates, R. F. (1950). *Interaction Process Analysis: A Method for the Study of Small Groups.* Cambridge, MA: Addison-Wesley.

Berg, B. L. (2001). *Qualitative Research Methods for the Social Sciences,* 4th edition. Boston: Allyn and Bacon.

Brown, S. R., and Melamed, L. (1990). *Experimental Design and Analysis.* Newbury Park, CA: Sage.

Carmines, E. G., and McIver, J. P. (1979). *Reliability and Validity Assessment.* Newbury Park, CA: Sage.

Copeland, A. P., and White, K. M. (1991). *Studying Families.* Newbury Park, CA: Sage.

Drapper, T., and Marcos, A. C. (1990). *Family Variables: Conceptualization, Measurement, and Use.* Newbury Park, CA: Sage.

Hambleton, R. K., and Kanjee, A. (1995). "Increasing the Validity of Cross-Cultural Assessments: Use of Improved Methods for Test Adaptations." *European Journal of Psychological Assessment* 11(3):147–157.

Larzelere, R. E., and Klein, D. M. (1987). "Methodology." In *Handbook of Marriage and the Family,* ed. M. B. Sussman and S. K. Steinmetz. New York: Plenum.

Lee, G. R. (1999). *Comparative Perspectives,* ed. M. B. Sussman, S. K. Steinmetz, and G. W. Peterson. New York: Plenum Press.

Neilsen, J. M. (1990). Introduction to *Feminist Research Methods,* ed. J. M. Neilsen. Boulder, CO: Westview Press.

Roth, P. L. (1994). "Missing Data: A Conceptual Review for Applied Psychologists." *Personnel Psychology* 47:537–560.

Rothbaum, F.; Pott, M.; Azuma, H.; Miyake, K.; and Weisz, J. (2000). "The Development of Close Relationships in Japan and the United States: Paths of Symbiotic Harmony and Generative Tension." *Child Development* 71(5):1121–1142.

Rubin, A., and Babbie, E. (2000). *Research Methods for Social Work,* 4th edition. Belmont, CA: Wadsworth.

Rubin, D. B. (1987). *Multiple Imputation for Nonresponse in Surveys.* New York: John Wiley & Sons.

Schumm, W. R., and Hemesath, K. K. (1999). *Measurement in Family Studies,* ed. B. Sussman, S. K. Steinmetz, and G. W. Peterson. New York: Plenum Press.

Teachman, J. D.; Tedrow, L. M.; and Crowder, K. D. (2000). "The Changing Demography of America's Families." *Journal of Marriage and the Family* 62(November):1234–1246.

Van de Vijver, F., and Leung, K. (1996). "Methods and Data Analyis of Comparative Research." In *Handbook of Cross-Cultural Psychology,* 2nd edition, Vol. 3, ed. J. W. Berry, Y. H. Poortinga, and J. Padey. Needham, MA: Allyn & Bacon.

Ward, T. J., and Clark, H. T. (1991). "A Reexamination of Public-Versus Private-School Achievement: The Case for Missing Data." *Journal for Educational Research* 84:153–163.

ALAN ACOCK
YOSHIE SANO

RESILIENCY

See AFRICAN-AMERICAN FAMILIES; DEVELOPMENTAL PSYCHOPATHOLOGY; DISABILITIES; FAMILY STRENGTHS; INTERRACIAL MARRIAGE; RURAL FAMILIES

RESOURCE MANAGEMENT

Resource management is the process in which individuals and families use what they have to get what they want. It begins with thinking and planning and ends with the evaluation of actions taken. Three fundamental concepts in resource management are *values, goals,* and *decision making.* Values such as honesty and trust are principles that guide behavior. They are desirable or important and serve as underlying motivators. Values determine goals, which are sought-after end results.

Goals can be implicit or explicit. They can be short-term, intermediate-, or long-term. Decisions are conclusions or judgments about some issue or matter. Decision making involves choosing between two or more alternatives and follows a series of steps from inception to evaluation.

Through choices, individuals and families define their lives and influence the lives of others. The study of resource management focuses on order, choices, and control, and how people use time, energy, money, physical space, and information. As an applied social science, it is an academic field that is fundamental to our understanding of human behavior. "The knowledge obtained through the study of management is evaluated in light of its ability to make an individual's or family's management practice more effective" (Goldsmith 2000, p. 5).

Individuals and families have characteristic ways of making decisions and acting called their *management style.* Although similar styles are exhibited within families (such as a tendency to be on time or to finish tasks to completion), there are also wide ranges of styles within families making the study of management intrinsically interesting, especially from a *socialization* point of view. Why do such differences exist and how does the individual's style mesh with that of the other members' styles in the family?

Measuring devices, techniques, or instruments that are used to make decisions and plan courses of action are called management tools. For example, time is a resource and a clock or stopwatch is a management tool.

Resources can be divided up into human and material resources, assets that people have at their disposal. *Material resources* (e.g., bridges, roads, houses) decline through use whereas *human resources* (e.g., the ability to read, ride a bicycle) improve or increase through use. *Human capital* describes the sum total of a person's abilities, knowledge, and skills. Education is one way to develop human capital. Related to this is the concept of social capital. The term *social capital* is gaining in importance in the family-relations field and management is considered part of a person's or family's social capital. As a dynamic concept social capital can be considered a resource imbedded in the relationships among people that individuals,

groups, and communities create, in which they invest, and which can be used to provide or develop resources or facilitate social and personal well being (Bubolz 2002).

Conceptual Framework and History

Resource management has a long history and an interdisciplinary base borrowing from and contributing to such fields as economics, organizational behavior, anthropology, psychology, and sociology. The discipline was originally called home management—with an emphasis on work simplification and household efficiency—but since the postmodern period (beginning in the 1960s) the emphasis has been on viewing the family as a social system and resource management as one of the many functions of that system (Knoll 1963; Maloch and Deacon 1966; McGregor 2001). In recent years the most widely used term to describe the field is *family resource management* or more simply *management,* which will be a term used in the remainder of the entry. Although the family is recognized as the fundamental societal unit, it is recognized that management principles and techniques apply to singles as well as to families. Attention is also paid to the management styles and situations of different types of families besides the traditional two-parents-and-children configuration.

Management research studies are conducted worldwide and results are reported in journals and at conferences. Family functioning, time, and stress are common themes. For example, data-based studies have found that family resources play a critical role in the healthy family functioning of Korean immigrant families in the United States (Lee 2000). Multinational papers presented at the 1998 International Household and Family Research Conference held in Helsinki, Finland reinforced the importance of family resource management to the well-being of families including the pursuit of the ideal life (Turkki 1999; Fujimoto and Aoki 1999).

Several theories, most importantly systems and economic theories, influence the way management is taught, practiced, and studied. According to Deacon and Firebaugh (1988), the family's values, demands and resources are defined as inputs to the system. A leading management theorist in the twentieth century, Beatrice Paolucci, was especially interested in how family systems interact

FIGURE 1

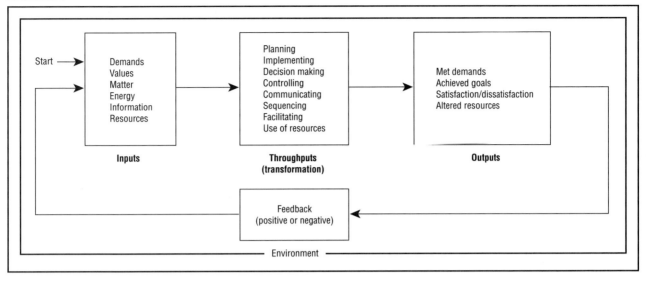

with their various near and far environments, which is termed the *human ecological approach*. Paolucci along with her coauthors Nancy Axinn and Olive Hall wrote:

> Things need not just happen in a family; they can be decided. The responsibility and the burden of choice are a particular attribute of humanness. The quality of human life and the prospect of the family's continued survival within limited environmental settings depends, in large measure, on the decisions made in daily family living (1977, p. 1).

For a history of her life and contributions to family resource management see *Beatrice Paolucci: Shaping Destiny through Everyday Life* (Bubolz et al. 2002). Economic theory assumes that people seek to maximize their satisfaction through the decisions that they make. In economics, individuals are seen as rational and acquisitive. Management recognizes that although individuals want to increase satisfaction, they often behave in nonoptimizing, less than rational ways. Unexpected events or reactions to events may require adjustments to plans and actions.

Family resource management differs from the way management is taught in business schools. In colleges of business, the application is mostly to employer/employee relationships in nonprofit and for-profit organizations. The fields are alike in that both are concerned with productivity and decision making but in family resource management the examples are more likely to be of a personal, home-based, or family nature. However, it should be pointed out that there are several cross-over topics such as time management and balancing work and family life and cross-field collaborations are common.

Practical Applications and a Model of Managerial Action

Because management explores the workings of everyday life, it is both complex and practical. To show the interaction of various management components, a model of managerial action using the systems approach is given in Figure 1.

In the model, for example, demands and values lead to planning and the use of resources ending with met demands, achieved goals, and feedback. In Africa, where many regions suffer from drought and food shortages, individuals and families have to plan wisely and use resources well in order to incrase their chances of survival. In management, wants and needs are differentiated from goals. Wants are specific and temporary, such as craving a certain food. Needs range from basic physiological needs to self-actualization (Maslow 1954). Within a family there can be conflicting needs. People arrive at their needs through a complex subjective assessment based on their inherent motivations and their perceptions of the external world (Foxall, Goldsmith, and Brown 1998). In today's fast-paced world, filled with competing demands, people do not have the time to carefully assess their needs or to plan effectively.

Situational factors, personality traits, and motivational forces affect plans. Individuals and families set standards within the context of existing demands and resource availability. Standards develop over time. People live in the present, but they are thinking about the future and developing plans based on their values and standards. "Planning is a thinking and information-gathering process involving a series of decisions. It is a process because formulating plans requires several steps, such as information gathering, sorting, and prioritizing; then, based on this information, the planner must decide which plan is most likely to succeed" (Goldsmith 2000, p. 125). Plans have purpose; they are taking the planner somewhere. To succeed, plans should be clear, flexible, appropriate, and goal-directed. People have primary plans and back-up plans. Implementing refers to putting plans into action. Evaluation is the end process of looking back, checking over, examining past decisions and actions and determining how they worked. Goal achievement should provide satisfaction.

Time, Work, Family, and Stress

Time use and the direction of human effort are integral to the study of management. Queen Elizabeth I said on her deathbed, "All my possessions for a moment of time." Time is generally considered the ultimate resource because it is a resource all people, rich or poor, share. In the discipline in the past there was debate about whether time is a "true" resource (Winter 1995).

As the Queen Elizabeth I quote shows we all share time but it is finite. Therefore, a critical management question is how do we make the best use of the time that we do have. One answer is through conscious control. In management studies, a person is trained to ask when confronted with competing activities, "What is the best use of my time right now?" Another question to ask is "Is the activity I am about to undertake consistent with my goals?" These questions address both quantitative time (measured units of time such as minutes and hours) and qualitative time (feelings about how

time is spent). Time perceptions vary widely by individual and by culture. For example, being on time in most North American cultures means five or ten minutes before the agreed upon time or being right on time. In other cultures, being an hour late may still be regarded as being on time. Discretionary time is free time one can use any way one wants. Nondiscretionary time is programmed by others or set by schedules and appointments. Everyday life is a combination of both. Stress is often caused by not having enough discretionary time. Over-programmed time is a problem for children as well as adults.

Few people are immune from the difficulties of trying to balance work and family life. Most controversy centers around managing hours and responsibilities, but it is also about one's priorities. Which is more important: work or family? When someone is asked to work overtime, this question becomes apparent. In *workaholism,* work is the most pleasurable part of life and family or personal life takes a back seat. On the other hand, procrastination is the postponement of work usually in favor of more pleasurable parts of family or personal life.

With improvements in technology, there has been a blurring of work and family roles and often less lag time. Email, cellular telephones, automatic teller machines, and the Internet have accelerated everyday life and have made people, information, and services more accessible. Work and family lives are becoming increasingly blurred and even may share the same physical space as one considers the growth in the number of home-based businesses.

The twenty-first century will be characterized by more family transformation and stress (McCubbin et al. 1997). Because the purpose of management is not only to describe problems, but also to present solutions, distress and fatigue are subjects of discussion in terms of what can be done to lessen them. Regarding getting more sleep, James Maas (1998) suggests getting an adequate amount of sleep every night, establishing a regular sleep schedule, getting continuous sleep, and making up for lost sleep. Another solution is the reestablishment of routines such as regular mealtimes as a way to simplify life. The simplification process may involve other steps such as pulling back on spending and building up more savings to provide for more leisure time in the future (Goldsmith 2001).

Family resource specialists strive to reach a stage called managerial judgment, defined as the ability to accept and work with change for the betterment of self and humankind. The ultimate goal of the management expert is the creation of a better tomorrow.

Conclusion

More could be said about managing human effort, environmental resources, and financial resources. This entry briefly touches the surface of a more than century-old discipline that affects every aspect of daily life. What management does is provide a framework, a way of looking at things that can be applied to a variety of situations. It is about life not just happening but happening in an orderly way. Humans are constantly seeking answers, making plans, and pursuing goals that bring desired results. Management provides insight into how this occurs. It is both simple and complex. Each day presents new challenges, new questions about how life should be and can be. Individuals are continually confronted with decisions to be made given scarce resources. This entry has endeavored to show the basics of the discipline and its application to everyday life. The greatest future challenge for the field will be the continued integration of management with other theories to address socially relevant issues as life becomes more complex and diverse.

See also: COHABITATION; DECISION MAKING; DIVISION OF LABOR; FAMILY LIFE EDUCATION; FAMILY SYSTEMS THEORY; FOOD; HOME ECONOMICS; HOUSEWORK; HOUSING; HUMAN ECOLOGY THEORY; POVERTY; POWER: MARITAL RELATIONSHIPS; PROBLEM SOLVING; RICH/WEALTHY FAMILIES; ROLE THEORY; SPOUSE ABUSE: THEORETICAL EXPLANATIONS; STRESS; TIME USE; WORK AND FAMILY

ELIZABETH BEARD GOLDSMITH

RESPITE CARE

ADULT *Karen A. Roberto*

CHILD *Stephen R. Block, April W. Block*

ADULT

Respite care refers to temporary, short-term supervisory, personal, and nursing care provided to older adults with physical and/or mental impairments. Programs provide respite services in the older person's home or at a specific site in the community (e.g., adult day center, nursing home, or hospital). Although older adults are the recipients of care, these dual-purpose programs provide relief for family caregivers from the constant responsibilities of caring for dependent older adults and allow both the caregivers and care receivers time for independent relationships and activities.

Users of Respite Care

Respite programs typically provide care for older adults with a wide range of physical and mental disabilities. Based on the small number of published reports that include data on client and family characteristics (Montgomery 1992), typical respite care users in the United States are around eighty years of age. Approximately 60 percent of the programs' participants are female who tend to be older than their male counterparts. More than 85 percent of the older adults live with their family caregivers, who are either spouses or adult children. Most older respite users have multiple impairments that limit their ability to perform routine daily activities such as bathing, eating, and dressing.

Types of Respite Programs

Various agencies operate respite programs, including both for-profit and nonprofit organizations. Programs differ with respect to their definitions of respite, target populations (e.g., persons with Alzheimer's disease; persons with developmental disabilities), eligibility criteria, and the amount and type of respite offered. Costs for respite services vary, depending on the type and intensity of care provided to participants. Most programs rely on contributions from participants, who pay a preset amount or on a sliding scale according to their financial resources. Many communities in the United States and abroad support agencies that help caregivers find respite care services for their family members. For example, *Carer Respite Centres,* located in fifty-eight regions across Australia, specialize in helping caregivers find and use respite services in their local area (Quality Care for Older Australians 2001).

In-home care. In-home respite care takes place in the home in which the older person lives. Depending on the needs of the caregiver, in-home respite can occur on a regular or occasional basis and can take place during the day or evening hours. Some programs provide personal and instrumental care for the older person, whereas others provide only companionship or supervisory services (Lawton, Brody, and Saperstein 1991). Professionals and paraprofessionals, employed by community-based agencies that offer respite services (e.g., home health agencies, senior support programs, and church-affiliated organizations), typically provide the care. Several communities have developed programs that rely on trained volunteers to provide in-home respite care. For example, the Visiting Nurse Association of America created a partnership with older adults in Senior Companion Programs in eighteen cities across the United States. The Senior Companion Program trains volunteers to assist older clients and their families by developing a relationship with dependent elders and, in the process, providing family caregivers much-needed respite (Fischer and Schaffer 1993).

Older adults who receive in-home care typically exhibit more frequent social and behavioral problems than do participants of other types of respite programs (Lawton et al. 1991). Their caregivers report a higher degree of burden and provide more intense care compared with caregivers using other types of respite. Caregivers using in-home respite services also spend fewer hours per day away from their care receivers than those using other types of respite services (Berry, Zarit, and Rabatin 1991).

In-home respite is the type of respite most acceptable to family caregivers (Conlin, Caranasos, and Davidson 1992; Lawton et al. 1991). It typically is more flexible than other forms of respite because it most easily accommodates to the specific day and time that the caregiver wants. Caregivers also view in-home respite as more acceptable than other types of programs because they do not have to take their care recipients out of the environment in which they are most comfortable. It also has its limitations because in-home respite services can be expensive, particularly if frequently used for several hours per day. Families also may be reluctant to use in-home respite services because they do not like having strangers in their homes or taking care of their loved ones.

Adult day care. Adult day care is a structured, community-based comprehensive program that provides a variety of health, social, and related support services in a protective setting during any part of a day, but less than twenty-four–hour care (National Council on the Aging 2001). These programs typically offer some combination of health and therapeutic services for participants while meeting their socialization needs through the provision of individual and group activities, and shared meals. Ninety percent of centers operate on a nonprofit or public basis. Regardless of the host agency, most centers are small, averaging twenty participants per day.

Most adult day care programs serve populations mixed in age and impairment. Findings from a nationwide study reported by the National Institute on Adult Day Care suggest that typical adult day care participants are women, in their mid-seventies, white, and living with a spouse, adult child, or other family and friends. Approximately 50 percent of adult day care participants need help with at least two activities of daily living and/or suffer cognitive limitations. The characteristics of caregivers who rely on adult day care services are more variable. For example, a comparative study of 118 female caregivers of persons with Alzheimer's disease found that caregivers of users of adult day care were younger, had higher education and income levels, were more likely to have children living in the household, and reported more symptoms of stress and depression than those caregivers who did not use this type of respite service (Guttman 1991). The forty-two caregivers who used a dementia-specific day program in New York, however, were more likely to be older, spousal caregivers, most of who have served as the primary caregiver for less than two years (Monaham 1993).

An advantage of day care over in-home respite care is that it provides important peer group support and greater opportunities for social interaction for the older adult. For the caregiver, adult day care offers freedom from caregiving responsibilities for potentially long, continuous blocks of time at a lesser cost than in-home services (Lawton et al. 1991). A disadvantage of using adult day care is the physical and emotional effort required to prepare care receivers to attend a day program. For example, transportation to and from the center is a major issue that caregivers and programs must resolve. Caregivers often view getting the family member ready to leave home more consuming and exhausting than providing the usual care. In addition, many caregivers and their care receivers have an adverse emotional reaction to the term *day care,* which they perceive is a program for children, not an appropriate setting for older adults (Bane 1992).

Residential respite care. Residential settings such as nursing homes and hospitals also provide respite services. In most situations, caregivers pay out-of-pocket for residential respite care. This type of respite care differs from in-home and adult day programs in that it provides overnight and/or extended services. Beds may be available for both emergency respite care (e.g., illness of a caregiver) and planned respite stays, such as when a caregiver plans a vacation or a short weekend of relaxation (Lawton et al. 1991).

Nursing homes indicate that almost 80 percent of their respite clients have functional impairments that would make them eligible for permanent residential care (Montgomery 1992). Caregivers of elders using residential respite services typically are older and spend more time in the caregiver role than caregivers using other types of programs. Perhaps, because these care receivers are at a point of requiring intense care and supervision, caregivers often use this type of respite service on a trial basis before permanent nursing home placement (Miller and Goldman 1989; Scharlach and Frenzel 1986).

Residential respite programs have their advantages and disadvantages with respect to cost, caregivers' perceptions of care and the facility's ability to provide care, and the additional burden of preparation required of the caregiver (Gonyea 1988; Rosenheimer and Francis 1992). Although

Adult day care offers support services in a protective setting during any part of a day, but less than 24-hour care. It provides peer group support and opportunities for social interaction. MEDIAFOCUS

residential programs offer respite care at costs comparable to similar amounts of in-home respite, caregivers still view it as a costly care alternative. Nursing homes and hospitals usually provide a supervised, professional setting equipped to handle emergencies, which may alleviate the family's anxiety about care. Caregivers, however, often try so hard to avoid nursing home placement that even a temporary placement evokes fear and guilt about future placement possibilities. In addition, although institutions typically can accept older individuals with a range of behavioral problems and functional disabilities, caregivers often fear that their elders will not receive proper individual attention and care. The preparation required for a nursing home or hospital stay (e.g., filling out forms, preparing

personal effects, explaining the situation to the care receiver, and transportation to and from the facility) and limitations on the number of days a person can stay in the program also discourage some caregivers from using this type of respite care.

Caregiver Outcomes and Respite Care Challenges

As a result of using respite services, family caregivers report enhanced levels of well-being, reduced feelings of burden and stress, and delayed placement of their loved one in a nursing home (Cox 1997; Kosloski and Montgomery 1995). In addition, most caregivers who use respite services report being highly satisfied with the program and the care their family member receives (Buelow and Conrad 1992; Henry and Capitman 1995; Jarrott et al. 1999).

Despite the potential for positive outcomes, and the growing availability of respite programs across the United States and internationally, caregivers are still reluctant to use any type of respite service. When caregivers do seek respite services, it is often at a time of crisis; their family situation escalates to a point at which they cannot continue providing care without some assistance. Family caregivers often view respite programs as a "last resort" or "end of the road" solution, rather than a preventive service. Respite services are more effective in alleviating the stress and strains of caregiving if providers can get caregivers to enroll in their programs earlier in the caregiving career.

To enhance program use by family caregivers, respite care programs must address both family-related and program-related issues. Family-related issues include caregivers' lack of awareness, apprehension, and attitudes about using respite services and the reactions of their care receivers (Schmall and Webb 1994). Many caregiving families have little or no contact with formal services; thus, they are often unaware of the availability of respite care in their communities. Even when caregivers are aware of such services, their fierce independence and personal beliefs about caregiving may hinder their use. It is common to hear caregivers say such things as "She's my mother, I am responsible for her care" or "No one can care for my husband better than I can." Family caregivers often feel guilty about leaving their care receivers and believe that using respite services is a sign of failure. They may be even more reluctant to use respite services if they see it as benefiting themselves, rather than their care receivers. In addition, some care receivers respond negatively to and resist respite care, thus reinforcing feelings of guilt often harbored by many caregivers.

Programmatic challenges related to the use of respite care services include lack of service availability when caregivers want or need them most and lack of control over who provides services (Malone-Beach, Zarit, and Shore 1992). For in-home respite users, having different workers every time they request help is a deterrent to the use of such services. Caregivers generally want to have more control over which respite care workers provide care for their family members. The limited availability (e.g., only weekdays) and time schedules (e.g., 8:00 A.M. to 5:00 P.M.) of many adult day care programs prohibit their use by some caregivers, particularly those who are working outside the home. Transportation is another major barrier to the use of respite services, particularly for adult day care. Many family caregivers find it difficult to get their care receivers to a center, and many centers have limited means of providing transportation for their participants. Finally, the lack of or limited government and private sources of insurance for respite care, especially for programs in the United States, also is perceived as a barrier for many families who may otherwise wish to use respite services.

See also: ALZHEIMER'S DISEASE; CAREGIVING: FORMAL; CAREGIVING: INFORMAL; CHRONIC ILLNESS; DEMENTIA; DISABILITIES; ELDER ABUSE; ELDERS; RESPITE CARE: CHILD; SUBSTITUTE CAREGIVERS

Bibliography

Bane, S. (1992). "Rural Caregiving." *Rural Elderly Networker* 3:1–6.

Berry, G.; Zarit, S.; and Rabatin, V. (1991). "Caregiver Activity on Respite and Nonrespite Days: A Comparison of Two Service Approaches." *The Gerontologist* 31:830–835.

Buelow, J., and Conrad, K. (1992). "Assessing the Influence of Adult Day Care on Client Satisfaction." *Journal of Health and Aging* 4:303–321.

Conlin, M.; Caranasos, G.; and Davidson, R. (1992). "Reduction of Caregiver Stress by Respite Care: A Pilot Study." *Southern Medical Journal* 85:1096–1100.

Cox, C. (1997). "Findings from a Statewide Program of Respite Care: A Comparison of Service Users, Stoppers, and Nonusers." *The Gerontologist* 37:511–517.

Fischer, L. R., and Schaffer, K. B. (1993). *Older Volunteers: A Guide to Research and Practice.* Newbury Park, CA: Sage.

Gonyea, J. (1988). "Acceptance of Hospital-Based Respite Care by Families and Elders." *Health and Social Work* 3:201–208.

Guttman, R. (1991). *Adult Day Care for Alzheimer's Patients: Impact on Family Caregivers.* New York: Garland.

Henry, M. E., and Capitman, J. (1995). "Finding Satisfaction in Adult Day Care: Analysis of a National Demonstration of Dementia Care and Respite Services." *Journal of Applied Gerontology* 14:302–320.

Jarrott, S. E.; Zarit, S. H.; Stephens, M. A. P; Townsend, A.; and Greene, R. (1999). "Caregiver Satisfaction with Adult Day Service Programs." *American Journal of Alzheimer's Disease* 14:233–244.

Kosloski, K., and Montgomery, R. (1995). "The Impact of Respite Use on Nursing Home Placement." *The Gerontologist* 35:67–74.

Lawton, M. P.; Brody, E.; and Saperstein, A. (1991). *Respite for Caregivers of Alzheimer's Patients: Research and Practice.* New York: Springer.

Malone-Beach, E.; Zarit, S.; and Shore, D. (1992). "Caregivers' Perceptions of Case Management and Community-Based Services: Barriers to Service Use." *Journal of Applied Gerontology* 11:145–159.

Miller, D., and Goldman, L. (1989). "Perceptions of Caregivers about Special Respite Services for the Elderly." *The Gerontologist* 29:408–410.

Monaham, D. (1993). "Utilization of Dementia-Specific Respite Day Care for Clients and Their Caregivers in a Social Model Program." *Journal of Gerontological Social Work* 20:57–70.

Montgomery, R. (1992). "Examining Respite: Its Promise and Limits." In *In-Home Care for Older People: Health and Supportive Services,* ed. M. Ory and A. Dunker. Newbury Park, CA: Sage.

Rosenheimer, L., and Francis, E. (1992). "Feasible with Subsidy: Overnight Respite for Alzheimer's." *Journal of Gerontological Nursing* 18:21–29.

Scharlach, A., and Frenzel, C. (1986). "An Evaluation of Institutional-Based Respite Care." *The Gerontologist* 26:77–82.

Schmall, V., and Webb, L. (1994). "Respite and Adult Day Care for Rural Elders." In *Providing Community-Based Services to the Rural Elderly,* ed. J. Krout. Thousand Oaks, CA: Sage.

Other Resources

National Council on the Aging. (2001). "Facts about Adult Day Services." Available from http://www.ncoa.org/nadsa/.

Quality Care for Older Australians. (2001). "Respite Care and Other Services for Carers." Available from http://www.health.gov.au/acc/.

KAREN A. ROBERTO

CHILD

Respite care refers to short-term care that is provided to children with special needs. The purpose of the short-term care is to give temporary relief to family members who need a break from the exceptional demands of their role and daily routine as primary caregiver of a child with special needs.

Respite care services are different from customary childcare or baby-sitting services provided to families whose children do not have special needs. For a child without special needs, usually a baby-sitter can be engaged within typical informal support systems such as a neighbor, a local teenager, or a relative. Whereas families of children without special needs may benefit from the break in their daily routine of childrearing, respite care is especially intended for families with children with excessive care needs who have disabilities, chronic disorders, or terminal illnesses. The demands of having a child with a disability, severe developmental delay, or terminal illness will often exacerbate stresses that exist even in normal family relationships. When their child has exceptional needs, families experience even greater levels of tension, anxiety, worry, and financial hardship than families that have children who are developing typically. If the pressures of stress are not managed, then the stability of the family unit can be jeopardized.

Providing personal care for a young dependent child who has special care demands is a daunting responsibility that can add unforeseen pressures and strain to a family's life. In virtually all families there is an understanding that in time of need the family may seek help from any of its relatives, such as a grandmother, sister, aunt, cousin, or others. However, due to the increased level of need that the extended family member might be asked to address, primary care families may feel stifled asking for respite support from extended family as often as their help might be needed. In addition, extended family members may be reluctant to volunteer if the child has significant developmental disabilities or delays, or has chronic or terminal illness for which special nursing skills and training may be necessary to adequately care for these children. The child's special needs may include the administration of oxygen, tube-feeding, frequent diapering, proper dosing of medication, or being properly managed if behaviors are extreme or particularly challenging for the caregiver. Some relatives are simply unable to cope with the extraordinary responsibilities of caring for a child that needs constant supervision, monitoring, and/or special personal care. Families may feel abandoned by their relatives who have fears about participating in the care of the child with special needs, even if those fears are understandable. In situations where relatives are unable or unwilling to provide the respite care, then a family must seek respite services outside the home from qualified individuals.

Respite Services throughout the World

Respite service is not just a U.S. phenomenon. The need for respite care knows no boundaries among families with children with developmental delays, disabilities, or serious illnesses. For instance, Johannes Schadler (1991) described the need for respite care services in the Federal Republic of Germany and efforts to develop a national organization called *Lebenshilfe*. Similarly, survey research conducted in North Wales reported that families caring for people with mental retardation expressed their greatest need as respite care services (Grant and McGrath 1990). Although there might be less publicized recognition of the need and benefits of respite care, the service is available in several countries that are visibly sensitive to providing services and supports to children with disabilities and their families. It is not altogether surprising that these countries include Canada, England, Ireland, Scotland, Wales, Australia, and New Zealand. Historically, professionals in these countries have tended to promote more inclusive or mainstream services for people with disabilities.

It is important to recognize that cultural diversity influences the variations of interaction among families from different parts of the world (Lynch and Hanson 1998). How a family responds to stress and the demands of caring for a child with exceptional demands may differ dramatically from culture to culture. The results of one study suggest that parents with more difficult children need and use respite care more than others. Nonusers of respite care reported a higher perception of social support than users of the service (Factor 1990). This finding suggests two additional points for consideration. First, comparing respite needs among inhabitants of different countries or cultural groups within a country requires an understanding of the group's mores and customs. Some groups may feel more comfortable in openly asking for help, whereas others may use more subtle signals to ask for help. Second, as discovered in one Australian study, the restricted use of respite services among

members of different ethnic communities may simply be a function of individuals not knowing that these services exist (Evert 1996).

State and local governments' abilities to support respite services have been inconsistent throughout the United States. In some states, state-funded services for people with mental retardation and other developmental disabilities have funds set aside for respite services. Some states have funded Family Resource Centers to support the respite care needs of families in specific neighborhoods or communities. Similar funded services are also available in other countries. Throughout Australia, for example, the Commonwealth Department of Family and Community Services provides a Special Needs Subsidy Scheme (SNSS) to support respite services and other childcare supports.

According to the U.S.-based National Respite Coalition, four states have adopted public policy provisions in order to create state or local infrastructures necessary for respite programs. Oregon, Nebraska, and Wisconsin developed services through the passage of *Lifespan Respite Acts*. Lifespan Respite is a network of community-based programs that provide scheduled or emergency-based respite care. By giving statutory authority to Lifespan services, a state is committing to fund respite services. Legislation is not the only route that can be used to develop a network of respite care programs. In Oklahoma, for example, a consortium of public and private organizations formed a coalition to provide a statewide information and referral service that can help Oklahomans with special needs find community resources.

In the early 1980s, many state-government agencies throughout the United States that were responsible for services to persons with developmental disabilities and mental retardation took an interest in Family Support Programs and launched these individualized services. Family Support services had greater flexibility than most traditional government-funded programs. This service could provide families with vouchers, direct subsidies, or reimbursements for expenditures on services or special equipment. The purpose of these programs was to keep a family intact and support the family who wanted to raise their child at home as an alternative to institutional care. One of the main provisions of Family Support was payment for respite care (Brown, Thurman, and Pearl 1993).

Types of Respite Care

Respite care services are provided in many countries. Over the years, in response to the varying needs of families, four models of respite care have been popularized throughout the world.

In-home care. In-home respite care is provided in the home of the child. In this format of respite care, the provider watches the child while the family members take a break to attend to other family or business interests. The family caregivers are given an opportunity to either relax, leave the house to run errands, or in some situations take a few days off as a brief vacation.

Host family care. Host family respite care is a service delivered in the home of another family. The respite services are provided in the same fashion and offer the same benefits as in-home respite care. In this format, however, the child is not in his/her familiar home environment. Some individuals believe that this model helps the development of the child through the opportunity to socialize. Others think that placing a child in an unfamiliar environment is unkind and may cause or exacerbate behavior issues. However, host family respite services should not automatically imply that the provider family is unknown to the child. The host family may be a close neighbor or relative.

Center care. Center care respite services are also provided in a setting outside of the child's home. The respite setting might be a medical clinic, school, a nonprofit (nongovernmental organization), or commercial day care setting. Generally, this form of respite service is not as individualized as the other two respite models. The center may be designed to take care of a number of children. Consequently, its staff may not be able to readily attend to the personal needs of each child. The availability of center care respite services may increase as an option for families in the United States as a result of the Americans with Disabilities Act (ADA) which requires childcare centers to make reasonable modifications in their policies in order to serve children with disabilities. Some center-based providers are equipped to provide respite care on an emergency or as-needed basis.

Cooperative care. Cooperative respite care is a service shared among several families. In this arrangement, families may take turns providing respite care for each other. Families who participate in this format of respite care believe there is an advantage of having another family provide the respite services (especially one that has first-hand experience in raising a child with a disability or serious illness). Parents believe that their children will receive better care through a cooperative since the families involved all have an appreciation for respite services. On the other hand, some think that this format may provide more opportunities for childcare errors and accidents. The concern is that the respite provider may experience unusual tension stemming from the number of details that they must manage in order to care for one or more children with special needs. This is, of course, in addition to providing direct care for one's own child with special needs.

The Effects of Respite Care

The opportunity to be relieved from the extraordinary tensions brought on by providing extra care for another person may have several social and societal benefits. Adverse side effects may be experienced by families who have children with special needs, but do not have adequate support such as the availability of respite care. These families face a significantly higher rate of divorce than families whose children do not have special needs (Hodapp and Krasner 1995). Consequently, the absence of support and the trigger of stress may lead to physical and/or verbal abuse (Epps and Jackson 2000). As a result of an abusive environment, families in these circumstances are likely to have sons or daughters in need of out of home placements, including costly tax-supported foster care placements or inhospitable institutional settings. Relief from the constant pressure of caregiving not only may protect the vulnerable child, but it also may prevent domestic violence against a spouse or other household members.

Respite services may also prevent other maladies to which primary family caregivers are prone. According to the National Family Caregivers Association, caregivers in need of supports experience more headaches, stomach disorders, sleeplessness, and depression. Even more seriously, the *Journal of the American Medical Association* (1999) reported that individuals experiencing caregiver strain had mortality risks that were substantially higher (by 63%) than noncaregivers.

Some researchers claim that the availability of respite services has enabled families to improve spousal relationships. Also, it has been reported that as a result of the relief of stress from respite care services, individuals have reported satisfaction with life in general and improved attitudes toward the child who requires intensive caregiving (Botuck and Winsberg 1991).

Although families who use respite services may potentially reap positive effects, the scope and availability of this important service remains insufficient. In fact, according to the National Respite Coalition (1998), approximately one-half of the families needing respite will find available services. Additionally, Jill Kagan (2001) reports that 1,500 families representing more than 3,000 children per week are unable to obtain respite services because of the limited pool of available services. Moreover, with the increasing number of aging adults, paid respite services—to support a family's care of an aging relative—may directly compete with the availability and supply of respite programs that would otherwise provide respite support to children's caregivers.

See also: CHILDCARE; CHRONIC ILLNESS; DEVELOPMENTAL DISABILITIES; DISABILITIES; SUBSTITUTE CAREGIVERS

Bibliography

Arsenault, C. C. *When Do I Get Some Time For Me?* Denver: Colorado Division of Child Care.

Blasco, P. M. (2001). *Early Intervention Services for Infants, Toddlers, and Their Families.* Boston: Allyn & Bacon.

Botuck, S., and Winsberg, B. G. (1991). "Effects of Respite on Mothers of School-Age and Adult Children with Severe Disabilities." *Mental Retardation* 29(1):43–47.

Braddock, D.; Hemp, R.; Parish, S.; and Westrich, J. (1998). *The State of the States in Developmental Disabilities: A Detailed State-by-State Analysis of MR/DD Services, Funding, and Trends.* Washington, DC: American Association on Mental Retardation.

Brown, W.; Thurman, S. K.; and Pearl, L F. (1993). *Family-Centered Early Intervention with Infants and Toddlers.* Baltimore, MD: Paul H. Brookes.

Epps, S., and Jackson, B. J. (2000). *Empowered Families, Successful Children.* Washington, DC: American Psychological Association.

Evert, H. (1996). "Ethnic Families, Their Children with Disabilities and Their Child Care Needs." *Australian Journal of Early Childhood* 21(3):20–27.

Factor, D. C. (1990). "Stress, Social Support, and Respite Care Use in Families with Autistic Children: Brief Report." *Journal of Autism and Developmental Disorders* 20(1):139–146.

Grant, G., and McGrath, M. (1990). "Need for Respite Care Services for Caregivers of Persons with Mental Retardation." *American Journal on Mental Retardation* 94(6):638–648.

Hodapp, R. M., and Krasner, D. V. (1995). "Families of Children with Disabilities: Findings from a National Sample of Eighth-Grade Students." *Exceptionality* 5(2):71–81.

Lynch, E. W., and Hanson M. J. (1998). *Developing Cross-Cultural Competence.* Baltimore, MD: Paul H. Brookes.

Salisbury, C. L., and Intagliata, J. (1986). *Respite: Support for Persons with Developmental Disabilities and Their Families.* Baltimore, MD: Paul H. Brookes.

Schadler, J. B. (1991). "Respite Care Services for the Family in Germany." *International Journal of Rehabilitation Research* 14(1):49–57.

Turnbull, A., and Turnbull, R. (2001). *Families, Professionals, and Exceptionality: Collaborating for Empowerment.* Upper Saddle River, NJ: Merrill Prentice Hall.

Other Resources

Kagan, J. (2001). "Lifespan Respite." Available from http://www.chtop.com.

National Respite Coalition. (1998). "Respite in Community Based Family Resource & Support (CBFRS) Grant Programs." Available from http://www.chtop.com/cbfrsfs.htm.

STEPHEN R. BLOCK
APRIL W. BLOCK

RETIREMENT

Family and work experiences are closely interwoven throughout adults' life course. Family relationships and obligations, both prior and current, shape the timing of retirement, retirement adjustment, and pensions; retirement can alter marital and kin interactions.

Definitions and Trends

The concepts *family* and *retirement* are understood by most people, yet scientific definitions of these concepts vary considerably. Definitions of family refer to household composition, common ancestry, childbearing and childrearing, and they can be restricted to nuclear family members (parents and their offspring) or can include other kin (Bundesministerium für Umwelt, Jugend und Familie 1999; Wingen 1997). Problems in defining retirement arise in regard to the exact timing of the retirement transition as well as the distinction between occupational retirement and withdrawal from the labor force (Ekerdt and DeViney 1990; Szinovacz and DeViney 1999). Some individuals retire gradually whereas others take up a second career in later life. Receipt of retirement benefits (Social Security, pensions) is not always tied to labor force withdrawal. Women may reject the retiree identity altogether due to their involvement in family work (Bernard et al. 1995; Onyx and Benton 1996).

The diversification of family experiences since the 1970s (especially increases in divorce and in women's labor force participation) has led to considerable variability in family structures (Teachman et al. 2000). These changes already shape retirement transition processes today and will become even more important as the post-World War II birth cohorts reach retirement age. For example, as more and more women participate in the labor force, more couples face the retirement of *both* spouses (Szinovacz and Ekerdt 1995).

Retirement as we know it today—the withdrawal of basically healthy individuals from the labor force at a certain age (typically between ages 55 and 65) and with the expectation of receiving Social Security and/or pension benefits—is a relatively new institution. In the United States, Social Security was created in 1935. Some European nations (for example, Germany) had already adopted old age pensions by the end of the nineteenth century, whereas many developing countries still lack public benefits for their elderly (Williamson and Pampel 1993). Prior to the creation of Social Security, old age economic security was often achieved through contributions from unmarried children, forcing some children to delay marriage and forego further education and, thus, the prospect of upward mobility. Those elderly who were unable to work and who could not rely on family funds sometimes found support from their communities and charities but were at considerable risk of poverty (Haber and Gratton 1994; Held 1982). In undeveloped countries that lack old age security programs, the elderly must still rely on their own wages and family support (Ngan et al. 1999; Social Security Administration 1999). Under these conditions, labor force participation often continues well into old age. For example, during the late 1990s, 75.7 percent of men aged sixty-five and over were still economically active in Zimbabwe as were 68.8 percent of men aged seventy to seventy-four in Bolivia and 52.7 percent of men aged sixty-five and over in Pakistan. This compares to 10.6 percent of men aged sixty-five and over in Canada, 1.9 percent in Belgium, and 14.7 percent in Poland (International Labour Office 1999). With the implementation of state- or employer-funded old age pensions, retirement has become an expected and accepted life transition. Social Security programs typically define windows for "normal retirement" based on individuals' age and employment history (Blöndal and Scarpetta 1998; Gruber and Wise 1999). However, generous provisions for "early" retirement and alternative pathways into retirement (e.g., through unemployment and disability benefits) resulted in a trend toward early retirement (Gruber and Wise 1999; Kohli et al. 1991).

Family Influences on the Retirement Transition

Old age security programs define age-based windows for retirement, but they usually allow some choice in the exact timing of the retirement transition (although sometimes at the cost of reduced benefits). Consequently, factors other than age and employment history can and often do affect retirement decisions. Studies addressing motives for retirement indicate that marital and family reasons play some role in retirement decisions, especially among women (Clemens 1997; Disney et al. 1997; Ruhm 1996).

The specific marital characteristics entering retirement decisions include marital status, spouse's employment/retirement status, spouse's health, spouse's economic situation, and the quality of the marital relationship. Marriage and marital history are pertinent for retirement benefits (spouses can rely at least partially on current or former partners' pensions), are linked to employment history, and influence individuals' attitude toward retirement. Most studies suggest that married persons are more prone to retire (Flippen and Tienda 2000; Miniaci 1998; Szydlik and Ernst 1996) although contrary evidence exists as well (Lindeboom 1998; Ruhm 1996) for married men.

Perhaps the most widely studied phenomenon is spouses' tendency toward joint retirement (All-mendinger 1990; Blau 1998; Disney et al. 1997; Henkens 1999; Miniaci 1998; Pepermans 1992; Zweimüller et al. 1996). Explanations for this trend refer to joint leisure preferences of spouses, shared economic restrictions, and similarity in spouses' background characteristics such as age and educa-tion, as well as traditional gender roles that pre-clude continued employment of typically younger wives after their husbands' retirement (Gustman and Steinmeier 1994; Henkens et al. 1993). Indeed, several studies show that already retired men pres-sure their employed wives to leave the labor force (Skirboll and Silverman 1992; Szinovacz 1989). However, there is also evidence for wives' influ-ence on their husbands' retirement decisions (Henkens and Siegers 1994; Smith and Moen 1998). Whether spouses are in fact able to imple-ment joint retirement depends on a variety of cir-cumstances, including the age difference between spouses, their economic situation, their health, and family obligations (Allmendinger 1990; Arber and Ginn 1995; O'Rand et al. 1992).

Research further suggests cross-influences of spouses' economic situation (wages, Social Secu-rity and pensions, Medicare eligibility) on each other's retirement timing, although these effects are often weak (Allmendinger 1990; Burkhauser et al. 1996; Madrian and Beaulieu 1998; Zweimüller et al. 1996). In addition, the spouse's health plays a role in retirement timing. A spouse's illness can either delay or hasten the partner's retirement depending on the balance between caregiver burden and fi-nancial needs associated with the spouse's disabil-ity (Hayward et al. 1998; Honig 1996; Szinovacz and DeViney 2000).

The attractiveness of retiring is also influenced by the quality of the marital relationship. Spouses who enjoy a close relationship, have joint hobbies, or desire more time with their partner are more in-clined to retire, whereas couples in conflict-laden relationships may dread spending more time to-gether and hence delay retirement (Henkens 1999; Honig 1998; Naegele and Voges 1989, as cited in Kohli et al.1989; Szinovacz and DeViney 2000). Some husbands also fear that retirement could un-dermine their power position in the marriage and

postpone retirement for that reason (Szinovacz and DeViney 2000).

Not only marital but also family circumstances can impinge on retirement decisions. Financial ob-ligations, especially for dependent children, may preclude early retirement (Miniaci and Stancanelli 1998; Pienta et al. 1994; Szinovacz, DeViney, and Davey 2001; Talaga and Beehr 1995), whereas the burden of care for frail relatives sometimes entices married women to retire (Miniaci and Stancanelli 1998; Zimmerman et al. 2000). Whether closeness of ties to relatives including adult children affects retirement transitions remains virtually unexplored. Preliminary evidence suggests that individuals who lack extended family ties (for instance, the child-less) may delay retirement (Szinovacz, DeViney, and Davey 2001).

Family Influences on Postretirement Well-Being

Marital and family circumstances not only influence retirement timing, but they also have an impact on postretirement well-being. Being married and hav-ing a high quality marriage contribute to well-being throughout the life span and may become especially important during the retirement years (Niederfranke 1989; Reitzes et al. 1996). Retirement satisfaction is also furthered when spouses concur in their evaluation of retirement (Buchmüller 1996), when the other spouse adjusts well to re-tirement (Haug et al. 1992), and when couples en-gage in joint leisure activities and decision-making (Dorfman and Hill 1986; Dorfman et al. 1988). In contrast, the number of contacts with relatives (in-cluding adult children) appears less important for well-being than contacts with peers (Lee and Ishii-Kuntz 1987). However, wives' involvement with friends may curtail their husbands' retirement satis-faction (Dorfman et al. 1988). Nevertheless, high-quality relations with relatives can enhance retire-ment satisfaction (Dorfman et al. 1988), and desired geographical proximity to relatives can mo-tivate relocation after retirement (Cuba 1992).

The realization of retirement plans is often contingent on family circumstances (Freericks and Stehr 1990). Continued economic responsibilities for children in the household and retirement prompted by family caregiving needs lead to the perception of retiring too early (Hardy and Quadagno 1995; Szinovacz 1989). Furthermore, the

Couples' interest in sharing hobbies and activities has led to the trend of joint retirement. WARREN MORGAN/CORBIS

illness of spouses and care for close relatives can spoil postretirement plans and reduce retirement satisfaction (Clemens 1993; Kolland 1988; Vinick and Ekerdt 1991a). However, some men seem to derive self-esteem from caring for their ill wives (Szinovacz 1992). Retirement adjustment is also hampered when negative family events, such as widowhood or illness or death of relatives, occur in close proximity to the retirement transition (Clemens 1993; Szinovacz and Washo 1992).

Retirement Influences on Marital and Family Relations

Despite the popular notion that retirement creates multiple marital problems (Harbert, Vinick, and Ekerdt 1992; Siegert 1994), there is considerable continuity in marital relations over the retirement transition (Atchley 1992; Ekerdt and Vinick 1991). Indeed, retirement tends to reinforce preretirement marital quality, and many marriages profit from retirement (Myers and Booth 1996; Rosenkoetter and Garris 1998). Improvements in postretirement marriages are linked to decreased stress, more time for companionship, and a more traditional division of household labor after wives' retirement (Szinovacz 1996; Vinick and Ekerdt 1991a, 1991b).

Nevertheless, some changes in marital relations do occur after retirement. Many wives expect retired husbands to contribute more to household work (Brubaker and Hennon 1982), and some studies suggest that husbands attempt to live up to this expectation, although they may focus their efforts on traditional male tasks such as home repairs (Niederfranke 1991; Schäuble 1989; Szinovacz 2000). Although many wives appreciate their husbands' efforts (Dorfman 1992; Vinick and Ekerdt 1991b), others perceive husbands' help as an interference in their domain and complain that their retired husbands are "underfoot" (Ekerdt and Vinick 1991; Kohli et al. 1989). Such perceptions prevail when husbands' housework is motivated by lack of other meaningful activities or when husbands criticize their wives' performance (Hill and Dorfman 1982; Vinick and Ekerdt 1991a).

Another concern in retirement marriages is the planning and coordination of spouses' time and leisure activities. Wives often adapt to their retired husbands' needs and negotiate the couple's leisure endeavors (Gilford 1986; Niederfranke 1991) but may resent increased demands by their retired husbands (Clemens 1993). Problems can also arise when spouses approach retirement with unrealistic or discordant expectations about joint endeavors (Caradec 1994; Ekerdt and Vinick 1991; Kohli et al. 1989; Vinick and Ekerdt 1992).

Lowered marital satisfaction often results if the husband retires prior to his wife and the couple abides by traditional gender role attitudes (Moen, Kim, and Hofmeister 2001; Myers and Booth 1996). In contrast, wives' retirement tends to reduce marital disagreements and arguments (Szinovacz and Schaffer 2000).

Retirement may further impinge on spouses' relative power in the relationship. Because a man's power is grounded in his status as provider, retirement can undermine his position in the marriage and render him more dependent on his wife (Kulik and Bareli 1997; Szinovacz and Harpster 1993).

Much speculation but little evidence exists concerning the effects of retirement on relationships to extended kin. Retirees seem to attach more importance to kin relationships (Niederfranke 1991) although this does not always result in more frequent contacts (Kremer 1985; Niederfranke 1991). Increased involvement seems to occur, especially in relations with grandchildren (Östberg 1992; Schäuble 1989), and men may catch up on previously neglected contacts with their children (Niederfranke 1991; Szinovacz and Davey 2001). On the other hand, retirees may be less able to provide financial support to children (Kremer 1985).

Retirement Programs and Social Change

Family and demographic change during the past decades (especially women's rising labor force participation, increases in divorces, and decreases in fertility after the baby-boom during the 1950s and 1960s) have unleashed debates about Social Security programs in many countries. Central to these debates are the call for adequate independent old age security for women and generational equity in social programs.

Social Security regulations in the United States and many other industrialized countries reflect a male provider-role ideology that is at odds with today's family values and behaviors (Arber and Ginn 1991; Rolf 1991; Sainsbury 1996). In most countries, old age security and private pension benefits are tied to continuous work histories (exceptions are countries with flat old age benefits such as Australia, but many of these countries have additional employment-based public or private pensions such as superannuation in Australia; see Social Security Administration 1999). Because it is primarily women who disrupt employment for child or elder care, their retirement benefits tend to be considerably lower than men's. Women's lower wages and employment in industries that are not covered by private pensions further aggravate this economic disadvantage (Gonnot et al. 1995; Kingson and O'Grady-LeShane 1993; Walker et al. 1993). Although a growing number of countries have begun to address this inequity by crediting some care years as "work" years in Social Security calculations (the United States does not have such credits), these credits rarely provide full compensation for lost work opportunities. Furthermore, most European Community countries have also implemented paid leave programs for mothers that encourage longer work disruptions (McMullen and Marshall 1999; Prinz and Marin 1999). Consequently, in countries both with and without childcare credits, many wives or widows must rely on their spouses' benefits (Hieden-Sommer 1994; Pampel 1998; Rosenman and Winocur 1990), an option that negates the value of women's own achievements in the labor force. Furthermore, reliance on spouses' benefits is limited for the growing number of retiring divorcees (for instance, in the United States, spouse benefits for divorcees are restricted to marriages lasting ten years or more, yet most divorces occur earlier), and some countries still disregard nonmarital unions.

Lower fertility, when combined with higher longevity, brings about increases in the old-age dependency ratio, that is, the number of persons

Retirees dancing outside the Cheshire Home for the Aged in Nairobi, Kenya. A/P WIDE WORLD PHOTOS

sixty-five and over as a proportion of the "working" population. Some argue that taxes that finance programs and benefits for the increasing number of elderly deplete the economic resources of relatively smaller younger cohorts, often at the expense of programs for children (for a review of these arguments see Kingson et al. 1986; Quadagno 1991), and advocate reductions in government spending for the elderly, including Social Security, or a shift to individually funded pension schemes. Nevertheless, opinion surveys show consistently high support for tax-funded old age pensions (Dekker 1993), and history—as well as evidence from present-day countries without old age pensions—tells us that family-funded support for the elderly is insecure and not conducive to intergenerational ties (Kingson et al. 1986; Ngan et al. 1999;). Indeed, as Alan Walker (1999, p. 10–11) notes, the generational contract inherent in tax-funded old age pension schemes implies "acceptance of the notion that generations are interdependent" and thus serves intergenerational solidarity and social cohesion. At a time when fam-

ilies are struggling to adapt to new societal and economic realities, retirement policies and programs are needed that further gender equality, incorporate alternative family life styles, and protect intergenerational ties.

See also: ADULTHOOD; ELDERS; FAMILY DEVELOPMENT THEORY; FAMILY POLICY; GRANDPARENTHOOD; HOUSEWORK; INTERGENERATIONAL RELATIONS; LATER LIFE FAMILIES; LEISURE; MARITAL QUALITY; POWER: MARITAL RELATIONSHIPS; STRESS; TIME USE; WIDOWHOOD; WORK AND FAMILY

Bibliography

Allmendinger, J. (1990). "Der Übergang in den Ruhestand von Ehepaaren. Auswirkungen individueller und familiärer Lebensverläufe." In *Lebensverläufe und sozialer Wandel,* ed. K. U. Mayer. Wiesbaden: Westdeutscher Verlag.

Arber, S., and Ginn, J. (1991). *Gender and Later Life.* London: Sage.

Arber, S., and Ginn, J. (1995). "Choice and Constraint in the Retirement of Older Women." In *Connecting*

Gender and Ageing, ed. S. Arber and J. Ginn. Buckingham, UK: Open University Press.

Atchley, R. C. (1992). "Retirement and Marital Satisfaction." In *Families and Retirement,* ed. D. Ekerdt and B. H. Vinick. Newbury Park, CA: Sage.

Bernard, M.; Itzin, C.; Phillipson, C.; and Skucha, J. (1995). "Gendered Work, Gendered Retirement." In *Connecting Gender and Ageing,* ed. S. Arber and J. Ginn. Buckingham, UK: Open University Press.

Blau, D. M. (1998). "Labor Force Dynamics of Older Married Couples." *Journal of Labor Economics* 16:595–629.

Blöndal, S., and Scarpetta, S. (1998). *The Retirement Decision in OECD Countries.* [Economic Department Working Papers No. 202]. Paris: OECD.

Brubaker, T. H., and Hennon, C. B. (1982). "Responsibility for Household Tasks: Comparing Dual-Earner and Dual-Retired Marriages." In *Women's Retirement: Policy Implications of Recent Research,* ed. M. Szinovacz. Beverly Hills, CA: Sage.

Buchmüller, R. (1996). "Ehepaare vor dem Ruhestand." In *Vor dem Ruhestand,* ed. R. Buchmüller, S. Dobler, T. Kiefer, F. Magulies, P. Mayring, M. Melching, and H. D. Scheider. Freiburg: Universitätsverlag.

Bundesministerium für Umwelt, Jugend und Familie. (1999). *Zur Situation von Familie und Familienpolitik in Österreich.* Vienna: Author.

Burkhauser, R. V.; Couch, K. A.; and Phillips, J. W. (1996). "Who Takes Early Social Security Benefits? The Economic and Health Characteristics of Early Beneficiaries." *The Gerontologist* 36:789–799.

Caradec, C. (1994). "Finding the Right Conjugal Distance Once Retired." *Revue française de sociologie* 35:101–124.

Clemens, W. (1993). "Verrentung und Ruhestand sanpassung von erwerbstätigen Frauen." *Zeitschrift für Gerontologie* 26:344–348.

Clemens, W. (1997). *Lebenslagen in spater Erwerbstatigkeit und fruhem Ruhestand. Frauen zwischen Arbeit und Rente.* Opladen, Germany: Westdeutscher Verlag.

Cuba, L. (1992). "Family and Retirement in the Context of Elderly Migration." In *Families and Retirement,* ed. M. Szinovacz, D. J. Ekerdt, and B. H. Vinick. Newbury Park, CA: Sage.

Dekker, P. (1993). "Image, Self-Image and Participation of the Elderly: An International Comparison." In *Report on the elderly 1993,* ed. J. M. Timmermans. Rijswijk, Netherlands: Social and Cultural Planning Office.

Disney, R.; Grundy, E.; and Johnson, P. (1997). *The Dynamics of Retirement: Analyses of the Retirement Surveys.* London: Stationary Office.

Dorfman, L. T. (1992). "Couples in Retirement: Division of Household Work." In *Families and Retirement,* ed. M. Szinovacz, D. J. Ekerdt, and B. H. Vinick. Newbury Park, CA: Sage.

Dorfman, L. T.; Heckert, D. A.; Hill, E. A.; and Kohout, F. J. (1988). "Retirement Satisfaction in Rural Hus bands and Wives." *Rural Sociology* 55:25–39.

Dorfman, L. T., and Hill, E. A. (1986). "Rural Housewives and Retirement: Joint Decision-Making Matters." *Family Relations* 35:507–514.

Ekerdt, D. J., and DeViney, S. (1990). "On Defining Persons as Retired." *Journal of Aging Studies* 4(3):211–229.

Ekerdt, D. J., and Vinick, B. H. (1991). "Marital Complaints in Husband-Working and Husband-Retired Couples." *Research on Aging* 13:364–382.

Flippen, C., and Tienda, M. (2000). "Pathways to Retirement: Patterns of Labor Force Participation and Labor Market Exit among the Pre-Retirement Population by Race, Hispanic Origin, and Sex." *Journal of Gerontology: Social Sciences* 55B:S14–S27.

Freericks, R., and Stehr, I. (1990). *Wann, wenn nicht jetzt?* Bielefeld, Germany: Institut für Freizeitwissenschaften und Kulturarbeit.

Gilford, R. (1986). "Marriages in Later Life." *Generations* 10:16–20.

Gonnot, J. P.; Keilman, N.; and Prinz, C. (1995). *Social Security, Households, and Family Dynamics in Aging Societies.* Dordrecht, Netherlands: Kluwer Academic.

Gruber, J., and Wise, D. (1999). *Social Security Programs and Retirement around the World.* Chicago: University of Chicago Press.

Gustman, A. L., and Steinmeier, T. L. (1994). *Retirement in a Family Context: A Structural Model for Husbands and Wives.* [Working paper]. Cambridge, MA: National Bureau of Economic Research.

Haber, C., and Gratton, B. (1994). *Old Age and the Search for Security: An American Social History.* Bloomington: Indiana University Press.

Harbert, E.; Vinick, B. H.; and Ekerdt, D. J. (1992). "Marriage and Retirement: Advice to Couples in Popular Literature." In *Qualitative Methods in Family Research,* ed. J. F. Gilgun, K. Daly, and G. Handel. Newbury Park, CA: Sage.

Hardy, M. A., and Quadagno, J. (1995). "Satisfaction with Early Retirement: Making Choices in the Auto Industry." *Journal of Gerontology: Social Sciences* 50B:S217–S228.

Haug, M. R.; Belgrave, L. L.; and Jones, S. (1992). "Partners' Health and Retirement Adaptation of Women and Their Husbands." *Journal of Women and Aging* 4:5–29.

Hayward, M. D.; Friedman, S.; and Chen, H. (1998). "Career Trajectories and Older Men's Retirement." *Journal of Gerontology: Social Sciences* 53B:S91–S103.

Held, T. (1982). "Rural Retirement Arrangements in Seventeenth-to-Nineteenth-Century Austria: A Cross-Community Analysis." *Journal of Family History* 7:227–254.

Henkens, K. (1999). "Retirement Intentions and Spousal Support: A Multi-Actor Approach." *Journal of Gerontology: Social Sciences* 54B:S63–S74.

Henkens, K.; Kraaykamp, G.; and Siegers, J. (1993). "Married Couples and Their Labour Market Status." *European Sociological Review* 9:67–78.

Henkens, K., and Siegers, J. (1994). "Early Retirement: The Case of the Netherlands." *Labour* 8(1):143–154.

Hieden-Sommer, H. (1994). "Männer Leistung— Frauen Liebe: Gespaltene Gesellschaft, gespaltenes Menschenbild, gespaltene Frauen." *Österreichische Zeitschrift für Politikwissenschaft* 22:327–341.

Hill, E. A., and Dorfman, L. T. (1982). "Reactions of Housewives to the Retirement of Their Husbands." *Family Relations* 31:195–200.

Honig, M. (1996). "Retirement Expectations: Differences by Race, Ethnicity, and Gender." *The Gerontologist* 36:373–382.

Honig, M. (1998). "Married Women's Retirement Expectations: Do Pensions and Social Security Matter?" *American Econmic Review* 88:202–206.

International Labour Office. (1999). *Yearbook of Labour Statistics.* Geneva: Author.

Kingson, E. R.; Hirshorn, B. A.; and Cornman, J. M. (1986). *Ties that Bind: The Interdependence of Generations.* Washington, DC: Seven Locks Press.

Kingson, E. R., and O'Grady-LeShane, R. (1993). "The Effects of Caregiving on Women's Social Security Benefits." *The Gerontologist* 33:230–239.

Kohli, M.; Gather, C.; Künemund, H.; Mücke, B.; Schürkmann, M.; Voges, W.; and Wolf, J. (1989). Je früher–desto besser? *Die Verkürzung des Erwrbslebens am Beispiel des Vorruhestandes in der chemischen Industrie.* Berlin: Sigma.

Kohli, M.; Rein, M.; Guillemard, A.; and Van Gunsteren, H. (1991). *Time for Retirement: Comparative Studies of Early Exit from the Labor Force.* Cambridge, UK: Cambridge University Press.

Kolland, F. (1988). "Nach dem Arbeitsleben Konzentration auf die Familie?" In *Arbeit–Freizeit–Lebenszeit. Neue Ubergange im Lebenszyklus,* ed. L. Rosenmayr and F. Kolland. Opladen, Germany: Westdeutscher Verlag.

Kremer, Y. (1985). "Parenthood and Marital Role Performance among Retired Workers: Comparison between Pre- and Post-Retirement Period." *Ageing and Society* 5:449–460.

Kulik, L., and Bareli, H. Z. (1997). "Continuity and Discontinuity in Attitudes toward Marital Power Relations: Pre-Retired vs. Retired Husbands." *Ageing and Society* 17:571–595.

Lee, G. R., and Ishii-Kuntz, M. (1987). "Social Interaction, Loneliness, and Emotional Well-Being among the Elderly." *Research on Aging* 9(4):459–482.

Lindeboom, M. (1998). "Microeconometric Analysis of the Retirement Decision: The Netherlands." [Working paper]. Paris: OECD.

Madrian, B. C., and Beaulieu, N. D. (1998). "Does Medicare Eligibility Affect Retirement?" In *Inquiries in the Economics of Aging,* ed. D. A. Wise. Chicago: University of Chicago Press

McMullen, J. A., and Marshall, V. M. (1999). "Structure and Agency in the Retirement Process: A Case Study of Montreal Garment Workers." In *The Self and Society in Aging Processes,* ed. C. D. Ryff and V. W. Marshall. New York: Springer.

Miniaci, R. (1998). "Microeconometric Analysis of the Retirement Decision: Italy." [Working paper]. Paris: OECD.

Miniaci, R., and Stancanelli, E. (1998). "Microeconometric Analysis of the Retirement Decision:United Kingdom." [Working paper]. Paris: OECD.

Moen, P.; Kim, J. E.; and Hofmeister, H. (2001). "Couples' Work/Retirement Transitions, Gender, and Marital Quality." *Social Psychology Quarterly* 64:55–71.

Myers, S. M., and Booth, A. (1996). "Men's Retirement and Marital Quality." *Journal of Family Issues* 17:336–358.

Ngan, R.; Chiu, S.; and Wong, W. (1999). "Economic Security and Insecurity of Chinese Older People in Hong Kong: A Case of Treble Jeopardy." *Hallym International Journal of Aging* 1:35–45.

Niederfranke, A. (1989). "Bewältigung der vorzeitigen Berufsaufgabe bei Männern." *Zeitschrift für Gerontologie* 22:143–150.

Niederfranke, A. (1991). "Lebensentwürfe von Frauen beim ‹bergang in den Ruhestand." In *Frauen-Alterrsicherung,* ed. C. Gather, U. Gerhard, K. Prinz, and M. Veil. Berlin: Sigma.

Onyx, J., and Benton, P. (1996). "Retirement: A Problematic Concept for Older Women." *Journal of Women and Aging* 8(2):19–34.

O'Rand, A. M.; Henretta, J. C.; and Krecker, M. L. (1992). "Family Pathways to Retirement." In *Families and Retirement,* ed. M. Szinovacz, D. J. Ekerdt, and B. H. Vinick. Newbury Park, CA: Sage.

Östberg, H. (1992). *Retirement, Health and Socio-Psychological Conditions.* Malmö, Sweden: Lund University.

Pampel, F. C. (1998). *Aging, Social Inequality, and Public Policy.* Thousand Oaks, CA: Pine Forge Press.

Pepermans, G. (1992). "Retirement Decisions in a Discrete Choice Model and Implication for the Government Budget: The Case of Belgium." *Journal of Population Economics* 5:229–243.

Pienta, A. M.; Burr, J. A.; and Mutchler, J. E. (1994). "Women's Labor Force Participation in Later Life: The Effects of Early Work and Family Experiences." *Journal of Gerontology: Social Sciences* 49:S231–S239.

Prinz, C., and Marin, B. (1999). *Pensionsreformen. Nachhaltiger Sozialumbau am Beispiel Österreichs.* Frankfurt: Campus.

Quadagno, J. (1991). "Generational Equity and the Politics of the Welfare State." In *Growing Old in America,* 4th edition, ed. B. Hess and E. W. Markson. New Brunswick, NJ: Transaction.

Reitzes, D. C.; Mutran, E. J.; and Fernandez, M. E. (1996). "Preretirement Influences on Postretirement Self-Esteem." *Journal of Gerontology: Social Sciences* 51B:S242–S249.

Rolf, G. (1991). "Ideologiekritik am Rentenrecht und ein Reformvorschlag zur eigenständigen Alterssicherung von Frauen." In *Frauen-Alterrsicherung,* ed. C. Gather, U. Gerhard, K. Prinz, and M. Veil. Berlin: Sigma.

Rosenkoetter, M. M., and Garris, J. M. (1998). "Psychosocial Changes following Retirement." *Journal of Advanced Nursing* 27:966–976.

Rosenman, L., and Winocur, S. (1990). "Australian Women and Income Security for Old Age: A Cohort Study." *Journal of Cross-Cultural Gerontology* 5:277–291.

Ruhm, C. J. (1996). "Gender Differences in Employment Behavior during Late Middle Age." *Journal of Gerontology: Social Sciences* 51B:S11–S17.

Sainsbury, D. (1996). *Gender Equality and Welfare States.* Cambridge, UK: Cambridge University Press.

Schäuble, G. (1989). *Die schönsten Jahre des Lebens?* Stuttgart: Enke.

Siegert, W. (1994). *Liebe in Pension. Wie sich Beziehungen nach dem Arbeitsleben ändern.* Reinbek bei Hamburg, Germany: Rowohlt.

Skirboll, E., and Silverman, M. (1992). "Women's Retirement: A Case Study Approach." *Journal of Women and Aging* 4:77–90.

Smith, D. B., and Moen, P. (1998). "Spousal Influence on Retirement: His, Her, and Their Perceptions." *Journal of Marriage and the Family* 60:734–744.

Szinovacz, M. (1989). "Decision-Making on Retirement Timing." In *Dyadic Decision Making,* ed. D. Brinberg and J. Jaccard. New York: Springer.

Szinovacz, M. (1992). "Is Housework Good for Retirees?" *Family Relations* 41:230–238.

Szinovacz, M. (1996). "Couple's Employment/Retirement Patterns and Marital Quality." *Research on Aging* 18:243–268.

Szinovacz, M. (2000). "Changes in Housework after Retirement: A Panel Analysis." *Journal of Marriage and the Family* 62:78–92.

Szinovacz, M., and Davey, A. (2001). "Retirement Effects on Parent-Adult Child Contacts." *The Gerontologist* 41(2):191–200.

Szinovacz, M., and DeViney, S. (1999). "The Retiree Identity: Gender and Race Differences." *Journal of Gerontology: Social Sciences* 54B:S207–S218.

Szinovacz, M., and DeViney, S. (2000). "Marital Characteristics and Retirement Decisions." *Research on Aging* 22:470–489.

Szinovacz, M., DeViney, S.; and Davey, A. (2001). "Influences of Family Obligations and Relationships on Retirement: Variations by Gender, Race, and Marital Status." *Journal of Gerontology: Social Sciences* 56B:S20–S27.

Szinovacz, M., and Ekerdt, D. J. (1995). "Families and Retirement." In *Handbook on Aging and the Family,* ed. R. Blieszner and V. H. Bedford. Westport, CT: Greenwood.

Szinovacz, M., and Harpster, P. (1994). "Couple's Employment/Retirement Status and the Division of Household Work." *Journal of Gerontology: Social Sciences* 49:S125–S136.

Szinovacz, M., and Schaffer, A. M. (2000). "Effects of Retirement on Marital Conflict Management." *Journal of Family Issues* 21:367–389.

Szinovacz, M., and Washo, C. (1992). "Gender Differences in Exposure to Life Events and Adaptation to Retirement." *Journal of Gerontology: Social Sciences* 47:S191–S196.

Szydlik, M., and Ernst, J. (1996). "Der ‚bergang in den Ruhestand in Westdeutschland Zwischen 1984 und 1992." In *Lebenslagen im Wandel: Sozialberichterstattung im Längsschnitt, ed.* W. Zapf, J. Schupp, and R. Habich. Frankfurt: Campus.

Talaga, J. T., and Beehr, T. A. (1995). "Are There Gender Differences in Predicting Retirement Decisions?" *Journal of Applied Psychology* 80:16–28.

Teachman, J. D.; Tedrow, L. M.; and Crowder, K. D. (2000). "The Changing Family Demography of America's Families." *Journal of Marriage and the Family* 62:1234–1246.

Vinick, B. H., and Ekerdt, D. J. (1991a). "The Transition to Retirement: Responses of Husbands and Wives." In *Growing Old in America,* ed. B. B. Hess and E. Markson, 4th edition. New Brunswick, NJ: Transaction.

Vinick, B. H., and Ekerdt, D. J. (1991b). "Retirement: What Happens to Husband-Wife Relationships?" *Journal of Geriatric Psychiatry* 24:16–23.

Vinick, B. H., and Ekerdt, D. J. (1992). "Couples View Retirement Activities: Expectation versus Experience." In *Families and Retirement,* ed. M. Szinovacz, D. J. Ekerdt, and B. H. Vinick. Newbury Park, CA: Sage.

Walker, A. (1999). "The Future of Pensions and Retirement in Europe: Towards a Productive Aging." *Hallym International Journal of Aging* 1:3–15.

Walker, A.; Alber, J.; and Guillemard, A. (1993). *Older People in Europe: Social and Economic policies. The 1993 Report of the European Observatory.* Brussels: Commission of the European Communities.

Williamson, J. B., and Pampel, F. C. (1993). *Old-Age Security in Comparative Perspective.* New York: Oxford University Press.

Wingen, M. (1997). *Familienpolitik.* Stuttgart: Lucius and Lucius.

Zimmerman, L.; Mitchell, B.; Wister, A.; and Gutman, G. (2000). "Unanticipated Consequences: A Comparison of Expected and Actual Retirement Timing among Older Women." *Journal of Women and Aging* 12:109–128.

Zweimüller, J.; Winter-Ebmer, R.; and Falkinger, J. (1996). "Retirement of Spouses and Social Security Reform." *European Economic Review* 40:449–472.

Other Resource

Social Security Administration. (1999). "Social Security Programs throughout the World." In *Social Security Administration Government Statistics.* Available from http://www.ssa.gov/statistics/ssptw/index.html.

MAXIMILIANE E. SZINOVACZ

RICH/WEALTHY FAMILIES

F. Scott Fitzgerald observed that "The very rich are different from you and me." His friend Ernest Hemingway quipped "Yes, they have more money" (Hemingway 1936). Hemingway envied the rich and coveted their money, but Fitzgerald knew wealth was not an unmixed blessing. Money, as he had learned from his flamboyantly spoiled wife Zelda, is only the starting point for a different functional relationship with the world, making the rich, like the poor, different from those of us who are driven by hope and go through life striving to improve our selves and our lot. Fitzgerald contemptuously described the rich couple in *The Great Gatsby* (1925): "They were careless people, Tom and Daisy—they smashed up things and creatures and then retreated back into their money or their vast carelessness, or whatever it was that kept them together, and let other people clean up the mess they had made." George Bernard Shaw, in *Candida* (1898), pronounced: "We have no more right to consume happiness without producing it than to consume wealth without producing it."

Wealth is certainly the stuff of envy. When the dispirited *have-nots,* despairing of their ability to create a better life for themselves, rebel, they are likely to massacre the *haves,* as they did during the French and Russian revolutions. Even if this does not enrich the rebels it compresses the distance between those on top and those on the bottom. Beheadings go a long way toward curing envy. In Cambodia in the late 1970s, Pol Pot and the Khmer Rouge evacuated the cities, killed off the middle and upper classes, moved the survivors out to rural farms, and destroyed the country's machines and motor vehicles. In Zimbabwe in first years of the twenty-first century, white farmers were killed and their land was confiscated and left to lie fallow as the country—both blacks and white—fell into famine. Envy destroys its subjects as well as its objects.

Despite the near-universal envy of the rich, family therapists and financial advisors to the rich observe daily that wealth does not make people happy (Pittman 1985.) This is not to suggest that poverty is the secret of universal happiness either, but those who long for riches and envy those who have it would be in for a shock if they ever achieved their heart's desire. The beaming winners of the lottery, the newly minted rock stars, or the blushing brides of billionaires, thrilled at their good fortune at the moment, are likely to sing a different tune a year or so later, after they have let their wealth do its work of depriving them of pride in their own usefulness, isolating them from everyone less fortunate, distorting relationships with their loved ones, and ultimately disillusioning them. Do the cheering throngs that follow them around or the greedy hands in their pockets love them or their riches? Their divorce rates, the likelihood of legal battles with their less "fortunate" family members, their rates of depression and suicide, and their general levels of misery go up beyond middle-class levels almost to the levels of the poor. As Cloe Madanes points out (1994), "wealth often appears to be cursed, bringing with it more misery than joy." Sooner or later they realize that the wealth is not going to make them happy, but they then are likely to seek out more intense and drastic pleasures, from taking more risks, finding new drugs, getting into machines that go too fast, or otherwise trying to intensify experiences in a life that is rapidly becoming jaded, exhausted from overindulgence.

It is often thought that a plethora of money in and of itself produces unhappiness but further examination of the matter suggests that it is not wealth that brings the unhappiness but the belief that wealth will bring happiness and the disillusionment that results when it fails to do so. It may be that the rich are more unhappy than those in the economic middle, but they may be unhappy because they are the children of the rich (which J. Sedgwick [1985] describes as a dispiriting and crippling burden), because they have married money (a cold bed at best), or because they have amassed wealth obsessively through their inability to be satisfied, their relentless need for competitive victory, and their willingness to commit the "great crime" that, presumably "lies behind every great fortune."

In other words, they are inherently unhappy and do what they do in hopes that more of something (or maybe even more of everything) will finally fill the void inside. It is their unhappiness (i.e., their inability to be easily satisfied) that has driven them to get rich.

Philip Slater (1980) points out the senseless greediness of the rich and continuation in the pursuit of wealth long past the point that it gives them pleasure. He writes:

> One of the main reasons wealth makes people unhappy is that it gives them too much control over what they experience. They try to translate their own fantasies into reality . . . an enervating and disappointing pastime . . . learning and growing are very difficult with wealth because they depend on experiences in real life, and wealth enables one to buy out of life. It provides the wherewithal to cling to every outworn fantasy, pathway, or goal—to grasp every outgrown security blanket more tightly—to control your input in such a way that you never need to change or develop.

Power (and wealth, whatever else it is, is power) bestows upon people the freedom to not change.

Marriage to someone rich is entry into an inherently unequal relationship, in which one spouse is essentially employed by the other, made even more unequal if there is some sort of prenuptial agreement to cement the basic inequality. Even without great wealth or a prenuptial agreement, some men believe the family money belongs to them (perhaps the paycheck has their name on it.) He may try to control the marriage and the family by controlling the use of the money. She may then have to gain equity in the relationship by spending the money he tries to control. His ploy is poor economy, because she is angry and resentful at his efforts at control, and she gets her only sense of power by blowing money foolishly. Poor wives of rich husbands are likely to be in a state of permanent rebellion. Marriage is not marriage, but some form of involuntary servitude—unless it is between equals. Equality usually means equal access to money. The more money there is, the more crucial this equation becomes.

Wealth is not good for children. As Andree Aelion Brooks (1989) noted, it creates a lifetime dependency upon rich parents, belittles children's own accomplishments, distorts their relationships with their peers, makes them distrustful of friendships, and increases their sense of what is enough.

There is no correlation between the skills necessary to acquire wealth and those required to raise children. Robert S. Weiss (1985) found success-oriented men to be emotionally unexpressive, controlled, and distant from their own emotions and those of others. Their lives and concerns seemed separate from those of their families. They turned childraising over to their wives. The fathers therefore had little impact on their children—except to deprive them emotionally and set grand and ambivalently held ideals for them. Success-driven women are little different, but they may be cued by the culture to feel guilty about it, whereas men more often than not have been praised for abandoning their families in the pursuit of various varieties of glory.

Successful men may bow out of active parenting, hiring in effect a wife or ex-wife to raise their children for them. Unfortunately, the children of these ever-present mothers and ever-absent fathers are not likely to get to know the creator and/or steward of the family wealth and therefore do not benefit from his wisdom—what he has learned from his failures and his successes—which would be his irreplaceable heritage. Because children learn about money and values from the parent who raises them, they identify with their angry, emotionally and often financially deprived mothers. These children are likely to develop selfish, short-term goals and objectives, far different from the long-term goal of their wealth-producing or wealth-protecting parent. They rarely develop skills at making or keeping money, merely skills at throwing it away—the skills that are least likely to produce long-term happiness or solid relationships.

Children of the rich, as described by Robert Coles (1997), may grow up with a strong sense of entitlement, enormous self-esteem, and a self-conscious belief in their own importance and visibility in the universe, but no self-confidence, no belief that they can do anything of value for themselves or anyone else. It should come as no surprise that rich kids, with all their privileges in health and education, usually turn out fairly well. Most rich parents, like most poor parents, are sane, sensible, caring people, and the rich may have

even more time and energy to invest in their children. However, although there is a high level of success, there are prominent failures as well. Rich kids may have to blow their inherited wealth before they can move on toward their own successes.

Certain defects are characteristic of the rich. The rich, even those acutely attuned to the rules of fashion, are often shockingly naïve, unaware of the emotional and interpersonal rules by which the rest of the world operates. For instance, rich and powerful men may think they have special sexual privileges and free sexual access to potential partners who are of lower status than they.

The rich may be far more concerned with what is stylish than with what is safe, sane, or sensible. Rich parents may go into battle to get their alcoholic son out of a drunk-driving charge, with great concern for how it would look on his record and little concern with the reality of his alcoholism.

Stylish, shallow, pampering parents can encourage style without content, charm without discipline, competition without function, and arrogance without confidence in any child—the addictive craving for wealth without enough exposure to it to know its dangers. Children of the rich can turn out a great deal better or a great deal worse than normal kids from normal families. There is little middle ground.

Children of the rich are deprived of the chance to become self-made men and women. And their parents, envisioning them as senators rather than dishwashers, may resist letting them start at the bottom.

The standards by which the child of the super-successful is judged may have little to do with the child's stage of functional development, and the parents themselves may have little value as role models. Much of the corrective therapy with the rich involves teaching them how to be more middle-class, just as financial planning focuses on teaching them how to live within their means.

People living on trust funds are in much the position of people on disability or welfare. Functioning is optional. A frequent suggestion to the rich, from both therapists and financial advisors, is not to turn bigger than life amounts of money over to children but set it up in foundations, put the children on the boards, and let them have the pride and pleasure of giving it away to worthy causes and to those who would appreciate it, rather than destroying themselves as they blow it on extravagant pursuits of pleasure or artifacts of affluence. As J. E. Hughes points out (1997), making money is one thing, knowing how to use it for the benefit of the family is another. "The problem with most families' images of wealth . . . is that they are limited to the preservation of the family's financial capital and give little or no thought to the preservation of the family's most important capitals—human and intellectual." Hughes points out that inherited wealth and lottery winnings last an average of about eighteen months. With the appropriate intellectual capital the same wealth could last indefinitely. The difference between the haves and the used-to-haves is a cohesive family understanding of how the financial capital can be deployed for the long-term benefit of the family members and of the larger society. Family fortunes that last for many generations only do so when they benefit the society and the economy that supports them, and when that benefit outweighs the envy the fortune engenders. Meanwhile, one's own successes and good deeds are far more closely correlated with happiness than an extravagant lifestyle.

Wealth is addictive. It enticingly offers happiness, but it cannot provide satisfaction, so those who have gotten a whiff of wealth may imagine that more money will finally provide the satisfaction. Withdrawal from wealth (or the hope of it) can be jolting and can produce panic and drastic behavior.

The problems of the rich—whether the Kennedys, the Windsors, or the lottery winners—are rarely caused just by the money. No amount of money can create good genes or good parents or good relationship or even good luck. Wealth alone can neither cause nor cure the pains of life—it can just make them inexplicable to the envious. Although the rich are as much in need of help as anyone else, they are an overlooked phenomenon in the psychotherapy literature. David W. Krueger refers to money as *The Last Taboo* (1986) of psychotherapy. Likewise, the danger of money is overlooked in the financial literature. Perhaps we have little patience with their seemingly enviable problems. They deserve our understanding and even sympathy. Anything that prevents people from developing a functional reciprocity with the world is destructive. Both the rich and the poor

can grow up without exposure to functional people and realistically attainable goals and acquirable skills. Both therapists and financial advisors need to overcome their envy long enough to understand the problem. Money is powerful. It can do good or it can do harm.

See also: FAMILY BUSINESS; POWER: MARITAL RELATIONSHIPS; RESOURCE MANAGEMENT; WORK AND FAMILY

Bibliography

Brooks, A. A. (1989). *Children of Fast-Track Parents.* New York: Viking.

Coles, R. (1977). *The Privileged Ones,* Vol. 5: *Children of Crisis.* Boston: Little, Brown.

Fitzgerald, F. S. (1925). *The Great Gatsby.* New York: Scribner's.

Hemingway, E. (1936). "The Snows of Kilimanjaro." *Esquire* (August).

Hughes, J. E. (1997). *Family Wealth: Keeping It in the Family.* Princeton: NetWrx.

Krueger, D. (1986). *The Last Taboo.* New York: Brunner-Mazel.

Madanes, C. (1994). *The Secret Meaning of Money.* San Francisco: Jossey-Bass.

Pittman, F. S. (1985). "Children of the Rich." *Family Process* 24:461–472.

Sedgwick, J. (1985). *Rich Kids.* New York: Morrow.

Shaw, G. B. (1898). *Candida.* Reprint; New York: Penguin, 1950.

Slater, P. (1980). *Wealth Addiction.* New York: Dutton.

Weiss, R. S. (1985). "Men and the Family." *Family Process* 24:49–58.

FRANK S. PITTMAN III
FRANK S. PITTMAN IV

RITES OF PASSAGE

Writing in French in 1909, the European comparative sociologist Arnold van Gennep (1873–1957) delineated in *Les rites de passage* (published in English in 1960) a structure for transformative ritual practices he considered universal and common to all cultures. Although they vary greatly in intensity, specific form, and social meaning, rites of passage are ceremonial devices used by societies to mark the passage or transition of an individual or a group from one social status or situation to another. Rites of passage resolve *life-crises*; they provide a mechanism to deal with the tension experienced by both individuals and social groups during ambiguous occasions including, but not limited to, birth, puberty, marriage, and death.

By facilitating these life course transitions, rites of passage hold considerable emotional importance for both the individual and society. To take on a new social identity, the former must negotiate an often-arduous status passage. Furthermore, society must assist individual members in accomplishing these rites and, when these occasions are complete, recognize the new standing of the initiate.

By adopting a comparative approach to develop his taxonomy of social rites, van Gennep noted that these social customs are used to mark specific moments of the life course. Many societies use these ceremonies to articulate events that hold significance not only for individuals and families but the larger society as well. Associated with each life stage is a specific social status and a definitive set of obligations and responsibilities that the incumbent is expected to fulfill. As the individual advances the normative, sequential stages of the life course—generally from infant, adolescent, spouse, parent, elder, to deceased—taking on a new social role at each phase. Rites of passage function to accomplish status transitions; they provide a mechanism for individuals and their societies to recognize those who negotiate the rites as intrinsically *different* beings.

Although rites of passage are used to accomplish a wide variety of different social transitions, van Gennep found that they typically involve a tripartite structure involving three sequential stages. During rites of separation (*séparation*), initiates are removed physically from the social group. Mortuary or funeral rituals, for example, are used to achieve the distinction between the world of the living and the realm of deceased ancestors.

Transition (*marge*) or liminality rites accentuate the often-profound changes an initiate undergoes. The debutant undertaking transition typically experiences a condition of liminality, a marginal status that is socially *betwixt and between* the former status and an uncertain future. Transitional rites are ambiguous periods. The initiate may receive special instruction and knowledge essential for those reincorporated within the society. Often

during the liminal stage, the human body is itself the object of ritual process. A young person, for example, may be required to undergo painful surgical procedures such as body piercing, scarification, or circumcision. The healed wounds permanently signify the status change.

The third stage is that of incorporation (*agrégation*) or reaggregation. This phase involves the reintegration of the transformed individual into the social group, albeit in a new capacity. Van Gennep underscored that this tripartite pattern of human transitions mimics the pattern of nature and the cosmos, a continuous sequence of birth, being, and rebirth. As the earth regenerates through the passing seasons, the new growth of spring following the dead of winter, so too do families and societies.

Rites of Passage Cross-Culturally

Birthing and pregnancy rites. Pregnancy and childbirth are often associated with rites of separation; pregnant women may be viewed as dangerous, or capable of polluting men and sacred objects and places (Douglas 1966). Commenting on birthing rites, van Gennep cites at length W. H. R. Rivers's 1906 ethnography of the Tonga of India. Among these people a series of pregnancy rites are performed, first to separate the pregnant woman from her village. After an extended liminal period, a ceremony is held in which the woman drinks sacred milk to purify her, her husband, and their child. Subsequently, the family is reintegrated into their social group. No longer a polluting women, she is re-established in her village as a mother.

Peter Loizos and Patrick Heady (1999) recently co-edited a compilation of essays on the relation of symbolic practice and pregnancy and childbirth among mainly contemporary European peasant societies and from communities in Africa, Asia-Pacific, and Latin America. Consistent with the findings of van Gennep, members of these diverse societies used different means to mark the status transition of pregnancy and the birth of a new human being. The physical birth of the infant may in fact not be the moment at which a status change takes place. Conducting ethnographic research among Indians and non-Indians in the Bolivian Andes, Andrew Canessa (1999) observed that the designation of personhood was not achieved at birth but rather emerged through other ritual practices throughout the life course.

Among a Flemish population of mixed religious background in Flanders, Belgium, Anne van Meerbeeck (1995) found that the rite of baptism was considered a highly desirable ceremony through which to integrate newborn babies into the community. Regardless of their affiliation with the Catholic Church, parents sought its assistance in marking an important stage in the life course of their infant.

Initiation rites. Puberty rites for van Gennep demark social rather than biological events. These initiation rites signify a departure from the asexual world of the child and are followed sequentially by rites of incorporation into the sexual world of the adult. Depending on the society, these ceremonies may take place either prior to attainment of sexual maturity or, alternatively, long after physiological puberty has occurred. These rites are extremely important in that they signify that the initiate is capable of upholding the office of an adult member of the social group. He or she is prepared to take a spouse, meet the occupational demands as a full member of the community, and to parent children.

Anthropologist Audrey Richards (1982) details through rich ethnographic description the *chisungu,* the month-long initiation rite for young Bemba females of Zambia. In matrilineal societies such as the Bemba, young men leave their families and join their wives' lineages. For Richards, Bemba social structure is reproduced through the *chisungu.* The female initiation ceremonies place initiates (and their future husbands) within the power structure of the matriarchy.

The circumcision ritual is the key component of the male initiation ritual for the Merina of Madagascar. According to Maurice Bloch (1986), the circumcision ritual represents, on the one hand, a *blessing* that is bestowed on the young initiate through a connection with his ancestors. Juxtaposed to this act of love and kindness, however, circumcision is also for the young male an extreme act of violence. As Madagascar has undergone considerable change, Bloch analyzes how the circumcision rite prevails through changing sociopolitical contexts. Despite shifting circumstances, Bloch finds an inherent stability to these rituals.

A contemporary classic ethnography is Gilbert Herdt's (1994) description of male initiation practices among the Sambia of the Papua New Guinea Highlands. The first European to observe these

A boy reads from the Torah during his Bar Mitzvah. Initiation rites such as the Bar Mitzvah signify that the initiate is capable of acting as an adult member of the social group. NATHAN NOUROK/PHOTO EDIT

rites, Herdt found that Sambian males must undergo a long, arduous, ritual process through which to transcend feminized boyhood to ultimately achieve masculinity. "This is ritual custom: it is what men must do to be men, even if they must be dragged into manhood screaming all the way" (Herdt 1994, p. 253).

Betrothal and marriage rites. The anthropological record reveals tremendous variation in marriage patterns. Robin Fox condenses what he calls the "facts of life" for kinship and marriage to four axioms (Fox 1983, p. 31):

- Principle 1: The women have the children;
- Principle 2: The men impregnate the women;
- Principle 3: The men usually exercise control;
- Principle 4: Primary kin do not mate with each other.

Although Fox's approach is extremely reductionist, his point would seem to be well taken that there are few universals relative to kinship and marriage with the exceptions of gestation, impregnation, a tendency toward male dominance, and incest avoidance. (For an alternative perspective, see Levi-Strauss 1949.)

Similarly, Lucy Mair (1977) documents a multiplicity of marriage practices while providing limited evidence for universal patterns. Mair does, however, include an illuminating discussion of the rites of marriage and divorce.

Mortuary rites. When a person dies, both the deceased and the survivors typically undergo a rite of passage. The dead are separated from the world of the living and incorporated into the domain of the ancestors. This is a significant status passage. Although the deceased may walk with the living as spiritual beings (or not infrequently efforts are made to ensure that they do not), they are, nevertheless, of the afterworld. Likewise, for the living there is the task of separating oneself from the relationship with deceased. One frequently mourns the passing of the relative or loved one. Property must be redistributed. Reincorporation for the survivors into the community often brings with it a new status, one of widow, widower, or orphan.

Annette Weiner (1976) depicts a lengthy, elaborate funeral ritual celebrated by the villagers of Kwaibwaga in the Trobiand Islands of Papua New Guinea. The funeral ritual exerts considerable effort to restore social harmony, the extent of which varies according to the social status of the deceased. Ceremonial clothes are donned. The spouse straps on a mourning neckband, a ritual object he or she will wear for approximately two years. As the dead body is wrapped, men and women sob and moan. The Kwaibwaga engage in a lengthy, highly structured mortuary ritual in which kinfolk and other villagers exchange gifts. For Weiner, the mortuary ritual provides a dramatic process through which social relationships are articulated and social harmony restored.

In some societies, the period of transition may be very brief. In her moving but deeply disturbing study of mothers in Brazil, Nancy Scheper-Hughes (1992) details the everyday struggles of women experiencing high rates, up to 25 percent, of infant mortality. Rather than to express sorrow, the

mother is expected to articulate her joy. Her dead infant—an *angel-baby*—will have a happy future. As one grandmother put it, "[m]an makes; God takes" (Scheper-Hughes 1992, p. 418). Yet in Bom Jesus da Mata, Scheper-Hughes found little celebration through funeral rituals for angel-babies. Ritual practice did not resolve the rupture in the social fabric caused by the recurring deaths of infants.

Cultural Performance, Social Drama, and Rites of Passage

The analytical framework for rites of passage—the parsing of the process into the stages of separation, liminality, and reaggregation—has also found its way into the analysis of cultural performance. Milton Singer proposed the theory of cultural performance, and it was adopted by anthropologists and folklorists to refer to a unit of analysis to circumscribe "[p]lays, concerts, and lectures . . . but also prayers, ritual readings and recitations, rites and ceremonies, festivals, and all those things we usually classify under religion and ritual rather than with the cultural and artistic" (Singer 1972, p. 71). This concept of cultural performance is essentially similar to what Turner calls "social drama," but it is Turner who adapted the rite of passage stages to the analysis of cultural performance. Both Turner (1990) and Singer (1972) wrote about social dramas and performances and the extension of these in technologically complex societies. These dramas share with ritual the properties of liminal events and social metacommentary. Modern social drama, says Turner, contains the components of separation, liminality, and incorporation that define a rite of passage.

Ritual, Performance, and Rites of Passage

Ritual behavior as classically applied to humans has four characteristics. First, ritual is a stylized or stereotyped, repetitive, pattern of behavior. Second, it is associated with religious beliefs and practices and in some sense deemed to be sacred. Third, it contains a temporal element in that rituals are held at set times and have a liturgical order. Last, ritual has a spatial element because it often takes place in a specified location with actors also being spatially coordinated. Sometimes, however, the second and third characteristics are rather loosely interpreted so that secular events like graduations, installation of officers, the visit of foreign dignitaries, and pilgrimages to Disneyland can be described in ritual terms (Kertzer 1988). In this expanded interpretation, what is deemed to be sacred spreads beyond religion to what is valued in secular life. Turner wrote about theater performance much in the same way as he interpreted Ndembu religious practices (Turner 1977), as a social and ritual drama, symbolically rich in expressing cultural meanings and indications for how a society structures the lives of its people. Rituals are for Turner always associated with rites of passage that mark a transition from one status state to another.

The extension of ritual performance to modern life has its most extensive expression in performance theory, especially the writings of Turner himself and those of Richard Schechner. The collection of works found in *By Means of Performance: Intercultural Studies of Theatre and Ritual,* (edited by Richard Schechner and Willa Appel) is the best source for the extension of the analysis of ritual into contemporary practice. Schechner organizes the range of performance events subject to this type of analysis into an event-time-space chart that includes, among many others, sporting events, executions, and hostage crises. This model for cultural analysis has also found its way into folklore studies as found, for example, in the analysis by Liz Locke (1999) of the *Rocky Horror Picture Show* as a social drama and as containing the three central elements of rites of passage.

Turner's model for cultural performance in complex societies suggests that the performance event can be parsed into ritual stages that mimic what occurs during a rite of passage. These are the stage of *separation,* a *liminal* stage, and a stage of *reaggregation.* The value of this partition is that it is a way of organizing symbolic data and because symbols evoke emotion, the analysis heightens the awareness of the undercurrents that drive the passions of the performance. As Turner phrases it, there is an effort in such symbolic expression to unite the organic with the sociomoral order. Examples are in courts of law (Garfinkel 1956), but also in the vast infrastructure of quasi-judicial bodies that regulate everything from global trade to health and the environment (Adam 1999).

Although the elements of separation and reintegration in the ritual process of social dramas are similar to those of nontechnological societies, Turner does find a degree of difference for the liminal stage. The overriding characteristic of being in the liminal state is the status of ambiguity, of being betwixt and between. In what Turner refers to as technologically simpler societies, the liminal state is associated with transformative creatures, with monsters and chimera. Masks are a usual ritual element, as are drugs and states of trance. There is an exchange of communication, conversations between those in the liminal state and the mixed-up creatures and figures inhabiting the netherworld. This has overtones in theater but can be extended also to sporting events (Bromberger 1995).

Turner does make the distinction between obligatory rites of passage as are found in less technological societies and those of a secular industrialized world where participation is voluntary. He refers to this voluntary aspect as *liminoid,* and it is in this venue in which the various genres of cultural performance, like theatre, festivals, parades, public executions, sporting events, and so on, are occasioned.

The Persistence of Rites of Passage

Martha and Morton Fried (1980) surveyed rites of passage associated with the transitions of birth, puberty, marriage, and death in eight societies of different levels of technological advancement. Although these cultures have significant differences, the Frieds have found that the persistence of these ceremonies is not a function of the political system or economy. Social controls were implemented in China, Cuba, and the former members of the Soviet Union to define rites of passage in terms of the communist state. As the Frieds note, these attempts failed. There appears to be a persistence to rites of passage, particularly those associated with life-crises that other mechanisms of the social system cannot efficiently or effectively transport social members through.

Although globalization has compressed both time and space on a world scale (Soja 1989), despite these homogenizing influences cultural distinctiveness at the local level continues to assert itself. For example, African American youth, generally males, are developing meaningful rites of passage to experience and exert a positive sense of self-identity (Brookins 1996; McKenry et al. 1997).

Yet there are other ways rites of passage are being used. Emma Ogilvie and Allan Van Zyle (2001) recently considered incarceration of Aboriginal youth in the remote Northern Territory of

Australia as a rite of passage for these young men. In discussing the experience of criminal offending and imprisonment among informants, aged eighteen to twenty-five, from twelve isolated communities, Ogilvie and Van Zyl found that imprisonment "provided access [to] resources unavailable within the original communities . . . The interviews point to detention as an opportunity for a *different experience* from that available in the remote communities . . . detention provides something new" (2001, p. 4). This is indeed a disturbing reminder that ritual practice is neither always positive nor celebratory.

See also: CHILDHOOD, STAGES OF: ADOLESCENCE; LIFE COURSE THEORY; MARRIAGE CEREMONIES; MENARCHE; SOCIALIZATION

Bibliography

Adam, B. (1999). "Radiated Identities: In Pursuit of the Temporal Complexity of Conceptual Cultural Practices." In *Spaces of Culture: City, Nation, World,* ed. M. Featherstone and S. Lash. London: Sage.

Bennett, J. F. (1988). *Events and Their Names.* Oxford: Clarendon Press.

Bloch, M. (1986). *From Blessing to Violence: History and Ideology in the Circumcision Ritual of the Merina of Madagascar.* Cambridge, UK: Cambridge University Press.

Bromberger, C. (1995). "Football as World-View and as Ritual." *French Cultural Studies* 6(3):293–311.

Brookins, C. C. (1996). "Promoting Ethnic Identity Development in African American Youth: The Role of Rites of Passage." *Journal of Black Psychology* 22(3):388–417.

Canessa, A. (1999). "Making Persons, Marking Differences: Procreation Beliefs in Highland Bolivia." In *Conceiving Persons: Ethnographies of Procreation, Fertility, and Growth,* ed. P. Loizos and P. Heady. London: Athlone.

Davidson, D. (1980). *Essays on Actions and Events.* Oxford: Clarendon Press.

Douglas, M. (1966). *Purity and Danger: An Analysis of Concepts of Pollution and Taboo.* New York: Praeger.

Fox, R. (1983). *Kinship and Marriage: An Anthropological Perspective,* American edition. Cambridge, UK: Cambridge University Press.

Fried, M. N., and Fried, M. H. (1980). *Transitions: Four Rituals in Eight Cultures.* New York: Norton.

Garfinkel, H. (1956). "Conditions of Successful Degradation Ceremonies." *American Journal of Sociology* 61:420–424.

Herdt, G. H. (1994). *Guardians of the Flute: Idioms of Masculinity,* Vol. 1, rev. edition. Chicago: University of Chicago Press.

Kertzer, D. I. (1988). *Ritual, Politics, and Power.* New Haven, CT: Yale University Press.

Levi-Strauss, Claude. (1949, 1969). *The Elementary Structures of Kinship,* trans. J. H. Bell and J. R. von Sturmer. Boston: Beacon Press.

Loizos, P., and Heady, P., eds. (1999). *Conceiving Persons: Ethnographies of Procreation, Fertility, and Growth.* London: Athlone.

Mair, L. P. (1977). *Marriage,* rev. edition. London: Scholar Press.

McKenry, P. C.; Kim, H. K.; Bedell, T.; Alford, K. A.; and Gavazzi, S. M. (1997). "An Africentric Rites of Passage Program for Adolescent Males." *Journal of African American Men* 3(2):7–20.

Richards, A. I. (1982). *Chisungu: A Girls' Initiation Ceremony among the Bemba of Zambia,* 2nd edition. London: Routledge.

Rivers, W. H. R. (1906). *The Todas.* London: Macmillan.

Sanday, P. R. (1990). *Fraternity Gang Rape: Sex, Brotherhood, and Privilege on Campus.* New York: New York University Press.

Schechner, R., and Appel, W., eds. (1990). *By Means of Performance: Intercultural Studies of Theatre and Ritual.* Cambridge, UK: Cambridge University Press.

Scheper-Hughes, N. (1992). *Death without Weeping: The Violence of Everyday Life in Brazil.* Berkeley: University of California Press.

Singer, M. B. (1972). *When a Great Tradition Modernizes: An Anthropological Approach to Indian Civilization.* New York: Praeger.

Soja, E. W. (1989). *Postmodern Geographies: The Reassertion of Space in Critical Social Theory.* London: Verso.

Turner, V. (1977). *The Ritual Process: Structure and Antistructure,* First Cornell edition. Ithaca, NY: Cornell University Press.

Turner, V. (1986). "Dewy, Dilthey, and Drama: An Essay in the Anthropology of Experience." In *The Anthropology of Experience,* ed. V. Turner and E. M. Bruner. Urbana: University of Illinois Press.

Turner, V. (1990). "Are There Universals of Performance in Myth, Ritual, and Drama?" In *By Means of Performance: Intercultural Studies of Theatre and Ritual,* ed. R. Schechner and W. Appel. Cambridge, UK: Cambridge University Press.

van Gennep, A. (1960). *The Rites of Passage*. [Originally published in 1909 in the French as *Les rites de passage*]. Chicago: University of Chicago Press.

van Meerbeeck, A. (1995). "The Importance of a Religious Service at Birth: The Persistent Demand for Baptism in Flanders (Belgium)." *Social Compass* 42(1):47–58.

Weiner, A. B. (1976). *Women of Value, Men of Renown: New Perspectives in Trobriand Exchange*. Austin: University of Texas Press.

Other Resources

Locke, L. (1999). "'Don't dream it, be it': The *Rocky Horror Picture Show* as Cultural Performance." *New Directions in Folkore* 3 [E-journal]. Available from http://www.temple.edu/isllc/newfolk/journal_archive.html.

Ogilvie, E., and Van Zyle, A. (2001). *Young Indigenous Males, Custody and the Rites of Passage*. Canberra: Australian Institute of Criminology. Available from http://www.aic.gov.au/publications/tandi/ti204.pdf.

BRUCE FREEMAN
USHER FLEISING

ROLE THEORY

Role theory is not one theory. Rather, it is a set of concepts and interrelated theories that are at the foundation of social science in general, and the study of the family in particular. The ideas and concepts formulated in the development of role theory continue to inform family theory and research more than half a century later. This is apparent in past and current research on the merging of family and work.

Roles are the building blocks of social institutions and social structures. Although numerous perspectives and terms have developed around the concept of *role*, Ivan Nye (1976) has divided the perspectives into two general approaches: structural and interactionist.

Roles as Structure

From the structural perspective, roles are the culturally defined norms—rights, duties, expectations, and standards for behavior—associated with a given social position (Linton 1945). In other words, one's social position is seen as influencing one's behaviors. In addition, statuses such as gender, ethnicity, sexual orientation, and social class also shape roles (Lopata 1991).

For example, as a mother, a woman is expected to place the care of her child above all other concerns. Although this normative expectation varies across cultures, with some cultures expecting mothers to be paid workers as well, opinion surveys show that the majority of people in countries as diverse as Australia, Japan, and Poland believe that women with preschool-age children should not work outside of the home and that their children will suffer if they do.

The actual enactment of role behavior, however, may not correspond to the role expectations. *Role competence*, or success in carrying out a role, can vary depending on social contexts and resources. In countries with strong normative expectations for women to be full-time mothers, single mothers and low-income mothers often have to violate these role expectations and have been criticized as less competent mothers as a result.

Indeed, there is pressure to conform successfully to roles. Sanctions are used as tools of enforcement. Punishments for not following the role of mother can range from informal sanctions, such as rebukes from neighbors, to formal sanctions, such as the intervention of child welfare services. An example is found among women who choose not to take the role of mother and remain voluntarily childless. In a study of Swedish couples without children, researchers found that women, in particular, felt alienated from the majority of women in their community, friendship networks, and at work who were mothers (Wirtberg 1999).

The social pressure to confirm to roles can be negative for individuals. *Role captivity* refers to the unwanted participation in a particular role (Pearlin 1983). Betty Friedan's *The Feminine Mystique* (1963) is probably one of the most well-known and influential works on role captivity. She found that many women, prohibited by the threat of sanctions from taking a role other than mother and wife, felt trapped and experienced depression and frustration as a result.

Despite sanctions, roles do not remain static, but change and evolve over time (Turner 1990). Roles *crystallize* when they are widely recognized and deemed important by those who share a culture (Nye 1974). Yet not all roles are equally crystallized, and highly crystallized roles can decrystallize over time. Since Friedan's work in the early 1960s, it has not only become socially acceptable for women in the United States to have other roles beside those in the family, but being "only a housewife" has become stigmatized (Rothbell 1991). As roles change, there can be shifts in *clarity*, or the extent to which roles have clearly defined, unambiguous expectations (Cottrell 1942). The clarity of well-established roles is often high, while newer roles can be met with uncertainty and confusion.

Roles as Interaction

The *interactionist* perspective focuses on how individuals adopt and act out roles during interaction. Individuals perform their roles to others in a social context (*role-performing*), analogous to actors on a stage (Goffman 1959). Individuals also take on the role of others in order to anticipate their actions and perspectives (*role-taking*) and continually produce and reproduce roles (*role-making*) (Turner 1956). As an outcome of these interactions, individuals identify themselves and are identified by others as holding particular social statuses or positions (Stryker 1968). For example, the action of caring for a child confirms a woman's identity as a mother.

Research has uncovered the complex relationship between roles in interaction and the construction of identity. In a study of women hospital workers, Anita Garey (1999) found that women use the night shift as a way to publicly perform the dual, otherwise mutually exclusive roles of stay-at-home mom and full-time worker. This performance is done at a great cost to the women, most of whom get only a few hours of sleep each day. In another study, Cameron Macdonald (1998) showed how employed mothers and paid caregivers both acted in a way to ensure that the biological mother remains the "mother," although the two share the responsibilities and duties associated with the role.

Individuals do not equally embrace all identities associated with roles. Individuals vary in the extent to which they are committed to or identify with their different roles. Sheldon Stryker (1968) spoke of a *salience hierarchy*, or the probability of role expectations associated with an identity being

displayed in a role performance. Ralph Turner (1978) wrote of *the role-person merger*, the process through which the person becomes what his or her role is, rather than merely performing a particular role in a given situation. Incongruity between a person's identity and roles results in person-role conflict. Erving Goffman (1961) spoke of *role distance*, or the way in which individuals separated themselves from particular roles that conflict with their identities.

Accumulating and Changing Roles

Individuals accumulate different roles at any given stage within the life course. Throughout life, individuals transfer into and out of different roles, keeping some, leaving others behind, and beginning new roles (Burr 1972). These *role transitions* accompany transitions through life stages and can be easy or difficult, depending on the timing and social context (Rodgers and White 1993). In addition, the transition into one role can affect the transition into another. For instance, women in Germany and other European countries are delaying their transition to the roles of wife and mother as they extend their time in the role of student. It is concluded that remaining a student delays the transition to adulthood and likewise to normatively associated adult roles (Blossfeld and Huinink 1991).

Within each life stage, individuals also simultaneously hold many different roles. One reason for this is that individuals hold multiple social positions at one time. When a woman becomes a mother, she can also continue to have the roles of daughter, wife, and daughter-in-law. In addition, each position is associated with a *role set*, an individual's range of role relationships that accompany any social status (Merton 1957). As a mother, a woman manages unique expectations from her child, her parents and in-laws who have become grandparents, the father, and her child's teachers and doctors. A *role cluster* refers to the interconnection between roles that occur within the same social institution (Lopata 1991). A woman's roles within the family are related and often different in important ways from her roles in the workplace, such as business owner, manager, and colleague.

Research finds multiple roles to be associated with both positive and negative consequences. Much attention had been given to the problems associated with multiple roles. Role overload and role conflict are two of the most well-known role theory concepts. *Role overload* refers to the experience of lacking the resources, including time and energy, needed to meet the demands of all roles. *Role conflict* describes an incongruity between the expectations of one role and those of another. Role overload and conflict often lead to difficulties with meeting role expectations, known as *role strain* (Goode 1960). Various negative psychological and physical problems can follow from role strain. In many cultures, including Japan, Singapore, and China, women experience stress, distress, and burnout as a result of combining work and family roles (Aryee 1993; Lai 1995; Matusi, Oshsawa, and Onglatco 1995). Levels of conflict, however, vary across cultures as a result of perceptions of gender roles and the subsequent amount of time given to work and domestic roles (Moore 1995).

At the same time, some evidence suggests that multiple roles provide opportunities and advantages. In their theory of *role balance*, Stephen Marks and Shelley MacDermid (1996) found that people who are able to fully participate in and perform a number of different roles experience not only less role strain but also lower rates of depression and higher self-esteem and innovation. Rose Laub Coser (1975) argues that it is among multiple roles that individuals are able to express individuality and act autonomously in accordance with or in opposition to normative expectations. Thus, multiple roles are important for the development of personality and intellect. Lois Verbrugge (1983) found that women who hold the multiple roles of mother, wife, and paid worker have better health than women holding none or only some of these roles.

Phyllis Moen (1992) has examined the potential positive and negative consequences for women of combining paid work and family roles. She concludes that whether multiple roles are positive or negative for women depends on many factors in women's lives, such as conditions of the work, conditions of their family roles, including the number and age of children, and extent to which women view themselves as captives or committed to their work and family roles.

Role sharing is likely a means through which the positive aspects of multiple roles can outweigh potential negative consequences. Individuals with different social statuses and social positions, or even across social institutions, can share the same role. For example, the care of children is often

considered to be the role of mothers. However, fathers, employers, and government can all adopt the caregiving role (Drew, Emerek, and Mahon 1998). When they do, women are better able to competently fill and benefit from roles as both workers and mothers and experience less role strain, overload, and conflict. In China, while the father role is still viewed as primarily teacher and disciplinarian and mothers are viewed as the physical caregivers, fathers are increasingly participating in the caregiver role. This change is attributed to government-sponsored parental education and contact with Western culture (Abbott, Ming, and Meredith 1992). The International Labour Organization calls for employers to take on the responsibility of helping employees combine work and family (Derungs 2001). As they learn the benefits of fulfilling this role, employers are committing to this role. Governments, on the other hand, seem to be moving in an opposite direction. European welfare states previously embraced the role of contributing to the care of children by providing policies that aided women and later men in combining work and family. However, recent years have seen a change in the role of the state, with less emphasis on ensuring public childcare for all citizens (Jenson and Sineau 2001).

See also: FAMILY ROLES; FAMILY THEORY; RESOURCE MANAGEMENT; SYMBOLIC INTERACTIONISM; TRANSITION TO PARENTHOOD

Bibliography

Abbott, D. A.; Ming, Z. F.; and Meredith, W. (1992). "An Evolving Redefinition of the Fatherhood Role in the People's Republic of China." *International Journal of Sociology of the Family* 22:45–54.

Aryee, S. (1993). "Dual-Earner Couples in Singapore: An Examination of Work and Nonwork Sources of Their Experienced Burnout." *Human Relations* 46:1441–1468.

Blossfeld, H. P., and Huinink, J. (1991). "Human Capital Investments or Norms of Role Transition? How Women's Schooling and Career Affect the Process of Family Formation." *American Journal of Sociology* 97:143–168.

Burr, W. R. (1972). "Role Transitions: A Reformulation of Theory." *Journal of Marriage and the Family* 34:407–416.

Coser, R. L. (1975). "The Complexity of Roles as a Seedbed of Individual Autonomy." In *The Idea of Social Structure*, ed. L. Coser. New York: Harcourt.

Cottrell, L. S. (1942). "The Adjustment of the Individual to his Age and Sex Roles." *American Sociological Review* 7:617–620.

Derungs, F. (2001). Die Vereinbarkeit von Familien- und Erwerbsleben: Eine Untersuchung von Dokumenten der Internationalen Arbeitsorganisation (The Reconciliation of Family and Work Life: A Study of Documents from the International Labour Organization). Unpublished Thesis. Switzerland: University of Fribourg.

Drew, E.; Emerek, R.; and Mahon, E., eds. (1998). *Women, Work, and the Family in Europe.* London: Routledge.

Friedan, B. (1963). *The Feminine Mystique.* New York: Norton.

Garey, A. (1999). *Weaving Work and Motherhood.* Philadelphia: Temple University Press.

Goffman, E. (1959). *The Presentation of Self in Everyday Life.* New York: Doubleday.

Goffman, E. (1961). *Encounters.* Indianapolis, IN: Bobbs-Merrill.

Goode, W. (1960). "Theory of Role Strain." *American Sociological Review* 25:483–496.

Jenson, J., and Sineau, M. (2001). *Who Cares? Women's Work, Childcare, and Welfare State Redesign.* Toronto: University of Toronto Press.

Lai, G. (1995). "Work and Family Roles and Psychological Well-Being in Urban China." *Journal of Health and Social Behavior* 36:11–37.

Linton, R. (1945). *The Cultural Background of Personality.* New York: Appleton-Century-Crofts.

Lopata, H. Z. (1991). "Role Theory." In *Social Roles and Social Institutions*, ed. J. Blau and N. Goodman. Boulder, CO: Westview Press.

Macdonald, C. (1998). "Manufacturing Motherhood: The Shadow Work of Nannies and Au Pairs." *Qualitative Sociology* 21:25–53.

Marks, S. R., and MacDermid, S. (1996). "Multiple Roles and the Self: A Theory of Role Balance." *Journal of Marriage and the Family* 58:417–432.

Matsui, T.; Oshsawa, T.; and Onglatco, M. (1995). "Work-Family Conflict and the Stress-Buffering Effects of Husband Support and Coping Behaviors among Japanese Married Working Women." *Journal of Vocational Behavior* 47:178–192.

Merton, R. K. (1957). *Social Theory and Social Structure.* New York: Free Press.

Moen, P. (1992). *Women's Two Roles: A Contemporary Dilemma.* New York: Auburn House.

Moore, D. (1995). "Role Conflict: Not Only for Women? A Comparative Analysis of Five Nations." *International Journal of Comparative Sociology* 36:17–35.

Nye, F. I. (1974). "Emerging and Declining Family Roles." *Journal of Marriage and the Family* 36: 238–245

Nye, F. I. (1976). *Role Structure and Analysis of the Family.* Beverly Hills, CA: Sage.

Pearlin, L. (1983). "Role Strain and Personal Stress." In *Psychosocial Stress*, ed. H. B. Kaplan. New York: Academic Press.

Rodgers, R. H., and White, J. M. (1993). "Family Development Theory." In *Sourcebook of Family Theories and Methods*, ed. P. Boss, W. Doherty, R. LaRossa, W. Shumm, and S. Steinmetz. New York: Plenum Press.

Rothbell, G. (1991). "Just a Housewife: Role-Image and the Stigma of the Single Role." In *Social Roles and Social Institutions*, ed. J. Blau and N. Goodman. Boulder, CO: Westview Press.

Stryker, S. (1968). "Identity Salience and Role Performance: The Relevance of Symbolic Interaction Theory for Family Research." *Journal of Marriage and the Family* 30:558–564.

Thomas, E., and Biddle, B. (1966). "The Nature and History of Role Theory." In *Role Theory: Concepts and Research*, ed. B. Biddle and E. Thomas. New York: John Wiley & Sons.

Turner, R. H. (1956). "Role Taking, Role Standpoint, and Reference-Group Behavior." *American Journal of Sociology* 61:316–328.

Turner, R. H. (1978). "The Role and the Person." *American Journal of Sociology* 84:2–23

Turner, R. H. (1990). "Role Change." *American Review of Sociology* 16:87–110.

Verbrugge, L. (1983). "Multiple Roles and Physical Health of Women and Men." *Journal of Health and Social Behavior* 24:16–30.

Wirtberg, I. (1999). "Trying to Become a Family; or, Parents without Children." *Marriage and Family Review* 28:121–133.

CARRIE L. YODANIS

ROMANIA

Located in southeastern Europe between the Carpathian Mountains, the Danube River, and the Black Sea, Romania has a population of 22.5 million, with 90 percent identifying themselves as Romanian, 7 percent as Hungarian, and 3 percent as belonging to other ethnic groups (NIS 2001). Romanians are proud of their two-thousand-year history. The formation of Romanian language began in the year 100 C.E. when the Roman Empire conquered the local population, the Geto-Dacians, establishing a province covering much of the current Romanian territory. Following hundreds of years of foreign influence and organization in smaller principates, present-day Romania took shape in two stages by the union of Moldavia and Wallachia Provinces (1859) and Transylvania (1918).

Political, Social, and Economic Setting

At the beginning of the twentieth century Romania was an agrarian society, with a traditional social structure that was not given to rapid progress (Zamfir 2001). The communist development program implemented between the 1950s and the 1970s brought significant changes by emphasizing urbanization and industrial modernization. Officially promoted by the regime was the uniform distribution of the rather limited resources available, the goal being to create an "egalitarian" society in which each member had decent living circumstances (Zamfir 2001). However, communism provided Romania with an economy that was underdeveloped and inefficient. Based on a state-owned monopoly of the internal market, modest technologies, and large enterprises, Romanian economy suffered from important structural and functional distortions, creating a crisis that started in 1970s, worsened in 1980s, and led to a sharp decline in people's standard of living (Zamfir 2001).

In December 1989, the dictatorial regime of Ceausescu was overthrown. Since then, Romania moved from a communist regime to a democratic political system, from a state-planned to a market economy, and from a state-governed and controlled family life to independently functioning family systems. The transformation into a democratic setup and a market economy was not smooth. The breakdown of the economic and social infrastructure resulted in worker unemployment, underemployment, and job insecurity, all of which translated in economic hardships for many families and communities. Thus, between 1991 and 2000 an average of 70 percent of Romanians estimated their income as barely sufficient or insufficient to cover basic necessities (RIQL 2001). Household composition is an important indicator correlating with poverty. For example, households

with five family members face a more than 50 percent chance of being poor (Tesliuc and Pop 2001), and each child that is born increases the poverty risk by almost 50 percent (RIQL 2001). Poverty rates vary by region as well: In 1998, the poverty rate in rural areas was 50 percent higher than in urban areas (RQIL 1998).

Family Evolution

The Romanian family has emerged as an institution with high stability, based on the principles of synchronicity and the complementary natures of gender roles (Mitrofan and Ciuperca 1997). The political, social, and economic setting has significantly influenced the structure and the functions of the family system.

The totalitarian society imposed outside pressure on the family, making its space very constrained (Mitrea 1993). Both spouses had to work full-time since this was the most acceptable family model. Family planning was strongly restricted, couples being encouraged to have as many children as possible.

Some of these pressures disappeared after 1989 with the transformation of many aspects of life in Romania. The state is no longer directly involved in family life. Contemporary family members have more choices in terms of individual interests. The family can regulate its own internal life and functions. For example, family planning has become easier and more accessible, allowing people to have more control over their lives. When family self-determination increased through modernization, however, the individual's environment became less secure. Increased liberty is paid for with a growing feeling of insecurity and greater efforts to adapt to unknown social dynamics (Mitrea 1993). Employment of both spouses remains predominant after 1989, mostly because few families can get by on a single income.

Change in the family structure itself has also occurred. Urbanization is responsible for the transition from an extended, multigenerational family pattern to a nuclear one (parents and their children), which maintains significantly strong relationships with the family of origin. In 2000, the urban population was 55 percent, reflecting a trend of migration towards the cities (from 18 percent in 1912) (INS 2001). Family solidarity plays an important role in family life; the term *family* includes parents, grandparents, aunts, uncles, cousins, and godparents.

Family Structure

Most Romanian families are traditional, married couples with children. In 2000, the marriage rate was 6.1 marriages per 1,000 inhabitants, the lowest level since the 1950s, but still relatively high among the European countries (NIS 2001; UNDP 2000). The average age at marriage was relatively young in 1998—28.4 years for men and 24.9 years for women (NIS 1999). The proportion of first marriages was over 80 percent, and, on average, marriages lasted twenty-two years, indicating a high level of family stability (UNPD 1996). The divorce rate remained relatively steady—around 1.3 divorces per 1,000 inhabitants (in the European context, this level is below average) (NIS 2001).

The number of children per family depended on educational background and region. People with higher educational levels and those living in the cities tended to have fewer children (Ilut 1995; UNDP 2000). Most of the families in the cities had one or two children. In the year 2000 the total fertility rate per woman was 1.3 (UNDP 2000).

Family Values

Romanian families place a high value on children; their protection and well-being are considered to be parents' primary responsibilities. Considerable efforts are made to provide children with what they need. Parents' hope and pride are focused on children's successes. Interdependent and reciprocal relationships are encouraged among members of the Romanian family. Parents provide care for their children and in return, children are expected to be obedient and respectful and, in later life, to care for their parents.

Dedication to extended family and friends is another important value. A complex system of rules and obligations regulates each individual's relations and responsibilities within the extended family. For example, in many cases, grandparents assist parents in raising their children. During the communist regime, the social networks of friends were an important source of emotional and intellectual support. In the transition period accompanied by financial strain, this support has often become financial. In addition, in one-child families, friends often become substitute siblings.

Education is very important, with the school holding a central role in the life of children. During the school years, children are expected to perform well, and parents try their best to help them. Success in school is prized because of its relation with economic advancement. Therefore, play and the other leisure activities are usually subordinated to studying.

Religion has always been an important value for Romanians. The majority of the population (70%) is Christian Orthodox, with the rest divided among other religions (Roman Catholics 6%, Protestants 6%, others and unaffiliated 18%). Religion has been one of the strengths of families, providing them with spiritual sustenance. Many family practices and customs are related to religion. Rites of passage, baptisms, weddings, and funerals are rich in rituals, and they are celebrated with the extended family and friends. Other important celebrations are Christmas, Easter, and name-days. Many people are given saints' names, and their name-days coincide with the celebration of the patron saint's day.

Conclusion

During Romania's long history, although exposed to many political, social, and economic challenges, family life has shown a high level of resiliency. Confronted at times with stressful life events, Romanians present personal and family protective factors that offer buffers against those vulnerabilities, at the same time promoting the well-being of children. Among these resiliency factors, the most widely manifested are empathy, problem-solving skills, realism, caring relationships, and positive family environments. Family activities communicate a feeling of solidarity and continuity, adding to a sense of security and predictability that encourages resilience. Moreover, Romanians have a strong sense of self-efficacy, of being able to deal with whatever situation arises.

Bibliography

Ilut, P. (1995). *Familia—cunoastere si asistenta*. Cluj-Napoca, Romania: Argonaut.

Mihailescu, I. (1995). "Politici sociale in domeniul populatiei si families. Politici Sociale." In *Romania in a European Context*, ed. E. Zamfir and C. Zamfir. Bucharest: Alternative.

Mitrea, G. (1993). Functiile familiei ieri si azi. *Calitatea vietii 2–3.*

Mitrofan, I., and Ciuperca, C. (1997). *Psihologia relatiilor dintre sexe.* Bucharest: Alternative.

National Institute of Statistics. (1999, 2001). Yearbooks. Bucharest: Author.

Research Institute for Quality of Life. (1992–1999, 2001). *Quality of Life Diagnosis.* Coordinator I. Marginean.

United Nations. (2000). Executive Board of the United Nations Development Programme and of the United Nations Population Fund. Geneva: Author.

United Nations Developmental Program. (2000). *Human Developmental Report 2000.* Oxford: Oxford University Press.

United Nations Development Programme and Romanian Academy. (1996). *Human Development Report, Romania.* Bucharest: Expert Publishing House.

Voinea, M. (1994). "Restructurarea familie: modele alternative de viata." *Sociologie Romaneasca* 5.

Zamfir, C. (2001). Introduction. In *Poverty in Romania,* ed. C. Zamfir, K. Postill, and R. Stan. United Nations Human Development Report.

Other Resource

Tesliuc, C. M., and Pop, L. (2001). "Poverty, Inequality, and Social Protection." Available from http://www.worldbank.org.ro/ECA.

MIHAELA ROBILA

RUNAWAY YOUTHS

Throughout history, runaways have persisted as a formidable presence on the social landscape. Leaving behind families and friends for any number of reasons, these youths are quickly and almost invariably exposed to the brutal reality of a harsh life on the streets. Idealized images of adventure-loving adolescents seeking an escape from the monotony of suburban life are quickly replaced by the more realistic and horrific images of physical and sexual abuse, exploitation, sexually transmitted diseases, hunger, and criminal activity. There are an estimated 1.3 million runaways on the streets of the United States, and the social consequences associated with this population extend far beyond these individuals and their immediate experiences. Families, communities, and the society as a whole are affected by this ever-increasing population of at-risk youths. With one child out of every seven running away from home at least once, it is likely that almost everyone has either experienced or knows someone who has experienced the running away of a child or adolescent. What is more, running away from home is coming to be regarded as a major international problem with children from all countries running away from home for a variety of substantiated and unsubstantiated reasons. As such, stringent efforts have been made to understand this unique subpopulation of youth within contemporary society.

Defining the Concept of a Runaway

Providing an effective definition for what constitutes a runaway, or what the act of running away involves, has proven difficult for many researchers. Although generic definitions do exist, many are fraught with ambiguity or lack the clarity necessary for a genuine empirical analysis. For this reason, there have been multiple attempts to create typological classifications of runaways in an effort to provide a foundation upon which to develop more lucid descriptions and definitions of what this phenomenon actually entails. The National Center for Health Statistics (NCHS) defines the act of running away as "leaving or staying away on purpose, knowing you would be missed, and intending to stay away from home for at least some time" (Gullotta 1978, p. 544). Although this definition does provide a thorough description of what an individual must do and feel to be labeled a runaway, it does not distinguish between the nature of the runners and their psychological and contextual motivations for doing so.

To remedy the problems associated with generic operational definitions, attempts have been made to systematically develop typologies of runaway youth. These devices, which provide information on subgroups of the population, are useful with more precise conceptualizations of the population, thus allowing for more effective empirical analysis.

Categories of Runaways

Four distinct types of runaways have been identified: running to, running from, thrown out, and forsaken (Zide and Cherry 1992; Cherry 1993). *Running to* individuals are those seeking the adventure of life on their own. These are the flower children of the 1960s who left home in search of the excitement of a life outside of the mundane confines of suburbia. These are the children who leave home for the excitement and adventure of a new life in a new city: they crave "limitless pleasures, instant gratification and freedom from parental attempts to set control or limits on them" (Zide and Cherry 1992 p. 158). They believe that the world that awaits them outside of the confines of their parents' rules and regulations is one that is far superior to the one that they are leaving. These kids are not leaving because of some intrafamilial trauma or negative dynamic, nor are they leaving abusive or neglectful parents. In fact, most of these youth come from a normal type of family, and positive familial supports await their return home (Zide and Cherry 1992; Cherry 1993). Another type within the runaway population is the *running from* subgroup. These are the youth who are seeking to escape something negative within their homes. Many times, these children are running from physical, sexual, or emotional abuse, from the neglect of an alcoholic parent or stepparent, or from extreme financial hardship within the family. Unlike the running to youths, they are not searching for excitement outside of the home: they are searching for a life that is more tolerable than the one from which they escaped. Although their parents may wish them to return, they cannot return home to a positive support system and are thus in a far more dismal predicament than their running to counterparts (Zide and Cherry 1992; Cherry 1993).

A third type within the runaway population consists of youths who are forced to leave home as a result of intense alienation with their families. These *throwaways* differ from other runaways in that their parents express little or no desire for their return home. Many times, these emotionally distraught youths are leaving a situation that "has been preceded by years of failures, not only within the home, but also within the school system and community" (Zide and Cherry 1992, p. 158). These kids are typically more assertive, engage in considerable amounts of criminal activity, and are more antisocial than their runaway counterparts (Zide and Cherry 1992).

Finally, a fourth type consists of those *forsaken* children who are forced to run away as a result of the inability of their family to support them financially. These youths generally leave homes with

large families with whom they have only the slightest of social bonds, and they also have very few peer relationships. Put simply, these children have little or no social, emotional, or economic support system at home. Thus, these children are more likely to be exploited upon their runs and are considerably more prone to feelings of victimization and poor self-concepts (Zide and Cherry 1992; Cherry 1993).

Other attempts at classification have yielded similar results. However, unlike the statistically driven approach of the previous typology (Zide and Cherry 1992; Cherry 1993), these attempts have created types based on intuition gained from experience working with the population. For this reason, the generalizability of these classificatory devices is questionable, at best. Still, they have merit in that they provide a means for more precisely understanding the nature of the runaway population. Specifically, one study isolated six subgroups of runaway children: (1) self-confident and unrestrained runaway girls; (2) well-adjusted runaway youth; (3) double failures, high delinquency involvement; (4) fleeing youth; (5) young, highly regulated, and negatively influenced youth; and finally, (6) young and unrestrained youth (Dunford and Brennan 1976). Although this typology has more groups, most of the groups included in the earlier typology exist within this one as well.

Historical Patterns of Runaways

Although there is a considerable body of research devoted to the analysis and classification of runaway behavior, attempts at placing this activity into its proper historical context have been scarce (Wells and Sandhu 1986; Chapman 1978; Minehan 1934). Researchers have emphasized that such efforts allow for a comprehensive understanding of the changing nature of this phenomenon. Any consideration of runaway behavior necessitates an inquiry into its origin and development (Wells and Sandhu 1986). However, runaway behavior is a direct consequence of the origin of the family: a social construction that necessarily implies the dependency and devotion of a child to his or her parents. Under this pretense, the origin of runaway behavior can be traced to no earlier than that of the origin of the family as it is known today.

Throughout history, there have been multiple waves of increased runaway behavior and activity.

During these times, the rates of runaway children and adolescents soared, and their presence on the social landscape presented a formidable social problem for parents and policy makers. The first of these waves was precipitated by the Industrial Revolution of the eighteenth and nineteenth centuries. Thousands of children, unprotected by restrictive labor laws and compulsory education, sought to escape the penury of rural life by obtaining factory jobs in the dense urban jungles of Europe and the United States. Leaving behind large families, many of these children left home with the consent of their parents and were forced into a new, urban poverty without the support of families and close-knit communities. The presence of this burgeoning population of young, urban independents activated protective legislation to strengthen and sustain the "dependency relationship" between parents and children (Wells and Sandhu 1986). Most influential to the problem of runaway youths was the early twentieth century emergence of the status offense: the criminalization of childhood and adolescent disobedience, including the act of running away (Wells and Sandhu 1986).

The second major wave of increased runaway activity occurred during the Great Depression of the 1930s. Children, once again with the consent of their parents, left their homes in search of economic opportunity. So pervasive was the problem of runaway youths during this time, that children were forced to travel from town to town in boxcars on freight trains in search of any available financial or material assistance (Minehan 1934; Wells and Sandhu 1986). Although boys considerably outnumbered girls as runaways, girls were more frequently jailed and were sometimes forced into prostitution to pay for food and shelter. Male runaways were sometimes forced to steal and beg for all of their necessities (Minehan 1934). Following the Great Depression, and especially during World War II, runaways maintained their presence on the social landscape, causing a great deal of pressure to create social policy capable of eradicating, or at least decreasing, the negative effects of this activity on individuals, families, and communities (Wells and Sandhu 1986).

Finally, the third major wave of runaway behavior corresponded with the emergence of the counterculture of the 1960s. No longer were runaways seeking to escape the hardships of home, nor were their runs sanctioned by their parents:

these runners flocked to hippie havens such as San Francisco to live as flower children and escape the "hypocrisies of a materialistic culture" (Chapman 1978, p. 18). Idealistic images of the adventurous and carefree hippies and yippies enticed many youths to abandon suburbia in search of the communal existence of brotherly and sisterly love. These images, however romanticized and picturesque, remained just beyond the grasp of many of these adventure-seekers, forcing them into a far more dismal reality: one characterized by drug use, sexually transmitted disease, exploitation, and criminality (Chapman 1978).

Demographic Considerations

Runaways continue to represent a significant social problem. In 1998, approximately 86 percent of the runaways in the United States were between fourteen and seventeen years of age. Calls to the National Runaway Switchboard indicate that 3 percent of calls are from throwaways, 1 percent are from homeless youth, 22 percent are from runners from, 10 percent are from potential runaways, and 61 percent are runners to. Nearly 74 percent of this population is female, a marked difference from the male domination of the earlier waves of runaway behavior and activity (National Runaway Switchboard 1998).

Most runaways are white and from two-parent households. Topping the list of motives for running away is an unpleasant family dynamic (40%), followed by issues with peers and school (15%), and abuse (8%). Almost 35 percent of these kids have run away before, and only 40 percent have crossed state lines (National Runaway Switchboard 1998).

One out of every seven children will run away at some point, and some five thousand of these children will fall victim to assault, illness, or suicide each year (National Runaway Switchboard 1998). For this reason, there have been many attempts, both public and private, to assist these children. The National Runaway Switchboard (NRS), for example, was created in 1971 to give "help and hope to [runaway] youth and their families by providing non-judgmental, confidential crisis intervention and local and national referrals through a 24-hour hotline" (National Runaway Switchboard 1998). Also, a plethora of homeless shelters and other nonprofit crisis organizations designed to assist the runaway population have

Seeking refuge from the materialistic culture of the 1960s, a wave of runaways—predominately male—loitered U.S. streets. TED STRESHINSKY/CORBIS

Young runaways, like this girl, are at risk for becoming involved in drug abuse and crime since they are unable to find jobs. ROBERT ESSEL/CORBIS

originated in the past thirty years as the reality of the horrors associated with this runaway lifestyle have become evident.

Covenant House, started in 1972 by Sr. Mary Rose McGeady, is a privately owned chain of shelters for runaway youths with locations throughout the United States. Here, any homeless child or adolescent can receive room, board, mental health care, and a number of other crisis-related services (Covenant House 2002). Also, many communities sponsor independent runaway shelters for these at-risk homeless children. Although some house children only temporarily, many others are designed to integrate these children into society by teaching them basic life skills and providing them with assistance in obtaining apartments and other living accommodations.

International Perspectives

It is important to recognize that the act of running away among children and adolescents is not confined to the borders of the relatively affluent countries of Europe and North America. Large runaway populations affect many, if not most, countries throughout the world, with developing and impoverished countries experiencing larger populations of these youths (Rodwell and Cavalcanti 1998; Wright, Wittig, and Kaminsky 1993). In these developing countries, the causes, consequences, and characteristics associated with runaways and their respective activities are considerably different. In many cases, there is a clear distinction between homeless runaways and throwaways, and street kids. Homeless youths tend to live on the streets for economic reasons and maintain ties with their families and friends back home. Researchers in this area have frequently referred to this distinction as that of "children of the streets" and "children on the streets" (Lugalla and Mbwambo 1999). Whereas children on the streets are the street kids who work all day on the streets and have homes to return to at night or on the weekends, children of the streets consider the streets a permanent residence, and have maintained little or no family contact since their initial run. These children pose a considerable problem for third-world policy makers and planners because their presence is pervasive, and their problems are various. In countries characterized by intense and abject poverty, social programs designed to administer to these socially, emotionally, and physically needy children are scarce. As a result, many of these countries have recently experienced a dramatic increase in the size of their runaway population, and are clearly ill-prepared to effectively and appropriately manage the problems associated with these youths.

In Brazil, for example, runaways represent a sizeable population of children, many of whom are forced to leave their homes for the same reasons as their North American and European counterparts. For these children, "life in the streets is the outcome of [a] perverse combination of factors: the situation at home becoming too unbearable and the appeal and freedom found in the streets becoming too enticing to be ignored" (Rodwell and Cavalcanti 1998, p. 33). However, the social context within which Brazilian children exist differs in that it is characterized by difficult, if not unbearable, living conditions and social policies that do little to protect and assist the impoverished. The decision to leave the home is exacerbated in that little can be done to improve the quality of life within the home. In addition to their intense family turmoil, many (37%) of these children experience both physical and sexual abuse within the home. Thus, these children clearly fit into many of the typological descriptions articulated earlier, but their experiences are considerably more intense, unsolvable, and undeniably more turbulent (Rodwell and Cavalcanti 1998).

The presence and pervasiveness of gangs of homeless youth and runaways on the streets of Honduras is likewise an all-too-familiar reality. Much like in the United States, there are multiple categories of street children within this country: some youths are forced to leave their homes, and some leave their homes voluntarily in an effort to provide economic assistance to their poor families. Although all of these children present a social problem for this impoverished, developing country, some runaway behavior is encouraged as a result of its contribution to the economy. Many *market children,* as they are appropriately named, are forced to drop out of school to assist their families economically. These youth relocate from the vast rural hinterlands of this mountainous country and congregate in the shanty-areas surrounding the major cities of Tegucigalpa and San Pedro Sula. It is here that they attempt to earn enough money to provide for themselves and their families. Their

presence, although unsupervised, plays an important role in the labor market of the country as these children work for low wages and long hours as market vendors and market aids. However, within Honduras, there is an additional population of street kids who are not classified as market children. These runaways are usually teenagers who have been orphaned or who have been abandoned by their families. Unable to enter the workforce, many of these children engage in delinquent activities such as theft and drug use. They consider the streets their home, and do not have families upon whom they can rely for social and emotional support. These are the truly homeless children who are in desperate need of any and all kinds of physical, emotional, and economic assistance. They pose a considerable threat to the cultural stability of this country, and thus present a major social problem (Wright, Wittig, and Kaminsky 1993).

In Tanzania, the presence of runaways on the streets of the major cities increased dramatically at the close of the twentieth century. Responding to the social and economic crises afflicting this Eastern African country, many of these children run away from home for economic reasons. The economic opportunity that awaits them in the city is more appealing than the poverty that exists within their homes. Many, if not most, of these children are leaving behind families whose primary economic support stems from primitive agricultural production and maintenance. In a semidesert country that is prone to frequent droughts and land that is only occasionally fertile, the economic promise of this endeavor is weak, at best. Children whose families cannot support them are forced to leave their rural communities and embark on a trek to Tanzania's largest city, Dar es Salaam. Most of these children are between the ages of eight and ten years old, and most come from large families with six or eight children. Few have permanent accommodations on the streets, and many are employed only informally as car-parking boys and car washers. As a result of their unsanitary and unhealthy living conditions, these youths experience infectious diseases on a continual basis, rarely receiving medical attention. Also, many of these children become sexually vulnerable as a result of their situation. Both males and females frequently engage in prostitution to obtain money for food and shelter, and they are unlikely to practice safe sex because they cannot afford condoms, nor are condoms readily available in this country. Because of the dangers inherent in this lifestyle, many children join gangs for protection. These groups are highly organized and territorial, providing children with the social and emotional support lost as a result of their running away. Unfortunately, little is done to remedy the problems associated with these children. With only few financial resources, Tanzania is ill-prepared to manage this ever-increasing population of at-risk youths (Lugalla and Mbwambo 1999).

Social service programs designed to administer to these needy children, although scant, have arisen in recent years with mixed results. Proyecto Alternativos, a health education and social service program for the street children of Tegucigalpa, is a prime example of a program that effectively addresses the situation of runaways in developing countries or children of the streets (Lugalla and Mbwambo 1999). This program attempts to assist these street children by providing "health education, a feeding program for the otherwise undernourished, nonformal educational and recreational activities, and primary health care" (Wright, Wittig, and Kaminsky 1993, p. 84). These services are designed to provide children with an alternative to the delinquency associated with life on the streets, and to assist them in establishing a permanent residence and obtain employment. In many Latin American, African, and Asian countries, the Peace Corps sponsors Urban Youth Development workers who organize and facilitate similar programs in an attempt to decrease many of the problems associated with the runaway population. These workers initiate programs with the hopes that the host community will maintain them after their service commitment is complete (Peace Corps 2002). Unfortunately, however, there is little information available regarding the effectiveness of these programs and others similar in scope.

The Psychology of the Runaway

Runaways represent a unique population among adolescents; whether this is a cause or a consequence of running away is unknown. Studies have shown that runaways are less adjusted than their nonrunaway peers, have lower achievement levels, are more frequently depressed, have poor family relations, and engage in more delinquent activities (Rohr 1996). Other researchers have suggested that runaways are sociopaths—that is, they refuse to commit to or believe in the traditional values and norms of the society within which they live. In addition, runaways have been portrayed as impulsive loners who are prone to excessive aggression when frustrated. They can also be passive-aggressive and possess several different personality disorders. Because the act of running away frequently involves feelings of intense alienation between children and their families, these children are, many times, quite exploitative and manipulative of other people. They do not trust others, thus they do not feel any obligation to treat others with respect. For this reason, many social programs designed to administer to this population focus on the provision of psychiatric care and counseling.

Conclusion

The problems associated with running away are multifaceted. Children and adolescents who leave home in the hopes of a better life on their own lose far more than a mere roof over their head. They lose the social and emotional support that comes with a loving family; they lose the feelings of security that only parents can provide. As education becomes a distant and fleeting memory, these children likewise lose the desire and opportunity to excel and compete with others from their own age cohort. They are truly the forgotten children, and attempts to understand and accommodate these vulnerable youths should be imperative. Running away is not an idyllic rite of passage for young people. It is not Huckleberry Finn floating down the Mississippi on a homemade raft. It is a harsh and brutal reality for millions of children worldwide, and it is a reality that needs to be addressed immediately. Programs such as the National Runaway Switchboard have made great strides in understanding and assisting these youngsters, but more attention must be paid to the international runaway problem, as the experiences of these impoverished children are far more intense and undoubtedly more dismal.

See also: CHILD ABUSE: PHYSICAL ABUSE AND NEGLECT; CHILD ABUSE: PSYCHOLOGICAL MALTREATMENT; CHILD ABUSE: SEXUAL ABUSE; CHILDHOOD, STAGES OF: ADOLESCENCE; CHILDREN OF ALCOHOLICS; CONDUCT DISORDER; GANGS; GRIEF, LOSS, AND BEREAVEMENT; JUVENILE DELINQUENCY; MISSING CHILDREN; POVERTY

Bibliography

Chapman, C. (1978). *America's Runaways*. New York: William Morrow.

Cherry, A. (1993). "Combining Cluster and Discriminant Analysis to Develop a Social Bond Typology of Runaway Youth." *Research on Social Work Practice* 3(2):175–190.

Dunford, F. W., and Brennan, T. (1976). "A Taxonomy of Runaway Youth." *Social Service Review* 50(3):457–470.

Gullotta, T. P. (1978). "Runaway: Reality or Myth." *Adolescence* 13(52):543–549.

Lugalla, J. L. P., and Mbwambo, J. K. (1999). "Street Children and Street Life in Urban Tanzania." *International Journal of Urban and Regional Research* 23(2):329–344.

Minehan, T. (1934). *Boy and Girl Tramps of America*. New York: Farrar and Rinehart.

Rodwell, M. K., and Cavalcanti, H. B. (1998). "Unstructured Childhood: Life on the Street in Rio Vermelho, Brazil." *International Review of Modern Sociology* 28(2):29–44.

Rohr, M. E. (1996). "Identifying Adolescent Runaways: The Predictive Utility of the Personality Inventory for Children." *Adolescence* 31(123):605–623.

Wells, M., and Sandhu, H. (1982). "The Juvenile Runaway: A Historical Perspective." *Free Inquiry in Creative Sociology* 14(2):143–147.

Wright, J. D., Wittig, M., and Kaminsky, D. C. (1993). "Street Children in North and Latin America: Preliminary Data from Proyecto Alternativos in Tegucigalpa and Some Comparisons with the U.S. Case." *Studies in Comparative International Development* 28(2):81–92.

Zide, M. R., and Cherry, A. L. (1992). "A Typology of Runaway Youths: An Empirically Based Definition." *Child and Adolescent Social Work Journal* 9(2):155–168.

Other Resources

Covenant House. (2002). Available from http://www.covenanthouse.org.

National Runaway Switchboard. (1998). Available from http://www.nrscrisisline.org.

Peace Corps. (2002). Available from http://www.peacecorps.gov.

SARAH MICHELLE STOHLMAN
ROBYN BATEMAN DRISKELL

RURAL FAMILIES

The concept of rural families is, at best, a slippery one. This is because both aspects—*family* and *rural*—are today continuously being redefined. Further, in taking an international perspective, how family is defined varies regionally and from nation to nation. How family and *rurality* are defined differs depending on the theoretical context as well. For example, feminist thinkers have reconstructed what constitutes a family and what rural work for women involves.

Even the U.S. Census Bureau had to rethink its 1990 definition of family, "a domestic group of two or more people united by bonds of blood, adoption or marriage" (U.S. Bureau of Census 1990). In the 2000 census, families were allowed much more freedom to self-define; even the overall designation of "Households and Families" changed to "Families and Living Arrangements."

Janet Bokemeier (1997), president of the Rural Sociology Society, says of families: "Families live together; share economic resources; act as cooperative, caring social units; and provide environments for the emotional, social and economic well being of family members." She goes on to talk about how families share a space—the home or domicile or unit of co-residence. This allows for the wide variety of new forms of families, which range from single-parent households including fathers as primary caregivers, cohabiting families, blended families, gay and lesbian families, foster families, and traditional nuclear and extended families (Gottfried and Gottfried 1994).

Whichever definition is used to describe rural families, it becomes clear that the rural family that was defined in the mid-twentieth century—the intact, large, hardworking, dirt-smudged, patriarchal farm family—if it exists at all today, is only one of a diverse and rich variety of families that live in rural regions of all countries.

The factors that seem to define families in most nations are economic, social, and emotional support among several individuals who live together in a household (or even a tribal village). Judith Stacey (1991), who has studied postmodern families, says it very well: "No longer is there a single culturally dominant family pattern, like the modern one, to which the majority of Americans conform and most of the rest aspires. Instead Americans today have crafted a multiplicity of family and household arrangements that we inhabit uneasily and reconstitute frequently in response to changing personal and occupational circumstances."

Defining Rurality

Any discussion of rural families requires first a definition of *rural* and some debate about the difference between rural versus urban lifestyles. Most discussions of rural populations in the United States define rural settings as encompassing those people living in places with fewer than 2,500 residents, or what has been called open countryside. In contrast, urban areas are defined as places that are composed of 2,500 or more residents in a region of at least 50,000 residents (U. S. Bureau of the Census 2002). A simple explanation of a rural-urban contrast does not fully define rurality or begin to demonstrate the various family lifestyles between the two.

According to O. William Farley (1982) and his colleagues, rural families have, over time, continued to function in a predominantly conservative style. These families participate in many religious and educational activities. The family often uses farmland for much of its income and resources. The nuclear family with traditional parental roles continues to exist. These families tend to spend more quality time together.

However, many families in rural areas often conceal their needs and disadvantages, which in turn does not allow their strengths to be fully known. Said differently, rural and urban areas, or the families that live in these respective areas, can no longer be characterized by definitions that use population density as the standard. Rather, the lifestyles and economic conditions of these families should be emphasized. No one universally accepted definition of rural areas exists; there is a great variance among rural communities, and poverty in rural areas tends to be long-standing and generational (Ginsberg 1998).

The great variation in what defines rural communities (and thus rural families) is important. Although the most often conceived and discussed impression of the rural family might be represented by the farming family, Leon Ginsberg's useful view could include people living in remote Zimbabwean villages, First Nations people living on rural reservations in the United States or Canada, native Alaskans in an iced-in polar village, the forest dwellers of Brazil, nomadic Bedouin tent dwellers in rural deserts of Northern Africa, citrus plantation families in Belize, or high Himalayan shepherd families in Nepal or Tibet. Is there any common ground for this wide divergence of family clusters and clans? If there is, it is that they are rural; they are not city dwellers, they occupy less dense living spaces, and they live closer to the land (whether they farm it or not) than their urban counterparts.

The Gemeinschaft concept (a community or society characterized by relationships) of sociologist Ferdinand Tonnies has traditionally been used to describe the small town, a community rooted in a sense of mutuality (efforts of two or more people to act together in ultimate harmony to achieve benefits for each), common destiny, and the resulting common bonds and obligations. Personal relationships are more informal and relaxed.

The advantages of rural life for families have sprung from this Gemeinschaft view: the interdependence and mutuality among extended family, clan, or tribal members; the harmony with nature; the link with friendship and neighboring networks; the strengths provided by rural places of worship; and the intrinsic satisfaction of working on the land and seeing an end product, the harvest of one's labors. A newer positive factor that now attracts young families to rural communities is the relative safety of rural schools and playgrounds as compared to urban institutions and parks.

Disadvantages for rural families have been viewed primarily as the lacks: lack of social and cultural opportunities, of high-paying jobs, of qualified teachers, of a larger worldview, of and adequate health care and social services.

Changes in Rural Life

From 1900 throughout the first half of the twentieth century, a massive migration from rural to urban areas took place in most developed countries. Even in less developed countries, farm families fled to cities for economic survival. Between 1960 and 1980 in the United States and Canada, a turnaround occurred (Fulton et al. 1997) in which families began to return to rural areas, attracted by the slower pace of life and the ideal of quiet rural life.

The family farm crisis of the 1980s slowed that trend between 1980 and the early 1990s. Early census configurations from the U.S. 2000 census suggest that another trend, a return of large populations to nonmetropolitan areas, is underway.

Although the rural family is difficult to define from an international perspective, clearly it is not the cherished mid-twentieth century prototype: intact, large (five to twelve farm-laboring children), tradition-bound, earth-bound, living in a rambling farmhouse on inherited acreage. The rural family of the beginning of the twenty-first century is smaller, lives a more mechanized life, is, at the least, exposed to modern media and technologies, is more likely to hold nonfarm jobs or jobs not related to farms, is more educated, and is in many ways more like its urban counterpart than the rural family of one hundred years ago.

Poverty and Economic Struggle

Understanding rural poverty has never been easy. Internationally, one out of every five individuals is affected by poverty (Lipton and Ravallion 1995). Whether a person is poor is influenced by whether one is male or female, cultural background, where one lives (rural versus urban), and age. We now know that in families, children and mothers usually are more likely to be impoverished than are fathers (Khan 2000). In small country areas, minority and small church groups face more poverty than the majority groups. Rural families have often had more economic challenges than their urban counterparts. According to Mahmood Hasan Khan (2000) most of the poverty in the world (63%) is located in rural areas. Internationally, in China and Bangladesh, rural poverty has at times increased to 90 percent and has fluctuated from 70 to 90 percent in parts of Africa.

Agricultural centers are characteristic of rural communities that are making limited industrial or professional progress (MacNair 1999). Agricultural companies in these settings often are combined with small processing plants and distribution centers. Small businessmen generally provide the local leadership and traditionally have family ties to the community. Endeavors to change or bring in new industry are often attempted by local businessmen and women and community planners, but these efforts are short lived and seldom successful. Conversely, religious institutions may provide resources, hope, and a sense of working together against the poverty that is indicative of rural life for many families.

Poverty, historically, has been an ongoing theme for many rural families both in the United States and internationally. In the United States rural poverty endures on small family farms, in remote county communities, and in a multitude of trailer parks (Fitchen 1998).

Ginsberg (1998) reports that poverty for minority populations remained about the same during the last decade of the twentieth century. The overall poverty rate in the United States in 1990 was mostly linked to whites: 71.3 percent of the people living in poverty are white, 25 percent are African American, and 5.6 percent are Hispanic. The rural population stands in exception to these general figures; poverty rates are altogether different among rural populations. The poverty rate for rural whites is 13.5 percent; for rural African Americans, 40.8 percent; for rural Hispanics, 32 percent; and for rural Native Americans, 30 percent. These statistics take on new meaning when rural families are headed by women.

In rural areas families with a female head of household are generally very poor (Lichter and Eggebeen 1992). Families headed by women in rural settings are living in poverty, and this population has increased internationally by almost 50 percent in the last two decades of the twentieth century. This growing poverty has many implications for all rural families. These statistics, however, may have different implications culturally. For example, Brazilian children have a 20 percent better chance of living longer when the family income is in the hands of rural mothers rather than in the hands of fathers (Speth 1997).

In the case of African Americans and poverty, rural and urban differences are related to the increased frequency of mother-headed families in rural settings. According to Hayward Derrick Horton and Beverly Lundy Allen (1998), family status for African Americans continues to be one of the main influences in understanding poverty status. For these families, marital status affects the chances for living in poverty. However, being a mother-headed family was not a significant factor in relation to increased poverty rates in 1980. By 1990 the poverty rates for African-American mother-headed families had dramatically increased. In the United States since 1980, African Americans have constantly had a total family income that is approximately one-third that of white families. According to Horton and Allen, this trend of poverty has remained consistent whether the African-American families were rural (35%) or urban (27%) in 1990 and continues to be a problem for rural families and their children.

Among children, the rates for rural minorities remain three times higher than for rural whites in the United States. By 1997 over three million rural children were growing up in families with income below the poverty level. The overall poverty rate for all rural children is 22.4 percent, compared with rates for rural African-American and Hispanic children, which are two times that rate at over 46 percent. In addition, approximately 62 percent of poor rural children grow up in single-parent families. More than 50 percent of these rural families in poverty are headed by mothers or female caregivers (Poverty and Well-Being in Rural America 1999).

Those rural families who are not considered poor still face a profound economic struggle. Sociologists have documented the dynamics of the changes in rural life as farming has moved from family-owned small enterprise to the large complex industrial and corporate farming giants (Jackson-Smith 1999). These marked changes in the economic organization of food production over the last fifty years have left farm families bewildered, depressed (both economically and emotionally), and frequently deprived of long-held family lands. More rural families have members working in nonagricultural jobs commuting further to solidify family income, or spending longer spans of time living away (either in urban industrial areas, offshore drilling sites, or remote foresting camps) in order to provide for their rurally based families. Yamu Karewa, an instructor in the Social Work Program at Bennett College in North Carolina, reports that in her native small rural Zimbabwean village, men frequently go to work in the cities to support their families. Texas and California are greatly affected by young male Mexican laborers who come to the United States for temporary work to support their families in rural villages in remote regions of Mexico.

This temporary absence of fathers has a profound effect on the families left behind in villages. Children grow up disconnected from their absent dads, and rural women are forced to assume roles previously held by male heads of households—disciplinarian, role model, family carpenter, decision maker. Eldest children frequently become begin to act as parents as well.

Changes in Gender Roles

Feminist writers have begun to examine the roles of women who live on farms or in rural towns and villages (Wright 1995; Fortmann et al. 1997). They have focused on nonpaid and often undervalued work done by women (housework, gardening, milking cows or goats, raising chickens, corn grinding, food preparation and preservation, laundry work, and garment construction, for example). A new view of the vital contributions rural women are making to family economics has emerged in the last two decades. The invisible farmers have now come to the forefront (Haney and Knowles 1988).

Rural women in Canada have taken a proactive view, organizing themselves to have a voice in addressing issues on their training needs (Rock 1996) and on their economic and social concerns. "In their search for solutions, (rural) women are themselves becoming the leading edge for positive change in rural Canada" (Wolfe-Keddie 1996).

Rural women have also entered the marketplace and are more likely to hold part-time or even full-time jobs that help to stabilize the family economy (Wright 1995). This increase in out-of-home labor by rural women creates problems of inadequate daycare, limited reliable transportation, and need for afterschool programs in rural areas for the children of working mothers.

Pace and Rhythm of Rural Life

One constant of rural regions and one continuing attraction for urban-to-rural migrant families is the slower pace and the rural rhythm of life. Rural families have traditionally lived at a slower pace than that of urbanites. Centers of life continue to be the village marketplace (whether that is a farmer's market, an African marketplace bazaar, a flea market, or a town square); the town café or eating place; and the sports arena (Friday night football in the United States, sandlot soccer in Mexico, or the frozen pond in Canada and the northern rural United States). Rural families continue to live closer to the land, to nature, and to the changing seasons. The rhythm of rural life has a slower beat, and involves different sensations: aromas, textures (new-mown hay), and sounds. Rural families are more likely to pause and listen to the sounds of dogs barking, roosters crowing, nightingales or parrots or owl sounds.

Whether rural families retain more quality time to spend together is up for debate. Certainly Nintendo and Saturday morning cartoons courtesy of satellite dishes have reached even the remotest rural areas. But family farming activities and family outdoor activities (family hog and calf raising as 4-H and Future Farmers of America [FFA] activities, for example) continue to be cherished activities among rural families.

In summary, the definitions of rural families have been evolving over many generations. A global perspective on families who live in rural areas must consider the wide diversity that is found from region to region and nation to nation. Issues of poverty, gender, and social justice for rural populations are issues that must not be overlooked when examining international rural families. Resilience—an incredible ability to survive against odds—continues to be the constant and defining feature among rural families.

See also: FAMILY ROLES; INDUSTRIALIZATION; MIGRATION; POVERTY; URBANIZATION

Bibliography

Becker, G. S. (1981). *A Treatise in the Family.* Cambridge, MA: Harvard University Press.

Bokemeier, J. L. (1997). "Rediscovering Farms and Households: Restructuring Rural Society and Rural Sociology." *Rural Sociology* 62:1–20.

Farley, O. W.; Griffiths, K. A.; Skidmore, R. A.; and Thackeray, M. G. (1982). *Rural Social Work Practice.* New York: Free Press.

Fitchen, J. M. (1998). "Rural Poverty and Rural Social Work." In *Social Work in Rural Communities,* 3rd edition, ed. L. Ginsberg. Washington, DC: Council of Social Work Education.

Fortmann, L.; Antinori, C.; and Nabane, N. (1997). "Fruits of Their Labors: Gender, Property Rights, and Tree Planting in Two Zimbabwe Villages." *Rural Sociology* 62:295–314.

Fulton, J. A.; Fuguitt, G. V.; and Gibson, R. M. (1997). "Recent Changes in Metropolitan–Non-Metropolitan Migration Streams." *Rural Sociology* 62:363–384.

Ginsberg, L. H. (1998). *Social Work in Rural Communities,* 3rd edition. Washington, DC: Council of Social Work Education.

Gottfried, A., and Gottfried, A. W. (1994). *Redefining Families: Implications for Children's Development.* New York: Plenum Press.

Gumbrium, J., and Holstein, J. (1995). "Deprivation and the Construction of Domestic Life." *Journal of Marriage and Family* 57:894–908.

Haney, W. G., and Knowles, J. B. (1988). *Women and Farming: Changing Roles, Changing Structures.* Boulder, CO: Westview Press.

Horton, H. D., and Allen, B. L. (1998). "Race, Family Structure and Rural Poverty: An Assessment of Population and Structural Change." *Journal of Comparative Family Studies* 29:397–406

Jackson-Smith, D. B. (1999). "Understanding the Microdynamics of Farm Structural Change: Entry, Exit, and Restructuring among Farm Families in the 1980s." *Rural Sociology* 64:66–91.

Khan, M. H. (2000). "Rural Poverty in Developing Countries." *Finance & Development* 37:26–29.

Lasch, C. (1977). *Haven in a Heartless World: The Family Besieged.* New York: Basic Books.

Lichter, D. T., and Eggebeen, D. (1992). "Child Poverty and the Changing Rural Family." *Rural Sociology* 57:151–172.

Lipton, M., and Ravallion, M. (1995). "Poverty and Policy." In *Handbook of Development Economics,* Vol. 3B, ed. J. Behrman and T. Srinivasan. Amsterdam: Elsevier.

MacNair, R. H. (1999). "The Family in the Community." In *Working with Families; An Integrative Model by Level of Need,* 2nd edition., ed. A. C. Kilpatrick and T. P. Holland. Boston: Allyn and Bacon.

"Poverty and Well-Being in Rural America." (1999). *Family Economics and Nutrition Review* 12:93–95.

Rock, C. (1996). "Training Needs of Canadian Farm Women." *Women and Environments* 38:11–12.

Speth, J. O. (1997). "Tend to Those Who Tend the Future." *Choices* 6:19.

Stacey, J. (1991). "Backward toward the Postmodern Family: Reflections on Gender, Kinship and Class in the Silicon Valley." In *America at Century's End,* ed. A. Wolfe. Berkeley: University of California Press.

U. S. Bureau of the Census. (1990). "Household and Family Characteristics: March 1990 and 1989." *Current Population Reports, Series P-20,* No. 447. Washington, DC: U. S. Government Printing Office.

Wolfe-Keddie, J. (1996). "Farm and Rural Business Women in Canada." *Women and Environments* 38:3–35.

Wright, M. M. (1995). "I Never Did Any Fieldwork, But I Milked an Awful Lot of Cows!: Using Rural Women's

Experience to Reconceptualize Models of Work."
Gender and Society 9:216–235.

Other Resource

U.S. Bureau of the Census. (2002). "United States Census 2000." Available at http://www.census.gov/main/www/cen2000.html.

LINDA B. MORALES
SAM COPELAND

RUSSIA

The collapse of the Soviet Union in 1991 has been followed by years of economic, political, and cultural tumult with serious repercussions for individuals and families. As the country struggles to privatize industries and services, jobs have been lost, workers have gone unpaid, inflation has skyrocketed, crime rates have multiplied, and people have discovered that attitudes and skills that garnered good positions in the former socialist command-economy do not always bring success in the new world of competitive business. Although well-heeled *new Russians* symbolize the wealth that can be achieved under capitalism, poverty rates have soared and the gulf between rich and poor has widened dramatically. Hand-in-hand with the economic revolution are shifts in ideology concerning the degree to which government may interfere in interpersonal matters. This has meant the easing of controls on a variety of details concerning marriage and childrearing, but it has also meant a much weakened social safety net.

The Demographic Crisis

The social costs of the country's political and economic upheaval since the Soviet collapse are sharply conveyed by figures reflecting the demographic crisis of the decade that followed. Between 1992 and 2000, Russia's population declined by more than three million people. Birth rates trail mortality rates. In 1989, Russian women had an average of 2.0 children; today, the average family has only 1.3 children. (Replacement requires 2.2 children per family.) Low birth rates are blamed on young spouses' reluctance to have children in challenging times and on infertility resulting from previous abortions and poor maternal health (*Russian Life* 2001; Bubnova et al. 2000).

Malnutrition and deficiencies in the health care system contribute to high infant mortality rates (an average of 16.7 infant deaths per 1,000 live births from 1995 to 2000) and poor health in children. For adults, drinking, smoking, lack of exercise, and stress are additional risk factors (Breeva 2000a; LaFraniere 2001; United Nations Population Division 2000). In 1987, the life expectancy of Russian men and women was 64.9 and 74.6 years, respectively. In 1998, these numbers had dropped to 61.3 and 72.9 years (Veselkova and Zemlianova 2000). The greater vulnerability of males creates a sex ratio that is among the most unbalanced in the world.

The Family in Soviet Times

Before the Revolution of 1917 (that replaced tsarist rule with Soviet rule), arranged marriages were common and family life was heavily patriarchal. Early Soviet law reflected more egalitarian beliefs. Marriages were to be voluntary and based on mutual respect and love. On paper, men and women were given roughly equal rights. However, in reality, discrimination at work and at home continued. Though Soviet ideology and financial need led virtually all women into the workplace, few held positions of prestige or equal pay. At home, the *double-shift* prevailed—employed women returned home from work to a full measure of housework and little participation by their husbands (Ispa 1984; Boss and Gurko 1994).

On the positive side, important supports for families were put into place. Partially because the government wanted to increase the birth rate and partially because such practices fit with socialist ideology, liberal maternity leave policies were put into place, families with small children were paid stipends, families with three or more children were given priority access to some goods and services, and the availability of childcare centers and after-school programs was widened. At the same time, the government did little to make safe, reliable birth control available. Many women resorted to abortion (legalized in 1955) as a form of birth control.

Soviet ideology stipulated that the family existed to serve the state. In that vein, the Marriage and Family Code of 1969 promoted government oversight of important marital and childrearing decisions. Parents were to obey the prescriptions of teachers and pediatric health care providers and to foster *communist morality* in their children (putting the collective interest above personal concerns). Coworkers, teachers, and others who detected breaches of proper parenting strategies or marital relations were encouraged to intervene.

Post-Soviet Legal Codes Affecting the Family

Soviet family law was thus contrary to democratic views that a partnership should exist between individuals and the state and that family privacy should be respected. After the collapse of Soviet rule, authoritarian laws pertaining to the family were therefore scrapped. The Family Code of 1995, which was partially modeled after the United Nations Convention on the Rights of the Child, outlawed "arbitrary intervention" by outsiders in family matters. Parents have clear obligations to care for their children, but only in the case of child maltreatment do others have the right to intervene. Even then, every effort must be made to preserve the family unit. Removing the child is to be a last resort. Moreover, children now have the right to voice their opinions. Their preferences are to be taken seriously during custody hearings and other disputes.

The new code also supports self-determination in marriage. Engaged couples may write their own marriage contracts specifying the percentage of income and property to be shared. (Soviet family law did not deal with property rights because, according to socialist ideology, citizens were not supposed to concern themselves with material possessions.) Another innovation in the 1995 Family Code was the explicit recognition of fathers' rights to participate in parental decision-making, to take parental leaves, and to win custody after divorce (Butler and Kuraeva 2001).

The 1995 code also abandons the Soviet view that, when children are involved, judges decide if a marriage may be dissolved. Now, when desire for divorce is mutual, judges must grant the request regardless of spouses' motives; the court's role is limited to decisions regarding custody and protection of children's property interests. When only one spouse desires divorce, the couple may opt for a court hearing. However, if either spouse refuses to air private difficulties in court, the judge's only option is to give the couple three months to reconcile. After three months, the divorce is granted even if only one spouse wants it. Lawmakers reasoned that children's interests are

A Russian family toasts a member of the family who, having emigrated to the United States, has returned for a visit. DAVID H. WELLS/CORBIS

not served by the maintenance of unhappy marriages. The only exceptions involve cases in which the husband wants a divorce but the wife is pregnant or they have child who is less than a year old (Antokolskaya 1996; Dyuzheva 1995).

The 1995 Family Code is also notable for its stance regarding individuals' responsibility for the well-being of extended family members. It continues Soviet tradition in requiring financial support not only of one's own children, but also of needy parents, siblings, grandchildren, and grandparents. This includes the legal right of relatives to live in the family home no matter what their age or marital status and no matter what the size of the dwelling. Post-Soviet price inflation coupled with stagnant pensions has seriously affected the quality of life of the aged; many couples must help elderly relatives with financial support, if not with daily care.

Even before the 1995 Family Code, the 1992 Education Law had sought to democratize relationships between parents, teachers, the community, and students. Whereas during Soviet times, schools were expected to guide and, where necessary, instruct, parents on *vospitanie* (moral upbringing) (Grigorenko 2000), the 1992 law gave parents the right to use their discretion in accepting or rejecting teachers' and health care workers' instructions. Moreover, parents have the right to be informed about school educational philosophies and strategies and may choose preferred types of schooling (public, private, religious, or at home) for their children.

Accordingly, the Parents' Committee, which had operated since Soviet times, appears to have changed in nature from being a vehicle for teachers to enlist parental support with *vospitanie,* to one that assists in the daily life of school, helps with children's education, and serves a platform for the voicing of complaints. In addition, a new School Council composed of parents, teachers, students, and community representatives has been introduced. However, the relationship of this body to other decision-making bodies has not been clearly spelled out and it seems that, in many cases, its function has been limited.

It must be said that, realistically speaking, it will be years before most Russian families feel these legal changes in practice. Many parents, teachers, and health care workers are unaware of parents' new rights. Second, for most families, especially for those living outside of the major large cities, choices of educational institutions are limited. Third, though some educators are indeed engaging in a more collaborative effort with parents than ever existed during Soviet times, creating new types of relationships is often difficult for parents and professionals socialized in different times according to different standards. Fourth, the age-old priority of the mother-child over the father-child relationship will be difficult to rebalance, as evidenced by the fact that, in the vast majority of cases, mothers are still awarded custody after divorce (Butler and Kuraeva 2001).

Common Patterns in Contemporary Marital and Parent-Child Relationships

Russians tend to marry and bear children young. The average age at marriage in the late 1990s was 22, and the peak childbearing years were from 20 to 24. There is strong social pressure to marry; both sexes tend to believe that women in particular cannot be fulfilled if they never marry. In surveys, husbands and wives tend to rate their marriages as satisfactory and to explain that their families provide a haven in which one can be oneself, express opinions openly, and find emotional support (Goodwin and Emelyanova 1995b; Vannoy et al. 1999). Yet divorce rates are among the highest in the world and have been increasing since 1991 (Bubnova et al. 2000; Dyuzheva 1995). Alcohol abuse is blamed in a large number of the cases. Family tensions arising from unemployment, poverty, labor migration, disagreements about gender roles, and improved housing access (allowing divorcing couples to move apart) contribute as

well. Also troublesome are high rates of spouse abuse, often rooted in alcoholism and patriarchal tradition (Vannoy et al. 1999).

Olga Zdravomyslova (2000) calls Russian families *quasi-patriarchal.* Her research shows that, though husbands and wives rely on one another for emotional support and help in decision making, men nonetheless have higher status, expect to be the main breadwinners, and leave most housework and childcare to their wives. Surveys suggest that preference for the egalitarian distribution of household labor is rising, especially among young couples, but in the majority of families, traditional gender roles are maintained. As in many parts of the world, more people espouse egalitarianism than actually practice it, and men tend to be more traditional in this regard than women. This means that, in general, men handle repairs and women are in charge of day-in-and-day-out domestic tasks, including the nurturing of children (Vannoy et al. 1999). Elena Breeva (2000b) found that, accordingly, adolescents indicated that they felt much closer to their mothers than to their fathers.

Although it is not unusual cross-culturally for children to feel closer to their mothers than to their fathers, the Russian situation has some unique features. As demonstrated in centuries of literature, art, and folklore, motherhood in Russia is held in special reverence. Even today, the traditional Russian image of *mother* is of a woman who is ever-loving and always ready to sacrifice for her children. Her ability to endure endless work and hardship in order to provide for family needs has earned her adjectives such as *virtuous* and *strong* (e.g., Hubbs 1988; Young 1996). Moreover, according to Russian sociologists, during the Soviet period, wives and mothers came to be the de facto family heads because their contributions—financial support plus domestic labor—were greater than men's financial support only. The Soviet socialist command economy further undermined men's position because at work there were few opportunities to exercise initiative. Their status at home thus could not benefit from prestige garnered at work. This pattern has persisted into the post-Soviet era (Zdravomyslova 2000).

At the same time, a backlash against maternal employment that began in the Soviet years has since accelerated. Having a stay-at-home wife has become a status symbol for young businessmen, and many young women would prefer to stay home if they could afford it. The difficulties post-Soviet women face in finding satisfying, well-paying employment and good quality child care are certainly factors. In post-Soviet Russia, women have suffered unemployment and underemployment even more than men. Moreover, cuts in state support to childcare centers and after-school programs have led to thousands of closings. High fees at remaining programs make them inaccessible for many families. As a result, across Russia, only 50 percent of young children attend preschool programs (Fillipov 2001). Contemporary messages from the mass media glorifying sexiness and passive femininity contribute to the devaluing of female employment. In addition, family histories are at play. Generations of Soviet children grew up with limited availability to their mothers and keen awareness of their mothers' exhaustion from coping with dual roles. Since the 1970s, the envisioned—but hard to attain—solution in many minds has been for fathers to earn enough to permit mothers to stay home (Attwood 1996; Ispa 1988; Vannoy et al. 1999).

In 1970, after several visits to the USSR, Urie Bronfenbrenner wrote about the devotion to children he detected everywhere he turned. In general, Russians are indeed a child-loving people. Family relationships tend to be close and children in particular are cherished. Yet economic hardship and the strain of parents' heavy workloads have had negative implications for a growing number of children. In 2001, childcare providers and teachers told Jean Ispa that, although most parents are committed to doing everything possible for their children, many are too harried. The educators worried about children from low-income families, where resources are stretched, but also about neglected children of the new class of well-to-do entrepreneurs. Many such parents spend long hours establishing and managing their businesses—and therefore very little time at home.

Another concern voiced by many adults reflect the belief that the advent of a "predatory capitalism" (Lisovskii 1999, p. 58) and increasing social polarization have challenged the traditional value systems and led to anomie and a "spiritual vacuum," particularly among the young. Oleg Karpukhin (2000a, 2000b) believes that many young Russians have become alienated from the cultural and historical values the Russian people have lived by

and this has resulted in widespread anxiety and depression. In their place, he argues, has been the formation for youth of value systems gleaned from mass culture and mass media and at odds with traditional parental values. For many Russian commentators, such developments have resulted in a shift from consideration for family and others to a preoccupation with the well-being of oneself, a growth of immorality, and a loss of spirituality. Others note that many children, particularly in the large cities, are more independent, self-confident, relaxed, and entrepreneurially inclined than their Soviet-era predecessors.

As everywhere in the world, family attitudes and behavior in Russia differ according to adult educational level and occupational prestige as well as according to the personalities of the individuals involved. For example, when compared to manual workers, educated individuals and entrepreneurs tend to have more liberal attitudes toward divorce, to share more of their most intimate thoughts with their spouses, and to be more likely to espouse goals for children that are centered on developing curiosity and independence of thought rather than on winning obedience (Ispa 1994; Goodwin and Emelyanova 1995a; Vannoy et al. 1999).

It is also necessary to recognize the relativity of perceptions about value changes among Russian youth. Although Russian commentators worry about increases in anti-intellectual, instrumental attitudes, international studies suggest that many Russian young people still reflect traditional respect for parents and scholarship, especially when compared with their Western peers (Elliott et al. 1999, 2001).

Stability and Reform in Compulsory and Higher Education

The Russian educational system provides free and compulsory education from the age of six or seven to fifteen years. Two more years of upper secondary schooling are available for those who wish it, thus providing a ten-year education. It is intended that the addition of an eleventh year at age seventeen will soon make the age of school leaving the same as that of most other industrialized nations.

An outstanding feature of the system of compulsory education in Russia, in comparison with most other countries, has been its durability. In the half century between the mid-1930s and mid-1980s, the basic system changed only in minor ways by gradual evolution. (It should be noted that many of the moral and social precepts outlined in Soviet documentation would be shared by contemporary U.S. and U.K. readers.) Nonetheless, pressure for educational democratization mushroomed during the time of Gorbachev's *glasnost.* At the national level, pressure for decentralization brought republics more independence and control over management and curriculum content. At the local level, democratization and decentralization led to demands for schools to have increased bureaucratic and budgetary freedoms. At the level of the student, individual needs were increasingly recognized and concern was voiced about the rigid system of schooling and heavy workload that, it was argued, served to alienate and overly stress many students. Reforms centered around six key concepts: *decentralization* (of regions and of schools), *de-ideologization* (removal of communist ideology from schools), *democratization* (giving greater freedoms for educational decision-making to teachers, parents and students), *diversification* (allowing the development of different school types), *humanization* (placing greater emphasis upon student individuality and needs), and *humanitization* (increasing the proportion of time allocated to arts and humanities in the curriculum).

The above elements of reform were realized through the 1992 Law on Education and its 1996 amendment. Education was now seen to include both *obuchenie* (instruction) and *vospitanie*—though the latter was downgraded from preeminent to subsidiary status in order to avoid any redolence of Soviet indoctrination. This was a reversal of Soviet policy wherein *obrazovanie* (education) was seen as a component of all-important *vospitanie* and individual differences were seen as elements to be overcome through the influence of education.

Greater emphasis on competitiveness and individualism have been reflected in the education system by a plethora of structural and pedagogic reforms, many of which have resulted in the development of socially divisive educational hierarchies and inequalities (Konstantinovskii and Khokhlushkina 2000). If the 1980s was the era of many innovatory and experimental teaching approaches, the 1990s was a time of diversification and differentiation in the type and roles of schools (Sutherland 1999). Although the expected increase

in private and religious schools largely failed to materialize (Galina Cherednichenko [2000] lists only ninety-eight such schools in Moscow for the 1997–98 school year), there has been a mushrooming of *gymnasia,* schools that are approved to run specialized programs for more able students, and schools that offer intensive instruction in one or more specialized subjects. In 1991, there were 100 *gymnasia* in Russia; by 1998, there were 1,013. In 1999, some 15 percent of the school population was attending specialist schools. Not surprisingly, the most able students and the most skilled teachers gravitate to these well-resourced schools. Many specialist schools require entry examinations and admit only top scorers.

The result is polarization: Although attendance at institutes and universities has increased, so have dropout rates among secondary students. Students for whom learning is a struggle and who find themselves in unfashionable schools have become increasingly alienated. Increasing disenchantment with schooling appears to be partially due to student concern that school curricula have changed too little to prepare them for the new economic pressures that will mark their passage into adulthood. Alienation is exacerbated by massive curriculum overload that leaves many students exhausted and allows little time for socialization and leisure (Andriushina 2000; Fillipov 2001).

Vladimir Lisovskii (1999) notes that under socialism, one could feel socially protected, education was free, and employment was guaranteed. *Honest poverty* and concern for country and one's collective traditionally underpinned much Russian behavior (van der Wolf and Roeser 2000). Opportunities for advancement and remuneration were made available irrespective of the individual's level of education (Kopytov 2000). Many now worry that the highly unstable economic situation, in which entrepreneurial skills can bring about immense wealth, has resulted in a shift from the traditional regard for education as intrinsically valuable to a focus on education as a means for achieving the individualistic goals of success and prosperity (Nikandrov 1995).

This value shift is seen in higher education. For some, further study is a means to avoid conscription in the army, whereas for the majority it is primarily a means to economic security. Because not all academic disciplines are well-rewarded and high levels of education do not necessarily result in material gain (Zubok 1999), the most popular courses are those that promise the greatest financial rewards such as economics, finance, law, and foreign languages (Rutkevich 2000). Those who have graduated in other subjects are increasingly turning their backs on their disciplines in the search for greater income.

In a study of fourteen- and fifteen-year-olds in two cities, Moscow and Ivanovo, Irina Shurygina (2000) identified three categories of adolescent attitudes toward higher education. The traditional Soviet model was one whereby success was primarily related to having a higher education and an "intellectual" profession. Families that are relatively impoverished but that have a history of high educational performance still tend to reflect this model. The second model is that of the entrepreneur, where high earnings are seen to have little or no connection to one's education or the intellectual demands of one's career. Here, one might anticipate finding a high proportion of less educated, but comparatively more affluent, families. A third model, new to Russian society, involves the assimilation of both the above involving a combination of education and money and power.

Russia has long enjoyed a reputation for high educational standards, something echoed both by the World Bank (Canning, Moock, and Heleniak 1999) and the Organization for Economic Cooperation and Development (1998). Several international comparisons in mathematics and science indicate performance largely superior to that of the United States, particularly for the most able graduates, where Russian students perform close to the top of the international league. Despite their many economic and social difficulties, massive cuts in spending on education throughout the 1990s (falling five-fold between 1991 and 1995), and growing concern within the country about a perceived decline in educational standards (e.g., Dolzhenko 1998), levels of educational performance, classroom behavior, academic engagement, and motivation continue to impress Western educationalists (cf. Hufton and Elliott 2000; Alexander 2000; Bucur and Eklof 1999). Their observations have tended to take place in larger cosmopolitan cities, however, and it is likely that educational standards are declining in more poorly resourced small town and rural areas (Sinagatullin 2001; Tarasov 2000).

Child Homelessness and Orphanage Care

One outcome of the economic upheavals of the post-Soviet period is a great increase in the number of homeless children. The Russian government and UNESCO estimate that in 2001, there were up to three million homeless children in Russia (Harrigan 2001; Tretyak 2001). Some are children of parents who have died or been imprisoned, some are abandoned, and some have run away from conflict-, abuse-, and alcohol-ridden homes. To survive, many become involved in begging, petty crime, and prostitution. Drug use and suicide are also serious problems. Russian children's charities and organizations such as the U.S.-based Love's Bridge and the Red Cross are working to provide shelters and other services to homeless children, but the need still far outweighs available help.

Approximately 1.5 percent of all Russian children are orphaned (Facts and Figures 2001). Between 600,000 and 700,000 children (90% of whom have a living parent) live in orphanages. Concern about orphanage conditions came to a head when Human Rights Watch (1998) published reports describing inhumane care in understaffed and underfunded institutions. Although the quality of care varies from orphanage to orphanage, the report exposed poor living and learning conditions and stigmatization based on notions about the heritability of mental deficiencies and social incompetence. A network of smaller family-like homes for orphans is in its infancy but holds promise of higher quality care. A significant proportion of children are now adopted by foreigners, many of whom are resident in the United States.

Bibliography

Alexander, R. (2000). *Culture and Pedagogy: International Comparisons in Primary Education*. Oxford: Blackwell Press.

Andriushina, E. V. (2000). "The Family and the Adolescent's Health." *Russian Education and Society* 42:61–87.

Antokolskaya, M. V. (1996). "The 1995 Russian Family Code: A New Approach to the Regulation of Family Relations." *Review of Central and East European Law* 22:635–660.

Attwood, L. (1996). "The Post-Soviet Woman in the Move to the Market: A Return to Domesticity and Dependence?" In *Women in Russian and Ukraine,* ed. R. Marsh. Cambridge, UK: Cambridge University Press.

Boss, P. G., and Gurko, T. A. (1994). "The Relationships of Men and Women in Marriage." In *Families Before and After Perestroika: Russian and U.S. Perspectives,* ed. J. W. Maddock, M. J. Hogan, A. I. Antonov, and M. S. Matskovsky. New York: Guilford Press.

Breeva, E. B. (2000a). "Zdorov'e Detei: Problemi i Puti Reshenia" [The Health of Children: Problems and the Paths to Solutions]. *Narodo Nacelenie* 4:111–116.

Breeva, E. B. (2000b). "Deti v Semie: Gendernie Aspekti Vospitania" [Children in the Family: Gendered Aspects of Upbringing]. *Narodo Nacelenie* 2:62–69.

Bronfenbrenner, U. (1970). *Two Worlds of Childhood: US and USSR.* New York: Russell Sage Foundation.

Bubnova, E. M.; Rusanova, N. E.; Andriushina, E. V.; Katkova, I. P.; Kulikova, O. A.; and Oskolkova, O. B. (2000). "Demographicheskie Protsessi" [Demographic Processes]. In *Rossia–1999: Sotsial'no-Demograficheskaia Situatsia* [Russia–1999: The Sociodemographic Situation], ed. N. M. Rimashevskaya. Moscow: Institute for Socio-Economic Problems of Population, Russian Academy of Science.

Bucur, M., and Eklof, B. (1999). "Russia and Eastern Europe" In *Comparative Education: The Dialectic of the Global and the Local,* ed. R. F. Arnove and C. A. Torres. Lanham, MD: Rowman and Littlefield.

Butler, A. C., and Kuraeva, L. G. (2001). "Russian Family Policy in Transition: Implications for Families and Professionals." *Social Service Review* 75:195–226.

Canning, M.; Moock, P.; and Heleniak, T. (1999). *Reforming Education in the Regions of Russia.* World Bank Technical Paper No. 457. Washington, DC: World Bank.

Cherednichenko, G. A. (2000). "School Reform in the 1990s." *Russian Education and Society* 42:6–32.

Dolzhenko, L. (1998). "The College Student Today: A Social Portrait and Attitudes Toward Schooling." *Russian Education and Society* 40:6–15.

Dyuzheva, O. A. (1995). "International Marriage and Divorce Regulation and Recognition in Russia." *Family Law Quarterly* 29:645–653.

Elliott, J. G.; Hufton, N.; Hildreth, A.; and Illushin, L. (1999). "Factors Influencing Educational Motivation: A Study of Attitudes, Expectations and Behaviour of Children in Sunderland, Kentucky and St. Petersburg." *British Educational Research Journal* 25:75–94.

Elliott, J. G.; Hufton, N.; Illushin, L.; and Lauchlan, F. (2001). "Motivation in the Junior Years: International Perspectives on Children's Attitudes, Expectations and Behaviour and Their Relationship to Educational Achievement." *Oxford Review of Education* 27:37–68.

Facts and Figures. (2001). *Russian Life,* May/June, p. 7.

Fillipov, V. (2001). "Education in Russia: Current State Problems, and Prospects: Report at the All-Russian Conference of Workers in Education." *Russian Education and Society* 43:5–27.

Goodwin, R., and Emelyanova, T. (1995a). "The Privatization of the Personal? I: Intimate Disclosure in Modern-Day Russia." *Journal of Social and Personal Relationships* 12:121–131.

Goodwin, R., and Emelyanova, T. (1995b). "The Privatization of the Personal? II: Attitudes to the Family and Child-Rearing Values in Modern-Day Russia." *Journal of Social and Personal Relationships* 12:132–138.

Grigorenko, E. L. (2000). "Psychology and Educational Practice: Snapshots of One Relationship." *Educational and Child Psychology* 17:32–50.

Hubbs, J. (1988). *Mother Russia: The Feminine Myth in Russian Culture.* Bloomington: Indiana University Press.

Hufton, N., and Elliott, J. G. (2000). "Motivation to Learn: The Pedagogical Nexus in the Russian School: Some Implications for Transnational Research and Policy Borrowing." *Educational Studies* 26:115–136

Ispa, J. M. (1984). "A Comparison of Soviet and American Women's Perceptions of the Postpartum Period." *Journal of Comparative Family Studies* 15:95–108.

Ispa, J. M. (1988). "Soviet Immigrant Mothers' Perceptions Regarding the First Childbearing Year: The 1950s and the 1970s." *Slavic Review* 47:291–306.

Ispa, J. M. (1994). "Child Rearing Ideas and Feelings of Russian and American Mothers and Early Childhood Teachers: Some Comparisons." In *Advances in Early Education and Day Care,* Vol. 6: *Topics in Early Literacy, Teacher Preparation, and International Perspectives on Early Care,* ed. S. Reifel. Greenwich, CT: JAI Press.

Karpukhin, O. I. (2000a). "The Young People of Russia: Characteristics of Their Socialization and Self-Determination." *Russian Education and Society* 42:47–57.

Karpukhin, O. I. (2000b). "Young People's Self-Assessment as an Indicator of Their Sociocultural Identification." *Russian Education and Society* 42:49–59.

Konstantinovskii, D. L., and Khokhlushkina, F. A. (2000). "The Formation of the Social Behaviour of Young People in the Sphere of Education." *Russian Education and Society* 4:26–58.

Kopytov, A. D. (2000). "Problems of Young People's Employment: The Regional Approach." *Russian Education and Society,* 42:15–28.

LaFraniere, S. (2001). "Hard Living is Making for Unhealthy Russia." *Washington Post,* August 25, A01.

Lisovskii, V. T. (1999). "Young People Talk about Themselves and the Times." *Russian Education and Society* 41:48–61.

Nikandrov, N. D. (1995). "Russian Education after Perestroika: The Search for New Values." *International Review of Education* 41:47–57.

Organization for Economic Co-operation and Development. (1998). *Reviews of National Policies for Education: Russian Federation.* Paris: Author.

Rutkevich, M. (2000). "Change in the Social Role of the General Education School in Russia." *Russian Education and Society* 42:5–25

Shurygina, I. I. (2000). "The Life Strategies of Adolescents." *Russian Education and Society* 42:5–24.

Sinagatullin, I. M. (2001). "Expectant Times: Rural Education in Russia." *Education Review* 53:37–45.

Sutherland, J. (1999). *"Schooling in the New Russia: Innovation and Change, 1984–95."* London: Macmillan.

Tarasov, A. (2000). "Young People as the Object of Class Experimentation." *Russian Education and Society* 42:5–36.

United Nations Population Division. (2000). *World Population Prospects,* rev. edition. New York: Author.

Van der Wolf, K., and Roeser, R. W. (2000). "Comparisons of Russian, American and Dutch Adolescents' Self-Reports on Social-Emotional and School Functioning."
Paper presented at the annual meeting of the European Conference on Educational Research, September 20–23, Edinburgh, Scotland.

Vannoy, D.; Rimashevskaya, N.; Cubbins, L.; Malysheva, M.; Meshterkina, E.; and Pisklakova, M. (1999). *Marriages in Russia: Couples During the Economic Transition.* Westport, CT: Praeger.

Young, K. (1996). "Loyal Wives, Virtuous Mothers." *Russian Life* (March):4–15.

Zdravomyslova, O. M. (2000). "O Voozmozhnosti Izmenenia Statusa Zhenshchini v Sem'e [About the Possibility of Changing the Status of Women in the Family]. *Narodo Nacelenie* 2:56–61.

Zubok, I. A. (1999). "Exclusion in the Study of Problems of Young People." *Russian Education and Society* 4:39–53.

Other Resources

Harrigan, S. (2001). "'Child by Child,' Group Aids Homeless Street Kids." In CNNfyi.com. Available from http://fyi.cnn.com/2001/fyi/news/07/02/russian.kids/index.html.

Human Rights Watch. (1998). "Abandoned to the State: Cruelty and Neglect in Russian Orphanages." Available from http://www.hrw.org/reports98/russia2/Russ98d.htm.

Tretyak, L. (2001). "'Street Children' March Through Russia." In UN in Russia. United Nations Development Program. Available from http://www.undp.ru/eng/Newsletter/01_2001/Page1.htm.

JEAN M. ISPA
JULIAN G. ELLIOTT

SANDWICH GENERATION

In the United States, from 1900 to 2000, life expectancy increased from 47 to 76 years. Similar improvements in the human life span occurred in other developed countries, such as Japan and Sweden. One consequence of humans living longer is an expanded population of older adults. This remarkable growth in the aging population has resulted in concern about the availability of family caregivers. Researchers consistently report that family members, especially female family members, provide the majority of instrumental and expressive care to their aging loved ones. Due to the social patterns of delayed parenting and increased female labor-force participation, a generation of middle-aged adults are becoming increasingly caught between the demands of child rearing and providing care to their aging parents. This trend, identified as the *sandwich generation* phenomenon, has become a topic of considerable research interest.

Definition

In 1981, Dorothy Miller coined the term *sandwich generation* to refer to inequality in the exchange of resources and support between generations (Raphael and Schlesinger 1994). Specifically, Miller was referring to a segment of the middle-aged generation that provides support to both young and older family members yet does not receive reciprocal support in exchange. Miller emphasized the unique stressors of multigenerational caregiving and the lack of community resources available to assist the middle generation. Because multigenerational caregivers are most often women dealing with the complex role configurations of wife, mother, daughter, caregiver, and employee, some researchers use the phrase *women in the middle* interchangeably with the *sandwich generation* (Dautzenberg et al. 1998).

Despite the importance of the experiences of middle-aged adults and their caregiving responsibilities, some variation in the conceptualization and definition of sandwich generation families exist. Conceptually, some researchers emphasize the demographic implications of this family type, whereas others point to the consequences of this family arrangement on individual well-being and family functioning (Dautzenberg et al. 1998). A number of researchers define this population as middle-aged adults caring for young children (less than the age of 18) and aging parents simultaneously. Other researchers, however, insist this population consists of middle-aged parents caring for aging parents as well as young adult children (18 years of age or older) (Chisholm 1999). Finally, in addition to disagreement over the age of the child or children, there is also disagreement as to whether the youngest generation must be living in the home or not, or if providing financial support to children is sufficient for middle-aged adults to be considered sandwich generation members (Nichols and Junk 1997).

Prevalence

Most likely as a result of this definitional inconsistency, some controversy exists over the prevalence of a middle generation sandwiched between younger and older family members. Elaine Brody (1985, 1990) suggests that due to increased life expectancy and the need to provide care to aging parents, many middle-aged women will inevitably spend time as women in the middle. Brenda Spillman and Liliana Pezzin (2000) reviewed the 1994 National Long Term Care Survey and found approximately 3.5 million individuals, primarily women, were responsible for both an aging parent and a dependent child. In contrast, other researchers, (Spitze and Logan 1990; Ward and Spitze 1998) consider the sandwich generation phenomenon to be a gerontological myth. Because child care and elder care generally occur sequentially rather than simultaneously, some researchers view the sandwich generation family form as an exception rather than the norm (Loomis and Booth 1995). The majority of empirical studies examining multigenerational caregiving have been conducted using samples that are often small and non-representative. As a result, more nationally representative studies, both in the United States and in other developed countries, are needed to assess the likelihood of families experiencing multigenerational caregiving and the impact these responsibilities may have on family relationships and family functioning.

International Comparisons

Few international studies have been conducted on multigenerational caregiving. One study conducted by Maaike Dautzenberg and colleagues (1998) examined the prevalence of women in the middle in the Netherlands. Limiting their population-based sample to women aged 40 to 54, the authors found that 29 percent of respondents cared for children in the home as well as parents or parents-in-law. Moreover, these mothers also provided care to adult children living outside of the home and to grandchildren. If a broader definition of care were utilized, 34 percent of the sample would have met the criteria of multigenerational caregiving. Other studies involving small non-representative samples of women from Canada (Raphael and Schlesinger 1994; Schlesinger and Raphael 1992) and Israel (Remennick 1999) also provide documentation of women caring for both aging parents and children of varying ages.

Impact on the Family

Research investigating the effect of multigenerational caregiving on family relationships and family functioning is limited. Laura Loomis and Alan Booth (1995) looked at a national sample of middle-aged married persons to document the effect of multiple caregiving responsibilities on individual caregivers. The authors found that multigenerational caregiving had little to no effect on the dependent variables of psychological well-being, satisfaction with leisure time, financial resources, or marital quality. Russell Ward and Glenna Spitze (1998) investigated the frequency of multigenerational caregiving and the impact of these responsibilities on perceived marital quality. Even though women provided more assistance to children and parents than men, marital happiness was shown to increase with age. Berit Ingersoll-Dayton, Margaret B. Neal, and Leslie Hammer (2001) examined the beneficial aspects of receiving help from the aging parents to whom sandwich generation members were providing care. Results indicated that receiving help from aging parents was both positive and negative for sandwich generation members. Emotional support was consistently beneficial, whereas instrumental support (i.e., financial assistance, help with child care and domestic tasks) was problematic.

A small number of researchers have examined the effect of multigenerational caregiving on the well-being of children and adolescents. Jacob Kraemer Tebes and Julie T. Irish (2000) evaluated the impact of support interventions for multigenerational caregiving mothers on the behavior of their children. The authors found that children of intervention participants displayed reduced depression and increased social competence. Sharon Hamill (1994) evaluated parent-adolescent communication among middle generation caregivers and found that strain between caregiving mothers and aging parents was associated with poor communication with adolescent children.

Conclusion

Although researchers disagree about the prevalence of the sandwich generation phenomenon, the demographic trends of delayed parenting and increased life expectancy are irrefutable. In order to accurately estimate the frequency of multigenerational caregiving and analyze the impact of this caregiving arrangement on the family system, a universal definition and more representative sample studies are needed.

See also: ADULTHOOD; FILIAL RESPONSIBILITY; INTERGENERATIONAL PROGRAMMING; INTERGENERATIONAL RELATIONSHIPS; LATER LIFE FAMILIES

Bibliography

Brody, E. M. (1985). "Parent Care as a Normative Family Stress." *The Gerontologist* 25:19–29.

Brody, E. M. (1990). *Women in the Middle: Their Parent-Care Years.* New York: Springer.

Chisholm, J. F. (1999). "The Sandwich Generation." *Journal of Social Distress and the Homeless* 8:177–191.

Dautzenberg, M. G. H.; Diederiks, J. P. M.; Philipsen, H.; and Stevens, F. C. J. (1998). "Women of a Middle Generation and Parent Care." *International Journal of Aging and Human Development* 47:241–262.

Hamill, S. B. (1994). "Parent-Adolescent Communication in Sandwich Generation Families." *Journal of Adolescent Research* 9:458–482.

Ingersoll-Dayton, B.; Neal, M. B.; and Hammer, L. B. (2001). "Aging Parents Helping Adult Children: The Experience of the Sandwiched Generation." *Family Relations* 50:262–271.

Loomis, L. S., and Booth, A. (1995). "Multigenerational Caregiving and Well-Being: The Myth of the Beleaguered Sandwich Generation." *Journal of Family Issues* 16:131–148.

Miller, D. (1981). "The 'Sandwich' Generation: Adult Children of the Aging." *Social Work* 26:419–423.

Nichols, L. S., and Junk, V. W. (1997). "The Sandwich Generation: Dependency, Proximity, and Task Assistance Needs of Parents." *Journal of Family and Economic Issues* 18:299–326.

Raphael, D., and Schlesinger, B. (1994). "Women in the Sandwich Generation: Do Adult Children Living At Home Help?" *Journal of Women and Aging* 6:21–45.

Remennick, L. I. (1999). "Women of the 'Sandwich' Generation and Multiple Roles: The Case of Russian Immigrants of the 1990s in Israel." *Sex Roles* 40:347–378.

Schlesinger, B., and Raphael, D. (1992). "The Sandwich Generation: The Jewish Woman in the Middle: Stresses and Satisfaction." *Journal of Psychology and Judaism* 16:77–96.

Spillman, B. C., and Pezzin, L. E. (2000). "Potential and Active Family Caregivers: Changing Networks and the 'Sandwich Generation.'" *Milbank Quarterly* 78:347–374.

Spitze, G., and Logan, J. (1990). "More Evidence on Women (and Men) in the Middle." *Research on Aging* 12:182–198.

Tebes, J. K., and Irish, J. T. (2000). "Promoting Resilience Among Children of Sandwiched Generation Caregiving Women Through Caregiver Mutual Help." *Journal of Prevention and Intervention in the Community* 20:139–158.

Ward, R. A., and Spitze, G. (1998). "Sandwiched Marriages: The Implications of Child and Parent Relations for Marital Quality in Midlife." *Social Forces* 77:647–666.

CHRISTINE A. PRICE

SCANDINAVIA

The Scandinavian peninsula is made up of Denmark, Norway, and Sweden. Sometimes these countries are linked with the *Nordic countries*—traditionally including Finland and Iceland—and in the late twentieth century these countries were sometimes linked with the three Baltic states of Estonia, Latvia, and Lithuania, as well as England and Scotland. This entry will examine marriage and family in Scandinavia, Finland, and Iceland, using Sweden for comparisons.

Defined by the number of inhabitants, all these countries are small. Sweden is the largest, with a population of 9 million and Iceland is the smallest, with a population of approximately 250,000.

Historically, Scandinavia and Iceland were known for the Vikings, famous for their fighting and conquering habits. However, the Vikings—in the eighth through the tenth centuries—were mostly farmers and tradesmen. Since that time the population remained fairly homogeneous, with some immigration, mainly from Germany and France, between the fifteenth through the nineteenth century. However, the population has become less homogeneous with immigration, mainly refugees, from the near and far East.

Around year 1000 CE, a number of Scandinavian kingdoms converted to Christianity—but it was many years before they became fully Christian.

FIGURE 1

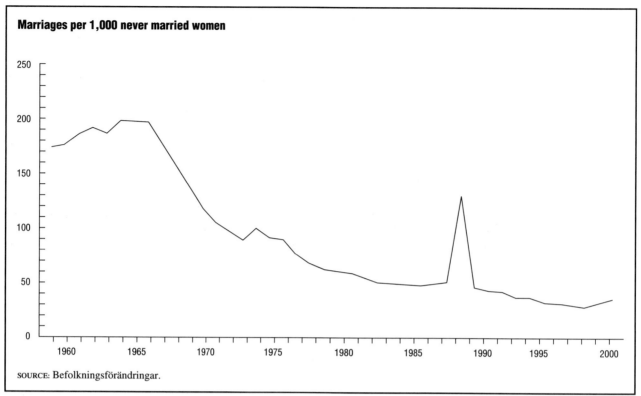

Marriages per 1,000 never married women

SOURCE: Befolkningsförändringar.

Martin Luther was a powerful influence in the sixteenth century, and the Lutheran Church became the sole religion until freedom of religion became the norm in the mid-nineteenth century. Nevertheless, non-Christians and non-Lutherans remain small minorities in Scandinavia.

Marriage

During pre-Christian times the process of becoming husband and wife was a five-step process following the courtship period. The first step was the *betrothal,* when what was already known was announced: the couple was going to marry. The second step was the *marriage ceremony,* when the father of the bride gave the bride to the groom and the bride's parents gave a party. The third step was the trip from the bride's home to the groom's home, which was dangerous because of the risk of bandits. The fourth step was the *wedding party* to which all important persons—friends and relatives of the bride's parents—were invited. The final step was the *bedding,* when the guests at the wedding party followed the newly married couple home and watched them go to bed (Carlsson 1965). The two were now a married couple.

These pre-Christian rules remained intact for several centuries after Christianity became the official religion. The pope sent papal bulls to the bishops demanding them to keep order, get rid of pre-Christian habits, and introduce the Christian ceremonies, but the changes took a long time.

For centuries, the mortality rate was high—especially for men—and therefore the marriage rate was much lower for women than for men; far more women than men never married. That contrasts with the twentieth century: By 1960 the marriage rate was higher than ever before.

However, the marriage rate suddenly decreased in Sweden the mid-1960s (see Figure 1). The decrease in the marriage rate was much more gradual in other Scandinavian countries, and did not appear until the early 1970s.

During the 1960s, many changes followed the relatively calm (for Scandinavia) postwar period. For example, the Vietnam War became a major political issue, neo-Marxists criticized the model nuclear family as well as marriage, and new contraceptives became available and socially acceptable. In Sweden, there was no need to import

A family celebrates Midsummers Eve in Stockholm. The Midsummers Eve holiday occurs on the longest day of the year (summer solstice) and was originally a celebration of fertility and harvest. MACDUFF EVERTON/
CORBIS

labor because many housewives could enter the labor market.

Criticism against traditional family and marriage resulted in the then-radical idea of cohabiting without marrying (Trost 1980). Not until the mid-1970s was it clear that *nonmarital cohabitation* had arrived as a social institution. Initially, cohabitation was a deviant phenomenon, but it rapidly became so common that eventually almost no couple married without having cohabited for some time (see Figure 2). Some couples moved in together early in the courtship period, some later, but virtually no one waited until they married to live together. For some couples, nonmarital cohabitation is *premarital cohabitation,* whereas others have no intention to ever marry.

Another way of showing the impact upon cohabitation is to look at the number of children born to unmarried women. Before the changes, about 10 percent of all children born were born by unmarried women. In 1975, this had increased to 32 percent, 46 percent in 1985, 53 percent in 1995,

and 55 percent in 2000. The other Scandinavian countries have followed the same trend, although at a slower pace (Befolkningsförändringar).

Thus, nonmarital cohabitation became a social institution alongside marriage in Scandinavian society. Viewing that society longitudinally, however, shows a slightly different picture. A young couple will start by living together for a few years—if they do not separate, they may marry. If they separate, both will find another partner with whom they will cohabit relatively soon. Thus, in this respect, the marriage and cohabitation are not parallel institutions.

What is different? Is the only difference the absence of the marriage ceremony? Superficially, it is tempting to say that nothing has changed except the rituals. However, previously there were four elements tightly connected and related to marriage: (1) the wedding ceremony and party; (2) the moving in together in a home of their own; (3) the initiation of a sex life together; and (4) a new born child, expected after about a year (Trost 1993).

FIGURE 2

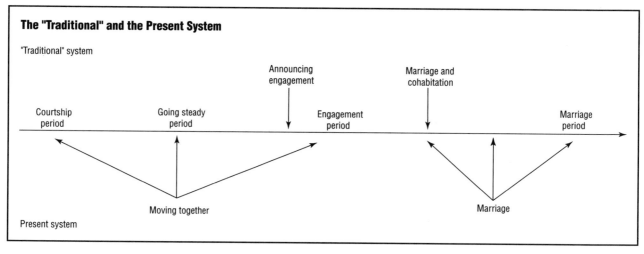

The "Traditional" and the Present System

There were normative connections between these four elements and couples were not supposed to violate them. The prohibition against premarital sex was what sociologists call an *ideal norm* and not a real behavioral norm—at least not in Denmark and Sweden. Everyone knew that almost all couples engaged in premarital sex, but it should be hidden—proper people should not share rooms in hotels, for example. Moreover, there should be no visible result of the common sexual behavior. If a woman became pregnant, she should either have an abortion (even though abortions were illegal until the 1930s) or the couple should marry as soon as possible. In Sweden in the 1950s, at least one bride out of three was pregnant at the time of her wedding (Historisk statistik 1967).

Most couples feel that if they cohabit they should get married eventually. It is important to note that these are two different statements. The first statement is a comment concerning a long-term situation and the other is about an occurrence—a wedding ceremony and party. The latter is particularly interesting because it demonstrates a remarkable change.

Before the meaning of marriage changed—namely, breaking the normative connections of the four elements mentioned above—the traditional wedding party was an occasion when the bride's parents celebrated—with friends and relatives—the occasion of their daughter leaving the parental home. Now the wedding party is primarily organized for the friends of the bride and the groom. (Typically, the couple has been invited to many wedding parties to the effect that they have to

marry in order to "pay back" for all the wedding parties to which they have been invited.) Relatives come next and then, if space allows, the parents' friends are invited. Furthermore, couples marrying are often around thirty years of age and well established in their lives. Thus, the parents play a subservient role.

Thus, the marital system changed—but what happened in 1989? (See Figure 1.) One can see the marriage rate increased and then almost immediately decreased again. What cannot be seen in the diagram is that there were no changes in the marriage rate during the months January through October. However, in November the number of marriages doubled—as compared to marriages in previous years—from 2,000 to 4,000 marriages. One would expect to see another 2,000 marriages in December—but there were 64,000 marriages during that month. In January 1990, the marriage rate was back again to the historically low level.

Why this totally unexpected rush to the altar (or the civil marriage official)? During the summer of 1989 the Swedish Parliament decided to eliminate the widow's pension (ordinarily provided by the government) after January 1, 1990. However, the old rules (somewhat modified) would remain in force for those women who were married at that time, and had a child when the husband died. One of the more important modifications was that the size of the pension would be dependent not only upon income of the deceased husband but also of the new widow. Thus, few widows would receive any pension and those who did would receive a minimal one. The result was that by the end of 1989 there were almost no housewives in Sweden. Thus, one answer to the question of the marriage boom is: the law changed.

Revising the widow's pension had been discussed for decades, and the issue was not considered a particularly interesting topic. Moreover, because the decision was made in the summer, few noticed what happened. However, a journalist wrote about it, and noted that quite a few couples would marry before the end of the year. Other stories followed in the print media, radio, and television discussing the rush to find appointments in the churches. This was actually not the case when the stories appeared, but it became a self-fulfilling prophecy. Thus, another answer is that mass media changed the marriage rate.

A third way of looking at the marriage boom of 1989 to consider unmarried couples. As mentioned above, many couples believe they should eventually get married. When a cue came—stories in the popular press—they took the opportunity to marry. As so often happens in decision making, there is a need for a cue if a decision is to be made.

For example, a woman and a man had been living together for almost twenty years, and they had two teenage children. One day in the middle of December 1989 the woman came home to their town house and met a neighbor. They began talking, and the neighbor asked what they would be doing for Christmas. The woman replied that her mother would be visiting (from far away in Northern Sweden) and this would probably be the last time she could take such a long journey because she was old and not doing well. Thus, this was a special occasion and they had to do something special for the mother. One of the two mentioned something about the possibility getting married and having a party—being traditional, the mother would be happy to see her daughter married. The neighbor, who was a minister, immediately said that even if there were problems with time slots in his church he could make some arrangements. Thus, the cohabiting couple married. (Later the mother recovered, and some years later the couple divorced.)

Sociological analysis suggests that the 1989 marriage boom was related to the large pool of cohabiting couples that grew during all the years since nonmarital cohabitation became common—and the

couples' idea that one should eventually get married. Thus, a boom could occur again with a strong enough cue: not only in Sweden, but in any part of the world where cohabitation is common.

Living Apart Together

All known societies are built upon some sort of marriage—and some have also constructed nonmarital cohabitation as a social institution. In the 1970s, the concept of *Living Apart Together* (LAT) relationships appeared in some countries. This was first identified in the Netherlands. The term *LAT relatie* first appeared in a newspaper article in 1978 (Levin and Trost 1999) and has since become the international term in English.

An LAT relationship is a couple, same or opposite gender, who lives together but does not share the same home. The two are defined by their social standing as a couple and treated in the same manner as married or cohabiting couples. They have two separate homes and households in which other persons may live, such as children or parents. The phenomenon of LAT relationships is clearly different from *commuting marriages/cohabitation*—the latter have a common home, whereas the LAT couples have one each.

One can ask what the difference is between couples *going steady* and the LAT couples. In countries such as Sweden, Denmark, and Norway, the phenomenon of a going-steady couple is more or less outdated. The difference is that, traditionally, the going-steady couple did not share a bed at anytime (at least not openly). LAT couples are allowed to do so.

Of course, LAT couples have always existed, as have cohabiting couples: but they were deviant cases. LAT couples tended to be among the more affluent, such as Simone de Beauvoir and Jean-Paul Sartre (Rodman 1966; Trost 1980).

In the early twenty-first century, LAT relationships could hardly exist had not nonmarital cohabitation come in existence along with the weakening of traditional prohibitions against nonmarital sex. Because the four elements mentioned above lost their connection, cohabitation and LAT relationships (somewhat later) became possible.

Information about the frequency of LAT relationships is limited. A 1993 study in Sweden showed that approximately 2 percent of the

FIGURE 3

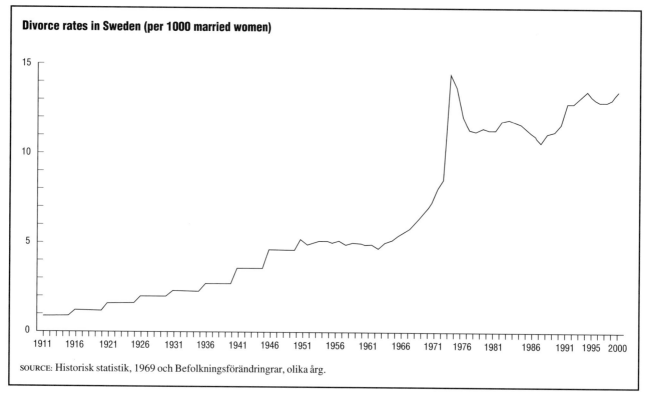

Divorce rates in Sweden (per 1000 married women)

SOURCE: Historisk statistik, 1969 och Befolkningsförändringrar, olika årg.

Swedes ages eighteen to seventy-four (35,000 couples or 70,000 individuals) were living in LAT relationships. By 2001 this had increased to over 5 percent (75,000 couples/150,000 individuals). For the purposes of comparison, if the percentages were the same in the United States, there would be four to five million people living in LAT relationships.

What are the reasons for couples not to follow the old norm that one should live together under such circumstances?

First, there are couples living relatively far from each other who have jobs at their respective locales. To quit a good job in order to take a job at the other place might be impossible or too risky. Many of these couples look forward to the time when one of them retires so that they can move in together. However, when that time comes, they might not move in together for various other reasons.

Next are those couples who have children at home—from a previous relationship—and who do not want to live in a stepfamily household (Levin 1994). Concerns about the children's well-being may preempt other desires. If individuals care for both their children and the new relationship, and are reluctant to risk either, they may decide to stay

apart but together. Both persons in the LAT relationship might have children at home and if they move in together the children of one of them would be forced to deal with various changes, such as the move itself, changing school, or missing friends and playmates. Couples in this situation might have elderly parents to care for and cannot, or do not wish to, move.

A third situation concerns those who have had bad experiences from previous cohabitation (e.g., a traumatic divorce or separation), and they do not wish to make the same mistake they made in a previous relationship. One woman remarked: "He found a younger and more attractive woman after we had been married for 25 years. I had become too boring and taken for granted. I don't want to run that risk again. This way with living apart we have more fun and might be able to keep the relationship alive in a positive way."

Finally, retired couples may prefer an LAT relationship. There can be various reasons for this. As mentioned above, it may have to do with the perceived risk of falling into a boring routine if they cohabit. Alternatively, one or both members of the couple may have children and/or grandchildren nearby, and they may wish to remain close to

FIGURE 4

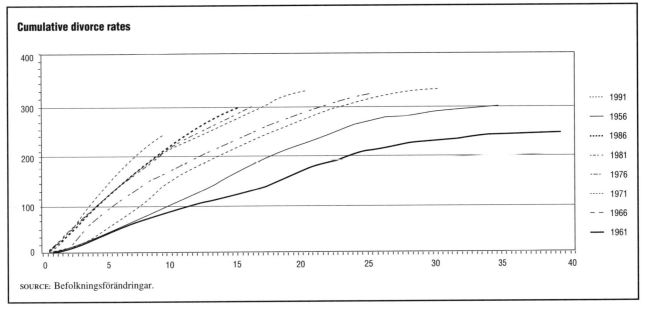

Cumulative divorce rates

------- 1991
——— 1956
••••• 1986
-- -- 1981
—·—· 1976
····· 1971
– – 1966
——— 1961

SOURCE: Befolkningsförändringar.

them, especially if the other member of the couple lives far away. For others there can be questions about which of one's belonging should be brought to a new home. Such decisions can be so difficult that the decision is to remain as a couple in an LAT relationship.

Divorce

In the Scandinavian countries, like the rest of the Western world, divorces were rare a century ago. Legislation prohibited divorces almost everywhere. Moreover, shorter lifespans left many women and men widows and widowers, respectively. As the mortality rate dropped, and lifespans became longer, fewer marriages were ended by death, and there was a need for more liberal divorce laws.

In 1916, Sweden became the first Scandinavian country with a liberal—for that time—divorce law (modified somewhat in 1920). The other Scandinavian countries followed with similar laws within few years. These laws allowed essentially two grounds for divorce: irretrievable breakdown, with a minimum of one year's separation, or a fault on the part of a spouse, such as adultery or alcoholism, in which case the divorce could be granted immediately. These laws remained on the books without any significant changes until the mid-1970s.

Figure 3 shows that the divorce rate in Sweden increased slowly at first and then more rapidly until about 1950, after which it remained stable for

about fifteen years. This trend is the same for other Scandinavian countries, although the number of divorces is fewer, especially in Finland and Norway, less so in Denmark. The divorce rates increased again—simultaneously with appearance of nonmarital cohabitation. However, research has not shown a direct connection. The sudden jump in divorces in the early 1970s is mostly due to technical changes of the legal system.

The late 1960s saw Scandinavian governments overhauling matrimonial laws, particularly divorce laws. In the early 1970s, new laws allowed for quick, *no-fault divorces*. However, if there is a child in the home the couple must wait six months and reflect upon the reasonability of a divorce. The same rule applies when only one of the spouses wants to divorce.

As nonmarital cohabitation became common, one might think that divorce statistics would no longer be of interest, and the simple divorce rates shown in Figure 3 support this view. However, examining marriage cohorts (Figure 4), one can see that of those who married in 1956, 25 percent were divorced after thirty-five years (the rest are either still married or one of the spouses has died). For those who married in 1991 it took only about eight years to reach to the same percentage. Thus, one can conclude that the divorce rates have continued to increase.

It would be interesting to compare divorce rates with those of cohabiting couples who have chosen to separate. Unfortunately, such comparisons are hard to make. Even if nonmarital cohabitation is a social institution like marriage, the two forms are not parallel. Nonmarital cohabitation can become marital cohabitation but marital cohabitation cannot become nonmarital cohabitation—almost no married couple divorces in order to live as nonmarital cohabitants, at least not in the Scandinavian countries. It is conceivable that in other countries there could be cases due to taxation or economic considerations.

Furthermore, many cohabiting couples may be compared with couples *going steady* (see Figure 2) and such couples also face the possibility of dissolution of the relationship. Thus, there is no reason to compare divorce rates with separations of nonmarital cohabitation.

When cohabitation was a new and relatively unknown phenomenon many believed that divorces among marriages preceded by cohabitation would be less common than those in which the couples did not cohabit before marriage. Such an assumption does not hold for Scandinavian countries, because almost no one marries without premarital cohabitation.

See also: GERMANY

Bibliography

Befolkningsförändringar (Vital statistics). (Various years). Stockholm: Statistiska Centralbyrån.

Caradec, V. (1996). "Les Formes de la vie conjugales des 'jeunes' couples 'âgés.'" *Population* 51: 897–928.

Carlsson, L. (1965). *Jag giver Dig min dotter* (I give you my daughter). Lund: Rättshistoriskt bibliotek, åttonde bandet.

Historisk statistik. (1967). *Historisk statistik för Sverige.* (Historical Statistics for Sweden). Stockholm: Statistiska Centralbyrån.

Levin, I. (1994). *Stefamilien—variasjon og mangfold.* Oslo: Tano.

Levin, I., and Trost, J. (1999). "Living Apart Together." *Community, Work and Family* 2:279–294.

Rodman, H. (1966). "Illegitimacy in the Caribbean Social Structure: A Reconsideration." *American Sociological Review* 31:673–683.

Trost, J. (1980). *Unmarried Cohabitation.* Västerås, Sweden: International Library.

Trost, J. (1993). *Familjen i Sverige.* Stockholm: Liber.

JAN TROST

SCHIZOPHRENIA

Schizophrenia is a debilitating, often chronic, mental disorder characterized by disturbances in thinking, perception, emotion, and social relationships. The term *schizophrenia,* which literally means "split mind," was first applied by Swiss psychiatrist Eugen Bleuler in 1911 to describe individuals whose thoughts were split from their emotions, leading to a disintegration of normal personality. Unfortunately, Bleuler's intended meaning is often lost on the lay public, which tends to equate schizophrenia with *multiple personality disorder* (also called *dissociative identity disorder*), an unrelated condition that typically shares few features with schizophrenia.

Nature of Schizophrenia

To be diagnosed with schizophrenia, an individual must demonstrate a six-month period of marginal functioning accompanied by a mixture of psychotic symptoms (delusions and hallucinations), disordered speech, disorganized behavior, emotional disturbance, and motivational impairment. *Hallmark delusions* (false beliefs) involve the conviction that individuals are conspiring to harm the patient and bizarre beliefs such as that one's thoughts are being broadcast or controlled by an external force. *Auditory hallucinations* (false sensory experiences) such as hearing voices are typical, but *unusual bodily sensations* (e.g., the perception that one is being touched) and *visions* (e.g., the image of the Virgin Mary) are also possible. Speech may be vague and difficult to follow, at times becoming incomprehensible. Normal variation in facial expressions may be restricted with the patient seldom smiling or displaying appropriate anger. Reduced ability to experience pleasure, a lack of drive and initiative, an absence of close friends, neglect of personal hygiene, and inappropriate behavior—such as public masturbation or childlike silliness—also comprise the symptom picture (American Psychiatric Association 1994). No one individual is likely to have all or even most of these symptoms, thus complicating diagnosis and leading to great heterogeneity in the clinical picture.

People with schizophrenia often have other problems as well. Despite the debilitation accompanying schizophrenia, many patients lack insight that they have a problem or are so mistrustful that they will not seek treatment. Depression often accompanies schizophrenia, with approximately 10 percent of patients committing suicide. Substance abuse, including nicotine addiction and alcoholism, is common. Medical conditions can result from poor self-care and chronic substance use. Unfortunately, the most effective drugs used to treat schizophrenia sometimes have deleterious health consequences, including excessive weight gain, diabetes, and an irreversible, involuntary movement disorder called *tardive dyskinesia.*

Schizophrenia afflicts slightly less than one out of every 100 people. Studies conducted with the sponsorship of the World Health Organization (WHO) suggest that when uniform diagnostic criteria are used to identify cases, the prevalence of schizophrenia varies little across cultures as diverse as the United States, Japan, and India (Jablensky et al. 1992). However, the content of delusions may vary across countries, emphasizing regionally popular themes. There may be some cultures where the prevalence varies slightly from the averaged estimate. For instance, African Caribbeans in the United Kingdom appear to have higher rates of schizophrenia than other inhabitants of this European country.

Schizophrenia typically begins during adolescence or early adulthood, with females lagging behind the average age of onset in males by about five years. Although the disorder can begin abruptly, most individuals experience an extended period of impairment characterized by mild symptom expression and a decline in social, educational, or occupational functioning. The course is variable, with a minority of individuals recovering whereas most experience recurrent episodes interspersed with periods of partial remission or a chronic course characterized by incoherence, unwavering delusions, and recurring hallucinations. Although the prevalence of schizophrenia in men and women is believed to be the same, men appear to experience a more chronic course and are thus more likely to be hospitalized and included in research investigations. The course and outcome

of schizophrenia may be more favorable in developing than developed nations, perhaps because the cultures of developing countries are characterized by more intact families and community networks, fewer job related demands, and greater acceptance of the unconventional beliefs and behavior characteristic of affected individuals.

Risk for Disorder

Numerous twin, family, and adoption studies from around the world indicate a familial basis for schizophrenia and point to a genetic influence. The first-degree biological relatives (parents, siblings, and children) of a person with schizophrenia have about a 10 percent chance of having the diagnosis whereas the risk for second-degree relatives (uncles, aunts, cousins, and grandparents) drops by more than half. The risk to the co-twin of an identical twin with schizophrenia is about 50 percent (Gottesman 1991). Findings such as these hold even when individuals are not raised by their biological relatives and clearly indicate that the risk of having schizophrenia is a function of the degree of genetic overlap with an affected person. If schizophrenia were due only to heredity, then because identical twins share all of their genes in common, both members of a pair would be affected if one develops the disorder. When both are affected, the pair is said to be *concordant.* The fact that identical twins are often discordant for schizophrenia confirms the important role environmental factors play in its genesis. These findings have given rise to a *diathesis-stress model* positing that it is the risk for schizophrenia (the *diathesis*) that is inherited, not schizophrenia per se. Whether schizophrenia arises in an individual with the diathesis depends on other factors, including the nature of environmental stress encountered over the lifespan.

Various research strategies have taken advantage of the familial nature of schizophrenia risk in an effort to elucidate causal mechanisms. One approach has been to study prospectively the young children of those with schizophrenia. As adults, study participants can be divided into those who did and those who did not develop schizophrenia and can be compared on measures collected before the onset of illness. Several of these investigations, called longitudinal high-risk studies, have been launched in different countries including Denmark, Israel, Sweden, and the United States (see Erlenmeyer-Kimling 2000). Compared to children of healthy participants, children of schizophrenic parents tend to have neurological, motor, social, memory, planning, and attentional dysfunctions that precede illness and are similar to those seen in adult schizophrenia (Erlenmeyer-Kimling 2000).

No genes for schizophrenia have been found, and the genetic mechanism by which the diathesis for schizophrenia is transmitted is unknown. There is growing concern that this state of affairs will persist as long as the identification of gene carriers depends on diagnosing schizophrenia based on the self-report of symptoms. The symptoms of schizophrenia are not present in all gene carriers (as the findings of discordant identical twins illustrate). Moreover, these symptoms may not be directly reflective of the biological underpinnings of the disorder. Because biological relatives of schizophrenia patients share genes with the patient, it is possible that many of them, even though they are not symptomatic, will exhibit neurobehavioral characteristics that are manifestations of the genetic diathesis. Many such characteristics have been documented in schizophrenia families, including difficulty producing certain kinds of simple eye movements and poor performance on tasks of attention and memory (Kremen et al. 1994). These investigations, like the high-risk studies mentioned above, are producing promising results, but much remains to be done before the biological mechanisms underlying the diathesis are clearly understood.

Environmental risk factors investigated in schizophrenia can be broadly grouped into social and neurobiological factors. Early theories of schizophrenia positing social influences, such as rearing by a cold and domineering (*schizophrenogenic*) mother (Fromm-Reichmann 1948), have not been supported by the results of controlled scientific investigation. The evidence that stressful life events contribute to the development of schizophrenia, as opposed to being a consequence of its early manifestation, is also limited. A correlation has been observed between social class membership and schizophrenia, with schizophrenia predominating in the underclass. This observation has been used to advance the hypothesis that the stresses associated with underclass rearing contribute to the development of schizophrenia. Investigations of this hypothesis have shown that this correlation is due in part to the debilitating consequences of schizophrenia leading to social migration from the upper classes into the underclass (Gottesman 1991). Nevertheless, schizophrenia patients are disproportionately born into the underclass, an observation that may reflect the likelihood that the accomplishment of the parents of schizophrenia patients is compromised because they too carry the genetic diasthesis for schizophrenia.

Birth complications constitute a neurobiological factor associated with the risk for schizophrenia. Schizophrenia has been associated with an excess of winter births. This finding is consistent with results from other investigations suggesting that events that are more likely to occur during winter pregnancies, such as viral infections, may affect the prenatal development of schizophrenia-prone persons (Torrey et al. 1994).

Investigations of risk factors have supported neurodevelopmental theories of schizophrenia. These theories hypothesize that schizophrenia develops from deleterious events early in life that disrupt pre- and post-natal brain development. This disruption may lead to poor communication among different brain regions, dysregulation of particular neurotransmitters such as the chemical messenger *dopamine,* and many of the neurobehavioral deviations associated with schizophrenia (Weinberger and Lipska 1995). Investigations with identical twins who are discordant for schizophrenia have indicated that a twin with schizophrenia can have abnormalities in brain structures that are not observed to the same degree in the healthy cotwin. Because identical twins have the same genetic diathesis for schizophrenia, this finding is consistent with the hypothesis that birth complications or *in-utero* viruses could, in a genetically vulnerable individual, constitute environmental stressors leading to disruptions in brain development.

Treatment

The aims of schizophrenia treatment are to reduce the severity and frequency of active episodes and to maximize healthy functioning between episodes (American Psychiatric Association 1997). Medications that reduce psychotic symptoms have been available since the 1950s and have contributed substantially to the deinstitutionalization of schizophrenia patients over the last half-century. Unfortunately, the medications do not provide a cure and have unpleasant side effects that, along with denial of illness, homelessness, cultural beliefs, and the stigma associated with the diagnosis, can reduce treatment compliance. Enhancement of medication treatment compliance is often a goal of psychosocial treatment. Psychosocial treatment is also intended to enhance occupational and social functioning by providing ongoing outpatient care following hospitalization that emphasizes vocational and social skills training.

When family members participate in programs combining education about the illness with training in problem solving skills, family support, and crisis intervention, relapse rates for schizophrenia patients are significantly reduced (Lauriello, Bustillo, and Keith 1999). Several studies support the role of specific relational influences on the risk for recurrence of active schizophrenia symptoms. *Expressed emotion* refers to the level of criticism, emotional overinvolvement, and hostility held about a psychiatric patient by another individual, typically a family member. Schizophrenia patients who have been hospitalized and return to households characterized by a high level of expressed emotion have increased likelihood of relapse. Cultural factors or ethnicity may mediate the impact or nature of expressed emotion (Butzlaff and Hooley 1998). *Communication deviance,* or the degree to which a relative's communication is unclear, fragmented, or disruptive, also increases relapse risk. When minimized, these factors, which may be related to the stress and burden of coping with a patient's illness, have been found to protect against relapse.

Because family members may be directly involved in the care of an affected relative, they can experience difficulties such as disruptions to family relationships, constraints on social leisure and work, financial problems, and feelings of loss, depression, anxiety, or embarrassment. As a result, various family and relative self-help group treatments have been developed to improve family members' knowledge of schizophrenia and available coping strategies and to enhance involvement in patient treatment. Despite the availability and efficacy of individual and family interventions, services to patients and family members appear to be underimplemented, with families of older patients and African-American families being among those least likely to take advantage of such services (Lehman, Steinwachs, and Co-Investigators 1998).

See also: CHRONIC ILLNESS; DEVELOPMENTAL PSYCHOPATHOLOGY; HEALTH AND FAMILIES

Bibliography

American Psychiatric Association. (1994). *Diagnostic and Statistical Manual of Mental Disorders: DSM-IV.* Washington, DC: Author.

American Psychiatric Association. (1997). *Practice Guideline for the Treatment of Schizophrenia.* Washington, DC: Author.

Butzlaff, R. L., and Hooley, J.M.. (1998). "Expressed Emotion and Psychiatric Relapse: A Meta-Analysis." *Archives of General Psychiatry* 55(6):547–552.

Erlenmeyer-Kimling, L. (2000). "Neurobehavioral Deficits in Offspring of Schizophrenic Parents: Liability Indicators and Predictors of Illness." *American Journal of Medical Genetics* 97(1):65–71.

Fromm-Reichmann, F. (1948). "Notes on the Development of Treatment of Schizophrenics by Psychoanalysis and Psychotherapy." Psychiatry 11:263–273.

Gottesman, I. I. (1991). *Schizophrenia Genesis: The Origins of Madness.* New York: Freeman.

Jablensky, A.; Sartorius, N.; Ernberg, G.; Anker, M.; Korten, A.; Cooper, J. E.; Day, R.; and Bertelsen, A. (1992). "Schizophrenia: Manifestations, Incidence and Course in Different Cultures. A World Health Organization Ten-Country Study." *Psychological Medicine* 20(Monograph Supplement):1–97.

Kremen, W. S.; Seidman, L. J.; Pepple, J. R.; Lyons, M. J.; Tsuang, M. T.; and Faraone, S. V. (1994). "Neuropsychological Risk Indicators for Schizophrenia: A Review of Family Studies." *Schizophrenia Bulletin* 20:103–119.

Lauriello, J.; Bustillo, J.; and Keith, S. J. (1999). "A Critical Review of Research on Psychosocial Treatment of Schizophrenia." *Biological Psychiatry* 46(10):1409–1417.

Lehman, A. F.; Steinwachs, D. M.; and Survey Co-Investigators of the PORT Project. (1998). "Patterns of Usual Care for Schizophrenia: Initial Results from the Schizophrenia Patient Outcomes Research Team (PORT) Client Survey." *Schizophrenia Bulletin* 24(1):11–20.

Torrey, E. F., Bowler, A. E.; Taylor, E. H.; and Gottesman, I. I. (1994). *Schizophrenia and Manic-Depressive Disorder: The Biological Roots of Mental Illness as Revealed by the Landmark Study of Identical Twins.* New York: Basic Books.

Weinberger, D. R., and Lipska, B. K. (1995). "Cortical Maldevelopment, Anti-Psychotic Drugs, and Schizophrenia: A Search for Common Ground." *Schizophrenia Research* 16(2):87–110.

MONICA E. CALKINS
WILLIAM G. IACONO

SCHOOL

Educational leaders and policy makers have called for revolutionary changes in schools. National and international school reform initiatives involve more challenging expectations for learning, high-stakes accountability, high performance standards, collaboration, and new roles for teachers and students (Adler and Gardner 1994).

A growing number of children, youth, and families are being affected by persistent poverty, unemployment, and discrimination. These same factors predict child abuse, including needs for child protective services and out-of-home placements. Children's learning barriers, emotional difficulties, and health risks also stem from these problems. The education system not only has a special interest in the well-being of children and youth, but it also shares an interest in the health and well-being of families, neighborhoods, and communities.

During the closing decades of the twentieth century, schools in the United States were being pushed to dramatically change the way they operated. Similarly, schools outside of the United States began to examine their formal policies in close cooperation with families and the communities in which they lived. In the 1980s shifts in Norwegian economics influenced the business of education (Hagan and Tibbitts 1994). Concern about international competitiveness and higher levels of unemployment resulted in a combination of child-centered policy, curriculum reform, new roles for teachers, and respect for the autonomy of parents and the local community.

The unique cultural history of Norway has resulted in child-centered policy that focuses on family support and community education. Educational reform in the United States relies on themes similar to those of Norway's grass-roots movement: parent and community involvement, a holistic approach, and collaboration between the school system and community-based organizations (Hagan and Tibbitts 1994).

Shifting social and economic realities have called into question the fundamental role that schools play in serving the growing number of vulnerable children and youth. To a large degree, in the United States and in Norway, the role of the teacher has always been premised on parents being actively responsible for the well-being of their children. However, when parents behave irresponsibly, teachers are being called upon to intervene. For some teachers, this has resulted in role conflict. Already overburdened and lacking resources, teachers continue to question the limits of their role as educators and the role they can play in coordinating services for children.

Although both Norway and the United States have acknowledged the need to form partnerships with parents and the community for the welfare of the children, neither country, in examining the role that families and teachers play in restructuring, has explicated the changing role of the student and the implications of school culture during educational reform.

School Culture

The latest wave of school reform in the United States has emphasized a change in the way organization of school cultures. A common theme throughout the literature on the subject in the United States is a redefining of the roles and relationships embedded in school cultures with the goal of improving learning conditions for all students and reducing student alienation.

Philip Cusick's *Inside High School* (1973) focused on a large semiurban public school to determine what students do in school and how they make sense of their lives in school. He concluded that the school organization was failing its students:

> It has not accepted them as active participants in their own education; rather it has systematically denied their involvement in basic educational processes and relegated them to the position of watchers, waiters, order-followers and passive receptacles for the depositing of disconnected bits of information. They, in turn, have responded by paying only minimal amount of forced attention to the formal educational processes. . . . (p. 221)

Surprisingly, the literature on school reform reflects little on the role of student. Michelle Fine (1991) has taken this criticism further by suggesting that schools take part in a "ritual of silencing" which is "a systematic commitment" (by the school) to "not name those aspects of social life or school that activate social anxieties or engage in conversations about controversy, inequity, and critique"

Elementary students in class at a rural school near Guilin, China. KEREN SU/CORBIS

(p. 33). Critics of education reform have challenged teachers to examine their own attitudes toward those excluded from power and authority and provide a voice for silenced groups (Lowe 1998).

In the 1990s the central focus of American education was economic growth, equality of opportunity, and meeting the basic academic and psychological needs of students. International economic competition with Germany and Japan and educating the workforce were also concerns. For example, nations are often engaged in educational competition. International competition has resulted in beliefs about one nation being better in some areas than other nations. Educators argue that Americans are more creative and innovative than are other nations. Some educators, however, assume that the Japanese approach of rote learning inhibits creativity and individual thought (Westbury 1993).

A closer examination reveals quite the opposite. Qualitative research studies provide evidence for the student-centered nature of Japanese classrooms (Letendre 1999). Teachers appear highly sensitive to student interests, emphasize creative problem-solving, and work to increase students' curiosity about their world. It has also been argued that Japanese schools provide more equal access to a problem-solving curriculum than do their American counterparts. Little evidence supports the claim that the Japanese focus on the elite class. Compared to Germany and the United States (where formal tracking and ability grouping occur very early), the Japanese system is more egalitarian regarding issues of creative problem-solving. The first step towards using comparative educational data more effectively would be to abandon beliefs about the superiority of one country's schools (Letendre 1999). International comparisons can lead to a more critical awareness of educational practices without such judgments.

During the mid-1980s the U.S. National Center on Effective Secondary Schools reported that "the effective schools literature in the U.S., and indeed most of the rhetoric about school improvement, had neglected the most salient issue (student disengagement) for both teachers and students each hour of the day" (Newmann 1992, p. 2). According to Fred Newmann (1992):

> The most immediate and persisting issue for students and teachers is not low achievement, but student disengagement. The most obviously disengaged students disrupt classes, skip them, or fail to complete assignments. More typically, disengaged students behave well in school. They attend class and complete the work, but with little indication of excitement, commitment, or pride in mastery of the curriculum. In contrast, engaged students make a psychological investment in learning. (p. 3)

Schools must deal with such issues as cultural diversity, the special needs of students, school violence, and distractions that compete with a student's emotional investment. For example, the problems facing U.S. and Japanese educational systems are deeply rooted in the social and economic structure of each nation. As evidenced by trends in teen pregnancy, substance abuse, and school violence, the United States has significant problems to deal with, as do Japan and other countries.

Overall social conditions such as poverty appear to have a significant impact on student achievement. Increasing student academic motivation is supported or constricted within a given organizational setting, family, and community (Letendre 1999). Finally, when students are not engaged in the learning environment, they are more likely to drop out of school. The problems facing schools today that have been identified by educational policy makers (i.e., attendance rates, drop-out rates, low student achievement) are not the actual problems, but the consequences of other fundamental issues within and outside of school.

Truancy and School Dropouts

Truancy is defined as being absent from school without permission. The education of adults and the presence of a school in the community have a significant impact on school attendance. According to UNICEF and World Bank policy research, females and the poor in Niger, Egypt, Morocco, India, and Pakistan are disadvantaged in their opportunity for education. India has a 17 percentage point difference between the school enrollment of girls and boys from the ages of six to fourteen. In Benin, the enrollment rate for boys is 63 percent higher than girls aged six to fourteen. In Colombia, the enrollment rate is 98 percent higher than that of girls (Filmer 1999). Morocco has 538,000 child laborers in the country, and most of these children are under fifteen years old and follow the tradition of working in the fields. Tens of thousands of these children are sold as domestic servants in the cities. More than half of the child laborers in Morocco are female. News reports suggest that the government is trying to return children to the classroom (BBC News 1999).

The World Declaration on Education for All (1990), issued in Thailand, affirmed a commitment to universal primary education. Access to education is seen as a prerequisite for progress in developing countries and in the reduction of poverty everywhere. However, more children are working rather than learning. As described by Clare Short, Secretary of State for International Development, "one hundred and thirty million children around the world do not or cannot go to school" (BBC News 1999).

The combination of low school enrollments and a lack of access to quality education restricts progress towards improved literacy in developing countries. Programs such as the Heavily Indebted Poor Countries Initiative—launched in 1996 by UNICEF—have begun to establish comprehensive poverty reduction strategies geared toward the creation of conditions for economic development and universal access to education and basic social services (UNICEF 1999).

In comparison, in the United States, school for some students has no intrinsic value, and it has no connection to the larger social context within which students live. In some classrooms, students are not provided with the opportunity to use personal experiences as a context for applying knowledge. The education movement of the 1990s valued the premise that "all students can learn." But many teachers failed to believe in this philosophy of education. There is often a lack of understanding about different cultures and the lives of students outside the classroom.

Nearly half of black children in the United States are poor, and more than one-third of Hispanic children live in poverty. Minority group students have higher drop-out rates regardless of socioeconomic status (Steinberg; Blinde; and Chan

1984). There appears to be a strong association between race and ethnicity and the likelihood of dropping out of school. What has become increasingly clear to education professionals is that children have multiple needs.

The United States, Norway, and Canada, among other countries, have begun to examine more closely the cost of traditional programs that only address truancy and dropouts by imposing laws and standards. Educators and health and social service providers are forming new partnerships to help improve the lives of children, youth, families, and communities (Adler and Gardner 1994). Educational leaders are also increasingly aware of the connection between a child's success in school and individual and family empowerment. Some nations have realized that it makes better sense to develop programs that focus on retaining youth in school rather than dealing with the costs later.

A key objective in school improvement efforts is raising the levels of achievement of underperforming groups of students. Increasingly, educators are realizing that the factors that put children at risk are varied and cumulative. Canadian and American critics point out that schools and human service agencies cannot work in isolation. Schools alone cannot solve the multiple needs of at-risk children. Critics of the American educational system conclude that traditional approaches pervasive in educational policy and children's services have resulted in fragmented responses doomed to fail. To address the need for integration of services, collaborative community programs are being developed.

Collaboration: Linking Schools with Social Services

The incentive for collaboration in Canada arose from similar problems to those that established the context for proposed joint efforts in the United States. In Canada, an estimated 30 to 40 percent of children in urban schools are at risk and have special needs; in rural schools, the figure is 15 to 20 percent (Mawhinney 1994).

According to the Ontario Ministry of Community and Social Services (1992), one in every six children in Ontario is in a family receiving social assistance. Mirroring efforts to improve education for all students through holistic approaches that integrate social services currently being practiced in the United States, several Canadian provinces have developed policies for interagency collaboration.

Collaborative practices in both the United States and Canada have documented the need for more inclusive, capacity-building strategies that result in shared outcomes for children, youth, and families, along with responsibility and accountability for the stategies. Successful collaborations such as California's State Partnership for School Linked Service involves schools and community partners in restructuring services to children and families. Schools must be prepared to nurture the healthy development of all children and their families. In the future, educational initiatives will ask teachers, parents, community members, health and social service workers, and students to be the lead designers of changes that occur within school walls. Communities need to remove the barriers that prevent children and their families to receive the support, resources, and services that they need.

Since the 1980s, Japan has experienced much social change. As in the United States, family structure and social conditions have both been modified. Japan is experiencing increasing urbanization, and more women are joining the paid workforce. Many of the social changes experienced by Japan are common to other nations making the transition to a postindustrial economy. Similarly, the People's Republic of China has been undergoing a shift towards a market-oriented economic system. The United States, Japan, and the People's Republic of China have acknowledged the importance of equal educational opportunity for all students and universal education (Cleverly 1985). Researchers bear the responsibility of documenting the impact of social change on cultural values and education.

Further research is needed to identify aspects of classroom and school processes that encourage student engagement. This research should focus on factors that affect the perseverance of engaged behavior in relation to those students who have been labeled at-risk. The effects of inviting marginalized students to become involved with school-change initiatives should be explored. In sum, priority should be given to understanding why many students disengage from school and to increasing efforts to involve students in school change initiatives (Lowe 1998).

Conclusion

As nations continue to examine the goals of education, systemic reform will encompass a variety of strategies that will require everyone in the educational system to change their roles and relationships. There are cross-national perspectives that present models from research that encompass collaboration and integrative services. The challenge for policy makers and educational leaders is to develop programs that will create, nurture, and sustain healthy learners, families, schools, and communities throughout the world.

Neither top-down nor bottom-up approaches to reform will, alone, effect reform. Genuine reform cannot be forced. Reform strategies must be tailored to political environments. Each country is different; consequently, each country engages in reform for different reasons.

See also: ACADEMIC ACHIEVEMENT; ATTENTION DEFICIT HYPERACTIVITY DISORDER (ADHD); CHILDHOOD; DISABILITIES; FAMILY LITERACY; HOMESCHOOLING; INTERGENERATIONAL PROGRAMMING; LEARNING DISORDERS; SCHOOL PHOBIA AND SCHOOL REFUSAL; UNEMPLOYMENT

Bibliography

Adler, L., and Gardner, S. (1994). *The Politics of Linking Schools and Social Services.* Washington, DC: The Falmer Press.

Cleverley, J. F. *The Schooling of China: Tradition and Modernity in Chinese Education.* London: Allen and Unwin.

Cusick, P. (1973). *Inside High School: The Student's World.* New York: Holt, Rinehart and Winston.

Fine, M. (1991). *Framing Dropouts: Notes on the Politics of an Urban High School.* Albany: State University of New York Press.

Hagan, U., and Tibbitts, F. (1994). "The Norwegian Case: Child-Centered Policy in Action." In *The Politics of Linking Schools and Social Services,* eds. L. Adler and S. Gardner. Washington, DC: The Falmer Press.

Letendre, G. (1999). "The Problem of Japan: Qualitative Studies and International Educational Comparisons." *Educational Researcher* 28(2):38–45.

Lowe, M. (1998). "The Phenomenology of Student Engagement during High School Restructuring." Ph.D. Dissertation. Lexington: University of Kentucky.

Mawhinney, H. (1994). "Discovering Shared Values: Ecological Models to Support Interagency Collaboration." In *The Politics of Linking Schools and Social Services,* eds. L. Adler and S. Gardner. Washington, DC: The Falmer Press.

Newmann, F. (1992). "Authentic Work and Student Engagement." In *Hands on Teachers Reader,* eds. H. Smith and H. Walker. Mountain City, GA: The Foxfire Fund Inc.

Ontario Ministry of Community and Social Services (1992). *Time for Action, Towards a New Social Assistance System for Ontario.* Toronto: Queens Printer.

Steinberg, L.; Blinde; P. L.; and Chan, K. S. (1984). "Dropping Out among Language Minority Youth." *Review of Educational Research.* 54:113–32.

Westbury, I. (1993). "Comparing American and Japanese Achievement: Is the United States Really a Low Achiever?" *Educational Researcher* 21(5):18–24.

Other Resources

"Child Labor Rife in Morocco." (1999). *BBC News Online: World. United Kingdom.* Available from http://news.bbc.co.uk.

"Children in Jeopardy." (1999). *United Nations Children's Fund, New York.* Available from www.unicef.org.

Filmer, D. (1999). "The Structure of Social Disparities in Education: Gender and Wealth." *World Bank Policy Research Report.* Available from http://www.worldbank.org/gender/ppr.

MITZI A. LOWE

SCHOOL PHOBIA AND SCHOOL REFUSAL

The term *school phobia* reflects the terminological and conceptual confusion that has plagued the problem of excessive school absenteeism since it was first introduced as a *phobia* by Adelaide M. Johnson and her colleagues (1941). Most investigators currently working in the area, therefore, have come to view school phobia as a subset of school refusal behavior. As a consequence, the more comprehensive term, *school refusal behavior* (SRB), has come to be preferred over *school phobia* (Hansen et al. 1998). Even the term *SRB* has its difficulties, however, as it may be taken to imply a conscious decision on the part of the child to refuse to go to school—a perspective that clearly is not appropriate to all cases (Wicks-Nelson and Israel 1997). Truancy usually is characteristic of children who are absent from school on an intermittent basis, usually without parental knowledge. Children with SRB are absent for extended durations, such as consecutive days, weeks, or months, and usually with parental knowledge. Truancy also is usually associated with other externalizing child behavior problems (e.g., conduct problems) as well as poor academic performance.

Clinical Picture

There is no one picture of the *school-refusing child*. Some children who display SRB fail to attend school fully and completely. Other children may initially attend school in the morning but call their parents to be picked up early, frequently because they have somatic complaints (e.g., nausea, headaches). Another group of children who display SRB may attend school and even manage to stay there all day. However, it is a chore each morning to get these children to school because of the severe problem behaviors (e.g., temper tantrums, crying, pleading) exhibited. Another group of children with SRB similarly attend school, but they experience high levels of distress while in school, leading to regular pleas to remain home in the future. These are not distinctive patterns of SRB, however; it is not uncommon for children to display more than one such pattern at a given time. Nor is it uncommon for children to move in and out of varying patterns over time.

The heterogeneity of SRB also is manifested in the diagnostic picture. Research has documented the clinical features of children who display SRB by evaluating these children with structured diagnostic interviews and deriving *Diagnostic and Statistical Manual* (DSM) diagnoses. For example, Cynthia G. Last and Cyd C. Strauss (1990) investigated DSM-III-R anxiety disorder diagnoses in sixty-three school-refusing youth (ages seven to seventeen years). The most common primary diagnosis was *separation anxiety disorder* (n=24), followed by *social phobia* (n=16), and *simple phobia* (n=14). Children with SRB also frequently display multiple (comorbid) diagnoses (Kearney, Eisen, and Silverman 1995). The main implication of these findings is that a number of the clinical features that characterize SRB are the same as those that characterize diagnoses that accompany a given SRB case (e.g., excessive avoidance if criteria for phobic disorder are met).

Even more heterogeneity may exist among children who meet criteria for a particular DSM diagnostic category. For example, although *school*

might be considered a circumscribed and specific stimulus for children with SRB who meet primary diagnosis for specific phobia, school phobia actually covers several different types of specific stimuli, such as hallway, classroom, gymnasium, pool, fire alarm, or school bus (Kearney, Eisen, and Silverman 1995). Identifying the specific phobic object or event thus also becomes important to consider when assessing SRB in children with a primary diagnosis of specific phobia.

Heterogeneity among children with SRB also is apparent in terms of the presence (yes/no) and types of somatic symptoms or complaints that children may report. Although somatic symptoms or complaints are frequently the main reason why parents feel they need to keep their children at home rather than force attendance, not all children report somatic symptoms. In a sample of adolescent school refusers (n=44) who were comorbid with anxiety and depression, many (32%) but not all participants reported somatic complaints (Bernstein et al. 1997). The specific somatic complaints varied across the youth and included autonomic (e.g., headaches, sweatiness, dizziness) and gastrointestinal (e.g., stomachaches) symptoms. These findings highlight the importance of inquiring about somatic complaints (presence/absence and type) among children with SRB.

Contributing Factors

Christopher A. Kearney and Wendy Silverman (1993) suggested that SRB may be maintained by at least one of the following functions or motivating conditions: (1) avoidance of objects or situations provoking specific fearfulness or generalized anxiety; (2) escape from aversive social or evaluative situations; (3) attention-getting behavior (analogous to traditional externalizing symptoms of separation anxiety, such as tantrums); and (4) positive tangible reinforcement (analogous to truant behavior, or preferring to stay home and play or avoiding school for reasons other than fear or anxiety). The first two refer to school refusal behavior maintained by negative reinforcement; the latter two refer to school refusal behavior maintained by positive reinforcement.

Distal factors also may spur SRB. Such factors include homelessness, maltreatment, school victimization, teenage pregnancy, divorce, and child self-care (Kearney 2000). Kearney, for example, indicated that homelessness in youth has been linked to educational problems such as school dropout, severe absenteeism, expulsion, higher risk of school failure, and poor achievement in reading and arithmetic.

Age and Gender

Research evidence suggests that the most common age of onset for SRB is generally in early adolescence, though this may simply reflect age at the time of referral. Last and Strauss (1990), for example, reported that onset of school refusal was, on average, about one to two years prior to referral. In terms of gender, SRB occurs fairly evenly across boys and girls (Kearney 1995).

Culture/Ethnicity and Race

According to the U.S. National Center of Education Statistics, 5.5 percent of students are absent from school on a typical school day. However, only a small number of studies have examined cultural/ethnic or race variations in SRB. Elena Granell de Aldaz and her colleagues (1984) examined the prevalence of school refusal and school-related fears in 1,034 Venezuelan children (ages three to fourteen years). Results indicated that children were generally afraid of test failure (35%), poor grades (33.4%), visiting the principal (29.7%), tests (18.4%), going to the blackboard (13.5%), talking to a group or class (13.4%), being called on unexpectedly in class (12.5%), becoming ill at school (11.2%), and waiting to be picked up at school (11.0%). In a subsequent study Granell de Aldaz and her colleagues (1987) further classified fifty-seven Venezuelan school-refusing children (ages three to fourteen years) based on presenting problems (i.e., adaptation problems [49.1%], phobia [42.1%], and *emotional problems* [8.8%]). Among these children, common but different fears emerged, including fear of the teacher (43.9%), other children (21.1%), and separation from parents (21.1%). Angelica Hibbet and Ken Fogelman (1990) found that 19.4 percent of sixteen-year-old adolescents in Great Britain displayed regular unexcused absences.

Although there is evidence that school dropout rates are substantially higher among Hispanic (29.4%) than African-American (13.0%) or white students (7.3%) (see www.nces.ed.gov for recent updates), some studies have shown that absence from school is higher among African-American students and those students with lower family income

(Berg et al. 1993). It is not clear however whether minorities and socioeconomic status were well represented in these studies.

Family Factors

Specific family factors have been linked with SRB. These include birth order, family size, marital problems and status, and parental psychopathology (Kearney 2000). In terms of birth order, several studies indicate that children with SRB tend to be the youngest in two-child families (Kearney 2000). For example, Ian Berg, Alan Butler, and Ralph McGuire (1972) found that 55 percent of their sample of 100 youth with SRB were either only or youngest children, and the average number of children in these families was 2.93. In terms of marital problems, Duane Ollendick (1979) reported that from a sample of 177 fourth-grade students, boys from single-parent families were absent from school significantly more than boys from two-parent families. In terms of parent psychopathology, Last and her colleagues (1987) found in their clinical school phobia sample that 57.1 percent of the mothers met DSM-III criteria for an anxiety disorder and 14.3 percent met criteria for an affective disorder. Kearney and Silverman (1995) provided a summary of the research literature relating to the family environments of children with SRB and concluded that five environments were most common: (1) *enmeshed*, (2) *conflictive*, (3) *detached*, (4) *isolated*, and (5) *healthy*. Kearney and Silverman (1995) also provided additional empirical support for these family environments based on the responses of sixty-four parents to the *Family Environment Scale* whose children (ages seven to sixteen years) displayed SRB.

Psychosocial Interventions

Generally, all psychosocial treatment approaches stress the importance of getting the child back to school, and thus in parents taking an active approach in returning the child to school (Wicks-Nelson and Israel 1997). Controlled clinical trials provide empirical evidence for the efficacy of this approach. Nigel Blagg and William Yule (1984), in a study comparing behavioral treatment condition, in-patient condition, and home schooling-psychotherapy condition with sixty-six youths (ages eleven to sixteen years) with SRB, found that more youth in the behavioral treatment condition returned to school (93.3%) compared with youth in the in-patient (37.5%) and home schooling-psychotherapy groups (10%). Blagg and Yule concluded that behavior therapy produced rapid and successful outcomes for most of the cases. More recently, Neville King and his colleagues (1998) randomly assigned thirty-four children (mean age=11.0 years) with SRB to two groups: cognitive-behavioral treatment and a wait-list control condition. Results indicated that youth in the cognitive-behavioral treatment group improved significantly more with respect to school attendance, fear, anxiety, depression, general internalizing behavior, and global clinician ratings.

Two studies have compared exposure-based *cognitive-behavioral treatment* to an attention-placebo control condition. Specifically, Cynthia G. Last, Cheri Hansen, and Nathalie Franco (1998) assigned fifty-six youths (age six to seventeen years) with school phobia to one of two groups: cognitive-behavioral treatment and an education support condition that did not involve therapist prescription for child exposure to school stimuli. Although children in the cognitive-behavioral treatment showed significant improvement, including increased school attendance, children in the education support condition showed similar improvement. A similar pattern of findings was found by Silverman and her colleagues (1999) in a treatment study for child phobic disorders (n=104; age six to sixteen years), including SRB. In this study education support also was used and contained no therapist prescription for child exposure to phobic stimuli. The two experimental conditions were a behavioral condition (i.e., *contingency management*) and a cognitive condition (i.e., *self-control*). Although some exceptions were found, overall, on most of the main outcome measures, similar patterns of improvements were found across conditions, including the education-support condition. Taking the findings of Last and her colleagues and Silverman and her colleagues together, the implications are that further psychosocial intervention research is needed for use with children with SRB that moves beyond wait-list control design, and that focuses particularly on investigating mediators or mechanisms of change.

In addition to cognitive behavioral interventions, family-based psychosocial intervention approaches are widely used by practitioners, including structural, strategic, experiential, and behavioral (Kearney 2000). Unfortunately, we are not aware of randomized controlled trials that have investigated the efficacy of treating SRB using family-based psychosocial therapy.

Using Kearney and Silverman's (1993) functional motivational approach to SRB, described earlier, in which SRB is conceptualized as maintained by positive and/or negative reinforcement, Kearney and Silverman (1999) used single case study design methodology in which children and their parents were assigned to either *prescriptive treatment,* based on the functional motivational condition as measured by the *School Refusal Assessment Scale* (Kearney and Silverman 1993) or *nonprescriptive treatment,* not based on the functional motivational approach youth. For youth who refused school for the functional motivational condition relating to attention-getting behavior, for example, parent training in contingency management was used to establish clear parent commands, regular evening and morning routines, and consequences for compliance and noncompliance. In contrast, youth who were assigned a *nonprescriptive* treatment (i.e., received a treatment based on their lowest-rated functional condition), these children showed worsened percentage of time out of school and daily ratings of anxiety and depression. Prescriptive treatment immediately following the nonprescriptive treatment was found to be effective, however. In summary, there is a need for further psychosocial intervention research for children who display SRB. Of particular importance will be examining the role of family factors in terms of both development/maintenance of SRB as well as SRB's treatment.

See also: ACADEMIC ACHIEVEMENT; ANXIETY DISORDERS; DEVELOPMENTAL PSYCHOPATHOLOGY; SEPARATION ANXIETY; SCHOOL

Bibliography

Berg, B.; Butler, A.; Franklin, J.; Hayes, H.; Lucas, C.; and Sims, R. (1993). "DSM-III-R Disorders, Social Factors and Management of School Attendance Problems in the Normal Population." *Journal of Child Psychology and Psychiatry* 34:1187–1203.

Berg, B.; Butler, A.; and McGuire, R. (1972). "Birth Order and Family Size of School Phobic Adolescents." *British Journal of Psychiatry* 121:509–514.

Bernstein, G. A.; Massie, E. D.; Thuras, P. D.; and Perwein, A. R. (1997). "Somatic Symptoms in Anxious-Depressed School Refusers." *Journal of the American*

Academy of Child and Adolescent Psychiatry 36:661–668.

Blagg, N. R., and Yule, W. (1984). "The Behavioural Treatment of School Refusal: A Comparative Study." *Behaviour Research and Therapy* 22:119–127.

Granell de Aldaz, E.; Feldman, L.; Vivas, E.; and Gelfand, D. M. (1987). "Characteristics of Venezuelan School Refusers: Toward the Development of a High-Risk Profile." *Journal of Nervous and Mental Disease* 175:402–407.

Granell de Aldaz, E.; Vivas, E.; Gelfand, D. M.; and Feldman, L. (1984). "Estimating the Prevalence of School Refusal and School-Related Fears." *Journal of Nervous and Mental Disease* 172:722–729.

Hansen, C.; Sanders, S. L.; Massaro, S.; and Last, C. G. (1998). "Predictors of Severity of Absenteeism in Children with Anxiety-Based School Refusal." *Journal of Clinical Child Psychology* 27:246–254.

Hibbet, A., and Fogelman, K. (1990). "Future Lives of Truants: Family Formation and Health-Related Behaviour." *British Journal of Educational Psychology* 60:171–179.

Johnson, A. M.; Falstein, E. I.; Szurek, S. A.; and Svendsen, M. (1941). "School Phobia." *American Journal of Orthopsychiatry* 11:702–711.

Kearney, C. A. (2000). *School Refusal Behavior in Youth.* Washington, DC: American Psychological Association.

Kearney, C. A.; Eisen, A. R.; and Silverman, W. K. (1995). "The Legend and Myth of School Phobia." *School Psychology Quarterly* 10:65–85.

Kearney, C. A., and Silverman, W. K. (1993). "Measuring the Function of School Refusal Behavior: The School Refusal Assessment Scale." *Journal of Clinical Child Psychology* 22:85–96.

Kearney, C. A., and Silverman, W. K. (1999). "Functionally-Based Prescriptive and Nonprescriptive Treatment for Children and Adolescents with School Refusal Behavior." *Behavior Therapy* 30:673–695.

King, N. J.; Tonge, B. J.; Heyne, D.; Pritchard, M.; Rollings, S.; Young, D.; Myerson, N.; and Ollendick, T. H. (1998). "Cognitive-Behavioral Treatment of School-Refusing Children: A Controlled Evaluation." *Journal of the American Academy of Child and Adolescent Psychiatry* 37:395–403.

Last, C. G.; Francis, G.; Hersen, M.; Kazdin, A. E.; and Strauss, C. C. (1987). "Separation Anxiety and School Phobia: A Comparison Using DSM-III Criteria." *American Journal of Psychiatry* 144:653–657.

Last, C. G.; Hansen, C.; and Franco, N. (1998). "Cognitive-Behavioral Treatment of School Phobia." *Journal of the American Academy of Child and Adolescent Psychiatry* 37:404–411.

Last, C. G., and Strauss, C. C. (1990). "School Refusal in Anxiety-Disordered Children and Adolescents." *Journal of the American Academy of Child and Adolescent Psychiatry* 29:31–35.

Ollendick, D. G. (1979). "Some Characteristics of Absentee Students in Grade 4." *Psychological Reports* 44:294.

Silverman, W. K.; Kurtines, W. M.; Ginsburg, G. S.; Weems, C. F.; Rabian, B.; and Serafini, L. T. (1999). "Contingency Management, Self Control, and Education Support in the Treatment of Childhood Phobic Disorders: A Randomized Clinical Trial." *Journal of Consulting and Clinical Psychology* 67:675–687.

Wicks-Nelson, R., and Israel, A. C. (1997). *Behavior Disorders of Childhood,* 3rd edition. Upper Saddle River, NJ: Prentice-Hall.

XIMENA FRANCO
WENDY K. SILVERMAN

SCOTLAND

See GREAT BRITAIN

SELF-DISCLOSURE

Disclosure as a phenomenon was first investigated by Sidney Jourard (1971). The process was originally defined as telling others about the self. Since then, an extensive amount of information about disclosure has been produced, leading to significant shifts in the way we think about this phenomenon (Derlega et al. 1993; Petronio in press). One change has been to consider disclosure as a process of revealing and concealing private information. Making this change raises many questions about how people decide to disclose or remain private and helps us better understand the process within romantic relationships, marriage, and families (Burgoon 1982; Holtgraves 1990; Petronio 1991, 2000).

Decision making behind the act of disclosing private information is an extremely complicated process, especially when we are considering close personal relationships and family interactions. For instance, we know that although intimacy often increases the possibility of revealing information, there are times when disclosure is counterproductive for the marital relationship or family. Soliciting disclosive information about a partner's health—such as asking about his or her level of pain—can actually increase the severity of pain a partner feels (Cutrona 1996). The more people disclose about their discomfort, the more they pay attention to the chronic pain. On the other hand, keeping secrets like sexual abuse can be destructive to a family and its members. Likewise, marital partners who are seriously ill with cancer, for instance, may find that the belief in self-sufficiency means the cancer patient is unable to disclose to his or her partner feelings of stress and discomfort (Pearlin and McCall 1990).

Because marital partners and families regulate both disclosure and privacy, it helps to have a framework to understand how people make decisions about this process. The theory of *Communication Privacy Management* (Petronio, in press) defines our revealing through the process of balancing disclosure and privacy. Briefly, the theory proposes that we manage the flow of our private information in relationships by constructing personal, dyadic, and group boundaries around private information. These metaphorically constructed boundaries allow us to identify who has ownership rights and control over the information; who does and does not have access to it; and how it should or should not be protected from those outside the boundary.

Because each of us simultaneously manages multiple boundaries with many individuals, the number of boundaries that we regulate increases exponentially with the number of individuals with whom we choose to disclose. To ensure our boundaries are protected, rules are enacted for revealing (disclosure) or concealing (privacy). Additionally, sanctions are established for any violation of a boundary rule. As information is shared to others outside of these co-constructed boundaries, additional rules emerge that govern this newly shared information. Individuals within the boundary become linked by the knowledge of the information disclosed (Petronio and Kovach 1997). The development of these rules forms the foundation for each of our boundary management systems.

Through these systems, we individually and with others coordinate and manage the private information that is contained within our boundaries.

For those in close relationships, such as marital couples, there exists a critical need to manage shared private information because it plays a functional role in the relationship (Derlega 1984). Thus, through the regulation of privacy boundaries and coordination of rules, the partners are able to reduce ambiguity about the meaning of behavior and determine insights into a partner's intentions. However, partners must come to a mutually agreed upon set of rules so that they can coordinate the management of the private information effectively. For example, on a night out with another couple, the husband of one of the couples begins to give a detailed description of pet names he has for his wife to the other husband. After the evening ends, the wife directly informs her husband that the pet names he calls her should be kept only between the two of them. This information is not for anyone else to know. She is operating under the boundary rule that such information should be kept private between the couple. In his defense, the husband explains that while growing up his parents used the pet names they had for each other in public frequently, and he did not consider it of any significance. Here is a communication event in which turbulence occurred because of a failure by the couple to coordinate a privacy boundary around this information. As a result, the rules that maintain this information are necessarily renegotiated and new boundary rules are formed to manage access to the information. The adjustment is essential for both the husband and wife to have the same definition of "pet names" as private information.

When there is a disparity in expectations for disclosure, the result can have a significant negative impact on the relationship. For example, in one study, it was found that couples experienced problems in marital adjustment when there was an inequality in the amount of disclosure expressed compared to the amount of disclosure received (Davidson, Balswick, and Halverson 1983). Along these lines, Jourard (1971) suggests that people expect to receive rates of disclosure similar to that which they give to others. If there are different criteria for disclosure between partners, expectations can go unfulfilled, resulting in relational dissatisfaction (Jorgensen and Gaudy 1980).

Gender Differences

Framed within the privacy management theory, an abundance of research has shown that men and women use different criteria for deciding to open or close their boundaries. Consequently, they tend to depend on different rules to reveal or conceal. The outcome of these rules is that women more than men tend to disclose overall (though there are situations where the reverse is also true). Women more than men also tend to talk about intimate or personal topics with each other. In addition, women prefer disclosing to same-sex friends while men prefer to disclose while engaging in some activity (Caldwell and Peplau 1982; Dindia and Allen 1992).

Men have a greater need to control their privacy (Petronio, Martin, and Littlefield 1984; Rosenfeld 1979). Men also report expecting greater negative ramifications when disclosing about life expectations (Petronio and Martin 1986). Men and women who enter into a marital relationship often have to change their personal rules to coordinate with their partners. Thus, although they still maintain the same rules around private information that is personal, once information becomes shared and defined as belonging to the couple collectively, new mutually held rules must be determined. If the couple is not able to agree on ways to mutually manage their shared boundary, conflict might erupt.

Family Privacy

Family boundary rules play a significant part in partners' coordination of private information. So much so that before entering into a partner relationship, each person brings with her or him specific boundary management rules that are inherited or learned from the way their parents managed such information. Similar to passing on rituals, parents often hand down family boundary access rules.

Karpel (1980) argues that for family secrets, there are those that are kept internally and those that are kept within the family as a whole but not given to outsiders. Similarly, members as a whole may develop an orientation to privacy and related boundary rules that apply to managing private information not only internally within the family, but also externally to others outside of the family. These family privacy orientations are passed down

from one generation to the next. In general, families may be more open than closed, or they may be secretive. Sometimes, whether family members reveal these secrets often depends on the function of keeping the secret, their level of family satisfaction, and the relationship they have with the targeted confidant (Vangelisti and Caughlin 1997). For the most part, families expect a certain degree of privacy so that they can test out ideas, opinions, or beliefs in a more secure environment (Berardo 1974). Nevertheless, each family has its own way of defining the boundaries of privacy.

Parents and Child Privacy

Similarly to relational partners, if boundary issues are not resolved between family members, discontent can occur within the family, particularly between the privacy demands of children and parents. Not only can the boundary regulation of the family and others outside of the family be difficult to attempt to manage, but also the management within can be disappointing if the boundary rules are not negotiated. Consider the privacy dilemma that often occurs about a child's bedroom. Prior research has shown that children allow parents wide latitude in encroaching on their personal space and invading their privacy (Burgoon et al. 1989). Nevertheless, when children feel that their parents have stepped over that line, violating their privacy boundaries, they react negatively. The children feel a need to have some control over possessions, space, and private information.

To avoid this dilemma, the parents and children need to negotiate exactly when the parents might enter the room, granting the children the ability to control the space. Continuous violations of personal space could eventually result in defense actions on the part of the child (Petronio 1994). Privacy issues are particularly salient for adolescents (Youniss and Smollar 1985). The children's claim of privacy rights tends to mark their need to separate from the parents. As they grow older, children declare the right to more privacy and control over their personal information, space, and possessions. When parents do not allow them jurisdiction over these things, it interferes with the child's ability to become a mature adult (Youniss and Smollar 1985).

This issue often becomes salient when adult children, who have gone away to college, return home to face issues of boundary management with their parents. In the first of four studies, Sandra Petronio (1994) uncovered a number of ways parents invade the privacy boundaries of their college-age children (mean age was nineteen years old). For example, the parents often violate the privacy of their adult children by entering bedrooms without knocking, attempting to overhear telephone conversations, asking personal questions, opening personal mail, infringing on personal time, giving unsolicited advice, and going through personal possessions.

These invasions within the home create a dilemma for the children. As a result, they react with protective strategies. For example, to manage their privacy, they tend to lock or close doors when in their parents' home, make calls away from home, hide personal items, confront their parents with violations, refuse to disclose personal information, express disappointment in parents, and meet friends outside of the home (Petronio 1994).

Within families, issues of privacy extend far beyond invasions of college children. Entire families can experience privacy boundary predicaments, such as when private information about one or more family members is exposed. The family member who learns this information is caught in a predicament that forces him or her to decide whether to maintain the existing boundaries around the information or breach confidences. For example, while cleaning the garage, a nineteen-year-old college sophomore comes across a series of love letters less than a year old addressed to his mother from a man who is neither his father nor married to his mother. The son is forced to grapple with the issue of concealing or revealing this private information to the other family members. He has possession of the information without the knowledge of his mother. He, alone, has to decide the way he is going to manage the boundary around this information.

Faced with the dilemma of two equally unsatisfying alternatives, such as above, the family member usually must juxtapose the desire to maintain the boundary with what she or he believes is the most appropriate course of action, which may be to disclose to others within or outside the family. In either event, one choice will be good for the family member whereas the other will not. In weighing their decisions to break the boundary, family members often consider the consequences of their revealing.

However, managing family boundaries around private information is often not a sole family member's responsibility. Because family members often serve as confidants for each other, the way they manage the co-ownership of disclosed information matters to their ongoing family relationships. When family members are told about a private problem, there is a certain responsibility for the information told. For example, a sibling tells her sister she thinks she might be pregnant. Since being able to disclose high stress information is beneficial to one's health, knowing that her sister will treat the information with respect is critical (Pennebaker 1990).

At times, only a few family members will co-own information. When family members share information with only one other member, a dyadic boundary is formed. On this level, the two family members co-own the information and establish coordinated rules as to the protection of or the access to the information by others. For example, a mother and daughter may protect the boundary around the fact that the mother has a secret checking account separate from her husband. Both mother and daughter establish boundary rules as to how to protect this private information from others in the family. As a result, the target of a disclosure, even among family members, can significantly influence the way people reveal and conceal certain information (Tardy, Hosman, and Bradac 1981). Interestingly, the most frequently selected confidant in families is the mother (Derlega et al. 1993). Fathers are chosen less often than mothers, either because they are less accessible or form a different type of relationship with their children.

The same process takes place when the entire family owns the information; all members are expected to take responsibility for managing the boundaries around access to and protection of the information. The maintenance of privacy is critical to the functioning of the family members. This is seen in the way families may place a boundary around the private information that one of the children is gay. When protection is working, all family members are expected to share in guarding this information from others outside of the family. However, if one member decides to disclose this to an outsider, others in the family may punish him or her by refusing to talk or through open confrontation about breaking the family rule.

Conclusion

Because disclosure is fundamental to family and personal relationships, identifying why it is expressed and how it is managed is critical for human understanding, especially within families. Since families provide a buffer zone for their members, a safe haven within which to learn and gain social support, understanding how disclosure functions is essential to the growth and development of the members.

See also: COMMUNICATION: COUPLE RELATIONSHIPS; COMMUNICATION: FAMILY RELATIONSHIPS; CONFLICT: COUPLE RELATIONSHIPS; CONFLICT: FAMILY RELATIONSHIPS; CONFLICT: PARENT-CHILD RELATIONSHIPS; FAMILY AND RELATIONAL RULES; FRIENDSHIP; HOUSING; INTIMACY

Bibliography

Berardo, F. M. (1974). "Family Invisibility and Family Privacy." In *Privacy,* ed. S. Margulis. Stony Brook, NY: Environmental Design Research Association.

Burgoon, J. K. (1982). "Privacy and Communication." In *Communication Yearbook* 6, ed. M. Burgoon. Beverly Hills, CA: Sage.

Burgoon, J. K.; Parrott, R.; Le Poire, B. A.; Kelley, D. L.; Walther, J. B.; and Perry, D. (1989). "Maintaining and Restoring Privacy Through Communication in Different Types of Relationships." *Journal of Social and Personal Relationships* 6:131–158.

Caldwell, M. A., and Peplau, L. A. (1982). "Sex Differences in Same-Sex Friendship." *Sex Roles* 8:721–732.

Cutrona, C. E. (1996). *Social Support in Couples.* Thousand Oaks, CA: Sage.

Davidson, B.; Balswick, J.; and Halverson, C. (1983). "Affective Self-Disclosure and Marital Adjustment: A Test of Equity Theory." *Journal of Marriage and the Family* 45:93–102.

Derlega, V. J. (1984). "Self-Disclosure and Intimate Relationships." In *Communication, Intimacy, and Close Relationship,* ed. V. J. Derlega. Orlando, FL: Academic Press.

Derlega, V. J.; Metts, S.; Petronio, S.; Margulis, S. T. (1993). *Self-Disclosure.* Newbury Park, CA: Sage.

Dindia, K., and Allen, M. (1992). "Sex Differences in Self-Disclosure: A Meta-Analysis." *Psychological Bulletin* 112:106–124.

Holtgraves, T. (1990). "The Language of Self-Disclosure." *Handbook of Language and Social Psychology.* New York: John Wiley and Sons.

Jorgensen, S. R., and Gaudy, J. C. (1980). "Self-Disclosure and Satisfaction in Marriage: The Relation Examined." *Family Relations* 29:281–287.

Jourard, S. (1971). *The Transparent Self.* New York: Van Nostrand.

Pearlin, L. I., and McCall, M. E. (1990). "Occupational Stress and Marital Support: A Description of Microprocesses." In *Stress between Work and Family,* ed. J. Eckenrode and S. Gore. New York: Plenum.

Pennebaker, J. (1990). *Opening Up: The Healing Power of Confiding in Others.* New York: Avon.

Petronio, S. (1991). "Communication Boundary Management: A Theoretical Model of Managing Disclosure of Private Information Between Marital Couples." *Communication Theory* 1:311–335.

Petronio, S. (1994). "Privacy Binds in Family Interactions: The Case of Parental Privacy Invasion." In *The Darkside of Interpersonal Communication,* ed. W. R. Cupach and B. H. Spitzberg. Hillsdale, NJ: Lawrence Erlbaum.

Petronio, S. (in press). "The Boundaries of Privacy: Praxis of Everyday Life." In *Balancing the Secrets of Private Disclosures,* ed. S. Petronio. Hillsdale, NJ: Lawrence Erlbaum.

Petronio, S., and Kovach, S. (1997). "Managing Privacy Boundaries: Health Providers' Perceptions of Resident Care in Scottish Nursing Homes." *Journal of Applied Communication Research* 25:115–131.

Petronio, S., and Martin, J. (1986). "Ramifications of Revealing Private Information: A Gender Gap." *Journal of Clinical Psychology* 42:499–506.

Petronio, S.; Martin, J.; and Littlefield, R. (1984). "Prerequisite Conditions for Self-Disclosing: A Gender Issue." *Communication Monographs* 51:268–273.

Tardy, C.; Hosman, L. A.; and Bradac, J. J. (1981). "Disclosing Self to Friends and Family: A Reexamination of Initial Question." *Communication Quarterly* 29:263–268.

Vangelisti, A. L., and Caughlin, J. P. (1997). "Revealing Family Secrets: The Influence of Topic, Function, and Relationships." *Journal of Social and Personal Relationships* 14:679–705.

Youniss, J., and Smollar, J. (1985). *Adolescent Relations with Mothers, Fathers, and Friends.* Chicago: University of Chicago Press.

SANDRA PETRONIO
JACK SARGENT

SELF-ESTEEM

Self-esteem refers to the evaluative and affective aspects of the self, to how "good" or "bad" we feel about ourselves. It is a consequence of the self's capacity for reflexivity, that is, the ability to look at oneself and to evaluate what one sees. Self-evaluations typically give rise to positive or negative self-feelings, such as pride or shame. These self-feelings make self-esteem important both experientially (i.e., they constitute some of our strongest emotions) and motivationally (i.e., people are motivated to seek positive self-feelings and to avoid negative self-feelings). Self-esteem can change over time, but individuals tend to maintain a consistent view of their self-worth due to the need for psychological consistency and the need to resolve cognitive dissonance.

The motivation to maintain and enhance a positive conception of oneself is a major dynamic of many contemporary self-theories (Gecas 1991). Such theories suggest that self-conceptions are valued and protected. Thus, a low self-evaluation on criteria that matter is an uncomfortable condition people are motivated to avoid. Avoiding low self-evaluations may occur through increased efforts at self-improvement or, more typically, through such self-serving activities as selective perception and memory, various strategies of impression management, and restructuring the environment and/or redefining the situation to make it reflect a more favorable view of self (Rosenberg 1979). These manipulations and distortions may raise self-esteem, but at the price of self-deception.

There may be optimum levels of self-esteem beyond which the consequences for individuals are negative. Overly low levels of self-esteem are associated with depression and self-defeating behavior including suicidal ideation, but excessively high self-esteem may be associated with arrogance, egoism, and even aggression. Ray Baumeister (2001), for example, hypothesizes that narcissistic individuals may react aggressively to criticism because their brittle self-esteem is too high, not too low. In terms of competent performance, high self-esteem individuals expect to perform well, whereas those with low self-esteem expect to do more poorly. The self-esteem literature generally indicates that low self-esteem individuals depend more on and are more influenced by external cues that provide self-relevant information about performance than high self-esteem individuals (Tice 1993).

Development of Self-Esteem

Several processes have been identified as important to the development of self-esteem: *reflected appraisals, social comparisons,* and *self-attributions.* Within sociology, reflected appraisals is the most important process because of its emphasis within symbolic interaction theory. The *reflected appraisals* process states that we come to see ourselves and to evaluate ourselves as we think others see and evaluate us. Based on Charles Cooley's (1902) influential concept of the *looking-glass self* and George H. Mead's (1934) theory of role taking as a product of symbolic interaction, reflected appraisals emphasize the essentially social character of the self (i.e., that our self-conceptions reflect our perceptions of the judgments of others, especially significant others, in our environment). Empirically, however, there is not much congruence between self-appraisals and the actual appraisals of us by others (Gecas and Burke 1995). This suggests that the appraisals of others are not very accurately perceived, and if accurately perceived, may not be believed. There are a number of reasons for this disparity. One is the difficulty of getting honest feedback from others, especially if it is negative. The norms of social interaction typically emphasize tact and proper demeanor, which serve to protect self-esteem. Another reason is that the feedback from "significant others" may be suspect. For example, parents and teachers and others who seek to boost self-esteem may overemphasize the importance of praise in developing self-esteem in children. Although praise and encouragement may be important for children's self-esteem, successful performance at activities that children value may be more important because they constitute more credible evidence of competence and worth. In fact, Baumeister (2001) suggest that society is doing more of a disservice by not tying praise to performance, and by doling out praise when it is not earned. Baumeister (2001, p. 101) aptly states: "one should beware of people who regard themselves as superior to others, especially when those beliefs are inflated, weakly grounded in reality or heavily dependent on having others confirm them frequently. Conceited, self-important individuals turn nasty toward those who puncture their bubbles of self love." Finally, the self-esteem motive has a distorting effect on all three processes of self-esteem development. To the extent that the self-esteem motive is operative, we are more likely to selectively perceive and remember favorable feedback and ignore or discredit unfavorable feedback from others. For these and other reasons it is important to emphasize that the reflected appraisals process operates primarily through our *perceptions* of the appraisals of others.

A second process important to the development of self-esteem is *social comparison*. This is the process in which individuals assess their own abilities and virtues by comparing them to those of others. According to Leon Festinger's (1954) theory, as well as much of the contemporary theory and research on social comparisons (see Suls and Wills 1991 for a review), the main function of this process is *reality-testing*. This is most likely to occur in situations where knowledge about some aspect of oneself is ambiguous or uncertain. Local reference groups are most likely to be used as standards for these comparisons, especially under conditions of competition, such as athletic contests and classroom performance. Individuals tend to compare themselves with others who are doing slightly better than themselves (*upward social comparisons*) as a means of gathering information about a specific task. As with reflected appraisals, the reality-testing that occurs by means of social comparisons is biased by the self-esteem motive: we are likely to seek out favorable comparisons, avoid unfavorable comparisons, or to try to neutralize unavoidably unfavorable comparisons with various disclaimers and excuses. Research has also shown that individuals often compare themselves with others who are performing poorly (*downward social comparisons*) to enhance their self-images (Spencer, Josephs, and Steele 1993).

A third process, *self-attributions,* refers to the tendency to make inferences about ourselves from direct observation of our behavior and its consequences. Daryl Bem's (1972) *self-perception theory* proposes that individuals acquire knowledge about themselves in the same way they acquire knowledge about others: by observing behavior and making inferences about internal dispositions and states (e.g., motives, attitudes, self-esteem) from these observations. Self-perception theory can be subsumed under the more general *attribution theory,* which deals with how individuals make causal attributions about their own and others' behavior.

Again, we are hardly neutral observers of what we see. Research suggests that our causal attributions tend to be self-serving. For example, we are more likely to make internal causal attributions for our behavioral successes and external attributions for our failures.

Although all three of these processes are important to the development and maintenance of self-esteem, at any one time one may be more relevant to self-esteem than the others. Also, it is evident that the self does not passively respond to processes that affect it. Rather, it actively shapes and influences these processes in the interests of protecting self-esteem and other self-motivations. In this sense, self-esteem is both a product of social forces and an agent in its own development (Gecas 2001).

Family Interaction and Self-Esteem

One of the most important social contexts for the development and expression of self-esteem is the family. For children, the family is the most important context because its major function is the socialization and care of children. The family is the first primary group that we experience—the place where some of our most important identities take shape (e.g., male/female, boy/girl, son/daughter, and sister/brother). Assessments of role performances based on these identities become early sources of self-esteem. Mead's (1934) discussion of the early stages of role-taking and role-playing, processes essential in the development of the self, occur within the context of family interactions. Parents typically serve as mentors and as significant others for children. The intimate, extensive, and relatively enduring relationships characteristic of the family as a primary group make it an important context for the self-esteem of children as well as adults.

All three processes of self-esteem formation are pervasive in family life. We frequently make self-attributions on the basis of our role performances and interactions with family members, feeling good or bad about ourselves depending on what inferences we draw. Social comparisons are also a common feature of family life, particularly among siblings. Notions of fairness or injustice initially develop within sibling relations, as do comparisons of various competencies and virtues, with inevitable implications for self-esteem. Reflected appraisals are ubiquitous among family members.

All family members have opinions about one another and are typically less reticent to express them to each other than is the case outside of family relations. Siblings, especially, may be only too eager to give critical feedback regarding each other's behavior, appearance, social skills, and intelligence. Not all of these appraisals, of course, are equally significant for one's self-esteem. Both what is being appraised (with regard to its importance for one's self-concept) and who does the appraising, are important qualifiers. For children, on most things, the reflected appraisals of their parents may matter much more than those of their siblings.

Reflected appraisals has been the main process examined in studies of self-esteem within families. The bulk of this research has focused on the effects of parental behavior on children's self-esteem. In general, these studies find that parental support and encouragement, responsiveness, and use of inductive control are related positively to children's self-esteem (Gecas and Seff 1990). Most of these parental variables could be considered indicators of positive reflected appraisals of the child. They are also the parental behaviors found to be associated with the development of other positive socialization outcomes in children and adolescents (such as moral development, prosocial behavior, and academic achievement).

Not surprisingly, these relationships are much stronger for the child's perceptions of parental behavior and his or her self-esteem than for actual parental behavior or parental reports of their behavior (Gecas and Schwalbe 1986). Furthermore, this research indicates that there is not much overlap between parental reports of their behavior and children's perceptions of this behavior. Evidently a good deal of selectivity and bias in recall and perception are reflected in these studies.

Birth order and sibling relations may also be consequential for children's self-esteem. On the basis of both reflected appraisals and social comparisons, we would expect first-borns to have higher self-esteem than later-born children. The greater attention and encouragement from parents should contribute to first-borns' greater sense of worth and importance; and first-borns' typically greater power and competence compared with younger siblings should result in more favorable social comparisons. Research, however, provides only modest (and inconsistent) support for these

expectations (Blake 1989). Oldest and only children do seem to have higher self-esteem than later-born children, but the differences are not significant. The effects of birth order may be suppressed or mitigated by the influence of several other features of the sibling system, such as sex composition of the sibling order, child spacing, family size, age and sex of target child, and age and sex of next oldest sibling. Without taking into account the effect of these other variables, the influence of birth order on self-esteem may largely disappear (Gecas and Pasley 1983).

Other structural variations within families (e.g., single-parent families, stepparent families, extended families) may affect children's self-esteem, if they have an impact on reflected appraisals, social comparisons, or self-attributions. There has not been much research on the effects of these family structural variations on children's self-esteem. What research there is does not report much variation. The quality of family relations does not seen to vary consistently enough across these structural variations for them to show significant and consistent differences in children's self-esteem.

For children's and adolescents' self-esteem the most relevant domains of evaluation are academic competence, athletic competence, social acceptance, physical appearance, and behavioral conduct. Interestingly, among all these domains, the evaluation of one's physical appearance takes precedence over other domains of self-esteem, especially for girls (Harter 1993). Parents, and others, begin to react to the physical self when one is an infant and toddler. Critical feedback on one's appearance negatively affects self-esteem. Moreover, self-esteem is implicated in various eating disorders (such as *anorexia, bulimia,* and binge eating), especially among adolescent girls (Heatherton and Baumeister 1991). Parents place greater emphasis on the academic competence and behavioral conduct of their children, whereas peers place the most importance on physical appearance, likeability, and athletic competence of others their age.

Family relations are also important for parents' and spouses' self-esteem, although these have not received the attention given to children's self-esteem. Husbands and wives are typically *significant others* for each other, and the reflected appraisals received from these sources should matter a great deal for spouses' self-esteem, even more so now than in the past. As the institution of marriage/family continues to evolve from a traditional pattern (characterized by multiple functions and a segregated division of labor), to a *companionship* pattern (characterized by fewer functions, but greater emphasis on love, emotional support, and nurturing socialization), the quality of the marital bond becomes increasingly relevant for the self-esteem of husbands and wives. As the high divorce rate attests, however, the family as a "haven in a heartless world" (Lasch 1975) is an increasingly fragile emotional anchor for the self in contemporary society. Along with the loss of functions, there has also been a decline in traditional social supports (such as religion and extended kin networks) for marriage and family. Consequently, a premium is placed on love and affection. It becomes the raison d'être for marriage. And when love and affection declines, as it often does under the stresses of contemporary life, divorce is a common solution. This too has serious consequences for self-esteem.

Along with the marital bond, the parental bond is a major source of self-conception and self-esteem for most adults. It may even be a more enduring source of self-definition than marriage, because people typically do not divorce their children. The identities of "mother" and "father" are among the most important in the self-conceptions of parents. How parents perform the roles associated with these identities, how their children respond to them, and the quality of the parent-child relationship have major implications for parents' self-esteem.

Research on parenthood suggests that it is a rocky road for parents' self-esteem. The transition to parenthood is itself a major event, typically a source of joy and stress, with significant consequences for the marital bond and for family patterns (Demo and Cox 2000). Children provide numerous occasions for both parental satisfaction and distress. They are a source of parental pleasure and pride, increasing parents' self-esteem, as well as a source of frustration, anger, and distress, decreasing parents' self-esteem. Research on parental satisfaction across the various stages of parenthood suggests that the positive experiences are more frequent when the children are young, and the negative experiences increase in frequency when children get older, with adolescence reported as the most difficult time for parents (Gecas and Seff 1990). Maternal self-esteem has long been associated with the quality of mother-child interactions.

Research indicates that low self-esteem mothers are more likely to engage in child abuse (Oates and Forrest 1985) and neglect (Christensen et al. 1994). There are, of course, numerous factors that qualify or mitigate this pattern, such as number and sex of children, personalities of the children and the parents, and economic and occupational stresses on the family.

Culture: Ethnicity and Self-Esteem

Most research and theory on self-concept and self-esteem is based on Western cultures and populations, whereas increasing attention to cross-cultural differences is expanding our view of self processes. Harry Triandis (1989) distinguishes between *individualistic* cultures, such as the United States, and *collectivistic* cultures, such as China and other Asian cultures. Self-esteem in the former is more likely to be based on the achievement of personal goals, whereas in the latter self-esteem is derived from the achievement of collective goals, such as those of family or society. Hazel Markus and Shinobu Kitayama (1991) propose a similar distinction between Western and Eastern cultures in their conceptualization of "independent" versus "interdependent" selves. *Independent self-conceptions* emphasize the uniqueness of the individual and the separation of self from others. *Interdependent self-conceptions* stress the connectedness of the person to the group and to fitting in with one's group. The same processes of self-concept formation may apply in both types of cultures, but with different emphases. For example, in collectivist cultures, such as those of Japan or China, the reflected appraisals from one's family, work group, or peer group are the primary sources of self-esteem and concomitant emotions such as shame and pride. By contrast, in the more individualistic Western cultures, self-attributions based on individual achievement may be a more important process for self-esteem.

These distinctions between Western and Eastern cultures are instructive for understanding self-processes, but it should also be noted that there is considerable variation *within* each culture regarding self-processes. For example, within the United States and other Western countries women are more likely to have an interdependent self-concept and men are more likely to emphasize an independent self-concept (Markus and Oyserman 1989). A more collectivist or interdependent self is also characteristic of ethnic and racial minorities in the United States. Although the level of self-esteem does not seem to vary much by race or by ethnicity (Gecas and Burke 1995), various social factors related to race and ethnicity (such as social class and racial composition of schools and communities) do affect self-esteem. For example, African-American students who attend predominantly African-American high schools report higher self-esteem than African-American teenagers who attend predominantly white high schools (Ross 1995).

Is There Too Much Emphasis on Self-Esteem?

Self-esteem has become the most popular aspect of personality studied, and a major emphasis of various family and individual therapy programs. The popularity of self-esteem is due largely to its perceived salutary consequences for individual functioning, and to the perceived strength and pervasiveness of the self-esteem motive. In the minds of many (scholars as well as the general public), high self-esteem has come to be associated with numerous "good" outcomes for individuals (e.g., academic achievement, popularity, personal success, health and happiness), whereas low self-esteem is associated with various "bad" outcomes (e.g., delinquency, academic failure, and depression). For example, the California Task Force to Promote Self-Esteem and Personal and Social Responsibility (1990, p. 4) concludes: "Self-esteem is the likeliest candidate for a social vaccine, something that empowers us to live responsibly and that inoculates us against the lures of crime, violence, substance abuse, teen pregnancy, child abuse, chronic welfare dependency, and educational failure. The lack of self-esteem is central to most personal and social ills plaguing our state and nation."

Scholarly research on self-esteem gives a much more qualified and equivocal picture. Although there is a tendency for high self-esteem to be associated with some positive outcomes, and low self-esteem with negative outcomes, the relationships tend to be modest, often mixed or nonsignificant, and specific to certain conditions (see Mecca, Smelser, and Vasconcellos 1989). Reasons for the low associations and mixed results are common to much of the research in the social sciences: problems of measurement (validity and reliability); problems of conceptualization (relating a global variable to a specific behavioral outcome); failure to control for other confounding variables; and reliance on cross-sectional research designs.

Nevertheless, self-esteem has come to be perceived, particularly by family practitioners, as the key solution of most personal and interpersonal problems. Programs to "raise self-esteem" are common in our society—in classrooms, rehabilitation centers, workplaces, and, of course, families (Hewitt 1998). The research evidence by itself does not seem to warrant this kind of advocacy in the applied sphere. This emphasis on self-esteem with family therapy is probably less a consequence of persuasive scientific research than an expression of some of our central cultural values, such as individualism. Some scholars have expressed concern about this over-emphasis on self-esteem (Baumeister 2001; Hewitt 1998), viewing it as detrimental to the maintenance of interpersonal and family bonds. Wesley Burr and Clark Christensen (1992) argue that the emphasis on self-esteem in the helping professions may contribute to selfishness, self-centeredness, and excessive individualism, which undermines commitment to families and the health of family processes.

Self-esteem is an important aspect of individual experience and it does have consequences for individual and family functioning. But it is no panacea for personal or social ills. No variable is. It should be viewed in the proper scientific perspective—an important social psychological variable that, like a number of others (e.g., commitment, altruism, gender identity), has been found to affect individual functioning and family relations.

See also: ATTRACTION; ATTRIBUTION IN RELATIONSHIPS; BIRTH ORDER; CHILDREN OF ALCOHOLICS; DEPRESSION: ADULTS; DEPRESSION: CHILDREN AND ADOLESCENTS; DEVELOPMENT: SELF; DEVELOPMENTAL PSYCHOPATHOLOGY; DIVORCE: EFFECTS ON CHILDREN; EATING DISORDERS; GIFTED AND TALENTED CHILDREN; JUVENILE DELINQUENCY; MENOPAUSE; PARENTING STYLES; POWER: MARITAL RELATIONSHIPS; SCHOOL; SIBLING RELATIONSHIPS; SUICIDE; SYMBOLIC INTERACTIONISM; THERAPY: FAMILY RELATIONSHIPS; TRANSITION TO PARENTHOOD; WIDOWHOOD

Bibliography

Baumeister, R.F. (2001). "Violent Pride." *Scientific American* 384(4):96–101.

Bem, D. (1972). "Self-Perception Theory." In *Advances in Experimental Social Psychology,* ed. L. Berkowitz. New York: Academic Press.

Blake, J. (1989). *Family Size and Achievement.* Berkeley: University of California Press.

Burr, W. R., and Christensen, C. (1992). "Undesirable Side Effects of Enhancing Self-esteem." *Family Relations* 41:460–464.

California Task Force to Promote Self-Esteem. (1990). *Toward a State of Self-Esteem.* Sacramento: California State Department of Education.

Christensen, M. J.; Brayden, R. M.; Dietrich, M. S.; McLaghlin, F. J.; Sherrod, K. B.; and Altemeier, W. A. (1994). "The Prospective Assessment of Self-Concept in Neglectful and Physically Abusive Low Income Mothers." *Child Abuse & Neglect* 18(3):225–232.

Cooley, C. H. (1902). *Human Nature and the Social Order.* New York: Scribners.

Demo, D. H., and Cox, M. J. (2000). "Families with Young Children: A Review of Research in the 1990s." *Journal of Marriage and the Family* 62:876–895.

Festinger, L. (1954). "A Theory of Social Comparison Processes." *Human Relations* 7:117–140.

Gecas, V. (1991). "The Self-Concept as a Basis for a Theory of Motivation." In *The Self-Society Dynamic, ed.* J. A. Howard and P. L. Callero. Cambridge, UK: Cambridge University Press.

Gecas, V. (2001). "The Self as a Social Force." In *Extending Self-Esteem Theory and Research,* ed. T. Owens, S. Stryker, and H. Goodman. Cambridge, UK: Cambridge University Press.

Gecas, V., and Burke, P. (1995). "Self and Identity." In *Sociological Perspectives on Social Psychology,* ed. K. Cook, G. A. Fine, and J. House. Boston: Allyn and Bacon.

Gecas, V., and Pasley, K. (1983). "Birth Order and Self-Concept in Adolescence." *Journal of Youth and Adolescence* 12:521–535.

Gecas, V., and Schwalbe, M. (1986). "Parental Behavior and Adolescent Self-Esteem." *Journal of Marriage and the Family* 48:37–46.

Gecas, V., and Seff, M. A. (1990). "Families and Adolescents: A Review of the 1980s." *Journal of Marriage and the Family* 52:941–958.

Harter, S. (1993). "Causes and Consequences of Low Self-Esteem in Children and Adolescents." In *Self-Esteem: The Puzzle of Low Self-Regard,* ed. R. Baumeister. New York: Plenum.

Heatherton, T. F., and Baumeister, R. F. (1991). "Binge Eating as Escape From Self-Awareness." *Psychological Bulletin* 110:86–108.

Hewitt, J. P. (1998). *The Myth of Self-Esteem.* New York: St. Martin's Press.

Lasch, C. (1975). *Haven in a Heartless World.* New York: Basic Books.

Markus, H. R., and Kitayama, S. (1991). "Culture and the Self Implications for Cognition, Emotion, and Motivation." *Psychological Review* 98:224–253.

Markus, H. R., and Oyserman, D. (1989). "Gender and Thought: The Role of the Self-Concept." In *Gender and Thought,* ed. M. Crawford and M. Hamilton. New York: Springer.

Mead, G. H. (1934). *Mind, Self and Society.* Chicago: University of Chicago Press.

Mecca, A. M., Smelser, N. J., and Vasconcellos, J. (eds.) (1989). *The Social Importance of Self-Esteem.* Berkeley: University of California Press.

Oates, R. K., and Forrest, D. (1985). "Self-Esteem and Early Background of Abusive Mothers." *Child Abuse & Neglect* 9:89–93.

Rosenberg, M. (1979). *Conceiving the Self.* New York: Basic Books.

Ross, L. E. (1995). "School Environment, Self-Esteem, and Delinquency." *Journal of Criminal Justice* 23:555–567.

Spencer, S. J.; Josephs, R. A.; and Steele, C. A. (1993). "Low Self-Esteem: The Uphill Struggle for Self-Integrity." In *Self-Esteem: The Puzzle of Low Self-Regard,* ed. R. Baumeister. New York: Plenum Press.

Suls, J., and Wills, T. A., eds. (1991). *Social Comparison: Contemporary Theory and Research.* Hillsdale, NJ: Lawrence Erlbaum Associates.

Tice, D. M. (1993). "The Social Motivations of People With Low Self-Esteem." In *Self Esteem: The Puzzle of Low Self-Regard,* ed. R. Baumeister. New York: Plenum.

Triandis, H. C. (1989). "The Self and Social Behaviors in Differing Cultural Contexts." *Psychological Review* 96:506–520.

VIKTOR GECAS
MONICA LONGMORE

SENEGAL

Marriage patterns in contemporary Senegal derive from Islamic, Western, and local traditions. This situation, which has prevailed for centuries, results from secular borrowings from the Arab world and

European colonizers. Senegal embraced Islam more than a thousand years ago, mainly through early contacts with traders from Northern Africa. The trans-Saharan trade did not survive French colonization, but its effects on the Senegalese society's religious landscape prevails to date. Although less than half of the Senegalese population was Muslim at the turn of the century, now more than 90 percent are. Scholars of Senegalese sociopolitical history recognize that the country's local social, political, and educational systems are at the crossroads of European and Islamic civilizations (Gellar 1995).

Before Senegalese independence from French colonization in 1961, marriage law followed an *Islamicized* Wolof custom—that is, a set of rules and regulations drawn from both Islamic law and local traditions. However, Senegalese with French citizenship were allowed to rely on French marriage law (Sow 1985). Customary and civil marriage still co-exist in Senegalese society, and neither is more valued than the other, although the educated elite is more likely to opt for the latter. These two forms of marriage differ mainly in that customary marriage does not require any registration through the official legal system, while civil marriage does. In addition, there are various forms of consensual unions that are often not considered as marital unions in official statistics. Current Senegalese marriage laws allow men to opt for either monogamy or polygamy, but the wife's consent is required. In either case, marriage is the only socially accepted context for sexual relations and procreation.

Current Senegalese marriage patterns reflect diverse influences. These shape the contours of entry into union and the prevalence of endogamous and polygamous marriages. However, Westernization, through rising levels of education, urbanization, and the diffusion of modern ideas, is likely to induce new forms of marriage that depart significantly from the prevailing ones.

Entry into Union

As in most sub-Saharan African societies, marriage in Senegal involves more than only the bride and groom, but also their families and kinships. It is a multistage process generally sealed with the payment of dowry in the form of cash, cattle, and other goods of a symbolic nature. Often, however, dowry payment may be made by installments before and after the spouses have started living together (Meekers 1992). In low-income families,

such as those living in rural Senegal, dowry payment may involve saving over several years on cash earned from farming activities. With irregularities in rainfall, many young males from rural areas migrate to town to search for employment opportunities that would allow them to meet rising dowry levels.

Marriage is almost universal in Senegal. All nationally representative demographic surveys conducted since the 1980s have consistently shown that more than 90 percent of women get married by the age of fifty. Less than 1 percent of women remain single by the time they are fifty years old (Ndiaye et al. 1997).

Women usually enter marriage at a young age. The median age at first marriage for the late 1990s was estimated at eighteen years, which means that more than half of the women within the reproductive ages (fifteen to forty-nine years) marry by the time they are eighteen years of age (Ndiaye et al. 1997). In certain ethnic groups such as the Tukuler and Peulh of North and East Senegal, parents often give away their daughters for marriage when they are as young as eight to twelve. In such instances, sexual intercourse may occur several years after the marriage has been celebrated. This practice of early marriage is sustained by the need to reduce financial burden on the family (through dowry for the bride's family), strengthen ties between the families involved, and ensure that the young bride is a virgin.

The age gaps between husbands and wives is usually large. An in-depth study of the Senegalese marriage market shows that, on average, husbands are eight years older than their wives (Diop 1980). Given that younger generations in developing countries such as Senegal are always larger than the older ones, the age gaps imply that the number of potential brides is always larger than the number of grooms. These mismatches sustain the practice of endogamy and polygamy because celibacy is not socially accepted.

Endogamy

Endogamous marriages are those that occur between spouses who are related by blood. In Senegal, most endogamous marriages are between paternal and maternal cousins. The 1986 Senegalese Demographic and Health Survey data reveal that women first marrying do so with paternal or maternal cousins or other relations. About 70 percent of married women are related to their husbands. This pattern has not changed much since 1970, although there are variations among ethnic groups. The lowest prevalence of endogamous marriages (50% to 60%) are found among the Manding and Diola, who live in the southern and Eastern parts of the country, while the highest levels (between 65% and 80%) prevail among the Wolof, Pulaar, and Serer. In most cases, women are married to paternal cousins, except among the Serer, where preference is given to maternal cousins.

In Senegal, endogamy cannot be explained by the matrilineal or patrilineal nature of the society. One purely demographic factor is the large age differences between spouses. Another important factor that encourages and sustains endogamous marriage is the permanent quest for cohesion and close ties between families, which in turn contributes to marriage stability.

Polygamy

The most distinctive pattern of Senegalese marriage is polygamy, a marital state in which a man is married to more than one wife. In principle a man may have as many wives as he wishes, although most polygamous males follow the Islamic rule that limits the number of wives to four. Senegal has the highest polygamy rate—the percentage of polygamous marriages among all married couples—in West Africa: Close to half of the women are married to polygamous husbands. Even for the youngest generations (fifteen to nineteen years old), polygamy rates are about 25 percent, suggesting that about one in four women first marries into a polygamous union (Pison et al. 1995).

The main social factors underlying the high polygamy rates are religion, pronatalism, high mortality, and levirate. Having more than one wife is authorized under Islamic law, and men often invoke their religious beliefs to explain their practice of polygamy. In 1997, about one-third of married Senegalese men had more than one wife, with one in four married men having two wives and one in ten men married to more than two wives (Ndiaye et al. 1997). The bulk of the Senegalese population (70%) lives in rural areas, with agriculture as their main economic activity. Polygamous marriage is, therefore, the expression of men's desire to have a large number of children to help on the farm. In such settings where overall mortality rates are extremely high, couples have many children in order to ensure that a few of them to survive to the productive years and, thus, serve as old-age security for parents through intergenerational wealth transfers. Finally, levirate, the possibility of inheriting the wives of deceased brothers, is a common practice in Senegal, and this too has contributed to the observed high polygamy rates.

Although at the aggregate level, polygamy certainly contributes to larger family sizes, research has demonstrated that Senegalese women in polygamous unions have on average a lower number of children than their counterparts in monogamous marriages. Michel Garenne and Etienne van de Walle (1989), studying the Serer of central Senegal, explain these differentials by the fact that women in polygamous marriage exhibit lower than average frequency of sexual intercourse because a polygamous "husband has to distribute his sexual activity between his wives." Also, polygamous husbands are on average older and thus less fertile than monogamous men. It has been shown, however, that lower fertility of polygamous marriages may be due to infertility problems encountered by first wives. Ndiaye (1985) argues that monogamous husbands are often obliged to marry a second wife when the first wife is infertile.

Polygamy has had major influences on the living arrangements of Senegalese families. In rural areas, all wives usually live together with their polygamous husband in the same compound, a group of adjacent rooms with a common fence and entry. Typically, the husband spends a certain number of nights with each wife, and the wives rotate cooking and other household chores. These living arrangements lead to large average compound size (more than ten people per household) and to the cohabitation of several nuclear families. Almost one out of six compounds is formed by three cohabiting family members, and more than one-third of Senegalese families are neither the wife nor the children of the household head. In such households with more than one male, household headship is determined mainly by age—the elder male is usually designated as the head.

Impact of Westernization

Westernization, or the adoption of ideas and lifestyles from the developed world, is the major

A Senegalese family shares a meal together on the Ile de Goree. Western influence, spread mainly through education and the mass media, is affecting the marriage patterns of the Senegalese, but endogamy and polygamy are still widely practiced. OWEN FRANKEN/CORBIS

factor that has been reshaping the characteristics of Senegalese marriage systems. Westernization is diffused mainly through education, urbanization, and the mass media. New ideas publicizing the benefits of small families and late marriage, and those condemning polygamy, are major channels for change. Progress in education for women and rural-to-urban migration sustain these sociocultural shifts.

Since the mid-1970s, when the first nationally representative demographic and health data became available, the social norm of universal marriage has been progressively fading. In the late 1970s, national surveys showed that about 13 percent of women aged fifteen to forty-nine years were not married. This percentage increased to 19 percent in the late 1980s and has been estimated at 25 percent during the early 1990s (Ndiaye et al. 1997). This clear indication of lower values attached to marriage is corroborated by a rise in the age at first marriage. While the 1978 national World

Fertility Survey yielded a median age at first marriage of sixteen years, the corresponding figure from the 1997 national Demographic and Health Survey was eighteen years. These surveys do not show a marked downward trend in polygamy rates. However, there is a reason to believe that ongoing societal changes are working against the practice of polygamy, as suggested by a landmark official report that concluded that "polygamy is considered by educated women as being a barrier to their social aspirations" (République du Sénégal 1981, p. 81). Women's protests over polygamy are also reflected in the high divorce rates of first wives when their husbands marry a second wife. Philippe Antoine and colleagues (1998) provide evidence of this using retrospective survey data collected in Dakar in 1989.

Changes in marriage patterns in Senegal are also visible in the large differentials observed in the late 1990s between urban and rural areas, and between educated and noneducated women (Ndiaye et al. 1997). High polygamy and endogamy rates and early age at first marriage are more prevalent among rural and less-educated women.

Almost half of marriages in rural areas are endogamous, compared to 28 percent in urban areas. With respect to educational levels, the percentage of endogamous marriages decreases from 44 percent among women with no formal education to 26 percent among those with primary schooling. It then falls to 18 percent for women who have reached secondary school.

The polygamy rates exhibit the same patterns; half of married uneducated women live in polygamous unions, against one fourth for those with at least secondary school education. But the difference in polygamy rates between urban (40%) and rural areas (50%) is not substantial.

In rural areas, girls marry on average at sixteen years of age; the corresponding figure for urban areas is twenty years. The largest effect on age at first marriage remains formal schooling; women with no education and those with at least secondary education first marry at sixteen and twenty-three years, respectively.

The transition to late age at marriage and lower levels of polygamy and endogamy is irreversible given rising levels of urbanization and female education. This modern feature of Senegalese marriage systems will loosen the strength of kinship ties, facilitate the spread of the nuclear family, and thus hasten the emergence of a more individualistic society.

See also: ISLAM

Bibliography

Antoine, P.; Ouédraogo, D.; and Piché, V. (1998). *Trois générations de citadins au Sahel: Trente ans d'histoire sociale à Dakar et à Bamako.* Paris: l'Harmattan.

Diop, A. K. (1980). "Nuptialité et fécondité au Sénégal." Ph.D dissertation. Paris: Université René Descartes, Paris V.

Garenne, M., and van de Walle, E. (1989). "Polygyny and Fertility Among the Sereer of Senegal." *Population Studies* 43(2):267–283.

Gellar, S. (1995). *Senegal: An African Nation between Islam and the West.* Oxford, UK: Oxford University Press.

Meekers, D. (1992). "The Process of Marriage in African Societies." *Population and Development Review* 18(1):61–78.

Ndiaye, K. L. (1985). "Polygamy et fécondité." In *Nuptialité et fécondité au Sénégal,* ed. Y. Charbit and S. Ndiaye. Paris: Presses Universitaires de France.

Ndiaye, S.; Ayad, M.; and Gaye, A. (1997). *Enquête démographique et de santé (EDS-III) 1997.* Calverton: Macro International Inc.

Pison, G.; Hill, L; Cohen, B.; and Foote, K., eds. (1995). *Population Dynamics of Senegal.* Washington, DC: National Academy Press.

République du Sénégal (1981). *Enquête sénégalaise sur la fécondité, 1978 : Rapport national d'analyse.* Dakar: Ministère de l'Economie et des Finances, Direction de la Statistique.

Sow, F. (1985). "Muslim Families in Contemporary Black Africa." *Current Anthropology* 26(5):563–570.

PIERRE NGOM

SEPARATION ANXIETY

Separation anxiety is defined as feelings of negative emotions such as loss, loneliness, and sadness that are experienced by individuals when they are separated from an important person in their life. Separation anxiety is typically used to describe the reaction of an infant who is separated from a major caregiver such as the mother or father. Separation anxiety, however, has also been noted to occur at other times during an individual's life. For example, the term is used to describe parents' reactions to leaving their young infant (Hock, McBride, and Gnezda 1989). Separation anxiety may also be experienced, at any age, when a significant person in one's life is lost due to death.

Theoretically, separation anxiety in a young infant is considered to be a normal process of development which helps ensure the infant's survival (Bowlby 1969). According to the ethological theory, an infant experiencing a separation from a caregiver will produce behaviors such as crying, following, and calling, which have the goal of ending the separation from the caregiver and allowing the infant to stay in close proximity to the caregiver. By staying close to the caregiver the infant increases the likelihood that he or she will be nurtured and protected and therefore will survive.

The infant's cognitive development is important in the development of the infant's separation anxiety. The development of the infant's memory and the ability to recognize when someone is familiar—or unfamiliar—is a key component in the development of the infant's separation anxiety and protest. Infants show a strong preference for people with whom they are familiar. Once the infant can recognize a familiar caregiver the infant will protest the separation from that caregiver and show a wariness of people who are strangers.

Separation anxiety develops over the infant's first year of life. Initially, a young infant does not differentiate between those persons who are familiar and those who are unfamiliar and therefore shows no sign of anxiety during separations from their major caregivers. At this early age infants readily accept the interaction of strangers and do not protest separation from caregivers. At approximately seven months of age the infant begins to recognize caregivers and it is at this time that the infant will begin to express separation anxiety and direct proximity seeking behavior (e.g., cries, smiles, and coos) toward familiar caregivers (Shaffer and Emerson 1964).

When the infant becomes mobile he or she becomes more active in contact-seeking and separation protest behavior. With the development of creeping and crawling the young infant, instead of just calling and crying, will follow a major caregiver when he or she leaves the room. Ethological theory assumes that the development of separation anxiety serves a functional purpose of causing the now mobile child to stay in contact with the caregiver.

The overt manifestations of separation anxiety (e.g., crying, calling, and following) typically peak between twelve and eighteen months of age. As the toddler matures, usually after the child's second birthday, he or she begins to develop cognitive and behavioral means to cope with separations and separation anxiety decreases. Examples of methods used by older children to cope with these separations are maintaining a mental picture of their caregiver and keeping themselves busy during separations. Older children also are beginning to understand that separations are temporary and that their caregiver will return shortly.

The development of the infant's caregiver-directed separation protest and contact-seeking behavior coincides with the development of the infant's attachment to his or her major caregivers. It is over the course of the infant's first year that the quality of the infant's attachments to major caregivers develops. The quality of the infant's attachment to major caregivers does not influence the development of separation anxiety, but it may influence the infant's overt separation protest behaviors and the child's ability to cope during separations. Insecurely attached infants may have heightened or decreased levels of separation protest and their separation anxiety may not be reduced when their caregiver is present. Though infants who are securely attached to their caregivers also protest separation, their separation anxiety decreases with the presence of their caregiver (Ainsworth et al. 1978).

The infant's security of attachment originates within the interactions of the infant-caregiver dyad during the infant's first year of life. For example, when the caregiver is sensitive to the infant and responds appropriately to the infant, the infant will develop a secure attachment. A securely attached infant is confident that their caregiver will be available when they need the caregiver and separation anxiety is decreased. However, if the infant has experienced rejection from a caregiver or is unsure of the caregiver's responsiveness the infant may develop an insecure attachment. The insecurely attached infant's separation anxiety will be enhanced due to the infant's lack of confidence in the caregiver's availability.

The degree to which the infant experiences separation anxiety is influenced by many factors besides quality of attachment. For example, the caregiver's behavior immediately proceeding the separation will influence how long the infant protests the separation (Field et al. 1984). Preparing a child for the separation by letting the child know that the separation is going to occur and that the caregiver will return, instructing the child on what to do during the separation (e.g., play with the toys), and making the leave-taking short has been found to decrease overt signs of separation anxiety.

Infants also display greater separation anxiety when they have less experience with separation from their caregiver (Jacobson and Wille 1984). When an infant has multiple caregivers (e.g., mother, father, grandparents, and baby-sitters) less separation protest is observed. It is assumed that children with multiple caregivers are familiar with what occurs during separations, understand that these separations are temporary, and have learned how to cope with these separations. These children may also have developed attachments to multiple caregivers and/or may have learned to gain comfort from other adults.

The level of separation anxiety expressed by infants is also influenced by cultural practices. Typically, Japanese infants have little or no experience with maternal separation. Japanese mothers also give their infants their total attention and positive regard. Japanese infants have an immediate and negative response to separation from their mothers. These infants appear to have a high level of separation anxiety (Van Ijzendoorn and Sagi 1999).

Separation Anxiety Disorder

Though separation anxiety is considered to be part of normal development, when a young child's separation anxiety is severe and prolonged he or she may by diagnosed with *Separation Anxiety Disorder* (American Psychiatric Association 1994). Separation Anxiety Disorder is diagnosed when a child, under the age of eighteen years, shows excessive anxiety about separation from a primary attachment figure or home which lasts for at least four weeks. Some of the symptoms associated with this disorder are unrealistic worry that either the child or the caregiver will be harmed during separation, refusal to go to school, and becoming physically ill or complaining of illness before or during the separation. This disorder is estimated to occur in approximately 4 percent of children (Anderson et al. 1987). It is assumed that Separation Anxiety Disorder may manifest itself in other psychological disorders when the child becomes an adult; however, little research has been completed to support this hypothesis (Majcher and Pollack 1996).

The symptoms associated with Separation Anxiety Disorder may decrease the number of positive interactions that the child has with his or her parents. For example, a child's school refusal may lead to daily prolonged negative interactions, with the parent attempting to get the child up and ready for school and the child refusing to cooperate and complaining of physical illness as a means to avoid school. Parents may respond to school refusal with increased harshness and develop feelings of guilt because of their child's behavior and their inability to manage this behavior.

The possible causes of Separation Anxiety Disorder are diverse and it is often difficult for the therapist to determine the exact cause. Cases of Separation Anxiety Disorder have been noted due to prolonged parental separation (e.g., if parent or child is hospitalized) and death of a significant figure in the child's life (e.g., grandparent). In some cases, the parents have also been found to have experienced a high level of anxiety as a child. Though theory and research show a connection between separation anxiety and protest and the child's quality of attachment, research is still needed to determine if the quality of the child's attachment relationships has an impact on the development of Separation Anxiety Disorder (Greenberg 1999).

There are several treatment options available for children with Separation Anxiety Disorder. Research is still needed to determine the most effective method to treat this childhood disorder. Therapies used to treat Separation Anxiety Disorder include behavioral therapy and cognitive-behavioral therapy, which have been found to be effective in decreasing the level of anxiety and overt separation protest behaviors produced by children (Mash and Barkley 1998). Examples of behavioral and cognitive-behavioral therapy include rewards for appropriate behaviors, modeling of appropriate behavior, and systematic desensitization.

With systematic desensitization the child is exposed to a series of events with each event in this series eliciting more separation anxiety than the preceding event. The first event usually causes the child to experience very little separation anxiety, the next event would cause the child to experience a little more separation anxiety, and so forth. These events may be imagined by child, if they are old enough and have the cognitive ability to imagine events, or the environment is manipulated so that the child actually experiences the events. Starting with the least anxiety producing event (e.g., the child imagines his/her mother explaining that she will need to go to the store to get an item of food for dinner or the mother actually explains to the child that she will need to go to the store to get an item of food for dinner), the child is taken through relaxation steps or counter conditioning (child receives a positive reward) that leads to a decrease in the anxiety. Once the child is experiencing little or no anxiety to this stimulus the next separation anxiety producing event is presented.

Family therapy and pharmacological interventions have also been used to treat Separation Anxiety Disorder. Family therapy may include child management training and parent education. The parents are given information about the disorder, how to manage their child's reactions to separations and school refusal, and how to support their child's emotional needs. In most cases family therapy is provided together with individual therapy for the child. Pharmacological interventions for Separation Anxiety Disorder are relatively recent and are usually integrated with the other forms of therapy described above. More research is needed to determine the effectiveness of pharmacological interventions on Separation Anxiety Disorder (Allen, Leonard, and Swedo 1995).

Treatment for school refusal, one of the possible symptoms of separation anxiety, varies depending upon how quickly the child develops this symptom. For children who develop this symptom quickly, a method developed by Wallace Kennedy (1965) appears to be effective. Kennedy's approach is to get the child into school, keep them at school, and provide them with positive reinforcement for attending school as well as modeling appropriate behavior. For other children, the development of school refusal occurs over an extended period of time and many different factors may play a role in the development of this symptom. In these cases treatment usually consists of individual therapy for the child as well as family therapy.

See also: ANXIETY DISORDERS; ATTACHMENT: PARENT-CHILD RELATIONSHIPS; DEVELOPMENT: COGNITIVE; DEVELOPMENTAL PSYCHOPATHOLOGY; LONELINESS; SCHOOL PHOBIA AND SCHOOL REFUSAL; SEPARATION-INDIVIDUATION; SHYNESS: THERAPY: FAMILY RELATIONSHIPS; THERAPY: PARENT-CHILD RELATIONSHIPS

Bibliography

Ainsworth, M.; Blehar, M.; Waters, E.; and Wall, S. (1978). *Patterns of Attachment: A Psychological Study of the Strange Situation.* Hillsdale, NJ: Erlbaum.

Allen, A.; Leonard, H.; and Swedo, S. (1995). "Current Knowledge of Medications for the Treatment of Childhood Anxiety Disorders." *Journal of the American Academy of Child and Adolescent Psychiatry* 34:976–986.

American Psychiatric Association (1994). *Diagnostic and Statistical Manual of Mental Disorders,* 4th edition. Washington, DC: Author.

Anderson, J.; Williams, S.; McGee, R.; and Silva, P. (1987). "DSM-III Disorders in Preadolescent Children: Prevalence in a Large Sample from the General Population." *Archives of General Psychiatry* 44:69–76.

Bowlby, J. (1969). *Attachment and Loss: Attachment.* New York: Basic Books.

Field, T.; Gewirtz, J.; Cohen, D.; Garcia, R.; Greenberg, R.; and Collins, K. (1984). "Leave-Takings and Reunions of Infants, Toddlers, Preschoolers, and Their Parents." *Child Development* 55:628–635.

Greenberg, M. (1999). "Attachment and Psychopathology in Childhood." In *Handbook of Attachment: Theory, Research, and Clinical Applications,* ed. J. Cassidy and P. Shaver. New York: Guilford Press.

Hock, E.; McBride, S.; and Gnezda, M. T. (1989). "Maternal Separation Anxiety: Mother-Infant Separation from the Maternal Perspective." *Child Development* 60:793–802.

Jacobson, J., and Wille, D. (1984). "Influence of Attachment and Separation Experience on Separation Distress at 18 Months." *Developmental Psychology* 20:477–484.

Kennedy, W. (1965). "School Phobia: Rapid Treatment of 50 Cases." *Journal of Abnormal Psychology* 70:285–289.

Majcher, D., and Pollack, M. (1996). *Do They Grow Out of it? Long-Term Outcomes of Childhood Disorders.* Washington, DC: American Psychiatric Press.

Mash, E., and Barkley, R. (1998). *Treatment of Childhood Disorders.* New York: Guilford Press.

Schaffer, H. R., and Emerson, P. E. (1964). "The Development of Social Attachments in Infancy." *Monographs of the Society for Research in Child Development* 29(3):1–77.

Van Ijzendoorn, M., and Sagi, A. (1999). "Cross-Cultural Patterns of Attachment: Universal and Context Dimensions." In *Handbook of Attachment: Theory, Research, and Clinical Applications,* ed. J. Cassidy and P. Shaver. New York: Guilford Press.

DIANE E. WILLE

SEPARATION-INDIVIDUATION

Margaret Mahler (1897–1986) represents a group of ego psychologists whose interest focuses on the development of psychic structures, as outlined in Sigmund Freud's ([1923] 1990) structural theory, the id, ego, and superego. Mahler's interest in the developing ego centered on its development within the context of object relationships. *Object relations* refers to how experience with another comes to be represented in the mind. Mahler shifted the focus away from the Freudian emphasis on the gratification of instincts or biological needs as the basis for mental life, to an emphasis on how interpersonal relationships become internalized within the ego or self.

As a former pediatrician and child analyst, Mahler sought, through the study of normal development, to understand how inner representations of the self and other develop within the context of interpersonal interactions between the caregiver and child, resulting in an integrated sense of self. *Separation-individuation* is the name she gave to the process by which internal maps of the self and of others are formed. These experiential maps, or internal representations, are built up through interactions with caregivers during the period spanning birth to three years of age, and consist of both positive and negative aspects of experience within the relationship. According to Mahler, it is the ability to integrate frustrating and pleasurable aspects of experience with another person that leads to a stable sense of self that can tolerate fluctuating emotional states within the self and with others. The inability to integrate these aspects of experience can lead to psychopathology (Mahler, Pine, and Bergman 1975).

Mahler and her research team studied caregivers and their children, in a naturalistic setting, from birth through three years of age and noted age-specific, regularly occurring behaviors that marked changes in the child's behavior in relationship to the caregiver and to the outside world. Mahler divides the early forerunners of the separation-individuation process into two phases, the *autistic* state and the *symbiotic* state. The separation-individuation process proper is broken down into four sub-phases: *differentiation, practicing, rapprochement,* and *on the road to object constancy. Separation* refers to the child's emergence from a symbiotic state with the caregiver, while *individuation* consists of individual achievements and characteristics that define identity.

Precursors to Differentiation

Normal autism. During the autistic stage—the first four weeks of life—the infant spends more time in sleeplike states than in states of arousal (Mahler 1967). The infant is thought to operate in a closed system, not distinguishing inner from outer, and to be protected by a *stimulus barrier,* a hypothesized protective shield against overwhelming stimulation. Experience centers on internal stimuli such as hunger, elimination, and bodily comforts. Infant life is concentrated on the satisfaction of needs and on the reduction of unpleasant tensions that relate to these internal states. The caregiver's gratification of the baby's needs is central, and it is out of this experience of gratification that the infant begins to differentiate "good" pleasurable experiences and "bad" painful experiences (Mahler 1967). At this stage feelings are islands of experience not yet held together by a sense of self or other.

Attachment, an intense emotional bond with the mother, begins to consolidate experience for the infant. The ability to attach to the caregiver and others is essential for emotional health. The absence of attachment-seeking behaviors such as smiling, reaching out, and anticipatory nursing postures are felt to be the result of constitutional or basic cognitive defects that interfere with the infant's ability to organize experience. Clinically, the absence of these behaviors can also be tied to profound environmental stress (Mahler 1952; Rutter 1971). Children who are unable to form attachments, or whose attachments have been ruptured though separations or abuse, are withdrawn and suffer from depression (Spitz 1965).

Clinical issues include panic states arising over loss of the self, or, alternatively, a wish to deny any differences between self and other (Pine 1979). The failure to establish an attachment is often seen in psychopathic characters where there is simultaneously an inability to keep rules, a lack of empathy for others, and a craving for affection, along with an inability to form lasting relationships (Bowlby 1944).

Normal symbiosis. The normal symbiotic stage, starting in the third to fourth week, results from maturation of sensory processes. The infant shows increased awareness of the outside world, as indicated by states of *alert inactivity*. During this period there is an increased responsiveness to the caregiver, who acts as an *auxiliary ego* in regulating internal states. Memory traces of the caretaker's ministrations help the infant become aware of the differences between inside and outside. *Mutual cueing,* the way in which the caretaker selectively responds to the infant's needs, sets up a process of interpersonal relating that leads to the development of a core concept of the self (Mahler and Furer 1963). The *social smile* is the developmental milestone of this period, indicating the infant's attachment to its caregiver.

Clinically, disturbances in ongoing consistent care can lead to deficits in the organization of the self. In the absence of this care, infants may precociously develop their own resources defensively, developing a *false self* (Winnicott 1953). Attachment is affected when there is difficulty in establishing self-object differentiation. Individuals with these issues lack a core sense of self and manifest a defensive detachment to others, low self-esteem, and a grandiose self structure, that is, a pseudo self-sufficiency to compensate for a lack of connection with another (Horner 1984).

The First Subphase: Differentiation

The first stage of differentiation is called *hatching* and spans four to ten months of age. Hatching, or *psychological birth,* is the phase in which the infant differentiates out of the symbiotic unit (Mahler, Pine, and Bergman 1975). It is characterized by a more alert state, with distinct periods of wakefulness. At about six months the infant begins to engage in exploratory behaviors of the caregiver, a process Mahler describes as *customs inspection* (Mahler, Pine, and Bergman 1975). This consists of visual and tactile exploration of the caregiver's face and body. It is the beginning of peek-a-boo games and of physical separation through crawling away, venturing back, and playing nearby. Throughout this process infants engage in a *visual checking back,* which serves the developmental function of discriminating the familiar from the unfamiliar (Mahler, Pine, and Bergman 1975). This is seen in *stranger anxiety,* the developmental landmark of this period. The *transitional object,* a soft blanket or other object that the infant chooses for comfort in the absence of the caretaker, becomes important

at this period of separation from the caregiver since it represents the comforting functions of the caretaker that the infant can now use on its own terms (Winnicott, 1953). It is important that the mother be available to the infant during these early attempts at separation so that the infant can build up a *confident expectation* and *basic trust* in the caregiver and in the outside world (Benedek 1938; Erikson 1950).

Clinically, issues arising from this period involve borderline phenomena, which are characterized by an unstable sense of self, unstable relationships with others, and chaotic, fluctuating internal states, with chronic feelings of emptiness. There is intense separation anxiety, the inability to be alone, and the constant concern about the availability of others to help manage intense internal tension (Horner 1984).

The Second Subphase: Practicing

The practicing subphase occurs from about six to ten months and up to eighteen months of age. It represents a shift to more autonomous functioning and is divided into two parts, early practicing and practicing proper (Mahler, Pine, and Bergman 1975). In the early practicing subphase, which overlaps differentiation, the infant is able to move away from the caretaker by crawling, climbing, and pulling itself up and holding on to a supporting object. During its explorations, the infant checks back to the caregiver to *emotionally refuel,* using the caretaker as a *secure base*—in other words, is reassured about the availability of the caretaker (Bowlby 1958). During practicing proper, the infant is upright and walking, seemingly impervious to bumps and falls. This period has been called the toddler's *love affair with the world,* in that a sense of omnipotence prevails with regard to newfound skills and functioning (Greenacre 1957). Games reflect a growing awareness of separateness and also the need to be reassured of the caregiver's availability for support, seen in games in which the infant runs away only to be quickly caught. Mahler (1972) noted that children at this age often show a preoccupation, an attempt to create a mental image of their caregivers when they are not available. The major shifts in cognition from sensorimotor to representational thought, and the beginnings of language and symbolic play, add to the child's increased autonomy in interacting with the outside world (Piaget [1936] 1992). The achievement of this period is a healthy sense of narcissism and a beginning sense of self-esteem, fueled by pleasure in one's own abilities and autonomous functioning.

Clinical issues arising from this level of development often reflect issues related to premature object loss. Instead of taking pleasure and delight in their newfoundskills, children worry over the loss of the primary object whose care they need. In narcissistic phenomena, there are disturbances in the ability to maintain self-esteem. Individuals often have an inordinate need for outside validation and admiration of their abilities to reassure themselves of their value. They often create an inflated sense of importance—of being "special"—and feel grandiose as a defense against not feeling valued. These feelings also defensively ward off the need for others, while simultaneously craving constant admiration and reassurance from them. Narcissistic individuals feel entitled, yet dependent on others, with whom they often demonstrate a lack of empathy and concern. Disappointment in others leads to rage.

Phase Three: Rapprochement

The period of rapprochement spans the ages of approximately fifteen to twenty-four months and is characterized behaviorally by an active approach back to the caregiver. Children begin to realize the limits of their omnipotence and have a new awareness of their separateness and the separateness of the caregiver. Increases in cognition and motor development lead to *ambitendency*—shadowing and darting away from the caretaker. These behaviors reflect the child's simultaneous need for autonomy and need for support. An increase in aggression is seen in behaviors such as pushing away while whining and clinging. These behaviors represent the struggle to reconcile the good and bad aspects of the self and the other, with the need of the other. Toilet training often begins at this stage, leading to further struggles with autonomy and control. The verbal *no,* the developmental milestone of this phase, acts as a metaphor for the issues of autonomy that characterize this stage (Erikson 1950).

Clinically, the rapprochement period is often cited in conjunction with borderline phenomena, which are characterized by unstable inner states, unstable relationships, and a fragile sense of self. In borderline phenomena there are feelings of loss

of support and approval of the other, as well as aggression and anger which arise out of intense feelings of vulnerability and dependency. The major defenses employed in borderline phenomena are those of splitting and projection. Splitting keeps the "good" and loved aspects of the other separate from the "bad" and hated aspects of the other. Projection is used to rid oneself of felt unwanted "bad" aspects of the self by attributing those unwanted parts to another. Internally, because of the lack of integration of the good and bad internal representations of the self and other, individuals with this defensive structure are subject to fluctuating internal states, feelings of disorganization, and low self-esteem.

Phase Four: Consolidation of Individuality, or on the Road to Object Constancy

This period spans the ages of twenty-four to thirty-six months and involves all aspects of previous stages, in particular the trust and confidence of the symbiotic phase (Mahler 1972). There are advances in cognition with representational thought and the use of language. Children have an inner picture of the caretaker and their relationship with the caretaker, which has formed has formed as a result of the soothing, gratifying, and organizing functions that the caretaker provides (Tolpin 1971). Internalization is the process of recovering what has been lost in the actual relationship with the mother, so that the toddlers carry around an internal picture of a gratifying mother that is now part of their internal structure (Mahler, Pine, and Bergman 1975). The developmental achievement is an individual identity with stable internal representations of self and others. This achievement is a prerequisite for the capacity to form one-to-one relationships where separation is not abandonment and closeness does not represent engulfment.

The clinical issues seen in this stage of developmental have to do with ambivalence toward caretakers and their functions, and with how needs have been met or not met. At times there can be depression associated with threatened object loss and the sense that important needs may never be met (Horner 1984).

Fathers

The role of the father changes during the different phases of separation-individuation.

In the early stages of homeostasis he provides a complement to the mother in understanding the infant's behavior patterns and, in his help with soothing and regulating behaviors, offers an added stimulus to the baby's experience. During the symbiotic period, the father is available as another love object, adding depth to new sets of experience. In the differentiation phase, the father engages his infant in interactive ways that complement the mother's more comforting functions. During practicing, fathers are the *significant other* that help modulate aggression and offer additional security as a base to return to in the toddler's forays out and back. Fathers also provide another gender for comparison and identification during the period where gender differences are being discovered. The availability of the father during rapprochement helps the child organize and modulate feelings of frustration and aggression, adding to emotional and cognitive growth. By setting limits while supporting autonomous strivings, fathers help children tolerate and integrate ambivalent feeling states (Greenspan 1982). In general, fathers' play and interaction with their children tends to be more active and exciting as compared with mother's soothing. When infant care is divided between both parents, comforting and active interactions may be associated with both. The experience of personality differences with both caregivers gives the infant varied experiences, allowing them a fuller expression of emotions and participation with others (Burlingham 1973).

Critique of Mahler's Theory

Critiques of Mahler's theory of separation-individuation come from the fields of infant and attachment research (Lyons-Ruth 1991; Stern 1985). Infant research demonstrates that infants are pre-wired for relatedness from birth and do not experience an autistic or symbiotic phase. From birth infants experience a subjective sense of self and other from which experience is organized, structured, and restructured according to cognitive and affective developmental levels (Stern 1985). Attachment theorists also cast doubt upon the validity of the symbiotic phase, pointing to infants' readiness to interact from birth with evolutionary behaviors such as crying, sucking, and smiling that elicit the caregiver's attention and care. (Bowlby 1969). There are points of convergence between Mahler and attachment theorists. The concepts of *internal working models* and *self-other representations* both demonstrate how early relationships become internalized and form expectations of relationships in general (Main, Kaplan, Cassidy 1985). Similarly, both Mahler's concept of *emotional refueling* and Bowlby's notion of the *secure base* underscore the need for the caregiver's availability during exploratory behavior. They come to different conclusions, however, regarding behaviors seen from nine to eighteen months. Mahler sees the practicing and rapprochement phases as characterized by active separations, with ambivalence toward reunions with the caregiver as a threat to emerging autonomy. Attachment theorists, on the other hand, see this period as an increase in the awareness of and interest in the caregiver's availability during exploratory behaviors. Infants seek proximity to caregivers, as opposed to the clinging, ambivalence, and aggression described by Mahler. To attachment theorists these behaviors represent problematic interactions between infant and caregiver and characterize problems in the quality of the attachment (Lyons-Ruth 1991; Tyson and Tyson 1990).

Cross-Cultural Issues

Cross-cultural studies attest to the normality and universality of attachment (van IJzendoorn and Sagi 1999). However, there are variations within and across cultures in how attachment behaviors are viewed (Matsumoto and Lynch 1994). The achievement of separateness and independence spelled out in Mahler's theory reflects the value of a separate self, functioning independently of others, a view characteristic of Western cultures. In non-Western cultures, however, interdependence and connection to others are valued. Conscious experience focuses on the intersubjective awareness of the self with others. Self-esteem is connected to the ability to fit in and to promote cultural tasks that keep relationships harmonious. In contrast, conscious experience in Western culture focuses on the subjective awareness of the self, with less attention paid to others' subjective states. Similarly, self-esteem is tied to the achievement of individual goals. Cross-cultural perspectives shed light on how culture shapes the ways the self, in its relationship to others, is defined (Matsumoto, Kitayama, and Markus 1994).

Conclusion

While many of Mahler's theoretical formulations of infant mental life have been revised by infant and attachment research, Mahler's influence has been far-reaching. Her pioneering observational studies alerted analytic and developmental theorists to the importance of the infant-caregiver relationship in the development of the self. Her clinical observations in early childhood have led to new understandings in the disturbances of the self, seen in psychotic, narcissistic, and borderline phenomena. Theoretically, she shifted the focus away from attachment as an emotional connection occurring from the satisfaction of hunger and other biological needs, by placing relationships in a central role in development. The task now is to continue the revision and extension of psychoanalytic thought in light of infant and attachment research. Researchers will then be in a better position to understand how the self evolves and develops within the cultural contexts that shape its development.

See also: ATTACHMENT: PARENT-CHILD RELATIONSHIPS; BOUNDARY DISSOLUTION; CHILDHOOD, STAGES OF: INFANCY; CHILDHOOD, STAGES OF: MIDDLE CHILDHOOD; CHILDHOOD, STAGES OF: PRESCHOOL; CHILDHOOD, STAGES OF: TODDLERHOOD; CHILDREN OF ALCOHOLICS; DEVELOPMENT: SELF; FATHERHOOD; MOTHERHOOD; SEPARATION ANXIETY

Bibliography

Benedek, T. (1938). "Adaptation to Reality in Early Infancy." *Psychoanalytic Quarterly* 7:200–214.

Bowlby, J. (1944). "Forty-Four Juvenile Thieves: Their Characters and Home Life." *International Journal of Psychoanalysis* 39:211–221

Bowlby, J. (1958). "The Nature of the Child's Tie to his Mother." *International Journal of Psychoanalysis* 39:350–373

Bowlby, J. (1969). *Attachment and Loss,* Vol. 1: *Attachment.* New York: Basic Books.

Brody, S. (1982). "Psychoanalytic Theories of Infant Development." *Psychoanalytic Quarterly* 51:526–597.

Burlingham, D. (1973). "The Preoedipal Infant-Father Relationship." *The Psychoanalytic Study of the Child* 28:23–47.

Erikson, E H. (1950). *Childhood and Society.* New York: Norton.

Freud, S. ([1923] 1990). *The Ego and the Id. Standard Edition,* ed. J. Strachey, trans J. Riviere. New York: Norton.

Greenacre, P. (1957). "The Childhood of the Artist: Libidinal Phase Development and Giftedness." *Psychoanalytic Study of the Child* 12:47–72. Reprinted in *Emotional Growth,* Vol. 2. New York: International Universities Press.

Greenspan, S. I. (1982). "The Second Other: The Role of the Father in Early Personality Formation and the Dyadic-Phallic Phase of Development." In *Father and Child,* ed. S. H. Cath, A. R. Gurwitt, and J. M. Ross. Boston: Little Brown & Company.

Horner, A. J. (1984). *Object Relations and the Developing Ego in Therapy.* Northvale, NJ: Jason Aronson.

Lyons-Ruth, K (1991). "Rapprochement or Approchement: Mahler's Theory Reconsidered from the Vantage Point of Recent Research on Early Attachment Relationships." *Psychoanalytic Psychology* 8:1–23.

Main, M.; Kaplan, N.; and Cassidy, J. (1985). "Security in Infancy, Childhood, and Adulthood: A Move to the Level of Representation." In *Growing Points of Attachment Theory and Research,* ed. I. Bretherton and E. Waters. *Monographs of the Society of Research in Child Development* 50 (1–2, Serial No. 209):66–104.

Mahler, M. (1952). "On Child Psychosis and Schizophrenia: Autistic and Symbiotic Infantile Psychoses." *Psychoanalytic Study of the Child* 7:286–305.

Mahler, M. (1967). "On Human Symbiosis and the Vicissitudes of Individuation." In *The Selected papers of Margaret Mahler,* Vol. 2: *Separation-Individuation.* Northvale, NJ: Jason Aronson.

Mahler, M. (1972). "On the First Three Subphases of the Separation-Individuation Process." In *The Selected Papers of Margaret Mahler,* Vol. 2: *Separation-Individuation.* Northvale, NJ: Jason Aronson.

Mahler, M., and Furer, M. (1963). "Certain Aspects of the Separation-Individuation Phase." *Psychoanalytic Quarterly* 32:1–14.

Mahler, M. S., Pine, F.; and Bergman, A. (1975). *The Psychological Birth of the Human Infant*; New York: Basic Books.

Matsumoto, D.; Kitayama, S.; and Markus, H. (1994). "Culture and the Self: How Cultures Influence the Way We View Ourselves." In *People,* ed. D. Matsumoto. Pacific Grove, CA: Brooks/Cole.

Matsumoto, D. , and Lynch, M. (1994). "Developmental Psychology." In *People,* ed. D. Matsumoto. Pacific Grove, CA: Brooks/Cole.

Piaget, J. ([1936] 1992) *The Origins of Intelligence in Children.* Madison, CT: International Universities Press.

Pine, F. (1979). "On the Pathology of the Separation-Individuation Process as Manifested in Later Clinical Work: An Attempt at Delineation." *International Journal of Psychoanalysis* 69:225–242.

Rutter, M.(1971). *Maternal Deprivation Reassessed.* Harmondsworth, Middlesex, UK: Penguin.

Spitz, R.A. (1965). *The First Year of Life: A Psychoanalytic Study of Normal and Deviant Development of Object Relations.* New York: International Universities Press.

Stern, D. (1985). *The Interpersonal World of the Infant.* New York: Basic Books.

Tolpin, M. (1971). "On the Beginnings of a Cohesive Self: An Application of the Concept of Transmuting Internalization to the Study of Transitional Objects and Signal Anxiety." *The Psychoanalytic Study of the Child* 26:316–352.

Tyson, P., and Tyson, R. (1990). *Psychoanalytic Theories of Development: An Integration.* New Haven, CT: Yale University Press.

Van IJzendoorn, M.H., and Sagi, A. (1999). "Cross-Cultural Patterns of Attachment: Universal and Contextual Dimensions." In *Handbook of Attachment: Theory, Research, and Clinical Applications,* ed. J. Cassidy and P. R. Shaver. New York: Guilford Press.

Winnicott, D. W. (1953). "Transitional Objects and Transitional Phenomena; A Study of the First Not-Me Possession." *International Journal of Psychoanalysis* 34: 89–97.

MERYL J. BOTKIN

SEX ROLES

See FAMILY ROLES; GENDER; GENDER IDENTITY

SEXUAL COERCION

See CHILD ABUSE: SEXUAL ABUSE; RAPE

SEXUAL COMMUNICATION

COUPLE RELATIONSHIPS *Sandra Metts*

PARENT-CHILD RELATIONSHIPS *James Jaccard*

COUPLE RELATIONSHIPS

The notion that relational partners can talk their way to better sex is a common theme in the print media of U.S. society. Even a cursory review of the

article titles in popular women's and men's magazines reveals an array of communication "do's and don'ts" for sex talk in the bedroom. For example, consider the following titles:

- "Pillow-talk Taboos" (*Cosmopolitan,* January 2001).
- "6 Things He's Scared to Tell You" (*Cosmopolitan,* January 2001).
- "Dirty Talk 101" (*Redbook,* September 2000).
- "Blab Your Way to Better Sex" (*Cosmopolitan,* August 2000).
- "Sex Signals: Give Him a Clue" (*Cosmopolitan,* July 1998).
- "Sex Talk Made Easy" (*Mademoiselle,* September 1997).
- "The Sexiest Things You Can Say in Bed" (*Redbook,* September 1996).
- "Let's Talk About Sex, Baby" (*Muscle and Fitness,* June 1996).
- "Talking Dirty" (*Glamour,* April 1996).
- "How to Really Talk to a Man About Sex" (*Glamour,* October 1995).
- "How to Ask for a Blow Job" (*Playboy,* January 1999).

The assumption that communicating to one's partner about sex can facilitate more mutually satisfying sexual activity is a reasonable assumption. Ironically, the need to address this issue is necessitated to some degree by the idealized depictions of sexual episodes in film and print fiction. In most depictions, when two people are in love (or at least sexually attracted to each other), they simply fall into each other's arms and with words unspoken achieve unparalleled sexual fulfillment. In reality, however, the needs of two people may not be in perfect harmony and the respective visions of what counts as satisfying sexual activity may be quite different. Hence, the advice offered in popular magazines for how to talk about sex seems to offer some degree of guidance for couples who might feel the need to improve their sexual communication. In the view of some social scientists (e.g., Simon and Gagnon 1986, 1987; Metts and Spitzberg 1996), when the sexual script portrayed in a culture's messages and images does not provide sufficient detail about how to enact a sexual episode at the interpersonal level, people will seek ways to fill in the missing information.

Unfortunately, the advice given in magazines, in self-help books, and on talk shows is largely simplistic and formulaic. It does not account for the full scope of what the term sexual communication includes, the complexity of how effective sexual communication might be accomplished, and how it affects, or is affected by, other relationship elements (e.g., overall satisfaction in the relationship). The purpose of this entry is to present an overview of the research conducted by social scientists and clinicians who carefully and systematically study the processes and consequences of sexual communication.

Areas of Research in Sexual Communication

Early stages of relationships. Some scholars are interested in how sexual scripts (on the cultural level) guide interactions in newly forming or potentially sexual relationships (for a review see Metts and Spitzberg 1996). For example, studies of flirting and the negotiation of initial sexual involvement can be found under the general rubric of sexual communication. This area of research suggests that, in most cases, these episodes are mutually enacted and proceed without incident. Flirting enables people to display their interest in another person and to determine whether their attraction is reciprocated. Sexual negotiation enables people to determine whether and to what degree they will participate in sexual activity.

On occasion, however, these episodes are miscued in some way and the episode becomes problematic (Frith and Kitzinger 1997). For example, when flirting is done inappropriately (e.g., as a display of power in the workplace) and/or is persistent but not reciprocated, it can take the form of sexual harassment (Bingham, 1991; Keyton 1996). Likewise, the negotiation of sexual involvement can become problematic. Given the role of men in many cultures as sexual initiator and the role of women as sexual "gatekeeper," women sometimes adopt a communication strategy of saying "no" when they are, in fact, willing to engage in sexual activity. Charlene Muehlenhard and her colleagues (Muehlenhard and Hollabaugh 1988; Muehlenhard and McCoy 1991) refer to this practice as "token resistance" and suggest that it may be employed by women to avoid appearing "easy" or promiscuous. Indeed, research suggests that this practice is not limited to U.S. women. In a cross-cultural study of

sexual attitudes and behaviors, Susan Sprecher and her colleagues (1994) found that almost 40 percent of U.S. and Japanese women reported using token resistance at least once, and almost 60 percent of Russian women reported using token resistance at least once. Although token resistance is not necessarily problematic, it can sometimes be confused with a sincere expression of intent not to engage in sexual intercourse. When a woman says "no" to sex and means it, but a man interprets it as token resistance and continues to pursue sexual activity, negotiation is no longer collaborative but coercive (Krahe, Scheinberger-Olwig, and Kolpin 2000). In these instances his continued pursuit becomes sexual intimidation, aggression, and may even lead to date rape (Abbey 1991; Muehlenhard 1989).

Sexual communication and health. Other scholars who work within the realm of sexual communication direct their attention to questions about how effective communication can contribute to sexual health. As the rates of sexually transmitted diseases, especially HIV and AIDS, continue to rise, the ability to engage in open dialogue about safer sex practices becomes increasingly important (Amaro and Raj 2000; Quina et al. 2000). In particular, scholars in this area explore the types of communication skills necessary to introduce the topic of safer sex with a new partner (Cline, Johnson, and Freeman 1992) and to convince a possibly reluctant partner to use a condom (De Bro, Campbell, and Peplau 1994). These scholars note that a number of challenges face sexually active individuals who wish to practice safer sex but are given little guidance from cultural level scripts in how this might be done (Edgar and Fitzpatrick 1993). For example, to explicitly and unequivocally insist that condoms be used can imply that the other person is a sexual health risk or that oneself is a sexual health risk. Or, to avoid open discussion of condom use until the passionate moments just prior to sexual intercourse may compromise the levels of arousal for one or both partners. It is not surprising that the types of strategies used by sexually active individuals tend to moderate the directness of the request, for example, by hinting first, embedding it within a humorous exchange, making references to the importance of the relationship or concerns for mutual well being, and providing or offering assistance with the condom (Metts and Cupach 1991), or by incorporating condoms as one element of erotic play (Adelman 1992).

Sexual communication in established relationships. The term sexual communication is, perhaps, most often used in scholarly and everyday discourse to refer to the range of expressive behaviors we find in established couples, both dating and married, that enables them to achieve satisfying sexual relationships. The research tends to focus on two areas: the terms or sexual vocabulary that partners use to discuss sex, and the types of communication skills that are needed to achieve mutually satisfying sexual activity.

Research findings suggest that men and women use different terms to describe aspects of their sexual experience. For example, when speaking to each other, men seem to communicate frequently about a wide range of sexual experience, but with a vocabulary that lacks terms for the quality of the experience. They also tend to use words that are referred to as *power slang* (Sanders and Robinson 1979; Simkins and Rinck 1982). By contrast, females discuss sex less often in same gender groups and seem to prefer clinical and/or "cute" sexual slang (Sanders and Robinson 1979; Simkins and Rinck 1982). These differences in vocabularies for talking about sex may influence early patterns of sexual talk in heterosexual dating couples. When men use sexual terms, they may sound rough, demeaning, or non-romantic to women; when women use sexual terms, they may sound too cute, silly, or clinical (non-erotic or impersonal) (Cornog 1986; Simkins and Rinck 1982). Thus, the intent to be open about the sexual relationship may be subverted by the need to first build a common vocabulary. This is often accomplished by the creation of what scholars call a couple's unique *personal idioms,* especially those idioms for genitalia, sexual rituals, and routines (Bell, Buerkel-Rothfuss, and Gore 1987). Because these idioms are spontaneously and jointly created, they represent a couple's shared meanings within their sexual relationship.

Considerable scholarly attention has been directed to the question of how couples use (or fail to use) communication to facilitate the accomplishment of mutually satisfying sexual encounters. One approach to this question is to assess the extent to which partners disclose information about their sexual attitudes and preferences to each other (Cupach and Metts 1991; Metts and Cupach 1989). Based on the findings in this research, some scholars suggest

that couples may share a general agreement about their sexual relationship (or believe they do), but may not have fully disclosed their sexual likes, and even less fully disclosed their sexual dislikes to their partner. In a study of dating couples in college, Sandra Byers and Stephanie Demmons (1999) confirmed their assumption that individuals were not necessarily fully disclosive about their sexual likes and dislikes, but also demonstrated that as sexual self-disclosure increased, so too did sexual satisfaction (see also, Ross, Clifford, and Eisenman 1987).

A second approach to the question of how couples use communication to accomplish satisfying sexual encounters shifts the focus from the individual level of self-disclosure to the dynamics of the couple. Typical of this approach, for example, is the position of Anthony D'Augelli and Judith D'Augelli (1985) who argue that people not only need to be able to express their own needs, describe behaviors that increase or inhibit their arousal, and indicate when sexual behaviors are being performed successfully, but also need to be able to solicit this same information from their partner. It is important that they must also be able to accept feedback from their partner without defensiveness or resentment. Engaging in this type of open communication about sex requires high levels of trust and acceptance. It is not surprising that much of the research in this area explores the associations between a couple's satisfaction with their sexual communication and their satisfaction in the relationship. Several of these studies are described in the following section.

Sexual Communication and Other Relationship Variables

Research on relationship satisfaction has found strong and consistent associations between sexual satisfaction, sexual frequency, and relationship satisfaction (for a review, see Christopher and Sprecher 2000). Interestingly, this association seems to be true in sexually conservative cultures as well, such as married couples in China (Renaud, Byers, and Pan 1997) and India (Kumar 1995). Although studies that also include measures of sexual communication and satisfaction with sexual communication are less common, in general they indicate that the quality of communication about sex is related to sexual satisfaction and the overall quality of the relationship. For example, in a study of married

As couples build sexual relationships they need to develop a common vocabulary. This is often accomplished by the creation of unique personal idioms, *especially idioms for genitalia, sexual rituals, and routines.* MARK HANAUER/ CORBIS

college students, William Cupach and Jamie Comstock (1990) found that sexual communication satisfaction contributes to sexual satisfaction, which in turn increases dyadic adjustment. In a study comparing couples who were in marriage counseling to couples who were not, John Banmen and Noelle Vogel (1985) found that inhibited sexual communication was associated with marital distress. In a similar comparison of couples who were attending sex therapy clinics with couples who were not, Alan Chesney and his colleagues (1981) found that the two groups differed significantly on measures of general communication quality, sexual communication, and dyadic adjustment. Lawrence Wheeless and Lonnie Parsons (1995) found that when persons in dating relationships had high levels of apprehension about sending or receiving sexual messages, they also had lower sexual communication satisfaction. In a study of immigrant and nonimmigrant families living in Australia, Ludwig Geismar (1984) found that ethnicity had little effect on sexual communication, but that verbal communication focused on goals and problems was related to a more satisfying sexual relationship.

Taken together, these representative studies underscore the complicated role of expressive and receptive communication skills in sexual communication. They suggest that sexual communication increases sexual satisfaction only to the extent that it is positive and rewarding to the couple. And this

point brings us back to the advice columns in popular magazines. The suggestion to "talk dirty in bed" or to role play sexual fantasies may work for some couples, but for others who have incorporated traditional sex role scripts into their marriage, these practices may be extremely uncomfortable (Cado and Leitenberg 1990). This discomfort may serve to inhibit, rather than facilitate, sexual enjoyment. Moreover, these studies suggest that sexual communication is not only associated with sexual satisfaction, but also with overall relationship satisfaction and adjustment. Because this association is reciprocal, it means that happy couples communicate in ways that make sex enjoyable and thereby further enhance (or maintain) the satisfaction in their relationship. Unfortunately, it also means that when couples are unhappy, they tend to have less effective sexual communication (either as cause or effect) and less enjoyable and less frequent sexual activity, which in turn contribute to less overall satisfaction in the relationship. The cycle is not an easy one to break and some couples seek the intervention of marital or sex therapy to help them develop more effective communication skills (Chesney et al. 1981; Cooper and Stoltenberg 1987).

Conclusion

This entry has attempted to foreground both the complexity and the importance of sexual communication in dating and married relationships. Although early phases of sexual intimacy are relatively constrained by shared culture scripts, as relationships develop, couples find it increasingly necessary to develop their unique interpersonal sexual script. In order to do this, they need to be able and willing to express their own sexual preferences and to appreciate the sexual preferences of their partner (i.e., the intrapsychic or personal level script). When such efforts fail, relationship quality diminishes. Scholarly research has provided substantial information about how this process works, but much remains to be done. Of particular importance is the need to complement the wealth of existing cross-sectional data with longitudinal data (see Christopher and Sprecher 2000). Following the same couples over time would provide researchers with greater detail about the direction of causality (e.g., does poor sexual communication cause lower relationship satisfaction or vice versa?) as well as greater detail about how over time couples discover the types of nonverbal and verbal messages that accomplish their sexual goals without doing collateral damage to the self-esteem of their partner. In addition, greater attention must be directed to those couples who find themselves in the difficult position of negotiating their sexual relationship while at the intersection of different and possibly competing cultural mandates. The work of Jung Ah Song, M. Betsy Bergen, and Walter R. Schumm (1995), investigating the sexual and communicative challenges of Korean couples who have immigrated to the United States, is an example of this type of research.

Finally, this entry has also raised the issue of sexual communication as a critical factor in controlling the level of sexual involvement in dating relationships and implementing safer sex practices. Again, existing research provides extensive information about how couples attempt to manage these episodes. However, there is a critical need to know more about these practices in non-Western cultures, particularly those that privilege male power and status. The recently published research of Brent Wolff, Ann Blanc, and Anastasia Gage (2000) on the negotiation of sexual activity in Uganda, of Bodil Frederiksen (2000) on the transformation of the family system in Kenya, and of Caroline Osella and Filippo Osella (1998) on friendship and flirting in South India are promising contributions. More research of this type will help scholars and practitioners understand the extent to which aspects of sexual communication processes and outcomes are culture-specific, cross-cultural, and subject to historical and political change.

See also: ATTRACTION; COMMUNICATION: COUPLE RELATIONSHIPS; DATING; DECISION MAKING; INFIDELITY; MARITAL QUALITY; MARITAL SEX; SEXUAL COMMUNICATION: PARENT-CHILD RELATIONSHIPS; SEXUAL DYSFUNCTION; SEXUALITY; SEXUALITY IN ADULTHOOD; SEXUALLY TRANSMITTED DISEASES; THERAPY: COUPLE RELATIONSHIPS

Bibliography

Abbey, A. (1991). "Misperceptions as an Antecedent of Acquaintance Rape: A Consequence of Ambiguity in Communication between Men and Women." In *Acquaintance Rape: The Hidden Crime*, ed. A. Parrot and L. Bechhofer. New York: Wiley.

Adelman, M. B. (1992). "Healthy Passions: Safer Sex as Play." In *AIDS: A Communication Perspective*, ed. T. Edgar, M. A. Fitzpatrick, and V. S. Freimuth. Hillsdale, NJ: Erlbaum.

Amaro, H, and Raj, A. (2000). "On the Margin: Power and Women's HIV Risk Reduction Strategies." *Sex Roles* 42:723–749.

Banmen, J., and Vogel, A. (1985). "The Relationship Between Marital Quality and Interpersonal Sexual Communication." *Family Therapy* 12:45–58.

Bell, R. A.; Buerkel-Rothfuss, N. L.; and Gore, K. E. (1987). "'Did You Bring the Yarmulke for the Cabbage Patch Kid?' The Idiomatic Communication of Young Lovers." *Human Communication Research* 18:88–115.

Bingham, S. G. (1991). "Communication Strategies for Managing Sexual Harassment in Organizations: Understanding Message Options and Their Effects." *Journal of Applied Communication Research* 18:88–115.

Byers, E. S., and Demmons, S. (1999). "Sexual Satisfaction and Sexual Self-Disclosure within Dating Relationships." *Journal of Sex Research* 36:180–189.

Cado, S., and Leitenberg, H. (1990). "Guilt Reactions to Sexual Fantasies during Intercourse." *Archives of Sexual Behavior* 19:49–63.

Chesney, A. P.; Blakeney, P. E.; Chan, F. A.; and Cole, C. M. (1981). "The Impact of Sex Therapy on Sexual Behaviors and Marital Communication." *Journal of Sex and Marital Therapy* 7:70–79.

Chesney, A. P.; Blakeney, P. E.; Cole, C. M.; and Chan, F. A. (1981). "A Comparison of Couples Who Have Sought Sex Therapy with Couples Who Have Not." *Journal of Sex and Marital Therapy* 7:131–140.

Christopher, F. S., and Sprecher, S. (2000). "Sexuality in Marriage, Dating, and Other Relationships: A Decade Review." *Journal of Marriage and the Family* 62:999–1,017.

Cline, R. J. W.; Johnson, S. J.; and Freeman, K. E. (1992). "Talk among Sexual Partners about AIDS: Interpersonal Communication for Risk Reduction or Risk Enhancement?" *Health Communication* 4:39–56.

Cooper, A., and Stoltenberg, C. D. (1987). "Comparison of a Sexual Enhancement and a Communication Training Program on Sexual and Marital Satisfaction." *Journal of Counseling Psychology* 34:309–314.

Cornog, M. (1986). "Naming Sexual Body Parts: Preliminary Patterns and Implications." *Journal of Sex Research* 22:393–398.

Cupach, W. R., and Comstock, J. (1990). "Satisfaction with Sexual Communication in Marriage: Links to Sexual

Satisfaction and Dyadic Adjustment." *Journal of Social and Personal Relationships* 7:179–186.

Cupach, W. R., and Metts, S. (1991). "Sexuality and Communication in Close Relationships." In *Sexuality in Close Relationships,* ed. K. McKinney and S. Sprecher. Hillsdale, NJ: Erlbaum.

D'Augelli, A. R., and D'Augelli, J. F. (1985). "The Enhancement of Sexual Skills and Competence: Promoting Lifelong Sexual Unfolding." In *Handbook of Social Skills Training and Research,* ed. L. L'Abate and M.A. Milan. New York: Wiley.

De Bro, S. C.; Campbell, S. M.; and Peplau, L. A. (1994). "Influencing a Partner to Use a Condom: A College Student Perspective." *Psychology of Women Quarterly* 18:165–182.

Edgar, T., and Fitzpatrick, M. A. (1988). "Compliance-Gaining in Relational Interaction: When Your Life Depends on It." *Southern Speech Communication Journal* 53:385–405.

Frederiksen, B. F. (2000). "Popular Culture, Gender Relations and the Democratization of Everyday Life in Kenya." *Journal of Southern African Studies* 26:209–222.

Frith, H., and Kitzinger, C. (1997). "Talk about Sexual Miscommunication." *Women's Studies International Forum* 20:517–528.

Geismar, L. L. (1984). "Contextual Aspects of Sexual Communication in Marriage." *Journal of Comparative Family Studies* 15:345–353.

Keyton, J. (1996). "Sexual Harassment: A Multidisciplinary Synthesis and Critique." In *Communication Yearbook 19,* ed. B.R. Burleson. Thousand Oaks, CA: Sage.

Krahe, B.; Scheinberger-Olwig, R.; and Kolpin, S. (2000). "Ambiguous Communication of Sexual Intentions as a Risk Marker of Sexual Aggression." *Sex Roles* 42:313–337.

Kumar, P. (1995). "Comprehensive Sexuality Scale: Its Development and Standarization." *Journal of Personality and Clinical Studies* 11:1–4

Metts, S., and Cupach, W. R. (1991). "Plans for Seeking and Resisting the Use of Condoms." Paper presented at the annual meeting of the International Communication Association, Chicago, IL, May.

Metts, S., and Cupach, W. R. (1989). "The Role of Communication in Human Sexuality." In *Human Sexuality: The Societal and Interpersonal Context,* ed. K. McKinney and S. Sprecher. Norwood, NJ: Ablex.

Metts, S., and Spitzberg, B. H. (1996). "Sexual Communication in Interpersonal Contexts: A Script-Based Approach." In *Communication Yearbook 19,* ed. B.R. Burleson. Thousand Oaks, CA: Sage.

Muehlenhard, C. L., and Hollabaugh, L. C. (1988). "Do Women Sometimes Say No When They Mean Yes? The Prevalence and Correlates of Women's Token Resistance to Sex." *Journal of Personality and Social Psychology* 54:872–879.

Muehlenhard, C. L., and McCoy, M. L. (1991). "Double Standard/Double Bind: The Sexual Double Standard and Women's Communication About Sex." *Psychology of Women Quarterly* 15:447–461.

Osella, C., and Osella, F. (1998). "Friendship and Flirting: Micro-Politics in Kerala, South India." *Journal of the Royal Anthropological Institute* 4:189–206.

Quina, K.; Harlow, L. L.; Marokoff, P. J.; Burkholder, G.; and Deiter, P. J. (2000). "Sexual Communication in Relationships: When Words Speak Louder than Actions." *Sex Roles* 42:523–549.

Renaud, C.; Byers, E. S.; and Pan, S. (1997). "Sexual and Relationship Satisfaction in Mainland China." *Journal of Sex Research* 34:399–410.

Ross, J. L., Clifford, R. E., and Eisenman, R. (1987). "Communication of Sexual References in Married Couples." *Bulletin of the Psychonomic Society* 25:58–60.

Sanders, J. S., and Robinson, W. L. (1979). "Talking and Not Talking about Sex: Male and Female Vocabularies." *Journal of Communication* 29(2):22–30.

Simkins, L., and Rinck, C. (1982). "Male and Female Sexual Vocabulary in Different Interpersonal Contexts." *Journal of Sex Research* 18:160–172.

Simon, W., and Gagnon, J. H. (1986). "Sexual Scripts: Permanence and Change." *Archives of Sexual Behavior* 15:97–120.

Simon, W., and Gagnon, J. H. (1987). "A Sexual Scripts Approach." In *Theories of Human Sexuality,* ed. J. H. Geer and W. O'Donohue. New York: Plenum.

Song, J. A; Bergen, M. B; and Schumm, W. R. (1995). "Sexual Satisfaction Among Korean-American Couples in the Midwestern United States." *Journal of Sex and Marital Therapy* 21:147–158.

Sprecher, S.; Hatfield, E.; Cortese, A.; Potapova, E.; and Levitskaya, A. (1994). "Token Resistance to Sexual Intercourse and Consent to Unwanted Sexual Intercourse: College Students' Dating Experiences in Three Countries." *Journal of Sex Research* 31:125–131.

Wheeless, L. R., and Parsons, L. A. (1995). "What You Feel Is What You Might Get: Exploring Communication Apprehension and Sexual Communication Satisfaction." *Communication Research Reports* 12:39–45.

Wolff, B.; Blanc, A. K.; and Gage, A. J. (2000). "Who Decides? Women's Status and Negotiation of Sex in Uganda." *Culture, Health and Sexuality* 2:303–322.

SANDRA METTS

PARENT-CHILD RELATIONSHIPS

Communication between parents and children about matters related to sex has received considerable attention by social scientists, program planners, and policy analysts alike. Most of the empirical literature on this topic has focused on the adolescent years, as children approach puberty and transition to young adulthood. Although there have been some cross cultural studies, the vast majority of research has focused on communication dynamics within the United States.

Some scientists study parent-adolescent communication as a means of developing family based interventions for combating unintended pregnancies and the spread of sexually transmitted diseases (STDs). Such interventions teach parents how to communicate with their children about sex and help parents acquire information and skills that make them more effective at helping their adolescent avoid adverse sexual outcomes. Other scientists study parent-child communication from the broader perspective of sexual socialization. As parents guide their children towards independent and healthy adult lives, helping their child understand his or her sexuality and adopting perspectives that lead to healthy sexual attitudes and orientations later in life are of prime importance. Sexual socialization is an important developmental process that encompasses research on parent-adolescent communication.

Do Parents Talk with Children about Sex?

Although almost all parents engage in informal and superficial discussions of reproduction with their children across the early childhood years, many parents do not talk about sex with their adolescent-aged children. Studies have indicated that adolescents most commonly rely on peers for information about sexual matters (e.g., Thornburg

1981). However, parents also tend to be mentioned as being important, sometimes prominently so (Shields and Adams 1995; Kaiser Foundation 1996). Averaging across a wide range of studies, about 70 percent of parents in the United States indicate that they have talked with their adolescents about sex, whereas about 50 percent of adolescents report engaging in such conversations with their parents. These rates, however, vary considerably from one study to the next. Not only are the rates dependent on who is reporting (parent or adolescent), but estimates also vary as a function of the wording and format of the questions, the specificity of the topic studied, and the year in which the study was conducted.

An important issue in parentadolescent communication is determining why parents fail to engage in meaningful discussions with their children. Research has suggested five classes of concerns that parents express about engaging in such conversations (Jaccard, Dittus, and Gordon 2000):

(a) Not having the requisite knowledge/skills to explain things;

(b) Concern that the adolescent will not take the parent seriously;

(c) Concern with whether the communication will make a difference;

(d) Difficulties in finding the right time and place; and

(e) Fear of encouraging sexual activity.

Many parents forsake conversations because their adolescents tell them they already know what they need to know. Research has found, however, that adolescent perceptions of their knowledge about sex and birth control is only weakly correlated with their performance on knowledge tests about these topics, suggesting that adolescent claims of high knowledge levels should not be trusted (Radecki and Jaccard 1995).

Just as parents have reservations about talking with adolescents about sex, so do adolescents have reservations about discussing sex with their parents. It is important to identify such reservations for both of the involved parties, as lack of interest by either hinders effective communication. Adolescents sometimes feel that their parents do not treat them as equals and that parents fail to have adequate knowledge about current adolescent lifestyles and peer pressures (Pistella and Bonati 1999). Several studies have noted complaints by adolescents that their parents are not sufficiently open, supportive, trusting, and empathic, nor do parents sufficiently respect their privacy (Neer and Warren 1988; Nolin and Petersen 1992; Warren, 1995). Adolescents also express concern about sexual conversations being embarrassing, both to the adolescent as well as the parent (Jaccard, Dittus and Gordon 2000).

Do Parental Discussions Lessen Adolescent Sexual Risk Behavior?

Considerable research has addressed whether parent communication with their children about sex actually impacts adolescent sexual activity. Most of this research has been correlational in nature. Early studies tended to find no significant associations between parent-adolescent communication and sexual risk behavior, whereas more recent studies have observed such links (see Jaccard and Dittus 1993 for a review of this literature as well as Jaccard, Dodge and Dittus 2002). The general finding in more recent studies has been that higher levels of parent-adolescent communication are associated with reduced sexual risk taking on the part of the adolescent. In addition, parent-adolescent communication has been found to moderate relationships between other variables and sexual activity. For example, peer norms have been found to be more influential for those adolescents who have not discussed sex with a parent as opposed to those who have (Whitaker and Miller 2000). A small group of studies has found higher levels of communication are associated with higher levels of adolescent sexual activity (Darling and Hicks 1982; Widner 1997). These findings could be the result of parents deciding to talk with their children about sex after learning about or anticipating sexual activity on the part of their child (so that behavior influences communication rather than vice versa). Or, it could be that such discussions encourage subsequent adolescent sexual risk taking. Conclusive research on these alternative explanations is lacking. There are a sufficient number of correlational studies as of early 2002 to conclude with a reasonable degree of confidence that parent-adolescent communication is indeed associated with reduced sexual risk activity in some populations. Further research is

needed, however, to permit stronger statements of causal impact.

A Communication Framework

Classic conceptualizations of communication distinguish five core components of a communication: the source of a communication, the communication itself (often referred to as the message), the medium or channel through which the message is transmitted (e.g., face-to-face, written materials, recorded messages), the recipient or audience of the communication, and the context in which the communication occurs. Each of these components of communication has subcomponents. For example, sources of a message (in this context, the parent) differ in their age, gender, expertise, and trustworthiness. Recipients of communications (in this context, the child) differ in their motivational states, their emotional states, their past experiences, and their expectations. The surrounding environment varies in terms of its temporal, physical, social, and cultural features. Variations in the five factors affect how adolescents respond to parental communications. Thus, the impact of a parental message on adolescent sexual risk taking may vary as a function of characteristics of the parent, characteristics of the message that the parent conveys, characteristics of the channel through which the message is delivered, characteristics of the adolescent, and characteristics of the context in which the communication occurs.

Source variables in parent-adolescent communication about sex. Studies of the effects of source variables have focused most often on how the gender of the parent affects communication. Although there are some exceptions, studies have tended to find that mothers are more likely than fathers to talk about sex and birth control with their children (Raffaelli, Bogenschneider, and Flood 1998; Rosenthal and Feldman 1999). Some theorists suggest that gender differences occur because mothers are better at communicating in general, because mothers are the agents of intimacy, and/or because mothers can discuss sexual matters more safely than fathers. Adolescent evaluations of their parents as sex educators tend to vary as a function of the gender of the parent, with mothers being evaluated more positively than fathers (Feldman and Rosenthal 2000). Research on the differential impact of mother and father communication on adolescent sexual risk taking has tended to find that mother-based variables are more predictive of adolescent risk taking than father-based variables (Jaccard and Dittus 1991; Dutra, Miller, and Forehand 1999). However, there also is evidence that father-based variables account for unique variance in adolescent behavior independent of mother-based variables (Dittus, Jaccard and Gordon 1997).

Demographic characteristics of the source other than gender also have been studied. For example, research has found that Latino parent-adolescent dyads exhibit somewhat different conversational dynamics than European American dyads and that social class is predictive of different communication styles with respect to sexual discussions (Lefkowitz et al. 1998). However, other studies have failed to find consistent relationships between non-gender based demographic characteristics of the source and communication variables (e.g., Raffaelli, Bogenschneider and Flood 1998). As of 2002, this literature is somewhat mixed and inconsistent.

General communication research suggests two source dimensions are of prime importance, the perceived expertise of the source and the perceived trustworthiness of the source. Expertise refers to knowledge, expert status, and familiarity with the topic. Trustworthiness refers to sincerity, honesty, and good intentions. How adolescents perceive parents in terms of expertise has not been explored with any degree of theoretical sophistication. Such judgments are likely to vary as a function of the topic area, with parents being seen as more expert in some areas than others. Studies suggest that adolescents sometimes see parents as being out of touch with current adolescent lifestyles and pressures, hence parental expertise may be undermined accordingly. In terms of trustworthiness, some research suggests that adolescents tend to perceive parents as trustworthy in their discussions about sexual matters. However, adolescents sometimes point out that their parents are judgmental, overly protective of them making mistakes, and that parents often fail to respect their privacy and desire for autonomy. Such factors may undermine the perceived trustworthiness of the parent as an information source.

Message variables in parent-adolescent communication. One of the more widely studied message variables in the literature on parent-adolescent communication is message content, (i.e., what parents and adolescents talk about when they engage

in conversations about sex). Characterizations of such discussions tend to differ depending on whether the parent or the adolescent is doing the characterizing. Some studies suggest that parent-adolescent discussions about sex are more often indirect than direct (Philliber 1980; Fox 1981). Other studies indicate biology rather than sexual decision-making are the primary topics of conversation (Baldwin and Baranoski 1990). Studies also report an emphasis on physical development and maturation as well as the dangers associated with STDs and the occurrence of an unintended pregnancy (Miller et al. 1998; Whitaker et al. 1999). Not surprisingly, studies find individual differences in the topics that parents think should be discussed with their adolescents, with some endorsing the inclusion of sensitive topics such as abortion and birth control and others preferring to omit such topics (Silverstein and Buck 1986; Foley 1986). Several studies have found that topics aimed at daughters tend to stress negative, problematic aspects of sexuality more so than communications aimed at sons (Darling and Hicks 1982; Kirby 1995). Adult females who recall their discussions with their parents tend to characterize them as somewhat negative, focusing on rules and warnings. Studies also suggest that fathers tend to deal with less intimate topics than mothers, that is that message content differs as a function of the gender of the source (Rosenthal, Senserrick and Feldman 2000).

One message-related variable that has been the subject of considerable study is the extent to which parents convey disapproval of the adolescent engaging in sexual intercourse (Dittus and Jaccard 2000). Early research on parent-adolescent communication assumed that parents are uniformly opposed to their adolescent engaging in sexual intercourse. Several researchers, however, have argued that parental disapproval of an adolescent engaging in sexual intercourse is a continuum, with some parents being strongly opposed to their adolescent engaging in sex and others being less opposed. Across a wide range of studies, some 15 percent to 20 percent of parents indicate that it is permissible for their teenaged son or daughter to engage in sexual intercourse under certain circumstances (e.g., with a close and steady boyfriend or girlfriend who is well known to the parents). The more the parent is perceived by the adolescent as disapproving of sexual intercourse has been found to be predictive of lower levels of future adolescent sexual activity (Dittus and Jaccard 2000). Adolescents may misperceive the extent to which their parents disapprove of them engaging in sexual intercourse, underscoring the need for parents to communicate effectively their orientations (Jaccard, Dittus and Gordon 1998).

Social scientists emphasize the importance of the frequency and timing of parent-adolescent communications. Too many parents feel that their job is finished once they have had "the big talk" in early adolescence. Studies suggest that communication needs to be an ongoing process. Many parents rely on fear-arousing strategies to motivate their child to avoid sexual risk taking by emphasizing the negative consequences of unintended pregnancy and the consequences of contracting a sexually transmitted disease. Extensive literature in social psychology suggests that such appeals are less effective than parents might think.

Audience variables in parent-adolescent communication. Audience variables focus on characteristics of the recipient of the communication that influence exposure, attention, comprehension, acceptance and retention of message contents. Often, characteristics of the recipient that maximize one of these processes will minimize another. For example, research has shown that intelligent recipients are more likely to comprehend the contents of a complex message, but that they also may be more likely to counter argue its contents and fail to accept it.

Among the most extensively studied audience characteristics in research on parent-adolescent communication about sex is the gender of the adolescent. Although there are exceptions, discussions about sex are more likely to occur with daughters and are more extensive for daughters as opposed to sons (Jaccard and Dittus 1991; Raffaelli, Bogenschneider and Flood 1998). Research suggests that daughters tend to evaluate mothers more positively as sex educators than do sons (Youniss and Smollar 1985; Feldman and Rosenthal 2000). Sons and daughters, however, have been found to have comparable evaluations of fathers (Feldman and Rosenthal 2000). Research also has suggested that the puberty status and prior sexual activity on the part of the adolescent may impact the nature and extent of parent-adolescent communication (Whitaker and Miller 2000).

An audience variable that has received limited attention in parent-adolescent communication literature is the developmental status of the adolescent (i.e., early adolescence, middle adolescence and late adolescence). Analyses of adolescent development typically focus on five broad areas: physical development, cognitive development, emotional development, moral development, and social development. Adolescent experiences in each of these domains differ for early, middle, and late adolescents. For example, during early adolescence, most adolescents undergo their most dramatic physical changes during the adolescent growth spurt. Most of these changes have transpired by late adolescence. The physical changes during early adolescence often are accompanied by heightened sensitivity to physical appearance, which, in turn, influences the kinds of information and arguments that an adolescent is receptive to. With respect to cognitive development, early adolescents tend to exhibit more concrete thinking. They have difficulty thinking abstractly. This is less true of older adolescents. Memory processes are still developing in adolescence, with older adolescents exhibiting more efficient strategies for storing and retrieving information from memory than early adolescents. Socially, early adolescents are less prone to see things from other people's point of view and tend to have difficulty imagining different perspectives for solving social problems. The nature of friendships also differs considerably for early and late adolescents. In terms of moral development, early adolescents are more likely to blame behavioral transgressions on extenuating circumstances and less likely to accept personal responsibility for their actions. All of these developmental differences have potentially important implications for strategies parents should use to discuss sexuality with their children, yet few studies have explored these implications.

Channel variables in parent-adolescent communication. Channel variables refer to the medium used to convey a message and how this affects message exposure, attention, comprehension, acceptance, retention and retrieval. A common channel used by parents is that of verbal communication through face-to-face interaction. However, there are other mechanisms by which parents communicate information that is sexually relevant, including various forms of non-verbal communication and parental behaviors that the adolescent observes (e.g., television-viewing habits of the parent). Studies have observed associations between adolescent beliefs about the advantages and disadvantages of engaging in sexual intercourse with maternal beliefs about the advantages and disadvantages of their child engaging in sexual intercourse, holding constant the extent to which the mother and child have talked about such advantages and disadvantages (Dittus, Jaccard and Gordon 1999). This suggests that factors other than direct communication may underlie parent-child similarity in belief structures.

Contextual variables in parent-adolescent communication. A large number of studies have examined the impact of the family context on adolescent sexual risk behavior, but relatively few studies have examined how family contextual variables impact parent-adolescent communication. Variables such as family structure (one versus two parent families; blended families; presence of grandparents or other relatives in the household), social class, marital status, presence of siblings, and psychosocial characterizations of the general family environment all are of potential relevance. Several studies have explored the general communication environment in the family and have found it to be associated with effective parental communication about sex (Fisher 1990; Jaccard, Dittus and Gordon 1998; Feldman and Rosenthal 2000; Lefkowitz et al. 2000). However, research on contextual variables and how they affect parent-adolescent communication about sex is limited.

Conclusion

Communication dynamics between parents and adolescents are far more complex than depicted here. The emphasis in this entry is on characterizing communication in a unidirectional fashion in which the parent attempts to convey meaning structures to the adolescent in hopes of influencing the knowledge, values, attitudes, intentions, and/or behavior of the adolescent. However, parent-adolescent communication about sex is an emotion-laden, dynamic, reciprocal exchange of information and feelings that unfolds over time (sometimes unpredictably so). Parents have sex-related issues they want to discuss with their children and children often have sex-related issues they want to discuss with their parents. Parents and children alternate between the roles of communicator and listener, or "source" and "audience."

Sometimes interaction is premeditated and planned by one of the participants. Other times it occurs spontaneously, perhaps in response to some event that has occurred. Communication may be direct or indirect, verbal or nonverbal. It may have persuasive intent and/or informative intent. Adolescents communicate with both mothers and fathers and hear multiple messages about topics. Sometimes these messages conflict, not only between parents but with other sources of information as well (e.g., peers, siblings). Indeed, conflicting messages sometimes occur from the same parent, such as when adolescents are told to abstain from sex while at the same time to use birth control if they do engage in sex.

Recognition of these complexities of communication dynamics, when juxtaposed against the extant literature on parent-adolescent communication, illustrates just how much work is yet to be done to gain a true understanding of parent-adolescent communication in the sexual domain.

See also: MENARCHE; MENSTURAL TABOO; SEXUAL COMMUNICATION: COUPLE RELATIONSHIPS; SEXUALITY; SEXUALITY EDUCATION; SEXUALITY IN CHILDHOOD

Bibliography

Baldwin, S. E., and Baranoski, M. V. (1990). "Family interactions and sex education in the home." *Adolescence* 25:573–582.

Darling, C. A., and Hicks, M. W. (1982). "Parental influences on adolescent sexuality: Implication for parents as educators." *Journal of Youth and Adolescence* 11:231–245.

Dittus, P., and Jaccard, J. (2000). "The Relationship of Adolescent Perceptions of Maternal Disapproval of Sex and of the Mother-Adolescent Relationship to Sexual Outcomes." *Journal of Adolescent Health* 26:268–278.

Dittus, P.; Jaccard, J.; and Gordon, V. (1997). "The impact of African–American fathers on adolescent sexual behavior." *Journal of Youth and Adolescence* 26:445–465.

Dittus, P.; Jaccard, J.; and Gordon, V. (1999). "Direct and indirect communication of maternal beliefs to adolescents: Adolescent motivations for premarital sexual activity." *Journal of Applied Social Psychology* 29:1927–1963.

Dutra, R.; Miller, K. S.; and Forehand, R. (1999). "The process and content of sexual communication with adolescents in two-parent families: Associations with sexual risk-taking behavior." *AIDS and Behavior* 3:59–66.

Feldman, S., and Rosenthal, D. A. (2000). "The effect of communication characteristics on family members' perceptions of parents as sex educators." *Journal of Research on Adolescence* 10:119–150.

Fisher, T. D. (1990). "Characteristics of mothers and fathers who talk to their adolescent children about sexuality." *Journal of Psychology and Human Sexuality* 3:53–70.

Foley, D. (1986). "How (and why) to teach your child about sex." *Prevention* 38:126–140.

Fox, G. L. (1981). "The Family's Role In Adolescent Sexual Behavior." In *Teenage Pregnancy in a Family Context,* ed. T. Ooms. Philadelphia, PA: Temple University Press.

Jaccard, J., and Dittus, P. (1991). *Parent-Teenager Communication: Towards The Prevention of Unintended Pregnancies.* New York: Springer-Verlag.

Jaccard, J., and Dittus, P. (1993). "Parent-adolescent communication about premarital pregnancy." *Families in Society* 74:329–343.

Jaccard, J.; Dittus, P. J.; and Gordon, V. V. (1998). "Parent-adolescent congruity in reports of adolescent sexual behavior and in communications about sexual behavior." *Child Development* 69:247–261.

Jaccard, J.; Dittus, P. J.; and Gordon, V. V. (2000). "Parent-adolescent communication about premarital sex: Factors associated with the extent of communication." *Journal of Adolescent Research* 15:187–208.

Jaccard, J.; Dittus, P.; and Litardo, H. (1999) "Parent-adolescent communication about sex and birth control: Implications for parent based interventions to reduce unintended adolescent pregnancy." In *Advances in Population Research: Psychosocial Perspectives,* ed. W. Miller and L. Severy. London: Kingsley.

Jaccard, J.; Dodge, T.; and Dittus, P. (2002). "Parent-adolescent communication about sex and birth control: A conceptual framework." In *Out in the open: Parent-teen communication about sexuality.* New Directions in Child and Adolescent Development, ed. S. Feldman and D. A. Rosenthal. San Francisco: Jossey-Bass.

Kahlbaugh, P.; Lefkowitz, E.S.; Valdez, P.; and Sigman, M. (1997). "The affective nature of mother-adolescent communication concerning sexuality and conflict." *Journal of Research on Adolescence* 7:221–239.

Kaiser Foundation. (1996). *Kaiser Family Foundation survey on teens and sex: What they say teens today need to know and who to listen to.* Menlo Park, CA: Henry Kaiser Family Foundation.

Kirby, D. (1995). *Parent-Child Communication about Sexuality.* Report to the Kaiser Foundation. Santa Cruz, CA: ETR Associates.

Lefkowitz, E. S.; Kahlbaugh, P.; and Sigman, M. D. (1996). "Turn-taking in mother-adolescent conversations about sexuality and conflict." *Journal of Youth and Adolescence* 25:307–321.

Lefkowitz, E. S.; Romo, L. F.; Corona, R. A.; Au, T. K.; and Sigman, M. (1998). *How Latino-American and European-American adolescents discuss conflicts, sexuality, and AIDS with their mothers.* Pennsylvania State University and University of California, Los Angeles.

Miller, K. S.; Kotchick, B.; Dorsey, S.; Forehand, R.; and Ham, A. (1998). "Family communication about sex: What parents are saying and are their adolescents listening?" *Family Planning Perspectives* 30:218–222.

Neer, M. R., and Warren, C. (1988). "The relationship of supportive communication to sex discussion in the home." *Communication Research Reports* 5:154–160.

Nolin, M. J., and Petersen, K. K. (1992). "Gender difference in parent-child communication about sexuality: An exploratory study." *Journal of Adolescent Research* 7:59–79.

Philliber, S. G. (1980). "Socialization for childbearing." *Journal of Social Issues 36:*30–44.

Pistella, C. L. Y., and Bonati, F. A. (1999). "Adolescent women's recommendations for enhanced parent-adolescent communication about sexual behavior." *Child and Adolescent Social Work Journal* 16:305–315.

Radecki, C. M., and Jaccard, J. (1995). "Perceptions of knowledge, actual knowledge and information search behavior." *Journal of Experimental Social Psychology* 31:107–138.

Raffaelli, M.; Bogenschneider, K.; and Flood, M. F. (1998). "Parent-teen communication about sexual topics." *Journal of Family Issues* 19:315–333.

Rosenthal, D. A., and Feldman, S. S. (1999). "The importance of importance: Adolescents' perceptions of parental communication about sexuality." *Journal of Adolescence* 22:835–851.

Rosenthal, D.; Senserrick, T.; and Feldman, S. (2000). *A typology approach to describing parents as communicators about sexuality.* Unpublished Manuscript, Stanford University, Palo Alto, CA.

Shields, G., and Adams, J. (1995). "HIV/AIDS among youth: A community needs assessment study." *Child and Adolescent Social Work Journal* 12:361–380.

Silverstein, C. D., and Buck, G. M. (1986). "Parental preferences regarding sex education topics for sixth graders." *Adolescence* 21:971–980.

Thornburg, H. D. (1981). "Adolescent sources of information on sex." *Journal of School Health* 51:274–277.

Warren, C. (1995). "Parent-child communication about sex." In *Parents, children, and communication: Frontiers of theory and research,* ed. T. L. Socha and G.H. Stamp. Hillsdale, NJ: Erlbaum.

Whitaker, D. J., and Miller, K. S. (2000). "Parent-adolescent discussions about sex and condoms." *Journal of Adolescent Research* 15:251–273.

Whitaker, D. J.; Miller, K. S.; May, D.; and Levin, M. (1999). "Teenage partners' communication about sexual risk and condom use: The importance of parent-teenager discussions." *Family Planning Perspectives* 31:117–121.

Widner, E. D. (1997). "Influence of older siblings on initiation of sexual intercourse." *Journal of Marriage and the Family* 59:928–938.

Youniss, J., and Smollar, J. (1985). *Adolescent relations with mothers, fathers and friends.* Chicago: University of Chicago Press.

Yowell, C. M. (1997). "Risks of communication: Early adolescent girls' conversations with mothers and friends about sexuality." *Journal of Early Adolescence* 17:172–196.

JAMES JACCARD

SEXUAL DYSFUNCTION

Psychosexual disorders were listed for the first time in 1980 in the third edition of the American Psychiatric Association's Diagnostic and Statistical Manual of Mental Disorders (DSM-III), a handbook used by almost all mental health professionals. This listing has led to an increasing medicalization of sexual problems that can allow individuals to avoid examining their own attitudes and experiences that could have contributed to their dysfunction. If the source of the problem is "medical," the individuals may not see the need to take responsibility for their problems. If the problem is a lack of desire, the medical diagnosis can be used as a rationale to continue to avoid sexual activity.

The DSM-IV (the fourth edition of the DSM, published in 1994) classifies sexual dysfunctions as primary or secondary. A *primary dysfunction* occurs when an individual has never experienced one of the phases of the sexual response cycle. A *secondary dysfunction* refers to a situation in which a person has been able to respond in the past to one of the phases but is not responsive at the current time, or can experience one of the phases only in certain circumstances.

It is important to remember that many people do not neatly fit into any of the diagnostic categories described. In many cases, problems with desire, excitement, and orgasm overlap. (Everaerd and Laan 2000)

There has been very little systematic survey information on the prevalence of sexual dysfunction. Robert Francouer (1977) edited three volumes that covered 170 countries and cultures. Almost all of the accounts were anecdotal or based on data collected in various types of clinics. In those countries that did have information based on representative samples of their population (Czech Republic, Slovakia, Denmark, Finland, France, Iceland, and Sweden), it is difficult to make comparisons because of methodological differences in how these studies were carried out.

An overview of the National Health and Social Life Survey (NHSLS), which was the first to question a nationally representative sample of U.S. adults about their sexual attitudes and behaviors, reveals that sexual problems are most common among young women and older men (Laumann, Park, and Rosen 1999). Low sexual interest and problems with erection tend to become more common as men age probably due to the physiological changes that occur over time. Young women "are more likely to be single, their sexual activities involve higher rates of partner turnover as well as periodic spells of sexual inactivity. This instability, coupled with inexperience, generates stressful sexual encounters, providing the basis for sexual pain and anxiety"(p. 9).

The effects of race and ethnicity on the prevalences of sexual dysfunction are fairly modest. Hispanic women report lower prevalence of sexual dysfunction than do African-American or white women. White women are more likely to experience sexual pain then are African-American women, whereas African-American women report experiencing less pleasure with sexual experience and sexual desire more frequently than white women. Differences between men roughly follow those among women but the differences are not as large. Generally, Hispanics are less likely to report sexual problems whereas African Americans report more sexual problems across the spectrum of sexual dysfunction (Laumann, Park, and Rosen 1999).

Sexual Desire Disorders

The DSM-IV divides desire disorders into two categories: hypoactive sexual desire disorders and sexual aversion disorders. The first of these, *hypoactive sexual desire disorder,* is defined as deficient or absent sexual fantasies and desire for sexual activity with anyone. The judgment of deficiency or absence is made by the clinician, taking into account factors that affect sexual functioning such as age, sex, and the context of the person's life. The deficiency may be selective: a person may experience erection or lubrication and orgasm but derive little pleasure from the physical feelings and thus have little interest in sexual activity. In other cases, the individual's desire is at such a low ebb that he or she has no interest in self-stimulation or in participation in sexual interaction that might even lead to arousal. Some people can be described as asexual; in other words, they do not experience desire for any kind of sexual activity. This is not considered a dysfunction if the individual is satisfied with not engaging in sexual activity.

The sources of sexual desire disorder have not been well clarified. Most current knowledge of the causes of low sexual desire is based on clients who are seen in therapy and thus must be viewed with caution until more objective research has been conducted using nonclinical samples. With that caveat in mind, low sexual desire has been associated with such factors as anxiety, religious orthodoxy, depression, habituation to a sexual partner, fear of loss of control over sexual urges, sexual assault, side effects of medication, marital conflict, and fear of closeness. (Allgeier and Allgeier 2000).

In the general population, 16 percent of men and 33 percent of women aged eighteen to fifty-nine reported that they lacked interest in sex for a period of several months or more in the year before they were interviewed (Laumann et al. 1994). The suppression of sexual desire is, of course, not dysfunctional in and of itself. Most of us learn scripts to suppress sexual desire for inappropriate partners, such as parents, close relatives, and children, and in inappropriate situations.

Sexual aversion disorder is a persistent aversion to almost all genital sexual contact with a partner. Whereas individuals displaying hypoactive sexual desires are often indifferent about sexual interaction, sexual aversion reflects fear, disgust, or anxiety about sexual contact with a partner. An individual with sexual aversion disorder may still engage in autosexual behaviors such as masturbation and fantasy, while avoiding interpersonal sexual behavior.

Excessive sexual desire is often associated with *paraphilias.* Preliminary evidence indicates that men with paraphilic disorders are two to three times more sexually active than men in the general population (Kafka 1997).

Sexual Arousal Disorders

Some people feel deep sexual desire and want to make love with their partners but experience little or no physical response (erection or vaginal lubrication and swelling) to sexual stimulation. Sexual arousal disorders are diagnosed when there is recurrent or persistent failure by a woman to attain or maintain the lubrication and swelling response or failure by a man to attain erection during sexual activity. Such a diagnosis is made only when the clinician is sure that the difficulty does not stem from physical disorders or medication and when the amount of sexual stimulation provided should be adequate to produce *vasocongestion.* Sometimes failure to respond results from insufficient stimulation rather than from inhibition of excitement.

Women's reactions to an inability to respond to erotic stimulation show much greater variation than do men's responses. Most men react to erectile dysfunction as if it were a disaster, whereas women's responses range from anxiety or distress to casual acceptance of the difficulty. To some extent, cultural expectations are responsible for these differences. In most cultures, men are expected to be sexually active and to perform satisfactorily. Women are not generally subjected to the same performance pressures and, in some cultures, are not expected to be sexually responsive. The restrictiveness of a culture is linked to the incidence of difficulties in a man's getting or maintaining an erection. In an examination of thirty preindustrial and industrializing countries, Michael Welch and Pamela Kartub (1978) found that the more restrictive a society was regarding such behaviors as premarital, marital, and extramarital sex, the greater was the number of reported problems with erectile functioning.

Erectile dysfunction is generally the most common complaint among men seeking sex therapy. In a more representative sample, however, about 10 percent of men report experiencing erectile dysfunction (Laumann et al. 1994). Some men with erectile dysfunction never have more than a partial erection during sexual activity. Others become erect, only to lose firmness when they attempt to have intercourse. Some men have erection problems with one partner but not with another.

Most men who experience problems with erection after a period of normal responsiveness respond well to treatment. The prognosis is not so good for men who have never been able to attain or maintain an erection with a partner.

About 20 percent of women and 10 percent of men aged eighteen to fifty-four in the general population reported arousal problems in 1992. Often the problem stems from the combination of widespread ignorance in our culture regarding women's sexual anatomy and the socialization of women to attend more to others' needs then to their own.

Orgasm Disorders

Some people have orgasms within minutes of sexual interaction. Others engage in sexual stimulation for an hour or more before having orgasm. Some people never have orgasms. Nowhere else is the problem of defining sexual dysfunction more evident. In fact, except in extreme cases involving orgasm within seconds or no orgasm at all, the main difficulty is a difference in the speed of the partners' responsiveness rather than any dysfunction.

The fact that one person responds quickly and his or her partner responds more slowly does not necessarily imply that either is dysfunctional. Although orgasmic and ejaculatory dysfunctions do exist in some people, simple differences between partners in the timing of orgasmic release are not necessarily problematic or indicative of sexual dysfunction.

Perhaps the most useful definition of *premature ejaculation* is ejaculation before the man wants it to occur. Speed of ejaculation is related to age (older men have fewer problems with ejaculatory control than do younger men, particularly adolescents), sexual inexperience, and novelty of the sexual partner.

The diagnosis of premature ejaculation is not appropriate unless the speed of a man's ejaculation becomes a regular, unwanted aspect of a couple's sexual activity. Ejaculation is a reflex that is difficult to control once it has been activated. The key to learning control is to recognize the signals that occur just before ejaculation, an awareness that can be difficult for young, inexperienced men. Roughly 30 percent of men report that they ejaculate more rapidly than they would like. Some men who continue to have problems with premature ejaculation after they have become sexually experienced may be hypersensitive to penile arousal and predisposed to early ejaculation (Slob, Van Berkel, and van der Werff ten Bosch 2000).

In clinical studies, inhibited male orgasm (also known as *retarded ejaculation* or *ejaculatory incompetence*) accounts for about 3 to 8 percent of men seeking treatment, and this rarer form of sexual dysfunction has been found to occur in about 3 to 10 percent of men in nonclinical samples (Simons and Carey 2001). The inhibition of orgasm may include delayed ejaculation or a total inability to ejaculate despite adequate periods of sexual excitement. As with the other dysfunctions, a diagnosis of inhibited male orgasms is not made when the problem stems from side effects of medication or some physical disorder.

In a physical condition known as *retrograde ejaculation,* the usual expulsion of ejaculate through the urethra is reversed. The neck of the bladder does not contract, so the semen is expelled into the bladder rather than out through the urethral opening in the penis. The condition usually results from surgery involving the genitourinary system or can be a side effect of some medications.

Some women suffer from inhibited orgasm, a condition that prevents them from having orgasm despite adequate sexual stimulation. Difficulty with orgasm is one of the most common sexual concerns among women

Women with this dysfunction may look forward to sex, and many experience high levels of sexual excitement with vaginal swelling and lubrication, but they are usually unable to have orgasm. Sexual arousal causes congestion of the pelvic blood vessels, and without orgasm, the congested blood remains for a while (analogous to the congestion in the testes associated with the absence of orgasmic release in highly aroused men). Consistent arousal in women without orgasmic release can result in cramps, backache, and irritation. Prevalence rates have ranged between 4 and 24 percent in European and U.S. studies (Simons and Carey 2001)

It is debatable whether a dysfunction exists when a woman does not have orgasm during coitus but does climax during other kinds of stimulation—oral or manual stimulation, for example. Calling this pattern a sexual dysfunction and assuming that it requires sex therapy would dictate treatment for a large number of women, given that fewer than 50 percent of women consistently have orgasm during coitus.

Sexual Pain Disorders

Sexual pain disorders include *dyspareunia,* which males and females can experience, *vaginismus* and *vulvodinia,* which are exclusively female complaints.

Dyspareunia is the technical term for recurrent and persistent genital pain in a man or woman before, during, or after sexual intercourse. They may experience the pain as repeated, intense discomfort; momentary sharp sensations of varying intensity; or intermittent twinges and/or aching sensations. Dyspareunia in men, who may experience the pain in the testes and/or the glans after ejaculation, appears to be much less common than painful intercourse in women

In a study by Edward O. Laumann and colleagues (1994), U.S. women reported prevalence rates of almost 15 percent. A large study in France found that 5 percent of the sexually active female respondents indicated that they had often experienced pain during sexual relations (Spira, Bajos, and LeGroupe 1993). The discrepancy between these prevalence rates may result, in part, from different methodologies and/or cultural differences.

A wide variety of disease and disorders of the external and internal sex organs and their surrounding structures can make intercourse painful for men and women. When physical disorders have been ruled out, psychological factors are assumed to be the cause.

Vaginismus refers to the involuntary spasm of the pelvic muscles surrounding the outer third of the vagina. Women who experience these spasms of the *pubococcygeus* (PC) and related muscles may be quite capable of becoming sexually aroused, lubricating, and experiencing orgasm but cannot have intercourse. The partner of a woman with this dysfunction who tries to have intercourse with her may have the sensation that his penis is hitting a rigid wall about an inch inside her vagina. Vaginismus rates have ranged from 0.5 to 30 percent of the women treated at clinics (Simons and Carey 1990).

Treatment ranges from the medical correction of physical problems to the use of psychotherapy, although it is sometimes difficult to determine the precise source(s) of the vaginismus. Relaxation training and gradual insertion of successively bigger dilators into the vagina appear to be highly effective in curing vaginismus. It is very important, however, that the woman (rather than a therapist or her partner) control the pace of treatment and the size of dilator (Heiman and Metson 1997)

Vulvodinia is characterized by a painful burning sensation in the vulvar and vaginal area. Also called *burning vulva syndrome,* the presenting complaint of women with this problem is burning and painful intercourse. The syndrome is associated with a history of vulvo/vaginal infection, microorganisms that cause *dermatosis,* and early contraceptive use (Binik et al. 1999). Current treatments include laser surgery, topical preparations, dietary restrictions, physical therapy, and pain reduction techniques such as self-hypnosis.

From this review of sexual dysfunctions, it should be clear that whatever the original source (biological, psychosocial, or both) of a person's inability to respond as he or she wishes, the problem may be aggravated by the development of fear of failure in future sexual contacts. Such fear can produce self-fulfilling prophecies; in other words, an intense focus on whether a person will respond adequately can reduce the likelihood that healthy sexual feelings and responses will unfold. No matter what particular treatment procedures sex therapists use, they should also identify and attempt to eliminate both clients' fears of sexual inadequacy and their tendency to engage in distracting and maladaptive thoughts during sexual intimacy.

Sex Therapy

Although sexual dysfunctions have been treated by a wide array of different therapies, this entry concentrates on the most commonly used techniques in sex therapy. Until the 1960s, the predominant approach to the treatment of sexual dysfunction was psychoanalysis. Sexual problems were viewed as symptoms of emotional conflict originating in childhood.

Cognitive-behavioral psychologists have long taken issue with the psychoanalytic approach. They believe that a person can be emotionally healthy and still have sexual difficulties. Maladaptive sexual functioning is learned, they believe, and it can be unlearned without extensive probing into a client's past.

Masters and Johnson's approach. The treatment program that William Masters and Virginia Johnson developed is a two-week process, conducted by a man and a woman. Both partners in the couple seeking treatment are given a thorough medical examination and interviewed by the therapist of the same sex, followed by an interview with the other therapist. All four people (the couple and the two therapists) then discuss treatment goals.

Masters and Johnson recommended the use of both a male and a female therapist to provide a "friend-in-court" for the client of the same sex. They stressed the treatment of specific symptoms rather than extensive psychotherapy aimed at determining potential underlying, unconscious sources of difficulty.

Kaplan's approach. Helen Singer Kaplan (1974) developed an approach to sex therapy that combined some of the insights and techniques of psychoanalysis with behavioral methods. Her approach begins at the *surface* or behavioral level, and probes more deeply into emotional conflicts only if necessary.

Many sexual difficulties stem from superficial causes. If a sexual difficulty is rooted in a lack of knowledge, for example, information and instruction may be all that are needed to treat it. If the trouble is of recent origin, a series of guided sexual tasks may be enough to change patterns of response. If deep-seated emotional problems exist, the therapist may use more analytic approaches to help clients obtain insight into the less-conscious aspects of their personality. This last approach has been designated as psychosexual therapy to distinguish it from sex therapy.

Nondemand pleasuring and sensate focus. In exercises involving *nondemand sensate focus,* the clients initially avoid sexual intercourse. In fact,

couples are forbidden to engage in any sexual activity until the therapist instructs them to do so. Over the course of treatment, they receive homework assignments that gradually increase their range of sexual behaviors. Initially, only kissing, hugging, and body massage may be allowed.

The partners are instructed to take turns in the roles of giver and receiver as they touch and caress each other's body. When playing the role of giver, the person explores, touches, and caresses the receiver's body. In applying this technique, called *nondemand pleasuring,* the giver does not attempt to arouse the receiver sexually. In an exercise called *sensate focus,* the receiver concentrates on the sensations evoked by the giver's touch on various parts of the body. In these exercises, the giver's responsibility is to provide pleasure and to be aware of his or her own pleasure in touching. The receiver's role is to prevent or end any stimulation that he or she finds uncomfortable or irritating by either telling or showing the partner his or her feelings.

The next step is to engage in nondemand breast and genital caressing while avoiding orgasm-oriented stimulation. If the partner or the person who is experiencing sexual difficulty becomes highly aroused during this exercise, that partner may be brought to orgasm orally or manually after completion of the exercise.

Other sexual behaviors are gradually added to the clients' homework. Successive assignments may include nongenital body massage, breast and genital touching, simultaneous masturbation, penile insertion with no movement, mutual genital manipulation to orgasm, and, finally, intercourse.

Masturbation training. Most treatment programs for orgasmically inhibited women include training in masturbation, particularly if the woman has never had an orgasm. This approach is used mainly in cases of primary orgasmic dysfunction and female hypoactive sexual desire. In this approach women are encouraged to learn about their bodies and relax to the point where they can experience orgasm.

The approach most commonly employed for premature ejaculation is the *squeeze technique* (Masters and Johnson 1970). The partner circles the tip of the penis with the hand. The thumb is placed against the frenulum on the underside of the penis, while the fingers are placed on either side of the corona ridge on the upper side of the penis. When the man signals that he is approaching ejaculation, his partner applies fairly strong pressure for three to five seconds and then stops with a sudden release. The partner stimulates his penis again after the sensations of impending ejaculation diminish, usually within twenty to thirty seconds. Typically, the man is told that he should not try to control his ejaculation but should rely instead on the squeeze technique. The entire process is usually repeated twice per session before ejaculation is allowed.

Some couples prefer to apply the squeeze technique as close as possible to the base of the penis rather than the tip. This variation has the advantage of being easier to do during intercourse, but for some couples it does not work.

Numerous other therapy formats and techniques are sometimes used in conjunction with the foregoing approaches to the treatment of sexual dysfunctions. For example, for women who have primary or secondary orgasmic dysfunction, group therapy is effective and less expensive than individual therapy (LoPiccolo and Stock 1986; McCabe and Delaney 1992).

Various approaches involving surgery and mechanical approaches, hormones, and drugs have been used in the attempt to treat sexual dysfunctions. The fact that most of these treatments have been developed for male sexual difficulties probably reflects the cultural emphasis on male sexual performance. In general, before permitting these kinds of treatment, the client should make sure no other type of treatment is effective for him and obtain a second opinion.

Surgical procedures, including implants, have been used in the treatment of erectile dysfunction. There are two basic types of plastic or silicone implants. One is a semirigid rod that keeps the penis in a constant state of erection but can be bent for concealment under clothing. The other type of silicone or plastic (polyurethane) implant an inflatable device surgically implanted under the skin of the penis; to achieve erection, the man presses a pump implanted in the scrotum. The pump forces fluid from a reservoir put under the abdominal muscles into cylinders implanted in the penis. Complications of this method include infection and mechanical failure. Follow-up studies of prosthesis recipients and their partners have indicated that they were generally satisfied with the choice to have the surgery.

The vacuum pump has been used as a nonsurgical method to treat erectile difficulties. The penis is inserted into an acrylic tube while a handheld vacuum pump draws blood into erectile tissue. A rubber band holds the blood in place for up to thirty minutes.

Hormone administration, principally testosterone, has been used for years to treat erectile dysfunctions. If the problem is not due to hormone deficiency, however, hormones can increase sexual arousability without improving performance, which can result in further deterioration of the client's condition. Testosterone treatment also increases the risk of coronary thrombosis, atherosclerosis, and cancer of the prostate.

The use of testosterone-estrogen pills, creams, and gels have been used to try to increase women's sexual desire. It is unlikely that these medications are helpful except, perhaps, for women with abnormally low levels of testosterone and without other complicating factors (e.g., anxiety, stress, guilt, or anger at partner) that are inhibiting their sexual response. Research is badly needed on the effectiveness of this approach as well as possible side effects. For example, the dosage level is presumably important; high levels of testosterone might increase sexual desire in some women, but they also would tend to masculinize women, producing unwanted body hair and the like.

A number of drugs can create pharmacological erections through injection into the penis by relaxing the smooth muscle of the corpora cavernosa. They appear to be most useful for men with irreversible biological erectile dysfunction. The client can be taught to inject the drug himself. Erection usually occurs within ten minutes and lasts about two hours. There is some risk with this treatment, which has a number of side effects such as penile scarring, priapism, cardiac irregularities, and changes in the liver with long-term use.

A recent drug, sildenafil citrate, approved by the Food and Drug Administration in 1998, is taken orally as a pill. Sildenafil is marketed as Viagra. Used by men who have erectile difficulties, it is taken one hour before the man wants to have an erection and the erection can last for up to four hours following administration. Unlike other treatments, Viagra does not work unless the person is experiencing sexual arousal. It works by blocking an enzyme that allows blood to flow out of the penis.

Irwin Goldstein and his colleagues (1998) reported in a study of 532 men that 70 percent of all attempts at sexual intercourse with an erect penis were successful for men taking Viagra, whereas only 22 percent of attempts were successful when men were administered a placebo. Other studies have shown the effectiveness of Viagra for men with erectile dysfunction. Viagra's effectiveness for women with sexual arousal difficulties has been more mixed but there has been less research conducted with women.

Effectiveness of Sex Therapy

One of the most impressive aspects of Masters and Johnson's (1970) therapeutic approach with almost 800 people with sexual problems was that they reported success in treating more than 80 percent of their clients who experienced various types of sexual dysfunction. Of the successful clients who could be found five years later (313 couples), only 5 percent reported recurrence of the dysfunctions for which they had obtained treatment. The therapeutic community was quite impressed with the success of Masters and Johnson's approach, and for years other therapists used modified versions of many of their methods.

Gradually, however, outcome statistics reported from clinical practice revealed overall improvement in only about two-thirds of cases. The improvements obtained from controlled treatment studies have all been more modest than the proportions Masters and Johnson reported. Do these finding indicate that the only reliable source of sex therapy is Masters and Johnson? Probably not. Instead, differences between the failure rates that Masters and Johnson reported and those that other sex therapists and researchers reported probably stem from a combination of factors other than Masters and Johnson's skills as therapists.

In addition, many of the problems that Masters and Johnson's clients experienced stemmed from misinformation and ignorance. People in the 1950s and 1960s did not have the easy access to information about sexuality that exists today. Clients today whose problems stem from a lack of information may be "curing" themselves instead of seeking professional treatment. The caseloads of sex therapists today may include a greater proportion of clients with sexual difficulties resulting from deeply rooted emotional problems or from conflicts within their relationships—sexual problems that are often difficult to treat. This factor would, of course, result in lower success rates and higher relapse rates.

Another question that must be addressed in the evaluation of any sex therapy is whether the treatment yields sustained change over the years. There is very little available research on this subject. Summarizing what is known, Keith Hawton (1992) reported that the successful short-term results of sex therapy for erectile dysfunction was maintained in the long-term (one to six years), whereas those for premature ejaculation were less permanent. Men with low sexual desire had a fairly poor response to treatment in the short- and long-terms. Sex therapy for vaginismus was highly effective in the short- and long-terms, whereas the long-term results of treatment for low sexual desire in women were fairly poor. Interestingly, there was improvement in the way a number of clients felt about their sexuality, despite the fact that some had returned to pretreatment dysfunctions in sexual behavior. If these clients had received occasion clinical "booster" sessions over the years, their post-treatment improvement would perhaps have been maintained through preventive measures.

See also: CONFLICT: COUPLE RELATIONSHIPS; INTIMACY; MARITAL SEX; SEXUAL COMMUNICATION: COUPLE RELATIONSHIPS; SEXUALITY; THERAPY: COUPLE RELATIONSHIPS

Bibliography

Allgeier, E. R., and Allgeier, A. R. (2000). *Sexual Interactions,* 5th edition. Boston: Houghton Mifflin.

American Psychiatric Association. (1994). *Diagnostic and Statistical Manual of Mental Disorders,* 4th edition. Washington, DC: American Psychiatric Press.

Binik, Y. M.; Meana, M; Berkeley, K.; and Khalife, S. (1999). "The Sexual Pain Disorders: Is the Pain Sexual or is the Sex Painful." *Annual Review of Sex Research* 10:210–213.

Everaerd, W., and Laan, E. (2000). "Drug Treatment for Women's Sexual Disorders." *Journal of Sex Research* 37:195–204.

Francouer, R. T., ed. (1997). *The International Encyclopedia of Sexuality,* Vols. 2–3. New York: Continuum.

Goldstein, I.; Lue, T. F.; Padma-Nathan, H.; Rosen, R. C.; Steers, W. D.; and Wicker, P. A, for the Sildenafil Study Group. (1998). "Oral Sildenafil in the Treatment of Erectile Dysfunction." *New-England Journal of Medicine* 338:1397–1404.

Hawton, K. (1992). "Sex Therapy Research: Has it Withered on the Vine?" *Annual Review of Sex Research* 3:49–72.

Heiman, J. R., and Meston, C. M. (1997). "Empirically Validated Treatment for Sexual Dysfunction." *Annual Review of Sex Research* 8:148–194.

Kafka, M. P. (1997). "Hypersexual Desire in Males: An Operational Definition and Clinical Implications for Paraphilias and Paraphilia-Related Disorders." *Archives of Sexual Behavior* 26:505–526.

Kaplan, H. S. (1974). *The New Sex Therapy.* New York: Brunner/Mazel.

Laumann, E. O.; Gagnon, J. H; Michael, R. T.; and Michaels, S. (1994). *The Social Organization of Sexuality: Sexual Practices in the United States.* Chicago: University of Chicago Press.

Laumann, E. O.; Park, A.; and Rosen R. A. (1999). "Sexual Dysfunction in the United States: Prevalence and Predictors." *Journal of the American Medical Association* 281:537–544.

LoPiccolo, J., and Stock, W. (1986). "Treatment of Sexual Dysfunction." *Journal of Consulting and Clinical Psychology* 54:158–167.

McCabe, M. P., and Delaney, S. M. (1992). "An Evaluation of Therapeutic Programs for the Treatment of Secondary Inorgasmia in Women." *Archives of Sexual Behavior* 21(1):69–89.

Simons, J. S.; and Carey, M. P. (2001). "Prevalence of Sexual Dysfunctions: Results from a Decade of Research." *Archives of Sexual Behavior* 30(2):177–219.

Slob, A. K.; van Berkel, A; and van der Werff ten Bosch, J. J. (2000). "Premature Ejaculation Treated by Local Penile Anesthesia in an Uncontrolled Clinical Replication Study." *Journal of Sex Research* 37:244–247.

Spira, A.; Bajos, N.; and LeGroupe, A. C. S. F. (1993). *Les comportements sexuels en France* Paris: La documentation Francaise.

Welch, M. R., and Kartub, P. (1978). "Sociocultural Correlates of Impotence: A Cross-Cultural Study." *Journal of Sex Research* 14:218–230.

A. R. ALLGEIER

SEXUALITY

Sexual behavior is behavior that produces *sexual arousal* and increases the chance of *orgasm* (Hyde and DeLamater 2003). *Sexuality* refers to sexual behavior, and the thoughts and feelings the person has in relation to that behavior. Every society controls the sexuality of its members, by embedding it in the institutions of family, religion, and law. The core social arrangement within the institution of the family is the marital relationship. The right to engage in sexual activity is a defining characteristic of marriage in all cultures; at the same time, marriage limits sexuality, separating the couple from all other sexually active adults in the society (Potts and Short 1999).

Contemporary analyses of sexuality emphasize that sexuality is not merely a biological phenomenon whose character is the same across time and space; it is also a cultural construct (DeLamater and Hyde 1998). Who engages in sexual behavior with whom and under what circumstances reflect cultural norms and values; even the behaviors in which partners engage reflect social and cultural influence (Gagnon and Simon 1973). The meaning of sexuality in contemporary society is situated "in a dense network of interrelated categories, including the body, maleness and femaleness, reproduction, sensuality, health, selfhood and so on" (Seidman 1991, p. 3).

Certain constructions are found in most or all societies. "Even in the face of great international diversity, . . . rules for sexual behavior often are found to be rigidly defined, strictly enforced, and ultimately used to uphold heteronormative family relations" (Nagel 2000, p. 114). In other words, sexuality is hetero, marital, and oriented toward reproduction.

Despite this normative framework, there is variation. Sexuality varies in its specifics by culture, by race/ethnicity, and by subgroups (e.g., religions) within society. Within each group, there is a perspective on sexuality. Michel Foucault (1978) refers to a way of thinking and talking about sex as a *discourse*. The discourse gives meaning to sexual behavior and relationships, and is the basis of norms that are policed by group members. The meaning of sexuality for particular persons reflects the discourses with which they have come in contact.

Cross-Cultural Variations

Social norms and practices related to love, sex, and marriage vary across cultures. A valuable reference is *The International Encyclopedia of Sexuality*, Vols. 1–4, edited by Robert Francoeur.

The role of the ideology of *romantic love* varies widely across societies. Love is typically the basis for the formation of long-term relationships in the United States and other Western developed societies. Love is less relevant or irrelevant to mate selection in Iran, China, and many South American and African societies (Francoeur 1997). In these societies, especially in rural areas, marriages are influenced or arranged by parents, based on the interests of families, clan, and class. This variation has been interpreted as reflecting an *independence-interdependence* dimension. Cultures that emphasize the individual and his/her goals encourage mate selection based on individual attraction and love, whereas cultures that emphasize the person's dependence on the collective or family will encourage arranged marriages (Hatfield and Rapson 1996). Societies experiencing westernization, such as Russia and urban areas of China, appear to accord increasing emphasis on love. The acceptance of romantic love as a basis for mate selection appears to be associated with greater sexual permissiveness, the acceptance of sexual intimacy before marriage, and with a single standard for the sexual behavior of both men and women.

The meaning of sexual behavior also varies across societies. The dominant discourse in some societies defines sexual activity as an important means of fulfilling the person's emotional and physical needs. This perspective places great value on the person's sexual satisfaction. This leads in turn to a concern with foreplay and the occurrence of orgasm for both parties. In such societies, there will be a concern with sexual technique, and perhaps the development of goods and services to enhance sexual pleasure. This pattern is observed,

for example, in the United States, Sweden, Mexico, and urban areas of Russia. In other societies, such as China and Iran, the discourse that defines sex as procreative persists. Sexual behavior is primarily vaginal intercourse, often with little or no foreplay, and perhaps therefore painful for the female.

Finally, there is variation across societies in the social organization of long-term relationships, especially in whether lifestyles other than marriage are accepted. In some societies, the only acceptable arrangement is marriage. In Iran, for example, most young people live at home until they marry, and mothers of the bride and groom live with the newly married couple, exercising continuing surveillance over their behavior. This leads to infrequent and hurried sexual interactions. (Drew 1997). In other societies, cohabitation is accepted as a prelude to marriage; these are societies, like the United States, where couples can be economically independent and have access to housing. In Sweden, most couples live together before marriage, and most marry. There seems to be great flexibility in Mexico, where marriage may be civil, religious, or both, cohabiting is an alternative to marriage for some couples, and men with sufficient economic resources may have a *second family,* supporting a second woman and their children.

The Ideology of Romantic Love in the West

The understanding of contemporary sexuality is enhanced by reviewing the changes that have occurred in views of sexuality, love, and marriage in Western developed societies since the Victorian era. In the 1800s, sexuality, love, and marriage were seen as distinct and separable experiences. Between 1880 and 1940, they came to be defined as integrated, with the emphasis on marriage. Since 1940, sexuality has gradually been separated from marriage.

Sexuality was severely repressed in the West during the Victorian era. Both sexual behavior and public discussion of topics related to sexuality were suppressed. Women were thought to have no sexual desire. The only legitimate reason for engaging in sexual behavior was to reproduce, and the only acceptable behavior was heterosexual vaginal intercourse, because only that behavior can result in conception. Furthermore, reproduction was to be limited to married couples; the only acceptable partner was one's spouse. Thus, sexuality was tied to the family, a system of marriage, kinship, and inheritance. Nonprocreative sexual activity was prohibited (Foucault 1978).

One of the first empirical studies of sexuality was carried out between 1885 and 1915 by Clelia Mosher (Jacob 1981). Contrary to the discourse of the time, most of the forty-seven women who completed her questionnaire reported that they experienced sexual desire and orgasm. Mosher's research shows that sexual behavior may deviate from social norms. Much information about sexuality in the past is from written documents, which tend to reflect norms and not necessarily behavior.

A new construction of love, the *romantic love ideal,* gained currency in the West during the nineteenth century (Lantz, Keyes, and Schultz 1975). This ideal includes five beliefs: (1) love at first sight; (2) there is one "true love" for each person; (3) love conquers all; (4) the beloved is (nearly) perfect; and (5) one should marry for love. The growth of this ideal can be seen in the increased number of references to it in popular magazines from 1740 to 1865. This ideal encourages people to marry for love.

At the beginning of the twentieth century, another change in construction occurred, the *sexualization of love.* Eroticism came to be seen as an appropriate basis for or component of love. People who were in love were expected to be sexually attracted to each other (and people who were sexually attracted to each other were expected to be in love). Sexual gratification became a goal of romantic relationships. "Mutual sexual fulfillment was intended to enhance intimate solidarity in a social context where other unifying forces (e.g., kinship, patriarchy, economic dependency) were losing their power" (Seidman 1991, p. 2).

These changes reshaped marriage. "Duty, moral character, personal sacrifice, and spiritual union were fast losing their appeal as the defining characteristics of . . . the conjugal relationship" (D'Emilio and Freedman 1988, p. 265). Instead, men and women sought happiness and mutual sexual gratification. Closely related was the gradual acceptance of sexual interest and motivation in women, at least within the marital relationship. The effect of these changes was to increase the expectations of and the demands made on marriage.

During the 1920s, numerous social changes occurred in the United States that both reflected and encouraged these new constructions of love and sexuality. The pursuit of love became a major theme in popular culture, especially in magazines and films. Young people gained autonomy and financial independence, which they used to create their own culture. Erotic themes and expression in art, music, and film created a new, more open public discourse. A popular, if minority, view uncoupled sexual behavior from marriage. Sexual expression was seen as legitimate in its own right. This view led to the creation of new types of relationships and lifestyles. These changes were not universally accepted; there was and is continuing support for the old discourse that limits sexual behavior to marriage.

The institution of dating was established during the 1920s and 1930s in the United States, primarily by white, middle-class youths in cities (D'Emilio and Freedman 1988). Large numbers of these people came together at work, in schools and colleges, and in leisure settings. With help from advice columns, they developed norms about various aspects of these interactions, especially the extent to which sexual intimacy was appropriate. *Necking* and *petting* were generally accepted and practiced. Some observers believe that up to 50 percent of young men and women engaged in intercourse (Smith 1973), although most women had intercourse only with the man they expected to marry (D'Emilio and Freedman 1988). Dating and sexual intimacy gradually diffused to high-school-age and lower-class youths in cities.

Literature giving advice regarding sexuality, much of it by physicians, has been available since the early 1800s in the United States. In the 1920s, this literature extolled physical pleasure as the goal of marital sexual expression. It provided elaborate instruction in sexual technique (Seidman 1991). Male sexuality was portrayed as quickly aroused and physical in nature, whereas female sexuality was slowly aroused and diffuse. Since simultaneous orgasm was the goal, the male was instructed to exert self-control and engage in the elaborate foreplay necessary to arouse his wife. If a couple did not experience mutual fulfillment, this was attributed to poor technique, and at least implicitly was the man's responsibility. This demonstrates the effect of beliefs about gender on public discourse about sex within marriage.

These major changes in the construction of marriage, love, and sex in the United States from

1850 to 1940 increased the demands on the marital relationship; in addition to the traditional expectations, husbands and wives were now expected to love each other and to provide mutual sexual gratification. Falling out of love or failing to experience sexual gratification were defined as problems. These problems became the bases for seeking help (from books, marriage counselors, or sex therapists) or for divorce.

Changing Views of Sex

Social constructions of sex continued to evolve throughout the twentieth century in Western societies. The pioneering surveys conducted by Alfred C. Kinsey and his colleagues (Kinsey et al. 1953; Kinsey, Pomeroy, and Martin 1948) found widespread premarital and extramarital sexual behavior among both men and women. This challenged the popular view that women were not interested in sex, or less interested in it than men. The work of William Masters and Virginia Johnson (1966) demonstrated that the processes of sexual arousal were similar for men and women, in contrast to the earlier view that they were different. These findings led to what has been termed the "eroticization of female sexuality" (Seidman 1991), the view that men and women were equally erotic. However, there are some gender differences in sexual behavior. Surveys in the United States (Smith 1991), Britain (Johnson et al. 1994), and France (Spira et al. 1992) find that men report a larger number of sexual partners than women, both lifetime and in the recent past. Studies also find that men are more accepting of sexual activity in casual relationships than are women (Oliver and Hyde 1993).

A major change in the discourse about sex is the uncoupling of sex from marriage. As sexual gratification became accepted as an end in itself, people began to challenge the belief that intimate sexual activity should be limited to marriage. A liberal discourse emerged, which argued that sexual intimacy involving consenting people who are not married nor planning to marry is acceptable. In the 1970s, some argued that extramarital sexual intimacy is acceptable if the spouse approves (O'Neill and O'Neill 1972). This discourse led to expansion of available sexual lifestyles, including *nonmarital relationships, cohabitation,* and *open marriage.*

Since the mid-1960s, in the United States and elsewhere in the West, a minority discourse has developed that separates sex from love. According to this view, engaging in sexual intimacy for physical pleasure, or to express affection for one's partner, is legitimate. This discourse is the basis of a best-selling sexual advice book of the 1970s, *The Joy of Sex* (Comfort 1972), and its sequel, *The New Joy of Sex* (Comfort 1991). This discourse views male and female as essentially equal in sexual potential and in the right to sexual gratification. It challenges the double standard that sexual intimacy outside marriage or a committed relationship is acceptable for men but not for women. This discourse is consistent with the view that sex need not be limited to heterosexual couples. Thus, it facilitated the movement toward acceptance of casual heterosexual and homosexual contacts and living in committed gay and lesbian relationships.

The most visible change in the United States and other Western cultures since the mid-1970s is the increasing explicitness of public discourse about sexuality. Explicit sexual representations are found in newspapers, magazines, novels, and films. The individual's desire for sexual fulfillment is used to sell lipstick, colognes, beer, clothing, travel, and automobiles. Personal advertisements, singles magazines, and dating services cater to the desire to find the (nearly) perfect spouse or the perfect sexual partner. The sex industry provides lubricants, vibrators, erotic clothing, and explicit videos to people seeking sexual fulfillment. Thus, stimuli associated with arousal are almost everywhere, creating a culture in which the sexual is ever-present. This *sexualization of the culture* undoubtedly contributes to the occurrence of sexual activity in places and among persons formerly prohibited.

The Social Organization of Sexual Relationships

Scientific knowledge about and research on sexuality have developed since 1950. Data on the sexual behavior of various groups have been obtained via surveys, often using self-administered questionnaires. However, the samples surveyed often do not represent the population as a whole and thus yield biased results. The bias is typically in the direction of inflated estimates of sexual behavior.

A variety of sexual lifestyles are evident in the late twentieth-century United States. Data from the National Health and Social Life Survey (NHSLS) (Laumann et al. 1994), based on a representative sample of persons aged eighteen to fifty-nine, indicates that 24 percent (29% of men, 20% of women) are single and never married. Some persons in this group intentionally choose this lifestyle and affiliate with the singles' subculture; others have been unable to form a live-in relationship. Twenty-five percent of this group had no sexual partners in the preceding year, whereas 9 percent reported five or more partners in the preceding year. Number of partners is negatively related to age; older men and women are much more likely to report having no partners.

Seven percent of the respondents were cohabiting (living with a person of the other gender). Most cohabiting couples (94%) expect sexual exclusivity and some consider themselves married; several studies report, however, a higher rate of infidelity among cohabitors, suggesting lower levels of commitment compared to married couples (Treas and Giesen 2000). A few cohabitors report no sexual partners, in other words, no sexual activity, in the past year.

A relationship with a *same-gender partner* was reported by 2.7 percent of the men and 1.3 percent of the women. Survey data suggest that 40 to 60 percent of gay men and 45 to 80 percent of lesbians are involved in a steady romantic relationship (Patterson 2000). Limited data suggest that members of lesbian couples are as faithful as members of heterosexual couples, whereas gay men are less likely to be monogamous. Regardless, both gay and lesbian couples report levels of satisfaction with their sexual relationships that are as high as married and cohabiting couples.

Almost 54 percent of the participants in the NHSLS were married. Virtually all of these persons expect the partner to be faithful, and most are; only 4 percent of the married respondents reported more than one partner in the preceding year. Data from the National Survey of Families and Households indicates that the average couple engages in sexual activity 6.3 times per month (Call, Sprecher, and Schwartz 1995). According to the NHSLS, 95 percent of the married men and women engaged in vaginal intercourse the last time they had sex. Sexual behavior within marriage became more diverse between 1940 and 1990. Compared to the data reported by Kinsey and his colleagues, subsequent surveys (Blumstein and Schwartz 1983;

Johnson et al. 1994) have found that married persons are more likely to engage in oral-genital activity and that they use positions other than man-above during intercourse. The incorporation of these practices into sexual expression reflects acceptance of the belief that sexual activity should be pleasurable for both men and women. Although marriage sanctions sexual intimacy, not all married couples are sexually active; 2 percent of the married respondents in the NHSLS reported no sexual intimacy in the past year. If one broadens the definition of a nonsexual marriage to engaging in sexual intimacy less than ten times per year, 20 percent of the couples in the NHSLS would be in the category (McCarthy 1999); such infrequent physical intimacy may threaten the marital bond.

Fifteen percent were *separated, widowed,* or *divorced.* Forty to 58 percent of these persons reported one sexual partner during the preceding year, suggesting an on-going relationship. One-third of these people reported no sexual partner in that period, with the number increasing sharply for older respondents.

Among married couples, there have been studies of the impact of normative transitions on sexual expression and satisfaction. The transition into a marital or live-in relationship may be associated with an increase in the frequency and variety of sexual expression. This reflects both the social legitimacy of sexual activity in these relationships and the opportunity afforded by ready access to the partner. Several studies report that frequency of activity is high in the first three years of marriage (the *honeymoon effect*), and then declines; the decline probably reflects habituation to the partner and the couple's sexual script (Call, Sprecher, and Schwartz 1995). A similar effect has been noted following remarriage. A normative transition experienced by many couples is the transition to parenthood, via birth or adoption. Research on heterosexual couples indicates that pregnancy and the birth of a child is associated with a reduced incidence of sexual activity at one month postpartum, and an increase in frequency over the following year; satisfaction with the sexual relationship of both men and women follows the same pattern (Hyde et al. 1996). Many contemporary couples fall in the dual-earner category, creating concern about the impact on sexuality; research utilizing two large samples finds that hours of work per week of one or both persons is not related to sexual behavior or satisfaction with the sexual relationship (Hyde, DeLamater, and Durik 2001). A transition experienced by many cohabiting (both heterosexual and same gender) and married persons is the termination of the relationship; research using data from the NHSLS finds that such persons report an increase in number of partners and frequency of activity during the year following dissolution (Wade and DeLamater 2001).

Conclusion

The connections observed between sexuality and marriage in any society reflect the social constructions of love, sexuality, and marriage found in that society. The individual's experience of love, sexuality, and marriage reflects the public discourse about these phenomena. This experience may result in sexual fulfillment or frustration, marital satisfaction or dissatisfaction, seeking counseling/treatment or engaging in adultery, or divorce. Therefore, the health of the institution of marriage reflects, in part, beliefs about sexuality.

See also: ABSTINENCE; ACQUIRED IMMUNODEFICIENCY SYNDROME (AIDS); ATTRACTION; CIRCUMCISION; COHABITATION; DATING; FAMILY PLANNING; GENDER; GENDER IDENTITY; INFIDELITY; INTIMACY; LOVE; MARITAL SEX; MENSTRUAL TABOO; SEXUAL COMMUNICATION: COUPLE RELATIONSHIPS; SEXUAL COMMUNICATION: PARENT-CHILD RELATIONSHIPS; SEXUAL DYSFUNCTION; SEXUALITY EDUCATION; SEXUALITY IN ADOLESCENCE; SEXUALITY IN ADULTHOOD; SEXUALITY IN CHILDHOOD; SEXUALLY TRANSMITTED DISEASES; SEXUAL ORIENTATION; SINGLES/NEVER MARRIED PERSONS

Bibliography

Blumstein, P., and Schwartz, P. (1983). *American Couples: Money, Work, Sex*. New York: Morrow.

Call, V.; Sprecher, S.; and Schwartz, P. (1995). "The Incidence and Frequency of Marital Sex in a National Sample." *Journal of Marriage and the Family* 57: 639–652.

Comfort, A. (1972). *The Joy of Sex*. New York: Crown.

Comfort, A. (1991). *The New Joy of Sex: A Gourmet Guide to Lovemaking for the Nineties*. New York: Crown.

DeLamater, J., and Hyde, J. S. (1998). "Essentialism vs. Social Constructionism in the Study of Human Sexuality." *Journal of Sex Research* 35:10–18.

D'Emilio, J., and Freedman, E. (1988). *Intimate Matters: A History of Sexuality in America*. New York: Harper and Row.

Drew, P. (1997) "Iran." In *The International Encyclopedia of Sexuality,* Vol. 2, ed. R. T. Francoeur. New York: Continuum.

Foucault, M. (1978). "An Introduction." In *The History of Sexuality,* Vol. 1, trans. R. Hurley. New York: Pantheon.

Francoeur, R. T., ed. (1997–2001). *The International Encyclopedia of Sexuality,* 4 vols. New York: Continuum.

Gagnon, J., and Simon, W. (1973). *Sexual Conduct: The Social Origins of Human Sexuality*. Chicago: Aldine.

Hyde, J. S., and DeLamater, J. D. (2003). *Understanding Human Sexuality,* 8th edition. New York: McGraw-Hill.

Hyde, J. S.; DeLamater, J. D.; and Durik, A. M. (2001). "Sexuality and the Dual-Earner Couple. Part II: Beyond the Baby Years." *Journal of Sex Research* 38:10–23.

Hyde, J.; DeLamater, J.D.; Plant, E.A.; and Byrd, J. M. (1996). "Sexuality During Pregnancy and the Year Postpartum." *Journal of Sex Research* 33:143–151.

Jacob, K. A. (1981). "The Mosher Report." *American Heritage* (June/July):56–64.

Johnson, A.; Wadsworth, J.; Wellings, K.; and Field, J. (1994). *Sexual Attitudes and Lifestyles*. Oxford, UK: Blackwell.

Kinsey, A. C.; Pomeroy, W. B.; and Martin, C. E. (1948). *Sexual Behavior in the Human Male*. Philadelphia: Saunders.

Kinsey, A. C.; Pomeroy, W. B.; Martin, C. E.; and Gebhard, P. H. (1953). *Sexual Behavior in the Human Female*. Philadelphia: Saunders.

Lantz, H. R.; Keyes, J.; and Schultz, H. (1975). "The American Family in the Preindustrial Period: From Baselines in History to Change." *American Sociological Review* 40:21–36.

Laumann, E. O.; Gagnon, J. H.; Michael, R. T.; and Michaels, S. (1994). *The Social organization of Sexuality: Sexual Practices in the United States*. Chicago: University of Chicago Press.

Masters, W., and Johnson, V. (1966). *Human Sexual Response*. Boston: Little, Brown.

McCarthy, B. W. (1999). "Marital Style and Its Effects on Sexual Desire and Functioning." *Journal of Family Psychotherapy* 10:1–12.

Nagel, J. (2000). "Ethnicity and Sexuality." *Annual Review of Sociology* 26:107–133.

Oliver, M. B., and Hyde, J. (1993). "Gender Differences in Sexuality: A Meta-Analysis." *Psychological Bulletin* 114:29–51.

O'Neill, G., and O'Neill, N. (1972). *Open Marriage: A New Lifestyle for Couples.* New York: Evans.

Patterson, C. J. (2000). "Family Relationships of Lesbians and Gay Men." *Journal of Marriage and the Family* 62:1052–1069.

Potts, M., and Short, R. (1999). *Ever Since Adam and Eve: The Evolution of Human Sexuality.* Cambridge: Cambridge University Press.

Seidman, S. (1991). *Romantic Longings: Love in America, 1830–1980.* New York: Routledge.

Smith, D. (1973). "The Dating of the American Sexual Revolution: Evidence and Interpretation." In *The American Family in Social-Historical Perspective,* ed. M. Gordon. New York: St. Martin's Press.

Smith, T. W. (1991). "Adult Sexual Behavior in 1989: Number of Partners, Frequency of Intercourse, and Risk of AIDS." *Family Planning Perspectives* 23:102–107.

Spira, A.; Bajos, N.; Bejin, A.; Beltzer, N.; Bozon, M.; Ducot, B. et al. (1992). "AIDS and Sexual Behavior in France." *Nature* 360:407–409.

Sprecher, S., and McKinney, K. (1993). *Sexuality.* Newbury Park, CA: Sage.

Treas, J., and Giesen, D. (2000). "Sexual Infidelity Among Married and Cohabiting Americans." *Journal of Marriage and the Family* 62:48–60.

JOHN DELAMATER
JANET SHIBLEY HYDE

SEXUALITY EDUCATION

There is little debate that the words *sex* and *sexuality* produce immediate attention. Researchers and teachers in this area have also come to employ the terms *family life education, human growth and development,* and *human sexuality* to describe instruction in human reproduction and sexuality (Roth 1993). The Sex Information and Education Council of the United States (SIECUS) recommends the term *sexuality education* (1992). This term refers to a comprehensive curriculum of instruction addressing not only sexual anatomy and physiology but also reproduction, contraception, sexually disseminated infections (SDIs), and related topics. Sexuality education is viewed by SIECUS as "a lifelong process of acquiring information and forming attitudes, beliefs, and values

about identity, relationships, and intimacy." These programs commonly address issues of personality, value formation, decision-making, peer and social pressures, affection, intimacy, body image, gender roles, communication strategies, and various sexual behaviors (Haffner and de Mauro 1991).

There continues to be wide variation in results from various sexuality education interventions in the United States as well as in other countries (Dryfoos 1985; Ekstrand, Siegel, and Krasnovsky 1994). Some have had positive results on actual sexual behavior while others have failed to attain favorable outcomes (Kirby, Short, and Collins 1994). Because a clear means for designing or implementing preventive sexuality education programs has not emerged, researchers and teachers need to remain current on which approaches work best for which students under which circumstances.

Sexuality Education and Development Stages

For clarity, the developmental stages are classified into four very broad categories: younger children (five to seven), intermediate children (eight to ten), older children (eleven to twelve), and teenagers. Education regarding sexuality in children one to four years of age is not examined, since little data exists on sexuality during these ages (Borneman 1983). It is important to note, however, that these children do receive "education" in the form of modeling from their caregivers.

Younger children (five to seven). Children five to seven years of age do not see the distinction between causes and their effects. The process of thinking is centered around themselves, and they have difficulty seeing the perspectives of others (Piaget 1930; Werner 1948). From a sexual standpoint, young children at this stage generally have a clear sense of the basic anatomical distinctions between the sexes. There is typically modesty regarding public exposure of their bodies. Not surprisingly, parents and other adults exert a strong influence regarding issues such as nudity in the home (Masters, Johnson, and Kolodny 1992). At the same time, children have a natural curiosity about their bodies. Since the child considers the parent to be the main guide for appropriate behavior, it is critical that parents not overreact to catching the child in various sexual exploration games such as playing "doctor" or "house" with peers.

By the time the child enters first grade, the frequency of exploration games decreases, and exchange of sex information emerges in the form of sexual jokes, riddles, and rhymes (Borneman 1983). Children become fascinated with the new array of words that have sexual or forbidden connotations. Researchers have studied this phenomenon in children and have suggested that when information on sexuality is not clearly provided by adults (e.g. parents and teachers), sexual jokes become the primary source of such knowledge (Money 1980). Sexuality education at this level requires an emphasis on the importance of knowing and being comfortable with one's sexual self while simultaneously avoiding negative modeling. A sound educational foundation at this level can foster greater social and sexual maturity at later stages.

Intermediate children (eight to ten). During this period, thinking is characterized by the ability to differentiate between self and others, between internal and external bodily events, and by an ability to comprehend cause-and-effect relationships. Sexuality education at this age can illustrate causality and thus more complex information. At this stage, children become intrigued with reproductive mechanisms. The idea of hormones as crystal-like structures flowing through one's blood is not abstract or unbelievable at this stage. Sexuality programs during this period have a twofold purpose: (1) provision of relevant, as well as scientifically correct, knowledge and language usage; and (2) instruction that facilitates the child's ability to understand causation and thus help them act to prevent future problems.

The goal of preventive sexuality education at this stage is important in view of AIDS/HIV in the United States and in other countries, such as those in southern and central Africa. Various medical and scientific authorities agree that the most promising method for controlling this crisis is early preventive and developmentally appropriate sexuality education (Greenberg, Bruess, and Hafner 2000).

Older children (eleven to twelve). During this time children integrate internal and external phenomena into one system. Their level of cognitive sophistication is also more intricate. They can easily see how one factor (lack of knowledge) may interact or combine with another factor (lack of self-esteem) to produce risky sexual acts and teenage pregnancies. Such interactive relationships are crucial in sexuality education designed to foster self-protective thinking among students. In contrast to prior stages, however, the biological side of development now begins to play a major role. There is a strong sense of one's external appearance and how it may be perceived as significant by others. Most children experience puberty at this age. Sex hormones begin to increase in activity and stimulate bone growth. This "growth spurt" typically occurs two years earlier for females than males (on average, age twelve versus fourteen).

Sexuality education is of crucial importance during this time. For girls, there is a need to know about breast development (*phelarche*), appearance of pubic and axillary hair (*pubarche, thelarche*), and the onset of menstrual cycles (*menarche*). There is also a need to know about vaginal secretion changes that may occur (*transudation*) and, most importantly, that these body changes are part of normal sexual development. In boys, there is a need for information on genital growth and ejaculation. Although males do not have a direct counterpart to menarche in females, the first nocturnal ejaculation of a young boy can cause the same psychological concern. Boys, like girls, also need to know about the onset of pubic and facial hair and how it is a biologically normal process. A condition known as *gynecomastia* or breast enlargement occurs in many young males whose hormonal systems are still trying to find their balance. Boys need clear and compassionate information that assures them this condition is not life threatening or cancerous and that it typically disappears within a year or two without any harmful effects.

Physical changes are also part of sexual differentiation at this period of development. Young girls tend to be overly concerned with the shape, texture, and general aesthetic of their bodies as estrogen causes fat to accumulate under the skin to produce the classic female figure. Boys, conversely, are more fixated on height and muscle mass comparisons as testosterone production begins to influence muscles that eventually produce the male physique.

Teenagers. By the time young people reach fourteen or fifteen years of age, their biological development is established. Most pubertal changes have

A public health worker gives a demonstration on the use of condoms at a family planning clinic in Gambia. LIBA TAYLOR/
CORBIS

occurred, and most of their physical attributes are set. Still, the teen years are considered by most authorities in development to be the most stressful. Personal appearance and social popularity grow to be overwhelming forces in teens' daily life. Teenagers naturally make sexual behavior a part of attaining peer affirmation. A teen may be asked, dared, or even belittled into proving solidarity with the peer group by performing sexual acts (Lewis and Lewis 1984; Duryea 1994). Research studies have shown that teenagers consistently submit to these pressures even *without* any inducement from peers (Duryea 1991; Saarni 1989).

Sexuality education for teens must present material perceived as relevant to them, in a factual manner that avoids the appearance of preaching or admonishment. Teenagers at this level possess a strong sense of autonomy. They easily detect in adults, especially their teachers, hidden strategies designed to alter their behavior or thinking. Course material and exercises examining reproduction,

contraception, and communication are among the more meaningful at this stage, but prevention of sexual assault and information on sexual varieties also generate interest among teenagers. At this age students require contemporary information and skills to form a thorough knowledge base from which to make complex and pressure-filled health-related decisions. Some research evidence suggests, however, that while sexuality programs do provide this information and these skills, they are not consistently decreasing risky sexual behavior (Frost and Forrest 1995; Kipke, Futterman, and Hein 1990).

Contexts and Types of Sexuality Education

Over the past twenty years sexuality education in the United States has experienced four distinct generations of school-based programs. In the first generation the focus was on providing students with knowledge of basic sexual anatomy and the risks and consequences of pregnancy. The context

An instructor teaches sex education in Mexico. Topics generally covered in sex education include value formation, decision-making, peer and social pressures, intimacy, body image, gender roles, and various sexual behaviors, among a range of other issues. KEITH DANNEMILLER/ CORBIS SABA

for such approaches was that information was the main objective and that students would apply it as needed. This approach was consistently criticized for not showing any linkage between increasing knowledge and reducing risky sexual behavior. The second generation of programs emphasized values, communication skills, and decision making in one's personal life. This approach was based on the assumption that such areas, if enhanced using sexuality education, would inevitably produce healthier young people. Many of these efforts were also criticized for not addressing a wider range of sexuality concepts (e.g. contraception options). Although students demonstrated enhanced communication and decision-making skills, there did not appear to be any relationship with decreased sexual risk especially with regard to actual sexual behavior. The third generation currently promotes "abstinence only" and in its most strict form omits examination of various contraceptive options. Its context is conservative and often grounded in religion. It proposes that offering students too many options about contraception—and thus "safer sex"—actually encourages risky sexual actions. Their critics argue that such a philosophy ignores the reality of adolescent sexuality: a large number of youth will engage in sex and that they need to do it safely (with effective and consistent contraception). The latest generation is referred to as *comprehensive sexuality education* which emphasizes abstinence as the best choice but also trains

students in refusal skills, assertiveness, communication strategies, and related areas. These programs revolve around acknowledging and addressing all of the major factors seen by adolescents as both real and important. This approach incorporates information about contraceptive options and even where teens can get access to contraceptives in their schools and community. Unsurprisingly, their opponents are abstinence-only advocates who suggest that including how to purchase contraceptives in a school curriculum is not only immoral and irresponsible but illegal, since students—by law—should not be having sexual relations. Conversely, in most European countries, Australia, and Canada, there is no such debate. Instead, many countries prefer to treat contraceptive access as a normal part of adolescent social development.

Since the mid-1980s, one trend in preventive sexuality education in the United States has been peer-based programs. These curricula are jointly designed and taught by well-respected, older-age peers in collaboration with the teacher. The rationale for using peers to help conduct these programs is student desire for ownership of this instruction. Peer leaders also tend to increase the credibility by which such instruction is viewed by students. Increased credibility is linked to greater student interest and ultimately to more meaningful learning. Such curricula are helpful to teachers responsible for teaching this class but who are uncomfortable with the content. Popular students recruited to help teach these programs often lessen this uneasiness and facilitate topical discussion. Results of such peer-based strategies, particularly if followed up with "booster" programs, have been variable but generally seen as favorable (Grunseit 1997).

Peers can enhance sexuality education programs, but parents and legal guardians remain the major sexuality teachers of their children. Research published by the Henry J. Kaiser Family Foundation (1999) estimated that 59 percent of youth ten to twelve years of age reported that they personally learned the "most" about sexuality from their parents. Seventy percent of parents of youth thirteen to fifteen years of age reported that they had spoken with their children regarding relationship issues and becoming sexually active. With or without parental support most communities in the United States have institutionalized sexuality education within school-based curricula. This allows teachers an opportunity to integrate parents into the curriculum content on a regular basis. The question to parents and teachers is no longer *if* sexuality education should be taught but *how* such material should be taught. Unfortunately, a number of studies indicate that relatively few parents systematically and comprehensively educate their children in sexuality (Cross 1991; Kallen, Stephenson, and Doughty 1983). Research suggests that open communication between parents and children helps develop enhanced self-confidence, caring relationships, and the skills needed to make healthy sexuality decisions later in life (Centers for Disease Control and Prevention 2000). Experts also suggest that young people who talk with their parents about sexuality are more likely to postpone first sexual activity and to use protection if and when they do become sexually active (Pike 2000; Darroch 2000). Canada, Britain, and the United States each emphasize the inclusion of parents in the schools sexuality education curriculum. They also emphasize delay of first intercourse as a major curricular theme. Such a theme is not emphasized in various European nations such as the Netherlands, Denmark, and France. Some research suggests specific areas that should be addressed in sexuality discussions within the family. These include delivering comprehensive messages, parental communication skill and sensitivity in discussing sexuality, and the timing of communication. Comprehensive messages foster discussion on a range of topics such as decision making, menstruation, reproduction, physical and sexual development, the age when one should assess whether or not to become sexually active, birth control methods, choosing partners, masturbation, and STD/HIV prevention strategies (Whitaker et al. 1998). Parental communication ability and sensitivity to difficult topics are consistently emphasized in successful school-based programs.

A recent study conducted by the Epidemiological Branch of Center for Disease Control's (CDC) Division of HIV/AIDS Prevention examined how selected individual, familial, peer, and environmental factors influence HIV risk and risk-reduction behaviors among adolescents age fourteen to seventeen. Interview data were collected from adolescent-mother pairs recruited from various public high schools and locations. The study focused on the role of mother-child communication regarding sex. The investigators examined how the content, process, and timing of this communication related to the child's later sexual risk behaviors. They found that adolescents who talked with their mothers before their first sexual encounter were three times more likely to use a condom than adolescents who did not talk with their mothers. Such a finding is critical because condom use at first intercourse strongly predicts future use. In fact, adolescents who used condoms at first intercourse were twenty times more likely to use condoms regularly in subsequent acts.

The World Health Organization's Expert Committee on Comprehensive School Health Education and Promotion released a report with recommendations that could enable schools to promote healthy lifestyles. Some of the key recommendations emphasize implementation of community and family involvement. Such involvement could serve as reinforcement for young people to adopt healthy sexual behavior throughout their adolescence and well into marriage.

Unlike their European counterparts, however, relatively few U.S. fathers play an active role in providing their children with age-appropriate sex information. Fathers who fail to participate in such education run the risk of allowing their children to interpret what they view in the media as accurate depictions of sexuality. This neglect can and often does produce negative consequences. Even when there exists a progressive, comprehensive, and developmentally sound school curriculum, parental involvement at home is needed to reinforce and support the skills, information, and viewpoints being explored at school. How to consistently foster this parental reinforcement is a dilemma for sexuality programs in U.S. schools. With the possible exception of Poland and Ireland, both Catholic countries, this dilemma does not pervade European countries. Since sexuality education is viewed the same way as any other education area such as mathematics or history, parental support and inclusion is not the major barrier it is in the United States.

There is a growing movement to implement sexuality education within various medical settings (Mansfield, Conroy, Emans, and Woods 1993). Such education is implemented in physicians' offices or hospitals during patient visits. Normally, a nurse conducts the education although health educators, or even a physician, can be employed.

Mansfield and associates (1993) studied the effects of one such physician-delivered HIV education program for high-risk adolescents. After thorough counseling and preventive education in the medical office, sexual behaviors of these adolescents were not significantly changed. Other research teams (Rickert, Gottlieb, and Jay 1990) have had similar difficulty altering sexual behavior of female adolescents in clinic-based interventions. Many health maintenance organizations (HMOs) routinely employ health educators to implement sexuality programs for youth. These interventions employ interactive videos, reading material, and counseling to motivate youth to make responsible choices in sexuality areas. The effectiveness of these education efforts is clear. While knowledge and skill levels are favorably enhanced, the degree to which they prevent later risky sexual *actions* is not known.

Since the mid-1980s, various religious organizations have instituted their own sexuality or family life education programs. Whereas schools and medical settings tend to emphasize personal responsibility in sexual behavior, religious programs are more likely to emphasize abstinence, a choice included in most major sexuality programs. The curricula offered in more conservative and/or religious areas usually have prohibitions against specific topics and language.

Despite the wide range of contexts, settings, and types of sexuality education in the United States, programs are implemented with the goal of providing relevant knowledge and training so that such education is internalized by students and that they will, therefore, act to avert potential sexual problems (Zabin and Hayward 1993). One specific area which received attention in the 1990s is preventive sexuality education in diverse student populations. The higher epidemiologic rates of teenage pregnancy, HIV, and SDIs in minority students continue to receive significant study and support.

Approaches and Controversies in Other Countries

Similar to young people in the United States, youth around the world are curious about sexual information and experiment with sexual behaviors. Not surprisingly authorities in other countries responsible for sexuality education have different ways of approaching such education. Unlike the United

States, most western European countries and Canada have neither racial heterogeneity nor the poverty the United States has (MacFarlane 1997). Program implementation under such constraints is much more difficult for U.S. educators. In many European nations, such as Sweden, France, and the Netherlands, governments—and thus social policy in this area—tend to be more liberal and better financially supported than in the United States. The conservative religious lobby in these countries is not nearly as evident, vocal, or powerful as in the United States. The focus in these nations is on reducing unprotected intercourse rather than trying to completely eliminate sexual behavior among the young (Greenberg, Bruess, and Hafner 2000). Due to the absence of an organized or persuasive opposition many European countries have little difficulty routinely offering students sequential sexuality education throughout their adolescent years—not just during a select few years. The philosophy underlying many curricula is that sexuality education should be considered as important to a young person's education as science, literature, language, or mathematics. In sharp contrast to the United States, most European countries, as well as Canada and Australia, offer access to contraceptives both in school clinics and in the community. In the Netherlands, for example, the various family planning organizations throughout the country develop curricula and advertise the availability of contraceptives. Essentially, the European approach is two-pronged: ongoing education in a variety of crucial areas (anatomy, sexual health, reproduction, contraception) and easy access to contraceptive clinics and contraceptives. Comparable to the United States, however, is the almost universal problem, even in Sweden, concerning the lack of teacher training in sexuality content.

In Francophone Africa, a girl's access to higher education is often halted by early pregnancy and consequently by early family responsibilities. Thus, the government has recognized the need for reproductive health education among this group. Although the government has tried to implement programs in sexuality courses, the students receive information only in their biology classes. One group, the Ministry of Youth and Sports, has implemented the Youth Promotion Program that conducts counseling life education. In other parts of Africa, such as Cameroon, the law states that, "Sex education for girls—especially information on contraceptive methods, STDs, and AIDS—receive special emphasis." Unfortunately, the reality is that education concerning young girls' sexuality remains taboo, except in the Muslim community, which teaches only from the religious perspective (Center for Reproductive Law and Policies 1999).

Over the past several years, the Catholic Church in Poland has played a major role in the teaching of young people in the schools. The availability of information related to sexuality has been restricted to sexual relations *after* one is married. Due to the lack of sexual information, and a religious prohibition against practicing birth control, many women use natural family planning methods, which increase their chances of an unwanted pregnancy (Nowicka 1996). Wanda Nowicka states: "Although the exact figures do not exist, it is estimated that there are from 180,000 to 300,000 unwanted pregnancies per year and, the sex education program under preparation by the ministry of Education, encompasses Catholic teaching on sexuality and a patriarchal model of the family in which a woman's main role is that of mother and wife, and that the only contraception that is recommended as acceptable is natural family planning."

Religious convictions also play a crucial role in the delivery of sexuality education in the Dominican Republic. As Article XII of the Concordato guarantees, the cardinal not only has the right to question state policy regarding sex education of students, but also can dictate this policy and even decide who teaches such courses (Women's Health Journal, 2000). As it is currently formulated, the public schools "have to conform to the Catholic morals and doctrine" (p. 2).

Although many countries strive to increase young people's access to sexuality information, Chile has recently regressed in this area due to pressure from several conservative groups. Currently in Chile, there are over 40,000 adolescent pregnancies every year, which comprise 20 percent of all pregnancies in the country. Moreover, AIDS continues to escalate at a rate that requires urgent solutions. Despite such trends the Chilean government has changed their curriculum to a more conservative program that focuses on how to "avoid shortcomings in the formation of values." It replaced the previous curriculum which emphasized a program for "dialogue on feelings and sexuality" (Gonzalez 1996).

There are considerable differences between countries and how they view and implement sexuality education for youth. Some nations have strong and vocal religious forces that dictate morality, and thus policy, and ultimately educational instruction. Others view sexuality education as just one of many life skills that young people require education in and thus permit greater freedom in accessing information and contraceptives. Regardless of the country, culture, or language, however, the impact of the family and marriage is crucial to the sexuality education of all young people.

The Family and Marriage

The family and the institution of marriage have changed dramatically throughout the world in the past few decades due to social, economic, technological, and medical influences. The traditional "nuclear" family of western nations where neither parent had ever been divorced, there were two to four children, and they lived in a different geographic region than their relatives, is a thing of the past (Greenberg, Bruess, and Hafner 2000). One out of every three children in the United States now resides with a stepparent. People getting married now face a 33 percent probability that the marriage will end in divorce. Gay marriages are the subject of federal litigation in various states, and court cases emerge regularly concerning which parent owns embryos, sperm, and egg donations. A child in today's society could theoretically count five "parents": legal mother and father, sperm and egg donors and the surrogate mother who carries and delivers the child. Children in Africa routinely see their families deteriorate as siblings, relatives, and parents die from AIDS. Amidst this complex and threatening landscape children must somehow be educated on the foundations of healthy human sexuality.

Schools cannot and should not be held solely responsible for this part of their education. U.S. schools, for instance, have eliminated much of their traditional sexuality education curricula (safe sex, condom use, birth control methods) and have replaced it with programs that pledge abstinence only (Hazelwood 1993). Federal funding guidelines, stemming from the 1996 Welfare Reform Act, prohibit many programs from providing students with information about contraception and contraceptive access (Sheer 2001). The debate over the place of moral and behavioral norms in sexuality education, and particularly how they influence family and marriage continues to be contentious.

In Europe, with the exception of Britain, this debate does not generate much controversy. Most European countries acknowledge that portraying sexual relations among young people as shameful makes contraceptive use also shameful. The result can only be that students will not be protected from unwanted pregnancy, HIV, and STDs. Such outcomes most certainly harm marriages as well as the family (Furedi 2001). Britain conversely *does* have a conservative and vocal representation and has many of the same family and morality debates as the United States. In India, with its population crisis, the State Institute of Education stipulated that children need "scientific knowledge of the process of growing up, drug addiction, bad effects of population explosion, family life and quality of life" (Indian Express 1999). While family integrity and the sanctity of marriage is a top priority, the population problem has caused Indian authorities to relax religious restrictions in order to control the birth rate and its harmful effects on the quality of life.

The specific effects of sexuality education on the institution of marriage are not fully documented. There is evidence that young, newly married couples that are able to plan their families (skill in contraception) experience greater success in avoiding divorce and economic hardship (Fielding and Williams 1990). Because couples who are skillful in negotiating the emotional stresses of early marriage will have a greater chance of remaining married, previous exposure to effective sexuality curricula or programs that help prepare youth for these challenges may foster a more successful marriage. Around the world, societies which support respectful, caring, and thus stable marriages also tend to produce these same types of families. Such families subsequently foster in their children these same traits. Ultimately, young people with these traits increase the quality of life for all members of the society.

See also: ABSTINENCE; ACQUIRED IMMUNODEFICIENCY SYNDROME (AIDS); ADOLESCENT PARENTHOOD; ASSISTED REPRODUCTIVE TECHNOLOGIES; BIRTH CONTROL: CONTRACEPTIVE METHODS; BIRTH CONTROL: SOCIOCULTURAL AND HISTORICAL ASPECTS; CIRCUMCISION; FAMILY LIFE EDUCATION; FAMILY PLANNING; MENARCHE; RELIGION; SEXUAL COMMUNICATION: PARENT-CHILD RELATIONSHIPS; SEXUALITY; SEXUALITY IN ADOLESCENCE; SEXUALITY IN CHILDHOOD; SEXUALLY TRANSMITTED DISEASES; SEXUAL ORIENTATION

Bibliography

Borneman, E. (1983). "Progress in Empirical Research on Children's Sexuality." *SIECUS Report* 12: 1–6.

Center for Reproductive Law and Policy. (1999). "Women of the World: Laws and Policies Affecting Their Reproductive Lives-Francophone, Africa." Washington, DC: Author.

Centers for Disease Control and Prevention. (2000). "Reducing the Risk: Building the Skills to Prevent Pregnancy, STD's and HIV." Atlanta, GA: Author.

Croft, C., and Asmussen, L. (1991). "A Developmental Approach to Sexuality Education: Implications for Medical Practice." *Journal of Adolescent Health* 14:109–114.

Cross, R. (1991). "Helping Adolescents Learn about Sexuality," *SIECUS Report* (April–May).

Darroch, J. E.; Landry, D. J.; and Singh, S. (2000). "Changing Emphases in Sexuality Education in U.S. Public Secondary School 1988–1999." *Family Planning Perspectives* 32:204–211.

D'Augelli, A., and D'Augelli, J. (1994). "The Enhancement of Social Skills and Competence: Promoting Lifelong Sexual Unfolding." In *Handbook of Social Skills Training and Research,* ed. L. L. Abate. New York: John Wiley and Sons.

Dryfoos, J. (1988). "School-based Health Clinics." *Family Planning Perspectives* 20:193–200.

Duryea, E. J. (1994). "Attack and Counter-Attack in Nonverbal Sexual Communication Among Adolescents: Relevance and Applications for Preventive Sexuality Programs." Paper presented at the Annual Meeting of the Society for the Scientific Study of Sexuality, Miami, November 3–6.

Duryea, E. J. (1991). "Principles of Nonverbal Communication in Efforts to Reduce Peer and Social Pressure." *Journal of School Health* 61:5–10.

Ekstrand, M.; Siegel, D.; and Krasnovsky, F. (1994). Paper presented at the Second International Conference on Biopsychosocial Aspects of HIV Infection. Brighton, United Kingdom.

Firestone, W. A. (1994). "The Content and Context of Sexuality Education." *Family Planning Perspectives* 26:125–131.

Greenberg, J.; Bruess, C.; and Haffner, D. (2000). *Exploring the Dimensions of Human Sexuality.* Sudbury, MA: Jones and Bartlett Publishers.

Grunseit, A. (1997). "Sexuality Education and Young People's Sexual Behavior: A Review of Studies." *Journal of Adolescent Research* 12:421–453.

Haffner, D., and de Mauro, D. (1991). *Winning the Battle: Developing Support for Sexuality and HIV/AIDS Education.* New York: Sex Information and Education Council of the United States.

Hazelwood, K. (1993). "No Sex is the Safest Sex." *Alberta Report/Magazine* 20:26.

Henry J. Kaiser Family Foundation. (1999). "Talking With Kids About Tough Issues: A National Survey of Parents and Kids." Menlo Park, CA: Author.

Kallen, D.; Stephenson, J.; and Doughty, A. (1983). "The Need to Know: Recalled Adolescent Sources of Sexual and Contraceptive Information and Sexual Behavior." *Journal of Sex Research* 19:137–159.

Kipke, D.; Futterman, J.; and Hein, J. (1990). "HIV Infection and AIDS During Adolescence." *Medical Clinics of North America* 74:1149–1167.

Kirby D. J.; Short, L.; and Collins, J. (1994). "School Based Programs to Reduce Sexual Risk Behaviors: A Review of Effectiveness." *Public Health Reports* 109:339–360.

Lewis, C., and Lewis, M. A. (1984). "Peer Pressure and Risk-Taking Behaviors in Children." *American Journal of Public Health* 74:580–584.

MacFarlane, R. (1997). "Summary of Adolescent Research: Implications for Prevention." *Prevention Researcher* 4:5–7.

Mansfield, C.; Conroy, M. E.; Emans, J.; and Woods, E. (1993). "A Pilot Study of AIDS Education and Counseling of High-Risk Adolescents in an Office Setting." *Journal of Adolescent Health* 14:115–119.

Masters, W.; Johnson, V.; and Kolodny, R. (1992). *Human Sexuality.* 4th Edition. New York: HarperCollins.

Money, J. (1980). *Love and Sickness.* Baltimore, MD: Johns Hopkins University Press.

Nowicka, W. (1996). "Roman Catholic Fundamentalism Against Women's Reproductive Rights in Poland." *Reproductive Health Matters* 8:1–7.

Pike, L. B.; Berger, T.; Rea-Halloway, M. (2000). "Conducting Adolescent Sexuality Research in Schools: Lessons Learned." *Family Planning Perspectives* 32:245–251.

Roth, B. (1993). "The School Nurse as Adolescent Health Educator." *Journal of School Nursing* (December Supplement):1–15.

Saarni, C. (1989). "Children's Understanding of Strategic Control of Emotional Expression in Social Transactions." In *Children's Understanding of Emotion,* ed. C. Saarni and P. Harris. Cambridge, UK: Cambridge University Press.

Sheer, S. (2001). "Effect of Highly Active Antiretroviral Therapy on Diagnoses of Sexually Transmitted Diseases in People With AIDS." *Lancet* 357:432–436.

SIECUS Fact Sheet. (1992). "Comprehensive Sexuality Education." *SIECUS Report* (August–September).

SIECUS Fact Sheet. (1993). "Comprehensive Sexuality Education: Guidelines for Comprehensive Sexuality Education, Kindergarten–12th Grade." *SIECUS Report* (April–May).

Stevens, S. C.; Dolgan, J. I.; Kelly, L.; and Singer, D. (1997). "The Effect of Monetary Incentives and Peer Support Groups on Repeat Adolescent Pregnancies." *Journal of the American Medical Association* 277:977–982.

Werner, H. (1948). *Comparative Psychology of Mental Development.* New York: Science Editions.

Whitaker, D. J.; Miller, K.; Levin, M.; and Xu, X. (1998). "Patterns of Condom Use Among Adolescents: The Impact of Maternal-Adolescent Communication." *American Journal of Public Health* 88:1542–1544.

Zabin, L., and Hayward, S. (1993). "Adolescent Sexual Behavior and Childbearing." In *Developmental Clinical Psychology and Psychiatry,* ed. A.E. Kazdin. Newbury Park, CA: Sage Publications.

Other Resources

Centers for Disease Control and Prevention. (2000). "Reducing the Risk: Building the Skills to Prevent Pregnancy, STD's and HIV." Available from http://www.cdc.gov/nccdphp/dash/rtc/curric3.htm.

Furedi, F. (2001). "Sex Education Without the Prejudice: Why the Government-Sponsored Sex Education Campaigns Have Had No Impact on the UK's High Rate of Teenage Pregnancies." Available from http://www.independent.co.uk/news/UK/Education/2001–01/sexed110101.shtml.

Gonzalez, G. (1996). "Chile-Population: School Sex Education Program Stalls." Available from: http://newfirstsearch.oclc.org.html.

India Express Newspapers. (1999). "Adolescents to be Educated on Sexual Development." Available from: http://www.expressindia.com/ie/daily/19990429/ige29157.html.

ELIAS J. DURYEA
KARI L. KUKA
DENISE E. HERRERA

SEXUALITY IN ADOLESCENCE

Research about adolescent sexuality has tradition-ally emphasized sexual intercourse. Most studies have focused on whether teenagers have had in-tercourse, how often, and with how many part-ners. Such simple measures of sexual behavior, narrowly defined as coitus, do not properly ac-knowledge the varied dimensions of adolescent sexual development. Sexuality, as opposed to sex, includes a wide range of attitudes, emotions, ex-pectations, sexual orientation, and both coital and noncoital behaviors. Although sexual behavior can be distinct and separate from romantic or emo-tional relationships, they often develop together, and are frequently dependent on each other (Miller and Benson 1999).

Sexual Intercourse Patterns in the United States

As depicted in Figure 1, about 50 percent of girls and 56 percent of boys in the United States age fif-teen to nineteen have had sexual intercourse at least once (Alan Guttmacher Institute 1999). Of course the percentages increase dramatically with age. Among fifteen-year-old youths, sexual intercourse experience is still unusual (22% for girls and 27% for boys), whereas more than half of seventeen-year-olds have had intercourse. Among nineteen-year-olds, the large majority (76% of females and 85% of males) are sexually experienced regardless of gen-der. About 20 percent of teenagers (15% of males and 24% of females) do not have sexual intercourse during their teenage years (Alan Guttmacher Insti-tute 1999). Intercourse among teenagers is most often voluntary but not always welcome. About one in four women report that their first coital experi-ence was unwanted, but the proportion is 70 per-cent unwanted among those whose first intercourse experience occurred before age thirteen. Adolescent females tend to be involved sexually with young men near their own age: 61 percent have partners who are within two years of their own age, 27 per-cent have partners who are three to four years older, and 12 percent have partners who are five or more years older. Conversely, teenage males tend to have sexual partners younger than themselves. Among nineteen-year-old males, 76 percent had seventeen-to eighteen-year-old partners, 13 percent had

FIGURE 1

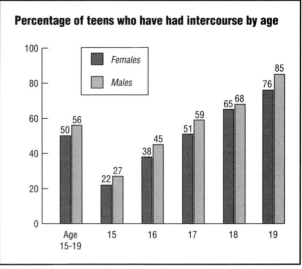

Percentage of teens who have had intercourse by age

sixteen-year-old partners, and 11 percent had thirteen- to fifteen-year-old partners (Alan Gutt-macher Institute 1999). Sexual intercourse is spo-radic and infrequent for most sexually experienced teenagers. In one study (De Gaston, Jensen, and Weed 1995), half of sexually experienced teenagers had been involved with only one partner, and many of them reported regrets about not having waited. According to Debra Haffner (1998), 65 percent of adolescent girls and 45 percent of boys felt that their sexual debut occurred too early.

Racial, National, and Ethnic Diversity

Sexual intercourse experience among female ado-lescents in the United States tends to be compara-ble to other industrialized nations, below rates of many sub-Saharan African nations, and higher than most Latin American nations. About 81 percent of females in the United States experience sexual in-tercourse before the age of twenty compared to 81 percent in Germany, 73 percent in France, and 87 percent in Britain (Alan Guttmacher Institute 1998). In sub-Saharan Africa, a higher proportions of fe-male adolescents have sexual intercourse: over 90 percent experience intercourse in nations such as Botswana and Uganda (91%), Burkina Faso, Niger, and Togo (92%), Cameroon and the Central African Republic (94%), Côte d'Ivoire (Ivory Coast) and Mali (95%), and Liberia (98%) (Alan Guttmacher Institute 1998). Females in Burundi and Rwanda differ from other African teenagers, with only 46 percent and 43 percent respectively having intercourse before age twenty. The percentage engaging in sexual intercourse as teenagers seems to be linked with patterns of early or delayed marriage in several of these African nations. In Botswana and Burkina Faso, the percentage who have sex before age twenty is similar, but marital status is very different: 81 percent of female Botswanans first have intercourse as teenagers *before* marriage, whereas only 25 percent of women in Burkina Faso experience sexual debut before marriage. In Latin American countries, lower percentages of young women are sexually experienced before age twenty than in either sub-Saharan Africa or the United States. From lowest to highest, the percentages are Peru (45%), Mexico (46%), El Salvador (49%), Dominican Republic (50%), Ecuador (51%), Trinidad and Tobago (57%), Bolivia (58%), Paraguay (61%), Brazil (62%), Colombia (62%), and Guatemala (64%) (Alan Guttmacher Institute 1998). Table 1 summarizes percentages of teenage sexual intercourse in select Latin-American, sub-Saharan African, and developed nations (Alan Guttmacher Institute 1998).

Premarital adolescent sexual intercourse varies widely between the various racial and ethnic groups within the United States. In the United States 79 percent of African Americans and 54 percent of Latinos between fifteen and nineteen years of age have had sexual intercourse (Perkins et al. 1998). European-Americans have a much lower rate of sexual intercourse experience (37%) and Asian-Americans have the lowest rate (16%). Among teenagers age fifteen to nineteen years, African-American and Latino teenagers tend to have the earliest sexual debut, greatest number of sexual partners, and highest frequency of intercourse (Perkins et al. 1998). Such findings are explained, at least in part, by racial/ethnic differences in socioeconomic status and other demographic factors.

Relationships and Sexual Activity

Patterns of physical maturation are parallel throughout the world, but the development of sexuality varies dramatically from culture to culture. As seen in Table 1, the timing of marriage and sexual intercourse varies widely. Cross-cultural differences in marriage patterns, courtship rituals and sexual norms are also related to differences in adolescent sexual behavior (Miller and Benson 1999).

TABLE 1

Percentage of women ages 20–24 sexually experienced by age 20

	Total	Premarital	Marital
Developed nations			
Poland	40	25	15
France	73	38	35
Germany	81	71	10
United States	81	75	6
Great Britain	87	64	23
Mean	72.4	54.6	17.8
Latin American nations			
Peru	45	27	53
Mexico	46	11	35
El Salvador	49	14	38
Dominican Republic	50	10	40
Ecuador	51	19	32
Trinidad and Tobago	57	14	43
Bolivia	58	28	30
Paraguay	61	34	27
Brazil	62	40	22
Columbia	62	35	27
Guatemala	64	16	48
Mean	55	22.54	35.9
Sub-Saharan African nations			
Rwanda	43	12	31
Burundi	46	10	36
Uganda	91	48	43
Botswana	91	81	10
Niger	92	5	87
Burkina Faso	92	25	67
Togo	92	68	24
Cameroon	94	40	54
Central Afr. Rep.	94	47	47
Mali	95	20	75
Cote d'Ivoire	95	64	31
Liberia	98	67	31
Mean	85.25	40.58	44.66

SOURCE: Alan Guttmacher Institute, *Into a New World*, 1998.

Social and cultural norms can either encourage or inhibit romantic and sexual behavior; the cultural context in which sexuality develops is important to the outcomes of that development. Romantic love has been associated more with Western cultures than traditional cultures, but romantic love (intense attraction that involves the idealization of the other within an erotic context, with the expectation of enduring some time into the future) is found in 88.5 percent of cultures (Jankowiak and Fischer 1994). Despite the prevalence of romantic love, the ways in which it is expressed varies widely. In the United States, sexual behaviors are normatively experienced in dating relationships; that is, adolescents usually first engage in sexual intercourse as part of romantic, dating relationships. Romantic feelings become prominent among adolescents by the mid-teenage years, and for most adolescents, especially females, these feelings are the basis for entry into sexual experience. Casual or nonromantic sexual experiences are also part of the teenage sexual landscape (Miller and Benson 1999). Although the double standard allowing males but not females to pursue purely sexual relationships is disappearing, gender-based differences remain in what is considered most important in a relationship. Females are likely (75%) to first engage in coitus in a relationship they characterize as being serious or steady, whereas males more often report (50%) that their first coitus was in a casual dating relationship. Males choose partners based on physical attractiveness, whereas females tend to associate sex with commitment. Dating relationships tend to follow a natural progression from casual to steady to permanent, although sequential stages have become less predictable in recent years (Miller and Benson 1999).

Noncoital sexual activity. Although adolescent coitus patterns mentioned previously provide important facts about teenage sexual behavior, adolescents usually do not go from being nonsexual to having sexual intercourse. Couples tend to follow a continuum from embracing and kissing to fondling, then petting, and finally more intimate behaviors that include vaginal intercourse (Miller and Benson 1999). Haffner (1998) reported that nearly 90 percent of teenagers say they have a boyfriend or girlfriend and that they have kissed someone romantically. By age fourteen, half of the boys reported having touched a girl's breasts and a quarter have touched a girl's genitals, and 75 percent report heavy petting by age eighteen. As many as half of the adolescents in the United States report experiencing *cunnilingus* or *fellatio* (oral sex) (Haffner 1998) with very little known about the percentage who experience sexual behaviors with partners of the same sex. Although most teenagers move through a progression of sexual behaviors, adolescents living in poverty are more likely to move directly from kissing to intercourse. Older teenagers tend to behave more responsibly in romantic relationships, basing relational decisions on mutual feelings, long-term plans, and commitment rather than desire for sexual relations (Miller and Benson 1999). Recent studies also have shown that early age of first romantic relationship is associated with early age at first intercourse (Flanigan 2001). Internationally, little information is available on the noncoital sexual activities of adolescents.

Although the majority of teenagers in the United States follow the patterns mentioned above, some do not. Sexual coercion is one possible explanation of why some move more quickly to sexual intercourse without first developing romantic attachments. About 22 percent of women and 2 percent of men in the United States report being forced into unwanted sexual acts at some time in their lives (Michael, Gagnon, Laumann, and Kolata 1994). Women who have intercourse in early adolescence are much more likely to have been coerced. Three out of four women who first had intercourse before age fourteen, and three out of five of those experiencing intercourse before age fifteen, reported doing so against their will. Having a coerced sexual experience can have long lasting effects on young women. Brent C. Miller and Brad Benson (1999) summarized studies that women who experienced forced sex at an early age also tended to be younger at first voluntary intercourse, less likely to use contraceptives, had more frequent sexual experience, greater numbers of sexual partners, higher incidence of drug and alcohol abuse, and greater risk of emotional problems. Those coerced into early sexual intercourse are also more likely to trade sex for money, drugs, alcohol, or a place to stay. Other research has reported similar outcomes (Miller, Monson, and Norton 1995). These patterns are apparent among African Americans, Latinos/Latinas, and European Americans (Perkins, Luster, Villarruel, and Small 1998).

Correlates and Outcomes

A wide range of factors influence and are affected by the timing and frequency of adolescent sexual activity (Kirby 2001). Neighborhood characteristics, socioeconomic status, parent's marital status, sibling characteristics, sexual abuse, and biological factors all have been shown to be related to teenage sexual behavior (Miller, Benson, and Galbraith 2001). Living in neighborhoods with low socioeconomic status (Ramirez-Valles, Zimmerman, and Newcomb 1998), high disorder or hazards (Upchurch et al. 1999), or in predominantly African-American neighborhoods (Sucoff and Upchurch 1998), is associated with higher risk sexual behavior whereas high neighborhood monitoring and high neighborhood religious practice are associated with lower sexual risk behavior.

High socioeconomic status of parents most often has been found to be associated with lower risk of having had intercourse and later sexual debut for adolescents (Taris and Semin 1997; Ramirez-Valles, Zimmerman, and Newcomb 1998; and Upchurch et al. 1999). Kathleen E. Miller and her colleagues (1998) found no relationship between family income and teenage sexual behavior and other investigators reported mixed results; parents socioeconomic status was related to lower risk for teenage pregnancy among Latinos and higher risk for African Americans.

Brent C. Miller and colleagues (2001) also reported that in most studies, living in other than a two-parent home (e.g., single parent, step, divorced, or other nontraditional family setting) is associated with increased risk of adolescent sexual intercourse. Miller and Benson (1999) reported that this trend was less evident among African-American and Latino samples. Also, having sexually active, pregnant, or parenting older siblings was found to be related to younger sibling's more risky sexual behavior (East 1996; Whitbeck et al. 1999), although this effect may be mediated by a positive sibling relationship.

Several biological factors also predict adolescent sexual behavior, including young age of menarche, high androgen levels in males and females, early pubertal development, and higher free testosterone levels (Miller, Benson, and Galbraith 2001). Miller and colleagues (2001) synthesized research on family factors influencing teenage pregnancy. Across the various studies, parent/child closeness was remarkably consistent in its inverse relationship to adolescent sexual behavior. Measures of parent/child closeness were positively related to at least one of the following outcomes: increased probability of abstinence, later sexual debut, fewer sexual partners, or increased use of contraceptives (Jaccard, Dittus, and Gordon 1998; Miller et al. 1998; Ramirez-Valles, Zimmerman, and Newcomb 1998; Rodgers 1999; Upchurch et al. 1999; and Whitbeck et al. 1999).

Parental control and monitoring were generally found to be related to decreased probability of sexual intercourse among teenagers (Miller, Benson, and Galbraith 2001). Parental rules, monitoring and presence were related to decreased and more responsible sexual activity (Perkins et al. 1998; Miller, Benson, and Galbraith 2001; Rodgers 1999; and Whitbeck et al. 1999). Les Whitbeck and colleagues (1999) found a mixed outcome by age, with parental monitoring of younger adolescents leading to decreased sexual activity and among older adolescents leading to increased sexual activity. In another study (Rodgers 1999), parental monitoring was associated with lower risk sexual behavior, but parent's psychological control was related to higher risk sexual behavior. Dawn Upchurch and colleagues (1999) also found that intrusive control by parents was linked to increased sexual behavior among teenagers.

The relationship between parent/child communication and adolescent sexual activity is less well understood. Although several studies report that frequent and positive parent/child communication about sex is related to less risky adolescent sexual behavior (East 1996; Miller, Benson, and Galbraith 2001), others report no relationship (Chewning and Koningsveld 1998; Rodgers 1999), and a few even reported a positive association between parent/child communication and riskier sexual behavior in teenagers (Miller, Benson, and Galbraith 2001). These counterintuitive findings could be due to methodological problems of the research.

Parent's values relating to teenage sexual activity are clearly associated with teenager's reported sexual behavior. Recent research shows that teenagers whose parents disapprove of teenage sex are less likely to have intercourse (Jaccard, Dittus, and Gordon 1998; and Miller, Benson, and Galbraith 2001). Conversely, mothers' permissive attitudes were found to be related to increased adolescent sexual intercourse (Taris and Semin 1997). Parents' attitudes alone are not responsible for this effect, because some studies suggest that adolescents' perception of their parents' attitudes is more important than the parent's actual attitude.

Conclusion

Much of the interest in adolescent sexual intercourse is driven by several of its serious consequences, including sexually transmitted diseases (STDs), unwanted pregnancy, and birth. The rate of sexual intercourse among teenagers varies a great deal between cultures. Even within the United States there is considerable variation according to age, socioeconomic status, geographic location, and race/ethnicity. Most of these differences can be attributed to a wide range of biological and social factors. Rates of sexual activity among teenagers leveled off in the United States during the 1990s, and teenage pregnancy declined, a fact that is partially attributable to less teenage sexual intercourse and an increase in the use of contraceptives among sexually active adolescents (Flanigan 2001). Adolescent sexuality is less often studied than sexual intercourse. As a result, the wide range of noncoital sexual activity that adolescents experience is less understood. Continued research can create a better understanding of sexual activity and the factors that influence it, and provide a scientific basis for policy to more effectively encourage responsible sexual behavior among adolescents.

See also: ABSTINENCE; ADOLESCENT PARENTHOOD; CHILDHOOD, STAGES OF: ADOLESCENCE; EATING DISORDERS; FAMILY LIFE EDUCATION; GENDER IDENTITY; INCEST; INCEST/INBREEDING TABOOS; MENARCHE; NONMARITAL CHILDBEARING; SEXUALITY; SEXUALITY EDUCATION; SEXUALITY IN ADULTHOOD; SEXUALITY IN CHILDHOOD; SEXUAL ORIENTATION

Bibliography

Alan Guttmacher Institute. (1998). *Into a New World: Young Women's Sexual and Reproductive Lives.* New York: Author.

Alan Guttmacher Institute. (1999). *Teen Sex and Pregnancy. Facts in Brief* series. New York: Author.

Chewning, B., and Koningsveld, R. V. (1998). "Predicting Adolescent's Initiation of Intercourse and Contraceptive Use." *Journal of Applied Social Psychology* 28:1245–1285.

De Gaston, J. F.; Jensen, L.; and Weed, S. (1995). "A Closer Look at Adolescent Sexual Activity." *Journal of Youth and Adolescence* 24:465–479.

East, P. L. (1996). "The Younger Sisters of Childbearing Adolescents: Their Attitudes, Expectations, and Behaviors." *Child Development* 67:267–282.

Flanigan, C. (2001). *What's Behind the Good News: The Decline of Teen Pregnancy Rates During the 1990s.* Washington, DC: National Campaign to Prevent Teen Pregnancy.

Haffner, D. W. (1998). "Facing Facts: Sexual Health for American Adolescents." *Journal of Adolescent Health* 22:453–459.

Jaccard, J.; Dittus, P.; and Gordon, V. V. (1998). "Parent-Adolescent Congruency in Reports of Adolescent Sexual Behavior and in Communication about Sexual Behavior." *Child Development* 69:247–261.

Jankowiak, W. R., and Fischer, E. F. (1994). "A Cross-Cultural Perspective on Romantic Love." *Ethnology* 31:149–155.

Kirby, D. (2001). *Emerging Answers: Research Findings on Programs to Reduce Teen Pregnancy.* Washington, DC: National Campaign to Prevent Teen Pregnancy.

Michael, R. T.; Gagnon, J. H.; Laumann, E. O.; and Kolata, G. (1994). *Sex in America.* Boston: Little, Brown.

Miller, B. C., and Benson, B. (1999). "Romantic and Sexual Relationship Development During Adolescence." In *The Development of Romantic Relationships in Adolescence,* ed. W. Furman, B. B. Brown, and C. Feiring. Cambridge, UK: Cambridge University Press.

Miller, B. C.; Benson, B.; and Galbraith, K. A. (2001). "Family Relationships and Adolescent Pregnancy Risk: A Research Synthesis." *Developmental Review* 21:1–38.

Miller, B. C.; Monson, B. H.; and Norton, M. C. (1995). "The Effects of Forced Sexual Intercourse on White Female Adolescents." *Child Abuse and Neglect* 19:1289–1301.

Miller, B. C.; Norton, M. C.; Curtis, T.; Hill, E. J.; Schvaneveldt, P.; and Young, M. H. (1997). "The Timing of Sexual Intercourse among Adolescents: Family, Peer, and Other Antecedents." *Youth and Society* 29:54–83.

Miller, K. E.; Sabo, D. F.; Farrell, M. P.; Barnes, G. M.; and Melnick, M. J. (1998). "Athletic Participation and Sexual Behavior in Adolescents: The Different Worlds of Boys and Girls." *Journal of Health and Social Behavior* 39:108–123.

Perkins, D. F.; Luster, T.; Villarruel, F. A.; and Small, S. (1998). "An Ecological Risk-Factor Examination of Adolescents' Sexual Activity in Three Ethnic Groups." *Journal of Marriage and the Family* 60:660–673.

Ramirez-Valles, J.; Zimmerman, M. A.; and Newcomb, M. D. (1998). "Sexual Risk Behavior among Youth: Modeling the Influence of Pro-Social Activities and Socioeconomic Factors." *Journal of Health and Social Behaviors* 39:237–253.

Rodgers, K. B. (1999). "Parenting Processes Related to Sexual Risk-Taking Behaviors of Adolescent Males and Females." *Journal of Marriage and the Family* 54:142–152.

Sucoff, C. A.; and Upchurch, D. M. (1998). "Neighborhood Context and the Risk of Childbearing among Metropolitan-Area Black Adolescents." *American Sociological Review* 63:571–585.

Taris, T. W., and Semin, G. R. (1997). "Parent-Child Interaction during Adolescence, and the Adolescents' Sexual Experience: Control, Closeness, and Conflict." *Journal of Youth and Adolescence* 26:373–398.

Upchurch, D. M.; Aneshensel, C. S.; Sucoff, C. A.; and Levi-Storms, L. (1999). "Neighborhood and Family Contexts of Adolescent Sexual Activity." *Journal of Marriage and the Family* 61:920–933.

Whitbeck, L. B.; Yoder, K. A.; Hoyt, D. R.; and Conger, R. D. (1999). "Early Adolescent Sexual Activity: A Developmental Study." *Journal of Marriage and the Family* 61:934–946.

BRENT C. MILLER
SPENCER C. LEAVITT

SEXUALITY IN ADULTHOOD

Since the early part of the twentieth century, sex and sexuality have been crucial elements of both private and public discourse. From the bedroom to the living room to the classroom, from religious venues to the streets, and via television, movies, magazines, and other media, sex and sexuality are prevalent topics.

Although there are many facets of sexuality in adulthood, the available research tends to be focussed on Western countries and white populations. It is important to recognize that other cultures may view this topic differently. The interactions of women and men from cultures other than the dominant Euro-American needs further investigation with an openness that does not deem them to be other, less than, or somehow deviant from the so-called Western norm.

Why has so much stress been placed on sexual performance, satisfaction, and identity? One reason may be that for the majority of people in Western cultures, sex is a life-long interest. Although it may be a life-long interest for most people, what constitutes sex and sexuality can vary considerably (Aiken 1998; Francoeur 1987; Lauer and Lauer 1997). Part of that variation stems from cultural, ethnic, class, religious, cohort, and gender differences. The time period in which people reach adulthood, what they learn from their elders, what they learn from their peers, cultural and religious expectations/norms, as well as gender identity, all influence how people perceive themselves and interact with others as sexual beings. What has helped to form many of these perspectives, in modern times, are social movements and technological advances that have made sweeping changes to concepts of sex and sexuality.

Sexual Revolution

Throughout the nineteenth and onset of the twentieth century, sex was not a socially acceptable topic of conversation (Abramson and Pinkerton 1995; Scanzoni 2000). Sex was seen as a means of procreation. Couples, within the bounds of marriage, engaged in sexual intercourse for the sake of reproduction (Abramson and Pinkerton 1995; Scanzoni 2000; Francoeur 1987; Tuttle 1984). Men could enjoy it, whereas women needed to endure it.

When did sex and sexual interaction become a means of expression and pleasure? According to John Scanzoni (2000), it was not until the 1920s that terms such as *necking, petting,* and *french kissing* found their way into the U.S. vernacular. This coincided with the practice of *dating.* What was new about this practice was that those involved were not necessarily planning to marry the person that they were dating. Couples shared some physical intimacies without the expectation of marriage. Although sexual intercourse, prior to marriage, was still a social taboo, these couples engaged in activities that could be considered *foreplay.* This meant that women and men were more likely (or at least had the opportunity) to experience, even if to a limited degree, sexual intimacy with someone other than the person they would marry. This is not to suggest that males and females, prior to this time, had never engaged in sexual activities but now many of these activities were more socially acceptable. A girl was not necessarily doomed for life because she engaged in necking with a boy that she was not engaged to, although there was still a double standard as to what was acceptable behavior for boys/men and girls/women (Scanzoni 2000).

The ability to date and explore one's sexuality, to a limited degree, continued in this manner for some time. It was not until the 1960s that there was a dramatic shift in sexual practices among late adolescents and adults (Abramson and Pinkerton 1995). This shift occurred not only in dating practices but in marital sexuality as well. The sexual revolution not only opened the doors for sex outside of marriage, it also liberated sexual practices within marriage (Aiken 1998; Scanzoni 2000; Tuttle 1984). Up to this point, procreation was still the focus of sexual intercourse within marriage. Now a shift in emphasis—or at least an addendum to that focus—became sex for the sake of pleasure. It was to be enjoyed by both men and women. Sexual intercourse no longer had to be the only venue of married sexual expression. Foreplay made its way into the marital sexual domain. Mutual stimulation and *oral sex* became components of married sexual relationships.

Although the sexual revolution may have been liberating to many, the concept of sex for pleasure also placed a tremendous amount of pressure on married couples and singles alike. Sexual performance was essential to pleasure. Advice columns appeared in a variety of places such as women and men's magazines. In addition, sex therapy became a viable component of marriage counseling. Discussions of sex and sexuality became part of the public discourse.

Women's Movement

Coinciding with the sexual revolution was the women's movement, which urged women to look beyond the bounds of motherhood and housewifery to discover their untapped potential. This potential was to be sought in the classroom, boardroom, courtroom, and the bedroom.

What the women's movement added to the sexual revolution was the concept of women being equal partners in the bedroom. Women no longer had to wait for a man to initiate sex and it was important that the experience be filled with as much pleasure for her as it was for him.

It is interesting to note that the concept of women enjoying sex and the importance of a woman experiencing orgasm is not a phenomenon of either the sexual revolution or the women's movement. In the 1600s it was believed, throughout much of Western Europe, that in order for a woman to become pregnant she must experience orgasm. Just as a man ejaculates sperm it was believed that a woman only releases her "seed" when she experiences an orgasm (Szuchman and Muscarella 2000). Therefore, it was imperative that a man did all that he could to ensure that this happened.

As medical knowledge advanced this concept was disproved. Foreplay and a woman experiencing orgasm were no longer an integral function of reproduction and therefore not deemed necessary. Sexual intercourse once again became primarily a venue for procreation (Szuchman and Muscarella 2000).

Three hundred years later women were demanding, not asking, that sex and pleasure no longer be mutually exclusive or a male prerogative. Sexual intercourse was not to be considered a wife's duty. Women could be the initiator, instructor, and full participant.

This change created further possibilities for sexual activity outside of marriage. For many it was no longer a necessity for a woman to be a virgin when she married. In the past those that "lost" their virginity prior to marriage were considered abnormal, whereas today maintaining one's virginity until marriage may be looked at as aberrant (Scanzoni 2000). Of course these trends are often mediated by an individual's moral, religious, cultural, and ethnic/racial affiliation. This is especially significant as many women delay marriage to build a career. Many women and men may be more reluctant to wait to engage in sexual intercourse until they marry.

In addition to delaying marriage, women are also delaying childbirth. The advent of *the pill* made it more possible for women and men to engage in sexual intercourse without the fear of pregnancy.

Contraception

There have always been means of trying to prevent pregnancy. From herbal applications to understanding the cycles of the moon and fertility, to sexual positions and praying, men and women have sought to engage in sexual intercourse without consequent pregnancy. Diaphragms, intrauterine devices (IUDs), and condoms have been available for a long time. However, these do not always work, can inhibit spontaneity, and therefore are not always used. It was not until the development of the contraceptive pill that women were able to take real control of reproduction (Abramson and Pinkerton 1995; Francoeur 1987; Montague 1969). Women could be sexually active without worrying about pregnancy. Couples could plan when to have a family and could engage in intercourse without being concerned about the time of the month. Of course a woman had to remember to take the pill for it to be effective. As with diaphragms and condoms it only works if you use it. There was also the possibility of side effects. These had to be taken into consideration when deciding what form, if any, of contraception would be used.

Of course not everyone who is sexually active worries about getting pregnant nor sees sexual activity as a means of reproduction. There is a bias, in Western culture in particular, of viewing sex and sexual intercourse as synonymous (Abramson and Pinkerton 1995; Aiken 1998; Tuttle 1984). The fact that foreplay is the prelude to intercourse is a prevalent notion. But what some may consider foreplay may be the mainstay of sexual expression for others and intercourse does not always involve a man and a woman.

Same-Sex Relationships

Along with the sexual revolution and the women's movement, the advent of the *Gay Rights movement* brought the notion of same-sex relationships "out of the closet." Women fall in love with and are attracted to women just as men fall in love with and are attracted to men. The Gay Rights movement provided a venue for gays, lesbians, bisexuals, and transgendered persons to meet, discuss issues, and advocate for their rights. These rights have included same-sex marriage and benefits for same-sex partners.

Heterosexual couples often take for granted the social acceptability for them to be openly affectionate. To hold hands and to kiss in public is not shunned. Except for a few localities this is not the case for same-sex couples. Same-sex relationships are part of the modern fabric of sex and sexuality. Within the medical and mental health fields, homosexuality is no longer listed as aberrant or deviant. It is no longer listed as criminal activity, although certainly many people are still persecuted for being openly gay.

Although there are still immense barriers, same-sex relationships have greater potential for flourishing today than in previous years. Although their union is not often recognized legally, it has not deterred couples from forming committed relationships, which often includes the raising of children.

A condom poster warns against the dangers of unprotected sex. Older adults are one of the faster growing populations being infected by HIV/AIDS. This could be due to a lack of continuing sex education for adult populations. A/P WIDE WORLD PHOTOS

The evolution of sexuality continues over the course of our adulthood. This will include changes that may occur with children, length of a relationship, aging, and health (including prevalence of sexually transmitted diseases).

Children

Although many view children as a blessing and a natural progression or outcome of a committed relationship, they can have a formidable affect on a couple's intimate relationship. Marital satisfaction tends to decrease with the advent of children (Aiken 1998). This fact does not imply that children are not wanted or loved but that their presence can change the nature of an intimate relationship. Focus can shift from *we* (meaning two) to *us* (meaning family). In lives that are already complicated by work and social obligations children can take what little time a couple may have reserved for one another. Infants need constant attention and as they get older the demands that children place on parents' time do not necessarily diminish. Although parents may be happy to fulfill the parental role, it can erode the sexual intimacy they once experienced. If a couple wants to enjoy intimacy they must make time for it.

Sexual expression is an important part of communication that must be accommodated (Coltrane 1998; Higgins and Tuttle 1984; Scanzoni 2000). If it was important before the advent of children into their lives, a couple should ensure its continuation. Frequency may decrease but that does not mean that satisfaction and pleasure has to as well.

Length of a Relationship

Often when a couple first gets together there is urgency for sexual expression. There is the thrill of exploration, finding what pleases the self and one another. They make being together a priority. As time passes and there is an increased familiarity and comfort, some of the urgency and intensity may diminish. The majority of studies conclude that sexual frequency decreases the longer a couple has been together (Aiken 1998). These findings include heterosexually married and cohabitating couples as well as same-sex couples (Edwards and Booth 1994; Kurdek 1991). One should not necessarily conclude that the couple's love for one another has decreased because they engage in sexual intercourse less frequently. In fact, studies show that when a couple is in the earlier stages of a relationship sexual frequency is higher than in the later stages regardless of age (Aiken 1998; Edwards and Booth 1994).

Aging

A prevalent stereotype suggests that individuals lose interest in and ability to engage in sexual intimacy once they reach later adulthood (Aiken 1998; Brecher 1984; Higgins and Tuttle 1984; Levy 1994). This stereotype is particularly reinforced in Western popular culture. Television shows and movies ridicule older adults that engage or try to engage in sexual activity. Men have heart attacks because they are too excited and women are grateful that anyone shows an interest in them. Even language connotes this behavior as aberrant. If an older man is sexually interested or active he is called a *dirty old man*. This is considered so abnormal for women that there is not an equivalent term for

older women. Rather the language for older women is sexless. *Crone, hag, biddy,* and *spinster* conjure up a picture of one who is sexually unattractive and undesirable.

Sexuality and aging is similar to most aspects of aging (Aiken 1998; Utley 1984). Age does not necessarily change our need or desire to be sexually expressive (Higgins and Tuttle 1984; Kaye 1993; Levy 1994; Willert and Semans 2000). If a couple is in a long-term relationship their frequency may decrease but not necessarily their satisfaction. Many couples find that the mode of expression may change and that with age and length of relationship there is increased intimacy. If sex and sexual intimacy are important aspects in one's life during young and middle adulthood they will continue to be factors in older adulthood (Aiken 1998; Kaye 1993; Levy 1994; Utley 1984).

One aspect of aging that is particular to a woman's experience is *menopause*. This process, which occurs with age, has also been imbued with myth. Many women are made to feel that because they are no longer able to reproduce they are no longer able to be sexual (Doress-Worters and Siegal 1994). Some women may experience a decline in sexual desire, whereas many others report an increase in desire and activity. There is no longer a concern about pregnancy, children are generally self-sufficient and the postmenopausal woman may even be more assertive in expressing her needs. Changes that women need to pay attention to are a decrease in vaginal lubrication as well as a thinning of the vaginal walls (Doress-Worters and Siegal 1994). These changes can be accommodated through the use of lubricating gels and sexual positioning.

Although men do not experience the same physical changes that women do with menopause they do experience physical changes with age that can affect their sexuality. Erections may not be as firm or last as long, and there may be a longer waiting period between erections (Aiken 1998). Once again these changes can be accommodated by increased manual stimulation and other modes of expression in addition to intercourse.

What can impact sexuality in old age is partner availability and health (two factors that have an impact throughout the lifespan). For older heterosexual women partner availability is a crucial issue

(Brecher 1984). Women outnumber men by increasingly larger proportions as they age. The available pool of heterosexual males decreases with age. Many divorced, widowed, and never-married older heterosexual women may find themselves alone and looking increasingly more towards masturbation for sexual gratification (Brecher 1984).

There are certain diseases, health situations, and medications that can have an impact on sex and sexual expression. There are ways to accommodate these changes. Medications can be altered and the way we express ourselves sexually can be changed to accommodate physical limitations. The need for intimacy continues throughout the lifespan. This need does not necessarily change with age. The myths, mentioned above, not only permeate the popular culture but have also seeped into the medical and mental health arena. Children and young adults have venues for getting information about sex but there are few avenues for the older adult. This is not just a matter of life satisfaction but as older adults are one of the faster growing populations being infected by HIV/AIDS it can be a matter of life and death (Lauer and Lauer 1997).

Sexually Transmitted Diseases

Although sexually transmitted diseases are unfortunately not a new concern, the deadly nature of a disease like acquired immunodefiency syndrome (AIDS) is. Certainly one could die from syphilis or gonorrhea if left untreated, but if diagnosed early enough both diseases are treatable. AIDS has had an impact on how and with whom individuals engage sexually. The condom is no longer primarily a means for the prevention of pregnancy. It has become a primary tool in the prevention of AIDS.

The fact of a disease like AIDS has had an impact on the concept of casual sex. Once again heterosexuals and gay male singles may be waiting to be in a committed relationship before being sexually intimate. Fear of pregnancy has been replaced by fear of death.

Other Influences

There are several other factors that influence sexual identity and how it is expressed. Religion, ethnicity, culture, and gender can have an overwhelming effect (Aiken 1998; Coltrane 1998; Francoeur 1987; Lauer and Lauer 1997; Sterk-Elifson 1994). These factors may determine how individuals respond to any or all of the areas mentioned previously. If one is religious what does the religion teach about sexuality and sexual practices? Are birth control, premarital sex, heterosexuality, and/or homosexuality sanctioned? People learn what is expected of them as well as what they are not supposed to do. How they interpret religious teachings can be influenced by their ethnicity and cultural and gender identities (Coltrane 1998; Francoeur 1987; Lauer and Lauer 1997; Sterk-Elifson 1994). This influence is a reciprocal one. Everyone is influenced by many different factors and to different extents.

Conclusion

Human sexuality is an intricate and integral component of adulthood. For most people it is essential for physical and mental well-being. The nature of sexuality has evolved to include the concept of mutual pleasure. Sexual practices are not limited to intercourse regardless of one's sexual orientation. Self-pleasure is also a component of human sexuality. Many people no longer consider masturbation deviant behavior. In fact it is suggested as a means to discover what one finds pleasurable. Oral sex and mutual stimulation are now more common sexual practices both within heterosexual and same-sex relationships. This coincides with the advent of viewing sex as something more than intercourse and something more than a means of reproduction.

Sex and sexuality may mean different things and be practiced in different ways according to a number of influences that people encounter. What is right for one person or group may not be right for another. The majority of people need to be in close contact with other people. They need to touch and be touched. This need does not end simply because they get older.

See also: ABSTINENCE; ADULTHOOD; ASSISTED REPRODUCTIVE TECHNOLOGIES; ELDERS; FERTILITY; GENDER IDENTITY; INCEST; INCEST/INBREEDING TABOOS; LATER LIFE FAMILIES; MENOPAUSE; SEXUAL COMMUNICATION: COUPLE RELATIONSHIPS; SEXUAL DYSFUNCTION; SEXUALITY; SEXUALITY IN ADOLESCENCE; SEXUALITY IN CHILDHOOD; SEXUAL ORIENTATION

Bibliography

Abramson, P. R., and Pinkerton, S. D. (1995). *With Pleasure: Thoughts on the Nature of Human Sexuality.* New York: Oxford University Press.

Aiken, L. R. (1998). *Human Development in Adulthood.* New York: Plenum Press.

Brecher, E. M. (1984). *Love, Sex, and Aging: A Consumers Union Report.* Boston: Little, Brown.

Coltrane, S. (1998). *Gender and Families.* Thousand Oaks, CA: Pine Forge Press.

Doress-Worters, P. B., and Siegal, D. L. (1994). *Experiencing Our Change of Life: Menopause.* In *The New Ourselves, Growing Older: Women Aging With Knowledge and Power,* ed. P. B. Doress-Worters and D. L. Siegal. New York: Simon and Schuster.

Edwards, J. N., and Booth, A. (1994). *Sexuality, Marriage and Well-being: The Middle Years.* In *Sexuality across the Life Span,* ed. A. S. Rossi. Chicago: University of Chicago Press.

Francoeur, R. T. (1987). *Human Sexuality.* In *Handbook of Marriage and the Family,* ed. M. B. Sussman and S. K. Steinmetz. New York: Plenum Press.

Higgins, L. P., and Tuttle, B. (1984). *Development of a Sexual Being: Growing Up Female.* In *Human Sexuality across the Lifespan: Implications for Nursing Practice,* ed. L. P. Higgins and J. W. Hawkins. Monterey, CA: Wadsworth.

Kaye, R. A. (1993). "Sexuality in the Later Years." *Ageing and Society* 13:415–426.

Kurdek, L. A. (1991). *Sexuality in Homosexual and Heterosexual Couples.* In *Sexuality in Close Relationships,* ed. K. McKinney and S. Sprecher. Hillsdale, NJ: Erlbaum.

Lauer, R. H., and Lauer, J. C. (1997). *Marriage and Family: The Quest for Intimacy,* 3rd edition. Madison, WI: Brown and Benchmark.

Levy, J. A. (1994). *Sexuality in Later Life Stages.* In *Sexuality across the Life Span,* ed. A. S. Rossi. Chicago: University of Chicago Press.

Montague, A. (1969). *Sex, Man and Society.* New York: Putnam.

Scanzoni, J. (2000). *Designing Families: The Search for Self and Community in the Information Age.* Thousand Oaks, CA: Pine Forge Press.

Sterk-Elifson, C. P. (1994). *Sexuality among African American Women.* In *Sexuality across the Life Span,* ed. A. S. Rossi. Chicago: University of Chicago Press.

Szuchman, L. T., and Muscarella, F. (2000). *Psychological Perspectives on Human Sexuality.* New York: Wiley.

Tuttle, B. (1984). *Adult Sexual Response.* In *Human Sexuality across the Lifespan: Implications for Nursing Practice,* ed. L. P. Higgins and J. W. Hawkins. Monterey, CA: Wadsworth.

Utley, O. E. (1984). *Sexuality and the Older Adult.* In *Human Sexuality across the Lifespan: Implications for Nursing Practice,* ed. L. P. Higgins and J. W. Hawkins. Monterey, CA: Wadsworth.

Willert, A., and Semans, M. (2000) "Knowledge and Attitudes about Later Life Sexuality: What Clinicians Need to Know about Helping the Elderly." *Contemporary Family Therapy* 4:415–435.

PHYLLIS A. GREENBERG

SEXUALITY IN CHILDHOOD

Because children are naturally sexual human beings, gaining a better understanding of childhood sexuality is important for parents, educators, and developmentalists. However, research in this field has been limited because of a culture that is profoundly ambivalent about human sexuality in general and, more specifically, reluctant to recognize the existence of children's sexuality. In fact, compared to other areas of child development, sexuality is one of the least discussed topics and was wholly unrecognized until Sigmund Freud's (1963, 1965) research in the early 1900s disputed the traditional image of children as asexual beings (Heiman et al. 1998).

Formation of Sexuality in Childhood

Although each child comes to form his or her sexuality in a unique way, there are patterns of sexuality formation common for both boys and girls. At an early age, children begin to form an understanding of the ways that bodies look and function for both sexes, often through a process of body discovery in which children become aware of their bodies as part of themselves and part of their identity (Schuhrke 2000). As children become aware of their own body parts, specifically their genitals, fundamental learning about sexuality begins. During the first year of life, the mouth is the main zone in which children derive pleasure as they associate comfort with feeding and often explore their world by using their mouth as a "third hand." From ages one to three, toilet training becomes the source of sexual information as children frequently come into contact with their genitals through this learning process. Children that are three to six years old often masturbate to gratify their increasing sexual desires although this is not a means of sexual expression at this age but simply a means of deriving pleasure. From ages six to twelve, children often explore their bodies and have a great deal of sexual curiosity even though they may not express their sexuality overtly. However, sexual and obscene language is often prevalent among this age group, a covert signal that this sexual curiosity is present (Renshaw 1971).

Through the early years of childhood, children's understanding of their sexuality focuses on visible body parts and functions, making diapering and toilet training opportune times to speak with children about sexuality and sexual functioning (Couchenour and Chrisman 1996). However, children often receive mixed messages about their sexuality. For example, touching their genitals feels pleasurable, yet they frequently receive negative feedback when exploring their bodies. In providing feedback about genital exploration, parents have a major influence on children's sexuality formation.

Janet Kahn (1985) explains:

Parents play a role in a child's learning about what it means to be a male or female, what are appropriate ways to express intimacy, affection, and other interpersonal or individual emotions, how a child feels about his or her body both in terms of its appearance and its capacities for pleasure and accomplishment, the ideas the child forms about family roles and other aspects of lifestyle, as well as all of the issues related to reproductive and erotic behavior and their social consequences. (p. 262)

Children also begin to recognize the way others evaluate and handle their own bodies and integrate this information into the ways in which they see their own bodies (Schuhrke 2000). Because children learn predominantly through observation, their parents are the conveyers of the messages they receive about sexuality: from how they are touched to what sexual topics are appropriate to discuss to the sexual behaviors that are rewarded or punished (Kahn 1985). Close and nude physical contact with parents brings attention to children's bodies and sparks sexual interest. For example, exposure to nudity within the home and sleeping in the parental bed is correlated with higher comfort levels with physical contact and affection, self-esteem, and sexual activity (Schuhrke 2000), whereas secrecy, disapproval, and inhibition in parents about sexuality may breed guilt in children (Renshaw 1971). Cross-cultural studies have shown that children are not born with sexual guilt or anxieties; they acquire them (Tannahill 1992).

Childhood Sexuality and Later Sexual Behavior

Healthy sexual interactions in childhood set the stage for healthy relationships in adolescence and adulthood. For example, parent-child communication during childhood about sexuality appears to have a significant influence on adolescent and adult sexual behavior. However, much of this communication comes in the form of silence about sexuality, and "one of the clearest messages received by many children from their parents' silence about or discomfort with discussing sexuality is that the issue should not be raised" (Kahn 1985, p. 268). When communication does take place about sexuality, it is often between mothers and daughters with sons getting less sexual information in the home and fathers being almost entirely absent during this type of parent-child communication (Kahn 1985).

Despite the infrequency of communication about sexuality with children, there are many ways in which parental communication with children concerning this issue affects later sexual behavior. Parents have less and less influence on their children's sexual information as children get older but can have a profound effect on children's sexuality if they speak to them when they are younger. Parents who speak to their children about sexuality have a strong influence on the development of their children's values concerning homosexuality, abortion, sex roles, and nudity. Children who feel free to speak to their parents about issues surrounding sexuality are more likely to come to their parents if they are sexually abused and also have an increased ability to resist sexual coercion (Kahn 1985). In addition, if sexuality is learned in the home, intercourse is likely to be delayed, whereas in homes where sexuality is not discussed, early coital experience and promiscuity is more common among adolescents and young adults (Kahn 1985).

Another major factor that influences later sexual behavior is the type and frequency of sexual behavior in childhood. Although negative sexual experiences in childhood, such as those that are not mutual or are painful, may have negative effects on adolescent and adult sexual functioning, positive sexual experiences in childhood, often in the form of sex play, have positive benefits for later sexual functioning. Young adults who reported exclusively positive and consensual sexual experiences before age sixteen reported less anxiety and more current sexual arousal and pleasure than those who had no childhood sexual experiences (Bauserman and Davis 1996). In general, a child's perception of early sexual experiences as either negative or positive, consensual or nonconsensual, is most significant in relation to later sexual functioning and attitudes about sexuality, and the frequency of some early sexual activities is positively correlated with frequencies at later ages (Bauserman and Davis 1996).

Gender Issues

Two key issues related to gender are gender identity and gender roles. *Gender identity* refers to the ways in which people come to recognize themselves as male or female. For young children, identity as a boy or girl is typically based on clothing (Couchenour and Chrisman 1996), hair length, and toy and game preferences (Byer, Shainberg, and Galliano 1999). For example, Johnny wears pants so he must be a boy, and Susie has a pink coat so she must be a girl. As children grow and develop, however, they often enhance their identities by comparing their bodies with other children's and adults' bodies and learning to more strongly identify themselves with people of their same sex based on the physical aspects they have in common (Schuhrke 2000). Although researchers originally thought gender identity was an inborn, genetic factor, it is now commonly understood that gender identity is greatly influenced by environmental experiences, specifically parental response. Many researchers have also found that the sense of maleness or femaleness a child has is established by the age of three (Renshaw 1971).

Gender roles, as defined by Curtis Byer, Louis Shainberg, and Grace Galliano (1999), are the totality of social and cultural expectations for boys/girls, men/women in a particular society at a particular time in history. Through gender role socialization, culture, conversation, and interactions significantly affect children's ideas about appropriate gender roles (Couchenour and Chrisman 1996). A major source of information concerning gender roles comes from within the home and often involves parents' nonverbal communication, as children are just as likely to learn from parents' behavior and expressions as they are to learn from verbal communication. In many ways, parents nonverbally communicate to their children that males and females are different. One way in which this difference may be communicated is in the ways parents deal differently with sons and daughters. From the time of birth, boys are generally handled more roughly, girls are spoken to more gently, each are given sex-stereotyped toys to play with, and are encouraged to play in different ways with girls playing in small groups and boys playing in larger groups (Kahn 1985). A second way in which gender roles are conveyed nonverbally is through modeling. Parents often demonstrate a differentiation of sex roles in their division of household labor which gives children a "strongly sex-differentiated view of family life" (Kahn 1985, p. 282). Bettina Schuhrke (2000) asserts that as parents teach their children about sexuality, "they are transmitting expectations of future ability to perform traditional sex roles skillfully and vigorously" (p. 29). Thus, parents repeatedly, though often inadvertently, reinforce the idea that males and females are different and should act according to their prescribed gender roles.

Exploring Sexuality in Childhood

Children often explore sexuality through sex play, for example, by "playing doctor." Sex play refers to sexual peer interactions in childhood that are participated in on a voluntary basis with children of similar age, size, and developmental status (Cavanagh Johnson 1999). This sex play generally takes place among peers (children within three years of one another of similar size and developmental status) and are voluntary experiences (Bauserman and Davis 1996; Byer, Shainberg, and Galliano 1999). Although these early sexual experiences within the context of play tend to be fairly routine, information about sexuality can be gathered from these encounters. Through sex play, children participate in information exchange in which they learn to label their sexual thoughts and functions (Langfeldt 1990). By looking and touching, children start to build an understanding of "what the body looks like, what differences exist between boys and girls, and what it feels like to touch another's body" (Cavanagh Johnson 1999, p. 12). Childhood sex play can also have an effect on later adult sexual functioning as these early experiences can later influence the adults' ability to achieve orgasm and reduce sexual dysfunction because they have learned early on how to manage their sexuality (Langfeldt 1990). If parents are supportive of sex play, children can learn the guidelines for social behavior concerning sexuality in terms of appropriate time and place for expression of sexuality (Langfeldt 1990).

Toni Cavanagh Johnson (1999) explains that children also frequently use their own bodies as a map and have a natural interest in discovering the different functions of their body parts. When children do explore their bodies, they not only learn about their bodily functions but also begin to understand what various people think about sexuality based on their reactions to the child's exploration. These reactions also provide children with rules for physical interaction (Schuhrke 2000). Based on adults' responses to their body exploration, children learn if their behavior is considered "good" or "bad," which will have an effect on the frequency with which they will engage in body exploration.

Another way that children explore their sexuality is through bathroom humor and games in which children begin to learn about the capabilities of their bodies (Cavanagh Johnson 1999). The most common situations in which genital nudity occurs, such as bath times or toilet training, are significant moments in the child's learning process as children discover their parents' or caregivers' openness to nudity and sexuality (Schuhrke 2000). Furthermore, because humor provides information to children regarding sexuality, a good deal of sexual information comes from sexual jokes, stories, and songs (Langfeldt 1990).

Children also gather information about sexuality through the media (Cavanagh Johnson 1999). Books, magazines, videos, and the Internet are all sources of material with sexual content whose messages tend to be indirect, nonverbal, ambiguous, or inconsistent. However, parents and caregivers can turn the discovery of sexual material into a constructive opportunity for sex education.

Conclusion

It is important to note that there are wide differences in the sexual development and interest of children (Cavanagh Johnson 1999). Also, curiosity about sexuality is just part of the whole picture; children are also curious about other parts of the universe. Nevertheless, the more children feel free to explore the characteristics of their bodies and therefore learn about sexuality and body functioning, the easier it may be for them to understand information that is given to them pertaining to reproduction and birth (Schuhrke 2000). Although children's exploration of their own bodies and others' bodies may seem abnormal, body exploration is natural, and curiosity is an important part of any child's sexual development (Schuhrke 2000) and should be accepted and fostered.

See also: CHILDHOOD; GENDER; GENDER IDENTITY; INCEST; INCEST/INBREEDING TABOOS; SEXUAL COMMUNICATION: PARENT-CHILD RELATIONSHIPS; SEXUALITY; SEXUALITY EDUCATION; SEXUALITY IN ADOLESCENCE; SEXUALITY IN ADULTHOOD; SEXUAL ORIENTATION

Bibliography

Bauserman, R., and Davis, C. (1996). "Perceptions of Early Sexual Experiences and Adult Sexual Adjustment." *Journal of Psychology and Human Sexuality* 8(3):37–59.

Byer, C.; Shainberg, L.; and Galliano, G. (1999). *Dimensions of Human Sexuality,* 5th ed. Boston: McGraw-Hill.

Cavanagh Johnson, T. (1999). *Understanding Your Child's Sexual Behavior: What's Natural and Healthy.* Oakland, CA: New Harbinger.

Couchenour, D., and Chrisman, K. (1996). "Healthy Sexuality Development in Young Children." *Dimensions of Early Childhood* 24(1):30–36.

Freud, S. (1963). *Three Essays on the Theory of Sexuality.* New York: Basic.

Freud, S. (1965). *Normality and Pathology in Childhood.* New York: International Universities Press.

Heiman, M.L.; Leiblum, S.; Esquilin, S.C.; and Pallito, L.M. (1998). "A Comparative Survey of Beliefs About 'Normal' Childhood Sexual Behaviors." *Child Abuse and Neglect* 22(4):289–304.

Kahn, J. (1985). "Sexual Messages: Parental Influences on Children's Sexual Development." In *Contemporary*

Marriage: Special Issues in Couples Therapy, ed. D. Goldberg. Homewood, IL: Dorsey.

Langfeldt, T. (1990). "Early Childhood and Juvenile Sexuality, Development and Problems." *Handbook of Sexology* 7:179–200.

Renshaw, D.C. (1971). "Sexuality in Children." *Medical Aspects of Human Sexuality* 5(10):62–74.

Schuhrke, B. (2000). "Young Children's Curiosity about Other People's Genitals." *Journal of Psychology and Human Sexuality* 12(1–2):27–48.

Tannahill, R. (1992). *Sex in History,* rev. edition. New York: Scarborough House.

SARA MOORHEAD PHILLIPS
DEBRA L. BERKE

SEXUALLY TRANSMITTED DISEASES

The world continues to live with the ironic realization that the most intimate form of human relations, that of sexual interactions, carries the threat of serious disease. *Sexually transmitted diseases* (STDs), once known as venereal diseases, have menaced humankind since the dawn of recorded history. There are references to STDs in Egyptian papyri dating to 1550 BCE, and according to biblical scholars, there are similar references in the Old Testament (Holmes et al. 1999). STDs operate at the intersection of individual human behaviors, collective sociodemographic trends, and specific disease pathogens. They are diseases caused by bacteria, viruses, protozoa, fungi, and ectoparasites. In society and within the lives of families and individuals, STDs continue to inflict considerable suffering, trauma, serious medical conditions, and medical expense. They can often stigmatize the infectee; they also can cause death. Despite powerful treatments including newer antibiotics, better diagnostic tools using advanced technologies, extensive prevention programs, and increased international awareness, STDs remain among the most common reported diseases.

Tragically, they have a global reach that in many countries dwarfs the burden in the United States. The World Health Organization estimated that in 1999, among women and men aged fifteen to forty-nine years, there were approximately 340 million new cases of the most common, nonviral,

sexually transmitted diseases that occurred throughout the world. They were syphilis (12 million), gonorrhea (62 million), chlamydia (92 million), and trichomoniasis (174 million). STDs most commonly affect people when they are between the ages of fifteen and forty-four, during their peak years of economic production (Ober and Piot 1993). This is of particular concern to developing countries.

For these four STDs and several others (there are more than twenty-five pathogens that can be transmitted by sexual intercourse), their spread in a population is a function of the average number of new cases caused by an infected person (often referred to as *the force of infectivity*). This number is the product of the efficiency of transmission of the STD, the average duration of infectiousness of the STD, and the mean number of different sexual partners per unit time (Anderson and May 1991). The use of numerical methods using this kind of methodology has allowed population- and country-specific estimates for incidence and prevalence of the most common STDs.

The three most common and threatening sequelae (i.e., after-effects) of STDs to infected individuals are impaired fertility for women, adverse pregnancy outcomes, and increased susceptibility to the *human immunodeficiency virus* (HIV), the virus that causes *acquired immunodeficiency syndrome* (AIDS). STDs cause acute illnesses, long-term suffering and disability, and infertility. Related psychological and medical consequences have an enormous global economic impact.

Since World War II, advances in epidemiology, disease surveillance, behavioral and social sciences, demographics, and medical science have greatly contributed to a better understanding of how STDs occur, are sustained, and shift into new populations in society; how they interact with each other; how several STDs can be successfully treated and cured (although many still cannot); and, importantly, how they and their most common sequelae can often be prevented. Despite these modern advances, STDs continue to imperil society, families and other loved ones, and individuals.

Although difficult to estimate (approximately 12 million infections from STDs occur annually in the United States), two-thirds of the infections from STDs occur among people less than twenty-five years of age (Noegel et al. 1993). Women and the poor suffer disproportionately, and it is estimated that one of every four people in the United States will have an STD in his or her lifetime. STDs are most commonly transmitted either from males to their female sex partners or from females to their male sex partners. Male to male transmission occurs often with some STDs, whereas female to female transmission occurs infrequently with nearly all STDs. Of the more than twenty-five known pathogens that are classified as causing STDs in humans, only the most important will be addressed here.

Bacterial STDs

Though readily curable, these STDs (sometimes referred to as *Sexually Transmitted Infections,* or STIs) account for considerable morbidity, ranking among the most frequently reported communicable diseases. *Chlamydia* and *gonorrhea* pose threats to the reproductive health of women and are readily transmitted between sex partners. These and many other bacterial STDs influence adverse pregnancy outcomes, either during fetal development or during birth. No effective vaccines exist for these diseases.

Chlamydia. This disease is thought to be the most common of all STDs in the United States. Between 20 percent and 40 percent of sexually active women have been exposed; they have chlamydial antibodies. Since the 1970s, the pathogenesis (i.e., production and development) of and threats to reproductive health from chlamydia have become better understood; it has emerged as an STD with major consequences. It has been estimated that more than $2 billion is spent each year in the United States on treatment of chlamydia and its complications (Noegel et al. 1993). The most common clinical manifestations of chlamydial infections in women are *salpingitis* and *mucccopurulent cervicitis,* with the *endocervix* being the most common site of infection. Chlamydia is a particularly insidious STD because women with active infections usually have minimal or no symptoms. Most women are unlikely to be treated unless: (1) they undergo a screening test (a rapid, inexpensive diagnostic test has only recently become widely available in the United States, but is still unavailable in many parts of the world) that specifically cultures the pathogen; or (2) their male sex partner develops a symptomatic infection and the woman

is informed. Seven-day oral antibiotic regimens of either *doxycycline* or *azithromycin* are effective treatment of chlamydia in men and women. A single dose azithromycin regimen is equally effective, and, though more expensive, is now available.

Gonorrhea. This disease is the second most commonly reported STD in the United States (approximately 350,000 cases per year are reported [approximately 260 cases per 100,000 U.S. population for men and women combined; many more are thought to occur]). The highest age-specific rates are for women ages fifteen to nineteen and for men ages twenty to twenty-four (Centers for Disease Control and Prevention 2000). For women, gonococcal infection occurs primarily in the cervix, although the pharynx, rectum, and urethra can also be infected. Approximately 40 percent to 60 percent of women with gonorrhea have symptoms, sometimes painful. Gonorrhea, which is less "silent" than chlamydia, can cause a purulent vaginal discharge, *dysuria,* and frequent urination. Cervical gonococcal infection is usually diagnosed via an endocervical culture. Most infected men have painful symptoms, usually pain and discharge upon urination, which cause them to seek treatment. Several antibiotic regimens (e.g., a single oral dose of *cefixime*) are safe and effective for most cases (Centers for Disease Control and Prevention 1993). Ominously, about one-third of all gonococcal isolates now manifest some degree of resistance to this conventional therapy, thus causing reliance on more expensive antibiotics and creating concern that some emerging gonococcal strains may soon be resistant to all known forms of antibiotics.

Comparison of chlamydia and gonorrhea. About 25 percent to 40 percent of women with gonorrhea also have a concurrent chlamydial infection. Yet the percentage of women with gonorrhea who also have a concurrent chlamydial infection varies dramatically by subpopulation (Holmes et al. 1999). (Since 1975, trends in reported U.S. gonorrhea rates have steadily declined.) Chlamydia is thought to be homogeneously distributed in the population, although focused in those who are younger, yet sexually active, whereas gonorrhea disproportionately affects minority populations. (In 2000, the ratio of U.S. gonorrhea cases reported in African Americans to whites was five to one; in Hispanics to whites, one to two; [Centers for Disease Control and Prevention 2000]). However, these differences should be viewed cautiously. Research analyzing population-based survey data suggests that the real differences may be less striking (Anderson, McCormick, and Fichtner 1994). Case reporting from publicly funded medical facilities tends to be more complete than that from private facilities, and minority populations disproportionately use publicly funded facilities. All states legally require the medical reporting of most STDs, but inconsistent adherence as well as frequent self-treatment of STDs prevent more accurate estimates of the incidence of STDs in the United States and thereby inhibit a better understanding of their respective epidemiologies.

Pelvic inflammatory disease (PID). PID broadly defines an array of inflammatory conditions, the most common of which are *endometritis* and *salpingitis,* which affect the upper reproductive tract of women. Symptoms are often pain with concurrent fever. (There are approximately 2.5 million symptomatic outpatient visits to medical facilities for PID annually in the United States. Nearly 300,000 women are hospitalized annually, and more than 100,000 associated surgical procedures need to be performed [Centers for Disease Control and Prevention 2000]). Most cases of PID are caused, directly or indirectly, by gonococcal and chlamydial infections. PID is frequently episodic, with initial acute episodes being directly caused by untreated or repeat infections of gonorrhea or chlamydia. Subsequent episodes can be caused by nonsexually transmitted pathogens or intrauterine contraceptive devices. Infertility caused by occlusion of the *fallopian tubes,* chronic pelvic pain, and *ectopic pregnancy* is the most frequent and serious complication of repeat episodes of PID. A diagnosis of PID is often difficult because there is a wide range of signs and symptoms—or none at all. Women and health care providers should be suspicious of symptoms, especially if there is a history numerous sex partners. A variety of antibiotic therapies (e.g., cefoxitin plus doxycycline) are available for PID; most require aggressive, extended regimens, usually up to fourteen days, for maximum effectiveness.

Syphilis. This disease has been central to the development of the practice of medicine and was the basis for *venereology,* an early medical subspecialty. Epidemic and a scourge in Europe in the fifteenth century, its symptoms, natural history, and transmission dynamics have fascinated students of medicine for years; its malevolence has caused great personal suffering; and it continues to be a prevention and treatment challenge. In the late 1970s and early 1980s, syphilis in the United States was at moderate levels and was primarily a disease that occurred in homosexual men (Fichtner et al. 1983). However, in the late 1980s, there was a surge in the reported incidence of syphilis in the United States, peaking at about 135,000 cases in 1990. About 50,000 of those cases in 1990, up from approximately 27,000 cases in 1985, represented occurrences of syphilis in primary or secondary stages, when the disease is infectious (i.e., transmissible). From 1990 to 2000, the rate of infectious syphilis declined by 89.2 percent. In 2000, only 5,979 cases were reported in the United States, the lowest since reporting began in 1941 (Centers for Disease Control and Prevention 2000).

About one-third of persons exposed to infectious syphilis acquire it. Within twenty-one days, primary, relatively painless lesions (ulcers or chancres) usually appear. Often these lesions disappear (after ten to ninety days) if the disease is untreated. The disease then reemerges in a secondary stage characterized by more disseminated symptoms, usually malaise, sore throat, and *adenopathy* (sore lymph glands). During this secondary stage, the classic rash of syphilis appears, often visible on the palms of the hands and soles of the feet. If the disease is still untreated in the secondary stage, a latent period of variable duration is entered by the patient. Subsequently, approximately 15 to 40 percent of the untreated patients develop tertiary syphilis, and small numbers of those (approximately 5–20%) develop serious neurological and/or cardiovascular manifestations that can become life-threatening (Holmes et al. 1999). These late manifestations are rarely seen in the United States.

Untreated pregnant women who are infected with syphilis have a 50 percent change of transmitting the disease to their newborns. About half of these women deliver a preterm baby or a still birth. Throughout the world, this is the most serious direct outcome of syphilis. (The rise of syphilis in U.S. women in the late 1980s, cresting in 1990, increased the concern for preventing cases of congenital syphilis. A peak in reported cases [approximately 4,400] of congenital syphilis occurred in 1991. [Centers for Disease Control and Prevention 2000]).

Syphilis is readily diagnosed by *serologic* (blood) testing; screening tests are inexpensive and routinely performed in a variety of settings. In the United States, premarital screening is required in nearly all states, a reminder of the history of the disease. One intramuscular injection of *benzathine penicillin* is the usual, effective treatment for syphilis during its early stages.

Viral STDs

These diseases are incurable, but during the 1980s and 1990s, many technological advances led to improved diagnostic tools, thus enabling a clearer understanding of the distribution of these diseases in the world. For some of the viral STDs, therapies to minimize symptoms exist. *Hepatitis B virus* (HBV), which is often but not always sexually transmitted, is the only STD for which an effective vaccine has been developed and is readily available.

Herpes simplex virus (HSV) infection. Herpes (from the Greek, *to creep*) is another STD with a long history. There are two major types of HSV: HSV-1 and HSV-2. *Genital herpes,* the clinical condition, is most often caused by HSV-2, and caused much less frequently by HSV-1. A prior history of HSV-1 appears to increase the risk of acquiring HSV-2. Herodotus, a Roman physician, described cold sores (from HSV-1) in the second century, and genital herpes was first described by John Astruc, a French physician in the eighteenth century, Shortly thereafter, other physicians noted that genital herpes often afflicted a patient shortly after the onset of syphilis or gonorrhea. Genital herpes results in painful ulcers that last about ten to fourteen days; both men and women can be affected. These ulcers can be treated by antiviral agents to ease discomfort and shorten periods of symptoms, but the infection persists in the body and symptoms are likely to reoccur. HSV-2 is most frequently transmitted by viral shedding from ulcers during sex, but transmission can occur even when no genital ulcer is evident. It can be acquired by the infant from its mother during child birth.

Both HSV-1 (much lower worldwide prevalence) and HSV-2 are widespread throughout the world. Surveys conducted in the United States have led to the approximation that about 20 percent of persons fifteen to seventy-four years of age have antibodies to HSV-2. From a survey conducted in the United States in the early 1990s, it was approximated that 31 million persons living in the United States are infected, as determined by the prevalence of serum antibodies, and it is estimated that approximately 20 to 25 percent of persons living in the United States will contract diagnosable (via symptoms) genital herpes sometime in their lives. Numerous studies have associated the presence of HSV-2 with the lifetime number of sex partners, history of other STDs, and age at first sex (i.e., sexual debut).

Several studies have linked HSV-2 with genital cancers in women (Holmes et al. 1999), and this is an area of intense epidemiological and clinical research. Unlike gonorrhea and syphilis, HSV seems to be distributed homogeneously in the sexually active population. Together with syphilis and chancroid, genital herpes forms a group of diseases called *genital ulcer disease* because of the dermatological eruptions they can cause. Patients with symptomatic genital herpes can be treated topically with *acyclovir* to moderate severity and duration of symptoms. Most often, genital herpes is a fairly benign STD; however, it can be of urgent concern during pregnancy when there can be danger of transmission of the infection to the newborn. *Neonatal herpes* causes frequent morbidity and even mortality, but infants who are delivered by cesarean section avoid risk of transmission, as do infants born to women with no recent symptomatic outbreaks.

Human papillomavirus infection (HPV). This disease, most often manifested as genital warts, is the most common viral STD. Although case surveillance of HPV is relatively poor worldwide, physicians report seeing increases in numbers of cases. The wart (*condyloma acuminata*) that is seen in about 30 percent of all HPV patients is usually a small, pimply tumor, pigmented or nonpigmented, with fingerlike projections. In women with HPV, it is commonly seen in the lower genital tract; in men, it can appear at various sites in the genital region. The presence of HPV in the cervix and vulva is cause for concern. Certain HPV DNA types have been found in more than 90 percent of patients with certain forms of genital tract cancer, and it is therefore thought that the HPV infections caused by these HPV DNA types are precursors of later cancers in women. Although the clinical management of HPV varies greatly, several therapies, including physical agents (e.g., *electrocautery*) and immunotherapy, are available and widely used.

HIV and other STDs. HIV (technically, also an STD when it is, in fact, sexually transmitted) and AIDS disproportionately affected white homosexual and bisexual men in the early stages of the epidemic (early 1980s) in the United States, but as the epidemic was spread and diagnosed around the world, the epidemiology of the disease varied by geographical region, influenced greatly by cultural differences. In the United States, the epidemic later appeared in subpopulations of injecting drug users, most of whom were members of racial/ethnic minorities. Since 1989, the group in the United States showing the greatest increase in reported HIV infection has been the group infected through heterosexual transmission, especially in subpopulations in which STDs are most prevalent (Wasserheit 1994). Persons with STDs, especially those infected with genital ulcer disease, appear to be at elevated risk for acquiring an HIV from an infected sex partner. A person who is co-infected (HIV and an STD) is also more likely to transmit HIV to a sex partner than one who is infected with HIV alone. Thus, an important strategy for modulating the HIV epidemic throughout the world is the successful prevention of all STDs and the successful treatment of curable STDs.

Another Important STD

Trichomoniasis is caused by *trichomonas vaginalis,* a protozoan pathogen, or type of parasite. Despite being the most common of all STDs of consequence, data on its global occurrence are badly inadequate. This disease, transmitted mainly by sexual intercourse, is manifested by vaginitis in women (approximately 50% of those infected have symptoms) and urethritis in men. Men have symptoms for only a brief period, but can easily transmit the parasite to their female sex partners during that period. *Metronidazole,* usually as a single oral dose, is the effective treatment of choice for trichomoniasis. This common disease, despite seldom resulting in clinical complications, has recently increased in priority for clinicians and prevention programs as new studies have shown that genital inflammation associated with trichomoniasis greatly increases the risk of acquiring other STDs, including HIV. It is thought, that in some populations of the world, the high prevalence of trichomoniasis may explain the explosiveness of the HIV epidemic they have experienced.

Unfortunately, laboratory tests for diagnosis are not always available in developing nations.

Global Distribution and Epidemiology of STDs

The World Health Organization estimated that 340 million new cases of curable STDs (limited to gonorrhea, syphilis, chlamydia, and trichomoniasis) occurred in the world in 1999 (Table 1). The largest number of new cases (incidence) occurred in the region of the world denoted by South and Southeast Asia. But, the highest prevalence (number of cases at any point in time per 1,000 population, ages fifteen to forty-nine) occurred in sub-Saharan Africa, meaning that at any random time during 1999, approximately 119 out of 1,000 persons, ages fifteen to forty-nine, were infected with one of these four STDs, or nearly one out of every nine people.

To understand why the global distribution of STDs is so highly differentiated and why cases occur in such geographically and culturally focal patterns is not a straightforward challenge. There are so many factors involved from which to hypothesize, even in industrialized countries. Two recent surveys of sexual behavior conducted in the United States and United Kingdom, where STD and HIV rates are lower, provide useful information, and clues, for comparison purposes. In both countries, the overwhelming majority of the population does not engage in high-risk sexual behaviors. Both surveys reported nearly identical mean numbers of sexual partners, but, in the United States, there were greater proportions of those who reported no or a high number of sex partners, and further, sexual behaviors and attitudes were more polarized in the United States. It was conjectured that the higher rates of STDs, including HIV, in the United States were attributable to the higher proportion of the population with greater numbers of sex partners and to restricted attitudes toward sexuality that made prevention efforts difficult (Michael 1998).

Because not all STDs are widely reportable in many countries, the task of understanding the worldwide epidemiologies of STDs is made more complex. Data on STDs from most of the world is incomplete at best, and in industrialized nations, is limited. In general, data on STDs from many European countries, the United States, Australia, and New Zealand showed increasing incidences of STDs in the 1960s and 1970s, with the bacterial

TABLE 1

Estimated* worldwide prevalence and incidence of curable STDs # (1999)

Region	Population 15–49 (million)	Prevalence (million)	Prevalence per/1000	Annual Incidence (million)
North America	156	3	19	14
Western Europe	203	4	20	17
North Africa and Middle East	165	3.5	21	10
Eastern Europe and Central Asia	205	6	29	22
Sub Saharan Africa	269	32	119	69
South and Southeast Asia	955	48	50	151
East Asia and Pacific	15	6	7	18
Australia and New Zealand	11	0.3	27	1
Latin America and Caribbean	260	18.5	71	38
Total	**3040**	**116.5**		**348**

*From the World Health Organization, based on population level methodologies.
#Curable STDs limited to gonorrhea, syphilis, chlamydia, and trichomoniasis.

countries that are manifested in mass media interventions, school-based sexual education, and public discussion about sexual health. It can be hypothesized that this openness also translates into openness between parent and child, and between sex partners. This may be relevant to understanding relative low STD and unintended pregnancy rates observed in these countries.

Another possible factor that may partially explain differences in STD rates among industrialized countries is access to medical care. In the United States, many young people who are at elevated risk for STDs do not have medical care, and thus do not routinely access clinical services where regular STD screening tests and counseling can occur. This factor is given credibility by the scant differences in viral STD rates between the United States and other industrialized countries, and larger differences in rates of curable STDs. Other possible factors include the higher use of crack cocaine in the United States, often strongly associated with STD risk, occurrences of sexual violence toward women, and the lack of regulation, or legalization, of prostitution in the United States.

STDs leveling off then declining since then, but the viral STDs continuing to increase. Of course, the extent of diagnoses and the technologies available to make diagnoses must be seriously taken into consideration in any examination of temporal STD trends. Syphilis probably fluctuates in incidence more widely than any other STD, with cyclic epidemics, in particular, seen in the United States nearly every decade since the discovery of penicillin. Since the dissolution of Russia, an explosive outbreak of STDs has occurred in its respective states, including large syphilis epidemics in the late 1990s in Belarus, Ukraine, and Kyrgyzstan (Eng and Butler 1997).

Openness about sexuality may be a crucial factor in prevention of STDs, an observation from industrialized nations that may be applicable to developing countries. For example, Scandinavia and some northern and western European countries have levels of sexual activity comparable to those reported in the United States, but these countries report much lower rates of unintended pregnancies and STDs. This may be attributable to the pragmatic, open attitudes toward sexuality in these

Conclusion

Recent calls for changes in public policy in the United States have cited the "hidden epidemic" of STDs in the United States, an epidemic that is characterized as hidden from view, cloaked in nondisclosure, stigmatizing attitudes, avoidance of medical care, and a byproduct of a society not prone to discuss sexual behaviors and sexuality openly (Eng and Butler 1997). This hidden epidemic is fortified by social norms that do not promote healthy, sexual behavior. If true, this realization may explain differences in reported STD rates among industrialized nations and may be instrumental in elevated STD rates in many developing countries. Bringing the hidden epidemic out into the open may be the key to major progress in STD prevention in the United States and in other parts of the world.

However, there are other related and unrelated factors to consider when trying to understand why these ancient diseases continue to plague the globe, despite the fact that nearly all are preventable and most are curable. People throughout the world are becoming sexually active at younger ages, having more sex partners earlier in life, getting married later in life, and, in general, exposing themselves more often to the risk of acquiring STDs. World governments, by means of acceptance, greater commitment, and enlightened policies, and through better health care and expanded prevention programs, must address STD epidemics on multiple fronts. Despite the responsibilities of governments, international health organizations, and faith and volunteer-based organizations, individuals must also shoulder responsibilities and be sexually cautious, decrease their risks of acquiring and transmitting STDs, and access routine medical care to protect their own health and that of their sex partners and children.

See also: ACQUIRED IMMUNODEFICIENCY SYNDROME (AIDS); FAMILY PLANNING; RAPE; SEXUAL COMMUNICATION: COUPLE RELATIONSHIPS; SEXUALITY; SEXUALITY EDUCATION

Bibliography

Anderson, J.; McCormick, L., and Fichtner, R. (1994). "Factors Associated with reported STDs: Data from a National Survey." *Sexually Transmitted Diseases* 21: 303–308

Anderson, R. M., and May, R. M. (1991). *Infectious Diseases of Humans: Dynamics and Control.* Oxford: Oxford University Press.

Centers for Disease Control and Prevention. (1993). "1993 Sexually Transmitted Diseases Treatment Guidelines." *Morbidity and Mortality Weekly Report* 42(RR-14).

Centers for Disease Control and Prevention. (2000). *Sexually Transmitted Disease Surveillance 1992.* Washington, DC: Government Printing Office.

Eng, T. R., and Butler, W. T., eds. (1997). *The Hidden Epidemic: Confronting Sexually Transmitted Diseases.* Washington, DC: National Academy Press.

Fichtner, R.; Aral, S.; Blount, J.; Zaidi, A.; Reynolds, G.; and Darrow, W. (1983). "Syphilis in the United States: 1967–1979." *Sexually Transmitted Diseases* 20(10):77–80.

Holmes, K. K.; Sparling, P. F., Mardh, P.-A., ; Lemon, S. M.; Stamm, W. E.; Piot, P.; and Wasserheit, J. N. (1999). *Sexually Transmitted Diseases,* 3rd edition. New York: McGraw-Hill.

Michael, R. T. (1998). "Private Sexual Behavior, Public Opinion, and Public Health Policy Related to Sexually Transmitted Diseases." *American Journal of Public Health* 88(5):749–754.

Noegel, R.; Kirby, J.; Schrader, M.; and Wasserheit, J. N. (1993). "Sexually Transmitted Disease Accelerated Prevention Campaigns." *Sexually Transmitted Diseases* 20:118–119.

Ober, M., and Piot, P. (1993). "HIV Infection and Sexually Transmitted Diseases." In *Disease Control: Activities in Developing Countries,* ed. D. T. Jamieson, W. H. Mosley, A. R. Measham, and J. L. Bobadilla. New York: Oxford University Press.

Wasserheit, J. N. (1994). "Effect of Changes in Human Ecology and Behavior on Patterns of Sexually Transmitted Diseases, including Human Immunodeficiency Virus Infection." *Proceedings of the National Academy of Science of the United States* 91:2430–2435.

Other Resources

National Center for HIV, STD, and TB Prevention. (2002). "Sexually Transmitted Disease Facts and Information." Available from www.cdc.gov/nchstp/dstd/disease_info.htm.

World Health Organization. (2001). "Global Prevalence and Incidence of Selected Curable Transmitted Infections—Overview and Estimates." Available from www.who.int/emc-documents/STIs/whocdscsredc200110c.html.

RONALD R. FICHTNER

SEXUAL ORIENTATION

Sexual orientation is defined by the sex of those to whom a person is attracted. In most societies, people are classified as homosexual, heterosexual, bisexual, or asexual. *Heterosexual* is the term applied to those attracted to the other sex; *homosexual* covers those attracted to the same sex; *bisexual* applies to those attracted to both men and women; and *asexual* individuals profess to no sexual attractions at all. Heterosexuals are, in slang parlance, referred to as *straight* people; homosexuals often prefer the terms *gay* (for men) and *lesbian* (for women) because the word *homosexual,* a nineteenth-century construct, has, for some, a medical or negative cast to it.

Terms such as *transsexual* and *transgender* are often mistakenly used as sexual orientation categories when they actually refer to other things. Transsexuals, people who have surgical procedures to change their sex from male to female or female to male, assume a new sex and gender identity and usually have sexual relations with someone of the sex they were before surgery.

Transgender is a term that has transplanted the term transsexual and added to it. It refers both to transsexuals and to those who enjoy wearing the clothing of the other sex on occasion—also known as cross-dressers or transvestites. In broad terms, transgender refers to anyone who transgresses societal sex/gender categories and can include a wide array of people who resist or simply do not fit narrow boundaries of gender identity, appearance, or behavior. In the 1990s, activists in the Gay Liberation Movement, particularly in the United States, began to speak of a transgender community or *transgender identity*. A transgender community refers, in general, to those living a life with a gender identity other than the one to which they were born. This identity does not, however, indicate what a transgendered person's sexual orientation is, beyond how they themselves determine it.

An intersexual person, called a hermaphrodite in the past, refers to someone born with sex characteristics of both women and men. Typically, a child born with dual sex characteristics is treated with surgical and hormonal therapy. Known as sex reassignment (or in this case, initial assignment) a choice is made to have the child made into either a male or female. Sex assignment is embedded in binary sex/gender categorization and demonstrates that most societies are uneasy with blurred sex/gender characteristics (Dreger 1999).

Essentialism or Social Construction

The biologist Anne Fausto-Sterling examined the social nature of biological knowledge about human sexuality. She contends that the act of labeling a person a man or a woman or heterosexual/homosexual is a social decision. Fausto-Sterling acknowledges the importance of scientific knowledge, but considers our beliefs about gender to be the foundation that defines sex and sexual behavior, even affecting the kinds of knowledge scientists produce about sex (Fausto-Sterling 2000).

Cross-cultural and multicultural comparisons show that sexuality encompasses a wide range of behaviors and practices that are selectively chosen and conditioned by individual societies. Categories are coded as acceptable or not acceptable, even as those categories can, and often do, change over time. Thus, where one is born and when, leads to differing experiences of sexuality.

This range of *meanings* provides insight into sexuality and sexual orientation as social constructions and as arenas of social control. For example, before the forced assimilation of the Pueblo peoples in the nineteenth century, the Zuni included a category known as the *berdache* (or third gender people), providing an alternative role for homosexual and bisexual males and females (Roscoe 2000). Similarly, knowledge of boy-wives and female-husbands in Africa reveals a spectrum of sexual desires and behaviors beyond binary sex and gender categories (Murray and Roscoe 1998).

Variances in identity and behavior, however, do not establish sexual orientation as a social construction beyond categorization and social meaning. Moreover, socially defined characteristics are problematic because categories are determined by humans and open to misinterpretation. As Charlene Muehlenhard argues, categorization of sexual orientation is not objective or universal; these categories have political implications (Muehlenhard 2000).

Where does sexual orientation come from—is it innate or chosen? This is the question that lies at the heart of controversies over sexual orientation. Because most people are heterosexual and because the majority's sexual orientation is seen as the norm, this question is really asking, "What causes homosexuality?" Heterosexuals do not typically think of themselves as having a sexual orientation or wonder where it comes from. If asked, most would say, "That's just how I am," as if it was so much the natural order of things that it seems ludicrous to ask. But just as being white is a racial category, heterosexuality is a sexual orientation category.

Asking a causal question regarding homosexuality can be considered "politically suspect and scientifically misconceived." (Bem 2000, p. 91). Political motivation is linked to agendas for prevention/cure or justification to discriminate. The scientific flaw is found, as noted above, in the fact that heterosexual origins are also not understood. Nevertheless, countless researchers, political pundits, and religious zealots have authoritatively pronounced that sexual orientation equals homosexuality and homosexuality equals perversion, sickness, evil, and a threat to the social order.

Early Sex Research

Some of the earliest sex research that centered on homosexuality was done in 1864 by Karl Ulrichs who postulated a "third sex" and called them urnings—those that loved others of the same sex. Later in the nineteenth century, Magnus Hirschfeld, a founder of sexology studies, embraced the idea of an inborn sexual orientation. In 1919 he founded the Institute for Sexual Science and was at the center of the first modern gay rights movement. Some later researchers, finding that a large number of people had sexual experiences at least once with a member of their own sex, argued that one's sexual orientation was fluid and could change over the course of a lifetime. Alfred Kinsey suggested that everyone was bisexual but, because of social conditioning, most people chose heterosexuality. He felt it would be good for society if people experimented with both same sex and cross-sex partners, as these practices would promote tolerance for difference (Kinsey 1953).

Studies that have tried to link sexual orientation to genetic or hormonal factors have been inconclusive. Nevertheless, the Sexuality Information and Education Council of the United States (SIECUS) does not consider sexual orientation to be a choice, and current scientific explanations leave open the possibility that sexual orientation may well be something one is born with, indicating the possible existence of a gay or straight gene (Stein 2001).

Consideration of a biological link to the formation of sexual orientation has conflicting implications. A positive aspect of a genetic cause is the loss of a foundation to discriminate against gay men and lesbians because of something they have no control over. A negative consideration might be that science will look for a genetic marker that can be changed so no one in the future would be born with a homosexual gene.

No one knows with certainty the answer to the nature/nurture debate, but in 1973 the American Psychiatric Association (APA), based on clinical experience, removed homosexuality from its list of disorders. Since that time it is considered ethically questionable for psychiatrists and psychologists to attempt to alter a trait that is not a disorder and that is an essential component of identity and sexual health.

Given the agreement of SIECUS, the APA, and others that sexual orientation is, in general, not flexible, the study of sexual orientation must take into account the knotty problems of public self-identification and why people are often forced to live a dual life. Consider, for example, the problem of choosing a same sex partner while still identifying as a heterosexual person. Under conditions in which sexual behavior is situational, such as in prison populations, the term sexual orientation does not apply because the behavior is brought on by the impossibility to engage in any other consensual sexual acts. Beyond restricted settings, there are those who do not wish to be labeled bisexual or gay and may even feel convinced that they are not, yet lead a double life with regard to their sexual practices. For instance, a study by Laud Humphreys, *Tearoom Trade* (1970), revealed the lives of men who practiced anonymous sex with other men in public bathrooms but who otherwise led traditional lives with wives and children where they publicly identified as a heterosexual. Another example was the rise of political lesbians in the 1970s when feminism was developing a strong sex/gender consciousness in the women's liberation movement. By the 1990s, though, many of these women were leading heterosexual lives (Stein 1997).

Some researchers have suggested that biological arguments of sexual orientation apply to men to a much larger degree than to women (Veniegas and Conley 2000). A close look at gender shows social, cultural, and experiential differences account for women's often late recognition of same-sex desires. A primary explanation for gender differences between gay men and lesbians is the recognition that women's relationships (gay and straight) have been guided by cultural scripts that are deeply heterosexist (Rose 2000). This fact should be kept in mind when speaking in generic terms of homosexuality (or heterosexuality). When lesbians and gay men are studied together, the gay male experience becomes the norm, and the unique aspects of lesbian's lives get ignored (Garnets and Peplau 2000; Rothblum 2000).

Sexual behavior both within and beyond orientation often resembles a continuum, particularly for women. There is also no doubt that for most people (gay and straight), sexual orientation is experienced as set, not flexible, and nonchanging.

The conflicting beliefs in essentialism and fluidity serve different purposes. Essentialism, the claim of biological origin, highlights the lack of preference in orientation. Fluidity calls for acceptance of diversity and, conversely, rejection of privileged hierarchies in sexual orientation, practices, and lifestyles.

Where sexual orientation comes from is not important except in how those beliefs are used. If the majority of people in society establish categories that fit their experience and draw lines that fail to account for difference, a sexual orientation that differs from the majority leaves the minority vulnerable to prejudice and discrimination.

Family and Social Relations

Awareness of sexual orientation usually occurs early, more so for men than for women, and often is established by adolescence, even before sexual activity begins. It is usually preceded by an awareness of attraction to one sex or the other. But acting on sexual attraction is more difficult, at least initially, for homosexuals than for heterosexuals because of social stigma, legal sanctions, and religious beliefs. Social conditioning from family and society toward heterosexuality acts as a constraint, leaving many youths and adults fearful of acknowledging their attraction to members of the same sex. The teen years are often a confused and anxious time; thus, it becomes particularly difficult for adolescents when their feelings contradict the social norms they have learned about sexuality. Indeed, gay, lesbian, and bisexual youths have been found to be three times more likely to attempt suicide as heterosexual youths (SIECUS 2001).

Passing, a tool for avoiding harm and gaining access to services, jobs, and housing, risks negative psychological affects including internalized oppression. Yet, once through the troubling period of recognition, teens and adults are able to construct a positive sense of self in spite of what they have been taught. An important part of this process is the support found in the gay and lesbian community. Acceptance, most importantly self-acceptance, allows people to feel comfortable with who they are.

Telling parents is often the hardest part of *coming out,* a term used to describe the open acknowledgement of one's homosexuality, to no longer keep it hidden, or in the closet, the common term for unacknowledged homosexuality.

Today, in many societies, family members are more educated on sexual identity issues than in the past, and parents are more likely to be accepting of their adult children's lifestyle choices. European and North American popular cultures have produced positive images in literature, theatre, and television that increase acceptance of diversity, including sexual orientation, such as the television show *Will and Grace,* which normalizes homosexuality. Going beyond normalization is the Showtime cable program *Queer as Folk* that originated in England before coming to the United States. This show fits the militant gay message "We're Here, We're Queer, Get Used to It."

A police raid on a gay bar in Greenwich Village in 1969 led to the Stonewall Riots and the Gay Liberation Movement. Since that time, Gay Pride Parades can be found in every major city of Europe and North America. Lesbian/gay/bisexual/transgendered (LGBT) people in other countries, including most developing countries, have not attained that level of visibility yet. Urban areas, where a mixture of individuals from diverse cultural, racial, economic, and social backgrounds live in close proximity, are where lesbian and gay communities are found.

A major difference between heterosexual and homosexual couples is the kind of support they get from their extended families, institutions, and communities. Insurance eligibility, tax exemptions, and inheritance rights have a different legal standing based on marital status. Marriage is restricted almost universally to heterosexual couples, even though lesbian and gay couples often maintain long-term relationships (Blumstein and Schwartz 1983; Peplau 1991). Not only are gays unable to marry, but in many societies they must also lead clandestine lives as couples, as it is not only laws that prevent them from declaring their love, but cultural restrictions. His or her most important relationship is given no recognition or status. Holidays and visits from friends and relatives often necessitate the exclusion of a partner. In those places where a gay/lesbian community exists, couples might make up a family network, constructing their own kinship ties (Weston 1991).

Cross-Cultural Sexual Diversity

Cross-cultural data shows that sexuality changes its form and meaning in accordance with cultural context. The evidence reveals a wide range of sexual terms did not exist to describe it as we do today. Neither the term heterosexuality nor the term homosexuality existed before 1890.

In societies where women have control over their productive activities, both formal and informal lesbian relations may occur. Where women lack control over their lives, particularly in male-dominated class and caste societies, only informal lesbian ties, unrecognized by the larger society, may form. A formal lesbian relation is one that is recognized as part of the social structure and includes a bond of friendship. Azande women, or co-wives, in Sudan formalize their relationship with ritual. Chinese sisterhoods exist in the province of Kwangtung, where groups of women take vows not to marry and to live together. There are examples of age-defined relations among blacks in South Africa and in the Caribbean between older married women and younger women who are usually not married. Woman-marriage is a type of marriage in some parts of Africa in which a childless woman marries another woman to bear her a child (Evans-Pritchard 1970; Gay 1986; Sankar 1986; Smith 1962). Native North Americans called individuals who expressed both masculine and feminine attributes two-spirited people. They often co-habitated and had sexual relations with someone of the same sex but different gender (Williams 1986).

As the above and other research shows, sexual behavior and gender are social constructions, but sexual orientation probably is not. It is important to note the distinction between these related but distinct concepts.

Sexual Orientation and Social Policy

Heterosexuals tend not to question their sexual orientation, nor do they question or even notice the privileges and protections they enjoy because of it. Another question remains, however: although no one knows where sexual orientation comes from, and most researchers agree that it is a basic emotional need that persists even in the face of repression, why is there so much anger, prejudice, and discrimination against people who are homosexual, bisexual, or transgendered? Homophobia, an irrational fear and hatred of same-sex relations, is found in societies around the world, although the degree of hostility towards people in same-sex relationships varies considerably. Homophobia is a

Members of the University of Sussex Lesbian, Gay, and Bisexual Society participate in a gay-pride march in Brighton, UK. HOWARD DAVIES/CORBIS

behaviors, even if the society itself may legitimate only a limited range of sexual expression. Many non-Western societies allow for some form of homosexual practice. In the early 1950s a survey found 64 percent of societies sampled considered homosexual behavior to be normal and socially acceptable (Ford and Beach 1951). More recent work has found homosexual practices and relationships play an acknowledged role in both the social and religious domains (Blackwood 1986).

Transgenerational homosexual relations are found in a number of societies such as has been found in some African groups where soldiers were given young boys to provide domestic and sexual services for them. Ritual homosexuality is found in New Guinea based on a belief that boys do not develop strength or masculinity until inseminated by older males (Herdt 1984). This belief supported a similar practice in ancient Greece, although the social construction; it is hatred "produced by institutionalized biases in a society or culture" (SIECUS 1993, p. 1).

As gays became more public and their homosexuality was more accepted by loved ones, the focus of activism changed from familial relations to public legal issues. Variance in laws and restrictions based on sexual orientation can be found around the world. Markers can be found in legal marriage, adoption, and military service. Inclusion in civil rights and human rights legislation are additional areas of contention.

LGBT people existed in every society before the 1970s, but gay identity and community did not. Even in those societies that formally legalized homosexuality, openness and the formation of gay groups often took longer. For example, homosexuality was legalized in Slovenia in 1974, yet it was 1984 before the first gay men's organization emerged and 1988 before the establishment of the first lesbian group. After the fall of the Soviet Union in 1990, dozens of gay groups organized in Eastern Europe. In the 1990s, gay life became visible in some form, such as organized groups, newsletters, or Gay Pride Parades in countries as diverse as Pakistan, Bolivia, Curacao, Kenya, Moldova, Portugal, South Korea, Sri Lanka, Japan, Turkey, Nicaragua, Mexico, Estonia, Hong Kong, Brazil, Czech Republic, and Zimbabwe. Decriminalization occurred earlier in Germany, the United Kingdom, and in twenty-seven states in the United States.

A number of countries have national laws that protect gays, lesbians, and bisexuals from discrimination, including Canada, Denmark, Finland, France, Iceland, Ireland, Israel, The Netherlands, New Zealand, Norway, Slovenia, South Africa, Spain, and Sweden. Australia bans employment discrimination and has some states that provide legal protection. Nine states in the United States have civil rights laws that include sexual orientation, and the U.S. Supreme Court has ruled that an amendment in Colorado disallowing an antidiscrimination law on sexual orientation was unlawful. Still, there are seven states that ban the practice of certain sexual acts between adults of the same gender; sixteen states include heterosexual couples in the same ban of specific sexual acts (SIECUS 1998/1999).

International organizations have become active in protecting sexual orientation through human rights policies. The United Nations, through programs and commissions such as The International Labour Office, The Development Program, and the U.N. High Commission for Refugees, are involved in promoting and monitoring the rights of gays and lesbians. United Nations Conference Resolutions, such as from the Fourth World Conference on Women, call on nations to recognize that women and men must be able to decide freely all matters relating to their sexuality. There are also nongovernmental organizations such as Amnesty International and Human Rights Watch that monitor states' repressive measures related to sexuality and sexual orientation.

Groups exist in countries with formal resistance, as in Nicaragua where same-sex relations were criminalized in 1992, and Zimbabwe, where the president in 1995, Robert Mugabe, called homosexuals subhuman animals who deserve no rights at all. In India, the topic of homosexuality has been one that is not spoken of, although by the end of the twentieth century, this forbidden subject began to slowly receive more attention. In China, homosexuality is not illegal, but it is seen as an illness.

The Gay Liberation Movement, as noted earlier, is a primary cause of increased social and self-acceptance. The greater access to education, particularly higher education, leads to generally more acceptance of difference (Gerek 1984). The Internet, which has made possible contact with others even when living in a remote environment, has played an important role in breaking down feelings of isolation. Also, there have been health concerns related to the spread of HIV, the virus that causes AIDS, which have led governments to be more open, particularly as gay groups have demanded government health services.

Even as greater tolerance and acceptance around the world increased in the late twentieth century, repressive societies remained, as did resistance to full equality in those countries that have become more progressive. The Islamic world is not accepting, nor is much of Africa. Early into the twenty-first century, Egypt sentenced twenty-three men to five years in prison for defaming Islam by their homosexual lifestyle (Schneider 2001, p. A11). Homosexuals can be jailed in Romania, the Caribbean, and Malaysia. In Saudi Arabia, homosexuals can be put to death. Indeed,

Susan Greenberg makes the point that in spite of rhetoric and sometimes in spite of equality laws, "there are few societies around the world where homosexuals are not persecuted in some way" (Greenberg 2001, p. 28).

Marriage laws are a major area of discrimination by sexual orientation. Norway has recognized same-sex marriages since 1993, The Netherlands and Germany since 1991. Canada, Norwegian, and Danish laws permit registrations of homosexual partnership that are identical to legal marriage except that they must be done in a civil context, and the couple is not allowed to adopt children. Iceland, Hungary, and Sweden enacted legislation allowing couples to register their partnerships.

The rest of the world basically does not recognize marriage or legal partnerships between same-sex couples. Many countries provide some level of economic and inheritance benefits, but not on the same level that is granted to legally married couples. In the United States, Vermont is the only state that provides legal same-sex ceremonies with domestic partner benefits. Some activists have come to feel that civil unions rather than marriage may be a more realistic goal, resulting in equality by practice, even if not equality in principle. However, not everyone in the LGBT community agrees with gay marriage. As some activists see it, marriage, as practiced by heterosexuals, is an oppressive institution to individual freedom and women's rights.

Adoption is another issue the LGBT community has struggled with, and for the most part, lost. Even countries like Denmark, which allow registered partnerships with all the rights associated with marriage, make an exception for the adoption of children. Remarkably, the right to artificial insemination is also disallowed. Other countries that allow officially recognized same-sex unions modeled their adoption policy on Denmark's conditions. Although gay men and lesbians are allowed to raise children as foster parents, full adoption rights are not granted. There have also been cases of divorce when biological parents have been denied custody because of their sexual orientation.

Gays in the military is an issue that has international differences. In 1993 the Israel Defense Force established an antidiscrimination policy and in 1997 the Tel Aviv Military Court recognized a gay male as the legal widower of a male officer (Gamson 1999). Israel's policies contrast sharply

A homosexual couple celebrates their marriage. Homosexual marriages are recognized in Norway, The Netherlands, and Germany. Several other countries, including Canada, recognize homosexual civil unions. REUTERS NEW MEDIA INC./CORBIS

with the United States's government response to the September 11, 2001, terrorist attacks in New York and Washington, DC, where surviving gay partners were denied recognition from the Victim Compensation Fund, or the "Don't Ask, Don't Tell" policy of the U.S. military.

The number of countries that ban homosexuals from serving in the military is declining. Australia no longer excludes gays, nor does Canada. The United Kingdom decriminalized homosexual acts in the military in 1992, but still regards homosexuality as incompatible with military service and can use a sexual orientation argument as grounds for dismissal. Italy followed suit and has a policy similar to the United Kingdom. Most NATO countries do not, as a matter of policy, exclude homosexuals from military service, with the exceptions of Turkey and Greece. Germany, in practice, has a highly exclusionary military, even though official policy states that homosexuals are fit for service and cannot be discharged for their sexual orientation. Countries that have decriminalized homosexuality in the military are Spain, France, Belgium,

Switzerland, and Poland. The Netherlands represents the most tolerant position on gays in the military (Segal, Gade, and Johnson 1993).

Policies and practices in the military appear to follow social norms of each country, and heterosexuality is clearly the norm. Thus, almost everywhere in the military, homosexuals keep their sexual orientation hidden except around people and situations where they know they are free to be themselves, express their desires, and behave in similar ways that heterosexuals have been allowed to do.

Conclusion

Sexual orientation is not something the heterosexual majority often thinks about simply because they are the mainstream. But for those whose sexual orientation lies at either end of the bell curve of sexual behavior, thinking about sexual orientation is a matter of survival. Livelihoods, family relationships, social contacts, even life itself can be imperiled if one transgresses what is considered the norm. To love someone of the same sex in some societies is to risk their very lives; in other societies they risk imprisonment along with the loss of the comforts of family and friends, and the ability to hold a job; in still other places they risk discrimination both blatant and subtle. The desire to live an open life, the need to live with integrity, and the hope to love the person of their choice is at best a daily struggle in most societies in the world.

Integral to the idea of sexual orientation is the idea of love; human beings are attracted to others and are brought to those others through the biological, psychological, and emotional aspects of sex. This initial physical attraction can lead to love. It is not solely whom people are attracted to sexually but whom they love that makes sexual orientation a controversial issue. Same sex marriage is contentious and divisive not because legalizing such unions will confer financial and legal benefits upon same sex partners, but because it validates a love that is outside the mainstream; it equalizes the love of same sex couples with the love of heterosexual couples.

Learning about the dynamics of sexual orientation and developing an appreciation of the differences and diversity in that field will help to deepen understanding of others, to change attitudes and, eventually, to make life better for people of all sexual orientations.

See also: FAMILY LAW; FAMILY POLICY; GAY PARENTS; GENDER; GENDER IDENTITY; LESBIAN PARENTS; SEXUALITY; SEXUALITY EDUCATION; SEXUALITY IN ADOLESCENCE; SEXUALITY IN ADULTHOOD; SEXUALITY IN CHILDHOOD

Bibliography

Bem, D. J. (2000). "The Exotic-Becomes-Erotic Theory of Sexual Orientation." In *The Gendered Society Reader,* ed. M. S. Kimmel and A. Aronson. New York: Oxford University Press.

Blackwood, E. (1986). "Breaking the Mirror: The Construction of Lesbianism and the Anthropological Discourse on Homosexuality." In *The Many Faces of Homosexuality: Anthropological Approaches to Homosexual Behavior,* ed. E. Blackwood. New York: Harrington Park Press.

Dreger, A. D. (1998). *Hermaphrodites and the Medical Invention of Sex.* Cambridge, MA: Harvard University Press.

Evans-Prichard, E. E. (1970). "Sexual Inversion Among the Azande." *American Anthropologist* 72:1428–1434.

Fausto-Sterling, A. (2000). *Sexing the Body: Gender Politics and the Construction of Sexuality.* New York: Basic Books.

Ford, C., and Beach, F. (1951). *Patterns of Sexual Behavior.* New York: Harper & Brothers.

Gamson, J. (1999). "The Officer and the Diva: Despite a Still-Powerful Closet, Israel has Granted Gay Civil Rights." *The Nation.* 268(24):19.

Garnets, L., and Peplau, L. (2000). "Understanding Women's Sexualities and Sexual Orientations." *The Journal of Social Issues* 56(2):181–92.

Gay, J. (1986). "Mummies and Babies' and Friends and Lovers in Lesotho." In *The Many Faces of Homosexuality: Anthropological Approaches to Homosexual Behavior,* ed. E. Blackwood. New York: Harrington Park Press.

Greenberg, S. H. (2001). "Punishable by Death." *Newsweek International,* July 9:28.

Herdt, G. (1984). *Ritualized Homosexuality in Melanesia.* Berkeley: University of California Press.

Herek, G. M. (1991). "Myths About Sexual Orientation: A Lawyer's Guide to Social Science Research." In *Law* and Sexuality: A Review of Lesbian and Gay Legal Issues, Vol. 1. New Orleans: Tulane University School of Law.

Humphreys, L. (1970). *Tearoom Trade: Impersonal Sex in Public Places.* Chicago: Aldine.

Kinsey, A., and Staff of the Institute for Sex Research at Indiana University. (1953). *Sexual Behavior in the Human Female.* Philadelphia: W. B. Saunders.

Muehlenhard, C. L. (2000). "Categories and Sexuality." *The Journal of Sex Research* 37(2):101–107.

Murray, S. O., and Roscoe, W., eds. (1998). *Boy-Wives and Female-Husbands: Studies of African Homosexualities.* New York: St. Martin's Press.

Murray, S. O., and Roscoe, W., eds. (1997). *Islamic Homosexualities: Culture, History, and Literature.* New York: New York University Press.

Roscoe, W., ed. (1988). *Living the Spirit: A Gay American Indian Anthology.* New York: St. Martin's Press.

Rothblum, E. D. (2000). "Sexual Orientation and Sex in Women's Lives: Conceptual and Methodological Issues." *The Journal of Social Issues* 56(2):193–204.

Rose, S. (2000). "Heterosexism and the Study of Women's Romantic and Friend Relationships." *The Journal of Social Issues* 56(2):315–328.

Sankar, A. (1986). "Sisters and Brothers, Lovers and Enemies: Marriage Resistance in Southern Kwangtung." In *The Many Faces of Homosexuality: Anthropological Approaches to Homosexual Behavior,* ed. Evelyn Blackwood. New York: Harrington Park Press.

Segal, D. R.; Gade, P. A.; and Johnson, E. M. (1993). "Homosexuals in Western Armed Forces." *Society* 32(1):37.

Schneider, H. (2001). "Egypt Jails 23 Men in Gay Case." *The Philadelphia Inquirer,* November 15: A11.

Sexuality Information and Education Council of the United States. (2001). "Lesbian, Gay, Bisexual and Transgender Youth Issues." *SIECUS Report.* 29(4):1–11.

Sexuality Information and Education Council of the United States. (1998/1999). "Worldwide Discrimination: Laws and Policies Based on Sexual Orientation." *SIECUS Report* 27(2): 1–6.

Smith, M. G. (1962). *Kinship and Community in Carriacou.* New Haven, CT: Yale University Press.

Stein, A. (1997). *Sex and Sensibility: Stories of a Lesbian Generation.* Berkeley: University of California Press.

Stein, E. (1999). *The Mismeasure of Desire: The Science, Theory, and Ethics of Sexual Orientation.* New York: Oxford University Press.

Veniegas, R. C., and Conley, T. D. (2000). "Biological Research on Women's Sexual Orientations: Evaluating the Scientific Evidence." *The Journal of Social Issues* 56(2):267–282.

Weston, K. (1991). *Families We Choose: Lesbian, Gays, Kinship.* New York: Columbia University Press.

Williams, W. L. (1986). *The Spirit and the Flesh: Sexual Diversity in American Indian Culture.* Boston: Beacon Press.

Other Resources

American Civil Liberties Union (ACLU). (2002). Web site. Available from www.aclu.org.

Gay and Lesbian Alliance Against Defamation (GLAAD). (2002). Web site. Available from www.glaad.org.

International Gay and Lesbian Human Rights Commission (IGLHRC). (2002). Web site. Available from www.iglhrc.org.

Lombardi, Chris. (2002). "Partners of Sept. 11 Victims Denied Compensation." *Women's E-News,* January 25. Web site. Available from http://www.womensenews.org/article.cfm?aid=789.

Queer Resources Directory. (2002). Available from www.qrd.org.

Sexuality Information and Education Council of the United States. (2002). Web site. Available from www.siecus.org.

Sexuality Information and Education Council of the United States. (1993). "Sexual Orientation and Identity." *SIECUS Report,* February/March: 1–6. Available from www.siecus.org/pubs/fact/fact0006.html.

BARBARA RYAN
JOSEPH R. G. DEMARCO